Humor in Twentieth-Century British Literature

Humor in Twentieth-Century British Literature

A Reference Guide

DON L. F. NILSEN

GREENWOOD PRESS
Westport, Connecticut • London

Library of Congress Cataloging-in-Publication Data

Nilsen, Don Lee Fred.
    Humor in twentieth-century British literature : a reference guide / Don L. F. Nilsen.
      p. cm.
    Includes bibliographical references and index.
    ISBN 0–313–29424–0 (alk. paper)
    1. English wit and humor—History and criticism—Bibliography. 2. English
literature—20th century—History and criticism—Bibliography. 3. Humorous stories,
English—History and criticism—Bibliography. 4. Humorous poetry, English—History and
criticism—Bibliography. 5. English drama (Comedy)—History and
criticism—Bibliography. 6. Comic, The, in literature—Bibliography. I. Title.
Z2014.W57 N565   2000
[PR927]
016.827′9109—dc21   99–054482

British Library Cataloguing in Publication Data is available.

Library of Congress Catalog Card Number: 99–054482
ISBN: 0–313–29424–0

First published in 2000

Greenwood Press, 88 Post Road West, Westport, CT 06881
An imprint of Greenwood Publishing Group, Inc.
www.greenwood.com

Printed in the United States of America

The paper used in this book complies with the
Permanent Paper Standard issued by the National
Information Standards Organization (Z39.48–1984).

10 9 8 7 6 5 4 3 2 1

435993

Contents

Preface

This book is a survey of humor in British literature during the twentieth century starting with Sir Arthur Wing Pinero (1855-1934), and ending with Douglas (Noel) Adams (1952-). Each chapter discusses the humor, satire, parody, irony, comedy, and wit of individual authors, and gives extensive bibliographical information about other critics who have done the same. The book is arranged chronologically according to the birth year of the author being discussed. Note that for ease of reference the birth and death dates of the various authors are given both in the text and in the index. The chronological arrangement was chosen so that the reader would be able to trace the evolution of British literary humor over time.

The main body of the book is divided into ten chapters with the first chapter covering a decade and a half (1855-1869), and all of the other nine chapters covering one decade each. What I expected to find is that each decade would be special and have its own particular sense or "Zeitgeist." What I found instead is that each decade was somewhat heterogeneous. But I also found that certain trends that were started in the nineteenth century and earlier continued through the twentieth century, and can be found represented in each of the various decades. But although each decade did not have a particular feel as distinct from other decades, it nevertheless had a particular impact on each of the trends that was passing through. These trends included the Comedies of Manners, the Mystery-Adventures, the Benign Fantasies, the Horatian Political Satires, the Fabular Animal Stories, the Light Verse, the Colonial Humor, the Irish Humor, the domestic comedy.

Chapter One is about the Comedies of Manners of George Bernard Shaw; the comic and ironic mysteries of Sir Arthur Conan Doyle's mystery novels; the physical, almost slapstick, humor of Jerome Klapka Jerome's; the fantasy-adventure humor of James Barrie; the just-so stories of Rudyard Kipling; and the benign animal stories of Kenneth Grahame and Beatrix Potter. Chapter Two is about the humorous poetry of Hilaire Belloc, Walter de la Mare, and Edmund Clerihew Bentley, the political humor of Sir Winston Churchill, the Comedies of Manners of W. Somerset Maugham, and the humor of the Raj of E. M. Forster. Chapter Three is about the Irish-posturing humor of Sean O'Casey, and the humor that celebrates what it means to be Irish that appears in the writings of James Joyce, and P. G. Wodehouse's benign Bertie Wooster and Jeeves Comedies of Manners, and A. A.

Milne's benign Winnie the Pooh Stories, and in contrast, Virginia Woolf's more aggressive feminist and shape-shifting humor.

Chapter Four is about the mystery-adventure amateur-detective humor of both Agatha Christie and Alfred Hitchcock, and about the religious and symbolic humor of J. R. R. Tolkien with his hobbits on adventures, and C. S. Lewis with his science fiction and allegorical stories, and Aldous Huxley's utopia-turned-dystopia Horatian satire, and Noel Coward's modern extension of Comedies of Manners. Chapter Five is about the domestic rural comedy of Stella Gibbons, the fantasy, mystery, adventure humor of Ian Fleming, the minimalistic and absurdist humor of Samuel Beckett, the chivalric, Canterbury, King-Arthur humor of T. H. White, the benign fantasy Mary Poppins humor of P. L. Travers, the colonial satires of Graham Greene, the dystopian satires and autobiographical humor of George Orwell, and finally Evelyn Waugh's satires about Catholicism, war, colonization, politics, journalism, and death. Chapter Six is about the benign nonsense of Stefan Themerson, and the domestic commonplace "Milkwood" humor of Dylan Thomas, and the naughty boy and girl humor of Roald Dahl, and James Heriot's rural real-animal, real-life humor, and Anthony Burgess's Juvenalian-satirical Clockwork-Orange humor, and Muriel Spark's understated feminist Prime-of-Miss-Jean-Brodie humor, and the beginning of the Spike Milligan Goon-Show, silly slapstick humor.

Chapter Seven is about Brendan Behan's Irish prison humor, and Alan Sillitoe's ironic and haunting humor. It is also about the campus humor of Kingsley Amis's Lucky Jim and Tom Sharpe's Porterhouse Blues. Kingsley Amis was one of the angry young men of the beat generation. Tom Sharpe wrote totally uninhibited, hilarious, outrageous humor about African colonization. Chapter Eight continues the tradition of mystery adventure humor with John le Carré, and the tradition of colonial humor with V. S. Naipaul's Indian humor, and the tradition of campus and academic humor with David Lodge, and the tradition of feminist shape-shifting humor with Fay Weldon, and the tradition of slapstick with Michael Frayn's Noises Off, and Joe Orton's Loot, and Tom Stoppard's Rosencrantz and Guildenstern Are Dead, and the appearance of John Cleese and the rest of the Monty Python group. This is also the decade of Alan Ayckbourn's continuation of the tradition of Comedy of Manners, and Comedy of Humors, and of Harold Pinter's witty and ironic plays like The Dumb Waiter. Chapter Nine is about Martin Amis's satires. It is also about Salmon Rushdie's political and religious satires like Shame, and Satanic Verses, and about his fantasy humor for children. But more importantly it is about Terry Gilliam, Graham Chapman, Terence Jones, Eric Idle, and Michael Palin, and such Monty Python events as The Life of Brian, The Meaning of Life, and The Holy Grail. Chapter Ten is about A. N. Wilson's farcical novels which mock British life. It is also about the humor of developing science, technology, and space travel in the form of Douglas Adams's Hitchhiker's Guide trilogy, and the adventures of Dirk Gently in Outer Space.

If the reader wants to read about the humor of a particular author, that reader should turn to the Index, where the authors are listed alphabetically. Extensive bibliographies are given after the discussion of each author's humor to allow the reader easy access to other books and articles that discuss the humor of these various authors. Special attention is given to earlier books written by the present author, since many of the authors discussed in this book are also mentioned or discussed in Humor in Eighteenth- and Nineteenth-Century British Literature: A Reference Guide (Greenwood, 1998), Humor in British Literature, From the Middle Ages to the Restoration: A Reference Guide (Greenwood, 1997), and especially in Humor in Irish Literature: A Reference Guide (Greenwood, 1996). Many of the Irish authors merely contain cross-reference information; however, for some Irish authors additional criticism was found and is written-up in this book. The information on Irish authors that is found in this book should therefore be considered as incomplete and supplemental to my earlier book, Humor in Irish Literature: A Reference Guide.

Acknowledgments

I would like to express my appreciation to Peter Lafford, Faye Verska, and members of the Arizona State University Humanities Computing Facility--Francis Larscheid, Ahmad Rafiq, Glenn Trombley, and Gary Walker--for managing the facility in such a way as to make it convenient to provide high quality camera ready copy to the publisher. I would also like to express my appreciation to Karen Adams, Dawn Bates, Lee Croft, Montye Fuse, Nancy Gutierrez, Marysia Johnson, Barbara Lafford, Neal Lester, Roy Major, Elly van Gelderen, and Wendy Wilkins, for their encouragement and support of scholarly research.

I would like to thank the A.S.U. students and T.A.s who have worked most closely with me on this project, namely, Stacie Anfinson, Julia Angelica, Margaret Baker, Barbara Bennett, Katie Bradford, Dan Breazeale, Maureen Chancy, Diane Clark, Melinda Collins, Clay Conner, Jeanice Conner, Larry Connolly, Gail Dadik, Barbara Daines, Bruce Davis, Chitra Duttagupta, F. Wayne Ellis, Pamela Erramuzpe, Edward Fredericks, Andrea Graham, Diane Harley, Michelle Hudgins, Frank Katz, Zsolt Klamar, Jim Koncz, Janet McConnell, Kristine McCrady, Elizabeth McNeil, Sandra Nagy, Chad Nilep, Roger Pearce, Sean Pollack, Michaela Safadi, Ronald Schott, B. J. Segura, Gene Valentine, Elizabeth Vanderlei, Linda Vander Wall, Teresa Wells, Jennifer Wilhoit, Anne Winter, and Maryln Zupicich.

I would also like to thank A.S.U. professors Paul Cook, Jeanne Dugan, Karen Dwyer, Greg Glau, Maureen Goggin, Beckian Goldberg, George Herman, James Janssen, Mark Lussier, Susan McCabe, Anita Obermeier, Melissa Pritchard, Jewell Parker Rhodes, Duane Roen, Robert Shafer, Laura Tohe and Jacqueline Wheeler for their important input that has resulted in various expansions and revisions.

Special thanks goes to A.S.U. professors Bert A. Bender, Jay M. Boyer, O. M. (Skip) Brack, Willis J. Buckingham, Cordelia C. Candelaria, Ron Carlson, Gregory Castle, Frank D'Angelo, Kenneth L. Donelson, Jeannine Savard Dubie, Norman Dubie, James L. Green, Donald C. Haberman, John Hakac, Mark Harris, Elizabeth Horan, James G. Janssen, Delmar G. Kehl, Marjorie J. Lightfoot, Keith Miller, Thais Morgan, J. Lynn Nelson, William T. Ojala, Thelma Shinn Richard, Alberto A. Rios, Nick Salerno, Kathleen M. Sands, Judith L. Sensibar, and Michael Vanden Heuvel for reading various sections of the manuscript, and for offering important suggestions for expansion and revision. Extra special thanks goes to my wife, Alleen, who has seen or heard the manuscript in many forms and has offered all of the constructive criticism I asked for--and more.

Without the above support, and without a sabbatical leave from Arizona State University, there is little hope that this project would ever have been completed.

1

Introduction

David Hirst traces the development of comedy of manners from the second half of the seventeenth century, through Richard Brinsley Sheridan and Oliver Goldsmith of the eighteenth century, through W. S. Gilbert and Oscar Wilde in the nineteenth century, through the inter-war comedies of Somerset Maugham, Noel Coward, and Frederic K. Lonsdale, and finally to Joe Orton, Harold Pinter, and John Osborne, who have "achieved a more marked dramatic precision by adopting the features of this comic mode" (Hirst 1). David Hirst notes that from the time of Wilde, the comedy-of-manners genre has frequently been the province of homosexual writers. Wilde, Coward, Maugham, and Orton "translated their life-style into their plays, whilst the nature of homosexual relationships features repeatedly in the work of Pinter and Osborne" (Hirst 3-4). Hirst also considers it significant that Wilde and Orton, who most fully exploited the savage satiric potential of the comedy-of-manners mode, wrote as they lived--dangerously--should have had such "short and tragic lives" (Hirst 5). In his Comedy of Manners, Hirst concentrates on the five plays which are the finest examples of this important comic tradition, namely, The Way of the World (William Congreve), The Importance of Being Earnest (Oscar Wilde), Design For Living (Noel Coward), Loot (William Wycherly), and The Homecoming (Harold Pinter).

Hirst marks 1924 as the watershed year for the return of comedy of manners in the twentieth century. That is the year in which Bonamy Dobree's Restoration Comedy was published. It is the year in which The Way of the World was revived by Nigel Playfair at the Lyric. And it was the year in which Noel Coward's Hay Fever was first performed. In the twentieth century, it is the comedy of manners of Noel Coward, Somerset Maugham, and Frederick Lonsdale which best represents a new brittle social drama, and it was Shaw who was still the most important of the serious dramatists. The lightness and wit which are constant in the work of Wilde and Coward (Shaw's contemporaries) are absent from Shaw's drama (Hirst 58-59).

Stephen Potter describes the late nineteenth and early twentieth century as the "Age of Humour." "It was a reaction against the unmeaning seriousness of the Queen Victorian age" (Potter 29). Richard Carlson notes that during this period a small group of writers developed a new genre which Carlson considers to be inventive, congenial, and accomplished. Carlson calls this genre "Benign Humor," and the genre is represented by such authors as Lewis Carroll, Edward Lear, Beatrix Potter, A. A. Milne, P. G. Wodehouse, Kenneth Grahame, and Walter de la Mare. The humor which these authors developed was very different from the humor of wit and satire which prevailed in nineteenth and twentieth-century England (Carlson ix). Unlike the literary wits and satirists who felt it incumbent upon themselves to comment on the problems and changing institutions of the new century, the benign humorists refused to deal with cultural and societal issues. They wrote about times past and about imaginary times and places (Carlson x). In this vein, Lewis Carroll wrote Alice in Wonderland; Edward Lear wrote verses and limericks; Kenneth Grahame wrote The Wind in the Willows; P. G. Wodehouse wrote about Bertie Wooster and Jeeves; Walter de la Mare wrote fantastic verses and songs; and Beatrix Potter wrote fantastic animal adventures. The benign humorists produced a kind of rescuing literature which promised to provide a respite from twentieth-century social and cultural problems. The benign humorists joined with such escapist writers as Dorothy Sayers (Lord Peter Whimsey and Bunter), P. G. Wodehouse (Bertie Wooster and Jeeves), and Arthur Conan Doyle (Sherlock Holmes and Watson) in offering the twentieth-century reader "a way to get well, a way to stay well" (Carlson xi).

In a book entitled, In Defence of Fantasy, Ann Swinfen says that it was J. R. R. Tolkien with his Lord of the Rings who first made fantasy "respectable." After Tolkien, British and American writers with a serious purpose could employ fantasy in a way that they had not been able to do since the growth and dominance of the realistic novel (Swinfen 1). But even though fantasy was respectable for these authors, most of them were obliged to write their first books as children's books; only later could Tolkien and these other writers establish themselves as writers of adult books. Swinfen argues that any prolonged study of what she calls "high fantasies" reveals that they should not be labeled as children's books. These books operate on an adult level of meaning, metaphor, and symbolism (Swinfen 2).

In an article entitled " 'Between the Gaps': Sex, Class and Anarchy in the British Comic Novel of World War II," Phyllis Lassner discusses Evelyn Waugh's Put Out More Flags (1942), Marghanita Laski's Love on the Supertax (1944), and Beryl Bainbridge's Young Adolf (1978), saying that these three novels are all comic fantasies which generate "alternate visions of a world known and all too well." These novels raise questions about the origins and destiny of the world at that time, and they "use its familiar signifiers to defamiliarize it through satire, parody, and mockery" (Lassner 206).

In a book entitled Comedy and the Woman Writer, Judy Little says that authors of feminist comedy "draw upon festive images of a world overturned." They provide structure and narrative substance to the "radical laughter of Wittig's guerrilla warriors and Lessing's Kate Brown, who found the concepts of obedience, anatomical destiny, wife, and husband to be extremely funny." For such feminist comic authors as Virginia Woolf, Muriel Spark, Margaret Drabble, Jean Rhys, Iris Murdoch, and Penelope Mortimer, there is a lack of closure. According to Judy Little, "At its best, feminist comedy deals with absolutes, but not absolutely. The novelists discussed here use liminal imagery to mock long-standing social and psychological situations" (Little Comedy 187-188).

Robert Ronning feels that Oscar Wilde, W. Somerset Maugham, Noel Coward, and Ben Travers all continue the seventeenth-century tradition of comedy of manners. A common point of view and comic sensibility are present in their plays. Each accepts the world as it is--conventional and conversational, rather restricted and more than a trifle stuffy--and each proceeds to subvert that world by creating an ironic, urbane tone, and by introducing conventional characters who act as eccentrics and who commit little outrages in word or deed. This subverting of the system, this inverting of the conventions of polite society, has always been a purpose of humor and its peculiar manner in these comedies is very English (Ronning 57). Hamilton Fyfe claims that the Victorians "have evolved, during the past generation, two art-forms which are distinctively English--the savoy opera and Mr. Pinero's farces of character" (Ronning 58).

Another trend in twentieth-century British writing is that of the "Angry Young Men" led by such authors as Kingsley Amis, John Osborne, John Wain and David Benedictus. Many of these angry young men turned to humor as a way of venting their disgust, and this can be seen in Amis's Lucky Jim, Osborne's Look Back in Anger, and Benedictus's The Fourth of June (Batts 51).

In a book entitled Three Modern Satirists: Waugh, Orwell, and Huxley Stephen Jay Greenblatt tells what these three satirists have in common. They have all three "witnessed the same historical developments, lived through the same national and international crises, been influenced by the same culture, grown up in the same society." Nevertheless, their satires reflect "a remarkable diversity of interest, prejudice, and temperament." In fact, in their satires, the only thing which unites them is that "there is something dreadfully wrong with society" (Greenblatt 22).

In "The Mythos of Spring: Comedy," Northrop Frye describes the "Old Comedy" that was prevalent before the twentieth century.

> What normally happens is that a young man wants a young woman, that his desire is resisted by some opposition, usually paternal, and that near the end of the play some twist in the plot enables the hero to have his will.... At the beginning of the play the obstructing characters are in charge of the play's society, and the audience recognizes that they are usurpers. At the end of the play the device in the plot that brings hero and heroine together causes a new society to crystallize around the hero. (Frye 163)

However, during the twentieth century, such American authors as Henry James, and such English authors as George Bernard Shaw developed a new kind of comedy which can be labeled as "tragicomic" (Kaul 3). A. N. Kaul suggests that before the twentieth century tragedy and comedy were separate and distinct genres. He adds, however, that, "the most striking contemporary [twentieth-century] writers have in fact tended to identify the two so increasingly that the most dominant literary form today is neither tragedy nor comedy, but tragicomedy." Thus, the tendency in twentieth-century literature is "to erase the line between tragedy and comedy" (Kaul 45).

Morris Beja agrees with Erich Auerbach that "epiphany," through which minor, unimpressive and random events are shown to be significant, is "one of the hallmarks of twentieth-century literature" (Beja 17), pointing to the "astonishing frequency with which sudden moments of intuitive insight appear in twentieth-century fiction, a frequency unmatched and even unapproached in the fiction of the past" (Beja 18). Beja notes that the epiphany as an aspect of the twentieth-century novel, borrows many characteristics, techniques, and standards from poetry. These epiphanies display great interest in apparently insignificant objects and trivial events, and are extensions of the spiritual tradition of Marvell and Hopkins as well as the Romantic tradition of Blake and Wordsworth (Beja 22).

Paul Grawe points out that throughout history tragedy has been considered a more significant genre than has comedy. He feels that critics have normally assumed that tragedy is the "serious" genre, the one more deserving of critical attention than comedy, which has generally been cast aside as the trivial genre that appeals to the masses. In the twentieth century, however, many prominent critics, theorists, and playwrights have questioned the majority opinion, and have demanded that we take another more-critical look at comedy. They have demanded that we accept comedy's potential in presenting the most serious and philosophical, even the most pessimistic, of literary insights. Grawe suggests further that no one can review the long tradition of comedy without recognizing the fact that,

> comedy has been by far the most widely developed, most enjoyed, and most financially successful of all literary genres. Tragedy may be more exalted in criticism, but comedy has always enlisted the predominant number of playwrights, procured more time on the boards, and enthralled the greater audiences. (Grawe 183)

In a personal letter dated April 28, 1994, Brian Lile, a librarian at the National Library of Wales indicated that virtually all of the writings of Gwyn Thomas are humorous, and that this can be demonstrated by reading his Meadow Prospect Revisited, edited by Michael Parnell. Lile adds that Dylan Thomas's most humorous short story is "A Story," also known as "The Outing," and is included in his Collected Stories. Other humorous Welsh writers include Alun Richards, whose two volumes of short stories are The Former Miss Merthyr Tydfil, and Dai Country, Harry Secombe, and Glyn Jones, who have written several humorous novels, and John Morgan who wrote The Small World. Lile also notes that Kingsley Amis's Lucky Jim, though not written by a Welsh author, is set in south Wales. But some of the best humor in Welsh literature is written in Welsh rather than English. Brian Lile writes the following:

> A most relevant work in Welsh is T. Mardy Rees's Hiwmor y Cymro, sef, Hiwmor mewn llenyddiaeth Gymraeg (Humour in Welsh Literature), Liverpool, 1922, while there have been several anthologies of jokes, including: Y Cydymaith Difyrus (1815), The Welsh Jester (1892), William Davies's Casgliad o Ffraethebion Fraethebydd (ca. 1880), Digrifwch, (1882), Gwreichion (1904), Y Ffraethebwr (1908), Ffraethebion y Glowr Cymreig (1928), John Williams Jones's Y Fainc 'Sglodion (1953), and J. Ellis Williams's Glywsoch chi hon? (1968). Two English anthologies are Humour of the Underground (i.e. coal mines) (1945), and Tales from Wales (1946).

R. Tudor Jones, a Professor of Religious Studies at the University of Wales in Bangor goes so far as to say that such authors as Dylan Thomas and Gwyn Thomas should not be considered as typical authors of humorous Welsh literature because they wrote in English, not Welsh, because neither of them spoke Welsh, and because both of them had a "marked prejudice towards it and consequently there is a strong element of mockery and parody in their treatment of their fellow countrymen."

Hugh Walker contrasts Scottish and English satire in the following way:

> It is remarkable that the same instinct [concreteness] shows itself in all the Scottish satirists from Dunbar to Burns; while the English satirists, from Piers Plowman to the close of the Elizabethan age, are, with few exceptions, far more abstract. The difference is all the more striking in view of the reputation of the northern people for metaphysical speculation, and that of the southern, one for practicality and a belief in that which can be seen and handled, and, it seems to be thought, in that alone. (Walker 56)

Humor in Twentieth-Century British Literature Bibliography

Batts, John Stuart. "The Humor of Anger: Looking Back at Amis and Company." WHIMSY 4 (1986): 51-54.

Beja, Morris. Epiphany in the Modern Novel. Seattle, WA: University of Washington Press, 1971.

Brown, Ivor. "British Comedy." Theatre Arts Monthly 19 (1935): 585-593.

Burgess, Anthony. "The Writer as Drunk." Urgent Copy: Literary Studies. London, England: Jonathan Cape, 1968, 98-102.

Carlson, Richard S. The Benign Humorists. New York, NY: Archon Books, 1975.

Cazamian, Louis. The Development of English Humor. Durham, NC: Duke University Press, 1952.

Charney, Maurice. Comedy High and Low: An Introduction to the Experience of Comedy. New York, NY: Oxford University Press, 1978.

Churchill, Thomas. "Loving: A Comic Novel." Critique: Studies in Modern Fiction 4

(1961): 29-38.

Eliot, Robert C. The Power of Satire. Princeton, NJ: Princeton University Press, 1968.

Esslin, Martin. The Theatre of the Absurd. Garden City, NY: Doubleday, 1961.

Fawkes, Richard. Fighting for a Laugh. London, England: Macdonald and Jane's, 1978.

Fisher, John. Funny Ways to be a Hero. London, England: Frederick Muller, 1973.

Frye, Northrop. "The Mythos of Spring: Comedy." Anatomy of Criticism. Princeton, NJ: Princeton University Press, 1957, 163-186.

Gilliatt, Penelope. Unholy Fools, Wits, Comics, Disturbers of Piece: Film and Theater. New York, NY: Viking Press, 1973.

Gindin, James. "Well Beyond Laughter: Directions from Fifties' Comic Fiction."Studies in the Novel 3 (1971): 357-364.

Grawe, Paul H. Comedy in Space, Time, and the Imagination. Chicago, IL: Nelson-Hall, 1983.

Greenblatt, Stephen Jay. Three Modern Satirists: Waugh, Orwell, and Huxley. New Haven, CT: Yale Univ Press, 1965.

Hall, James. The Tragic Comedians: Seven Modern British Novelists. Bloomington, IN: Indiana University, 1963, 3-10.

Hendrickx, Johan Remi. Ben Travers and the English Farce Tradition. Dissertation Abstracts International 42.1 (July, 1981): 226A.

Hirst, David L. Comedy of Manners. New York, NY: Methuen, 1979.

Innes, Christopher. "The Comic Mirror--Tradition and Innovation." Modern British Drama, 1890-1990. Cambridge, England: Cambridge University Press, 1992, 260-267.

Johnson, Bruce. "Henry Green's Comic Symbolism" Ball State University Forum 6.3 (1965): 29-35.

Jones, R. Tudor. Personal Letter. Dated April 19, 1994.

Kaul, A. N. The Action of English Comedy: Studies in the Encounter of Abstraction and Experience from Shakespeare to Shaw. New Haven, CT: Yale University Press, 1970.

Kennedy, Dennis. "Granville Barker's Sexual Comedy." Modern Drama 23 (1980): 75-82.

Kitchin, George. "Burlesque of the 'Aesthetes' and Prose Parody of To-day." Survey of Burlesque and Parody in English. London, England: Oliver and Boyd, 1931, 348-376.

Lassner, Phyllis. " 'Between the Gaps': Sex, Class and Anarchy in the British Comic Novel of World War II." Look Who's Laughing: Gender and Comedy. Ed. Gail Finney. Amsterdam, Netherlands: Gordon and Breach, 1994, 205-220.

Lile, Brian. Personal Letter. Dated April 28, 1994.

Little, Judy. Comedy and the Woman Writer: Woolf, Spark, and Feminism. Lincoln, NE: University of Nebraska Press, 1983.

Lowrey, Burling, ed. Twentieth Century Parody: American and British. New York, NY: Harcourt, 1960.

Marcus, Frank. "Comedy or Farce?" London Magazine 6 (February 1967): 73-77.

Moseley, Merritt. "Humor and the British Academic Novel." WHIMSY 6 (1982): 55-56.

Nathan, David. The Laughtermakers: A Quest for Comedy. London, England: Peter Owen, 1971.

Nilsen, Alleen Pace, and Don L. F. Nilsen. Encyclopedia of Humor and Comedy: Patterns, Trends, and Connections. Phoenix, AZ: Oryx, 1999.

Nilsen, Don L. F. Humor in Eighteenth- and Nineteenth-Century British Literature: A Reference Guide, Westport, CT: Greenwood, 1998.

Nilsen, Don L. F. Humor in Irish Literature: A Reference Guide. Westport, CT: Greenwood, 1996.

Nilsen, Don L. F. Humor British Literature, From the Middle Ages to the Restoration: A

Reference Guide. Westport, CT: Greenwood, 1997.

Nilsen, Don L. F. Humor Scholarship: A Research Bibliography: A Research Bibliography. Westport, CT: Greenwood, 1997.

Palmer, Jerry. "Humor in Great Britain." National Styles of Humor. Ed. Avner Ziv. New York, NY: Greenwood, 1988, 85-111.

Petro, Peter. Modern Satire: Four Studies. Berlin, Germany: Mouton, 1982.

Potter, Stephen. Sense of Humour. New York, NY: Henry Holt and Company, 1954.

Previté-Orton, C. W. "Satire under the Despots: Development of Modern Verse." Political Satire in English Poetry. New York, NY: Russell and Russell, 1968, 31-55.

Price, R. G. G. A History of "Punch." London, England: Collins, 1957.

Pritchett, V. S. "The Comic Element in the English Novel." Listener LI, 1320 (June 17, 1954): 1047-1049, 1053.

Rademacher, Frances. "Violence and the Comic in the Plays of Edward Bond." Modern Drama 23 (1980): 258-268.

Richter, Richard H. "Humor and the British Academic Novel: What is the British Academic Novel?" WHIMSY 6 (1988): 55-56.

Risden, E. L. "The Owl and the Nightingale: Postmodernism Play and Medieval Stand-up Comedy." WHIMSY 7 (1989): 48-49.

Robinson, Fred Miller. The Comedy of Language. Amherst, MA: University of Massachusetts, 1980.

Ronning, Robert. "The Eccentric: The English Comic Farce of Sir Arthur Pinero." Quarterly Journal of Speech 63 (1977): 51-58.

Stubbs, John Heath. "The Moderns." The Verse Satire. London, England: Oxford University Press, 1969, 106-115.

Swinfen, Ann. In Defence of Fantasy: A Study of the Genre of English and American Literature since 1945. London, England: Routledge and Kegan Paul, 1984.

Tinsley, James R. "A Middle Class Comedy of Manners?" Satire Newsletter 5 (1968): 38-43.

Took, Barry. Laughter in the Air. London, England: Robson/BBC, 1976.

Van O'Connor, William. The New University Wits and the End of Modernism. Carbondale, IL: Southern Illinois University Press, 1964.

Walker, Hugh. English Satire and Satirists. London, England: J. M. Dent, 1925.

Williams, Pat. "My Kind of Comedy." Twentieth Century. (July, 1961): 46-50.

Wilmut, Roger. From Fringe to Flying Circus: Celebrating a Unique Generation of Comedy, 1960-1980. London, England: Eyre Methuen, 1980.

Wilmut, Roger. The Goon Show Companion: A History and Goonography, with a Personal Memoir by Jimmy Grafton. London, England: Robson, 1976.

Wilmut, Roger. Kindly Leave the Stage! The Story of Variety, 1919-1960. London, England: Methuen, 1985.

Winkler, Elizabeth. The Clown in Modern Anglo-Irish Drama. Bern, Switzerland: Herbert Lang, 1977.

2

Authors Born between
1855 and 1869

Sir Arthur Wing Pinero (1855-1934)

Robert Ronning feels that Arthur Pinero's most lasting contributions as an author were the development of native English comedy and the perfection of the English eccentric character on the stage. "With the eccentric as the centerpiece of his comic farce, Pinero's humor was indigenously English and his form distinctively original" (Ronning 51). Pinero's new genre was not exactly comedy of manners; rather it was a kind of modern "comic farce," the twentieth century equivalent of this earlier genre. Ronning says that Pinero's comic farce had its roots in Robertson's early comedies of plain domestic life, and in Gilbert's farces depicting a world of cynicism and fantasy, and even in the French "well-made play."

Pinero's comic court farces include The Magistrate (1885), The Schoolmistress (1887), Dandy Dick (1887), The Cabinet Minister (1890), and The Amazons (1893). In these plays, the eccentric qualities of the principal character is usually elaborately drawn, and the characters represent an English-type person who finds himself caught up in unusual circumstances. "Pinero's eccentrics, paradoxically, are drawn from conventional Victorian society. It is through Pinero's magic that he transforms an English magistrate, an impoverished aristocrat, and a village clergyman--types normally regarded as conventional, rather dull personages--into finely drawn and unusual comic creations" (Ronning 52). Pinero's eccentrics are reminiscent of earlier eccentrics such as Lord Ogleby in The Clandestine Marriage, Mr. Hardcastle in She Stoops To Conquer, and Sir Peter Teazle in The School for Scandal. Like these earlier characters, Pinero's characters exhibit such qualities as self-deception, playful deceit, role-playing, and self-dramatization. But these earlier eccentrics were peripheral characters, while Pinero's eccentrics are at the center of his plots. "Pinero uses his eccentric characters to invert the traditional forms of duty, respectability, and compromise which were the code words of the Victorians" (Ronning 52). According to Ronning, prototypical eccentrics either defy or ignore their humanity, and they always refuse to compromise. They are headstrong in their obsession to continue a collision course which may be absurd and destructive to the audience but which is perfectly logical and consistent from the eccentric's point of view.

In The Rocket (1883), and In Chancery (1884), Pinero burlesques the earlier stereotyped farces of James Kenney and John Maddison Morton. Both of these plays contained reference to contemporary Victorian events, and in In Chancery, the character of McCafferty is a stage Irishman who is ridiculed mercilessly (Hendrickx 55).

The venerable Aeneas Posket of The Magistrate (1885) is another of Pinero's eccentrics. Mr. Posket can be described as "silly" as he struggles to preserve his respect and decorum. As Mr. Posket and his wife, Agatha, are hiding under a table at the hotel, he assures her that he is "entirely the victim of circumstances." The Magistrate is as smooth as a French farce, but it is less moral. This play reintroduces the idea of the farce of character which is based on incongruity. This farce demonstrates in a light-hearted and entertaining way how true-to-life people can do un-true-to-life things. In fact, Piner's formula for farce might be, "possible people doing improbable things." In The Magistrate, Mr. Posket is a bumbling, soft-hearted judge who has trouble condemning criminals in his police court. The conflict between his soft heart, and his position as a judge becomes even more intense when he has to condemn his wife and his sister-in-law to jail (Hendrickx 55).

In The Schoolmistress (1887), both Admiral Rankling and Reginald Paulover are humours characters (Hendrickx 58). The title character is Miss Constance Dyott, the principal of the Volumnia College for Daughters of Gentlemen. She is married to the snobbish Honorable Vere Queckett, an eccentric who is not able to earn any money because he is a gentleman of leisure. Vere Queckett conceals his own poverty and his wife's financial support in a continuing charade meant to preserve a pride and dignity he finally realizes he never had in the first place. In Act II of The Schoolmistress, Queckett's friends are suspicious; the guests are angry; and the dinner party is in shambles. When Queckett enters, his hair is disarranged, and his appearance is generally wild. He says merely, "I can't help it! I am in the hands of fate." The Reverend Augustin Jedd, another humours character, leads a life of pompous self-deception in which he hypocritically tries to save the church fund by secretly betting on a racehorse. He ends up in jail (Ronning 53), where Rev. Jedd, like Queckett, remarks that he is, "the victim of a misfortune only partially merited." According to Robert Ronning, the eccentricities of these characters in Pinero's comic farces is a "principal delight" (Ronning 54). In order to keep her husband happy, Constance Dyott takes on the role of Queen Honorine in a new comic opera (Hendrickx 56). She thus has three alternate identities in the play. As Miss Dyott, she is a respectable schoolmistress. As Mrs. Vere Queckett, she is a dutiful wife, and as Constance Delaporte, she is a queen of the "opera buffa." Schoolmistress Dyott, however, must be absent from school in order to star in the theatre, and this is the comic mechanism of the farce. The school is accidentally set on fire, and this brings the deception into the open. "Here Pinero creates one of the most striking images of farce literature, as Miss Dyott in full costume as Queen Honorine comes to the rescue of her tiny husband, Vere, and carries him bodily through the window down the ladder." The cynical spirit that pervades this play is also shown in the denouement, where everyone is happily paired off, and Miss Dyott strikes a blow for freedom as she ceases to continue as schoolmistress, and chooses instead to pursue her lucrative role as Constance Delaporte. At the end of the play, Constance Delaporte continues the comic tradition by speaking directly to the audience (Hendrickx 57).

The Very Reverend Augustin Jedd, Dean of St. Marvells Church, is an eccentric victim in Pinero's Dandy Dick (1887). Reverend Jedd has two rebellious daughters by the names of Salome and Sheba, who sneak off to a fancy dress-ball and in general bring disgrace to their "saintly" father. Reverend Jedd is so pious that he does not even allow card-playing in his house, but he is forced by capricious fate to place a bet on a horse named "Dandy Dick" which is partially owned by his "horsy" sister Georgia Tidman, who is known on the track as George Tidd. At the beginning of the play, Reverend Jedd's family is lounging after a boring dinner, and everyone seems to be at ease. But the various family members reveal their true thoughts by expressing revealing asides to the theatre audience. Reverend Jedd is worried about his money problems. Salome and Sheba are dreaming about the forbidden but alluring fancy ball. And the girls' suitors are thinking about their hatred for each other (Hendrickx 58). The language of Dandy Dick, "sparkles like champagne and overflows with good-natured wit" (Hendrickx 59). Each of the characters is given a unique language style, as Pinero burlesques the use of contemporary language. For example, "Dean Jedd speaks inflated patter faintly echoing the pulpit; and Georgina joyfully expresses herself in the vernacular of the track to the consternation of her stuffy brother and fussy nieces" (Hendrickx 59).

The Cabinet Minister (1890) is a farce which lacks a hounded victim, since the play is broader in its scope. It gives an ironic view of London society and its social season (Hendrickx 59). The Amazons (1892) is the final farce which Pinero wrote for the Court Theatre (Hendrickx 60). Pinero gives The Second Mrs. Tanqueray (1893) the label of "a farcical romance." The humours characters in this play include the sickly Earl of Tweenwayes, and the Count de Grival, a stage-Frenchman (Hendrickx 60). Pinero's Trelawny of the Wells (1898) is a sentimental comedy. Johan Hendrickx indicates that some critics consider Child Man (1928) to be a "sedate farce" (Hendrickx 60).

Oscar Wilde wrote elegant society dramas and comedies; George Bernard Shaw wrote clever thesis comedies and dramas; however, Sir Arthur Pinero wrote eccentric comic farce and manners comedy that would continue into a later tradition called "light comedy" (Ronning 55-56). Arthur Pinero's development of eccentric characters had an important influence on W. Somerset Maugham. Both Pinero and Maugham mixed sentiment and cynicism in their work through the controlling sensibility of their eccentric characters. Pinero's point of view was essentially Victorian. "His stuffy magistrates and deans attempt to extricate themselves from compromising situations--whereas Maugham's view was Edwardian and essentially modern--a manners comedy emerges as the characters reflect a freer, more brittle and urbane wartime and postwar culture" (Ronning 56). Walter Lazenby says that Pinero was the only English farceur to invent "a new formula for farce based on showing possible people doing improbable things" (Hendrickx 54).

Sir Arthur Wing Pinero Bibliography

Hendrickx, Johan Remi. "Pinero's Court Farces: A Reevaluation." Modern Drama 26.1 (1983): 54-61.
Ronning, Robert. "The Eccentric: The English Comic Farce of Sir Arthur Pinero." Quarterly Journal of Speech 63 (1977): 51-58.

F. Anstey (1856-1934)

F. Anstey wrote a series of lampoons of music-hall music for Punch entitled "Model Music Hall Songs." Laurence Senelick says that Anstey's humorous works, which are also his "most enduring" works, fall into four categories: "parodies, 'overheard' dialogues, fantastic romances, and social satires" (Senelick 35). Anstey had a formula for writing plays in which ordinary middle-class life is turned topsy-turvy by the interference of some supernatural force. The lowly barber in The Tinted Venus, a Farcical Romance (1885) is able to make a statue of Venus come to life, but after he does so, Venus gets the barber into one embarrassing situation after another. This play served as the source for One Touch of Venus, a play and a movie that were co-written by American humorists S. J. Perelman and Ogden Nash. A Fallen Idol (1886) is about an evil Asian effigy that curses the protagonist's existence. There is a magic flask in The Brass Bottle (1900) that produces a genie; the genie in turn upsets the career and the love life of an aspiring architect. The Brass Bottle was later made into a movie staring Tony Randall as the architect and Burl Ives as the genie. In Tormalin's Time Cheques (1891) there is a mechanism that allows the protagonist to return to past experiences for limited periods of time. And in The

Talking Horse and Other Tales (1892) the horse manages to wreck the life of its owner. (Senelick 36-37).

Many of Anstey's humorous pieces are of some significance. Burglar Bill and Other Pieces (1892) is a satire blasting "rhetorical sentimentality." In The Travelling Companions (1892), there are two disagreeable gentlemen who are compelled to share each other's company on a European tour. Voces Populi (1892) demonstrates Anstey's fine ear for capturing colloquial speech. In order to appropriately capture the vernacular language in these plays, Anstey would visit public events. Laurence Senelick noted that Anstey was much like Dickens in his ability to "distill character into a memorable phrase of speech" (Senelick 36). The Man from Blankley's (1893) is considered by Senelick to be a "delightful tour de force" which describes a dinner party with hired waiters. It is a Comedy of Manners (Senelick 37). Mr. Punch's Pocket Ibsen (1893) is a satiric attack on the Henrik Ibsen productions that were being dramatized by the Independent Stage Society. Anstey didn't approve of Ibsen's "ponderous absurdities" (Senelick 36).

Lyre and Lancet (1895) contains mistaken identities during a countryhouse weekend, and it is crisp and sparkling because it is played almost entirely in dialogue (Senelick 37). In Baboo Jabberjee, B.A. (1897), and in A Bayard from Bengal (1902), Baboo Jabberjee is portrayed as an over-educated and conceited Bengali whose attempts to break into English society are often comic, but Laurence Senelick notes that much of the buffoonery is overdone, and much of the comedy is racist (Senelick 37). Sir John Squire said that the collection of sketches contained in Salted Almonds and Other Tales (1906) is important because it bridged "the gulf between Mark Lemon and Burnand on the one hand and A. A. Milne and A. P. Herbert on the other" (Senelick 37).

Vice Versa, a Farcical Fantastic Play in Three Acts (1910) is about Mr. Bultitude who is a humorless businessman. The story becomes topsy-turvy, as a magical "Garuda stone" metamorphoses Mr. Bultitude's body into that of his son. In his new body, Mr. Bultitude is forced to undergo the humiliations of a school boy while he still retains his old memories and obligations as a businessman. As part of the transformation, the son now is forced to inhabit the body of his father as he, "romps through the mysteries of high finance." Without giving any credit to Anstey, Hollywood made a film from this plot, as they modernized it and Americanized it. The Hollywood film starred Judge Reinhold and Fred Savage and was entitled Vice Versa (Senelick 36). Three other Anstey plays which include important elements of humor are The Brass Bottle, a Farcical Fantastic Play in Four Acts (1911), The Man from Blankley's, A Comedy of the Early Nineties (1927), and Four Molière Comedies, Freely Adapted (1931)

F. Anstey Bibliography

Anstey, F. Humour and Fantasy: Vice Versa, The Tinted Venus, A Fallen Idol, The Talking Horse, Salted Almonds, The Brass Bottle. New York, NY: E. P. Dutton, 1931.

Senelick, Laurence. "F. Anstey." Encyclopedia of British Humorists, Volume I. Ed. Steven H. Gale. New York, NY: Garland, 1996, 35-38.

Edmund Downey (1856-1937) IRELAND

See Nilsen, Don L. F. "Edmund Downey." Humor in Irish Literature: A Reference Guide. Westport, CT: Greenwood, 1996, 91.

George Bernard Shaw (1856-1950) IRELAND

Paul Grawe feels that George Bernard Shaw's plays exhibit a kind of "female chauvinism," in that Shaw often creates a "laughable reversal of the typically male-oriented social values of the post-Victorian world." Grawe feels that Shaw developed this reversal of gender roles philosophically in Back to Methuselah, and Man and Superman (Grawe 137). He developed it whimsically in Arms and the Man. And he developed it socially in Major Barbara and Pygmalion. Grawe says that this role reversal is a "surefire basis for provocative theatre" (Grawe 138).

There is a comic contrast in Arms and the Man (1894) between Bluntschli and Sergius, Raina's suitor. Bluntschli is a Swiss mercenary and experienced soldier, more interested in survival than in heroics, while Sergius wants to be British, and therefore he mistakes heroic posturing and disastrous cavalry charges for heroism and warfare. Another comic contrast in Arms and the Man is that between the sophisticated Raina and her earthy servant, Louka (Richardson 961).

In The Devil's Disciple (1896), Dick Dudgeon at first represents the Devil, but then there is a comic reversal where he turns out to be, "the man of a higher god than the American Puritans know." Anthony Anderson also breaks reader expectations, for he is more than the preacher of the play; he turns out to be an effective secular leader as well, and a very good organizer of men (Richardson 962).

Betty Richardson says that many critics have termed Shaw's Widowers' Houses (1893), The Philanderer (1898), and Mrs. Warren's Profession (1898) to be "blue-book" plays. This is because during Shaw's time, the British Parliament published their official public reports in a blue binding, and the unflattering term "blue-book" plays was therefore applied to Shaw's plays because their political bias tended to be as strong as these official Parliamentary publications. In Widowers' Houses (1893) Shaw forced both the characters and the audience to share the guilt for slum land-lordism. In Widowers' Houses there is an exaggeration of stage gesture which makes the play more of a farce than a high comedy. The heroine is Blanche, and she stalks her prey (future husband) in the same way that a cat would stalk a bug (Richardson 960-961).

In a similarly political vein, Shaw uses The Philanderer (1898) to reveal various odd sexual compacts made between men and women. Both Dr. Harry Trench in The Widower's Houses, and Leonard Charteris, the philanderer in The Philanderer become comically frustrated when "instead of being the manipulators, they are systematically manipulated by seemingly modest, cliché-spouting heroines" (Richardson 960).

In Mrs. Warren's Profession (1898), Shaw forces actors and audiences to see the economic basis of prostitution. The Second Act of Mrs. Warren's Profession, "mocks every melodramatic reconciliation scene and, probably, every second-rate printing of Madonna and child that Shaw winced at in the Dublin galley (Richardson 960-961). It is in these three plays that Shaw develops many of the comic techniques that he would later use more effectively in his later plays. These techniques include reversal of stock stage stereotypes, and reversal of stock male and female linguistic expressions and physical gestures (Richardson 960).

Man and Superman (1903) is a comedy in many senses. It is a romantic comedy, but it is also a parody of romantic melodrama with brigands and chases across the country of Spain. It is an intellectual comedy, but it is also a drama of ideas, and in spite of its belonging to all of these classifications, it is a farce as well (Richardson 962). In the Second Act of Major Barbara (1905), there is a vivid Bacchaean procession when the musical instruments of the Salvation Army end up in the hands of Untershaft and Euripides (Major Barbara's suitor Adolphus Cusins), who has been newly converted (Richardson 962).

Eliza Doolittle in <u>Pygmalion</u> (1913) is the Cockney flower girl who represents Galatea of the Greek myth.   She is transformed into a lady by Henry Higgins to demonstrate Shaw's socialist belief that the upper classes are not naturally superior, but rather that their social advantage is the result of having had good food, healthy living, decent clothes, and training in the proper way to move and to talk. In the play, Eliza slips and uses the British Cockney term, "bloody likely," but even this is misinterpreted by Freddy Eynsford-Hill, who is sure that he is hearing one of the latest expressions in fast-set slang (Richardson 960).

Paul Grawe gives evidence that Higgins has to marry Eliza at the end of <u>Pygmalion</u>. Freddie is developed as a bumbling boob who in the opening scene of the play is not even able to secure a cab for his mother and sister. He is, "henpecked beyond any rational man's endurance," and is sent wandering into the rain in search of a cab all the way from Charing Cross to the Strand. His search is not so much to secure a cab as it is to appease his womenfolk (Grawe 141). Even though Freddie is much higher than Eliza in the social register, he is presented as a fool, and as no real match for Eliza (Grawe 142). Eliza and Higgins, on the other hand, are a perfect match. Eliza has been used by Higgins, and she wants to get back at him. She is an "endangered heroine," who has "truly unparalleled verve and social genius." She is twenty years younger than her teacher, yet she is attracted enough to him to become the object of his experiments. Eliza explains why she allowed herself to be part of Higgins's experiment: "What I done [correcting herself] what I did was not for the dresses and the taxis: I did it because we were pleasant together and I come-- came--to care for you; not to want you to make love to me, and not forgetting the difference between us, but more friendly like."Through the play, she becomes increasingly hostile to him as she realizes how little Higgins is willing to learn about basic human kindness.   Nevertheless, as her antagonism increases, her fascination increases correspondingly. Finally, she sees her opportunity to get even, or as she says, "to get a bit of her own back," by making Higgins into a man in the same way that he has made her into a woman. She realizes that Higgins is emotionally a child, but Eliza is smart, is driven, and is a glutton for hard work (Grawe 143).

<u>Heartbreak House</u> (1917) is a Chekhovian play of disillusion. Like many of Shaw's other plays, it is also a comedy with socialist themes (Richardson 959-960). Heartbreak House is shaped like a ship, because it represents the "ship of state." It is in Heartbreak House that the "sophisticated classes" meet, people who are preoccupied with their personal relationships and love affairs, or with horses and the great outdoors, or with playing their petty games while the ship of state is floundering around them (Richardson 963).

<u>Back to Methuselah</u> (1920) is a cycle of five plays telling about the history of humans from the time of the Creation until 30,000 years beyond the date of the play (Richardson 963). Lileth, the first mother, whose voice ends the play, provides much of the warmth and the humor (Richardson 964). The comedy in <u>Saint Joan of Arc</u> (1923) comes from the fact that Joan is a peasant who is able to perceive events with clear common sense, while more sophisticated perceptions of the church and state become banal because the perceptions lack true insight (Richardson 963). <u>In Good King Charles's Golden Days</u> (1939) is a short play filled with wit, especially in the dialogues of Charles II, George Fox (founder of the Quakers), Sir Isaac Newton, Catharine of Braganza (Charles's Queen), and a number of Charles's mistresses, such as Nell Gwynn, Barbara Villiers, and Louise de Keroualle (Richardson 964).

See also Nilsen, Don L. F. "George Bernard Shaw." <u>Humor in Irish Literature: A Reference Guide</u>. Westport, CT: Greenwood, 1996, 5-6, 54, 81-82, 91-111, 215-216.

George Bernard Shaw Bibliography

Couchman, Gordon W. "Comic Catharsis in Caesar and Cleopatra." Shaw Review 3.1 (1960): 11-14.

Crane, Gladys. "Shaw's Comic Techniques in Man and Superman." Educational Theatre Journal 23 (1971): 13-21.

Crane, Gladys. "Shaw's Misalliance: The Comic Journey from Rebellious Daughter to Conventional Womanhood." Educational Theatre Journal 25 (1973): 480-489.

Frank, Joseph. "Major Barbara--Shaw's Divine Comedy." Publication of the Modern Language Association 71 (1956): 61-74.

Furlong, William B. GBS/GKC Shaw and Chesterton: The Metaphysical Jesters. University Park, PA: Pennsylvania State University Press, 1970.

Ganz, Margaret. "Humor's Devaluations in a Modern Idiom: The Don Juan Plays of Shaw, Frisch, and Montherlant." Comedy: New Perspectives. Ed. Maurice Charney. New York, NY: New York Literary Forum, 1978, 117-138.

Gatch, Katherine Haynes. "The Last Plays of Bernard Shaw: Dialectic and Despair." English Stage Comedy: English Institute Essays 1954. Ed. W. K. Wimsatt, Jr. New York, NY: Columbia Univ Press, 1955, 126-147.

Gibbs, A. M. "Comedy and Philosophy in Man and Superman." Modern Drama 19 (1976): 161-175.

Grawe, Paul H. "Romantic Comedy in Perspective: Shaw." Comedy in Space, Time, and the Imagination. Chicago, IL: Nelson-Hall, 1983, 131-148.

Hobson, Harold. "George Bernard Shaw." English Wits. Ed. Leonard Russell. London, England: Hutchinson, 1940, 279-306.

Holroyd, Michael, ed. The Last Laugh: Bernard Shaw, Volume 4. London, England: Chatto, 1992.

Kaul, A. N. The Action of English Comedy: Studies in the Encounter of Abstraction and Experience from Shakespeare to Shaw. New Haven, CT: Yale Univ Press, 1970.

Kornbluth, Martin L. "Shaw and Restoration Comedy." Shaw Bulletin 2.4 (1958): 9-17.

McDowell, Frederick P. W. "Politics, Comedy, Character, and Dialectic: The Shavian World of John Bull's Other Island." Publication of the Modern Language Association 82 (1967): 542-553.

Mills, John Arvin. Language and Laughter: Comic Diction in the Plays of Bernard Shaw. Tucson, AZ: University of Arizona Press, 1969.

Nilsen, Don L. F. "The Pygmalion Story: A Recurring Theme." The Leaflet 90.2 (1991): 34-47.

O'Farrell, Padraic. G. B. Shaw: Gems of Irish Wisdom. Cork, Ireland: Mercier, 1980.

Park, Bruce R. "A Mote in the Critic's Eye: Bernard Shaw and Comedy." University of Texas Studies in English 37 (1958): 195-210.

Pearson, Hesketh. "Bernard Shaw." Lives of the Wits. New York, NY: Harper and Row, 1962, 248-268.

Potter, Stephen. "S.B. and G.B.S." Sense of Humour. New York, NY: Henry Holt, 1954.

Rayner, Alice. "Shaw's Paradox: Use in Dystopia." Comic Persuasion: Moral Structure in British Comedy from Shakespeare to Stoppard. Berkeley, CA: University of California Press, 1987.

Reardon, Joan. "Caesar and Cleopatra and the Commedia dell'Arte." Shaw Review 14 (1971): 120-136.

Richardson, Betty. "George Bernard Shaw." Encyclopedia of British Humorists, Volume II. Ed. Steven H. Gale. New York, NY: Garland, 1996, 957-967.

Shaw, Bernard. "Tolstoy: Tragedian or Comedian." The London Mercury 4 (1921), 32.

Speckhard, Robert R. "Shaw and Aristophanes: Symbolic Marriage and the Magical

Doctor/Cook in Shavian Comedy." Shaw Review 9 (1966): 56-65.
Watson, Barbara Bellow. "The New Woman and the New Comedy." Fabian Feminist:
     Bernard Shaw and Women. Ed. Rodelle Weintraub. University Park, PA:
     Pennsylvania State Univ Press, 1977, 114-129.
Whittemore, Reed. "Shaw's Abstract Clarity." Comedy: Meaning and Form. Second
     Edition. Ed. Robert W. Corrigan. New York, NY: Harper and Row, 1981, 415-246.
Winsten, Stephen. Jesting Apostle: The Private Life of Bernard Shaw. New York, NY: E.
     P. Dutton, 1957.

Brandon Thomas (1856-1914)

     Brandon Thomas wrote three comic plays: Charley's Aunt (1892), Women Are So
Serious (1901), and A Judge's Memory (1906). In Charley's Aunt, the humor of Lord
Babberly's predicaments is mainly based on mistaken identity, chasing and hiding behind
bushes, broadly defined character types, and the general slapstick of farce. These farce
devices were developed by the French, but were transferred to the English setting and were
provided with a special brand of English wit and repartee by Thomas. Nevertheless, Robert
Ronning feels that Thomas's Charlie's Aunt, "seemed like hack work compared to Pinero's"
(Ronning 55).

Brandon Thomas Bibliography

Ronning, Robert. "The Eccentric: The English Comic Farce of Sir Arthur Pinero."
     Quarterly Journal of Speech 63 (1977): 51-58.

Joseph Conrad (né Teodor Józef Konrad Korzeniowski)(1857-1924)

     It was Joseph Conrad who said that caricature is, "putting the face of a joke upon
the body of truth" (Auerbach-Levy 54). However Elsa Rael considers Joseph Conrad's
"caricature" to be of a special sort, as she considers Conrad to be a "master absurdist,"
adding that "The Secret Sharer" contains a number of choice examples of absurdity, and
that absurdity runs through Heart of Darkness like a consistent thread. Ukrainian born
Joseph Conrad once wrote to Hugh Clifford that, "in human affairs the comic and the tragic
jostle each other at every step" (Gerard 217). To many critics Joseph Conrad was an
enigma. Galsworthy, Graham, Forster, Ford, and Symons, Conrad's literary friends, have
all noted Conrad's comic sensibilities; however most modern critics, in their high
seriousness, have failed to see the humor. H. L. Mencken could hear Conrad's "harsh roars
of laughter, and considered Conrad to be a "Herculean Humorist." Galsworthy said that
Conrad had the "humor to perceive" both sides of a serious issue. Edward Garnett wrote
about Conrad's "flashing wit, his humor, often playful, often fiercely sardonic." This
unique Conradian sense of humor can be found throughout the Conrad letters, and a close
examination of the comedy in his fiction forces the reader to reevaluate the brooding
novelist (Lincoln 184).
     In 1890 Joseph Conrad took a voyage up the Congo, and on May 15th of that year
he wrote a letter his aunt in the style of Heart of Darkness (1902) in which he referred to
a particular Congo outpost as, "that comedy of light at the door of darkness" (Lincoln 184).
Marlow is the narrator of Heart of Darkness, and he describes numerous scenes of comic
incongruity. Marlow describes the freaks and the caricatures of humanity that appear at
every station along the Congo. He describes the pilgrims in pink pajamas firing

Winchesters into the undergrowth with "a glorious lot of smoke," as they cavort in "the jolly lark of slaughtering natives" (Lincoln 185). Stanton de Voren Hoffman discusses the farce and the purposeless absurdity that occurs throughout Heart of Darkness, adding that Marlow's comic resilience is what allows him "at least a choice of nightmares" (Hoffman "Hole" 113-123).

In discussing Conrad's absurdist vision, Elsa Rael tells about Marlow's coming upon the "knitting fates" in the whited sepulchre city. There were two women, one fat and the other one slim, and they sat knitting black wool. "The slim one got up and walked straight at me--still knitting with downcast eyes--and only just as I began to think of getting out of her way, as you would for a somnambulist, stood still and looked up" (Rael 163). As Marlow is preparing to go into the jungle, an "unshaven little doctor" confronts him with a pair of calipers. Although he is surprised by the procedure, Marlow allows the doctor to measure his skull, "back and front and everyway" while being assured that it was in the interest of science that they measure the crania of "those going out there." This was an understated way of questioning Marlow's sanity, and Marlow's submitting to the meaningless examination is in the tradition of absurdist literature. This episode also foreshadows some of the blacker comedy that is to come later in the novel (Rael 164).

As Marlow comes up to the French man-of-war, he passes Gran' Bassam, and Little Popo. And then, as he rounds the bend he sees the warship, "incomprehensible, firing into a continent. Pop, would go one of the six inch guns...and nothing happened. Nothing could happen. There was a touch of insanity in the proceeding, a sense of lugubrious drollery." There was no resistance, and Marlow concluded that there was in fact no enemy. There was only the apathetic little vessel, "flying a limp flag, ridiculously shooting a pop-gun, and voila!--French Equatorial Africa." A bit later in the novel Marlow comes to a mountain that is being leveled out. The explanation is that they are building a railway, but the mountain is not in the way of anything. The incident is symbolic of the objectless blasting that was trying to level out all of Africa (Rael 164).

Marlow then meets a white man in elegant dress. He had a, "high starched collar, white cuffs, a light alpaca jacket, snowy trousers, a clean necktie and varnished boots...under a green parasol." This is the chief accountant, and Marlow said of him, "He kept up his appearance." Later, on his way to the Central Station Marlow met another white man, who was assigned to keep the road in good repair. "Can't say I saw any road or any upkeep, unless the body of a middle aged Negro, with a bullet hole in the forehead...three miles farther on, may be considered a permanent improvement." The mordant irony of this statement may evoke an involuntary laugh (Rael 164). Marlow then meets the manager, a man of no learning and no intelligence. At the end of each of his speeches, he has a "stealthy smile, like a seal applied to the words to make the meaning of the commonest phrase appear absolutely inscrutable." And finally, there is the "Brickmaker," who has still another meaningless title, since he is really a spy, who is in league with the manager.

Then the steam gets underway, crawling determinedly toward Kurtz. In this surreal scene, Marlow would like to, "go ashore for a howl and a dance," but cannot because of the demands of the leaky steamer (Rael 165). Marlow is very pleased with the "restraint" of his cannibal crew, and he hopes he doesn't appear too appetizing to them. Before the reader meets Kurtz, Marlow describes him in absurdist terms. His voice is "a dying vibration of one immense jabber"; his head is, "a lofty frontal bone...impressively bald...an ivory ball." Kurtz has a very possessive air about him. He says, " 'my ivory.... My intended...my station, my river, my---' everything belonged to him!" Kurtz's physical appearance is described as, "covered with bright patches, blue, coloured binding around his jacket, scarlet edging at the bottom of his trousers, looking in the sunshine extremely gay and wonderfully neat withal" (Rael 166). He has the appearance of a clown. Marlow describes him as looking "at least seven feet long," thereby contradicting the name of "Kurtz," which in German means "short" (Rael 167). The reader learns that Kurtz has been preparing a report for the "International Society for the Suppression of Savage Customs." This is seventeen pages of close writing, "eloquent, vibrating with eloquence...burning noble words." Here Conrad is the "master absurdist."

Heart of Darkness contains a large number of social caricatures and comic grotesques. There is a chief accountant with nothing to account for; there is a stout firefighter with a hole in his water bucket. There is a brickmaker with no straw for bricks. There is a harlequin disciple who claims to be the son of a Russian arch-priest. And presiding over this "dance macabre" there is "Mistah Kurtz," a hollow man who knows music, painting, journalism, poetry, and philosophy. It is ironic that the most civilized characters in Heart of Darkness are the thirty cannibals on Marlow's tin-can steamer. Marlow is unable to rely on his fellow Europeans, but he finds these thirty cannibals perfectly dependable (Lincoln 192). The irony becomes even greater still when Marlow realizes that imperial England, "was once a heart of darkness for Roman conquerors" (Lincoln 196).

Another irony results from the disparity between Marlow's conversational voice and the grotesque vision he is describing. "There it was, black, dried, sunken, with closed eyelids--a head that seemed to sleep at the top of that pole, and, with the shrunken dry lips showing a narrow white line of the teeth, was smiling too, smiling continuously at some endless and jocose dream of that eternal slumber" (Lincoln 194).

Marlow's meeting with "the Intended" is also absurd. She "almost smothers Marlow in her demand for romantic lies. Marlow keeps trying to evade, but she will now allow him to. Marlow is talking with her about Kurtz's last words. "The Intended" says, "Repeat them. I want--I want--something--something--to--to live with." Then we have Marlow's thoughts: "I was on the point of crying at her, 'Don't you hear them?' The dusk was repeating them in a persistent whisper all around us, in a whisper that seemed to swell menacingly like the first whisper of a rising wind. 'The horror! The horror!' " In The Heart of Darkness, the last word uttered by Kurtz is "Horror." Kenneth Lincoln considers this to be a pun based on the similarity of the words "horror" and "whore." Supporting this association, Lincoln points out that the purpose of Conrad's novel was to expose the various ways that Europeans were "prostituting" Africa. Also supporting this association is the fact that in his Last Essays (1924), Conrad alludes to the rape of Africa as "the vilest scramble for loot that every disfigured the history of human conscience and geographical exploration" (Conrad Last Essays 17).

"The Intended" proudly wears black for an entire year after Kurtz's death, in a bit of gallows humor that "rattles through a symbolic background of artificial mourning and mocks the self-emulating 'grief' of the Intended" (Lincoln 187). "The Intended" intrudes into Marlow's thoughts: " 'His last word--to live with,' she insisted. 'Don't you understand I loved him--I loved him--I loved him!' " Marlow pulls himself together and speaks slowly, "The last word he pronounced--your name." On hearing this, "the Intended" "utters a cry of inconceivable triumph" (Rael 168). Lincoln describes the poignancy of this scene. Conrad had a penchant for le mot juste, and this scene is filled with "word play, intricate symbolism, obscure irony, and dark comedy." Lincoln adds that, here, Conrad, "has played one of the most shadowy jokes in prose fiction. It is a hidden but audacious pun, which triggers a network of images whispering of whoredom throughout" (Lincoln 188).

Conrad called his Under Western Eyes (1911) a, "comedy of errors in which no one escapes the tragic ironies of mistaken judgment." Camille LaBossière said that in Under Western Eyes "Berthoud ironically provides a convenient point of departure for an examination of the logic of tragi-comedy." LaBossière says that Under Western Eyes like Chance (1913) should be classified as, "tragi-comedy slipping between frank laughter and unabashed tears" (LaBossière 37).   Albert Guerard contrasts Heart of Darkness (1902) with "The Secret Sharer" (1950), saying that Heart of Darkness is Conrad's most "intense expression of mature pessimism," while "The Secret Sharer" is, "a good-humoured and joyful paean to youthful idealism, its optimistic aspirations, and its not infrequent success" (Guerard 15). Dinshaw Burjorjee would agree with Guerard, since he considers comedy to be a vital element in Conrad's "The Secret Sharer." "Few will deny that there is a current of humour in this perhaps most happily civilized and youthfully exuberant of his sea stories which Conrad has imbued with, one might say, a Meredithian spirit" (Burjorjee 51). The two most obvious comic devices in "The Secret Sharer" are the concealments or surprises, and the happy ending, two qualities often found in comedies of intrigue (Burjorjee 52). In addition, the characters in "The Secret Sharer" tend to be depicted with caricatured oddities (Burjorjee 53); the characterizations are often comic, and the young Captain describes himself as "the only stranger on board" (Burjorjee 54). Much of the humor is a result of the disparity between the crew's conception of the young Captain, and his own self-appraisal of his personality. The Captain's chief mate is an "absurdly whiskered" eccentric, and to such questions as, "Are you aware that there is a ship anchored inside the Islands?" he responds, with his usual ejaculations, "Bless my soul, sir! You don't say so!" (Guerard 21-22).

There is much linguistic humor in "The Secret Sharer". For example, there are often nonsequiturs in Leggatt's logic, and there is eccentric diction both in the descriptions and in the dialogues (Burjorjee 53). Dinshaw Burjorjee suggests that many of Archbald's phrases suggest "lumbering comic inflections" in their readings. Burjorjee is referring to such phrases as "Painful duty," "Such a young man, too!" "God's own hand in it," and "Sui-cide! That's what I'll have to write to my owners directly I get in" (Guerard 39, 41, 42). Burjorjee goes so far as to say, "Practically all of Archbold's lines beg the same kind of delivery" listing the following as examples (Burjorjee 58):

> "What would you think of such a thing happening on board your own ship? I've had the Sephora for these fifteen years.   I am a well-known shipmaster"; "I have been at sea now, man and boy, for seven-and-thirty years, and I've never heard of such a thing happening in an English ship. And that it should be my ship. Wife on board, too," and "He looked very smart, very gentlemanly, and all that, But do you know--I never liked him, somehow. I am a plain man." (Guerard 40-41, 44)

Burjorjee agrees that Archbold may be "a plain man," but he also has a "unique, guilty conscientious manner of sticking to the point," and he is unable to complete his parting remark to the Captain, saying, "I say...you...you don't think that--" (Guerard 44). "Archbald ends with a comic whimper" (Burjorjee 59). Much of the humor in "The Secret Sharer" comes from the comic counterpoint that brings into sharp relief the Doppelgänger and his antithetical counterpart (Burjorjee 60).

In "The Secret Sharer," the captain walks about the quarter deck in his "sleeping suit...barefooted, a glowing cigar in his teeth." In this comic outfit, the captain sees a "corpse" "complete but for the head." The captain gasps, and his cigar drops from his "gaping mouth with a tiny plop and a short hiss" into the water. Then the "corpse" regains his head, and asks the time before he comes aboard. There are also what Elsa Rael calls "wry evasions of truth" in "The Secret Sharer." The chief mate speculates on Leggatt's fate: "I suppose he did drown himself. Don't you sir?" "I don't suppose anything." "You have no doubts in the matter, sir?" "None, whatever" (Rael 169).

Morris Beja notes that much of Joseph Conrad's writing is epiphinal, though Conrad himself used the term "moments of awakening" (Beja 20). In Lord Jim, for example, Marlow is sensitive to the, "light of glamour created in the shock of trifles." He tells of a conversation with a French officer:

I kept him company; and suddenly, but not abruptly...he pronounce, "Mon Dieu! How the time passes!" Nothing could have been more commonplace than this remark; but its utterance coincided for me with a moment of vision...there can be only few of us who had never known one of these rare moments of awakening when we see, hear, understand ever so much--everything--in a flash--before we fall back again into our agreeable somnolence. (Beja 17)

Joseph Conrad (né Teodor Józef Konrad Korzeniowski) Bibliography

Auerbach-Levy, William. The Art of Caricature. New York, NY: Watson-Guptill, 1947.

Beja, Morris. Epiphany in the Modern Novel. Seattle, WA: University of Washington Press, 1971.

Burjorjee, Dinshaw M. "Comic Elements in Conrad's The Secret Sharer." Conradiana 7.1 (1975): 51-61.

Bush, Roland. "Tragic Versus Comic Vision: Joseph Conrad's Heart of Darkness and Lamara Laye's Le Regard du Roi." CLA Journal 34 (1990): 81-98.

Conrad, Joseph. Last Essays. London, England: Dent, 1963 (originally published in 1924).

Covino, William A. "Lugubrious Drollery: Humor and Horror in Conrad's Fiction." Modern Fiction Studies 18.2 (1975): 183-197.

Gerard, Jean-Aubry. Joseph Conrad: Life and Letters. (Garden City, NY: Doubleday, 1927.

Guerard, Albert J., ed. "Heart of Darkness" and "The Secret Sharer". New York, NY: Signet/New American Library, 1964.

Hoffman, Stanton de Voren. Comedy and Form in the Fiction of Joseph Conrad. The Hague, Netherlands: Mouton, 1969.

Hoffman, Stanton de Voren. "The Hole in the Bottom of the Pail: Comedy and Theme in Heart of Darkness." Studies in Short Fiction 2 (1965): 113-123.

Hoffman, Stanton de Voren. "Scenes of Low Comedy: The Comic in Lord Jim." Ball State University Forum 5.2 (1964): 19-27.

Knoepfmacher, U. C. "The Secret Agent: The Irony of the Absurd." Laughter and Despair: Readings in Ten Novels of the Victorian Era. Berkeley, CA: University of California Press, 1971, 240-273.

LaBossière, Camille R. " 'A Matter of Feeling': A Note on Conrad's Comedy of Errors in Under Western Eyes." Thalia: Studies in Literary Humor 2.1-2 (1979): 35-38.

Land, Stephen K. Conrad and the Paradox of Plot. London, England: Macmillan, 1984.

Land, Stephen K. Paradox and Polarity in the Fiction of Joseph Conrad. New York, NY: St. Martin's Press, 1984.

Lincoln, Kenneth R. "Comic Light in Heart of Darkness." Modern Fiction Studies 18.2 (1972): 183-197.

Rael, Elsa. "Joseph Conrad, Master Absurdist." Conradiana 2.3 (1969-1970): 163-170.

Simmons, Kenneth. The Ludic Imagination: A Reading of Joseph Conrad. Ann Arbor, MI: UMI Research Press, 1985.

Smith, J. Oates. "The Existential Comedy of Conrad's 'Youth.' " Renascence 16 (1963): 22-28.

Winner, Anthony. Culture and Irony: Studies in Joseph Conrad's Major Novels. Charlottesville, VA: University Press of Virginia, 1988.

Ella D'Arcy (1857-1937)

Ella D'Arcy liked to add ironic touches to what are in the main very tragic stories

(Fisher 301). D'Arcy improved her ability to develop biting ironies regarding the interactions of humans from reading Guy de Maupassant. In fact, D'Arcy's stories often highlight such ironies (Fisher 297).

"An April Folly" (1891) is a short story which first appeared in Argosy. In this story, the narrator is in love with Katherine, who tells him on April 1st (1890) that she doesn't "like" him. On hearing this, he retreats to the country, where he is charmed by Annie, the attractive daughter of the farmer in whose house he is living. The narrator thinks about marrying Annie, and he is therefore shocked when he learns that Annie is engaged to a young neighbor whom she has known all her life. In the meantime, Katherine tells the narrator that she actually dearly loves him, and had only been teasing when she had told him that she did not, so the narrator prepares to return to marry Katherine. Much of the comedy of "An April Folly" comes from the reader's seeing the disparities between the narrator's outward demeanor of calm and his stoicism as contrasted with the inner turmoil he must be feeling (Fisher 297).

"The Elegie" (1891) originally appeared in Blackwood's Edinburgh Magazine. It deals with the ironies that develop when the protagonist attempts an artistic life at the expense of his humanity (Fisher 297-298). "A Modern Incident" (1891) appeared in Argosy, and is about an ocean voyage, a shipwreck, and the aftermath of the shipwreck. Appropriately, the name of the First Mate is Fleet. The officer who is in charge of the commercial cargo is also appropriately named: "Tennyson Tupper bears names that hit satirically at two extremely influential Victorians, the Poet Laureate, Lord Tennyson, and Martin Farquar Tupper, another popular poet of the times." Tennyson Tupper's conversation is very much like that of both the poet Tupper and the poet Tennyson in its lofty platitudes about spiritualizing the conduct of everyday life, and also is much like the language of Tupper and Tennyson, in D'Arcy's view, in that it offers, "second-rate verse as a panacea for the world's trials." It is ironic that only Tupper and the stowaway survive the ship wreck, because these are the two characters that appear to be the least suited to survival (Fisher 298).

"Kensington Minor" (1893) appeared in Argosy, and is about a secretary who pretends that he is the master, and that his employer is his servant. This pretense is unmasked, and his hopes for a good marriage are frustrated (Fisher 297). "Kathleen, Maid of All Work" (1894) appeared in Good Words. This is one of the most cheerful of all of D'Arcy's short stories. It is about a strong-willed Irish girl who isn't very bright, who is propelled into a number of hilarious situations. Her vernacular dialect "intensifies the comic substance" in this story (Fisher 297).

In 1892, Blackwood Publishers in Scotland agreed to publish The Bishop's Dilemma (1898), and commented specifically on the fine humor in the piece. But, for some reason or other, D'Arcy decided to delay publication until 1898 (Fisher 296). The Bishop's Dilemma contains much mordant humor. In this book, the Catholic Bishop sends one of his priests, who goes by the name of Young Father Fayler, to a country chapel which is dominated by the elderly and bigoted Lady Welford. Young Father Fayler falls in love with Lady Welford's ward, Mary. About Young Father Fayler's name, and about the situation described above, Benjamin Fisher remarks that, "his name may be yet another of D'Arcy's well-chosen ironic transparencies. The cruel ironies that ruin the young lovers are balanced by comedy in the drunken antics of another priest with whom Fayler had earlier worked and who visits him in his country residence" (Fisher 299). Fisher notes that "Irremediable" (1894), which appeared in The Yellow Book contains a number of biting ironies as well (Fisher 299). There are also several bits of humor in "Poor Cousin Louis" (1894) which was published in The Yellow Book, in which Margo has sadistic tendencies for playing horrible jokes on a feeble and senile old man, thus bringing about his early death. "Her red hair and rampant sexuality mark her out as a devil figure" (Fisher 300).

"An Engagement" (1896), which also appeared in The Yellow Book, also contains a number of humorous bits, again related to Margo, Dr. Owen's sexually rampant mistress" who ruins his relationship with the young, pretty, and innocent Agnez Allez (Fisher 300). Finally, Benjamin Fisher believes that "The Pleasure-Pilgrim" is a satiric thrust both at Henry James, and at the "New Woman" figure that was so popular during this time (Fisher 301).

Ella D'Arcy Bibliography

Fisher, Benjamin F. "Ella D'Arcy." Encyclopedia of British Humorists, Volume I. Ed.
        Steven H. Gale. New York, NY: Garland, 1996, 296-302.

Allan Monkhouse (1858-1936)

Allan Monkhouse was the Manchester playwright who wrote The Education of Mr. Surrage (1912). Newell Sawyer describes Mr. Surrage as a wealthy widower who had retired to his country estate. Into this small and sedate world, Mr. Surrage's children bring a group of Bohemians who profoundly disturb Mr. Surrage's conventional views of life. Mr. Surrage is baffled, but he does try to understand his guests, and in the attempt he finds a stimulation that rejuvenates his mind (Sawyer 237).

Allan Monkhouse Bibliography

Sawyer, Newell W. "The Comedy of Manners from Sheridan to Maugham: The Study of
        the Type as a Dramatic Form and as a Social Document." Unpublished Ph.D.
        Dissertation. Philadelphia, PA: University of Pennsylvania, 1931.

Edith Nesbit (1858-1924)

As a child, Edith Nesbit was a hot-tempered and rebellious tomboy. She hated going to school, and she once declared that she had, "never been able to love a doll" (Moore 25). Doris Moore says that Nesbit, "had all the caprices, the little petulances, the sulks, the jealousies, the intolerances, the selfishnesses of a child; and with them went a child's freshness of vision, hunger for adventure, remorse for unkindness, quick sensibility, and reckless generosity" (Moore 208-209). Nesbit was Bohemian in appearance. She was quite untidy, and wore a loose and trailing kind of dress. Her arms were encircled by silver bangles, and she bobbed her abundant dark hair. At a time when it was only "fast women" who smoked, Nesbit always could be found with her tobacco and cigarette papers (Lurie 102).

Nesbit's books are not like other Victorian books. They take place in contemporary England and suggest socialist solutions to England's problems. They present a modern, not a Victorian, view of childhood. And they use magic, both as a comic device, and as a serious metaphor to represent the power of the imagination (Lurie 100). Nesbit feels that if any book is vivid enough, its contents will, "become real to us and invade our world for good or evil." Nesbit's "magic" is really "imagination," and this is what gives Nesbit's characters the power to journey through space and time (Lurie 111). And for Nesbit, comedy is the best ally of imagination (Lurie 112). At the ends of the journeys, in Nesbit's fairy tales, her kings and queens are comic bunglers, and her court officials are often two-faced frauds who use a sort of up-to-date smarmy political rhetoric (Lurie 106).

Edith Nesbit wrote many short stories, one of which is "The Cockatoucan" from Nine Unlikely Tales (1901), in which Nesbit explains why Matilda doesn't want to visit Great Aunt Willoughby:

> She would be asked about her lessons, and how many marks she had, and whether she had been a good girl. I can't think why grown-up people don't see how impertinent these questions are. Suppose you were to answer, "I'm top of my class, Auntie, thank you, and I'm very good. And now let's have a little talk about you. Aunt, dear, how much money have you got, and have you been scolding the servants again, or have you tried to be good and patient as a properly brought up aunt should be, eh, dear? (Nesbit Tales 7)

Nesbit's tone here is direct, humorous, and fast moving. Nesbit frequently blends comedy with metaphorical magic, and in "The Cockatoucan," "the laughter of a magical bird transforms everything and everyone, in the process revealing their true nature." For example, the unpleasant nursemaid, Pridmore, is changed into an "Automatic Nagging Machine." And the King of the country is exposed as a vulgar and undersized fraud (Lurie 113).

In Nesbit's short stories the serious, diffident, and well-behaved children that would be the heroes and heroines in most Victorian fairy tales, are portrayed as timid and dull (Lurie 104). In Nine Unlikely Tales is a story entitled "Fortanatus Rex & Co." in which Nesbit exhibits her Fabian point of view. For Nesbit, urbanization is always associated with capitalist greed, and the King in this story is one of the largest speculative builders in the world. The King and his speculators buy up all the beautiful woods and fields they can, and cut them all up into squares. They tear up the trees and the grass and build streets there and lamp-posts and ugly little yellow brick houses, hoping that people will come there to live, and sure enough, people do come there to live, and the King and his Company become rich. "It is curious that nearly all the great fortunes are made by turning beautiful things into ugly ones. Making beauty out of ugliness is very ill-paid work" (Nesbit Tales 205).

In Nesbit's stories about the Bastable Children, Nesbit presents herself as twins. She is both the morally courageous and determined Alice, and she is also her vulnerable brother Noel, who is subject to fits of poetry, fainting, and tears (Briggs 12). The Bastable stories are filled with wit, energy, and invention (Lurie 101). The Story of the Treasure Seekers (1899) is a lively, comic adventure of six London children who attempt to restore the family fortune, because their father's business partner got ill, and absconded with all of the firm's total assets. It is interesting to note that the same thing happened to Edith Nesbit. Her husband's partner had taken advantage of his illness to abscond with Edith and Hubert's money. The Bastable children are therefore placed into a position where they attempt to recoup the missing money. They sell patent medicine; they start a newspaper; they rescue an old gentleman from danger--in the form of their own pet dog; and they marry a princess (Lurie 104); all of these attempts prove to be comic disasters. According to proper Victorian standards, all of these children are behaving badly. They disobey their elders; they dig up gardens; they trespass; they play practical jokes. "But though they may be scolded and punished, they are always forgiven" (Lurie 105). The narrator is Oswald Bastable, a child who came out of the same mold as did Edith Nesbit herself. He is bold, quick-tempered, egotistic, and literary (Lurie 101).

Comedy and magic continue to be linked in The Wouldbegoods (1901), New Treasure Seekers (1904), and The Enchanted Castle (1907). The most striking incident in The Enchanted Castle is when Mabel and the other children decide to enact a play. Because there are only three grown-ups available to watch the play, they must construct an artificial audience out of old clothes, pillows, umbrellas, brooms, and hockey sticks (Lurie 113). They paint paper faces on the created bodies, and a magic ring brings all of these ungainly creatures to life, as they are transformed into grotesque caricatures of different types of adults the children know. Gerald calls these creatures the "Ugly-Wuglies," who finally become disenchanted and fall back into mere piles of clothes again (Lurie 114).

In Five Children and It (1902), the children have a number of wishes. First, they want to be "as beautiful as the day." Second, they want a sand pit filled with gold sovereigns. They also wish to be giants in size and strength, and wish to become adults. But each wish leads to an appropriate comic disaster. When they become beautiful, for example, their baby brother doesn't recognize them and bursts into howls of tears. In each case, the children are very much relieved at sunset when the spell cast by their wish comes to an end (Lurie 112).

The Queen of Babylon makes a rash wish that brings her to London in The Story of the Amulet (1906). In London, the Queen is shocked by the conditions of the working people. She tells the cab driver that she is appalled at how the slaves are treated in England. When the cab driver tells the Queen that these are not slaves, they're working people, she replies, "Of course they're working. That's what slaves are." Cyril, the cab driver, responds that they're not slaves because they can vote, at which point the Queen says, "What is this vote? Is it a charm? What can they do with it?" Cyril says, "I don't know. It's just a vote, that's all! They don't do anything particular with it," and the Queen concludes, "I see, a sort of a plaything" (Nesbit Amulet 196).

Nesbit tells fairy stories, but with a difference. In traditional fairy stories the princess is always the most beautiful, the prince is the bravest, and the witch is always the most wicked person in the land. For Nesbit reality was always creeping in, and whenever it did, the result was humor. Nesbit's The Magic World (1924) contains three fairy tales: "The Princess and the Hedge-Hog," "The Magician's Heart," and "Belinda and Bellamant" (Dorao 126).

"The Princess and the Hedge-Hog" is a Nesbit short story which opens with the dilemma of whom to invite to the christening of the daughter. If they invite the wicked fairies, these fairies would be in a position to cast a christening curse. If they don't invite the wicked fairies, they will be angry and will be even more likely to cast a christening curse. They decide not to invite the wicked fairies, but this means that the invitations have to be printed with invisible ink on the back of a baker's bill, and the guests have to go to the christening dressed as creditors. The Lord Chief Justice goes disguised as a shoemaker. "He still had his old blue brief-bag with him, and a brief-bag and a boot bag are very much alike." The Prime Minister went dressed as a tailor. "This required no change of dress and only a slight change of expression." The Lord High Admiral was not able to find butcher's clothing that was large enough, so parts of his uniform showed through his costume. His epaulette was peeping out, and the wicked fairy who was sitting at the palace back door, disguised as a dog, "started thinking that everything there was very strange," so she disguised herself as a toad, crept into a pipe and in that way entered the palace, just in time to give the baby a dreadful christening curse (Dorao 126).

The education of the princess in "The Princess and the Hedgehog" appears to be more appropriate for a boy than for a girl. She learns how to fence, how to ride, and how to shoot a crossbow, a long bow, pistols, rifles, and artillery. She also learns how to dive, and swim, and run, and jump, and box, and wrestle. Only a few princes go to the palace to ask for her hand, and these princes all turn away as soon as they find out how small her dowry is, "remembering suddenly something urgent they had to do in their own countries." The king's soldiers would not fight because their wages hadn't been paid for many years. The king loses his throne, and the princess goes to visit her aunt in a distant country. This country is so small that it doesn't have a Post Office, and the only person who will befriend her is the Baker's Boy who years before had delivered the invitations to her christening (Dorao 127). In the end the princess regains the throne, and the usurpers return to their former kingdom--by train--on Thursday (Dorao 128).

There is a wicked magician in "The Magician's Heart," who turns the royal baby into the most stupid prince in the world. This same magician turns the princess into the most ugly princess on the face of the earth. With the help of a powerful fairy, the King catches the wicked magician and has him locked up in an unaccessible tower. Because the wicked magician has no audience to see his tricks, he becomes bored. The magician's nurse visits him and suggests that he take on an apprentice so that he can have an audience, but the magician doesn't want anyone to learn his tricks. The nurse suggests that the Baker's Boy would make a fine apprentice because "he's completely stupid." The nurse asks the Baker's Boy if he wants to be apprenticed. When he says yes, she tells him to give the magician his money then. When he does this the magician is convinced that he is stupid enough to make a fine apprentice (Dorao 128). As the reader guesses, the Baker's Boy turns out to be the prince; he becomes no longer stupid; he marries the princess, who becomes no longer ugly. In order to get the evil out of the body of the wicked magician, he is turned into the, "babe in a plaid frock with the dearest little fat legs ever you see." Dorao suggests that these fairytales are based on traditional story-telling techniques, but in crucial places the traditions are left behind and more creative solutions are developed (Dorao 129).

Finally, there is the tale of "Belinda and Bellamant." A spell is cast on Princess Belinda which makes her more ugly each day that passes by--except on Sundays when she is seven times more beautiful than she had been on the previous Sunday. At first the king and queen thought they were seeing things. They thought it might be the light, or the curtains, or the color of her clothes, but they finally were able to figure out the nature of the curse. So on the bad days, the queen gave up putting frills and bows on the young princess's clothes, thinking that on these days it was better for her to wear plain clothes and a veil. But on Sundays, the princess was encouraged to wear her best frock, and a clean crown (Dorao 129). The queen suggested that maybe they could find a prince who would marry the princess on a Sunday, and not see her for the rest of the week, but the king thought that would be stretching it. Then the princess herself got the "Catalogue of Eligible Princes," a catalogue containing photos of princes who were of marriageable age, and also containing a little information about their incomes, hobbies, and favorite meals. On the bottom of the last page, in the corner, the princess found the photo of the most attractive prince she'd ever seen, and next to the picture was the following description: "Prince Bellamant, age 24. Wishes to find princess who doesn't object to a christening curse. Nature of curse only revealed in the strictest confidence. Good tempered. Comfortably off. Quiet habits. No relations." So the princess sent the prince a note saying that the christening curse wouldn't be a problem, and they set the wedding for the first Sunday in June (Dorao 130). But the prince absolutely refused to get married on that particular date. As it turned out, the christening curse over the prince caused him to appear very attractive during the week, but really ugly on Sundays. The only way that the prince's curse could be broken is if he could stay under water for five minutes. He had tried to do this many times, but had always failed. Since E. Nesbit's work is a parody, and since it has the benefit of a number of years of invention since the time that the fairy tale takes place, she offers the perfect solution. She produces a good magician, who is the godfather of the princess (note that in traditional fairy tales it would have been a fairy godmother rather than a godfather), and this godfather has a special talent for inventing things. He invents a diving bell (note that E. Nesbit was writing at the same time that H. G. Wells was publishing stories about journeys across time, etc.). And they lived happily ever after (Dorao 131).

In <u>Five of Us</u> (1925), Nesbit gives one of the many examples of her implicit feminism when in "The Last of the Dragons," the princess says, "Father, darling, couldn't we tie up one of the silly little princes for the dragon to look at--and then I could go and kill the dragon...? I fence much better than any of the princes we know" (172).

Edith Nesbit Bibliography

Briggs, Julia. A Woman of Passion: The Life of E. Nesbit. London, England: Century Hutchinson, 1987.

Dorao, Marisal. "E Nesbit's Smile (The Touch of Humour in Three Fairy Stories by E. Nesbit)." Literary and Linguistic Aspects of Humour. Barcelona, Spain: University of Barcelona Department of Languages, 1984, 125-132.

Lurie, Alison. "Modern Magic: E. Nesbit." Don't Tell the Grown-Ups: Subversive Children's Literature. Boston, MA: Little, Brown, 1990, 99-117.

Moore, Doris Langley. E. Nesbit: A Biography, Revised Edition. London, England: Ernest Benn, 1967.

Nesbit, Edith. The Magic World. London, England: Macmillan, 1924.

Nesbit, Edith. Nine Unlikely Tales. London, England: T. Fisher Unwin, 1901.

Nesbit, Edith. The Story of the Amulet. London, England: T. Fisher Unwin, 1906.

Edith Ann Oenone Somerville (1858-1949) IRELAND

Most of Edith Somerville's life was spent in Drishane, Castle Townshend, Ireland, her ancestral family home.   In her Irish Memories she tells about how she defied convention by studying art and music in Duesseldorf, Germany, and in Paris France in 1884 and 1885. "They said that Paris was the Scarlet woman embodied; they also said, 'The IDEA of letting a GIRL go to PARIS!' This they said incessantly in capital letters." But even though Somerville went to Paris, it was nevertheless something of a compromise, as she went with a bodyguard consisting of her mother, her eldest brother, a female cousin, and another girl (Woodall 1034).
See also Nilsen, Don L. F. "Edith Ann Somerville." Humor in Irish Literature: A Reference Guide. Westport, CT: Greenwood, 1996, 9, 11, 112-126, 154.

Edith Ann Oenone Somerville Bibliography

Cahalan, James M. " 'Humor with a Gender': Somerville and Ross and The Irish R.M." Éire-Ireland 28.3 (1993): 87-102.

Weekes, Ann Owens. "Somerville and Ross: Ignoble Tragedy." Irish Women Writers: An Uncharted Tradition. Lexington, KY: University Press of Kentucky, 1990, 60-82.

Woodall, Natalie Joy. "Edith Anna Oenone Somerville." Encyclopedia of British Humorists, Volume II. Ed. Steven H. Gale. New York, NY: Garland, 1996, 1034-1035.

Sir William Watson (1858-1935)

William Watson's satire is described by Previté-Orton as aloof and unworldly (Previté-Orton 230). Previté-Orton furthermore feels that Watson's major contributions to political satire have been in his assaults on the Sultan of Turkey during the Armenian massacres (Previté-Orton 231).

Sir William Watson Bibliography

Previté-Orton, C. W. "Algernon Swinburne." Political Satire in English Poetry. New York, NY: Russell and Russell, 1910, 226-229.

Sir Arthur Conan Doyle (1859-1930) SCOTLAND

In his writing style, Arthur Conan Doyle is a direct descendant of Edgar Allan Poe, and a contemporary of Robert Louis Stevenson, and like Poe and Stevenson, he is interested in the process of "doubling." "Watson and Holmes constitute one of the great pairs of literature, in the tradition of Sancho Panza and Don Quixote, Boswell and Johnson, Mr. Pickwick and Sam Weller. The conjunction of the tall, thin, angular man with the short, stocky, rotund companion usually serves as the visual equivalent of two contrasting but essentially harmonious temperaments" (Grella 92).

The name of Arthur Conan Doyle was derived from the name of "King Arthur," and the name of "Michael Conan," who was Arthur Conan Doyle's uncle. John Doyle, Arthur Conan Doyle's grandfather, was an artist and prominent political cartoonist of the Georgian and the early Victorian periods. Arthur Conan Doyle's uncle, Richard (Dickie) Doyle, became a leading artist for Punch (Grella 80), and in fact designed the famous cover which appeared on each issue for 100 years. Arthur Conan Doyle enjoyed reading Sir Walter Scott's historical novels, especially Ivanhoe, and he wanted to emulate the chivalry of Scott's works in his own writing. His characters, therefore, tend to have such knightly traits as courage, nobility, fairness, courtesy, respect for women, and a flair for protection of the poor (J. Randolph Cox 116).

For a short while, Arthur Conan Doyle was a friend of Harry Houdini, who at the time was specializing in exposing fraudulent spiritual mediums. Doyle was in favor of Houdini's exposés, because he felt that the spiritualist movement was constantly being compromised by charlatans. The friendship between Houdini and Doyle ended abruptly, however, when Jean Doyle told Houdini that she had communicated with his dead mother and had seen her wearing a crucifix. Houdini was insulted because both he and his mother were Jewish (Helfand 111).

In 1884, Doyle had an article entitled "J. Habakuk Jephson's Statement" accepted for publication in Cornhill Magazine. But the Advocate General of Gibraltar took Doyle's story to be factual, and sent telegrams to various major newspapers denouncing the story as "a fabrication." He followed this up with a written report to the government. Doyle, of course, considered this response to be a "triumph of his art" and this is what caused him to devote more of his time to writing fiction and less time to his medical practice (Helfand 99).

Arthur Conan Doyle was never very successful as a physician. During his first year in Southsea, Doyle declared on his income-tax form that he owed no taxes since he had earned only 154 English pounds sterling. The form was returned to Doyle with the comment, "Most unsatisfactory." Doyle returned the form the Internal Revue Service with the comment, "I entirely agree" (Grella 81). In Memories and Adventures (1924), Arthur Conan Doyle tells about his study of medicine at Edinburgh University (which began in 1876). One of his professors was a tall, hawknosed Scotsman by the name of Joseph Bell. Dr. Joseph Bell was a skilled surgeon who could not only diagnosis diseases, but also could diagnose a person's character or occupation. "Although he was sometimes incorrect, usually the results were dramatic and accurate. He could look at a former soldier, not long discharged, and tell him what regiment he had served in and where he had been stationed" (J. Randolph Cox 116). What made Bell's pronouncements so dramatic was not so much his empirical method of explanation, but that the conclusions were made before the explanations were given (Helfand 103). Dr. Bell was the model on which the character of

Sherlock Holmes was later to be formed (Grella 81). Michael Hardwick concurs that the character of Sherlock Holmes was modeled after Joseph Bell. Doyle was a clerk in Joseph Bell's ward, and a clerk's duties were to bring all the patients together and make a note of all the patients seen; there would often be seventy to eighty patients in a group. When everything was ready, Doyle would show the patients to Dr. Bell, who would have the students gather round him. Doyle notes, "His intuitive powers were simply marvelous;" and then he continues, "Another case would come forward. 'Cobbler, I see.' Then he would turn to the students, and point out to them the inside of the knee of the man's trousers was worn. That was where the man had rested the lapstone--a peculiarity found only in cobblers!" (Hardwick 73). In "The Boscombe Valley Mystery," Sherlock Holmes states, "You know my method. It is founded upon the observance of trifles" (Fromkin and Rodman 302).

The Adventures of Sherlock Holmes were written as a satire of events that were happening in London at the time. Jack the Ripper had been committing his London crimes only a few months when Doyle started to write these stories. Don Cox makes the connection:

> The bloody crimes of Jack the Ripper galvanized London [against crime], making the public aware of brutality in the streets and the need for efficient police work. The relatively ineffective actions of Scotland Yard one usually finds in the Holmes stories, in fact, may simply reflect what the public felt was all too true. Conversely, the ability of Holmes to foil every criminal made him the very figure that a crime-conscious England was seeking. (Don Cox 34)

Watson often teases the reader with hints of stories he and Holmes will shortly be investigating--stories about "the shocking affair of the Dutch steamship, Friesland," and about the "giant rat of Sumatra," and about "the notorious canary-trainer." Watson will say nothing more about these upcoming and intriguing adventures, because "the world is not yet prepared to hear" (Carlson 113). Richard Carlson is intrigued by the fact that Doyle writes the character of Sherlock Holmes as a sleuth who maintains a cocaine habit and an aversion to women. When Holmes himself is confronted by this question, his simple response is "imprecise thinkers" (Carlson 115).

English understatement is an important feature of Doyle's writing. When he is introduced to a man in "The Norwood Builder," Holmes responds, "You mentioned your name as if I should recognize it, but beyond the obvious facts that you are a bachelor, a solicitor, a Freemason, and an asthmatic, I know nothing whatever about you" (Fromkin and Rodman 187). In his English Humour, John Priestly says that irony, absurdity, reality, and affection are all qualities that add to humor, and Lucee Seiter says that Doyle is a "true humorist" in that he mixes irony, absurdity, reality, and affection to embody his character, Sherlock Holmes (Seiter 5).

There is quite a bit of anecdotal evidence that supports the suggestion that the Sherlock Holmes stories had an influence on real-life crime detection; however the claim that the French police, the Sureté named its crime laboratories in Lyons after the detective, and the story that the Egyptian police used the Sherlock Holmes stories as a sort of textbook in crime detection are both unsupported, and are probably apocryphal (J. Randolph Cox 118).

Some Sherlock Holmes readers claim that he was a real man, and they refuse to acknowledge that Arthur Conan Doyle exists. Some say that Doyle was Sherlock Holmes. Arthur Conan Doyle did receive many letters asking for help in personal matters, and to this very day the London Post Office still receives mail addressed to Sherlock Holmes, 221 Baker Street (Seiter 1).

Arthur Conan Doyle inherited a number of important elements from Edgar Allan

Poe as he reinvented the modern form of the detective story. Like Poe, Doyle's detective stories were in the Gothic tradition, but Doyle added his own special charm, wit, and energy (Grella 79). In 1886 Doyle began writing down ideas, names, and fragmentary bits of dialogue and description for a short story entitled "A Tangled Skein." The story was originally narrated by Ormond Sacker, who, like Doyle himself, was a doctor. "Originally he was named Ormond Sacker, but Conan Doyle changed this to John H. Watson. His detective also underwent a name change from first draft to finished work, becoming Sherlock--instead of Sherrinford--Holmes" (Grella 82). Ormond Sacker had lived in Afghanistan, and now lived at 221B Upper Baker Street. Sacker was to have had a friend by the name of I. Sherrinford Holmes. But these notes are in Doyle's handwriting, and there was no period after the letter "I." J. Randolph Cox asks whether Doyle merely forgot to include the period, or whether he intended the letter to stand for the first-person-singular pronoun, "I" (J. Randolph Cox 117-118). The name of Sherlock Holmes is probably derived from the name of an American author, "Oliver Wendell Holmes," and from the name "Sherlock," a sportsman whom Arthur Conan Doyle bowled against in various cricket matches (J. Randolph Cox 118).

Sherlock Holmes was a brilliant rationalist (Grella 92), but paradoxically, he was also afflicted by chronic melancholia. He had the mind of a scientist, but the soul of an artist. He was a strict logician who could deduce a life history from a hat, a pipe, and a watch, but he also dulled the harsh pain of reality by taking cocaine. Although he said that he despised the "softer emotions," he would lose himself for hours playing his beloved Stradivarius violin. There was thus an uneasy tension for Holmes between appearance and reality, and this is the type of double vision that pervades Doyle's fiction, and is firmly based in the Victorian mentality (Grella 93).

There are many humorous concepts in the Sherlock Holmes series. These humorous concepts include a league of red-headed men, a lovers' rendez-vous at the gasfitters' ball, Sherlock Holmes's comment in "The Man with the Twisted Lip" that what makes Watson such an invaluable companion is his "gift of silence," and the quest for the Blue Carbuncle lost in the crop of a goose (J. Randolph Cox 121). There are also references to other cases that have a humorous ring to them, cases like that of Wilson, the notorious canary trainer, or that of the Giant Rat of Sumatra ("for which the world is not yet prepared"), or the affair of the aluminum crutch, or allusions to "the politician," "the lighthouse," and "the trained cormorant" that are "dropped teasingly into the texts of stories." These allusions, "are tantalizing in their puckish humor and effective in the way they suggest a greater dimension to the career of the detective; there is a world beyond the confines of the present case" (J. Randolph Cox 123).

Sherlock Holmes's "deductive reasoning" (which is actually inductive reasoning) is used both for humorous effect, and to advance the story line. In "The Red-Headed League," Holmes surveys Jabez Wilson and concludes in an offhanded way that "he can deduce nothing beyond the fact that the man has done manual labor, takes snuff, is a Freemason, has been to China, and has done a lot of writing lately" (J. Randolph Cox 123). There are actually two stories in A Study in Scarlet (1887)(J. Randolph Cox 118). One of these stories is about a detective's investigation of a murder, and the other story is a detailed explanation of the family history, and the events that led up to the murder (J. Randolph Cox 119). It is in A Study in Scarlet that Sherlock Holmes and Watson first meet. To Watson's amazement, Holmes proposes that Watson has been in Afghanistan. Holmes and Watson decide to share rooms at Mrs. Hudson's establishment at 221B Baker Street. Watson learns that Holmes is the world's first "unofficial consulting detective," and Holmes and Watson share their first case when Holmes is called on by Inspector Lestrade and Inspector Gregson of Scotland Yard. They tell Holmes that a dead man has been found in an abandoned house, and that the dead man has no wounds on his body. They also tell

Holmes that a message has been left on the wall--written in blood (Grella 82).

The Sign of the Four (1890) is the second Sherlock Holmes novel. It is a story about an aboriginal dwarf, a stolen treasure, and murder by poison darts. At the end of the novel there is a thrilling chase down the Thames, after which Watson becomes engaged to marry Holmes's client; Scotland Yard has received the credit for having solved the crime; and Holmes turns to his cocaine bottle for solace (Grella 82).

When Arthur Conan Doyle completed the manuscript for The White Company (1891), "he was so elated that he threw his pen across the room, splashing the wall with ink, as he shouted, 'That's done it!'" (J. Randolph Cox 119). By November of 1891, Arthur Conan Doyle had become convinced that the character of Sherlock Holmes was keeping him in a rut as a writer, so he decided that he would have to kill off his detective. When his mother heard about his plan, she was horrified, "You won't!" she said. "You can't! You mustn't?" It was because of his mother's plea that Holmes's life was saved at this time (J. Randolph Cox 121). In the Gothic tradition, Sherlock Holmes is characterized as an eccentric, secretive, hero, but he is also a man of action who lives by the rules of chivalry. Nevertheless, Holmes is constantly putting Watson down. In "A Case of Identity" (1891), for example, Holmes gives the following left-handed compliment to Watson: "'Pon my word, Watson, you are coming along wonderfully. You have really done very well indeed. It is true that you have missed everything of importance, but you have hit upon the method" (Helfand 103).

The Adventures of Sherlock Holmes (1892) is a collection of twelve Sherlock Holmes short stories. Arthur Conan Doyle must have been aware that his short stories contain many of the basic devices that are fundamental to detective literature, and a case could be made that he was parodying his own genre. The obviously guilty person is usually found to be innocent, as in "The Boscombe Valley Mystery." If one of the characters is "too good to be true," this is a character to watch out for, as in "The Adventure of the Beryl Coronet." And of course there is the frequent clue that is to be found on a scrap of paper clutched in the dead man's hand, as in "The Reigate Squire." The characters also have imaginatively appropriate names, such as Dr. Grimesby Roylott, Charles Augustus Milverton, Flosmer Angel, Bartholomew Sholto, Professor James Moriarty, and Colonel Sebastian Moran. The name often communicates how the reader should feel toward the character, with the most villainous characters often having the most ornate and splendid names (J. Randolph Cox 123). Another dramatic device which Doyle used was understatement. In "The Adventure of Silver Blaze" (1892), for example, one of the key clues is not something, but is rather the absence of something--the absence of a dog's bark (Helfand 103).

In 1893, Arthur and Louise Conan Doyle travelled to Switzerland because they thought it would be good for Louise's tuberculosis. During this trip, Arthur Conan Doyle not only introduced skiing to the Swiss [he had learned to ski in Norway], but he also saw that Reichenbach Falls would be a good place for him to have Sherlock Holmes killed, thus allowing him to get on with his other writing. Sherlock Holmes and Professor James Moriarty went over Reichenbach Falls locked in mortal combat. As George Grella record the event,

> The plunge of Sherlock Holmes and the evil Professor Moriarty ("the Napoleon of crime"), locked in mortal combat, into the Reichenbach brought a tremendous outburst of public mourning for the sleuth. More than 20,000 readers canceled their subscriptions to the Strand; Conan Doyle received an avalanche of hate mail; and City businessmen went to their offices wearing black crepe around their top hats. (Grella 85)

Dr. Watson closed his casebook with a paraphrase of Plato's description of the death of Socrates, calling Holmes a person, "whom I shall ever regard as the best and wisest man whom I have ever known" (J. Randolph Cox 123). Sherlock Holmes's death was recorded in a story entitled "The Final Problem" (1893), and letters were sent to Holmes, to Watson, and to Doyle, offering to keep house for Watson when he retired. Years later, an organization was formed which called itself the Baker Street Irregulars. It is still functioning, and is dedicated to carrying on the pretense of Holmes's actual existence (Helfand 102).

In 1893, Arthur Conan Doyle wrote a comic opera entitled, Jane Annie; or, The Good Conduct Prize. In 1893 Doyle also wrote "Silver Blaze," a story in which Holmes makes his famous remark about "the curious incident of the dog in the nighttime." Someone responded, "The dog did nothing in the night-time," and Holmes replies, "That was the curious incident" (Grella 84). In 1893, Doyle also began writing a series of comic tails about the exploits of Etienne Gerard, a French colonel in the Napoleonic Wars (Helfand 102). And Gerard's activities were later expanded in The Exploits of Brigadier Gerard (1896). Gerard is a comic buffoon who boasts about his bravery, and his military and amorous successes in the exciting stories he tells. Sometimes he engages in "absurdly brave pranks." He fills the British reader with patriotic emotions as by representation of their image of the stereotypical French soldier. Etienne Gerard was one of Doyle's most popular characters, and he was based on a real-life French soldier by the name of General Baron de Marbot, who was heroic, comical, swaggering, and boastful (Grella 85). Gerard continues his escapades in Adventures of Gerard (1903) (Helfand 103). Brigadier Gerard is a strange blend of chivalrous heroics and comic high jinks, and this mixture appeals to British readers who have ambivalent feelings about the French. They would admire his bravery, but his overly amorous "French" nature also made him appear foolish to the British reader (Helfand 104).

Round the Red Lamp: Being Facts and Fancies of Medical Life (1894) is a collection of stories about doctors. The stories vary greatly in tone; some are comic, and others are starkly realistic. "A Straggler of '15" is considered by Michael Helfand to be, "sentimental, but is saved from mawkishness by the comic grotesque behavior of the old soldier" (Helfand 104). In Round the Red Lamp there are also stories about comic misunderstandings, and, "tales dwelling on the unlimited possibilities for strangeness in a post-Darwinian world." "The Los Amigos Fiasco" is a comic fantasy about the attempt to electrocute a man. Instead of killing him, however, the electricity makes him so strong that later attempts to execute him by hanging and shooting prove no match for his acquired strength (Helfand 105).

In The Hound of the Baskervilles (1902), a newspaper reports that Sir Charles Baskerville died of natural causes, but Dr. Mortimer notes that these are the "public facts," as he puts away the folded newspaper clipping. Dr. Mortimer is aware that there were a number of suspicious circumstances associated with the case. Mortimer then goes on to disclose the "private facts," based on his own observations. He ends his account with what J. Randolph Cox calls, "one of the most memorably chilling lines in all of literature," ranking with Robinson Crusoe's discovery of a footprint on an otherwise uninhabited island. He had seen traces around the body of Sir Charles, traces that no one else had observed: "Mr. Holmes, they were the footprints of a gigantic hound" (J. Randolph Cox 126).

Although The Hound of the Baskervilles was published in 1902, it was set in 1886, before Holmes's death in Reichenbach Falls in 1891. As in other Doyle novels, The Hound of the Baskervilles employs a Gothic setting, an inexplicable crime, a disguised hero, a bungling Watson, and an unusual villain. It is Dr. James Mortimer who comes to Baker Street and tells the legend of a ghostly demon-dog that is somehow linked to the recent mysterious death of Sir Charles Baskerville on his estate. Mortimer appeals to Holmes to protect Sir Charles's nephew, the heir to the estate. Holmes says that he is too busy right now to take on the case, but he will send Watson to Devonshire to perform the investigation. There are a number of suspicious events, and suspicious characters that appear on the sinister landscape of the moor. By letting Watson carry on the lion's share of the inquiry, Doyle builds the suspense, which climaxes with Holmes's unexpected appearance, in the nick of time to rescue the young heir, and unmask the villain (Grella 87). When Holmes and Watson get back to their home at Baker Street, Holmes recapitulates the intricate plot designed to illegally seize the Baskerville inheritance (Grella 88).

In 1894, Doyle was under great pressure to write more Sherlock Holmes mysteries. He realized that he had provided no witnesses to the death plunge of Holmes and Moriarty into Reichenbach Falls, and he further realized that Holmes's and Moriarty's bodies had never been found, so Doyle started a new series of stories with "The Adventure of the Empty House" (1894). In this story, Holmes reappears after an absence of three years. The period between Holmes's death and his reemergence is known to Holmes scholars as "The Great Hiatus." Holmes tells Watson that he had never fallen into the Reichenbach at all, but had decided that he had reasons for wanting the world to think that he was dead. In the meantime, Watson's wife has died, so now Holmes and Watson can move back in together in their old residence at 221B Baker Street. Many critics feel that the Sherlock Holmes stories were not the same after the Reichenbach fall as they had been before. One Cornish boatman said to Doyle, "I think, sir, that when Holmes fell over that cliff he may not have killed himself, but he was never quite the same man afterward." It is true that Doyle wrote some weak stories after the Reichenbach incident, but many critics feel that some of his best stories were also written after this time, stories like "The Adventure of the Dancing Men" (1903), "The Adventure of the Devil's Foot" (1910), and The Valley of Fear (1914) (Grella 88).

In 1911, Conan Doyle took Jean as a passenger as he competed in an Anglo-German automobile race around England and Germany. The British team won, and the Doyles went to Denmark for Conan Doyle's brother Innes's wedding to a Danish woman. At the reception Innes was forced to make a speech, and to prove that he was thoroughly an Englishman, his speech in its entirety was, "Well...I say, don't you know! By Jove! What!" (Grella 89).

The Lost World (1912) is a story about Professor George Edward Challenger, who discovers a lost race of dinosaurs that exist in the twentieth century on a plateau in South America. The Lost World was originally published serially in the Strand, and was illustrated with photos of himself made up as Professor Challenger. Doyle was so proud of his disguise that he drove thirty miles in costume to meet with E. W. Hornung, the husband of his sister Connie, the creator of a "gentleman burglar" named Raffles. He talked with Hornung for several minutes before Hornung realized that he was the butt of a joke (J. Randolph Cox 129). In his autobiography, Arthur Conan Doyle wrote about an incident that may have inspired the writing of The Lost World. In the waters near Aegina in Greece, Doyle and his wife saw, "a creature which has never, so far as I know, been described by Science. It was exactly like a young ichthyosaurus, about 4 feet long, with thin neck and tail." When he discovered that two years later an admiral had seen a similar creature, Doyle remarked that, "this old world has got some surprises for us yet" (Helfand 108). It is worth noting that The Lost World has been made into a motion picture about a fantastic journey to a remote region, where the historic past becomes the present (Grella 93).

In 1913, Doyle wrote an article for the Fortnightly Review entitled "Great Britain and the Next War" which was about a possible war between England and Germany. In this article, Doyle argued that the major German weapons in this war would be submarines and airships. In this same article Doyle strongly argued for the construction of a tunnel to be built under the English Channel. The British military ignored Doyle's warnings because they did not believe that the Germans would sink nonmilitary ships. The British navy did, however, take up Doyle's suggestion to create inflatable life preservers (Helfand 110).

The Valley of Fear (1915) contains a great deal of what J. Randolph Cox calls "puckish humor" (J. Randolph Cox 130). Some of Doyle's science fiction stories are comic. "The Great Keinplatz Experiment" (1923), for example, describes a farcical confusion that results when the personalities of a professor and his student are exchanged by a machine which the professor has invented (Helfand 109).

The Maracot Deep and Other Stories (1929) is a book of short stories, two of which are about Professor George Edward Challenger. These two stories are entitled "The Disintegration Machine" and "When the World Screamed" and both had appeared earlier in the Strand Magazine. Both of these stories show Professor Challenger to be a humorous, brash, bullish, and likeable person. In "When the World Screamed," Challenger shoots an iron dart into the nerve ganglion of old Mother Earth. Old Mother Earth howls with pain, anger, and menace, "and the outraged majesty of Nature all blended into one hideous shriek." This is nature's defense against such intrusions as that imposed by Challenger, but Michael Helfand asks, "Is the story a joke, an attempt to show the absurdity of Challenger's ego?" and then Helfand answers his own question, "Perhaps" (Helfand 111). The last two stories in The Maracot Deep and Other Stories also demonstrate that Arthur Conan Doyle's puckish humor is still intact (J. Randolph Cox 131).

During the last decade of his life, Arthur Conan Doyle became an ardent propagandist in favor of spiritualism. Because of his Celtic background, it was easy for him to believe in fairies and goblins, and he inserted his beliefs into his stories. In The Land of Mist (1926), Professor Challenger is skeptical at first, but is converted into believing in communication with the dead. Nevertheless, Doyle never made Sherlock Holmes a believer in spiritualism, not even in "The Adventure of Shoscombe Old Place" (1927), the last Holmes story Doyle ever wrote. In fact, in "The Adventure of the Sussex Vampire" (1924), Holmes says, "This Agency stands flat-footed upon the ground, and there it must remain. The world is big enough for us. No ghosts need apply" (Grella 92).

In 1925 P. G. Wodehouse wrote a letter to W. H. Townsend about Arthur Conan Doyle: "I'm having lunch with Conan Doyle. Conan Doyle, a few words on the subject of. Don't you find as you age-in-the-wood, as we both are doing, that the tragedy of life is that your early heroes lose their glamour? Now with Doyle, I don't have this feeling. I still revere his work as much as ever. I used to think it swell, and I still think it swell" (Carlson 112).

On July 7, 1930, Arthur Conan Doyle died and he was buried on his estate in Windlesham. The inscription on his headstone reads "Steel True, Blade Straight." In 1912, Ronald Knox had written a satire entitled "Studies in the Literature of Sherlock Holmes," in which he commented on "the higher criticism as applied to the Bible." At the time he had to invent titles and authors for the "learned publications" he had invented. "Today, so many of the same topics have been the subject of real publications that no writer need invent sources to cite" (J. Randolph Cox 132).

A few years after his death, Sherlock Holmes, the character which Doyle had created, took on an immortality which may be unequaled in literary history. In his "The Bowling Green" column of the Saturday Review of Literature, Christopher Morley proposed an organization of the followers of Sherlock Holmes to be called the "Baker Street Irregulars." The society was formed to study the sixty stories of Arthur Conan Doyle that had come to be called the "Sacred Writings." "In emulation of other learned societies and in a spirit of fun, the members began to exchange notes and write 'scholarly' papers concerning the minutiae of the stories. Eventually these 'scholarly' activities came to form a sort of satire on the world of academic research" (J. Randolph Cox 131).

At about this same time, 1933, Vincent Starrett, a Chicago critic, novelist, and short-story writer, published a book entitled The Private Life of Sherlock Holmes, which was a loving tribute to Arthur Conan Doyle. This book further intensified the growing interest in having fun with the character of this great detective. Since 1934 there has been an annual dinner in New York City on or near January 6th, which Christopher Morley had established as the birth date of Sherlock Holmes, who had by then come to be known as "the Master." Scholarly papers are presented at this convention, which is designed to be as much as possible like annual conferences of scholars in any other discipline (J. Randolph Cox 132). The joke became more and more elaborate when Edgar W. Smith, an executive for General Motors, began collecting material about Sherlock Holmes. He published his collection entitled Profile by Gaslight in 1944, and two years later, he founded and edited a quarterly journal devoted to the study of Sherlock Holmes entitled The Baker Street Journal (J. Randolph Cox 131).

Sir Arthur Conan Doyle Bibliography

Carlson, Richard S. "Benign Humor and Escape Literature: Wodehouse, Doyle, and Sayers." The Benign Humorists. New York, NY: Archon, 1975, 111-123.

Cox, Don Richard. Arthur Conan Doyle. New York, NY: Frederick Ungar, 1985.

Cox, J. Randolph. "Sir Arthur Conan Doyle." Dictionary of Literary Biography, Volume 70: British Mystery Writers, 1860-1919. Eds. Bernard Benstock and Thomas F. Staley. Detroit, MI: Gale (1989), 112-134.

Fleissner, Robert F. "Sherlock Holmes and Shakespeare's Second Most Famous Soliloquy: The Adventure of Hamlet's Polluted Flesh." Thalia: Studies in Literary Humor 10.1 (1989): 43-47.

Fromkin, Victoria, and Robert Rodman. Introduction to Language. Third Edition. New York, NY: Holt, Rinehart and Winston, 1983.

Grella, George. "Sir Arthur Conan Doyle." Dictionary of Literary Biography, Volume 18: Victorian Novelists After 1885. Eds. Ira B. Nadel and William E. Fredeman. Detroit, MI: Gale, 1983, 77-94.

Hardwick, Michael. The Complete Guide to Sherlock Holmes. New York, NY: St. Martin's, 1986.

Helfand, Michael S. "Sir Arthur Conan Doyle." Dictionary of Literary Biography, Volume 156: British Short-Fiction Writers, 1880-1914: The Romantic Tradition. Detroit, MI: Gale. Ed. William F. Naufftus, 1996, 94-113.

Knox, Ronald A. "Studies in the Literature of Sherlock Holmes." Blue Book 1 (1912): 111-132.

Priestly, John Boynton. English Humour. New York, NY: Stein and Day, 1976.

Rosenberg, Samuel. Naked is the Best Disguise: The Death and Resurrection of Sherlock Holmes. New York, NY: Bobbs-Merrill, 1974.

Seiter, Lucee. "Humor and Wit in Sherlock Holmes." Unpublished Paper. Tempe, AZ: Arizona State University, 1989.

Kenneth Grahame (1859-1932) SCOTLAND

Pagan Papers (1893), Kenneth Grahame's personal essays, represent the first stage of his writing. The Golden Age (1895), and Dream Days (1898), Grahame's stories, represent the second stage of his writing. And The Wind in the Willows (1908), a beast fable and a mock-epic novel, represents the third and most mature stage of his writing. The language in Pagan Papers is that of upper class, late Victorian England. It includes Latin and Greek tags, frequent allusions to classical literature, and an incessant use of puns. These reflections and personal essays demonstrate the "gentle humor of a sensitive writer" (Mellown 459). Pagan Papers is filled with anecdotes and humorous reminiscences of the childhood experiences of five brothers and sisters--Edward, Harold, Charlotte, Selina, and "the unnamed narrator" (Mellown 460).

In The Golden Age (1895), Grahame considers the childhood world of imagination to be equal in value to the adult world of reality. In fact, Grahame uses his gentle wit and humor to persuade the reader that "it may even be more valuable" (Mellown 460). In Dream Days (1899), there is a story entitled "The Reluctant Dragon" in which Grahame retells in modern form the story of St. George and the dragon. "While an obvious example of Victorian whimsy, the story also has satiric intentions, with national and cultural ideals being the subject of the author's humor" (Mellown 461).

Richard Carlson classifies Kenneth Grahame as a teller of fantastic beast fables. adding that Grahame created one of the classic pieces in the genre of benign humor entitled, The Wind and the Willows (1908). Grahame's story is filled with "fabulously human beasts" who live in what Carlson calls the "netherland" (Carlson 63). Grahame's major characters are four--Toad, Water Rat, Mole, and Badger. These "fur people" have human qualities. Toad, the central character, is brusque, vain, and boisterous. He enjoys stealing automobiles, which he drives with, "admirable abandon into walls and onto front lawns." In The Wind and the Willows, Toad is sentenced to jail after one such crack up, but Toad escapes from jail and "with Homeric determination, he finds his way, like Ulysses, across incident-filled lands" until he arrives back home at Toad Hall. In the meantime, some ferrets, weasels, and squirrels have taken over Toad Hall. So Toad enlists the help of his friends, Water Rat, Mole, and Badger to join him in a display of swaggering "bluff bravado" and "military acumen" to recapture Toad Hall (Carlson 64).

According to Alison Lurie, Toad in The Wind and the Willows is more than foolish, rash, or boastful; he is, "incorrigibly criminal--a kind of Edwardian upper-class juvenile delinquent, with a passion for flashy clothes and fast cars" (Lurie 8). As a secretary for the Bank of England, Grahame lived a quiet and respectable life, but Lurie suggests that he identified with Toad, the snatcher of a motor car, the prisonbreaker, "the Toad who always escapes" (Lurie 9).

In a sense, The Wind and the Willows is a comedy of manners in that the animals have a social structure which clearly reflects a human class system. Badger is upper-upper class; Toad is upper class; Rat and Mole are Middle Class; and the ferrets and weasels are lower class. Their class is established by social presentability, the quantity and quality of their rhetoric, and their leadership capabilities (Carlson 67). The Wind and the Willows is also realistic in that the animals suffer cuts and bruises, and they fall prey to brittle egos and personality faults. There is much infighting between and among Toad, Mole, Rat, and Badger, but at the same time they realize that the fighting only helps them to love each other better (Carlson 67).

There are various themes which emerge throughout Grahame's writing. One of these has to do with the despoiling of the environment; another is a yearning for the halcyon delights of a "golden past"; still another is the efficacy of remaining loyal in a rigid class system. Another recurring theme is the Homeric struggle (Carlson 64). Grahame was pained whenever he saw man ruining the environment, and in The Wind and the Willows Grahame is gently but surely chiding those who leave, "brambles and tree roots behind them, confusedly heaped and tangled" (Carlson 67).

Grahame's writing is filled with sensuous and tactile pleasures, as Grahame specializes in allowing the reader to hear, see, and smell the story.

Willows is replete with "crackling-fresh" grass and "dewy-sweet" gardens.

In addition, the book is fragrant with food. Smell is everywhere as "...she carried a tray with a cup of fragrant tea steaming on it; and a plate piled-up with very hot, buttered toast, cut thick, very brown on both sides, with the butter running through the holes in it in great golden drops."
In a passage such as this, Carlson suggests that, "the reader feels tempted to chew on its sound" (Carlson 65).

The visual imagery is just as intense. The Wind and the Willows tells about a, "'hummocky' pastoral land spread in 'purple loose-strife where the willow herb is...tender and wistful,' and 'where pink clouds and sunsets' go hand in hand with 'amber jerkins,' 'shepherd boys,' and 'nymphs.' "

> Stores...are visible everywhere...piles of apples, turnips, and potatoes, baskets full of nuts and jars of honey; but the two little white beds on the remainder of the floor looked soft and inviting and the linen on them, though coarse was clean and smelt beautifully of lavender, and the Mole and the Water Rat, shaking off their garments in some thirty seconds, tumbled in between the sheets in great joy and contentment. (qtd in Carlson 65)

Grahame's fantasy woods lack any real fear or terror. The homes of the animals are small and dear, and they are set in holes along river banks and in sides of snow banks and they have solid doors with iron bell-pulls hanging next to small brass plates on which the animals' initials are engraved. Grahame's humor comes from, "the emotion and flow of a sudden discovery of descriptive prose," what Carlson calls the "epiphany." An example involves Mole, standing in the road with, "his heart torn asunder, and a big sob gathering...leaping up...in passionate escape." Carlson describes The Wind and the Willows as both "ecstatic and melancholy," as both "mystical and real," as both "sweet and aching," as both "innocent and knowing." Carlson feels that such contradictions, or paradoxes, make the book "difficult to get at" but they also add much to the humorous or unorthodox perspective (Carlson 66).

Grahame provided some significant insights into the nature of nature, and what is especially ironic is the environment in which Grahame did this extremely sensual writing. As mentioned before, Grahame was the Secretary of the Bank of England, and he often indulged his imagination while on the job. Some of his friends once asked him why he wanted to "get mixed up with beauty" (Carlson 67).

Many critics have denegrated "light literature"; however, Toad could tell these critics a thing or two, if only they could "grow tails and sport fur."

> And then they heard the angels tell,
> Who were the first to cry Nowell?"
> Animals all, as it befell,
> In the stable where they did dwell!
> Joy shall be their's in the morning! (Carlson 68)

While most critics consider The Wind in the Willows to be a beast fable, Elgin Mellown says that it is much more than this. It is a mock-epic allegorical saga, in which much of the charm of the piece comes from Grahame's "unique blend of anthropomorphism and naturalism." The novel can be divided into twelve units equivalent to the twelve units that are often found in the classical epic. Furthermore, Chapters 1 and 7 of The Wind in the Willows resemble the invocations at the beginning and at the middle of the classical epic. Mellown notes that although the animals have engaging personalities, they do not have personal names, because Grahame doesn't want readers to think of a single animal that would be limited in time and space. Rather he wants the reader to think of, "creatures from the world outside the boundaries of time who, having escaped individuality, have also escaped mortality." But Mellown further notes that The Wind in the Willows is not a true epic; rather it is the epic turned upside down, the mock epic (Mellown 461).

Mellown suggests that The Wind in the Willows has elements of farce, such as Toad and his motor car; tragedy, such as the references to the deaths of small animals in traps; pathos, such as Mole's longings for his home; and satire, such as Toad's experiences in the law courts. These elements would all be consistent with the mock-epic reading. There are also stylistic incongruities that are necessary to the mock epic, incongruities in which serious and important matters are treated with nonchalance, and trivial and minor matters are treated with very inflated language. Furthermore, Toad epitomizes the mock-epic hero. Toad is denigrated by being disguised as a washerwoman and humiliated by being hurled overboard by the barge-woman: "The water...proved quite cold enough for his taste, though its chill was not sufficient to quell his proud spirit, or slake the heat of his furious temper." These adjectives would be appropriate for an "epic hero in a moment of triumph" (Mellown 462).

Also consistent with the mock-epic reading are the numerous parodies that can be found throughout The Wind in the Willows. These parodies range in length from sentence-long echoes of classical or traditional pieces to almost entire chapters. When Rat and Mole are lost in the Wild Wood, Mole becomes Dr. Watson, and Rat becomes Sherlock Holmes. When Mole cuts his shin in the snow he proclaims, "It's a very clean cut," and Rat examines the cut carefully and adds, "That was never done by a branch or a stump. Looks as if it was made by a sharp edge of something in metal. Funny!" This observation causes him to search for and find the door-scraper; and this leads to the door-mat, and finally to the brass plate beside the door that says, "MR. BADGER." Just as Watson would have done for Holmes, Mole comments on Rat's methods of detection: "I see it all now! You argued it out, step by step, in that wise head of yours, from the very moment that I fell and cut my shin, and you looked at the cut, and at once your majestic mind said to itself, 'Door-scraper!'" As another example of an extended parody, Mellown points to the retaking of Toad Hall in the final chapter of The Wind in the Willows. This chapter is appropriately entitled, "The Return of Ulysses" (Mellown 462).

Peter Green says that Grahame's "inner purpose throughout [The Wind in the Willows] was threefold: to satirize contemporary society, to sublimate his personal life, and to construct an ideal model of the Good Life" (141). Mellown notes that Grahame's satire is not just political satire, but includes personal satire as well. Many of Grahame's contemporaries could easily see that Toad's imprisonment was an allusion to Oscar Wilde's imprisonment, and that the Sea Rat was a symbol for his bohemian existence (Mellown 463). All of the creatures in The Wind in the Willows are symbolic.

> Rat is the artist who sublimates his longings in the act of artistic creation; Toad is the unrepressed, boisterous child still living in the man; Badger is the ideal, strong male, the archetypal father-figure who is at once both longed for and feared; Otter is the loving father, who is also the clever provider. Together they might be considered to form Grahame's ideal male figure. (Mellown 464).

Kenneth Grahame Bibliography

Carlson, Richard S. "Kenneth Grahame's The Wind in the Willows." The Benign Humorists. New York, NY: Archon, 1975, 63-78.

Green, Peter Morris. Kenneth Grahame, 1859-1932: A Study of His Life, Work, and Times. New York, NY: World, 1959.

Lurie, Alison. "Kenneth Graham." Don't Tell the Grown-Ups: Subversive Children's Literature. Boston, MA: Little, Brown, 1990.

Mellown, Elgin W. "Kenneth Grahame." Encyclopedia of British Humorists, Volume I. Ed. Steven H. Gale. New York, NY: Garland, 1996, 458-464.

Alfred Edward Housman (1859-1936)

In Housman's Poems, John Bayley comments on the way that Housman mingles the "weighty" and "the deadpan" throughout his poetry (Bayley 15). Benjamin Fisher suggests that Housman's "The Shades of Night Were Falling Fast," "Fragment of a Greek Tragedy," and "Purple William or, The Liar's Doom" are typical of Housman's poetry in that this poetry is deliberately light, comic, and parodic in tone (Fisher 547). In his A. E. Housman: Collected Poems and Selected Prose, Christopher Ricks says that since Housman wrote such nonsense verse during most of his life he should be classified with such late nineteenth-century nonsense poets as Edward Lear, Lewis Carroll, C. S. Calverley, and W. S. Gilbert. Housman's poetry exhibits a playful intention, a razor wit, and is satirically directed at the deficiencies in the work of other scholars (Fisher 547).

A Shropshire Lad (1896) contains a number of different types of humor, as the,"ironies sound from first to last among the sixty-three poems." According to Benjamin Fisher, Housman's, "vision encompasses oscillations between comic and tragic aspects of life." Number V is a typical representation of Housman's understated poetic humor that dramatizes the encounter between a would-be seducer and this would-be seducer's mistress (Fisher 547). Comic undercurrents are to be found throughout A Shropshire Lad. Innuendo and exquisite wordplay are evident in No IX of A Shropshire Lad, and are also especially effective in Number VI of Last Poems (1922). There are many incongruities in A Shropshire Lad that form the foundation for humor. In Number LXII, we read, "Terence, this is stupid stuff." In Number LXII, Terence, the poet, is taunted by his friend, who suggests that Terence could find relief, and could write better poetry if he were to indulge in "worldly pleasures." Terence responds that his poetry expresses his preparations to confront the "saddening events that life brings," and he concludes by retelling the story of King Mithridates (Fisher 548), who incessantly ingested small amounts of poison to keep from being poisoned. Thus Terence answers a would-be humorist with an astringent irony (Fisher 549).

In Last Poems (1922), Housman writes, "Half the night he longed to die." This statement, "may insinuate his urgent sexual desires or fantasies, however, especially since the stanza, after the comment that there are daytime pleasures to distract him, concludes 'Ere he longs to die again,' and since the final stanza reveals that during the past night the scornful girl has been sleeping with someone else" (Fisher 548).

Alfred Edward Housman Bibliography

Bayley, John. Housman's Poems. Oxford, England: Clarendon, 1992.
Fisher, Benjamin F. IV. "A. E. Housman." Encyclopedia of British Humorists, Volume I. Ed. Steven H. Gale. New York, NY: Garland, 1996, 546-550.
Ricks, Christopher. A. E. Housman: Collected Poems and Selected Prose. Englewood Cliffs, NJ: Prentice-Hall, 1968.

Jerome Klapka Jerome (1859-1927)

Jerome K. Jerome was the leading figure in the "New Humor" that developed during the 1880s and 1890s. His popularity is a direct result of his early humorous books, and his editorships of The Idler, and To-Day. His comic novel Three Men in a Boat is a classic. Because Jerome's humor differed so markedly from the norms of Victorian humor, it earned the label of "New Humor" (Hall 574). Much of Victorian humor was playful mockery of institutions such as the Courts of Chancery, or of individuals. Marriage, family life, men's clubs, the pretentious ineffectuality of the House of Lords, the self-serving qualities of lawyers and politicians and the bumblings of various admirals and generals were also targets of mockery and satire. Jerome's humor dealt with domestic matters, as he used slang and vernacular language to write about everyday middle-class life. His humor very much appealed to the growing anti-Victorianism of the 1880s and 1890s (Hall 575).

During Jerome's time, the letters that were written to The Times symbolized Victorian earnestness and high-mindedness, and Jerome was therefore determined to have a letter printed in The Times that showed his irreverence and iconoclasm. At that time there was a debate going on about the propriety of displaying paintings of nude figures at the Royal Academy's Summer Exhibition, so Jerome had The Times publish the following for him:

> Sir--I quite agree with your correspondent, "A British Matron," that the human form is a disgrace to decency, and that it ought never to be seen in its natural state. But, "A British Matron" does not go far enough, in my humble judgement. She censures the painters who merely copy Nature. It is God Almighty who is to blame in this matter for having created such an indelicate object. (Hall 575)

Jerome signs the letter as follows, "I am, Sir, your obedient servant, Jerome K. Jerome." In this way, Jerome is able to deconstruct the high moral outrage of "A British Matron." As Peter Hall states, "This kind of facile mocking of Victorian values and pretentiousness is endemic in the 'New Humor.' From the perspective of Jerome's contemporary reviewers, who were steeped in traditional Victorian humor, this material was not only considered unfunny but it was also seen as a sign of a poor, narrow, and decidedly vulgar approach to life" (Hall 575).

The name of "Jerome K. Jerome" sounds just too perfect to be a real name, but John Batts assures us that it is neither a nom-de-plume, nor a pseudonym. Since Jerome Klapka Jerome's father was named Jerome Clapp Jerome, his mother called him "Luther" to avoid confusion. Batts says that Jerome K. Jerome's persistent use of humor is born out of an upbringing in which he was constantly surrounded by failure. In his autobiography, he is bitter in recalling how his manuscripts were constantly being turned down:

> With appalling monotony [the scripts] had been returned to me again and again: sometimes with the Editor's compliments and thanks, and sometimes without: sometimes returned with indecent haste, seemingly by the next post; sometimes kept for months--in a dustbin, judging by appearances. My heart would turn to lead whenever the dismal little slavey would knock at the door and enter with them.... I shunned the postman when I saw him in the street, feeling sure he knew my shame. (Batts 57)

Jerome's first humorous series of essays was entitled, On the Stage--And Off (1885) was an immediate success. It is subtitled The Brief Career of a Would-be Actor, and is based on Jerome's acting experiences in London and with stock companies touring England in the late 1870s. The essays are colloquial and friendly. The stories contain a blend of broad realism and satire much in the style of the picaresque novel. The structure is basically episodic as Jerome's various ambitions, misadventures, and disappointments are recounted. Most of the humor derives from Jerome's ironic deflation of his own pretensions. He creates a genuine pathos by faithfully recording the little incidents of jealousy, and grief, and the sacrifices that have to be made among second-rate, but earnest, actors (Hall 575).

On the Stage--And Off was followed by The Idle Thoughts of an Idle Fellow, (1886) a second series of humorous essays (fourteen of them) that first appeared serially in Home Chimes in 1886. Algernon Swinburne considered these essays to be "fresh and joyous." Jerome dedicates Idle Thoughts to "a very dear and well-beloved friend," whom the reader soon discovers to be his pipe. This is typical of the air of irreverence of self-deprecating wit, and of mock-philistinism that pervades the book and that is so identifiable as the "New Humor" (Hall 576).

Woodbarrow Farm: A Comedy in Three Acts (1888) is a comedy targeting and satirizing the same stock characters and stage devices that Jerome mocks in the essays of Stage-Land (1889), Jerome's third series of humorous essays. These essays had originally appeared serially in The Playgoer magazine in 1886. In virtually all of these essays, failure was a constant theme. Usually things start to go wrong, and then they gain momentum as they go from bad to worse. In Stage-Land, the term "hero" takes on an ironic meaning. He views a hero as someone who is not able to take care of himself for even a day, someone upon whom "troubles shower with persistence." He is always hanging around, getting into trouble, and being accused of crimes he didn't commit. He sometimes muddles things up with a corpse in some complicated way, so as to be mistaken for the murderer (Batts 58).

Stage-Land is a gentle satire that targets the stock characters and shopworn devices of Victorian melodrama. The comic-satiric device which Jerome uses to make his point is his innocently refusing to separate the stage from reality. Jerome's "Stage Villain," for example, "wears a clean collar, and smokes a cigarette; that is how we know he is a villain.... It is well that the rule does not hold off the stage, or good men might be misjudged. We ourselves, for instance, wear a clean collar--sometimes." Stage-Land is beautifully illustrated by Bernard Partridge, who later became an important illustrator for Punch (Hall 576).

Jerome's typical heroine in Stage-Land and elsewhere is equally surrounded by failure. She sees the many woes around her, and she weeps a good deal. The heroine's husband is either sentenced to prison on their wedding morning, or remains to make their marriage into some sort of a failure. The heroine's father is normally a financial failure, or has heart failure, or both. The heroine's child is often chronically ill, and lingers only to die. Her brother is also a failure, and is sometimes mistaken to be her lover. The narrator advises the stage heroine to dump the hero, marry the villain, and go and live abroad (Batts 58).   Jerome thought he was writing a serious travel book when he began The Three Men in a Boat--To Say Nothing of the Dog (1889). Jerome tells about the writing process as this book is developing:

> There was to be "humourous relief"; but the book was to have been "The Story of the Thames," its scenery and history.... About the "humorous relief" I had no difficulty. I decided to write the "humorous relief" first--to get it off my chest, so to speak. After which in a sober frame of mind, I could tackle the scenery and history. I never got there. It seemed to be all "humorous relief." (Batts 58)

There are three characters in this story, and one of the characters is the narrator. He is called "J", which is actually "Jerome" in thin disguise. Three Men in a Boat is a series of escapades involving the difficulties of rowing a boat upstream, major embarrassments in the locks, problems with tow lines, and with other boats, and general ineptitude in trying to get their act together. They have brought with them clothes they don't need, and they have left behind utensils that are essential. Even a simple task like putting up a canvas awning over the boat on their first night proves to be an epic struggle:

> We took up the hoops, and began to drop them into the sockets placed for them. You would not imagine this to be dangerous work; but, looking back now, the wonder to me is that any of us are alive to tell the tale. They were not hoops, they were demons. First they would not fit into their sockets at all, and we had to jump on them, and kick them, and hammer at them with

the boathook; and, when they were in, it turned out that they were the wrong hoops for those particular sockets, and they had to come out again. But they would not come out, until two of us had gone and struggled with them for five minutes, when they would jump up suddenly, and try to throw us into the water and drown us. (Batts 57)

The humor of Three Men in a Boat comes from the true-to-life quality of the misadventures. It also comes from a "thoroughly anthropomorphized dog named Montmorency." The narrator, "J," gives the reader Montmorency's innermost thoughts and opinions about the events, and some of the most amusing episodes are about Montmorency's preoccupation with chasing rats or fighting with cats. Jerome uses a combination of overstatement and understatement to develop the satire (Hall 576).

The Diary of a Pilgrimage (1891) is a utopian satire. The late Victorians were very fond of writing utopian literature. It was during this period that Samuel Butler wrote Erewhon, and William Morris wrote News from Nowhere, and America's Edward Bellamy wrote Looking Backwards. Jerome is therefore poking fun at these late-Victorians in "The New Utopia" (Hall 577).

Jerome enjoyed writing about trios of men. A decade after writing Three Men in a Boat he wrote Three Men on the Bummel (1900), and Three Men on Wheels (1900). Three Men on the Bummel and Three Men on Wheels are about the same three men of Three Men in a Boat on a bicycling tour of Germany, but the men are older and more settled. Again the humor sparkles in what Peter Hall calls a "very shrewd analysis of various facets of turn-of-the-century German society" (Hall 577). Batts notes that the book was not very popular with readers--except for those in Germany (Batts 57).

New Lamps for Old: A Farcical Comedy in Three Acts (1890) and The MacHaggis: A Farce in Three Acts (1896) are written in the tradition of the "New Humor," but they also contain some conventional forms of late-Victorian farce. Jerome's Social Comedies include Miss Hobbs: A Comedy in Four Acts (1902), which addresses the question of the role of the "New Woman" in late-Victorian society, The Prude's Progress: A Comedy in Three Acts (1895), which is a comedy of manners, Fanny and the Servant Problem (1909) which is concerned with English class-consciousness, The Master of Mrs. Chilvers: An Improbable Comedy (1911), which has a plot rooted in the Suffragist movement, and The Celebrity (1926), which is a comedy exposing the pretentiousness and the hypocrisy of the social reformers from the upper classes (Hall 577).

Exaggeration is an important aspect of Jerome's writing. Another important aspect is the endowment of human traits to inanimate objects. There is also much linguistic humor in terms of verbal infelicities, and one-liners (Batts 57).

Jerome Klapka Jerome Bibliography

Batts, John Stuart. "The Comedy of Failure: J. K. Jerome." WHIMSY 3 (1985): 57-59.
Hall, Peter C." Encyclopedia of British Humorists, Volume I. Ed. Steven H. Gale. New York, NY: Garland, 1996, 573-579.
Hutchenson, Robert, Ed. The Humorous World of Jerome K. Jerome. New York, NY: Dover, 1962.
Paton, George E. C. " 'Cruising Down the River': Jerome K. Jerome's Three Men in a Boat and the Victorian Comic Novel." Le Fleuve et Ses Métamorphoses. Paris, France: Didier Érudition, 1992, 459-466.

James Matthew Barrie (1860-1937) SCOTLAND

Because James Barrie used dialects, provincialisms, and gentle irony to present a sentimental view of Scotland, he came to be classed with the Kailyard (cabbage-patch) writers (Athey 86). James Barrie had a brilliant older brother by the name of David. The Barrie parents clearly favored David, and Mrs. Barrie was determined that David would attend Edinburgh University, and become a famous minister, which, according to Alison Lurie, was, "the highest reward on earth any mother could hope for" (Lurie 119). But on the day before his fourteenth birthday, David was killed in a skating accident. On hearing the news, his mother took to bed, and stayed there for a solid year. Jamie's older sister, who was now the mother of the family, told Jamie to go to his mother and tell her that she still had another boy, so he decided to do that. He went into the dark room and when he heard the door shut he was afraid. He stood still for a while. Finally he heard a listless voice ask, "Is that you?" Jamie thought it was the dead boy she was speaking to, and he said in a small and lonely voice, "No, it's no' him; it's just me." At this point, James felt an intense desire to "take the place of his dead brother," to become so much like him that even his mother would not be able to see the difference, and he promised her that, "he too would be a famous man, and make her as proud as David would have done. At this point, Jamie became David, and he remained David exactly as he had been on the day he died" (Lurie 120). Because of a glandular deficiency which very well may have been psychological in origin, James Barrie as an adult remained just over five feet in height, the height of a child. In addition, he was extremely slight and youthful in appearance. He was thin and had a small voice. "In photographs taken during his twenties and early thirties he looks like a thirteen-year-old wearing a false mustache" (Lurie 121). Just as David would have done if he had lived, James graduated from Edinburgh University (in 1883), and became successful (first as a journalist and essayist and later as an author) (Lurie 121). Harry M. Geduld says that in Peter Pan, the scene in which Wendy reattaches Peter's shadow is symbolic of the fact that James Barrie wanted Margaret Ogilvy to "fuse her dead and her living son" (Lurie 129). Margaret Ogilvy (1896), by the way, is an autobiographical sketch of Barrie's early life; it is also a panegyric that Barrie wrote to his mother (Athey 86).

Tommy and Grizel (1890), and Sentimental Tommy (1896) are both subtly autobiographical novels. In them, Tommy Sandys is a boy who cannot grow up. The narrator of these two books is James Barrie's other self, the coolly ironic London journalist. "Tommy is an inspired liar and fantasist for whom the world of his imagination is realer than the drab, untidy one he lives in" (Lurie 122). In these two works, the emphasis was on loss, pain, and deception; later in Peter Pan, the emphasis would change to pleasure and discovery. Sentimental Tommy was written at a time that James Barrie was going through a failed marriage. Peter Pan was written during one of the longest and most intense personal relationships of Barrie's adult life (Lurie 124).

In 1897, the small and childlike James Barrie would walk Porthos, his large and adult Saint Bernard dog, through Kensington Gardens. "The tiny man and the huge dog made friends with two little boys, George and Jack Davies, then aged five and four, who were playing in the park, accompanied by their nurse and baby brother." James met the Davies boys on many occasions, and played fun games with the boys as he told them exciting stories (Lurie 124). During holiday time in 1901 the Davies family decided to rent a country cottage on Black Lake in Surrey. The cottage they rented was very close to the Barrie's cottage, so that for six weeks they saw each other almost every day. During that summer, James Barrie was forty-one, but he nevertheless looked more like an adolescent boy than a grown man, and he was often taken to be one of the Davies boys. To the Davies boys, James came across as a "wonderfully clever older brother," who could lead them in exciting games of invention and discovery in the woods and on the shores of the lakes. These games involved pirates, indians, shipwrecks, and desert islands. James recorded these adventures with his camera, and after the holidays were over he made two copies of a photograph album entitled <u>The Boy Castaways of Black Lake Island</u>. The photo album had imaginary chapter headings and adventurous captions like, "We prepared for the pirates by making spears and other trusty weapons." James kept one of these copies for himself, and gave the other copy to Arthur Davies, the father of the Davies boys. In Freudian fashion, Arthur soon left his copy on a train, and it was never recovered (Lurie 125). Another sadness is that the Davies children, unlike James Barrie, did grow older, and as they did they began to find Barrie's games and his jokes embarrassing and to resent his presence in the household (Lurie 132).

Barrie's comic masterpiece, and his best work of social commentary, was <u>The Admirable Crichton</u> (1902). In this work he satirized the master-servant relationship, a relationship which Conan Doyle had questioned earlier. Barrie poses a situation where a king and a servant are stranded on an island. In such a case, Barrie asks the question of who would be the ruler. In <u>The Admirable Crichton</u>, Lord Loam, his daughter Lady Mary, and his son Ernest are shipwrecked on an island with their servants Crichton and Tweeny. Since it is nature who makes decisions in such cases, Crichton becomes the "Gov" within two short years (Althey 86).

James Barrie started writing <u>Peter Pan</u> in 1903, but didn't publish all five acts of the play until 1928. <u>Peter Pan</u> was originally written as a pantomime. "A pantomime had several stock characters: a young hero and heroine, the Principal Boy and Principal Girl, both always played by young actresses; the Good Fairy (and sometimes a Bad Fairy as well); the principal villain, or Demon King; and the Dame, an old woman portrayed by a male comic in drag" (Lurie 126). In writing <u>Peter Pan</u>, Barrie followed the pattern of the pantomime in all details. The role of Peter Pan is always given to a young woman in tights, and this is the Principal Boy of the pantomime. Wendy is the Principal Girl. Captain Hook is the Demon King. And Nana, the dog-nurse (usually played by a man) is the Dame. Tinker Bell is both the Good Fairy and the Bad Fairy. She has a loving and protective attitude toward Peter, but she is murderously jealous of Wendy. In the tradition of the pantomime, there is also a transformation scene. In <u>Peter Pan</u> this is the flight to Never-Never Land, when the walls of the nursery set melt away into the wings. Also in the tradition of the pantomime, which follows the earlier tradition of the old mystery and morality plays, the villains all enter from stage left, and the good characters all enter from stage right. There is one scene which gave James Barrie a great deal of apprehension not only on opening night, but during many later performances as well. This is the scene in which Tinker Bell is dying, and Peter calls on everyone in the audience who believes in fairies to save her life by clapping their hands. Barrie used to pace nervously at the back of the auditorium, waiting to see if the audience would answer Peter's appeal (Lurie 127).

<u>Peter Pan</u> is a five-act play that, "delightfully demonstrates Barrie's grasp of a child's sense of humor and fair play." Peter Pan, with his wood sword, tights, and mask, is clearly in the tradition of the harlequin. In a 1913 production of <u>Peter Pan</u>, it was Noel Coward who played the title role. For children, the penalty must fit the crime, as when Mr. Darling does penance in Nana's dog house, or as when Hook explains, "Pan flung my arm to a crocodile that happened to be passing by." In <u>Peter Pan</u>, Hook may be a pirate, but he is a very courteous pirate. When he prods his victims along the plank, he always says, "Sorry." He has a Thesaurus in his cabin, and is a pretty good performer on the flute. So he is not totally evil. In fact, in one adventure of murder and mayhem he exclaims, "Split my infinitives, but 'tis my hour of triumph!"

Time, which is the enemy of Hook, is signalled by the ticking clock in the crocodile's stomach. But Time is the enemy not only of Hook; he is the enemy of us all. The crocodile that follows Captain Hook has swallowed not only Hook's right hand, but it has swallowed a clock as well, and Alison Lurie considers this to be, "one of the wittiest and most sinister symbols ever created," because Time is chasing in an attempt to devour all of us, and this is especially frightening to people who are trying to cling onto their lost childhood. Lurie suggests that in <u>Peter Pan</u>, James Barrie is not only represented by Peter; he is represented by Captain Hook as well. Peter Pan is a rival of Captain Hook because they both want to have possession of Wendy. But neither Peter Pan nor Captain Hook wants Wendy as a lover. Captain Hook, like Peter Pan, wants to kidnap Wendy so that he and the other pirates can have a mother (Lurie 130). As further evidence that the character of Captain Hook is one of James Barrie's alter egos, she notes that Hook, like Barrie, loved cigars. In one sense, then, Peter Pan and Captain Hook are opposites, but in another sense, they are "two sides of the same coin." "The whole play is an elaborate dream fulfillment of intense but contradictory childhood wishes--to be grown up at once and never to be grown up; to have exciting adventures and be perfectly safe; to escape from your mother and have her always at hand." But one side has to win: "When the clock stops, Hook is outfought and devoured, after which Peter assumes Hook's role, cigar, hat, and hook" (Lurie 131).

Part of the reason that children in the audience are so glad when Peter Pan slays Hook is that the same actor who plays Mr. Darling also plays Hook. This gives the action something of an Oedipal shape. At one point in the play Wendy kneels at the kennel and tells Mr. Darling that Nana is crying. Mr. Darling responds, "Coddle her; nobody coddles me. Oh dear no. I am only the bread-winner; why should I be coddled? Why, why, why?" After quoting from this scene Alison Lurie remarks, "That is what you get for leaving people's precious photograph albums in trains" (Lurie 129).

"Peter Pan" has entered the English language as a symbol for the boy who refuses to grow up. The name is a reincarnation of the Greek god Pan, ironically an important symbol of fertility during late Victorian and Edwardian times. Pan was the spirit of the woods who, "embodied natural energy and sexual passion. He was represented as a man with goat's legs, and pointed ears, and he played music on a reed pipe" (Lurie 128). Joel Athey says that Peter Pan imagery is a very important aspect of contemporary American life, so important in fact that in Steven Spielberg's movie <u>E.T.</u>, the bedtime story that inspires the children to save E.T. is the episode from <u>Peter Pan</u> in which the boys have to believe in Tinkerbell in order to save her life (Athey 87).

After he had written <u>Peter Pan</u>, James Barrie developed a severe pain and case of writer's cramp in his right hand and arm, in what Alison Lurie considers to be an "uncanny imitation of Captain Hook." But Barrie had an unusual strength of will, and with great difficulty, he trained himself to write with his left hand, and it was with his left hand that he wrote <u>Mary Rose</u> (1920). Barrie remarked that his affliction had made him into two authors, since <u>Mary Rose</u>, written with the left hand, "was more sinister" (Dunbar 326). Mary Rose is the only child of a timid and silly English couple who love her so much that they can't bear to have her grow up. In many ways, <u>Mary Rose</u> is a darker version of <u>Peter Pan</u>. It is about a boy lost on an enchanted island. There are temporarily bereaved parents, and there are children who never grow up. But the mood of the play is melancholy, weird, and sometimes frightening rather than being joyous (Lurie 133).

James Matthew Barrie Bibliography

Athey, Joel. "James Matthew Barrie." <u>Encyclopedia of British Humorists, Volume I</u>. Ed.
    Steven H. Gale. New York, NY: Garland, 1996, 85-89.
Dunbar, Janet. <u>J. M. Barrie: The Man Behind the Image</u>. Boston, MA: Houghton, Mifflin,
    1970.
Lurie, Alison. "The Boy Who Couldn't Grow Up: James Barrie." <u>Don't Tell the Grown-
    Ups: Subversive Children's Literature</u>. Boston, MA: Little, Brown, 1990, 118-135.

Douglas Hyde (1860-1949) IRELAND

See Nilsen, Don L. F. "Douglas Hyde." Humor in Irish Literature: A Reference Guide. Westport, CT: Greenwood, 1996, 4, 112.

Patrick Joseph McCall (1861-1919) IRELAND

See Nilsen, Don L. F. "Patrick Joseph McCall." Humor in Irish Literature: A Reference Guide. Westport, CT: Greenwood, 1996, 112.

Owen Seaman (1861-1936)

Owen Seaman was a devoted editor of Punch and a prolific writer of light verse. Many critics dismiss him as being ultra-conservative and dull, but he often had a kind of natural exuberance that triumphed over his puritanical and snobbish upbringing, and according to John Adlard, he "produced a good deal of work that is pure delight" (Adlard 916). Archibald Philip (1847-1929), 5th Earl of Rosebery, who declared himself to be charmed, was the target of the satire in Tillers of the Sand (1895) C. L. Hind considered "A Ballad of a Bun," which was published in The World on March 13, 1895, to have "confirmed Owen Seaman's career as a parodist." It is a parody of John Davidson's "Ballad of a Nun." The Battle of the Bays (1896) was another successful volume of parodies (Ablard 925). In 1908, the Times Literary Supplement saw Owen Seaman as, "a kindly uncle of middle age, ready with a smile at his own weakness, and a good humoured laugh at the follies which his shrewd eye detects in his nephews and nieces" (Adlard 926).

Owen Seaman Bibliography

Adlard, John. "Owen Seaman." Encyclopedia of British Humorists, Volume II. Ed. Steven H. Gale. New York, NY: Garland, 1996, 924-926.

Violet Florence Martin (1862-1915) IRELAND

Sir Patrick Coghill says that both Edith Ann Somerville and Martin Ross (Violet Martin) "had a blazing sense of humour, the golden gift of sympathetic conversation and cast-iron memories" (Coghill 56). Coghill tells about a humorous dog name Maria in "The House of Fahy." "The House of Fahy" is hilarious because it is filled with so many incongruities. Not only does this story tell about Maria, the retriever, but it also tells about a shipwreck, an insane asylum, and an aggressive cockatoo. Maria is constantly fighting to get into the house, and when Sinclair and Philippa board a yacht to go on a weekend holiday, Maria decides to join them and swims to the ship. Philippa allows Maria to board the ship, against the protestations of Yeates, who says at this point, "the element of fatality had already begun to work." The second "element of fatality" was when everyone aboard ship, including Maria, become seasick. The next "element of fatality" is when the yacht runs aground in the dark, and begins to sink. This forces all of the passengers, including Maria, to abandon ship and look for a new shelter. The next "element of fatality" is when the only shelter they can find is a local insane asylum. It is soon discovered that Mrs. Buck, one of the inmates, owns a nasty cockatoo that attacks the intruding passengers, causing them to flee to another room. Still another "element of fatality" occurs the next morning when Maria is found holding the corpse of the cockatoo between her paws. After this, Maria buries the bird in the garden for a while, and this sets up the final "element of fatality" which occurs when the passengers are trying to make their escape back to the ship, and are overtaken by Maria, with the dead cockatoo in her mouth (Coghill 56).

Through Connemara in a Governess Cart (1893) is a collection of articles that first appeared in The Ladies' Pictorial. Typical of the humor of Through Connemara in a Governess Cart is when the narrator says, "I'd be ashamed to show such weather to a Connemara pig," and then adds, "Now Connemara is a sore subject with my second cousin, who lives within sight of its mountains" (Woodall 1035). The second cousin then says, "Well, let's go to Connemara!" so they go on a trip through Connemara that has not only its share of adventures, but also has stubborn horses and mules, and aggressive beggar women who are said to be cousins of Ross, and of "mad dogs" (Woodall 1036).

Major Sinclair Yeates is the protagonist in Some Experiences of an Irish R.M. (1899). Yeates is an Irish Royal Magistrate who, "describes with droll humor the people, animals, and events with which he comes into contact in his official capacity as royal magistrate and leader...of the local social set." Since he is a member of the gentry, Yeates is automatically an avid hunter. But he encounters disasters on most of his hunts, and most of these disasters are directly related to his "tongue-in-cheek aplomb." Yeates describes one of his typical episodes, this one being a duck hunting expedition. "I had left Mrs. Brickley's house a well-equipped sportsman, creditably escorted by Peter Cadogan and the widower. I returned to it a muddy and dripping outcast, attended by two little girls, two goats, and her own eight ducks whom my hand had widowed" (Woodall 1036).

The character of Philippa Yeates provides even more humorous opportunities for Somerville and Ross. Consider, for example, the time when Philippa evicts her houseguests and enthusiastically welcomes the chimney-sweep, Cantillon, who has treated her with great respect and dignity, in "Harrington's." "My poor friends," she says, "this means a cold luncheon for you and a still colder reception for me from Mrs. Cadogan [the housekeeper], but if I let Cantillon escape me now, I may never see him again--which is unthinkable." Thus, Philippa Yeates treats the chimney-sweep with exaggerated courtesy and at the same time humorously points out the importance of chimney sweeps in nineteenth-century Ireland, where fireplaces are so important in both the heating and the cooking for the family. Thus, "Philippa's reception of Cantillon must have been duplicated many times over with similar fervor throughout the countryside" (Woodall 1037).

In Irish Memories (1917), Martin describes her mother's "common sense," by telling how she solved the problem of what to give an elderly servant for Christmas. Her mother suggested, "Give her a nice shroud: There's nothing in the world she'd like as well as that" (Martin Irish Memories 89). On the subject of aunts, Martin tells about a woman who was asked the question of which she loved best, her husband or her son. She replied without hesitation, "Me son of course! Why wouldn't I love me own son better than a strange man!" (Woodall 1038).

See also Nilsen, Don L. F. "Violet Florence Martin." Humor in Irish Literature: A Reference Guide. Westport, CT: Greenwood, 1996, 9, 11, 112-116, 154.

Violet Florence Martin Bibliography

Cahalan, James M. " 'Humor with a Gender': Somerville and Ross and The Irish R.M." Éire-Ireland 28.3 (1993): 87-102.
Coghill, Sir Patrick. "Somerville and Ross." Hermathena 79 (1952), 47-60.
Martin, Violet Florence. Irish Memories. London, England: Green, 1917.
Woodall, Natalie Joy. "Violet Florence Martin." Encyclopedia of British Humorists:

Geoffrey Chaucer to John Cleese, Volume 2: L-W. New York, NY: Garland, 1996, 1035-1041.

Oliver Herford (1863-1935)

In Oliver Herford's A Child's Primer of Natural History can be found such humorous poems as the following:
>Children, behold the Chimpanzee:
>>He sits on the ancestral tree
>>From which we sprang in ages gone.
>I'm glad we sprang: had we held on,
>We might, for aught that I can say,
>Be horrid Chimpanzees to-day. (Fromkin and Rodman 353)

Oliver Herford Bibliography

Fromkin, Victoria and Robert Rodman. Introduction to Language. Third Edition. New York, NY: Holt, Rinehart and Winston, 1983.

Anthony Hope (1863-1933)

In The Dolly Dialogues (1894), the small talk of Lady Mickleham and Mr. Samuel Carter is often elliptical and somewhat trivial, as they comment on the concerns of London society. Lady Mickleham is a flirtatious society lady who is known to her friends as Dolly. Dolly thinks that it is bourgeois for a person to go to the theater with her husband if there is some other gentleman who is available (Hall 544). The Dolly Dialogues became so well-known in England that parodies of them in Punch were easily recognized. The Dolly Dialogues contains much banter and delicate wit in the conversations that Mr. Carter has with Lady Mickleham, and these conversations also expose many facts about the traditions and behaviors of late-Victorian society (Hall 545). When The Prisoner of Zenda (1894) appeared, it was praised by many critics for its "snap and humor." The hero is a suave, nonchalant, and urbane English gentleman who is both witty and irreverent (Hall 545). Anthony Hope also wrote Comedies of Courtship (1896).

Anthony Hope Bibliography

Hall, Peter C. "Anthony Hope." Encyclopedia of British Humorists, Volume I. Ed. Steven H. Gale. New York, NY: Garland, 1996, 543-546.

William Wymark Jacobs (1863-1943)

John Cloys categorizes W. W. Jacobs with Barry Pain and Jerome K. Jerome as one of the "New Humorists," who were noted for their use of vernacular and their lower-class subject matter. Jacobs is skilled at developing the plot reversal, so that in the end the reader receives the opposite of what is expected (Cloy 565). In an article entitled, "The Humor of W. W. Jacobs," Robert Whitford tells about the unaristocratic approach that Jacobs has to humor (Cloy 568).
Many Cargoes (1896), Light Freights (1901), Odd Craft (1903), and Short Cruises

(1907) are all concerned with what goes on in the dock area of London. Many of the characters are ne'er-do-well country eccentrics much in the tradition of Charles Dickens. In the world which Jacobs creates, the tragedy is comic, and pain is laughable, and is not to be taken too seriously. The narrator is a night-watchman who works on the docks. He speaks in dialect, and his speech is "dry, matter-of-fact, and flatly comic." Two other Jacobs characters are Ginger Dick and Peter Russett, both of whom are hard-drinking seamen (Cloy 566).

"The Money Box" is an episode in Odd Craft (1903), in which Dick and Peter are outwitted by an old seaman named Isaac. The two young sailors ask Isaac, the more experienced tar to hold their wages while they are on leave and to give them only small amounts of their money. This is to keep them from quickly squandering all of the money. Much of the humor comes from the young sailors' attempts, while drunk, to recover their money from the stolid Isaac. All of their pleas for money are in vein. "The Persecution of Bob Pretty" is another episode in Odd Craft. Bob Pretty is a country poacher who is crafty enough to fool sheriffs, gamekeepers, and country squires with "effortless finesse," and this is a constant source of humor. "The Persecution of Bob Pretty": also has a comic denouement (Cloy 566)

Dialstone Lane (1904) is an amusing story about a buried treasure and the people who are forced to change their lives in order to look for it (Cloy 567). John Cloy says that Jacobs's drama is like his fiction in that it is essentially comic in tone. Jacobs's characters are what Cloy calls "amiable miscreants." They tend to be petty domestic tyrants, or lazy seamen who work very hard trying to get out of work (Cloy 567).

William Wymark Jacobs Bibliography

Cloy, John "W. W. Jacobs." Encyclopedia of British Humorists, Volume I. Ed. Steven H.
      Gale. New York, NY: Garland, 1996, 565-568.
Whitford, Robert C. "The Humor of W. W. Jacobs." South Atlantic Quarterly 18 (1919):
      246-251.

Barry Eric Odell Pain (1864-1928)

In the 1890s, everything had to be "new," and during the 1890s, Barry Pain was regarded as one of the leading exponents of the "New Humor" (Adlard 831). His humor would just "come bubbling up" (Adlard 830). Pain was an excellent parodist, and his targets included such "fashionable" authors as Margot Asquith, A. S. M. Hutchinson, and Michael Arlen (Adlard 830).

In a Canadian Canoe (1891) is a mixture of, "lighthearted meditation, shameless puns, youthful parody, bleak naturalism, dream-sequences, and a happy surrealism" (Adlard 830). In Playthings and Parodies (1892), Pain made fun of John Ruskin, Walter Pater, and R. D. Blackmore (Adlard 830). Eliza (1900) is reminiscent of George and Weedon Grossmith's Diary of a Nobody, which had been published eight years earlier. But Eliza is more subtle. Eliza's husband is a complacent suburban office-worker who writes, "I believe there are but few people who could give you an accurate description of themselves." Eliza's husband has perfect confidence that he is one of the few who could, but Eliza and her mother know that he is not. The two ladies deal with Eliza's husband with stoic patience. Eliza was so successful that a number of sequels had to be written, including, Eliza Getting On (1901), Eliza's Husband (1903), Exit Eliza (1912), and Eliza's Son (1913). "The comedy of Eliza's husband is the comedy of self deception." But Eliza knows the truth, and so does the reader, who sees Eliza's husband through Eliza's eyes.

In contrast to Eliza's husband, the title character in The Memoirs of Constantin Dix (1905), is not self deceived. Rather, he is a cheeky rogue, a criminal who poses as a social worker, and rather than being deceived, he is a deceiver of others. This novel was also very successful (Adlard 830).

Barry Eric Odell Pain Bibliography

Adlard, John. "Barry Eric Odell Pain." Encyclopedia of British Humorists, Volume II. Ed. Steven H. Gale. New York, NY: Garland, 1996, 829-832.
Lawrence, Arthur H. "The Humour of Women: Mr. Barry Pain, His Work and His Views." The Young Woman 6 (1898): 129-132.
Noyes, Alfred, ed. Barry Pain's Humorous Stories. London, England: Werner Laurie, 1930.

Rudyard (Joseph) Kipling (1865-1936)

Occasionally Rudyard Kipling becomes patriotically vehement as he satirizes the home-staying Englishmen and his pursuit of pleasure and frivolity, describing them with such phrases as "flannelled fools," and "muddied oafs." According to C. W. Previté-Orton, Kipling's ideal is the rule of the adventurous Anglo-Saxon over other races (Previté-Orton 229). Like most celebrities, Kipling abhorred autograph seekers. One disgruntled collector complained to Kipling, "I have written to you five times for your autograph without success. I hear you get five dollars a word for every word you write. Enclosed is $5. Send me one word." Kipling put the five dollars in his pocket, and wrote a single-word on a sheet and sent it unsigned to the autograph seeker; the word was "Thanks" (Wallace et. al. 154).

Esther Smith says that Kipling had the word power of a poet and the philosophy of a humorist. She further remarks that his writing is in the tradition of the masters. It reflects the style and tone of Ancient Rome, the style and tone of the Bible, the style and tone of Muslim thinking. Kipling's stories are from the heart of his Soldiers Three (Irish Mulvaney, Cockney Ortheris, and Scotch Learoyd). He wrote satiric stories about the "naughty" Simla; he wrote romantic and heroic stories about charming Indians, Anglo-Indians, Americans, Englishmen, and Frenchmen; he wrote stories about animals, machines, prehistory, and science fiction. He wrote parables and allegories. His range was impressive (Smith 628).

"His Wedded Wife" is one of the stories in Plain Tales from the Hills (1887). A youthful subaltern earns the nickname of "The Worm" because he is not able to master the social skills that are expected of an English officer, and also because he is so often to be found writing letters to his mother and sisters at home. When a practical joke is played on him, he challenges the practical joker to a bet that he will be able to return the humiliation. He is considered to be a "pretty boy" because he doesn't have any facial hair, and he has a waist like that of a girl, but these traits are later used to his advantage. He is able to masquerade as the Senior Subaltern's wife, who has come all the way from England because she has been so neglected. The Junior Subaltern is so convincing in his performance that he not only teaches the Senior Subaltern a lesson, but he is also made head of the drama club (Smith 629).

"False Dawn" is also a story in Plain Tales from the Hills. This story is about a midnight picnic that takes places in the ruined gardens of an old tomb. Saumerez, a civil servant, plans to propose to Edith Copleigh, but a dust storm blows up, and in the "roaring, whirling darkness" he proposes instead to Maud, Edith's older sister. Edith hears about the proposal and flees, but Saumerez rides after her. He brings her back to correct the mistake, but the mistake cannot be corrected. Saumerez learns the deep and sad lesson that trying to stage picnics and fancy courtships in ruins, and in violent weather is doomed to disaster. From a different perspective, the story is even more sad, "There is a woman's version of this story, but it will never be written...unless Maud Copleigh cares to try" (Gray 188).

"A Second Rate Woman" is one of the Simla stories in Under the Deodars (1888). There are many clever and witty exchanges between Mrs. Hauksbee and her housemate, the lazy Mrs. Mallowe. Mrs. Delville, who dresses so badly that she is nicknamed "The Dowd," is a newcomer that Mrs. Hauksbee is not able to welcome (Smith 629). In the first paragraph, Mrs. Hauksbee describes Mrs. Delville as follows: "Dressed! Don't tell me that woman ever dressed in her life. She stood in the middle of the room while her ayah--no, her husband--it must have been a man--threw her clothes at her. She then did her hair with her fingers, and rubber her bonnet in the flue under the bed. I know she did, as well as if I had assisted at the orgie" (Smith 629).

T. R. Henn considers "Judson and the Empire" to be an "intensely funny story." He also considers some of Department Ditties, Barrack Room Ballads and Other Verse (1890) to be "extremely funny" (Henn 65). The title character in "Mulholland's Contract" in Seven Seas (1896), is a sailor who is on the lower deck of a freighter during rough weather. Mulholland makes a contract with God that if he is saved, he will exalt the Name of God and praise His Holy Majesty. He is saved, but it is with reluctance that he becomes a preacher to his unenlightened ship mates. He is frequently attacked, "as warned would be the case, / An' turned my cheek to the smiter exactly as Scripture says; / But, following that, I knocked him down an' led him up to Grace" (Kipling Seven 62).

Kim (1900) is a picaresque novel which illustrates Kipling's great sense of detail. Kim has memorable characters, and a compelling theme, and it is filled with wit, exaggeration, disguise, mirth, and most importantly the exposure of ignorance and pomposity. Kim becomes a skillful player of "The Great Game." He earns the love and respect of a wide range of other characters, a Tibetan lama, a Moslem horsetrader, a Bengali scholar, and a Hill Country widow. Kim is a bildungsroman in which Kimball O'Hara, the son of an Irish soldier who has become orphaned and street wise, turns himself into a "chela," or "servant-disciple" of the saintly Teshoo Lama (Smith 630).

In both The Jungle Book (1894), and The Second Jungle Book (1895), the boy Mowgli learns the law of the jungle and becomes the leader of the jungle's creatures before he marries and settles down on the boundary of the forest. Mowgli thus becomes the master of two cultures, the wild and the civilized. In The Jungle Book, The Second Jungle Book, and The Just So Stories (1902), Kipling changes from the farce of his adult stories to the exaggeration and word play of his stories written for children. There are pranks, and challenges to adults that are somehow appropriate, and that are possible through the world of Kipling's imagination. These features are illustrated by the "satiable curiosity" of "The Elephant's Child," that gets the young elephant into and out of trouble. They are also illustrated in the "great grey-green, greasy Limpopo River" that is part of his adventures (Smith 631). After the "Jungle Books," and the "Just So Stories," Kipling continued to write for children and adolescents. His Puck of Pook's Hill (1906), and Rewards and Fairies (1910) were fanciful retellings of stories taken from British history (Gray 190).

"My Sunday at Home" was published as a farce in The Day's Work (1898). Here, an American doctor makes a mistake in administering a purgative to a perfectly healthy laborer. At the end of the story, the enraged laborer is approached by another doctor who wants to do him some good. Kipling ends the story with the lightly ironic comment about "man who is immortal and master of his fate" (Gray 192).

"Below the Mill Dam" is a story in Traffics and Discoveries (1904) in which Waters and the Spirit of the Mill discuss the innovation of having a mill. Everybody is in favor of the mill except for an old English rat, who is discovered when the electric lights come on as the mill starts running (Gray 191). "They" is another story in Traffics and Discoveries. The narrator of "They" is clattering through the magical southern English landscape in his car when he comes upon a lovely Elizabethan house with the shrubbery shaped as knights and ladies. There is a gracious blind lady who lives alone in the house, and she is accompanied by some children. Gradually the narrator comes to realize that these children are ghosts, summoned by the need of the blind lady. Donald Gray points out that Kipling's young daughter, Josephine, had died during his visit to the United States in 1899. The story is therefore made even more poignant by Kipling's Preface, which included a poem in which, "the Virgin Mary releases children from heaven so that their spirits will comfort people on earth" (Gray 192).

"Mrs. Bathurst" is also published in Traffics and Discoveries. Donald Gray says that this is one of Kipling's best short stories. It starts out with a group of people who are reminiscing about various farcical episodes they had as youths, but it turns into a ghost story and ends up with reality almost gone from the story. Vickers is a Warrant Officer in the Navy who is haunted by something he sees in the movies during carnival time at Cape Town. Because of his haunted feeling, Vickers takes Pyecroft, one of the other story tellers, night after night to watch a woman get out of a train at Paddington Station and walk toward the camera looking straight at them until she melts out of the picture. There are two other people who help Pyecroft tell the story. One of them has known Ada Bathurst, who is a generous proprietor of a small hotel near Aukland. The other is aware of what happened to Vickers. But none of them know what Mrs. Bathurst is doing in London. "She's lookin' for me," Vickers says. Donald Gray describes Kipling's process of story telling in "Mrs. Bathurst:" "The artful ramble of the story, as its several tellers exchange information and opinions that end without resolving its plot, testifies both to the ambition of realistic narrative to take in everything and to the futility of that ambition" (Gray 192-193).

"Little Foxes" is a story from Actions and Reactions (1909) in which British administrators in Africa put on ingeniously organized fox hunts while they are supposed to be settling land disputes. The general attitude is that, "one gets at the truth in a hunting-field a heap quicker than in your law courts" (Gray 191). "The Mother Hive" is another story in Actions in Reactions. In this story a wax moth flies into "The Mother Hive" and subverts the work of the hive so much that a batch of Oddities are created. These Oddities will destroy the hive because they feel that the honey combs should be built in "democratic circles." They furthermore believe that the bees can live on the honey of the hive without producing any more honey (Gray 191). Still another story in Actions and Reactions is "With the Night Mail: A Story of 2000 A.D." This is a fantasy story about airplanes, and about the Aerial Board of Control which regulates the airplanes. The story even has mock news reports, a book review, and an advertisement for used dirigibles and aerial chauffeurs. Anyone who applies to the advertisement must be a member of the Church of England, and must be able to make himself useful in the garden (Gray 191).

"The Puzzler" is a farce published in Actions and Reactions. The title alludes to a very densely branched tree, but it is meant to be taken both literally and metaphorically. In the story, a group of important politicians and government ministers set a monkey loose in the tree to see how penetrable it is. But the monkey escapes into a house, and one puzzle is how to catch the monkey after it has escaped. A more metaphorical puzzle is how the colonies can be governed through the dense thicket of British governmental bureaucracy. The irony is that the solution to the first puzzle is also the solution to the second one. Bonded by the fun of their adventure in catching the monkey and facing down the indignant residents of the house, the politicians and government ministers work together to obtain a solution. What they come up with is a good idea, even though it is, "a little chipped at the edges" (Gray 192).

France at War (1915) is a factual account, but the visual imagery is sometimes as great as it is in Kipling's fiction. Talking about a gun, Kipling said that "she spoke" with a higher pitch than that of the men, and he said that she spoke, "with a more shrewish tang to the speeding shell." He added that, "her recoil was as swift and as graceful as the shrug of a French-woman's shoulders" (Smith 631).

"The Legend of Mirth" is a poem in A Diversity of Creatures (1917) in which Kipling uses humor in the same way that he believes God uses humor. Raphael, Gabriel, Michael, and Azreal are four archangels that have discovered that the burdensome troubles on earth are too much for their lofty sense of duty. So God sends the Seraph of Mirth to meet them, and to help them in developing the sense of humor that is necessary for them to function effectively (Kipling Diversity 289-292). "Mary Postgate" is another story in A Diversity of Creatures. Here, a middle-aged spinster lady finds an injured German pilot in her garden. At the time, the spinster is grieving over a young friend who had just been killed while training to be a pilot. "She lets the German die, takes a hot bath, and comes down looking quite handsome" (Gray 194).

"The Village that Voted the Earth Was Flat" is also collected in A Diversity of Creatures, and it is a story about an elaborate hoax. A journalist, a Member of Parliament, and the proprietor of a music hall are caught in a speed trap in a small village, and they combine their efforts in order to seek revenge. They conspire to concoct various newspaper stories, to commission a music-hall song, and to arrange a question in Parliament to convince the public that the villagers of Huckley are fools who have voted their belief that the earth is flat. In this story, Kipling is showing his scorn at how easy public opinion can be created and swayed by powerful people in politics and popular culture (Gray 195).

"The Necessitarians" is a poem in The Years Between (1918) which demonstrates that Kipling believed that God included humor as part of his Divine Plan. It is argued that it was the same Power that shaped our planet and the rose that also provided us with "Urns of Mirth" (Kipling Years Between 102). Kipling's satire is more humorous than it is bitter. His poem "Natural Theology" points out that humans like to blame God for their misfortunes, and that this has been happening through "Primitive," "Pagan," "Medieval," "Material," and "Progressive" times.

> I ate my fill of whale that died
> And stranded after a month at sea...
> There is a pain in my inside.
> Why have the Gods afflicted me?

Kipling presents a number of such complaints, and after each he applies the "Conclusion."

> This was none of the Good Lord's pleasure,
> For the Spirit He breathed in Man is free;
> But what comes after is measure for measure,
> And not a God that afflicteth thee. (Kipling Years Between 399-401)

"The Miracle of St. Jubanus" is a story in Limits and Renewals (1932) in which there is a young shell-shocked Frenchman. He, like everyone else in the church, is overcome with laughter when they see the village's only atheist forced to participate in church services by becoming entangled in the ritual equipage carried by the acolytes (Kipling Limits 277-295). "Fairy-Kist" is another story in Limits and Renewals. It is an ironic story about a man who has been wounded and gassed and developed gangrene during the war, and his obsession to go around England planting flowers (Gray 194). "The Tender Achilles" is still another story in Limits and Renewals. It is about a member of Lodge 5837 who returns to his important work as a research scientist after he has become unstrung by memoires of his numerous failures as a surgeon in various field hospitals during the war. "Everything that a man's brain automatically shoves into the background was out before the footlights, and dancing Hell's fox-trot, with drums and horns" (Gray 194). "Dayspring

Mishandled" is a story about a practical joke gone awry; it also appeared in Limits and Renewals. In the 1890s, Castorley had been writing for a fiction syndicate, but he had risen from that position to become an expert on Geoffrey Chaucer. Menallace writes historical novels, and Castorley says something insensitive about a paralyzed woman whom Manallace loves and cares for. Manallace spends years thinking of a way to get even with Castorley. He finally arranges for a manuscript to be discovered that is supposedly a lost Chaucerian tale. Castorley reviews the manuscript, and publishes a book supporting its authenticity. The irony of the story is that Manallace, who has been lying in wait, waiting to ambush Castorley's research, dies (Gray 195).

Kipling's humor was a tool that he used to talk about both the exalted and the mundane (Smith 632). In her The Art of Rudyard Kipling (1965), J. M. Tompkins devotes an entire chapter to "Laughter" (Tompkins 33-54). Kipling used a wide range of literary techniques in his development of humor, all the way from sophisticated wit to Rabelaisian farce (Smith 632). Although Kipling's poems and stories are serious exposés, there is frequently a mask of wit, ambiguity, oversimplification, mistaken identity, paradox, exaggeration, and sometimes even slapstick. Kipling writes comedies in that there is usually the reversal of an unjust situation by the exposure of some kind of injustice. In many of his poems and stories there is a vengeance or poetic justice involved (Smith 632).

J. M. Tompkins has discussed in detail Kipling's sophisticated uses of irony, and Elliot K. L. Gilbert has commented on Kipling's notion of, "the irrationality of the universe and man's need to find some order in it" (Gray 196). Kipling was continually experimenting with various voices, and various points of view. Kipling liked to let his manuscripts, "lie by to drain as long as possible" before revising them. He frequently read his writing aloud, testing the, "weights, colours, perfumes, and attributes of words in relation to other words.... There is no line of my verse or prose which has not been mouthed till the tongue has made it all smooth" (Gray 197).

Rudyard (Joseph) Kipling Bibliography

Bromwich, David. "Kipling's Jest." Grand Street 4 (1985): 150-179.
Gray, Donald. "Rudyard Kipling." Dictionary of Literary Biography, Volume 156: British Short-Fiction Writers, 1880-1914: The Romantic Tradition. Ed. William F. Naufftus. Detroit, MI: Gale, 1996, 181-199.
Henn, T. R. Kipling. New York, NY: Barnes and Noble, 1967.
Kipling, Rudyard. A Diversity of Creatures. London, England: Macmillan, 1917.
Kipling, Rudyard. The Just So Stories. London, England: Macmillan, 1902.
Kipling, Rudyard. Limits and Renewals. Garden City, NY: Doubleday, Doran, 1932.
Previté-Orton, C. W. "Algernon Swinburne." Political Satire in English Poetry. New York, NY: Russell and Russell, 1910, 226-229.
Smith, Esther M. G. "Rudyard Kipling." Encyclopedia of British Humorists, Volume I. Ed. Steven H. Gale. New York, NY: Garland, 1996, 624-633.
Tompkins, J. M. The Art of Rudyard Kipling. Lincoln, NE: University of Nebraska Press, 1965.
Wallace, Irving, David Wallechinsky, Amy Wallace, and Sylvia Wallace. The Book of Lists 2. New York, NY: William Morrow, 1980.

Ada Leverson (1865-1936)

In an article entitled "The Sphinx Goes Wild(e): Ada Leverson, Oscar Wilde, and the Gender Equipollence of Parody," Osbert Sitwell describes Ada Leverson as, "quite alone, but shaking with quiet, irrepressible laughter" (Sitwell 136); Harold Acton remembers her "chuckling to herself [in] sneezes of laughter," and remarks that, "it was comforting to know that she had died in a good humour" (Burkhart 28); and Corinna Rohse notes that the lasting image of Leverson as a laughing Sphinx, still delighting in friends and jokes, is captured in Osbert Sitwell's poem:

> Great loyalty, great wit:
> (Each strives against the other)
> Both win, both lose; both benefit
> In laughter none can smother. (Wyndham 102)

Ada Leverson is Oscar Wilde's "partner in the equipollence of parody" (Rohse 134). As Wilde himself says, "You are the most wonderful Sphinx in the world." He telegrams her, "Rely on you to misrepresent me" (Hart-Davis 380, 383).

Ada Leverson Bibliography

Burkhart, Charles. Ada Leverson New York, NY: Twayne, 1973.

Hart-Davis, Rupert, ed. The Letters of Oscar Wilde. London, England: Rupert Hart-Davis Ltd., 1962.

Rohse, Corinna Sundararajan. "The Sphinx Goes Wild(e): Ada Leverson, Oscar Wilde, and the Gender Equipollence of Parody." Look Who's Laughing: Gender and Comedy. Ed. Gail Finney. Amsterdam, The Netherlands: Gordon and Breach, 1994, 119-138.

Sitwell, Osbert. Noble Essences or Courteous Revelations: An Autobiography. London, England: Macmillan, 1950.

Speedie, Julie. " 'Wonderful, Witty, Delightful Sketches': Ada Leverson's Periodical Contributions to 1900, A Checklist and an Introduction." Turn-of-the-Century Women 4.2 (1987): 11-22.

Wyndham, Violet. The Sphinx and Her Circle. New York, NY: Vanguard Press, 1963.

Frank Mathew (1865-1924) IRELAND

See Nilsen, Don L. F. "Frank Mathew." Humor in Irish Literature: A Reference Guide. Westport, CT: Greenwood, 1996, 116.

Arthur William Symons (1865-1945) WALES

Arthur Symons was a renowned critic of the arts, but he was also a famous "Decadent," who frequented London's risqué music halls, especially the Alhambra and the Empire Theatre. Symons was often seen in the company of "immoral" actresses and dancers. He was said to have had no interest in what was proper, regular, or virtuous. Instead, he was "attracted by everything that is unusual, Bohemian, eccentric." "Symons even tends to identify abnormality, the grotesque or the perverse, with artistic quality, emphasizing the importance of unconscious impulses in all artistic creations" (Snodgrass 1096).

Between 1895 and 1896, Symons was the literary editor of The Savoy (Snodgrass 1097). During this time, Symons was quite solemn, and was not generally known as a humorist. Nevertheless, he had a keen wit, and a dry irony. He was often facetious and self-deprecating, both in speech and in writing. He especially targeted the moralistic Philistine press, and the public with his keen ironic wit. Some of his best examples of humor occurred while he was with The Savoy. He wrote "Being a Word on Behalf of

Patchouli" in February of 1896. It was the preface to the second edition of Silhouettes (originally published in 1892). Here Symons wryly argues that, "art is artifice and so logically should be judged on its quality of craftsmanship rather than merely on the morality of its subject matter" (Snodgrass 1098).

The satirical journal Punch lampooned the first issue of The Savoy for its "immoral tone." Punch sarcastically declared that, "There is not an article in the volume that one can put down without feeling the better and the purer for it." Punch then continues in the same sarcastic vein, "This book should be on every schoolroom table; every mother should present it to her daughter, for it is bound to have an ennobling and purifying influence" (Punch February 1, 1896, 49). It is amusing that in the second issue of The Savoy, Symons published an advertisement excerpting the above quote, and placing it, out of context, at the beginning of a series of press notices which praised The Savoy (Snodgrass 1098).

During the mid 1890s, Symons spent time with his friend William Butler Yeats, who was instrumental in getting Symons to shift his emphasis from "Decadent" to "Symbolist," and in an important work entitled The Symbolist Movement in Literature (1899) Symons redefined "Decadence" as being primarily stylistic. He said it was a "'deliberately abnormal' distortion of the organic and unified relationship between language and literary form." Symons was attracted to Impressionism, Decadence, and Symbolism, because he believed in epiphanies, or, "intense moments through which the poet could snatch an experience of beauty from the jaws of time and decay." In The Symbolist Movement, Symons showed how dreams, religion, and art are used to escape the oppression of both life and death, and Chris Snodgrass feels that Symons profoundly influenced the careers of such notable authors as William Butler Yeats, James Joyce, Ezra Pound, and T. S. Eliot (Snodgrass 1099).

In a play entitled The Fool of the World (1906), Symons ironically portrays Death as a blind jester, who at the end of the play reveals herself as a woman, and pleads for pity (Snodgrass 1100). Outlaws of Life (1925) and The Last Day of Don Juan (1926) are two satiric plays that are motivated by Symons's personal sense of failure. There are characters in both of these plays that are satires of Symons himself. One is a perverse poet who is obsessed with death, and who writes very sensual verse. The other is an egocentric Symbolist named Don Juan, who is dying. Symons quoted William Blake when he wrote the following about himself, "I was born 'like a fiend hid in a cloud,' cruel, nervous, excitable, passionate, restless, never quite human, never quite normal" (Beckson 56). Chris Snodgrass says of Arthur Symons, "his was a paradoxical, even bifurcated, temperament quite typical of the Victorian 1890s. Most of his wit and humor grows out of and reflects that fundamental irony" (Snodgrass 1101).

Arthur William Symons Bibliography

Beckson, Karl, ed. The Memoirs of Arthur Symons: Life and Art in the 1890s. University Park, PA: Pennsylvania State University Press, 1977.

Snodgrass, Chris. "Arthur William Symons." Encyclopedia of British Humorists, Volume II. Ed. Steven H. Gale. New York, NY: Garland, 1996, 1093-1102.

William Butler Yeats (1865-1939) IRELAND

See Nilsen, Don L. F. "William Butler Yeats." Humor in Irish Literature: A Reference Guide. Westport, CT: Greenwood, 1996, 6, 82, 100, 114, 116-120, 144, 155, 215-216.

Beatrix Potter (1866-1943)

When Alison Lurie first read Beatrix Potter's Peter Rabbit books, and looked at the artwork, she had no idea that Potter was a grown-up woman. She thought that Potter must be a little girl, small enough to look at the hollyhocks and tables and big dogs from below, and to see everything from such a close vantage point (Lurie 94-95).

Richard Carlson considers Beatrix Potter to be what he calls a "benign humorist." Carlson says that Potter's stories have a "teardrop at the center of each laugh." In each story there is a melancholy shift. Potter's rabbits and squirrels go about all day in work and play until their resources of cheer are exhausted by the end of the day. Even though they know that night can bring disappointments, Potter's animals enjoy many hours of sunshine each day (Carlson 47). In such stories as Tale of Peter Rabbit (1902), The Tailor of Gloucester (1902), Squirrel Nutkin (1903), and The Tale of Jemima Puddle-Duck (1908) there is a curious distance between the writer and the material. Potter writes from the point of view of an observer; her treatment is almost clinical (Carlson 55). Margaret Lane goes so far as to say that Potter's treatment has a, "seam of toughness running just below Potter's dewy-fresh surfaces." Themes in Potter's writing include nature's deep secrets, the survival of the fittest, and how animals are misused by humans, who somehow believe that their interests are more important than are those of the animals (Carlson 56).

Beatrix Potter's titles may be amusing to English ears; however, they become much more amusing and intriguing when they are translated into various foreign languages. Jemima Puddle-Duck (1908) is translated into French as Sophie Canetang, and into Welsh as Hanes Dili Minllyn. When Squirrel Nutkin (1903) is translated into French, it becomes Noisy-Noisette. In French, The Tale of the Flopsy Bunnies (1909) becomes La Famille Flopsaut, but in German it becomes more Germanic--Die Geschichte der Hasenfamilie Plumps. The Tale of Jeremy Fisher (1906) becomes Jeremie Pêche-à-la-Ligne in French and Jeremias de Hengelaar in Dutch. The Tale of Tom Kitten (1907) is Tom Het Poesje in Dutch. Mrs. Tiggy-Winkle (1905) is Hanes Meistres Tigi-Dwt in Welsh and Die Geschichte von Frau Tigge-Winkel in German. Finally, The Tale of Peter Rabbit (1902) becomes Il Coniglio Pierino in Italian, and Sagan Om Pelle Kanin in Swedish. Thus translation adds a new element of humor to Beatrix Potter's delightful stories (Potter 110).

Ruth MacDonald feels that The Tale of Peter Rabbit (1902), which is a story about a rabbit family that lives in a parallel universe to that of humans, but is mainly not noticed by the humans in the other parallel universe is "entirely convincing and endearing" (MacDonald 233). The person who reads The Tale of Peter Rabbit superficially will see the book as a recommendation for restraint and obedience. At the end of the book, Peter Rabbit is sent to bed in disgrace, while all of the "good little Bunnies," (Flopsy, Mopsy, and Cottontail) have bread and milk and blackberries for supper. But Alison Lurie asks us to remember that Peter's adventures were exciting, and that he learned something from having the adventures. Alison Lurie's class, after having read the book, were asked which character in the book they would prefer to have been, and without exception they all voted to have been Peter, recognizing that the real moral of the story was not the obvious one. The real moral was that, "disobedience and exploration are more fun than good behavior, and not really all that dangerous, whatever Mother may say." Lurie continues, "Consciously or not, children know that the author's sympathy and interest are with Peter, and with Tom Kitten and the Two Bad Mice; with impertinent, reckless Squirrel Nutkin, and not with the other timid, good squirrels or with obedient, dull little Flopsy, Mopsy, and Cottontail" (Lurie 95).

The Tailor of Gloucester (1902) is about a tailer who is ill and not able to do his work. In the tradition of "The Shoemaker and the Elves," one of the fairy tales collected by the Brothers Grimm, the mice finish the Lord Mayor's waistcoat in time for his wedding on Christmas Day. Since this happens on Christmas Eve, a time when animals have traditionally been given special gifts in honor of their presence during the birth of Jesus in Bethlehem, the magic becomes more "credible," or at least more appropriate (MacDonald 235).

The Tale of Squirrel Nutkin (1903) is about a naughty squirrel, who is more of a tempter of fate than is Peter Rabbit. Peter simply reacts without thinking, while Squirrel Nutkin deliberately taunts an owl by the name of Old Brown by chattering riddles and jokes. The other squirrels seek Old Brown's permission to scavenge for nuts in his territory, and offer him tasty gifts in return for his favors. Squirrel Nutkin, on the other hand, offers not tasty gifts, but jests and offenses. In the end, Squirrel Nutkin gets his just deserts, however, in an incident that could have cost him his life, but instead costs him only the loss of part of his tail (MacDonald 235).

The Tale of Two Bad Mice (1904) was probably written in reaction to what was happening in Beatrix Potter's real life. She had fallen in love with her editor, Norman Warne, and had decided to marry him. But her parents did not approve of the marriage. They were shocked and furious that Beatrix would marry someone who was not a gentleman because he was "in trade." They therefore refused to give their consent. But by then, Beatrix was an independent woman, so she announced her engagement nevertheless. The names of the protagonists in The Tale of Two Bad Mice are Tom Thumb, and Hunca Munca, the same names that Beatrix had given to her own pet mice. Tom and Hunca go inside a large and pretentious dollhouse, and taste the fancy food. But the fancy food is made out of painted plaster, so they become angry and vandalize the doll house, and carry off part of the contents. Suzanne Rahn suggests that, "the dollhouse, with its useless luxuries and stiff, helpless inhabitants, represents the Potter residence in South Kensington and that the two lively and destructive intruders--who at the end make partial restitution--are Beatrix and Norman Warne" (Rahn 91).

Ribby is the protagonist in The Pie and the Patty-Pan (1905). Ribby is a striped cat who invites Duchess, a Pomeranian dog, to tea. The dog finds out that mouse pie is what they are going to have for dinner, and she decides to substitute a veal and ham pie, which she has discovered in the oven while Ribby is shopping at the store for some last minute purchases. There are two complications in the story. One complication results from the fact that Ribby has only one patty pan (a patty-pan is a metal liner used to give baked pies their shape), and this patty-pan has been switched from one pie to the other. When Duchess sees the patty-pan under the pie she has not eaten, she gets sick because she assumes that there was a patty-pan under the other pie as well, the pie she has eaten--patty-pan and all. But then Dutchess is told that there was only one patty-pan and that this patty-pan is under the other pie--the one not eaten. And this makes her feel better, until she then discovers that it was not the veal-and-ham pie that she ate, but rather the mouse pie. Ruth MacDonald describes the dénouement to the story as follows: "A rushed visit from the doctor and the revelation of the veal pie's existence in the remaining oven does not reassure the dog, since she now feels ill at the thought of having eaten mouse" (MacDonald 240).

The title character in The Tale of Jeremy Fisher (1906) is an eighteenth-century gentleman frog, dressed in waistcoat and pumps. Jeremy Fisher likes to fish, and he has many fishing adventures. He catches a stickleback. He hooks a game fish that gets away. And he is nearly eaten by a trout. This last catastrophe causes Jeremy to resolve that he will never go fishing again. The clothes that Beatrix Potter puts on Jeremy Fisher give him both human qualities, and antique (eighteenth-century) qualities. He is in full dress regalia (MacDonald 238), wearing not only a waistcoat and pumps, but long stockings as well. His dress accents Jeremy's skinny legs. Since Jeremy Fisher is a frog, he has no neck, so he must express much of his emotion through his shoulders. Ruth MacDonald describes the frog, and his two friends, the newt, and the tortoise in the following way: "The newt's waistcoat takes advantage of the naturally colorful pigmentation of his underbelly, and the cravats of the frog, newt, and tortoise make their heads seem more human than animal. Like gentlemen on permanent vacation, these three are dining partners and tellers of tall tales about the fish that got away." They are, in Ruth MacDonald's words, three eighteenth-century "dandies." Jeremy and his friends are, "somewhat ridiculous in their clothing, which is unsuitable for rough, wet sporting, and their highly proper manners are a comment on Potter's father and his cohort of gentlemen on permanent vacation from care and from the realities of early-twentieth-century life" (MacDonald 239).

The Tale of Tom Kitten (1907) is about small-town ladies and their pretentious manners and their overly correct etiquette. Tabitha Twitchit has a number of playful kittens in her family. She tries to keep her kittens "proper" by keeping them washed, and keeping them dressed in party clothes. At the beginning of the story, Potter shows the kittens dressed in Little Lord Fauntelroy outfits, all stiff and upright, with pained looks on their faces. After some rough-and-tumble play, Tom Kitten finds himself without any of his clothing. At the end of the story, Potter pictures Tom Kitten as dirty, kitten-like, and without clothes. Tabitha exclaims that she is "affronted," because some of her neighbors will soon be coming over for tea, and the kittens are no longer "fit for exhibition as proper kittens." The reader realizes what Tabitha does not realize--that it is she herself who is responsible for their undoing by dressing them inappropriately and by having unreasonable expectations. The readers' sympathies are totally with the playful kittens, and not with the "twitchy, nervous, overbearing mother" (MacDonald 240).

The title character in The Tale of Jemima Puddle-Duck (1908) is so muddle-headed that when she goes off looking for a good nesting spot, she finds herself in the territory of a "sandy-whiskered gentleman." When this "gentleman" invites Jemima to join him for an omelette, she accepts, not realizing that it is her own eggs that will provide the ingredients for the main course. She doesn't even catch on when the "gentleman" asks her to bring some herbs that are usually associated with omelettes and with roast duck. In the gentleman's house, Jemima finds a great place for a nest, not realizing that the feathers there have been left as the remains of previous house guests. It is finally a neighboring farm dog that meets Jemima, and realizes what is happening. He brings together the hounds from other nearby farms and they go to destroy the fox and his home, but the fox escapes. Finally, Jemima has an opportunity to lay and brood her eggs, but even at the very end of the story she is, "none the wiser as to the close circumstances of her life" (MacDonald 242).

The Tale of the Flopsy Bunnies (1909) is about Flopsy Rabbit, Peter Rabbit's sister, who marries Benjamin Bunny to form a new family called the "Flopsy Bunnies." Their babies are caught in a burlap sack by Mr. McGregor, and when the parents notice that their babies are missing, they call on Peter to rescue them. Peter foils Mr. McGregor by changing the contents of the sack, and all of the rabbits live happily ever after, while Mr. and Mrs. McGregor bicker over a sack of rotten vegetables that Mr. McGregor has given her by mistake, thinking that the sack was full of baby rabbits (MacDonald 242).

The "sandy-whiskered gentleman" from The Tale of Jemima Puddle-Duck reappears in The Tale of Mr. Tod (1912), which is the last installment of the Peter Rabbit saga. The "gentleman" is still wild, and foxy, and still has a special liking for bunnies. By now, Flopsy and Benjamin Bunny have had another litter of bunnies, and Tommy Brock, the badger, steals this litter, puts them in a bag, and takes them to the home of Mr. Tod. Benjamin and Peter try to rescue the baby bunnies by digging a tunnel under the house. In the meantime, Tommy Brock has taken over Mr. Tod's house, and when Mr. Tod returns home, Mr. Tod and Tommy Brock battle it out for possession of the fox's home, Peter and Benjamin rescue the baby bunnies and return them home for a happy family reunion (MacDonald 245). The Peter Rabbit series, but especially The Tale of Peter

Rabbit, continue to be purchased and read extensively, "at least partly because of the growing gift trade during the Easter season and Potter's tie-in with rabbits and other springtime animals" (MacDonald 248).

Thomas Peter Piperson, the protagonist in The Tale of Pigling Bland (1913) has a name that conflates to two different nursery-rhyme characters, "Tom, Tom, the Piper's Son," and "Peter Piper." Old Man Piperson shuts Pigling up in a house with a little girl black Berkshire pig named Pigwig, but Pigwig and Pigling escape and run away into the next county. In the last picture, they are dancing together in a traditional country dance, "high-spirited and clearly in love." This story reflects what was happening in Beatrix Potter's life at the time. She was engaged to marry a country lawyer, but her parents objected, so the couple planned to escape to her country farm. The name of "Pigling Bland" is somehow appropriate, because Potter, "knew her husband was not spectacularly exciting or a prime candidate for marriage" (MacDonald 246).

Ginger and Pickles (1919) is about a general store that is run by a cat named Ginger, and a terrier dog named Pickles (MacDonald 242). Since these two entrepreneurs don't understand how the profit motive works, they extend unlimited credit to their animal customers, many of whom are characters in Beatrix Potter's other books. They end up by having to close up shop and eat into their own stock in order to survive. This book, "gently chides small-town life while glorifying in the simple pleasures of neighborliness and material comforts as provided by a country general store" (MacDonald 243).

The Tale of Little Pig Robinson (1930) is a take-off on Daniel Defoe's Robinson Crusoe (1719). Little Pig Robinson is sent to market, but on the way, he is, "pressed into naval service, not so much to perform nautical duties as to provide an eventual meal for the sailors." When Little Pig Robinson figures out his fate, he escapes on a lifeboat to the Land where the Bong Tree grows. It was Edward Lear who made the Land of the Bong Tree famous, as the destination of the Owl and the Pussy-Cat. When he arrives at his destination, Little Pig Robinson sets up a leisure chair on the beach under a Bong tree, and lives happily ever after (MacDonald 247).

Beatrix Potter Bibliography

Carlson, Richard S. "Benign Humorists of Children's Literature: Milne, Potter, and Wooster." The Benign Humorists New York, NY: Archon, 1975, 46-62.
Lurie, Alison. "Animal Liberation: Beatrix Potter." Don't Tell the Grown-Ups: Subversive Children's Literature. Boston, MA: Little, Brown, 1990, 90-98.
MacDonald, Ruth K. "Beatrix Potter." Dictionary of Literary Biography, Volume 141: British Children's Writers, 1880-1914. Ed. Laura M. Zaidman. Detroit, MI: Gale, 1994, 230-248.
Potter, Stephen. "On Beatrix Potter Translated." Sense of Humour. New York, NY: Henry Holt, 1946, 109-111.
Rahn, Suzanne. "Tailpiece: The Tale of Two Bad Mice." Children's Literature 12 (1984): 78-91.

Herbert George Wells (1866-1946)

During his early period, H. G. Wells wrote in the tradition of the "New Humor" of the 1880s and 1890s. His Certain Personal Matters (1897) is a collection of much of this "New Humor" which he had written earlier. Many of these humorous pieces were originally published in the Pall Mall Gazette, and Wells wrote them in response to the ready market for such essays during this period. In the tradition of Jerome K. Jerome and other writers of "New Humor," Wells's early essays depict the quirks, annoyances, and vagaries of lower-middle-class London life. They tend to be light, humorous, and irreverent. "The Art of Staying at the Seaside" is a breezy and facetious essay which examines the problems associated with a holiday at the sea shore. "The Shopman" is about exasperating confrontations with shop clerks. And "Of Blades and Bladery" instructs the person who wants to be a man-about-town how to wear his hat with the proper rakish angle. It tells him how to tie his cravat in the proper careless way, and how to use the latest slang when ordering drinks at a bar. In "The Jilting of Jane," as in Wells's other short fiction of this period, Wells is attempting to show how members of different social classes perceive the same event in very different ways. A maid says the following in trying to explain the nature of her relationship with a certain young suitor.

> "He is second porter at Maynards, the drapiers'" said Jane, "and gets eighteen shillings a week--nearly a pound a week, m'm; and when the head porter leaves he will be head porter. His relatives are quite superior people, m'm. Not labouring people at all. His father was a greengrosher [sic], m'm, and had a tumour, and was bankrupt twice. And one of his sisters is in a Home for the Dying. It will be a very good match for me, m'm," said Jane, "me being an orphan girl." (Hall 1197)

This passage demonstrates how effectively Wells is able to blend humor with genuine pathos (Hall 1197).

The Wonderful Visit (1895) is a wide-ranging satire on the human condition. Wells uses humor and charm to tell about the appearance of an angel and his stay with the local vicar of a small English village (Hall 1197).

According to Peter Hall, The Wheels of Chance (1896) is Wells's only completely comic novel; Hall considers it to be a minor comic classic. The influence of Jerome K. Jerome's Three Men on a Bummel (1900) is obvious, as Wells's protagonist, Mr. Hoopdriver goes on an extended bicycle tour to escape from his regular life as a draper's assistant. Hoopdriver crashes into an experienced woman cyclist in gray bloomers. Mr. Hoopdriver notices the bloomers immediately, and realizes that bloomers are associated with "New Women"--women who hold "advanced" ideas (Hall 1197).

Although his Edwardian novels are not totally comic, they are nevertheless comic in places. In such novels as Love and Mr. Lewisham (1900), The Sea Lady (1902), Kipps: The Story of a Simple Soul (1905), Tono-Bungay (1908), and The History of Mr. Polly (1910), there are moments of genuine humor and pathos about the characters' sense of dislocation and need for adjustment in lower-middle-class life. The characters in Wells's Edwardian novels are Dickensian both in their humor and in their pathos (Hall 1198). In The Sea Lady, Wells uses the same device of an alien visitor, but this time it is a mermaid rather than an angel. It is through the mermaid's eyes that Wells is able to comment on the social and sexual morés of Edwardian England (Hall 1197). In The History of Mr. Polly Mr. Polly is described as follows:

> Mr. Polly went into the National School at six and left the private school at fourteen, and by that time his mind was in much the same state that you would be in, dear reader, if you were operated upon for appendicitis by a well-meaning, boldly enterprising, but rather overworked and under-paid butcher boy, who was superseded towards the climax of the operation by a left-handed clerk of high principles but intemperate habits--that is to say, it was in a thorough mess. (Hall 1198)

Herbert George Wells Bibliography

Hall, Peter C. "H. G. Wells." Encyclopedia of British Humorists, Volume II. Ed. Steven

H. Gale. New York, NY: Garland, 1996, 1195-1199.

Edward Frederic Benson (1867-1940)

Dodo (1893) is the first of Edward Benson's social satires (Lundin 137). It is a light social satire based on the life of Margot Tennant, later to become the Countess of Oxford and Asquith (Lundin 136). Benson delighted English readers with his satires of English village life during the 1920s and the 1930s (Lundin 136). The style of Benson's social satires is derived from what Deanne Lundin calls "a nicely balanced disparity," and "an inversion of 'high' and 'low.'" "Petty struggles for social supremacy in two tiny, insular English villages receive the treatment of military campaigns, and serious ethical questions are made to seem, if not positively pretentious, at the least irrelevant" (Lundin 135).
　　　Emmeline Lucas, who goes by the name of Lucia, and Miss Elizabeth Mapp, who, "might have been forty, and had taken advantage of this opportunity by being just a year or two older," are two of the major characters of Edward Benson's social satires. These social satires include the following: Queen Lucia (1920), Miss Mapp (1922), The Male Impersonator (1929), Lucia in London (1927), Mapp and Lucia (1931), Lucia's Progress (1935), and Trouble for Lucia (1935). Make Way for Lucia (1977) contains all of the Mapp and Lucia social satires that were originally published between 1920 and 1939 (Lundin 137). Emmeline Lucas, Lucia, lives in Riseholme, and Elizabeth Mapp lives in Tilling. Even though these stories are satires, they are not satires of high moral outrage. Instead, the reader has no desire for these characters to develop morally. Benson exposes the vices and follies of society, but merely makes the characters look ridiculous, and he does so with warmth and sympathy. Lucia is colonizing London by slicing through divorce cases, art movements, developments in psychology. "All are mere rungs on the dizzying climb of her social advancement." Benson's social satires are in the tradition of "Comedy of Manners" which was first developed in England by Ben Jonson and George Chapman in the sixteenth century, and later revived by Oliver Goldsmith and William Congreve. Benson's Comedy of Manners takes place in the tiny villages of Riseholme first, and then later in Tilling. Benson is like Oscar Wilde in deflating the pretensions of "serious art." The driving force of Benson's art is the fundamental comic device of exploiting the incongruity between what a character pretends to be and what the viewer knows to be "true" (Lundin 134).
　　　Miss Mapp (1922) is about Captain Puffin's and Major Flint's quarrel with each other. The quarrel is over a trivial offense, but the excited Tillingites, led by Miss Mapp, escalate the quarrel to the point that a duel is necessary. In fact, however, the scandalous duel never takes place. In Lucia in London (1927), Benson mocks the avant-garde of his day. Sophy Alingsby is, "tall and weird and intense, dressed rather like a bird-of-paradise that had been out in a high gale" (Lundin 134).
　　　Ironically, Benson delivered Final Edition (1940) to his publisher only ten days before he died. Virginia Woolf wrote the following in her diary: "My Times [Book Club] book this week is E. F. Benson's latest autobiography--in which he tried to rasp himself free of his barnacles" (Lundin 136).

Edward Frederic Benson Bibliography

Lundin, Deanne. "E(dward) F(rederic) Benson." Encyclopedia of British Humorists, Volume I. Ed. Steven H. Gale. New York, NY: Garland, 1996, 132-138.

Norman Douglas (1868-1952)

South Wind (1917) is very similar to, and probably a bit derivative of, the conversational novels of Thomas Love Peacock. It is also similar to Ford Madox Ford's satirical novel that appeared during the war years, The Good Soldier (1915). The basic difference between The Good Soldier and South Wind is that Ford's novel concentrates on four or five characters, and uses satire to target the British upper class, while Douglas's novel is peopled with many characters, very Dickensian in mold, and he uses satire to target a multitude of social and cultural institutions simultaneously. Norman Douglas's humor ranges all the way from silly to scholarly, but he is always able to remain in the context of the novel's themes. In South Wind, a bishop goes to Nepenthe and while he is there he meets "all sorts of perfection." The bishop's motto is, "Be perfect of your own kind, whatever that kind may be." In Nepenthe the bishop finds many kinds of perfection; there are "perfect fools," "perfect villains," even "a perfect murderess." Ironically, instead of overturning the bishop's motto about perfection, the novel confirms it (Mesher 332). South Wind is about the residents of Nepenthe, many of whom have personalities that are very similar to that of Douglas. One of these characters is a "loquacious epicure." Another is a Jewish geologist, and a third is an old con-man, but there are others as well, such as Miss Wilberforce who is often inebriated and sexually promiscuous, and the members of the Russian immigrant sect known as "Little White Cows." David Mesher says that In Douglas's "overpopulated little paradise," "there is something for almost everyone to make fun of." South Wind contains a chapter-long parody of the "history of Saint Dodekanus and the origin of his cult on Nepenthe," in which Dodekanus grows restless after he has received many "visions," containing a beautiful young woman. Dodekanus is not able to determine whether this was a woman of flesh and blood, or merely an angel (Mesher 331).

Douglas is spoofing religion in general and the lives of the saints in particular in the episode about the equinoctial feast in South Wind. "On the evening of that day they sawed the whole [saint], superstitiously, into twelve separate pieces, one for each month of the year; and devoured of the saint what was to their liking" (Douglas South Wind 20). David Mesher considers South Wind to be a combination of brilliant social satire and verbal slapstick. It is a tongue-in-cheek modern tour-de-force (Mesher 332).

Norman Douglas Bibliography

Douglas, Norman. South Wind. London, England: Martin Secker, 1917.
Mesher, David. "Norman Douglas." Encyclopedia of British Humorists, Volume I. Ed.
    Steven H. Gale. New York, NY: Garland, 1996, 329-333.

St. John Hankin (1869-1909)

St. John Hankin wrote many local-color satires and parodies and published them in Punch. He parodied well-known plays , novels, and poetry of his day, and was thus a typical mainstream turn-of-the-century contributor to Punch, which Peter Hall describes as "the bastion of British humor." Hankin's satires targeted the dress regulations of the Royal Navy, the problems of the London telephone exchange, scholarship, motor racing, and West-End theatrical productions. His tone was playful, mocking, and filled with goodhearted fun, very similar to the burlesque tone that W. S. Gilbert and Arthur Sullivan developed for their comic operas (Hall 512).

Mr. Punch's Dramatic Sequels (1901), and Lost Masterpieces and Other Verses (1904) contain Hankin's best contributions to Punch and to the St. James's Gazette. Mr.

Punch's Dramatic Sequels is a collection of fourteen of Hankin's dramatic parodies. His parody of William Shakespeare's The Tragedy of Hamlet is entitled "The New Wing at Elsinore," and in the parody, it is Horatio rather than Fortinbras who has taken possession of the throne of Denmark, and the Grave-digging clowns, now called the "Master Builders" are renovating the castle under his supervision. In like manner, Arthur Wing Pinero's The Second Mrs. Tanquery, becomes "The Third Mrs. Tanquery" in the Hankin's parody. In "The Third Mrs. Tanquery," Aubrey Tanquery marries still another time, this time to a reform-minded feminist who is able to dominate Aubrey, and alienate all of his friends. Pinero's The Notorious Mrs. Ebbsmith becomes "The Unfortunate Mr. Ebbsmith," which is presented as a prologue to the original play. In Hankin's parody prologue, the eight years of Agnes Ebbsmith's life before her marriage are shown, and these eight years show her development as a feminist zealot (Hall 512).

      Lost Masterpieces and Other Verses (1904) contains light verse, and parodies of verse that Hankin had originally written for Punch and the St. James Gazette. Many prominent authors of Romantic poetry are parodied, such as William Wordsworth, Lord Byron, Percy Bysshe Shelley, and Robert Burns. Important Victorian poets are also parodied, such as Alfred, Lord Tennyson, Robert Browning, Gabriel Rossetti, Algernon Swinburne, and Matthew Arnold. A satiric device which Hankin often uses is the ironic deflation of theme and manner. "Home Thoughts from Abroad," for example is a parody of a nostalgic poem about how beautiful England is in the springtime entitled, "Home Thoughts from at Home." The parody reduces the poem to "a suburban complaint about the dismal weather of England in the fall" (Hall 513).

      The Cassilis Engagement (1912) is a parody of such Victorian plays as Tom Taylor's New Men and Old Acres, and T. W. Robertson's Caste, whose misalliances between the social classes are resolved by conventional and sentimental plots. The Last of the De Mullins (1912) is a reversal of the fallen woman motif so common in Victorian drama, and The Two Mr. Wetherbys is a parody of Oscar Wilde's The Importance of Being Earnest (Hall 513).

St. John Hankin Bibliography

Drinkwater, John, ed. The Dramatic Works of St. John Hankin, 3 Volumes. London, England: Martin Secker, 1912.

Hall, Peter C. "St. John Hankin." Encyclopedia of British Humorists, Volume I. Ed. Steven H. Gale. New York, NY: Garland, 1996, 511-513.

Seamus MacManus (1869-1960) IRELAND

Nilsen, Don L. F. "Seamus MacManus." **Humor in Irish Literature: A Reference Guide.** Westport, CT: Greenwood, 1996, 120.

3
Authors Born between 1870 and 1879

Joseph Peter René Hilaire Belloc (1870-1953)

Hilaire Belloc wrote epigrams. Once he designed a Christmas card which read, "May all my enemies go to hell; Noel, Noel, Noel, Noel" (Kennedy 83). As his epitaph, he suggested, "When I am dead, I hope it may be said; 'His sins were scarlet, but his books were read'" (Peter 211). Belloc also wrote nonsense verse. One of his poems is entitled, "The Frog." It reads as follows:

> Be kind and tender to the Frog,
>> And do not call him names,
> As "Slimy-Skin," or "Polly-wog,"
>> Or likewise, "Uncle James,"
> Or "Gape-a-grin," or "Toad-gone-wrong,"
>> Or "Billy-Bandy-Knees;"
> The Frog is justly sensitive
>> To epithets like these.
>
> No animal will more repay
>> A treatment kind and fair,
> At least, so lonely people say
> Who keep a frog (and, by the way,
>> They are extremely rare). (Wells 207)

Some of his nonsense verse is written for more rare animals like "The Yak."

> As a friend to the children command me the yak,
>> You will find it exactly the thing:
> It will carry and fetch, you can ride on its back
>> Or lead it about with a string.
>
> A Tartar who dwells on the plains of Tibet
>> (A desolate region of snow)
> Has for centuries made it a nursery pet,
>> And surely the Tartar should know!
>
> Then tell your papa where the Yak can be got,

And if he is awfully rich,
He will buy you the creature--or else he will not,
(I cannot be positive which). (Wells 208)

Belloc was the antithesis of George Bernard Shaw, who said of him: "Like most anti-Socialists, Belloc is intensely gregarious. He cannot bear isolation or final ethical responsibility: he clings to the Roman Catholic Church: he clung to his French nationality because one nation was not enough for him: he went into the French army because it gave him a regiment, a company, even a gun to cling to" (Pearson 269). In the early nineteen hundreds Belloc and Shaw had great public debates. Belloc was joined in these debates by Gilbert Keith Chesterton, and in fact, Sturge Moore once described Belloc and Chesterton as "two buttocks of one bum" (Potter 29).

Belloc wrote many verses for children. The Bad Child's Book of Beasts (1896), is filled with the kind of manic violence that children can easily relate to. Examples include "Jim, Who ran away from his Nurse, and was eaten by a Lion," and "Henry King, Who chewed bits of String, and was early cut off in Dreadful Agonies." In this tradition, Belloc also wrote More Beasts for Worse Children (1897), A Moral Alphabet (1899), Cautionary Tales for Children (1907), and More Peers (1911). Later, he wrote two more books in this same tradition, New Cautionary Tales (1930), and Ladies and Gentlemen (1932). The language in these books of verses for children is a form of parody that frequently deconstructs itself, as in the following poem:

The vulture eats between his meals,
And that's the reason why
He very, very rarely feels
As well as you and I.
His eye is dull, his head is bald,
His neck is growing thinner.
Oh! what a lesson to us all
To only eat at dinner! (Jago 131)

Belloc used inconsequential titles for his ten collections of essays that came from his original journalism pieces. Four of these are On Nothing (1908), On Everything (1909), On Anything (1910), and On Something (1910). At this point he had run out of titles, so in desperation he finally entitled the fifth one simply On (1923) (Jago 130). Other "insignificant" titles which Belloc used to mark his humor were First and Last (1911), and This and That (1912), and One Thing and Another (1955). Belloc also published a series of conversation books, including Short Talks with the Dead (1926), A Conversation with an Angel (1928), and A Conversation with a Cat (1931) (Jago 132). Belloc's A Conversation with a Cat follows Jonathan Swift's A Tale of a Tub (1704) in style and tone. Here he describes Swift's essay as "immortal," and here he also mocks the Protestant who believes that Christ died specifically in order to save his particular skin (Jago 131). The most enduring of Belloc's humorous works are his fourteen satirical novels, starting with Emmanuel Burden (1904), and ending with The Hedge and the Horse (1936) (Jago 130).

According to Hesketh Pearson, the platform battles of political idealogy waged by Belloc and Shaw provided "the best intellectual entertainments of the time." This was a battle of giant proportions. One such debate took place shortly after the publication of Belloc's The Cruise of the "Nona" (1925). Magnanimously, Shaw referred to Belloc's new book three times during his speech, and each time he did so, Belloc looked severely at the audience and ejaculated, "Buy it!" almost as if Shaw were advising them to borrow it from their public libraries. On another occasion, there was a debate between Shaw and Chesterton, and Belloc was sitting in a chair, acting as referee. After introducing the speakers, Belloc said, "They are about to debate. You are about to listen. I am about to sneer." And at that point he threw a savage glance at Shaw and returned to his seat (Pearson 270).

According to David Jago, Belloc's humor is a weird mixture of aggressiveness and melancholy. Paradoxically, Belloc had fierce religious convictions, but at the same time he was very skeptical of religion. His essay entitled "On Irony," which is published in On Anything gives an estimate of what Belloc thought of his own contribution and that of other "ironists." "No man possessed of irony and using it has lived happily; nor has any man possessing it and using it died without having done great good to his fellows and secured a singular advantage to his own soul" (Jago 132).

Joseph Peter René Hilaire Belloc Bibliography

Jago, David. "Joseph Peter Rene Hilaire Belloc." Encyclopedia of British Humorists, Volume I. Ed. Steven H. Gale. New York, NY: Garland, 1996, 128-132.
Kennedy, X. J. Tygers of Wrath. Atlanta, GA: University of Georgia, 1981.
Pearson, Hesketh. "Hilaire Belloc." Lives of the Wits. New York, NY: Harper and Row, 1962, 269-285.
Peter, Laurence J. The Laughter Prescription. New York, NY: Ballantine Books, 1982.
Potter, Stephen. Sense of Humour. New York, NY: Henry Holt and Company, 1954.
Wells, Carolyn, comp. A Nonsense Anthology. New York, NY: Scribner's, 1915.

Saki (Hector Hugh Munro)(1870-1916)

In an article entitled, "Saki: Practical Jokes as a Clue to Comedy," Miriam Cheikin argues that Saki is better skilled at developing comic characters than he is at mere satire (Cheikin 137). George Spears wrote a book entitled, The Satire of Saki, in which he investigated the satiric elements in Saki's stories, plays, novels, and political articles (Donnelly 922). Hector Munro got his pen-name of "Saki" from the companion who is addressed in The Rubáyát of Omar Khayyám. His stories are filled with, "epicine audacities, bizarre twists, hints of the supernatural, flashes of wit, and clever paradoxes." His satirical short stories, such as "Tobermory," "The Open Window," "Sredni Vashtar," and "The Schwartz-Metterklume Method" tend to be very short (rarely over 3,000 words), and are therefore very distilled and focused. His heroes in Reginald (1904), Reginald in Russia (1910) and Beasts and Super-Beasts (1914) tend to be prankish aristocratic youths who dislike the "beastly stuffiness of the bourgeoisie (Donnelly 920).

The title character of "Sredni Vashtar" is a ferocious ferret which a small boy loves and hides in the potting shed where Mrs. de Ropp, his overbearing cousin and guardian, won't find him. But Mrs. de Ropp goes to the potting shed to find out what is so much engaging the boy's attention, and as she is snooping through the shed, the ferret kills her. The adults in the story are concerned over who will break this bad news to the poor child, and as they are debating the matter among themselves, "Conrad made himself another piece of toast." William Donnelly comments on this story: "The icy irony of that conclusion puts it on the border between humor and horror, a territory pioneered by Saki and more fully explored by later writers such as John Collier, Evelyn Waugh, and Aldous Huxley" (Donnelly 921).

"The Strategist" is a story about a woman who is very protective of her money. She, "adopted a protective, elder-sister attitude towards money in general, irrespective of the nationality or demonination. Her energetic intervention had saved many a ruble from dissipating itself in tips in some Moscow hotel, and francs and centimes clung to her instinctively under circumstances which would have driven them headlong from less sympathetic hands" (Donnelly 921). William Donnelly points out that in this passage the word-play on the word "denomination" is skillfully done. "Denomination" can refer to monetary denomination (rubles, francs, centimes), but it can also refer to religious denomination. These coins, then, are more than mere money; they are religious icons (Donnelly 921).

John Gore calls Saki a "literary Peter Pan" because neither he nor his wit ever grew up. His wit remained that of an undergraduate. He wrote many books, and most of them "sparkled," but John Gore feels that his first book, a compilation of short stories entitled, Reginald (1904), was one of his best (Gore 311). Hector had a sister who supplied many of the biographical notes we now use to reconstruct Hector Munro's life. Hector had two Aunts, one of them named Aunt Augusta, and the other Aunt "Tom." Hector's sister considered them to be "gorgons"; however Gore says that they were probably no worse than other middle-aged, middle-class maiden ladies in the Victorian age: "That is to say, narrow, ignorant, self-willed, quarrelsome, jealous, domineering, stuffy, females, ill-qualified to bring up imaginative children" (Gore 312). Thus, when Saki began to write for a living, he aimed some of his earliest and sharpest barbs at Aunts. This is what he said about Aunts at Christmas time:

> Then there are Aunts, always a difficult class.... The trouble is that one never catches them really young enough. By the time one has educated them to an appreciation of the fact that one does not wear red woollen mittens in the West End, they die or quarrel with the family or do something equally inconsiderate. That is why the supply of trained aunts is always so precarious. (qtd. in Gore 312)

As can be seen in this excerpt, Saki's writing was light in tone, and satirical in effect. His sketches were lively, and they contained pithy and insightful legends (Gore 313). Saki was the kind of person who was "utterly incapable of boring a fellow-creature--man or dog or woman or cat or child of any age." His keen sense of honor, his strength of purpose and his stark simplicity defined his writing style (Gore 324-325). He made many political statements, many of them in the form of aphorisms such as "An army moves at the rate of its slowest unit; it is the fate of a Coalition to move at the rate of its most headlong section." Saki also said, "There seems to be some confusion of mind in these circles of political thought between a nation of shop-keepers and a nation of shop-lifters. If these men are on the side of the angels, may I always have a smell of brimstone about me" (qtd. in Gore 315).

Conrad Bassington, the protagonist of The Unbearable Bassington (1912), has adventures that bring him into contact with virtually everyone and everything that Saki dislikes from gossip mongers to women novelists to voguish foreign painters to a pretentious popular playwright by the name of "Sherard Blaw" (Donnelly 920).

When William Came (1913) is more of a series of satirical sketches than it is a novel. It predicts the fall of England to Kaiser Wilhelm, saying that in Saki's time British society had become so effete that England could offer no resistance to the conqueror, except the resistance that could be given by the Boy Scouts. Saki tells what life would be like under German occupation, saying that there would be a continuation of the "comical pettiness and imperturbability," that would keep the English from realizing what a humiliating disaster they had undergone (Donnelly 920).

Saki patterned his writing after that of Oscar Wilde. In the tradition of Wilde, Saki's short stories have epigrams, witticisms, and inversions of pious platitudes, like, "Scandal is merely the compassionate allowance which the gay make to the humdrum," which is patterned after Wilde's "Hypocrisy is the tribute vice pays to virtue." Elements of Wilde's "Decay of Lying," can be seen in Reginald's remarks on a truthful woman. "It is so easy to slip into the habit of telling the truth in little matters. And then it becomes difficult to draw the line at important things, until at last she took to telling the truth about her age." It was under the apprenticeship of Wilde that Saki developed his ear for paradox, oxymoron, understatement, anticlimax, and "le mot juste" (Donnelly 920).

Saki wrote quickly and without correction, and this is one reason why his writing has such a great sense of mental energy, playfulness, and spontaneity. The editor of Spectator, a paper for which Saki wrote, said that Saki had the great gifts of, "wit, mordant irony, and a remarkable command of ludicrous metaphor" (Donnelly 921). Saki's satiric targets would no longer be considered "politically correct;" he targeted Jews, suffragettes, pacifists, reformers, and the poor. But in the opinion of William Donnelly, Saki's, "humor redeems the satire, and it is the humor of delight." A. J. Langguth said of Saki, "He reached the degree of proficiency where the humor came less from his jokes than from the precision of each sentence. The reader laughs with delight at the absolute rightness of his language. Wit may be rebellious in its intent but in its perfection of expression it upholds a universal order" (Donnelly 920). One critic said that Saki's perfectly honed style was "smooth as a shave with a new razor-blade" (Donnelly 920).

Saki (Hector Hugh Monro) Bibliography

Cheikin, Miriam Quen. "Saki: Practical Jokes as a Clue to Comedy." English Literature in Transition 9 (1980): 121-137.
Donnelly, William. "Saki." Encyclopedia of British Humorists, Volume II. Ed. Steven H. Gale. New York, NY: Garland, 1996, 919-922.
Gore, John. "Saki." English Wits. Ed. Leonard Russell. London, England: Hutchinson, 1940, 307-326.
Spears, George J. The Satire of Saki. New York, NY: Exposition, 1963.

John Millington Synge (1871-1909) IRELAND

See Nilsen, Don L. F. "John Millington Synge." Humor in Irish Literature: A Reference Guide. Westport, CT: Greenwood, 1996, 5, 7, 9-10, 121-126, 144, 155.

Sir Henry Maximilian Beerbohm (1872-1956)

Hilaire Belloc and Max Beerbohm were opposites. Belloc was, "passionately prejudiced, noisily fanatical, a terrific talker, a great walker, restlessly active and variable in expression." In contrast, Beerbohm was, "genially tolerant, quietly skeptical, a good listener, a non-walker, physically lazy and uniform in expression." Because they were so different from each other they very much enjoyed the pleasure of each other's company. Hilaire Belloc, Max Beerbohm, and Max's brother Herbert Beerbohm Tree used to eat lunch together at the Continental Hotel, near the Haymarket Theatre, which H. Beerbohm Tree managed. It was here that many of Oscar Wilde's plays were being performed, and it was here that Beerbohm met not only Oscar Wilde, but also Aubrey Beardsley, Reginald Turner, Robert Ross, Lionel Johnson, Charles Conder, Lord Alfred Douglas, and other notables (Pearson 289). Beerbohm was usually so quiet that Oscar Wilde once quipped, "He is jealous of his wit and keeps it to himself," to which Max replied, "If I did not, it might prove unfaithful to me" (Pearson 286).

Beerbohm was noted for the brevity of his artistic creations. He specialized in the caricature, the parody, and the personal essay (Owens 115). Beerbohm did excellent caricatures and parodies of many famous literary figures. In one series of caricatures, entitled "The Young and the Old Self," Beerbohm gives his idea of what such figures as H. G. Wells, George Bernard Shaw, Joseph Conrad, and Arnold Bennet would look like as old men. Many of the pictures are prophetic. In many of his caricatures, Beerbohm would provide captions denoting very specific fantastic events, such as "Henry James" (c 1904) a humorous portrayal of Henry James kneeling in front of a closed apartment door inspecting two pairs of shoes, one male, and one female. Other fantastic caricatures include "Walt Whitman, inciting the bird of freedom to soar" (1904), and "Mr. W. B. Yeats, presenting Mr. George Moore to the Queen of the Fairies" (1904), and "Mr. Henry James Revisiting America" (1905) and "Some Persons of 'the Nineties'" (1925).

Of himself, Max Beerbohm wrote, "I was a modest, good-humoured boy," but then with tongue in cheek, he added, "It is Oxford that has made me insufferable" (Hopkins 259). Gerard Hopkins notes that it is no accident that Beerbohm's appreciation of dandyism should be the subject of his first published volume, "Dandies and Dandies" (1895). Beerbohm loved the fun and marshalling of words. For Beerbohm, it was not uncommon for a word to "kick up its heels in exuberant fantasy." He could play with such phrases as "the inilluminate parchment," "the scud-a-run of quivering homuncules over the vert on horses," and words like "comprimend" and "couth" (Hopkins 260).

When asked about his hobbies, Beerbohm once said, "I suppose I may claim one hobby of which I have never tired. I enjoy looking at things and people, especially people," and when he was told that he had been very lucky throughout his life, Max agreed, but with a slant. "I have been lucky...yes...once." When asked, "Only once?" Max replied, "Once is enough. I was lucky to be born" (Pearson 287). Max Beerbohm had the ability of putting a positive slant on even the most unpleasant of events. He didn't like school, and he once said of Charterhouse, "My delight in having been at Charterhouse was far greater than had been my delight in being there" (Pearson 288). This same type of slant can be seen in Beerbohm's description of the year 1880. "To give an accurate and exhaustive account of that period would need a far less brilliant pen than mine" (Hopkins 261).

Beerbohm was a story-teller, a draughtsman, and a parodist, but above all, he was a dramatic critic (Hopkins 262). In responding to works by Kipling, or Conrad, or Hardy, works he viewed with patience and mild dislike, Beerbohm was only slightly clever; however, in responding to the works of James, Meredith, Moore, or Chesterton, works he loved, his joking tended to be "superbly brilliant" (Hopkins 276). Gerard Hopkins feels that Beerbohm's wit vitalizes everything that Beerbohm touches, and this is as true of his art as of his writing. "The nimbleness of line, sensitiveness of observation, dislike of crude exaggeration, scrupulous choice, are as evident in his caricatures as in his essays" (Hopkins 276). Beerbohm's personal essays tended to concentrate on the commonplace. He wrote about household fires, about seeing friends off on trips, and about names given to streets. What is humorous about these essays is that he always saw things from an unusual perspective. In his "An Infamous Brigade," for example, he tells a fireman who is pouring water on the fire to "desist from his vandalism. I told him that I had driven miles to see this fire, that great crowds of Londoners, poor people with few joys, were there to see it also, and I asked him who was he that he should dare to disappoint us" (Owens 116). Beerbohm's tone was mock serious. He wrote about hatboxes (in "Ichabod") about books mentioned in other books (in "Books within Books"), and about a piece of a fan (in "The Relic") as if they were matters of high seriousness (Owens 117).

Beerbohm's criticism tended to be extremely mild. In critiquing Madame Bernhardt's playing of Shakespeare, Beerbohm said, "the only compliment one can conscientiously pay her is that her Hamlet was, from first to last, très grande dame". This gentle tone was also used in reference to George IV, who, at the end of his life, looked at all of his old coats, and laughed and sobbed according to the memories which they brought back to him. About this event, Max Beerbohm said, "It is pleasant to know that George, during his long and various life, never forgot a coat, however long ago worn, however seldom (Pearson 289).

Roger Henkle considers Max Beerbohm to have been "the avatar of turn-of-the-century sophisticated humor. His essay entitled, "A Defense of Cosmetics" which appeared in The Yellow Book (1894) established Beerbohm as a Decadent writer and a dandy. Wilde had influenced his writing style, and his caricatures of Wilde are among his best known. But although "A Defense of Cosmetics" established Beerbohm's reputation, it also elicited a great deal of spirited criticism (Owens 115). The Happy Hypocrite (1897) is a parody of Oscar Wilde's The Picture of Dorian Gray. In Beerbohm's parody, the roguish hero wears a saintly mask in order to win his lover, and he takes on the good qualities of the mask by wearing it (Owens 117). Zuleika Dobson (1911) is Beerbohm's single novel. It is a sustained satiric fantasy in which a femme fatale by the name of Zuleika "conquers Oxford and leads all of the undergraduates to commit suicide." Jill Owens says that Oxfordians "delight in the satire of university customs, types, and rituals of a by-gone day." The parody of Henry James in A Christmas Garland (1912) entitled "The More in the Middle Distance" may be Beerbohm's best known piece, but his parodies of the rhythms and eccentricities of Rudyard Kipling, H. G. Wells, Joseph Conrad, George Meredith, and twelve other authors are also well done (Owens 116).

"Enoch Soames," which appeared in Seven Men and Two Others (1919) is interesting to modern critics because of the circularity of its plot line (Owens 117). Soames "was a stooping, shambling person, rather tall, very pale, with longish and brownish hair. He had a thin vague beard--or rather, he had a chin on which a large number of hairs weakly curled and clustered to cover its retreat." "I was sure he was a writer." Soames is such a marginal person that there is a distinct possibility that he will disappear from minds altogether. He ineptly begins conversations with something like, "You don't remember me!" and his opinions disintegrate in the telling. His poetry, which is very bad, is fixated on nonexistence: "Thou art, who has not been! Thou hast not been nor art!" When Rothenstein, the portrait painter, does a painting of Soames, it is done in pastels, and Beerbohm observes, "it 'existed' so much more than he; it was bound to" (Henkle 332-333). However, things are different when Soames is transported into the next century. Here he discovers that the only reference to him is in Beerbohm's satiric short story, "Enoch Soames," and this makes him angry, because in the story he is described as an imaginary character. He returns to the nineteenth century and confronts Beerbohm, reproaching him for having incompetently deprived him of his existence. "You aren't an artist.... And you're so hopelessly not an artist that, so far from being able to imagine a thing and make it seem true, you're going to make even a true thing seem as if you'd made it up. You're a miserable bungler. And it's like my luck" (Henkle 333-334).

Sir Henry Maximilian Beerbohm Bibliography

Beerbohm, Max. Caricatures of Twenty-Five Gentlemen. London, England: Leonard
      Smithers, 1896.
Beerbohm, Max. A Book of Caricatures. London, England: Methuen, 1907.
Beerbohm, Max. Fifty Caricatures. London, England: Heinemann, 1913.
Caesar, Terry. "Betrayal and Theft: Beerbohm, Parody, and Modernism." Ariel 17.3 (1986):
      23-32.
Felstiner, John. The Lies of Art: Max Beerbohm's Parody and Caricature. New York, NY:
      Knopf, 1972.
Hart-Davis, Rupert, comp. A Catalogue of the Caricatures of Max Beerbohm. London,

    England: Macmillan, 1972.
Henkle, Roger B. "Wilde and Beerbohm: The Wit of the Avant-Garde, The Charm of
    Failure." Comedy and Culture--England--1820-1900. Princeton, NJ: Princeton
    University Press, 1980. 296-352.
Hopkins, Gerard. "Max Beerbohm." English Wits. Ed. Leonard Russell. London, England:
    Hutchinson, 1940, 257-278.
MacDonald, Dwight, ed. Parodies: An Anthology from Chaucer to Beerbohm--And After.
    New York: Random House, 1960.
Owens, Jill Tedford. "Max Beerbohm." Encyclopedia of British Humorists, Volume I. Ed.
    Steven H. Gale. New York, NY: Garland, 1996, 114-118.
Pearson, Hesketh. "Max Beerbohm." Lives of the Wits. New York: Harper and Row, 1962,
    286-301.
Riewald, J. G., ed. Beerbohm's Literary Caricatures. Hamden, CT: Archon Books, 1977.

Bertrand Arthur Russell (1872-1970)

        Bertrand Russell was a philosopher, a wit, and an epigramist. In a very short space
he was able to jar the listener, to make him stand back and look again at something he
thought he already knew, but really didn't. "What is wanted," Russell said, "is not the will
to believe, but the wish to find out, which is the exact opposite" (Peter 95). Russell also
said, "Laughter is the most inexpensive and most effective wonder drug. Laughter is a
universal medicine" (J 6). He said "The armed forces of one's own nation exist--so each
nation asserts--to prevent aggression by other nations. But the armed forces of other
nations exist--or so many people believe--to promote aggression" (Peter 158). In a letter
to Will Durant, Russell discusses the nature of truth: "I do not see we can judge what
would be the result of the discovery of truth since none has hitherto been discovered"
(Stearns 58). And he has also discussed the nature of man--by comparing him to a dog.
"No matter how eloquently a dog may bark, he cannot tell you that his parents were poor
but honest" (Cross 70; Fromkin and Rodman 346).
        Bertrand Russell's writings have often been compared to those of François Marie
Arouet Voltaire (1694-1778), because for both of these writers philosophical discussions
so often appear in their non-philosophical writings. Both Russell and Voltaire have a
graceful writing style and a sophisticated and delightful sense of humor that is sometimes
biting, but is more often gentle. Both Russell's and Voltaire's humor tends to be based on
absurd hyperbole, unexpected changes in thought, comic juxtapositions, and calculated
irreverence. Russell's books and essays are sprinkled with whimsicality, with pithy
statements, and with "intolerable incongruities" (Pratt 910).
        The Conquest of Happiness (1930) contains much understated humor, and amused
self-effacement. Russell said that during adolescence, he hated life and was continually on
the verge of committing suicide. He was restrained from suicide, however, by "the desire
to know more mathematics." Russell attacks the notion of "sin" by saying that from
infancy the sinner is taught that "swearing is wicked; drinking in wicked; ordinary business
shrewdness is wicked; above all, sex is wicked," but then with wry truth, he continues, "He
does not, of course, abstain from any of these pleasures" (Pratt 910). In The Conquest of
Happiness, Russell wrote, "Certain things are indispensable to the happiness of most men,
but these are simple things: food and shelter, health, love, successful work and the respect
of one's own herd. To some people parenthood also is essential" (Russell 186). The use
of the word "herd," and the tacking on of "parenthood" are both subtle but effective
communication strategies (Russell Conquest 19; Peter 95).
        Alan Pratt says that some of Russell's most delightful occasional pieces can be

found in his Praise of Idleness (1935), and Unpopular Essays (1950) (Pratt 911). Nightmares of Eminent Persons (1953) is a collection of thirteen amusing fables which attack a number of Russell's "bêtes noires." In the introduction, Russell says that the nightmares function as "Signposts to Sanity." He says that "every isolated passion is, in isolation, insane; sanity may be defined as a synthesis of insanities." In this collection, censorship, psychiatry, existentialism, politics, and technology all become satiric targets for Russell's wit. "These nightmares include, in part, President Dwight D. Eisenhower's vision of Senator Joseph McCarthy on friendly terms with the Russians, a metaphysician's visit to Hell, an existentialist who finally convinces himself that he exists, Stalin's sentence to live among Quakers, and the apocalyptic vision of Dean Acheson, President Harry Truman's Secretary of State" (Pratt 911).

Satan in the Suburbs (1953) is a collection of five short stories, all five of which are comic, and revolve around themes dealing with the nature of evil (Pratt 911). In Fact and Fiction (1962), Russell uses parody to spoof the maxims of François de La Rochefoucauld. "The purpose of morals is to enable people to inflict suffering without compunction," or "Liberty is the right to do what I like, license, the right to do what you like" (Russell Fact and Fiction 205). In an essay on "Cranks," Russell says, "I have long been accustomed to being regarded as a crank, and I do not much mind this except when those who so regard me are also cranks, for then they are apt to assume that I must of course agree with their particular nostrum" (Russell Fact and Fiction 177). Fact and Fiction also contains another essay entitled, "The Theologian's Dream," in which Russell uses dreams to place plausible characters in implausible situations. He does this to illustrate their follies and their obsessions. In a particular dream, a theologian dies and goes to heaven where he meets a janitor who has never heard of him. They consult the heavenly librarian, who is also baffled. The heavenly librarian enlists the help of 5,000 galactic sub-librarians, and after years of research they determine that the theologian comes from Galaxy XQ321,726, where there is an insignificant star called "Sun," around which spin some planets that are even more insignificant still. At this point, one of the sub-librarians is able to report, "I discovered that some, at least, of these planets have parasites, and I think that this thing which has been making the inquiries must be one of them" (Russell Fact and Fiction 215).

In Autobiography, Volume III (1969), Russell explains that his stories were the best release he had discovered for expressing difficult-to-express feelings. With his typical good sense of humor, Russell goes on to say that it is sad that his nightmares were never choreographed as ballets. Alan Pratt suggests that Russell's droll nature, and his sparkling wit "helped make of him one of the most widely read philosophers of the twentieth century" (Pratt 911).

Bertrand Arthur Russell Bibliography

Cross, Donna W. Word Abuse. New York, NY: Coward/McCann, 1797.

Green, Jonathan. The Cynic's Lexicon. New York, NY: St. Martin's Press, 1984.

Organ, Troy. "The Humor of Bertrand Russell." The Humanist 46 (1986): 24-32.

Pratt, Alan. "Bertrand Arthur Russell." Encyclopedia of British Humorists, Volume II. Ed. Steven H. Gale. New York, NY: Garland, 1996, 908-912.

Peter, Laurence. The Peter Plan. New York, NY: Morrow, 1976.

Russell, Bertrand. The Conquest of Happiness. London, England: Unwin, 1975.

Russell, Bertrand. Fact and Fiction. New York, NY: Simon and Schuster, 1962.

Stears, Frederic R. Laughing. Springfield, IL: Charles C. Thomas, 1972.

Walter de la Mare (1873-1956)

Richard Carlson says that Walter de la Mare in some sense believes in ghosts and spectres, and that he "humorizes" them in his literature. For Walter de la Mare, death is merely the harbinger for another born spirit, brought to populate his slowly diminishing faery-world. Walter de la Mare's Songs for Childhood (1902) is his best written example of benign humor. Here there are ethereal songs which seem to float on angel hair as the writer presents verses which are "magic, easy, precise, and fair" (Carlson 69).

Walter de la Mare writes what Carlson calls "beauty-humor." His humor is filled with fantasy, but it is nevertheless unforced. It is also unpredictable as it flits from purple bushes to cameo clouds to wildflowers to skunk cabbages, and to floating seeds which are growing just above the ground in soil which is farmed by a "vaporous and almost indolent magic." Critics have called Walter de la Mare's verses "dusty," "rare," "quaint," and "filigree." Following is an example:

> Down-adown-derry
> Sweet Annie Maroon,
> Gathering daisies
> In the meadowes of Doone,
> See a white fairy
> Skip buxom and free
> Where the waters go brawling
> In rills to the sea;
> > Singing down-adown-derry. (Carlson 73).

Here there is a "sense of sound," and there is also a "modest and gracious humor in the flow of lines" (Carlson 72). In his Stuff and Nonsense, and So On (1927) there is what Richard Carlson calls "humor-in-dotage, smiles in senescence":

> There was a young lady of Tring,
> There was an olde Fellow of Kello.
> And she-she did nothing but sing,
> And he-he did nothing but bellow:
>
> Now I think (and don't you?),
> That the best thing to do
> Were to marry these two;
> Then maybe the one would sing no more in Tring,
> Or the other not bellow in Kello. (Carlson 76).

Carlson says that De la Mare, like most of the more accomplished benign humorists, enjoys the coining of words. Examples include "momotumbo," "manaqua," "desdado," "tim-tam," "yookoo," "clutemnacious," and "chalatenanaga" (Carlson 78).

Walter de la Mare Bibliography

Carlson, Richard S. "The Inner Visions of Walter de la Mare." The Benign Humorists New
      York: Archon, 1975, 63-78.

Ford Madox Ford (1873-1939)

When he was a boy, Ford Madox Ford's nurse had told him frightening stories, since she had "a predilection for tales of violence and disaster." Ford wanted to spare his children this same experience, so his writings often lead the readers to brief shallow and whimsical stories of a type that was very common during Ford's time. In Ford's tales, the fairies are "tiny, silly, helpless creatures who wear cowslip caps and whisper in seashells." The fairies are so small that one of them gets caught in the fur of the family dog, named Cromwell, and it is only when Cromwell is sprayed with flea powder that the fairy gets noticed (Lurie 85). Jonathan Alexander points to Ford Madox Ford's attention to detail, his symbolism, and his shifts in point of view to place him into the camp of "Impressionism" (Alexander 383). Ford's humor is often hyperbolic and satiric. His laughter is frequently strained, but this may be his best way of maintaining personal control and perspective in a world that is falling apart (Alexander 387).

Ford's style in The Brown Owl (1892) varies from flowery-elaborate to comic-realistic. Alison Lurie considers The Brown Owl to be a "rather heavy-handed farce about such disparate objects as the court doctor, his umbrella, a dwarf, and a giant." For the amusement of the reader, Ford also makes many ironic asides and references to contemporary events (Lurie 76). The story is about Princess Ismara, who looks very much like Ford's sister Juliet. They both have blue eyes, and long rippling golden hair. Princess Ismara is a typical Victorian heroine--extremely active, courageous, and enterprising. Modern feminists would be proud of the fact that the Princess refused to be addressed as a child. "Now I won't be called a girl, for I'm nineteen, you know. His Majesty the Emperor of India there insulted me by calling me a girl, and I have not forgiven him yet" (Hueffer 66). Ford's tone here is gently mocking, but it is clear here as elsewhere that Ford admired independent and outspoken women. Princess Ismara is protected by an old brown owl. This "brown" color may show that the owl represents Ford Madox Brown, who did the illustrations for the book (Lurie 77). At first the owl is ill tempered, just as Ford Madox Brown, Juliet's grandfather, had been. Ford was to write later that Brown "had his irasibilities, his fits of passion when, tossing his white head, his mane of hair would fly all over his face, and when he would blaspheme impressively" (Ford Memories 246). It is interesting that the two illustrations which Ford Madox Brown did for the book make Princess Ismara look very much like a grown-up Juliet, and the spectacles on the eyes of the owl resemble his own spectacles. Even the wicked chancellor who disguises himself as the "Knight of London" and who tries but fails to take King Intafernes's place is grounded in reality. He is a caricature of Ford's uncle William Rossetti (Lurie 78).

The Feather (1892) is like The Brown Owl in having an independent princess, a kingdom ruled by a wicked usurper, a giant, and a prince. In this story, the magic device is an eagle's feather that has the ability to make someone invisible, and can also make it possible for the princess to go on a voyage to the moon, save the prince's life, and play a number of practical jokes on both friends and enemies. There are episodes in The Feather involving the goddess Diana, the Three Fates, and the Man in the Moon. In the story, Diana lives in a Greek temple made completely out of green cheese, and this temple is, of course, located on the moon. When the prince brings the princess home, and is congratulated by the "populace," Ford remarks, "This is a habit of populaces, they are fond of congratulating anyone who is successful--but they never assist anyone to success if they can help it" (Ford The Feather 182; Lurie 78-79).

The Queen Who Flew (1894) is antiaristocracy, and antimilitary in its tone. Queen Elrida has led such a sheltered life that when someone proposes that she give her worn-out stockings to the poor, she asks, "What are the poor?" (Lurie 79). Lord Blackjowl replies that, "The poor are wicked, idle people--too wicked to work and earn the money, and too dirty to wear stockings" (Ford The Queen Who Flew 59). The ending to The Queen Who Flew is rather contrary to the traditions of "old fairy lore." The queen does not marry the king. She is not restored to her own kingdom. Instead, she goes to the country, where she is taken in by a blind plowman and his mother. There she makes tea out of her wreath of magic flowers and gives the tea to the blind man, whose sight is immediately restored. She

appoints the bat as the king in her place, and goes off to marry the plowman and live
happily ever after--in his cottage (Lurie 82).

Alison Lurie says that Christina's Fairy Book (1906), "has moments of wit and
charm" (Lurie 84). Mr. Apollo (1908) is a social satire. The Portrait (1910) is a mild
satire on the late seventeenth century. The Panel (1912) is a comedy of modern times; it
is also a satire on literary tastes. The New Humpty-Dumpty (1912) is a weak satire set in
the fictional republic of Galizia. Mr. Fleight (1913) is a satire about English party politics
(Alexander 384). The Good Soldier (1915) has drawn a great deal of critical attention from
critics interested in humor and comedy because of its prevailing ironic tone, that saturates
not only the story, but the narration as well. The Good Soldier uses irony to mix comic
and tragic elements. This irony keeps the reader from sure footing, and leads to "comic
uneasiness," as the reader is tempted to laugh at the short-sightedness of the narrator while
at the same time being drawn into the tangle of adulterous affairs that are going on in the
text. Ann Snitow says, "the collapse of the comic into nightmare, pathos, or grief is an
increasing tendency as the novel proceeds" (Snitow 180).

A Little Less than Gods (1928), No Enemy (1928), and Vive Le Roy (1936) all
employ a clever mixing of comedy and tragedy (Alexander 387). Parade's End (1950)
deals with serious and weighty matters, but it does so with comic sketches and comic
undertones. Ann Snitow says, "for all the suffering and despair [that Ford] presents [in
Parade's End, it] is essentially a comic work" (Snitow 217. Jonathan Alexander says that
Ford's brilliance in Parade's End, like his brilliance in The Good Soldier comes from his
ability to use irony as a way of mixing comedy and tragedy. The Good Soldier may have
tragic events, such as various aspects of the war, that are being described, but the book
nevertheless sustains a comic tone throughout (Alexander 386).

In Some Do Not (1950), Ford uses the dialogue of an afternoon tea party to develop
his comic and satiric structures. Jonathan Alexander says that the exchanges between the
vulgar Mr. Duchemin and the other guests, who are very polite and proper, creates a
comedy of manners that is comparable to Oscar Wilde's The Importance of Being Earnest
(Alexander 386).

Ford Madox Ford Bibliography

Alexander, Jonathan. "Ford Madox Ford." Encyclopedia of British Humorists, Volume I.
    Ed. Steven H. Gale. New York, NY: Garland, 1996, 382-388.
Ford, Ford Madox. The Brown Owl, A Fairy Story. London, England: T. Fisher Unwin,
    1892.
Ford, Ford Madox. Memories and Impressions. London, England: Chapman and Hall, 1911.
Ford, Ford Madox. The Feather. London, England: T. Fisher Unwin, 1892.
Ford, Ford Madox. The Queen Who Flew. London, England: Bliss, Sands, and Foster,
    1984.
Lurie, Alison. "Ford Madox Ford's Fairy Tales." Don't Tell the Grown-Ups: Subversive
    Children's Literature. Boston, MA: Little, Brown, and Company, 1990, 74-89.
Snitow, Ann Barr. Ford Madox Ford and the Voice of Uncertainty. Baton Rouge, LA:
    Louisiana State University Press, 1984.

Dorothy Miller Richardson (1873-1957)

Kristin Bluemel indicates that there is a gentle and subversive parody at work
throughout Dorothy Richardson's Pilgrimage (1919). She compares Pilgrimage with James
Joyce's Ulysses saying that in both novels, "deployment of parody typically links its

challenges to literary convention with the reader's participation in its humor" (Bluemel 166).

Dorothy Miller Richardson Bibliography

Bluemel, Kristin. "The Feminine Laughter of No Return: James Joyce and Dorothy Richardson." Look Who's Laughing: Gender and Comedy. Ed. Gail Finney. Amsterdam, The Netherlands: Gordon and Breach, 1994, 161-172.

Gilbert Keith Chesterton (1874-1936)

As a child, G. K. Chesterton enjoyed practical jokes. Sometimes he would knock at a door and then run away. Sometimes he would lie down across a threshold to trip whoever came out, but these were crimes of imagination and humor, not crimes of malice (Pearson 302). In school, Chesterton would fill his schoolbooks with drawings that obliterated the text, and he just couldn't take the school routine seriously. Often, he would mutter to himself and laugh. He later referred to his school days as, "the period during which I was being instructed by somebody I did not know about something I did not want to know." Chesterton sometimes forgot to do his home-work, and sometimes he even forgot to attend school. One day he was discovered wandering about on the playing-field when he should have been at his desk, and he said that he thought it was Saturday (Pearson 305).

As a child Chesterton loved fairy-tales, and when he grew older he wrote fairy tales. His stories were fantastic, and his characters were fabulous (Pearson 303). At the age of sixteen Chesterton wrote essays for The Debater, one of which was entitled "Dragons" and described them as resembling "an intoxicated crocodile." Chesterton went on to say that the modern dragon has grown prudent:

> He doesn't see the good of going about as a roaring lion, but seeks what he may devour in a quiet and respectable way, behind many illustrious names and many imposing disguises. Behind the scarlet coat and epaulets, behind the star and mantle of the garter, behind the ermine tippet and the counsellor's robe, behind, alas, the black coat and white tie, behind many a respectable exterior in public and in private life, we fear that the dragon's flaming eyes and grinning jaws, his tyrannous power, and his infernal cruelty, sometimes lurk. (Pearson 304)

Chesterton was an epigramist. About Christianity, he wrote "The Christian ideal has not been tried and found wanting; it has been found difficult and left untried." About individuality, he wrote, "Do not free a camel of the burden of his hump. You may be freeing him from being a camel" (Katz and Arbeiter 195). Chesterton wrote mainly between 1900 and World War I. During this time he wrote a series of stories, novels, and poems that, "place him among the greatest of British literary humorists." His work is filled with wit, paradox, verbal play, and intensely visual imagery. Although the paradox and word play continue after World War I, "Chesterton's later work considered on the basis of his humor and verbal art is generally of less interest" (Richardson 246).

The Man Who Was Thursday: A Nightmare (1908) is a melodramatic spy story; it is also a religious allegory and a fantasy. Gabriel Symes, the protagonist, is an undercover policeman who is also a poet. In his undercover work he finds himself with a bunch of anarchists who would like to overthrow all order. Each of these anarchists takes on the name of a day of the week, and in this way, Symes becomes Thursday. The leader of the group is Sunday. As each of the anarchists is unmasked, he turns out to be an "undercover policeman." The anarchists get together in a subterranean crypt that is filled with bombs that look, "like the bulbs of iron plants, or the eggs of iron birds." This is a funny description. Also funny is when Sunday escapes from the London Zoo by riding an elephant; he is pursued by six detectives in a cab. The ending of the novel is also funny. At the final scene, in which Sunday is unveiled, there is a masquerade ball with dancers dressed in various strange costumes. There is a man dressed as a windmill with enormous sails, a man dressed as an elephant, and a man dressed like an enormous hornbill, with a beak that is huge. "Every couple dancing seemed a separate romance; it might be a fairy dancing with a pillar-box or a peasant girl dancing with the moon; but in each case it was, somehow, as absurd as Alice in Wonderland, yet as gay and kind as a love story" (Chesterton Thursday 186).

The first collection of Father Brown stories was published as The Innocence of Father Brown (1911). The Father Brown stories were continued in The Incredulity of Father Brown (1926), The Secret of Father Brown (1927), and The Scandal of Father Brown (1935). These were later collected in The Father Brown Omnibus (1982). The humor in the Father Brown stories is gentle, charming, and witty (Richardson 246).

Gilbert Keith Chesterton Bibliography

Barnes, Lewis W. "Christopher Fry: The Chestertonian Concept of Comedy." Xavier Review 2 (1950): 30-47.
Chesterton, G. K. The Man Who Was Thursday: A Nightmare. London, England: Simpkin, 1908.
Chesterton, G. K. What's Wrong with the World. New York, NY: Cassell, 1910.
Furlong, William B. GBS/GKC Shaw and Chesterton: The Metaphysical Jesters. University Park, PA: Pennsylvania State University Press, 1970.
Katz, Marjorie, and Jean Arbeiter. Pegs to Hang Ideas On. New York, NY: M. Evans, 1973.
Kenner, Hugh. Paradox in Chesterton. New York, NY: Sheed, 1961.
Pearson, Hesketh. "Gilbert Keith Chesterton." Lives of the Wits. New York, NY: Harper and Row, 1962, 302-318.
Richardson, Betty. "G K. Chesterton." Encyclopedia of British Humorists, Volume I. Ed. Steven H. Gale. New York, NY: Garland, 1996, 243-248.

Sir Winston Churchill (1874-1965)

Winston Churchill once said, "In my belief, you cannot deal with the most serious things in the world unless you also understanding the most amusing" (Athey 251). Churchill's humor was like that of Samuel Johnson's. It was a bluffing masculine kind of humor that dealt with individual ethics, the qualities of leadership, and the enhancement of the British Empire. His attitudes about empire were basically those of Rudyard Kipling. He also had the "Bully spirit" of Teddy Roosevelt, the machismo of Ernest Hemingway, and the frontier spirit of Mark Twain (Athey 249). Churchill viewed life as an aristocrat, and a controlling metaphor for him was the "white man's burden" philosophy that is so closely associated with the British Empire. The effectiveness of Churchill's wit is that it is grounded in a sense of family, class, history, and empire (Athey 250).

James Athey feels that Churchill's humor is very consistent with what James Beattie said in An Essay on Laughter and Ludicrous Composition (1776): "Laughter arises from the view of two or more inconsistent, unsuitable, or incongruous parts or circumstances, considered as united in complex object or assemblage, or as acquiring a sort of mutual relation from the peculiar manner in which the mind takes notice of them." It is also consistent with what William Hazlitt said in "On Wit and Humour" (1819), which describes humor as "the incongruous, the disconnecting of one idea from another, or the jostling of one feeling against another." Furthermore it is consistent with what George Meredith said in On Comedy and the Uses of the Comic Spirit (1897) when he talked about humor being a "social corrective" (Athey 250). Churchill liked to mock his foes, and a good example of this appeared in 1942 when Churchill used sarcasm and a childlike tone to talk about Adolf Hitler: "Then Hitler made his second great blunder. He forgot about the winter. There is a winter, you know, in Russia. For a good many months the temperature is apt to fall very low. There is snow, there is frost, and all that. Hitler forgot about the Russian winter. He must have been very loosely educated. We all heard about it at school, but he forgot it. I have never made such a bad mistake as that!" (Athey 250).

Churchill was a true wit. In The Last Lion: Visions of Glory 1874-1932 (1984), William Manchester explains how he would build up to a witticism, saying that this was an entertainment in itself. Manchester is quoting Hugh Massingham, a peer of Churchill, who described this recurring event as follows:

> One always knew it was coming...the bubble of mirth was slowly rising through his body. The stomach would swell; a shoulder heave. By this time, the audience would also be convulsed, although it had no idea what the joke was going to be. Meanwhile, the bubble had ascended a little farther and had reached the face.... Finally, there would be the explosion, the triumphant sentence of ridicule." (Manchester 34)

Churchill was aware of his own genius, and once said, "We are all worms. But I do believe that I am a glow worm" (Halle 49). When a particularly gushy woman asked him, "Doesn't it thrill you to know that every time you speak the hall is packed to overflowing?" Churchill replied, "It is quite flattering, but whenever I feel this way, I always remember that, if instead of making a political speech, I was being hanged, the crowd would be twice as big" (Manchester 810). Churchill enjoyed analogies, and once said that there are only two things that are more difficult than making after-dinner speeches. "One is climbing a wall leaning toward you, and the other is kissing a girl leaning away from you" (True 163). Churchill also compared politics with war, saying that, "Politics are almost as exciting as war, and quite as dangerous. In war you can only be killed once, but in politics many times" (Bartlett 743).

Churchill had many verbal duels with other wits. When American-born Lady Nancy Astor entered the British Parliament as its first woman member, she and Churchill cultivated a friendship that was based partly on their regular matching of wits. Lady Astor once told Churchill, "Winston, if I were your wife, I'd put poison in your coffee," to which Churchill replied, "Nancy, if I were your husband, I would gladly drink it" (Adler 35; Halle 72). Another of Churchill's delightful feuds was with George Bernard Shaw. One time Shaw sent Churchill tickets to two seats to his new play and invited him to attend the opening night and to, "bring a friend--if you have one." Churchill promptly wired back, "Impossible to be present for the first performance. Will attend the second performance--if there is one" (Adler 35).

Churchill also had some witty encounters with America's President Franklin Delano Roosevelt. Once, when President Roosevelt was tiring, he suggested to Churchill that a conference should last for five days, or six days at most. Churchill responded, "I do not see any way of realizing our hopes about a world organization in five or six days. Even the Almighty took seven" (Halle 208). At another time, while he was visiting America, Churchill was conferring with President Roosevelt on the rising threat of Hitler to international security and about Europe's need for America's military assistance. Churchill stepped from his bathroom--naked--just as Roosevelt was wheeling his chair into the room for a meeting. The startled Roosevelt began to apologize and leave, but Winston said solemnly, "The Prime Minister of Great Britain has nothing to hide from the President of the United States." According to Bill Adler, "it was that month that Britain had a new ally--the United States--and Churchill had a new friend--Roosevelt" (Adler 76).

Churchill gained some notoriety for being unfaithful to any particular political party. He started out as a Conservative, but he disagreed with their platform and joined the Liberals. Then he rejoined the Conservatives again. When asked about his fickleness, he responded, "Anybody can rat, but it takes a certain amount of ingenuity to rerat" (Halle 42). Churchill was in favor of having a strong military, saying that England would not be likely to get into trouble by having an extra thousand or two up-to-date airplanes at their disposal. His questionable and no-longer-humorous comparison was to the man whose mother-in-law had died in Brazil, and who had replied when asked how the remains should be disposed of, responded, "Embalm, cremate and bury. Take no chances" (Adler 3).

It is because Winston Churchill dictated most of his books that they have "the orator's ring to them." This "orator's ring" tends to give them a scintillating style with sharp, pungent phrases. Much of Churchill's humor resulted from his "philosophy of the individual." He advocated the role of the individual in shaping his environment, and this gives his writing a spirit of, "optimism, with its romantic blush of ardor and courage, denied absolutes and a required comic view to delineate the complexity of the world and improve the lot of mankind." Churchill had a very succinct way of catching the essence of the situation. About Clement Attlee, his political opponent, he said, "He is a sheep in wolf's clothing" (Athey 249). Churchill liked aphorisms because they were so effective in getting his point across in a succinct and powerful way. He said, "To jaw-jaw is better than to war-war." He also said, "It is a good thing for an uneducated man to read books of quotations" (Athey 250). When a particular bureaucrat accused Churchill of ending a sentence with a preposition, Churchill responded, "This is the sort of English up with which I will not put." On another occasion, Churchill was at a gathering of dignitaries, and a matron patronizingly admonished the cigar-smoking Churchill by saying, "I am shocked, sir, that you are so drunk." Churchill responded, "Madam, tonight I am drunk and you are ugly, but tomorrow I shall be sober." This response was typical of Churchill; it was offensive, rough, course, and bullying. Such episodes as these capture the essence of Winston Churchill (Athey 251).

Churchill did not lose his wit in later years. On his eighty-fifth birthday, he delivered a powerful retort at the House of Commons, and a young politician who thought he was out of Churchill's hearing range said to the man beside him, "They say the old man is getting gaga." Without turning his head, Churchill responded, "Yes, and they say he's getting deaf, too" (Manchester 34). Still later in life Churchill was talking about his own impending death and quipped, "I am prepared to meet my Maker. But whether my Maker is prepared for the great ordeal of meeting me is another matter" (Keller 110). Sir Winston Churchill's last words, on his deathbed, were, "I am bored with it all" (Athey 251).

Sir Winston Churchill Bibliography

Adler, Bill. The Churchill Wit. New York, NY: Coward-McCann, 1966.

Athey, Joel. "Winston S. Churchill." Encyclopedia of British Humorists, Volume I. Ed. Steven H. Gale. New York, NY: Garland, 1996, 248-252.

Bartlett, John. Bartlett's Familiar Quotations. 15th edition. New York, NY: Little Brown, 1980.

Halle, Kay. The Irrepressible Churchill: A Treasure of Winston Churchill's Wit. Cleveland, OH: World Publications, 1966; London, England: Robson, 1985.

Keller, Mollie. Winston Churchill. New York, NY: Franklin Watts, 1984.

Manchester, William. The Last Lion: Winston Spencer Churchill, 3 Volumes. Boston, MA: Little, Brown, 1983-1990.

True, Herb. Humor Power. New York, NY: Doubleday, 1980.

Willans, Geoffrey, and Charles Roetter. The Wit of Winston Churchill. London, England: Parrish, 1956.

W. Somerset Maugham (1874-1965)

Betty Richardson is impressed by the versatility of W. Somerset Maugham's wit and humor. In Maugham's writing, "wit flashes through his non-fiction; aphorisms reminiscent of Oscar Wilde's illumine his comedies of manners; and sardonic twists of plot and character make his fiction memorable" (Richardson 739). Richardson continues that Maugham's principal theme is the entrapment of men and women by the social codes and institutions, and the ways they try to escape from these entrapments. Maugham constantly develops the paradox that his characters need the very codes and institutions that imprison them. They are not able to cope with the freedom that liberation from these bourgeois rules gives (Richardson 740).

One of Maugham's best plays is Lady Frederick (1907)(Richardson 741). It is a play about the comic qualities that emerge when male and female roles are reversed. The most famous scene in the play is frequently associated with the satire of Jonathan Swift. In this scene, Lady Frederick has changed her mind about seducing the Innocent, and has therefore allowed him to see her without makeup and in early morning disarray. The Innocent is startled by her artificiality. Lady Frederick has been observed in her indiscretions, and she must therefore maneuver her way through, "a minefield of would-be bribers, blackmailers, and suitors" in order to bring herself to the end of the play in an appropriate marriage with a husband equal in status to herself (Richardson 741).

Of Human Bondage (1915) is a coming-of-age novel about Philip Carey, who is very much like Maugham himself, except that he has a club foot instead of a stutter. Philip's narrow upbringing, and his physical handicap keep him from exploring. Nevertheless he is in love with Mildred Rogers. This love is debasing, because Mildred is stupid, greedy, and conventional (Richardson 740).

Sir Arthur Pinero's immediate successor in the development of eccentric characters was W. Somerset Maugham. In 1907 Maugham wrote Loaves and Fishes in which,

> a clergyman--in the best Pinero tradition of eccentric conduct--is the object of comedy. Maugham's affinity to Pinero was not only apparent in subject matter, but also in his rather brittle tone, unusual characterizations, and deft, often witty, dialogue; and especially in his successful manners comedies of the 1920s--beginning with the light and trivial Home and Beauty and the elegant manners tone of The Circle--he showed a debt to Pinero and the tradition of English eccentricity. (Ronning 56)

Maugham's Freddy and Bill in Home and Beauty (1919) are earthy types who try to free themselves from the gentle clutches of the callous but entertaining Victoria. The tone is cynical as the characters alternate between quaint sentiments and drollery, in their enactments of a series of boldface hypocrisies and indiscretions (Ronning 56).

Thirty years before the curtain rises in the play The Circle (1920), Lady Kitty Champion-Cheney has left a note on her pincushion, and has run off with Porteous, her husband's best friend. Between that time and the time of the opening of the play she has not seen her husband or her son, but now the son is thirty-five, and he is married, and Lady Kitty has been asked for a visit. When her husband and her son arrive, Lady Kitty, who thirty years earlier had been one of the great beauties of England, now rouges her cheeks and dyes her hair, and is filled with airs and pretentions. And the love of Lord Porteous has grown cold, and he is snappish and pompous, and choleric. Lord Champion-Cheney, the deserted husband, who has been greatly wronged is amused by this scene, and he realizes that after these thirty years, he is the one who has been the least hurt (Kronenberger 297). In The Circle there is a kind of sad fun, a kind of rueful amusement. "If Time heals all wounds, it equally mars all loveliness." The Circle demonstrates how similar high comedy and tragedy are on the surface, and yet how different they are in their effect. "For high comedy is tragedy stripped of all that is heroic and exalted and affirmative. There is indeed...something joyous about tragedy, because something exultant." High Comedy, "is concerned with something infinitely sadder than the death of people: with the death of their dreams, the débris of their aspirations, the pressed leaves of their high impassioned vows. Tragedy carves out in granite the fact that Character is Fate; but high comedy knows that everything is writ in water" (Kronenberger 298).

According to Louis Kronenberger, The Circle is one of the few creditable "high comedies" written in English in the twentieth century. Both Our Betters and The Circle are drawing-room comedies, and both are concerned with how people behave in certain ticklish, complicated, or embarrassing situations; however Our Betters could not exist outside of the drawing room, because the central theme of Our Betters is Grayston's drawing-room (Kronenberger 294). If you remove the drawing-room from the play, it becomes meaningless. Although the drawing room plays a large and special role in The Circle, the play could still exist perfectly well without the drawing room. "The Circle represents a real clash between worldly advantage and personal emotion. In Our Betters, people sacrifice all they are to ambition; in The Circle, they sacrifice all they have, for love." Although the drawing room is a very natural setting for The Circle, the action, "could take place equally well in a middle-class living room or a lower middle-class parlor" (Kronenberger 295). While Our Betters is nothing but drawing-room comedy, or comedy of manners, The Circle is this plus something more. It is "high comedy," which cuts across circumstances to character. In high comedy there is a constant spraying of wit and irony. In high comedy there is something that reaches the audience through the mind. The Circle is well written. There is a neat story fully developed. There is a dry, worldly, wellbred tone that is a little bit brittle, a little bit mocking, and yet never just frivolous. The Circle is too serious a play to be considered merely a sentimental comedy (Kronenberger 296).

In Our Betters (1923), Maugham assaulted the London social scene, but with an important precaution. He made the targets of his satire Americans rather than English. Therefore, when English audiences heard the word "slut," on stage they found consolation in the fact that it was spoken by one American about another American (Kronenberger 290). Our Betters is a testimonial to American push--to aggressive social climbing. There is a millionaire American lover who is courting Pearl Lady Grayston. Lady Grayston does love him, but she wants to inherit his fortunes since she herself has only a scant million dollars, and since she wants to be able to maintain herself as the formidable hostess she has become. Lady Grayston is young and attractive, in contrast to the Duchesse de Surennes, "formerly Minnie Somebody-or-Other," who is middle-aged, sadly rouged, and struggling to hold onto the, "good-looking good-for-nothings she has bought herself." In addition to the Americans, these are Maugham's chief targets. A younger sister of Lady Grayston and her former fiancé have just arrived from America (Kronenberger 291). In this satire, Maugham makes fun of the coronet-crazed Americans by, "satirizing their methods of getting on, beyond pointing up the differences between America and England." Thus Maugham is a direct descendent of Restoration comedy. "His characters are not mere hummingbirds and peacocks, but foxes and even birds of prey" (Kronenberger 292).

The Trembling of a Leaf (1921), and Ashenden; or, The British Agent (1928) are collections of stories based on Maugham's intelligence work. "Rain" is a short story in The philosophers (Homer, Petronius, Plato), Irish authors (George Bernard Shaw, Edmund Spenser, Jonathan Swift), Italian authors, statesmen, and inventors (Dante, Machiavelli, Mussolini, Marconi), Norwegian musicians and authors (Edvard Grieg, Henrik Ibsen), Russian leaders (Karl Marx), Scottish authors (Bobbie Burns, Sir Walter Scott), Spanish authors (Miguel de Cervantes), world leaders (Cleopatra), world explorers (Columbus, Sir Walter Raleigh), and World Military Leaders (Alexander of Macedon, Attila, Hannibal, Zinghis Khan). But Bentley's favorite target was English authors (Jane Austen, Frances Bacon, The Venerable Bede, Hillaire Belloc, Robert Browning, John Bunyan, Thomas Carlyle, Lewis Carroll, Geoffrey Chaucer, Noel Coward, Charles Dickens, Desiderius Erasmus, John Gay, John Keats, John Milton, Alexander Pope, William Shakespeare, Alfred, Lord Tennyson, and H. Beerbohm Tree) (Ewart ix).

The index in The Complete Clerihews is not an index at all, but is rather a parody of an index. The heading "Absurdity" will take the reader to "George III." The heading "Zulus, table manners of, resort to" takes the reader to the Duke of Fife. Other entries include the following:

Day, rainy, preparedness for (FORD)
Dejection, stanzas written in, nowhere near Naples (MILTON)
Delicacy (BRIGHAM YOUNG)
Diet, indiscretion in (MILTON, HENRY I); morbid delicacy in matter of (DAVY, BESANT, MARCONI, but cf. BUNYAN)

Nancy Cohen is correct when she says, "This index is of little use in finding a clerihew on Miguel de Cervantes or Savonarola, but it aims a number of very funny barbs at the practice of indexing" (Cohen 140).

In his clerihews, Bentley treated Karl Marx with humor, not disapproval. He refers to the Primrose League only obliquely, as an "unburied ichthyosaurus." Henry Ford is "another millionaire" who is satirized for his meanness. In a clerihew devoted to Goering, Hitler is only treated facetiously (Ewart xiii). Bentley's clerihews tend to be free from malice. "Bentley probably thought that Beit was a villain, but he doesn't say so. The illustration is far more outspoken; Chesterton was a great arguer and far more of a polemicist. The clerihew could easily be used for satire, and even satire of great bitterness, but as far as I know it never has been." Instead, the clerihew is an absurdity in which the author is challenged to find rhymes for the names chosen, and the names are often selected because they are hard to rhyme. The general tone of the clerihew is both "civilized and dotty." "It is a humorous pseudo-biographical quatrain, rhymed as two couplets, with lines of uneven length more or less in the rhythm of prose. It is short and pithy, and often contains or implies a moral reflection of some kind" (Ewart xiv). Gavin Ewart says of Edmund Bentley that, "I think it gave him more pleasure than anything else he achieved in life that he lived to see the word 'clerihew' " enshrined in the Oxford Dictionary as part of our language" (Ewart x).

The only way to get a true sense of Bentley's clerihews is to sample them personally; therefore three examples follow. The samples are representative in being doggerel verse written in mock invective tone:

When their lordships asked Bacon
How many bribes he had taken
He had at least the grace
To get very red in the face. (Ewart 6)

What I like about Clive
Is that he is no longer alive
There is a great deal to be said
For being dead. (Ewart 30)

Trembling of a Leaf which is about the complex relationship between freedom and convention. In "Rain" there is a sardonic twist whereby a prostitute gains victory over a self-righteous missionary. Rather than converting a particular prostitute, The Reverend Davidson succumbs to her. Since the Reverend is not able to tolerate freedom, he kills himself, and the prostitute becomes permanently embittered. The humor of this piece is grimly ironic, as when the Reverend Davidson boasts on the eve of his seduction that, "Last night I was privileged to bring a lost soul to the loving arms of Jesus" (Maugham East and West 30).

The Constant Wife (1927) is a play which represents Maugham's comedy at its best. The early dialogue is epigrammatic, written very much in the style of Oscar Wilde. Constance Middleton is met by her sister at the beginning of The Constant Wife. Her sister is anxious to inform Constance of her husband's adultery with her best friend. This gossiping sister is the type of idle, bored, manipulative women that Maugham abhorred. Constance becomes bored with her life of idleness, and before long she takes on the roles, the responsibilities, and the stage dialogue of a man. She enters a friend's business and is able to earn enough money to pay her husband for her last year's room and board, and after doing this she takes off to Italy for a six-week trip with a man who had once proposed to her. In the meantime, her husband is reduced to, "drooling conventional inanities of a melodramatic heroine." Constance, who has escaped her prison is now unrepentant, but her husband has now become more attracted to her than when she was a conventional woman, and he wants her to return to him when her trip is over (Richardson 741).

"Mr. Harrington's Washing" from Ashenden (1928), illustrates the irony that we need a kind of imprisonment in order to be free. Ashenden is a secret agent who ends up in Petrograd at the time when Aleksandr Kerensky and his troops are overpowered by the Bolshevik forces of V. I. Lenin and Leon Trotsky. John Quincy Harrington is a tidy New Englander who is a slave to his habits, but Harrington is a hero to Ashenden because Harrington refuses to, "let the Russian revolution interfere with his proper breakfast, his seat on a train, and his clean laundry." Even at a time when soldiers are randomly shooting in the streets, Harrington is fussing at the hotel management because they have not returned his washing. Harrington goes after the laundry, and Ashenden and his Russian friend follow Harrington wanting to see this "helplessly conventional man" safely out of Russia, but when they find him, he is laying with his face in a pool of blood. In his hand he clenches a parcel containing four clean shirts, two union suits, a pair of pyjamas, and four collars. "Mr. Harrington had not let his washing go" (Maugham East and West 640).

Cakes and Ale (1930) is both comic and scandalous. It is about Edward Driffield, a character who is probably modeled on Thomas Hardy. Driffield's first wife, Rosie, is one of Maugham's "exuberantly earthy women." The novel is also about Alroy Kear, a character unflatteringly modeled after Hugh Walpole. Willie Ashenden is the narrator of this novel, and Ashenden's reminiscences are, of course, filled with the paradoxical and ironic relationships between convention and freedom, between careerism and creativity, and between genuine women and artificial ones. The humor comes from developing these contrasts, and it also comes from Ashenden's dry irony, and the satiric depictions of such figures as Kear. Rosie is at the center of the story. Rosie had been married to Driffield, and this fact must be concealed by Driffield's second wife and by members of the London literary establishment, but this is hard to do because of Rosie's life-enhancing qualities and her vibrant energy. Rosie's liberating qualities are the opposite of the, "careerists of literary London whose self-serving concern with propriety is rendered comic by [the] contrast" (Richardson 741). The Summing Up (1938), and Writer's Notebook (1949) contain occasionally witty remarks. They are frank discussions of Maugham's experiences, and the conclusions at which Maugham has arrived. They give insights not only into the personality of Somerset Maugham, and Maugham's writing, but also into the nature of writing in general. This is especially true of Writer's Notebook, "which shows how a writer's eye works as it records the sights and sounds that lead to stories" (Richardson 742).

Art Buchwald interviewed W. Somerset Maugham during one of his visits to Paris. The interview happened on the very same day that the musical version of Maugham's Sadie Thompson was opening in New York, and so of course Buchwald and Maugham talked about this famous character. When Buchwald asked Maugham if he ever returned to Pango Pango, Maugham replied, "I'm too old for those trips. Besides, all those places have become far too civilized for me. Did you know, the house where we all stayed on my original trip is now all dolled up and called 'The Sadie Thompson Hotel'?" (Buchwald 152).

Somerset Maugham's style was quite straight forward. He once said,

> I look upon readableness as the highest merit that a novel can have. They say that it is better for a women to be good than to be clever; that is a point upon which I have never been able to make up my mind; but I am quite sure that it is better for a novel to be readable than to be good and clever. (Towne 51)

Claude Searcy McIver makes an insightful comparison between a particular quote from Oscar Wilde, and a similar quote from Somerset Maugham. One of the characters in Wilde's play, A Woman of No Importance (1839) says, "The advantage of playing with fire, Lady Caroline, is that one never gets even singed. It is the people who don't know how to play with it who get burned up." On the surface, this is very different, but in terms of meaning, Wilde is saying something quite similar to Maugham, when Maugham says in Merry-Go-Round "There are three good maxims in the conduct of life: Never sin; but if you sin, never repent; and above all, if you repent, never, never confess" (McIver 17). In a way, Maugham's quote would be more typical of Wilde than it is of Maugham. Yet, it is very appropriate for Maugham as well, for it was also Maugham who has Rose say in Lady Frederick (1947), "When a man's in love he can only write sonnets to the moon. When a woman's in love she can still cook his dinner and darn her own stockings" (Maugham 26).

Forrest Burt says that Maugham had a strong feeling of inferiority; he felt like an outsider. "Standing outside he could more easily observe the foibles and weakness of others. It is little wonder that his stylistic tendency was toward the comic and satiric" (qtd in Roby 96). Burt continues that Archie Loss also made similar comments: "The emotional distance characteristic of Maugham gives rise, in his best work, to an ironic and sometimes witty view of human experiences" (Loss 114). "As a humorist, he [Maugham] demonstrates an unusually great range of techniques: aphorisms and turns of phrase that evoke the memory of Wilde or of the Enlightenment, ironies of situation and character that evoke memories of the Greeks, and social satire purely modern in its force and directness" (Richardson 742).

W. Somerset Maugham Bibliography

Barnes, Ronald E. The Dramatic Comedy of William Somerset Maugham. The Hague, The Netherlands: Mouton, 1968.

Buchwald, Art. Art Buchwald's Paris. Boston, MA: Little, Brown and Co. 1954.

Kronenberger, Louis. The Thread of Laughter: Chapters on English Stage Comedy from Johnson to Maugham. New York, NY: Hill, 1970.

Loss, Archie K. W. Somerset Maugham. New York, NY: Ungar, 1987.

McIver, Claude Searcy. William Somerset Maugham: A Study of Technique and Literary Sources. Unpublished Ph.D. Dissertation. Philadelphia, PA: University of Pennsylvania, 1938.

W. Somerset Maugham (1874-1965)

Maugham, W. Somerset. East and West, Volume 1 of The complete Short Stories of W. Somerset Maugham. Garden City, NY: Doubleday, 1952.

Maugham, W. Somerset. Lady Frederick: A Comedy in Three Acts. London, England: Samuel French, 1947.

Maugham, W. Somerset. Six Comedies. Garden City, NY: Doubleday, 1937.

Richardson, Betty. "William Somerset Maugham." Encyclopedia of British Humorists, Volume II. Ed. Steven H. Gale. New York, NY: Garland, 1996, 738-744.

Roby, Kinley E., ed. W. Somerset Maugham. Boston, MA: Twayne, 1985.

Ronning, Robert. "The Eccentric: The English Comic Farce of Sir Arthur Pinero." Quarterly Journal of Speech 63 (1977): 51-58.

Sawyer, Newell W. The Comedy of Manners from Sheridan to Maugham: The Study of the Type as a Dramatic Form and as a Social Development. Unpublished Ph.D. Dissertation. Philadelphia, PA: University of Pennsylvania, 1931.

Towne, Charles Hanson, et. al. W. Somerset Maugham: Novelist, Essayist, Dramatist, with a Note on Novel Writing by Mr. Maugham. New York, NY: George H. Doran, 1977.

Edmund Clerihew Bentley (1875-1956)

The clerihew, invented by Edmund Clerihew Bentley, is designed to satirize historical, political, and literary figures (Cohen 141). In Those Days (1940), Edmund Clerihew Bentley tries to explain the nature of the clerihew by giving examples and explaining why they are good or bad examples. As an example of a bad clerihew, Bentley gives the following:

> Frederick the Great
> Became King at twenty-eight.
> In a fit of amnesia
> He invaded Silesia.

Bentley suggests that the reason this clerihew fails is that, "there is nothing with which the dry-as-dust historiographer could possibly quarrel." Bentley says that this bad clerihew is, "truthful and reliable--yes, even slavishly so. But where is the human appeal? Where is the probing psychological touch?" (Bentley Those Days 157). In contrast to the failed clerihew given above, Bentley gives what he considers to be a near-perfect clerihew below:

> Mr. Philip Snowden
> Was rarely mistaken for Woden.
> People as a rule were much more
> Apt to mistake him for Thor. (Bentley Complete Clerihews xiii)

In this clerihew, the rhyme and meter are stretched. There is also an enormous improbability of the pairings, with the second couplet taking the outrageous statement of the first with "polite credulity." The tone of this good clerihew is "both civilized and dotty" (Cohen 140).

Edmund Bentley's "clerihews" tend to be inconsequential, anachronistic, biographical, benignly satirical, and absurdly amusing (Ewart ix). In The Complete Clerihews of E. Clerihew Bentley (1981) there are 141 clerihews which target American authors, cult figures, and Presidents (Edgar Allan Poe, H. G. Wells, Henry Ford, General Sherman, Brigham Young, Calvin Coolidge, Herbert Hoover, Franklin Roosevelt), artists (Leonardo de Vinci), Biblical characters (Job, Methuselah), English Kings and Dukes (King Edward, George III, Henry I, Henry VIII, King John, the Duke of Wellington), French authors and kings (Victor Hugo, Voltaire, Louis XI, Louis XVIII), German musicians (Johannes Brahms, George Frederick Handel, Franz Liszt), Greek authors, leaders, and

> George the Third
> Ought never to have occurred.
> One can only wonder
> At so grotesque a blunder. (Ewart 49)

Nancy Cohen believes that Bentley's clerihews reflect a schoolboy taste for secret codes, inside jokes, and a depiction of silly elders. Late in his life, Bentley was told that he had never written a clerihew about the queen, so he did:

> What fools we've been!
> We've forgotten the Queen!
> She removes her crown, it is said,
> When she goes to bed. (Cohen 140)

Nancy Cohen suggests that the clerihew is a very close ancestor of the light verse form called the "double dactyl" which was invented in the twentieth-century and was used extensively by Anthony Hecht and John Hollander (Cohen 141).

Edmund Clerihew Bentley Bibliography

Bentley, Edmund Clerihew. The First Clerihews. Oxford, England: Oxford University Press, 1982.

Bentley, Edmund Clerihew. Clerihews Complete. London, England: T. W. Laurie, 1951.

Bentley, Edmund Clerihew. The Complete Clerihews of E. C. Bentley. Oxford, England: Oxford University Press, 1981.

Bentley, Edmund Clerihew. Elephant's Work, an Enigma. New York, NY: Knopf, 1950.

Bentley, Edmund Clerihew. Those Days. London, England: Constable, 1940.

Cohen, Nancy. "Edmund Clerihew Bentley." Encyclopedia of British Humorists, Volume I. Ed. Steven H. Gale. New York, NY: Garland, 1996, 138-142.

Ewart, Gavin, ed. The Complete Clerihews of E. Clerihew Bentley Oxford, England: Oxford University Press, 1981.

Gilmour, John, and Nicholas Wall. "The Clerihew: Its History and Bibliography." The Book Collector 29.1 (1980): 23-35.

Russell, Leonard, ed. "E. C. Bentley: Greedy Night." Parody Party. Plymouth, England: Mayflower Press, 77-96.

Edward Morgan Forster (1879-1970)

Edward Morgan Forster's name is the result of a comedy of errors. Forster was born in London, and his name was officially registered as "Henry Morgan Forster." In March of 1879 the baby Forster was taken to the church of Clapham Commons, and on the way to the church the old verger asked the future-novelist's father for the name. Misunderstanding the intent of the question, the novelist's father, whose name was "E. M. Forster" gave his own name, so the babe was christened "Edward Morgan Forster." About this event, the novelist comments: "I had been registered in one way, and christened another. What on earth was to happen! It turned out after agitated research that the christening had it, so Edward I am" (qtd. in Shahane 15). In 1897, Forster entered King's College, Cambridge, and he was pleasantly surprised by the cordiality and the intellectual playfulness of this "enchanting institution" (Shahane 16).

In the Clark Lectures, E. M. Forster notes that he sees the writing of novels as "serious work." He also notes, however, that he believes that it can be fun. In the Clark Lectures, he explains the importance of plot, but he scoffs at the notion, calling it "a sort of higher government official" that tells the author what to do. In his own novels, humor plays a central part in every one of them. In order to amuse the reader and vary the tone, Forster creates comic characters. In order to poke fun at some of the characters he has created, characters who have allowed their estimates of themselves to get a bit out of hand, Forster devises humorous situations, or employs satire. Throughout his canon, the interplay of the serious and the comic gives his work a special charm (Williams 391).

Paradoxically, Forster was both a romantic and an anti-romantic. J. B. Beer compares Forster's writing with that of such romantics as Blake, Coleridge, and Shelly, in that all four writers shared an intense love of nature, deep feelings for the English countryside, and a fondness and nostalgia for old England. But unlike the romantics, Forster had a keen awareness of the vital function of money. In this respect, Forster was more like Wallace Stevens, the modern American poet, who made the witty and profound remark that "money is a kind of poetry" (qtd. in Shahane 28).

Vasant Shahane is struck with the charm of E. M. Forster's writing, and with his fascinating personality. He considers these two qualities to be both rare and special (Shahane 13). Bob Trevelyan, one of Forster's friends, objected to those qualities which the modern reader most admires in Forster, his "cool, hard, comic tone." Trevalyan found Forster's writing to be "too conversational and even slangy," and he considered this inappropriate even for "a slight and comic narrative." Trevelyan tried to convince Forster of the importance of "dignity" for an author (Herz 4). But Trevelyan did not have Forster's sense of humor. Judith Herz tells of a conference in which Elizabeth Spencer read a passage from Where Angels Fear to Tread (1905). In this passage, Harriet gets smut in her eye, and the audience laughed heartily. "We obviously heard something Trevelyan had not, for one of the passages he had singled out for special disapproval moved from the waltzing train to Harriet's notorious smut. The passage was completely familiar to most of us; yet the laughter was the response of a new delight" (Herz 7).

Nevertheless, Herz agrees with Trevelyan that in his early novels, Forster sometimes lapses into silliness. John Lehmann describes E. M. Forster as having an appearance of retiring diffidence, adding that he desired only to be gentle, and charming, and amusing, but from this stance he used his satire to take deadly aim (Lehmann 327). Forster's voice of judgmental assurance is a comic one, as it uses playfulness and charm to undermine and unmask. This voice can suddenly turn to somber tones, but it never loses the balance between the somber and the comic. This voice, "always produces a widening out of perception unlike many comic strategies which tend to work reductively" (Herz 4). Forster's humor was like that of Jane Austen, for both of these authors developed language nuance, surprise, and verbal wit which directly attack traditional "truths." Even the sentence and paragraph rhythms of these two writers create a comic depth that frequently make the surface actions of the various characters resemble pantomime (Herz 5).

Forster had a number of unpleasant experiences in his school life, and these experiences later found impassioned expression in his writings. In The Longest Journey (1907), Forster tells about Sawston School and expresses his adverse reaction to the entire system of public school education in England, a system which operated against Forster's creed of personal relations. Forster considered the notion of "public school" to be rather misleading since these schools are "exclusive and private in character" (Shahane 15-16). In The Longest Journey, Forster is as much concerned with the temporal as he is with the spiritual, and this creates a paradox, for it is the contrary pull of these two antithetical notions that give rise to Forster's aesthetic ambivalence and complexity. In The Longest Journey Forster raises a question that is opposite to the one that is usually asked, "Will it really profit us so much if we save our souls and lose the whole world?" (Shahane 27).

Lucy Honeychurch is the heroine in A Room with a View (1908). This is a domestic romance about her meeting of George Emerson in Italy, and according to Edwin Williams contains some of Forster's best humor. Miss Lydia Lavish is writing a novel about Englishmen living in Florence, and she says that this novel will contain "some humorous characters." She even warns that she plans, "to be unmerciful to the British tourist." The Reverend Mr. Eager, who is the head of the English colony in Florence, scoffs at the various tourists as they, "go from city to city and pension to pension until they are thoroughly confused." This reminds Reverend Eager about the American girl in <u>Punch</u> who says, "Say, poppa, what did we see at Rome?" The father replies, "Why I guess Rome was the place where we saw the yaller dog." Lydia Lavish's and Reverend Eager's opinions of English tourists are very similar to the opinions of E. M. Forster. Forster has said that when the English go abroad, their first consideration is finding a hotel as similar to London as possible. In <u>A Room with a View</u>, they find the Pension Bertoline, which is very English in atmosphere and even has a Cockney landlady (Williams 391).

Our attitudes regarding some of the characters in <u>A Room with a View</u> change as the novel progresses. At the beginning of the novel, the Reverend Beebe seems to be more caring than are the other characters, but later we discover that he is basically superficial. Early in the novel, George Emerson seems to be comic, ill-bred, and a bit childish. He is too quick and too frank with his opinions. But later we learn that he speaks from the heart. Cecil Vyse is another comic character who seems to change during the progress of the novel. Society has decided that Cecil is the best choice for Lucy Honeychurch to marry. Cecil insists on propriety and has difficulty relating to other people. His way of getting close to other people is to play a joke on them. Later, he goes too far with a practical joke, and Lucy tells him she can't marry him. At this point, he begins to realize that he is the type of person who cannot be intimate with anyone. He thanks Lucy for showing him his true character, and the reader feels that Cecil has some hope for progress. <u>A Room with a View</u> is a Comedy of Manners, and as such it has many comic characters. "In <u>A Room with a View</u>, Forster is having fun with the characters. He is amused by them, but the reader knows that he likes them" (Williams 392).

In <u>Howard's End</u> (1910), Forster characterizes Margaret as being deeply committed to art and ideas, and Henry, her husband, as being committed to business and finance. The novel is about the small skirmishes that result from these two very-different ideologies. Forster juxtaposes comic characters with more serious characters. Aunt Juley Munt is one of Forster's most successful characters. She always has good intentions, but she nevertheless bungles everything that she attempts to do. Bast is another comical character who gains the sympathy of the reader. Bast is a complex character (Williams 392). He is both a hero and a clown. Although he is poor, he is trying to improve himself through self-education, and participation in the arts. Leonard is idealistic, comic, and tragic; Edwin Williams considers him to be a Don-Quixote character. "The most pronounced example of mixed heroism and comedy, however, is Leonard's death.... In a parody of the ceremony of knighthood, Charles grabs old Mr. Schlegel's sword and strikes Leonard with the flat of the blade. As Leonard stumbles, a bookcase falls on him, causing his heart to fail. Thus, Leonard is clearly a victim of the very culture that he sought so desperately as a means to a rich and better life" (Williams 393).

Narayana Menon considered Forster to be, "witty, humane, mischievous, lovable, sensitive to music and to art, and what is not widely understood, or accepted, a man of tremendous guts" (qtd. in Shahane 17). Mulk Raj Anand admired Forster's "ever-pleasant, benevolent, slightly cynical smile" (qtd. in Shahane 18). Vasant Shahane says that even when Forster was not in affluent circumstances he would often invite friends to dinner in a restaurant and then order very expensive dishes for them, while at the same time ordering only the cheapest items on the menu for himself (Shahane 18). Shahane considers Forster "rare" because he is partly a late Victorian, partly an Edwardian, and partly a modern. "His life extends over a long period--from 1879 to 1970--marked by rapid and radical social change" (Shahane 19).

Shahane considers Forster to be an absorbing narrator, a perceptive symbolist, and a writer of revealing social comedy that is filled with tragic prophecy. Shahane also notes that there is a felt sense of duality in Forster's writing, out of which Forster's synthesis emerges. Forster was noted for his "double vision." It is this double vision that explains the complexity of Mrs. Moore's experience in the Marabar Caves (A Passage to India). "She had come to the state where the horror of the universe and its smallness are both visible at the same time--the twilight of the double vision in which so many elderly people are involved" (Shahane 25). Forster's writing, like that of James Joyce and D. H. Lawrence has a vision which, "is as complex as it is elusive and it defies the critical chemistry of pre-fabricated formulae" (Shahane 25).

Edwin Williams says that Forster uses humor to make many serious points in A Passage to India (1924). In this novel there is, "a satirical treatment of characters that holds them up to ridicule." Mrs. Turton is the wife of the head of the British colony, and she assures a newcomer that the English are superior to everybody in India merely by the fact that they are English. The only words of Urdu that she learns are what she will need to give orders to her servants. She never learns any of the politer forms, and she only knows how to use the verbs in their imperative mood. Mrs. Callendar, the wife of the Chief Surgeon, has a similar attitude about the natives. "Why, the kindest thing one can do to a native is to let him die." When the Turtons host a Bridge Party to introduce Adela and Mrs. Moore to the Indian community, it is a total failure. Although the party had been designed to bridge the distance between East and West, the Indian guests group together at the "Indian" end of the lawn, and the hosts group together at the "English" end, and "each group talked about the other group in unflattering terms" (Williams 394).

One of the ironies in A Passage to India occurs when a subaltern condemns the depraved Indian accused of attacking Miss Quested and wishes that all Indians were like the one he played polo with. This is ironic for two reasons. First the Indian did not attack Miss Quested, and second, this Indian was the one that the subaltern played polo with, Dr. Aziz. Another example of ironic racism relates to Police Superintendent McBride, who appears to be rational, fair, and competent, until he tells his theory that the dark races are criminals at heart who are prone to succumb to their sexual drives. The irony is that Aziz is innocent of sexual misconduct, but McBride is at the time having an extramarital affair (Williams 394).

Elizabeth Barrett considers A Passage to India to be a comedy about domesticity (Barrett 77). Wilfred Stone considers the last section of this book to be filled with "spiritual gusto and mud-bespattered hilarity" that somehow unites the book's sense of prophesy, and its sense of humor (Stone 303). Kenneth Burke considers A Passage to India to be a "social comedy" revolving largely around the social mysteries and social embarrassments that are often the result of colonization.

> The muddle of castes and classes in India itself, capped by the essential conflict between the natives, and the British officials...allows for a maximum number of interesting embarrassments in personal relations. Everybody is subtly at odds with everybody else; every situation treated by Forster acutely involves the "mysteries" that result from marked social differentiation--and these are further accentuated by the fact that, since India is in a state of acute transition, along with the traditional formalities due to such a clutter of social ratings there is much improvising of protocol. (Burke 225)

The important point here is that when A Passage to India is read as social comedy, the secondary characters become larger than they would be otherwise (Barrett 91).

The visual imagery of Mrs. Moore and Mohammed Latif sleeping together as they return after their expedition to the Marabar Caves is laughable. "Mrs. Moore slept, swaying against the rods of the howda, Mohammed Latif embraced her with efficiency and respect"

(Passage 150). Here there is a juxtaposition of English and Indian cultures. The embrace here is not an erotic oriental embrace, but is rather an embrace that is both efficient and respectful. Mohammed Latif must modify his embrace to the English standard where respect becomes a surrogate for affection (Barrett 79-80).

Elizabeth Barrett feels that there are three important aspects of domestic comedy to be found in A Passage to India and for each of these aspects there is an incongruity which results from the transportation of English values to the Indian setting. The first aspect of comedy is about the rituals of invitation and withdrawal that relate to the concept of the "invited guest" Much of the humor here is the result of misfiring expectations and the embarrassments that result (Barrett 81). When Ronny takes Adela for a drive with the Nawab Bahadur, for example, there develops a clash between Indian courtesy and English chivalry. It is Indian courtesy that prompts the Nawab to offer his car; it is English chivalry that has Ronny suggest that Adela might enjoy the ride. Adela is being chivalrous when she attempts to shake the Nawab's hand, but her act is extremely discourteous because it is sexually embarrassing. Ironically, she is not even aware that the Nawab is sexually embarrassed (Barrett 84).

The second aspect of comedy relates to the buffoons. These buffoons must not only expose ridiculousnesses, but they must heal these ridiculousnesses as well (Barrett 81). In A Passage to India there are three important buffoons: Mohammed Latif, Panna Lal, and Professor Godbole (Barrett 85). There is one comic scene which involves Mohammed Latif's loading of the purdah carriage in order to prepare the carriage to take Mrs. Moore and Miss Quested to the caves. "Much had still to enter the purdah carriage--a box bound with brass, a melon wearing a fez, a towel containing guavas, a step-ladder and a gun" (Passage 121). This juxtaposition of strange and disparate objects is very comic to the English mind, but is in no way comic to the Indian mind which perceives this not as a muddle of disparate objects in a strange country, but rather as some of the mysteries of English domesticity (Barrett 86). The function of Mohammed Latif in A Passage to India is to increase the "mood of festivity." He is a parasite in Hamidullah's household, and according to Northrop Frye, the parasite is one of the oldest and most prototypical types of buffoon. Aziz and Hamidullah sat down to eat with Mohammed Latif, who, "lived on Hamidullah's bounty and...occupied the position neither of a servant nor of an equal." Mohammed Latif was a gentle and happy man, but he was also a dishonest man, a man who throughout his lifetime had never done a bit of work (Barrett 87). Panna Lal is the second buffoon. He is the Hindu doctor who is introduced into the novel by going smash into the hollyhocks during the Bridge Party. Panna Lal has a peripheral status. He never seems to quite belong to any group, and when he intentionally says "mislaid" instead of "misled," his, "'error' in pronunciation comically articulates the seriousness of the colonial dilemma." This is how Forster describes the situation in which Panna Lal makes the "error."

> Agitated, but alert, he saw them smile at his indifferent English, and suddenly he started playing the buffoon, flung down his unbrella, trod through it, and struck himself upon the nose. He knew what he was doing, and so did they.... When he found they wanted Nureddin, he skipped like a goat, he scuttled like a hen to do their bidding, the hospital was saved, and to the end of his life he could not understand why he had not obtained promotion on the morning's work. (Passage 89)

It is ironic that Panna Lal gains status by deliberately humiliating himself. Panna Lal's "mislaid" is not the only example of a calculated mispronunciation in A Passage to India. There is also Mohammed Latif's "You spick a lie" (Passage 122), and Ram Chand's "You will make yourself chip" (Passage 30). Such errors, "bring into focus the falseness and debasement that characterizes the relationships of colonizer and colonized" (Barrett 91).

Professor Godbole is the third buffoon. His taking of tea is simultaneously a participation, and a lack of participation (Barrett 87).

> [Godbole] took his tea at a little distance from the outcasts, from a low table placed slightly behind him, to which he stretched back, and as it were encountered food by accident; all feigned indifference to Professor Godbole's tea.... The ladies were interested in him, and hoped that he would supplement Dr. Aziz by saying something about religion. But he only ate--ate and ate, smiling, never letting his eyes catch sight of his hand.
> (Passage 65)

At the end of the meal everyone stood up except for Professor Godbole, who was still eating his banana (Barrett 88). Professor Godbole is the most fully developed buffoon in A Passage to India. His presiding over the birth of Krisha is filled with an atmosphere of comic celebration. "There is fun in heaven. God can play practical jokes on Himself, draw chairs away from beneath His own posteriors, set His own turbans on fire, and steal His own petticoats when He bathes" (Passage 279). Edwin Williams says Forster uses humor to show that Professor Godbole's spiritualism is flawed. Godbole is clearly a ridiculous character. "There is something ludicrous about him whether he is taking tea and 'encountered food by accident' or interrupting Fielding on the day of Aziz's arrest to secure suggestions for the name of a nonexistent school that he hopes to found" (Williams 395).

The third aspect of comedy lies in the surrogate action of the characters, and in the fact that old concepts take on new and sometimes unexpected dimensions (Barrett 81). According to Elizabeth Barrett, social gestures are inextricably rooted in linguistic expression in A Passage to India. Syed Mohammed vigorously denunciates the Hindus, for example (Barrett 82). "His outburst took some time, and in his excitement he fell into Punjabi (he came from that side) and was unintelligible" (Passage 96). Syed Mohammed's bigotry is rendered comically deflated by the unintelligibility of his speech. For the English, one of the most salient aspects of India is the "muddle of language." Even the Indian insult has to be framed in extremely polite terms. There can be no direct accusation, for example, and this fact results in much linguistic indirection. Panna Lal's statement, "I beg pardon, but some might say your leg kicks," is filled with hedges. He begins with "I beg pardon." From there he goes to the intentionally vague expression "some might say," and only then can he make an accusation (Barrett 83). "How is stomach...? how head?" (Passage 99) is also a subversive insult. Because politeness is necessary, Lal must inquire about the other person's health. But his inquiry is perfunctory. Furthermore, he leaves out the pronoun "your," thereby not distinguishing Aziz's state of health from the health of anyone in the world who has a stomach and a head. The expression is thereby reduced to the insignificance of total genericness (Barrett 84).

In Aspects of the Novel (1927), Forster compars and contrasts two types of novels-- the fantastic, and the prophetic. They are both concerned with human problems, but in fantasy a more humorous view of reality is presented. Fantasy, "has an improvised air about it, and it involves slips of the memory, all verbal coincidences, Pans, and puns" (Williams 393).

Maurice (1971) is a novel about Maurice Hall's inward struggles to accept who he is. He is normal in all ways, except that he is homosexual. He thinks that his homosexuality might just be a passing phase, as it had been for Clive Durham, his first lover at Cambridge. "As sensitive as the subject was for Forster, he was still able to employ his sense of humor. Most of the treatment of Clive is very serious, but there is also an element of satire, especially in the way that Clive glorifies homosexuality in literature but hedges at the borders of lasting commitment in real life" (Williams 395). Some of the ironic humor in Maurice occurs when Maurice is attempting to develop his heterosexuality. He escorts Miss Tonks to a concert that featured Peter Ilyitch Tchaikovsky's Symphonie

Pathétique. Maurice is more moved by the music than he is by Miss Tonks, and he later finds out that Symphonie Pathétique had originally been written when Tchaikovsky had fallen in love with a nephew. It was dedicated to the nephew. Thus Maurice's attempt to encourage his heterosexuality by taking Miss Tonks to a concert, in truth makes him more sure that he was homosexual (Williams 396).

Edward Morgan Forster Bibliography

Barrett, Elizabeth. "Comedy, Courtesy, and A Passage to India." English Studies in Canada 10 (1984): 77-93.

Bell, Vereen M. "Comic Seriousness in A Passage to India." South Atlantic Quarterly 66 (1967): 606-617.

Burke, Kenneth. "Social and Comic Mystery: A Passage to India." Language as Symbolic Action: Essays on Life, Literature and Method. Berkeley, CA: University of California Press, 1966, 233-239.

Forster, E. M. A Passage to India. London, England: Macmillan, 1970.

Herz, Judith Scherer. "Introduction: In Search of the Comic Muse." E. M. Forster: Centenary Revaluations. Eds. Judith Herz and Robert K. Martin. Toronto, Canada: Univ of Toronto Press, 1982, 1-11.

Johnstone, J. K. The Bloomsbury Group: A Study of E. M. Forster, Lytton Strachey, Virginia Woolf and Their Circle. New York, NY: Farrar, Straus, 1978.

Lehmann, John. In My Own Time. Boston, MA: Little Brown, 1969.

Shahane, Vasant A. E. M. Forster: A Study in Double Vision. New Delhi, India: Gulab Vazirani/Arnold-Heinemann, 1975.

Stone, Wilfred. The Cave and the Mountain. Stanford, CA: Stanford University Press, 1966.

Wallace, Ronald. "The Inclusion of Merriment: Comedy in A Passage to India. Essays in Literature 4 (1977): 37-48.

Williams, Edwin W. "E. M. Forster." Encyclopedia of British Humorists, Volume I. Ed. Steven H. Gale. New York, NY: Garland, 1996, 389-398.

4

Authors Born between
1880 and 1889

Sir Henry Howarth Bashford (1880-1961)

In 1988, an anonymous reviewer for The New Yorker said that Augustus Carp, Esq, By Himself, Being the Autobiography of a Really Good Man (1924) was "a sublime ferocious farce." This critic continued, "Some of the best lines, delivered deadpan, are given to drinkers, smokers, dancers and adulterers" (Batts 92). In that same year, an anonymous reviewer from The Bookman said that Augustus Carp contained "elephantine attempts at humor." The theme of Augustus Carp is hypocrisy. One of the targets of the satire is the father Carp, who wants to be an independently-minded member of lower-middle class society, but manages to bring up his son "in his own obnoxious image." Pa Carp is pompous in his speech, in his dress, and in his manners. He "cuts a preposterous figure" with his "lower middle height," his "large and well modelled nose," his "massive ears," and his "powerful voice." Part of the ironic humor lies in the fact that he is oblivious to the harsh and un-Christian way that he treats his wife, his sisters-in-law, and his temporary charlady. Another irony is that Augustus Carp is totally against swearing, drinking, dancing, and smoking, and he battles with his schoolmasters and fellow students over their blasphemies, cheating, and worldliness, but he himself is given to inflated diction, and extravagant hates. One of the best sustained pieces of humor in the book is when Alexander Carkeek donates a brass lectern to the church, resulting in droll narration, mock-heroic diction, and exaggeration (Batts 90). Henry Bashford's description of the Xtian lads deserves special comment. Augustus describes them as being about his own age, and says that both of them have a speech impediment, and explains that they "were destined on this account for eventual ordination in the Church of England" (Batts 91).

Augustus Carp is a series of anecdotes that conforms to Stephen Leacock's observation that, "for the English the point lies in the humorous telling rather than in some culminating fireworks" (Batts 91). Bashford often creates humor by juxtaposing surprising ideas or language. John Batts says that Augustus Carp is filled with humorous episodes, hyperbole, parodies, comic analogies, inversions, and bathos. It is Mary Moonbeam who introduces Augustus to a cordial health drink named "Portugalade." Augustus finds the drink to be "peculiarly attractive to the nostril," and "no less grateful to the tongue." Days later, Mary invites Augustus to dinner, and she serves him this same beverage, and since it now is brought to him in a wine glass Augustus now realizes why the beverage had tasted so good. John Batts says that Henry Bashford is a fairly good humorist, but he nevertheless concludes, "among Bashford's shortcomings is an English reliance on pun and hidden quotation which ranges from silliness to pedantry" (Batts 91).

Sir Henry Howarth Bashford Bibliography

Batts, John S. "Sir Henry Howarth Bashford." Encyclopedia of British Humorists, Volume I. Ed. Steven H. Gale. New York, NY: Garland, 1996,89-92.

Sean O'Casey (1880-1964) IRELAND

John Frayne and Bobby Smith say that Sean O'Casey "was always a humorist, always a satirist, always a vigilant, angry artist lashing out against those who would destroy life, either literally or by repressing the human spirit.... O'Casey's wonderful sense of humor informed every line that he wrote. His autobiographies, short stories, essays, poems, songs, and letters are as open, direct, and exciting as his plays" (Frayne and Smith 795). O'Casey wrote tragedies that contain both humor and comedy. Most of his comic heroes foster grandiose illusions of themselves in spite of the evidence of their squalid lives, their doubting friends, and their outraged families. Frayne and Smith add that O'Casey's humor supports the idea that Ireland, is "the land of the tear and the smile." This supports Richard Brinsley Sheridan's quip about Ireland as, "the land of merry wars and sad love songs." One of O'Casey's stock characters is the "Stage Irishman," with his distinctive brogue, his blarney, his boastfulness and extravagance, his wit, his charm, and the twinkle in his eye. Fluther Good in The Plough and the Stars, and Joxer Daly and Captain Boyle in Juno and the Paycock are good examples of "Stage Irishmen." They, "have most of the major traits of the stage Irishman, including vainglory, exaggeration, and the comic repetition of tag lines or words. Fluther has his 'derogatory' and Joxer has his 'daarlin,' for instance" (Frayne and Smith 789). Sean O'Casey is a humorist and a satirist who deals with both laughter and tears. He is a master humorist who, "uses laughter as a weapon to unmask and ridicule pretense and to attack evil in all its forms" (Frayne and Smith 790).

The Shadow of a Gunman (1923) explores the gap between patriotic rhetoric like "Dyin' for Ireland" and the grim realities of political violence. Donal Davoren, a poet and dreamer, is the anti-hero of the novel. As a resident of a working-class tenement, he suddenly discovers that he is thought to be a famous IRA gunman. At first, Davoren is dubious about his sudden fame and respect, but he soon discovers that he likes it, especially when it involves the hero worshiping of the pretty Minnie Powell. Seumas Shields, Davoren's roommate, is a lazy peddler who gives a comical and a cynical commentary on the relationship between patriotic rhetoric and terrorist fact. A lot of the humor in Shadow of a Gunman is verbal, as when the slovenly Shields says, "I don't think I need to wash myself this morning; do I look all right." Seumas is contemptuous of Maguire even though Maguire has all of Seumas's faults. On one occasion Maguire is late, and just before he arrives, Seumas proclaims him to be "almost too lazy to wash himself" (Frayne and Smith 790).

Adolphus Grigson is another comic character in The Shadow of a Gunman. Adolphus is a coward and a drinker. According to Mrs. Grigson, "No matter how much he may have taken, when he's taken more he'll always say, 'Here's the first to-day.'" Mrs. Grigson describes her husband Adolphus as "far gone in the horns," and "always fumblin'." When he misses curfew, she asks him, "Do the insurance companies pay if a man is shot after curfew?" (Frayne and Smith 790).

In The Plough and the Stars (1926), as in other O'Casey plays, most of the humor is verbal. But there are also some visual scenes that are hilarious, such as those involving the prepared shopping lists, the use of prams, and Mrs. Gogan's search for Cuban shoes with pointy heels as she is looting the shoe store. These scenes are made all the more hilarious by the poverty, the looting, and the carnage that is going on around them. The Clitheroes in The Plough and the Stars are depicted as having what Frayne and Smith call "middle-class aspirations." The uppitiness of the Clitheroes is contrasted with the working-class behavior of Fluther Good, the carpenter, Bessie Burgess, the loud-mouth loyalist, and Jinny Gogan, Bessie's Catholic antagonist who has a babe in one hand, and a bottle of malt in the other. Fluther Good, Bessie Burgess, and Jinny Gogan are all humors characters, and as such they are comic figures. Fluther Good, for example, is in many ways the "Stage Irishman" of Irish comedy. Time and time again, he gives the temperance pledge: "No more dhrink for Fluther. It's three days now since I've touched a dhrop, an' I feel a new man already." A little bit later, however, he feels dizzy, and says, "I hope I didn't give up th' beer too suddenly" (Frayne and Smith 792). One of the major ironies in The Plough and the Stars occurs when the loyalist Bessie is shot by a British soldier who thinks that she is a sniper. The final image of the play is of a group of British soldiers who are brewing tea and watching Dublin burning in the background as they are singing, "Keep the 'Ome Fires Burning" (Frayne and Smith 792).

Juno and the Paycock (1934) is a tragi-comedy that shows how the humor of the slums allows people to transcend the carnage. Sons lose their hips or their arms, or are killed and buried, or are executed. But the humor is a continuing reminder that the survivors must acclimate themselves to what is left for them (Frayne and Smith 792). O'Casey develops a number of stock or "humors" characters in Juno and the Paycock. Juno is the universal mother. Captain Jack is the braggart soldier, the alizon. Mary is the wronged daughter (the maiden in distress). Joxer is the parasite. Much of the humor in Juno and the Paycock is verbal, as when Joxer utters line after line in repetition of something that has just been said by another character (Frayne and Smith 791). Joxer Daly and Captain Boyle are good examples of characters who play off from each other (Frayne and Smith 789) The novel is about the comic antics and tragic destinies of the Boyle family; Captain Jack Boyle is the arrogant and drunken head of this family. Captain Boyle is a comic figure whose legs, or whose back, or whose mental attitude prevent him from taking any of the jobs that his friends and the local priests are continually finding for him. Joxer Daly is a "pilot fish," similar to the clever ironic slaves of Roman drama. It is Joxer's function to, "echo the vainglorious monologues of his comrade and to feed the Captain cue lines to flesh out his heroic fantasies." The leitmotif word that is constantly coming from Joxer's lips is "darlin," as in "D'jever rade Willie Reilly an' his own Colleen Bawn? It's a darlin' story, a daarlin' story." Another example is "Ah, a cup o' tay's a darlin' thing, a daarlin' thing." For Captain Boyle, the leitmotif word is "chassis" (crisis), as in, "I'm telling you, Joxer, the whole worl's in a terrible state o' chassis!" (Frayne and Smith 791).

In Juno and the Paycock, the Boyle family receives a fairly-large bequest from a distant relative, and this reinforces their belief that they are the "darlings of the gods." Of course the promise of money brings out the worst in them. It changes their working-class directness and simplicity into petty bourgeois extravagance and pretentiousness. Juno's final speech in Juno and the Paycock develops a tragic tone which O'Casey then contrasts with the one last drunken scene and comic romp of the Captain and Joxer. Frayne and Smith ask, "Is this a tragi-comic comment on the folly of it all or, especially from the point of view of Dublin tenement dwellers, is it one last comic turn by these lovable fools?" This is a good example of O'Casey's double vision. On the one hand he accepts human frailty, but on the other hand he is protesting against the cruelty of evil social conditions (Frayne and Smith 791).

Purple Dust: A Wayward Comedy in Three Acts (1940) is a morality play, and a farce, and a fantasy, in which Englishmen who are escaping the blitz in World War II become conned and victimized by the, "wily, cunning, yet smooth-talking local Irishmen." Frayne and Smith say that some of the Irish tricksters in Purple Dust are similar to tricksters created by Dionysius Boucicault (Frayne and Smith 789). In Purple Dust, O'Casey uses humor to attack a wide array of enemy targets. A giant roller for leveling the lawn goes out of control and crashes through the wall of the already-crumbling mansion. A cow is mistaken for a bull, and is shot, and when Poges asks the questions, "Where the hell did that bull come from? Who owns her?" the audience knows that O'Casey has "John Bull" in mind. "The Englishmen are gulls and fools, though in their own minds they are inherently and permanently superior to the primitive Irish." The humor in this play ranges from slapstick to satire. The Tudor mansion is the British Empire in miniature. It is already decrepit as the play begins, but by the end of the play, all symbols of British power have either disappeared or have self destructed. These include, "cows, enterprising hens, startling cocks, bathrooms, antiques, and efficiency experts" (Frayne and Smith 794).

In Red Roses for Me (1943), O'Casey is displaying his sardonic sense of humor in almost every line of dialogue. "The play itself is a gallery of portraits--all satiric" (Frayne and Smith 793). Ayamonn Breydon, for example, is full of blarney. Frayne and Smith suggest that the blarney of this character is not intended so much as comic exaggeration as it is a parody of Irish verbal inflation (Frayne and Smith 790). At more than one point, O'Casey makes the argument that all marriages are mixed marriages, since they consist of a woman and a man (Frayne and Smith 794).

Cock-a-Doodle Dandy (1949) is O'Casey's favorite play. The play is a comic treatment of, "the goodness of the sexual urge in the face of clerical Puritanism." It is dedicated to James Stephens, another Irish humorist, "the jesting poet / with a radiant star / in's coxcomb." In Cock-a-Doodle Dandy, O'Casey shows his skill in combining magic and slapstick humor, as religious pictures become turned toward the wall, sexy and beautiful women grow the horns of devils, a whiskey bottle becomes a demon, a hat walks, chairs collapse, and geese or ducks transport fools away. The final image, which involves the confusion of a hat and a cock, is especially hilarious (Frayne and Smith 794). There is much slapstick humor, and much verbal humor in Cock-a-Doodle Dandy. The characters in this play feel that if song and dance and joy and life are devil inspired, then, "th' devil's not a bad fella either." This play foreshadows The Drums of Father Ned (1960), in which Father Ned, who represents the Devil, calls for song, dance, joy, and life (Frayne and Smith 795).

Frayne and Smith consider the humor in The Bishop's Bonfire (1955) to be "delicious." The humor becomes increasingly darker as the young leave Ireland. The establishment is afraid of art and want to destroy it, but at the same time, they don't want to admit that they are censoring it (Frayne and Smith 795). In an essay entitled, "St. Pathrick's Day in the Morning," which appeared in The Green Cow (1956), O'Casey describes the Irish sardonic sense of humor as, "the only thing we Irish have in full measure" (Frayne and Smith 793).

See also Nilsen, Don L. F. "Sean O'Casey." Humor in Irish Literature: A Reference Guide. Westport, CT: Greenwood, 1996, 7, 9, 127-136, 191.

Sean O'Casey Bibliography

Coakley, James, and Marvin Felheim. "Thalia in Dublin: Some Suggestions about the Relationships between O'Casey and Classical Comedy." Comparative Drama 4 (1970): 265-271.

Cowasjee, Saros. "The Juxtaposition of Tragedy and Comedy in the Plays of Sean O'Casey." Wascana Review 2.1 (1967): 75-89.

Daniel, Walter C. "Patterns of Greek Comedy in O'Casey's Purple Dust." Bulletin of the New York Public Library 66 (1962): 603-612.

Frayne, John P. and Bobby L. Smith. "Sean O'Casey." Encyclopedia of British Humorists, Volume II. Ed. Steven H. Gale. New York, NY: Garland, 1996, 787-798.

Mercier, Vivian. The Irish Comic Tradition. Oxford, England: Clarendon Press, 1962.

Mikhail, E. H., and John O'Riordan, eds. The Sting and the Twinkle: Conversations with Sean O'Casey. New York, NY: Barnes and Noble, 1974.

Pasachoff, Naomi. "O'Casey's Not Quite Festive Comedies." Éire-Ireland 12.3 (1977): 41-61.

Smith, B. L. O'Casey's Satiric Vision. Kent, OH: Kent State University Press, 1978.

Waters, Maureen. "The Paycocks of Sean O'Casey." The Comic Irishman. Albany, NY: State Univ of New York Press, 1984, 149-160.

White, M. C. "Language and Humour in O'Casey's Abbey Plays." Literary and Linguistic Aspects of Humour. Barcelona, Spain: Univ of Barcelona Dept of Languages, 1984, 285-290.

Lytton (Giles) Strachey (1880-1932)

Lytton Strachey wrote witty and ironic portraits of an earlier time in history (Mullen 1079). Strachey is an "ironic stylist" who was a champion of such witty epigrams as, "We do not reflect that it is perhaps as difficult to write a good life as it is to live one." Strachey modeled his writing style not after English writers, but after French writers. He borrowed his tone of satirical mockery from François Marie Arouet Voltaire (1694-1778), and he borrowed his interested in psychological manners from Marie Henri Beyle Stendhal (1783-1842) (Mullen 1077). Like E. M. Forster and Virginia Woolf, Lytton Strachey was a member of the Bloomsbury group, and it is possible that Strachey loathed the Victorians even more than Forster and Woolf did (Mullen 1078).

In 1912, Strachey wrote to Lady Ottoline Morrell that he was beginning a new experiment. This experiment was to be a condensed biography of Cardinal Manning "written from a slightly cynical standpoint." When he finished his piece, he called it Eminent Victorians (1918), and it caused quite a stir. At the beginning of Eminent Victorians (1918), Strachey establishes as his motto Voltaire's aphorism, "Je n'impose rien; je ne propose rien; j'expose," which translates into English as "I don't impose. I don't propose. I expose." According to Alexandra Mullen, Strachey fully intended all of the spicy double entendre of the word "expose" (Mullen 1077). Although Strachey was not the first writer to expose Victorian stuffiness, hypocrisy, and religious peculiarity, "his ironic malice struck a new note." Realizing that he had the final say, he was quite frank to admit that his decisions were irreverent, arbitrary, and final. Strachey set up new standards for judgment. No longer would people be judged only on their works or on their faith, but now in addition, they would be judged on their aesthetics and their humor. Strachey took special joy in making the insidious comparison. Much of his humor is also the result of his debunking-metaphors that "mention the unmentionable." Alexandra Mullen suggests that, "the more serious and august the institution, the more extreme his tropes." Strachey was a master at comic elevation, and comic deflation. He posed loaded questions, he quoted droll diary entries, he recreated inner monologues (Mullen 1078). Mrs. Humphry Ward, the granddaughter of Thomas Arnold, was one of those who were shocked by the novel. Herbert Henry Asquith, who had just stepped down as Prime Minister, was one of those who were amused. And Bertrand Russell, who had just been imprisoned as a conscientious objector, was one of those who were very amused. He said, "It caused me to laugh so loud that the officer came to my cell, saying I must remember that prison is a place of punishment" (Mullen 1078).

In Queen Victoria (1921), Strachey's used light comedy and sympathetic humor in his treatment of the Queen. The few times when he used sarcastic barbs, they were aimed at the "Teutonic Albert," and the faithful servant, John Brown (Mullen 1079).

Lytton (Giles) Strachey Bibliography

Johnstone, J. K. The Bloomsbury Group: A Study of E. M. Forster, Lytton Strachey, Virginia Woolf and Their Circle. New York, NY: Farrar, Straus, 1978.
Mullen, Alexandria. "Lytton Strachey." Encyclopedia of British Humorists, Volume II. Ed. Steven H. Gale. New York, NY: Garland, 1996, 1075-1080

William Stanley Houghton (1881-1913)

Stanley Houghton wrote in the tradition of "comedy of manners." His writing is concerned with ordinary people of Lancashire country, and is infused with the spirit of revolt. His first two comedies of manners were Independent Means (1909), and Marriages in the Making (1909), both of which give evidence of his gift for bringing his characters into an intimate relationship with his audience (Sawyer 233). Edgar Forsyth in Independent Means has been brought up in a well-to-do, but not-well-managed upper-middle-class home. He is a "gentleman," but is trained for nothing further. Sidney is a spirited girl of advanced ideas who marries Edgar and insists on living her own life. The conflict of these two forces is inevitable. It is perfectly appropriate that in this struggle, the wife triumphs (Sawyer 234).

Newell Sawyer considers The Younger Generation (1910) to be Houghton's most successful play next to Hindle Wakes This is a play about parents and children, and it is like Houghton's previous comedies in that it inveighs against the bigotry that age often breeds. The domination by the parents force the children, Arthur, Reggie, and Grace Kennion, into chronic fibbing. (Sawyer 234). James Kennion, the father, reprehends the children for lying, but ironically the children force him into a falsehood that he tells in order to hold the moral victory he thinks he has gained. In The Younger Generation, Houghton is skillful as he plays each of three generations off against the others. The staid grandmother is played against the rebellious grandchildren. "The old lady is as displeased with her son for his laxity as a parent, as his children are for his own severity to them" (Sawyer 235).

Partners (1911) is Houghton's closest approach to true comedy of manners because of its immorality and its complete surrender to the "spirit of banter and badinage." It is a delicious play filled with entertaining exchanges of flirtations between two married couples. A critic who wrote during Houghton's time said of this play, "It is a little gem, and it has all the elfin grace, the elusiveness, the unexpected turnings of Oscar Wilde" (Sawyer 235).

William Stanley Houghton Bibliography

Sawyer, Newell W. The Comedy of Manners from Sheridan to Maugham: The Study of the Type as a Dramatic Form and as a Social Development. Unpublished Ph.D. Dissertation. Philadelphia, PA: University of Pennsylvania, 1931.

Frederick Lonsdale (1881-1954)

Frederick Lonsdale's plays sparkle with his brilliant dialogue. His themes were rarely fresh since he simply rewrote old ideas, but he rewrote these old ideas in exciting dialogue, with thrilling twists. He wrote them in ways that amused and even engrossed the theater audiences. Lonsdale wrote comedies, often musical comedies, about matrimony, aristocratic negligence, and the flighty upper class. His comedies are light and tightly structured, and they often have far-fetched plots, and much witty, satirical dialogue. There is usually a pair of lovers who misunderstand each other, but nevertheless end up either reconciled or married. Examples include, The Early Worm (1908), The King of Cadonia (1908), co-authored with Sydney Jones, and The Best People (1908), which are drawing room comedies highly reminiscent of the style of Oscar Wilde's Comedies of Manners (Lambdin 702). High Jinks (1916), and The Maid of the Mountain (1917), co-authored with Harold Fraser-Simson and Harry Graham are also comedies (Lambdin 704). The Last of Mrs. Cheyney (1925) is a witty satire of human nature, which may be a little bit melodramatic, but which nevertheless has swift action, a number of unexpected twists, and great satirical lines about the lifestyles of the rich and famous (Lambdin 702).

David Hirst says that epigrammatic speech distinguishes the characters in Lonsdale's plays, and adds that this quality places Lonsdale clearly in the tradition of Oscar Wilde. In the first scene of The Last of Mrs. Cheyney (1925), Charles, the butler sums up one of the guests: "He's my lord Dilling. Young, rich, attractive and clever...! I would describe him as a man who has kept more husbands at home than any other man of modern times" (qtd. in Hirst 64).

On Approval (1926) is more biting than Lonsdale's other works. According to Laura Lambdin, it contains sparkling dialogue and is brilliantly constructed. The title alludes to two trial marriages in which the people are treated like commercial products that can be returned if they are unacceptable. Mrs. Wislake is very selfish. Her first husband had not been the lackey that she had wanted, so she wants to be sure that her second husband will be more pliable. Richard Halton is this second husband, and Mrs. Wislake agrees to try him out for a month to find out if he will do. The other trial marriage involves the pompous Duke of Bristol. He wants to sell off his title for cash and marry a rich lady by the name of Helen Hayle, the daughter of a pickle millionaire. Both couples move to Scotland for their trial marriages. But in Scotland, Richard and Helen discover not only how very selfish their partners are, but they also discover how much they love each other. So they run away to get married, and the pompous Duke is left behind with the catty Mrs. Wislake, and they end up having only each other to be hateful to. On Approval contains much witty banter, and also contains suspense, and some titillating situations (Lambdin 703).

Frederick Lonsdale Bibliography

Hirst, David L. Comedy of Manners. New York, NY: Methuen, 1979.
Lambdin, Laura. "Frederick Lonsdale." Encyclopedia of British Humorists, Volume II. Ed.
    Steven H. Gale. New York, NY: Garland, 1996, 701-704.

Pelham Grenville Wodehouse (1881-1975)

P. G. Wodehouse created a number of buffoons, but all of his buffoons were sympathetic characters, with redeeming qualities. Wodehouse exaggerated the traits of his characters for humorous effect. He made them larger than life, and paradoxically, this makes them easier to sympathize with because the reader does not view them as real people. No real person could be this bad, or this stupid. Once the readers realize that Wodehouse's characters are caricatures, then these readers can accept the fact that they could be a little bit like these characters in certain ways. Wodehouse also exaggerates the situations in which the characters find themselves. In Wodehouse's writings, there are typically two diametrically opposed forces at work--the trivial, and the exaggerated. "The trivial tone is used to present even the most ludicrous events and make them seem natural and banal. At the same time, there is exaggeration of events and people's characteristics. The power of the stories is derived from the paradoxical tension which exists between the humorous surface events and the serious issues beneath them" (McLure 1220).

Wodehouse wrote during the period between the two world wars, a time when spats, morning coats, tea time, valets, and endless social engagements were the vogue. Wodehouse writes in a matter-of-fact style, which can lead the reader to think that the events being discussed are trivial. But beneath the informal tone, and the trivial exterior, Wodehouse is dealing with many serious issues. Like Charles Dickens, Wodehouse created memorable eccentrics. They included Lord Elmsworth, the patriarch of Elmsworth Castle, Mr. Mulliner, a permanent fixture of the Angler's Rest Pub, Psmith, and the team of Bertie and Jeeves. All of Wodehouse's important characters are loveable, somewhat eccentric, and prone to finding themselves in the middles of complex situations. Bertie and Jeeves are opposites. "Bertie is rather casual in his manner, while Jeeves is decidedly stuffy. Bertie is likely to consider lavender spats an appropriate article of dress; Jeeves would rather die than have them in the house. Bertie is constantly getting into difficult situations and Jeeves is constantly extricating him from them" (McLure 1218).

In the tradition of Gilbert and Sullivan's "The Sorcerer," and also in the tradition of Anthony Trollope's Barchester novels, P. G. Wodehouse is satirizing the hierarchy of the Anglican church, "by abusing all offices with equal zeal. He begins with the pale, young curates and moves upward through the ranks, raking vicars and bishops over the coals." Wodehouse is very aware of the hierarchy of offices, as he pits the lowest members of the order, the clerics, against the next in line, the vicars. The vicars are caught in the middle. They are pitted against the clerics below them, and against the bishops above them. Wodehouse's clerics are pale. His vicars are loud, and his bishops are fat and jolly. (McLure 1219).

When Mary Lydon was asked to write an article for Profession 94 defining the essence of language and literature, she turned to P. G. Wodehouse, and especially his character named Jeeves. Bertie Wooster says, "I remember Jeeves saying to me once, à propos of how you can never tell what the weather's going to do, that full many a glorious morning had he seen flatter the mountain tops with sovereign eye and then turn into a rather nasty afternoon" (Wodehouse Code 60). Lydon notes that this joke depends on the reader's recognizing Shakespeare's sonnet, and further notes that on first reading this line at the age of fourteen she burst into laughter because at the time she was being required to learn large chunks of Shakespeare by heart, and therefore her laughter was the "laughter of recognition" (Lydon 23). In another passage of this same novel, Bertie Wooster's friend, Gussie Finknottle has stolen a police officer's helmet as a prank, and during Gussie's arraignment Bertie asks why the judge let Finknottle off with only a fine. Jeeves responds, "Possibly the reflection that the quality of mercy is not strained, sir." When Bertie Wooster says, "You mean it droppeth as the gentle rain from heaven?" Jeeves continues, "Precisely, sir. Upon the place beneath. His worship would no doubt have taken into consideration the fact that it blesseth him that gives and him that takes and becomes the throned monarch better than his crown" (qtd in Thompson 298).

Jeeves is always able to make the appropriate literary allusion, and always able to use "le mot juste." He is also able to clean up any malapropisms that happen to be in the air. "Just as Wodehouse's deployment of quotation teaches what reading is, so his handling of idiom reveals his uncanny ability, as he pursues his meditation on language and literature in a popular form, to teach one how to write." Whenever Mary Lydon reads a student paper and sees a mangled cliché like "heralds back," she is reminded of Jeeves, and is tempted to say to the student, "Harks back, I believe, is the expression you are seeking, sir" (Lydon 24).

P. G. Wodehouse had a flawless sense of comedy. His characterization is enchanting, and his wit is everpresent. His name was Pelham Grenville, but his friends called him "Plum." "His gentle humor and effervescent faith in human beings have enriched the literature of the world" (Kneen 78). Everyman's Dictionary of Literary Biography calls Wodehouse, "the greatest humorous novelist of our time" (Priestley 108). His novels are filled with "sexless young women" running around breaking off their engagements, and with "formidable bullying aunts," and with eccentric and dotty dukes and earls (Priestley 109). Edward Galligan suggests that the excitement of Wodehouse's writing comes not from the originality of his message, but from the freshness of his images (Galligan 616). Robert Hall says that Wodehouse specializes in double meanings (one figurative and one literal) as when Leonard Q. Ross, one of his characters says, "If your eye falls on a bargain, pick it up" (Hall 88). Whatever his appeal, by the time he died, on St. Valentine's Day in 1975, he had become one of the most prolific writers of all time. He lived for ninety-five years, and during this time he published more than ninety-five novels, more than three hundred short stories, twelve plays, forty-eight films, and about five hundred articles, essays, and humorous verses. He also co-wrote or collaborated on sixteen plays, and provided lyrics for forty-five musical comedies mostly in collaboration with his friend, Jerome Kern (Reese 2). Commenting on why he waited until he was five before he began to write, Wodehouse said that, "before that time I suppose I just loafed." The first recorded example of Wodehouse's writing reads as follows:

> About five years ago in a wood there was a thrush, who built her nest in a poplar tree and sang so beautifully that all the worms came up from their holes and the ants laid down their burdens and the crickets stopped their mirth and moths settled all in a row to hear her. She sang a song as if she were in heaven--going up higher and higher as she sang. At last the song was done and the bird came down panting. Thank you said all the creatures. Now my story is ended. Pelham G. Wodehouse. (Heineman 59)

Most Wodehouse titles give the reader a clue as to what is to be expected. He wrote and edited books like Louder and Funnier (1932), Laughing Gas (1936), Joy in the Morning (1946), Methuen's Library of Humour (1934), A Century of Humour (1936), The Best of Modern Humor (1951), The Week-End Book of Humor (1952), and A Carnival of Modern Humor (1968). He collaborated with Ian Hay on Baa, Baa, Black Sheep: A Farcical Comedy in Three Acts (1930), A Damsel in Distress: A Comedy of Youth, Love, and Misadventure in Three Acts (1930), and Leave It to Psmith: A Comedy of Youth, Love and Misadventure in Three Acts (1932). He collaborated with Guy Bolton in Anything Goes: A Musical Comedy (1936), and Come On, Jeeves: A Farcical Comedy in Three Acts (1960). And Wodehouse adapted other people's work. He adapted Good Morning Bill: A Three-Act Comedy (1928) from Siegfried Gleyer. He adapted Don't Listen, Ladies: A Comedy in Three Acts (1952) from Stephen Powys and Guy Bolton. And he adapted O Clarence!: A Comedy (1969) from John Chapman (McLure 1224).

"The Fiery Wooing of Mordred" is about the Sprockett-Sprocketts who try to burn down their ancestral home because its taxes are so high. This is Wodehouse's way of amusing the reader while at the same time presenting the reader with important social issues. It is true that Mordred's plight is funny (McLure 1218). It is also true, however, that many landed gentry in England are in the same situation of wanting to simply be rid of their ancestral homes which are eating up all of their income. Since the Sprockett-

Sprocketts want their house to burn down, and since they know that Mordred had managed to set a wastebasket full of paper on fire while waiting for the same dentist that Annabelle Sprockett-Sprockett used, they simply invited Mordred to their estate, and gave him an ample supply of cigarettes, matches, and ash trays. Mordred does manage to set a wastebasket on fire; however, the other swains who have also been invited to the house, manage to put out the fire. Wodehouse's matter-of-fact tone in recounting this story contributes greatly to the funniness. His characters are light and fluffy, and they provide a great deal of verbal humor (McLure 1219).

The humor of Wodehouse stories is based on the eccentric characters he created, but it is also based on the marriage of disparate situations and the "rhythmical harmonizing of words." The humor is also the result of pithy approaches to succinctness and clarity of expression. Many of his sentences are a blend of the true and the unlikely, such as the following: "Beach the butler entered the room a dignified profession of one"; and "He talks French with both hands"; and "He gazed at the girl like an ostrich goggling at a brass door knob"; there is also the description of, "a fruity voice, like old tawny port made audible" (Heineman 60-61). Sometimes the "epitomes" are more developed as in, "If a girl thinks you're in love with her and says she'll marry you, you can't very well voice a preference for being dead in a ditch" (Kneen 77).

Richard Carlson considers Wodehouse's Bertram Wilberforce Wooster to be a fascinating character, and as benignly innocent as any character in all of English comic literature. He hates no one and is always chivalrous and gallant. He is completely ignorant of how to employ hurtful gossip or spiteful revenge. He listens to an assortment of aunts who call him "an excrescence," a "blot on the globe," but Bertie bears them no malice, and loves them all (Carlson 61-62).

Wooster's valet, Jeeves, is the dignified embodiment of reserve and understatement (Kneen 77). Jeeves is such a powerful literary force that even Wodehouse himself seems sometimes to loose control. In fact, Wodehouse once said that he never meant to continue the character of Jeeves, but he did continue. According to Wodehouse, the character of Jeeves "just took hold and held on" (qtd. in Carlson 61). Jeeves is the real power behind the throne. Wodehouse's novels are "delightfully gothic," filled with "eerie passages of melancholic detachment--Bertie Wooster is little more than an impressionistic puff of fun, sun, and light wind. Wodehouse creates ticklish but easy dilemmas for Wooster and Jeeves" (Carlson 57). Like Arthur Conan Doyle's adventures of Sherlock Holmes and Watson, P. G. Wodehouse's adventures of Bertie Wooster and Jeeves are in the category of escapist literature (Carlson xi). It is uncanny how much the team of Bertie Wooster and Jeeves has in common with the team of Sherlock Holmes and Watson. They both love the intrigue of the chase. They also love opera, sea cruises, and "small libations at Covent Garden." P. G. Wodehouse, like Sir Arthur Conan Doyle, also made outrageous use of hyperbole and of "missed thoughts" (Carlson 113). At the end of Wodehouse's stories, as at the end of Doyle's stories, there is the predictable gathering of all suspects and participants in the adventures, as they line leathery dens to hear detectives' final resolutions. Furthermore, both Sherlock Holmes and Jeeves are "practicing misogynists." In a book entitled Wodehouse at Work, Richard Usborne further develops the similarities between Arthur Conan Doyle and P. G. Wodehouse:

> The Bertie-Jeeves [stories] may be an echo of the Sherlock Holmes stories...blackmail, theft, revolver shots in the night, air-guns shot by the day, butlers in dressing gowns, people climbing in at the bedroom windows, people dropping out at the bedroom windows, people hiding in bedroom cupboards, the searching of bedrooms for missing manuscripts, cow-creamers and pigs. (Carlson 114)

Mary Jane Kneen notes that the stories of P. G. Wodehouse are filled with frolicking joy, and says that "Wodehouse is to literature what 'Saturday Night Live' is to television, quintessential humor." His stories contain whimsical names like "Gussie Fink-Nottle," "Boko Fittleworth," and "Galahad Threepwood" (Kneen 77). Some of Wodehouse's characters have aristocratic first names like "Algernon," or "Mortimer," but it is their nicknames that are the most humorous. Frederick Fotheringay Widgeon is called "Fungy." Claude Cattermole Potter-Pirbright" is known as "Catsmeat." And G. D'Arcy Cheesewright goes by the nickname of "Stilton." "Pongo," "Bingo," and "Beefy" are nicknames of three other characters who wander through Wodehouse novels. The girls that these Wodehouse men fall in and out of love with are frequently deemed "gooey," and are therefore not given nicknames, but a few of the more spirited women are honored by such names as "Stiffy," or "Nobby." Even the old and dignified men have somewhat discourteous names in Wodehouse novels, names given them at school that they are never allowed to forget. Major Brabzon-Plank is called "Bimbo," and George Pyke, a "Lord of the Realm" is generally known as "Stinker." Some Wodehouse characters get their names from events that are associated with these particular characters. "John San Francisco Earthquake Mulliner" got his name because the San Francisco Earthquake is what brought his parents together (Reese 5).

The English countryside that Wodehouse wrote about is dotted with towns and hamlets often with names that are long and odd and dear to the British people. Wodehouse's imaginary names of towns, therefore, are only slight exaggerations of the real names. Wodehouse created such imaginary places as Wockley Junction, East Wobsley, Blotsam Regis, Blicester Regis, Eggmarsh St. John, and Lower Smattering-on-the-Wissell. Wodehouse's Rudge-in-the-Vale is a town that is, "so quiet that it is nearly unconscious" (Reese 3). In these imaginary towns and villages there are country estates and homes at which Wodehouse's characters spend a week or two playing golf, visiting, getting engaged, getting unengaged, and making fools of themselves in gentle and harmless ways. The names of some of these places frequently imply more than merely lovely old homes. "Bludgleigh Court" is the estate of a family that likes to hunt and shoot all kinds of wildlife. A country home by the name of Matcham Scratchings is filled with family pets. While staying at such homes, the Wodehouse characters pass the time by reading such popular detective stories as "Blood on the Banisters," "Strychnine in the Soup" or "Mystery of the Pink Crayfish." The evenings of Wodehouse characters are spent at restaurants or nightclubs like "The Feverish Cheese," "The Startled Shrimp," "The Mottled Oyster," or "The Puce Ptarmigan." There is even a pub by the name of "The Caterpillar and Jug" (Reese 3-4).

Even the objects in various Wodehouse stories are given silly names. There is a patent medicine for nervous ailments called "Sugg's Southine," another called "Doctor Smythe's Tonic Swamp-Juice," and a third named "Mulliner's Buck-U-Uppo." There are dog biscuits named "Donaldson's Dog Joy," and others named "Todd's Tail-Wagger's Tid-bits." A snoring bulldog is called "Lysander," and a particular sheep dog is named "Mittens." "Wing-Fu" and "Ping-Poo" are the names of a pair of Pekinese dogs, and there is an unnamed Aberdeen terrier which mutters Gaelic under its breath. The most famous of Wodehouse animals is a prize-winning pig named "The Empress of Blandings." This pig is adored by her owner, the dyspeptic and grumpy Earl of Elmsworth of Blandings Castle. The Empress of Blandings is the focus of three of Wodehouse's novels, including one in which she is kidnapped and later saved (Reese 4).

Arthur Conan Doyle is frequently alluded to in P. G. Wodehouse's early stories and novels, including such public-school novels as The Pothunters (1902), A Perfect Uncle (1903), and The Gold Bat (1904). There are numerous reference to Doyle's "Rodney Stone," and two of Wodehouse's public school boys name their pet ferrets after Sir Nigel (from Doyle's The White Company). In Mike at Wrykn, a young boy refuses to leave his home to go to a rugby game until his revered copy of Doyle's "The Adventure of the Speckled Band" arrives. Furthermore, Wodehouse's most developed character, Bertie Wooster, uses a kind of language that seems to have been inspired by the rhetoric of Conan Doyle's Dr. Watson. "Both Wooster and Watson juggle colloquialisms and idiom, and none too successfully. Both men wait for some client to creep up the stairs to seek a resolution to their problem. And the resolution comes not from Wooster and Watson, but rather from Jeeves and Sherlock Holmes." Finally, Dr. Watson has the same sense of whimsey that Bertie Wooster has (Carlson 113). According to Richard Voorhees, Wodehouse's language, "is admirably clear, a mad and marvelous variegation." Richard Usborne says that Wodehouse has. "taught the English language to turn hand-springs for him, to lift weights, and to walk a tight-rope letting off fireworks" (qtd. in Carlson 58). Richard Carlson says that the most significant feature of Wodehouse's language is its coziness. It is a language that looks good, feels right, and is both familiar and comfortable (Carlson 83). "Wodehouse has learned his literary lessons, not only from past epochs and comic masters, but from other benign humorists as well. He has, in fact, taken Lewis Carroll's echoing images, de la Mare's 'faery flutters,' Milne's pristine evocations, and Beatrix Potter's ambivalence, and stripped and redressed them in the crazy quilt of Bertie's glen-plaid confusion" (Carlson 85).

Like Lewis Carroll and Edward Lear, Wodehouse used inventive language, but Wodehouse's language was different in that it depended not so much on the originality of the words themselves as it depended on the placement of these words into bizarre situations. Wodehouse had the ability to "flair a word." He was able to "probe deep into the mottled oyster." "While others can't wait to say 'goodbye' to him, Bertie exhibits the easy, if unrelaxed sophistication of the dilettante as he responds with a "pip-pip," a "teuf-teuf," and a "tinkerty-tonk" (Carlson 60).

Wodehouse's zany Bertie-Jeeves stories have been collected in such books as The Inimitable Jeeves (1923), Ring for Jeeves (1923), Carry On, Jeeves (1925), Thank You, Jeeves (1934), Very Good, Jeeves (1930), How Right You Are, Jeeves (1960), The Girl in Blue (1970), Much Obliged, Jeeves (1971), and Jeeves and the Tie That Binds (Kneen 77). Robert Hall considers many of Bertie Wooster's comments to contain a special type of personification which Hall calls the "transferred epithet." In Uneasy Money (1917) Bertie Wooster says that he was, "smoking a sad cigarette and waiting for the blow to fall" (Uneasy 93). In Big Money (1931) there is an irate house owner who replaces the word "bloody," a word considered taboo in British English with a number of inappropriate synonyms. "I catch you in my hall, sneaking my ensanguined hats, and you have the haemorrhagic insolence to stand there and tell me it's quite all right" (Big Money 129).

Wodehouse's Mulliner stories are about two pale young curates by the names of Augustine and Anselm. They are endearing to the reader because they are the underdogs among the clerical caste system. They are automatically at the bottom of all clerical scales (McLure 1219). Meet Mr. Mulliner (1925) is filled with delightful places like Higgle-ford-cum-Wortelbury-beneath-the-Hill," and people like "Catsmeat Entlwhistle," "Isadore Zinzinheimer," "Lord Biddlecomb," "Mrs. Postlethwaite," and "General Bloodenough" (Kneen 78).

In The Code of the Woosters (1938), Bertie is attempting to recover from an evening of drinking when he calls on Jeeves for one of his great hangover cures: "I loosed it down the hatch and, after undergoing the passing discomfort, unavoidable when you drink Jeeves's patent morning revivers, of having the top of the skull fly up to the ceiling and the eyes shoot out of their sockets and rebound from the opposite wall like racquet balls, felt better" (McLure 1221). In The Code of the Woosters, Tuppy Glossip says to Bertie Wooster, "You're a pig, Bertie," and Bertie Wooster calmly replies, "A pig maybe, but a shrewd, level-headed pig" (Code 45). In this same novel, Bertie Wooster also forms an analogical neologism by saying, "I could see that, if not actually disgruntled, he was far from being gruntled" (Code 84). In The Code of the Woosters, Bertie Wooster engages in his typical "Woosterisms," as he says, "The well-dressed man does not go around with kippered herrings in his pocket" (Code 45). In The Code of the Woosters there is a revealing dialogue between Bertie Wooster and Jeeves. Jeeves suggests to Bertie that, "the trousers, perhaps a quarter of an inch higher, sir. One aims at the carelessly graceful break over the instep. It is a matter of the nicest adjustment." Bertie is put off by Jeeves's fastidiousness and responds, "There are moments, Jeeves, when one asks oneself, 'Do trousers matter?'" and Jeeves, always able to get the last word calmly says, "The mood will pass, sir" (Carlson 84-85). Richard Carlson suggests that American readers and British readers read this passage differently. American readers, who have been taught to expect a punch line in their comic literature, hear it in Bertie's "Do trousers matter?" But the British reader better realizes that the dialogue is not really over until Jeeves says, "The mood will pass, sir" (Carlson 85).

In Joy in the Morning (1947) Bertie says that he, "balanced a thoughtful lump of sugar on the teaspoon" (Joy 56). In Jeeves in the Offing (1960) Bertie Wooster says, "It was plain that I had shaken him. His eyes widened, and an astonished piece of toast fell from his grasp" (Jeeves 18). In Uncle Dynamite (1948) Sir Aylmer is confused by the ambiguity of the word "by." When he is told, "I was assaulted by the duck pond," he responds with his eyes widening, "By the duck pond? How the devil can you be assaulted by a duck pond?" (Uncle 20). In A Pelican at Blanding (1969) Wodehouse implies that Lord Emsworth is a sensitive man, and then he continues: "To a sensitive man, the spectacle of a cascade of people falling downstairs is always disturbing" (Pelican 158). The relationship between Bertie Wooster and Jeeves is nicely illustrated in Very Good Jeeves (1958).

> "What-Ho, Jeeves," I said, entering the room where he waded knee-deep in suitcases and winter suitings like a sea-beast among the rocks. "Packing?"
> "Yes, sir," replied the honest fellow, for there are no secrets between us.
> "Pack on!" I said approvingly, "Pack, Jeeves, pack with care. Pack in the presence of the passenjare." And I rather fancy I added the words "tra-la" for I was in a merry mood. (qtd. in Carlson 60)

Wodehouse developed a kind of humor which critics have called "unconscious humor," and this can also be found in Very Good Jeeves: "If you were your aunt, and you knew the sort of chap you were, would you let a fellow you knew to be your best pal tutor your son?" (Very Good Jeeves 13). Unconscious humor is a special subset of dramatic irony.

The Bertie Wooster and Jeeves stories started in 1917 with My Man Jeeves and continued into the 1970s with Jeeves and the Tie That Binds (1971) using the same loony tone (Carlson 57). Wodehouse remained, "untouched by the twentieth-century maladoption of sexuality, technology, and cultural fall-out and litter" (Carlson 58). In The Performing Flea, Wodehouse said that when he is sent an unfavorable press clipping "an icy-look comes into my hard grey eyes and I mark my displeasure by not pasting it in my scrapbook." Wodehouse prefered clippings like that of the lady who considered Shakespeare to be "grossly materialistic and much overrated," and who "greatly prefers P. G. Wodehouse." About this comment, Wodehouse wryly remarked, "Shakespeare's stuff is different than mine, but that is not necessarily to say that it is inferior. There are passages in Shakespeare to which I would have been quite pleased to put my name.... The man may have been 'grossly materialistic,' but he would crack through the cover all right, when he got his eye in. I would definitely place him in the Wodehouse class" (qtd. in Carlson 121).

Pelham Grenville Wodehouse Bibliography

Benson, Donald R. "Exclusive Interview with P. G. Wodehouse: Two Comic Works." Writer's Digest 51 (1971): 22-24, 43.

Bowen, Barbara C. "Rabelais and P. G. Wodehouse: Two Comic Works." Esprit Createur 16 (1976): 63-77.

Carlson, Richard S. "Benign Humor and Escape Literature: Wodehouse, Doyle, and Sayers." The Benign Humorists New York, NY: Archon, 1975, 112-123.

Galligan, Edward L. "P. G. Wodehouse: Master of Farce." Sewanee Review 93.4 (1985): 609-617.

Hall, Robert A. Jr. The Comic Style of P. G. Wodehouse. Hamden, CT: Shoe String/Archon Press, 1974.

Heineman, James. "P. G. Wodehouse: An Unique Humorist." WHIMSY 4 (1986): 59-61.

Kneen, Mary Jane. "Recommended: P. G. Wodehouse." English Journal 73.1 (1984): 77-78.

Lydon, Mary. "First Love: Reading with P. G. Wodehouse." Profession 94. Ed. Phyllis Franklin. New York, NY: Modern Language Association, 1994, 21-25.

McCracken, George. "Wodehouse and Latin Comedy." The Classical Journal 29 (1934): 612-614.

MacDermott, Kathy. "Light Humor and the Dark Underside of Wish Fulfillment: Conservative Anti-Realism." Studies in Popular Culture 10.2 (1987): 37-53.

McLure, Victoria E. "P. G. Wodehouse." Encyclopedia of British Humorists, Volume II. Ed. Steven H. Gale. New York, NY: Garland, 1996, 1217-1227.

Mikes, George. "P. G. Wodehouse." Eight Humorists. London, England: Allan Wingate, 1954, 153-175.

Muggeridge, Malcolm. "The Wodehouse Affair." Tread Softly for You Tread on My Jokes. London, England: Collins, 1966, 83-93.

Olson, Kirby. "Bertie and Jeeves at the End of History: P. G. Wodehouse as Political Scientist." HUMOR: International Journal of Humor Research 9.1 (1996): 73-88.

Priestley, J. B. "Wodehouse, Beachcomber, and Waugh." English Humour. New York: Stein and Day, 1976, 108-114.

Reese, Margaret. "The Humor of P. G. Wodehouse." Unpublished Paper. Tempe, AZ: Arizona State University, 1993.

Thompson, Kristin. Wooster Proposes, Jeeves Disposes; or, Le Mot Juste. New York, NY: Heineman, 1992.

Voorhees, Richard J. "The Jolly Old World of P. G. Wodehouse." South Atlantic Quarterly 61 (1962): 213-222.

Wodehouse, Pelham Grenville. Big Money. New York, NY: Doubleday, Doran, and Co., 1931.

Wodehouse, Pelham Grenville. The Code of the Woosters. London, England: Herbert Jenkins, 1938.

Wodehouse, Pelham Grenville. Jeeves in the Offing. London, England: Herbert Jenkins, 1960.

Wodehouse, Pelham Grenville. Joy in the Morning. London, England: Herbert Jenkins, 1947.

Wodehouse, Pelham Grenville. A Pelican at Blanding. London, England: Herbert Jenkins, 1969.

Wodehouse, Pelham Grenville. Uncle Dynamite. London, England: Herbert Jenkins, 1948.

Wodehouse, Pelham Grenville. Uneasy Money. London, England: Methuen, 1917.

Wodehouse, Pelham Grenville. Very Good, Jeeves. New York, NY: Penguin, 1958.

Harold Brighouse (1882-1958)

Newell Sawyer says that Harold Brighouse belongs to the "drama of revolt." His Odd Man Out (1912) is a modestly entertaining country-house comedy in which Barbara has been raised by a dour and sanctimonious stepfather. He has brought her up to feel obliged to marry a cousin like himself. Her real father is a beloved vagabond, who returns home in time to confound the schemers and to help Barbara gain the man of her choice. Garside's Career (1914) is the story of a young Socialist who considers himself to be another Napoleon, and who gets himself elected to Parliament. Lady Mottram represents the archetype of the haughty matron. Her son, Freddie is saved from foppishness by his rich sense of humor, which gives him a more realistic perspective on class distinctions (Sawyer 236). Hobson's Choice (1915) became popular because the characterizations were genuine, and because the humor was breezy (Sawyer 237).

Harold Brighouse Bibliography

Sawyer, Newell W. The Comedy of Manners from Sheridan to Maugham: The Study of the Type as a Dramatic Form and as a Social Development. Unpublished Ph.D. Dissertation. Philadelphia, PA: University of Pennsylvania, 1931.

James Joyce (1882-1941) IRELAND

James Joyce loved diametric opposition. This is why he created such pairs as Bloom and Molly, Stephen and Buck Mulligan, Humphrey and Anna, and Shem and Shaun. John Slack says that Joyce had a "comic flair" that can best be described as what Mikhail Bakhtin calls "lower body humor," or "grotesque realism." "The essential principle of grotesque realism is degradation, that is, lowering of all that is high, spiritual, ideal, abstract; it is a transfer to the material level, to the sphere of the earth and body in their indissoluble unity." This "grotesque realism" is seen in writers like Geoffrey Chaucer, Miguel de Cervantes, François Rabelais, Jean Baptiste Molière, Giovanni Boccaccio, Jonathan Swift, Henry Fielding, Laurence Sterne, and Nikolai Gogol. In the "grotesque realism" school of writing, taboo subjects like sex, sexuality, digestion, elimination, and other physiological functions are considered to be fitting topics for humorous treatment. Rather than being shunned, these topics are highlighted in "grotesque realism." These same subjects are, of course, shunned in the "high comedy" school of writing.

Mary T. Reynolds argues that each of the stories in Dubliners (1914) is an allusion to a particular episode in Dante's Inferno, and that the book as a whole is an indication of Dublin's "moral death." Thus, she sees Dubliners as a kind of parody of Inferno, with the comic targets being such Irish people as the young students, the priests, the merchants, the artists, the minor politicians, the hangers-on, the ne'er-do-wells, the welshers, the salesmen, the newspapermen, and the office workers (Reynolds 159). The story entitled "Two Gallants," is about Lenehan and Corley. John Slack describes Corley as a "walking, tumescent phallus" (Slack 612). "He walked with his hands at his sides, holding himself erect and swaying his head from side to side. His head was large, globular, and oily; it sweated in all weathers; and his large round hat, set upon it sideways, looked like a bulb which had grown out of another" (Joyce Dubliners 51). Another story in Dubliners is entitled "Grace." In this story, Tom Kernan is a serious alcoholic who is in need of help, so his friends coax this former Protestant to attend a Catholic retreat for businessmen, because they believe that this will keep him away from alcohol for a while. It is ironic, then, when the retreat turns into a, "typical Irishmen's drinking bout, made hilarious by all of the participants' spouting of faulty knowledge of the history of their religion" (Slack 612). "The Dead" is still another story in Dubliners. Slack says that "The Dead" can, "tickle the funnybone of its readers, even as it touches the heartstrings with fond memories." The reader smiles at Aunt Julia's inability to understand the connection between guttapercha galoshes and prophylactics, rubber once being the main ingredient of both. Julia's sister exclaimed, "Galoshes, Julia! Goodness me, don't you know what galoshes are? You wear them over your...over your boots, Gretta, isn't it?" (Joyce Dubliners 181). The reader also laughs at the drunken antics of Freddy Malins, but Slack feels that it is the "authorial mocking of the mildly pompous Gabriel" that, "best marks the comedy of the story." Even though Gabriel is putting on airs of superiority and aloofness, he frequently, "falls dismally short of grasping the truth of a given situation" (Slack 612).

Although A Portrait of the Artist as a Young Man (1916) is more subtle than Joyce's other works, the humor nevertheless shines through at times. At the Christmas Dinner scene in Chapter 1, for example, the high rhetoric and the blasphemous speech compete with each other for dominance. There are also a number of lighter scenes, as when Mr. Casey is teasing Stephen about the "purse of silver in his throat" (Joyce Portrait 28), or when Simon takes off on the hotelkeeper and both Stephen and Mr. Casey join in on the merriment (Joyce Portrait 29), or the father's perfectly timed wry statement about the "pope's nose" (Joyce Portrait 32), or Mr. Casey's spitting story, which Slack considers to be the closest approximation to "eliminative comedy" that appears in the novel (Slack 613).

Slack says that Ulysses and Finnegans Wake "altered our understanding of what constitutes a funny novel" (Slack 611). Maureen Waters says that Joyce heaped scorn on the writings of W. B. Yeats, Augusta Gregory and John Synge (Waters 104). Mulligan in Ulysses (1922), "mocks the new art as pretentious, hence 'snot green'" (Waters 104). Even Stephen Dedalus announces that Irish art is "the cracked looking glass of a servant." "The culminating effect of the combined mockery of the two young men is to dismiss the work of the Revival as effete and pretentious" (Waters 107).

Joyce's Ulysses is a parody of Homer's Odyssey even though, "the author's parodic intent is not to write a modern sequel to that Greek epic, but merely to pepper his narrative with Homer's ghostly presence." The final effect is

> ...purely comic, since Stephen-Telemachus is less than enthusiastic to find another father to replace his already drunken one; Molly-Penelope is less than patiently faithful in her affair with Blazes Boylan; and Bloom-Odysseus, although a wanderer on this and every day (he is an advertising canvasser for a daily Dublin newspaper), is less than heroic in demeanor as he fights his minor battles and encounters his own psychological demons, sirens, and harpies. (Slack 614)

But Joyce's Ulysses is more than just a parody Homer's Odyssey; for the parody is much more extensive than this. Michael White says the following:

> One of the features which immediately attracts our attention is the prevalence of parody in this [the Cyclops] episode. The numerous Homeric parallels are quite often tantamount to a parody of the Greek text--especially in the second narrative (for example Bloom's "knockmedown cigar," the numerous incoherent lists or the biscuit-box affair)--while the whole second narrative is one continuous parody of the first. The very English language itself suffers varied and constant parody, both in the hands of Nameless and in the second narrative. Both narratives can in turn be seen as a parody of nineteenth-century "realist" narration. (White 190)

On the surface there is the banter of a drinker, and the story hinges on the presentation of the claustrophobic oppressive confinement of domineering partisan nationalism, but the structure of the episode transcends this ideas in two ways, one "incoming" and the other "outgoing" (White 191). Michael White says, "The proliferation of parody and jest in this episode, rather than just parody or jest, is at the same time the vehicle by which Joyce is unobtrusively and apparently effortlessly carrying out his revolution in narration." White continues, "The coexistence of two narratives, two views of the same events which run parallel courses, is the object lesson in undermining any possible claim to objectivity on the part of 'realist' narration." As Joyce would say, "There's many a true word spoken in jest" (White 192).

The first half of the "Nausicaa" episode of Ulysses is told by an omniscient narrator whose language is very much like that to be found in the glamour and beauty magazines that Gerty MacDowell reads, but then in the second half of "Nausicaa", the reader is suddenly hit with Bloom's very long interior monologue which is accompanied by very little narrative interruption or explanation.   The reader is thus given two hilariously contrasting views of the events which have just taken place. Gerty's perception is that she has been in the environment of "a sterling man, a man of inflexible humour to his fingertips," a man whose "hands and face are working" all the while that she is leaning back to observe the fireworks, thus exposing her "graceful beautifully shaped legs" (Joyce Ulysses 365). Only a couple of pages further along, Bloom reveals a number of things that the reader had not been able to determine for sure from the first account. "He is, naturally, the dark gentleman about whom Gerty has over-romanticized; she is in fact lame ("Glad I didn't know it when she was on show. Hot little devil all the same"); and Bloom's gestures have been onanistic rather than chivalrous" (Slack 614).

In Ulysses the "Veiled Sibyl" proclaims that Bloom is "the funniest man on earth" (Joyce Ulysses 491). Readers may not agree with this assessment; they would, however, agree that he is, "imbued with a true comic spirit." In "Ulysses" as a Comic Novel, Zack Bowen sees Bloom as "a sort of common man's Ulysses." He is a schlemiel figure, with whom the average reader can identify, or even feel superior to. In addition, "as spiritual misfit, Bloom embodies the traditional comic salvation of the powerless against the powerful, the individual against the social order" (Bowen 11). Slack says that Bloom also is the comic foil to the melodramatic Stephen (Slack 615).

In his Finnegans Wake (1939), James Joyce follows the structure of Giambattista Vico's Scienza Nuova. The first eight chapters (Book 1) tell about the period of Viconian time when God ruled. The next three chapters (Book 2) tell about the period of Viconian time when the Heroes ruled. The next three chapters (Book 3) tell about Vico's democratic period of Human rule. And the final chapter (Book 4) is Vico's "ricurso," or the transitional period before the return to the first age.

Chapter 2 of Finnegans Wake begins with a parody of a playbill that includes a cast of characters and an acknowledgement of everybody who helped in the production, including "jests, jokes, jigs, and jorums for the Wake" that were, "lent from the properties of the late cemented Mr. T. M. Finnegan R. I. C." (Joyce Finnegans Wake 26-27). This chapter is filled with puns, riddles, nursery rhymes, and children's fun and games. It is a chapter about the twins Shem and Shaun, and about their sister Issy, who is paired with her own image, (her sister reflection in the mirror). According to Robert Polhemus, Shem and Shaun are, "quintessential comic opposites, reverberating as significantly as Yin and Yang or cerebral bipolarity. They create each other, [and] play off each other" (Slack 616).

In Finnegans Wake, James Joyce deals with actual events; nevertheless, he twists the spellings and sounds of the words around to acquire new meanings.   Joyce defamiliarizes conventional associations with these events by comic distortion, where The Duke of Wellington becomes "Slaughter Willingdone," and Saint Patrick, the patron saint of Ireland, becomes "Flop Hattrick." Brian Boru, Ireland's last king has his name changed into "Brewinbaroon" (Trosky 209). Through such word play, Joyce is able to associate the Duke of Wellington with a ruthless murderer, and the patron saint of Ireland with a Shakespearean-like fool (Goldman 7).

Like Lewis Carroll before him, Joyce used many "portmanteau" words in <u>Finnegans Wake</u>, to tease the reader into making verbal associations between the spoken and the written word. An example is "psocoldlogical," which relates graphically to "psychological," but relates phonologically to "so-called logical." "Joyce's neologism is not only funny, it is also economical! Indeed, constant poetic explication like the above is an intrinsic part of the process of reading <u>Finnegans Wake</u> (Slack 615). Beckett explains that <u>Finnegans Wake</u> "is not <u>about</u> something; <u>it is that something itself</u>.... When the sense is dancing, the words dance" (Beckett 14).

See also Nilsen, Don L. F. "James Joyce." Humor in Irish Literature: A Reference Guide. Westport, CT: Greenwood, 1996, 1-2, 6-7, 9, 81, 137-153, 164-165, 168-169, 181-182, 187, 191, 211, 213, 215-216.

James Joyce Bibliography

Beckett, Samuel, et. al. <u>Our Exagmination round his Factification for Incamination of Work in Progress</u>. Paris, France: Shakespeare and Company, 1929.

Bell, Robert H. <u>Jocoserious Joyce: The Fate of Folly in Ulysses</u>. Ithaca, NY: Cornell University Press, 1991.

Bluemel, Kristin. "The Feminine Laughter of No Return: James Joyce and Dorothy Richardson." <u>Look Who's Laughing: Gender and Comedy</u>. Ed. Gail Finney. New York, NY: Gordon and Breach, 1994 161-172.

Bowen, Zack R. <u>Ulysses as a Comic Novel</u>. Syracuse, NY: Syracuse University Press, 1989.

DiBernard, Barbara. "Parallax as Parallel, Paradigm, and Paradox in <u>Ulysses</u>." <u>Éire-Ireland</u> 10.1 (1975): 69-84.

Goldman, Ben. "Conventions of Joycean Humor." Unpublished Paper. Tempe, AZ: Arizona State University, 1997.

Howarth, Herbert. "The Joycean Comedy: Wilde, Jonson, and Others." <u>A James Joyce Miscellany. Second Series</u>. Ed. Marvin Magalaner. Carbondale, IL: Southern Illinois Univ Press, 1959 179-194.

Ingersoll, Earl G. "Irish Jokes: A Lacanian Reading of Short Stories by James Joyce, Flann O'Brien, and Bryan MacMahon." <u>Studies in Short Fiction</u> 2 (Spring, 1990): 237-245.

Joyce, James. <u>Dubliners</u>. London, England: Grant Richards, 1914.

Joyce, James. <u>Finnegans Wake</u>. London, England: Faber and Faber, 1939.

Joyce, James. <u>A Portrait of the Artist as a Young Man</u>. New York, NY: B. W. Huebsch, 1916.

Joyce, James. <u>Ulysses</u>. Paris, France: Shakespeare and Company, 1922.

Klug, Michael A. "The Comic Structure of Joyce's <u>Ulysses</u>." <u>Éire</u> 11.1 (1976): 63-84.

McCarthy, Patrick A. <u>The Riddles of "Finnegans Wake</u>." Rutherford, NJ: Fairleigh-Dickinson University Press, 1980.

MacNicholas, John. "Comic Design in Joyce's 'The Dead.' " <u>Modern British Literature</u> 1.1 (1976): 56-65.

Maher, R. A. "James Joyce's <u>Exiles</u>: The Comedy of Discontinuity." <u>James Joyce Quarterly</u> 9 (1972): 461-474.

Polhemus, Robert M. "Joyce's Finnegans Wake (1924-39): The Comic Gospel of 'Shem'." <u>Comic Faith: The Great Tradition from Austen to Joyce</u>. Chicago, IL: Univ of Chicago Press, 1980, 294-337.

Reynolds, Mary T. <u>Joyce and Dante: The Shaping Imagination</u>. Princeton, NJ: Princeton University Press, 1981.

Robinson, Marian. "Funny Funereels: Single Combat in <u>Finnegans Wake</u> and the <u>Táin Bó</u>

Cuailnge." Éire-Ireland 26.3 (1981): 96-106.

Santos, Antonio Raul de Toro. "Algunas Consideraciones sobre el Humorismo de James Joyce." Literary and Linguistic Aspects of Humour. Barcelona, Spain: Univ of Barcelona Dept of Languages, 1984, 233-238.

Schlossman, Beryl. Joyce's Catholic Comedy of Language. Madison, WI: University of Wisconsin Press, 1985.

Slack, John S. "James Joyce." Encyclopedia of British Humorists, Volume I. Ed. Steven H. Gale. New York, NY: Garland, 1996, 608-620.

Trosky, Susan M. ed. Contemporary Authors. Detroit, MI: Gale, 1989.

Waters, Maureen. "James Joyce and Buck Mulligan." The Comic Irishman. Albany, NY: State Univ of New York Press, 1984, 95-109.

White, Michael C. "'Cyclops': Beyond Parody." James Joyce: A New Language. Eds. Francisco Garcia Tortosa, Manuel Almagro Jimenez, Jose Carnero Gonzalez, and Paul Witkowsky. Seville, Spain: Publicaciones de la Universidad de Sevilla, 1982, 189-192.

Wyndham Lewis (1882-1957)

Wyndham Lewis is a paradox. One indication of his paradoxical nature is that the writers he most attacked were the expressionists. He attacked them because of the violence that he saw as a necessary aspect of expressionism. But paradoxically, Lewis "produced energetically expressionist creative works in his three major novels" (Paton 681). About Lewis's writing, Julian Symons says, "Mr. Lewis's style sometimes gets in the way of his satire." He continues by saying, "there is so much style that one can see nothing else. With Swift this is never so" (Gross 113). In Men Without Art (1934) Lewis argues that the best satire is nonmoralistic and therefore the best satirists always find themselves the enemies of society. "There is laughter and laughter, and that of true satire is as it were tragic laughter" (Lewis Men Without Art 113). Lewis continues, "the greatest satire cannot be moralistic at all: if for no other reason, because no mind of the first order, expressing itself in art, has ever itself been taken in, nor consented to take in others, by the crude injunction of any purely moral code" (Paton 680).

According to George Paton, Tarr (1918) is both an "intellectual comedy of art," and a, "comedy of sex, set in the bohemian and cosmopolitan student life of pre-1914 Paris." In the Preface to Tarr, Lewis wrote, "if you look closely at my grin, you will perceive that it is a very logical and deliberate grimace." Tarr, the narrator, is a detached observer who makes fun of Kreisler, the other main male character. Kreisler is a wild and bourgeois bohemian who is portrayed as a "would-be artist with no talent." He is seen as a, "comic automaton spasmodically embodying the ideas of Teutonic Romanticism and militarism." Tarr, nevertheless, is both contemplative and sardonic. In Tarr, there is also an antithesis developed between the two main women characters, Bertha and Anastasya, as, "Lewis gives comic expression to his own misogynist and sexist leanings" (Paton 674).

"Wildboy" (1927) is an essay in which Lewis explicates his comic aesthetic, and his theory of laughter (Paton 679). In Time and Western Man (1927) Lewis discusses being vs. non-being, or self vs. non-self. He says that laughter is a hysterical attempt to bridge this gap (between being and non-being), and that it anticipates the existential concerns of Sartre's Being and Nothing (Paton 681).

The Human Age is a trilogy of novels which includes The Childermass (1928), Malign Fiesta (c1928) co-authored with D. G. Bridson, and Monstre Gai (1955) co-authored with D. G. Bridson. Daniel Schenker suggests that the paradox of Lewisian satire is very well illustrated in this trilogy. George Paton considers The Childermass (1928) to be

Lewis's, "best fictional satire written from a surrealistic and obscure style of a philosophical extravaganza dealing with a journey through a fantastic and macabre Heaven." Frederic Jameson considers The Childermass to be "theological science fiction" (Jameson 6). It is set outside the gate of a fictional Heaven in a wasteland that is to represent the afterlife. The "emigrant mass" of humanity is waiting at the gate to be interrogated by the Bailiff. Two of the characters, Pullman and Satherwaite, are talking with each other sometimes in "highly and deliberately flourished anglicisms," and sometimes in an English colloquial slang that includes such words as "fuss," "toddle," "beastly," and "strapping." The character of Pullman is the type of "intellectual" that Lewis hated, and is probably modeled on James Joyce. Lewis was satirizing authors who used the stream-of-consciousness style of writing, which Lewis considered to be barbaric. In discussing the "comic obedience" to the archetypes of the novel, Frederic Jameson brings attention to the conventionalized roles (Keystone Cops, and Jack the Giantkiller), and the archetypal circus clowns and Pierrots. Jameson considers Lewis's style to be a "satire-collage." Lionel Stevenson further notes that there is a, "wild phantasmagoria of broad farce, poetic symbolism, and philosophical subtlety" (Stevenson 172). Stevenson says that the Bailiff is a cartoon character who is acting as what Jameson calls the "household bogeyman." "The Bailiff conducts his inquisition from a Punch-and-Judy booth, evoking roars of laughter from the mob of working-class peons (or 'herd,' as Lewis dismissingly calls them--the 'sham-puppet victims of his satire'" (Jameson 161).

Lionel Stevenson says that Lewis described The Apes of God (1930) as "pure satire." Lewis savagely satirizes the wealthy dilettantes, or "Apes" of art, and their "frivolous and self-indulgent lifestyles." Lewis especially targets the bourgeois-bohemians of London, and the leading members of the Bloomsbury Group (Stevenson 183). Almost all of the characters in The Apes of God are described as an "animal," or a "machine," or a "dummy," or a "split-man." The "split-men" are "alienated from their true selves by the pressures of 'group-rhythm' and drifting with the flux of contemporary fads" (Stevenson 176-177). Lewis uses the term "romantics" to describe his principle antagonists. James Joyce, Virginia Woolf, George Sitwell, Edith Sitwell, and Vanessa Bell (the Bloomsbury painter) were his main satiric targets. He attacked homosexuality, burgeoning feminism, militarism, nationalism, the cult of youth, leftist political radicalism, and the adulation of the colored races. He also targeted people who espoused Freudian theories of the unconscious (Paton 676). In The Apes of God, Dan Boleyn is depicted as an imbecilic, childish, would-be poet who is the apprentice ape-hunter. He is introduced into the world of "Apes" by Sir Horace Zagreus, his mysterious patron. Zagreus is androgynous, and is both a non-ape, and an anti-ape. He is a loquacious character who enjoys staging elaborate practical jokes for his friends. James-Julius Ratner, a self-promoting author who is a caricature of James Joyce, is "singled out for particular satirical demolition" (Paton 677).

In Wyndham Lewis's autobiography, Blasting and Bombardiering (1937), he explains that it was his political education in the trenches during the First World War that convinced him to become a social critic and satiric novelist during the 1920s and 1930s. He wrote, "That we were all on a fool's errand had become plain to many of us" (Lewis Blasting 187).

Lewis's fourth novel, entitled The Snooty Baronet (1932), is Lewis's funniest, lightest, and most complex novel, and it marks the apex of his literary career (Paton 679). The Snooty Baronet is a fast-paced picaresque novel which Daniel Schenker considers to be a "Religious Satire." Schenker points out that is filled with "self-consuming ironies." It is a diary, or a picaresque travelogue in which Snooty is being transported from New York to Persia via Mayfair and Martigues, in the South of France (Paton 678). Lionel Stevenson considers it to be, "a masterpiece of Hogarthian comedy and the author's nearest approach to a 'comic romp'" (Stevenson 178). George Paton points out that the first-person narrator, Sir Kell-Imrie (nicknamed Snooty) is both sardonic and ironic. He is a war veteran with an artificial leg, and a silver plate in his skull. Since The Snooty Baronet is a parody of cheap novelettes, it contains chatty and impulsive dialogue and anonymous quotations, and allusions to songs, nursery rhymes, limericks, puns, and popular sayings of the day that are "used to telling comic and satiric effect" (Paton 678).

According to Bernard Lafourcade, The Snooty Baronet has many comic scenes, one of which involves Snooty's unscrewing his artificial leg so that he can have sex with his aging mistress, Val. Lafourcade calls this scene, "existential farce": "She grappled with me at once, before the words were well out of my mouth, with the self-conscious gusto of a Chatterly-taught expert. But as I spoke I went to meet her--as I started my mechanical leg giving out an ominous creak (I had omitted to oil it; like watches and clocks these things require lubrication" (Lewis Snooty 48). Lafourcade says that The Snooty Baronet is a, "dehumanized-machine-age version of the comedy of manners" (Lafourcade 265).

In Monstre Gai (1955), co-authored with D. G. Bridson, Lewis evokes a grotesque hellishness in which Sammael (the Devil) provides a tour of Dis (Hell) for Pullman. In Sammael's car there is a captive French woman who is about to be given to the "beasts."

> He flung the door open, getting bitten in the hand by one of the ravening beasts. There burst into the car the fearful stench, there was a scarlet flash of sexual monstrosity, the whining and snorting of a score of faces--the beasts leaping on one another's backs, so that several appeared to be about to spring on to the roof of the car.--Scores of sinewy arms terminating in claws shot into the car, and snatched the woman out of it. (Lewis Monstre Gai 371)

Wyndham Lewis felt that men were really machines pretending to be human, and he coined the term "wild body" to symbolize this notion. Lewis's view is, "a peculiar inversion of Henri Bergson's influential theory of laughter which Bergson developed in Le Rire." In A Soldier of Humour (1966), Lewis describes workers as "cogs," "bobbins," and "puppets," because workers exist only in the context of the dynamics of the group (Paton 681).

According to Anthony Bertram, "Lewis never achieved sustained greatness in any work: he was a master of the sentence, the paragraph, even the scene; but never the whole book" (Bertram 628). Lewis may have been paranoid, but his paranoia was not without grounding. Julian Symons says of him,

> It is startling, sixty years later, to see how prophetically right he was in relation to the demise of the family, the standardization of clothing and its unisexual nature, the rise of feminism and homosexuality, the immense growth of what he called "associational life" through the development of specialized interests, and the control exerted over all our lives by gigantic international cartels and the press. (Symons 7)

Wyndham Lewis Bibliography

Bertram, Anthony. "Lewis, Percy Wyndham." Dictionary of National Biography. Oxford, England: Oxford University Press, 1971, 626-629.

Chapman, Robert. Wyndham Lewis: Fiction and Satires. London, England: Vision Press, 1973.

Gross, John, ed. "Wyndham Lewis." The Modern Movement. London, England: Harvill, 1992, 101-114.

Henkle, Roger B. "The 'Advertised Self': Wyndham Lewis's Satire." Novel 13 (1979): 95-108.

Jameson, Frederic. Fables of Aggression: Wyndham Lewis, the Modernist as Fascist.

Berkeley, CA: University of California Press, 1979.

Lafourcade, Bernard. "Afterword." The Snooty Baronet. Auth. Wyndham Lewis. Santa Barbara, CA: Black Sparrow Press, 1984, 264-265.

Lewis, Wyndham. Blasting and Bombardiering. London, England: Eyre and Spottiswoode, 1937.

Lewis, Wyndham. Men Without Art. London, England: Cassel, 1934.

Lewis, Wyndham. Satire and Fiction. London, England: Arthur Press, 1930.

Lewis, Wyndham. The Snooty Baronet. London, England: Cassell, 1932.

Lewis, Wyndham. Tarr. London, England: Methuen, 1928.

Paton, George E. C. "Wyndham Lewis." Encyclopedia of British Humorists, Volume II. Ed. Steven H. Gale. New York, NY: Garland, 1996, 671-684.

Rosenthal, Raymond, ed. A Soldier of Humour and Selected Writings of Wyndham Lewis. New York, NY: New American Library, 1966.

Schenker, Daniel. Wyndham Lewis: Religion and Modernism. Tuscaloosa, AL: Alabama University Press, 1992.

Stevenson, Lionel. The History of the English Novel, Volume XI--Yesterday and After. New York, NY: Barnes and Noble, 1967.

Symons, Julian. "The Thirties Novels." (Wyndham Lewis Issue). Agenda 7.3-8.1 (1969): 37-48.

Alan Alexander Milne (1882-1956)

A. A. Milne was a prolific writer of light verse and whimsical essays. He was often criticized that his writing was too childlike, and that he should try to make his subject choices more sophisticated and his plots more dramatic. Milne responded to this criticism very poignantly:

> When I am told, as I so often am, that it is time I "came to grips with real life"--preferably in a brothel or Public Bar where life is notoriously more real than elsewhere, minds more complex, more imaginative, more articulate, souls near the stars--I realize sadly that, even if I made the excursion, I should bring back nothing but the same self to which objection had already been taken. (qtd. in Haring-Smith xxxv)

James Heineman says that Milne was not a much liked man, and that Wodehouse, who had known him for about forty years, decided to start a "Try to Like A. A. Milne Club." Wodehouse found it hard to find members to join the club. Finally, one man joined, but he resigned within a week stating, "Since joining the association, I have met Mr. Milne" (Heineman 60).

Frederick Crews says that a major error in much of Milne criticism results from the fact that the critics aren't careful enough in distinguishing between Milne the writer and Milne the narrator, nor are they careful enough in distinguishing between Christopher Robin the listener and Christopher Robin the character (Crews 5). Crews says that Milne, "conceals his own desire to publish a book by making himself appear simply as the reluctantly obliging father (the Milnean voice) who must humor his son with stories, and whose stories, indeed, lie open to the direction of that son, nay, of that son's teddy bear" (Crews 7). Crews utilizes the Great Chain of Being Metaphor to explain how the Pooh books should be read. At the top of this Great Chain of Being is A. A. Milne, who rules the hierarchy and has absolute control over everything that happens. Milne the person, however, delegates some of his authority to Milne the Narrator, who in turn grants considerable privilege to the "Christophoric ear." Number four in this Great Chain of Being is Christopher Robin the character, and under him is Pooh, Christopher's favorite animal. Piglet, as Pooh's best friend is number six. There is a competition between Owl and Rabbit for the number seven position, each trying vainly to dominate the action, but each doomed to failure by their low ranking. Number nine is Eeyore, the archetypal outsider, and below Eeyore there is a vast array of, "virtually vegetal nonentities, concluding with one of Rabbit's least imposing friends-and-relations, Small and Alexander Beetle" (Crews 8).

Some of the phenomenal popularity of When We Were Very Young (1924), Winnie-the-Pooh (1926), Now We Are Six (1927), and The House at Pooh Corner (1928) is based on E. H. Shepard's illustrations which capture, "the subtle humor, the generous spirit, and the amiable style of the author" (Otten 179). When We Were Very Young (1924) is a book of poems that are anti-didactic, written from the child's point of view. The children in these poems are in control, and break rules, conventions, prudential restrictions and regulations of obedience that are imposed by adults. These poems are subversive in the sense that they encourage bad habits and disobedience in children, and some adults, therefore, want them censored. The problem for the censors is that not only are the rules broken, but the rules are broken without disaster following. "Teddy Bear" is about a person who is short and stout, and proud of it. "If I Were a King" is about a child who has the fantasy of being powerful enough to demolish adult restrictions. "The Dormouse and the Doctor" is considered by Trivizas and Davies to be "Milne's subversive masterpiece." At first the dormouse is unable to resist the doctor's forced prescriptions for good health, but then he turns to his imagination. By using his imagination he is able to change the hateful chrysanthemums that the doctor had prescribed into the delphiniums and geraniums that he wanted. There are other subversive children as well. Emmeline is a child whose hands aren't very clean, and Mary Jane obstinately refuses to eat the rice pudding that is good for her. Even the titles of the poems suggest subversiveness: "Politeness," "Independence," "Disobedience." Such titles, "suggest a thoroughly enjoyable reveling in an imaginary anarchic carnival" (Trivizas and Davies 773).

"Vespers" is a poem in When We Were Very Young in which the child first prays for Mummy, and then prays for Daddy, and then for Nanny. Then he spreads his fingers apart and opens his eyes and sees Nanny's dressing gown through his parted fingers. He prays that God should "make her good," which may have been as much for his own benefit as for hers. Then he associates the dressing gown, which he sees through his parted fingers, with his own hood, which he pulls over his head to make himself invisible (Otten 180). Finally, he remembers to pray for himself, "Oh! Now I remember. God bless me." Charlotte Otten suggests that in "Vespers" Milne is capturing, "not so much the egotism of a child at prayer but the erratic concentration of all people at prayer, whether child or adult" (Otten 181). In "Disobedience," the child inverts the mother-child relationship. The child assumes his mother's power and says to his mother, "You must never go down to the end of the town, / if you don't go down with me." Of course the mother disobeys, and goes down to the end of town alone, and "James James / Morrison's mother / Hasn't been heard of since" (Otten 181). In A. A. Milne, The Man Behind Winnie-the-Pooh, Ann Thwaite explains the effect that Milne's poetry can have on people. She tells about the Honorable Edwin Samuel who had read some Milne poetry at a Chamber of Commerce lunch in Jaffa, Israel. Samuel later recounts the event: "All those busy Arab merchants took the afternoon off for endless repeats of 'Christopher Robin goes hoppity, hoppity, hop.'" Another incident involved a New York woman who reported, "We had to hop. We kept it up until I was overcome by exhaustion" (Otten 181).

Three years after Milne wrote When We Were Very Young (1924), he wrote Now We Are Six (1927). He uses the dual voice of himself and Christopher Robin. As he explains, "We have been nearly three years writing this book. We began it when we were very young...and now we are six. So, of course, bits of it seem rather babyish to us (Otten

185). At the end of Now We Are Six, Christopher Robin writes a poem which is entitled, "The End." "But now I am Six, I'm as clever as clever as clever. / So I think I'll be six now for ever and ever" (qtd. in Otten 186).

It is interesting to note that Christopher Robin called himself "Billy Moon," the "Moon" part being a child's pronunciation of "Milne" (Otten 181). It is also interesting to note that children who have read the Winnie-the-Pooh books are very much confused when they meet the real Christopher Robin in the flesh and discover that he is "even older than their parents." Winnie-the-Pooh (1926) was written by "dual authors," and dedicated to the "wife/mother of the dual authors." "Hand in hand we come / Christopher Robin and I / To lay this book in your lap." Charlotte Otten comments on this strange authorial perspective: "One of the most complex approaches to narration in all of children's literature is Milne's use of the child who is narrator to the father, who then recounts what the child has told him back to the child and to all the readers" (Otten 183).

Winnie-the-Pooh begins as follows: "Once upon a time, a very long time ago now, about last Friday, Winnie-the-Pooh lived in a forest all by himself under the name of Sanders." At this point Christopher Robin asks, "What does 'under the name' mean?" and he is given the answer, "It means he had the name over the door in gold letters, and lived under it" (qtd. in DeLuca and Natov 40; Winnie 4-5). Winnie-the-Pooh is described as "the Bear of Very Little Brain." But in the Pooh stories, not having a brain is not a bad thing, since it is equated with the, "surer power of nature and primitive intelligence." As Piglet says, "Owl hasn't exactly got Brain, but he knows Things" (qtd. in Carlson 52).

Winnie-the-Pooh contains six animals that were actual toy animals that Christopher Robin played with as a child. These are Pooh, Piglet, Eeyore, Kanga, Roo, and Tigger. Pooh is unintelligent; little Piglet is apprehensive; Eeyore is pessimistic; Kanga is overprotective of her baby; and little Roo is stifled by his mother. The other two animals are provided by A. A. Milne's own imagination. Rabbit is dictatorial; and Owl is pseudointellectual (Otten 185). Kanga is the fussy mother, or the nanny archetype. She is continually saying, "We'll see, dear," and the only two things that she is interested in are children and numbers. She wants to know how many pieces of soap are left, and she points out the two clean spots in Tigger's feeder (Milne House 58). The two children in this scenario are Tigger, who is always bouncing, and Roo, who is always asking questions. Tigger and Roo are, "always pushing themselves forward in a noisy, simpleminded way, but are of no use in serious matters" Eeyore is the total pessimist who says, "I shouldn't be surprised if it hailed a good deal tomorrow" (Milne House 66). Tigger feels it is impossible for him to make a mistake. When he loses his tail, he says, "Somebody must have taken it," and then he continues, "How like them" (Milne Winnie 45). Alison Lurie suggests that the character of Eeyore may have been modeled after Owen Seaman, an editor of Punch during 1906-1914 when Milne was working there (Lurie 149). According to Milne, Seaman was a strange and unlucky man who was always dissatisfied and suspicious, and always blaming his errors on "extraneous circumstances." Once when Seaman lost a golf match, he threw down his putter and said, "That settles it. I'll never play in knickerbockers again" (Milne Autobiography 230). Christopher Robin is the child-as-God archetype, while Winnie-the-Pooh is the child-as-hero archetype (Lurie 151). Winnie-the-Pooh represents the Innocent, or the Child Archetype. He has the virtues and faults that are common to all children. He is simple, natural, and affectionate. He is a "Bear of Very Little Brain." He is so greedy that he eats Eeyore's birthday jar of honey as he is on his way to deliver it. But all of these faults are endearing. As Milne has remarked, children combine natural innocence and grace with "brutal egotism" (Milne Autobiography 9). When Christopher Robin says, "Oh, Bear! How I do love you!" Pooh responds, "So do I." (Milne Winnie 69; Lurie 150-151).

The incident of Roo falling into the river brings out the salient characteristics of all of the characters:

> Everybody was doing something to help. Piglet...was jumping up and down
> and making "Oo, I say" noises; Owl was explaining that in a case of Sudden
> and Temporary Immersion the Important Thing was to keep the Head Above
> Water; Kanga was jumping along the bank, saying "Are you sure you're all
> right, Roo dear?" ...Eeyore had turned round and hung his tail over the first
> pool into which Roo fell, and with his back to the accident was grumbling
> quietly to himself.... "Get something across the stream lower down, some
> of you fellows," called Rabbit. (Milne Winnie 121-121)

But it is finally Pooh who actually rescues Roo (Lurie 151).

Winnie-the-Pooh, the title character of the Winnie-the-Pooh books, has an insatiable
appetite.

> PIGLET: When you wake up in the morning, Pooh, what's the first thing
>   you say to yourself?"
> POOH: What's for breakfast? What do you say, Piglet?
> PIGLET: I say, I wonder what's going to happen exciting to-day?
> POOH: It's the same thing. (qtd. in Otten 185)

Pooh is enigmatic. Although he is inventive, he's not very smart. Although he's
adventuresome, he blunders a lot. Although he's the most faithful friend a child ever had,
he's obtuse. At the end of the first chapter, Milne explains how Pooh got his name.
Because Pooh had been holding onto the string of a balloon in order to reach a tree with
honey in it, his arms had to remain straight up in the air for more than a.week. During this
time, whenever a fly came by and settled on his nose, he had to blow it off. "And I think--
but I am not sure--that that is why he is always called Pooh." Later chapters in the book
include one about catching a woozle, one about meeting a heffalump, one about leading an
exposition to the North Pole, one about rescuing Piglet who is entirely surrounded by
water, one about getting Pooh out of a tight place, one about helping Eeyore find his tail,
one about celebrating Eeyore's birthday, one about observing how Kanga and Baby Roo
relate with each other, one about giving a Pooh Party, and one about saying "Good-bye"
(Otten 183).

In Winnie-the-Pooh, the everyday rules of communication break down. When Roo
is talking with Tigger, he wants to know all of the things that Tiggers can do (Trivizas and
Davies 771). He asks Tigger, "Can they fly?" and Tigger responds, "Yes, they're very
good flyers." Roo then asks, "Can they fly as well as Owl?" and Tigger says, "Yes, only
they don't want to." When Roo asks if they can jump as far as Kangas, Tigger replies,
"Yes, when they want to." Another dialogue in which the rules of communication break
down involves Owl and Rabbit. Rabbit challenges Owl to read a notice that has been left
by Christopher Robin on the door of his house. "Owl took Christopher Robin's notice from
Rabbit and looked at it nervously. He could spell his own name WOL, and he could spell
Tuesday so that you knew it wasn't Wednesday, and he could read quite comfortably when
you weren't looking over his shoulder and saying 'Well?' all the time, and he could--"
"Well?" says Rabbit. Still another dialogue in which the rules of communication break
down involves Pooh and Piglet. Pooh hurried back to his house and suddenly saw Piglet
sitting in his best arm-chair. Pooh stood there rubbing his head and wondering whose
house he was in. "Hallo, Piglet. I thought you were out," says Pooh. Piglet responds,
"No, it's you who were out, Pooh" (qtd. in Trivizas and Davies 772). "'So it was,' said
Pooh. 'I knew one of us was.'" As a last example the rules of conversation breaking down,
consider a dialogue between Piglet and Tigger that takes place at Pooh's house.

> PIGLET: Hallo, Pooh.
> TIGGER: Hallo, Piglet. This is Tigger."
> PIGLET: Oh, is it? I thought Tiggers were smaller than that.

TIGGER: Not the big ones. (qtd. in Trivizas and Davies 773)

Pooh has a penchant for honey that is so strong that it sometimes reveals a selfish streak. When Winnie-the-Pooh is looking for a birthday present for Eeyore, the first place he goes to is his cupboard to see if he has "quite a small jar of honey" (Winnie 78). On his way with the honey to Eeyore's house, Pooh decides that he is feeling "a little eleven o'clockish," and this is a condition which requires a bit of honey to remedy. The honey jar is soon empty, and then Winnie-the-Pooh remembers that the honey was to be his gift to Eeyore. He quickly recovers, however, by giving Eeyore a "Useful Pot to Keep Things in" (Winnie 81).

In Winnie-the-Pooh, the animals are robust and careless as they, "careen and bump delightfully off each other" (Carlson 46). A. A. Milne writes in the tradition of "Comedy of Humours," as each animal emphasizes a dominant characteristic. Winnie-the-Pooh is noted for his appetite, Owl for his pedantry, Piglet for his timidity, Tigger for his unabashed energy, and Eeyore for his misanthropic attitude. Then there is the sensitive Christopher Robin (Milne's son's alter ego), and the innocuous Kanga and Roo, and the deliberately absent "Heffalump" (Carlson 47).

Much of the entertainment of Winnie-the-Pooh is that we can see ourselves in the characters. Winnie-the-Pooh is often placed into embarrassing situations in which he needs to save face, as when Pooh is stuck in Rabbit's hole. He is asked if he is stuck, and he responds, "No, just resting and thinking and humming to myself" (Winnie 28). Another time that Winnie-the-Pooh must save face is when he refuses to admit that he doesn't know how to read. He says that the reason he cannot read a letter he has received is that he has some water in his eyes (qtd. in Carlson 50). Piglet, Pooh's friend, often disguises his embarrassment in a similar way: "Suddenly Winnie-the-Pooh stopped, and pointed excitedly in front of him. 'Look!' 'What?' said Piglet, with a jump. And then, to show that he hadn't been frightened, he jumped up and down once or twice in an exercising sort of way" (Winnie 39).

Winnie-the-Pooh is also filled with puns and word play. When Winnie-the-Pooh asks "And how are you?" Eeyore shakes his head from side to side. "Not very how," he says. "I don't seem to have felt all that how for a long time" (Winnie 43). When Pooh is acting mysteriously and tells Piglet that he is "tracking," Piglet asks, "Tracking what?" Pooh answers, "That's just what I ask myself, What?" at which point Piglet wryly responds, "What do you think you'll answer?" (qtd. in Carlson 50). In Winnie-the-Pooh there is also a sketch about Eeyore, in which Owl has appropriated Eeyore's tail to use it as a bell-rope. " 'Owl,' said Pooh solemnly, 'you made a mistake. Somebody did want it.' 'Who?' 'Eeyore. My dear friend Eeyore. He was--he was fond of it.' 'Fond of it?' 'Attached to it,' said Winnie-the-Pooh sadly' " (Milne Winnie 54).

A. A. Milne was a frustrated philosopher who liked to express himself in syllogisms. Thus, when Pooh hears "buzzing" noises in a tree, he assumes that the only reason for any buzzing noise is, "because you're a bee." He further concludes that the only reason for being a bee is, "to make honey." And for Pooh, it necessarily follows that, "the only reason for making honey is so as I can eat it." Another example of syllogistic reasoning is when Pooh sees a hole in the river bank and says, "If I know anything about anything, that hole means Rabbit...and Rabbit means company, and Company means Food and Listening-to-me-humming" (qtd. in Carlson 49).

Like Winnie-the-Pooh, The House on Pooh Corner (1928) has ten chapters. The first chapter is about building a house for Eeyore on Pooh Corner. Then there are nine more chapters in which Tigger is welcomed to the forest; the characters almost encounter the Heffalump again; they discover that tiggers can't climb trees; they follow Rabbit and Christopher Robin to see what they do; they observe Pooh inventing a game; they assist in the unbouncing of Tigger; they applaud Piglet as he does a very nice thing; Eeyore finds the Wolery for Owl to move into; they discover the Enchanted Place where Christopher Robin and Pooh promise that they will never forget each other. In The House on Pooh Corner, "Pooh is still addicted to honey and is just as addle-brained. Eeyore is just as gloomily self-effacing and pessimistic. Rabbit is still the quintessential organizer. Owl is just as skillful in disguising his intellectual vacuities. Piglet is as faithful and as fearful. Tigger is a new, uncontrollably bouncy presence. And Christopher Robin remains the companion, savior, and friend of them all." In The House on Pooh Corner, as in Winnie-the-Pooh, the humor springs from the situations (Otten 187).

Like Winnie-the-Pooh, The House on Pooh Corner is filled with tangled thoughts, logical illogic, deductive reasoning, euphoric-blending, and coined language. In The House on Pooh Corner the reader will encounter such words as "smackeral," "worraworroworra," "skoos-e," "stripy," "golollop," "organidized," "sterny," "jagulars," "hooshing," "coffy," "squoze," "squch," and "spudge." When Pooh looks into Piglet's home and sees that Piglet is not there, he keeps searching and peering into the home, "and the more he looked inside, the more Piglet wasn't there" (qtd. in Carlson 52). In The House on Pooh Corner Milne is a bit literary and self-conscious. For example, Pooh-bear, the poet laureate of the Hundred Acre Woods, alludes to the importance of prose music and poetic melody, as he explains that "poms" were put into his song "to make them more hummy." He continues that "Poetry and Hums aren't things which you get, they're things which get you. And all you can do is to go where they can find you" (qtd. in Carlson 53).

In The House on Pooh Corner, Pooh explains why Tigger is constantly jumping out from behind bushes and trees in order to "scare the daylights and nightlight" out of Rabbit. " If Rabbit / was bigger / And fatter / And stronger, / or Bigger / than Tigger, / If Tigger was smaller, / The Tigger's bad habit / of bouncing at Rabbit, / Would matter / No longer / if Rabbit / was taller" (qtd. in Carlson 54). At one point in The House on Pooh Corner, Christopher Robin sighs and tells Pooh-bear, "What I like doing best is Nothing." When Pooh-bear asks, "How do you do nothing?" Christopher Robin, who is tired from lying in the sun and picking buttercups answers, "Well, it's when people call at you just as you're going off to do it." This is a very strange and enigmatic kind of logic (Carlson 54).

By the end of The House on Pooh Corner Christopher Robin is "threatened by adolescence." Therefore, he has to leave the enchanted woods of Pooh and his friends. Knowledge and insight have tainted Christopher Robin so that he can no longer live a pure and primitive existence free from earthly concerns. Christopher Robin learns that unlike the Hundred Acre Woods, the real world demands his work and participation (Carlson 54). Almost every moment in the Pooh books is filled with rollicking in rolling green meadows which trail off into the horizon. In Milne's world the adult business goes unconducted. "Things there are small and the stresses of larger, adult lives are absent and unimportant. In these woods, there are no bad spellers, only those who spell in ways that, "wobble and get in the wrong places." In Milne's world Pooh is right when he proclaims, "Nobody can be uncheered with a balloon" (qtd. in Carlson 51).

Winnie-the-Pooh and House on Pooh Corner are satires in which Tigger represents verbal hypocrisies, Piglet represents cowardice, and Rabbit represents polite etiquette (Lurie 152). But more importantly, Winnie-the-Pooh and House on Pooh Corner represent a modern version of an archetypal legend. Like the Garden of Eden, the story of Winnie-the-Pooh is about a peaceful animal kingdom ruled by a single benevolent human being. Like Adam, Christopher even gives the names to his animals. "It seems no accident, therefore, that the threat of change and loss enters this Eden in the shape of a tree of knowledge. One day, Christopher Robin is discovered to be missing from the Forest. He has gone to school for the first time and is learning his alphabet, beginning with the letter A. Piglet comes across this letter A, arranged on the ground out of three sticks, and thinks "that perhaps it was a Trap of some kind" (Milne House 84; Lurie 154-155).

Most critics very much like the Winnie-the-Pooh stories and songs, but Dorothy Parker did not. Assuming the name of "Constant Reader," she wrote a review which was especially critical of the songs. One song which Pooh had devised was entitled "Outdoor Song which Has To Be Sung In the Snow," and Pooh tells Piglet about the part that goes, "The more it snows, tiddely pom---." Piglet asks "Tiddely what?" and Pooh responds, "Pom." "I put that in to make it more hummy." Parker didn't like the word "hummy." And in her review of The House on Pooh Corner she uses the child-parody-voice of "Constant Reader" to say, "And it is that word 'hummy,' my darlings, that marks the first place in The House on Pooh Corner at which Tonstant Weader fwowed up." A. A. Milne later wrote a reaction to Dorothy Parker's criticism: "No writer of children's books says gaily to his publisher, "Don't bother about the children; Mrs. Parker will love it." As an artist one might genuinely prefer that one's novel should be praised by a single critic, whose opinion one valued, rather than be bought by "the mob;" but there is no artistic reward for a book written for children other than the knowledge that they enjoy it" (Otten 187).

In a chapter entitled "Back to Pooh Corner," of Don't Tell the Grown-Ups: Subversive Children's Literature, Alison Lurie explains some of the impact of the Winnie-the-Pooh books on the "Now Generation." Milne's books have been published in a large number of languages, including Serbo-Croatian and Esperanto, and the Russian and Latin editions are both used as texts in college language courses. Benjamin Hoff's The Tao of Pooh is sometimes used as a text book for courses in Chinese philosophy (Lurie 145). Lurie says that when her former husband was in prep school, he was called "Piglet" because he was apprehensive. His two friends were called "Pooh" and "Eeyore" because the first one was paradoxical and the second was pessimistic. When she was going to college, Alison Lurie had a girl friend named "Tigger" because she was confident, and another one named Roo because she was inquisitive. She notes that on some college campuses, the school grounds and the surrounding countryside are remapped to correspond to the hundred-acre woods (Lurie 144).

Lurie discusses the pleasure that a child must feel by imagining himself to be larger, wiser, and more powerful than all of the adults near by. Christopher Robin may be a small boy in a world of adults, but in the Pooh books, he is the ruler. In the illustrations, for example, he towers over the society of smaller beings he associates with (Lurie 145). In the Winnie-the-Pooh books, Milne is writing about the world of Christopher Robin who was six at the time of the books, but Milne was also writing about his own childhood. The setting of the books could easily be pre-1900 Essex and Kent, where Milne spent his holidays as a child. This landscape is much like that of the hundred-acre woods. It is quite bare and uncultivated, and consists mostly of heath and woods and marshes. There are quite a few pine trees, and gorse and thistles are very common. Rain, wind, fog, and snow are not at all uncommon in this area (Lurie 146).

Both A. A. Milne's and Christopher Robin's perceptions of their fathers changed over time. At first they both believed that their fathers, "knew everything there was to know" (Lurie 147). But they later both found their fathers to be more pedantic than wise. In his Autobiography, Milne writes, "Later on...I formed the opinion that, even if Father knew everything, he knew most of it wrong" (Milne Autobiography 38). Milne's father was therefore Owl in the Winnie-the-Pooh books. "If anyone knows anything about anything..., it's Owl who knows something about something" (Milne Winnie 43). Like Milne's father, Owl is pompous and pedantic. He appears very literate, but he turns out to be almost illiterate, not even able to spell his own name (Lurie 148). The other character that Milne invented (rather than discovering in Christopher Robin's bedroom) was Rabbit, and Rabbit represented Milne's mother. Milne's mother could cook better than the cook, and she could dust better than the parlour-maid (Milne Autobiography 35). And like

Rabbit, Milne's mother lived constantly in a state of, "preoccupation with small responsibilities and bossy concern for the duties of others" (Lurie 148).

A. A. Milne has a distinctive writing style that is very easy to parody. Frederick C. Crews wrote The Pooh Perplex: A Freshman Casebook (1963) which Eugene Trivizas and Christie Davies describe as a very funny set of parodies of literary critics attempting to analyze the Pooh books (Trivizas and Davies 775). Charlotte Otten says that The Pooh Perplex created such a significant market for Winnie-the-Pooh on college campuses that many Pooh Societies sprang up, and Hummalongs and Heffalump hunts became regular features of campus life. In the Preface to The Pooh Perplex, Crews writes, "Winnie-the-Pooh is, as practically everyone knows, one of the greatest books ever written, but it is also one of the most controversial. Nobody can quite agree as to what it really means." In The Pooh Perplex, fictitious critics, "dazzle their readers with the brilliance of their readings and the ingenuity of their interpretations." These critics represent the various approaches to literary criticism that are represented at the Modern Language Association--psychoanalytic, biographical, materialistic, stylistic, cultural, archetypal, etc. (Otten 185).

Benjamin Hoff has written another parody under the title of The Tao of Pooh (1982). Trivizas and Davies say about The Tao of Pooh that, "The title either is or isn't self-explanatory" (Trivizas and Davies 775). The following passage reveals the tone of the parody:

> "What's this you're writing?" asked Pooh, climbing onto the writing table.
> "The Tao of Pooh," I replied.
> "The _how_ of Pooh?" asked Pooh, smudging one of the words I had just
>   written.
> "The _Tao_ of Pooh," I replied, poking his paw away with my pencil.
> "It seems more like the _ow!_ of Pooh," said Pooh, rubbing his paw.
> "Well, it's not," I replied huffily.
> "What's it about?" asked Pooh, leaning forward and smearing another word.
> "It's about how to stay happy and calm under all circumstances!" I yelled.
> "Have you read it?" asked Pooh. (Hoff x)

This passage is about "Taoism," and it is meant to establish Hoff's book; it is clearly written in the style of A. A. Milne. Later, Hoff quotes from Milne, and says that Milne's passage is also about "Taoism."

> "When you wake up in the morning, Pooh," said Piglet at last, "what's the
>   first thing you say to yourself?"
> "What's for breakfast?" said Pooh. "What do _you_ say, Piglet?"
> "I say, I wonder what's going to happen exciting _today_?" said Piglet.
> Pooh nodded thoughtfully.
> "It's the same thing," he said. (Hoff xi)

Hoff parodies the above quote from Milne to prove that Milne was actually talking about "Taoism," though he may not have known it.

> "What's that?" the Unbeliever asked.
> "Wisdom from a Western Taoist," I said.
> "It sounds like something from Winnie-the-Pooh," he said.
> "It is," I said.
> "That's not about Taoism," he said.
> "Oh, yes it is," I said.
> "No, it's not," he said.
> "What do you think it's about?" I said.
> "It's about this dumpy little bear that wanders around asking silly questions,
>   making up songs, and going through all kinds of adventures, without
>   ever accumulating any amount of intellectual knowledge or losing his

simple minded sort of happiness. That's what it's about," he said. "Same thing," I said. (Hoff xii)

In addition to the Winnie-the-Pooh books, A. A. Milne also wrote a number of comedies, some of which are, To Have the Honour: A Comedy in Three Acts (1925), Miss Marlow at Play: A One-Act Comedy (1936), Sarah Simple: A Comedy in Three Acts (1940), and Prince Rabbit and the Princess Who Could Not Laugh (1966) (Otten 177-178). Like Lewis Carroll, Kenneth Grahame, Edward Lear, and Beatrix Potter, A. A. Milne was a "Benign Humorist," whose works appeal as much to adults as to children. In fact, A. A. Milne adapted Grahame Greene's The Wind in the Willows for the stage, and it turned out to be a very successful play for children. Milne's adaptation was entitled Toad of Toad Hall (1929) (Trivizas and Davies 771). Like Lewis Carroll, Milne was a mathematician; in fact, he studied mathematics under the tutelage of H. G. Wells, who taught mathematics at Henley House, where Milne's father was headmaster (Otten 179). As a mathematician, Milne was fascinated with rules and the breaking of rules. He was interested in "humorous nonsense." As Trivizas and Davies note,

> mathematicians live in a world of precise and explicit rules, [a world] that progresses by breaking them to form new rules, by creating and then explaining paradox. For mathematicians, ideas and concepts such as irrational numbers, imaginary numbers, the division of one infinitely small entity by another, the set of things that do not belong to a set or the impossibility of completing mathematics and resolving the problem of the nature of mathematics itself, lie at the core of their work. (Trivizas and Davies 771)

Alan Alexander Milne Bibliography

Carlson, Richard S. "Benign Humorists of Children's Literature: Milne, Potter, and Wooster." The Benign Humorists. New York, NY: Archon, 1975, 46-62.

Crews, Frederick C. The Pooh Perplex: A Freshman Casebook. New York, NY: E. P. Dutton, 1963.

Haring-Smith, Tori. A. A. Milne: A Critical Bibliography. New York, NY: Garland, 1982.

Heineman, James. "P. G. Wodehouse: An Unique Humorist." WHIMSY 4 (1986): 59-61.

Hoff, Benjamin. The Tao of Pooh. New York, NY: Penguin, 1982.

Hoff, Benjamin. The Te of Piglet. New York, NY: Dutton, 1992.

Lurie, Alison. "Back to Pooh Corner: A. A. Milne." Don't Tell the Grown-Ups: Subversive Children's Literature. Boston, MA: Little, Brown, 1990, 144-155.

Milne, A. A. Autobiography. New York, NY: Dutton, 1939.

Milne, A. A. The House at Pooh Corner. New York, NY: E. P. Dutton, 1928.

Milne, A. A. Winnie-the-Pooh. New York, NY: E. P. Dutton, 1926.

Otten, Charlotte F. "A. A. Milne." Dictionary of Literary Biography, Volume 160: British Children's Writers, 1914-1960. Eds. Donald R. Hettinga and Gary D. Schmidt, Detroit, MI: Gale, 1996, 177-188.

Thwaite, Ann. A. A. Milne, The Man Behind Winnie-the-Pooh. London, England: Faber and Faber, 1990.

Tremper, Ellen. "Instigorating Winnie the Pooh." The Lion and the Unicorn: A Critical Journal of Chilcren's Literature 1.1 (1977): 33-46.

Trivizas, Eugene, and Christie Davies. "A. A. Milne." Encyclopedia of British Humorists, Volume II. Ed. Steven H. Gale. New York, NY: Garland, 1996, 770-775.

Virginia (Adeline) Woolf (1882-1941)

From an early age Virginia Woolf had an eye for the ludicrous, and Clive Bell, her brother-in-law said that she was, "a born and infectious mocker" (Donaldson 206). Virginia Woolf once said, "The capacity to criticize the other sex had its share in deciding women to write novels, for indeed that particular vein of comedy has been but slightly worked, and promises great richness" (Woolf Contemporary 26-27). Woolf also said, "Thus, when a woman comes to write a novel, she will find that she is perpetually wishing to alter the established values--to make serious what appears insignificant to a man and trivial what to him is important" (Collected, Volume 2, 146). Judy Little suggests that Woolf's most devastating laughter targets essential features of the male monomyth such as the questing hero, the scapegoat, an "Angel" in the house, or in the soul (Little Comedy 22). Woolf's feminist tracts, A Room of One's Own, and Three Guineas show that politics and wit can reinforce each other (Little Comedy 23). When she was young, Virginia Woolf and some of her friends impersonated a delegation of Abyssinians in order to get a tour of the HMS Dreadnought. Virginia herself was disguised as an African man, and spoke in a low, gruff voice, as she worked very hard to restrain her laughter, especially when she greeted the flag commander, who happened to be her cousin, William Fisher. "In this escapade, the elements of disguise, of sex-role reversal, and of impudent mockery of a respected institution such as the British navy, all expressed the festive and revolutionary import typical of liminal celebrations" (Little Comedy 27).

In Comedy and the Woman Writer: Woolf, Spark, and Feminism, Judy Little indicates that especially in Woolf's first five novels the questing male scholar is a source of amusement both to the narrator and to various woman characters. In contrast, the ritual activities of women are viewed as occasions for celebration and even for some anti-male sentiments (Little Comedy 26). Little suggests that Virginia Woolf and Muriel Spark capitalize on the times of transition and rebellion in which they live. "When they undertake to tansform these commonplace patterns, their comedy mocks established values, and the roots of their mockery go all the way down to myth, that is, to the archetypes expressive of 'God,' or to our biological and social chemistry.... Their laughter is not content to tease follies and flail vices, or to urge a little common sense. Their laughter instead demands a radical 'new plot' " (Little Comedy 178). Little suggests that the outsider in Woolf's novels, "celebrates, offers her gift, and keeps open the possibility of psychological and political change. The jungle laughs; the wild goose of truth flies; the woman in the garden writes, and frightens observers as she does so" (Little Comedy 187).

B. H. Fussell writes about the effect of Virginia Woolf's work: "Both detractors and admirers tend to mistake the degree of Woolf's satiric and ironic tone. She is still critically patronized and extolled not as a comic writer but as a novelist of sensibility or, even worse, of female sensibility--A Sensitive Plant drooping in a Bloomsbury hothouse" (Fussell 264). Denise Marshall states that Virginia Woolf parodies, puns, burlesques and mimes everything. Woolf's comedy is quick, flashing, and various. She wields comedy in all its grinning and grimacing distortions (Marshall 171). Woolf combines aesthetic scorn with extremely funny, laugh-out-loud comedy, as when she suggests that women should take to wearing tufts of hair on their shoulders to represent each child they have given birth to; this image is hilarious (Marshall 169). Wordplay, redundancy, and aesthetic punning are to be found throughout Virginia Woolf's writing (Marshall 167). She adds that, "for Woolf, wit shatters illusions and bowls over the current conversation as a cannon ball lays low the violets and the daisies exposing society's intricate hypocrisies" (Marshall 156). Denise Marshall feels that it is anger which motivates Woolf's humor, and which fuels its energy (Marshall 157). There are numerous comic moments in Woolf's novels, moments when, "women bond, totally confusing the men around them." Woolf seems to encourage such breakage and confusion, and she splits images and presents them so that they are viewed as if from a cracked mirror. "Hers is a funhouse mirror which distorts to extravagant grotesqueness on one side and withers on the other" (Marshall 158).

> One of the cultural ironies Woolf uses in her books is the conventional refuser of festivity. This refuser is usually a male who needs to be coaxed into a good humor, who mutters and mumbles to himself, who denies that he has had a good time, or who spends the time throwing around as many monkey wrenches as he can lay his hands on. These males have a long history in Woolf's novels, but come more center stage in her later works. Mr. Ambrose (Voyage Out) is one, so is Mr. Hillbery (Night and Day). Mr. Ramsay is the first of the more vivid figures whose misanthropic/misogynist behavior is amply rounded out by Bart and Giles in Between the Acts. (Marshall 159)

Virginia Woolf laughingly pointed out on a number of occasions that men, "hate to be told that any cause to which they have given their affection has, after all, a tinge of absurdity" (Martin 8). "Woolf's humor, her comedic range, her scorn, her sardonic funny satire, her anger became invisible because she pinned the patriarchy to the wall. Her feminist humor and her feminist theory threatened the order of things" (Marshall 175). B. H. Fussell says that laughter shook Virginia Woolf: "Elizabeth Bowen recalls her 'whoops of laughter,' while Clive Bell affirms that 'she was about the gayest human being I have known'..., and all who knew her remarked that fun and gaiety [was] her most identifying characteristic" (Fussell 265). Denise Marshall says that her favorite photograph of Woolf, which is in Ottoline Morrell's album of Garsington guests, shows her surrounded by people, all laughing, as she is herself. "She is dressed in the most vivid dress, and her head is thrown back in a full laugh" (Marshall 175).

The comic devices used by Virginia Woolf range from the "outlandishly wild social fireworks" of Orlando to the "sardonic insight with the overall sardonic dynamism" of Room of One's Own and Three Guineas to the "surrealistic puzzles" of The Waves, The Years, and Between the Acts (White 5-7). Virginia Woolf's power as a writer increased her personal sense of detachment from the "masculinist" culture, but it also increased her power in this culture (Marshall 149). It gave Woolf not only the power of the word, but the power of the pocketbook as well. As Woolf stated it, "If one has five hundred a year there is no need to tell lies, and it is much more amusing to tell the truth" (Marshall 150). The targets of Virginia Woolf's sardonic grotesque comedies include women's education, women's networks, the lives of the obscure, the fabric of daily life, power, influence, authority, honesty, madness, and absurdity. Her satiric comedy is sometimes harsh. "This comedy is cuttingly double-edged and decisively anti-romantic. Its tone and surface may be comic, but its text is essentially serious, full of semi-tragic anti-climaxes" (Marshall 152). Beverly Ann Schlack says that Woolf's satiric laughter is scornful and that her target is the patriarchy. This scorn is at the highest aesthetic level. Furthermore, it is, "succinct of form and irrefutable of content, an attitude utterly unanswerable by serious debate or clever retorts." This type of comedy invokes laughter which, "is often rather grim, gargoyle-faced, and many-clawed" (Schlack 147).

In a speech given in 1931, Virginia Woolf said, "The villain of my story was a woman...the Angel in the House" ("Speech xxix). Woolf claimed that, "almost every respectable Victorian house had its angel" ("Speech xxxi). According to Woolf, this "Angel" is "intensely sympathetic."

> She was immensely charming. She was utterly unselfish. She excelled in the difficult arts of family life. She soothed, conciliated, sacrificed herself, took the hash if there was only chicken enough for one, and in short was so constituted that she never had a wish or a mind of her own but preferred to sympathize with the wishes and minds of others. Above all--I hope I need not say it--she was pure. There were a great many things that one could not

say without bringing a blush to her cheek. ("Speech" xxx).

Since this Angel was "dangerous to Woolf's comedy" (Marshall 150), she, "swoops onto this ideal of woman with murderous talons," because this Angel tried to dictate how a woman should write. The Angel advised, "Never disturb them [men] with the idea that you have a mind of your own. And above all be pure" ("Speech xxxi).

Freshwater, A Comedy (1923) has six characters, all based on people with whom Woolf was actually acquainted--Ellen Terry and her elderly husband Watts, Mr. and Mrs. Cameron, Alfred Lord Tennyson, and Lieutenant John Craig. Woolf exaggerates the features of these characters to emphasize the inanity of their "illustrious" professions, a painter, a model, a philosopher, a photographer, a poet, and a lieutenant in the Navy respectively. She mocks these individuals while at the same time endorsing the liberation of women by attacking the traditions of marriage and chastity (Fakoury 1). Woolf says that Alfred Lord Tennyson's skin is, "like a crumpled rose leaf" (Fakoury 7), and she expresses her dissatisfaction with his character, his poetic ineptitude, his primitive and unjust regard for women, and his pride. She portrays him as an, "inattentive, dramatic persona who fades in and out of conversation, blurts out quotes, and pivots on the recognition of a single word, ignoring its context (Freshwater 36). Although Tennyson prides himself on his poetic abilities, the script of the play testifies otherwise. For example, he compliments Ellen by calling her a "beautiful wench," a phrase which clearly lacks both in eloquence and appreciation (Fakoury 2). As a model and as a woman, Ellen must play the roles that society has given her. "Sometimes I'm Modesty. Sometimes I'm Poetry. Sometimes I'm Chastity. Sometimes, generally before breakfast, I'm merely Nell" (Freshwater 24). Watts wants to paint Ellen as "Abstract Modesty," so he feels that she should be at the same time both veiled and absolutely naked. His solution is to paint her in a veil that is composed of stars, which, by the way, symbolize fertility (Woolf 18; Fakoury 6).

In "Mr. Bennett and Mrs. Brown" (1924), Virginia Woolf writes that whereas the typical French novelist would focus on the general qualities of human nature, and the typical Russian novelist would probe the soul, the typical English novelist would exaggerate a character's eccentricities, giving us Mrs. Brown, for example, "in all her particularity, her oddities and mannerisms, her buttons and wrinkles, her ribbons and warts" (Kolodny 45).

In Mrs. Dalloway (1925), "Woolf's comedy is basically satiric in nature, with one of the comic targets being a patriarchal figure who holds a position of leadership in society" (Cuddy-Keane 276). Septimus may be a Christ figure, but if he is, he is a "comic Christ." The "crucifixion" of the comic Christ occurs in a context of satire, the target of the satire being both society in general and the Christ-figure convention in particular. Mrs. Dalloway refuses to take seriously the archetype of the scapegoat. Mrs. Dalloway and Septimus both mock society's very idea of tragedy. In Mrs. Dalloway, Woolf is mocking the male idea that in war a person should make some heroic sacrifice, and that this sacrifice, though it may be painful, is necessary. At the same time that Woolf is denigrating the male war metaphor, she is elevating Clarissa's party metaphor. Woolf is suggesting that wars and revolutions are not the only solution when groups disagree with each other. She suggests that we try the "way of the hostess" asking the question, "Could we learn to value joy as much as we now treasure suffering?" Clarissa's flowers, and parties are symbolic of comedy, hope, and communication (Little Comedy 55). Many critics have suggested that Woolf's depiction of Dr. Bradshaw in Mrs. Dalloway is too severe; however, Little points out that, "one of the traditional elements of comedy is the ritual of harsh rhetorical attack on the life denying forces whose presence threatens the festive gaiety and the hope of fertility" (Little 56).

To the Lighthouse (1927) is a "savage comedy" in which Mr. Ramsay is a grotesque who makes everybody feel vaguely uncomfortable because of his sarcastic grinning (Marshall 154). Mr. Ramsay strides up and down embarrassing his wife and guests as he recites Tennyson's <u>Charge of the Light Brigade</u>. The rhythm of the poem, the emphatic repetitions, and the crude patriotism, "accurately express Mr. Ramsay's bullying nature and self-indulgent emotionality. In fact it sums up a whole ideology of militarism that was so often the object of Virginia Woolf's satire: the swashbuckling derring-do combined with 'dulce et decorum est' idealism so harshly exposed to the canons in the First War" (Tylee 261). It is Virginia Woolf's hatred of paternalism that causes her to caricature Mr. Ramsay as both ridiculous and grotesque. But the balancing effect of Woolf's humor is essential to the perception of <u>To the Lighthouse</u> in enabling the reader to recognize and accept something which is so unpalatable (Tylee 263).

Mrs. Ramsay has a joyful but absurd hope for the future, as she knits a stocking that will certainly not be finished in time for the promised trip to the lighthouse, and will probably never be finished. Mrs. Ramsay is also a humours character--a stock comic mother. She has grey hair, and eight children, and at the age of fifty she is forever exaggerating and fussing as she knits (Tylee 260).

> Much of our respect for Mrs. Ramsay stems from her sense of humour, the way she laughs at her own vanity, and from the way she works to counter the grotesque emotional clumsiness of her husband, who reminds her on one occasion when he disturbs the calm beauty of the evening "of the great sea-lion at the Zoo tumbling backwards after swallowing his fish and walloping off so that the water in the tanks washes from side to side" (Tylee 261).

<u>To the Lighthouse</u> is epiphanal not in the Biblical sense, or in the Flannery O'Connor sense, but rather in the James Joycian sense of the epiphany of the mundane. The novel is a "celebration of the commonplace" in which Lily Briscoe, a painter, observes, "One wishes to feel simply that's a chair, that's a table and yet at the same time, it's a miracle, it's an ecstacy." At another place in the novel she says, "The great revelation had never come. The great revelation perhaps never did come. Instead, there were little daily miracles, illuminations, matches struck unexpectedly in the dark" (Shloss 106). Claire Tylee says that the caricature in <u>To the Lighthouse</u> establishes Virginia Woolf into the comic tradition starting with Chaucer and continuing through Jonson, Fielding, Austen, Thackeray, and Dickens (Tylee 257).

There is an antithetical relationship in <u>To the Lighthouse</u> between the cluster of feminine imagery associated with Mrs. Ramsay and the cluster of masculine imagery associated with Mr. Ramsay. In between the two there is a cluster of androgynous imagery associated with Lily Briscoe (Little <u>Comedy</u> 57). Judy Little considers <u>To the Lighthouse</u> to be powerful, yet subtle, comedy. The voice of the narrator sometimes is mingled with the voice of the characters to reinforce the mockery in this comedy of manners. The novel is indeed a comedy of manners in the tradition of Jane Austen, but it is also a comedy of myth, because the mocking voice frequently satirizes well-established traditions by critically examining the mythic metaphors (Little <u>Comedy</u> 58).   <u>To the Lighthouse</u> is somewhat episodic both in its physical and in its psychological development. In melodramatic fashion, Mr. Ramsay attempts to do a recitation of "The Charge of the Light Brigade" as he strides across the lawn in an alphabetical fantasy, "progressing through the alphabet of knowledge from A to Z, but sticking at Q, unable to push on to R" (Little <u>Comedy</u> 58). At another time Mr. Ramsay imagines himself the leader of a party of mountain climbers who have gone too high and are in danger of perishing. Thinking that he is about to freeze to death, Mr. Ramsay raises his fingers to his brow, "so that when the search party comes they will find him dead at his post, the fine figure of a soldier. Mr. Ramsay squared his shoulders and stood very upright by the urn." Mr. Ramsay, who envisions himself dying carefully arranges his body into a noble posture so that the search party will, "at least reap the fine figure of a hero for their pains" (Little <u>Comedy</u> 59).

The visual imagery of Mr. Ramsay in armor is also comic, as he goes mentally clanking around in the heavy gear of Western chivalry. Mr. Ramsay's extravagant language matches his extravagant dress: "the waste of ages and the perishing of the stars" provides a comically grand frame to such a humble gesture as putting his pipe in his pocket. Mr. Ramsay's gesture described as "bending his magnificent head" is also mocked by the narrator. Little notes that if the word "magnificent" is the narrator's word, it is truly ironic, and if it is Mr. Ramsay's word it is humorously consistent with his vanity and with his gesturings as a "hero" (Little Comedy 61).

Orlando (1928) is a description of a "semimystical" woman, but the story becomes a "semipicaresque" and "semibiographical" fantasy of a sixteen-year-old man who doesn't age during the sixteenth century, and who becomes a woman late in the seventeenth century (but a woman who still sometimes wears men's clothing when she ventures into London's rough neighborhoods). In the nineteenth century, Orlando marries and has a child, and finally, in the twentieth century she wins a prize for a poem it has taken her more than three centuries to write. Little notes that in Orlando many things are being mocked, including the authors own writing style (Little Comedy 68).

The first sentence in Orlando develops an ambiguous cause-effect relationship: "It was not Orlando who spoke, but the spirit of the age. But which ever it was...." Judy Little considers this to be a deconstructive sentence. "The very first sentence asserts Orlando's gender, and then betrays the assertion all in one breath: "He--for there could be no doubt of his sex, though the fashion of the time did something to disguise it--was in the act of slicing at the head of a Moor which swang from the rafters." The first word establishes a masculine subject, but this is contradicted by evidence later to come (Little "Laughter" 182-183). As Orlando kneels on the window sill, realizing that she must obtain a wedding ring and learn to depend on a man, and as she is kneeling physically, she is considering whom she can lean on figuratively (Little "Laughter" 179). A lot of the comic sentences in Orlando only pretend to be true--in order to be insightfully false. "And sometimes the truths that they pretend to are royal and noble ones, exactly those (assumed) realities of gender and nature that less subversive writers of comedy have allowed to stand as norms (Little "Laughter" 181).

Concerning Orlando's gender ambivalence, Judy Little states:

> From the first sentence onward..., this particular myth is comically re-politicized. That is, its political quality of being the spirit and rhetoric of an era, is exposed by the narrator's language and by the record of Orlando's transitions from several different kinds of men to several different kinds of women. The very "nature" of Orlando as a young man must "belong" to the nineteenth century (when she is a woman), because of "the indomitable nature of the spirit of the age." (Little "Laughter" 186-187)

Orlando's meeting with her husband at the end of the biography is ecstatic, but it is deflated by Orlando's exclamation, "It is the goose!" referring to the single bird over Shelmerdine's head as "the wild goose." There is an ambiguity in the word "it." "It" could refer to the bird, to Shelmerdine, or to the centuries-long adventure, and this is, "an effective reminder that the entire text has been spoken, assigned; it has been a wild goose chase, in which 'truth' was written by the reader-narrator and by Orlando's reading of an age" (Little "Laughter" 188). Orlando is playing with the concept of the "nature of things," or the "nature of human beings," or the "nature of gender." Little states that "the comedy engendered by Orlando resists--indeed mocks--the temptations to 'gender' human beings into absolute roles" (Little "Laughter" 188).

The laughter in Orlando connected Woolf intricately with a wider audience than she had ever enjoyed before (Marshall 149). In Orlando, Woolf considers what it would have been like to have been really witty in the eighteenth century. "What might it have been like to have a Wit and his/her tribe to dinner?" (Marshall 155). Orlando, the protagonist, has, "inherited a drop too much of that black humour which ran in the veins of all her race" (Orlando 195). The comic monologue is the turning point in Orlando. Here Woolf abandons her lack of direction and begins to use comedic forms to grapple directly with issues (Marshall 158).

Orlando the character is a female jester, and Orlando the novel is a burlesque of many different genres. To some extent, the novel is a caricatured biography of Vita Sackville-West, one of Virginia Woolf's close friends. But Orlando is not really a biography. Rather it is a mock biography. The characters in the novel tend toward caricature, and toward the end of the book they even become allegorical. Orlando is a picaresque novel, in which social institutions are attacked. Its basic function is to remind the readers that, "norms are fictions and made by mere humans." As with other picaresque heroes, Orlando is never reintegrated into society (Little 68). The major point of the joke of the sex change is that this change actually makes very little difference in Orlando's character. By implication, Woolf is saying that, "most expressions of sex differences are culturual and not biological" (Little Comedy 70).

In A Room of One's Own (1929) Woolf contrasts women's and men's views of the world. Denise Marshall considers Room of One's Own to be, "revolutionary in its pervading comedic stance, and in its discourse about the hypocrisies and deprivations of women spoken by a woman to women" (Marshall 157). One of the men's voices in A Room of One's Own is that of hypothetical novelist "Mr. A" who presents only opinion to his readers. "Mr. A's vigorously unrelenting and didactic voice casts on his text a sterile shadow 'shaped something like the letter 'I' " (Woolf Room 150).

There are monsters in The Waves (1931) which appear in various and ambiguous guises. This monster is Louis's, "great beast's foot [as it] stamps, and stamps," It is Bernard's, "fin in a waste of water." And it is also, "the gardeners sweeping the lawn with giant brooms" (Waves 180, 307, 307). The Waves is a comedy of grotesquerie. It is a, "riddle of misfortunes which must be accepted but before which one must not capitulate." It is a novel in which, "obsessional characters mock themselves and their obsessions" (Marshall 153).

The parties in The Years (1937) and in Between the Acts can be described as disharmonious. The party in The Years is held in Delia's London home, and it overwhelms several floors of the house which has been converted into an estate agent's offices and various rooms for solicitors. This party brings together an extremely divergent set of people who are, "in an odd but real sense--family" (Marshall 163). It is because of this divergence and incongruity that Maggie knows that when it is her turn to give a speech she will be interrupted, and so she laughs: "Laughter took her and shook her. She laughed, throwing her head back as if she were possessed by some genial spirit outside herself that made her bend and rise, as a tree.... No idols, no idols, no idols, her laughter seemed to chime as if the tree were hung with innumerable bells, and he laughed too" (Years 425). The Years also uses scorn and grotesque imagery as rhetorical devices. In the 1880 section, the rain, "slid down, till, reaching the mouths of those fantastic laughers, the many-clawed gargoyles, it splayed out in a thousand odd indentations" (Years 47).

Dale Spender considers Three Guineas (1938) to be a very funny book, and Woolf's, "most outspoken denunciation of patriarchy had disappeared" as well (Spender 673). In both The Years and in Three Guineas, Virginia Woolf plays with her irreverence for party conventions. Here she juxtaposes satiric images of human behavior in a sort of bizarre paradox. She also uses scorn as an offensive strategy, as a way of challenging the "patriarchal cosmos." The Years frequently disguises the enormous amount of mischief going on in the text, but Three Guineas is more direct and compressed. Joanna Lipkin says that here Woolf is exhibiting a "flaring red cape" (Lipking 142). Both in The Years and in Three Guineas, Woolf dissects and minutely examines the patriarchy, employing many strategies of laughter and scorn as she

> parodies the dominator's style, not only by restating her feminist themes in Aristotelian syllogisms which make a travesty of masculinist logic, mocking and destroying the patriarch's explanation of "mankind"; but also by using their footnoted dissertationese which is supposed to overwhelm with unanswerable evidence, and is as biased in its choice of evidence as the logical propositions. (Marshall 167)

Woolf subjects her target to, "murderous verbal invective full of lethal alliteration and disdainful caricatures" in such titles as "His Magesty's Royal Regiment of Ratcatchers" (Guineas 314). "The Angel," "Arthur's Education Funds," "Oxford," "Cambridge," "Miss," and "Mrs." are also words which have "certain odors attached" (Marshall 168)--"or shall we call it 'atmosphere'?" (Guineas 52). These words combine, "in a surreal chaos where all juxtapositions are paradoxical and laughable" (Marshall 168). Woolf's comedy in The Years and in Three Guineas represents, "feminist guerilla warfare, lobbing jokes and puns, heaping scorn and derision, claiming in Ciceronian humility that as a daughter of an educated man, she must speak only tentatively to these issues" (Marshall 168).

Three Guineas gives the readers a glimpse of what a new plot might be if it were designed by women. "If the state, for instance, paid women a living wage for rearing the children, the men would no longer need to be such struggling heroes of the business world. Their financial burden would be eased, and 'culture would thus be stimulated.' " A further advantage would be that medals, gowns, and symbolic public ceremonies of the war culture could also be eliminated, and replaced by the beauty of spring, summer, and autumn--the beauty of flowers, silks, and cloths (Little Comedy 94). The utopean society in Three Guineas is one in which both sexes are mainly occupied with increasing the, "private beauty of silks, flowers, season-watching, and child-raising." This new society would affirm the significance of immediacy, of perception, and of sensuous relationships, values and activities which either are not valued or are relegated to women (Little Comedy 97).

David McWhirter considers Between the Acts (1941) to be, "quite literally both a novel and a play, for its action consists mainly in the characters' attendance at the comic pageant written and staged by Miss La Trobe" (McWhirter 197). Virginia Woolf means Miss La Trobe's pageant to be a burlesque of all such pageants. In addition, the meal (the "sacramental" tea) which is served in the barn is a burlesque of a ceremony in a Greek temple; however the cakes are fly-blown, and the tea tastes like "rust boiled in water" (Little Comedy 93).

Denise Marshall says that Between the Acts is, "a fulfillment of Orlando but at Woolf's most sardonic and savage comedic stretch" (155). Marshall describes Old Bart Oliver as a grotesque. Bart is making facial contortions in trying to make his grandson laugh, but instead he frightens the daylights out of the child (Marshall 154). The sense of family in Between the Acts is interrupted by disunities, bitternesses, and burlesques which add up to lack of unity, and a "confused but tumultuous clamor." In the novel it is described as "a melee; a medley; an entrancing spectacle" and also as "skimble-skamble" (Acts 68-69). Since Woolf was a lover of the music hall, she has converted an English "panto," ("a British tradition combining vaudeville, satire and music") into prose (Nemy C2).

In Between the Acts, "scorn is interlaced inextricably with affectionate mockery and a wry almost exasperated amusement." Woolf's humor has asperity, and her comedy has violent images. The structure of Between the Acts, is "a multi-tiered parodic burlesque of just about everything." The action takes place in an English country house, the standard setting for Restoration comedies of manners. Here Patriarchs have defined which acts are "worthy," for history and for novels, but for Woolf, life is not these acts of significance. "Woolf's history book, as she pointed out more than once, would be lives of the obscure.

Real life occurs between the acts, in the intervals" (Marshall 169).

The words in Between the Acts are constantly being lost and drowned out by "laughter, loud laughter." The words are, "swallowed by the speakers, blown away by the wind, or scratched to insensibility by a creaky gramophone" (Marshall 170).

> Illusion had failed.... Then suddenly, as the illusion petered out, the cows took up the burden. One had lost her calf. In the very nick of time she lifted her great moon-eyed head and bellowed.... From cow after cow came the same yearning bellow.... The cows annihilated the gap; bridged the distance; filled the emptiness and continued the emotion., Miss La Trobe waved her hand ecstatically at the cows. (Acts 99)

The play is a sort of a joke, but with no definitive ending to any act, except when the audience "goes to feed." "The eternal human comedy shreds the masculinist attempt to contain humans in the bounds of civilization. Woolf places the obscure onto center stage-- and by doing so ridicules the concept of the famous, the infamous, the significant (Marshall 170).

In a diary entry of 1935, Woolf was struck by the idea that the more complex a vision is, the harder it is to turn it into satire. Therefore, in the more complex parts of Between the Acts, Woolf abandons the pure satire, and, "adopts a qualified satire that embraces even the threatening element within the new inclusive community" (Cuddy-Keane 276-277). Melba Cuddy-Keane considers Between the Acts to be a subversive comedy in which the leaderless and fragmented community offers a direct challenge to the powerful, leader-centered group postulated by Sigmund Freud and his followers (Cuddy-Keane 274). She further compares the communal chorus of Between the Acts to the communal chorus of Greek drama where their chants interrupt the action. "In fact, the Oxford English Dictionary's entry for chorus--which Woolf might well have read--describes the Greek chorus as appearing 'between the acts.' " The rhetorical act of combining all of the voices into a single chorus is political in that, "it subverts the habitual dominance of the leader figure and introduces a new concept of community" (Cuddy-Keane 275). Woolf's suggestions become more compelling because she replaces the voice of the leader with the voice of the community. It is paradoxical that this collective voice, which is communal without being coercive, tends to be more individualistic than the voice of the spokesperson. By using the community-as-chorus voice, Woolf implies that the overturning of the existing order has resounding support. Instead of using fragmentation to represent disintegration, this communal voice investigates fragmentation as a new way of seeing. "In this way it has affinities with the subversive forms of absurdist and ironic comedy, which similarly function to deconstruct a prevailing world" (Cuddy-Keane 283).

Between the Acts exploits three important comic modes--the satiric, the amiable, and the liminal. "Woolf inhibits her satiric impulse by modifying the satire with elements of amiable comedy and expands the amiable comedy with elements of liminality to create a subversive and revisionary mode, the art of the whole community" (Cuddy-Keane 276). Concerning the relationship of the liminal mode to comedy, Cuddy-Keane notes that she has modified the term "liminal" which in common usage refers to "limen" or threshold, and implies a transitional period and an eventual return to order. Woolf's comedy, however, is not liminal in this latter sense, since it, "celebrates the dismantling of order and actually advocates a permanent instability." Destablizing comedy has the effect of blocking the establishment of norms, and offers a vision of society that, "accomodates fragmentation, paradox, ambiguity, and contradiction" (Cuddy-Keane 280).

"Festive Comedy" tends to end with everyone being happily married, but in this particular regard, Between the Acts should not be classified as "Festive Comedy." Many readers note that Between the Acts is written as a comedy, and they are frustrated when it does not end like a comedy should end (Little Comedy 92).

In "The Man at the Gate" (1942) Virginia Woolf says, "The only way of getting at the truth [is] to have it broken into many splinters by many mirrors and so select" (Woolf "Man" 72). Most of Virginia Woolf's readers are aware of her madness, her frigidity, her delicacy, her lack of stamina, her melancholy and her general fragility (Marshall 173); however, Nigel Nicolson, who was an early friend of Virginia Woolf, describes her as follows: "She was Virginia. Virginia who was fun, Virginia who was easy..., and who floated in and out of our lives like a godmother" (Nicolson 216).

The hotel guests at Santa Marina in The Voyage Out (1948) are comic stock figures. They are the bored British tourists who show up so often in English satire. They represent the comic caricatures which identify certain things as good and reasonable, and other things as peculiar or grotesque (Little Comedy 25).

Virginia (Adeline) Woolf Bibliography

Comstock, Margaret. "George Meredith, Virginia Woolf, and Their Feminist Comedy." Ph.D. Dissertation. Stanford University, 1975.

Cuddy-Keane, Melba. "The Politics of Comic Modes in Virginia Woolf's Between the Acts." PMLA 105.2 (1990): 273-285.

Donaldson, Ian. The World Upside Down: Comedy from Jonson to Fielding. Oxford, England: Clarendon Press, 1970.

Fakoury, Monica. "Freshwater, A Comedy: A Fresh Look at the Master of Caricatures, Virginia Woolf." Unpublished Paper. Tempe, AZ: Arizona State University, 1997.

Fry, Christopher. "Comedy." Comedy: Meaning and Form. Ed. Robert W. Corrigan. San Francisco, CA: Chandler, 1951, 15-17.

Fussell, B. H. "Woolf's Peculiar Comic World: Between the Acts." Virginia Woolf: Revaluation and Continuity. Ed. Ralph Freedman. Berkeley, CA: Univ of California Press, 1980, 263-283.

Johnstone, J. K. The Bloomsbury Group: A Study of E. M. Forster, Lytton Strachey, Virginia Woolf and Their Circle. New York, NY: Farrar, Straus, 1978.

Kolodny, Annette. "Some Notes on Defining a Feminist Literary Criticism" Feminist Criticism. Eds. Cheryl Brown and Karen Olson. Metuchen, NJ: Scarecrow, 1978, 42-45.

Lipking, Joanna. "Looking at the Monuments: Woolf's Satiric Eye." Bulletin of the New York Public Library 80 (1977): 141-145.

Little, Judy. Comedy and the Woman Writer: Woolf, Spark, and Feminism. Lincoln, NE: Univ of Nebraska Press, 1983.

Little, Judy. "(En)gendering Laughter: Woolf's Orlando as Contraband in the Age of Joyce." Last Laughs: Perspectives on Women and Comedy. Ed. Regina Barreca. New York, NY: Gordon and Breach, 1988, 179-193.

McWhirter, David. "Feminism/Gender/Comedy: Meredith, Woolf, and the Reconfiguration of Comic Distance." Look Who's Laughing: Gender and Comedy. Ed. Gail Finney. New York, NY: Gordon and Breach, 1994, 189-204.

Marcus, Jane. "Enchanted Organs, Magic Bells: Night and Day as Comic Opera." Virginia Woolf: Revolution and Continuity. Berkeley, CA: University of California Press, 1980, 97-122.

Marshall, Denise. "Slaying the Angel and the Patriarch: The Grinning Woolf." Last Laughs: Perspectives on Women and Comedy. Ed. Regina Barreca. New York, NY: Gordon and Breach, 1988, 149-178.

Martin, Robert Bernard. The Triumph of Wit: A Study of Victorian Comic Theory. Oxford, England: Clarendon, 1974.

Myers, Robert Manson. From Beowulf to Virginia Woolf: An Astounding and Wholly

Unauthorized History of English Literature. Urbana, IL: University of Illinois Press, 1984.

Nemy, Enid. "A 'Panto' called 'Poppy' to Open in November." New York Times 19 April, 1985: C2.

Nicolson, Nigel. Portrait of a Marriage. New York, NY: Bantam, 1974.

Schlack, Beverly Ann. "Virginia Woolf's Strategy of Scorn in The Years and Three Guineas." Bulletin of the New York Public Library 80: (1977): 146-150.

Shloss, Carol. Flannery O'Connor's Dark Comedies: The Limits of Inference. Baton Rouge, LA: Louisiana State University Press, 1980.

Tylee, Claire Margaret. "Virginia Woolf and the Art of Caricature." Literary and Linguistic Aspects of Humour. Barcelona, Spain: Univ of Barcelona Dept of Languages, 1984, 257-264.

White, Kenneth S. ed. Savage Comedy: Structure of Humor. Amsterdam, The Netherlands: Rodopi, 1978.

Woolf, Virginia. Between the Acts, 1941. Hamondsworth, England: Penguin, 1953.

Woolf, Virginia. Collected Essays, 4 Volumes. London, England: Hogarth Press, 1966-1967.

Woolf, Virginia. Contemporary Writers. New York, NY: Harcourt, Brace and World, 1966.

Woolf, Virginia. "The Man at the Gate." The Death of the Moth. London, England: Hogarth, 1942, 69-73.

Woolf, Virginia. Mrs. Dalloway. London, England: Hogarth, 1963.

Woolf, Virginia. Orlando. New York, NY: Harvest/Harcourt, Brace Jovanovich, 1928.

Woolf, Virginia. Room of One's Own. New York, NY: Harvest/Harcourt, Brace, Jovanovich, 1929.

Woolf, Virginia. "Speech Before the London/National Society for Women's Service. January 21, 1931." The Pargiters. Ed. Mitchell Leaska. New York, NY: Harvest/Harcourt, Brace, Jovanovich, 1977.

Woolf, Virginia. Three Guineas, 1938. New York, NY: Harvest/Harcourt, Brace, Jovanovich, 1977.

Woolf, Virginia. The Years. New York, NY: Harvest/Harcourt, Brace, Jovanovich, 1937.

David Herbert Lawrence (1885-1930)

In the 1975 Penguin edition of Lady Chaterley's Lover (1928), Hoggart notes that the book has been widely censored, frequently because of its obscenities. He then makes the following comment:

> Most of us know these "four letter words" from an early age. We know them as swear words or as parts of dirty jokes. If we wish to speak simply and naturally about sex we are baffled. We tend to take roundabout ways, most of which are ashamed escape-routes. There is an old war-time story which illustrates both these characteristics. A soldier on leave from abroad was charged with assaulting another man. He explained why he had done it: "I came home after three fucking years in fucking Africa, and what do I fucking-well find? My wife in bed, engaged in illicit cohabitation with a male." (Hoggart ix)

In a poem entitled "Conundrums," Lawrence showed his disgust for our inability to talk about the perfectly natural functions of sex: "Tell me what's wrong / with words or with you / that you don't mind the thing / yet the name is taboo" (qtd. in Rosenthal 14). In his "Introduction to Pansies Lawrence answers his own question:

> What is obvious is that the words in these cases have been dirtied by the

mind, by unclean mental associations. The words themselves are clean, so are the things to which they apply. But the mind drags in filthy association, calls up some repulsive emotion. Well, then, cleanse the mind, that is the real job. (qtd. in Rosenthal 15)

In a poem entitled "13,000 People" Lawrence takes on a tone of mock innocence to talk about people who will swarm to an art exhibit of nude paintings, "as though nudity were unknown to them." At this exhibit, the people "blushed, they giggled, they sniggered, [and] they leered" (Rosenthal 15). In a poem entitled "No! Mr. Lawrence!" Lawrence uses the technique of ironic reversal as Lawrence appears to address himself, saying that life is not as he (Mr. Lawrence) supposes. The narrator of the poem says that he doesn't mind telling D. H. Lawrence that he is rather well versed on matters of love, and he chides Lawrence that perhaps he knows more than Lawrence does. This is ironic because Lawrence is writing to Lawrence. Then Lawrence the narrator says to Lawrence the audience that the problem that Lawrence the audience has is that he makes love all too nice, and too beautiful. Lawrence the narrator says that love is really not like that, and the reason we think it is is that people fake the glitter. Lawrence the narrator says that in truth, love is truly "rather dull." (Rosenthal 16).

Lawrence wrote his poems in hopes of convincing people that they should change and reform, and Lawrence considered this to be a sympathetic mission, one that required provocation rather than entreaty, humor rather than discourse, and satire rather than invective (Rosenthal 17). Lawrence considered satire to be a form of sympathy. "When Lawrence satirizes, in verse, the industrialization of England, he does so out of hatred for machines. But his antipathy arose originally from his commiseration for the factory workers and his conviction that machines dehumanize, a basic sympathetic stance" (Rosenthal 11). "Oh Wonderful Machine!" uses savage irony to expose what Lawrence believed to be, "the blasphemous nature of the creed of the intellegent-matchine." He considered this to be a, "modern religion of nothingness that has reduced man from the more than human being he might have become to the less than human creature he is" (Rosenthal 12).

Rae Rosenthal laments the fact that Lawrence's poetry has for so long not been considered an important part of his writing. Now his poetry is getting the respect it deserves; nevertheless, Lawrence's achievement as a verse satirist is only now beginning to be recognized. Lawrence's Complete Poems is over 1,000 pages in length, and much of his poetry is satire. Lawrence wrote most of his satiric verse between 1925 and 1930. The poetry of the last two years of his life was published in collections with antithetical names--Pansies and Nettles. Much of the poetry in these volumes is bitter and petty, but much of the satire is also significant. Rosenthal feels that satire by definition is insincere, and she suggests that Lawrence is a master at, "speaking in a voice while simultaneously ridiculing it" (Rosenthal 17). Furthermore, Lawrence is not seeking mere understanding or acceptance in his poetry. Like other satirists, he is seeking change in the form of solutions. His verse is bitter only because Lawrence has difficulty understanding the smallness of people's lives. He wants more for them, and he wants more for himself. After Lawrence's death some more satiric verse was found, and this was published in the "More Pansies" section of Last Poems, and in the "Uncollected" section of his Complete Poems (Rosenthal 10).

David Herbert Lawrence Bibliography

Galenbeck, Susan Carlson. "A Stormy Apprenticeship: Lawrence's Three Comedies." D. H. Lawrence Review 14 (1981): 191-211.
Hodgkins, William. "Vulgarity in Humour" It's a Funny Thing, Humour. Eds. Antony J.

Chapman and Hugh C. Foot. New York, NY: Pergamon Press, 1977.

Rosenthal, Rae. "D. H. Lawrence Satire as Sympathy." Studies in Contemporary Satire 11 (1984): 10-19.

(Arthur Annesley) Ronald Firbank (1886-1926)

Because of his outrageous circumstances of plot, the comic names of his characters, his "camp repartées," and his sexual innuendos, Ronald Firbank has been compared with Oscar Wilde. Cyril Connolly labeled him one of the "breed of the permanent giggle." Like Wilde, Firbank was also concerned with homosexual issues ranging from lesbian nuns to pederastic priests. And like Wilde, Firbank's dialogues are highly dramatic, and the source of much of his humor. For example, the following dialogue occurs in The Flower Beneath the Foot (1923): "Did you hear what the dear King said?" "No." "It's almost too appealing. Fleas have been found at the Ritz." "...!...?...!!" The Flower Beneath the Foot uses comedy to express the malaise and futility of modern life that comes from lack of hope. The novel offers a good example of how loss and despair can be hidden beneath the manic humor common to Firbank's fiction (Barnhill 370). The Flower Beneath the Foot contains many scatological jokes, and much frivolity, but there is nevertheless a sense of the apocalyptic gloom that covered Europe after World War I (Barnhill 371).

The odd behavior of the title character in Concerning the Eccentricities of Cardinal Pirelli (1926) includes the baptizing of a German shepherd puppy named Crack. This is considered to be an ecclesiastical faux pas with serious consequences for the Cardinal, and in the closing scene, the Cardinal has been summoned to the Vatican to hear what his punishment will be for canine baptism. Unfortunately, however, before he can make the trip to Rome, the Cardinal drops dead of a heart attack, that is brought on by his ardent chase after a choirboy by the name of Chicklet (Barnhill 370). Because of Firbank's twisted logic and nonsequiturs, Sarah Barnhill compares his writing to that of Lewis Carroll, and would place him among, "the notable eccentric comic writers of British fiction" (Barnhill 371).

(Arthur Annesley) Ronald Firbank Bibliography

Barnhill, Sarah. "Ronald Firbank." Encyclopedia of British Humorists, Volume I. Ed. Steven H. Gale. New York, NY: Garland, 1996, 369-371.

Ben Travers (1886-1980)

Most of Ben Travers's farces have the kind of setting that is conducive to ironic play and farcical humor. The plays are usually set in the two-level interior of a home. At the top of the stairs there are normally two bedroom doors to allow for the innuendos associated with sexual hide-and-seek. There are also several other doors and quiet passageways, and niches, where various characters can see without being seen, and where they have quick exits and entrances available to them. Often, one door closes just as another door opens. All of the ingredients of stage farce are therefore provided (Gale 1139). Christopher Innes has suggested that the hectic pacing is a reflection of one of farce's basic themes, "man as helpless victim of circumstances" (Innes 260). Innes goes on to talk about the absurdity and improbability of the on-stage actions which mirror the, "incongruity between the obvious innocence of his protagonists, and their unambiguously compromising situations" (Innes 263).

The person who probably had the most influence on Ben Travers's play writing was

Arthur Wing Pinero, considered by Shannon Gale to be "England's foremost farceur." Travers explains Pinero's formula as follows: "Act 2--the sympathetic and guileless hero is landed into the thick of some grievous dilemma or adversity. Act 1--he gets into it. Act 3--he gets out of it" (Gale 1139). Johan Hendrickx, in Ben Travers and the English Farce, and Christopher Innes, in "The Comic Mirror," and Horace Richards, in "Being Funny Is No Joke!" and Leslie Smith, in "Ben Travers and the Aldwych Farces" all discuss how Ben Travers fits into the English farce tradition (Gale 1141). Based on this evidence, and evidence of her own, Shannon Gale concludes that, "Travers's farces constituted some of the most popular theater of the early twentieth century." Travers's plays were originally being produced during the 1920s and 1930s, but there have also been a number of recent revivals of his plays. Travers developed a formula for the writing of farces that has become the model for such subsequent British farce pieces as Joe Orton's What the Butler Saw, and Loot; Alan Ayckbourn's Bedroom Farce and The Norman Conquests; and Tom Stoppard's Dirty Linen. According to this formula, the characters are developed as familiar stereotypes, and then these stereotypes are developed as highly exaggerated caricatures. Travers explained that the characters in his plays are, "recognizable types of human beings. The funniness must be in the situations and circumstances...and these are only funny because the characters are so recognizably human" (Travers Vale 92-93). Travers has two main leads in his Aldwych Farces--Walls and Lynn, and there was an agreement between author and actors that whenever the two characters appeared in the same scene, each was to have the same number of laughs (Gale 1137). It was further agreed that Walls would be the deceiving ladies' man, and that Lynn would be the asinine simpleton (Gale 1138). But there was still one more aspect to the formula. The farces were to have another character, Hare, and they also had to, "contain a situation in which Hare stood between an inexorable Walls and a more plausible, but no more ruinous Lynn, to be fleeced of his fair repute, of his cash, of his trousers" (Travers Vale 124). Many of Travers's characters are given outrageous and punning names like "D'Arcy," "Tuck," "Putz," "Cherry," "Buck," "Clive Popkiss," and "Poppy Dickey" (Gale 1138).

Putz, a Yiddish insult expression, is the name of the person who represents the archetype of the domineering German father in Rookery Nook (1926) (Gale 1138). Putz usually makes a quirky bob whenever he gets excited, and this is amusing to the audience. It is interesting that in Rookery Nook the momentum of the play is based on the attempt to convince everyone that nothing happened between Rhoda and Gerald while at the same time suggesting that something did happen. This is because this play was written before the Licensing Act of 1737 was abolished in 1968. During this period, "all drama was strictly regulated by censorship laws. Political topics, sexual subjects, and profane language were disallowed, and Travers's plays sometimes seem to be a series of things that don't happen" (Gale 1139).

In Thark (1927), as in other Travers plays, the characters often dance around the truth:

> BENBOW: I've had some very awkward--news, my boy. Your aunt's
> coming back home to-night.
> RONNY: What? And Kitty?
> BENBOW: No. Just your aunt--that's enough, ain't it?
> RONNY: I say, why is auntie coming home? Has she heard something
> about you?
> BENBOW: Wat d'yer mean? There is nothing to hear about me.
> RONNY: I know. That's why I asked in that surprised way.
> BENBOW: There's nothing to hear, I tell you....
> RONNY: I know--that's just what I say. And very glad I am of it.
> BENBOW: Glad of what?

RONNY: Glad that she heard nothing--because she can't have, because
there's nothing to hear.... (Gale 1138)
Most of Travers's plays contain an unbelievably ugly and meddling woman. In
Plunder (1928), this is Mrs. Leverett, whose clothes could be sold, "to a man who makes
circus tents!" (Travers Plunder 20). Some of the insults that occur in Travers's exchanges
are also humorous.
> JOAN: ....My grandfather married you?
> MRS. HEWLETT: ....He did.
> JOAN: He must have been mad.
> D'ARCY: He must have been blind. (Gale 1138)
One of the humorous techniques which Travers frequently uses is to put his
characters into quite unusual locations. In Plunder, for example, no one is where he or she
ought to be. "The housekeeper has become the mistress of the house while the dead
master's daughter has been turned out with nowhere to go, and the respected members of
high society have grown rich by practicing thievery" (Gale 1138).

The Bed Before Yesterday (1975) is about a woman's late discovery of the joys of
sex. It is also about a lying whore and an immoral, drunken, swearing young man. Here,
Travers drew his humor out of the fact that things were not said, and did not happen, even
though the censorship laws had been abolished in 1968. Travers was using innuendo not
because he was afraid to openly discuss sexuality and profanity, but because he felt that the
innuendo made better drama (Gale 1139).

Ben Travers Bibliography

Gale, Shannon. "Ben Travers." Encyclopedia of British Humorists, Volume II. Ed. Steven
H. Gale. New York, NY: Garland, 1996, 1136-1141.
Hendrickx, Johan Remi. Ben Travers and the English Farce Tradition. Dissertation
Abstracts International 42.1 (July, 1981): 226A.
Innes, Christopher. "The Comic Mirror--Tradition and Innovation." Modern British Drama,
1890-1990. Cambridge, England: Cambridge University Press, 1992, 260-267.
Richards, Horace. "Being Funny Is No Joke! Says Ben Travers in an Interview with Horace
Richards." Theatre World 30 (December, 1938): 248.
Smith, Leslie. "Ben Travers and the Aldwych Farces." Modern Drama 27 (September,
1984): 429-448.
Travers, Ben. Plunder. London, England: Bickers, 1931.
Travers, Ben, ed. Pretty Pictures, Being a Selection of the Best American Pictorial
Humour. London, England: John Lane, 1932.
Travers, Ben. Vale of Laughter. London, England: Bles, 1957.

Edith Sitwell (1887-1964)

When Edith Sitwell was asked why she preferred to dress all in black, she
responded, "I'm in mourning to the entire world." This is an example of Sitwell's mordant
humor. G. A. Cevasco comments on the brilliance and the wit of Edith Sitwell's poetry.
Cevasco says that there is a great deal of humor, burlesque, ridicule, and satire scattered
throughout not only her poems, but also her works of fiction, biography, autobiography,
and social history (Cevasco 1009).

One of the poems in The Mother and Other Poems (1915) is entitled "Aubade."
This poem portrays the sad stupidity of a servant girl who lives on a farm, and who each
morning rises from bed to go down and light the morning fire:
> Jane, Jane

> Tall as a crane,
> The morning light creaks down again;
> Comb your cockscomb-ragged hair,
> Jane, Jane come down the stair. (Cevasco 1009)

Cevasco says that the intellectual play that can be seen in "Aubade" can also be seen in Sitwell's Clowns' Houses (1918), her The Wooden Pegasus (1920) and her Bucolic Comedies (1923). But it is even more prevalent in Façade (1922). The title of Façade comes from a snide remark which Sitwell overheard. Someone was talking about Sitwell's work, and complained, "Very clever, no doubt--but what is she but a Façade." Sitwell chose this title to imply that something may have a superficial meaning at first glance, and it is only through closer inspection and reflection that the humor, the wit, and the real significance are revealed (Cevasco 1010).

Sitwell's first public performance of Façade was very controversial. During the reading, she sat behind a transparent curtain adorned with a painted moonface, and she sat with her back to the audience. The moonface was symbolic of the dreamlike world of apes, ducks, grotesque lords and ladies, clowns, peasants, and servant girls that were the subjects of her poems. In order to magnify her voice above the accompanying music during the reading Sitwell employed the use of a Sengerphone, which had been invented by George Senger, a Swiss opera singer to approximate the voice of a dragon. The general reaction of the audience to this performance was quite hostile. Even though the performance contained much humor and gaiety, many subtle criticisms of modern life, many innuendoes of despair, decay, and death, the audience mainly only heard a kind of gibberish. Sitwell was attacked by the press as an, "ostentatious fool, an eccentric avant-garde iconoclast, and worse" (Cevasco 1010).

Nevertheless, Façade is quite funny. Sitwell placed two rhymes immediately together at the end of each two lines, rhymes like "Fox trot," which Cevasco describes as "leaps in the air." An example is "Sally, Mary, Mattie what's the matter, why cry? / The huntsman and the reynard-coloured sun and I sigh" (Cevasco 1010). One of the poems in Façade is entitled "Trio for Two Cats." In addition to its amusing title, this poem has a fast rhythm that creates an eerie mood, and that mood is accentuated by the accompanying castanets. The rhythms of Sitwell's other poems are also entertaining. "I Like to Do Beside the Seaside" is read to a tango rhythm. "Scotch Rhapsody" begins with "Do not take a bath in Jordon, Gordon," and is read to a heavy drum beat throughout the poem. "Polka" has cleverly strange rhymes like "Robinson Crusoe rues so" and "the proxy, doxy dear." "Popular Song" is joyful and carefree, and is about "Lily O'Grady / Silly and Shady, / Longing to be / a lazy lady." Although Sitwell's poetry is rather good, she tended to accompany her poems with statements rebutting the critics and giving long and instructive analyses of her individual poems. "Sitwell's long and profuse explanations of the aural techniques and technicalities contribute little to the average person's enjoyment of the humorous quality of many of the poems in Façade." Cecil Beaton agreed that Sitwell's long explanations were a waste of time, but he loved to hear her recite her lines. Beaton described her poetry as follows: "Edith could make any rubbish sound like poetry" (Cevasco 1011).

Edith Sitwell Bibliography

Cevasco, G. A. "Edith Sitwell." Encyclopedia of British Humorists, Volume II. Ed. Steven H. Gale. New York, NY: Garland, 1996, 1007-1013.

(Arthur) Joyce (Lunel) Cary (1888-1957) IRELAND

Joyce Cary was a "jaunty, gay, vital little Englishman in cap and tweeds." Lord David Cecil said that Cary made a picturesque and exhilarating first impression, with his elegant, virile handsomeness, and his racy, vivid, appreciative conversation. It was partly because of his personal charm and ebullience that Cary was so often classed as a "comic novelist." For people who liked him he was one of the outstanding humorous writers of the century. For those who didn't like him he was a minor humorist. "But large or small, humorist he is" (Yeager 141). Many critics consider Cary's writing to be a continuation of such eighteenth-century comic and picaresque authors as Daniel Defoe, and Henry Fielding; however Cary himself says that the most important influences in his life have been Joseph Conrad, Henry James, and Thomas Hardy. Rosenthal says that Cary's writing has Conrad's dignity and moral sense, James's vision of the fragility of innocence, and Hardy's sense of tragic fate (Rosenthal 338). Cary's humor relates to the, "cosmic comic structure of life," and the "ironic divergence between the official record and the actual events." His novels are filled, therefore with contradictions and paradoxes (Smith 220).

Joyce Cary wrote three great trilogies. The first was a trilogy of ethnicity (Aissa Saved [1932], An American Visitor [1933], and The African Witch [1936]). The second was a trilogy of art (Herself Surprised [1941], To Be a Pilgrim [1942], and The Horse's Mouth [1944]). The third was a trilogy of politics (Prisoner of Grace [1952], Except the Lord [1953], and Not Honour More [1953])(Smith 221). Cary's first great trilogy is Aissa Saved (1932), An American Visitor (1933), and The African Witch (1936). Here, a single person describes two other persons, but in the descriptions, the reader can see the discrepancy between one person's point of view, and the private views of the people he is describing. Thus, much of the humor results from the difference between the objective truth (whatever that is), and the subjective truth. "Most hilarious and pathetic is the divergence between the official record and the actual event" (Smith 220). In Aissa Saved (1932), Aissa is a Christian missionary convert, who has been maimed, whose child has been beheaded, whose husband has been slain, and who is eaten alive by soldier ants. The word "Saved" that occurs in the title means "saved" in the evangelical sense of the word, as Aissa has been listed in London as a "triumphant missionary convert" (Smith 220). There is therefore a comic divergence between the fact and the reporting. Cary himself was a mild, patient, and benevolent man with his family and friends, but his books are nevertheless filled with violence, disaster, and horrible deaths. Cary patiently explains that this is all to be expected, and that in fact it could not have been otherwise (Smith 221).

Joyce Cary's comic novels were mainly written during the middle of his career. These four comic novels (out of a total of fifteen) are Mister Johnson (1939), Charley Is My Darling (1940), Herself Surprised (1941), and The Horse's Mouth (1944) (Rosenthal 337). Cary's comic novels are all constructed on the opposition of the hero and conventional society from which this hero is alienated. "Cary's heroes are outcasts, rejected by a society that does not understand them. Mr. Johnson, Charley, Sara, and Gulley manifest the unfitness for social living in various ways: they are impoverished, frequently immoral, invariable criminal--cheating, lying, and stealing their ways through the world." But at the same time they have such life-affirming qualities as spontaneity, kindness, and imagination. They may be immoral rogues, but they embrace life joyously, thereby, "coming closer to the secrets of life than the decorous representatives of society who frown at them and put them in jail" (Rosenthal 342). D. M. Yeager notes, however, that Gulley Jimson is not a conventional rogue hero, and he is also not a facetious clown. Rather, he is a "comic hero" (Yeager 141).

Michael Rosenthal describes Mister Johnson (1939) as, "the best of Cary's early novels, at once poignant and funny." Herself Surprised (1941), To Be a Pilgrim (1942), and The Horse's Mouth (1944) are described by Charles Hoffman as "the Gulley Jimson trilogy." Gulley Jimson is an artist who has given up a career in commerce in order to paint the things he really believes in. He is poor, unrecognized, misunderstood, and totally irresponsible toward society. He is immoral, disrespectful, and a bit crazy. He is the stereotype of the typical bohemian. In addition, society feels that Gulley Jimson is not even able to paint "pretty" pictures (Hoffman "Comic Mask" 135). Gulley Jimson

> is the artist forever at odds with society, forever leaving taste behind to create new things in a new way. Whether he is successful or not by society's standards does not matter, nor does it matter to him whether posterity might eventually catch up to what he is already finished with; he has gone on to something else, or his wall falls down and posterity never catches up. All he wants is enough canvas (or wall space) and paint; all he needs is enough freedom and ideas. (Hoffman "Comic Mask" 136)

Sara (Monday) Jimson is the title character in Herself Surprised (1941); she is an earthy woman who lives by a code of natural morals, but she also has a particular capacity for love and forgiveness. Sara comes from a good home. Her father is a freeholder and a working foreman, and her mother is a teacher. Sara has won prizes for recitation and for Scripture in school, and has even been granted a certificate for sewing. But it is this same Sara who is later castigated by the judge at her trial for stealing from Tom Wilcher. Her actions are described by the judge as an "unhappy example of that laxity and contempt for all religious principle and social obligation which threatens to undermine the whole fabric of our civilization" (Cary Herself Surprised 1).

Tom Wilcher in To Be a Pilgrim (1942) is a man who has not been able to keep up with change; thus, he is a pilgrim who is wandering about aimlessly in a modern world that has passed him by. "He is the unchanging pilgrim in the land of unfulfilled promise. He is the voice of moral and religious conscience that says to be a pilgrim is to know where one is going" (Hoffman "Comic Mask" 140). Tom cannot stop the younger generation:

> "And where are they going?" I thought. "Do they know? When Chaucer wrote of pilgrimage, in England, then every man knew where he was, and where he could go. But now all is confusion and no one has anywhere to go. They leave home only to sit under glass roofs, in black overcoats and black hats, with faces so private and cunning that you are afraid of them." "A pilgrim is not a lost soul," I thought, "nor a wanderer. He is not a tramp. But these are lost souls who don't even know that they are lost." (Hoffman "Comic Mask" 142)

Tom doesn't resist the change of the modern world so much as he resists lack of purpose or direction in this world (Hoffman Comedy of Freedom 410). Hoffman considers both Tom Wilcher and Gulley Jimson to be pilgrims, because they know where they are going. "If Tom Wilcher had known Gulley Jimson, he would approve of him, as he did of Sara, perhaps not as a person, perhaps not even as an artist, but as a pilgrim believing in himself, journeying on to the promised land of fulfillment" (Hoffman Comedy of Freedom 142).

Michael Rosenthal considers The Horse's Mouth (1944) to be Joyce Cary's funniest novel, and in fact, "one of the outstanding comic novels of the century." Joyce Cary explains how he first got the idea for writing The Horse's Mouth:

> I met this man who'd been a well-known painter in England.... I've never met a man in such misery and despair, because his family was starving. The impressionists had knocked him right out, and he couldn't sell a picture. He hadn't sold a picture for years, some years.... And of course he thought the impressionists were daubs. He couldn't see anything in impressionists. And there you have the tragedy.... I was practicing impressionism myself, and I understood the old man's misery and despair and pitied him. I thought,

poor old fellow: he's no good and never was any good. You see, what a tragedy. (qtd. in Rosenthal 341)

Charles Hoffman suggests that Gulley Jimson in The Horse's Mouth (1944) is the voice for the author, Joyce Cary. Gulley is a reprobate, but he is nevertheless correct in his assessment of how badly society treats a creative artist. Since Gulley the narrator is himself a creative artist, a painter, the novel is entitled The Horse's Mouth. Charles Hoffman considers The Horse's Mouth to be filled with comic verve and wit, and with freshness of satiric vision. He feels that the first-person narrative sets the tone of comedy and satire for the novel (Hoffman "Comic Mask" 137). Society does not respect Gulley Jimson's ability as an artist. One of his paintings is used to mend a hole in the roof. He is forced to support himself by selling "art" in the form of "dirty postcards." And he is even beaten up because he infringes on another salesman's territory (Rosenthal 342).

D. M. Yeager feels that the positive and life-affirming qualities of Christian comedies like The Horse's Mouth make them better examples of comedy than they would be if they were non-Christian. It is as if there were a double dénouement, the hopeful dénouement of the novel itself, and the hopeful dénouement of the hereafter as well, but Yeager feels that non-Christians are not able to appreciate the full impact of this second dénouement.

> The statement embedded in the book is a religious one which cannot be fully grasped apart from the Christian concepts of consent to being and selfless love; to the degree that critics are reluctant or unable to bring such concepts to bear on the novel, they miss the affirmation that the novel offers and the framework within which the very real suffering of the characters is accommodated.... The novel is a brilliantly achieved comedy, but it is high comedy--and high comedy is not easily accessible to the late twentieth-century consciousness. As secular humanism has tightened its grip on Western culture, the notion of high comedy has been eroded to such a degree that for most of us the term comedy is now synonymous with what used to be called low comedy. (Yeager 132-133)

Because Gulley Jimson suffers from high blood pressure, he realizes that if he fights for what he terms a "sense of justice" he will probably have a stroke. Therefore he spends the last two years of his life in an effort to avoid "getting up a grievance." Since he is unable to avoid situations that provoke grief, anger, and despair, he decides that he will deal with this grief, anger, and despair by developing a sense of humor. Thus, he is able to turn his tormentors into objects of ridicule. He learns to laugh at his own tendency toward seriousness, and develops the capacity to appreciate the incongruities of life (Yeager 137).

Michael Rosenthal notes that for Joyce Cary, the laughter is never far from tears (342). On the last page of The Horse's Mouth Gulley Jimson is lying in an ambulance on his way to the hospital and a nun tells Gulley not to talk. "It's dangerous for you to talk, you're very seriously ill." Gulley responds, "Not so seriously as you're well. Why don't you enjoy life, mother. I should laugh all round my neck at this minute if my shirt wasn't a bit on the tight side." The nun says, "It would be better for you to pray." And Gulley responds, "Same thing, mother" (Carey The Horse's Mouth 345).

L. A. G. Strong says that "everywhere and always," Cary was engaged in "the Comedy of Freedom." Cary was a master of the unexpected simile, the fantastic plot structure slowed down by the intrusive author lecturing on every conceivable subject. He was a master of the extended hyperbole, and the basic assumption that, "justice is a mental concept unknown in actual experience." In commenting about Joyce Cary's comedic style, Andrew Wright notes, "the Smollettesque dialogue, the Shandean capital letters, the Dickensian names, the brackets (and brackets within brackets), the historical present tense, the abrupt chapter divisions, above all the picaresque structure" (Smith 222).

(Arthur) Joyce (Lunel) Cary Bibliography

Cary, Joyce. A Fearful Joy. London, England: Michael Joseph, 1949.
Cary, Joyce. Herself Surprised. New York, NY: Riverrun, 1941.
Cary, Joyce. The Horse's Mouth. London, England: Michael Joseph, 1944.
Hoffman, Charles G. Joyce Cary: The Comedy of Freedom. Pittsburgh, PA: University of
    Pittsburgh Press, 1964.
Hoffman, Charles G. "Joyce Cary and the Comic Mask." Western Humanities Review 13.2
    (1959): 135-142.
Rosenthal, Michael. "Joyce Cary's Comic Sense." Texas Studies in Literature and Language
    13 (1971): 337-346.
Smith, Elton E. "Joyce Cary." Encyclopedia of British Humorists, Volume I. Ed. Steven
    H. Gale. New York, NY: Garland, 1996, 219-222.
Wright, Andrew. Joyce Cary: A Preface to His Novels. New York, NY: Harper and
    Brothers, 1958.
Yeager, D. M. "Love and Mirth in The Horse's Mouth." Renascence 33.3 (1981): 131-142.

Thomas Stearns Eliot (1888-1965)

Robert Kantra describes both Samuel Beckett and T. S. Eliot as religious satirists. Both of these writers intentionally mixed tragedy and comedy in a relatively simple way to produce a dramatically power feeling (Kantra 158). William Arrowsmith says that much of T. S. Eliot's writing contains two apparently disparate orders which tend to intersect happily and comically when the death of the desiring of the worldly self yields to the dedication of a person's thoughts and deeds to others (Arrowsmith 162). It was Eliot's intention that his plays should be both teasing and unsettling, but it was also his intention that they should be evocative, and that in the end they should be satisfying (Arrowsmith 166). In other words, he wanted to use the precision and richness of Christian doctrine and mystery to create plays that were true "comedies of reconciliation." He wanted to begin with secular disorder, but end with "a genuine order, complete at every point" (Arrowsmith 167).

In an article entitled "The 'Comic Spirit' and The Waste Land," Patricia Galivan presents evidence that while Eliot was working on The Waste Land (1922) he viewed it as a comedy, not a tragedy. It was only after Ezra Pound's influence that he changed the poem to its more tragic form.

> Eliot's own conception of comedy is decidedly dismissive of the idea that it exists primarily to be funny. But both in its order and in the kind of material it includes, the early version of The Waste Land aims to do, I think, what Eliot thought comedy should do. That, it seems to me, is why he showed a degree of caring for the first plan and that is the conception of the poem which Pound persuaded him to abandon. (Gallivan 36)

Part of Gallivan's evidence comes from the fact that the essays that Eliot was working on in 1921 have an obvious relationship to The Waste Land, and these essays were ironic in tone; they were, "mocking versions of lines which show up in the poem.... Sometimes they preview images we find in the poem...and one essay sees Stravinsky and Rubenstein through the superimposition and fadeout lenses which structure The Waste Land." Furthermore, he was writing these essays during the same period that he was composing The Waste Land (Gallivan 36-37).

In 1919, Eliot wrote an essay on Ben Jonson in which he discusses the impossibility of distinguishing between tragedy and comedy. Eliot says that both tragedy and comedy are appropriate to dramatic literature, but the rigid separation of comedy and tragedy that was common in Elizabethan times, is no longer viable (Gallivan 41). In 1921, Eliot wrote formal essays on Marvell, on Dryden, and on the Metaphysical Poets in which he again discussed comedy, and in fact, "showed the degree to which his considerations of the comic are at the centre of Eliot's view of poetry." Eliot felt that what prevented the wit of the metaphysical poets from descending into mere funniness is that it is critical in tone. As Eliot notes, "It implies a constant inspection and criticism of experience" (qtd. in Gallivan 42).

In 1921 Eliot wrote nine essays, showing three converging areas of interest. They continue Eliot's review of contemporary criticism; they turn around the issue of the fusion of disparate elements in poetry; and they, "declare the focussed intensity of Eliot's inquiry into comedy." In one of these essays, entitled "The Romantic Englishman, the Comic Spirit, and the Function of Criticism," Eliot states that the romantic Englishman is "in a bad way," for he lacks both a "myth," and a "corporately-held moral character" (Gallivan 39). Furthermore, on the dramatic stage, man is portrayed as a caricature: "Man desires to see himself on the stage, more admirable, more forceful, more villainous, more comical, more despicable--and much more else than he actually is" (qtd. in Gallivan 40).

In the June, 1921 issue of "London Letter" which Eliot wrote for Dial, Eliot discusses the national character of the comic. He says that readers love to observe the comic clash of opposites. They like to see a conflict between the "ideal" and the "actual." Eliot says that the Lancashire comedian is at his best when he is pitting himself against a suitable audience in what he calls the "fierce talent of Nellie Wallace" (Gallivan 41). It is clear that Eliot takes the comic seriously. However, he sees comedy as only loosely related to what is funny, and he considers comedy to represent, "an extremely modern type of beauty." For Eliot, comedy represents the, "vital relationship between the real and the transmuted" (Gallivan 41).

The opening section of "The Burial of the Dead," in The Waste-Land Manuscript, uses old jokes about the man who is too drunk, and the retiring madam. The protagonist in this piece is a Bergsonian caricature who...

> lists with mechanical energy, the events of a night out, which includes drink, food, cigars, a show, a brothel, a brush with the law, and more than one kind of violence. He finds it all terribly funny, and Eliot intended him at various stages to have "a good laugh" or "a couple of laughs" or a "real laugh." Indeed the passage is packed with matter for raucous laughter. (Gallivan 45)

The Waste-Land Manuscript also contains a comic poem about a ship wreck in which Eliot turns the "comic gonorrhea" into something great. The poem tells about sailors who experience such bad storms and who become so concentrated on the charts and sheets of the ship, and so worn down by the storms that even when they come ashore, they appear somewhat inhuman in the cleanliness and dignity they display in streets and in public bars. These sailors, who have been sobered by the storm provide a stark contrast with the drunken ruffians who descend from backstreet stairs after indulged in illicit activities. It is the drunken sailors who deride their sober friends, as they stager or limp around with a kind of "comic gonorrhea." The clean and dignified sailors who have arrived on land from their experience with wind and sea are "much seen and much endured," but they are also seen as foolish, as impersonal, as innocent, as gay. They provide a surreal element to the bawdy environment in their wish to be shaved, combed, scented and manicured (Gallivan 46).

Gallivan suggests that Eliot here is aiming at an "effect which is far from laughter," an effect where "the comic is the material," and where the result is a kind of poetry. Gallivan further contends that in the final version of The Waste Land Eliot does not abandon the comic spirit. Gallivan notes however that, "what the systematic revision did to the poem...was to shift the balance." Gallivan further notes that, "to the degree that the revisions tipped the poem towards the mythic, they tipped it away from its comic material" (Gallivan 47).

Based on such evidence as that mentioned above, Patricia Gallivan concludes that while he was writing The Waste Land (1922) Eliot was, "seriously preoccupied with various manifestations of the comic." It was during this period that he wrote his "London Letter," in which he discussed the nature of caricature and the music hall. He also mentions Bergson, and quotes from Baudelaire's essay on laughter (Gallivan 43).

Murder in the Cathedral (1935), a comedy written in blank verse is described by Robert Kantra as Eliot's "Canterbury play" (Kantra 162). In addition to being a comedy, it is also a tragedy. Robert Kantra feels that the quadruple dialogues of Thomas with the Tempters and the Knights are crucial to an understanding of the central theme and structure of the play. Kantra further feels that these dialogues can be identified as an imaginative mode which Northrop Frye calls "Menippean satire" (Kantra 163).

In the play, Saint Thomas of Canterbury is murdered by four knights, and although these four knights may not have been comic in history, they are (according to Kantra) comic in the play. Nevertheless, their function in the play is much more than the mere providing of simple comic relief, because the play has a structure similar to the structure of a medieval morality play (Kantra 167). The basic theme of Murder in a Cathedral is satire, and the play is formally symmetrically composed of two parts, about equal in length. As dramatis personae, there are the Four Tempters and the Four Knights, whose dialogue with Thomas contributes significantly to sustain a satire that is structurally balanced. Furthermore, in Part II, the Knights, "are riduculous past the point of comic relief" (Kantra 168).

The Cocktail Party (1949) is a problematic comedy because Eliot attempted to treat high moral seriousness in the light comedic style of Noel Coward. But as Eliot himself observed, laughter can occur in the play only when there is detachment and objectivity. He feels that detachment from self is the, "first requisite to salvation--Christian or otherwise" (Davenport 301). During 1910 and 1911 Eliot had heard Bergson's lectures on laughter, and Bergson had talked about the "negation of ego," an idea which was totally compatible with the Christian meaning of The Cocktail Party. Eliot is almost paraphrasing Bergson when he says, "We laugh every time a person gives us the impression of being a thing." Eliot talks about going down a staircase. "When you come to the bottom step there is one more step than your feet expected. And you come down with a jolt. Just for a moment you have the experience of being an object at the mercy of a malevolent staircase" (qtd. in Davenport 302).

The Cocktail Party was originally named "One-Eyed Reilley," and received its present title at a later stage of composition. William Arrowsmith explains the earlier title as relating to the "one-eyed vision of Julia and Reilly as a metaphor for their spiritual 'half-sight' " as distinct from the total blindness of Edward and the total vision of Celia. Eliot realizes that the most important disadvantage of one-eyed vision is the loss of perspective, that is, the inability to see things in three dimensions. The Christian reading of the play relates to individualism and lack of social perspective. When the individual is relinked to his friends, his vision becomes whole again. And the test of this relinking is laughter and the comic spirit. "If one cannot laugh, he has not attained the state. The same two-eyed vision which brings laughter brings salvation from the prison of self" (qtd. in Davenport 306).

W. K. Wimsatt Jr. talks about the "one-eyed foolery" in The Cocktail Party, and associates it not only with Reilly, but with Julia Shuttlethwaite as well. Julia is wearing spectacles with only one lens, and these one-lens spectacles are alluded to repeatedly in various dialogues. She is constantly misplacing them; one time she finds them in her purse, and another time she leaves them at Edward's house. When the one-lens glasses are first mentioned, a drunken guest, who is later identified as Reilly, bursts into song. He sings about drunking gin and water, and he also sings about being the "One Eyed Reilley. He sings about how he cam in the room in order to court the landlord's daughter, and that she totally stole his heart (Davenport 304).

Thomas Stearns Eliot Bibliography

Arrowsmith, William. "The Comedy of T. S. Eliot." English Stage Comedy: English Institute Essays 1954. Ed. W. K. Wimsatt, Jr. New York, NY: Columbia Univ Press, 1955, 148-172.

Baroody, Wilson G. "Corrective Irony and Hope in T. S. Eliot's The Wasteland. WHIMSY 1 (1983): 164-165.

Collins, Philip. "A Twinkle in the Narratorial Eye: Dickens, Thackeray and Eliot." Literary and Linguistic Aspects of Humor. Barcelona, Spain: Univ of Barcelona Dept of Languages, 1984, 9-25.

Davenport, Gary T. "Eliot's The Cocktail Party: Comic Perspective as Salvation." Modern Drama 17 (1974): 301-306.

Gallivan, Patricia. " 'The Comic Spirit' and The Waste Land." University of Toronto Quarterly 45 (1975): 35-49.

Gardner, Helen. "The Comedies of T. S. Eliot." Essays by Divers Hands, 3rd Series 34 (1966): 55-73.

Kantra, Robert A. "Waiting for Gödel: Beckett and Eliot." All Things Vain: Religious Satirists and Their Art. University Park, PA: Penn State University Press, 1984, 154-173.

Wimsatt, W. K., Jr. "Eliot's Comedy." Southern Review 58 (1950): 666-678.

Enid Algerine Bagnold (1889-1981)

Enid Bagnold is a keen observer of British life and character, and she is skilled at sharp characterization and believable dialogue both of which create a humor that is born out of the accuracy of her observations (Gazeley 76). In A Diary Without Dates (1918) Bagnold uses a fragmentary style that gives it the feel of being a documentary. Here Bagnold clearly has a special facility with language, and she is good at providing strong visual imagery. A Diary Without Dates is filled with pathos, but it also has many instances of understated humor that come across as very British. Bagnold describes different types of hospital visitors in A Diary Without Dates. One woman visitor acts as if the hospital were a school treat. Another woman asks the soldiers about their friends, "exactly as though she was talking about Cairo in the season." There is still another visitor who embarrasses the author with compliments in front of the men. When she leaves, she says she hopes to come again, and Bagnold wryly remarks, "And she will" (Gazeley 74). Serena Blandish, or the Difficulties of Getting Married (1924) is a bitter parody that captures the hard gaiety of the post-war period. It is described in the Times Literary Supplement (December, 1924) as "a brilliant tract for the times" (Gazeley 76).

Bagnold liked to create masculine women, matriarchal figures who are immensely strong emotionally, and Mrs. Brown in National Velvet (1935) is one such woman. She is the wise, calm cornerstone of the family, and although she speaks very little, she fights, "quietly but inexorably for her children and their dreams." When her husband wouldn't let Velvet enter the horse in the race, she, "rose like a sea monster from its home" (Gazeley

75). There is a great deal of humor in National Velvet, a book about family life and the rituals and trials of small children. The daughters quickly rise from the meal table, and mutter without thinking, "For whatayave received, thank God!" The little boy, named Donald, collects his spit in a bottle, and is perhaps the greatest source of humor (Gazeley 74). When Velvet wakes him and tells him that he has slept too long, the dialogue goes as follows: "'I've slept too long,' moaned Donald.... Slept too long," he wailed self-pityingly. Mrs. Brown washes him and he returns. 'I've slept too long,' he said in quite a different voice, engagingly, socially. 'Yes, we heard,' said Mr. Brown" (Gazeley 75). This demonstrates the fact that National Velvet develops down-to-earth characters and shows how they relate to each other. There is also a strong sense of place, as a young girl rides her horse in the Grand National Steeple Chase (Gazeley 74).

The Squire (1938) provides many important and humorous insights into what it was like to live in an English country house (Gazeley 76). The Chalk Garden (1956) is Bagnold's most successful play. In The Observer (April 15, 1956), Kenneth Tynan describes it as, "the finest artificial comedy to have flowed from an English pen since the death of Congreve." The Chalk Garden contains many witty exchanges, as when Laurel asks, "Was she hung?" and Mrs. St. Maugham responds, "Hanged, my darling, when speaking of a lady." The Chalk Garden, like Bagnold's other plays is filled with epigrams, which she called her "plums" (Gazeley 75). The brothers Bibesco are the leading characters in The Last Joke (1970). In the Evening Standard (September 29, 1960), Milton Shulman says that in The Last Joke, Bagnold explores aging and death, but these subjects become softened by the richness of Bagnold's idiom, her lush metaphors, and her exotic imagery (Gazeley 75).

Enid Algerine Bagnold Bibliography

Bagnold, Enid. The Happy Foreigner. London, England: Heinemann, 1920.
Gazeley, Helen. "Enid Algerine Bagnold." Encyclopedia of British Humorists, Volume I. Ed. Steven H. Gale. New York, NY: Garland, 1996, 73-76.

5

Authors Born between 1890 and 1899

Agatha Christie (Mary Clarissa Miller)(Mary Westmacott)(1890-1976)

Agatha Christie's novels are intricate puzzles that are designed to misdirect the reader's attention away from the most important clues. "The solution of the puzzle is invariably startling, although entirely logical and consistent with the rest of the story." Anthony Lejeune of The Spectator said that there were basically three qualities which made Agatha Christie's writing so great. The first quality was the texture of her writing, a texture which Lejeune considers "as smooth and homely as cream." A second quality was Christie's ability to "buttonhole a reader," her ability to make each page serve as a hook to the next page. The third quality was her "coziness." One reviewer for the Times Literary Supplement provides a fourth important quality of Christie's writing--that she, "never excluded any characters from possible revelation as murders, not the sweet young girl, the charming youth, the wise old man, not even the dear old lady" (Lesniak 84).

Agatha Christie believed in the theater of entertainment and escape. She wrote to delight and to entertain. She defined her work as, "halfway between a crossword puzzle and a hunt in which you can pursue the trail sitting comfortably in a theater seat" (Athanason 117). Agatha Christie's world was that of cozy upper-middle-class English gentility. This is a world that is normally consciously devoid of the gruesome and the sordid, and it is this gruesomeness and sordidness that Christie depicts so charmingly and invitingly in such plays as The Mousetrap (Athanason 118). Christie, who also wrote under the pseudonym of Mary Westmacott, is considered by Arthur Athanason to be the "undisputed Queen of Crime," though Christie herself preferred the title of "Duchess of Death" (Athanason 112). John Heideury of Commonweal explains the process of reading an Agatha Christie novel by describing how he read a particular one: "On page 35 I had guessed the identity of the murderer, by the next page knew the victim, and on page 112 deduced the motive. (On page 41 I had changed my mind and reversed murderer and victim, but on page 69 returned steadfast to my original position).... I was wrong on all counts at book's end" (Lesniak 85).

The Mysterious Affair at Styles (1920) is Agatha Christie's first mystery novel featuring Hercule Poirot. The character of Hercule Poirot was developed as an eccentric and amusingly pompous Belgian detective. Christie described him in The Mysterious Affair at Styles as, "an extraordinary-looking little man. He was hardly more than five feet, four inches, but carried himself with great dignity. His head was exactly the shape of an egg. His moustache was very still and military. The neatness of his attire was almost incredible. I believe a speck of dust would have caused him more pain than a bullet wound" (Lesniak 84). In <u>Autobiography</u> (1977), Christie made it clear that the team of Hercule Poirot and Captain Hastings is modeled after Arthur Conan Doyle's famous team of Sherlock Holmes and Dr. Watson (Keating 72). Christie wrote that her detective should have, "rather a grand name--one of those names that Sherlock Holmes and his family had.... How about calling my little man Hercules?" Christie then altered the name to the more euphonious "Hercule." At first, Christie was going to give Hercule Poirot a mysterious brother by the name of "Achille," because, as Poirot himself says, "all celebrated detectives have brothers who would be even more celebrated were it not for constitutional indolence." Poirot had a number of leitmotifs associated with him. He regularly referred to "the little grey cells" of his brain, and he almost always wore a black jacket, correct striped trousers, and a bow tie. In order to accommodate her readers, Christie had him use French only for the easy phrases, and English for anything more complicated (Keating 73).

David J. Grossvogel said that Agatha Christie was very aware of the faintly ridiculous figure cut by Poirot. After all, she named him after a vegetable; "poireau" means both "leek," and "wart" in French. She gave him the Christian name of Hercule, which comes from the name of "Hercules." Each of these names, therefore, plays off from the other, and ridicule is therefore cast in both directions. This ridiculous name is supported by Poirot's being Belgian, not French, and by his fastidiousness and his mincing ways. The fact that he is patronizingly dismissed until the very end of the novel or play, when only he is able to solve the crime, makes the dénouement all the more entertaining (Lesniak 85).

In <u>The Secret Adversary</u> (1922), Christie introduced two young people, Thomas Beresford (Tommy), and Prudence Cowley (Tuppence) who would reappear in Christie works over the years. In <u>The Secret Adversary</u>, Christie developed her gifts for deceiving the reader, and for writing a swift narrative that makes the book fun to read (Keating 74). <u>The Murder of Roger Ackroyd</u> (1926) is a mystery novel featuring Hercule Poirot. The way Christie tricked the reader in this novel is to make the narrator turn out to be the murderer. The story is told entirely in the words of the narrator, and Christie contrived his narration so that everything he says is misleading but everything he says is also true (Keating 74). This novel created a sensation because many critics felt it was not kosher of Christie to have the narrator be the murderer. Critics called the novel everything from "a rotten, unfair trick" to "a brilliant, psychological tour-de-force" (Keating 75).

After the publication of <u>The Murder of Roger Ackroyd</u>, things were not going well in Agatha Christie's life. Her mother died, and she went to Ashfield, her family home in Torquay to straighten things out. She was thus separated from her husband and her young daughter for a long time, and when she returned home she learned that Colonel Christie wanted a divorce from her so that he could marry someone else. These events caused Agatha to have a breakdown, and after an especially bitter quarrel with Colonel Christie, Agatha left her husband and went to the Yorkshire spa town of Harrogate, where she checked into a hotel using the last name of the woman her husband planned to marry. There was a great deal of publicity in the papers about her disappearance, and after nine days, she was recognized at her hotel (Keating 75).

It was shortly after these events, that Christie wrote <u>The Murder at the Vicarage</u> (1930), Christie's first mystery novel featuring Miss Jane Marple (Keating 75). One of the parishioners of the Vicarage described Miss Marple as "that terrible Miss Marple," but Len Clement, the vicar and the narrator of the novel pointed out that in the end, "Miss Marple had been right on every count." The character of Miss Jane Marple was written in contrast to the character of Hercule Poirot. Whereas Poirot is, "an embodiment of so many eccentricities that he seems unreal," Miss Marple, "has a credibility derived in part from her prototype, Caroline Sheppard, and in part from Christie's grandmother, on whom Miss Marple is partly modeled." Where Poirot works by at least the appearance of logic and reasoning, Miss Marple works largely by intuition. Miss Marple has five distinct qualities. First, she has an extensive knowledge of people; second, she believes that gossip, or "tittle-tattle" is more-often-than-not true; third, she has a gift for making connections between people's minor misdemeanors and their capacity for bigger ones; fourth she has her intuition; and fifth she is pessimistic, cynical, and untrusting of people. This last quality prevents Miss Marple ever from taking anything or anyone at face value (Keating 76).

The A.B.C. Murders (1936) is a mystery novel featuring Hercule Poirot which became retitled as The Alphabet Murders (1966). Here, there is a series of murders that have apparently been committed by a madman with an alphabet obsession. This murderer has started by killing Alice Ascher in Andover. Next, he kills Betty Barnard in Bexhill. Then he kills Sir Carmichael Clarke in Churston. And each of these murders is accompanied by a taunting letter to Poirot that is signed, "A.B.C." The dénouement shows that the killer was not a madman, but rather a calculating murderer named Franklin Clarke, who wanted to kill his brother, Carmichael Clarke, who just happened to live in Churston. Franklin Clarke devised the alphabet murders as a way of diverting attention away from the only "real" murder. H. R. F. Keating notes that this is a variation on the device that Edgar Allan Poe used in The Purloined Letter. Poe had "hidden" a crucial letter among some other uncrucial letters (Keating 77). Here, Christie was hiding a crucial murder among some other uncrucial murders. In order to hide his motive, Franklin Clarke, "provides a ready-made suspect, a feeble individual saddled with the name of Alexander Bonaparte Cust. Franklin Clarke happens to have become acquainted with him and persuades him to answer an advertisement for a salesman's job. His unknown employer (Clarke himself) then directs him to each of the towns where a murder is about to take place." The Alphabet Murders thus demonstrates one of Agatha Christie's most important techniques as a mystery/detective writer. According to Julian Symons, she offers the reader not one or two clues, but, "a dozen clues of which eleven are misleading while a true interpretation of the twelfth will lead to the heart of the maze--and then of course to try to make sure that this twelfth clue is not interpreted rightly" (Keating 78).

Ten Little Niggers (1939) is a play which became retitled as And Then There Were None (1940), and finally became Ten Little Indians (1944). It is about ten people who have been invited to a small island off the coast of Devonshire. A mysterious loud speaker tells them all that each of them has been associated with the death of one or more persons at some previous time, and that each of them is on the island to meet his or her proper fate. The boat has left; a storm has come up; and there is no escape from the island. Even the telephone is out of commission. The title is based on the macabre nursery rhyme, "Ten Little Niggers," which is named "Ten Little Indians" in the United States, and which gradually reduces the number until the concluding line which reads, "And Then There Were None." Arthur Athanason considers the mystery to be "clear, straightforward, and baffling," so baffling that there needed to be an epilogue in order to explain it (Athanason 113). Each person on the island is being murdered one by one. Ten Little Niggers offers a combination of predictability and suspense. Part of the suspense relates to which guest is to be murdered next, and another part of the suspense relates to which of the last two remaining guests will prove to be the murderer, and how the final death will take place (Keating 79). In all but the first version, the last two "victims," who also represent the romantic interest, manage to solve the mystery and effect their own escape (Athanason 114).

Evil under the Sun (1941) is a mystery novel featuring Hercule Poirot, in which Agatha Christie uses one of her typical methods of character development--comparing people to dogs. Miss Brewster is a tough, athletic woman with a pleasant, but weather-beaten face; Christie compares her to a sheepdog. In contrast, the loquacious American guest, Mrs. Gardener, is compared to a yapping Pomeranian (Keating 80). Poirot comments on how much the sunbathers' motionless bodies on Smugglers Island would resemble those of murdered corpses. When one of the guests at the hotel on Smugglers Island remarks to Poirot that he should be able to enjoy his vacation because there shouldn't be any bodies for the detective to be concerned with, Poirot turns to the sunbathers and says, "Ah, but that is not strictly true" (Keating 79). He continues, "Regard them there, lying out in rows. What are they? They are not men and women. There is nothing personal about them. They are just--bodies!" (Keating 80).

Five Little Pigs (1942) is very much grounded in the realities of Agatha Christie's true life. Christie's famous disappearance had happened exactly sixteen years earlier, and in Five Little Pigs, Poirot is retained to investigate a murder that had taken place just sixteen years in the past. As had been true for Agatha Christie sixteen years earlier, in the story of Five Little Pigs, there is a wife, and a young daughter, and a husband in love with a much younger woman. Finally, Amyas Crale, the self-centered painter in the story who was murdered, had the same initials as did Christie's first husband (Keating 80). H. R. F. Keating notes that The Crooked House (1949) is a mystery novel that contains two of Christie's favorite ingredients, a nursery rhyme ("There was a crooked man"), and a poisoning (Keating 80).

When Queen Mary was approaching her eightieth birthday, the British Broadcasting Company wanted to give her a royal birthday present, and therefore asked her what she would like them to produce for that event. She could choose anything from Shakespeare to opera, but what she did choose was an Agatha Christie play. At that point, Agatha Christie wrote a radio play entitled Three Blind Mice (1947). This became the novella Three Blind Mice (1950), and then the play The Mousetrap (1951) (Athanason 114). Christie gave the rights to The Mousetrap to her nine-year-old grandson when the play first opened in 1952. The Mousetrap then became the longest-running play in theatrical history, so that this gift to her grandson has earned him well over fifteen million pounds, and is continuing to earn him more money every year (Lesniak 85).

The Mousetrap is about some middle-class strangers who are isolated in an English manor house during a severe storm. They are cut off from all communication with the outside world, and one of the group is discovered to be a murderer. In the Gothic tradition, the English manor house is named "Monkswell Manor," and the killer, who is an escaped psychopath, likes to recite the macabre nursery rhyme, "Three Blind Mice." This murderer had strangled his first victim in London on the previous day, and is now in Monkswell Manor in pursuit of two more victims. Monkswell Manor is symbolic of the last glories of a dying empire in its artifacts, its remnants, and its dispossessed character types. But one member of the group is quickly identified as different. He has a cockney accent, and a working-class manner. He is clearly a social inferior who is trespassing, "into a world where he does not belong." His goal is to use murder and chaos in order to subvert the upper-middle-class social system (Athanason 115).

A Pocket Full of Rye (1953) is a mystery novel featuring Jane Marple. The word "rye" in the title has a double meaning. In the play entitled Spider's Web (1954), there is so much humor related to the disposal of the corpse that it is difficult to take the criminal proceedings seriously (Athanason 117). In The Unexpected Guest (1958), a stranger walks into a country house, and there finds a woman with a gun standing in front of her husband's corpse that is slumped in a wheelchair. The woman is dazed. She admits killing her husband. The stranger feels, however, that there is more to this scene than meets the eye, so he decides to help her blame the murder on an intruder. Although matters are complicated at this point, they become more complicated when the police find clues that implicate a man who had died two years earlier. "Then, just as the murder seems solved, there is an unexpected twist" (Athanason 117).

Poirot became such a strong and eccentric character that Christie began to very-much dislike him. She called him a "cocky Belgian," and in an interview with the Daily Mail in 1938 she said, "Why--why--why did I even invent this detestable, bombastic, tiresome little creature?" (Keating 75). Finally, in Curtain: Hercule Poirot's Last Case (1975), Poirot's sleuthing comes to an end. Curtain was written just before Agatha Christie's death, and she had placed the manuscript into a bank vault just after World War II, with instructions to publish it after her death. But Christie finally decided that she herself wanted to enjoy the ending of Poirot's career, and so she therefore published the book early (Lesniak 85). H. R. F. Keating remarks that Sleeping Murder (1976) is Miss Jane Marple's most typical case and that it is also her last case. Jane Marple had aged well: "Miss Marple was an attractive old lady, tall and thin, with pink cheeks and blue eyes, and a gentle, rather fussy manner. Her blue eyes often had a little twinkle in them" (qtd. in Keating 81).

Agatha Christie's novels, plays, and collections of short stories sold a phenomenal two billion copies, a number topped only by the Bible and the works of William Shakespeare. Christie's writings have been translated into 103 different languages, and her play The Mousetrap is the longest running play in theatrical history (Lesniak 83). On Monday, January 12, 1976, Agatha Christie died in her home in Wallingford, Oxfordshire. She was eighty-five years old when she died, and on the day of her death, The Mousetrap gave its 9,612th performance. On the day of her death, London theaters dimmed their lights in tribute to her (Athanason 118).

Agatha Christie (Mary Clarissa Miller)(Mary Westmacott) Bibliography

Athanason, Arthur Nicholas. "Agatha Christie." Dictionary of Literary Biography, Volume 13: British Dramatists Since World War II. Ed. Stanley Weintraub, Detroit, MI: Gale, 1982, 110-118.

Christie, Agatha. Autobiography. New York, NY: Dodd, Mead, 1977.

Grossvogel, David I. Mystery and Its Fictions: From Oedipus to Agatha Christie. Baltimore, MD: Johns Hopkins University Press, 1979.

Keating, H. R. F. "Agatha Christie." Dictionary of Literary Biography, Volume 77: British Mystery Writers, 1920-1939 Eds. Bernard Bernstock and Thomas F. Staley. Detroit, MI: Gale, 1989, 68-82.

Maida, Patricia D., and Nicholas B. Spornick. Murder She Wrote: A Study of Agatha Christie's Detective Fiction. Bowling Green, OH: Bowling Green University Press, 1982.

Lesniak, James G., ed. "Agatha (Mary Clarissa) Christie." Contemporary Authors, New Revision Series, Volume 37. Detroit, MI: Gale, 1992, 79-87.

Alan Patrick Herbert (Albert Haddock)(1890-1971)

From the age of sixteen on, Alan Herbert exhibited his natural aptitude for writing humorous poetry, and of course his talents were encouraged by Owen Seaman, the editor of Punch. The verse that Herbert wrote during the 1920s was about light flirtations of pretty young women. These verses would now be considered "offensively patronizing." Herbert's housemaids had their simple pleasures, their half-days off spent with boy-friends at the movies. Herbert wrote about comic charladies with hearts of gold. He had a sardonic appreciation of Britain as being "stodgy but dependable," and he was mildly xenophobic against America and Continental Europe. According to David Jago, Herbert was a bit philistine in his attitudes against arty Bohemians. Herbert was even a bit unsure about William Shakespeare, the national bard (Jago 521).

Herbert was famous for his private wit and for his public wit. On one occasion he addressed the House of Parliament in verse on the subject of population statistics. On another occasion Neville Chamberlain, the Prime Minister growled, "Say it in Punch!" (Jago 519). Herbert's literary output, especially his contributions to Punch, was impressive. He once boasted that no living Briton had written as much verse as he had (Jago 520).

Herbert's most important contribution to the genre of humorous writing was his long series of "Misleading Cases." Jago says that this will almost certainly ensure his lasting claim to fame. These "Misleading Cases" appeared in Punch between 1924 and 1970, and were collected in such titles as Misleading Cases in the Common Law (1927), More Misleading Cases (1930), Still More Misleading Cases (1933), Uncommon Law (1935), Codd's Last Case (1952), and Bardot MP? (1964). For Herbert, the law was a touchstone for the absurdities of life, and these volumes present some of the absurdities, ironies, contradictions, and paradoxes which Alan Herbert encountered as a lawyer. David Jago says that Herbert's various collections of "Misleading Cases" gives, "a genuinely humorous insight into the disparity between the manic unruliness of life and the desperate attempts to master it through the lucidity of legal language" (Jago 522). Herbert had one of his fictitious judges say, "the way to remove a fantastic measure from the Statute Book is not to evade or ignore but to enforce it" (Herbert Uncommon Law 313).

In Holy Deadlock (1934) Herbert demonstrates the absurdities of the divorce laws of England (Jago 520). In Uncommon Law, Herbert asked the question, "Is Marriage Lawful?" in order to ridicule the marriage laws. In answering this question, the person presiding over the divorce court feels obliged to say that,

> in all matrimonial transactions...the element of skill is negligible and the element of chance predominates. This brings all marriages into the category of gaming...and therefore I hold that the Court cannot according to law assist or relieve the victims of these arrangements, whether by way of restitution, separation, or divorce. Therefore it will be idle for married parties to bring their grievances before us, and, in short, this Court will never sit again. (Herbert Uncommon Law 99)

Under the name of Albert Haddock, his alter-ego, Herbert wrote much poetry for Punch which has since been collected in A Book of Ballads, being the Collected Light Verse (1931). A Book of Ballads, being the Collected Light Verse contains such humorous poems as "Laughing Ann" (1925), "She-Shanties" (1926), "Plain Jane" (1927), and "Ballads for Broadbrows" (1930) (Jago 522).

Alan Patrick Herbert (Albert Haddock) Bibliography

Herbert, Alan Patrick. Uncommon Law. London, England: Methuen, 1934.

Jago, David M. "A. P. Herbert." Encyclopedia of British Humorists, Volume I. Ed. Steven H. Gale. New York, NY: Garland, 1996, 518-522.

Price, R. G. G. A History of "Punch." London, England: Collins, 1957.

Thomas, W. K. "Satire for Those over Thirty: 'A. Herbert Come to Judgement.'" Dalhousie Review 55 (1975): 405-418.

Brinsley MacNamara (né John Weldon)(1890-1963) IRELAND

See Nilsen, Don L. F. "Brinsley MacNamara." Humor in Irish Literature: A Reference Guide. Westport, CT: Greenwood, 1996, 154-156.

Angela Margaret Thirkell (Leslie Parker)(1890-1961)

Donna Olendorf says that the setting of Angela Thirkell's novels is the same as that of Anthony Trollope's novels--Bartsetshire. Nevertheless, most critics compare her writings to those of a different eighteenth-century novelist, Jane Austen. Thirkell was also influenced by Rudyard Kipling, not only his writings, but also himself, since she was related to him, and spent a great deal of time with his daughter Josephine. The two girls were, in fact, the first audience for Kipling's Just So Stories (Olendorf 459).

Angela Margaret Thirkell (Leslie Parker) Bibliography

Olendorf, Donna. "Angela (Margaret) Thirkell. Contemporary Authors, Volume 140. Washington, DC: Gale Research, 1993, 459-460.

J. R. R. Tolkien (1892-1973)

While J. R. R. Tolkien was at Oxford University, during the 1930s, he helped form a literary society, named "The Inklings." This society included authors like Charles Williams, C. S. Lewis, and of course Tolkien himself (Kolich 522). Tolkien was a large man, but in every other way, he resembled a hobbit. In his garage study, he typed away on his old fashioned Hammond typewriter. "Professor Tolkien must have seemed like Bilbo Baggins himself in Rivendell, carefully chronicling in the Red Book of Westmarch his fantastic adventures" (Grotta 1). In Tolkien's "hobbit-hole," "books were everywhere, in stacks and on shelves, dark topped tobacco tins lined the shelves as well, and scattered about and stuffed into drawers were papers filled with Elvish scribblings, histories, and genealogies." Tolkien once indicated that his study was filled with "distinguished dust" (Grotta 9).

Tolkien laughed more than most men, and he frequently amused himself by making up jokes and stories, but his mind outraced his social skills. Whenever he told a joke or a story, he would always muff the punch line, or even forget to have a punch line at all, or he would swallow it in a mumble, or would laugh heartily in the middle of the story (Grotta 12). An English journalist once described Tolkien as a cross between Bilbo and Gandalf (Grotta 10). "Tolkien's love for the green, plush countryside of Oxfordshire and his distaste for the polluting extravagances of a world directed toward its own final destruction find representation in the contrasts between the Shire and Mordor of The Lord of the Rings trilogy" (Kolich 529). August Kolich says that Tolkien seems to be telling the reader that we cannot hide in our hobbit holes no matter how tempting that idea might be, for if we do, "the terror of modern self-destruction" is inevitable (Kolich 530).

Tolkien would not normally be classified as a comic or humorous writer. Nevertheless, there are many qualities that make his writing appropriate to this volume. His writing tends to be whimsical, satiric, ironic, parodic, and incongruous. His writing is both awesome and aweful. His fantasies are fantastic, and his fables are fabulous. And his characters are genuinely funny in both their looks and their demeanor. In an essay entitled "On Fairy-Stories," Tolkien explains something of his literary intentions: "The peculiar quality of the 'joy' in successful fantasy can...be explained as a sudden glimpse of the underlying reality or truth" (Kolich 522).

Tolkien created the Hobbits for his small children, as a holiday tradition. On Christmas, each of the Tolkien children would receive a letter from Father Christmas containing the adventures of Bilbo and his friends. Near the fireplace where Father Christmas had left the letter, his dirty footprints could be seen on the floor (Salu and Farrell 34). The faces of the hobbits are good-natured but not beautiful. They had round bright eyes, and red cheeks, and their mouths were shaped especially for laughing, eating, and drinking. "And laugh they did, and eat, and drink, often and heartily, being fond of simple jests at all times, and of six meals a day (when they could get them). They were hospitable and delighted in parties, and in presents, which they gave away freely and eagerly accepted" (qtd. in Grotta 10). Tolkien was himself a hobbit, for he said,

> I like gardens, trees, unmechanized farm lands. I smoke a pipe and like good, plain food--unrefrigerated--but I detest French cooking. I like--and even dare to wear in these dull days--ornamental waistcoats. I'm fond of mushrooms out of a field, have a very simple sense of humor (which even my most appreciative critics find tiresome). I go to bed late, and get up late, when possible. (qtd. in Grotta 10)

Tolkien's "fairy stories" are varied in characterization and action, detailed in description, and expansive in philosophy. Tolkien was constantly revising, correcting, and amending manuscripts in the interest of verisimilitude. August M. Kolich suggests that, "not since Milton has any Englishman worked so successfully at creating a secondary world." Tolkien's Middle-earth is a side-show of strangely humorous characters including hobbits, elves, dwarfs, orcs, and the men of Westernesse. Although his writing covers the full 10,000 years of Middle-earth history, he concentrates on the Third Age, the age which sets the stage for Man, which is to come in the Fourth Age (Kolich 521).

This Third Age is about three millennia in length and is treated chronologically in five books: 1). The Hobbit (1937), 2). The Fellowship of the Ring (1954), 3). The Two Towers (1955), 4). The Return of the King (1956), and 5). The Silmarillion (1977), with the middle three novels commonly referred to as "The Trilogy."

The Hobbit (1937) presents a world in which the forces of evil might at times overcome the forces of good, a world in which the true hero is not strong, or handsome, or aristocratic, or victorious in combat (Lurie 157).

In The Hobbit there is a humorous description of what hobbits look like.

> They are inclined to be fat in the stomach; they dress in bright colours (chiefly green and yellow); wear no shoes, because their feet grow natural leathery soles and thick warm brown hair like the stuff on their heads (which is curly); have long clever brown fingers, good-natured faces, and laugh deep fruity laughs (especially after dinner, which they have twice a day when they can get it). (The Hobbit 2)

Bilbo Baggins's adventure is also humorous from its beginning on: "Bilbo Baggins was standing at his door after breakfast smoking an enormous long wooden pipe that reached nearly down to his woolly toes (neatly brushed)" when Gandalf came by (The Hobbit 3).

The Hobbit establishes the battle between the forces of evil, led by the bad wizard Sauron, and the forces of good, led by the good wizard Gandalf. During the Elder days, Sauron tricked the Elf smiths at Eregion into making seventeen rings of power. Seven were to be for dwarfs; nine were to be for men; and then there was made "One Ring," the ring with the most power because it controls all of the other rings. But this One Ring is very seductive and very dangerous, because its power can be misused, and in fact tends to corrupt whoever is wearing the ring. So Gandalf wants the ring to be worn by someone who is not easily corruptible, and the race which is least corruptible on the earth is the race of hobbits (Kolich 523).

Hobbits are what Robley Evans calls "improbable heroes." They are "improbable" because they are unadventurous, small, peaceful, and devoted to such creature comforts as two dinners. But these hobbits have a large share in carrying on the adventures of Tolkien's novels because they are capable of great fortitude and endurance. Their inner, or hobbit-strength is related to their, "commitment to a greater vision of life than oneself" (Evans 15).

Hobbits resemble both an English countryman and a rabbit. They love peace and quiet and good tilled earth. Their lives are well ordered and the pastoral countryside is their favorite place to be. They are skillful with such tools as forge-bellows, watermills, or handlooms, but dislike anything more complicated than that. They have a strong sense of tradition, and are totally unobtrusive. Bilbo Baggins is small, frail, and under four feet tall. He loves the comfort of his own hole and has no sense of adventure. A Hobbit, especially Bilbo, would not abuse the power of the One Ring. Bilbo's transformation, his growing up, is the main point of The Hobbit. Gandalf knows that hobbits, although they tend to be quite domestic and unassuming, are capable of incredible feats. When a really difficult job needs to be done, a hobbit often has just the right size and temperament to do it properly, as when Bilbo climbs into a small passageway in Lonely Mountain to face the dragon, Smaug (Kolich 525).

Bilbo is a hero, though a reluctant one, and whenever he is provoked to action, he responds in a pragmatic, steadfast, and effective way. As Thorin says to Bilbo, "There is more in you of good than you know.... Some courage and some wisdom, blended in measure. If more of us valued food and cheer and song above hoarded gold, it would be a merrier world" (Kolich 525). Gandalf says it this way, "Mr. Baggins has more about him than you guess, and a deal more than he has any idea of himself" (Kolich 525).

The humor of The Hobbit can be seen as Bilbo confronts various other characters. When Bilbo first encounters the wizard Gandalf, for example, he describes him as being quite old and a bit decrepit looking, with an extremely long white beard and immense black boots. He addresses the wizard with "Good Morning," and Gandalf looks back at him through extremely bushy white eyebrows and asks, "What do you mean? ...Do you wish me a good morning, or mean that it is a good morning whether I want it or not; or that you feel good this morning, or that it is a morning to be good on?" (Hobbit 13).

When Bilbo confronts the evil dragon Smaug, he addresses the dragon thus, "O Smaug, the chiefest and Greatest of Calamities," and Smaug commends Bilbo on, "nice manners for a thief and a liar." What follows is an example of slippery talk. Bilbo dances around the subject of his true identity by calling himself a number of power-titles, such as, "he that walks unseen, ringbearer, luckwearer, clue-finder...." This, according to Bilbo, is "the way to talk to dragons" (Hobbit 190).

In "Farmer Giles of Ham" (1952), Tolkien's humor very much reflects his training as a linguist. Here Tolkien frequently plays the Latin against the Anglo Saxon as the story develops. When he first introduces the farmer, Tolkien says, "In full his name was Aegidius Ahenobarbus Julius Agricola de Hammo; for people were richly endowed with names in those days." He later adds, however that "in the vulgar form: he was Farmer Giles of Ham" ("Farmer Giles" 125). The dragon in this story was given a Latin name, "Chrysophylax Dives," and even Farmer Giles's sword was called "Caudimordax." This was, "the famous sword that in popular romances is more vulgarly called Tailbiter" ("Farmer Giles" 147).

Tolkien liked to play with Latin terminology. Farmer Giles's King was named "Augustus Bonifacius rex et basileus" ("Farmer Giles 161). After Farmer Giles had conquered the dragon, he was given the title of "Giles, Dominus de Domito Serpente, which is in the vulgar Lord of the Tame Worm" (183). At the end of the story, Giles becomes the King of his Little Kingdom of Ham. "He was crowned in Ham in the name of Aegidius Draconarius; but he was more often known as Old Giles Worming" ("Farmer Giles" 184). The final word of this story is "Finis," but of course Tolkien must translate this word for his readers as "The End" ("Farmer Giles" 187).

Farmer Giles's sword was humorous in that it would not stay sheathed if there was a dragon within five miles. The parson tried, for example, to sheath the sword with the following results: "He picked the sword up carefully and tried to put it back in the sheath;

but it would not go so much as a foot in, and it jumped clean out again, as soon as he took his hand off the hilt" ("Farmer Giles" 146).

In order to become a proper knight, Farmer Giles had to obtain some armour.

> The blacksmith shook his head. He was a slow, gloomy man, vulgarly known as Sunny Sam, though his proper name was Fabricius Cunctator. He never whistled at his work, unless some disaster (such as frost in May) had duly occurred after he had foretold it. Since he was daily foretelling disasters of every kind, few happened that he had not foretold. ("Farmer Giles" 149)

The armour which the blacksmith prepared for Farmer Giles was rather strange, and in it, Farmer Giles cut a humorous figure.

> They had stitched on the rings so that they overlapped, each hanging loose over the one below, and jingle they certainly did. The cloak did something to stop the noise of them, but Giles cut a queer figure in his gear. They did not tell him so. They girded the belt round his waist with difficulty, and they hung the scabbard upon it; but he had to carry the sword, for it would no longer stay sheathed. ("Farmer Giles" 152)

When Farmer Giles meets the Dragon, the language of the Dragon is not that which would be expected of a Dragon. The Dragon says, "Excuse my asking, but were you looking for me, by any chance?" The Dragon later says, "Those are your holiday clothes, I suppose, A new fashion, perhaps?" Farmer Giles's felt hat had fallen off and his grey cloak had slipped open; but he brazened it out ("Farmer Giles" 154).

Tolkien confesses that The Lord of the Rings began as an exercise in "linguistic esthetics." "Not only does he play endless verbal games and make inside philological jokes, but he has created and annotated a series of self-justifying alphabets and languages" (Stimpson 4). The Lord of the Rings is a journey and a quest. One of the songs of Middle-earth says,

> The Road goes ever on and on
>> Down from the door where it began.
> Now far ahead the Road has gone,
>   And I must follow, if I can....

As Bilbo says to Frodo, "It's a dangerous business...going out of your door" (Duriez 13). When Sam asks, "Don't adventures ever have an end?" he is able after a moment's reflection to answer his own question, "I suppose not. Someone else always has to carry on the story" (Evans 14).

At first Tolkien had no intention of writing The Lord of the Rings, but Stanley Unwin, Tolkien's publisher, wanted another book about the Hobbit. Tolkien responded that, "Mr. Baggins began as a comic tale among conventional Grimm's fairy-tale dwarves, and got drawn into the edge of it--so that even Sauron the terrible peeped over the edge. And what more can hobbits do?" (Helms Silmarils ix-x). The Lord of the Rings was therefore an afterthought, an accident of the success of The Hobbit. Once committed to the task of writing The Lord of the Rings, however, Tolkien decided to write a, "really long story that would hold the attention of readers, amuse them, delight them, and at times maybe excite them or move them" (Helms Silmarils xiii).

The Lord of the Rings trilogy is not designed for people who cannot come to grips with an author who would go to elaborate lengths to create an entire history, geography, literature, and language as a background for his work of fiction. Ironically however, it is precisely these features of The Lord of the Rings which readers find most appealing (Duriez 8). Tolkien's readers and Tolkien's characters are worlds apart. Nevertheless readers can identify with the characters' feelings, and share their dreams and fears. "Heart in mouth, we follow Frodo and Sam on their struggle through the ash-pits of Mordor towards Mount Doom." Duriez continues, "The presiding virtue of Tolkien's tales is hope. Always, even in the longest and darkest night of Middle-earth, there glimmers a light--however small and flickering--of humanity, compassion and courage" (Duriez 9-10). These are features which would help to define Lord of the Rings not as a tragedy, but as a comedy, since the literary world acknowledges that a "comedy" may be mostly serious or even grim, but the story moves from ironic chaos to a renewal of human hope and spirit.

Tolkien follows Horrace's statement that, "the aim of the poet is to inform and to delight; he will succeed at the former only insofar as he succeeds at the latter" (Flieger viii). Flieger believes that Tolkien puts us in touch with the supernatural by opening our eyes to wonder. Tolkien gives us a glimpse into the universe of beauty and meaning and purpose, but then Flieger goes on to say, "Whether there really is such a universe is less important than the undeniable truth that we need one badly" (Flieger viii).

The Fellowship of the Ring (1954) is the first book in The Lord of the Rings trilogy. It begins in pretty much the same way as The Hobbit does. There is a party in which Bilbo is celebrating his "eleventy-first birthday." It is a huge party during which he gives away most of his wealth and possessions that he obtained during his quest to the Lonely Mountain. In The Fellowship of the Ring, Bilbo passes the one ring, the ring of invisibility on to his nephew, Frodo. Frodo, like Bilbo, is a reluctant hero, and as such he is the perfect candidate to be the guardian of the ring. His band of adventurers includes Samwise, Pippins, and Merry (Kolich 525).

The Two Towers (1955) is the second book in The Lord of the Rings trilogy. In this book all of the hobbits are separated as they all have to perform their individual tasks of glory. Sauron's flaw is that he cannot understand how it would be possible for someone having the power of the One Ring to want to destroy it rather than using this power to enhance his own glory; Sauron therefore fails to understand the mind of his opponent. Sauron thus underestimates the hobbits. He believes that they are too small and insignificant to be able to harm him. Therefore, Frodo's journey into Mordor catches Sauron off guard. Sauron has a garrisoned fortress, and seems to be ready for anything but the brave, self-sacrificing dedication of a four-foot-tall hobbit, and this proves to be his vulnerability (Nilsen 1126).

Frodo and Sam were separated in The Two Towers, but they are reunited in The Return of the King (1956), the third and last book in The Lord of the Rings trilogy. In The Return of the King, Sauron's demonic rule has been total and relentless, and the Mere of Dead Faces has become a surrealistic and horrible battlefield where the faces of the fallen soldiers are mirrored in the swamp water. "Here nothing lived, not even the leprous growths that feed on rottenness. The gasping pools were choked with ash and crawling muds, sickly white and grey, as if the mountains had vomited the filth of their entrails upon the lands about" (Kolich 529). This visual imagery describes what the entire world would become if Frodo failed his task. At the end of The Return of the King, Frodo does finally succeed in throwing the ring into the fires of Mount Doom. This ending of the Lord of the Rings trilogy is what Tolkien calls a "Eucatastrophe," or a "good catastrophe." "The joy of...victory blends with the forlorn sadness created by the terrible cost of all catastrophes." The hobbits, dwarfs, elves, and wizards all sail off into "the Uttermost West" (Kolich 529). Like all of Tolkien's fairy stories, The Lord of the Rings demonstrates that, "the virtues of every happy ending are poised with the potential of absolute defeat. There are no easy solutions, no dream or hope that is not qualified by the possibility of a nightmarish defeat" (Kolich 530). "Through Frodo's effort, Middle Earth is freed from the demonic will of Sauron, who vanishes into the sky. But the scars remain" (Kolich 529).

Tolkien loved to parody linguistic scholarship, and at one point he discusses the possible sources and meanings of "Hey Diddle Diddle." One possible source is ancient Greek, but Tolkien also suggests five other possible sources. The best evidence forces

Tolkien to conclude that Bilbo Baggins wrote it. Tolkien explains that the reason the cat and the cow and the little dog, and the dish and the spoon are all behaving so strangely is that there is an old inn beneath an old grey hill in Middle-earth where they brew a very powerful beer. And this inn is located very close to where they found the "Red Book of Westmarch." Tolkien explains that the expression "hey diddle diddle" is "Bilbo's onomatopoeic representation of the fiddle's squawk," and Tolkien even goes so far as to say that Bilbo is not the original source, for in fact he received much of his inspiration from an even earlier source--Gondor, thus providing an excellent satiric exposé on the way in which literary scholarship is conducted, and the nature of the evidence and the conclusions (Helms "Gleanings" 141). Unaware that many of Tolkien's writings are parodies of scholarly writings, many scholars have traced Tolkien's words back to legitimate sources. In an article entitled "Tolkien's Elvish," Thomas Donahue points out that various scholars have traced Tolkien's "alcar," "amhar," "anar," "certa," and "cor" to Kenyan words meaning "glory," "world," "sunk" "rune," and "circle" respectively. Different scholars have traced these same words to Welsh words meaning "reindeer," "greensward," "uncultivated," "cart," and "dwarf" respectively. And these scholars, unlike Tolkien, were making no attempt to be humorous, and were in fact unaware of each other's work. Donahue says that Tolkien, "just knew that some day someone would spend a real nerd of an afternoon with Celtic and Kenyan dictionaries, proving <u>nothing</u>." In fact, Donahue suggests that chasing these words back and forth through the <u>Lord of the Rings</u> is, "like wading waist deep in a wet and soggy marsh. In fact there is such a marsh in the story, a bog certain to mire hobbits down waist-deep. The name of the marsh is "Wetwang" (Donahue 64).

The Red Book of Westmarch is a parody of the Welsh version of <u>The Red Book of Hergest</u>. In addition to being a parody of the book, it is a parody of the poor research methods of its editor, William F. Skene. Tolkien presents <u>The Red Book of Westmarch</u> as if it were a true document. It is a red, leather-bound volume, and it contains a large number of verses. It is, "an exquisite parody of scholarly introduction to a long-lost manuscript." Tolkien takes a mock scholarly stance as he theorizes about the authorship of the manuscript, the sources, and the linguistic relationships in what Helms describes as, "one of the best jokes in recent literary history." The preface parodies the methods of textual and philological scholarship, and many of the poems parody scholarly themes that were common during Tolkien's time. "With loving humor, he greatly deflates some of the more puffy parts of two things dear to him, his hobbit creations and his profession of literary and philological scholarship" (Helms "Gleanings" 126). <u>The Red Book of Westmarch</u> contains many doggerel poems about elves, gold-lust, journeys into an unknown land, and passage into the West. Much of the humor of the poems comes from the readers' recognition of the limitations of the Hobbits' grasp of the subjects they wrote about.

Tolkien was using a kind of self-parody by passing off his bad poetry as having been written by Hobbits. But in addition to being a writer of bad poetry, Tolkien is also an amused critic, as he explains exactly why the poems are so bad. The Hobbits considered strange words and rhyming or metrical tricks as poetic virtues (Helms "Gleanings" 128). Tolkien criticizes the Hobbit verses, which are actually his own verses once removed, and this adds another level of irony as Tolkien criticizes the less-than-keen poetic minds of the Hobbit poets (Helms "Gleanings" 128). Even though the poetry is written in doggerel form, it is skillfully contrived and it presents excellent comic morals such as, "never kick a stone troll's behind, for you'll break your foot." The Hobbits especially enjoyed writing comic "circle" poems, such as "Errantry." These circle poems returned to their own beginnings, and therefore they may be recited continuously until the hearers finally revolt. In his preface, Tolkien compares the comic circularity of the poems to the comic circularity of the Hobbits themselves (Helms "Gleanings" 134).

According to Verlyn Flieger, the Silmarillion (1977) was written before, during, and after both The Hobbit and The Lord of the Rings. It subsumed The Hobbit, and engulfed The Lord of the Rings and turned the Hobbit sequel into an extension of the broader mythology. Though it took fifty years for Tolkien to write, he never finished it, and it was not published during his lifetime (Flieger x). Flieger notes that this body of myth, legend, folktale, and song imitated the primary mythologies of the world by later being collated, edited, and published in bits and pieces (Flieger xii). According to Flieger, "the governing principles of Tolkien's world are explicit in The Silmarillion, implicit in The Lord of the Rings. Without the one, the other could not exist" (Flieger xiii).

Ironically, although The Silmarillion is the most significant of Tolkien's works, it would have no audience at all had it not been for The Lord of the Rings. It is damped by biblical language and by a narrative that is, "constructed along the lines of the Old Testament." Time magazine said that Tolkien's prose here sounds like, "a parody of Edgar Rice Burroughs in the style of The Book of Revelation. The New York Review of Books predicted that many more people would purchase the book than would read it all the way through (Flieger xiv). Flieger's Splintered Light discusses The Silmarillion. Flieger's title is based on the fact that, "myth and language create one another." Flieger agrees with Owen Barfield that, "the polarities of light and dark, perceived through and expressed in language, define one another and develop Tolkien's world" (Flieger xx).

According to Neil Isaacs and Rose Zimbardo, The Lord of the Rings is filled with, "narrative power, droll charm, intricate playfulness, and physical and psychological detail." All this is substantially absent from the solemnly sacred text of The Silmarillion (Isaacs and Zimbardo 7). A major paradox of The Silmarillion is that, "those who are most eagerly drawn to the book as a major object of their cultic attention will most easily be put off by its remoteness from The Lord of the Rings" (Isaacs and Zimbardo 6).

Tolkien wrote The Silmarillion because he was enchanted by words. In Rivendell, Frodo hears a song sung in the Sindarin language about Elbereth Star-Kindler. Frodo is enraptured by "the elvish craft" of the song. "The beauty of the melodies and the interwoven words in the Elven-tongue...hold him in a spell.... Almost it seemed that the words took shape, and visions of far lands and bright things that he had never yet imagined opened out before him" (Helms Silmarils xii). Tolkien shows us time and time again that there are no easy solutions, no dreams or hopes that are not also fraught with the possibilities of nightmarish defeats. Aragorn, the first human ruler of the Fourth Age of Middle-earth says to his friends, "Ours is but a small matter in the great deeds of this time" (Kolich 530).

J. R. R. Tolkien Bibliography

Beard, Henry N. and Douglas C. Kenney. Bored of the Rings: A Parody of J. R. R. Tolkien's The Lord of the Rings. New York, NY: New American Library, 1969.

Donahue, Thomas S. "Tolkien's Elvish." WHIMSY 1 (1983): 64-65.

Duriez, Colin. The Tolkien and Middle-earth Handbook. Tumbridge Wells, England: Monarch, 1979.

Evans, Robley. J. R. R. Tolkien. New York, NY: Warner Paperback Library, 1972.

Flieger, Verlyn. Splintered Light: Logos and Language in Tolkien's World. Grand Rapids, MI: Eerdmans, 1983.

Grotta, Daniel. The Biography of J. R. R. Tolkien: Architect of Middle-Earth. Philadelphia, PA: Running Press, 1976.

Helms, Randel. "Last Gleanings from the Red Book: Scholarly Parody in The Adventures of Tom Bombadil." Tolkien's World. Boston, MA: Houghton Mifflin, 1974, 126-47.

Helms, Randel. Tolkien and the Silmarils. Boston, MA: Houghton Mifflin, 1981.

Isaacs, Neil D. and Rose A. Zimbardo, eds. Tolkien and the Critics: Essays on J. R. R. Tolkien's The Lord of the Rings. Notre Dame, IN: University of Notre Dame Press, 1968.

Kolich, August M. "J. R. R. Tolkien." British Novelists, 1930-1959. Ed. Bernard Oldsey. Detroit, MI: Gale, 1983, 520-530.

Lurie, Alison. "Heroes for Our Time: J. R. R. Tolkien and T. H. White." Don't Tell the Grown-Ups: Subversive Children's Literature. Boston, MA: Little, Brown, 1990, 156-168.

Nilsen, Don L. F. "J. R. R. Tolkien." Encyclopedia of British Humorists, Volume II. Ed. Steven H. Gale. New York, NY: Garland, 1996, 1122-1131.

Salu, Mary, and Robert T. Farrell, eds. J. R. R. Tolkien, Scholar and Storyteller: Essays in Memoriam. Ithaca, NY: Cornell University Press, 1979.

Scholz, Kristin. "J. R. R. Tolkien and his Comical Imagery, Character Description, and Scenarios." Unpublished Paper. Tempe, AZ: Arizona State University, 1989.

Stimpson, Catharine R. J. R. R. Tolkien. Columbia Essays of Modern Writers, No. 41. New York, NY: Columbia University Press, 1969.

Tolkien, J. R. R. "Farmer Giles of Ham." The Tolkien Reader. New York, NY: Ballantine Books, 1966, 121-188.

Tolkien, J. R. R. The Hobbit; or There and Back Again. London, England: Allen and Unwin, 1937; Boston, MA: Houghton Mifflin, 1938.

John C. A. B. Morton (Beachcomber) (1893-1979)

J. B. Priestley considers Beachcomber to be, "one of the best-known and most-loved humorous writers of our time, keeping up those high spirits during about forty years of daily journalism." Beachcomber was influenced by the writing style of Rabelais. Beachcomber's journalistic style can be seen in the "Epic of Mr. Justice Cocklecarrot and the Twelve Red-bearded Dwarfs":

> Mr. Justice Cocklecarrot began the hearing of a very curious case yesterday. A Mrs. Tasker is accused of ringing the doorbell of a Mrs. Renton, and then, when the door is opened, pushing a dozen red-bearded dwarfs into the hall and leaving them there. For some weeks Mrs. Renton had protested by letter and by telephone to Mrs. Tasker but one day she waited in the hall and caught Mrs. Tasker in the act of pushing the dwarfs into the hall. Mrs. Renton questioned them, and their leader said, "We know nothing about it. It's just that this Mrs. Tasker pays us a shilling each and every time she pushes us into your hall." "But why does she do it?" asked Mrs. Renton. "That's what we don't know," said the spokesman of the little men. (qtd. in Priestley 110)

This same reporting style can be seen in "The Unsavoury Saga of Captain Foulenough":

> News has just come in of the appearance of Captain Foulenough at Lady Drain's cocktail-party. He is said to have entered by the tradesman's entrance. Suspicions were aroused when he seized the arm of Aurora Bagstone, and holding it to his lips, in the manner of a flute-player, kissed it up and down the scale, from wrist to elbow. Aurora remarked afterwards, "One does like to know who is kissing one, after all." Meanwhile, Mr. Cowparsleigh had been flung down the steps of Mrs. Woodle's house in Crabapple Mews, and has threatened to make his uncle call in her overdraft.

(qtd. in Priestley 111)

Priestly remarks that "When Beachcomber is at his best--and his best is enormous--he is not a direct satirist but is the inspired creator of glorious and instantly laughable nonsense that just has some seasoning of satire" (Priestley 112).

John C. A. B. Morton (Beachcomber) Bibliography

Priestley, J. B. "Wodehouse, Beachcomber, and Waugh." English Humour. New York, NY: Stein and Day, 1976, 108-114.

Dorothy Leigh Sayers (1893-1957)

Dorothy Sayers's adventures of Lord Peter Whimsey and his butler, Bunter have been termed "escapist literature" (Carlson xi). Lord Peter Whimsey is the peer-detective who drops his g's, and shuffles his "aint's" and "gonnas" around in his mellifluous sentences. Whimsey is elegantly aloof, and his butler, Bunter, knows that it is, "inexcusable to contradict his master's speech" (Carlson 116). Dorothy Sayers, like Sir Arthur Conan Doyle, typically writes a rambling plot containing "intriguingly bloated but rich characterizations" (Carlson 111). Lord Peter Whimsey is a peer but he is also a sleuth. The humor is benign, and it is made light and gay by this "properly hedonistic peer" (Carlson 115). Dorothy Sayers's Clouds of Witness (1926), her The Unpleasantness at the Bellona Club (1928), and her The Five Red Herrings (1931) are the novels which established Dorothy Sayers's reputation both in England and in America. In contrast to such Arthur-Conan-Doyle titles as "The Adventure of the Devil's Foot," "The Adventure of the Engineer's Thumb," and "The Adventure of the Red Carbuncle," which are "resplendently mysterious," Dorothy Sayers's titles are playful and sly, and less malignant: "The Bibulous Business of a Matter of Taste," "The Piscatorial Farce of the Stolen Stomach," and "The Incredible Elopement of Lord Peter Whimsey." Furthermore, the crimes in Sayers's novels tend to be victimless crimes (Carlson 116).

Dorothy Leigh Sayers Bibliography

Carlson, Richard S. "Benign Humor and Escape Literature: Wodehouse, Doyle, and Sayers." The Benign Humorists. New York, NY: Archon, 1975, 111-123.
Sandoe, James, ed. Lord Peter: A Collection of All the [Dorothy Sayers] Lord Peter Wimsey Stories. New York, NY: Harper and Row, 1972.

Aldous Leonard Huxley (1894-1963)

William Donnelly said that Aldous Huxley's writings, "crackled with lively modern personalities." He talked about Huxley's, "easy and good-humored erudition, his vividly sketched characters, and his detached ironic handling of the intrigues of his plots" (Donnelly 553). Huxley's early satirical novels create a strange blend of the comic novel and the novel of ideas. They are both brilliant and cynical in their approach (Donnelly 554). Huxley's dystopic Brave New World is more subtle and detached than is George Orwell's dystopic 1984. George Orwell's true feelings are obvious, while Aldous Huxley hides his true feelings behind a mass of contradictory opinions and emotions that are expressed in such satiric novels as Crome Yellow, Antic Hay, and Brave New World. The tone of these novels is somewhere in between anger and amusement, between disgust and fascination, but it can never be precisely fixed or characterized. Some Huxley critics have said that a major flaw in his writing is his "inability to adopt a clear position" (Greenblatt 78). But Huxley's writing displays a verbal brilliance, a precocity, and an encyclopedic mind (Greenblatt 82).

J. W. Burrow compares Aldous Huxley to H. G Wells, and to George Bernard Shaw, but adds that Huxley himself would have hated the comparison (Trenz 202). Peter Bowering says, "No one since Swift has viewed the totality of human activity with such complete skepticism." And Jerry W. Carlson divides Huxley's novels into two genres. Carlson considers Huxley's earlier novels to be "carnivalesque;" in these novels a number of characters are presented in conflict, but the novel does not attempt to resolve these conflicts. According to Carlson, Huxley's later novels are "apologues;" these novels present persuasive arguments that are disguised by the novel format (Trenz 203).

According to Brandan Trenz, Crome Yellow and Antic Hay are both written in the carnivalesque style. Jerry W. Carlson adds that Crome Yellow (1921) combines the grotesque with the beautiful, but tips the balance in the direction of the grotesque (Trenz 203). Crome Yellow is a satire targeting the venerable English institute of the week-end party. The party is held at a pleasant and isolated country estate; however there are sometimes reminders of the unpleasantnesses outside of the estate's walls, and these unpleasantnesses must be rationalized away:

> "At this very moment," Mr. Scogan went on, "the most frightful horrors are taking place in every corner of the world. People are being crushed, slashed, disemboweled, mangled: their dead bodies rot and their eyes decay with the rest. Screams of pain and fear go pulsing through the air at the rate of eleven hundred feet per second. After travelling for three seconds they are perfectly inaudible. These are distressing facts; but do we enjoy life any the less because of them? Most certainly we do not.... A really sympathetic race would not so much as know the meaning of happiness. But luckily, as I've already said, we aren't a sympathetic race. (Crome 77)

The residents of Crome Manor are thus aware of evil and suffering, but it does not affect them personally. It only establishes an ironic contrast to their little isolated society (Greenblatt 80).

Much of the charm of Crome Yellow derives from Huxley's wonderfully humorous caricatures, and Huxley's concise phrases which sum up his characters. "Barbeque Smith was a name in the Sunday papers. He wrote about the Conduct of Life. He might even be the author of What a Young Girl Ought to Know" (Crome 7). "Mary Bracegirdle's face shone pink and childish.... Her short hair, clipped like a page's, hung in a bell of elastic gold about her cheeks" (Crome 10). "In appearance Mr. Scogan was like one of those extinct bird-lizards of the tertiary" (Crome 10). In Crome Yellow, the self-conscious novelist Denis Stone makes a number of amusing and unsuccessful attempts to win the love of Anne, who is a shallow but charming hedonist. Stone finally sends a telegram to himself saying that he is needed back in London.

The lack of plot in Crome Yellow is an important characteristic of all of Huxley's satires. Huxley is writing about people who have lost all ability to act in any meaningful way. They can't create, or produce anything. They do nothing but expound clever theories, or make witty comments. They have all retreated into the artificial world of Crome Manor, and have thus cut themselves off from other humanity. As Denis says, "We are all parallel straight lines" (Greenblatt 82).

Many critics of Crome Yellow are disturbed by the strange and distracting "History of Crome" that appears throughout the novel in the form of intermittent anecdotes. Sisirkumar Ghose, for example, considers the Histories to be, "delicately spiced, funny, but altogether an interior piece. It has really no connection with the rest of the novel" (qtd. in

Greenblatt 83). Stephen Greenblatt, however, feels that these "Histories" are not distractions at all, but contain significant messages about the spirit of the times of each century mentioned.

The first "History" takes place in the seventeenth century, and tells about the laying of the massive cornerstone of the mansion. Sir Ferdinando Lapith was the builder and the architect, and he was so obsessed with the vulgarity of bodily functions that he built the water closet at the top of the house, so that it could be the room closest to heaven. He provided this water closet with a picture window that commanded an extensive and noble view of the countryside. The walls of this chamber were lined with bookshelves containing the most noble specimens of books. The satire here is targeting the seventeenth-century preoccupations with nature, and the lengths that these people would go to be natural (Greenblatt 83-84).

The second "History" takes place in the eighteenth century, and tells a strange story about Hercules Lapith, a dwarf who contrived to shield himself from the "scorn of the vulgar and insensitive giants" by marrying a beautiful Italian dwarf princess, and by converting Crome Manor into a miniature world of dwarf servants, tiny furniture, a string of Shetland ponies for rabbit hunting, and so on. The former lord of the country estate called Crome was only four feet tall, and he gathered a group of midgets around him to ride terriers in their hunt for rabbits (Donnelly 553). The dream of Hercules is shattered when their son, Ferdinando, turns out to be of "normal gigantic dimensions." So the story of Hercules, written in heroic couplets, is a delicate blending of irony and pathos in which Huxley targets the eighteenth century which Huxley felt was, "glorying in its artificiality, pleased with its pygmy stature" (Greenblatt 84-85).

Another "History" takes place in the nineteenth century, and is about the three beautiful daughters of Ferdinando. These girls are self-proclaimed romantics who are so completely immersed in meditations about Transcendence and the Soul that they totally ignore their physical existence. They wave away whatever is offered to them "with an expression of delicate disgust," saying, "Pray, don't talk to me of eating. We find it so coarse, so unspiritual, my sisters and I. One can't think of one's soul while one is eating" (Crome 94). Ironically, however, these sisters gorge themselves in secret with an, "earthy enthusiasm they would be ashamed to admit to in society" (Greenblatt 85). Huxley is here satirizing the nineteenth-century preoccupation with false modesty and superficial knowledge.

Another "History" takes place in the twentieth century, and suggests that it is better to travel by Tube than by Bus, because a person travelling by bus can't avoid seeing a few random works by God, such as the sky, an occasional tree, or some flowers in window boxes. A person travelling by Tube, on the other hand, sees nothing except things made by man such as iron riveted into various shapes, rows of concrete structures, and patterned expanses of tiles. Huxley is here satirizing the twentieth-century tendency to turn its back on nature, and to exalt "the falsehood which is Crome." Here Huxley is targeting the whole notion of progress, because, "Crome is no different in 1920 than in the seventeenth century, in that man has had no success in learning to live in and with nature" (Greenblatt 86-87).

According to Steven Greenblatt, then, these "Histories" are central to the satiric message of the novel.

> Behind a front of nostalgia and sheer fun, Huxley is presenting an allegory of man's relationship with nature through the centuries. From the insolence of the builder of Crome in the seventeenth century, through the delicate artificiality of the eighteenth, through the spurious romanticism of the nineteenth, and into the hyperintellectualism of the twentieth, man has been living on bad terms with nature and with himself. (Greenblatt 86)

William Donnelly says that in Huxley's later works, Antic Hay (1923), Those

Barren Leaves (1925), and Point Counterpoint (1928) the, "pattern of diverse characters discussing their theories of life, of sexual misadventures, of erudition and satire, remains the same" as in the earlier novels (Donnelly 553). Those Barren Leaves (1925) is the last of Huxley's purely carnivalesque novels (Trenz 204). Sybille Bedford says that Antic Hay (1923), "is intended to reflect--fantastically, of course, but none the less faithfully--the life and opinions of an age which has seen the violent disruption of almost all the standards, conventions, and values current in the previous epoch" (Trenz 204). Stephen Greenblatt considers Antic Hay to be, "significant only in its insignificance." There are no plot, no unified adventures, no meaningful actions, no climax, no dénouement. It is a, "gruesome picaresque piece with separate scenes connected only by the consistent tone of bitterness and disillusionment and by the central characters" (Greenblatt 90). Coleman is a satanist who devotes himself to masochistic debauchery. He cultivates the most unpleasant habits in order to attain the delicious pleasure of punishing himself, and he even cultivates a belief in God so that he can truly know the anguish of the sin he is wallowing in. Shearwater is a physiologist who is totally devoted to science. His experiments involve albino guinea pigs that peer through the meshes of their hatches with red eyes like the rear lights on bicycles, and a cock into which Shearwater has grafted an ovary, which comes out not knowing whether to crow or cluck, and some beetles which have had their heads cut off and replaced by the heads of other beetles and don't know whether to obey their brains or their genital organs (Greenblatt 92).

Beneath the slick surface of wit in Antic Hay there is a brilliant, a powerful, a cold and bitter examination of a sick society. Antic Hay is a brutal slap at accepted values. Many critics have commented on the comicality of the novel. Philip Henderson says that it is "all rather good fun," but Stephen Greenblatt says that the laughter is, "alternatingly delirious, hysterical, sinister, cynical, diabolical, false--anything but happy." One of the characters in the novel remarks, "Everyone's a walking farce and a walking tragedy at the same time. The man who slips on a banana-skin and fractures his skull describes against the sky, as he falls, the most richly comical arabesque" (Antic 275). The main theme of Antic Hay is the disintegration of values, and the resultant meaninglessness of existence. The characters run pall mall from one scene of debauchery to the next in a frantic search for diversion. The title of Antic Hay comes from Christopher Marlowe's couplet, "Men like satyrs grazing on the lawns / Shall with their goat-feet dance the antic hay" (qtd. in Greenblatt 89).

In Point Counter Point (1928) Huxley explains how each of the eccentric characters in his discussion of ideas "picks up on a challenging theme and distorts it through the narrowness and obsessiveness of his own solipsistic orientation, like instruments in an orchestra (Donnelly 553-554). Jerry W. Carlson says that in Point Counter Point each character is placed in counterpoint to other characters, and thus is, "seen and heard with a multiplicity of eyes and ears" (Trenz 204). Philip Quarles, a character in Point Counter Point, is unable to determine which vision is truly his own:

> Pascal had made him a Catholic--but only so long as the volume of Pensées was open before him. There were moments when, in the company of Carlyle or Whitman or bouncing Browning, he had believed in strenuousness for strenuousness' sake. And then there was Mark Rampion. After a few hours in Mark Rampion's company he really believed in noble savagery.... But always, whatever he might do, he knew quite well in the secret depths of his being that he wasn't a Catholic, or a strenuous liver, or a mystic, or a noble savage. (Point 204-205)

Brave New World (1932) is a dystopic novel which uses "reductio ad absurdum" reasoning by proposing a scientific "utopia" in which compulsory euphoria, mandatory sex, hypnotic consumerism, and mindless conformity are imposed on the majority of the human race by a cadre of social engineers. Huxley's Brave New World was influenced by Evgeny Zamyatin's We (1920), a novel which described a totalitarian future in a dehumanized society. We showed Zamyatin's disenchantment with the new Soviet state, but he also had an unflattering description of England as he satirized middle-class conformity (Locher 551). The satire of Brave New World darkens after the light tone of the opening chapters (Donnelly 554). In Brave New World, Huxley is concerned that advances in science, medicine, and technology may not in fact be advances at all, because he felt that they were not balanced by equal responsibility on the part of those who would use them. Huxley says that Brave New World started out as a parody of H. G. Wells's Men Like Gods, but it gradually took on a life of its own, "and turned into something quite different from what I'd originally intended." Jerry Carlson says that the end result is a cautionary tale (Trenz 204). Brave New World demonstrates Huxley's foremost fear that the adoption of Henry Ford's assembly-line techniques would result in a race of robot-humans in what he ironically termed the "Model-T Utopia" (Trenz 205).

Brave New World takes place in the year 632 A.F. (After Ford), at which time copulation is no longer needed because a new process has been invented by the name of "Bokanovsky budding" whereby one sperm and ovum can yield ninety-six almost identical children. Very early in life, these children are divided into social and working classes, and sleep-teaching is used to teach them proper functions in society. By the time they reach adulthood, "Citizens perform their tasks without complaint and are rewarded with material comforts, with leisure activities such as 'Centrifugal Bumble Puppy' and 'Obstacle Golf,' and by guiltless group sex" (Trenz 204). They are further kept in check by being served liberal doses of an opium-like drug called "soma" (Trenz 205).

Brave New World is a bitterly funny futuristic novel in which Huxley employs delightful acerbity and urbane wit to indict twentieth-century Western culture by carrying contemporary trends to shocking, amusing, and fantastic extremes. Huxley could see that science and technology were advancing to a stage where they would soon be able to "solve" all of the social and material problems of mankind, but only at the expense of individual freedom, and beauty, and a sense of purpose. An important ironic message of Brave New World is that in spite of mechanized reproduction and constant conditioning, individualistic traits and inclinations still persist. Another important message, however is that in "Brave New World" many (perhaps most) people would actually prefer to live in such a society. "The savage" is the term used to refer to John, and this term is both ironic, and true, for it is John who has known the beauty of great art because of his reading of Shakespeare, and it is also John who has known the pain of loneliness because he has been ostracized by the natives on account of his light skin and his mother's loose morals. Lenina Crowne, whom John considers to be a goddess and a symbol of ultimate beauty is described by Stephen Greenblatt as, "generally a comic figure but with some tragic overtones" (Greenblatt 99).

In an article entitled "Our Ford, Our Freud and the Behaviorist Conspiracy in Huxley's Brave New World," Jerome Meckier suggests that the novel is satirizing technology in general, but in addition, there are two more specific targets, Henry Ford, who felt that the assembly-line was the answer to all problems, and Sigmund Freud, who felt that it was family relationships that were responsible for most neurotic behaviors. Brave New World used assembly-line techniques to produce a world of people who were happy with their lot, and these same techniques bypassed natural parenthood--and therefore got rid of most neuroses in the process. As Huxley says in the novel,

> Our Ford--or Our Freud, as, for some inscrutable reason, he chose to call himself whenever he spoke of psychological matters--Our Freud had been the first to reveal the appalling dangers of family life. The world was full of fathers--was therefore full of misery; full of mothers--therefore of every kind of perversion from sadism to chastity; full of brothers, sisters, uncles,

aunts--full of madness and suicide. (<u>Brave</u> 43-44)
The mass production of bottle babies, therefore, meant the "consequent abolition of the family and all the Freudian 'complexes' for which family relationships are responsible" (qtd. in Meckier 37).

In the Foreword to <u>Brave New World</u> Huxley said that he gave John only two choices:

> The Savage is offered only two alternatives, an insane life in Utopia, or the life of a primitive in an Indian village, a life more human in some respects, but in others, hardly less queer and abnormal. At the time the book was written, this idea that human beings are given will in order to choose between insanity on the one hand and lunacy on the other, was one that I found amusing and regarded as quite possibly true. (<u>Brave</u> vii)

In <u>Brave New World</u> the basic goal of the state is to provide happiness for everybody, even at the cost of imagination, discovery, free will, poetry, and pure science. There is a constant source of promiscuity and meaningless games, and there is liquid air, and television, and radio, and a vibro-vacuum massage, and boiling caffeine solution, and there are hot contraceptives, and eight different types of scent in every bedroom. There is even a wonder drug named "soma" that offers all of the advantages of Christianity and alcohol, but none of the disadvantages. The people in this world are, "doomed to be happy."

The tension in <u>Brave New World</u> is mainly caused by the confrontation of two equally powerful conflicting philosophies. The outcome of the debate is a stalemate. Near the end of the novel, the Savage argues with the World Controller, Mustapha Mond. The Savage tells Mond that what he needs is "something with tears." He argues that "nothing costs enough here." Mond responds that what the Savage is claiming is "the right to be unhappy," and John agrees that this is the case. Then Mond goes on. "Not to mention the right to grow old and ugly and impotent; the right to have syphilis and cancer; the right to be lousy; the right to live in constant apprehension of what may happen to-morrow; the right to catch typhoid; the right to be tortured by unspeakable pains of every kind." There is a long silence, and the Savage says, "I claim them all." Mond merely shrugs his shoulders and says, "You're welcome." The argument, then has no clearcut winner. There is as much of an irresolvable conflict after the argument as there was before (Greenblatt 100).

<u>After Many a Summer Dies the Swan</u> (1939) is a science-fiction novel in which the social satire lightens the burden of serious philosophizing. It is set in a millionaire's castle of the San Simeon sort, and satirizes Hollywood cemeteries, American science, sexual naiveté, and British scholarship among other things (Donnelly 554). <u>Ape and Essence</u> (1948) is a satire about a post-apocalyptic society of beastly human survivors, who are ruled over by an animal-like priesthood (Donnelly 554).

Sybille Bedford noted that decades after the initial publication of <u>Brave New World</u>, Huxley was alarmed at the degree of accuracy in which he had captured the future of American society (Bedford xx). In <u>Brave New World Revisited</u> (1960), Huxley expressed his alarm that the world was much closer to what he had depicted in his dystopian novel written twenty-nine years earlier than he had expected. "The prophecies made in 1931 are coming true much sooner than I thought they would" (Trenz 205). Gregory Castle gives some specific examples. Castle notes that sheep and other animals have been cloned, just as Huxley had envisioned. In addition, animals have been mass-produced; the Central London Hatchery has produced ninety-four chicks from a single egg. In addition, today contraception is possible by taking a pill and can be as unobtrusive as a capsule inserted under the skin. In <u>Brave New World</u>, women strap birth control belts to their waists. Today, depression is alleviated by any number of drugs, from Prozac to Valium to alcohol.

In <u>Brave New World</u> Soma was given to Huxley's protagonists, and this Soma took them on a virtual vacation of the mind, sparing them the realities of everyday life (Castle EV10).

Aldous Leonard Huxley Bibliography

Bedford, Sybille, ed. "Introduction." <u>Brave New World</u> by Aldous Huxley. London, England: The Hogarth Press, 1984, vii-xxii.

Castle, Gregory. "In Some Ways We're Already There, <u>Brave New World</u>." <u>The Arizona Republic</u> (24 August, 1997): EV10.

Donnelly, William. "Aldous Leonard Huxley." <u>Encyclopedia of British Humorists, Volume I</u>. Ed. Steven H. Gale. New York, NY: Garland, 1996, 552-555.

Greenblatt, Stephen Jay. "Aldous Huxley." <u>Three Modern Satirists: Waugh, Orwell, and Huxley</u>. New Haven, CT: Yale Univ Press, 1965, 75-102.

Huxley, Aldous. <u>Antic Hay</u>. New York, NY: Doran, 1923.

Huxley, Aldous. <u>Brave New World</u>. New York, NY: Harper and Brothers, 1932.

Huxley, Aldous. <u>Crome Yellow</u>. (1922). New York, NY: Bantam, 1959.

Huxley, Aldous. <u>Point Counter Point</u>. New York, NY: Harper and Row, 1928.

Kessler, Martin. "Power and the Perfect State: The Study of Disillusionment as Reflected in Orwell's <u>Nineteen Eighty-Four</u> and Huxley's <u>Brave New World</u>." <u>Political Science Quarterly</u> 72.4 (1957): 565-577.

Locher, Frances C. Ed. <u>Contemporary Authors, Volume 105</u>. Detroit, MI: Gale Research, 1982, 551.

Meckier, Jerome. <u>Aldous Huxley, Satire, and Structure</u>. London, England: Chatto and Windus, 1969.

Meckier, Jerome. "Our Ford, Our Freud and the Behaviorist Conspiracy in Huxley's <u>Brave New World</u>." <u>Thalia</u> 1.1 (1978): 35-60.

Trenz, Brandon. "Aldous (Leonard) Huxley." <u>Contemporary Authors, New Revision Series, Volume 44</u>. Ed. Susan M. Trotsky. Detroit, MI: Gale, 1994, 200-208.

John Boynton Priestley (1894-)

J. B. Priestley attended Cambridge University in 1919 where he won a considerable reputation as a parodist. From Cambridge he went to London, where he became the adviser for a large publishing house. Here he wrote witty reviews of contemporary novels, and became one of the favorite writers for <u>The Daily News</u>. Since then he has written a book entitled <u>English Humour</u>, and an anthology entitled, <u>Fools and Philosophers</u> (1925), which is made up of great comic passages from English literature. Priestley has written two biographies in the <u>English Men of Letters Series</u>, and both of these deal with authors devoted to comedy--<u>Thomas Love Peacock</u> (1927), and <u>George Meredith</u> (1926). Priestley has also written <u>The English Comic Characters</u> (1925), which is a study of the great comic figures in English Literature. According to Dorothea Mann, Priestley's <u>Adam in Moonshine</u> (1927), "is evidence of the author's own rollicking delight in telling a story" (Mann 242).

<u>The Good Companions</u> (1929) swept the country when it was published, and it became a good omen for shops, tea rooms, and other establishments to name themselves "The Good Companions." The immediate success and popularity of <u>The Good Companions</u> has been compared to the immediate success and popularity of Charles Dickens' <u>The Pickwick Papers</u>, and like <u>The Pickwick Papers</u>, it is filled with humor, has a wealth and variety of characters, and an originality of nomenclature. But there are differences between Dickens and Priestley as well. "Dickens burlesques his characters slightly so that you may

appreciate how funny they are. Priestley's characters are funny in being themselves and you realize in them just as they are how they differ from the norm which spells happiness and success for a man or woman" (Mann 243).

In Angel Pavement (1930) every character is a humours character who would have been very easy to burlesque. There is the well-meaning but unprogressive employer, and the careful and anxious cashier; there is Miss Matfield, who lives in her club for women, and who finds it difficult to make her life seem romantic to her companions; and there is Poppy, the ambitious cockney typist; there is also Turgis, the drab clerk who escapes from the dinginess of his life into rose-colored romantic dreams; and there is the office boy who wants to be a detective, and who is therefore always late in returning from his errands because he has been shadowing people. But unlike Dickens's characters, Priestley's characters are not so burlesqued nor caricatured, because Priestley's writing is in the tradition of realism (Mann 243). Dorothea Mann considers Miss Matfield to be one of the best women characters Priestly has depicted. "She is picked out with the beaming light of comedy which shows her folly without sentiment or pathos" (Mann 245).

Unlike Shaw, Wells, Belloc, Chesterton, and Bennett, Priestley was not a man of opinion. Dorothea Mann noted that these other authors were overwhelmed by dogmatism. She says that, "they always expressed themselves with utmost certainty. They changed their opinions at times but they were equally certain about their new opinions." Mann admits that Priestley was also a reformer at heart, and that he could become dogmatic, but his wit, his humor and his comedy have the effect of softening the dogmaticism (Mann 246).

John Boynton Priestley Bibliography

Mann, Dorothea Lawrence. "J. B. Priestly: Servant of the Comic Spirit." Bookman 73
     (1931): 241-246.
Priestley, J. B. English Comic Characters. New York, NY: Dutton, 1925.
Priestley, J. B. English Humour. New York, NY: Stein and Day, 1976.
Priestley, J. B. Fools and Philosophers: A Gallery of Comic Figures. London, England:
     John Lane, 1925.

Jean Rhys (1894-1979)

In After Leaving Mr. Mackenzie (1931) Sasha, "gets into the driver's seat of male power and adventure." She takes a sarcastic and brutal pleasure in her false position. A gigolo sees her fur coat, and assumes that she is rich and would be interested in his services, but Sasha is in disguise. Sasha relishes her position of inverted power and status, and especially enjoys the possibility of wounding someone who is, "just sensitive enough to get hurt," so the gigolo is somewhat jarred when Sasha praises his teeth in an act of play and mockery (Little 181).

The middle-age Sasha of Good Morning Midnight (1939) employs unsparing satire as she attacks her symbolic white male employer.

> Well, let's argue this out, Mr. Blank. You, who represent Society.... There
> must be the dark background to show up the bright colours. Some must cry
> so that others may be able to laugh the more heartily. Sacrifices are
> necessary.... Let's say that you have this mystical right to cut my legs off.
> But the right to ridicule me afterwards because I am a cripple--no, that I
> think you haven't got. And that's the right you hold most dearly, isn't it?
> You must be able to despise the people you exploit. (qtd. in Little 180)

Jean Rhys Bibliography

Little, Judy. Comedy and the Woman Writer: Woolf, Spark, and Feminism. Lincoln, NE: University of Nebraska Press, 1983.

Archibald Gordon Macdonell (1895-1941) SCOTLAND

An anonymous writer for The Springfield Sunday Union and Republic reviewed Archibald Macdonell's humorous sketches of social and sporting life, and said that they were, "brightly amusing if not new." This writer also said that Macdonell's work is filled with wit and has an ironically intellectual edge (Batts Encyclopedia 713). A different anonymous writer for the Times Literary Supplement dealt with the use of humor by various English novelists during the previous fifty years. Batts notes how this article is important to show how Macdonell fits in with other British humorists of the period (Batts Encyclopedia 713).

Archibald MacDonell achieved humor by his characterizations, his development of action, his descriptions, and his dialogues. "The humour is at its most illuminating when the beams of exaggeration intersect with these four, producing respectively caricature, then burlesque and farce through action, and often parody by description and dialogue. [MacDonell's] humour is supported by a texture of tropes, one-liners, puns, metaphors, similes, understatements, and allusions" (Batts England 49). John Batts notes, however, that much of MacDonell's humor is based on local color, and much of it has therefore been eroded by time and distance.

In an article in the Encyclopedia of British Humorists, John Batts says that Macdonell wrote at least four books that should be of interest to the student of literary humor: England, Their England (1933), How Like an Angel! (1934), Lords and Masters (1936), and The Autobiography of a Cad (1938). England, Their England (1933) is a parody of D. H. Lawrence's England, My England. Here MacDonell makes the point that in England, Scotts are considered to be outsiders. This book is considered a "straightforward novel" by some critics, a "fictionalized autobiography" by others, and "a satire" by still others. John Batts notes that England, Their England weaves in and out of its autobiographical framework, and has the curious Celtic combination of being about a Welshman urging a Scot to write a book about the English. Donald Cameron, the protagonist, is perplexed about the extraordinary contradictions of the English character. The book is episodic in nature as it tells about comic incidents happening to comic characters. The humorous names of some of the minor characters deserve special note. There is the Right Honorable Bob Bloomer, Captain de Weston-fallow, and Miss Prudence Pott. The novel is filled with lovable, old-fashioned English eccentrics who are devoted to endless cricket or to empty social rituals. "In strange contrast to these active young men was the vast, amorphous mass of American tourists who never had anything to do. They eddied about the streets in aimless shoals, like lost mackerel, pointing out celebrities to each other and always getting them wrong; taking endless photographs of obscure Genevese citizens in mistake for German Chancellors or Soviet Observers." (qtd. in Batts England 48).

John Batts notes that the mild satire of MacDonell's England, Their England lacks the consistent satiric bite of MacDonell's younger contemporary Evelyn Waugh. Nevertheless, Batts Considers England, Their England to be Macdonell's "humorous masterpiece" (Batts Encyclopedia 713). J. B. Priestly describes the writing in England, Their England as, "thinking in fun, while feeling in earnest." The theme of the book is the English at work and at play, and the satiric edge to the writing often shows through. The novel has an episodic structure that allows for much of the comic incident and also allows the development of comic characters. Mrs. O. K. Poop is the wife of an American stockbroker, and there are also caricatures of upper-class twits and politicians, and a trio of young diplomats. Many of these characters have, "double-barrel names and the aplomb of a Rolls-Royce." In the novel, the humor is especially sustained in the description of the cricket match in Chapter 7, and the golf game in Chapter 8. The novel amply illustrates that Macdonell has a gift for exaggeration and parody (Batts Encyclopedia 712).

Macdonell uses humor throughout How Like an Angel! (1934) to poke fun at English conventions, both domestic and national (Batts Encyclopedia 712). In Lords and Masters (1936), Macdonell's fiction is infused with satire against the background of European re-armament. Jack Crawford is much like a Waugh character. He is a cavalry officer and at the same time a super cad. The hero of this novel is Edward Percival Fox-Ingleby; about his father, he complains, "he developed a painful knack of espousing lost causes, and, worse, of subscribing to them" (Batts Encyclopedia 712). The Autobiography of a Cad (1938) is humorous, but it also has its ponderous moments (Batts Encyclopedia 712)

Archibald Gordon Macdonell Bibliography

Batts, John Stuart. "Archibald Gordon MacDonald." Encyclopedia of British Humorists, Volume II. Ed. Steven H. Gale. New York, NY: Garland, 1996, 711-714.
Batts, John Stuart. "England, Their England as National Humor." WHIMSY 6 (1988): 48-50.
Pritchett, V. S. "The Comic Element in the English Novel: 5. The Last Forty Years." Listener LI, 1320 (June 17, 1954): 1047-1049, 1053.
"Scotsman Humorously Portrays the English." The Springfield Sunday Union and Republican (August 6, 1933): 7E.
"The Uses of Comic Vision: A Concealed Social Point in Playing for Laughs." Times Literary Supplement, 3054 (September 9, 1960): ix.

Joe Randolph Ackerley (1896-1967)

Joe Ackerley's life was a rich source for black humor. "He began with every advantage--money, brains, spectacular good looks--and ended up a rather solitary eccentric, his life wrapped up in that of his dog" (Allen 4). Ackerley wrote about this absurdity of life that "Once upon a time, I was a handsome young man, regarded as one of the most promising writers of the day, much sought after by everyone, involved in countless exciting love affairs--and now look at me, grey-haired and going deaf, a dog lover and grovelling about...in a public park" (Parker 268). Brooke Allen said that Ackerley's writings tended to be black, sometimes farcical, humorous, and brutally honest (Allen 6).

Even though all of Ackerley's books have elements of black comedy of a deeply sardonic nature, Brooke Allen considers Hindoo Holiday: An Indian Journal (1932) to be Joe Ackerley's only "straightforwardly comedic" work. Hindoo Holiday contains a series of portraits, especially a portrait of the Maharajah himself. According to Brooke Allen, it is very funny, but at the same time a very moving portrayal (Allen 4).

My Dog Tulip: Life with an Alsatian (1956) is a detailed depiction of the life of Ackerley's dog, Queenie. Queenie is "a spoiled, capricious, feminine beauty," who resembles very closely many of the possessive women that Ackerley had known for many years; the book is deeply misogynistic (Allen 4-5). Tulip is portrayed as a typical romantic heroine. Ackerley extols her beauty and her goodness, but he also mischievously details all of her bodily functions, including the sexual and the scatological.   The book is intentionally written to provoke (Allen 5).

We Think the World of You (1960) is a fairy story for adults. It is also an ironic indictment of conventional Christian customs, and an argument for the individual, no matter how eccentric this individual may be, over the conventions of society and the family. It is written much in the manner and tone of Samuel Butler. The novel is narrated by Frank, a middle-aged civil servant, and Frank's judgments are frequently colored by his own neuroses. His misogyny and his misanthropy make him a comically unreliable narrator (Allen 5). As Ackerley himself put it, "Frank is an unstable, maladjusted man, obsessed and frustrated, and the story is subtly contrived to turn completely over so that his 'persecutors' can be viewed in a sympathetic light" (Parker 349). Brooke Allen considers My Father and Myself (1969) to be both deeply moving, and ludicrously funny (Allen 5).

Joe Randolph Ackerley Bibliography

Allen, Brooke. "Joe R(andolph) A(ckerley)." Encyclopedia of British Humorists, Volume I. Ed. Steven H. Gale. New York, NY: Garland, 1996, 3-6.
Parker, Peter. Ackerley: A Life of J. R. Ackerley. London, England: Constable and Co., 1989.

Archibald Joseph Cronin (1896-1981) SCOTLAND

In 1923, A. J. Cronin received his medical degree from Glasgow University. At this time he said that he discovered not only that he had passed, but that the governing board had given him honors as well. He felt proud even though his friend, "Doggy Chisholm" had passed as well, and had said, on seeing the results of the examination, "Slight lachrymal-gland activity this morning, Doctor. May I prescribe a hundredth of atropine? Or a good glass of beer?" Cronin commented on the incident, "He could afford to be lighthearted. His father, provost of Winton, owned the Laughlan steelworks" (Commire 66). A. J. Cronin wrote many darkly humorous pieces that later became movies, including The Citadel (1938), Hatter's Castle (1941), The Keys of the Kingdom (1944), The Spanish Gardener (1957), and The Green Years (1946). A. J. Cronin also wrote Jupiter Laughs (1940), which is a three-act play (Commire 47).

Archibald Joseph Cronin Bibliography

Commire, Anne. "A(rchibald) J(oseph) Cronin." Something about the Author, Volume 47. Detroit, MI: Gale Research Co., 1987, 47-72.

Kate O'Brien (1897-1974) IRELAND

See Nilsen, Don L. F. "Kate O'Brien." Humor in Irish Literature: A Reference Guide. Westport, CT: Greenwood, 1996, 156.

Clive Staples Lewis (1898-1963) IRELAND

Peter Schakel points out that there are many clues that C. S. Lewis's various writings are intended as satires. First of all, they are filled with ironies, and some of these ironies are gentle while others of them are not so gentle. Instead of becoming a prince and the heir to the White Witch, for example, Edmund is seized as her prisoner. Another irony is that Eustace, who has such a high opinion of himself, cannot even be given away as a slave. In addition to this, consider the disparaging descriptions of the 1920s flappers in The Pilgrim's Regress. Also consider Ransom's difficulty in translating Weston's unreasonable philosophy into the language of Malacandra in Out of the Silent Planet. This passage is highly reminiscent of Gulliver's struggle to make the Houyhnhnms understand English culture in part 4 of Gulliver's Travels. Consider also the humorous satire targeting modern thought and values throughout That Hideous Strength, especially the acronym N.I.C.E., which stands for the diabolical organization named "National Institute for Co-Ordinated Experiments" (Schakel 665). The Great Divorce has many examples of ironic humor, including the satire on the liberal theology of the bishop who considers the crucifixion to have been a disaster, and said, "What a tragic waste...so much promise cut short" This same bishop decides not to remain in Heaven because it lacks "an atmosphere of free inquiry" and because he has to be back in Hell on Friday to read a paper to a theological society on the topic of what Jesus's mature views might have been if he had not died so young. In Chapter 14 of Prince Caspian there is a satiric targeting of the schools and in chapter 4 of The Voyage of the "Dawn Treader," there is a satiric targeting of economic development. In Chapter 3 of The Last Battle there is also a satiric targeting of socialism and liberal theology (Schackel 666). In addition, there are many humorous and satirical names in The Chronicles of Narnia. In Prince Caspian and The Voyage of the "Dawn Treader" there are Trufflehunter, Trumpkin, Nikabrik, the three Bulgy Bears, Pattertwigg, Glenstorm, Wimbleweather, and Reepicheep. Prince Caspian also talks about Miss Prizzle, and The Voyage of the "Dawn Treader" about Coriakin, Ramandu, Eustace, Pug, Gumpas, and the Dufflepuds. The Horse and His Boy talks about Puddleglum. And The Magician's Nephew talks about Digory and Fledge.

The names in The Pilgrim's Regress: An Allegorical Apology for Christianity, Reason and Romanticism (1933) show that it is an allegory; Vertue, Media and Gus Halfways, Reason, Mr. Sensible, his servant Drudge, Mother Kirk, Mr. Broad, Mr. Wisdom, and Savage are examples. God is represented by the Landlord, and this is where John begins his journey. However after many trials and tribulations of his journey, John finally realizes that it is the Landlord (God) that he has been searching for the whole time (Kilby 28). In The Pilgrim's Regress, John (Everyman) makes a journey toward death. The island he is trying to reach is unattainable, even though he attempts many routes to attain it. His paths lead him through various sensuous and rationalistic sins; however, it is through the efforts of Mother Kirk (Christianity) and Reason that John is able to perceive that Desire (his goal) is not only unattainable, but that striving for it can only end in death. In his journey, John encounters the brown girls who represent the temptations of the flesh. He also meets Mr. Enlightenment, the Clevers, and Sigismund Enlightenment who represent the temptations of the intellect. In turn, he repudiates neo-Anglicanism, Classicism, Humanism, Marxism, and Fascism (Glover 67). The connections between C. S. Lewis's Pilgrim's Regress and John Bunyan's Pilgrim's Progress are obvious, and since Pilgrim's Regress is an allegory the author uses stock characters who personify virtues and vices. The journey itself consists of loosely integrated episodes as the narrator passes through various struggles on his way to salvation. Pilgrim's Regress offers more discourse than dialogue or narration, and is weak in the characterization, ambiguity, suspense, excitement, and vividness of description that is usually found in non-allegorical fiction (Glover 68). Excitement and suspense are minimal since the reader is never in any serious doubt that John will "see the light" (Glover 70).

Interest in the narration centers upon Lewis's imaginative forces as he places obstacles to impede John's conversion, and in his imagination as he skillfully writes how

John overcomes these obstacles (Glover 70). The novel also has its touches of humor, irony, and wit, as can be seen in Sensible's speech to Virtue (Pilgrim's Regress IV, 4): "Sense is easy, Reason is hard. Sense knows where to stop with gracious inconsistency, while Reason slavishly follows an abstract logic wither she knows not. The one seeks comfort and finds it, the other seeks truth and is still seeking" (qtd. in Glover 69). This same type of humor and irony can also be seen in many of the descriptive passages, as in the early description of Claptrap by Mr. Enlightenment (Pilgrim's Regress II,1 37-38).

Doris Myers suggests that the characters in The Pilgrim's Regress are of two types: archetypal characters, and humors characters (Myers 22). The archetypal characters can be identified by their appearances and action, while the most significant features of the humors characters are their catch phrases. Virtue, Mr. Sensible, and Drudge are humors characters. Virtue likes to say "Keep to the road," which is a reference to the Middle Way, and, "The great thing is to do one's thirty miles a day," by which he means that we should be self-determined in our persistence. Mr. Sensible can be identified by his misapplied Latin and Greek quotations; this illustrates that he has had a superficial classical education. Drudge's catch phrase is "Coming, sir!" and this identifies him as a perfect servant (Myers 23).

Out of the Silent Planet (1938) is a satiric science-fiction novel in the tradition of H. G. Wells. Elwin Ransom, the protagonist, in many ways resembles C. S. Lewis, or his friend J. R. R. Tolkien, and the book is about Ransom's being taken to the planet Malacandra (Mars), and finding there an ancient utopia which contrasts distinctly with the planet from which Ransom had originated, Earth (Schakel Encyclopedia 663). Earth is called "the silent planet" because it is cut off from Heaven--Malacandra (Schakel Encyclopedia 664). In Out of the Silent Planet, Elwin Ransom is abducted by Weston, a world-famous physicist who wants to help mankind spread to the other planets, and Devine, who is interested in the exploitation of natural resources and inhabitants of the various planets (McGovern 300). Out of the Silent Planet deals with the, "struggle of the Oyarsa to free the silent planet from the grip of the Bent One" (Glover 74). Out of the Silent Planet, like Pilgrim's Regress is about the journey of a Christian who must struggle with vices (both internal and external) in a search for truth. In both cases the protagonist must meet the "ultimate reality" at the conclusion of his spiritual and physical journey. "Out of the Silent Planet is Pilgrim's Regress in a new key" (Glover 76). In case there might be any ambiguity of interpretation, Lewis provides the reader with correspondences, saying that the "eldila" are the angels; "Maleldil" represents Christ; "Old One" is the Father, and "Bent One" refers to Satan (Glover 79).

The story of Out of the Silent Planet quickly progresses from the uninviting environs of Sterk, England to the pink and purple landscape of Malacandra (Mars) with its unnaturally elongated topographical features. The reader is pulled along by Ransom in his "love of knowledge--a kind of madness" into adventures with the hrossa, the sorns, and Oyarsa (Glover 80). The hrossa are like large black furred humans; the sorns are huge intellectuals, and the pfifltriggi are the mechanics and the artisans of the planet. Weston and Devine kill one of the inhabitants of Malacandra, and are brought to trial. Ransom serves as the interpreter in the court, and thus Lewis is able to satirize Ransom's translations of Weston's florid expression of ideas from George Bernard Shaw's Back to Methuselah (1922), and Olaf Stapelton's First and Last Men (1931) into simple language (McGovern 300).

Much of the humor of Out of the Silent Planet comes from the fact that the animals are both like humans and not like humans, but it also comes from the old hross sleeping through the trial, and Ransom's mistaken identification of Hyoi's accoutrements, and Weston's defense. There are also moments in the book which are awe inspiring, such as when Ransom perceives that earth is a gap and space is an intense and radiant reality (Glover 81). There is also episodic humor as Ransom encounters the hrossa, the sorns, the pfifltriggi, and Oyarsa (Glover 82), and there is the sophomoric humor of Weston and Devine's trial. Weston is in a position where he cannot win, and Donald Glover therefore considers him a comic character whom the reader should not take too seriously as either a villain or a buffoon. Glover feels, in fact, that in Out of the Silent Planet Lewis uses humor to balance the seriousness of his underlying message (Glover 83).

Donald Glover suggests that the animals in Out of the Silent Planet are very reminiscent of medieval England. Much of the satire of this novel targets the machine-age emphasis on "scientific progress," and on the inhumane aspects of scientific research, the greed of modern materialism, and on how the individual is often sacrificed for the "good" of general "progress" (Glover 76). Lewis hints that Ransom, the protagonist, was based on a humorous depiction of a man he knew, and Donald Glover suggests that this man was J. R. R. Tolkien. Lewis said that he made Ransom a philologist, "chiefly to render his rapid mastery of Old Solar more plausible. His friends in That Hideous Strength are a literary critic (Dimble), a Doctor (Miss Ironwood), an unspecified scientist (MacPhee), a scholar's wife, a charwoman, and a bear" (Glover 77).

The narrator in The Dark Tower (1938) picks up exactly where the last sentence of Out of the Silent Planet ends, with the suggestion that the next trip for Ransom would be time travel. In Chapter 2, all that we see of the other world is a massive building with a square tower. As more evidence is given, this "dark tower" is shown to be the Library at Cambridge University. We are introduced to an old sex maniac named Knellie, who is a graduate of Oxford University and a don at Cambridge University. He humorously confuses the chronoscope for a movie projector and "Othertime" with blue film "art" (Glover 85). The "dark tower" of the title is a clear reference to the symbolic "ivory tower," which is seen as a closed and inbred type of academic society, where, "the chosen leader infects his workers--automata, who think they are sacrificing themselves for a noble purpose--to enter the new religion's more intense life." In this satire, these "drones" attempt to exert a power they don't have and are forced to live lives of futile experimentation (Glover 90).

The Screwtape Letters (1942) was a best-selling satirical novel both in Britain and in the United States. Screwtape is a senior bureaucrat in Hell, and he is writing these imaginary letters to Wormwood, his nephew, telling him about how he can lead his "patient" to damnation. The book is filled with wit, with satire, and with keen psychological and theological insights (Schakel Encyclopedia 663). The Screwtape Letters is a collection of thirty-one letters of advice and guidance written by an experienced devil named Screwtape to a novice devil named Wormwood, who is dealing with his first human "patient." Screwtape, for example, reminds Wormwood that, "forgiveness has no place in the lowerarchy" (McGovern 302). Lewis said that he used humor as a rhetorical device in The Screwtape Letters because, "humor involves a sense of proportion, a way of seeing ourselves from the outside." Humor gave Lewis the objectivity he needed to allow him to approach war and death that was imminent to his English readers of 1942. It allowed them to see the humor of their situations, and to lighten their burdens, and to give them hope. The book is symbolic for believers, because they believe in Hell, and the words therefore carry a sense of immediacy and truth. For non-believers, the book is an allegory. But the widespread popularity of the book is not based on either of these factors, but is rather based on the book's humor, which undercuts the humorless antagonist, Screwtape (Glover 124). The Screwtape Letters is epistolary in its presentation. In his letters, Screwtape mocks the inefficiency of Wormwood and the inexplicable aims and methods of the Enemy. The inversion of meaning is sustained through the entire book, and this provides a witty bite which produces the effect which Lewis was after (Glover 125). "We laugh at Screwtape's peevishness, temper, and cringing fear of blackmail much as we laugh at Rumpelstiltskin stamping his way out of the story given his name" (Glover 127).

The Screwtape Letters presents a satiric portrayal of Hell as a gigantic modern and tyrannical bureaucracy. But instead of a "Hierarchy," Lewis's Hell has a "Lowerarchy." It also has a Training College, a Records Office, a Department of Research, and a Department of Secret Police. Screwtape is in correspondence with Wormwood, and the reader must invert the meanings of almost everything in order to discover Lewis's true meaning. Screwtape writes, "Of course a war is entertaining. The immediate fear and suffering of the humans is a legitimate and pleasing refreshment for our myriads of toiling workers. But what permanent good does it do us unless we make use of it for bringing souls to Our Father Below?" (Lewis Screwtape 30). In Letter number eleven, Screwtape is disparaging human laughter, saying that it is a "disgusting and a direct insult to the realism, dignity, and austerity of Hell" (Lewis Screwtape 58). Screwtape also disparages Joy and Fun, because they belong to the Enemy--God. Screwtape nevertheless believes that Jokes and Flippancy can be of some value, especially with the British, "who take their 'sense of humour' so seriously that a deficiency in this sense is almost the only deficiency at which they feel shame" (Lewis Screwtape 59). In The Screwtape Letters, Lewis even went so far in his satire as to target himself. Screwtape says, "As long as [the patient] does not convert it into action, it does not matter how much he thinks about this new repentance. Let the little brute wallow in it. Let him, if he has any bent that way, write a book about it" (Lewis Screwtape 70).

Perelandra (1943) is a satiric science-fiction piece which describes a place that very much resembles the Garden of Eden, as Ransom goes to Venus to help the "Eve" of that newly-created world resist the evil that was certain to be there (Schakel Encyclopedia 664). Perelandra illustrates C. S. Lewis's contention that, "a writer can smuggle any amount of theology into the reader's mind if he colors it with romance." This novel is written tongue-in-cheek, and highlights Lewis's view of literature as an evangelical tool. Earlier in his life, Lewis had been drawn to the Venus myth. As a young man he had written a Venus poem, and had admired Botticelli's "Venus," seeing this pagan goddess as symbolic of the creative imagination. Lewis indicates that the myth in Perelandra is a multiple allusion. It alludes to Tor and Tinidril, to Adam and Eve, and to Ask and Embla. "It is the creation myth of a new world, pagan or Christian" (Glover 93). The movement of the plot is slow and deliberate as Ransom comes out as a victor, as he is resurrected and reborn. Perelandra is what Tolkien would term a "eucatastrophe" (Glover 95). In this novel, Satan (in the form of Weston) tempts Eve (in the form of the Green Lady), but Christian (in the form of Ransom) helps her to resist, and he finally symbolically kills Satan (Glover 96). The reader is won over to the fantasy by being given Ransom's reasonable and perhaps humorous acceptance of such fantastic sights as the Oyarsa and the coffin spaceship (Glover 97). In Perelandra, as in Out of the Silent Planet, there are what Glover calls "stylized categories of experience built up for symbolic purposes." These include the development of the companionably shaggy hrossa with their primitive cult of hunting, singing and victory celebrations, the elongated and intelligent sorns who live in towers, and the squat pfifltriggi who are earth-dwelling artisans (Glover 101). Lewis's fertile imagination can also be seen in his fun descriptions of the sea world, the Lady, the bubble trees, and the dragon (Glover 104).

In That Hideous Strength: A Modern Fairy-Tale for Grown-Ups (1945), Ransom confronts a world-threatening totalitarian power that is headquartered, ironically enough, in a small university town, just a bit smaller than the city of Oxford. Lewis's satiric dystopia is very similar to that of George Orwell's in 1984 which would be published just a few years later--in 1948. As in Orwell's novel, the hideous threat came from the new resources that were being developed in the sciences and the social sciences (Schakel Encyclopedia 664). In That Hideous Strength the National Institute of Coordinated Experiments (NICE) enlists the aid of a young sociologist named Mark Studdock, so that they can approach his wife, Jane, who dreams that she is able to locate the grave of Merlin, the Magician. NICE wants to find the grave, to revive Merlin, and to use his magical powers for their own ends. Elwin Ransom enters the novel as the director of a company that is able to locate Merlin before NICE is able to do so. In That Hideous Strength the satire targets college politics, bureaucracy, journalism, married life, academic ambition, education in general, "equality," obedience, language abuses, scientism, social science, vivisection, magic, the legend of King Arthur, and medieval cosmology in general (McGovern 300). Another of Lewis's satiric targets is the genre of science fiction, as when Weston explains to Ransom that the spacecraft is powered by, "exploiting the less observed properties of solar radiation" (McGovern 301).

Irony is an important aspect in That Hideous Strength, since it is used to keep the parallels from becoming stiff and repetitious. Lewis uses humor in this novel to relieve the tension and the seriousness that is necessarily associated with his theme of cosmic conflicts. "Neither humor nor irony had been used as extensively before by Lewis, with the possible exception of The Screwtape Letters" (Glover 118). Minor comic characters in the novel include Ivy, Mother Dimble, MacPhee, and the tramp; these characters stop just short of silliness. Merlin, in contrast, "emerges as Lewis's triumphant balance of the serious and comic." Glover feels that Lewis approaches Merlin's development "with humor and relish," and he also feels that the humor heightens the plot before the apocalyptic dinner.

> Humor can be found relieving the tension of the final dinner at Belbury as Lewis, using the convenient device of Babel, engages in some amusing linguistic creativity and allows various major characters to reflect on the meaning of these unearthly events. The humor is like the woman guest's laughter which turns into hysterics. There is humor of a gentler sort to be found in the jovial banter of the company at St. Anne's when they chide MacPhee for his skepticism at the last supper. Here, however, it is tinged with sadness of Ransom's parting and is relieved only by the anticipated reunion of Jane with Mark as the book closes. (Glover 119)

In the end, Mark finds himself not a brilliant convert, but rather a humble lover, "between the angels who are our elder brothers and the beasts who are our jesters, servants and playfellows." There are some critics (e.g., Robson) who consider the ending to be "opera bouffe" (Glover 122).

There is a disillusioned ghost in The Great Divorce (1945) who is certain that all the places he has visited are tourist traps. These places are Peking, Niagara Falls, the Pyramids, Salt Lake City, the Taj Mahal, and Hell. He has come to the conclusion that all of these places are advertisement stunts, and they are all run by the same people. "There's a combine, you know, a World Combine, that just takes an Atlas and decides where they'll have a Sight. Doesn't matter what they choose: anything'll do as long as the publicity's properly managed" (Lewis Divorce 50). The Great Divorce like The Pilgrim's Regress is an allegory containing stock allegorical characters. These characters are engaged in encounters which provide them with information about their spiritual futures. One notable aspect of the book is the speech mannerisms which Lewis uses in the development of particular characters. The Great Divorce is a satire which attacks the liberalization and demythologizing movement of elements within the church (Glover 129). Donald Glover feels that Lewis has used traditional humor in his ironic treatment of the fashionable lady who refuses to be seen in Heaven, "but the lightness of observations on board the bus and on arrival fade into the instruction which the fictional Lewis receives and passes directly to us." Thus, The Great Divorce may contain wit, and humor, and irony, but it is not a legitimate debate, because all of the evidence presented is on one side (Glover 130).

The Chronicles of Narnia are C. S. Lewis satires which were published between 1950 and 1956. They include The Lion, the Witch and the Wardrobe (1950), Prince

Caspian (1951), The Voyage of the "Dawn Treader" (1952), The Silver Chair (1953), The Horse and His Boy (1954), The Magician's Nephew (1955), and The Last Battle (1956). The four Pevensie children, Peter, Susan, Edmund, and Lucy are introduced in The Lion, the Witch and the Wardrobe. They go through the back of a magical wardrobe to enter the land of Narnia where they help the animal inhabitants and other mythical creatures to defeat the evil White Witch. In Prince Caspian, the Pevensie children come back again to Narnia to help restore Prince Caspian to his rightful thrown, which has been usurped from him by his evil Uncle, Miraz. In The Voyage of the "Dawn Treader" Edmund and Lucy and Eustace Scrubb, their cousin, accompany Prince Caspian on a quest to the end of the earth in search of the Seven Lost Lords. In The Silver Chair, Eustace and Jill Pole rescue Caspian's son from his underworld imprisonment. And in The Horse and His Boy, there are two horses and two children who save Archenland and Narnia from the attack of the evil King of Calormene. In The Magician's Nephew and The Last Battle, Lewis describes the land of Narnia, and tells about its destruction by the Calormenes, and about how the children and good animals entered into the "New Narnia" (Schakel Encyclopedia 664).

The Chronicles of Narnia are romances that are filled with detail, action, excitement, adventure, and suspense. They are a blend of such familiar things as human children, British foods, and ordinary animals with such unfamiliar things as a world separated from our own, animals who think and talk like people, and mythical characters. There is also a blend of the ideal, a pastoral paradise without factories or cities, and the reality of evil forces and evil characters. Some of Lewis's characters are fascinating, such as the Marshwiggles in The Silver Chair who are described by Peter Schakel as "dour but good-natured." Puddleglum is one of these Marshwiggles; Puddleglum is always able to find a dark center in any cloud, no matter how bright and silver-lined it seems to be. Peter Schakel says that the Dufflepuds in The Voyage of the "Dawn Treader" are very similar to the Marshwiggles in The Silver Chair (Schakel Encyclopedia 665). The Chronicles of Narnia have many allegorical qualities, but Lewis preferred not to call them allegories because for Lewis, the term "allegory" could only be used when abstract qualities such as Faith, Hope, and Charity are given human shape (Schakel Encyclopedia 664).

All of the books in The Chronicles of Narnia were written expressly for children. Narnia is a world other than ours that

> ...can be entered only by certain children and only at certain times. Narnia time runs independently of English time: a Narnian year may be much longer or much shorter than an English year. Through each of the stories strides Aslan, a huge lion. It is Aslan who creates Narnia (in The Magician's Nephew), sacrifices his life for one of the human children (in The Lion, the Witch and the Wardrobe), protects Narnia in times of trouble, and draws the curtain at the close of Narnian history (in The Last Battle). (McGovern 302)

Aslan is a Christ figure, but Aslan does not do what Christ did. Rather, Aslan does what Christ might have done if Christ came to a world like Narnia. This is why C. S. Lewis became so frustrated when his stories have been used in Sunday School classes, and when students have been told to turn from The Voyage of the "Dawn Treader," to the Book of Luke, and from The Last Battle to the Book of Revelation (McGovern 303).

The Lion, the Witch and the Wardrobe (1950) is the novel which should be read first in this series of seven "children's" stories. In numerous letters Lewis wrote of his attempts to catch his readers, of all ages, off guard. "If I am now good for anything it is for catching the reader unawares--thro' fiction and symbol." Lewis continues, "The fairy-tale version of the Passion in The Lion etc. works in the way you describe because--tho' this sounds odd--it by-passes one's reverence and piety.... Make it a fairy-tale and the reader is taken off his guard (Unless ye become as little children...)"(qtd. in Glover 131).

Glover notes, by the way, that the two special qualities which best describe Aslan are his playfulness and his solemnity (Glover 142). Kim Kellso points out another type of play that Lewis uses, language play. When Lucy is first brought to Narnia, she encounters a faun by the name of Mr. Tumnus, who asks her how she came to Narnia. When Lucy tells the faun that she came from the spare room, through the wardrobe, the faun is fascinated, and asks Lucy to tell him more about the Land of "Spare Oom" and the city of "War Drobe" (Kellso 9-10).

In Prince Caspian: The Return to Narnia (1951) the readers are yanked into Narnia off from a railway platform along with the Pevensies. The Old Narnians who are encountered include Trufflehunter, who says, "I'm a beast, I am, and a Badger what's more. We don't change. We hold on." There is Trumpkin who tends to do "whistles and whirligigs." Then there is Nikabrik, who is the Black Devil and can be compared to Miraz in Old Narnia. Finally, there are the three Bulgy Bears, Pattertwig the squirrel, Glenstorm the Centaur, Wimbleweather the giant, and Reepicheep. These characters show both the humor and the gravity of courtly life, and will be even more significant characters in the next novel (Glover 144). The nature of the magic in Prince Caspian can be seen when Lucy calls the trees to life but then feels that she "had just missed something." She felt, "as if she had spoken to the trees a split second too soon or a split second too late, or used all the right words except one; or put in one word that was just wrong" (qtd. in Glover 147-148). Glover feels that Reepicheep is the "masterpiece" of this book. With this character Lewis, "hits that happy balance between humor and awe which is reflected even in Aslan's capitulation over the renewal of the tail" (Glover 148). In fact, Glover feels that the humor in this novel revolves around Reepicheep and Trumpkin, and that this humor tends to puncture the solemnity of the various ceremonies described in the book. Even Reepicheep's name is humorous, as it suggests a mouse's "squeaks" and it also suggests "cheek." The Bulgy Bears are also humorous characters. They represent "all the sleepy, comfortable virtue of an uncomplicated existence, hibernating and sucking honey from their paws even as marshals in the list." Prince Caspian does a good job of creating a fantasy land in the new reign of Old Narnia--"a Narnia that would belong to the Talking Beasts and the Dwarfs and Dryads and Fauns and other creatures quite as much as to man. The imagination and fancy are reënthroned as the Pevensies end another adventure" (Glover 149). Prince Caspian ends with a long romp which results in the liberation of the young school mistress and the old nurse and the appropriate punishment of Miss Prizzle and the, "dumpy and prim little girls with fat legs." Reepicheep becomes a star with his deathbed revival as he insists on having a tail. The ending of the book is happy, but a bit frivolous, as Susan and Peter, who have grown old, pass beyond Narnia, and Edmund and Lucy return to help Caspian find the seven lost lords in the next book, The Voyage of the "Dawn Treader" (Glover 147).

The Voyage of the "Dawn Treader" (1952) begins as follows: "There was a boy called Eustace Clarence Scrubb, and he almost deserved it" (Lewis Voyage 9). The basic spirit of The Voyage of the "Dawn Treader" is that of limitless expectation and fulfilling adventure. The book reawakens the reader's imagination with its exotic experiences involving dragons, sea serpents, Midas pools, fallen and retired stars, and lands where both our worst nightmares and our fondest heart's desires come true. In this novel, Coriakin and Ramandu are very old, and very wise, and very serious; yet, "there is little threat that they will step in to spoil the fun." Lewis is playing with time in this novel. Eustace is made old before he is young, and in fact he must grow young by symbolically shedding his skin and by bathing, with both of these acts representing his rebirth not only physically but to wonder and to goodness as well (Glover 150). The setting of The Voyage of the "Dawn Treader" is both impressionistic and symbolic, and, "the comic account of Eustace's dawning realization that the claws and fire are his own, blunts our self-righteous 'that's only what he deserves' attitude and prepares the way for his conversion." Glover sums up his evaluation of this novel by saying, "the creative imagination has given us a feast of possibilities, touched with gentle humor" (Glover 152).

Eugene McGovern says that the title of Mere Christianity (1952) is not meant to be ironic. "It is a phrase Lewis found in the works of Richard Baxter, a Puritan theologian. The 'mere' refers to that which is common to the beliefs of all Christians" (McGovern 302). "Mere" really means then "basic," or "essential," and before C. S. Lewis's talks were collected in Mere Christianity, they had been broadcast as a series of four talks over the BBC during World War II (Schakel Encyclopedia 663). Lewis's Broadcast Talks, which became his Mere Christianity, contain a great deal of wit. Consider the following excerpt, for example: "A man who was merely a man and said the sort of things Jesus said wouldn't be a great moral teacher. He'd either be a lunatic--on a level with the man who says he's a poached egg--or else he'd be the Devil of Hell. You must make your choice" (Lewis Broadcast Talks 50-51; Mere Christianity Book 2, Chapter 3).

Lewis once playfully remarked about the title of The Horse and His Boy (1954) that it might attract the "ponybook" reader (Glover 157). Lewis is also playful in the novel itself. Glover considers his description of the Great Snow Dance to be both, "comic and stately, rhythmical, orderly, and yet childlike in its simplicity and compelling movement." This is Lewis's counter ritual to the Witch's distorted logic. It is silly, and it is pointless. It serves no purpose other than that of expressing joy in life, which, according to Glover, "no amount of logic can express, define, or deny" (Glover 170).

As noted earlier, Uncle Andrew in The Magician's Nephew (1955) is described by Glover as "a comic masterpiece." Uncle Andrew is neither a good magician nor a good man. "Humor tempers awe as we pass on to the first joke and comic misunderstanding which constitutes Uncle Andrew's punishment" (Glover 177). The gentle punishment he receives is to be "beaten" by the paws and trunks of the talking beasts. This "beating" is aimed more at his dignity than at his soul or his body (Glover 175).

In many ways the structure of The Magician's Nephew parallels that of The Lion the Witch and the Wardrobe in that, here again, the reader sees the ironic antithetical contrasts of magic versus true creativity, the negative power of Jadis and the destructive force of the "Deplorable Word" versus the creative force of Aslan's song, the queens versus their subjects, the magicians versus their servants, and Aslan's talking animal friends versus the other non-talking beasts. The main message of The Magician's Nephew has to do with the distinction between magic and true creativity. The magician is not able to create anything; rather, he can only move already-created things around, combining them in unusual or striking ways (Glover 172). The power of Jadis, the magician, is that of destructive brute force. She represents Satan. She is an Amazonian figure of strength who destroys anything which is in her way; she is corrupted by her own power. In contrast, Aslan, the symbol of true creativity and originality, sings a song that is movingly described by Lewis as the, "archetype of all earthly literary or musical creations carrying only that hint of Joy and exaltation which the one act of creation, symbolized in the unfolding of Narnia, excites in the children." Still another contrast is the cold, sterile, and dead land of Charn as compared with the warm, fecund and growing land of Narnia. There is a wooded area between these two worlds that is a "limbo of drowsy inactivity" (Glover 173). The dénouement of The Magician's Nephew is the trailing off into a "happy-ever-after" type ending. But this ending has a minimum amount of sentimentality. The book itself is filled with life and vigor and hope, and the problems are just enough to make the hope more significant (Glover 177). While The Magician's Nephew is filled with dark symbolism, based on reflections on a decadent contemporary life and the final spiritual apocalypse, The Last Battle (1956) emphasizes the simplicity of goodness. These two books are antithetical in tone and location, but they should nevertheless be considered companion pieces (Glover

179).

    Till We Have Faces (1956) has surprised and puzzled many of C. S. Lewis's readers because it is not like the rest of C. S. Lewis's canon. In Till We Have Faces, pagan myths are not treated simply as falsehoods, but are rather considered to be "profoundly important bearers of truth." "The ambiguity of the story, the psychological emphasis on feelings, the importance given to subjective interpretations of events, the viewing of a world almost entirely through the mind of one character (and that character a woman)--all of this was a surprise, coming from Lewis" (McGovern 303).

    Wit is a very important aspect of C. S. Lewis's humor, and some of this wit is epiphenal in nature--especially some of that in his Poems (1964). In one of his poems C. S. Lewis wrote about the tombstone of Martha Clay which which had been erected by her brothers in memory of their sister. It expresses the sentiment that finally she is "in peace," and her brothers are "in peace" as well (Lewis Poems 134).

    Because C. S. Lewis's novels are accessible to the general public, they have not attracted much attention from the most celebrated critics like Lionel Trilling and Edmund Wilson. This is probably not because the novels are insignificant, but is rather because "they do not need the explication and analysis that have been found necessary, or useful, in dealing with the fiction of Charles Williams, Flannery O'Connor, to mention two other writers whose Christianity had an important place in their work." But some critics have sneered at Lewis's novels. In Language and Silence (1967), George Steiner says that Lewis was one of "The Enemy," who "divide study of literature with the pursuit of elegance or science fiction." Steiner says that Lewis can be considered to be "The Enemy" because his work exhibits "coziness, frivolity, mundane cliques, the uses of culture for mutual adulation or warmth." Steiner continues by saying that Lewis's, "brow is middle, and his tone is suave" (McGovern 305).

    Throughout his lifetime, humor was a significant aspect of his life and his literary style. From his father, he developed a love of what his family called "wheezes," which were humorous anecdotes (Lewis Surprised by Joy 12). C. S. Lewis loved conversations that involved either an intense discussion of ideas, or the telling of humorous stories. Owen Barfield tells about Lewis's "irrepressible feeling for comedy," without which, "one would miss altogether the typical flavor of his company" (Lewis Surprised by Joy 34). In fact, Peter Schakel considers comic story telling to be a central characteristic of Lewis as a humorist. Lewis had a great ear for dialogue, and great eye for absurd detail, and great timing that allowed him to effectively build toward a climax (Schakel Encyclopedia 665). His timing in life was as impressive as the timing in his novels. It is interesting to note that C. S. Lewis died on November 22, 1963, the same day that both John F. Kennedy, and Aldous Huxley died (McGovern 299).

Clive Staples Lewis Bibliography

Glover, Donald E. C.S. Lewis: The Art of Enchantment. Athens, OH: Ohio University Press, 1981.

Kellso, Kim. "C. S. Lewis: An Emphasis on His Children's Literature." Unpublished Paper. Tempe, AZ: Arizona State University, 1996.

Kilby, Clyde S. The Christian World of C. S. Lewis. Grand Rapids, MI: William B. Eerdmans, 1964.

Lewis, C. S. Broadcast Talks. London, England: Geoffrey Bles/The Centenary Press, 1942.

Lewis, C. S. The Great Divorce. London, England: Geoffrey Bles, 1945.

Lewis, C. S. Mere Christianity. London, England: Geoffrey Bles, 1952.

Lewis, C. S. Poems. Ed. Walter Hooper. London, England: Geoffrey Bles, 1964.

Lewis, C. S. Surprised by Joy. London, England: Geoffrey Bles, 1955.

Lewis, C. S. The Screwtape Letters. London, England: Geoffrey Bles, 1942.

Lewis, C. S. The Voyage of the "Dawn Treader." London, England: Geoffrey Bles, 1952.

McGovern, Eugene. "C. S. Lewis." British Novelists, 1930-1959. Ed. Bernard Oldsey. Detroit, MI: Gale, 1983, 520-530.

Myers, Doris T. C. S. Lewis in Context. Kent, OH: The Kent State University Press, 1994.

Schakel, Peter J. "C. S. Lewis." Encyclopedia of British Humorists, Volume II. Ed. Steven H. Gale. New York, NY: Garland, 1996, 661-670.

Schakel, Peter J. "The Satiric Imagination of C. S. Lewis." Studies in the Literary Imagination 22 (1989): 129-148.

Elizabeth Dorothea Cole Bowen (1899-1973) IRELAND

See Nilsen, Don L. F. "Elizabeth Bowen." Humor in Irish Literature: A Reference Guide. Westport, CT: Greenwood, 1996, 156-159.

Sir Noel (Pierce) Coward (Hernia Wittlebot) (1899-1973)

As a boy, Noel Coward was talented and attractive and he was asked by Miss Lila Field to appear in her all-children fairy play entitled, "The Goldfish." Coward played the part of Prince Mussel, and when he told his mother that the payment would be a guinea and a half a week, his mother sadly replied that they couldn't afford to pay that. Miss Field laughed, and explained that the guinea and a half a week was what Coward would receive for acting in the play. So Noel Coward became Prince Mussell, King Starfish's court jester in "The Goldfish" (Lesniak 114).

Coward later became world-famous not only as an actor, but also as a playwright, a director, a producer, a composer, a lyricist, a screenwriter, a nightclub entertainer, a novelist, a mesmerist, and a poet (Lesniak 34-35). Coward was a born wit. Once, when working with Mary Martin on a particular TV extravaganza, he said, "The show will be completely spontaneous, the kind of spontaneity I like best, the kind that comes after five weeks rehearsal" (Hirst 60). David Hirst suggests that it is Noel Coward who emerges as the best chronicler of the "gay" 1920s and the "turbulent" 1930s, as he was the most original and influential comic writer of the period (Hirst 59). Hirst suggests that it was Noel Coward who, "first crystallized the particular strength of English understatement in the brief exchanges so characteristic of his dialogues" (Hirst 112). Robert Ronning suggests that Noel Coward respected the graceful, well-behaved, and endearing conventions of Victorian and Edwardian society. "Indeed, his dependence on them for scandalous and shocking effects in his own comedies and dramas was as intense as, though different from, earlier masters." Coward concentrated on conversation rather than action (Ronning 57).

Sir Terence Rattigan said that Noel Coward always spoke and wrote with wit, and added that "wit is a quality that does not date." He continued that Coward is interested in, "humanity, its quirks and foibles, its vanities and idiocies, its prejudices and pomposities, and these things, as Congreve and Sheridan have taught us, are changeless" (Ashley 286). Noel Coward's comic vision comes from the love-hate relationship he has with the world as it is, and his disappointment in not being able to make the world change. He wanted to be part of the world but was not able to make a full connection; therefore, his writing changes from flip to cruel to romantic to realistic to gay to "gay." He had the ability to rise into high comedy or descend into camp (Ashley 280). Coward was able to put some of the sharpest and most scintillating dialogue ever written into the mouths of his characters. His song lyrics are also filled with word play, ranging from such poetic devices as alliteration and assonance to impudent and caustic wit, or ingenious rhymes and captivating rhythms. In his real life, Coward was as amusing as he was in his writings. In fact, "real life was part of his work, as it was with Wilde." When Gertrude Lawrence, his friend, got married, he sent her a doggerel telegram containing much wit, irony, and sexual innuendo, but also much true emotion. (Ashley 281)

One of the plays which Noel Coward wrote was described in various papers as being "tenuous," "thin," "brittle," "gossamer," "iridescent," and "delightfully daring," and Noel Coward suggests that all of these descriptors, "connoted, to the public mind, 'cocktails,' 'evening dress,' 'repartée,' and 'irreverent allusion to copulation,' thereby causing a gratifying number of respectable people to queue up at the box office." Noel Coward handled his sex drives the way Oscar Wilde did; he commented on the lives of more "normal" people in a way that was, "flip yet serious, cynical and whimsical," sometimes blasé, sometimes stinging, and sometimes sad (Ashley 282). Coward was himself an excellent critic. Evelyn Laye was an actress who was prone to wave her arms around, so Coward said she played "like a windmill." A. E. Matthews tended to be a bit shaky in his lines, so Coward said that he, "ambled through a play like a charming retriever who has buried a bone and can't quite remember where." Coward was angered when George Bernard Shaw rejected some complimentary tickets he had sent to one of his premieres, so for the opening to his next play, he sent Shaw tickets to a stage box that seated four people and said, "bring all your friends." When a particularly "dimwitted" Hollywood actor committed suicide by blowing out his brains, Coward said, "He must have been a wonderful shot" (Ashley 284).

Some critics called Coward cynical, sarcastic, or satiric; others called him brittle or sadistic; all critics called him controversial. He often had parts in various productions. In Around the World in Eighty Days (1956) the part he played was described as, "superior and ineffably smug." Coward joked that it was "typecasting." Although Shaw said it of himself first, Coward might just as well have said of himself, that he, "specialized in being right when other people are wrong" (Ashley 284). Noel Coward's writing has often been compared to that of Oscar Wilde and George Bernard Shaw, but unlike Wilde and Shaw, Coward was, "carefully self-deprecating in public" (Seymour 7). Noel Coward has written a large number of revues and plays, and has been given such titles as "superman of the theatre" and "the modern theatre's wonder boy" (Snider 99). His plays are filled with witty and amusing remarks, much like those of Oscar Wilde. Coward writes in the comedy-of-manners tradition. He writes about a section of society which is sophisticated, and cultivated. This section of society concentrates on nonchalance and gaiety and smart talk, all of which can easily be translated into satire (Snider 101). Coward's plays tend to be very witty, charming, and well-constructed (Ashley 283).

His musicals are clever and tuneful, and his books are no sillier than those of P. G. Wodehouse or Guy Bolton. His comic songs are hilarious, and his short stories are in places deft and very touching. There is a great deal of local color, and many local allusions to his own time and place, but nevertheless, his catty jabs and debonair and suggestive comments like "a roll in the hey-nonny-nonny" don't demand excessive background, and are still quite funny. Another reason that his comedies are timeless is that his punchlines have the advantage of being delivered by modern actors. Coward's comments carry a punch, but it is the punch of an iron fist in a velvet glove. "All of Coward's humor has an element of attack in it, a nastiness that saves it from the two great vices of British humor: whimsicality and sentimentality" (Ashley 283). Coward traveled extensively, and often entertained the troops during wartime or diverted sophisticated audiences during peacetime, and he made an important contribution to comedy in his sentimental and funny short stories and his witty popular songs. He carried a thesaurus and a rhyming dictionary everywhere he went, and any time he had an idea for a song or a dialogue or a plot, he would stop what he was doing and jot it down (Ashley 285).

Coward spent fifty years acting in comic films, usually playing the gentleman cad. Coward's first adult role was in Hearts of the World (1918). During the 1930s Coward can be seen playing the role of the gentleman cad in Private Lives (1931), Cavalcade (1933), Tonight Is Ours (1933), Bitter Sweet (1933), and Design for Living (1934). In The Scoundrel (1934), Coward played the starring role, an attractive-repulsive roué. During the 1940s Coward played in Blithe Spirit (1945), in This Happy Breed (1945), and in The Astonished Heart (1949). During the 1950s, he wore his comic mask in cameo roles in Meet Me Tonight (1950), Around the World in Eighty Days (1956), and Our Man in Havana (1959), where he was a British spy. During the 1960s he acted in Surprise Package (1960) and Paris When It Sizzles (1964). In Bunny Lake Is Missing (1965) he was the superior spy, who is a sinister pervert who wears a seedy bathrobe rather than his usual sleek silk dressing gown. In The Italian Job (1969) he was again the gentleman cad.

I'll Leave It to You (1920) is a light comedy which portrays a family of well-born young people suddenly confronted with the business of supporting themselves (Snider 99). The Young Idea (1921) is a satire which targets English country society (Snider 99). In 1923, Coward wrote a playlet by the name of The Swiss Family Whittlebot, which critics thought was a parody of Edith, Osbert, and Sacheverell Sitwell, one of England's premier literary families (Lesniak 115). The satire in The Vortex (1923) is light, flippant, and indulgent, and in this play there are many humours characters such as Pauncefort Quentin, and Clara Hibbart, the soprano, and Tom Veryan, Florence's young athlete, and Bruce Fairlight, the dramatist. These characters all have one thing in common; they are all consumed with the cosmetic and the superficial (Snider 106). Pauncefort, or "Pawnie" talks and acts very much like "Ernest" in Oscar Wilde's The Importance of Being Earnest; like Ernest, he makes an art of nonsense. "We are to laugh with Pawnie for his facetious comments on the follies of others, but we must laugh at him also for the feminine attributes with which Mr. Coward occasionally endows certain of his characters." Clara Hibbart has stage freight before her concert, but Pawnie gives her no sympathy, and in fact remarks, "she eternally labors under the delusion that she really matters" (Snider 107). Because Bruce Fairlight is a celebrity, he is a guest of Florence. "The idle rich cultivate celebrities as a matter of course, particularly because there are so many new ones forever cropping up that the novelty does not soon wear off." The seriousness of his manner is at odds with the trivialness of the manners of his hostess and her friends (Snider 108).

Noel Coward said that his main concern in writing The Vortex was to provide a play, "with a whacking good part in it for myself" (Snider 103). Much of the satire of the play comes through the characterization of Florence Lancaster, a middle-aged woman who still believes herself to be young, and who therefore encourages a bevy of youthful lovers. The entire play revolves around Florence's vanity (Snider 103). Florence's friend, Helen, has more common sense than Florence has. Helen says, "it's silly not to grow old when the time comes," but to Florence, who has made up her mind to be forever young, these words carry no significance (Snider 104). David Hirst says that the conversations between Florence's friends, the sincere Helen, the superficial Clara, and the bitchy Pawnie (who is described in the stage directions as "an elderly maiden gentleman") are as near as Coward ever got to copying the flamboyant verbal style of Oscar Wilde (Hirst 59).

The Vortex is the old story of age versus youth, and as usual, it is youth that wins out. Florence's son is Nicky, a young man of much musical talent, intelligence, and attractiveness. He doesn't blame his mother for her distorted vision, but rather, he blames the world in general, as he cries out, "It's not your fault--it's the fault of circumstances and civilization; civilization makes rottenness so much easier. We're utterly rotten--both of us-- How can we help ourselves? We swirl about in a vortex of beastliness" (Snider 105). It is this last statement which provides the title for the play. Coward's Fallen Angels (1925) is a three-act comedy which both shocked and entertained theatre goers. It is a play about two middle-aged women slowly getting drunk while waiting for a mutual lover (Lesniak 115).

Hay Fever (1925) is a farcical comedy about an actress named Judith, who is married to a novelist named David. They have a couple of madcap children named Sorel and Simon. And each of these characters invites a guest onto the family estate for the weekend, and "before the bohemian hijinks drive all of the guests away there is plenty of motion and emotion" (Ashley 285). Hay Fever is about how the various characters revile each others' guests (Lesniak 115). This play is probably the best known, and also the most characteristic of Noel Coward's comedies. The satire in Hay Fever is not as earnest as is the satire in The Vortex, but it is appropriate for a comedy-of-manners piece (Snider 113). Hay Fever is a comedy of bad manners about the customs of the 1920s by playing a flapper, a vamp, a sporty young chap, and a respectable businessman against the selfish and overbearing people who are their hosts (Hirst 60). There is no plot in this play, because a plot would distract from the steady stream of wit and nonsense that pervades it. And that's the point, because the satire targets the aimlessness of the activities of the "beau monde." Because the satire in Hay Fever is so determined by nonsense and farce, the resultant laughter may in fact hide the satire from the audience (Snider 108). The action of the play takes place in the home of Judith Bliss, who used to be a famous actress, and who is now always contemplating her return to the stage. Judith's husband is David, a novelist who spends most of his time on his new novel, The Sinful Woman. Judith Bliss is like Florence Lancaster in that neither of these women will accept the fact that they are no longer young, and both foolishly continue in their youthful ways. The fact that Judith used to be a great actress dominates Judith's every thought and action. She manages to hold the center of the stage at all times, and she also derives a strange sort of satisfaction from manufacturing grand tableaux and dramatic situations which strangers find quite bewildering (Snider 110). To illustrate Judith's ability to offer stage directions in real-life situations consider the time that she stumbles upon Sorel and Sandy in a casual embrace.

> SOREL (playing up): Mother--Mother, say you understand and forgive!
> JUDITH: Understand! You forget, dear, I am a woman.
> SOREL: I know you are, Mother. That's what makes it all so poignant.
> JUDITH (magnanimously, to Sandy): If you want Sorel, truly, I give her to
>   you--unconditionally.
> SANDY (dazed): Thanks--awfully, Mrs. Bliss. (Coward Hay Fever 172)

Judith continues in character when she later finds David kissing Myra, and Judith goes into her same act, at the end of which she gives David to Myra, again unconditionally.
Still later, Simon enters from the garden exclaiming that he is engaged to Jackie Coryton, and Judith, still in character, magnanimously gives Simon to the bewildered Jackie whose protestations are simply brushed aside (Snider 111).

At one point in Hay Fever at a particularly hectic time Richard enters and asks, "What's happened? Is this a game?" It so happens that these words are exactly the same as some lines in Love's Whirlwind, and recognizing this, the Blisses take this as a cue and begin other lines from Love's Whirlwind, as the guests look on in silent amazement. At this point, the curtain descends. Later, the Blisses observe that their guests have been very rude, and they continue their bickering during breakfast, and the play ends with Judith's final decision that she is really going to return to the stage (Snider 112).

The satire in Easy Virtue (1926) is designed to expose hypocrisy. With the exception of Colonel Whittaker, all of the members of the Whittaker family are hypocrites. Mrs. Whittaker and Marion use religious motives to rationalize their devoting of their lives to meddling in the affairs of other people (Snider 113). The Colonel describes the actions of Mrs. Whittaker and Marion in the following way: "They are always trying to help lame dogs over stiles--even if they're not lame and don't want to go" (Easy Virtue 19). Noel Coward considers Bitter Sweet (1929) to be his best work. "It combines my talents in almost perfect balance" (Ashley 286). In a 1929 musical review entitled "Bitter Sweet," Coward said, "The most I've had is just a talent to amuse" (Seymour 7).

In Private Lives (1930), Noel Coward himself played the role of Elyot Chase, and Gertrude Lawrence played the role of Amanda Prynne. Elyot and Amanda had once been married, but they have divorced, and have now remarried. They slowly discover that they are still very much in love with each other, though outwardly they can't stand each other (Lesniak 116). In Private Lives Amanda Prynne meets her first husband, Elyot Chase, on the night of her second honeymoon. Elyot Chase, the audience soon discovers, is also on his second honeymoon. The illicitness of this chance meeting rekindles the earlier flame they had for each other and Amanda and Elyot elope to Amanda's apartment in Paris, thereby jilting their new mates, Victor and Sibyl (Snider 118). In Private Lives, Elyot and Amanda "embody those very contradictions which Maugham in his comedies had claimed as essentially English in character." The brawl at the end of Act II between Elyot and Amanda is only one of many instances in which Coward uses blatant farce (Ronning 57).

Unlike the high-flown rhetoric of Wilde, Noel Coward's rhetoric demonstrates an ability to pare down comic dialogue to its bare essentials. In Private Lives this paring down can be seen in the deft badinage between Amanda and Elyot:

> AMANDA: Don't leave me until I've pulled myself together.
> ELYOT: Very well. (There is a dead silence.)
> AMANDA: What have you been doing lately? During these last years?
> ELYOT: Travelling about. I went round the world you know after--
> AMANDA: (hurriedly) Yes, yes, I know. How was it?
> ELYOT: The world?
> AMANDA: Yes.
> ELYOT: Oh, highly enjoyable.
> AMANDA: China must be very interesting.
> ELYOT: Very big, China.
> AMANDA: And Japan--
> ELYOT: Very small. (qtd. in Hirst 62)

Both Private Lives and Design for Living continue the comedy-of-manners tradition started by William Congreve. Both of these plays target Noel Coward's own social set, a social set in which the members are all very clever, and where wit and nonsense fill intriguing conversations. This is a social set of dilettantes, who have no responsibilities, and no real business worries. They have no exacting relatives to help them develop a code of responsible action, and they laugh at moral codes, at religion, at science, and at the conventions that seem so essential to the rest of humanity (Snider 116). In both of these plays, Coward satirically depicts the irregularities of these impulsive characters; he is, however, quite fond of such characters. By developing their points of views, Coward is also satirizing respected institutions and accepted conventions which his society finds of little value (Snider 117).

In both Private Lives and Design for Living marriage is ridiculed. In Private Lives Amanda and Elyot attribute their former marital misery to the fact that they were married in an ornate public ceremony, so now they decide that they are not going to, "let marriage again interfere with their love." In Design for Living, Ernest, the friend of Gilda, Otto, and Leo suggests that Gilda should marry one of the two, but Gilda explains that the only reasons to marry would be to have children, a home, social activities, and financial security, and she therefore says, "I don't like children; I don't wish for a home; I can't bear social activities, and I have a small but adequate income of my own" (Design 72).

Design for Living (1933), like Private Lives, involves a juggling of partners. The three principle characters in <u>Design for Living</u> are Gilda, Otto, and Leo. "They are like moths in a pool of light, unable to tolerate the lonely outer darkness, and equally unable to share the light without colliding constantly and bruising one another's wings" (<u>Play Parade</u> xv). Leo is a playwright who loves Gilda and Otto. Otto is a portrait painter who loves Gilda and Leo. And Gilda is an interior decorator who loves Otto and Leo (Snider 118). In <u>Design for Living</u>, Ernest is the effeminate art collector who feels that he should warn Gilda, Otto, and Leo about their life style, but they laugh at his admonitions until the place in the play where Gilda becomes so disgusted with Leo and Otto that she marries Ernest. Ernest, like Pawnie in <u>The Vortex</u> is a target of Coward's satire, since both Ernest and Pawnie go through life as spectators only (Snider 120).

The guests in <u>Design for Living</u> are uniformly dull. The Bliss family, on the other hand, are "artificial to the point of lunacy," but the sympathies of the audience go with the Bliss family because they are the most clever (Hirst 60). The Bliss family has a way of treating their guests like puppets, as they act through their own emotional tensions in much the same way as George and Martha manipulate their guests in Edward Albee's <u>Who's Afraid of Virginia Woolf?</u> (Hirst 61). Noel Coward said that <u>Design for Living</u> was, "liked and disliked, and hated and admired, but never, I think, sufficiently loved by any but its three leading actors." Coward said that he never intended that the "Design for Living" of the play should be meant to apply to anyone except Gilda, Otto, and Leo, three characters who are glib, overarticulate, and amoral, three characters who "force their lives into fantastic shapes and problems because they cannot help themselves" (Ashley 285).

Newspaper columnists and dramatic critics are two particular targets for the satire in <u>Play Parade</u> (1933). Here Coward mocks the stereotyped phrases they tended to use in describing his plays. The press had described <u>Hay Fever</u> as "thin," "tenuous," and "trivial," and so Coward took delight in its successful reception by large audiences. Coward suggested that drama critics liked to use negative stock phrases for anything later in date or lighter in texture than <u>The Way of the World</u>, and he was therefore very pleased when his play ran triumphantly for a full year (<u>Play Parade</u> xi).

<u>Point Valaine</u> (1935) is about Victor Prynne, Mr. and Mrs. Carver, and the various guests who sit on the porch of Linda Valaine's hotel, and chat. Victor is wooden, and pompous, and he is married to the exciting Amanda. Victor lacks imagination, and he can't play up to Amanda's mood changes, nor is he able to recognize when Amanda is joking, and so he has a constant intuitive suspicion that Amanda is making fun of him. He is not a sympathetic character, and the audience does not feel sorry for him when Amanda leaves him for Elyot. In <u>Point Valaine</u>, Coward continues his satiric targeting of the duller members of society, and he does this by, "recording in detail the insignificant dialogue and the trivial concerns of the guests at Linda Valaine's hotel." These guests talk about their liver pills, and about mosquitoes, and jellyfish, and Mortimer Quinn is delighted with this conversation since he is looking for material for a novel he has in mind. Part of the humor of the play lies in the contrast between the nonconsequential chatter of the guests about hats and young men as contrasted with the intelligent conversation of Linda Valaine and Mortimer Quinn. Many of the characters in <u>Point Valaine</u> are earthy and sensual. They illustrate the unpleasant aspects of life in the tropics, and because of their corruptness, and also because of the influence of the extreme climate, they are incapable of engaging in the banter and caprices of the smart set.

<u>Present Laughter</u> (1939) is one of Coward's broader comedies. It is a farce which deals with the domestic entanglements of a writer by the name of Garry Esseldine (Hirst 65). Tallulah Bankhead, after playing Amanda for more than two hundred weeks, said,

> I played it for an entire summer in Chicago, while racked with neuritis, and
> for an entire season in New York. I played it in summer theaters, in Shrine
> mosques, in school auditoriums, in a blizzard in Minneapolis, in a coma in

Westport. I played it in Passaic, in Flatbush, in Pueblo, in Cedar Rapids, in Peoria, in the Bronx, in Joplin, in 'thunder, lightning and in rain'...in towns known but to God and Rand McNally. (Ashley 286)

Blithe Spirit (1941) is about an author who is henpecked by his second wife, and also henpecked by Madame Arcati, an eccentric medium who raises his first wife's spirit from the dead. Blithe Spirit is a whimsical comedy of situations in which a ghost comes out of the past to disturb a marriage. This play is filled with wit and economy of verbal expression (Hirst 66). In Blithe Spirit, Charles Condomine has the problem of living with two wives, Ruth (who is living), and Elvira (who is a ghost). There is much sharp dialogue, and some of Coward's best characterizations. Margaret Rutherford played one of the roles, in the film version, and one of the comic images is of her bicycling away in an evening dress (Ashley 285).

In Noel Coward: A Biography (1996), Philip Hoare notes that Noel Coward's mother so thought of Noel as a star that she removed him from his first school because the teachers refused to tie his shoelaces. As an adolescent, Coward was a friend of Esme Wynne, "an exuberant girl who toured with Coward and even shared baths with him rather than miss a moment's conversation. In lighter moments, the two went shoplifting together. Hoare says that Noel Coward's writing was greatly influenced by the works of Saki (H. H. Munro), whom Hoare describes as, "the wittiest of the pre-World War I generation of English writers." Saki developed malevolently funny one-dimensional characters, and so did Coward (Seymour 7). About his contribution to writing, Noel Coward said, "If I can make people laugh, maybe I am not doing so very badly.... This is my job really, and will remain so through all wars and revolutions and carnage" (Lesniak 116). Near the end of Coward's life, a television biography was filmed in Switzerland. Coward was asked to sum it all up, and said, "Sum up? Well, now comes the terrible decision as to whether to be corny or not. The answer is in one word, 'Love'" (Ashley 286).

Sir Noel (Pierce) Coward (Hernia Wittlebot) Bibliography

Ashley, Leonard R. N. "Sir Noel Pierce Coward." Encyclopedia of British Humorists, Volume I. Ed. Steven H. Gale. New York, NY: Garland, 1996, 278-288.

Cole, Leslie. Remembered Laughter: The Life of Noel Coward. New York, NY: Knopf, 1976.

Coward, Noel. Bitter Sweet and Other Plays. New York, NY: Doubleday, Doran, and Co., 1929.

Coward, Noel. Blithe Spirit. New York, NY: Doubleday, 1941.

Coward, Noel. Easy Virtue. New York, NY: Benn, 1926.

Coward, Noel. Private Lives. New York, NY: Doubleday, Doran, and Co., 1930.

Coward, Noel. Design for Living. New York, NY: Doubleday, Doran, and Co., 1933.

Coward, Noel. Hay Fever. New York, NY: Doubleday, Doran, and Co., 1929.

Coward, Noel. Play Parade. New York, NY: Doubleday, Doran, and Co., 1933.

Hadfield, John, ed. Cowardy Custard. London, England: Heinemann, 1973.

Hirst, David L. Comedy of Manners. New York, NY: Methuen, 1979.

Kronenberger, Louis. Cavalcade of Comedy: 21 Brilliant Comedies from Jonson and Wycherley to Thurber and Coward. New York, NY: Simon and Schuster, 1953.

Lesniak, James G. "Noel Coward." Contemporary Authors, New Revision Series, Volume 35. Detroit, MI: Gale Research, 1992, 110-117.

Morley, Sheridan. Out in the Midday Sun. New York, NY: Philosophical Library, 1988.

Morley, Sheridan. A Talent to Amuse: A Biography of Noel Coward. New York, NY: Doubleday, 1969; London, England: Heinemann, 1969.

Morse, Clarence R. "Mad Dogs and Englishmen: A Study of Noel Coward." Emporia State

Research Studies 21.4 (1973): 5-50.

Richards, Dick. The Wit of Noel Coward. London, England: Ferwin, 1988.

Ronning, Robert. "The Eccentric: The English Comic Farce of Sir Arthur Pinero."
Quarterly Journal of Speech 63 (1977): 51-58.

Seymour, Miranda. "A Talent to Amuse." New York Times Book Review. August 25,
1996, 7.

Snider, Rose. "Noel Coward." Satire in the Comedies of Congreve, Sheridan, Wilde, and
Coward. New York, NY: Phaeton Press, 1972, 95-123.

Alfred (Joseph) Hitchcock (1899-1980)

At a very young age, Alfred Hitchock was placed by his Catholic family into St.
Ignatius College, a Jesuit school in London, England. Hitchcock considers this early
placement to have been an "eccentricity," adding that it was probably during this period
with the Jesuits that his strong sense of fear first developed. He had a, "moral fear--the
fear of being involved in anything evil." During those years, he also developed a "physical
fear" because whenever he did something wrong, the Jesuits would tell him to step in to
see the father as soon as classes were over. The father would then, "solemnly inscribe your
name in the register, together with the indication of the punishment to be inflicted, and you
spent the whole day waiting for the sentence to be carried out." The waiting was as much
of a punishment as was the punishment itself. In those days, the Jesuits often used a cane
made out of very hard rubber (Commire 113).

Hitchcock had important guidelines in the making of films. First, the film must be
both dramatic and human. "What is drama, after all, but life with the dull bits cut out."
He also needed to have a really bad villain. "The more successful the villain, the more
successful the picture. That's a cardinal rule." Nevertheless, Hitchcock's villains tend to
be charming and polite, because that makes them all the more villainous. Hitchcock's hero
is always an average man to whom bizarre things happen. Finally, he needed strong
characters, even though these characters seem to take the author places where he never
intended to go. Hitchcock says about the relationship between himself as author of the
novel and these characters, "I'm like the old lady with the Boy Scouts who're trying to help
her across the street: 'But that's not where I want to go!'" Another important guideline for
Hitchcock is that he reveals the villain early. "I've never used the whodunit technique."
"It is possible to build up almost unbearable tension in a play or film in which the audience
knows who the murderer is all the time, and from the very start they want to scream out
to all the other characters in the plot, 'Watch out for So-and-So! He's a killer!' For that
reason Hitchcock believes in giving the audience all the facts as early as possible"
(Commire 113). Hitchcock also says that he is not interested in content. "It's the same as
a painter not worrying about the apples he's painting--whether they're sweet or sour"
(Commire 117).

For his television trademark, Hitchcock did a minimalist self-portrait in caricature.
He did the artwork himself, later commenting on the three lines at the top of his head, "At
one time I had more hair. All three of them were wavy." Hitchcock loved practical jokes,
but in a late interview said, he had pretty much outgrown them but he still had fun in
elevators. "Sometimes in a crowded elevator I turn to someone with me and say, "Of
course, I didn't know the gun was loaded, but when it went off it blasted a great hole in
his neck. A flap of his flesh fell down, and I could see the white ligaments uncovered.
Presently I felt wetness around my feet. I was standing in a pool of blood." Everyone in
the elevator stiffens, and Hitchcock gets out and leaves them standing there. (Commire
117).

Hitchcock's fifty-four films are, "famous for their deft, haunting visual style," and for the, "carefully crafted balance struck between dramatic tension and comic relief" (Locher 249). Hitchcock made an appearance in all of his films. This tradition started with his first picture, when they had a shortage of extras, and they had Hitchcock in the film for a few seconds as an editor with his back to the cameras, but he says, "Since then I have been trying to get into every one of my pictures. It has an impelling fascination that I can't resist" (Commire 115).

Alfred (Joseph) Hitchcock Bibliography

Commire, Anne, ed. "Alfred (Joseph) Hitchcock." Something about the Author, Volume 27. Detroit, MI: Gale, 1982, 112-118.

Locher, Frances C. ed. "Alfred (Joseph) Hitchcock." Contemporary Authors, Volume 97-100, 1981, 249-250.

6

Authors Born between
1900 and 1909

Benn Wolfe Levy (1900-1933)

Benn Levy wrote twenty stage plays; they included traditional comedies, farces, melodramas, and social problem plays (Rusinko 656). Typical titles are the following: This Woman Business (1925), The Man with Red Hair (1928), which was adapted from Hugh Walpole's novel, Mud and Treacle (1928), Mrs. Moonlight (1928), The Devil (1930), Hollywood Holiday (1931), which was co-authored with John van Druten, Springtime for Henry (1932), The Poet's Heart (1937), Young Madame Conti (1938), which was co-authored with Hubert Griffith and was adapted from Bruno Frank's play, The Jealous God (1939), Clutterbuck (1947), Return to Tyassi (1951), Cupid and Psyche (1952), The Rape of the Belt (1957), and The Member for Gaza (1968) (Rusinko 661). These plays are all comic, but they are not the same kind of comic. This Woman Business, for example, is a Shavian comedy, while Springtime for Henry is a Restoration comedy of manners with farcical overtones, and Clutterbuck is a Cowardian-Wodehousian farce. The Rape of the Belt, in contrast is a high comedy of ideas (Rusinko 658).

This Woman Business (1925) contains more corrosive irony than festive laughter. In this play, there are witty debates in the tradition of George Bernard Shaw. In This Woman Business, a group of misogynists gather together away from the women of their lives who are so demanding. These misogynists are of various ages, and of various professions, and this battle of the sexes launched a theme that permeates the rest of Benn Levy's plays. Honey is the youngest member of the group. He is a would-be poet who appears to be a satiric version of Eugene Marchbanks of Shaw's Candida. Judge Bingham, the oldest member of the group, displays a dry wit and appears to be a new rendition of Shaw's Captain Overshot. Crawford is a female thief who intrudes into the group and manages to snare Hodges, the strongest of the misogynists. Crawford openly admits that she uses the three principle weapons of her sex, "the flaunting of her sex, lying, and cajolery." Crawford says that these are, "woman's only weapons in a male-created morality in which force is not considered as immoral as fraud." This Woman Business demonstrates Levy's talent for witty repartée and debate, and a critic for the Observer said that this play is, "an almost exhaustible flow of wit and humour" (Rusinko 657).

Mrs. Moonlight (1928) is a satire of the sentimental fantasy of James Barrie's "what-if" plays. It is a story about a woman with a wish-giving necklace who wishes to remain young forever. "The irony takes on a seriousness that is the premise for his later

Ibsen-like social problem plays The Jealous God and Public and Confidential" (Rusinko 660). The Devil: A Religious Comedy (1930) is a serious play with witty debate in the tradition of George Bernard Shaw (Rusinko 657). Here, a shadowy figure shows up at a country house while there is a gathering of artists and intellectuals there. This figure is trying to tempt each of them with a way of becoming famous, and much of the humor of the play is in the form of ironies (Rusinko 660).

Hollywood Holiday (1931), which was co-authored with John van Druten, is a farcical kaleidoscopic burlesque. Miss Pinner is an unaccomplished governess who finds herself away from her chintzy Bayswater boardinghouse, and in Hollywood, the land of moguls who are not able to control the tantrums of a temperamental actress appropriately named Hedda Maelstrom (Rusinko 659). High points in the farce are when Miss Pinner does a poor reading of an inferior script, and when there is a physical tussle between Miss Pinner and Hedda Maelstrom. After the fight, Miss Pinner goes back to her Bayswater boardinghouse where she is viewed by the boarders as some sort of a celebrity (Rusinko 660).

Springtime for Henry (1932) is a Restoration-type farce about two rakes who are business associates with old-school ties. In the New York Times, Brooks Atkinson describes this play as "enjoyably unscrupulous" and "hilariously impudent." He says that the humor of this comedy comes from the way in which, "well-bred Englishmen can insult each other with a perfect sense of decorum and without any sign of human emotion. It is high art" (Atkinson New York Times March 15, 1961, p. 36). Susan Rusinko considers the play to be sophisticated farce at its best. In this romp there is an inevitability that heads in the direction of a happy conclusion for everybody (Rusinko 657).

Clutterbuck (1947), like Noel Coward's Private Lives, is a play about two mismatched couples. One couple is a novelist husband and his not-very-intelligent wife. The other couple is an intelligent wife and her bumbling husband. The witty conversations and humorous situations develop out of their respective qualities, with one husband and one wife of each pair becoming the straight-man supporting the wit of the other half of the pair. Susan Rusinko considers the farcical doubling of Clutterbuck to be exquisite, but the comedy becomes even greater when a third couple is introduced. This third couple is named Clutterbuck and Melissa, and they are recognized both by Julian and Jane Pugh, and by Arthur and Deborah Pomfret, though everyone attempts to hide their recognition. The twist is that Melissa had been involved with both Julian and Arthur before their respective marriages, just as Clutterbuck had been involved with both Deborah and Jane at this same time (Rusinko 657).

In Clutterbuck, each character has speech habits that are associated uniquely with that character. Arthur is the Edwardian dandy who uses fumbling slang. In the tradition of a Wodehouse character, Arthur has trouble finishing, or even starting a thought, and he therefore relies on the mannered idiom of the time. Julian is constantly throwing ironic barbs at Arthur, but Arthur doesn't understand that they are barbs. Melissa is constantly adding syllables to words in a kind of schoolgirl talk. "Now, now, now, now, now! Peace upon earthle and good willikins among millikens! That's not a nice way to talk, Artle. I think you ought to apologize." When they all sail off at the end, Deborah resorts to her literary quotations like "How beauteous the morn!" Jane responds to the same view by using the stylish slang of the day, "Crikey, what a view!" (Rusinko 658).

Cupid and Psyche (1952) is a farcical romp by a group of young artists who are enjoying the freedom of the latest ideas of their times. They are involved in many prankish situations and farcical contrivances, such as the many well-timed exits and entrances, and withheld secrets, recognition scenes, etc. There are many hilarious complications that are only unraveled at the end of the play when a middle-aged feminist in the Pankhurst tradition appears (Rusinko 659).

The Rape of the Belt (1957), is about three sets of relationships, Zeus and Hera, Theseus and Hippolyte, and Heracles and Antiope. Just like in Aristophanes's Lysistrata, the females in The Rape of the Belt confront the males on issues of war and peace, and on the relative merits of civilized and so-called barbarian values, as these are translated into political ideologies that relate to patriarchy and to matriarchy. Zeus and Hera are spectators to the actions of Heracles and Theseus, as Heracles is carrying out his ninth labor--the wrestling of a girdle away from Antiope, Queen of the Amazons. Of course Zeus and Hera are in a continuing feud about Zeus's infidelities, so Hera changes the normally peaceful Amazons into a warring army. Later in the play, the Greek heroes are informed by Thalestris, the Minister of Maternity, that, "the men at the Farm are all properly labelled and numbered. And our girls MUST make a note of who they are mating with" (Rusinko 658). Finally, Heracles and Antiope engage in a battle of titans, and Heracles wins. He nevertheless decides to return the belt, but Antiope refuses his offer, because, "even if I took it, it would no longer be ours. We have betrayed it." Some of the most comic scenes in The Rape of the Belt are those in which Heracles and Theseus try unsuccessfully to provoke the Amazons. When it is clear that the Amazons have no intentions of fighting they leave their hostesses. This is one of the ironies. Another irony is that Hera questions the legitimacy of Zeus's claim that he is the father of Heracles. Zeus responds to Hera: "You raise a novel legal point. You mean to say, when I borrow Amphitryon's body to woo his wife, is the resulting progeny fathered by the body or the body's occupant, by the ground-landlord, as it were, or by the tenant? Fascinating. It should keep the lawyers busy" (Rusinko 659). Rusinko says that the play expresses Levy's disillusionments about Western civilization (Rusinko 658).

Benn Wolfe Levy Bibliography

Rusinko, Susan. "Benn Wolfe Levy." Encyclopedia of British Humorists, Volume II. Ed. Steven H. Gale. New York, NY: Garland, 1996, 656-661.

Stephen Meredith Potter (1900-1969)

During the early 1920s, Stephen Potter was so much influenced by George Bernard Shaw's Pygmalion that he placed an ad in the paper--"Cockney accents cured." Later, Potter began writing satires about such concepts as "one-upmanship," "gamesmanship," and even "lifemanship," and "supermanship." In Modern English Usage, H. W. Fowler acknowledged that Stephen Potter created, "the conceit of making facetious formations by treating -manship as a suffix." In a 1951 New-York-Times-Book-Review interview with Stephen Potter, Harvey Breit said, that Potter is, "one of the funniest men writing in the English language today" (Shaw 871). The Muse in Chains: A Study in Education (1937) is a work which satirically attacks the British educational system. He later wrote Potter on America (1956) which is a satirical look at America (Shaw 872). In between these two satires, Potter wrote a serious book entitled, Sense of Humour (1954), which is a critical work that deals with various forms of English humor through the ages (Shaw 872).

In 1943 Potter started working for B.B.C. on a series of "How to" programs. Various episodes involved "how to listen to radio," "how to throw a party," and in 1947 there was "how to be good at games." This series, with Potter as its leader, is considered by some critics to have, "introduced sophisticated humor to radio" (Shaw 873). The first of Potter's "one-upmanship" was Gamesmanship, or the Art of Winning Games Without Actually Cheating (1947). Then came One-Upmanship (1952), Supermanship (1958), and Golf Gamesmanship (1968). This was followed by Three-Upmanship: Gamesmanship, or

The Art of Winning Games Without Actually Cheating, Some Notes on Lifemanship, and One-Upmanship (1966). Finally there appeared The Complete Upmanship: Gamesmanship, or the Art of Winning Games Without Actually Cheating, Some Notes on Lifemanship, One-Upmanship, Supermanship (1970) (Shaw 872). According to Jason Shaw, Potter's one-upmanship strategies ranged from very humorous to outlandish to subtle. The presentation is wry, and textbooklike in form. "It is this manual-like presentation, with extensive footnotes and diagrams, which imbues much of his theory with its satirical, witty edge." One example of one-upmanship involves a tennis strategy in a game in which Potter and his partner, Dr. Cyril Joad, are outmatched by better opponents. In Gamesmanship, he tells how he and Joad unnerved the younger and more talented opponents by asking if Potter's own return of serve had landed in or out. It had clearly landed out. The younger players offer to play the point again, and Joad refuses, and replies, "I only want you to say clearly, if you will, whether the ball was in or out" (Shaw 872). Potter describes this scenario as follows: "There is nothing more putting off to young university players than a slight suggestion that their etiquette or sportsmanship is in question. How well we know this fact, yet how often we forget to make use of it." Of course the two younger players are taken out of their stride, and off their game, and they lose a match they should easily have won." Potter notes that in gamesmanship, the timing is absolutely essential, as is the apparent candor of the gamesman (Shaw 873).

Another example which Potter gives happens during a friendly game of golf. This time Dr. Joad discomforted even Potter himself, by slowly undressing and taking a dip in a nearby water hazard while being watched by two foursomes who had to play through. Potter, of course, lost the match. Another type of gamesmanship that can be used is to whistle some fragment of classical music over and over again while one's opponent is trying to swing. At the right time it is important to whistle one of the notes just a bit off key. Still another example of gamesmanship is to ask a friend for a favor at the third hole, but not to tell what the favor is until the sixteenth hole. Other techniques involve the wearing of mis-matched clothes, or the faking of minor injuries or ailments, or just simply delaying the game, rushing the game, or both (Shaw 873).

But Potter's one-upmanship is not just relevant to games. The name which Potter uses for the more general concept is "lifemanship," which involves such strategies as, "how to make an expert look like a fool, how to make people feel awkward, the art of conversation, various womansmanship ploys, and a plethora of other stratagems used to cause 'the eternal opponent...[to] feel that something has gone wrong, however slightly.'" Whenever a person is faced with a world traveler or expert on international affairs, for example, it is always possible to reply, "Yes, but only in the South." One-upmanship, or lifemanship can also occur in the doctor's office. If a physician is treating a patient as if he or she were ignorant, the patient can glance at the doctor's credentials that are hanging on the wall and ask, "I am, I suppose, right in calling you a Doctor?" When ordering dinner in a restaurant, it is possible to appear knowledgeable by saying something like, "Look, you've got a Chateau-Neon '45 somewhere secreted about the place, I know. Can you let us have a bottle?" (Shaw 873). Since you have already read the wine list, you know for a fact that they have do Chateau-Neon '45, and you furthermore know that it is the next-to-the-cheapest wine on the list. When the waiter leaves, you can turn to your dinner guests and say, "They keep a little cache for favored customers" (Shaw 874).

Potter's humor is pseudo-scholarly. It tends to be both deadpan and outrageous, and is often implemented best when no more than two people are present. One-upmanship is a great satirical device; however, many critics feel that the joke goes on too long. It is true that each book is cleverly written, and satirically charming, with footnotes and diagrams at first adding to, but later on detracting from the effect. After a while, the new "-manship" concepts become trivial. One or two of the volumes might be fun to read, but after that the level of saturation becomes exceeded (Shaw 874).

Stephen Meredith Potter Bibliography

Breit, Harvey. "Talk With Stephen Potter." New York Times Book Review (May 20, 1951): 23.

Fowler, Henry Watson. A Dictionary of Modern English Usage. Oxford, England: Clarendon Press, 1926.

Potter, Stephen Meredith. Sense of Humour. Darby, PA: Arden, 1954.

Shaw, Jason. "Stephen Meredith Potter." Encyclopedia of British Humorists, Volume II. Ed. Steven H. Gale. New York, NY: Garland, 1996, 871-875.

Sir Victor Sawdon Pritchett (1900-)

V. S. Pritchett was the son of Walter Sawdon Pritchett. Walter was a traveling salesman of Welsh descent who originally lived in Yorkshire. Walter was always pumped up with optimism, and he had strutting mannerisms, and laughable social pretensions. V. S. used to call his father a "bumptious cocksparrow." Beatrice Martin Pritchett was V. S. Pritchett's mother. Before marriage, she had been a Cockney shop clerk who loved to tell tall tales and later she delighted in composing popular comic fiction with her son (Stinson, 1994, 187). V. S. Pritchett's humor is not so much the result of his attempt to see the funny side of life, or to make readers laugh as it is an inevitable result of describing a disoriented age in great detail. In this disoriented age, no aspects of human behavior can be assumed, since the actions and attitudes of people are inscrutable, and unpredictable, and sometimes alarming (Jago 893).

In the Introduction to his Oxford Book of Short Stories (1981), Pritchett says, "Readers used to speak of 'losing' themselves in a novel or a story: the contemporary addict turns to the short story to find himself" (Jago 893). In the New York Times Book Review, Richard Locke says that Pritchett, "has the lower-middle Londoner's quick eye and sharp tongue and appetite for comedy." Locke also says that Pritchett is quick to spot pride, flummery, snobbery, and cant (Johnson 355). In Time magazine, Timothy Foote wrote that Pritchett's short stories, "regularly throb with the same grotesque scenes and sensuous memories as his life, recollected with a comic clarity and shrewd indulgence" (qtd. in Johnson 356). V. S. Pritchett's stories are often filled with love and erotic attraction, and they tend to be comic, ironic, and very emotional (Stinson 194). Just like people in real life, Pritchett's characters tend to reveal themselves by their posturing, their face-saving expressions, their hyperboles, their non-sequiturs, their quirky verbosities, and their digressions. Pritchett has a good ear for the odd and revealing phrase, and his writing tends to be filled with wit, pungency, and "general felicity of phrasing" (Stinson, 1994, 197). Harry Marks considers Pritchett's comedy to be noteworthy because of his, "sense of the comic, a comedy less exaggerated than Samuel Beckett's, for example, but nevertheless an effective and vivid comedy regarding the foibles of human nature" (Marks 465). From reading Thomas Hardy novels, Pritchett developed, "a lasting taste for the wry and ironical" (Marks 466).

Nothing Like Leather (1935) is a novel that tells about the tragedy that results when Mathew Burkle's moral character degenerates as his fortunes become greater. The main irony is that Mathew, the son of a strict English schoolmaster, has been trying to escape the influence of his father for years because of his moral character (Stinson 468). It is also ironic that, because of Mathew's drive for money and power, he fails to notice the pervasive unhappiness of the Petworth family (Stinson 469).

In "Sense of Humour," the first story in You Make Your Own Life (1938), Pritchett is at the height of his short-story-writing ability. "Sense of Humor" contains, "sharp, highly selective, individuated, totally convincing dialogue." Pritchett says that this story was originally intended as an ironic story about a dull man, but it turned out to be in its first version "simply a dull story." When he revised it, he changed it from third-person to first-person narration, and this allowed his insensitive traveling salesman to talk directly to the reader, and allowed all of the ironies to come to life. "Sense of Humour" is a combination of humor and satire. The humor is droll, and the satire is filled with sophisticated ironies that are, "so uninsistent that nonastute readers will miss them" (Stinson, 1994, 188). Arthur, the protagonist in "Sense of Humor" is a vulgar salesman who wants to win the affections of Muriel, the girl with a "sense of humor." Arthur and Muriel are eccentrics in the tradition of Charles Dickens. Muriel's eccentricity resides mainly in what she calls her "sense of humour." At a number of different places in the story she proudly proclaims, "I'm Irish. I've got a sense of humour." Muriel is a desk clerk at a small hotel, and Colin, her boyfriend, is an inarticulate garage mechanic who gets upset and follows Muriel on his motorcycle whenever she goes anywhere with Arthur. But one day as he is trailing the couple on their way to Arthur's home which is a considerable distance away, Colin loses control of his motorcycle, rides into the path of an oncoming bus, and is killed. This event so excites Muriel that she gives herself sexually to Arthur for the first time that night, and as they are in a passionate embrace, she cries out, "Colin! Colin!" In trying to figure out how to get the body back home, Arthur and Muriel decide that the easiest thing to do is to take it back in a hearse, provided by Arthur's father, who is an undertaker. On their way home, Arthur is the driver of the hearse. And Muriel is sitting next to Arthur, and Colin is behind them both, not on his motorcycle, but in his casket. Muriel notices this bizarre situation, and because she has a "sense of humor," she begins to laugh, but Arthur quickly responds, "Keep your sense of humour to yourself" (Stinson, 1994, 188).

The title story in You Make Your Own Life is mainly a monologue which blends satire, humor, and compassion as it investigates the intricacies of small-town life (Stinson, 1994, 189). William Peden considers the style of "You Make Your Own Life" to be Hemingwayesque, by pointing to, "the brevity, directness, understatement, and effective use of dialogue" (qtd. in Stinson, 1994, 189). In this story, the first narrator is a visitor to a small town, who sits down in a barber's chair to get a haircut. The second narrator is the barber whose monologue continues until the end of the story. The situation is very similar to that in Ring Lardner's "Haircut" (1925), and like Lardner's piece, it does well in capturing the colloquial speech of the period, employs ironic humor, and exposes false values (Stinson, 1994, 189).

"The Sailer," "The Saint," "It May Never Happen," "Many Are Disappointed," "The Night Worker," and "The Oedipus Complex" are six of the stories in It May Never Happen and Other Stories (1945). John Stinson says that the revelation of character through indirect means is one of the most significant contributions of this volume. Pritchett's style is often both subtle and ironic as he develops his characters. Another important quality of this volume is the development of eccentric features in the characters. Many of these eccentric characters are "Puritans." Pritchett was also effective at satiric exposure, while at the same time making the readers feel both compassion and amusement as they learn about the characters. Pritchett also uses what Stinson calls a "haze technique," which makes it difficult for readers to be certain whether they have, "taken full, final, and definitive measure of a character" (Stinson, 1994, 189). The structure of "The Sailer" has a certain "ease" to it. The tone is relaxed, and at times comical or whimsical. In "The Sailer," the first-person narrator gradually, subtly, and ironically exposes himself through the narration. The narrator takes a former sailor into his home, a former sailer who tends to get hopelessly, and blindly lost. The narrator has a certain affinity for the sailor, because he considers both of them to be "puritans" (Stinson, 1994, 189).

The humor is broader, the comedy is richer, and the satire is more obvious and pointed in "The Saint" than it is in "The Sailer" (Stinson, 1994, 190). "The Saint" is a poignant, comic, satiric story which was written shortly after V. S. Pritchett's father, Walter, had converted to Christian Science (Stinson, 1994, 187). In "The Saint," there is a sect which is called the "Church of the Last Purification," which denies the existence of evil. The narrator is seventeen years old, and he is having his doubts. "We regarded it as 'Error'--our name for Evil--to believe the evidence of our senses." "If we had influenza or consumption, or had lost our money or were unemployed, we denied the reality of these things, saying that since God could not have made them they therefore did not exist" (qtd. in Stinson, 1994, 190). Mr. Timberlake is the leader of the sect. He goes punting on a river with the doubting narrator in order to have a heart-to-heart talk with him. Pritchett first develops a pleasant tableau scene to frame this conversation, but it soon becomes clear to the reader that Mr. Timberlake is really not a very good punter, and he runs into the low overhanging branch of a willow tree. Pritchett wittily describes this scene as Timberlake clings to the branch as it slowly sinks into the water. Timberlake's black suit becomes gilded with buttercup pollen, and he later has to rest on the shore, totally soaked and disheveled, all the while "refusing to give any acknowledgement that he has met with a mishap." "The Saint" has what Stinson calls "a real touch of pathos," as the boy undergoes an initiation that day and comes to realize that the sect is a sham, and more (Stinson, 1994, 190).

"It May Never Happen" is a "comedy of humours," since it provides Dickensian character sketches of various eccentrics. Mr. Phillimore is constantly engaged in verbal impostures and theatrical scenes of his own making (Stinson, 1994, 190). "Many are Disappointed" is like a Chekhov play because of the precision of the structure, and because of the establishment of significance through the "deft control of mood and atmosphere" (Stinson, 1994, 191). Pritchett uses much comic irony in "The Night Worker," a story in which everything is "magnificently understated." It is about a seven-year-old boy who is not able to comprehend that he is unwanted by both of his parents. The sadness of the boy's plight is contrasted with the joyful impending wedding of his cousin, Gladys. At the end of the story there is the strong suggestion that the soon-to-be-married couple very well might adopt the young narrator (Stinson, 1994, 191). "The Oedipus Complex" is a comic story about a zany dentist who reveals his own character as he talks with Mr. Pollfax the patient in his dentist chair (Stinson, 1994, 191).

Phillip Beluncle is the chief protagonist in Mr. Beluncle (1951), but the rest of the Beluncle family are protagonists as well. In his own eyes, Phillip is the ideal father; he is self-sacrificing, generous, patient, and understanding. In the eyes of Ethel (his wife) and his children, however, Phillip is a short-sighted tyrant. Phillip tries to find ultimate answers in a succession of religious affiliations, but he never succeeds because he equates God with the fulfillment of material desires. It is extremely ironic, then, that Beluncle's religious beliefs provide a curtain to hide him from ordinary life, from his family, and from the world around him. "In his obsession with divine mind, Phillip Beluncle is totally unable to communicate with his family." Pritchett develops the character of Phillip Beluncle with skill and wit, though the wit seems, at times, to be forced. (Marks 470).

"The Wheelbarrow" is one of the stories in When My Girl Comes Home (1961). It is a convincing and comic story about a man and a woman who are separated from each other by class and background as well as by gender. They meet; they feel some sexual chemistry; they spar wittily; and they part. The man, who is a Welsh cabdriver and a lay preacher, is presented as charming, wily, brash, and hypocritical (Stinson, 1994, 191).

John Stinson considers The Key to My Heart: A Comedy in Three Parts (1963) to be a, "successful mix of character sketch, droll comedy of manners, and farce." The style is light and polished, and the characters are dotty and obsessed with social class, so that the book can be considered to be "very English" (Stinson, 1994, 192). The stories are about the English preoccupation with class distinctions. These stories can be classed as light social comedies (Stinson, 1994, 197-198).

The ten stories in Blind Love and Other Stories (1969) are all comedies, and all of them are about different kinds of love--unrecognized love, dammed up love, thwarted love, or misdirected love. "In the stories, 'blind love' can mean blind because of love, blind to one's own love or that of someone else, or a blind plunge into love." Some critics have expressed a mild surprise that an author in his sixties would still be so consumed with notions of erotic love (Stinson, 1994, 192). The stories in Blind Love and Other Stories can be considered to be "comedies of Eros," as the characters learn about their own self-deceptions, their hidden motives, and their fears. One of the protagonists in the title piece is a well-to-do lawyer who is totally blind. About twenty years before the story takes place, the lawyer's wife had deserted him, because he was going blind. The other protagonist is his thirty-nine-year-old secretary who was abandoned by her husband when he found out (only after their marriage) that she had a birthmark extending from her neck to below one of her breasts. Of course the blind lawyer is not able to see his lover's birthmark (Stinson 193).

The Camberwell Beauty and Other Stories (1974) is an allegory about male possessiveness, in which Isabel is the "Camberwell Beauty." She's a beautiful teenager who has three suitors, and ends up marrying the oldest of the three, an impotent man who wants to possess her in the same way that he possesses his porcelain "objets d'art." So he keeps her locked up, and every night he commands her to undress while he looks at her, "with the same pride of possession he reserves for his most prized porcelain objects." But when he is not home, he forces her to dress as a soldier and march around beating a drum and blowing a bugle to scare away anyone who would come around to rape or to seduce his beautiful wife (Stinson 193). "The Marvelous Girl" is another story in The Camberwell Beauty and Other Stories. The first part of the story is rather straight forward. The second half of the story, however, can be read either in a way that the readers share the excitement of a young man's romantic infatuation, or it can be read ironically. In fact, it can be given both readings at the same time, as Pritchett, "walks a fine line between romance and gentle mockery" (Stinson 194).

"The Fig Tree" is the story in On the Edge of the Cliff (1979) in which a wife named Sally has a sexual affair with Teddy, a nurseryman, because she finds her life to be unemotional and barren. The sweet revenge which the husband arranges at the end of the story is very ironic. He arranges to have Sally and Teddy work together in a continual condition of intimate contact every day. Soon the adulterous couple become completely bored with each other (Stinson 195).

"Cocky Olly" is one of the stories in A Careless Widow and Other Stories (1989) (Stinson 195). It is about a 54-year old woman named Sarah who wants to recapture her youth. Sarah was raised by conservative middle-class English parents who tended to be dull, suspicious, and timid. But a liberal family with "advanced" ideas bought an adjoining property, and Sarah became acquainted with their son, who was something of a mischievous and maladjusted boy. At the boy's home, all of the children used to play a game named "Cocky Olly" in which the children would race around the house, shouting and flinging all of the doors open, while the boy's parents seemed to be "perfectly and easily tolerant." John Stinson considers "Cocky Olly" to be a metaphor for the opening of doors, and for the breaking away from social constraints, but it is also a metaphor for neurosis and maladjustment resulting from unrestrained extravagances (Stinson 196).

"The Chain-Smoker" and "The Last Throw" are two of the stories in The Complete Collected Stories (1991) that are generally considered humorous. One of the descriptions in "The Last Throw," for example, is: "Chatty slipped into Karvo's room like a well-dressed fever." Another humorous line comes from "The Snag," "Our difficulty was the common one of turning a love affair into a marriage." Most of the humor is not this obvious, however, as it usually arises out of the sheer oddity of the human behavior that is being observed (Jago 892).

V. S. Pritchett wrote satirical sketches and situational comedy that could be compared favorably with the similar writings of other twentieth-century British novelists, especially Evelyn Waugh and Aldous Huxley (Marks 470). Pritchett was especially skilled with his characterizations, and with his ironic tone. Pritchett's most well-developed characters tend to be salesmen and garage mechanics, barmaids and sailors, preachers and accountants. He writes ironically, and with tartness and wit. The situations in which he places his protagonists evoke both sympathy and pity. His writing style is swift moving, and uses language economically while at the same time selecting significant details, and offering vividly descriptive passages. Most of his writing could be called "understated social commentary" (Marks 471).

Sir Victor Sawdon Pritchett Bibliography

Jago, David. "V. S. Pritchett." Encyclopedia of British Humorists, Volume II. Ed. Steven H. Gale. New York, NY: Garland, 1996, 889-894.

Johnson, Anne Janette. "V. S. Pritchett." Contemporary Authors, New Revision Series, Volume 31. Ed. James G. Lesniak, Detroit, MI: Gale Research, 1990, 354-358.

Marks, Harry S. "V. S. Pritchett." Dictionary of Literary Biography, Volume 15: British Novelists, 1930-1959. Ed. Bernard Oldsey, Detroit, MI: Bruccoli Clark/Gale Research, 1983, 464-471.

Peden, William. "Realism and Anti-Realism." The Teller and the Tale: Aspects of the Short Story. Ed. Wendell M. Aycock. Lubbock, TX: Texas Tech Press, 1982, 47-62.

Pritchett, V. S. George Meredith and English Comedy. London, England: Chatto and Windus, 1970; New York, NY: Random House, 1970.

Pritchett, Victor Sawdon. Oxford Book of Short Stories, Chosen by V. S. Pritchett. New York, NY: Oxford University Press, 1981.

Stinson, John J. "V. S. Pritchett." Dictionary of Literary Biography, Volume 139: British Short-Fiction Writers, 1945-1980. Ed. Dean Baldwin, Detroit, MI: Bruccoli Clark Layman/Gale Research, 1994, 185-198.

Stinson, John J. V. S. Pritchett: A Study of the Short Fiction. New York, NY: Twayne/Macmillan, 1992.

John Henry Noyes Collier (1901-1980)

During the 1930s, John Collier wrote such novels as His Monkey Wife, or, Married to a Chimp (1930), Tom's A-Cold (1933), and Defy the Foul Fiend, or, The Misadventures of a Heart (1934). These novels satirized London society during Collier's time. Collier later wrote many witty pieces for Playboy, Esquire, and the New Yorker. He also wrote teleplays for Alfred Hitchcock Presents (Donnelly 262). His Monkey Wife (1930) has a lighthearted and preposterous tone (Donnelly 262). In this story, an Englishman returns from Africa with a monkey bride, and this is a fascination to British society. Emily, the monkey bride, is a sensitive, warm, compassionate, and very educated chimpanzee who is contrasted to the hysterical women and the "neurasthenic" men of 1930s London society. In Tom's A-Cold (1933), Collier did a bit of conservative philosophizing that, "was an embarrassment to the author in his later years." Nevertheless, it is quite witty. Defy the

Foul Fiend (1934) is a picaresque novel about a naïve young man named Willoughby who goes through various phases of romantic love, radicalism, and decadent hedonism. He finally becomes a Tory. All of his various "enthusiasms" are doomed to ironic outcomes. The novel satirizes many aspects of modern English culture and society. William Donnelly says that Collier's novels are the work of a, "serious moralist with a taste for the absurd and an audacious wit" (Donnelly 263).

During the period between 1937 and 1939, Collier wrote many short humorous grotesque stories which are satiric, and are stylistically well conceived, with their careful plottings, and their economical characterizations (Donnelly 264). These short stories, which were later collected in Fancies and Goodnights (1951), The Devil and All (1954), and The Best of John Collier (1975), usually involve the romantic misadventures of naïve young men. There are also supernatural elements, grisly episodes, social satire, and parodies of myths, fairy tales, or serious literature. The main appeal of these stories is their tightly constructed style. Another appeal is that they tend to be very short, averaging usually only about 3,000 words (Donnelly 263). These short stories usually have macabre and fantastic plots, and were written in the refined elegant style that one critic has called a "strictly British genre of humor" (Donnelly 264).

The opening line of "The Devil, George and Rosie" is, "There was a young man who was invariably spurned by the girls, not because he smelt at all bad, but because he happened to be as ugly as a monkey." In this story, George is given an opportunity to get revenge on the female gender by being appointed as the "Chief Prosecutor of Women" in Hell. Rosie is in Hell by accident, but she agrees to stay there so as not to cause a fuss, and then George falls in love with her. The narrator of "Are You Too Late Or Was I Too Early" is a recluse who finds the footprint of a woman on his shower mat. As time goes on, he becomes more and more aware of her presence in his apartment. He sees her breath on his mirror. He sees flowers parting their petals for her unseen face. He hears and feels her breathing in his bed. Her presence becomes more and more vivid to him until he is finally able, through intense effort, to hear her voice. George explains, "I heard in a full opening of the sense, the delicate intake of her breath, the very sound of the parting of her lips. Each syllable was clear as a bell." It is the woman who speaks the last words in the story, "Oh, it's perfect. It's so quiet for Harry's work. Guess how we were lucky enough to get it! The previous tenant was found dead in his chair, and they actually say it's haunted" (Donnelly 263).

John Henry Noyes Collier Bibliography

Donnelly, William. "John Henry Noyes Collier." Encyclopedia of British Humorists, Volume I. Ed. Steven H. Gale. New York, NY: Garland, 1996, 262-264.

John William van Druten (John Harewood) (1901-1957)

John van Druten, who did most of his early publishing with London's Mercury, and Punch, has a reputation as a skillful writer in the comedy-of-manners tradition (Pedersen 191). Van Druten is known for his skill at dialogue, and at characterization. He has a special talent for subtle comedy, and for urbane wit (Pedersen 199). Diversion (1928) is a play about the relationship between a young man named Wyn Hayward, and his father. Wyn has killed an actress, and his father helps Wyn to commit suicide in order to spare him the public humiliation of a trial and execution. Many critics praised the play for its humor, but criticized it for its melodramatic qualities and for its failure to achieve credibility (Pedersen 192).

After All (1929) is notable for its gentle humor. Ivor Brown commended van Druten for his, "ability to elicit the comedy from domesticity instead of forcing 'laughs' on its surface" (Pedersen 193). London Wall (1931) is both a domestic comedy, and a comedy of manners. It is about the sex and love adventures among the members of the clerical and secretarial staff in a lawyer's office, with the main focus being on the women. One of the women, Pat Milligan, is naïve and innocent, and is almost taken in by the office cad but is saved by the timely intervention of Miss Janus. Miss Janus has given up looking for a lasting love, and is now interested in marriage to almost anyone, just so she will have a way of getting out of the office. Miss Hooper withholds sexual gratification from the man she loves in order to snare him and cause him to propose marriage. Miss Bufton is a "fluffy blonde" who "knows all of the rules" of the game she is playing. And Miss Willesden is a sixty-five-year-old eccentric client who wishes she had a love in her life rather than all of her money. Although the play is humorous, it is also a serious commentary about women who work in offices and the dreary lives not only of office women, but of all women who do not succeed in getting married (Pedersen 193).

There's Always Juliet (1931) is a comedy of manners about a woman who is leading such a boring life that she is happy to play the role of "Juliet" to a "Romeo" who is an American architect visiting in England. Within twenty-four hours, she is forced to make the choice of whether or not she will go off to America and marry her "Romeo." At first she is cautious and "sensible," but eventually, romance triumphs. And yet it is a romance that is tempered with a good deal of common sense (Pedersen 193). Hollywood Holiday (1931), which was co-authored with Benn Wolfe Levy, is an "extravagant comedy" about a silly and "twittery" middle-aged spinster from England who is a governess in Hollywood, and who survives in this "jungle" because she is a, "basically solid, kind, and good-natured person with integrity and a sense of self" (Pedersen 193).

The Distaff Side (1933) is another of van Druten's comedies (Pedersen 194), as is Most of the Game (1935). The three protagonists in Most of the Game are a successful writer, a young girl who loves him, and his secretary. The secretary is a cynical and wise-cracking man who is perfectly competent, but whose disillusionment has caused him to withdraw from active participation in the game of life (Pedersen 194). There is a friendship between two middle-aged women in Old Acquaintance (1940) which has endured from their childhood despite the fact that these two women have very different moral convictions, values, and ways of life. Their close relationship is a source of emotional support for both of them because their having known each other for such a long time has produced a lifetime of shared memories. Critics have praised Old Acquaintance for the believability of its character portrayals, for its skillful construction, and for its wit and irony (Pedersen 195). Burns Mantle considers The Voice of the Turtle (1943) to be a "tastefully staged sophisticated comedy." In this play, a promiscuous woman breaks a date with a soldier on leave, and a younger friend of hers, who is a bit more innocent, takes pity on the soldier and eventually allows him to spend the night with her. What starts out as a casual encounter ends up by being a real love for each other, and it is obvious that marriage will soon follow. The play is light and charming (Pedersen 196).

I Remember Mama (1944), which was adapted from Kathryn Forbes's Mama's Bank Account is a romantic comedy of humours. It was produced the year that van Druten became a naturalized citizen of the United States, and this may in part account for van Druten's, "swing from amoral and worldly sophistication to a touting of homely virtues of the immigrant families who built America." The mother in the play is very much romanticized and idealized. She is all-wise, understanding, and charitable. She denies pleasures to herself because she is always concerned for other people. She is hardworking, and humble, but despite her humility, she will oppose authority when this authority is wrong. The daughter in the family wants to become a writer, but in order to have anything worthy of writing about, she must learn how to value her family and her heritage. There is also a crusty old uncle in the play, who has a heart of gold, and two aunts who are caricatures of evil-mindedness, small-mindedness, and silliness. John Gassner, an American critic, says that the escapism in I Remember Mama was merely "justifiable human indulgence." British critics, on the other hand, have been a bit more objective, characterizing it as a "synthetic homespun" play that is full of "wishy-washy sentimentalizing," and the "corniest corn" (Pedersen 196).

The protagonist in The Mermaids Singing (1945) is a middle-aged playwright by the name of Clement Waterlow, who is going to have an affair with a young small-town girl who is attracted to him because he is a playwright. Because of the pleas of the girl's mother, and her fiancé, and because of some fortuitous occurrences in the play, however, he decides not to have the affair because it would result in great suffering for the girl. Jean Nathan listed The Mermaids Singing as the best new comedy of the 1945-1946 season (Pedersen 196). Make Way for Lucia (1948) is a farce which is based on the Lucia novels of E. F. Benson (Pedersen 196). It is about how two women use their wit and will in a battle for social domination of a small town in southern England ir 1912 (Pedersen 197).

Bell, Book and Candle (1950) is a play about a modern-day wı :h who has an affair in order to relieve the boredom of her mundane existence. But sh: ₁iscovers that she has fallen in love with her partner, and by so doing, has lost her powers as a witch. The characters in the play are both credible and amusing, and the play itself is entertaining. It reflects a theme that occurs in many of van Druten's plays--"that commitment to love of a man will save a woman, by giving her life purpose and filling its emptiness," and this principle evidently holds true not only for women, but for witches as well (Pedersen 197). John van Druten's most significant play, I Am a Camera (1951), was adapted from Christopher Isherwood's Berlin Stories, and it inspired the musical Cabaret (1966). There are two characters in the play. Christopher Isherwood is the "camera" of the title. He observes and records life around him without making any value judgments, without actively participating in this life, and without making any real effort to have an influence on this life. The other character is Salley Bowles, the promiscuous, pleasure-seeking, directionless poseur. She is a would-be actress who is in love with the glamorous side of show business (Pedersen 197).

John William van Druten (John Harewood) Bibliography

Kronenberger, Louis. Cavalcade of Comedy: 21 Brilliant Comedies from Jonson and
        Wycherley to Thurber and Coward. New York, NY: Simon and Schuster, 1953.
Pedersen, Lisë. "John van Druten." Modern British Dramatists, 1900-1945. Ed. Stanley
        Weintraub. Detroit, MI: Bruccoli Clark/Gale Research, 1982, 189-200.

Stella Dorothea Gibbons (1902-1989)

Stella Gibbons was a contributor to Punch, Tatler, and other magazines concerned with humor. Extracts from her Cold Comfort Farm (1932) have been anthologized in Modern Humor (J. Dent, 1940), in Phoenix Book of Wit and Humor (Phoenix House, 1949), and in Laughter in a Damp Climate (Jenkins, 1963) (Kinsman 114). Stella Gibbons's humor is much more savage and more outrageous in her early books, those written before 1940. After the war, however, her novels became serious explorations of human nature. During this period, they tended to be more sympathetic than skewering (MacPike 443). Marya Mannes says that Stella Gibbons's reputation as a humorist mainly comes from Cold Comfort Farm (1932). Mannes called this novel, "one of the most brilliantly funny books ever written" (Mannes 1). It is the story of an orphaned girl named Flora Poste, who has to stay for six months with her relatives, the Starkadders. The Starkadders live in what Loralee MacPike describes as, "the gloomiest imaginable reincarnation of a Sussex peasant farmhouse dating back to a swineshed of Edward the Sixth." But since Cold Comfort Farm is a parodic satire of the romance novel of the 1930s, Flora is able to tidy up the remarkably untidy lives of her cousins in short order. Brooding and sensual Seth is lured to Hollywood by Flora's friend, a movie producer who is looking for a new Clark Gable. Flora changes artsy Elfine into an elegant young lady who is able to convince the neighborhood squire to marry her. Urk, who had his eyes on Elfine, has to take second best, Meriam, a hired girl who has been pregnant every summer since puberty, and Urk is changed to become a doting father to her babies. In the meantime, Flora convinces Amos, the patriarch of the family to take his hell-fire-and-brimstone preaching on the road in a Ford van. This clears the way for Reuben, the only sensible Starkadder, to buy fertilizers and plows with the egg money that he has been hiding from Aunt Ada. Aunt Ada has been ruling the family with an iron fist because she saw something nasty happen in the woodshed as a child. Before Flora arrived, Aunt Ada had refused to let anyone leave the farm, but she finally succumbs to Flora's arguments, and flies away to Paris wearing a new leather trousers suit featured in Vogue. Her departure leaves the remaining sons free to bring their secretly-married wives onto the farm. In the end, Flora falls in love with her cousin Charles, and flies off into the sunset with him (MacPike 441).

Cold Comfort Farm is a satire of the turn-of-the-century British pastoral novel. "Gibbons pokes gentle fun at literary pretension by transforming Heathcliffish Urk into a paterfamilias and literary critic Mr. Mybug into an anachronistic advocate of the Branwell-Brontë-wrote-all-of-his-sisters'-novels school." By the time Elfine has her wedding reception, all of the Starkadders have reached the pinnacle of civilization. They are finally able to have a nice time in an ordinary human manner. They were, "not having it because they were raping somebody, or beating somebody, or having religious mania or being doomed to silence by a gloomy, earthly pride, or loving the soil with the fierce desire of a lecher, or anything of that sort." "She had accomplished a great work" (Gibbons Cold Comfort Farm 441).

Bassett (1934) presents Gibbons's view of what it is like when an impoverished and flighty aristocrat and a doughty pattern-cutter who has been fired from her job try to create a new life as owners of a boarding house. The novel portrays both the sad realities and the golden hopes of such an endeavor (MacPike 443). The humor in Miss Linsey and Pa (1936) is very gentle, although it is true that in this novel Gibbons skewers butch lesbianism and artsy downward mobility of the young intelligentsia. The charm of the novel comes from its empathy toward a silly and anachronistic old maid who is trying to survive in modern London. "We chuckle over the naïveté of Miss Linsey's cousin Len because he truly believes that he can find the girl he left behind in France two decades ago" (MacPike 443).

The satire of Ticky (1943) is darker than is that of the Cold-Comfort-Farm novels, but it has the same type of "funniness." The Colonel wants to appropriate a muddy acre of land which has been deeded to the waiters, and which is called "Pleasure Ground." The Colonel and his troupes invade and occupy the Pleasure Ground in order to find the Charter, and they finally find it; it was being used as a dishcloth. At the end of Ticky, the simple people retire to their rose-covered cottages, as the Colonel is still trying to figure out a way around the Charter (MacPike 443). It is important to note that in 1984, Ticky was reissued as part of Sutton's "Classics of Humor" series (MacPike 444).

In Conference at Cold Comfort Farm (1949), Flora, who has by now been married to Reverend Charles Fairford for sixteen years, returns to Cold Comfort Farm to help Mr.

Mybug plan a conference of the International Thinkers' Group. The farm has been "redone," so that in Mock-Middle-English style, every room is given a name like "Lytle Stille-Roome," or "Great Scullerie." The farm implements have been cleaned, shined, and hung as decorations. There are Toby jugs, peasant pottery, window seats and other elements of farm nostalgia sprinkled around generously to make the farm into a historic site, "exactly like being locked in the Victoria and Albert Museum after closing time" (Gibbons Conference 46). But the parody becomes even more grotesque than this, as modern music is satirized by the playing of Bob Flatte's latest opera, The Flayed, which is about a tanner who is torn between a love for his girl and a love for his craft (MacPike 442). "The grotesquely Freudian relationship between the tanner and his hides climaxes with an aria sung by his mother 'in which she confesses that Stan is the illegitimate son of a taxidermist who seduced her in early youth, thus accounting for her son's sadistic obsession" (Gibbons Conference 105).

The upper classes are also targets of the biting satire. There is a depressed girl chauffeur who is the daughter of an impoverished Lord, who has had to go to school and learn a Cockney accent and learn how to be tacky, in order to be successful in earning a living. The farm has become so extreme that it is now a caricature of itself, and the only way that it can be saved is to reinstitute the original Starkadderness. So the seven Starkadder cousins and brothers that are still alive are lured back to the homestead, and immediately they start to destroy the Victoria-and-Albert retreat in order to return the farm to its original fen-like state. The perfection that ended Cold Comfort Farm cannot be maintained. "Civilization must lose the battle between order and chaos for only then is there room for the talents of the Flora Postes (and the Britains) of the world" (MacPike 442).

Many of the characters in Here Be Dragons (1956) are compared to animals: "He looked like a saucy but well-meaning adolescent chicken" (Gibbons Dragons 301). In The Wolves Were in the Sledge (1964), ordinary language undergoes "comic scrutiny." Nancy Leland asks about the phrase "little baby," for example, "why do people call them little, by the way? They always are, and surely it could be taken for granted by now" (Gibbons Wolves 102). Gibbons is constantly making statements about the sexes in her novels. In The Charmers (1965), for example, she has one of the characters say, "Men! Why need there be any? Of course, you had to have them for other things, like looking at bodies when people were murdered, but if there weren't any men probably no one would get murdered" (MacPike 443).

Stella Dorothea Gibbons Bibliography

Gibbons, Stella Dorothea. Cold Comfort Farm. London, England: Longmans, Green, 1932.
Gibbons, Stella Dorothea. Conference at Cold Comfort Farm. London, England: Longmans, Green, 1949.
Gibbons, Stella Dorothea. Here Be Dragons. London, England: Hodder and Stoughton, 1956.
Kinsman, Clare D. Contemporary Authors, First Revision, Volumes 13-16. Detroit, MI: Gale, 1975.
MacPike, Loralee. "Stella Dorothea Gibbons." Encyclopedia of British Humorists, Volume I. Ed. Steven H. Gale. New York, NY: Garland, 1996, 440-445.
Mannes, Marya. "What Did Aunt Ada See?" New York Times (December 26, 1971, Sect II, 19:1).

George Orwell (1903-1950)

David Zehr considers George Orwell to have been a complex and paradoxical writer who once described himself as a "Tory anarchist." This is a phrase that expressed his, "complex unification of radical and conservative impulses" (Zehr 407). Emil Draitser used to write satire for Russia's best satiric publication Krokodil. It is therefore of interest to find on page 7 of his Forbidden Laughter an especially appropriate statement by George Orwell: "Every joke is a tiny revolution." Sant Singh Bal divides Orwell's writing career into two stages. During the 1930s Orwell was a social critic. In the 1940s he became an essayist and a political satirist. The writings published after his death in 1950 show him to be an austere yet gentle author. It was the real world which motivated Orwell to write his satires. He saw troops who had fought bravely denounced in the newspapers as cowards and traitors. He saw other troops who had never fired a shot hailed in the newspapers as heroes of imaginary victories. He saw, "history being written not in terms of what happened but of what ought to have happened according to various 'party lines'" (Beadle 13).

Because of Orwell's ambivalent social position during his formative years the extraordinary importance of money was a prominent theme in Orwell's first four books. This also explains why Orwell developed his strong attitudes in favor of the bourgeoisie and against the privileged intelligentsia. In the conflict between the society at large and the individual, Orwell always favored the individual. His love for individual freedom is demonstrated not only in the social subjects he chose to write about during the 1930s, but also in the political subjects of his writings during the 1940s. He strongly disliked favoritism, arbitrary rules, and the omnipotence of the system. Cyril Connolly, one of Orwell's colleagues at Eton remarked that Orwell rejected "the war, the Empire, Kipling, Sussex, and Character" (Zehr 408).

Orwell's Down and Out in Paris and London (1933) was initially entitled "A Scullion's Diary." It was written in diary form and blended imaginative fantasy with accurate reportage. The book is buoyant and lively. The Paris part is imaginative and evocative with a tenuous story line that bases the narrator's experiences on typical events experienced by Parisian low life. There is a sprinkling of queer tales and stories about individuals who lived "lives that were curious beyond words" (Zehr 410). The anecdotes and experiences are told in a vigorous and individualized voice with boyish glee. The London part of the book is less imaginative and has more detachment. The narrator is no longer a raconteur; he is rather a research worker and detached social critic, and he tells an honest and objective story about tramps and the social laws that serve to perpetuate their condition.

Burmese Days (1935) describes Burma as a multilingual country where class and language are interrelated. In Burma, a butler may be rebuked for learning his English too well, and an English woman may find it best not to learn anything more than "kitchen Urdu" (Bolton 19). John Flory, the protagonist of Burmese Days said, "Free speech is unthinkable. All other kinds of freedom are permitted. You are free to be a drunkard, an idler, a coward, a backbiter, a fornicator; but you are not free to think for yourself. Your opinion on every subject of any conceivable importance is dictated for you by the pukka sahib's code" (Zehr 411).

In A Clergyman's Daughter (1935), as in Down and Out, and in "Hop-Picking," Orwell is concerned with various non-standard varieties of English and how a dialect is related to the character and status of the individual who uses it (Bolton 19). At one point in the novel the clergyman's daughter finds herself homeless in Trafalgar Square on a freezing night with a bunch of characters just as lost and even more desperate than she is. Their talk is a kind of "litany of the damned." In the group there is a defrocked parson, and a woman whose husband has locked her out, and an old louse-infested tramp, and a bunch of children from the north who sing at the pubs for a living. To add to the pathos, every time they are beginning to experience an illusion of warmth and fellowship, a policeman stops by and moves them along. To demonstrate the grimness of the head mistress in the school where the Clergyman's Daughter eventually teaches, Orwell has her classify all of her pupils into three categories. The first category consists of pupils which may be ill-treated to any extent. The second category consists of pupils who should be treated with some care. And the third category consists of pupils who must not be touched for whatever reason, and whose work must be constantly praised. The placement of pupils into these categories is determined by how promptly and generously the parents pay their bills.

Keep the Aspidistra Flying (1936) is a gloomy novel about money. Gordon Comstock, the protagonist, is a struggling poet and angry young man who declares a war on money by giving up his position in an advertising firm to take a low-paying job as an assistant in a book store. He feels that by doing this he will have time for his writing. Ironically, his new poverty so dominates his thoughts that he cannot get on with his writing. Comstock has a manuscript rejected and thinks to himself, " 'The Editor regrets!' Why be so bloody mealy-mouthed about it? Why not say out-right, 'We don't want your bloody poems. We only take poems from chaps we were at Cambridge with' " (Hopkinson 275).

The first half of The Road to Wigan Pier (1937) documents the squalid living conditions that Orwell had encountered in the economically depressed areas of Yorkshire and Lancashire. His discussion tends to support his "incisive criticism of socialism." "Socialism, at least in this island, does not smell any longer of revolution and the overthrow of tyrants; it smells of crankishness, machine worship and the stupid cult of Russia." He then goes on to detail what this means in terms of his own sensibilities, "One sometimes gets the impression that the mere words 'Socialism' and 'Communism' draw towards them with magnetic force every fruit-juice drinker, nudist, sandal-wearer, sex-maniac, Quaker, 'Nature Cure' quack, pacifist and feminist in England" (Zehr 414). The Road to Wigan Pier is Orwell's first clear identification with the aims and ideals of socialism. The title is based on a North Country joke, for the word "Pier" suggests the seaside, holidays, and gaiety while "Wigan" is a forbidding inland town whose pier is a derelict wharf not on the seaside but on a canal.

In Orwell's Coming Up for Air (1939), protagonist George Bowling is a dull, sluggish, solitary, middle-aged, non-intellectual lower-middle-class insurance-salesman. George is fat and good natured and has a ripe and easy sense of humor. Although the life of George is dreary, he is not a dreary character himself, as the book is written with dash and enjoyment. George wins some money at the track and conceals his winnings from his wife, deciding instead that he will visit the little country town where he was raised. In his mind his former home was the symbol of idyllic peace and natural rural beauty. But when he arrives at his old home, he discovers that the sylvan setting has been replaced by a "hellish" development. According to Tom Hopkinson, Orwell here and in other places enjoys "rubbing the reader's nose in it." The reader must accompany George everywhere he goes as he sees what has happened to the old marketplace, to the old High Street, to the old horse trough, to the teashop, the corn merchant's, the churchyard, to the pool where the great fish used to be, and finally to the girl he had once loved.

One vivid scene of the novel describes the effects of bombing. A bomb has fallen on Lower Binfield. It is ironic that the bomb has fallen by accident and during peacetime. The result is nevertheless dramatic, as the bomb has sheared away the front of a house, leaving all of its contents exposed and strangely undisturbed, like an open-sided doll's house. This scene in Orwell's 1939 novel is a warning of the imminence of war.

Orwell's Animal Farm (1945) is a brilliant Swiftian satire about the Russian revolution. It was at first rejected by a number of publishers both in England and in

America. One American publisher rejected it because, "Americans were not in the mood for animal stories" (Zehr 418). Animal Farm tells how power corrupts. There is a betrayal of the revolution, and there is a gradual perversion of its ideals. Animal Farm is a rough approximation of what had happened during Orwell's time in Spain and in the Soviet Union (Beadle 13). Animal Farm is the one book which was able to achieve a level of detachment and admirable good humor that was largely missing from his other books. Tom Hopkinson suggests that one reason for this is Orwell's disillusionment with Socialism as a perfect political system. Another reason was Orwell's choice of animals rather than humans as his characters. Orwell had a sincere love for animals, and this was one of the reasons for the detachment and good humor of Animal Farm. Orwell suggests that there are a number of reasons for the perverse drive for power among those who already have power. One reason is that the animals below them lack the intelligence and the memory. Orwell says, "this makes them powerless against the autocracy of the pigs." Another reason is the shape of a society that is "insufficient as a revolutionary goal." Orwell said in 1947 that Animal Farm was, "the first book in which I tried, with full consciousness of what I was doing, to fuse political purpose and artistic purpose into one whole" (Zehr 419).

Animal Farm is an allegory which portrays the animals on Animal Farm as misled victims of a rising totalitarian dictatorship. Tom Hopkinson suggests that Orwell's study of Swift in an essay entitled "Politics vs. Literature" foreshadows Animal Farm. Orwell said that it was the only book he had ever really sweated over. Ironically, this is the novel that shows the fewest signs of being sweated over, since it flows smoothly and clearly from start to finish, as though all the author had done was copy it from another source. Animal Farm is written in the classic tradition of satire, the tradition of receding planes. There is a level for every reader, regardless of the reader's sophistication. Like Gulliver's Travels or Aesop's Fables, the novel can be read as a delightful children's story. But it is also an attack on Stalinism. At still another level, it is a lament on the fate of revolutions. And finally it is a profound and moving commentary on human interactions in general.

At the beginning of Animal Farm, which is also a fable, the animals on Manor farm are upset at the inequality of the system where the humans enjoy all the privileges and the animals do all the work. Old Major is the political visionary who represents Karl Marx. He describes the plight of the animals, their lack of freedom, their misery, and their powerlessness. As he declares the principle of "Animalism," it is clear that Orwell is allegorically describing the Marxist view of the relationship between the working class and the rich, landowning class of any society. So they take over the farm with the idea of making it into a utopian society, and they adopt as their motto, "All Animals Are Equal." It is not long until the animals discover that for everyone except the pigs, and their protectors the dogs, life is exactly as hard and as painful as it had been with Mr. Jones. Although "All Animals are Equal," the pigs argue that pigs must be in positions of leadership because of their superior knowledge and intellects. They must be the leaders in order to assure that Farmer Jones won't return and take back the farm. Furthermore, the pigs must be given the apples and the milk, not because they especially like apples and milk but because apples and milk are brain food, and sharp brains are needed for the survival of the group.

Orwell suggests that the socialistic structure on Animal Farm fails for three fundamental reasons: The first is the perverse drive for power among those who already possess it; the second is the lack of intelligence and memory (i.e., past) among the lower animals; the third is the idea that merely altering the superficial shape of a society (without changing the internal reasoning processes) is an inadequate revolutionary goal. Because the lower animals lack a verifiable historical consciousness, they are easy prey to the manipulative uses of language and power that repeatedly falsify their sense of history and their sense of identity. During the Battle of the Cowshed, Snowball

> had not paused for an instant even when the pellets from Jones's gun had
> wounded his back.... Snowball fought bravely at the Battle of the
> Cowshed.... Did we not give him "Animal Hero, First Class," immediately
> afterwards? (Orwell Animal Farm 80)

but Squealer responds simply, "That was our mistake, comrade, For we know now--it is
all written down in the secret documents that we have found--that in reality he was trying
to lure us to our doom" (Orwell Animal Farm 80). This is indeed dark and ironic humor,
as is the abolishment of the singing of Beasts of England. When asked why this
revolutionary song has been abolished, and why it is now forbidden to sing it, Squealer
says stiffly, "Beasts of England was the song of the Rebellion. But the Rebellion is now
completed" (Orwell Animal Farm 86). Again the humor is very dark. This becomes darker
still later, when the animals hear guns being fired, and ask what that means. "To celebrate
our victory!" (Orwell Animal Farm 99), cries Squealer. When Squealer is asked what
victory he is referring to he responds,

> "What victory, comrade? Have we not driven the enemy off our soil--the
> sacred soil of Animal Farm?" "But they have destroyed the windmill. And
> we had worked on it for two years!" "What matter? We will build another
> windmill. We will build six windmills if we feel like it" (Orwell Animal
> Farm 100)

The loss of historical memory is also demonstrated by the gradual rewriting of the
seven commandments of Animalism. Clover thought that she had remembered the Fourth
Commandment differently:

> "Muriel," she said, "read me the Fourth Commandment. Does it not say
> something about never sleeping in a bed?" With some difficulty Muriel
> spelt it out. "It says, 'No animal shall sleep in a bed with sheets,' " she
> announced finally. (Orwell Animal Farm 69)

After a number of animals have been executed, Clover again thinks that she has
remembered a commandment differently, so she asks Muriel to read the Sixth
Commandment, "No animal shall kill any other animal without cause." The novel
continues, "somehow or other, the last two words had slipped out of the animal's memory"
(Orwell Animal Farm 88). Toward the end of the novel, Muriel

> was reading over the Seven Commandments to herself and noticed that there
> was yet another of them which the animals had remembered wrong. They
> had thought the Fifth Commandment was "No animal shall drink alcohol,"
> but there were two words that they had forgotten. Actually the
> Commandment read; "No animal shall drink alcohol to excess." (Orwell
> Animal Farm 103)

Later the animals discover that the Seven Commandments have been reduced to a single
Commandment: "All Animals Are Equal" which has been extended to "But Some Animals
Are More Equal than Others" (Orwell Animal Farm 123). The animals return from the
fields one evening to discover that the pigs have taken to walking on two legs and carrying
whips (Orwell Animal Farm 123), and the sheep instead of bleating "Four legs good, two
legs bad" are bleating "Four legs good, two legs better. The great irony of Animal Farm
is that the Pigs, who were the leaders in the rebellion against the humans are becoming
more human every day.

In 1946 Orwell published Critical Essays. This was later republished in America
as Dickens, Dali and Others (1946). David Zehr considers this to be Orwell's finest
collection of essays. One of the pieces, "The Art of Donald McGill," is about the comic
post cards of Orwell's day each of which was simply an illustration to a joke; these cards
stood or fell by their ability to raise a laugh ("Art" 125). Orwell makes an important point
here about the nature of humor. Obscene remarks and gestures seem to be perfectly

acceptable orally and on stage, but if these same remarks and gestures are printed, there is usually a public outcry. However, the genre of the comic post card seems to be an exception to this rule, since. "Only in post cards and on the variety stage can the stuck-out behind, the dog and lamp-post, baby's nappy type of joke be freely exploited." Orwell suggests that these post cards give expression to what he calls the "Sancho Panza view of life."

> The Don Quixote-Sancho Panza combination, which of course is simply the ancient dualism of body and soul in fiction form, recurs more frequently in the literature of the last four hundred years than can be explained by mere imitation. It comes up again and again, in endless variations, Bouvard and Pécuchet, Jeeves and Wooster, Bloom and Dedalus, Holmes and Watson. ("Art" 135)

Orwell suggests that these representations merely reflect that in real life, the two principles, noble folly and base wisdom, exist side by side in every human being ("Art" 135). Donald McGill is our unofficial self. He is "the voice of the belly protesting against the soul. His tastes lie towards safety, soft beds, no work, pots of beer and women with 'voluptuous' figures" ("Art" 136). The Donald McGill postcards are a kind of saturnalia, a harmless rebellion against virtue. "They express only one tendency in the human mind, but a tendency which is always there and will find its own outlet, like water. On the whole, human beings want to be good, but not too good, and not quite all the time" (Art 138).

In 1984 (1949) Orwell wrote about a time in the near future when the world has been divided into three super states, and each of these states eliminates privacy, intellectual freedom, friendship, and individuality. Each state is systematically depriving its inhabits of "verifiable history," and of other resources that could develop a cultural consciousness. Orwell magnifies and distorts the disturbing tendencies he saw developing in the world so that these tendencies could be recognized and stopped. The dystopia presented in 1984 is more disturbing than is the dystopia presented in Aldous Huxley's Brave New World, or Zamyatin's We, because the dystopia in 1984 is set in the near future rather than in the distant future. In the world of 1984, virtually all private and subjective life has been erased. Winston Smith, however, begins writing a diary (which is a political crime), so that he can give shape to his "ancestral memory." In seeking to validate this "ancestral memory," he also collects some relics from the past, not only the diary, but also a paperweight, and Charrington's upstairs room, where Julia and he make love. For Winston, these are "pockets of the past" (Zehr 420).

England is the scene of 1984, but England is now known as "Airstrip One," and is part of a larger nation named "Oceania." There are three superstates; each of them is a system of oligarchical collectivism that has eliminated all intellectual freedom, and privacy. During the novel there is a ceaseless and pointless war that goes rumbling along. Sometimes Oceania is in alliance with Eastasia against Eurasia; at other times Oceania is in alliance with Eurasia against Eastasia. It doesn't seem to matter much who is fighting whom as long as the war prevails. Everything in Oceania is controlled by the Party, which has three slogans, "War Is Peace," "Freedom Is Slavery," and "Ignorance Is Strength." The Oceania government is divided into four ministries, the Ministry of Truth (concerned with propaganda), the Ministry of Love (concerned with law and order as controlled by the Thought Police), the Ministry of Plenty (concerned with rationing goods), and the Ministry of Peace (concerned with the conduct of war). Orwell uses "Doublethink" as a term to attack satirically the myopic intellectuals of his day. "Doublethink" is, "the power of holding two contradictory beliefs in one's mind simultaneously and accepting them both" (Calder, Chronicles 256). Orwell's protagonist, Winston Smith (named after Winston Churchill), works in the Ministry of Truth, and his job is to rewrite history to the benefit of the Party. But Winston is in secret revolt against the Party, and he illegally keeps a private diary in which he records his thoughts and feelings.

The choice of England as the setting of <u>1984</u> was made because Orwell wanted to emphasize that, "the English-speaking races are not innately better than anyone else and that totalitarianism, if not fought against, could triumph anywhere." When he wrote <u>1984</u>, the last thing Orwell was concerned about was literature. This is one reason why there are no credible or three-dimensional characters. Another reason is that Orwell was trying to present a world in which individuality had become obsolete and personality a crime. But many intellectuals feel, "embarrassed before the apocalyptic desperation of the book. They begin to wonder whether it may not be just a little overdrawn and humorless; they even suspect it is tinged with the hysteria of the death-bed" (Howe, <u>Politics</u> 236-237).

<u>1984</u> was written not as a prediction, but as a warning. On the dust jacket of the novel, Orwell writes, "I don't believe that the kind of society I describe will arrive, but I believe something resembling it could arrive." The primary purpose of the novel is to satirically magnify the disturbing conditions, tendencies and habits of thought that existed all around him, so that these tendencies could be recognized and arrested. The novel does not have a happy ending. Winston is obliterated, and the proles survive. This demonstrates Orwell's basic pessimistic nature, as expressed also in statements like, "When you are on a sinking ship, your thoughts will be about sinking ships" (Zehr 421).

Tom Hopkinson feels that Newspeak is the most important invention in <u>1984</u>, a language invented by Ingsoc [English Socialism] to make all unpatriotic thoughts impossible. In Newspeak, large amounts of vocabulary are systematically eliminated and words are stripped of any unorthodox connotations. The result has the effect of diminishing the range of thought possible, so that all unconventional ideas become by definition unthinkable. Orwell gives an example of how "Newspeak" works: "The word <u>free</u> still existed in Newspeak, but it could only be used in such statements as 'This dog is free from lice' or 'This field is free from weeds.' It could not be used in its old sense of 'politically free' or 'intellectually free,' since political and intellectual freedom no longer existed even as concepts, and were therefore of necessity nameless" (Hopkinson 285).

<u>England Your England and Other Essays</u> (1953) was republished in America as <u>Such, Such Were the Joys</u> (1953). It is ironic that the basic difference between the English and the American version is that the American version contains an article about England that the English version does not contain. This essay is entitled "Such, Such Were the Joys," and it is an autobiographical essay about Orwell's life in an English preparatory school. It is left out of the English edition because of the possibility of libel proceedings.

<u>Such, Such Were the Joys</u> is an attack on St. Cyprian's School and its proprietors, whom Orwell calls "Flip" and "Sambo." He is able to describe in detail the sour porridge clinging to the rims of the pewter bowls, and the smells of sweaty stockings and dirty towels in the corridors, and the cold, loneliness and lack of privacy. He also remembers the humiliating punishments and the pressures to conform.

> He felt ugly, cowardly, unpopular, and weak; he learned at first hand the injustice of class and snobbery. His emotions and ideals were manipulated to make him feel guilty and subservient.... The worst source of guilt was that while inwardly loathing and fearing Flip, he found himself desperately trying to please her. (Meyers <u>George</u>, 4)

Writing about <u>1984</u>, Anthony West says that the whole pattern of society shapes up along the same lines of fear which had been laid down in "Such, Such Were the Joys." Frederick Karl remarks that Orwell's description of his life at St. Cyprians school is very similar to the life in Oceana, and in both cases they have a Kafkaesque tone. According to Karl, both works deal with the pathos and terror which are involved when a man is caught between what he wants for himself and what the political system has to offer him. According to Karl, the political matter is secondary to the personal content (Carter 3-4).

Tongue in cheek, Lionel Trilling celebrates Orwell for, "the virtue of not being a genius." Arthur Koestler, suggests that we consider Orwell to be, "the only writer of genius among the littérateurs of social revolt between the two wars" and he further calls him "the missing link between Kafka and Swift" (Trilling 1). Orwell's satire can be best compared to that of Swift. It is a satire against mankind, and it is a satire against the frustrations of various personal experiences. In his essays, Orwell tends to choose subjects which other writers overlook, like the comics which are read by schoolboys and the humorous postcards that are sold at shops along the English seaside.

As soon as 1984 was written, it was claimed by the politically right, and in fact, Fredric Warburg, Orwell's publisher, said, "1984 is worth a cool million votes to the Conservative Party; it is imaginable that it might have a preface by Winston Churchill after whom its hero is named." In an article entitled "Arguments against Orwell," D. A. N. Jones notes that such anti-communist writers as Robert Conquest, Kingsley Amis, and Lincoln Barnett considered Orwell to be anti-communist as they were, and they often quoted Orwell to support their arguments in favor of the American war in Vietnam. However such American leftists as Noam Chomsky, Norman Mailer, and Arthur Schlesinger Jr. felt that Orwell was in their camp, and quoted Orwell in support of their position in opposition to the U.S. government's war policy.

It is Orwell's ability to speak to people of widely ranging political persuasions which makes him, "more widely read than perhaps any other serious writer in the twentieth century." George Woodcock says,

> When people of widely differing viewpoints--Conservatives and Anarchists, Socialists and Liberals, ageing academics and young writers born old--find encouragement for their attitudes in a single author's work, we can reasonably assume that each of them is missing something, and that the work, considered as a whole, must be a good deal more complex than it appears at first sight. (Carter 1)

Mark Connelly has observed that reading Orwell is like looking through a kaleidoscope or a series of distorted mirrors. "Catholics, anarchists, New Critics, Freudians, Marxists, and existentialists have probed Orwell's clear prose and written prolifically, each claiming Orwell as one of their own. Like Shakespeare, Orwell has become a handy source for quotes, which, taken out of context, are used to endorse almost anything" (Connelly 3).

Ironically, Orwell always considered himself to be a failure. In Such, Such Were the Days, he wrote, "Until I was about thirty I always planned my life on the assumption that any major undertaking was bound to fail." At the age of forty-six he wrote "There has literally been not one day in which I did not feel that I was idling, that I was behind with the current job, and that my total output was miserably small." When congratulated for being famous and successful, he responded, "I wonder if you know what my books sell-- usually 2000! My best book, the one about the Spanish war, sold less that 1000" (Shelden 1-2). In 1940, when Twentieth Century Authors asked him for a short summary of his life, he mentioned each of his major achievements and then followed this with some admission of failure or weakness. He was educated at Eton, BUT he did no work there and learned very little. He served with the Indian Imperial Police in Burma, BUT the climate ruined his health, and, "in any case there was no honour in having served the 'racket' of imperialism." He wrote fiction for a year-and-a-half in Paris, BUT, no publisher would accept any of his work. He fought in the Spanish Civil War, BUT the experience gave him a "horror of politics" (Sheldon 2).

George Orwell Bibliography

Bal, Sant Singh. George Orwell: The Ethical Imagination. New Delhi, India: Arnold-

Heinemann, 1981.

Beadle, Gordon. "George Orwell and the Spanish Civil War." Duquesne Review 16 (Spring, 1971): 3-16.

Bolton, W. F. The Language of 1984: Orwell's English and Ours. Oxford, England: Basil Blackwell, 1984.

Calder, Jenni. Chronicles of Conscience: A Study of George Orwell and Arthur Koestler. London, England: Secker and Warburg, 1968.

Calder, Jenni. Huxley and Orwell: "Brave New World" and "1984." London, England: Edward Arnold, 1976.

Carter, Michael. George Orwell and the Problem of Authentic Existence. London, England: Croom Helm, 1985.

Chilton, Paul, and Crispin Aubrey, eds. Nineteen Eighty-Four in 1984: Autonomy, Control and Communication. London, England: Comedia Publishing Group, 1983.

Connelly, Mark. The Diminished Self: Orwell and the Loss of Freedom. Pittsburgh, PA: Duquesne University Press, 1987.

Deutcher, Isaac. "1984--The Mysticism of Cruelty." Russia in Transition and Other Essays. Ed. Issac Deutcher. London, England: Hamilton, 1957, 230-45.

Friedman, Richard. "Predicting 1984: How Did Orwell Do?--Don't Ask." WHIMSY 3 (1985): 13-14.

Fyvel, T. R. George Orwell: A Personal Memoir. New York, NY: Macmillan, 1982.

Gottlieb, Erika. The Orwell Conundrum: A Cry of Despair or Faith in the Spirit of Man? Ottawa, Canada: Carleton University Press, 1992.

Greenblatt, Stephen Jay. Three Modern Satirists: Waugh, Orwell, and Huxley. New Haven, CT: Yale University Press, 1965.

Harris, Alan Charles. "I Wasn't Going to Talk about it, George...." WHIMSY 3 (1985): 14-16.

Hopkinson, Tom. "George Orwell (1903-1950)." British Writers. Ed. Ian Scott-Kilvert. New York, NY: Charles Scribner's Sons, 1983, 273-287.

Howe, Irving. Politics and the Novel. New York, NY: Horizon Press, 1957.

Kehl, D. G. "The Belletrist Looks--and Laughs--at Doublespeak: Beyond 1984." WHIMSY 3 (1985): 21.

Kessler, Martin. "Power and the Perfect State: The Study of Disillusionment as Reflected in Orwell's Nineteen Eighty-Four and Huxley's Brave New World." Political Science Quarterly 72.4 (1957): 565-577.

Meyers, Jeffrey, ed. George Orwell: The Critical Heritage. London, England: Routledge and Kegan Paul, 1975.

Nilsen, Don L. F. "George Orwell." Encyclopedia of British Humorists, Volume II. Ed. Steven H. Gale. New York, NY: Garland, 1996, 807-828.

Orwell, George. Animal Farm. New York, NY: Harcourt, Brace, 1950.

Orwell, George. "The Art of Donald McGill." Dickens, Dali and Others. New York, NY: Harcourt Brace Jovanovich, 1946, 124-139.

Petro, Peter. "George Orwell's Nineteen Eighty-Four: Anti-Utopian Satire." Modern Satire: Four Studies. Berlin, Germany: Mouton, 1982, 73-102.

Shelden, Michael. Orwell: The Authorized Biography London, England: Heinemann, 1991.

Thackeray, W. M. The English Humorists, Charity and Humour, The Four Georges. London, England: Dent, 1912.

Thale, Jerome. "Orwell's Modest Proposal." Critical Quarterly 9 (1962): 365-368.

Trilling, Lionel. "Introduction." Homage to Catalonia. Auth. George Orwell. Boston, MA: Beacon, 1952, v-xxiii.

Voorhees, Richard J. The Paradox of George Orwell. West Lafayette, IN: Purdue University Studies, 1961.

West, W. J. The Larger Evils: Nineteen Eighty-Four--The Truth behind the Satire. Edinburgh, Scotland: Canongate Press, 1992.
Zehr, David Morgan. "George Orwell." British Novelists, 1930-1959, Part 2: M-Z. Ed. Bernard Oldsey. Detroit, MI: Bruccoli Clark, 1983, 407-423.

Evelyn Arthur St. John Waugh (1903-1966)

Evelyn Waugh's first short story, entitled, "The Curse of the Race" was written at the age of seven, and was published in Little Innocents; Childhood Reminiscences by Dame Ethyl Smith and Others. It is about a man named Rupert who loses 500 pounds sterling to his friend Tom by betting on a horse that doesn't win. Rupert decides that he must kill Tom because he owes him money, but the attempted murder fails because Rupert's sword makes a noise in the dark and awakens Tom. Tom and a policeman pursue Rupert until Rupert kills the policeman and the policeman's horse and is forced to take refuge in a crowded inn. There he must share a room in the dark with Tom. Finally, Rupert is caught and hanged, and the last line of Waugh's story reads, "I hope the story will be a lesson to you never to bet." Another of Waugh's early short stories was entitled, "The Tutor's Tale: A House of Gentlefolks," and was published in The New Decameron: The Fifth Day. This is an amusing satire about the eccentricities and the foibles of the rich (Rogers 339). It is interesting to note that Waugh once made the statement that satire could not be written in the twentieth century because this genre, "presupposes homogeneous moral standards" (Doyle 573). Some of Waugh's favorite satirical targets were sex, authority, religion, suffering, and death (Swanson 1193).

Harold Acton notes that during his uproarious days at Oxford, Waugh's views were strongly tinged with irony as he revelled in the absurdities of his acquaintances, and the crankiness of some of the dons (Beaty 9). While at Oxford, Waugh would declare himself to be a Tory. At Lansing, he pretended to be a socialist, and at other times he indicated that he advocated the restoration of the Stuarts, along with anarchism and the rule of a hereditary caste. He always managed to take a stance that would startle his audience. Frederick Beaty notes that Waugh had a penchant for teasing and for deceptive play, and that his teasing on the personal level easily translated into the ironic rhetoric of his fiction (Beaty 10). Mark Amory has edited a volume entitled The Letters of Evelyn Waugh in which he says that Waugh wrote letters in the mornings, when he was sober, and he wrote his diary at night, when he was drunk. His letters to his children were delightful, "and if he describes them to others with ironic resignation there is also a gleaming humorous affection" (Wiloch 496).

Evelyn Waugh was something of a paradox. Steven Marcus notes that Waugh has been called, "nasty, hateful, snobbish, trivial, reactionary, vindictive, fawning, immature, pompous, and rude, ascriptions which are substantially true yet somehow beside the point." Marcus also notes that Waugh has been called a, "dandy, curmudgeon, wit, moralist, conservative, anarchist, Tory satirist, Catholic romancer, gentleman, snob, loyal friend, and, off the record, one mean son of a bitch" (Wiloch 496). Even though he was a devout Catholic, Waugh often made fun of Catholic practices, as when Cordelia makes a novena for her pig; Waugh also shows evil aspects and tendencies in many of his Catholic characters (Doyle 578). Waugh was such a complex individual that some critics consider him to be two different people. But Paul Doyle says, "Critics should not view Waugh as two different authors--a writer of comic novels and a writer of serious novels. Waugh can be understood fully and enjoyed most completely only when he is viewed as a writer of tragicomedy" (Wiloch 497).

Evelyn Waugh has been variously classed as a "humorist," a "satirist," a "writer of comedy," a "Catholic writer," and a "progressively misanthropic pessimist" (Swanson 1191). In Waugh's later works, his humor becomes more situational, as he becomes more of a satirist and a moralist, and less interested in the amusing side of the issue (Swanson 1192). In the opening passages of The Loved One and of Love Among the Ruins, Waugh misleads the reader into making false assumptions about the location, and he later takes delight in shattering the illusions which he himself has created (Beaty 10). Frederick Beaty says that Waugh frequently gives the impression of playing various theatrical parts rather than expressing a single consistent personality (Beaty 18). Jeffrey Heath viewed these various personas as, "designed to shield the diarist from the world's scrutiny and possibly even from his own" (qtd. in Beaty 19).

Waugh's early novels are satiric romances more than they are novels proper, while his later works (especially the Crouchback trilogy) are more realistic, and can therefore be described as a blend of the novel and the romance. The ironic attitude of his early works is associated with Menippean satire, a genre which tended to be assimilated by the romance form, and in this respect, Ronald Firbank a writer of satiric romances was a paramount influence on Waugh's development as an author (Carens xii). Firbank's writing tended to be objective and detached. He used the counterpoint or montage technique in his presentation, and his dialogue tended to be subtle, relying on understatement, suggestive emphasis, and sly innuendo. These rhetorical techniques provided the young Waugh with a model for, "an economical, destructive, and nondidactic satire" (Carens 10). Stephen Greenblatt would contrast Waugh's early satires as follows: The controlling device in Decline and Fall is "comic audacity;" the controlling device in Vile Bodies is "comic sadness;" the controlling device in Black Mischief is "comic cruelty;" and the controlling device in Handful of Dust is "comic bitterness" (Greenblatt 20, 28).

Waugh's novels of the 1930s could be classed as comedy, or even farce, but they nevertheless contains an underlying note of bitterness and ruthlessness and nerviness, and unhappiness, and lack of purpose, and lack of love for British life during this period. "Waugh has always been a writer whose surface--apparently gay, sometimes bizarre, often even wildly uproarious--has masked a devastating satirical vision of the modern world" (Carens 4). Roger Henkle notes that Evelyn Waugh's novels depict the frenzy of life after the "Great War" and provide, "hard, glossy, and often hilarious specimens of this kind of mordant, emotionless comedy" (Henkle 59). Evelyn Waugh's style of comedy can be traced back to early nineteenth-century satirists of the Regency, and to Romanticism--such predecessors as George Meredith, and Aldous Huxley. Like these earlier writers, Waugh wrote "comedies of ideas" which were based on the, "presentation and spoofing of various current philosophies and social and political positions" (Henkle 60). In 1946, when Evelyn Waugh, in an interview with a reporter for the "Fan-Fare" section of Life Magazine, was asked if his characters were drawn from real life, he said they were, and added, "My problem has been to distill comedy and sometimes tragedy from the knockabout farce of people's outward behaviour" (Stovel 15). In this same interview Waugh was asked if his novels were meant to be satirical, and he replied with an emphatic and unequivocal "No." Then he continued, "Satire is a matter of period. It flourishes in a stable society and presupposes homogeneous moral standards [such as existed in] the early Roman Empire and eighteenth-century Europe" (qtd. in Beaty 23). Frederick J. Stopp agrees that Waugh's novels are not satiric novels, even though they contain elements of farce, satire, and comedy of manners. They cannot be considered to be sustained satire because they are not impelled by any moral indignation on Waugh's part (Beaty 26). Frederick Beaty says that while Waugh used a number of the reductive techniques that are associated with satire, such as burlesque, caricature, exaggeration, and parody, his approach is nevertheless indirect and subtle, and his attitude is ambivalent, so that the reader frequently cannot determine exactly what the ethical stance of the narrator-persona is (Beaty 30). In addition, Waugh tended to separate himself from the issues which he discussed, and according to Ian Littlewood, he used five escape strategies in order to do this. "The earliest of these were detachment of tone and humor, followed more or less progressively by romanticism and nostalgia until religion ultimately became the strategy that not only diminished but subsumed all the previous ones in such a way as to alter quite radically the character of Waugh's writing" (Beaty 28).

In a book entitled Evelyn Waugh's Writings: From Joke to Comic Fiction, Leszek Kolek suggests that there is a joke pattern underlying all of Waugh's writing (Kolek 146), and he investigates the increasingly complex comic texts of Evelyn Waugh going from the joke to the short story to the novel, to Waugh's entire "oeuvre" (Kolek 5). Kolek says that Waugh's writings are prototypical of the modern comic novel, which Kolek describes as, "one of the most important phenomena in twentieth-century fiction. This modern comic novel which emerged during the decade of the 1920s is marked by the novelist's tragic view of the human condition, but it is also marked by the novelist's comic, grotesque, and absurd way of presenting this tragic view" (Kolek 6). Because of the paradoxical juxtaposition of the tragic and the comic in the modern comic novel, the genre is often described as some sort of hyphenated expression such as "comic-satiric," or "surreal-comic," or "modern-satirical" (Kolek 7). One Waugh critic felt obliged to add such qualifying adjectives as, "ironic, moral, didactic, grotesque, negative, destructive, [and] absurdist," and to these adjectives are added such qualifications as, "invective, picaresque, mock-heroic, broader satirical modes, low-keyed ironic realism," and so on. Thus a Waugh novel might be described not merely as a comedy, but as a "cosmic comedy," "solipsistic high comedy," "dry comedy," "social comedy," "comedy of manners," "surrealistic comedy of novelties," etc. (Kolek 16).

In a book entitled The Ironic World of Evelyn Waugh, Frederick Beaty says that irony is interwoven into the fabric of Waugh's writing much as it is interwoven into the universal condition of humanity. In this book, Beaty discusses Waugh's ironic development of theme, plot, and character (Beaty 3). Waugh uses such ironic rhetorical devices as understatement, overstatement, misrepresentation, ambiguity, double entendre, internal contradiction, innuendo, analogy, fallacious reasoning, caricature, parody, burlesque, and the mock heroic. He also develops the irony of the "ingénue," by allowing an innocent to speak the truth for him rather than using his own voice of pretended innocence.

> Other types of situational irony prevalent in Waugh's fiction are simple incongruity (mere juxtaposition of contraries), dilemma (choices appearing equally bad or equally good), irrationality or misapprehension (either a misuse of logic or a use of logic leading to an illogical conclusion), deliberate deceit (the irony of a lie being in its very plausibility), foreshadowing (something taking on a different meaning in the light of subsequent events than was originally intended or interpreted), self-deception (holding to a belief that is known or proved to be false), and self-betrayal (revealing the opposite of what one intends or expects to reveal). In these cases, too, there should be at least a shade of belief or expectation that something will not happen. (Beaty 5)

One ironic technique which Waugh mastered was to barely mention something, not mention it again for a long time, and then bring it up again in an entirely new context, at which point its significance, frequently ironic, would emerge. In The Flower beneath the Foot (1923), he used this ironic technique in his progressive references to fleas at the Ritz. In Concerning the Eccentricities of Cardinal Pirelli (1926), he used the same ironic technique with the baptism of dogs. In Decline and Fall (1928), he made a number of allusions to the seriousness of Lord Tangent's wound, and of course the seriousness of the wound becomes clear at the time of his eventual death (Beaty 14).

Waugh's essay entitled "What to Do with the Upper Classes: A Modest Proposal" uses irony and satire in an attempt to discredit the socialism which he feared was negatively affecting British society. The title alludes to Jonathan Swift's famous "Modest Proposal," and Waugh's "Modest Proposal" is like Swift's "Modest Proposal" in that they are both satires against various economic theories that were being proposed at the time. Waugh proposed designating certain affluent sections of London, as well as certain historic estates, certain universities, and certain areas of the countryside as "reservations," where, "nothing should be done to disturb their simple beliefs and natural piety" (Beaty 19). The reasons and methods which Waugh gives for preserving the upper classes are so preposterous, and his justifications are so trivial that his argument becomes invalid and satiric. Waugh mimics the shortsighted, and impractical schemes of socialism in order to pull the rug out from under the socialists' feet (Beaty 20).

Early in his career, Waugh wrote a play with an ironic cast entitled Conversion: The Tragedy of Youth in Three Burlesques (1921). In this play, an athlete denigrates scholarship, and leads a profligate life with his constant stealing. This athlete runs into a master who encourages him to new depths of depravity. In the concluding act of Conversion, a subtle irony develops as Waugh, "drives a wedge between educational theory and the reality of its application" (Beaty 11). The irony in The Balance (1926) is more sophisticated than that in Conversion. Frederick Beaty describes The Balance as one of Waugh's most daringly original works. The Balance contains a screenplay that is surrealistically intermingled with the actual theater-showing and the film's captions. The film characters have a kind of real-life status, as the camera captures divergent points of view and offers them without judgmental bias. In this way Waugh tried to present his fiction from various points of view (Beaty 12). The final dramatic irony occurs when Imogen insists on being introduced to Ernest; the reader realizes that Ernest is actually dead (Beaty 13).

In the "Author's Note" to the first edition of Decline and Fall, a Novel (1928), Evelyn Waugh wrote, "I hope that my publishers are wrong when they say that this is a shocking novelette. I did not mean it to be when I wrote it, and I do not believe that anyone with a sense of humor will find it so" (Phillips 9). The title of Decline and Fall is an allusion to Edward Gibbon's Decline and Fall of the Roman Empire, which had been a major influence on Waugh's writing. Waugh's Decline and Fall, like Gibbon's Decline and Fall was filled with ironic understatement (Beaty 15). "Waugh, in studying Gibbon, could have assimilated much about how to expose, without necessarily indicting, the follies, crimes, and misfortunes of a disintegrating culture" (Beaty 16). In Decline and Fall, there is a boy named "Little Lord Tangent," who is accidentally wounded in the foot by a starter's pistol during a school game (Henkle 59). He develops gangrene, and loses his foot, "all in a few witty textual asides" (Henkle 60).

Captain Grimes of Decline and Fall is always "in the soup" (Swanson 1192). He is described by Bruce Stovel as, "one of the world's great rogues, one of those whose serenity and bloomy sense of inner rightness almost persuade honest men that there is a strong moral case for roguery." Captain Grimes is based on the life (i.e. the career, the personality, and even the idiom) of a real-life rogue by the name of Richard Young. Young played a crucial role in helping Waugh to develop the comic outlook on life that characterizes his best fiction (Stovel 14). Still, a great many facts had to be changed in the process of distilling the, "knockabout farce of Richard Young's life into a comic elixir" (Stovel 15). What most struck Waugh about Young was his resilience. He had the strange ability to get better and better jobs in spite of his scandalous behavior (Stovel 17). Waugh was also fascinated by the fact that Young was a novelist. Young's first and only novel was entitled A Preparatory School Murder, and was published in 1934. Like Waugh's first novel, it was a detective story set in a disguised version of Arnold House, where both

Waugh and Young had taught school. The prime suspect in Young's novel was a, "young, confused, self-divided teacher who is clearly a portrait of Waugh himself" (Stovel 20). Their paths divided until 1963 when Waugh found Young living at the Saint Cross Alms Houses at Winchester. These alms houses were designed for "old men in noble poverty." Waugh's Captain Grimes, who is based on Richard Young, is a short, balding, one-legged man, who dominates Decline and Fall by providing the novel with its comic exuberance, and its outrageous playfulness. In the novel, Grimes "dies" and "is resurrected," as a parody of a Christ figure. Grimes is a satiric and a comic figure who demonstrates the blasphemous materialism of the society represented in the novel. He also provides a "psychic holiday" for readers of the novel, who unlike Grimes are not, "singularly in harmony with the primitive promptings of humanity" (Waugh Decline 45).

Paul Pennyfeather, the protagonist of Decline and Fall is a theology student at Oxford and the novel begins with the "breaking of glass" of the Bollinger Club banquet. During the festivities, Paul is forced to run the entire length of the quadrangle without any trousers, and he is therefore sent down for indecent behavior. This illustrates one of Waugh's favorite satiric devices, whereby a totally naïve character is catapulted into a grotesque and uncontrollable situation. By using this device, Waugh is able to expose both the corruption of society and the, "hopelessness of naïve goodness and simple-minded humanism" (Greenblatt 8). Paul Pennyfeather is an innocent in the tradition of Candide, as he watches the disturbing and corrupt events that occur around him. He notes that, "the evil prosper, the good are punished, and no standards of behavior are operable" (Wiloch 492).

In Decline and Fall, after being sent down from Oxford, Paul Pennyfeather becomes a "Master" at Llanabba Castle, a public school in Wales, where the headmaster, Dr. Augustus Fagan, Esquire, Ph.D. is a total sham. This castle used to be merely "Llanabba House," but during the cotton famine of the 1860s the owner decided to make it into a castle by adding a medieval façade, a mile of machicolated, crenelated, towered, and turreted wall which was decorated with heraldic animals, and a working portcullis. At an earlier time, these battlements and fortifications would have been useful in defending this lonely outpost from hordes of barbarians, but built during a later period they rather served only to show the ridiculous pretensions of the landlord, a prosperous owner of a Lancashire mill (Greenblatt 8). After the house had been transformed into a castle, it was usable only as a movie set, a prison, or a public school. In this house, there is Solomon Philbrick, a criminal who has become a butler, Captain Grimes, a schoolmaster, who is also a bigamist and a scoundrel, Prendergast, a chaplain who is tormented by "doubts" and who has no faith, and Doctor Fagan, a swindler who owns the castle (Greenblatt 9). Other characters in Decline and Fall include Flossy and Dingy, Augustus Fagan's ugly daughters, and Sebastian Cholmondley (pronounced Chumley, and called Chokey). One of the jokes here is that Waugh assumes that Americans will mispronounce the name. Cholmondley is Lady Margot Beste-Chetwynde's lover. He is not only black, but he is also a jazz musician, one of Evelyn Waugh's "bêtes noires." One of Chokey's speeches is a parody of Shylock's "do-we-not-bleed speech," in William Shakespeare's The Merchant of Venice. This is one of Waugh's most farcical paraphrases of a well-known speech (Swanson 1192).

Waugh's description of the Llanabba Silver Band which provides music for this area is a perfect example of the blurring of the line between animals and beasts.

> They were low of brow, crafty of eye and crooked of limb. They advanced huddled together with the loping tread of wolves, peering about them furtively as they came, as though in constant terror of ambush; they slavered at their mouths, which hung loosely over their receding chins, while each clutched under his ape-like arm a burden of curious and unaccountable shape. (qtd. in Greenblatt 7)

Margot Beste-Chetwynde, who has a child at Llanabba Castle is an attractive socialite who owns a chain of brothels in South America named the "Latin-American Entertainment Co., Ltd." She expands her business by buying a magnificent estate by the name of King's Thursday, an estate that had remained unchanged for about three hundred years. But this mansion has many inconveniences, since there is no electricity or hot water. So Margot contracts to have King's Thursday transformed into "something clean and square." Professor Otto Friederich Silenus is the architect who is given this delicate and difficult charge (Greenblatt 5). Professor Silenus may be a ludicrous and comic figure, but he is also a man of genius (Greenblatt 6).

In Decline and Fall, Margot Beste-Chetwynde hires Paul Pennyfeather to tutor her son, Peter Pastmaster on her estate (Swanson 1192). When Paul arrives at the Beste-Chetwynde estate, there is a party going on that is attended by social climbers, politicians, homosexuals, and other members of the "smart new set." Unaware that Margot is a drug addict, a nymphomaniac, and the owner of a prostitution business, Paul falls in love with her. Margot in turn hires Paul to ship girls to South America, but he is soon arrested for engaging in the white slave trade (Swanson 1193). When Paul moves to King's Thursday, Margot's estate, he finds that his experiences are basically the same as they had been in Wales. Even the characters are the same even though Solomon Philbrick is now the managing director of a disreputable cinema company, and Grimes is an employee of the Latin-American Entertainment Co., Ltd., and Prendergast is a "Modern Churchman" who is able to draw the full salary of a salaried clergy man without having to commit himself to any particular religious belief. And Sir Digby-Van-Trumpington, who had forced Paul to run trouserless across the quadrangle at Oxford, is now the best man at Paul's wedding to Margot. But the wedding is prevented by Arthur Potts, Paul's best friend at Scone, because Potts is now an investigator for the League of Nations, and he arrests Paul for his connections with the white slave market. At his trial, Paul is chastised for dragging down Margot. Of course Margot is not implicated in the trial. Paul is sent to prison, where Margot provides him with books, sherry, clothes, and oysters. After a while, he is mysteriously released and sent to a nursing home, run by Fagan, so that his appendix can be removed. However, Paul's appendix had already been removed years earlier. A doctor at clinic certifies that Paul died on the operating table, so Paul must wear a moustache as a disguise as he returns to Scone College to resume his position as a Professor of Theological Studies (Swanson 1193).

Waugh's satire is at its acrid best when the judge passes sentence on Paul Pennyfeather and at the same time berates him for attempting to tarnish the venerable aristocratic Margot Beste-Chetwynde by attempting to implicate a lady of beauty, rank, and stainless reputation in so base an enterprise (Phillips 13). Pennyfeather has to go to prison, where he again meets Philbrick, Grimes, and Prendergast. Sir Lucas-Dockery is the governor of the prison, and it is his belief that all crime is the result of the repressed desire for aesthetic expression, so he issues carpenter's tools to a maniac prisoner, who promptly cuts off Mr. Prendergast's head, thereby providing a hilarious and gruesome ironic twist in the plot (Greenblatt 10). The story comes full cycle when Paul finally returns to his room after attending a stimulating discussion of plebiscites in Poland, where once again he hears the "confused roaring and breaking of glass" which signal another Bollinger Club banquet (Greenblatt 12). Anthony Burgess says that the humor of Waugh's Decline and Fall is never flippant, and that this novel, "would not have maintained its freshness for nearly forty years if it had not been based on one of the big themes of our Western literature--the right of the decent man to find decency in the world" (Wiloch 492).

Manic humor so much prevails in Decline and Fall that John Priestly wrote in English Humour that the novel, "still holds up very well indeed, revealing all over again a new and original humorist with a very cool, impudent, deadpan manner, together with some excellent prose" (Swanson 1192). Much of the humor in <u>Decline and Fall</u> is based on word play, and on the suggestiveness of names, and on the discrepancies between how things appear and how they truly are. Waugh's deadpan narration uses dialogue to parody the "fashionable" speech of Waugh's time, and this is essential to the effect (Swanson 1192). Paul Doyle notes that when Waugh published <u>Decline and Fall</u>, he had to write a disclaimer in the preface that stated, "Please bear in mind throughout that it is meant to be funny." Doyle continues by saying, "Waugh was allowing all seven deadly sins to hold sway and was enjoying the triumph of evil and the decadence in the novel with the most carefree insouciance possible." The novel contains much disjointed dialogue and black humor which would years later come to be identified with the theater of the absurd. "Waugh is one of the first, if not the first, to blend these two elements successfully in one book" (Doyle 573).

The satire in <u>Decline and Fall</u> which exposed the follies of English society of the 1920s was quite detached. The satire in <u>Vile Bodies</u> (1930), written to satirize the same general target was equally detached. <u>Vile Bodies</u> is like <u>The Great Gatsby</u> in that it seems to define and to sum up the period--England during the 1920s (Wiloch 493). The satiric target in <u>Vile Bodies</u> is the frantic young set of "Bright Young People" which characterized the Roaring Twenties in England. These "Bright Young People" have names such as Miles Malpractice, Lady Circumference, the Duchess of Stale, Fanny Throbbing, and Agatha Runcible; There is a performing troupe named "Mrs. Ape and Her Angels," and these angels may be angels when they are on stage, but they are certainly not at other times. They have names like Chastity, Innuendo, Humility, Creative Endeavor, and Cross Examination. In <u>Vile Bodies</u> there is a former Prime Minister by the name of Outrage and a present Prime Minister by the name of James Brown who throws parties for the "Bright Young People" at Number 10 Downing Street. The male and female protagonists are named Adam and Nina (like Adam and Eve) and Nina lives at Doubting Hall (frequently pronounced as "Doubting 'All"). Waugh was chronicling the demise of the Jazz Age in England just as F. Scott Fitzgerald was doing it in America (Phillips 15). In <u>Vile Bodies</u> Adam Fenwick-Symes is shown to have a total lack of conviction, as is illustrated by his turning over of his fiancée, Nina Blount, to a rival in exchange for having his hotel bill paid for him, and by the fact that he later retrieves Nina with a worthless check. Adam leads a mad existence, but at one point the world becomes even too hectic for him, as he exclaims to Nina, "Oh, Nina, What a lot of parties" (Phillips 16).

> Masked parties, Savage parties, Victorian parties, Greek parties, Wild West parties, Russian parties, Circus parties where one had to dress as somebody else, almost naked parties in St. Johns Wood, parties in flats and studios and houses and ships and hotels and nightclubs..., parties at Oxford where one drank brown sherry and smoked Turkish cigarettes, dull dances in London and comic dances in Scotland and disgusting dances in Paris--all that succession and repetition of massed humanity.... Those vile bodies. (Waugh 14)

This list of parties seems to promise endless variety, but it also promises total sameness; it suggests pleasure, but it also suggests a deep weariness (Hopkins 216) <u>Vile Bodies</u> may be about the flux of modern culture, and the release from old traditions, however, it also is about possibility that such a release might be more terrifying than relaxing (Hopkins 217). In real life Waugh had been at some of these parties, and in the December 29, 1925 entry of his diary he described some "disgusting dances in Paris" where he had visited a dreary looking café called Roland. Here he was approached by a young man dressed up as Cleopatra. Waugh had found the whole thing revolting, and had ended his account by saying that he took a taxi home and "went to bed in chastity," adding, "I think I do not regret it" (Phillips 16).

One of the episodes in <u>Vile Bodies</u> occurs when a cigar-smoking Priest tells visitor to Doubting Hall that Colonel Blount, and some other Wesleyans are "being shot." The bishop continues, "I dare say you'd like to come round to the front and see the fun. There's been some damn bad management. Why, yesterday, they kept Miss LaTouche waiting the whole afternoon, and then the light was so bad when they did shoot her that they made a complete mess of her--we had the machine out and ran over all the bits carefully last night after dinner--you never saw such rotten little scraps--quite unrecognizable half of them. We didn't dare show them to her husband." The visitor later finds out that they had been "shooting a film" (Swanson 1193).

    <u>Vile Bodies</u> is a comedy that is haunted by inexplicable sadness. It is an experimental novel with practically no plot and no continuity of narrative. It contains disconnected and seemingly irrelevant scenes. Waugh uses chaos and disjointed structure in order to portray a chaotic land disjointed world, and according to Stephen Greenblatt, Waugh uses this device all too successfully (Greenblatt 13). In the preface to <u>Vile Bodies</u> there is a quote from Lewis Carroll's <u>Through the Looking Glass</u> which sets the tone of breathless futility: "It takes all the running you can do, to keep in the same place." In <u>Vile Bodies</u> the customs officials who destroy Adam Symes's manuscript are operating under the philosophy of, "If we can't stamp out literature in the country, we can at least stop its being brought in from outside" (Waugh 15). When Adam's manuscript is destroyed, he must figure out some other way to make a living as a writer so he becomes a journalist for a newspaper named <u>The Daily Excess</u>, writing under the name of Mr. Chatterbox. Here he writes columns like "Notable Invalids," and "Titled Eccentrics," and here he makes up names and personalities to make his column more readable. J. B. Priestley considers <u>Vile Bodies</u> to be broadly satirical. In this novel the antics in Lottie Crump's hotel and the eccentricities of Colonel Blount make for very good comic reading (Priestley 113). Colonel Blount is a trickster figure. Adam visits him in order to ask for money, but he evades Adam's requests with a wide range of avoidance strategies. When Adam finally does catch up with him, and Colonel Blount is finally forced to make out a cheque for a thousand pounds, he signs the check, "Charlie Chaplin" (Hopkins 213).

    When it was first published, many critics felt that <u>Vile Bodies</u> did not fit well into any genre. It was funny, but it was also serious. It was satire, but it was also comedy (Hopkins 207). Hopkins suggests that the novel is both funny and serious, both satire and comidy, and he furthermore suggests that it is the novel that challenges the genre categories rather than the reverse (Hopkins 208). Jeffrey Heath says that Waugh's, "hilarious comedy is at the same time serious business." He continues by saying that a, "moral dimension coexists with a deep strain of the most untamed anarchy" (Heath xiii). Waugh's characters are Humours Characters, and the names of his characters tell what humour each of his characters represents, either straightforwardly or ironically. There is Mrs. Ape, Faith, Charity, Divine Discontent, Miles Malpractice, and the Honorable Walter Outrage (Hopkins 209). The names of Mrs. Ape's angels are also significant, and allegorical. When Mrs. Ape does the roll call of her troupe, Faith and Fortitude answer promptly, but Chastity can not be found. When the other angels say that Chastity is not well, Mrs. Ape notes that Chastity is never well when there is packing to be done (Hopkins 210). Chris Hopkins says that <u>Vile Bodies</u> has an opportunistic narrator who will do anything for a laugh (Hopkins 209). The narrator tells the reader that Mrs. Ape, "watched them benignly, then squaring her shoulders and looking (except that she had really no beard to speak of) every inch a sailor, strode resolutely forward to the first class bar" (Waugh <u>Vile Bodies</u> 2). By saying that Mrs. Ape looks like a sailor except that she "had really no beard to speak of" is really saying that even down to the beard, she looked like a sailor (Hopkins 210).

    The major blocking characters in <u>Vile Bodies</u> are Mrs. Ape and Outrage. They stand in the way of the younger characters, and exhibit the "petrified falsity" of society.

Most of the older generation have comic names that establish them as blocking characters. There is Father Rothschild, and Mrs. Ape, and Sir Walter Outrage, and Lady Throbbing, and Mrs. Blackwater. In contrast, the young protagonists have non-comical names--Adam Fenwick-Symes, and Nina Blount. This comic naming of blocking characters is a device used frequently in romantic comedies. The novel is about Adam and Nina's attempts to get married, but their lack of money becomes associated in a number of ways with the various older, blocking characters (Hopkins 212). Clive James says that Vile Bodies, "remains one of the funniest books in the world" (Wiloch 493). Vile Bodies is a satiric comedy of errors which targets the defects of politicians, and also targets religion by introducing the evangelist Aimee Semple McPherson and her touring "Angels." But most of all, it targets the "Bright Young Things" who spent their lives in an endless round of going to parties, drinking, and sexual excess (Doyle 573). In Vile Bodies it is not only the senex figures that are rigid, but the junex figures as well. Ironically, however, it is the extreme flexibility of the younger generation which has become so rigid that their flexibility has become inflexible (Hopkins 214).

In Remote People (1931) Waugh ridicules the coronation of Haile Selassie as the emperor of Ethiopia as he describes a nightmare journey through East Africa (Carens vi). Black Mischief (1932) is a burlesque of the attempt of Africa to modernize itself. It takes place in a large imaginary island off the East coast of Africa named Azania (a blend of Zanzibar and Abyssinia not only phonologically, but in terms of its character and its history as well). Black Mischief is based on Waugh's first visit to Ethiopia, and it continues the themes of Waugh's earlier satires--the shabbiness of Western culture, the decline of institutions, and the savagery underlying the veneer of civilization and society (Greenblatt 16). The novel discusses the attempt to modernize the African Kingdom of Azania by its Emperor, Seth, who is called Chief of Chiefs of Sakuyu, Lord of Wanda and Tyrant of the Seas, in addition to being a graduate of Oxford University. Seth is a paradoxical blend of savagery and civilization as he vascilates between the cannibal feast and the drawing room. According to Stephen Greenblatt, he is, "unpredictable, cruel, naïve, insanely optimistic, lonely, [and] terrified." Seth is like Paul Pennyfeather in that he is the outsider in contact with an alien society, and Waugh uses this outsider-insider contrast as a means of satirizing that society (Greenblatt 17). Waugh's roguish hero Basil Seal tells Seth about his responsibilities: "We've got a much easier job now than we should have had fifty years ago. If we'd had to modernize a country then it would have meant constitutional monarchy, bicameral legislature, proportional representation, women's suffrage, independent judicature, freedom of the press, referendums...." "What is all that?" asked the Emperor. "Just a few ideas that have ceased to be modern." (qtd. in Greenblatt 18)

Basil Seal also convinces Seth that he should develop a birth control program in Azania, and Seth does so, renaming the Anglican cathedral "Place Marie Stopes" after the real-life Marie Stopes, a noted British advocate of birth control (Phillips 21). But Seth's birth control program ultimately fails because the ignorant poor for whom the program is designed pour into the capital, "eagerly awaiting initiation to the fine new magic of virility and fecundity" (Phillips 22). These examples show how Waugh uses Africa as a lens to give his readers a grotesque image of English institutions and social classes. The quote above demonstrates that Waugh is really not talking so much about Africa in Black Mischief as he is talking about England. According to Greenblatt, "the black faces and foreign dress heighten the ironic force of Waugh's biting scrutiny of his homeland" (Greenblatt 19).

In Black Mischief, the General of the army, Mr. Connolly, is married to a native woman whom he affectionately calls "Black Bitch," but he notes that particular term of endearment is no long appropriate when he becomes a Duke, and "Black Bitch" becomes the "Duchess of Ookaka". In Black Mischief, Dame Mildred Porch is a Comedy of

Manners "aristocrat" who comes to Azania in order to crusade for the more humane treatment of animals. She is comic in her extreme dedication to her cause. She writes cryptic letters to her husband; in one of these letters she tells how she fed some "doggies" in the market place, but the, "children tried to take food from [the] doggies. Greedy little wretches" (Greenblatt 19). There is a kind of comic cruelty which runs throughout Black Mischief. The references to starving children, executed men, and mutilated bodies, are quite hilarious in their context. As Seth becomes more and more infatuated with Western culture, the savageness underlying the calm surface of the superimposed English civilization becomes increasingly agitated, until it finally explodes in a revolt which overthrows the Emperor (Greenblatt 20). Stephen Greenblatt says that Black Mischief, "is not a statement of the African nation's inability to share in the glories of civilization but a sly and satiric examination of modernity itself" (Wiloch 493). Paul Doyle called Black Mischief a "wild, rollicking comedy" with a more savage note of satire than was found in Waugh's earlier novels (Wiloch 493). In Black Mischief, Basil has an affair with Prudence, the "sexually delicious" daughter of the British ambassador. "Near the novel's end, after the two have separated in the jungle, Basil, exhausted and starved, staggers into a remote native encampment where a jubilant and lavish banquet is being held. After satiating his hunger, Basil learns from the cannibals that his metaphorical desire to 'eat' Prudence has been fulfilled: he has literally eaten her" (Doyle 574).

A Handful of Dust (1934) gets its title from T. S. Eliot's The Waste Land. Tony is entrapped deep in the jungles by Mr. Todd, who is an insane settler who keeps Tony prisoner, and who forces him relentlessly to read aloud from the works of Dickens. The novel contains subtle satire and biting irony, and much of the comic satire is quite embittered in tone (Doyle 575). In A Handful of Dust (1934), Waugh's blending of the comic and the satiric can also be seen in the grotesque sermons delivered by Reverend Tendril, the vicar of Tony's church. This Vicar had composed his sermons while he was serving in India, and he had not adapted them to changing conditions, so that his sermons are a charming employment of Henri Bergson's image of "the mechanical encrusted on the living" (Greenblatt 26-27). Even though he was no longer in India, Reverend Tendril talked about having to spend Christmas under the, "harsh glare of the alien sun.... Instead of the ox and ass of Bethlehem...we have for companions the ravening tiger and the exotic camel." A special irony is added by the fact that the villagers don't find the vicar's sermons at all inappropriate, since, "few of the things said in church seemed to have any particular reference to themselves" (Phillips 30).

A Handful of Dust is filled with the comic bitterness, and the comic rigidity of betrayed ideals and unfulfilled dreams (Greenblatt 28). It has a plot similar to that of a bedroom farce about a stupid country squire who is married to a beautiful wife who has an affair with a younger man from the city. The husband in A Handful of Dust is called "old boy" by his friends, and is the only person who doesn't know that he is being cuckolded, though he does suspect something. The clever wife treats him very badly, and even chastises him for being such a suspicious old fool. A Handful of Dust is about Tony Last who lives with his wife, Brenda, and his son, John Andrew, at Hetton, a large ancestral estate which the county guide books describe as, "entirely rebuilt in 1864 in the Gothic style and is now devoid of interest." When Andrew is killed in a hunting accident and Brenda reveals her infidelity, Tony's, "whole Gothic world had come to grief," and he decides to go to Brazil (Greenblatt 22). However, the frequent juxtapositioning of a scene in Brazil with a similar scene in London makes it clear that the foul and inhuman jungle in Brazil is actually London transfigured (Greenblatt 31).

Waugh published a short story entitled "The Man Who Liked Dickens" in Hearst's International Combined with Cosmopolitan in 1933. It is about a naïve English explorer who is trapped in a South American jungle and is forced to read the novels of Dickens to his illiterate captor. Ironically, this ludicrous and macabre short story has come down to us not as a short story, but rather as the end of Waugh's novel, A Handful of Dust (Rogers 340). According to Paul Doyle, Handful of Dust is a novel of subtle satire and biting irony. It ends in tragicomedy, as the despairing Tony travels to the Brazilian jungle to forget his troubles, but is taken prisoner by a Mr. Todd. Todd is devoted to Charles Dickens, and therefore he forces Tony to read Dickens novels to him presumably for the rest of his life (Wiloch 493).

Lord Moping in Mr. Loveday's Little Outing, and Other Sad Stories (1936) always threatens to commit suicide on the occasion of his wife's annual garden party, and when he actually does attempt suicide, his wife has him committed to a local asylum for mental defectives. Lady Moping and her daughter Angela, then visit the institution and become acquainted with Mr. Loveday, an older inmate who is sweet, kind, and loved by everybody. When he was young, Mr. Loveday knocked a young lady off from her bicycle and strangled her. But Angela is a social reformer and she listens to Mr. Loveday as he tells her that there is just one thing that he often wishes that he could do, and it wouldn't take long. "But I do feel that if I had done it, just for a day, an afternoon even, then I would be more quiet." So she consults legal precedents, visits a member of Parliament, and after making a number of strenuous efforts on Mr. Loveday's behalf, she finally succeeds in getting Mr. Loveday freed from the asylum. He is gone only for a couple of hours, and then he returns to the asylum and informs the doctor that he has returned to the asylum now that he has had such an enjoyable holiday. Shortly thereafter, however, the body of a strangled young lady is discovered. The young lady was bicycling near the institution. "Waugh thus satirically indicts sociological and psychological professors and scientific experimenters who coddle the insane and the criminal without regard for common sense and public safety" (Rogers 340).

Another sad story in this collection is entitled "Bella Fleace Gave a Party." The story is about eighty-year-old Annabel Rochfort-Doyle-Fleace, an Anglo-Irish aristocrat who lives in an elaborate but decaying mansion in Ireland. She decides to give an elaborate Christmas party, and she prepares the invitations and does all of the details necessary in preparing for such a grand event. On the night of the party, however, nobody arrives except for the hired band, and so she decides to have the butler serve her. After the meal, two couples arrive, but neither of these couples were been invited to the party, so Bella refuses to receive them, and in fact is horrified at their presumption. A day after the "grand party," Bella Fleace dies, and later her heir, a distant cousin comes to sort out her effects. On her writing table he finds all of the party invitations, all of them addressed and stamped, but obviously never mailed (Rogers 341).

Still another sad story in this collection is entitled "Winner Takes All." In this story, Mrs. Kent-Cumberland consistently favors her older son, Gervase, over her younger son, Tom. She sends Gervase to a better school. She gives him better gifts. She even gives him credit for writing and publishing a monograph on which Tom had done all of the work. Tom is exiled to Australia to work on a sheep farm, and there he marries the daughter of a wealthy landowner. When Mrs. Kent-Cumberland realizes this, she decides that Bessie, Tom's fiancée, is the ideal rich wife for whom she has been looking for Gervase to marry, so she does what has to be done to alienate Bessie from Tom and get her married to Gervase. John Rogers notes that this story might be somewhat autobiographical, since Evelyn's relationship with his brother Alec, who was five and a half years older than he was, seems similar to the relationship between Tom and Gervase (Rogers 341).

"An Englishman's Home" was also published in Mr. Loveday's Little Outing, and Other Sad Stories. In this short story, there are two brothers who buy some land in England, and then spread rumors throughout England that they are planning to build an experimental industrial factory with two very large chimneys, and a number of other polluting features. They are hoping that the neighboring landowners and townspeople will put all of their funds together to buy the land back, and they, the brothers, will be able to make a huge profit. They reason that these neighbors will not want the beauty and tranquility of their countryside disturbed (Rogers 342). The neighbors and townspeople finally get enough money together to buy the land and build a Boy Scout meeting hall on it. In the meantime, Harwood-Hood and his brother use their huge financial profit in another part of England to maintain their mansion, which has fallen into difficulty because of increased property taxes (Rogers 343).

Scoop: A Novel about Journalists (1938) draws on Waugh's second visit to Ethiopia, and it, "freely transforms the Italian intervention in Ethiopia into a political spoof." The three principle targets of satire in Scoop are Newspapers, Africans, and Communists (Carens vi). In the preface to the 1964 edition of Scoop Waugh describes the novel as a "light-hearted tale" that he wrote because of the "peculiar personal happiness" he was feeling at the time (Phillips 33). He was referring to his happy marriage to Laura Herbert. Waugh, who served for some time as a foreign correspondent, felt that he had no talent for newspaper writing, but he did have a talent for studying the excesses of his colleagues, and these excesses became the basis for the humor of the novel, one of the funniest books he ever wrote. Waugh's eccentric hero is named William Boot, and lives with his equally eccentric family at Boot Magna. Waugh notes to his younger readers that they must accept his assurance that such people and their servants had actually existed and were not merely drawn from his imagination (Phillips 34). In Scoop, William Boot is a reporter for the Beast, and he is sent to cover a war in the mythical African country of Ishmaelia. Boot is an innocent who is thrown into a bizarre world where, "journalists fabricate news stories and rival nations engage in deadly competition for mineral resources." Scoop is based on real-life events, and William Deedes, a fellow correspondent with Waugh in Abyssinia, certifies its accuracy, and says that it is, "the ultimate comic satire on journalistic practices" (Doyle 575). Missionaries, ambassadors, tradesmen, prospectors, and natural scientists were all sent to Ishmaelia, but none of them returned. "They were eaten, every one of them; some raw, others stewed and seasoned--according to local usage and the calendar (for the better sort of Ishmaelites have been Christian for many centuries and will not publicly eat human flesh, uncooked, in Lent, without special and costly dispensation from their bishop)" (Swanson 1193).

There are many humorous events in Scoop, such as the hilarious scene when Mrs. Stitch loses control of her car and drives it into a men's public rest room, or the scene where a Spaniard confides in William Boot that he has brought along a good history of Africa written in German, so that when he has nothing to report he can translate passages from the book (Phillips 36). The entire reporting scene is extremely haphazard. When telegrams come, for example, they are delivered by messengers who can not read, and whose system of delivery therefore is to hand a bundle of envelopes to the first white man they come across, who in turn reads all of the telegrams that look promising, and then hands them back to the messenger. This method of distribution is not so different from real life. Waugh describes how telegrams were distributed when he was a novelist in Jacksonburg. They were, "delivered irregularly and rather capriciously, for none of the messengers could read. The usual method was to wait until half a dozen had accumulated and then send a messenger to hawk them about the more probable places until they were claimed" (Phillips 37). Waugh noted that in Jacksonburg there was a different standard for British and American journalists: "While the latter will not hesitate in moments of emergency to resort to pure invention, the former must obtain their lies at second hand. This is not so much due to lack of imagination, I think, as lack of courage" (Phillips 37).

In Scoop, when William gets involved in a story, he becomes an eager journalist.

He is filled with sentiments of patriotism and a zeal for justice as he puts his total energies into his typing. "One finger was not enough; he used both hands. The keys rose together like bristles on a porcupine, jammed, and were extricated; curious anagrams appeared on the paper before him; vulgar fractions and marks of punctuation mingled with the letters. Still he typed" (qtd. in Phillips 39). When William tries to find out which of the fighting factions in Ishmaelia is on the Patriot side, Mr. Salter, one of Lord Copper's subordinates, tells him that both sides consider themselves to be Patriots, and that both sides also claim all of the victories. Lord Copper confides in William that he shouldn't worry if his reports contradict those that are filed by the other correspondents, since all of the newspapers have different editorial policies, and therefore expect different news. But William becomes cynical about being a reporter, and at one point he refuses to join the other journalists on a trip that the Ishmaelian government has designated as a potential trouble spot, because he has learned from other sources that this place doesn't even exist. He confronts the government with this bit of news, and a government official merely shrugs his shoulders and says, "I see you are well informed about my country, Mr. Boot. I should not have thought it from the tone of your newspaper" (Phillips 38).

Talking about Work Suspended (1942), Waugh said, "So far as it went, it was my best writing." But it didn't go very far because with the coming of World War II, "the world in which and for which it was designed, has ceased to exist." Therefore, Waugh published it as a fragment. John Plant is the hero of Work Suspended. He is a writer of detective fiction, who has been trying unsuccessfully to finish his latest novel, and in that respect was much like Waugh himself (Phillips 42). Work Suspended ends where Put Out More Flags begins, with the coming of World War II, and the resultant change in the lives of the English people (Phillips 43).

A. A. DeVitis says that Put Out More Flags (1942) is a "dance macabre" which deals with the "Bright Young People grown old" (Doyle 577). Put Out More Flags is a broadly satirical novel that describes the first year of the war as it influenced the lives of a number of English types during the 1930s. Waugh used the expression "Churchillian renaissance" to describe the English spirit during this period of time (Carens vii). In this novel, Alastair Trumpington joins the army in atonement for his having had such a wild youth (Phillips 20). Put Out More Flags tells about some unruly children from the London slums who subvert the bureaucratic guardianship that marks the patriarchy's control over public and private space. The dreadful Connolly children, led by "ripely pubescent" Doris, wreak havoc on the conservative village of Malfrey. The Connolly children can be considered as "humours characters." Doris is the tomboy; Mickey is the delinquent, and Marlene is the mental defective (Phillips 44). The novel parodies the Dionysian fates, as the Connollies appear, "as an act of God apparently without human agency; their names did not appear on any list; they carried no credentials; no one was responsible for them" (qtd. in Lassner 207). Waugh is mocking the misguided good intentions of a paternalistic government that is defeated by its children. Waugh contextualizes his comic anti-hero, Basil Seal, who stands precariously between an uneasy peace and a purposeful war (Lassner 208).

Since none of the inhabitants of the village will have these horrible evacuee children, Basil Seal, the billeting officer, concocts a plan whereby he transports them to different homes around the countryside demanding a bribe from each resident to get him to transport the children on to the nearest neighbor. The longest that the Connolly children stay in any one place is ten days; the shortest is an hour and a half. Basil Seal makes a good bit of money in this enterprise, but he is running out of homes in his territory. Then he concocts another scheme whereby he turns the children over to Mr. Todhunter, the billeting officer in a nearby area, charging Mr. Todhunter a pretty good price for the children, because Todhunter will be able to carry on Seal's lucrative activities in his own territory (Phillips 44).

Ambrose Silk is the homosexual aesthete in Put Out More Flags. In the Religious Department of the Ministry of Information, Ambrose Silk is the sole representative of atheism. It is Ambrose's task to supply copy for periodicals like Free Thought, Atheist Advertiser, and Godless Sunday at Home (Phillips 45). It is interesting to note the similarities between Ambrose Silk's tragic friendship with a storm trooper named Hans, and Sebastian's tragic friendship with a German youth named Kurt in Brideshead Revisited. Hans is member of Hitler's youth comrades, and when he discovers that Ambrose is a Jew, Ambrose must leave him and return to England. In England, Ambrose becomes comic again, as Basil disguises him as an Irish Jesuit and sends him off to Ireland, so that he [Basil] can take over Ambrose's apartment (Phillips 46). Another humours character that is encountered in Put Out More Flags is a poet named Parsnip, who is probably a caricature of W. H. Auden. Parsnip is working on a poem to be entitled "Guernica Revisited" (Phillips 49).

Brideshead Revisited, or the Sacred and Profane Memories of Captain Charles Ryder (1945) is a novel which has aroused both passionate attacks, and passionate defense. Paul Doyle says that

> Blanche is one of the most fascinating characters in modern fiction. Based on Brian Howard and Harold Acton, Blanche is the aesthete par excellence. An intellectual in every sense of the word, a witty, cruel, gossiping commentator on the Marchmains and on all the events around him, he dazzles whenever he appears in the book. He has the attraction of a deadly but beautiful cobra; and his stuttering, his homosexuality, and his blending of several racial backgrounds add to the artistry of the picture. (Doyle 579)

According to Frederick Beaty, Brideshead Revisited contains a great deal of "vibrant irony" (Beaty 8). According to Gene Phillips, it was a great surprise to Waugh that Brideshead Revisited became the greatest popular success of his career. In a Life essay dated April 8, 1946, Waugh proclaimed, "Like a shy waterfowl who has hatched out a dragon's egg, I find that I have written a 'best-seller' " (Phillips 50). Waugh wrote Scott-King's Modern Europe (1947) shortly after he had visited Spain even though the satire targets a totalitarian Balkan state which is more like Yugoslavia than it is like Spain (Carens viii).

The Loved One: An Anglo-American Tragedy (1948) is a satire targeting Forest Lawn Memorial Park in Hollywood, California. According to Paul Doyle, Forest Lawn is "the world's most statued necropolis." It contains art, sculpture, loud speakers talking from the shrubbery broadcasting inspirational messages and funeral music. There are swans floating languidly in the ponds, and stunning gates at the entrance modelled after the gates of Buckingham Palace. "Every feature was designed to obliterate the reality of death" (Doyle 579). The Loved One features Dennis Barlow, a young English poet who has come to Hollywood in order to write for the movies. When he is unsuccessful in that endeavor, he becomes employed by the "Happier Hunting Ground," a pet cemetery which is an imitation of "Whispering Glades," which is an imitation of "Forest Lawn." Barlow quickly becomes enamored with Aimée Thanatagenos, a cosmetician working for Whispering Glades. The word "Tragedy" in the subtitle of The Loved One is one of Waugh's wilder flights of irony, since The Loved One is in fact one of the zaniest pieces of humor ever to come from Waugh's pen (Swanson 1191). Waugh was satirizing American refusal to recognize death by using games and euphemisms to deal with death when he told of the various sections at Whispering Glades--Eventide, Babyland, Graceland, Inspiration Slope, Slumberland, and Sweet Memories. At Forest Lawn and other places, death was just becoming another aspect of show business (Swanson 1193).

The Loved One tells us that Hollywood stars attend funerals not only to honor the dead, but also to promote themselves and their next films. Thus, Juanita del Pablo is a sexy starlet whose career has been personally developed by Sir Francis Hinsley, shows up at his funeral to sing "The Wearing of the Green." This particular song is one of the songs featured in her next movie. It is also a fiery IRA song which is symbolic of the Irish cause, and which is sung to denounce the British. It is ironic, then, that this song is sung at Sir Francis Hinsley's funeral, since Hinsley is English, not Irish. What results is an, "absurdity, incongruity, and irreverence which characterize the movie colony" (Doyle 580).

The Loved One is written by an author with religious conviction, but it nevertheless contains much graveyard humor (Beaty 9). The Loved One is an acerbic attack on the mortuary business of southern California, as Dennis Barlow sees his "loved one" transformed by the hands of the mortuary cosmeticians into a "painted and smirking obscene travesty." Here is death deprived of all of its dignity (Griffiths 165). But although Dennis is offended, he is also fascinated by death and its associated ambiance, as his love for Aimée Thanatagenos seems to be strengthened by her death (Griffiths 166).

At the Whispering Glades Mortuary, the "waiting one" is able to select which particular area of the Park to have his or her "loved one" occupy. Each area has its own special name, and its own special work of art, and the prices vary according to the zones, and according to the proximity of the work of art (Waugh The Loved One 43). Mr. Joyboy is an American who works at the Whispering Glades Mortuary. He takes pride in the fact that he is the Senior Mortician, and in the fact that his specialty is fixing "serene and philosophical" expressions on the faces of the deceased (Waugh The Loved One 67). It is ironic that the humans that Mr. Joyboy has embalmed and presented in the "slumber rooms" look more alive than they ever did. It is also ironic that in this discussion there is no reference to religion (Swanson 1194). Also, Mr. Joyboy plays little practical jokes, as when he poses Sir Francis for his final "appearance" not with his hands together in a sign of prayer, but rather with his hands folded one over the other in a sign of resignation (Waugh The Loved One 72).

Aimée is "the loved one," but this name is ironic, because Barlow is not very loving toward her. When Barlow tells Aimée that he has no problem with her earning enough money to keep them both, she responds that an American man might, "despise himself for living on his wife," but Barlow responds that that's not a problem because he's "European" (Waugh The Loved One 110). This satire targets Barlow, but it also targets Americans. A further attack on Americans occurs when Sir Ambrose says that in America, "they don't expect you to listen" because, "they talk entirely for their own pleasure; nothing they say is designed to be heard" (Waugh The Loved One 5). At the end of The Loved One, Aimée commits suicide by going to Mr. Joyboy's embalming room and giving herself a lethal injection of embalming fluid. Mr. Joyboy finds the body, and asks Dennis to help him dispose of the body, so Dennis takes Aimée's body to the Happier Hunting Ground, and blackmails Mr. Joyboy into giving him enough money to return to England. Then he takes care of Aimée's body as if it were someone's favorite pet. He leaves a notice in the files that on every anniversary of Aimée's death a card should be sent to Mr. Joyboy saying, "Your little Aimée is wagging her tail in Heaven tonight" (Swanson 1194).

Paul Doyle notes that when Evelyn Waugh writes about noncontemporary events, as he did in Helena (1950), his, "touch becomes uncertain, and the humor and satire become diffuse and often overly obvious" (Doyle 581). Love Among the Ruins: A Romance of the Near Future (1953) tells about a planned society of "womb-to-tomb welfare," a society where everything is done for everybody in the name of progress. Ironically, the people in this society become so bored that the most exciting and popular service, the only service that offers real security, is euthanasia, and many citizens elect this service in order to relieve the boredom of a life devoid of excitement or interest. The penal system in this Utopia/Dystopia is a "progressive" one in which no one is held responsible for his or her own acts. People who do wrong things are considered to be "victims of inadequate social services," or are considered to be "maladjusted." These wrongdoers are not called criminals, and in fact, they receive better treatment from the society than do the ordinary citizens. Some of the worst offenders are sent to "Mountjoy," a magnificent manor house with beautiful gardens. Waugh explains that the best rooms are along the garden front, and these best rooms are given to the murderers and sex offenders (Beaty 21).

John Verney, the husband in "Tactical Exercise," (published in Tactical Exercise [1954]) is planning to kill his wife Elizabeth, because he has grown to hate her during their seven years of marriage. When they go on vacation, they stay at an old house on the edge of a cliff, and part of the fence on the balcony that faces the living room is broken. In order to have an alibi, John spreads rumors around the town that his wife is a sleepwalker. He even goes to the local doctor , and there he learns that Elizabeth has already visited the doctor and told him that her husband is a sleepwalker. In the evening, John feels woozy, and falls asleep. Elizabeth has drugged his whiskey bottle, and as the story ends, it is obvious that she will succeed in murdering her husband (Rogers 343).

"Compassion" was another Waugh short story that was published in 1949. It is a satirical story which shockingly reveals the horrors and cruelties of war and of communism. "Basil Seal Rides Again" is a short story that was published in Esquire Magazine in 1963. Basil Seal is a highborn and well-educated cad who is totally unprincipled, but who always seems to be able to land on his feet. In this story, he is fifty-eight years old, and is not in good health. He and his wife go away to a spa, but Basil is soon discharged for violating the rules against drinking alcohol. Barbara, his daughter, has decided to marry her disreputable boyfriend, and Basil is determined to prevent the marriage. Therefore, through a clever ruse, he convinces Barbara that her boyfriend is his own illegitimate son, and it is this suspicion of incest that prevents the marriage. John Rogers considers the story to contain a great deal of "amusing dialogue" (Rogers 344).

In Officers and Gentlemen (1955), the satire is dominant. Thomas Wiloch says that this novel, "stimulates laughter again and again but its aftertaste is as bitter as the author meant it to be" (Wiloch 495). The Ordeal of Gilbert Pinfold: A Conversation (1957) is somewhat autobiographical, as Waugh masks himself as a combination of an eccentric don and a testy colonel (Carens x). The Life of the Right Reverend Ronald Knox: Fellow of Trinity College, Oxford, and Pronotary Apostolic to His Holiness Pope Pius XII (1959) is a biography of Waugh's friend, Monsignor Ronald Knox, who was a fellow convert to Catholicism, and a minor satirist in his own right (Carens viii).

In The End of the Battle, or Unconditional Surrender (1961), Guy Crouchback is given a leave from the military in order to attend his father's funeral. While attending the funeral, he becomes reacquainted with his family and with his religion, and he comes to embrace Catholicism with a renewed vigor. He develops a new sense of purpose that contrasts sharply with his unfocused past, and also with the lack of a sense of purpose of his directionless army buddies (Wiloch 495).

Sword of Honour (1965) is actually a trilogy of three novels, Men at Arms, Officers and Gentlemen, and Unconditional Surrender. In this trilogy, Guy Crouchback is transformed from an unloving "loner" into a man of compassion. "The trilogy combines Waugh's usual satire with an emotional depth not found in his previous works" (Wiloch 494). Most of the satire in Men at Arms (1952)is directed at the cynicism and the inefficiency of the military. The novel ends with Crouchback facing a court martial because, although he had successfully raided some enemy territory, he had not been authorized to perform the action (Wiloch 495). In Sword of Honour, Guy Crouchback is very honorable. It is ironic, then, that other characters who commit adultery, or display immorality and cowardice are more respected than Crouchback is. Sword of Honour contains a wide variety of Dickensian "Humours Characters." "Apthorpe is a formal, stiff, pompous braggart, yet he is a civilized figure who becomes a classic portrayal of self-assuredness and almost complete imperviousness. Ritchie-Hook is a fire-breathing warrior who loves offensive battle tactics and military carnage." Guy Crouchback joins Ritchie Hook in heroic action, as the two of them lead a brave and imaginative patrol raid on the Vichy French-held African coast, but their raid does not have official approval, so their action leads to temporary disgrace (Doyle 581). Ritchie-Hook and Crouchback are both censured for their actions, showing that, "in an unheroic age, genuine heroism must go unrewarded" (Doyle 582).

There is a further irony when a cowardly officer named Trimmer is chosen to lead a raid on a small unoccupied island in the English Channel. Trimmer performs this action with utmost incompetence, but due to the initiative of a sergeant under his command, and due to false publicity given to the episode, Trimmer is glorified by the popular press and becomes the hero of "The People's War," and he is sent on personal appearances around England and receives a great deal of national acclaim. Thus, "heroic actions are deplored while cowardly activity is applauded" (Doyle 582).

Waugh wrote A Little Learning; An Autobiography: The Early Years (1964) when he was at the top of his form. It is easy and natural, and it is also urbane, witty, allusive, precise, and graceful. According to James Carens it is, "responsive to every modulation of narrative and dialogue he wishes to express" (Carens ix). The novel treats Waugh's early years, the contended years of his nursery, and his shock when he departed from home to attend school. Waugh is delighted as he remembers his favorite house during childhood, and his mid-Victorian aunts. The book illustrates, "the importance of certain motifs of childhood innocence and symbolic architecture in his satires" (Carens ix).

Edmund Wilson said that Evelyn Waugh is, "the only first-rate comic genius that has appeared in English since Bernard Shaw" (Doyle 578). John Rogers said that Waugh's plots help to bring about some of the humor, and furnish some of the satiric foundation, but it is the "mot juste," or the cleverness of Waugh's descriptions and phrasings, and his genius in handling dialogue that play the biggest role in making Waugh's comedy and satire successful. David Lodge has pointed out that while reading Waugh, the reader often, "laughs without knowing why. One often laughs or at least smiles when one may not want to" (Rogers 342).

Waugh's life was a life of irony. In 1927 Evelyn Waugh married Evelyn Gardner but they remained married for less than a year. Alec Waugh, Evelyn Waugh's brother considered Evelyn Gardner to be a charming, pretty, neat, and gracious woman, and said, "She and Evelyn were a delightful team; they were so at ease, so affectionate together, their having the same Christian name was an amusing bond. They were called "He-Evelyn" and "She-Evelyn" (Phillips 27). J. B. Priestly says that Evelyn Waugh provided the world with a new and original type of humorous prose. He was an author with a cool, impudent, deadpan manner in the great tradition of comic story telling (Priestley 112). Paul A. Doyle suggests that Waugh was, "one of the most devastating and effective satirists in the history of English letters" (Wiloch 492). Evelyn Waugh wrote an epigraph which seems to sum up his own perception of his writing career: "To have been born into a world of beauty, to die amid ugliness, is the common fate of all us exiles" (Carens x).

Evelyn Waugh was a manic depressive who had a brilliant mind, and was exceptionally witty and humorous. He was always quick to observe the ludicrous and the comic aspects of every situation. When he arrived in Hollywood, he was beset by reporters and was asked about the state of creative writing in Hollywood. He replied, "Creative writing in Hollywood? I don't think it's ever been tried" (Doyle 584).

>Waugh's testiness and ennui increased and lasted until his sudden and unexpected death. When asked how he could behave nastily in person while being a practicing Catholic, Waugh remarked that if he were not a Catholic,

he would be much more critical and hostile.... Waugh, especially in later years, was a volcano of contradictions, paradoxes, biases, and unpredictability. He would criticize a person or a group--for example, Americans--and later defend or praise them. He appeared to enjoy agitating and creating controversies. Like Dr. Samuel Johnson he often took the opposite side of an issue just because it was the opposite side. In the notable history of British character oddities and great eccentrics, he must occupy a prominent place. (Doyle 583-584)

Evelyn Arthur St. John Waugh Bibliography

Amory, Mark, ed. The Letters of Evelyn Waugh. New York, NY: Ticknor and Fields, 1980.

Beaty, Frederick L. The Ironic World of Evelyn Waugh: A Study of Eight Novels. DeKalb, IL: Northern Illinois Press, 1992.

Carens, James Francis. The Satiric Art of Evelyn Waugh. Seattle, WA: University of Washington Press, 1966.

Doyle, Paul A. "Evelyn Waugh." British Novelists, 1930-1959. Ed. Bernard Oldsey. Detroit, MI: Gale, 1983, 570-586.

Doyle, Paul A. "Evelyn Waugh." British Short-Fiction Writers, 1915-1945. Ed. John H. Rogers. Detroit, MI: Gale, 1996, 337-345.

Doyle, Paul A. Evelyn Waugh. New York, NY: Eerdmans, 1969.

Farr, D. Paul. "The Novelist's Coup: Style as Satiric Norm in Scoop." Connecticut Review 8 (1975): 42-54.

Green, Martin. "Evelyn Waugh and the Commedia dell'Arte." New York Arts Journal 1.3-4 (1976): 25-28.

Greenblatt, Stephen Jay. Three Modern Satirists: Waugh, Orwell, and Huxley. New Haven, CT: Yale Univ Press, 1965.

Griffiths, Joan. "Waugh's Problem Comedies." Accent 9 (1949): 165-170.

Heath, Jeffrey. The Picturesque Prison--Evelyn Waugh and his Writing. London, England: Weidenfeld and Nicolson, 1982.

Henkle, Roger B. Comedy and Culture: England 1820-1900. Princeton, NJ: Princeton University Press, 1980.

Hopkins, Chris. "Comic Flexibility and the Flux of Modernity in Evelyn Waugh's Vile Bodies." HUMOR: International Journal of Humor Studies 10.2 (1997): 207-218.

Kleine, Don W. "The Cosmic Comedies of Evelyn Waugh." South Atlantic Quarterly 61 (1962): 533-539.

Kolek, Leszek S. Evelyn Waugh's Writings: From Joke to Comic Fiction. Lublin, Poland: Uniwersytet Marii Curie-Sklodowskiej Wydzial Humanistyczny, 1985.

Lassner, Phyllis. " 'Between the Gaps': Sex, Class and Anarchy in the British Comic Novel of World War II." Look Who's Laughing: Gender and Comedy. Ed. Gail Finney. Amsterdam, Netherlands: Gordon and Breach, 1994, 205-220.

Marcus, Steven. Representations: Essays in Literature and Society. New York, NY: Random House, 1975.

Meckier, Jerome. "Cycle, Symbol, and Parody in Evelyn Waugh's Decline and Fall." Contemporary Literature 20 (1979): 51-75.

Phillips, Gene D. Evelyn Waugh's Officers, Gentlemen, and Rogues: The Fact behind His Fiction. Chicago, IL: Nelson-Hall, 1975.

Priestley, J. B. "Wodehouse, Beachcomber, and Waugh." English Humour. New York, NY: Stein and Day, 1976, 108-114.

Rogers, John H., ed. British Short-Fiction Writers, 1915-1945. Detroit, MI: Gale, 1996,

337-345.

Stannard, Martin. Evelyn Waugh--The Critical Heritage. London, England: Routledge, 1984.

Stovel, Bruce. "The Genesis of Evelyn Waugh's Comic Vision: Waugh, Captain Grimes, and Decline and Fall" Thalia: Studies in Literary Humor 11.1 (1989): 14-24.

Swanson, Donald R. "Evelyn Arthur St. John." Encyclopedia of British Humorists, Volume II. Ed. Steven H. Gale. New York, NY: Garland, 1996, 1189-1195.

Waugh, Evelyn. Decline and Fall (1928). London, England: Chapman and Hall, 1962.

Waugh, Evelyn. The Loved One. New York, NY: Little Brown, 1977.

Waugh, Evelyn. Vile Bodies. Harmondsworth, England: Penguin, 1938.

Wiloch, Thomas. "Evelyn Waugh." Contemporary Authors: New Revision Series, Volume 22. Detroit, MI: Gale Research, 1988, 491-498.

Graham Greene (1904-1991)

In an interview with Marie-Françoise Allain, Greene suggests that some of his forays into Latin America were an example of the enemy of his enemy being his friend. In the 1950s, Greene would go out of his way to poke his, "feeble twig in the spokes of American foreign policy" (Nehring "Greene" 130). Even in Greene's darkest works there are comic scenes and comic characters. The reviewer for Time said that the humor of Greene's later fiction is, "best appreciated in relation to the earlier comic creations that have enlivened the population of Greeneland" ("Hamlet's Aunt" 68). Many critics have compared the writing of Graham Greene with that of T. S. Eliot, and David Higham parodies both Greene and Eliot in his play The Confidential Cleric or The Land Below the Waistline, which is published in his book, Literary Gent (1978) (Hindman 213). Graham Greene's works, especially his Catholic novels, have an allegorical, or double, meaning. There is the outward story about the novel's action, the crime and the punishment, but there is also the inner story of sin and its consequences, what Michael Rouch calls "the novel's moral center" (Rouch 182).

Graham Greene novels are about suffering, seediness, and sin. First, consider the suffering. In Dr. Fischer of Geneva; or, The Bomb Party, Dr. Fischer tells his wife, "If souls exist you certainly have one." When she asks him how he knows, he replies, "You've suffered." In The Power and the Glory, the whiskey priest says, "Pain is part of joy." And in The End of the Affair, Sarah says, "How good You [God] are. You might have killed us with happiness, but You let us be with You in Pain." Next, consider the seediness. In The Art of Graham Greene, Kenneth Allott and Miriam Farris say that seediness, "seems to Greene the most honest representation of the nature of things." In The Man Within, there is a bored and "shambling" priest who "sniffles his way through the burial service for Elizabeth's guardian." In Brighton Rock there is the wheezing old priest who smells of eucalyptus, in The Power and the Glory, there is the whiskey priest, and in The Potting Shed, there is the broken-down Father Callifer, who is described as having a "stubbly worn face," "bloodshot eyes," and a "dirty wisp of a Roman collar." Sin is the third important quality of Greene's trilogy. In A Gun for Sale, Raven is a protagonist who "had been marked from birth." In The Power and the Glory, there is the whiskey priest's illegitimate daughter; "the world was in her heart already, like the small spot of decay in the fruit." D., the "confidential agent" in The Power and the Glory thinks, "and I shall infect anything" (Rouch 183). Michael Rouch says that Greene is making the point that those who sin and suffer most are paradoxically, drawn closest to God. But John Atkins adds that Greene's, "concern with sin has become so intense he finds a life without sin to be devoid of meaning." George Orwell goes so far as to say that Graham Greene is the leader of the "cult of the sanctified sinner." Orwell says that Green has a sort of "Catholic snobbishness" about sin. "There is something distingué in being damned; Hell is a sort of high-class nightclub, entry to which is reserved for Catholics only." John Spurling suggests that Greene, "wanted this [religious] dimension in his novels not so much because he was converted to Catholicism at the age of twenty-two as for literary and temperamental reasons: without it the fictional stakes were not high enough, the action not important or significant enough" (Rouch 184).

The quixotic "whiskey priest" in The Power and the Glory (1940) is a sinner; he is inept as a priest and, "it is a patent absurdity that this man is chosen to serve and save The Faith and even attain martyrdom and sainthood." The description of the "whiskey priest" seems like something out of "Theatre of the Absurd": "He stood stiffly in the shade, a small man dressed in a shabby dark city suit, carrying a small attaché case. He had a novel under his arm: bits of an amorous scene stuck out, crudely coloured. He said: 'Excuse me. I thought just now you were talking to me.' He had protuberant eyes: he gave an impression of unstable hilarity, as if perhaps he had been celebrating a birthday...alone." (Sternlicht 430). The whiskey priest is in a dry province, but he is finally able to locate a bootlegger so that he can purchase some wine for the mass, but the corrupt cousin of the Governor drinks the wine before his very eyes. As the wine is being drunk, the priest sees hope, like the wine, dwindle before him, as he becomes drunk on the brandy he is forced by social conventions to drink; this is comedy blended with pathos (Sternlicht 430-431).

Peter Wolfe's Graham Greene the Entertainer is a study of the seven works that Greene originally called "entertainments" because they were lighter than his other writings. These included A Gun for Sale (1936) The Confidential Agent (1939), The Ministry of Fear (1943), Our Man in Havana (1958), and others (Mesher 485). Greene also wrote "comedies," such as The Complaisant Lover (1961), May We Borrow Your Husband? (1967), and The Return of A. J. Raffles: An Edwardian Comedy (1975). But the comedy varies. In Travels with My Aunt (1969), the comedy is explicit. In Doctor Fischer of Geneva, or the Bomb Party (1980) the humor is black. And in Monsignor Quixote (1982), much of the humor could be classified as "literate wit" (Mesher 479). David Mesher considers Graham Greene's three comic masterpieces to be Our Man in Havana (1958), Travels with My Aunt (1969), and Monsignor Quixote (1982). Mesher adds that in many others, such as A Burnt-Out Case (1961), and The Comedians (1966) "the comedy is more of a subject or a theme than a description" (Mesher 481). In The End of the Affair (1951), The Quite American (1955), The Burnt Out Case (1961), and The Comedians (1966) Graham Greene, "expresses a belief in the comic and absurd nature of human existence" (Sternlicht 427). Greene himself labels both A Complaisant Lover (1959) and The Return of A. J. Raffles (1975) as comedies, and in fact the subtitle of The Return of A. J. Raffles is, "An Edwardian Comedy in Three Acts Based Somewhat Loosely on E. W. Hornung's Characters in the Amateur Cracksman" (Hindman 209).

Orient Express (1932), which was published in England as Stamboul Train (1932), is a melodrama set in contemporary Europe. This "Entertainment" contains, "cloak-and-dagger intrigue, flight and pursuit, hair-breadth escapes, and a breakneck narrative pace," as Greene shifts the focus away from the hunter, the "hero" of the story, to the "villain" (Rouch 182). In Journey Without Maps (1936), Greene considers Africa not to be so much of a place as a shape--the shape of the human heart. Greene concludes this novel as follows: "This journey, if it had done nothing else, had reinforced a sense of disappointment with what man had made out of the primitive, what he had made out of childhood" (Rouch 186).

In Ways of Escape (1980), Greene says that the plot in his The Minister of Fear (1943) is "a funny one." Here, a man is acquitted of the murder of his wife by a jury. But the man believes in his own heart that he is guilty. Ironically, then, here is a man who is pursued for a murder which he did not commit, but believes he has committed (Greene Ways 101). In The Heart of the Matter (1948), Scobie is a total failure in all things, except that he has empathy. He fails as a policeman, and as a father, and as a lover, and as a husband, and in the end he fails even in his attempt to mask his suicide as a natural death so that he fails to keep from embarrassing his wife and her lover. As Scobie says, "I love failure" (Sternlicht 432). The misery and suffering of humanity that exist in the world that Scobie inhabits are found to be the universal condition, and that is "the heart of the matter" (Sternlicht 433). Charles Peguy in The Heart of the Matter says that the sinner, "stands at the heart of Christianity." James, one of Greene's "spoiled priests" in The Living Room says that his pious sisters, "are good people, I doubt if they've ever committed a big sin in their lives--perhaps it would have been better if they had. I used to notice in the old days, it was often the biggest sinner who had the biggest trust." Thus Greene felt justified in disagreeing with critics who felt his stories were pessimistic. He claimed that his novels were optimistic because they deal with the infinite mercy of God (Rouch 187).

One of the stories in Twenty-One Stories (1954) is entitled "The Destructors." This story makes the point that destruction, is in a way, a form of creation. This theme is adapted from Mikhail Bakhtin's famous anarchic statement that, "the passion for destruction is a creative passion, too!" (Nehring "Greene 131). In "The Destructors," the working-class boys are called "teddy boys" because they wear the Edwardian suit which had originally been fashioned by Saville Row tailors for upper-class young men, "as a nostalgic protest of the new social welfare state." The "teddy boys" are associated with delinquency and destruction, but they are very creative as well. In "The Destructors," the Wormsley Common Gang enjoys destroying a house designed by Christopher Wren, a symbol of the Edwardian upper class, But they destroy the house, "with the seriousness of creators--and destruction after all is a form of creation. A kind of imagination had seen this house as it had now become." Trevor, the gang's leader, is aware that the Wren house is "beautiful," but for him and for his gang, the word "beauty" belongs to, "a man wearing a top hat and a monocle with a haw-haw accent." It is because the concept of "beauty" is so associated with such people that Trevor has no difficulty in convincing his gang to destroy the house. Trevor explains to his gang, "We'd be like worms, don't you see, in an apple." It is from this statement that Greene's teddies allegorically become the "Wormsley Common Gang." "One moment the house had stood there with such dignity between the bombsites like a man in a top hat and then, bang, crash, there wasn't anything left--not anything" (Nehring "Greene" 133). In "The Destructors" the gang's elder adversary, Mr. Thomas, whom they call "Old Misery," is the owner of the house. He is a, "clear allegorical voice of authority in general" (Nehring "Greene" 132). The boys lock "Old Misery" up overnight in his outhouse, while they dismantle his house from the inside to the point where the touch of a truck the next morning will bring the entire house crashing down. When this happens, the lorry driver begins to laugh, and says, "I'm sorry. I can't help it, Mr. Thomas. There's nothing personal, but you got to admit it's funny" (Greene Collected Stories 346).

Another of the short stories in Twenty-One Stories is the comic "When Greek Meets Greek." It is about a young romantic couple who feel that the corruptness of society justifies the use of fraud. Both of their fathers were con men. Nevertheless, "there were bigger frauds all around them: officials of the Ministries..., controllers of this and that..., and men with the big blank faces of advertisement hoardings.... Their fraud was a small one by the world's standard." "When Greek Meets Greek" is a melodrama about a café owner's sudden conversion to the "brotherhood of man," after being invaded first by rioters and later by policemen who shoot up his bar and kill one of the communists. "They enter my café, he thought, they smash my windows, they order me about and think that all is well if they pay, pay, pay. It occurred to him that these men were intruders" (Nehring "Greene" 135).

        Paul O'Prey says that <u>Loser Takes All</u> (1955) is Greene's "first attempt at a sustained piece of humorous writing." He furthermore states that what follows, <u>Our Man in Havana</u> (1958), which appeared as a screenplay in 1960, is "a truly comic masterpiece" (O'Prey 110). Peter Wolfe says that <u>Loser Takes All</u> is Greene's only "entertainment" which, "bypasses the terror of the thriller in favor of light romantic comedy" (Wolfe 133).

        Kathleen Hindman considers <u>Our Man in Havana</u> (1958) to be "one of Greene's funniest entertainments," and she adds that Greene's play <u>The Complaisant Lover, A Comedy</u> (1959) displays Greene's hilarious and rather bizarre sense of humor (Hindman 214). <u>The Complaisant Lover</u> was easy for Greene to write since it displays a "satisfying blend of his manic and depressive moods." There are three characters who are involved in a love triangle. Victor Rhodes is a practical joker and a dentist who is insensitive and totally unromantic. Mary Rhodes is a competent mother and housewife who is dedicated to satisfying her husband's and her children's needs, but she no longer has a romantic attachment to her husband. Both Victor and Mary are in their forties. Clive Root is a seller of antique books who habitually falls in love with older married women only to loose out each time to their husbands. Clive is in his thirties (Hindman 214). In <u>The Complaisant Lover</u>, Clive Root is complaisant despite his lover's husband's demands. Victor Rhodes, the cuckolded dentist orders Clive, who is suffering from tooth-decay, to remain as his wife's lover at the end of the play, and at this point, Clive remains as complaisant as ever (Mesher 479). Clive Root in <u>The Complaisant Lover</u> sums things up this way, "We aren't allowed a tragedy nowadays, without a banana skin to slip on and make it funny" (Rouch 185). John Atkins considers <u>The Complaisant Lover</u> to be, "as vital as many of the restoration comedies" (Rouch 186).

        In <u>Brighton Rock</u> (1959), Fred Hale is a character described by Sanford Sternlicht to be "comic, pathetic, desperate, and doomed." Hale works for the <u>Daily Messenger</u> as a walking promotion. His face appears in the paper, and the lucky reader who is able to recognize him at the seaside resort of Brighton will receive a cash prize from the paper. But Hale is also being hunted by a mob which wants to kill him. So he faces an identity crisis: If he is discovered by a reader of the <u>Daily Messenger</u>, it would create so much attention that the mob would not be permitted access to him, but if found by Pinkie, he would be killed. Hale meets the intoxicated Ida, a good-hearted buxom girl, and stays with her, but when she goes to use the toilet, he is whisked away to his death by his pursuers (Sternlicht 429).

        In <u>A Burnt-Out Case</u> (1961), Greene claimed that he, "had discovered comedy." Querry is a "dubious hero" in this story. He has come to an African leper colony not for salvation, but for refuge, and there he "dies laughing." He looked down the barrel of a gun which is held by Rycker, his lover's husband, and "made an odd awkward sound which the doctor by now had learned to interpret as a laugh, and Rycker fired twice" (Greene <u>Burnt-Out Case</u> 243). As he is dying, Querry explains that he had not been laughing at Rycker, but was instead laughing at himself (Mesher 477). <u>Travels with My Aunt</u> (1969) is about the "seedy, fly-specked grimness" of the world of Greene's imagination which a number of critics have named "Greeneland." The comic tone ranges from lighthearted to slapstick. The reviewer for <u>Time</u> magazine said, "It is as if Shakespeare, after the tragedies, had chosen to write not <u>The Tempest</u> but <u>Charley's Aunt</u>" (Mesher 477).

        In his Introduction to <u>Collected Stories</u> (1973), Greene singles out "The Destructors," and "A Chance for Mr. Lever," from <u>Twenty-One Stories</u> (1954), "Under the Garden," from <u>A Sense of Reality</u> (1963) and "Cheap in August" from <u>May We Borrow Your Husband</u> (1967) and says "I have never written anything better" (Nehring "Greene" 131). "Under the Garden," from <u>A Sense of Reality</u> (1963) is about Wilditch, who has a dream about an eccentric, one-legged old man by the name of Javitt, who has a harelip wife named Maria. Javitt and Maria live underground both literally and figuratively. The story is about Javitt's tutoring Wilditch about people who refuse to conform, which he calls "rogues." "It's the hardest thing in the world for a rogue to survive. For hundreds of years now we've been living underground and we'll have the laugh of you yet, coming up above for keeps in a dead world." Javitt gives instructions for a rogue's conduct which is anarchic: "Riots...purge like a dose of salts;" "Be disloyal. It's your duty to the human race" (Nehring "Greene" 135). He continues, "The human race needs to survive and it's the loyal man who dies first from anxiety or a bullet or overwork." Wilditch is a rogue who has never taken his various professions seriously, "The refusal to take seriously the demands of work, in particular, as part of a general disavowal of institutional imperatives, make Wilditch's lifelong evasion of responsibility not some character dysfunction but an admirable pursuit of freedom" (Nehring "Greene" 136).

Graham Greene considers Carving a Statue (1964) to be a farce, but notes that farce and tragedy are closely related. This shimmering between comedy and tragedy can be seen in the fact that it is difficult to feel the humor (dark as it is) of the father's intimacy with the son's first girl friend or of the death of the young deaf and dumb second girlfriend, hit by a car and killed while trying to escape the embraces of the father's doctor (Hindman 215). The Comedians (1966) became a screenplay in 1967. A number of critics have suggested that the title of The Comedians is based on the narrator's observation that "Life was a comedy, not the tragedy for which I had been prepared, and it seemed to me that we were all...driven by an authoritative practical joker towards the extreme point of comedy" (Green Comedians 30).

The title piece of May We Borrow Your Husband? And Other Comedies of the Sexual Life (1967) takes place a year before the May Revolution in France. At that time, the expression "May We Borrow Your Husband?" was spray-painted by anarchists on many of the walls of Paris. The narrator of the story describes "Je ne regrette rien," a song which Edith Piaf used to sing, as embracing a phrase that is always sung or spoken in the spirit of defiance (Nehring "Greene" 130). "Cheap in August" from May We Borrow Your Husband is a comedy about the postwar period. John Spurling observes that comedy for Greene, "is bound up with antagonism to conventional society." In "Cheap in August," Mary Watson is an English woman who is married to a dull-but-successful American literary academic. Mary travels to Jamaica in hopes of having an affair, but she ends up with an elderly, overweight American by the name of Henry Hickslaughter who is afraid of the dark. The story reveals Greene's hatred of America not only by his characterization of Americans, but also in his treatment of Coca-Cola, television, shaving-cream ads, and fat tourists from Saint Louis. Greene is here satirically attacking American affluence and consumerism (Nehring "Greene" 137).

Another farce in May We Borrow Your Husband? is entitled, "Two Gentle People." Again it shows Greene's loathing for American culture. Again he writes about American icons like Coca-Cola and the Time-Life publishing conglomerate. The subtitle of May We Borrow Your Husband? is And Other Comedies of the Sexual Life, and "The Root of All Evil," is again about sexuality. At the end of the nineteenth century there was a drinking group, so the story goes, in a German village. This group is trying to conceal itself from a rather unpopular person who would like to join the group, and this unpopular person interprets the concealment of the group to mean that they are a secret society of anarchists, so he arranges for police surveillance of the group. The police have to cross-dress in order not to be discovered, and this results in a story that is more farcical than the other pieces in Greene's ouvre. But Greene is also making some serious points about authoritarianism. One policeman who balks at having to shave his moustache and wear a dress is simply told, "in the service of the law he should abandon any scruples." Neil Nehring says that the punchline to this story is more ironic than it is comic. The dialogue goes as follows: One policeman asks, "Subordination of authority?" and is answered, "Yes, men in women's clothes--the terrible sin of Sodom." The first one asks, "And what's that?" and is answered, "At your age, some things must remain secret" (Nehring "Greene" 137).

Another farce in May We Borrow Your Husband? is entitled, "Doctor Crombie." The narrator recalls an earlier period in his life when a school doctor had told him that sex causes cancer. Greene is satirizing the "abnormal fear of sexuality" that characterized the English public schools of Greene's youth (Nehring "Greene" 137). In "The Old School," Greene is criticizing England's authorities for their myopia. The targets include Greene's own father. Norman Sherry says, "One is alternately amazed at the unworldly innocence of the pedagogic mind and its tortuous obscenity," and of course these are exactly the same qualities that can be seen in the fictional character Dr. Crombie (Nehring "Greene" 137).

The Human Factor (1978) is a "spy spoof" about the absurdities in international espionage. Here the humor is both insightful and outrageous. One of the puns involves "Wormold," the name of a vacuum-cleaner salesman in Cuba who becomes a British operative. There is also visual humor, as when Wormold passes off the drawings of the various vacuum-cleaner parts as giant secret weapons. There is also slapstick, as when Wormold and the sinister Captain Segura play a game of checkers, with all of the pieces being represented by souvenir shot-sized bottles of liquor. Each man must drink down the bottle of liquor as soon as the piece has been captured (Mesher 478).

For Whom the Bell Chimes (1980) is a farce which contains a transvestite police officer, and a lascivious Scotsman. There are also a number of theatrical tricks as when the corpse is hidden in the folding bed which keeps falling down on stage (Hindman 216). Yes and No (1980) is a satire which targets the stage. It is about a rehearsal in which the director attempts to show a beginning actor the correct way to convey his bit part. The only words he has in his script are "Yes" and "No," and the description of the acting that must be used to accompany these two words depending on the situation in the play adds to the fun. In general critics agree that For Whom the Bell Chimes and Yes and No (1980) are both "hilarious comedy" (Hindman 216).

Monsignor Quixote (1982) is about the quixotic hope that there can be a "reasonable accord" between Catholicism and communism (Nehring "Greene" 130). It is a humorous adaptation of Don Quixote by Miguel Cervantes. Here the narrator tells about a simple, black-robed parish priest who is suddenly promoted to the purple-robed regal world of being a monsignor. This simple parish priest retraces the path of his namesake, Don Quixote, providing many opportunities for Greene to discuss politics and religion in a way that is filled with ironic humor. On his way toward Barcelona the priest confuses a brothel for a friendly hotel, and here he sees a pornographic movie because of the innocence of its title--"A Maiden's Prayer" (Champaign 62). In many ways Monsignor Quixote is like Don Quixote, but in many ways he is different. Don Quixote is a retired professor who assumes the title of a knight because he was thinking of bygone days of chivalry, while Greene's Father Quixote is a simple parish priest who assumes the title of monsignor because he is thinking of the bygone days of the Church prior to Vatican Council II, a time when dogmatic theology was much more in vogue. Don Quixote rides on his horse named Rocinante, is accompanied by Sancho Panza, and is guided by books on chivalry, while Father Quixote rides his decrepit Fiat 600, is accompanied by Enrique Zancas the former Mayor of El Toboso, and is guided by five holy books, one of which is the Communist Manifesto. Much of the humor of Monsignor Quixote is derived from the reader's making the various connections between Monsignor Quixote and the original Don Quixote. Monsignor Quixote, like Don Quixote, is totally naïve, as can be seen for example when he mistakes a condom for a balloon, or uses an outhouse for a confessional (Champaign 63).

Monsignor Quixote is Greene's last great comic novel. It represents the, "final reworking of Greene's most important themes as well as a last departure in his comedy."

Greene's Quixote figure is the priest of a village named El Toboso, in La Mancha of post-Franco Spain. Like the original Don Quixote, Monsignor Quixote is poor and his clothes are threadbare. His "steed" is a jalopy that is "little better than scrap," and in honor of the original story, he has named this jalopy, "My Rocinante" (Greene Monsignor Quixote 15). In contrast, the Bishop of Motopo drives a Mercedes. The bishop wonders, "How can he be descended from a fictional character?" (Greene Monsignor Quixote 16), and the answer to this question is a quote from Shakespeare's Hamlet, "There is nothing either good or bad, but thinking makes it so." There is jousting in Monsignor Quixote, but it is with La Guardia rather than with windmills. The galley slaves that are freed in Monsignor Quixote turn out to be a fugitive robber. Father Quixote's sidekick is the ex-Mayor of El Toboso. David Mesher feels that both the humor and the action in Monsignor Quixote is more philosophical than it is physical (Mesher 480). The ending of Monsignor Quixote is something of a switch: One of Greene's characters is "a Catholic in spite of the Curia," and the other is "a Communist who is still alive in spite of the Politburo" (Greene Monsignor Quixote 179).

One of the stories in The Last Word and Other Stories (1982) is entitled "An Appointment with the General." It is about the French editor of a "distinguished left-wing weekly," who waffled in his politics to accommodate changing attitudes. His most current attitudes are smugly delivered to a correspondent on her way to interview a character based on Torrijos. "The General, I think, could be a subject in your usual style. Suitable for your brand of irony." We "wonder whether his socialism is not rather skin-deep. He is no Marxist certainly" (Nehring "Greene" 130).

Graham Greene had suicidal tendencies, and during his last months at Berkhamsted and first months at Balliol College, Oxford, he experimented with Russian roulette (Mesher 473). During one of these episodes, Greene recounts, "I remember an extraordinary sense of jubilation. It was as if a light had been turned on. My heart was knocking in its cage, and I felt that life contained an infinite number of possibilities" (Greene Lost 175). But Greene's boredom and depression soon returned and he would do the Russian roulette again, until, finally, "as I took my fifth dose it occurred to me that I wasn't even excited: I was beginning to pull the trigger about as casually as I might take an aspirin tablet" (Greene Lost 176). This is a very interesting story; however Philip Stratford doubts its validity. Stratford warns that Greene had a passion for practical joking, and says therefore, "before making any neat biographical equation, one should at least entertain the possibility that the confessional essay is pure fantasy" (Sherry 87). In Ways of Escape (1980), Greene's second autobiography, Greene said that he was, "not a Catholic writer, but a writer who happens to be a Catholic." He says, "I'm not a religious man, though it interests me. Religion is important, as atomic science is" (qtd. in Rouch 184). In Ways of Escape, Green identifies his best pieces as "The Destructors," "A Chance for Mr. Lever," "Under the Garden," and "Cheap in August" (Rouch 185).

Graham Greene Bibliography

Atkins, John. Graham Greene. New York, NY: Roy, 1958.

Champagne, Roland A. "The Charm of Monsignor Quixote: Graham Greene's Art of Laughter." WHIMSY 3 (1985): 62-64.

Greene, Graham. A Burnt-Out Case. London, England: Heinemann, 1961.

Greene, Graham. Collected Stories. New York, NY: Viking Press, 1973.

Greene, Graham. The Comedians. New York, NY: Viking Press, 1981.

Greene, Graham. The Lost Childhood and Other Essays. London, England: Methuen, 1951.

Greene, Graham. Monsignor Quixote. London, England: Bodley Head, 1982.

Greene, Graham. Ways of Escape. London, England: Bodley Head, 1980.

"Hamlet's Aunt." Time 95 (January 19, 1970), 68.

Hindman, Kathleen B. "Graham Greene." British Dramatists Since World War II. Ed. Stanley Weintraub, Detroit, MI: Gale, 1982, 208-217.

Lewis, R. W. B. The Picaresque Saint. Philadelphia, PA: Lippincott, 1959.

Mesher, David. "Graham Greene." Encyclopedia of British Humorists, Volume I. Ed. Steven H. Gale. New York, NY: Garland, 1996, 473-485.

Nehring, Neil. "Graham Greene." British Short-Fiction Writers, 1915-1945. Ed. John H. Rogers, Detroit, MI: Bruccoli Clark Layman (Gale Research), 1996, 125-139.

Nehring, Neil. Flowers in the Dustbin: Culture, Anarchy, and Postwar England. Ann Arbor, MI: University of Michigan Press, 1993.

O'Brien, Conor Cruise. "A Funny Sort of God." New York Review of Books 18 (18, October, 1973): 56-58.

O'Prey, Paul. A Reader's Guide to Graham Greene. New York, NY: Thames and Hudson, 1988.

Rouch, Michael. "Graham Greene." Contemporary Authors, New Revision Series, Volume 35. Ed. James G. Lesniak, 1992, 179-188.

Sharrock, Roger. Saints, Sinners and Comedians: The Novels of Graham Greene. Notre Dame, IN: University of Notre Dame Press, 1984.

Sherry, Norman. The Life of Graham Greene, Volume 1: 1904-1939. New York, NY: Viking Press, 1989.

Sternlicht, Sanford. "Prologue to the Sad Comedies: Graham Greene's Major Early Novels." Midwest Quarterly 12 (1971): 427-435.

Sternlicht, Sanford. "The Sad Comedies: Graham Greene's Later Novels." Florida Quarterly 1.4 (1968): 65-78.

Wolfe, Peter. Graham Greene: The Entertainer. Carbondale, IL: Southern Illinois University Press, 1972.

Christopher Isherwood (1904-1986)

Much of Christopher Isherwood's humor is verbal. One of his characters, for example, is named "Herr Issyvoo," and this is a "wry Germanization" of Isherwood's own name. Isherwood's dialogue is sparkling, and has what Elton Smith considers to be a "verve and coruscating wit." Isherwood's characters are often innocent undergraduates who are contrasted against "middle-aged grotesques" (Smith 561). Isherwood's dialogue tends to be light, easy, and witty; nevertheless, underneath there is an irony that comes from the sharp differences between what the characters think and what the readers know. "The characters' lack of self-knowledge and understanding of others makes for constant comedies of error" (Smith 563).

All the Conspirators (1928) is a novel about a group in which Allen is the sanest member. But Allen has to suffer the ironic humiliation of Philip's patronizing advice which he gives with a wave of his mittened hand, and with his feet propped up by his sister and mother, "You see, Allen, what I really dislike about your attitude is that it gets you nowhere" (Smith 561). Mr. Norris Changes Trains (1935) was published in America as The Last of Mr. Norris (1954). Mr. Norris is a fussy and nervous man who wears a wig, and who spends hours every day putting perfume on his body. He has a collection of whips, and a pair of high crimson boots. He spends his days in orgies of luxury with wealthy young friends, but he chooses to spend his nights in squalid cellar clubs plotting with other conspirators to overthrow various governments (Smith 561).

Isherwood warns readers that Lions and Shadows: An Education in the Twenties (1938) is not an autobiography and that it should be read as a novel. Isherwood says that his characters are "caricatures" (Smith 560). Goodbye to Berlin (1939) contains a sharp contrast between the earlier lighthearted diary, and the later doom-laden diary. It contrasts heterosexual outlaws like Sally, with homosexual deviants such as those on Ruegen Island. It also contrasts a working-class family named the Nowaks with a wealthy Jewish family named the Landauers. It was in Goodbye to Berlin that Isherwood made the famous statement, "I am a camera with its shutter open, quite passive, recording, not thinking." This served as the basis for Van Druten's I Am a Camera, and also for a later musical comedy and movie named Cabaret (Smith 562).

Christopher and His Kind, 1929-1939 (1976) is an autobiography in which Isherwood takes the, "strident tone of the avowed gay activist who is determined to bare all." Although the book is written in first person singular, the narrator often describes Isherwood as if he were being observed from the outside, and as if the observer were not always totally pleased by what he saw. Isherwood uses comedy and irony to present his "pilgrim's progress" from "angry young man" to "gay liberation publicist" (Smith 561).

Christopher Isherwood Bibliography

Smith, Elton E. "Christopher Isherwood." Encyclopedia of British Humorists, Volume I. Ed. Steven H. Gale. New York, NY: Garland, 1996, 557-564.

Patrick Kavanagh (1904-1967) IRELAND

See Nilsen, Don L. F. "Patrick Kavanagh." Humor in Irish Literature: A Reference Guide. Westport, CT: Greenwood, 1996, 7, 161-162, 209.

Molly (Mary Nesta Skrine) Keane (1904-) IRELAND

See Nilsen, Don L. F. "Molly Keane." Humor in Irish Literature: A Reference Guide. Westport, CT: Greenwood, 1996, 163.

Nancy (Freeman) Mitford (Rodd) (1904-1973)

Frederick Karl says that reading Nancy Mitford is always great fun, because her truly English eccentrics are hilarious. Karl suggests that Mitford makes the outlandish seem natural, and she makes the natural sound bizarre, and Karl considers this to be a twin talent that is necessary for a really successful comic writer (Karl 276). Manuel Ben notes that whenever Nancy Mitford uses the term "society" in her novels she is referring to "High Society." The novels which Mitford wrote during the 1930s are light-hearted and ironic both about life in general, and about the class system in particular. Her novels of the 1940s and later are more polished, and her characterizations are especially improved. Mitford develops what Ben calls "Aristocratic Characters," and he also notes that the exaggerated portrayals of the ideas and the speech-patterns of these characters are often hilarious (Ben 175). Some critics have been harsh on Mitford because they feel that she encourages and applauds some of the glaring snobberies and prejudices of her characters. They have also accused her of "pandering to the status quo" (Ben 176). Nancy Mitford pokes fun at the upper classes, but she also pokes fun at the lower classes. Her favorite targets are the middle class trying to pass themselves off as aristocrats, or aristocrats playing at being workers (Ben 178). Most Nancy-Mitford critics emphasize her wit, her use of language, her sophistication, and her portrayal of the upper classes. Elizabeth Janeway described her writing as, "cunningly constructed, artfully written, echoing delightfully in the mind, purely frivolous, divinely farcical." V. C. Clinton-Braddeley said that her, "sense of humor is much deeper than her sense of the significant." And Honor Tracy says, "Miss Mitford's difficult art at its best is so fine, so beautifully a-shimmer with wit and nonsense and gaiety, that it creates a standard of its own" (Kinsman and Tennenhouse, 636).

Mitford's novels take place in an enchanted fantasy land of rich and witty aristocrats. Even though many critics have categorized Mitford as a satirist, Brooke Allen feels that it is her ability at writing romantic fantasy that makes her books so appealing. Mitford's friends included Evelyn Waugh, Robert Byron, John Betjeman, Harold Acton, and Raymond Mortimer, and it is clear that her writing was influenced by Evelyn Waugh's early novels, especially Vile Bodies (Allen 776). Brooke Allen says that both Nancy Mitford's pre-war and her post-war novels were influenced by her romanticism and her love for the French (Allen 777). Brooke Allen suggests that Mitford's wild generalizations, and her frothy style were not well suited to historical precision. Evelyn Waugh said that she wrote as if she were babbling into a telephone. It is probably this chatty and colloquial tone which provides Mitford's novels their intimate charm (Allen 778). In Highland Fling (1931) philistinism is targeted by a subtle form of ironic mimicry, and also by satirical characterization (Ben 177). In Wigs on the Green (1935), Mitford lampoons the Facist movement. She truly disliked Facism, and in Wigs on the Green she wanted to emphasize its absurdities (Allen 776).

The raging Uncle Mathew of The Pursuit of Love (1945) is a classic comic figure. He is a backwoods philistine who has read only one book--Jack London's White Fang. He loves blood sports and warfare, and he has a sign over his chimney piece that reads, "an entrenching tool, with which in 1915, Uncle Matthew had whacked to death eight Germans one by one as they crawled out of a dug-out" (Mitford Pursuit 3). Uncle Matthew also owned four huge bloodhounds with which he hunted his children (Allen 776). These chases caused quite a stir, especially with the Kentish weekenders on their way to church who, "were appalled by the sight of four great hounds in full cry after two little girls." Uncle Matthew was an exaggeration of everything that is British. Fanny said that although they feared Uncle Matthew, and disapproved of what he did, and sometimes hated him, he was nevertheless a, "criterion of English manhood. There seemed something not quite right about any man who greatly differed from him" (Mitford Pursuit 33). In the same way that Uncle Matthew was quintessentially English, Linda's lover, Fabrice de Sauveterre was quintessentially French. He was charming and sophisticated. He was romantic, passionate, cosmopolitan, and frivolous but erudite. He was the whole French nation rolled into a single character (Allen 777).

Uncle Matthew not only appeared in The Pursuit of Love, he also appeared in Love in a Cold Climate (1949). In both novels, he is depicted as a bumbling, ultra-conservative ignoramus. Therefore his views on the lexical differences between the Upper and the Middle (not Working) class must be rejected as coming from an uninformed character. Nevertheless, when Nancy Mitford herself expressed similar views (as a joke) in a 1954 issue of Encounter, these attitudes about the English aristocracy started a furor (Ben 176). There are two well-developed comic characters in Love in a Cold Climate. One of them is Lady Montdore, who says, "I think I may say we put India on the map. Hardly any of one's friends in England had ever even heard of India before we went there, you know" (Mitford Love 476). The other one is the homosexual, Cedric. Brooke Allen notes that many of Mitford's friends were homosexual, and that her novels, "were among the first to capture their idiom and humor in fiction" (Allen 777).

In The Blessing (1951) there is a scathing portrayal of a post-war pseudo-liberated avant-garde group of people who had an admiration for everything foreign, low, or socially depraved. Mitford wrote:

> The Crew only liked plays written by sad young foreigners with the sort of titles (This Way to the Womb, Iscariot Interperson) which never seemed to attract family parties out for a cheerful evening.... Sir Theseus was, in fact, Phedre written with a new slant, under the inspiration of modern psychological knowledge, by a young Indian. Phaedra was the oldest member of the Crew and really rather a terror, only kept on by the Captain because she was such an excellent cook. She was got up to look, as Sir Conrad said, like a gracious American hostess, with crimped blue hair and a housecoat. When she bore down upon Hyppolitus, whose disgust at her approach, as he cowered against the blackcloth, had nothing to do with histrionic art, Sir Conrad said in his loud, politician's voice, "She's got young Woodley on the ropes this time...." They could not be the clever girls they were without seeing life a little bit through Marx-coloured spectacles. (Ben 177-178)

The Blessing is about the very English Grace, who is Mitford's alter-ego. Grace is married to Charles-Edouard de Valhubert, and the plot is about Grace's coming to terms with her husband's incurable infidelity. "This infidelity is presented by Mitford as inseparable from the vitality and free spirits of French manhood." The Blessing is filled with pathos, but it is also wildly funny, especially in those places where Mitford describes the "unyielding Englishness" of characters who have been uprooted from England and placed in France. When the nanny of the Valhuberts's child, for example, is presented with a fine French cheese, she proclaims, "I wish you could have smelt it dear, awful it was, and still covered with bits of straw.... Funny-looking bread here, too, all crust and holes" (Allen 777).

Nancy (Freeman) Mitford (Rodd) Bibliography

Allen, Brooke. "Nancy Mitford." Encyclopedia of British Humorists, Volume II. Ed. Steven H. Gale. New York, NY: Garland, 1996, 775-779.

Ben, Manuel Miguez. "Humour in the Society Novels of Nancy Mitford." Literary and Linguistic Aspects of Humour. Barcelona, Spain: Univ of Barcelona Dept of Languages, 1984, 175-178.

Karl, Frederick R. The Contemporary English Novel. New York, NY: Farrar, Straus and Cudahy, 1962.

Kinsman, Clare D., and Mary Ann Tennenhouse. "Nancy Mitford." Contemporary Authors, First Revision, Volumes 9-12. Detroit, MI: Gale Research, 1973, 635-636.

Mosley, Charlotte, ed. A Talent to Annoy: Essays, Articles, and Reviews 1929-1968. London, England: Hamish Hamilton, 1986.

Mitford, Nancy. Love in a Cold Climate. London, England: Hamish Hamilton, 1949.

Mitford, Nancy. The Pursuit of Love. London, England: Hamish Hamilton, 1945.

Glyn Jones (1905-) WALES

In a personal letter dated April 28, 1994, Brian Lile has indicated that Welsh author Glyn Jones is a humorous writer. Anyone interested in the humorous writing of Glyn Jones and of other Welsh writers should consult the following works by and about Glyn Jones: The Dragon Has Two Tongues: Essays on Anglo-Welsh Writers and Writing (1968), Profiles: A Visitors' Guide to Writing in Twentieth Century Wales (1980), Selected Poems: Fragments and Fictions (1988), Goodbye, What Were You? Selected Writings of Glyn

Jones (1994), and The Collected Poems of Glyn Jones (1996). Please see the bibliography below for further details.

Glyn Jones Bibliography

Jones, Glyn. The Dragon Has Two Tongues: Essays on Anglo-Welsh Writers and Writing. London, England: Dent, 1968.
Jones, Glyn. Goodbye, What Were You? Selected Writings of Glyn Jones. Llandysul, Wales: Gomer, 1994.
Jones, Glyn. Selected Poems: Fragments and Fictions. Ogmore-by-Sea, Wales: Poetry Wales, 1988.
Jones, Glyn, and John Rowlands. Profiles: A Visitors' Guide to Writing in Twentieth Century Wales. Llandysul, Wales: Gomer, 1980.
Lile, Brian. Personal Letter Dated April 28, 1994.
Stephens, Meic, ed. The Collected Poems of Glyn Jones. Cardiff, Wales: University of Wales Press, 1996.

Anthony (Dymoke) Powell (1905-)

Anthony Powell's surname rhymes with "Noel" (Johnson 340). Powell is skilled at blending the, "ludicrous with the necessary" to show how people are from a number of different angles. From 1952 to 1958, Powell served as the literary editor of Punch (Tucker 442). Powell's comedies demonstrate awareness of the sadnesses of life--the depression, the coming war, the moral chaos. The characters arrange for entanglements and fruitless re-alignments. Their basic emotion is ennui giving them opportunity for little else than self gratification, and their basic charm, "lies in their powers of self-deception." Frederick Karl says that, "in Powell, we have the unique comic novelist who can write with wit and subtlety and still create not simple personality but character" (Karl 240). Powell's humor depends more on the qualities associated with normalcy than on those associated with eccentricities. Furthermore, Powell, unlike Waugh, doesn't rely on cultural prejudices or fixed beliefs in order to be funny. A lot of Powell's humor comes from the fact that characters keep re-appearing from the past, as if there were only a few individuals in the world, and these individuals keep being recycled. Thus, the distinction between the past and the present is blurred, and whenever anyone is mentioned, Nicholas Jenkins already knows who he is (Karl 242). Although he is trying to retain his individuality in the face of various social pressures, Nicholas Jenkins nevertheless succumbs to the loss of his own will. "This is, indeed, the paradox of the vapid age Powell describes. And whenever he suggests this paradox with all its sadness, he is writing the best type of comedy; for he has revealed the tragedy that lies beneath all serious social comedy" (Karl 244).

Afternoon Men (1931) is Powell's first novel, and the best known of his pre-war work. It is a satire about the upper-middle-class penchant for aimlessness. It begins and ends with party invitations. In this novel, Powell, "expertly depicts the banality of the lives under scrutiny by having characters talk with a remorseless, plodding simplicity, as if half-baked, half-drunk, or half-asleep after too many nights on the town" (Tucker 434). Powell felt that Afternoon Men was more a comedy than a satire, and was surprised when so many reviewers saw it as an attack on contemporary behavior. James Tucker says that Afternoon Men is funny and good humored, but he also feels that the aimless young people in the novel, who represent the middle- and upper-middle-classes, are being lampooned. Like Evelyn Waugh's Vile Bodies, Powell's Afternoon Men is a book mainly about parties and outings. The novel gets its title from the fact that these young men party so much in the evenings that on the next days they are not able to get out of bed until the afternoon. The book opens with an invitation to a party for William Atwater, and ends with an invitation to another party. Atwater is a mild and somewhat languid young man who works in a museum. The novel is about his search for love with a series of women. Atwater has a yearning for something profound, and this expectation fails throughout the novel in comic and grotesque ways (Tucker 434). In the novel, the tragic aspects are always overwhelmed by the comic. The novel is saying that, "life ought to be deeper and more purposeful than the norm here." The humor comes from the one or two clownish figures who are laconic, self-centered, and often abrasive in their conversations. Before writing Afternoon Men, Powell had read Hemingway's The Sun Also Rises (1926), and because of Hemingway's influence, Powell describes the dialogue in Messengers of Day as, "the naturalistic, vocable, banal, even inane, purposeless exchanges that are their own purpose, on account...of an undercurrent of innuendo and irony" (qtd. in Tucker 434).

Many reviewers have praised Venusberg (1932) for its humor. James Tucker considers Venusberg to be a, "lavishly ironic love story of great charm and delightful wry humor." "Count" Bobel is a comic creation who is both sinister and threatening. The tone of Venusberg moves from comedy to menace to melancholy to tragedy, and also contains tender love affairs. It is about Lushington, and the wife of a local professor who is hilariously ponderous, but endearing nevertheless. Frau Mavrin, the wife, is warm and sweet, but also strong (Tucker 435). From a View to a Death (1933) is, "wholeheartedly, even laboriously, devoted to comedy--comedy which at times approaches farce," especially in the first part, which is about a bunch of eccentric and half-witted rural characters who are very amusingly presented. The reviewer for the New York Evening Post said that From a View to a Death was, "brilliantly written, witty, and bitter" (qtd. in Tucker 436).

In Agents and Patients (1936) Powell is saying that some people are born to be led, to be milked, to be put-upon, and other people are born to lead, to milk, and to put-upon others, and each of these classes of people are destined to be what they are. At the beginning of the novel, Blore-Smith is a sucker, a victim, and at the end of the novel he is still paying for the debts of Maltravers and Chipchase, as Maltravers and Chipchase are becoming involved with new projects to be financed by other people (Tucker 436). Agents and Patients contains a number of comic incidents such as one where Blore-Smith is in a brothel, and others involving several, "magnificently bizarre minor characters" (Tucker 437). What's Become of Waring (1939) is an amusing novel in which the unnamed narrator has the role of observing the mild ironies and keeping the plot moving. The narrator is employed by a publishing house that wants him to discover the identity of one of the firm's most successful authors, an author who prefers to remain anonymous. James Tucker says that What's Become of Waring is a book of negations. There is an unnamed and featureless narrator, who is trying to find the identity of an unnamed author who has no discoverable identity, and who turns out to have done no writing on his own (Tucker 437).

Anthony Powell's A Dance to The Music of Time (1951-1976) is a, "Roman Fleuve," consisting of the following twelve books: A Question of Upbringing (1951), A Buyer's Market (1952), The Acceptance World (1955), At Lady Molly's (1957), Casanova's Chinese Restaurant (1960), The Kindly Ones (1962), The Valley of Bones (1964), The Soldier's Art (1966), The Military Philosophers (1968), Books Do Furnish a Room (1971), Temporary Kings (1973), and Hearing Secret Harmonies (1976) (Tucker 433). This twelve-volume "Roman Fleuve" allowed Powell to establish characters through successive volumes. The title is based on a painting by Nicolas Poussin entitled A Dance to the Music of Time, which is described by Nicholas Jenkins, the protagonist in A Question of Upbringing (1951) as, "The Seasons, hand in hand and facing outward, tread in rhythm to the notes of the lyre that the winged and naked graybeard plays" (qtd. in

Tucker 442). Powell considers Poussin's painting to be about how time and life, "bring people into contact with each other, separate them for a while, and then perhaps push them together again in evolutions that take recognizable shape." The major characters dance their ways in and out of each other lives, and each other's beds, in a style that seems to be random, but there is still some sort of order (Tucker 442).

James Tucker says that in A Dance to the Music of Time, Powell is not so interested in invention and making a striking presentation of important things that happened, but rather in the, "elaborate embellishment of generally quite small-scale events through discursive, even circuitous, witty prose" (Tucker 435). A Dance to the Music of Time represents the life of the narrator, Nicholas Jenkins, and the novels present a, "vivid, amusing, shrewd, and passably balanced account of upper-class Britain between 1914 and 1975." This series of books is about a rather small privileged social class, which Powell treats with, "perception, irony, and verve" (Tucker 433). A Dance to the Music of Time is, "the longest fictional work in the English language, published in installments over a period of almost twenty-five years" (Johnson 341). Anne Johnson describes A Dance to the Music of Time as a "roman fleuve" in which, "scores of major characters dance their way in and out of one another's lives--and especially one another's beds." The dance often seems random, but the music and dance metaphors imply that there is a system, a pattern, a harmony. This series of novels is a comedy of manners. Bernard Bergonzi indicates that A Dance to the Music of Time is, "a great work of social comedy in a central English tradition." But unlike many comedies of manners, this series also, "conveys the cumulative sense of a shabby and dispirited society" (qtd. in Johnson 342). A Dance to the Music of Time is a series of novels in which the "pushers" do well in the City, while Stringham, who is loyal to his heritage ends, up in a life of drink and wasted opportunities. "The offensive and mechanical Widmerpool becomes a hero of our time, the vulgar buffoon and clown now making his way through sheer will" (Karl 238). The Music of Time has a solid foundation of tragic events, but this is discussed with a kind of puckish humor (Karl 241).

A Question of Upbringing (1951), the first novel in the series, is a novel of wit and intelligence which treats the period between 1921 and 1924, the time when Jenkins attended public school, and the university, and went to France to improve his use of French. Jenkins also visits the homes of two of his school friends, Charles Stringham, and Peter Templer. These three characters are poised, casual, and high spirited, especially when contrasted with Kenneth Widmerpool, another student at the school, who is plodding, career oriented, and rather gauche. By the end of the series, Widmerpool has become a figure of evil, but a figure still touched by farce. Throughout the series, Widmerpool can be described as one of life's aggressors. Jenkins, Stringham, and Templer come from families either with lineage, or with money, or with both, but Widmerpool's father had operated a low-level company that sold liquid manure to the gentry (Tucker 442).

A Buyer's Market (1952) is largely about parties, dinners, and dances. Jenkins is now about twenty-one years old (Tucker 442), and works with a publishing house. He is thinking about writing a novel, but it is actually the nightlife that really matters to him. A Buyer's Market contains many social gaffes, as when a torrent of sugar falls from a sprinkler to cover poor Widmerpool, or as when Sir Magnus Donners, a rich and bourgeois industrialist, becomes morbidly gleeful as he talks about various punishments for young girls. A Buyer's Market is Powell's satirical statement on the fragility and the preposterousness of the pleasure-seeking world he is describing (Tucker 443).

At one point in The Acceptance World (1955) Nicholas Jenkins tells about the world in which he lives, a world very similar to that depicted in Evelyn Waugh's Vile Bodies: "I had enacted scenes with Jean: Templer with Mona: now Mona was enacting them with Quiggin: Barnby and Umfraville with Anne Stepney: Stringham with her [Anne's] sister Peggy: Peggy now in the arms of her cousin: Uncle Giles, very probably, with Mrs. Erdleigh: Mrs. Erdleigh with Jimmy Stripling: Jimmy Stripling, if it came to that, with Jean [Jenkins's own mistress]: and Duport [Jean's husband], too" (Karl 239).

And Frederick Karl notes that this is only a partial alignment of the various couples in the novel (Karl 239). In At Lady Molly's (1957), Jenkins's career changes for working with a publishing firm to writing scripts for films. By the end of At Lady Molly's, Jenkins has completed his second novel (Tucker 443).

A Dance to the Music of Time continues by showing the decline of Stringham. For Stringham, A Dance to the Music of Time is a Bildungsroman in reverse. He started out as an aristocrat with grace and savoir faire, a person who by comparison made Widmerpool look like a plodding fool. But in The Soldier's Art (1966), Stringham is a waiter in the officers' mess. He is debilitated by his alcoholism, and is being humiliated by crude officers in the mess. Even in this hostile environment, however, Stringham is able to retain his dignity and charm. As James Tucker says, "No amount of military rank can make Widmerpool his superior." As Stringham is declining in this Roman Fleuve, Widmerpool, who started out as a blundering clown, has by now become something considerably worse. Indirectly he will be the cause of Stringham's death, and possibly of Templer's death as well, in both cases because of his abuse of power (Tucker 445). There is one major female character in A Dance to the Music of Time, Pamela Flitton. In A Buyer's Market (1952) she is a child, but in The Military Philosophers (1968) she has become a, "fierce sexual predator, bedding with many of the male characters." Pamela Flitton provides much of the structure of the Roman Fleuve, since it is through her relationships that the reader can see the elaborate crisscrossing of lives. "Such interweavings are the very fabric of the Music of Time" (Tucker 445).

In the tenth and eleventh books of the series, Books Do Furnish a Room (1971), and Temporary Kings (1973), a large number of new characters are introduced, many of them, "brilliantly individual, vital, and--in some cases--comic." One of these characters is Lindsay Bagshaw, who is known as "Books-Do-Furnish-A-Room-Bagshaw." He is a complex and amusing figure, as is Daniel Tokenhouse, a retired army major in his seventies (Tucker 46). There is an interlacing flow of lives in volumes one through eleven of A Dance to the Music of Time. But it is the last volume, Hearing Secret Harmonies (1976), which brings order to the whole series. A Question of Upbringing (1951), had opened with Jenkins watching a bunch of street workmen hovering around a fire, and his mind was led to thoughts of the past, and went from there to wider speculations about the patterns and convolutions of time. Now Hearing Secret Harmonies (1976) ends with a similar scene. Jenkins is tending to a bonfire in the garden of his country house. "It is as if time pauses momentarily, having achieved some measure of order. The novel ends with a reference back to Poussin: 'Even the formal measure of the Seasons seemed suspended in the wintry silence'" (Tucker 446).

Anthony (Dymoke) Powell Bibliography

Bergonzi, Bernard. The Situation of the Novel. Pittsburgh, PA: University of Pittsburgh Press, 1970.

Hall, James. The Tragic Comedians. Bloomington, IN: Indiana University Press, 1963.

Johnson, Anne Janette. "Anthony Powell." Contemporary Authors, New Revision Series, Volume 32. Detroit, MI: Gale Research, 1991, 340-343.

Karl, Frederick R. "Chapter XIII: The Still Comic Muse of Humanity: The Novels of Anthony Powell, Angus Wilson, and Nigel Dennis." The Contemporary English Novel. New York, NY: Farrar, Straus and Cudahy, 1962, 254-273.

Powell, Anthony. Afternoon Men. New York, NY: Duckworth, 1931.

Powell, Anthony. The Fisher King. New York, NY: Norton, 1986.

Powell, Anthony. Messengers of Day. London, England: Heinemann, 1978.
Tucker, James. The Novels of Anthony Powell. New York, NY: Columbia University Press, 1976.

Rex Warner (1905-1986)

Rex Warner's novels are about the tension between private freedom and public authority, or between innovation and tradition, or between the individual and the socio-political system, or what he calls the "polis" (Cary 549). As a youth, Warner was an excellent athlete. He was unbeatable in pub sports, and was captain of his rugby teams both at St. George's and Wadham. When Warner was playing for the Gloucestershire rugby team, the Stroud News reported that he was, "perhaps the most dangerous man in the West of England" (Cary 550). Warner's novels are intellectually intense, but they also have a quality which Cecil Day Lewis calls "homeric boisterousness." This quality is especially prevalent in the stylistic highjinx of his first novel, The Wild Goose Chase: An Allegory (1937) (Cary 550). There are three brothers in The Wild Goose Chase who set off on bicycles in search of something they don't quite understand. Thus, they are off on a Wild Goose chase. Like Leda the swan of mythology, the mother of these three boys is rumored to have a red mark on her belly that is in the shape of a webbed foot. The plot is picaresque, and the characters are humours characters. Rudolph, the oldest brother, is a Blimpish gallant; he is brave but stupid. David is a sexual neuter who is an academic aesthete of the type that D. H. Lawrence called a "water spider." George is just an ordinary simpleton; he is the warm-blooded, easygoing hero, who enjoys his hobby of bird-watching. The boys have a series of comic misadventures. One of these is the lecture about Othello to a convent audience who are not able to understand the sexual passion or the human tragedy in the play. Another is when George referees a football match whose final score has already been posted. The book is filled with "ebullient inventiveness and sheer verve" (Cary 551).

The Aerodrome: A Love Story (1941) is a novel about the easygoing lifestyle of a Cotswold village with its squire, rector, and Bess, the landlord's daughter, as contrasted with the regimented and structured aerodrome which is adjacent. The aerodrome is an allegorical representation of a lifestyle which is utopian for some, but dystopian for most. It has been compared both with George Orwell's Nineteen Eight-Four (1949) and with Aldous Huxley's Brave New World (1932). The Air Vice-Marshall of The Aerodrome is trying to create a "conscious community," a community where it is possible, "to escape from time and its bondage, to construct around you in your brief existence something that is guided by your own will, not forced upon you by past accidents, something of clarity, independence and beauty." The Aerodrome is designed to be as different as possible from the "vague, amorphous, drunken, unwieldy, and unsatisfactory" life of the village. It is the function of the airmen to redeem the land, and if possible to subjugate the land, whether by guile or by force so that, "the supreme experiment may continue efficiently," and the world may be "clean." This noble end is so important to the Air Vice-Marshal that any means whatsoever are justified to achieve it (Cary 553). The Air Vice-Marshall feels that the historical past is a "cultural-genetic accident," and an obstacle to his perfect world (Cary 555).

On the dust jacket of Escapade (1953), Warner writes that this novel was composed "for no serious reason." It is written as a "holiday," in the tradition of P. G. Wodehouse, and is about the village of "Average," which is populated with endearing eccentrics that are precisely as political as are the characters in Wodehouse's Blandings Castle (Cary 556). The Young Caesar (1958), and its sequel, Imperial Caesar (1960) are Warner's "autobiographies" of Julius Caesar. In one of these books, Warner has Julius Caesar say, "I should not like to be described as either good or bad. It would be true to call me necessary, brilliant and, whenever possible, well-meaning" (Cary 557).

There are many places in Warner's novels which demonstrate Franz Kafka's theme that reality is in general unknowable. It is unknowable for Warner's "scholar-hermaphrodites in their convent;" it is also unknowable for Professor A. These two examples illustrate Warner's "consistently anti-academic satirical slant." They are presented in order to show "the perils of 'pure' intellect cut off from earthly phenomena" (Cary 553).

Rex Warner Bibliography

Cary, Joseph. "Rex Warner." Dictionary of Literary Biography, Volume 15: British Novelists, 1930-1959. Ed. Bernard Oldsey. Detroit, MI: Bruccoli Clark/Gale Research, 1983, 548-558.

Samuel Barclay Beckett (1906-1989) IRELAND

Samuel Beckett has been classed as a Proustian, a Joycean, a Sartrean, a Jungian, and even a Christian writer. His writings have been described as absurdist, experimentalist, existentialist, and "French nouveau romain" (Bair 15). In the late 1940s, Beckett began to write in French (Bair 25). Beckett preferred French, because the French "have no style." "They write without style; they give you only the phrase, the sparkle." Beckett said, "Perhaps only the French language can give you the thing you want" (Bair 21). When he was only fifteen, he won a position on the varsity cricket team at the Portora Royal School in Enniskillen County Fermanagh in Northern Ireland. Beckett is the only winner of the Nobel Prize to be listed in Wisden, the cricketer's annual (Bair 16).

Whoroscope (1930) is a poem, the title of which puns on the Greek word "horo" meaning "hour," and combines this idea with Descartes's belief that if he revealed the date of his birth, an astrologer would be able to use this information to create his "horoscope," and thereby predict the date of his death (Bair 18). In Proust (1931), Beckett says that the attempt to communicate when no communication is possible is very comic. It is like a mad man who holds a conversation with the furniture (Beckett Proust 103).

Beckett's More Pricks than Kicks (1934) suggests that suffering is "horribly comic." In this collection of short stories, Balacqua Shuah, the protagonist, is named after a character from Dante. Balacqua has "ruined feet," and a "spavined gait." He is a picaro who wanders around Dublin and Ireland, and his stories are told in a series of picaresque adventures arranged chronologically, but with no other link (Bair 22). One of the ironic stories of More Pricks than Kicks is entitled, "Love and Lethe." Here, Belacqua proposes to Ruby that they should commit suicide together, but Ruby would prefer to have an affair, because she is dying anyway (Jiji 103). In the end, the pistol misfires, so they just decide to have sex instead (Jiji 104). Another story in More Pricks than Kicks is entitled "Yellow." As Balacqua is waiting to have an operation he asks whether he should approach it with tears or with laughter, but then decides, "It came to the same thing in the end" (Beckett Pricks 163). Wanting to make a good impression on people, Belacqua chooses laughter, so he tries to remember a funny story about a priest who wants to be an actor, but doesn't want to take the Lord's name in vain. So the production company allows him to change the line "By God! I'm shot!" to "Upon my word!" But something went wrong with the scene, and the revolver actually went off and shot him, and he responded, "Oh! Oh...!...By CHRIST! I am SHOT!" (Beckett Pricks 172). Because his anesthesia mixture was too rich, Belacqua "bounced up on to the [operating] table like a bridegroom..., and, like the priest in the joke, 'By Christ! he did die!'" (Beckett Pricks 174).

Murphy (1938) was rejected by forty-one publishers before it was finally accepted by Routledge, the forty-second publisher to see it. Murphy is an Irish everyman; "Murphy" is the most common surname in Ireland. Beckett's Murphy lives with Celia Kelly, a temporarily-reformed streetwalker (Bair 22). Celia threatens to return to her profession unless Murphy is able to find work. But Murphy's horoscope tells him that he should not try to find work for another year. Nevertheless, Celia insists that Murphy should go job hunting, and he finds a job as an attendant in a mental hospital. The irony is that Murphy gets a job to be able to be with Celia, but the job he gets forces him to live at the mental institution, and therefore keeps them apart. Mr. Endon, one of the patients at the mental institution, likes to play chess. His chess strategy is to ignore the opposition, and to keep his chess pieces as close as possible to their initial positions on the board. There are many puns in Murphy. Celia's name in French is "S'y la," and there are also names like Ticklepenny, and Dr. Killiecrankie, and Miss Counihan, who is the love interest. Some of the incidental humor comes from parodies of Shakespeare, and from inappropriate diction, and from subtle references to esoteric subjects (Jiji 104). At the end of the novel, Murphy's funeral is long, and comically grotesque. Celia is left alive, wheeling her crippled kite-flying grandfather, Mr. Kelly, out of Kensington Gardens. She is on her way to resume her former profession after all (Bair 23).

Molloy (1951), Malone Meurt (1951), which was published in English as Malone Dies (1956), and L'Innommable (1953), which was published in English as The Unnamable (1958), were written as a trilogy (Bair 26). Molloy (1951) begins with the statement that it was midnight, and it was raining. It ends with the statement, "It was not midnight. It was not raining" (Bair 26). In Molloy, there are many grotesque bits of humor. For example, there are seven pages which Vera Jiji describes as the, "wonderfully absurd, perfectly logical, dead-pan pages devoted to explaining how Molloy distributes his sixteen sucking stones in four pockets so as to suck each in turn without repeating any before going the whole round." He finally throws away all but one of the stones, and then loses, or maybe swallows, the last one (Beckett Molloy 93-100). Another amusing scene in Molloy is the passage that explains that, "three hundred and fifteen farts a day [are] nothing [when] mathematics [are called on to] help you know yourself" (Beckett Molloy 39).

Malone Meurt (1951), which was published in English as Malone Dies (1956) is a parody of the "Bildungsroman." It uses such comic devices as parody of the Bible and of Shakespeare, incongruity, jargon, litotes, non sequiturs, etc. In Samuel Beckett: The comic Gamut, Ruby Cohn gives an example of Beckett's ironic tone: "Humbly to ask a favour of people who are on the point of knocking your brains out sometimes produces good results" (Beckett Malone Dies 238). About the stories that he has been told, Malone makes a contradictory comment, "all funny, not one funny" (Beckett Malone Dies 98). Valerie Topsfield considers Macmann's love affair with Moll to be a source of "bawdy humour" (Topsfield 84). Moll was degenerating. She was "beginning to smell." She was "subject to fits of vomiting," and "her hair began to fall out in abundance." "Her complexion also changed from yellow to saffron." "The sight of her so diminished did not damp Macmann's desire to take her, all stinking, yellow, bald and vomiting, in his arms. And he would certainly have done so had she not been opposed to it" (qtd. in Jiji 106). In Malone Dies, Malone is shown to be alone and dying, and he wants to continue writing his story as long as he is alive. Malone is between eighty and one-hundred years old, and a woman comes to his room every day to bring him soup and a chamber pot. He has a notebook and a pencil, but he can't move from his bed, so he has a stick with which he pokes through his stack of possessions (Bair 27).

The narrator of L'Innommable (1953), which was published in English as The Unnamable (1958), starts out as a rump and a head with weeping eye sockets, and ends up in a jar spewing out his consciousness in the only way available to him--by using words (Jiji 106). The Unnamable is thus about an unnamed person who lives in a jar that is placed in a window. He tells the first dozen stories in normal paragraphs, but by the end of the novel his telling becomes, "one continuous sentence, a desperate spew of words." Beckett said, "In L'Innommable, there's complete disintegration. No 'I,' no 'have,' no 'being,' no nominative, no accusative, no verb. There's no way to go on" (Bair 27).

En Attendant Godot (1952) was published in English as Waiting for Godot (1954). In 1955, Beckett won the "Award for Most Controversial Play" for Waiting for Godot (Bair 13). Raymond Williams notes that in Waiting for Godot there are three important qualities of the dialogue. First, the speech is very simple. The sentences are short and the words are also short and common. Second, Beckett uses a great deal of repetition in his sentences and in his situations. This repetition can be seen through the entire play. And third, Beckett leaves some of the dialogue unfinished, as when Vladimir says "Hope deferred maketh the something sick"; the reader is supposed to furnish the complete phrase taken from the Bible, "half reminiscence of hope deferred...." The repetition of the dialogue, as well as the repetition of the situations shows the boredom of the human condition and the mechanical gestures of humans. We are just passing time until we die (Williams 300-301; Cohn 65). One of the most powerful visual images of the play is expressed by Pozzo who believes that life is just an instant on earth. He says that women, "give birth astride of a grave, the light gleams an instant, then it's night once again" (Barnard 96).

In Waiting for Godot there are two sets of couples. In one set, Pozo is the master and Lucky is the slave. Vladimir and Estragon, on the other hand, are friends and equals. They call each other Didi and Gogo respectively (Jiji 107). The suffering on stage is farcical because it is being consistently undercut. Gogo's shoes are too tight, but only some of the time. Didi's torrential urination is too funny to be a tragedy. Lucky is treated as a slave, but this is undercut by his mechanical reactions and by his vaudevillian pratfalls. Pozzo's blindness and ridiculous helplessness is undercut by Didi's and Gogo's careless response to his cries for help. Didi and Gogo seem to be filled with angst, and they talk a lot about their discomfort, but this is undercut by the fact that they do nothing about it. They don't even get the rope that they will need to carry out their threat of suicide. "In Godot, all the mental sufferings of Beckett's tramps are made less real by their failure to do anything about them." We don't know who Godot is, or who he represents. We don't even know for sure that the tramps have an appointment with him. But we do know that they will continue to wait. Furthermore, "We know that Didi and Gogo will continue to think of suicide, of parting from one another, of going elsewhere, and that they will do none of these" (Grawe 240). Therefore, the survival of Didi and Gogo is guaranteed by the way the play is patterned, as demonstrated by the "virtual future" created by that pattern. So Waiting for Godot is a comedy and a farce, but more specifically, it is a prototypical example of "somber comedy," which Paul Grawe defines as, "comedy in which survival is possible only at continual cost" (Grawe 241). Grawe's position is a refinement of Ruby Cohn's position that Waiting for Godot is a comedy because of the jokes and the vaudevillian stage techniques (Cohn 283-299). Thus Grawe's analysis supports Cohn's analysis, but goes one step further (Grawe 242).

Paul Grawe also provides details for a Christian reading of Waiting for Godot, by showing how Waiting for Godot relates to Father William Lynch's Christ and Apollo. "The mud in man, the lowermost point in the subway, is nothing to be ashamed of. It can produce...the face of God...to recall this, to recall this incredible relation between mud and God, is, in its own distant, adumbrating way, the function of comedy" (Lynch 109). Didi and Gogo are "the mud in man." They are nobodies, doing nothing. They are beaten; they are tossed around; they are bewildered; they are irrational; they have lost their memory, their purpose, and much of their pride. Nevertheless, "despite their loss of rationality,

memory, purpose, and pride, Didi and Gogo maintain a wry sense of humor. They fight
back, if only by refusing to stop waiting" (Grawe 244). Grawe feels that in Waiting for
Godot, we find, "the mud in man, the lowermost point in the subway," but more
importantly, we find that this, "is nothing to be ashamed of" (Grawe 245).

Deirdre Bair describes Watt (1953) as a, "maddening fiction, filled with
mathematical games and lists of highly possible impossibilities." She considers this novel
to be deliberately obscure and puzzling, as it is filled with "biographical revelations which
are almost immediately undercut or denied outright by the narrator" (bair 25). Some of the
humor in Watt is very cruel, as when Sam and Watt feed frogs to rats, and then feed the
rats to their relatives, "watching with glee as the lucky relatives tear the rat apart, Sam
reflects, 'It was on these occasions, we agreed, after an exchange of views, that we came
nearest to God'" (Beckett Watt 156). Another example of cruel humor is Beckett's cruel
treatment of humanity's physical weaknesses, their disfigurements, diseases, aging, and
death (Jiji 104). Watt himself is physically grotesque, and so is Mrs. Gorman, his aging
paramour. They advertise for an aphrodisiac named "Bando"; Vera Jiji notes that the
French word "bander" means "to have an erection." Watt also contains many puns. "Watt"
is a pun on "What?" and Watt goes to work for a person named "Mr. Knott," who is "not
God," just as "Godot" is "not God." Mr. Graves, the gardener, says "turd" for "third," and
"fart" for "fourth," and there is a "hardy laurel" bush that laughs. The bush, of course, is
named after the American clowns, Stan Laurel and Oliver Hardy (Jiji 105). In Watt,
Arsene describes various types of laughter.

> The bitter laugh laughs at that which is not good, it is the ethical laugh.
> The hollow laugh laughs at that which is not true, it is the intellectual
> laugh.... But the mirthless laugh is the dianoetic laugh [i.e., the laugh of
> pure reason], down the snout--Haw!--so. It is the laugh of laughs, the risus
> purus, the laugh laughing at the laugh, the beholding, the saluting of the
> highest joke, in a word the laugh that laughs--silence please--at that which
> is unhappy. (Beckett Watt 48)

In Act Without Words: A Mime for One Player (1957), a carafe of water is hung
just out of the reach of the lone actor. He is encouraged to try to reach it by boxes which
magically appear on stage, but the carafe remains tantalizingly just out of his reach (Jiji
109). Part of the humor of All That Fall (1957), a radio play, comes from the visual
imagery of Mrs. Rooney's huge bulk, as, "her polite neighbor tries to hoist her into his car
without touching her body in a sexually suggestive way." The text contains one double
entendre after another (Jiji 109).

Fin de Partie (1957) was published in English as Endgame (1958) (Bair 27). It
takes place in a room that has two small windows that are placed high on the wall. The
setting is similar to the inside of a human skull. Hamm, the master, is crippled and blind,
and he is confined to his armchair which is on casters. He dominates Clov, the servant.
Nagg and Nell are Hamm's legless parents. They converse from the two ash cans in which
they have been placed. When Hamm asks Clov to get him ready for bed, Clov refuses,
saying, "I can't be getting you up and putting you to bed every five minutes. I have things
to do." After a short silence, Hamm says, "Did you ever see my eyes?". Hamm is saying
that his martyrdom is greater than is Clov's martyrdom. Hamm threatens not to feed
Clove, and Clov replies that that's OK; he'll just go ahead and die. He is implying that
he would then be free from Hamm's domination. So then Hamm threatens to feed Clov
just enough to keep him from dying (Jiji 108).

Paul Grawe points out that the chess match in Endgame has three possible
outcomes. One outcome is for one player to checkmate the king of the other player. The
other two outcomes are "Catch-22 situations." If there is no winner, there could be one of
two types of stalemate. In one type of stalemate, neither player has enough power to

checkmate the other player. In the other type of stalemate, the player who has the next move cannot move without putting his king in check. Since the rules of chess do not allow the king to commit suicide, the pieces are frozen and the players can't move (Grawe 246).

The title piece in Krapp's Last Tape and Other Dramatic Pieces (1958) is a mixture of humor and pathos that ranges from vaudevillian to existential. It is humorous that the protagonist is not able to give up such bad habits as his reliance on alcohol, or his passion for bananas; bananas, by the way are the reason for Krapp's constipation. These bananas are a constant source of humor, as they are locked in his desk drawer, and he is able to reach them only after much effort. The bananas also look funny as he eats them, and there is a subliminal reminder of the vaudeville term, "top banana." Krapp also slips on the skins of the bananas, and tosses the skins offstage, and so on (Jiji 109).

During the 1960s and 1970s, Beckett was experimenting with both form and substance in both his drama and his fiction. Sometimes he published his items in slim pamphlets with extra large type and wide margins (Bair 28). The publishers wanted to satisfy Beckett's readership, who were fascinated by Beckett's dramatic experiments.

> The brevity of the 1960s prose also signaled the beginning of a comparable brevity in Beckett's drama as well. Breath, first published in Oh! Calcutta! (1969), is 120 words and lasts thirty-five seconds; Not I (1973) should be played in no more than sixteen minutes; That Time (1976) should last between twenty-four and thirty minutes. The fiction continued with Fizzles (1976; published in French as Foirade, 1976), which Paul Gray called "slight to the point of frippery."

Bair continues,

> Throughout the late 1960s and the 1970s, the trend toward brevity continued with works such as Assez (1966; published in English as Enough, 1974), Sans (1969; published in English as Lessness, 1970), and Le Dépeupleur (1970; published in English as The Lost Ones, 1972). Now Beckett's characters were only voices recalling past lives, inhabiting cylinders, or divorced from recognizable landscape. They were sterile, passionless, resigned to nothingness. (Bair 30)

Deirdre Bair says that there has been a great deal of speculation about Beckett's purposes in these writings which become more and more diminished in both form and substance (Bair 31). Valerie Topsfield suggests that in Comment C'est (1961), which was published in English as How It Is (1964), Beckett resolves his, "conflicting feelings about tragedy and humor." Here, "the conflict between tears and laughter disappears; they are truly now the same" (Topsfield 130).

Happy Days (1961) is the epitome of "black humor." Winnie is buried up to her waist in Act 1, and up to her neck in Act 2, as she happily prattles away in a way that is reminiscent of an, "air-headed breakfast television talk show" where the hostess has been instructed, "to be upbeat at all cost, as she chats on about the increasing deaths from AIDS." Winnie's speech is filled with stale clichés like "can't be cured," "genuine pure," "nothing like it," "that is always what I say," and "another happy day." Her speech also contains much archaic diction, like "tis," "beseech," "enow," "God grant...," damask cheek," and "dire need." There are also many misquotations from Shakespeare. There is also humor in the way that Winnie tortures Willie by demanding his full attention, and hitting him on the head with her umbrella as he tries to resist her "relentless cheeriness" (Jiji 109).

Mercier et Camier (1970), which was published in English as Mercier and Camier (1974), is about the two halves of a single personality. There is the contrast of the optimist and the pessimist, of the mind and the body, and of the one who needs and the one who needs to be needed. Mercier wants Camier to obtain a sense of proportion, "When you fear for your cyst think of your fistula. And when you tremble for your fistula consider your chancre. This method holds equally for what is called happiness" (Beckett <u>Mercier</u> 58). Valerie Topsfield feels that by distancing themselves from the assaults of providence, Mercier and Camier are on their way to the "risus purus," which "laughs at fate" (Beckett <u>Mercier</u> 69).

In <u>The Lost Ones</u> (1972), a narrator takes inch-high white paper figures out of a case that he has brought onto the set. He sets these small paper actors into a miniature cylinder which represents the place where lost bodies roam around looking for their "lost one." The space is large enough that the search is always in vain. The audience is seated around this performance on bleachers that are covered with a dark gray felt. This same felt also covers the floor, the seats, and the ceiling. As members of the audience enter the theater, they are given pocket binoculars so that they can see the mannikin actors by looking through either end of the binoculars. At two different places in the recital the narrator [David Warrilow] strips down and becomes one of the characters. At another place in the recital the narrator places a figure in his left ear and pulls the figure out of his right ear, while at the same time describing how the climbers move through tunnels in the cylinder wall. The narrator maintains his dignity and equanimity by lifting one eyebrow and then the other to indicate some small amount of discomfort as the climber moves through his head. The size of the figures, the view through both ends of the binoculars, and the dispassionate text all give members of the audience the impression that they are mini-Gods (Jiji 102). The mannequins themselves are reminiscent not only of Dante's circles in Hell, but also of Wall Street tycoons and social climbers, or of scholars and students (Jiji 103).

<u>Company</u> (1980) is only sixty-three pages long. Beckett's narrator in <u>Company</u> is alone, on his back in the dark. He invents voices, and is a, "devised devisor devising it all for company" (qtd. in Bair 31). Martin Esslin has a chapter on Beckett's life and works in his <u>The Theatre of the Absurd</u>. In <u>Samuel Beckett: The Comic Gamut</u>, Ruby Cohn explains how Beckett's use of comic devices is easily explained by using Henri Bergson's categories. Cohn also says that Beckett, "reduces the comic to the hysterical, but also to the pathetic." The narrator in <u>The Unnamable</u> says, "I'll laugh, that's how it will end, in a chuckle" (Cohn 123). In <u>Comedy High and Low</u> (1978), Maurice Charney discusses comic theory that ranges in its sources from farce to film to the writings of Shakespeare (Jiji 113). In a book entitled, <u>The Last Modernist</u> (1997), Anthony Cronin classifies Samuel Beckett with such writers as Vladimir Nabokov, William Faulkner, Henry Miller, Witold Gombrowicz, Henry Roth, Nathanael West, and Louis-Ferdinand Céline. All of these writers are second-generation modernists who started writing in the late 1920s or early 1930s, just after T. S. Eliot, James Joyce, Franz Kafka, and Marcel Proust had written their major works. These authors were caught in the uncertainties and anxieties of political and economic crisis. They therefore turned toward a dark and mocking humor that became one of the literary vehicles of the depression years.

Maurice Charney says that Samuel Beckett is our best writer of "tragic farce," which he considers to be uterribly serious, and even savage, kind of comic humor. Charney places Beckett in the tradition of Ionesco, Friedrich Durrenmatt, Joe Orton, and Tom Stoppard (Charney 111). Beckett's humor results from his innovative characterizations, his innovative plot structures, his innovative literary style, and his obsessive desire to tell some hard truths about humanity. Part of the reason that Beckett's characters are funny is that they seem so mechanical, and thus conform to Henri Bergson's concept of humor. His characters are also as invulnerable as clowns or cartoon figures. The wide range of Beckett's humor is also amazing. "Some of it is based on bathroom jokes, on mild obscenities, on comic disgust with body smells, on pratfalls, trouser-dropping, flea scratching, Ireland, humanity's inability to control or do without material objects which resist human will, or the expression of childish hostility." Some of Beckett's humor is

based on the futility of humans to gather meaning from meaningless events, some of his humor is expressed from the lofty view he assumes to look at humanity's absurdities. Beckett uses puns, and parodies as he, "plays on the preposterousness of language and human logic." It was Samuel Beckett who said, "Nothing is funnier than unhappiness" (Jiji 110).
See also Nilsen, Don L. F. "Samuel Beckett." Humor in Irish Literature: A Reference
     Guide. Westport, CT: Greenwood, 1996, 5-9, 163-181, 216.

Samuel Barclay Beckett Bibliography

Bair, Deirdre. "Samuel Beckett." Dictionary of Literary Biography, Volume 15: British
     Novelists, 1930-1959. Ed. Bernard Oldsey. Detroit, MI: Bruccoli Clark/Gale
     Research, 1983, 13-32.
Barnard, G. C. Samuel Beckett: A New Approach. New York, NY: Dodd, Mead, 1970.
Beckett, Samuel. Comédie et Actes Divers. Paris, France: Editions de Minuit, 1966.
Beckett, Samuel. Malone Dies. New York, NY: Grove Press, 1956.
Beckett, Samuel. Molloy New York, NY: Grove Press, 1955.
Beckett, Samuel. More Pricks than Kicks. London, England: Calder and Boyars, 1970.
Beckett, Samuel. Watt. New York, NY: Grove Press, 1959.
Charney, Maurice. Comedy High and Low: An Introduction to the Experience of Comedy.
     New York, NY: Oxford University Press, 1978.
Coetzee, John M. "The Comedy of Point of View of Beckett's Murphy." Critique: Studies
     in Modern Fiction 12.2 (1970): 19-27.
Cohn, Ruby. Samuel Beckett: The Comic Gamut. New Brunswick, NJ: Rutgers University
     Press, 1962.
Cormier, Ramona, and Janis L. Pallister. "En attendant Godot: Tragedy or Comedy?"
     L'Esprit Créateur 11.3 (1971): 44-54.
Cronin, Anthony. Samuel Beckett: The Last Modernist. New York, NY: Harper Collins,
     1997.
Esslin, Martin. The Theatre of the Absurd. Garden City, NY: Doubleday, 1969.
Grawe, Paul H. "Beckett's Changing Faith." Comedy in Space, Time, and the Imagination.
     Chicago, IL: Nelson-Hall, 1983, 237-250.
Henkle, Roger B. "Beckett and the Comedy of Bourgeois Experience." Thalia 3.1 (1980):
     35-39.
Jiji, Vera. "Samuel Beckett." Encyclopedia of British Humorists, Volume I. Ed. Steven H.
     Gale. New York, NY: Garland, 1996, 99-114.
Kenner, Hugh. Flaubert, Joyce, and Beckett: The Stoic Comedians. Boston, MA: Beacon
     Press, 1962.
Kern, Edith. "Beckett and the Spirit of the Commedia dell'Arte." Modern Drama 9 (1966):
     260-267.
Lynch, William F. Christ and Apollo. New York, NY: Sheed and Ward, 1960.
Murray, Patrick. The Tragic Comedian: A Study of Samuel Beckett. Cork, Ireland: Mercier
     Press, 1970.
Orr, John. "Samuel Beckett: Imprisoned Persona and Irish Amnesia." Tragicomedy and
     Contemporary Culture: Play and Performance from Beckett to Shepard. Ann Arbor,
     MI: University of Michigan Press, 1991, 47-71.
Reid, Alec. "Comedy in Synge and Beckett." Yeats Studies 2 (1972): 80-90.
Robinson, Fred Miller. The Comedy of Language. Amherst, MA: University of
     Massachusetts, 1980.
Smith, Frederik N. "Beckett's Verbal Slapstick." Modern Fiction Studies 29 (1983): 43-55.
States, Bert O. The Shape of Paradox: An Essay on "Waiting for Godot." Berkeley, CA:

University of California Press, 1978.

Topsfield, Valerie. The Humour of Samuel Beckett. Basingstoke, England: Macmillan, 1988; St. Martin's Press, 1988.

Waters, Maureen. "Samuel Beckett's Murphy." The Comic Irishman. Albany, NY: State Univ of New York Press, 1984, 110-122.

Watson, David. Paradox and Desire in Samuel Beckett's Fiction. Basingstoke, England: Macmillan, 1991.

Williams, Raymond. Drama from Ibsen to Brecht. London, England: Chatto and Windus, 1968.

Winkler, Elizabeth. The Clown in Modern Anglo-Irish Drama. Bern, Switzerland: Herbert Lang, 1977.

Sir John Betjeman (1906-1984)

John Betjeman carefully cultivated his image as a, "bumbling, untidy, absent-minded, friendly old duffer," and this boosted his popularity among ordinary people. In spite of this image, or maybe because of it, Betjeman was appointed as the Poet Laureate of England (Smith 148). Most critics agree that John Betjeman is a skilled writer of light, humorous occasional verse. Philip Larkin, and W. H. Auden have said that Betjeman's writing is lucid, and has a delicate lyricism. They further say that he has a good ear for dialogue, and a good command of language, and metrical style. Auden especially liked his, "use of light, humorous verse as the vehicle for serious truth about himself and contemporary society" (Smith 150).

"Come, friendly bombs and fall on Slough" is a poem in Continual Dew: A Little Book of Bourgeois Verse (1937), in which Betjeman offers a savage invitation. He wants the bombs to fall on Slough because everything in Slough is "tinned." This includes the fruit, the meat, the milk, the beans, and even the minds and the breath (Smith 150).

"In Westminster Abbey," one of the poems in Old Lights for New Chancels (1940), has the sting of satire. The "lady of the glove," who wants to feel better about herself, has squeezed a quick prayer in Westminster Abbey into her busy schedule. She prays that the Gracious Lord will bomb the Germans and spare the British, especially the British residence located at 189 Cadogan Square, her own residence. She bargains with God for His favors, saying that she will attend Evening Service whenever she is able to find the time. She also says that she will send white feathers to all of the men who have not listed in the war effort, and she will interrupt her busy social calendar by joining the Women's Army Corps, though she will not go so far as to promise that she will actually serve in this corps (Smith 148). In "Trebetherick," also from Old Lights for New Chancels, Betjeman tells how the town of Trebetherick reminds him of the brutal past, a time when people on shore waited expectantly to plunder the ships that foundered on the rocky beach. In "Lake District," Betjeman says that times have changed so that instead of having real adventures, Ralph, Vasey, Alastair, Biddy, John, and "I" merely get sand in our sandwiches and wasps in our picnic tea. The entire Lake District, which had been so dear to Wordsworth, is now just a place where a person can drink "non-alcoholic wine," and shake the H.P. Sauce, and spill the Heinz's Ketchup on the tablecloth (Smith 150).

In "The Dear Old Village," which was published in A Few Late Chrysanthemums (1954), Betjeman shows his preference to the windows that "squint beneath thatch" as opposed to the "vita-glass" windows of the new school. Betjeman deplores the girls who clerk in Woolworth's and the boys who no longer have a warm plough horse, but instead have a smelly, noisy tractor. Betjeman uses a comic and satiric tone to describe the modern "improvements" which he hates, and to wryly show his nostalgia for the old things which he loves (Smith 150). Summoned by Bells (1960) is filled with rapidly moving blank verse, but the verse becomes rhymed whenever Betjeman's emotions become particularly aroused (Smith 149).

It was the Earl of Birkenhead who compiled the Collected Poems of John Betjeman (1971). And it was the Earl of Birkenhead who called John Betjeman "one of modern England's few upper-class licensed jesters." In the Introduction to this volume, the controversial poet Philip Larkin says in an epigram, "If the spirit of our century is onwards, outwards, and upwards, the spirit of Betjeman's work is backwards, inwards, and downwards" (Smith 149).

Sir John Betjeman Bibliography

Smith, Elton E." Encyclopedia of British Humorists, Volume I. Ed. Steven H. Gale. New York, NY: Garland, 1996, 146-151.

Catherine McMullen Cookson (Catherine Marchant) (1906-)

In an interview for the London Times (August 15, 1983), Catherine Cookson told Caroline Moorehead why she has never had difficulty coming up with ideas for her historical novels, "I've always been a jabberer. I just talked. I see everything in images. The plot sort of unfolds. Even the dialogue. In the morning, it's all there to put down." Anne Duchene says that Cookson, "writes stories in which her readers can gratefully recognize experiences and emotions of their own--heightened, to be sure, by greater comedy or greater violence than their own lives normally vouchsafe, but based on all their own affections, furies, aspirations and reactions" (qtd. in May and Lesniak 117).

Catherine McMullen Cookson (Catherine Marchant) Bibliography

May, Hal and James G. Lesniak, Eds. Contemporary Authors, New Revision Series, Volume 28. Detroit, MI: Gale Research, 1990, 116-117.

Pamela Lyndon Travers (1906-1996)

Like Mary Poppins, P. L. Travers is a story teller. As a story teller, she feels that "Old Wive's Tales" are great. They are the best stories in the world, and they have long memories. She feels that women are the best story tellers because they play the triple role of Maiden, Mother, and Crone. "Each of us, of course, begins as a maiden and whether she becomes a physical mother or not makes no difference, the role of mother is the next step, the flowering of the bud. Last of all comes the grandmother--again, not the physical grandmother, but the stage where the flower withers into seed pod. To become a crone, it seems to me, is the last great hope of woman, supremely worth achieving" (Commire 162).

A reviewer for the Times Literary Supplement describes Mary Poppins (1935) as, "the embodiment of authority, protection, and cynical common sense," adding that Mary Poppins's powers are magical, and that basically, she is the "Good Fairy" (Lesniak 448). There is much humor in the Mary Poppins books, as when Mary Poppins tells the older children as they crowd around to hear one of her stories, "Gently, please, gently! This is a baby, not a battleship!" (qtd. in Commire 150). One of Mary Poppins's important qualities is her tremendous vanity. Another important quality is that she never explains.

"I often wonder why people write and ask me to explain this and that. I'll write back and say that Mary Poppins didn't explain, so neither can I or neither will I." When they persist, Travers says, "I'm not going to write footnotes to Mary Poppins. That would be absolutely presumptuous." Only Mary Poppins knows the answers, and she's not saying. That's what makes her so intriguing to readers (Commire 159). In all, there are eight Mary Poppins books, Mary Poppins (1935), Mary Poppins Comes Back (1935), Mary Poppins Opens the Door (1943), Mary Poppins in the Park (1952), Mary Poppins from A to Z (1962), Mary Poppins in the Kitchen (1975), and Mary Poppins in Cherry Tree Lane (1982). After the third Mary Poppins book, a little boy wrote Travers a touching letter which began, "Madum: I have just finished reading Mary Poppins Opens the Door. She has gone away. Did you know? You are awful. You shouldn't have done that. You have made the children cry." Travers wrote back to the little boy, "I'm not surprised that you cried. I cried bitterly. My typewriter was rained with tears when I was writing it" (Commire 159). In 1981, Travers published a revised edition of Mary Poppins, but it was forced to be removed from the shelves of the San Francisco libraries because a "minority group" had pointed out that in the chapter entitled "Bad Tuesday," Mary Poppins went to the four points of the compass, where she meets a mandarin in the East, an Indian in the West, an Eskimo in the North, and blacks in the South. These blacks speak in a "pickaninny language." Travers quickly revised the offending chapter and substituted a Panda, a Dolphin, a Polar Bear, and a Macaw (Commire 161).

Professor McWhirter is portrayed as a "bad guy" in Friend Monkey (1971). In fact, P. L. Travers herself didn't know that he was actually not really a bad guy until she got to the end of the book. She had no idea. It came on her as a great shock (Commire 160). "He was not a villain, after all, but the rescuer." Then she adds, "Perhaps, in a sense, the villain is always the rescuer, the one who throws the story forward, like the Wicked Fairy in the Sleeping Beauty story" (Commire 161). P. L. Travers was influenced by the writings of D. H. Lawrence, and has quoted him again and again. Lawrence said that there are two kinds of truth, "truth of fact," and "truth of truth." Everybody sees Professor McWhirter collecting and stealing the animals; that's "truth of fact." But they don't realize until the end of the story that he's taking them to a secret island where they can run free; that's "truth of truth."

In an interview with the editors of Something about the Author, Travers said that as a child she found a book on her father's shelf entitled Twelve Deathbed Scenes. She read the book so often that she knew it by heart, "each death being more lugubrious and more edifying than the one before it." She loved the book so much that she longed to die, in order to see if she could, "pass away with equal misery and grandeur." But she wanted to die only on the condition that she could return to life again the next minute. She was also influenced by her mother's choice of books, and every afternoon she would slip into her mother's room while she was asleep and read for half an hour, and then sneak away just as her mother was waking up (Commire 150). P. L. Travers said that she looked forward to those stolen half-hours, "as a drunkard does to a drinking bout--not so much with pleasure as a kind of enthrallment." She was ensnared by reading, like a snake is ensnared by a snake charmer. Travers also liked to read the Bible,

> ...perhaps because there was an air about it as of something forbidden. I spurned the gutted children's version and went looking for enormous terrible facts. Tellings, anyway, are always diminishments. They present the lively plot of the story but omit the curious splendors--beheaded drunk in the pavilions; Jezebel eaten by dogs at the wall; the Beast that was, is not, yet is; harlots, unicorns. Don't think that I understood it--how could I? But the Bible's trumpets breached my inner walls and the potent brew came swirling in to mix with fairy tales and myths and whatever stuff was in me.

(Commire 151)

At one time, Travers considered adopting the pen-name of "Anon," because "Anon" is her favorite author. She says that if you go through an anthology of poems that go from the distant past to the present times, all of the best poems have been written by "Anon." On a slightly more serious note, Travers says that she always wanted to use initials, so that readers would not know whether she was a man, or a woman, a dog, or a tiger. She could hide from view, like a bat on the underside of a branch. C. S. Lewis went by initials, and so did A. A. Milne, and W. B. Yeats. And that's why she became P. L. Travers (Commire 159).

In 1941, P. L. Travers was not able to return to England because of the mine-infested waters, so John Collier, an Administrator for Indian Affairs said he would send her to live among the Indians. Travers said, "That's mockery. What good will that do me?" and he replied, "You'll see." So she went to Window Rock, Arizona to live on the Navaho Reservation. She told the Indian children about the children in England who had been evacuated from the cities, and she told of some of the experiences that the children had had. "At the end there was dead silence. I turned to the man who had introduced me and said, 'I'm sorry. I failed. I haven't got across.' and he said, 'You wait. You don't know them as well as I do.' And every Indian in that big hall came up and took me silently by the hand, one after another. That was their way of expressing feeling with me" (Commire 157).

P. L. Travers was a personal acquaintance of the poet Ae (George William Russell) and of William Butler Yeats as well. Travers says that it was Ae who showed her how to pay attention to detail in her writing. Ae always called her "Popkins," and he once said to her that if Popkins had lived in another earlier time she would have worn long golden tresses, and carried a wreath of flowers in one hand and a spear in the other. "Her eyes would have been like the sea, her nose comely, and her feet winged sandals." But Ae's description of Popkins was also a description of the Hindu Kali Yuga, who changes in modern times into habiliments that are suited to these more modern times. Travers (Popkins) said that it was only years later that she understood what Ae was saying--that she, "had come out of the same world as the fairy tales" (Commire 156).

Because of her admiration for Yeats, Travers once brought him a huge armful of rowan branches from the Isle of Innisfree. "...I carried the great branches to Yeats's house in Merrion Square and stood there, with my hair like rats' tails, my tattered branches equally ratlike, looking like Birnam come to Dunsinane and wishing I was dead. I prayed, as I rang the bell, that Yeats would not open the door himself." But Yeats did open the door, and he shouted a name into the dark, and someone came forward and took Travers down to the basement kitchen, where she was warmed and dried and given cocoa. The branches had been taken away. Travers was gathering herself together to leave when the maid came bustling in and said, "The master will see you now." Together they went up the stairs of what Travers calls the "seven-story mountain," and then they went into a room with blue curtains. She noticed that on Yeats's desk there was a vase of water, and in the vase was one sprig of the fruiting rowan. Through this incident, Travers learned an important lesson about writing. "The secret is to say less than you need. You don't want a forest; a leaf will do" (Commire 154).

Pamela Lyndon Travers Bibliography

Commire, Anne, ed. "P(amela) L(yndon) Travers." Something about the Author, Volume 54. Detroit, MI: Gale, 1989, 148-162.

Lesniak, James G. "P(amela) L(yndon) Travers." Contemporary Authors, New Revision Series, Volume 30. Detroit, MI: Gale, 1990 447-448.

Terence Hanbury White (James Aston) (1906-1964)

About his mother, T. H. White wrote, "She was clever and intelligent and wildly imaginative. You never knew who she was being--Joan of Arc on Monday, Cleopatra on Tuesday, Florence Nightingale on Wednesday. I adored her passionately until I was about eighteen" (Commire 230-231). Throughout his life, White had been subjected to various fears. He had suffered the fears of a menacing, psychopathic mother, the fears of the prefects at Cheltenham College as they rattled their canes, the fears of poverty, of tuberculosis, and of public opinion. But according to Sylvia Townsend Warner, White battled these fears with courage, levity, sardonic wit, and hard work (Lesniak 465). In 1931, White ironically wrote to L. J. Potts, his tutor, that snobbery is, "one of the best parlour games known to me--for persons not among the gentry." In fact, both role-playing, and making fun of role-playing were major aspects of T. H. White's personality (Keenan 309). T. H. White, like some of his protagonists, was "headstrong, eccentric, humorous, and kind" (Lesniak 465).

In March of 1935, White wrote in his diary that he had driven his Bentley automobile into a cottage in which there were two old people asleep in bed. About this incident, Anne Commire said that a number of legends have sprung from this accident. One legend says that the Bentley had to be jacked up in order to free the old man's beard; another legend says that the old man slowly got out of bed, put on his trousers, and called to his daughter, "I think there is somebody trying to get in" (Commire 232). In January of 1938, White made the following entry in his diary: "Writing books is a heartbreaking job. When I write a good one it is too good for the public and I starve, when a bad one, you and Mary are rude about it. This Sword in the Stone forgive my reverting to it--I have nobody to tell things to--may fail financially through being too good for the swine. It has (I fear) its swinish Milne-ish parts (but, my God, I'd gladly be a Milne for the Milne money)" (Commire 233).

Alison Lurie says that T. H. White was well born and well educated. Furthermore, he was, "large, handsome, courageous, witty, imaginative, and industrious" (Lurie 160). In The Sword in the Stone (1938), King Arthur as a child is known as "The Wart," and lives as a poor relative in the castle of Sir Ector, his guardian. He is bullied and disparaged by Kay, who is Sir Ector's son (Lesniak 466). However, when Merlyn becomes Arthur's tutor, Merlin is able to magically transform the Wart into various kinds of birds and beasts, and is able to send him among the animals of nature to develop the wisdom, courage, and virtue that would be required of a future king. Alison Lurie says that The Sword in the Stone is filled with energy and comic invention (Lurie 162). Lurie considers The Sword in the Stone to be "subversive without being hopeless." By this, she means, "The Wart, the shabby little boy who begins as the teased and scorned foster child of Sir Ector, becomes King Arthur, in the process enjoying many adventures, some of which take him into strangely twentieth-century surroundings, including an ice cream parlor with jazz music (For a child reader, the deliberate anachronisms are part of the subversive fun)"(Lurie 167-168). To a large extent, The Sword in the Stone is an anachronistic parody on medieval education. "On Mondays, Wednesdays and Fridays it was Court Hand and Summulae Logicales, while the rest of the week it was Organon, Repetition and Astrology." The book's point of view is constantly shifting back and forth between medieval and contemporary life. This is possible because Merlyn is a twentieth-century magician living in the fifteenth century (Keenan 310).

In The Sword in the Stone, the Questing Beast almost dies of a broken heart when King Pellinore stops chasing it. White's character of Merlyn is something of a bumbler. He sometimes says his spells incorrectly, and he gets a bunch of wrong hats and has to be corrected by Archimedes, the owl. There are also a number of inside jokes, such as the double entendre of the governess's muddle with her astrolabe, or Little John's insistence that Robin Hood's true name is Robin Wood; this last example was probably based on the name of "Robin de Bois." Another inside joke is when Kay and Wart are invited to dine, and are trapped in a cottage by Madame Mim. There is a veiled allusion here to the story of Hansel and Gretel, even down to the description of the temptations of sweets at the castle of Queen Morgan. On a wider scale, this is a burlesque of the excessive food imagery of many children's books. The Sword in the Stone also has many incongruities, such as the neon movie sign placed over Morgan's door which says, "THE QUEEN OF AIR AND DARKNESS, NOW SHOWING." Morgan's description is also incongruous; she is, "a very beautiful lady, wearing beach pajamas and smoked glasses." There are also incongruous quotes from the classics, as well as silly rhymes, and parodies of popular tunes. There is also an incongruity between Wart and Kay, who talk and act like young teenaged boys and the various adults who are mostly comic stereotypes (Keenan 310). Many of the details in The Sword in the Stone are autobiographical in nature. Merlyn's study is messy; it is full of books, animals, and insects. The same was true of White's study. In The Sword in the Stone there is an owl named Archimedes that sits on Merlyn's head. In White's real life this was true as well (Keenan 310).

The Book of Merlyn (1941) begins with an underground seminar in which Merlyn, Arthur, and all of the animals from The Sword in the Stone are attending. There is Archimedes, the owl, and the badger, and the hedgehog, and all of the rest. They discuss the patterns of aggression that are used by men and other species. Like other seminars, this one is composed in equal parts of, "pedantry, humor, interesting questions, stupid answers, amusing digressions, repetition, and boredom" (Lurie 163).

Mistress Masham's Repose (1946) is a comic children's novel about a ten-year-old orphaned heroine named Maria. Maria wears eye glasses and is a good student, but she is also impulsive and adventurous. She has dark hair, and pigtails, and brown eyes, and is very good at games. But she is afraid of cows, and she is also afraid of her mean governess, Miss Brown. The time is the eighteenth century, and Maria lives in Malplaquet, a Northamptonshire mansion that is four times longer than Buckingham Palace. It has fifty-two state bedrooms, and twelve company rooms. But only two of the many bedrooms don't leak when it rains, so Maria and her governess live in these two rooms. Mrs. Noakes, the cook, lives in the basement kitchen, and because the mansion is so huge, she has to pedal her bicycle through the corridor in order to wait on Maria and her governess. There are 365 windows in the mansion, one for each day of the year, but only six of the windows are unbroken. There are a number of incongruous scenes or jokes in Mistress Masham's Repose, such as when the Professor is chopping wood with a six-penny hatchet from Woolworth's under a marble monument to the theater that is dedicated, "to Congreve, or to somebody of the sort." Another example is the monument to Admiral Byng, who was court-martialed for cowardice, and "Mrs. Masham's Repose" which has been named after a bitter political enemy of Sarah Churchill, and a pyramid that is dedicated to John Burgoyne, who surrendered at Saratoga to the American army (Keenan 312).

Mistress Masham's Repose is a comedy of humours. The Cook's illiterate speech and writing remind the reader of Sheridan's Mrs. Malaprop in The Rivals. There is an old professor who lives in the gamekeeper's cottage, and is totally devoted to scholarship and his electric menagerie. Miss Brown is Maria's nemesis; she uses flowery speech and when she sits down, she, "spreads as a toad on one's hand." Her other nemesis is Mr. Hater, who is the local vicar and Maria's guardian. He is a schoolmaster who is very fond of caning boys. The title of the book comes from the time when Maria is invading an island as a "pirate." Near an ornamental lake, she discovers a classical summer pavilion that is the home of five hundred descendants of Jonathan Swift's Lilliputians. This pavilion has the name of "Mistress Masham's Repose" (Keenan 311). When Miss Brown and Mr. Hater learn about the Lilliputians they try to capture them so that they can sell them to the circus or to the movies, but in the end, Maria and the Professor join forces to prevent this from happening (Keenan 312). The Elephant and the Kangaroo (1947) is a satiric novel which borrows heavily from Chaucer's Miller's Tale.

The Once and Future King (1958) contains The Sword in the Stone, The Queen of Air and Darkness, The Ill-Made Knight, and The Candle in the Wind. The Once and Future King is based on T. H. White's early experiences teaching Sir Thomas Malory's Morte d'Arthur (1485). This experience, "led White to invent the comic and didactic details of Wart's education and to give Merlyn a more active role" (Keenan 308). Alison Lurie refers to The Once and Future King as "White's brilliant four-volume novel," which explores the same period as Sir Thomas Malory's Arthurian chronicles. In 1967, it was made into the Lerner and Lowe musical motion picture, Camelot (1960) (Lesniak 464). The Once and Future King is an amusing tale of magic and adventure for children, but it is also a sophisticated tragedy for adults (Lurie 159). The Once and Future King did not receive any real world-wide fame until it became a Broadway musical, and Hollywood film, and a presidential myth. "It is quite appropriate that John F. Kennedy's court, often at the time of his reign compared to the musical and film versions of Camelot, turned out in the end to have been more like White's chronicle, with its flawed heroes, its inspiring public rhetoric and scandalous private revelations--and, of course, its awful end" (Lurie 166).

Because T. H. White had strong homosexual tendencies, he was not able to develop a normal relationship with a woman, but he also refused to become active as a homosexual. What he did instead is to develop a very close relationship with and affection for animals, including badgers, owls, goshawks, grass snakes, and various red setters, especially one named Brownie. When Brownie died in 1944, White wrote that she, "was mother, child and mistress to me for fourteen years" (Keenan 309). About Brownie's death, White said, "She had a happy life, probably happier than most setters, except that the happier you are the more you want to be happy, so it evens out. Her major troubles were only being allowed to sit in my lap for six hours a day, and things like that" (Commire 236).

Terence Hanbury White (James Aston) Bibliography

Commire, Anne. "T. H. White." Something about the Author, Volume 12. Detroit, MI: Gale Research, 1977, 229-238.

Keenan, Hugh T. "T. H. White." Dictionary of Literary Biography, Volume 160: British Children's Writers, 1914-1960. Eds. Donald R. Hettinga and Gary D. Schmidt. Detroit, MI: Bruccoli Clark Layman/Gale Research, 1996, 307-314.

Lurie, Alison. "Heroes for Our Time: J. R. R. Tolkien and T. H. White." Don't Tell the Grown-Ups: Subversive Children's Literature. Boston, MA: Little, Brown, 1990, 156-168.

Shepherd, Kenneth R. "T. H. White." Contemporary Authors, New Revision Series, Volume 37. Ed. James G. Lesniak. Detroit, MI: Gale Research, 1992, 464-467.

Warner, Sylvia Townsend. T. H. White: A Biography. New York, NY: Viking, 1967.

Wyston Hugh Auden (1907-1973)

As a writer, W. H. Auden was satirical, chatty, serious, deliberately corny, slapstick, witty, self-deprecating, and pompously slick. His tongue was usually in his cheek (Adams 54). Auden believed that he could use comedy to reveal mankind's deficiencies and excesses "in all their farcical glory" (Adams 48). Auden had a reputation for his witty and incisive book reviews. He also had a reputation for writing intellectual poetry that explored the spiritual paradox of man, who is both fallen and free (Adams 47). Auden's sense of the comic came from his ability to see the ludicrous side of every situation. He understood the value of instructing by entertaining. Although his writing was light, ironic, playful, and parodying, it was also, "informed with a restless, probing intelligence." The sustained pastiche in Auden's "Letter to Lord Byron" and the parodies in The Age of Anxiety attest to Auden's wide range of comic expression (Adams 51). Auden also wrote ironic ballads, like "Victor," which is about a man who has murdered his unfaithful wife, and "Miss Gee," which is about an old maid whose, "virginity implodes into cancer which kills her." Such pieces are comic because they, "demonstrate the conflict between what is and what should be." Auden wrote comic sonnets, ballads, ironic odes, lyrical verse, the villanelle, "shorts," and "clerihews." He also wrote witty and pungent epigrams. He wrote so much in this vein that he was often dismissed as "a writer of pastiche and light colloquial verse" (Adams 52).

In his discussion of the relationship between authors and the language which authors use, Charles Feidelson notes that they are indistinguishable, and part of his support for this contention is W. H. Auden's not-entirely facetious comment, "How can I know what I think, till I see what I say?" (Feidelson 72). Frederick Buell called W. H. Auden a "Social Poet," and said that his terse style developed out of the cryptic, private, and codified language in which Auden and his circle of schoolboy friends communicated. About this private language, Christopher Isherwood said,

> We were each other's ideal audience; nothing, not the slightest innuendo or the subtlest shade of meaning, was lost between us. A joke which, if I had been speaking to a stranger, would have taken five minutes to lead up to and elaborate and explain, could be conveyed by the faintest hint. Our conversation would have been hardly intelligible to anyone who had happened to overhear it; it was a rigmarole of private slang, deliberate misquotations, bad puns, bits of parody, and preparatory school smut. (Guregian 29)

W. H. Auden specialized in interpreting the comic and comic responses from a religious perspective. Auden's comic theory dignified laughter, and comic situations which intimated or signalled the presence of moral conscience or sanctity. He focused not so much on what causes laughter, but rather on the ethical content of that laughter. He divided comedy into two mutually exclusive modes, "lower comedy," and "higher comedy." Timothy Green gives an illustration of this dichotomy: "If A does something comical, such as slip on a banana skin, and B laughs at A, B's unsympathetic laughter depicts the lower (aggressive, critical) mode of the comic. But if B laughs both at and with A's actions, B's laughter is of the higher comic mode. Or, if A laughs at himself, he represents the higher comic mode in which both the comic and the suffering or distress are present" (Green "Comic Theory" 86).

In an article entitled "Concerning the Unpredictable," Auden talks about the "spirit of Carnival" which he describes as "true laughter," or "belly laughter." This type of laughter is both with, and at. Auden notes, however, that the "Carnival solution" is subordinate to the "ultimate solution of religious faith," suggesting further that the comic celebration which is grounded in religious faith is a sane and healthy response to real-world difficulties such as the suffering and anxiety that result from our thinking that we are finite in our existence (Auden "Concerning" 471). But Auden doesn't separate the Carnival spirit from the religious spirit of comedy. Auden, in fact, considers the spirit of Carnival to be "sanctified laughter" (Green "Comic Theory" 89). For Auden, suffering is unavoidable, but it is also a promise of redemption. "There is...a particular religious form of the comic in which suffering is involved, i.e., a man may laugh at suffering on condition 1) that it is he who suffers, 2) he knows that, ironically, this suffering is really a sign that in truth, he who suffers is really blest" (Auden <u>Flood</u> 129-130).

What laughter does for Auden is to display an acceptance of the "insoluble contradictions of life," and it should therefore serve as a prelude to faith. Nevertheless, Auden does recognize some value in the satiric spirit in his poetry as such. In his "Under Which Lyre" for example, he slightly praises the followers of the god Hermes, saying that they are cheerful, cunning gadflies in contrast to the grave and practical followers of Apollo. Thus Auden approves of playful satire, but only so long as it resists the illusion that it is improving the world, and only so long as it stops short of mercilessly destroying its targets (Green "Comic Theory" 91).

Timothy Green says that the best encapsulation of W. H. Auden's comic theory is given in his "The Greeks and Us." Here Auden delineates three types of comedy: 1). primitive comedy which is associated with holidays of license, 2). aggressive comedy which originated with the Greeks and which later developed into the comedy of humors, the comedy of manners, and European problem plays, 3). sympathetic and reverent comedy exemplified by <u>Don Quixote</u> (Auden "Concerning" 29-31). It is the first of these three types which corresponds to the "spirit of Carnival," and it is the third type which corresponds to "religious humor" (Green "Comic Theory" 94). The second type, which is both aggressive and satiric, reflects, "the confident laughter of people who know their strength, that is, either the scorn of the normal majority for the eccentric or arrogant individual whose behavior is not so much above the law as outside it, or the polemical passion of one political party against its rival" (Auden "Concerning" 30).

In an article on Tolkien, Auden clearly explains the six essential elements of the prototypical quest story. First, there must be a precious object or person to be found. Second, the seeker must discover the whereabouts of the treasure and go on a long journey in that direction. Third, the treasure can be found only by a "hero," the only person who possesses the right qualities of breeding or character. Fourth, there is a test, or a series of tests which screens out the unworthy, and is passed only by the hero. Fifth, the hero must overcome the guardian(s) of the object. And sixth, there are "sages" who help the hero on various stages of the journey with knowledge or magical powers, without which even the hero would never succeed. These sages may appear either in human form, or in animal form (Auden "Quest" 44).

During Auden's first period, between 1930 and 1938, his poetry, "assumes the positions of smirking schoolboy and monitor, social critic and detached clinician, the diagnostician of the ills of a society in which he finds more to deplore than to admire" (Adams 47). During this period, his writing contained much schoolboy humor, many inside jokes, and he mostly wrote about revolutionary politics and psychological theory. Melinda Adams says that parody, satire, punning, and name-dropping regularly occurred during Auden's earliest period (Adams 50). The prose sections of <u>The Orators: An English Study</u> (1932), for example, were written with something of the smirk of a school boy (Adams 51).

Auden's second period, between 1939 and 1949, is called his "American period." It was during this period that Auden changed his preoccupation from the quest for physical love to the quest for a more Christian kind of love. During this second period, Auden's comic vision deals with his subjects with compassion and sympathy instead of judgment. For Auden, the decade of the 1930s was a decade of grimness and uncertainty. The times were desolate, and in spite of this desolation, or perhaps because of it, Auden wrote, "on the whole, I believe that in our time it is only possible to write comic poetry; not the <u>Punch</u> variety, but real slapstick" (Carpenter 129).

There is a humorous quality which Melinda Adams calls "Audenesque" in "The Question," which was published in <u>Another Time</u> (1940). This quality is achieved through Auden's skillful development of an ironic, witty, mocking, and sometimes campy tone, as can be seen in the following:

> All of us believe
> We were born of a virgin
> (for who can imagine
> his parents copulating?),
> And cases are known
> of pregnant Virgins.
> But the Question remains:
> from where did Christ get
> that extra chromosome? (qtd. in Adams 49)

Max Bluestone suggests that Auden's "Musée des Beaux Arts," which was published in Another Time, is an example of Horatian (as opposed to Juvenalian) satire. Bluestone further says that discrepancy between the persona's "calm voice" and the scenes of tragedy and torture the persona witnesses in this poem provides the poem with a "supremely ironic cast" (Wilson 2). The irony is enhanced by Auden's line, "About suffering they were never wrong The Old Masters." This is ironic because such an expansive statement would be extremely irregular for Auden to seriously propose. Auden, who was a careful recorder of detail, and excellent analyst, "would hardly allow himself the luxury of such claims as 'they were never wrong,' or 'there must always be,' or 'they never forgot.'" And Robert Wilson therefore concludes that "they were never wrong" is therefore intended to be read as ambiguous or sarcastic (Wilson 3). Robert Wilson also suggests an ironic reading of "The Massacre of the Innocents," a poem based on a painting by Breughel. The "dreadful martyrdom" which Auden describes takes place in a "corner," in "some untidy spot." Although "The Massacre" is vivid in its depiction of the helplessness of all innocents--humans and animals alike--when confronted by a pogrom, the horror of the moment is transcended by the condescendingly witty patter like, "dogs go on with their doggy life." (Wilson 5). "The Massacre" is like "Icarus," which has "humorous and ironic overtones." "Icarus" represents, "Breugel's satiric hit at Mediterranean art and classical mythology." (Wilson 6). There seems to be a great deal of sardonic humor in "Icarus" because it blatantly juxtaposes mundane and extraordinary events. Auden warns us, however that, "we cannot learn about human tragedy from an afternoon's visit to the museum" (Wilson 7).

The Age of Anxiety: A Baroque Eclogue (1947) contains a poem entitled, "The Age of Anxiety," which is a sympathetic satire about how human beings of the 1930s try to escape through their own efforts the anxiety in which they live. About his poetry, Barbara Everett has this to say: "In his verse, Auden can argue, reflect, joke, gossip, sing, analyze, lecture, hector, and simply talk; he can sound, at will, like a psychologist on a political platform, like a theologian at a party, or like a geologist in love; he can give dignity and authority to nonsensical theories, and make newspaper headlines sound both true and melodious" (Guregian 29). The Age of Anxiety has a pastoral form, that clashes with the poem's non-pastoral setting--a bar in New York. It is about four patrons of that bar during World War II, as Auden's, "imitation of the Old English metric patterns is counterpointed by the characters' catalog of modern-day pettinesses." There is an irony between the epicness of the form, and the banality of the subject. The "Baroque" aspect uses wit as a means of clarifying the issues (Adams 52).

During Auden's third period, between 1948 and 1973, Auden became more forgiving and less blaming. His tone changed from proclamation to celebration, as he realized that the cure for man's guilt and sinfulness is Christian grace. During this final period, Auden's poetry became more relaxed, more conversational, lighter in tone, and as a result, more comic (Adams 48).

"Squares and Oblongs" (1948) is an essay in which Auden takes the position that, "the only popular art will be comic art, like Groucho Marx or Li'l Abner, and this will be unpopular with the Management. Whatever their differences, highbrows and lowbrows have a common enemy, The Law (the Divine as well as the secular), and it is the Law which it cannot alter which is the subject of all comic art" (qtd. in Adams 54). The Rake's Progress (1951) was a play co-authored with Chester Kallman. Goodbye to the Mezzogiorno (1958), and About the House (1965) were all written during Auden's third period.

Auden's "For the Time Being," from his Collected Poems (1968) is a Christmas Oratorio which demonstrates a fresh use of comedy and humor, as can be seen in the following excerpt:

> Come to our well-run desert
> Where anguish arrives by cable,
>   And the deadly sins
>   May be bought in tins
> With instructions on the label. (Auden Collected Poems 457)

In "For the Time Being," Auden uses comedy to help in the development of his plots, to help in the development of his characters, and to help in clarifying his religious or theological stance. In "For the Time Being" he juxtaposes the ancient and modern, the biblical and the contemporary in order to expose human folly and the shortcomings of society. Auden uses wit and humor extensively, and the Oratorio's main theme is developed through Auden's use of "Christian Comedy," where man's pride and assurance are shown to be nothing more than foolish pretense when they are compared to God's miraculous acts of incarnation (Morse 35). Academic Graffiti (1971) is also written during Auden's third period.

Melinda Adams suggests that Auden is "dominantly a satirist" (Adams 59), and many critics would agree. In an article entitled "Notes on the Comic," in Dyer's Hand and Other Essays (1968), however, Auden himself said that he believed satire to be nothing more than one of the many types of comedy. In this essay, he makes a distinction between satire and comedy by noting the difference in their effects. In Shakespeare's Henry IV, Part 1, Act 5, Scene 2, Falstaff is comic because in his speech about honor there is a disparity between the way Falstaff sees himself, as "a daredevil who plays highwayman," and the way he really is, a coward who is afraid to die on the battlefield. Auden says that the speech is, "a comic criticism of the feudal ethic as typified by Hotspur," and this is true "irrespective of the speaker." In contrast to Comedy, Satire has the effect of demonstrating the guilt of both the object of the satire, and the victims of the satire, who share in their own victimization as a result of their own vices. For Auden, both are guilty. Auden concludes this essay by saying that formal literary satire is not possible in the modern world because the satirist and audience don't agree on how, "normal people can be expected to behave." Because of this, "satire cannot deal with evil and suffering" (qtd. in Adams 50). Auden suggests that both satire and comedy make use of the "comic contradiction," but he adds that the aims of satire are different from the aims of comedy. "Satire would arouse in readers the desire to act so that the contradictions disappear; comedy would persuade them to accept the contradictions with good humor as facts against which it is useless to rebel" (Auden "Notes" 388).

Auden realized that real satires couldn't be written during his lifetime because the artists and the audience diverged in issues of attitudes, common standards, and beliefs, and this is why he developed the "Lunatic Clergyman." Auden used the comic as a "better, gentler vehicle for truth (Adams 50). In "The Globe" (1988), Auden discusses what he calls "Christian comedy," a kind of comedy that is frequently found in Auden's works:

> Comedy...is not only possible within a Christian society, but capable of a much greater breadth and depth than classical comedy..., [for] Christian comedy is based upon the belief that all men are sinners; no one, therefore,

whatever his rank or talents, can claim immunity from the comic exposure
and, indeed, the more virtuous, in the Greek sense, a man is, the more he
realizes that he deserves to be exposed.... In Christian comedy the
characters are exposed and forgiven: when the curtain falls, the audience and
the characters are laughing together. (Auden <u>Dyers Hand</u> 177)

Auden's "The Aesthetic Point of View" is light and comic, but it is at the same time
instructive. The poem shocks as it amuses. The limerick first appears to be frivolous, but
in fact, the frivolity is the point of the poem, since it, "condemns frivolity and amorality
of an aesthetic point of view."

> As the Poets have mournfully sung,
> Death takes the innocent young.
> The rolling-in-money
> The screamingly funny,
> And those who are very well-hung. (qtd. in Adams 53)

Wyston Hugh Auden Bibliography

Adams, Melinda. "W(yston) H(ugh) Auden." <u>Encyclopedia of British Humorists, Volume I</u>. Ed. Steven H. Gale. New York, NY: Garland, 1996, 45-59.

Auden, Wyston Hugh. <u>Collected Longer Poems</u>. New York, NY: Random House, 1968; London, England: Faber and Faber, 1968.

Auden, Wyston Hugh. "Concerning the Unpredictable." <u>Forewords and Afterwords, Selected by Edward Mendelson</u>. New York, NY: Random House, 1973.

Auden, Wyston Hugh. <u>The Enchafed Flood: or, The Romantic Iconography of the Sea</u>. London, England: Faber and Faber, 1951.

Auden, Wyston Hugh. "Notes on the Comic." <u>The Dyer's Hand and Other Essays</u>. New York, NY: Knopf-Vintage, 1968, 371-385.

Auden, Wyston Hugh. "Squares and Oblongs." <u>Poets at Work</u>. Ed. Charles D. Abbott. New York, NY: Harcourt, Brace, Jovanovich, 1948, 165-181.

Auden, Wyston Hugh. "The Quest Hero." <u>Tolkien and the Critics</u>. Notre Dame, IN: University of Notre Dame Press, 1968, 40-61.

Bluestone, Max. "The Iconographic Sources of Auden's 'Musée des Beaux Arts.' " <u>Modern Language Notes</u> 76 (April, 1961): 331-336.

Callan, Edward. <u>Auden: A Carnival of Intellect</u>. New York, NY: Oxford University Press, 1983.

Carpenter, Humphrey. <u>W. H. Auden: A Biography</u>. Boston, MA: Houghton Mifflin, 1981.

Cook, F. W. "The Wise Fool: W. H. Auden and the Management." <u>Twentieth Century</u> 168 (1960): 219-227.

Fiedelson, Charles Jr. <u>Symbolism and American Literature</u>. Chicago, IL: University of Chicago Press, 1981.

Green, Timothy. "The Comic Theory of W. H. Auden." <u>Renascence</u> 29 (1977): 86-96.

Green, Timothy. "The Spirit of Carnival in Auden's Later Poetry." <u>Southern Humanities Review</u> 11 (1977): 372-382.

Guregian, Elaine. "Wyston Hugh Auden." <u>Contemporary Authors, New Revision Series, Volume 5</u>. Detroit, MI: Gale Research, 1982, 26-30.

Morse, Donald E. "Auden's Concept and Practice of Christian Comedy." <u>Michigan Academician</u> (1971): 29-35.

Replogle, Justin. "Auden's Homage to Thalia." <u>Bucknell Review</u> 11.2 (1963): 98-117.

Spears, Monroe K. "The Divine Comedy of W. H. Auden." <u>Southern Review</u> 90 (1982): 53-72.

Spears, Monroe K. "Late Auden: The Satirist as Lunatic Clergyman." <u>Sewanee Review</u> 59

(1951): 50-74.

Wilson, Robert F., Jr. "The Person and the Poem: Irony in Auden's Musée des Beau Arts." Studies in Contemporary Satire 3 (1976): 1-8.

Daphne du Maurier (1907-1989)

As an author, Daphne du Maurier is passionately devoted to Cornwall; she insists on the reader's participation in her novels and plays; her characters are a bit larger than life; their eccentricities enhance the drama; and they tend to represent people we all have met and know (Straub 146). Alfred Hitchcock adapted many of du Maurier's novels for the movies, including Jamaica Inn, Rebecca, and The Birds. Du Maurier's Gothic novel Rebecca (1938) begins with the words, "Last night I dreamt I went to Manderley again." In Spectator, Kate O'Brien described Rebecca as, "a Charlotte Brontë story minus Charlotte Brontë." Rebecca features, "an enigmatic heroine in a cold and hostile environment, a brooding hero tormented by a guilty secret, and a rugged seacoast setting, all staples not only of modern romantic novels, but especially features of the Gothic novel." V. S. Pritchett says that Rebecca moves at a fast pace from surprise to surprise. "From the first sinister rumors to the final conflagration, the melodrama is excellent" (Straub 145).

Daphne du Maurier Bibliography

Straub, Deborah A. "Daphne du Maurier." Contemporary Authors, New Revision Series, Volume 6. Ed. Ann Evory. Detroit, MI: Gale Research, 1982, 144-146.

Christopher Fry (né Christopher Harris) (1907-)

Christopher Fry was connected to the theater in many different capacities. He was an actor, a translator, a director, an adapter, a writer of radio plays, screenplays, and television plays, and of lyrics and music for musicals. But most of all, he was a successful playwright (Rippy 419). Both in his "Christopher Fry as Tragicomedian," and in his "Imagery in the Comedies of Christopher Fry," Emil Roy points out that Christopher Fry liks to write on serious themes, but with light overtones; he likes to write tragedy with a happy ending (Rippy 426). In "Christopher Fry: The Twentieth Century Shakespeare?" Earle Davis shows how Christopher Fry is centrally in Shakespeare's comic tradition. Their language is similar, since both of them like to use blank verse and metaphor; their plots are similar; their comedy is similar. Nevertheless, according to Davis, Fry has not yet "challenged Shakespeare in tragic utterance" (Rippy 424). The difference between tragedy and comedy, according to Fry, is that tragedy is experience while comedy is intuition (Corregon 16). For Christopher Fry, comedy is closely allied to tragedy, and springs from basically the same sources. In an article entitled, "Comedy," Fry said, "Comedy is an escape, not from truth but from despair: a narrow escape into faith. It believes in a universal cause for delight, even though knowledge of the cause is always twitched away from under us." He continued, "In tragedy every moment is eternity; in comedy eternity is a moment" (qtd. in Rippy 416).

Christopher Fry's characters are articulate, and witty, and they love to use apt metaphors. The world that these characters find themselves in is absurd. It is unnatural, illogical, and sometimes "mad." Frances Rippy says that Christopher Fry's comedies have six important characteristics. First, they demonstrate Fry's intimate experience as an actor and director in the theater and how this experience has affected his play writing. Second, they focus on natural settings which are established by the lines of the characters rather than by the stage directions (Rippy 416). An example of this is when Perpetua describes the greenness of England by talking about "this green and pleasant aquarium." Third, they demonstrate Fry's sophisticated sense of language. In "An Experience of Critics," for example, he says that critics think of him as, "a man reeling intoxicated with words." These words, "flow in a golden--or perhaps pinchbeck--stream from his mouth; they start out his ears; they burst like rockets and jumping crackers and catherine-wheels round his head." Fry says that in truth, however, he sits for hours in front of his typewriter, finally typing a word, as "the night wears dumbly on towards dawn." Such Characters as Ols Skips in The Lady's Not for Burning might use malapropisms. Words for Fry, and for his characters, always seem to have more than one meaning. As Reedbeck says, in Venus Observed, "A spade is never so merely a spade as the word spade would imply." Fourth, Fry is able to create very memorable female characters. These characters tend to be, "witty and wise and sensitive without making that male counterpart any less so." Fifth, Fry's comedies have two archetypal human themes, love and death, and these are bound inextricably together. "Death is a Kind of Love," is Tegeus's line in A Phoenix Too Frequent. Sixth, Fry's comedies contain much paradox and irony. His comedies demonstrate the complexity of words that never seem to operate to just a single purpose. For Fry, words are always "glancing off into a pun, a 'double entendre,' an imprecision" (Rippy 417).

Audrey Williamson says that The Boy with the Cart (1938) is humorous in its word usage, in characterization, and in its development of a religious theme (Williamson 187). A Phoenix Too Frequent (1946) is a comedy which was first produced in London at Mercury Theatre (Prescott 138). It is a comedy based on Petronius's story about the Ephesian widow. This play shows Fry's effective use of wit and lyrical metre (Williamson 187).

The Lady's Not for Burning was the first installment of a series of four tragi-comedies each representing a different season. The Lady's Not for Burning represents Spring. The series continued with Venus Observed (Autumn), The Dark is Light Enough (Winter), and A Yard of Sun (Summer). Frances Rippy says that Christopher Fry's four seasonal comedies are reminiscent of a "Frye with a different spelling." Rippy is referring to the Canadian Northrop Frye, who at this same time was writing The Archetypes of Literature which told how the four seasons appear philosophically in both folklore and literature (Rippy 419). In The Lady's Not for Burning (1948) Jennet is a wealthy young orphan who loves life, but because she has had a trumped-up witchcraft charge brought against her, she has been sentenced to burn at the stake. After she is dead, the town will inherit her property. "The play intertwines irony and comedy, with a dense mayor, his practical wife, and their two quarrelling sons all playing clownish roles." The humor is bawdy on occasions, since Fry has, "combined the robustness of the Elizabethans with touches of the cheerful blasphemy that mingled with piety in the medieval morality play. But the sense of the abundance, mystery, and poetry of life is unimpaired" (Prescott 140). The Lady's Not for Burning is a story about two contrasting characters. One character is a young soldier of fortune who is disillusioned with life and wants to die. The other character is a young woman who is a medieval alchemist's daughter and who is on the verge of arrest for being a witch, so she is passionately trying to stay alive (Williamson 187). The Lady's Not for Burning is a blank-verse comedy which was first produced in London at Arts Theatre (Prescott 138). It is a joyous medieval paradox which became an immediate success (Prescott 139). In The Lady's Not for Burning, Fry developed a kind of bawdy humor that often penetrated the "golden haze." There are such humours characters as the lute-playing Chaplain who says that legal matters are Greek to him, except, of course, that he understands Greek. He is placed beside the fussy Mayor, and the sarcastic, obese Judge (Williamson 187). In The Lady's Not for Burning, Alizon Eliot says that men are strange. She feels that it's almost strange to discover that they speak English. Richard, who is in love with Alizon responds, "Things happen to them." when Alizon asks, "What things?" Richard replies, "Machinations of nature." Alizon has difficulty agreeing with Richard, and says, "Show me daffodils happening to a man!" Richard responds, "Very easily," but then Thomas Mendip, the cynic, adds, "And thistles as well" (Rippy 418).

Venus Observed (1950) is a comedy representing the Autumn season. It is about an aging duke who has had many lovers, and who has decided to choose from among them, one to be his wife. But in the process, he falls in love with a young woman his son is also in love with. L. N. Roditte says that the character of the duke is mild and witty, but there is also an element of tragedy which surrounds this character (Prescott 140). On the surface, Venus Observed is a sophisticated amorous comedy; however the wit and the intelligence penetrate well below the surface (Williamson 189). This play is about public ceremonies that center around Halloween imagery, and about how a group observes the eclipse of the sun by the moon, and about a public conflagration which may suggest the Guy Fawkes bonfires on November 5th (Rippy 418).

The Dark Is Light Enough (1954) is a Winter comedy, and it was first produced on the West End at Aldwych Theatre (Prescott 138). This play begins with a quotation from Jean Henri Fabre, the French naturalist, about a butterfly which is not deterred by storm or night: "So well it directs its tortuous flight that, in spite of all the obstacles to be evaded, it arrives in a state of perfect freshness, its great wings intact.... The darkness is light enough." The countess in The Dark Is Light Enough is a woman of wit and courage, who has a special quality which she describes as a "disenchantment of the body" (Williamson 189). This play is a "winter comedy," and as such is the most nearly tragic of the four. "We should not have called it a comedy except that its author does. It is set in an Austrian country-house near the Hungarian boarder in the winter of 1848-1849, a year of revolutions (Rippy 418).

A Yard of Sun (1970) is a Summer comedy, and it was first produced at Nottingham Playhouse in Nottingham, England (Prescott 138). A Yard of Sun ends the quartet of Season Plays. It deals with a black sheep and a betrayed friend who absent themselves from their Italian family and later return to this family. The play has a "concentrated glow of language" which, "shimmers with poetry and affirms Fry's belief in a basically mystical Christian benevolence." Although Fry describes all of the plays in his quartet of the seasons as comedies, the "fall" and "winter" plays are much darker than the others. In A Yard of Sun, Cesare says, "A good idea, the sun," and Giosetta, his mistress, responds, "Yes, it helps" (Rippy 419).

Cyrano de Bergerac: A Heroic Comedy in Five Acts (1975) was adapted from Edmond Rostand's Cyrano de Bergerac. In Can You Find Me: A Family History (1978), Christopher tells about his childhood visions. After his father had died, he remembers seeing his father standing beside his bed, with the scene being lit by a tiny paraffin lamp. He called to his mother, "Daddy's here, daddy's here," but his mother, who was still half asleep, told him to go back to sleep. He had other visions as well. On one occasion, he saw an elf in the yard; on another occasion, he saw an underwater scene as though he were looking through the eyes of a fish (Olendorf 74).

Of Christopher Fry, the critic F. E. Faverty wrote, "In spite of the heavy themes, the dialogue is light and sparkling. There is a quotable epigram on every page." And John Mason Brown wrote, "Mr. Fry has a wit, nimble and original; an agile and unpredictable mind, as playful as it is probing; and a love of language which can only be described as a lust" (Prescott 140). In 1950, Christopher Fry made a statement on BBC Radio's Third Programme which expresses his view of the contemporary theatre. He says that the contemporary playwright "is exploring for the truth of the human creature, his truth in comedy or his truth in tragedy, because over and above the drama of his actions and conflicts and everyday predicaments is the fundamental drama of his ever existing at all" (qtd. in Williamson 191).

Christopher Fry (né Christopher Harris) Bibliography

Alexander, John. "Christopher Fry and Religious Comedy." Meanjin 15 (1956): 77-81.

Barnes, Lewis W. "Christopher Fry: The Chestertonian Concept of Comedy." Xavier Review 2 (1950): 30-47.

Collins, J. A. "Poet of Paradox: The Dramas of Christopher Fry." Literary Half-Yearly 12.2 (1971): 62-75.

Corrigan, Robert W. Comedy--Meaning and Form: Second Edition. San Francisco, CA: Chandler, 1981.

Davis, Earle. "Christopher Fry: The Twentieth Century Shakespeare?" Kansas Magazine (1952): 10-15.

"Enter Poet, Laughing." Time (November 20, 1950): 58-64.

Fry, Christopher. "Comedy." Adelphi 27 (1952): 27-29; also in Comedy: Meaning and Form. Second Edition. Ed. Robert W. Corrigan. New York, NY: Harper and Row, 1981, 15-17.

Oldendorf, Donna. "Christopher Fry." Something about the Author, Volume 66. Detroit, MI: Gale Research, 1991, 71-77.

Prescott, Jani. "Christopher Fry." Contemporary Authors, New Revision Series, Volume 30. Detroit, MI: Gale Research, 1990, 138-141.

Rippy, Frances Mayhew. "Christopher Fry." Encyclopedia of British Humorists, Volume I. Ed. Steven H. Gale. New York, NY: Garland, 1996, 409-428.

Roy, Emil Lawrence. "Christopher Fry as Tragicomedian." Modern Drama 11 (1968): 40-47.

Roy, Emil Lawrence. "Imagery in the Comedies of Christopher Fry." Modern Drama 7 (1964): 79-88.

Spanos, William V. "Christopher Fry's A Sleep of Prisoners: The Choreography of Comedy." Modern Drama 8 (1965): 58-72.

Spears, Monroe K. "Christopher Fry and the Reception of Joy." Poetry 78.1 (1951): 28-43.

Stanford, Derek. "Comedy and Tragedy in Christopher Fry." Modern Drama 2 (1959): 3-7.

Urang, Gunnar. "The Climate Is the Comedy: A Study of Christopher Fry's The Lady's Not for Burning." Christian Scholar 46 (1963): 61-86.

Vos, Nelvin. "The Comic Victim-Victor: His Passionate Action in the Drama of Christopher Fry." The Drama of Comedy: Victim and Victor Ed. Nelvin Vos. Richmond, VA: Knox, 1966, 74-99.

Williamson, Audrey. "Christopher Fry." Dictionary of Literary Biography, Volume 13: British Dramatists Since World War II. Ed. Stanley Weintraub, Detroit, MI: Gale, 1982, 185-192.

Helen MacInnes (1907-1985)

Helen MacInnes develops characters that are both good and bad, but all these characters tend to be well educated, and they have read widely, have a historical sense, and they speak refined English. Her agents make allusions to such authors as Shakespeare or Dante, and are at home in discussions of Vermeer, Turner, or Dali. Her characters also have a refined taste in music, and their rooms are elegant, the tailors are exact, and their jests are genteel (MacDonald 294).

MacInnes believed that in writing international intrigue, the author should not try to hide things from the reader in order to achieve suspense. For MacInnes, the important issue was not what is going to happen, but when and how it is going to happen so, "a reader may know everything, but still be scared stiff by the situation" (MacDonald 293).

Above Suspicion (1941) is about a young Oxford couple named Frances and Richard Myles. As they go for one last look at Europe in peacetime they appear to be "above suspicion" and therefore ideal to use as amateur agents who are advised to contact the underground and locate a British anti-Nazi agent. "Their wit, good humor, and courage help them through trying encounters with people who are powerless in the grip of 'the new order'" Critics praise the novel for its "technical smoothness," its "feminine insights," its "pervading atmosphere of suspense," and its "subtle humor," but they criticize its "simplified black and white portraits" (MacDonald 288).

Assignment in Brittany (1942) provides a collage of details of the Breton countryside, the seacoast villages, and the behavior of the inhabitants. St. Deodat is lovingly portrayed, and its ironic motto, "Nothing changes" is typical of MacInnes's understated humor (MacDonald 286).

In Rest and Be Thankful (1949), Margaret Peel is a harried New York writer who takes a much-needed vacation in Wyoming. The satire of the novel targets both the eastern literati and the western cowpokes as they come together to form a strained relationship.

> The ironic contrast between hardworking wranglers, worried about day-to-day practicalities and contemptuous 'dudes' who are physically inept, and the posing, egocentric easterners, with their pretentious literary allusions, their conversations about the nature of art, and their snobbish amusement at what for the cowboys is serious business is intensified by Margaret Peel's memories of the changes wrought in Europe, the old days gone, the old friends dead or imprisoned or embittered by postwar politics, by her fears of Communist propaganda undermining democratic values, and by her sense of being a stranger in her own country. (MacDonald 290)

Home Is the Hunter (1966) is a two-act comedy about Ulysses returning home from the Trojan War (MacDonald 285).

Helen MacInnes Bibliography

MacDonald, Gina. "Helen MacInnes." British Mystery and Thriller Writers Since 1940;
    Dictionary of Literary Biography, Volume 87. Ed. Bernard Benstock, and Thomas
    F. Staley. Detroit, MI: Gale, 1989.

Quentin Crisp (Denis Pratt) (1908-)

The Naked Civil Servant (1968) is Quentin Crisp's autobiography, and it presents him as a "flamboyant, effeminate homosexual." This book, which is sometimes shocking, sometimes absurd, recounts Crisp's psychological and social difficulties as a homosexual. The story is told in a candid and witty manner. In one particular passage, for example, Crisp describes himself as wearing, "as much makeup as the force of gravity would allow." In another passage he says, "My father won his great gamble with the future. He died" (Ross 90). In The Naked Civil Servant, Crisp says, "I now know that if you describe things better than they are, you are considered to be romantic; if you describe things as worse than they are, you will be called a realist; and if you describe things exactly as they are, you will be thought of as a satirist" (Crisp Naked 177). Crisp's persona in The Naked Civil Servant is humble, disarming, and charming. He is a man who has been alienated from most national and social conventions, but he is also a man who can offer, "shrewd, wise, and witty observations about the human animal" (Calhoun 291).

A critic for the New York Times Book Review said that Crisp's How to Have a Life-Style (1975) is a, "witty, aphoristic, outrageous, and often very acute description" (qtd. in Ross 90). Doing It with Style (1981) is co-authored with Donald Carroll. In a 1986 interview with Quentin Crisp, Jean W. Ross remarked that Crisp's lifestyle contained both humor and good sense, to which Crisp replied, "Yes, well, it's the essence of humor that it's true. In fact, nothing can be funny that isn't at least partially true" (qtd. in Calhoun 291).

In the Times Literary Supplement, Jennifer Uglow said about How to Become a Virgin (1981), that it is less flamboyant and acerbic than The Naked Civil Servant, but then added that it was "full of ridiculous anecdotes," and "nicely calculated extravagances" (Ross 90). In How to Become a Virgin, Crisp says, "Everything in America is on wide screen" (Crisp Virgin 152). In this same book, Crisp has an essay entitled "Reflections of the City of Angels," in which he says, "the Los Angeles airport, like so much in America, is in a chaos of improvement" (Crisp Virgin 93).

In Manners from Heaven: A Divine Guide to Good Behavior (1985), co-authored with John Hofess, Crisp demonstrates his keen wit and sense of the absurd as he targets etiquette. Crisp says, "The lie is the basic building block of good manners." In the Detroit Metro Times, Cal Burnette said that this book was, "brisk, witty, and brash, elegant but never marred by the faintest trace of stuffiness or self-importance" (Ross 90). In Manners from Heaven, Crisp says, "Having been the butt of mockery and abuse almost from birth I became well acquainted with humility and her twin, irony, even before my compulsory miseducation began in earnest" (Crisp Manners 90). Randall Calhoun considers Manners from Heaven to be cynical. He also considers it to be a, "shrewd guide for getting along in a world populated with rude people living in an impolite society" (Calhoun 291).

During his writing career, Quentin Crisp was an extravagant humorist who mainly wrote about himself (Ross 90). Crisp called himself "England's second reigning queen." It is Crisp's humility and his irony that best account for his effective humor. Crisp's satire is traditional (Calhoun 290). In "The Unlikely Hero Gets his Reward," Tom Shales notes the irony which Quentin Crisp had noted earlier--that the world later rewarded Crisp for what it had previously condemned him for. Crisp finds this situation to be a bit humorous (Calhoun 192).

Quentin Crisp (Denis Pratt) Bibliography

Calhoun, Randall. "Quentin Crisp." Encyclopedia of British Humorists, Volume I. Ed. Steven H. Gale. New York, NY: Garland, 1996, 289-292.

Crisp, Quentin. How to Become a Virgin. London, England: Duckworth, 1981.

Crisp, Quentin. Manners from Heaven: A Divine Guide to Good Behavior. New York, NY: Harper, 1985.

Crisp, Quentin. The Naked Civil Servant. (1968) London, England: Cecil Woolf, 1975.

Kettlehack, Guy, Ed. The Wit and Wisdom of Quentin Crisp. New York, NY: Harper, 1984.

Ross, Jean W. "Quentin Crisp." Contemporary Authors, Volume 116. Detroit, MI: Gale Research, 1986, 89-92.

Shales, Tom. "The Unlikely Hero Gets his Reward." The Washington Post Book World (October, 1978): D1.

Ian (Lancaster) Fleming (1908-1964)

Ian Fleming wrote the flamboyant James Bond, or Agent 007, into fifteen of his books: <u>Casino Royale</u> (1953), <u>Live and Let Die</u> (1954), <u>Moonraker</u> (1955), <u>Diamonds are Forever</u> (1956), <u>From Russia with Love</u> (1957), <u>Dr. No</u> (1958), <u>Goldfinger</u> (1959), <u>For Your Eyes Only: Five Occasions in the Life of James Bond</u> (1960), <u>Thunderball</u> (1961), <u>The Spy Who Loved Me</u> (1962), <u>On Her Majesty's Secret Service</u> (1963), <u>You Only Live Twice</u> (1964), <u>The Man with the Golden Gun</u> (1965), and <u>Octopussy, and The Living Daylights</u> (1966). The name "James Bond" came from Fleming's reading of nature books. "James Bond" was a well-known ornithologist who wrote <u>Birds of the West Indies</u> (1936), one of Fleming's favorite books (DelFattore 93). James Bond is an idealized adventurer. He is a very sophisticated spy-hero who is sexy, and exciting. The film series, which is now more than ten in number, exaggerates the "guns-gadgets-and-girls" aspects of Fleming's original stories (DelFattore 86). Much of the humor in Fleming's novels had been in the form of tongue-in-cheek exaggerations, but the film producers wanted a broader kind of humor, so they put in the "one-liners," and the "send-ups" which have become hallmarks of the Bond films. Fleming enjoyed much of the humor in the films, but he didn't like the jokes that detracted from Bond's status as a British gentleman. When Fleming read the script for <u>Goldfinger,</u> for example, he was annoyed by a scene in which Bond is looking into a woman's eyes and sees the reflection of an assailant approaching with a blackjack. Quickly Bond swings the girl around so that she is the one who receives the blow. Fleming wrote in the margin, "wouldn't do this to a girl!" (DelFattore 107). The <u>London Daily Express</u> offered Fleming fifteen hundred pounds sterling per book for permission to publish Bond's adventures in comic-strip form. Fleming agreed to this (DelFattore 101).

Ian Fleming wrote his James-Bond novels from a house named "Goldeneye," on the bay at Oracabessa in Kingston, Jamaica (DelFattore 92). Most critics report that the James Bond novels are, "entertaining, spectacularly imaginative, and highly readable." James Bond's appearance is very much like that of Ian Fleming. They both were tall and lean men with black hair, gray eyes, and high cheekbones. Bond also represented Fleming's drives and fantasies. Bond knows about and enjoys the finest in food and drink. He makes love to the most beautiful and affectionate of women, and he defeats the most fiendish of villains. "Bond's accomplishments do reflect a vivid wish-fulfillment fantasy" (DelFattore 94). Many of the incidents in the James Bond novels are romanticized versions from incidents in Fleming's personal life. "The autobiographical and psychological elements in these books are quite deliberate" (DelFattore 96). Fleming used formulas to write his escapist James Bonds books. These formulas included, "emphasis on expensive brand-name products; feminine capitulation (immediate or eventual) to Bond's charms; Bond's survival of fiendish tortures, deadly perils, acts of God, and assorted other unpleasantries; exotic, or seemingly exotic, settings; and the presence of outrageously ugly villains with grandiose schemes for world domination" (DelFattore 101). Much of the humor in the Bond books works for a general audience; however Fleming also had many "inside" jokes which are comprehensible only to people who are familiar with real-life people or events which Fleming was familiar with and was parodying (DelFattore 104).

It is interesting to note that shortly after writing   <u>Casino Royale</u> (1953), Fleming married Anne Rothermere at the Town Hall in Port Maria, Jamaica, and the principal witness in the marriage ceremony was Noel Coward (DelFattore 96). The film <u>Casino Royale</u> which was released by Columbia Pictures in 1967, is a spoof of the other Bond films. It features David Niven as an aging James Bond, and Woody Allen as his nephew, Jimmy Bond (DelFattore 99).

Fleming's puns are intentionally atrocious. In <u>Live and Let Die</u> (1954), Felix Leiter, Bond's American associate, is dropped into a shark tank, and his mauled body is returned to Bond in its bloody and maimed state with a note that says, "He disagreed with something that ate him." Bond retaliates against the author of this bitingly satirical note by kicking him into the same tank and listening to the grunts of the sharks as they strike. This is the kind of "poetic justice" that is characteristic in Fleming's novels (DelFattore 97).

In their advertisement campaign for Moonraker (1955), Macmillan ran a number of full-page full-color advertisements showing a cordial bottle. The name of the cordial was "Moonraker," and the advertisement said that it was, "the sensational new 100 proof spinechilling concoction." The ad also contained a warning label: "WARNING. Take dosage only in sitting, prone, or supine position. If apathy continues, consult your psychiatrist" (DelFattore 98).

Fleming got some of the material for Diamonds are Forever (1956) from Philip Brownrigg, a former schoolmate of Fleming's who was in 1955 and 1956 a senior executive with the world's largest diamond importer, De Beers. Brownrigg supplied Fleming with the information he needed about diamond mining and diamond smuggling, and Fleming added to this the, "gadgetry and glitter which were becoming increasingly important in his books" (DelFattore 98). Joan DelFattore says that Diamonds are Forever is neither logical nor probable, but it is exciting, and that accounts for its commercial success (DelFattore 99). Fleming enjoyed using adolescent sexual puns in his novels. An example in Diamonds are Forever is in reference to a jeweler's loop when Bond says, "Don't push it in. Screw it in" (DelFattore 104).

Before writing From Russia with Love (1957), Ian Fleming attended a conference of the International Police Organization Interpol in Istanbul, Turkey. There he met a Turkish businessman by the name of Nazim Kalkavan who showed him around Istanbul. Nazim Kalkavan provided the inspiration for the character of Darko Kerim in From Russia with Love. Kalkavan made a statement to Bond that Kerim later states in the novel, "But I am greedy for life. I do too much of everything all the time. Suddenly one day my heart will fail. The Iron Crab will get me as it got my father. But I am not afraid of The Crab." Kerim continues, "Perhaps they will put on my tombstone, 'This Man Died from Living Too Much'" (DelFattore 99). The basic premise of From Russia with Love is that the Russian Secret Service wants first to ruin Bond's reputation by filming him in bed with a female Russian spy, and wants second to ruin Bond himself by killing them both. Bond refers to his assignment in From Russia with Love as "pimping for England" (DelFattore 104). Darko Kerim has "a rudimentary philosophy of life," and "a rather eccentric sense of humor." Joan DelFattore says that Darko Kerim is, "one of Fleming's best characters, and, although none of his female characters is really well-rounded (in the literary sense), Tatiana Romanova is one of the most charming" (DelFattore 100). Fleming ends From Russia with Love with a scene in which a villainess stabs James Bond with a poisoned blade which has been built into the toe of her boot, and Bond crashes to the floor. This scene has been very controversial. Iain Hamilton, one of Fleming's friends, wrote him a jocular letter of protest, saying, "I have said harsh words about this fellow in the past but, by George, you can't go and let an ugly old trollop kick him to death with an absurdly poisoned boot. This won't do at all." Fleming replied, "Surely a man can have a dose of Fugu poisoning without at once being written off. Pray spare your tears." Fleming later made a more public explanation in the newspapers in the form of a medical bulletin from Sir James Molony, who is the physician to the British Secret Service in Fleming's books. Sir James declared that James Bond was alive and well and recovering from a dose of Fugu poisoning. This explanation was accompanied by ads in the "Personals" sections of various newspapers addressed to James Bond. They warn him that, "Rosa Klebb may have poisoned knife blade concealed in toe of shoe. Look alive" (DelFattore 101).

The most controversial scene in Dr. No (1958) is after Bond has been imprisoned by Dr. No, and escapes through a tunnel. During his escape, he is knocked down by an electric shock, and burnt by a heated section of pipe. He mashes twenty giant tarantulas into a "writhing, sickening mess of blood and fur." He crawls over this pulp of tarantulas and then stops to catch his breath before he tumbles headfirst down a shaft. He is knocked unconscious when he hits the sea at 40 miles per hour, but he manages to cling to a cable which has been strung across the inlet. He recovers consciousness just in time to see the fish eating his blood, and after this, a squid tries to eat the rest of him. This building of violence onto violence is similar to the humor-of-excess in Jonathan Swift's "A Modest Proposal" (DelFattore 103). Some critics have suggested that such violent scenes as these are not humorous; however Fleming himself, "often expressed disingenuous surprise at the seriousness with which some critics took scenes which he regarded as funny" (DelFattore 104). Grossness is often added to the violence in Fleming's novels, as when Dr. No meets his demise under a twenty-foot pile of guano (DelFattore 104).

In Oracabessa Bay of Kingston, Jamaica, where Fleming wrote his James Bond novels, he very much enjoyed underwater swimming. He took a personal interest in the flora and fauna of the bay, and in the bay there was an unusually friendly octopus which he named Pussy Galore. He later used this "Pussy Galore" as the name of one of his characters in Goldfinger (1959) (DelFattore 92). One of the best known and most popular scenes in all of the Bond novels is the golf scene that occurs in Goldfinger (DelFattore 105). Oddjob is an original character in Goldfinger; he kills people with his hat and eats pet cats (DelFattore 105). Many of the other scenes in Goldfinger are similar to scenes in Fleming's other novels and movies. There is the fight in a moving vehicle, the seduction of a woman who had previously been unresponsive, the castration-fantasy tortures. In Goldfinger, Fleming "carried such repetitions to the point of self-parody" (DelFattore 105).

In On Her Majesty's Secret Service (1963) there is a genealogist who tells James Bond that his family's coat of arms features three golden bezants (balls). Using adolescent sexual humor, Bond responds, "That is certainly a valuable bonus" (DelFattore 104). There are several exciting chase scenes in On Her Majesty's Secret Service, one of which became an important sequence in the filmed version (DelFattore 107). Ian Fleming was fascinated by the Japanese preoccupation with death, and his You Only Live Twice (1964) is filled with death scenes and death imagery (DelFattore 108). It may be Fleming's grimmest novel, but even here there is a scene where the lobster which Bond has been served by his Japanese host flips over and starts to wander off across the dinner table. Bond exclaims, "Good God, Tiger!... The damn thing's alive!" (DelFattore 104). The villain in You Only Live Twice is a nightmarish figure who creates a garden for suicides because he enjoys furnishing people with the opportunity to destroy themselves with poisonous plants, a pool filled with piranhas, or steaming fumaroles. In this novel, Bond is reflective, and at times, poetic. The title comes from a haiku verse which Bond recites, "You only live twice. Once when you're born, and once when you look death in the face" (DelFattore 108).

Ian Fleming's books may be, "superficial, implausible, and erratically structured," and the books may have been overshadowed in popularity by the films, which are "even more superficial, implausible, and erratically structured." Nevertheless, Fleming's writing is very imaginative, readable, and best of all, "outrageously entertaining." Ian Fleming died just after 1 AM on August 12, 1964. He was fifty-six, and the last words he said were in the form of an apology to the ambulance attendants for having inconvenienced them (DelFattore 110).

Ian (Lancaster) Fleming Bibliography

Commire, Anne, ed. "Ian (Lancaster) Fleming." Something about the Author, Volume 9. Detroit, MI: Gale, 1976, 67-69.
DelFattore, Joan. "Ian Fleming." Dictionary of Literary Biography, Volume 87: British Mystery and Thriller Writers Since 1940. Eds. Bernard Benstock and Thomas F.

Staley. Detroit, MI: Gale, 1989, 85-112.

Mary Margaret Kaye (Mollie Hamilton, Mollie Kaye) (c1909-)

Many critics have compared M. M. Kaye's The Far Pavilions (1978) with Rudyard Kipling's Kim. Like Kim, Kaye's The Far Pavilions is a picaresque novel which features a young British boy who is orphaned and is raised as a Hindu and as an Indian. Kaye's protagonist is named Ash, and when he is discovered to be English, he is sent to live with his aristocratic relatives in England, but when he later returns to India as a soldier, he finds himself torn between his two heritages. In the Washington Post Book World (November 11, 1984), Walter Shapiro says that Kaye's Trade Wind (1981) is well written and has good character development, clever plotting, and a slightly ironic narrative tone (Straub 261).

Mary Margaret Kaye (Mollie Hamilton, Mollie Kaye) Bibliography

Straub, Deborah A., Ed. "M. M. Kaye." Contemporary Authors, New Revision Series, Volume 24. Detroit, MI: Gale Research, 1988, 260-261.

7

Authors Born between
1910 and 1919

Stefan Themerson (1910-1988)

Wim Tigges defined literary nonsense as, "A genre of narrative literature which balances a multiplicity of meaning with a simultaneous absence of meaning;" Stefan Themerson's nonsense is consistent with this definition (Boelens 229). As an author, Themerson tended to oscillate between playful anarchy and the suggestion of meaning. Themerson even founded a publishing house in London and named it "Gaberbocchus Press," a Latinized version of the word "Jabberwocky," which published the surrealistic prose-poems of Henri Chopin, Patrick Fetherston, David Miller, and Oswell Blakeston.

Bayamus (1945) is an attempt by Themerson to provide a "semantic translation" of the famous nursery rhyme, "Taffy was a Welshman." The nursery rhyme is analyzed and paraphrased as follows: "Taffy was a male native of Wales. Taffy was a person who practiced seizing the property of another unlawfully and appropriated it to his own use and purpose. Taffy came to the structure of various materials, having walls, roof, door, and windows to give light and air. He came to that structure which was a dwelling to me. And there he appropriated to his own use one of the limbs of the dead body of an ox prepared and sold by a butcher." Tysger Boelens considers this parody to be above all, a criticism of political rhetoric (Boelens 233-234).

Wooff, Wooff, or Who Killed Richard Wagner? (1951) relies, to a very large extent, on the inversion of expectations. It is about a human being who bumps into a car, instead of a car which bumps into a human being. It is also about a human being who barks like a dog. It is a development of Anatole France's notion that even the smallest dog thinks that it is the center of the universe: "So I climbed on to my bench, and standing on all fours, I shyly tried to bark. It was a good bark" (Boelens 234).

The Adventures of Peddy Bottom (1951) is a children's book about Peddy Bottom who has an identity crisis. Peddy Bottom goes out into the world trying to discover who he is. At first, Peddy is depicted as a composite of things, among them, a fish and a dog (Boelens 236). Next, Peddy runs into a hypochondriac on top of a step-ladder by the name of Captain Metapherein (Greek for "to carry over"). The captain tells Peddy, "You are what you will be." But then the captain says that between the Red Lion Inn and the Black Lion Inn there were only five inches of space, where there used to be a whole city. He exclaims, "What has happened to geography?" The captain then goes to the top of the step ladder for a better view, and the step ladder keeps him from coming back down, saying, "a gentleman doesn't kick away the ladder by which he rose" (Boelens 237). Then the reader meets Mrs. Metapherein who says that she used to live in a very big city, but this city appears to have shrunk because of the rain. Mrs. Metapherein thus tells a story within a story. Next, Peddy visits a theatre, but this is really a "Theatre of War." And finally, Peddy asks Mrs. Goat whether the news in the newspaper she has in front of her might be good news. Mrs. Goat responds that the news is indeed not too bad. It is in fact extremely nutritious, especially the part between the lines (Boelens 238). In Chapter 7 of The Adventures of Peddy Bottom, Peddy meets a "non-contemporary, straightforward gentleman," who has a long beard plaited into a pigtail with a ribbon. This man says that only one road is the correct road forward" (Boelens 239). And finally, in Chapter 8, the reader is told that, "Camels have humps--one, two, three." But when Peddy Bottom tells a camel, "but you have only one hump," the camel simply responds, "I know that perfectly well" (Boelens 240).

Professor Mmaa's Lecture (1953) is a satire which exposes the political, sexual, religious, and scientific peculiarities of human societies. This novel is about a colony of termites which receives most of its information from the sense of smell; hence the book has been described as a "best smeller." In this book, "termitocentrism" is pushed to its extreme. Ertrand Bussell and Sigmund Krafft-durch-Freud are two scientists who help develop the plot. Boelens notes that in this novel so many points are parodied that, "the reader is left in doubt as to what, if anything, wins the author's assent" (Boelens 232).

The Life of Cardinal Polatuo; with Notes on his Writings, his Times and his Contemporaries (1954) is a satire targeting both science and religion. At the back of the book there is the "Dictionary of Traumatic Signs" which again ridicules Freud. Logic, Labels, and Flesh (1974) is a collection of satiric essays on such subjects as the "quantification of qualities." In this collection, the comedy of "The Anatomy of Laughter" attempts to capture incomprehensible thoughts by suggesting exact formulas. Factor T (1956) is another satire. In this novel, Themerson tries to resolve the conflict between need and conscience by stating the relationship in terms of an isosceles triangle (Boelens 233). Tom Harris (1967) appears at first to be a straightforward mystery as told by an unnamed narrator, but in fact, it is a spoof of several conventions of the novel form (May and Lesniak 468).

The Mystery of the Sardine (1986) is a strange combination of philosophy, humor, and suspense. The plot involves terrorists, but the novel is actually a, "comedy of erudition" because it, "provides side trips into the ironies of mathematics, philosophy, and political thought" (May and Lesniak 468). Neville Shack considers The Mystery of the Sardine to be "entertainment perhaps, at the expense of those who are educated above their intelligence." Shack adds that in this novel "there is a capacity to surprise, both through its transitions and its many rum non sequiturs." Selina Hastings said, "I admire Stefan Themeron's book; I can recommend it; but explain it--no." Publishers Weekly said that the book would, "appeal mostly to readers who truly care how many angels can dance on the head of a pin;" Victoria Glendinning said that reading this novel is, "like playing chess with someone who is better at it than you are;" and Robert Nye, after reading The Mystery of the Sardine, said that Stefan Themerson, "is a comedian whose favourite joke is the reader," adding that, "his wit apparently baffles critical measure." Nicholas Shakespeare described The Mystery of the Sardine as, "a shoal of red herrings, each one pursued as soon as it is spawned; and all of them, in the end, pulled together in one net and presented as inexorably linked." Tysger Boelens sums up his criticism of the novel by saying that in this novel, "the license to be far-fetched ensures a gusto and makes light of everything, even when it exasperates" (Boelens 231).

Stefan Themerson argued that gentleness is biological and aggression is cultural, not vice versa. He supports this opinion by saying, "My very presence here, in front of you, is the proof. The proof that when I was small and defenseless, my mother didn't eat me, even when she was very hungry" (Boelens 243).

Stefan Themerson Bibliography

Boelens, Tysger. "The Bad Manners of Nonsense: An Inquiry into the Nonsensical Orthodoxy of Stefan Themerson's The Adventures of Peddy Bottom." Explorations in the Field of Nonsense. Ed. Wim Tigges. Amsterdam, Netherlands: Rodopi, 1987, 229-244.
May, Hal and James G. Lesniak. "Stefan Themerson." Contemporary Authors. Detroit, MI: Gale Research, 1990, 467-468.
Themerson, Stefan. "On Nonsense and On Logic-Fiction." Explorations in the Field of Nonsense. Ed. Wim Tigges. Amsterdam, Netherlands: Rodopi, 1987, 3-16.

William Golding (1911-)

Lord of the Flies (1954) is an allegory of today's society, and the theme is that what we have come to call civilization is, at best, only skin deep. Lord of the Flies was a reaction to the popular notion that youth are innocents, and that they are basically the victims of adult brutality. Lord of the Flies, like J. D. Salinger's Catcher in the Rye, presents youth as much stronger than adults often give them credit for being. In this novel, Golding establishes the boys as "real" children by providing such details as Piggy's attitude toward his asthma, and the boys' joy in discovering Piggy's nickname (Lesniak 173).

Pincher Martin (1955) is about a naval officer whose ship is torpedoed in the Atlantic. He drifts around aimlessly before catching onto a barren rock. He clings onto the rock for days, eating sea anemones and trying to remain conscious. But delirium overtakes him, and his rambling thoughts tell the reader about his past. The sailor's corpse is discovered at the end of the story, so the reader must ask, "if the sailor is dead, who is telling the story?" This is Golding's "gimmick ending," and it gives the book a metaphysical turn, since the reader learns that the sailor has been dead from the beginning of the story. James Lesniak feels that this is the Creation Story in reverse--or a parody of the Creation Story. "What we watch is the unmaking process, in which man attempts to create himself his own God, and the process accelerates daily" (Lesniak 174). James Ginden further notes that at the end of each of Golding's first three novels there are metaphors so unique and striking that they turn into "gimmicks," into "clever tricks that shift the focus or the emphasis of the novel for a while" (Lesniak 175).

S. J. Boyd describes Golding's The Spire (1964) as "divine tragi-comedy." It can be compared to the main events of the divine comedy relating man's fall and redemption, "It's like the appletree!" is Jocelin's dying attempt to describe the spire and the terrible experience of building it. It is also like the Tree of Knowledge of Good and Evil. The Spire is a comedy because it describes the ultimate triumph of the central characters. Although the spire is far from perfect, it stands nevertheless. The beginning of The Spire is filled with innocence, joy, laughter, maybe even ecstasy, as this quote from early in the novel illustrates:

> He was laughing, chin up, and shaking his head. God the father was exploding in his face with a glory of sunlight through painted glass, a glory that moved with his movements to consume and exalt Abraham and Isaac and then God again. The tears of laughter in his eyes made additional spokes and wheels and rainbows. (qtd. in Boyd 86)

Jocelin is enthusiastic that the spire is reaching toward heaven not only because it thereby glorifies God, but because it glorifies himself as well. This strengthens the associations with the Tower of Babel in the Book of Genesis which was another monument to the folly of human pride. The varied languages of the masons who have come from distant lands to work on the spire, also help the reader make this comparison (Boyd 89). It is ironic that when the dumb stonecutter carves the gargoyle in the image of Jocelin with wide and blind eyes to represent his innocent naivety, Jocelin misinterprets the expression as a representation of his spiritual vision (Boyd 90). The spire is indeed a, "blatant image of Jocelin's desire for Goody Pangall" (Boyd 92). Later, an accident occurs which nails Jocelin to the ground at the crossways by the giant stone "hammer" of the spire, and ironically this image is strongly suggestive of the Crucifixion (Boyd 95).

Of course the spire is built on Christian faith, but it is also built on pagan human sacrifice. Pangall (Goody's husband) is the first victim. Even his name is suggestive of his role as, "bearer of all the cares and sorrows of the world" (Boyd 99). But when Pangall dies, the spire still continues to rise, at pagan hands, as, "the image of impotence is killed to bring new life in the sprouting wood of the timbers." The name of Pangall is also suggestive of Pan, the goatish deity of the pagans, who died, according to tradition, when Christ was born (Boyd 100). Pangall is the fool who is sacrificed to the pagan gods. Jocelin is the fool who offers himself to the Christian God and is crucified by the "stone hammer and nail." He is sacrificed on the great tree of the spire that grows out of these offerings. It is an extension of the eternal pattern of death and resurrection--death is necessary to the bringing of new life. "As far as some people were concerned, his eye had acquired a new facility. (Pain did it, pain did it, pain did it)" (qtd. in Boyd 101). The spire is "an upward waterfall." It is an impossible thing because it is, "a fall upwards, a happy fall, a miracle in stone" (Boyd 102). Thus Boyd supports the notion that The Spire is not a tragedy, but a comedy. "The tragedy of the cross transforms history to a comedy by establishing again for man a bridgeway to heaven" (Boyd 101).

Larry L. Dickson says that Barclay in The Paper Men (1984) is patterned after events in Golding's own life. Barclay, like Golding, "is a bearded, aging English novelist, who lives in an old house in the country, outside of London literary circles." There is much sustained humor in The Paper Men, though it tends to be bitter and sarcastic. Larry Dickson considers Golding to be, "normally one of the least humorous writers of the contemporary British novel;" but Dickson also feels that in The Paper Men Golding had lots of fun creating Barclay's cynical comments. Barclay always delivers these comments at the expense of the groveling Tucker. Many of the jokes in The Paper Men are directed at the academic world in the form of Rick L. Tucker, an Assistant Professor at the University of Astrakan in Nebraska (affectionately referred to as "Ole Ashcan"). Tucker even offers Barclay his dense but pretty wife, Mary Lou in order to win his favor. Mary Lou was Rick Tucker's student, and she explains to Mr. Barclay, "We worked together on you, sir." Mary Lou has not personally read any of Barclay's work, but she does know the titles of everything he had written. When Barclay asks her how this was so, Mary Lou replies, "I majored in flower arranging and bibliography" (Dickson 12).

In the "Foreword" to a book of interviews, Professor Jake Biles tells about an informal reception after one of his lectures at an American university. Golding said, "I was colloquial and witty; or, at least, those around me seemed to think so, laughing, as they balanced their cups of coffee" (Dickson 11).

William Golding Bibliography

Boyd, S. J. The Novels of William Golding. New York, NY: St. Martin's Press, 1988.
Dickson, Larry L. "American Yank Meets British Crank: The Humor of William Golding's The Paper Men." WHIMSY 6 (1988): 11-13.

Dickson, Larry L. "The Serio-Comic Vision of William Golding's The Brass Butterfly." West Virginia University Philological Papers 25 (1979): 61-68.

Golding, William. The Paper Men. New York, NY: Farrar, Straus and Giroux, 1984.

Lesniak, James G. "William Golding." Contemporary Authors, New Revision Series, Volume 33 1991, 172-178.

Skilton, David. "The Pyramid and Comic Social Fiction." William Golding: Some Critical Considerations. Eds. Jack I. Biles and Robert O. Evans. Lexington, KY: Univ Press of Kentucky, 1978, 176-187.

Brian O'Nolan (Flann O'Brien) (1911-1966) IRELAND

Brian O'Nolan's writing was all done under pseudonyms. He used the names Nolan, and Brian O Nuaillain and Myles na Gopaleen, but mostly he used Flann O'Brien. Peggy Broder suggests that this preoccupation with identity is a very regular part of the "Irish experience." O'Nolan also had a preoccupation with paradoxes (Broder 799). Brian O'Nolan himself was a paradox. He was raised in County Tyrone in Northern Ireland, but Strabane, his childhood city, was right on the boarder between Northern and Southern Ireland, so which was he, Northerner or Southerner? Geographically speaking he was a Northerner, but his being raised by a Catholic family made him a Southerner. His father was a customs and excise officer for the British crown, and this made him a Northerner, but his father insisted that Gaelic be spoken at home, so this made him a Southerner. In a "dizzying meditation," Brian O'Nolan asks, "Who am I?" and this leads to "Where am I?" and in The Third Policeman, the question goes even one step further, to "What am I, man or bicycle?" (Broder 799). There were two aspects of Brian O'Nolan's writing that are special, his parodies, and his wild fantasies. He also had a fondness for wordplay of every kind, but especially puns and malapropisms (Broder 800). John Fowles says, "Flann O'Brien was, I think, a genius at really absurd humour." However, Fowles adds, "I suspect his humour is very difficult indeed if you are not Irish. Even the English have a little trouble with it" (Fowles 72).

Much of O'Nolan's funniest writing appeared in the newspaper column which he wrote for Cruiskeen Lawn. He assumed the pen-name of Myles na Gopaleen in writing these columns, which frequently chronicled the activities of the fictional "Central Research Bureau," which became famous for its goofily impractical inventions. One of these was a plan to save on fuel costs by having all Irish trains run only across boglands. The trains would be equipped with a device that would scoop up the turf or the peat from the bogs, dry it, and burn it for fuel. Another project was an intoxicating ice cream, and still another was a plan to print the Irish Times in an ink that emitted an alcoholic vapor, thus giving the reader his quick pick-me-up in the morning. O'Nolan's columns also told about the poet John Keats and his friend George Chapman in their elaborate and amusing adventures. These stories always ended in a pun (Broder 801). O'Nolan often targeted the citizens of Dublin in Cruiskeen Lawn. His most devastating satire targeted "The Bore," whose sole occupation, enjoyment, and recreation is boring other people. The bore comes in many varieties. There is the man who is always telling the story about the watch he got eighteen years ago for only a few shillings; it has never lost a minute. There is the man who knows how to make a tuppenny razor blade last for five years. There is the man who always buys wholesale, and the man who never gives pennies to beggars. There is the man who does all of his own carpentry. And there is the man who, when he is asked if he has read Tolstoy's War and Peace, responds in the affirmative, and then adds that in fact he read T. Allstoy's Warren Peace when it was still in manuscript form. Then he asks, "Is it published yet?" (Broder 802).

At Swim-Two-Birds (1939) is a parody of many things, ranging from ancient Irish sagas to American Wild West adventures. The story is about Mad King Sweeny, who according to ancient Irish legend, flies from tree to tree around Ireland. "At Swim-Two-Birds" is one of the places which he visits. At Swim is written from the perspective of an anonymous college student, and it is about Dermot Trellis, who is writing a novel. Both the author and the narrator believe that novels should not be all good or all bad. Instead, the characters should have their own private lives and some significant input in their own destinies. The characters in Trellis's novels rebel against their author while he is asleep because he is causing them to do immoral things. They go so far as to take Trellis, the author, prisoner (Broder 800).

In The Hard Life (1961) the narrator's brother patents "Gravid Water," which is miraculously able to cure rheumatism. Unfortunately, however, one patient takes three times as much as is recommended, and he gains weight until he weighs more than 400 pounds. This is especially humorous because his 400-pound weight is contained by a body which has stayed the same non-overweight size (Broder 800).

An Beal Bocht (1964), which was translated as The Poor Mouth (1973), is probably O'Nolan's most hilarious novel. On the surface, the depiction is realistic, but only slightly beneath the surface the romanticized simple peasant is being satirized, as is the linguistic scholar who is visiting the area in order to record the rapidly disappearing Irish speech. This linguist mistakes the snorting and grunting of the family pig, who sleeps in the cottage with them, to be sounds in the Gaelic language (Broder 801).

In The Third Policeman (1967) there is a gradual transformation from man to bicycle. Late in the novel it becomes very difficult to tell whether the author is talking about a man or a bicycle. The reader begins to notice some sort of a transformation when a man is often seen leaning with one elbow against a wall, or he is standing, propped on one foot at a curb. Another comical aspect of The Third Policeman is O'Nolan's fascination with the infinitely small. There is a spear with a point that is so thin it is invisible to the human eye. There are also some boxes that nest inside each other until they become smaller and smaller. The last ones are too small to be seen even with a very strong magnifying glass (Broder 800). O'Nolan is also fascinated by possibilities of infinity. De Selby is a mad scientist who arranges mirrors very precisely so that they reflect backward to infinity. He claims that by the use of a powerful magnifying glass he has been able to see his own reflection at the age of twelve. In addition to Policeman MacCruiskeen's boxes which are smaller and smaller to the point of infinity, there is another example. MacCruiskeen is able to hear musical tones that are not audible to any other human beings (Broder 801).

See also Nilsen, Don L. F. "Flann O'Brien." Humor in Irish Literature: A Reference Guide. Westport, CT: Greenwood, 1996, 1-2, 181-190, 211.

Brian O'Nolan (Flann O'Brien) Bibliography

Broder, Peggy. "Brian O'Nolan (Flann O'Brien)." Encyclopedia of British Humorists: Geoffrey Chaucer to John Cleese. Ed. Steven H. Gale. New York, NY: Garland, 1996, 798-803.

Cronin, Anthony. No Laughing Matter: The Life and Times of Flann O'Brien. London, England: Grafton, 1989.

Devlin, Joseph. "The Politics of Comedy in At Swim-Two-Birds." Éire-Ireland 27.4 (1992): 91-105.

Fowles, John. "Fowles on Fowles: John Fowles Interviewed by Susana Onega." Actas del X Congreso Aedean. Zaragoza, Spain: University of Zaragoza, 1988, 72.

Ingersoll, Earl G. "Irish Jokes: A Lacanian Reading of Short Stories by James Joyce, Flann

O'Brien, and Bryan MacMahon." Studies in Short Fiction 2 (Spring, 1990): 237-245.

Lanters, José. " 'Still Life' Versus Real Life: The English Writings of Brian O'Nolan." Explorations in the Field of Nonsense. Ed. Wim Tigges. Amsterdam, Holland: Rodopi, 1987 161-181.

Power, Mary. "Flann O'Brien and Classical Satire: An Exegesis of the Hard Life." Éire-Ireland 13.1 (1978): 87-102.

Tigges, Wim. "Flann O'Brien." An Anatomy of Literary Nonsense. Amsterdam, Holland: Rodopi, 1988, 205-216.

Waters, Maureen. "Flann O'Brien and Mad Sweeny." The Comic Irishman. Albany, NY: State Univ of New York Press, 1984, 123-136.

White, Michael. "Observations on Flann O'Brien's At Swim-Two-Birds in Translation." Revista Alicantina de Esudios Ingleses 5 (1992): 155-161.

Terence Mervyn Rattigan (1911-1977)

Terence Rattigan used such comedic devices as plots built on misunderstandings and misadventures, confusions which result from the misuse of language, suspense and climax that are created by perfectly timed entrances or exits, and mixups of identity. The use of such devices resulted in a topsy-turvy world that remains topsy-turvy until the end of the play. Rattigan's later plays were character-centered comedies that featured Chekhovian irony (Rusinko 905). In addition to his many comedies, Rattigan wrote four farces, French Without Tears, Follow My Leader, While the Sun Shines, and Harlequinade, but the characters in these farces are sensitive and vibrant, unlike most formulaic farces where characters tend to be flat (Rusinko 907).

First Episode (1934), co-authored with Philip Heimann, is a rites-of-passage comedy about the lives of carefree undergraduates at Cambridge University. There are scenes of drinking, gambling, weekend romances, and cricket, and there are many undergraduate jokes that take serious turns. The comedy is about the male bonding that occurs after a visiting actress interrupts a male friendship by forming an obsessive attachment to one of the undergraduates. The tension that develops between what is said, and what is unsaid provides a "Chekhovian irony." The dialogue in First Episode is effective, as when the abandoned graduate student says of the actress who has come between them that, "Her eyes are too close together," and "her mouth [is] too small," and "I don't like her voice," and then he ironically asks, "Did you have a good rehearsal?" (Rattigan Episode 51).

French Without Tears (1936) is a farce which contains a great deal of witty dialogue that is reminiscent of George Bernard Shaw, as the students fumble around in their attempts to learn French. The humor of this dialogue is constant, as it, "steadily entertains from its opening to its closing lines" (Rusinko 905). Follow My Leader (1940), co-authored with Anthony Maurice, is a Chaplinesque farce about Adolf Hitler. Hitler is a dummy plumber who rises to power because of intra-party rivalry. This play contains such farcical scenes as that of "poor lumpen" Adolf Hitler yelling ferocious harangues into a microphone. His text is being provided by a secretary who dictates it to him sentence by sentence. The reviewer for the London Times (January 17, 1940, p. 6) said that this was "an amusing picture that the authors exploit to the fullest possible extent" (qtd. in Rusinko 905).

While the Sun Shines (1943) is a conventional and traditional farce that broke many box-office records (Rusinko 905). The plot is built around greatly improbable events that are exaggerated for dramatic effect. There were well-timed entrances and exits. There is a "hilarious" series of misunderstandings, and there is the predictable restoration of order at the end. The play is about three characters: An intoxicated Irish-American serviceman, a French officer, and, Lord Harpenden, an English sailor who is on leave in order to marry Elizabeth, a member of the Women's Air Force. One of the funniest scenes in the play is one involving these three men rolling dice for the opportunity to speak with Elizabeth on the phone. Later, two of the men (the American and the Frenchman) roll dice for the honor of being the best man at the wedding. Much of the laughter of While the Sun Shines, both in the plot and in the dialogue, comes from linguistic misunderstandings (Rusinko 906).

Harlequinade (1948) is Rattigan's last pure farce. It is about a theatrical company getting ready to present Romeo and Juliet on the road. This is a comedy of chaos. The plot is loose; the focus shifts, and there is not a single dominant character. All of the staging problems of a road performance are demonstrated, and there is the further complication of a local woman who appears, saying that her baby was fathered by one of the actors who had had a liaison with her the last time the troupe was in town. Harlequinade is a comic demonstration of how art gets entangled with life (Rusinko 906).

Who Is Sylvia (1950) is a blend of fantasy and comedy. The reviewer for the New York Times (October 25, 1950, p. 47) said that it demonstrates, "humorous invention at its freshest" (qtd. in Rusinko 907). Lord Binfield (Mark, to his friends) is the protagonist of this play. He has been trying for thirty years (three decades, each decade corresponding to one act in the play) to find his ideal woman. His concept of the ideal is based on a sculpture of "Sylvia" in his Knightsbridge apartment. Mark is joined in his rakish life by Oscar, his comic double. Each of the three acts is about a different "Sylvia" in "yet another romantic episode of a given decade." Mark's wife has known about his affairs, and she has noted to Mark that his first Sylvia, who was seventeen when Mark knew her, is now sixty three, and she wants Mark to invite this Sylvia to dinner (Rusinko 906).

The Sleeping Prince (1953) is a romantic comedy about a young Carpathian regent who comes to the coronation of King George V in 1911. It is ironic that in 1911, the actual year of the coronation of King George V, Vera Rattigan had had to miss the coronation in order to give birth to Terence. In The Sleeping Prince, there are again the typical misunderstandings that are caused by language difficulties, and these misunderstandings lead to farcical situations. The "femme fatale" of The Sleeping Prince is Mary Morgan. She is an American actress who is a seductress, but she is also an independently practical woman. One of the farcical series of events in the play is when she is given the same gifts (for services she has rendered) by three different members of the visiting royal family. A humorous line that occurs throughout the play is "himmel heilige bimbaum!" This is the line which is said in response to every new situation, and of course it is also the line which ends the play (Rusinko 907). In Praise of Love (1973) is not so much comic as it is ironic. There is much joking, playing games, and civilized wit in this play about a husband and a wife. The wife uses comic devices to deal with the physical and psychological pain of the cancer which is soon to kill her (Rusinko 907).

Terence Mervyn Rattigan Bibliography

Rattigan, Terence. First Episode. London, England: Hamish Hamilton, 1934.
Rusinko, Susan. "Terence Mervyn Rattigan." Encyclopedia of British Humorists, Volume II. Ed. Steven H. Gale. New York, NY: Garland, 1996, 904-908.

Geoffrey Herbert Willans (1911-1958)

In "Molesworth Rides Again," John Sisk places Willans into the British satirical tradition (Mullen 1212). Because of the influence of Aldous Huxley and Evelyn Waugh on Willans's writing, his humor was grounded in irony rather than in sentimentality or whimsy (Mullen 1209). Alexandra Mullen says that Geoffrey Willans wrote humor which was "highbrow high jinx." Willans's humor highlighted verbal twists, comic stereotypes, and parodic invention (Mullen 1208). Many of Willans's humours characters have a penchant for generalizations. There is an English naval man, for example, who is a caricature of the stereotypical Englishman, and who has a disdain for the French, "Just what you would expect from a navy which [keeps] chickens on board their ships" (Mullen 1209).

Some of Nigel Molesworth's parodies of academic conventions are masterful. Consider the following from <u>Down with Skool!</u> (1953):

> Proposition: Masters are swankpots.
> Proof: Wise boys like me use Flatery with masters from time to time....
>   [D]uring a bit of parsing or drawing a map of Spane you can just
>   look up and sa. "Did you have a tomy gun during the war sir?"
> "Get on with your map molesworth one."
> "No, but did you sir really?"
> "As a matter of fact i did molesworth."
> "gosh sir did you shoot many germans sir."
> "Get on with your map, boy."
> "No sir but did you?"
> "Altho it have nothing to do with the lesson i got 9 thousand with one burst
>   once...etc." Q.E.D. (Willans <u>Skool</u> 28)

Or consider Molesworth's recitation of Alfred, Lord Tennyson's "Charge of the Light Brigade" which goes, "Har fleag har fleag har fleag onward / Into the er rode the 100," or Shakespeare's soliloquy in "MacBeth," which begins, "Tomowandtomowandtomow / Creeps in this um um / Out! / Out! / brief candle" (Mullen 1210). Grimes, the headmaster, and Sigismund Arbuthnot, the mad math master, are especially menacing figures in the Molesworth novels, but all of the masters are menacing. Molesworth describes them as follows: "English master hav long hair red ties and weeds like wordsworth throw them into ecstasies." Molesworth himself can be described as a, "modern sceptic whose highly developed capacity for puncturing the absurd and embellishing the mundane makes him a classic comic figure" (Mullen 1211).

In Willans's <u>Whizz for Atomms</u> (1956), Nigel Molesworth considers the masters to be the chief drawback of school life. There are, "...thin ones fat ones little ones tall ones some with cranky cars others with posh ties, some you can rag and others who strike mortal fear into our tinyhearts it is cruelty to expose us to such monsters. Everywhere a boy goes at skool there is liable to be a master chiz chiz seeking you out with his fierce burning eyes" (Willans <u>Whizz</u> 57).

<u>Admiral on Horseback</u> (1954) is a humorous novel which draws from Willans's wartime experiences (Mullen 1208). It is about Rear-Admiral Sir Strangways Foxe-Forsyth who has an impressive oil painting of HMS Nelson at sea in bad weather (Willans <u>Admiral</u> 13). Admiral Foxe-Forsyth has many humorous adventures, one of which is when he visits Paris and buys tickets for <u>Phedre</u> instead of the <u>Follies Bergeres</u> (Mullen 1209).

In <u>How to be Topp</u> (1954), St. Custard's School is founded on the principle that "any skool is a bit of a shambles." It is here that Nigel Molesworth sardonically notes that "skool according to head-master's pi-jaw is like Life chiz if that is the case wot is the use of going on?" (Willans <u>Topp</u> 63). Molesworth especially hates the English game of cricket, and says, "Give me a thumbscrew or slo fire every time" (Mullen 1209).

<u>Fasten your Lapstraps!</u> (1955) is a comic guide to air travel and air travelers (Mullen 1208). <u>My Uncle Harry</u> (1957) is a book of humorous adventures in the form of sketches (Mullen 1208). Uncle Harry is a British Clubman who could be described as a "late Edwardian buck." The narrator, Uncle Harry's nephew, describes Uncle Harry as

follows: "It is said that the hall-mark of a gentleman is that he is only rude intentionally. One never knew with Uncle Harry whether he was rude intentionally or not, but he was certainly rude to nearly everybody" (Willans Harry 17). Geoffrey Willans teamed with Ronald Searle in the writing of The Dog's Ear Book (1958), a humorous collection of "doggy types" of both the two-legged and four-legged varieties (Mullen 1208).

Geoffrey Herbert Willans Bibliography

Mullen, Alexandra. "Geoffrey Willans." Encyclopedia of British Humorists, Volume II. Ed. Steven H. Gale. New York, NY: Garland, 1996, 1207-1212.
Susk, John P. "Molesworth Rides Again." Commonweal 63 (November 4, 1955): 123-124.
Willans, Geoffrey. Admiral on Horseback. London, England: M. Joseph, 1954.
Willans, Geoffrey. Down with Skool!. London, England: Max Parrish, 1953.
Willans, Geoffrey. How to be Topp. London, England: Max Parrish, 1954.
Willans, Geoffrey. Whizz for Atomms. London, England: Max Parrish, 1956.
Willans, Geoffrey. The Wit of Winston Churchill. London, England: Max Parish, 1956.

Ronald Frederick Delderfield (1912-1972)

R. F. Delderfield had a number of schoolmasters when he was in grammar school who either individually, or in composite form became characters in his novels. "I have used them all at one time or another, sometimes compounding three or four into a single character--the mild and courteous Bentley, who ruled like a cultured King Réné of the Two Sicilies, the informative Scott, who had a way of making English words perform the tricks of circus dogs, the grave and kindly Parkinson, the ironic and candid Barlow, and above all, the tempestuous Mr. Ferguson, who taught French" (Commire 35). In his autobiography entitled For My Own Amusement, Delderfield described himself as, "a lineal descendent of the medieval minstrel who trudged from castle to castle telling tales for his supper.... I am a compulsive teller of tales, a real chronic case" (qtd. in Dear 99). Give me a pen and some blank sheets of paper, and I am content to ply my craft in a hogshead, of the kind Huck Finn inhabited. Deny me the privilege and I would die of boredom and frustration in the Palace of the Doge set in the Garden of Eden" (qtd. in Commire 37).
There Was a Fair Maid Dwelling (1960), which was published in America as Diana (1960), is about the romance between a Cockney orphan and a wealthy heroine. Much of the charm of the novel comes from its understanding of the, "ironic predicaments of the lovers and in their identification with an enchanted setting" (Commire 37). The reviewer for the New York Times (June 27, 1972) said that God is an Englishman (1970) is "a cheerful anachronism in the world of letters." The reviewer adds that "Delderfield writes with vigor, unceasing narrative drive, and a high degree of craftsmanship," and concludes "although difficult to take seriously, [this book] provides a good bird's eye view of Victorian England and contains numerous snippets of social history.... There is a place for this conventional, traditional, lively and amusing sort of fiction" (qtd. in Commire 37).

Ronald Frederick Delderfield Bibliography

Commire, Anne. "R. F. Delderfield." Something about the Author, Volume 20. Detroit, MI: Gale Research, 1980, 34-37.
Dear, Pamela S. "R. F. Delderfield." Contemporary Authors, New Revision Series, Volume 47. Detroit, MI: Gale Research, 1995, 98-101.
Delderfield, R. F. For My Own Amusement. London, England: Hodder and Stoughton,

1968.

Nigel Dennis (1912-)

Nigel Dennis's plays are, "vastly entertaining and first-rate theater (Nasso 185). In A Sea Change (or Boys and Girls Come Out to Play) (1949) Nigel Dennis, "ironically draws the contrast between the heroic Max of the newspaper world and the puny Max as seen by Jimmy" (Karl 249). In Cards of Identity (1955) there is a broad range of satire. Nevertheless, Dennis maintains a sharp focus for his ironic view of the world as he describes "The Identity Club," which operates under the principle that, "Identity is the answer to everything. There is nothing that cannot be seen in terms of identity" (Karl 249). It is the function of this club to provide entirely new identities to its members. In one case, which is labeled "Dog's Way: A Case of Multiple Sexual Misidentity," the client had, early in life, heard his father say to his mother, "Let's always speak frankly about sex before the child, so that we don't give society a maladjusted dwarf." The client had remembered these words, and had taken them to heart, feeling compelled, therefore, always to speak frankly about sex so that he would not become a maladjusted dwarf (Karl 250). Dennis says that this client considered sex to be a kind of a doctor, sitting on a cloud. Being preoccupied with sex, this client confused Church services with sexual relief, and when he filled out the form to sign up for war service, he wrote "Church of England" in the blank which asked for his sex. Another case history of a person changing his identity involves a person who confuses religion and politics. This man works in a modern monastery devoted not to religious aspirations, but rather designed to help ex-communists write anti-communist pamphlets and histories. For example, he is working on the Encyclopedia Penitentia, which is a rewriting of history from an anti-communist perspective. The clients in this particular wing of the Identity Club are not referred to by name, but are rather referred to by the year in which they broke with the Communist Party (Karl 251).

Cards of Identity is a comic tour de force in which Dennis attacks all aspects of life. "He joins with the major satirists of the past, Voltaire among them, as a fearless castigator of social and political nonsense. As satire or comedy, Cards of Identity is trenchant." Frederick Karl says that the satirist should avoid the temptation to caricature, and notes that Dennis is unsuccessful in this regard. Nevertheless, "Dennis reveals the verbal and mental gifts as well as the ability to perceive levels of hypocrisy which are the essence of great comic novelists." In fact, Karl concludes that, "Of contemporary novelists still working seriously, few seem better qualified than Dennis to catch satirically the major currents of contemporary life" (Karl 252).

According to Christine Nasso, the two plays of Two Plays and a Preface (1956), "constitute the best that British drama has produced since the death of Shaw," and the preface is also "brilliantly witty" (Nasso 186).

Nigel Dennis Bibliography:

Karl, Frederick R. "Chapter XIII: The Still Comic Muse of Humanity: The Novels of Anthony Powell, Angus Wilson, and Nigel Dennis." The Contemporary English Novel. New York, NY: Farrar, Straus and Cudahy, 1962, 254-273.
Nasso, Christine. "Nigel Dennis." Contemporary Authors, First Revision, Volumes 25-28. Detroit, MI: Gale Research, 1977, 185-186.

Lawrence George Durrell (Charles Norden, Gaffer Peeslake) (1912-1990)

In the tradition of twentieth-century authors, Lawrence Durrell explores the interrelationships between space, time, consciousness, sexuality, and identity. His writing is lusty, vital, and affective. He is both a maverick and a paradox in that he is an exile who frequently writes about England and Englishmen. He is a journalist who, "calls for the destruction of the very structure which, for a very long time, supported him" (Begnal 88). About his paradoxical serious-but-comical style, Durrell wrote a note to Henry Miller in 1958, "All this is very perplexing to my fans who don't know whether I am P. G. Wodehouse or James Joyce or what the hell" (Begnal 89).

Lawrence Durrell calls The Black Book (1938), "a savage charcoal sketch of spiritual and sexual etiolation." The characters are "humours characters." Lobo is a Peruvian student who thinks about "tweed English women who wear padlocks between their legs." Tarquin is a homosexual who is in love with Clare, a black dancing master. Gregory considers himself to be "the average Englishman." He says, "I carry my virginity and my self-satisfaction on a string round my neck." When Gregory writes his last will and testament, he gives a bequest to himself: "I offer only the crooked grin of the toad, and a colored cap to clothe my nakedness" (Begnal 89). The title of The Black Book refers to a diary which was found, presented, and commented on by Lawrence Lucifer, the narrator of The Black Book. The diary recounts the life of Herbert "Death" Gregory, Esquire (Begnal 89). Cefalu (1947), which was renamed The Dark Labyrinth in 1958, is a social satire in the tradition of Aldous Huxley.

Justine (1957), Balthazar (1958), Mountolive (1959), and Clea (1960) are the four books in Lawrence Durrell's Alexandria Quartet (Trosky 107). Justine (1957) is filled with exotic imagery and sensuality (Begnal 91). In Balthazar (1958) Durrell states that his four-volume novel is based on Albert Einstein's theory of relativity. The first three volumes of the quartet are involved with space; the final volume is involved with time (Begnal 91). In the Alexandria Quartet, the reader faces many enigmatic questions, such as whether Balthazar is a sage or a fool, and who murdered Nessim's brother, Narouz, and whether Pursewarden committed suicide because he has compromised Nessim and Mountolive, the British Ambassador, or commited suicide because he wanted to free his sister, Liza, from an incestuous affair, and whether Justine and Nessim are patriots or traitors, and whether Pursewarden is a great novelist, or just a drunkard. Throughout the quartet, Durrell is making the point that truth is relative. As Darley wonders, "Perhaps then the destruction of my private Alexandria was necessary...: Perhaps buried in all this there lies the germ and substance of a truth--time's usufruct--which, if I can accommodate it, will carry me a little further in what is really a search for my proper self" (Begnal 91).

The Revolt of Aphrodite: Tunc (1968), and Nunquam (1970) is a "double-decker novel" based on Petronius's Satyricon: Aut Tunc aut Nunquam; the sub-title translates as "then or never." In Satyricon, a Roman character contrasts the fertile and spiritual past with the present, in which people are only concerned with profit. Felix Charlock is a detective who is sifting through his past for, "the key to where things all went wrong" (Begnal 93). Felix's life is defined by two women, Iolanthe, the prostitute who later becomes a film star, and Benedicta Merlin whom he marries. Iolanthe tells Felix as she is dying of cancer caused by an injection of paraffin into her breasts that, "only the free man can really be loved by a woman." Felix is certainly not free. His wife leaves him alone for years at a time, and in the reader's final view of her, she is, "standing naked in a mirrored hall in their country house, muttering the Lord's Prayer and blasting away at her multiple images with a shotgun" (Begnal 94). The plot is complicated by the fact that Julian, who is impotent, has fallen in love with Iolanthe, and her death has affected him deeply. At this point, "The Firm" constructs a new Iolanthe, who is so perfect in every detail that even she does not realize that she is a dummy. What Julian wants is, "a neo-Aphrodite--one who cannot eat, excrete, or make love," and Felix, with the help of Marchant, is successful--perhaps too successful, because Iolanthe, is so human in form and thinking that she demands freedom, and finally manages to escape from the Firm's control. "Ironically enough, the plastic Aphrodite achieves the freedom that the human being cannot" (Begnal 95).

Lawrence George Durrell (Charles Norden, Gaffer Peeslake Bibliography

Begnal, Michael H. "Lawrence Durrell." Dictionary of Literary Biography: British Novelists, 1930-1959, Volume 15. Detroit, MI: Bruccoli Clark/Gale Research, 1983, 87-97.
Trosky, Susan M. ed. "Lawrence (George) Durrell." Contemporary Authors, Volume 132. Detroit, MI: Gale Research, 1991, 107-108.

Pamela Hansford Johnson (Nap Lombard)(1912-1981)

Anthony Burgess described Johnson's novels as, "witty, satirical, and deftly malicious--some of her books characterized by a sort of grave levity, others by a sort of light gravity. Johnson's novels demonstrate an interest in the bizarre and the abnormal. They contain nymphomaniacs, and homosexuals, and old men and women painfully in love with young men and women. They also contain crazed passion, and murder" (Stephens 258).

Between 1959 and 1965, Pamela Hansford Johnson published a trilogy entitled, "Dorothy Merton Comedies." The Unspeakable Skipton (1959-) is about a picaresque rogue who lives in Bruges, and who tries to con his way through life. In this novel, Skipton is a writer who must live by his wits (Karl 275-276). The other two novels in the comic trilogy are Night and Silence, Who Is Here? An American Comedy (1963), and Cork Street, Next to the Hatters: A Novel in Bad Taste (1965) (Stephens 257). This trilogy of satiric novels comment on the literary life of both England and America. Critics have been impressed by Johnson's ability to write successful comic novels which were so different from her earlier works. According to Walter Allen, Johnson's paranoid artist, Daniel Skipton is "a superb comic creation." Daniel Skipton is developed as an English-born writer who is living in Belgium, and who is fully convinced that he is an unappreciated genius (Stephens 259).

Pamela Hansford Johnson (Nap Lombard) Bibliography

Karl, Frederick R. The Contemporary English Novel. New York, NY: Farrar, Straus and Cudahy, 1962.
Stephens, Kenneth R. "Pamela Hansford Johnson." Contemporary Authors, New Revision Series, Volume 28. Eds. Hal May and James G. Lesniak. Detroit, MI: Gale Research, 1990, 256-260.

Mary Lavin (1912-) IRELAND

See Nilsen, Don L. F. "Mary Lavin." Humor in Irish Literature: A Reference Guide. Westport, CT: Greenwood, 1996, 11, 190.

George Mikes (1912-1987)

George Mikes was a natural comic. "Humor was in his veins, laughter in his movements; his features included a small, rotund figure and a round head with a moon-like face, large but quickly darting eyes, and a ready, engaging smile." Mikes's best writing tends to be anecdotal and funny. Of the forty books he wrote, thirty-five of them are humorous. Mikes played senior tennis at the Hurlingham Club with such gusto and humor that he would often beat players who were much younger and better than he was. "They could not return his tricky balls for laughing" (Kabdebo 763).

How to Be an Alien (1946) was Mikes's first bestseller. In this novel, he presented himself as a bumbling alien and described the habits of the natives of the, "vast, strange but friendly country of London." He observed that the Continental people may have a better sex life, but the British people have better hot water bottles (Kabdebo 763).

George Mikes liked to travel to foreign countries and gather a book full of humor about each country he would visit, blending their local jokes with his own brand of humorous presentation. How to Scrape Skies (1948) is a humorous description of the United States; Milk and Honey (1950) is a humorous description of Israel; Über Alles (1953) is a humorous description of Germany; and The Land of the Rising Yen (1973) is a humorous description of Japan. Even Britain is not immune from Mikes's satiric observations. In How to Be Inimitable: Coming of Age in England (1960), and How to be a Brit (1987), Mikes presents a humor that is spicy, but not biting. Nicholas Bentley, who illustrated many of Mikes's books, was able to capture the essence of Mikes's humor in his drawings. In these books, Mikes was able to caricature the national stereotypes by bringing out their comic qualities. His French are "little cabbages;" Japan is the country of the "rising yen;" and everyone in the world seems to be related to one of Mikes's Hungarians. "Everybody is a Hungarian, but some people don't know it yet." Mikes depicts the English as eccentrics who only pretend to be interested in sex (Kabdebo 764).

George Mikes Bibliography

Kabdebo, Thomas. "George Mikes." Encyclopedia of British Humorists, Volume II. Ed. Steven H. Gale. New York, NY: Garland, 1996, 763-764.

William Sansom (1912-1976)

The Body (1949) is probably William Sansom's best novel. It is a "comedy of exacerbation" in which the vision of the hero-narrator is distorted. This vision is expressed mainly by minute renderings of the objects that make up his external world. Herbert Barrows says that in The Body, Sansom has combined a concentrated sense of humor with acute observations, and sound psychological insights to produce a "distinguished descriptive prose style" (Trosky 393).

The Cautious Heart (1958) is written in a colloquial style, and is filled with good-humored slang and nervous energy. Frederick Karl says that, "Sansom's comic talent is obvious (Karl 286), and that he has a special gift for narrative and for colloquial dialogue (Karl 287). Valerie Cunningham finds A Young Wife's Tale (1974) to be a "fetchingly jokey" novel (Trosky 394).

In conclusion, Elizabeth Young says that William Sansom, "writes like an angel, and his joy in the performance communicates itself directly to the reader." About Sansom's writing, J. J. Maloney adds, "It is all too seldom that one comes across a man who can tell a rattling good story and write like the devil" (Trosky 394).

William Sansom Bibliography

Karl, Frederick R. The Contemporary English Novel. New York, NY: Farrar, Straus and
    Cudahy, 1962.
Trosky, Susan M. "William Sansom." Contemporary Authors, New Revision Series,
    Volume 42. Detroit, MI: Gale Research, 1994, 392-394.

Benjamin Britten (1913-1976)

Albert Herring is about a town of do-gooders who are not able to find a suitable girl
to be the May Queen, and so instead they select Albert Herring as their "May King." The
opera is a comedy of humours which revolves around the overly pious townspeople, which
include Lady Billows and Florence Pike, Albert and his somber mum, and two flirty young
lovers by the names of Sid and Nancy. The May Queen committee has decided to honor
Albert Herring as May King for his chastity, and this is ironic because it is Herring's
chastity which precipitates his emancipation. The characters in this opera are stereotypes
very similar to those found in a Gilbert and Sullivan operetta; they include the overbearing
society matron, the old maid school teacher, the holier-than-thou minister, and the inept
British police officer (Hamilton-Smith 3).

Benjamin Britten Bibliography

Hamilton-Smith, Vicki. " 'Lyric Opera Theatre' Opens Season with Witty British Albert
    Herring." ASU Insight (September 23, 1994): 3.

Ralph Hammond Innes (1913-)

Ralph Hammond Innes is a master story teller. His novels tend to be exciting,
entertaining, and believable. High Stand (1913) is a book about environmental issues. In
the New York Times Book Review, Jack Sullivan says that High Stand is, "a book where
the nonhuman world is depicted as more admirable and more alive, than the human."
Hammond Innes is vitally concerned with environmental issues. He has been supporting
reforestation projects for more than twenty-five years, and it has been reported that he has
planted more than a million trees (Chapman and Dear 176). About his obsession with
reforestation, Hammond Innes told Alan Bestic, "I'm replacing some of the timber used up
by my books." In his writing, Hammond Innes seems to be more concerned with the forest
setting of his stories than he is with the characters or their actions (Chapman and Dear
177).

Ralph Hammond Innes Bibliography

Chapman, Jeff, and Pamela S. Dear, eds. "Ralph Hammond Innes." Contemporary Authors,
    New Revision Series, Volume 52. Detroit, MI: Gale, 1996, 174-177.

Barbara Pym (1913-1980)

In a book entitled The Pleasure of Miss Pym, Charles Burkhart provides a
stimulating discussion of the humor in Barbara Pym's fiction (Bellman 900). Burkhart tells

about Pym's fondness for demonstrating incongruities of behavior or situation in her writings. She also presents ludicrous misunderstandings, and various aspects of the absurd in everyday life. Burkhart finds a broad range of comic features exhibited by her characters. As Patricia Kane notes, "Barbara Pym's characters do ridiculous things" (Kane 16). In her novels dealing with anthropology her characters are seen to be prejudiced, ignorant, and just plain inaccurate. Many of her comic markers relate to the ways in which her characters distort reality, and include irrelevance, inconsequence, incongruity, and enlargement (Bellman 897). Samuel Bellman describe's Pym's style as spare, tellingly direct, ironic; Bellman also says that the cross-purposes of Pym's characters are developed by her skillful use of dialogue. Pym's narrators are keenly aware of domestic details relating to cooking, cats as household pets, furniture and antiques, female dress, etc. Her humours characters come from parochial country life, or from life in London or Oxford, and they range from droll churchmen, to self-centered spinsters, to academics, to office personnel, to effete unmasculine floaters, to women who want love in that "heaven they're dreaming of." Among academics, anthropologists specializing in African studies are especially targeted (Bellman 896).

   One of Barbara Pym's many examples of "incongruity" can be seen in Some Tame Gazelle (1950) when Bishop Grote returns home from the foreign mission he has been serving in the African country of Mbawawa. He is giving a slide lecture about the country of Mbawawa, and is telling the audience that the climate is temperate and that the soil is very fertile, but then feels that he must explain himself. "'When I say temperate,' went on the Bishop, 'I dare say many of you might find it rather hot.' He paused and tapped his pointer vigorously on the floor" (qtd. in Bellman 897). Samuel Bellman considers Some Tame Gazelle to be, "chock-full of Pym's typical comic types--aging, crotchety spinsters, pretentious pedants, and a gallery of prim clerics" (Bellman 899).

   The "Excellent Women" in Pym's Excellent Women (1952) are always doing "good works." They serve in the church; in fact the churches could probably not exist without them. And they also remain (ironically for Pym) as spinsters (Bellman 896). When excellent women marry, they often become typists for their husbands (Kane 17). Mildred Lathbury is the daughter of the clergyman in Excellent Women and she describes the Wednesday lunchtime service at St. Ermin's Church in the posh Belgravia part of London in the following way, "I always thought of us as being rather like the early Christians, surrounded not by lions, admittedly, but by all the traffic and bustle of a weekday lunch-hour" (Bellman 898). Samuel Bellman considers Julian Malory to be, "one of the most outrageously funny clergymen in Pym's spacious gallery." Father Malory is the High-Church Father who lives with his sister Winifred in Excellent Women (Bellman 899).

   One of Barbara Pym's many examples of "inconsequence" occurs in Jane and Prudence (1953) when Jessie Morrow, the companion to the wealthy Miss Doggett, accidently upsets a cup of tea on the lilac cotton dress of the self-conscious spinster Prudence Bates. Miss Doggett is concerned that the spill may have left a permanent mark on the dress. "'It seems to be leaving a mark already,' said Jessie in an unsuitably detached tone for one who had been responsible for the disaster; 'rather in the shape of Italy. I wonder if that can have any significance?'" (Bellman 897).

   Father Gemini is a missionary and a linguist in Less Than Angels (1955). He tends to overdress in musty black garments, and at times he throws off the layers of clothes, "in the manner of a strip-tease performer." Catherine Oliphant is a writer, and is Tom's lover. She is attracted to the tall and rugged Alaric, who has a grim, rough-hewn face. She thinks of Tom as one of those huge Easter Island statues that has been, "reduced to the level of a vulnerable, imposed-upon, poor old man" (Bellman 899). In Less Than Angels, there is a woman at an academic gathering who must listen to another woman after listening to a man describing his linguistic research. Mrs. Foresight remarks that, "it was a little hard that so much concentration should be called for when talking to a member of her own sex. It seemed, somehow, a waste of efforts" (Pym Angels 16). Later in the novel two young men decide to drop in on a lady friend at meal time because, as one of them says, "It's so depressing cooking for one person, or so one hears. Let's go and make it worth her while to prepare a good meal" (Pym Angels 25).

One of the many examples of irrelevance can be found in A Glass of Blessings (1958) in the scene when Wilmet Forsyth, the narrator, has attended the Ash Wednesday lunch service, and is chatting with Mr. Bason, the person in charge of domestic affairs at the clergy house. As Bason reaches into his pocket to take out a piece of paper, Wilmet notices that on the paper there appears to be, "a list, written in purple ink in a large bold hand." Then Wilmet tries to make sense of such a list. "It must be a Lenten laundry list-- the purple ink, of course, representing the liturgical color." Although Wilmet is wrong, the list turns out to be something equally intriguing. It is a list of clergy-house menus especially designed for the Lenten season (Bellman 897).

Monica Beltane teaches botany in a London University in No Fold Return of Love (1961), and when Monica meets a young innocent named Laurel, Laurel is greatly impressed that Monica teaches botany at the university. Mrs. Beltane, Monica's mother hears Laurel's praise, and says, "Yes, it is interesting to see how the same thing has come out in our family," explaining further that, "my husband was a great gardener and had a gift for water divining." Mrs. Beltane continued, "'Monica has this passion for botany--the scientific side, you see--while Paul is very artistic and loves flowers for their own sake. And Felix is very fond of nature too, aren't you darling?' She looked down at the poodle, who had lapsed into silence on his little cushion" (qtd. in Bellman 898).

Quartet in Autumn (1977) is about four office works, two men and two women. Both of the women retire, and one of them, Marcia Ivory, dies of cancer. Quartet in Autumn may treat dark and serious topics, but it nevertheless contains much comedy and irony (Bellman 896). Marcia Ivory is one of the four characters in Quartet in Autumn who have been working in their drab office. As Marcia, terminally ill, is lying in her hospital bed, the nurse brings her a card from the other three office workers which expresses good wishes and hopes for a speedy recovery (Bellman 897). The nurse tells Marcia that the card is signed by Letty, Norman, and Edwin, but in the nurse's mind, Letty and Norman were a married couple, and Letty and Norman must have had a little boy named Edwin (Bellman 898).

Leonora Eyre is the elegant-but-old-fashioned, egocentric protagonist of The Sweet Dove Died (1978). One night, Leonora is awakened by a sharp cry. Frightened, she huddles under her bed covers, but then she becomes aware that it was only the cat from next door. Still, she is unable to go back to sleep, and she goes down stairs to make a cup of tea, "a drink she did not much like because of the comfort it was said to bring to those whom she normally despised." This is another example of "irrelevance" as a comic device (Bellman 897). In both The Sweet Dove Died, and in A Glass of Blessings there is a woman who decides to have an interesting affair only to discover that the young man she has chosen has a preference for other men (Kane 17).

Daisy Pettigrew in An Unsuitable Attachment (1982) lives with her brother Edwin, a veterinarian who is thought by some of his clients to resemble the various animals he is treating. The particular animal he resembles changes with his mood as he changes from a marmalade cat to a sheep dog, etc. (Bellman 899). Sophia, the clergyman's wife in An Unsuitable Attachment has a special relationship with her cat. The cat, which is a mirror image of Sophia herself, has the complete run of the place. It gets its cat hair on the altar cloth. It jumps on tables to snatch bits of food. And it loves no one. Sophia is also a manipulator who tries to change other peoples lives for them. She is finally challenged by one of the people she has interfered with, who tells her that a person should not, "arrange other people's lives for them like that," and Sophia responds by brooding about whether or not she should have her cat neutered (Kane 17).

The title of Crampton Hodnet (1985) comes from an anecdote which appears in the novel involving a flimsy alibi of a new curate who is trying to explain why he had missed the evensong service. In fact he had been dallying with one of the lady parishioners in the countryside, but he says that the vicar in another parish had asked him to take evensong there. When he was asked for the name of that other parish, he improvised with "Crampton Hodnet." Hazel Holt considers Crampton Hodnet to be, "funnier than any of the writer's later works" (qtd. in Bellman 898).

In An Academic Question (1986), there is a woman who decides to do volunteer work and is encouraged by her husband to read to the residents of an old persons' home because "old people are in fashion now" (Kane 17). Cassandra Marsh-Gibbon in Civil to Strangers (1987) is married to Adam, who is described as not only "a gentleman of means," but "a very minor writer" as well (Bellman 898). Whenever Adam is in a bad mood, he quotes from Wordsworth to Cassandra, so in her mind, Cassandra associates Wordsworth with their domestic quibbles (Bellman 898).

Samuel Bellman says that Barbara Pym's writings are filled with her subtle and often elusive sense of humor. He says that the reader of Pym's fiction will be fascinated by the diversity of her satiric targets, her low-key manner, penetrating descriptions, and amusing social interactions, and her power to transform the commonplace into a "rich comic landscape" (Bellman 899).

Barbara Pym Bibliography

Bellman, Samuel I. "Barbara Pym." Encyclopedia of British Humorists, Volume II. Ed. Steven H. Gale. New York, NY: Garland, 1996, 894-900.
Burkhart, Charles. The Pleasure of Miss Pym. Austin, TX: University of Texas Press, 1987.
Holt, Hazel. A Lot to Ask: A Life of Barbara Pym. New York, NY: Dutton, 1991.
Kane, Patricia. "A Wry Outlook: Barbara Pym's Humor." WHIMSY VI. Eds. Don and Alleen Nilsen. Tempe, AZ: Arizona State University, 1988, 16-17.
Pym, Barbara. Less Than Angels. 1955, New York: Perennial Library, 1982.

Gwyn Thomas (1913-1981) WALES

Thomas's autobiography is entitled A Few Selected Exits: An Autobiography of Sorts, and Clive Barnes describes this work as, "an engaging book to be warmly recommended to anyone who has an affection for the frantic and untamed Celtic spirit." Philip Burton observed that, "Gwyn Thomas transmutes the commonplace into the delightfully grotesque by means of his keen perception, his twinkling compassion, his cartoon comedy, and his deft way with words" (Evory and Metzger 495).

In a personal letter dated April 28, 1994, Brian Lile indicated that almost all of the works of Welsh author Gwyn Thomas are humorous, but especially humorous is his most recent anthology entitled Meadow Prospect Revisited, and edited by Michael Parnell. Gwyn Thomas said, "My work is based on the humour of astonishment." His work reflects life in the South of Wales, an area which has been pulverized by a long and bitter slump that occurred during the years between the wars. The people became dislocated, and this provided the materials for Thomas's writing. Gwyn Thomas himself made a poignant observation about these people who, "distilled a laughter of ravelling delusions, gallows-humor, scored for a horde of gifted hymn-singers. They lost simultaneously their aboriginal language (Welsh), their major industry (coal) and most of their religion. They recovered from the shock of this only when the Second World War came along with its promise of atomic power and cheaper funerals" (Evory and Metzger 494).

Gwyn Thomas Bibliography

Evory, Ann, and Linda Metzger. "Gwyn Thomas." Contemporary Authors, New Revision
    Series, Volume 9. Detroit, MI: Gale Research, 1983, 494-495.
Lile, Brian. Personal Letter dated April 28, 1994.
Parnell, Michael, ed. Meadow Prospect Revisited. by Gwyn Thomas Bridgend, Wales:
    Seren Books, 1992.
Thomas, Gwyn. A Hatful of Humors. London, England: Schoolmaster Publishing, 1965.

Angus Wilson (Frank Johnstone)(1913-)

Angus Wilson has always been a natural maverick and mimic, and he continues to be so. Wilson began as a comic writer, and the comic tradition can be seen throughout his career. "He has always written with a strong sense of a tradition, yet in urgent dispute with it." In The Portable Dickens, Angus Wilson reprinted Dickens's Great Expectations in its entirety, and then gathered excerpts from other novels under such headings as "Crime, Murder and Pursuit," "Humor," and "Theater." About Dickens, Angus Wilson said, "Apart from the humour of Dickens which lies very close to a good deal of my humour, what is vital to his approach and to mine is that he sees his central features always in relation to, first of all, a group and then in relation to the whole of society" (Wiloch 488).

The Wrong Set and Other Stories (1949), Such Darling Dodos and Other Stories (1950), and A Bit Off the Map and Other Stories (1957) are collections of Angus Wilson short stories that are noted for their incisive wit and satire, and for their accurate portraits of postwar English society. In 1969, these short stories were collected into a large volume entitled, Death Dance: Twenty-Five Stories (Wiloch 485).

Angus Wilson has written some mature wit and direct dialogue in Hemlock and After, (1952), Anglo-Saxon Attitudes (1956), and The Middle Age of Mrs. Eliot (1958)(Karl 158). According to Frederick R. Karl, Anglo-Saxon Attitudes (1956) has a mature wit that gives tone and shape to the material. This wit explores every mood from that of high comedy to that of bitter melodrama (Wiloch 486). Both Anglo-Saxon Attitudes and The Middle Age of Mrs. Eliot contain, "whole sections of glittering dialogue, wonderfully satiric imitations of academics, politicians, diplomats, artists, and scientists." Wilson "probes the inner lives and especially the disappointments of the 'unheroic' figures who are the central characters in his fiction" (Wiloch 486).

Meg Eliot is a smart and attractive lady in The Middle Age of Mrs. Eliot (1958), but she is also a selfish and domineering woman who finds herself at the age of forty-three without a husband and without a position. When her husband dies, she must salvage her life without depending on anyone else. The problem of the novel, then, is how a woman who has never before relied on herself must suddenly survive entirely through her own devices (Karl 248).

The Old Men at the Zoo (1961) is the story of bickering zoo administrators who are caught up in a European invasion of England. This novel uses satire to contrast the treatment of animals in a zoo with the treatment of human beings in modern society (Wiloch 486). No Laughing Matter (1967) is about an eccentric family by the name of Matthews. They used to be wealthy, but are wealthy no longer, and their experiences echo those of twentieth-century England at large (Wiloch 487). Richard Mayne describes No Laughing Matter as revealing the, "complex responses, the image making, the mimesis, parody, and unconscious feedback that inform a family entity" (Wiloch 487). As If By Magic (1973) is about some magic rice that a scientist by the name of Hamo is going to use to feed the Third World. But his magic rice does not solve the Third World's hunger problems. Though acknowledging the novel's humor, Phoebe Adams of the Atlantic states that Wilson's "underlying purpose is serious. He is quite savagely out of patience with the fashion for magic shortcuts to Utopia and Nirvana" (Wiloch 487). According to critic Michael Ratcliffe, Setting the World on Fire (1980), "triumphs as a macabre cultural comedy of English family life" (Wiloch 487).

    Ann Tyler wrote the following about Angus Wilson:

> As a novelist, he is tireless in his pursuit of each and every character. He pounces upon the slightest tell-tale gesture or turn of phrase. He is meticulous, exhaustive in building up his scenes, word by word and clink of china upon clink of china. The result is people so firmly defined that you feel you could count the stitches in their English lawn dresses although, in fact, you could not, for it is by their speech and movements that he describes them. (Wiloch 489)

Angus Wilson (Frank Johnstone) Bibliography

Karl, Frederick R. "Chapter XIII: The Still Comic Muse of Humanity: The Novels of Anthony Powell, Angus Wilson, and Nigel Dennis." The Contemporary English Novel. New York, NY: Farrar, Straus and Cudahy, 1962, 254-273.
Wiloch, Thomas. "Angus Wilson." Contemporary Authors, New Revision Series, Volume 21. Detroit, MI: Gale Research, 1987, 484-490.

Patrick O'Brian (1914-) IRELAND

    Patrick O'Brian wrote more than fifteen books that follow the adventures of two friends named Jack Aubrey and Stephen Maturin in the Napoleonic Wars (Stephens 330). In The Thirteen-Gun Salute (1989), O'Brian said that Jack Aubrey was normally not aggressive, but was rather, "a cheerful, sanguine, friendly, good-natured creature, severe only in the event of bad seamanship--but when he was on a Frenchman's deck, sword in hand, he felt a wild and savage joy, a fullness of being, like no other, and he remembered every detail of blows given or received...with the most vivid clarity" (Stephens 331).

Patrick O'Brian Bibliography

Stephens, Aarti D. "Patrick O'Bian." Contemporary Authors, Volume 144, Ed. Donna Olendorf. Detroit, MI: Gale Research, 1994, 329-332.

Dylan Thomas (1914-1953) WALES

    In "The Comic Welshman in British Literature from Shakespeare to Dylan Thomas," Christie Davies does a humorous comparative study of the writings of Dylan Thomas with the writings of other Welsh authors. In "Ethnic Jokes and Social Change: The Case of the Welsh," Davies does a historical study of the comic images of the Welsh in their jokes and in the way their ethnic scripts are used by Welsh humorists. Both of these Davies pieces serve as a frame for analyzing Dylan Thomas's humor (Davies 1118). Davies considers Dylan Thomas to be, "Wales's national humorist in the same sense that Jaroslav Hašek

represents the Czechs, Miguel de Cervantes the Spaniards, or François Rabelais the French."
Davies considers Dylan Thomas's humor to be secure and cozy, sometimes even
sentimental, but he also thinks that Thomas had a, "profound and uneasy sense of the
mortality and mutability of all things" (Davies Encyclopedia 1117). Dylan Thomas was
obsessed with words. He enjoyed their sounds and rhythms, and he especially enjoyed the
richness of their multiple meanings, a richness which allowed Thomas to write an illogical
and revolutionary syntax. But this creative syntax, together with his cosmic and sexual
imagery made Thomas's early poetry very difficult to comprehend (Holborn 373). At
Swansea Grammar School, Thomas collaborated with a friend by the name of Daniel Jones.
Jones later became Thomas's editor. As a youth, Thomas wrote numerous childhood
poems, and about two hundred of these poems survive in the Dylan Thomas collection at
the Harry Ransom Humanities Research Center of the University of Texas. Many of these
poems were written in collaboration with Daniel Jones. Paul Ferris says that Daniel Jones
would often write the odd-numbered lines of the poem and Dylan Thomas would write the
even-numbered lines (Holborn 373).

In a personal letter dated April 28, 1994, Brian Lile indicated that all of the short
stories in Dylan Thomas's Collected Stories are humorous; however, he feels that the best
is the one entitled "A Story," which is also known as "The Outing." Walter Whittaker
would agree, stating that, "Throughout his prose, and, if one becomes sensitive to it, in his
poetry too, runs an almost compulsive streak of humor. Perhaps it springs from his
obsession with language--his delight in the sound of words and in the coining of new
combinations of words, creating new meanings for words, and even developing his own
special vocabulary" (Whittaker 349).

The linguist Samuel Levin has studied semantic violations in Dylan Thomas's
poetry, and says that these violations form strange and interesting aesthetic images. In
Thomas's expression "a grief ago," for example, "Ago is a word ordinarily used with words
specified by some temporal semantic feature: a week ago, an hour ago, a month ago, a
century ago, but not *a table ago, *a dream ago, *a mother ago. When Thomas used the
word grief with ago he was adding a durational-time feature to grief for poetic effect"
(Fromkin and Rodman 178). Thomas uses many such semantic clashes. In one poem, he
sets up a pattern by writing about the October wind, which has "frosty fingers." This wind
punishes his hair." Thomas then continues by saying that this is especially tru when the
October wind, which now has "fists of turnips" punishes the land (Brooke-Rose 197).

Leslie Whittaker feels that Dylan Thomas's writing has a child-like exuberance and
delight in life. Whittaker feels that Thomas reflects the tradition of the Welsh to enjoy the
exuberance of language. Thomas's words become, "pressed together to form a torrent of
sound with multiple levels of meaning which, like good wine, excites the mind as well as
delights the palate." Thomas has written, "glorious examples of puns, double entendres,
or just plain absurdities which challenge one's intellect and tickle one's comic fancy"
(Whittaker 349). Much of the humor of Dylan Thomas's stories come from the setting of
these stories in the peaceful frontier town of Swansea, Wales. Dylan Thomas had spent his
childhood, "in the safe and secure ambiguity of a predominantly English-speaking,
industrial town with a Welsh-speaking, rural hinterland where his relatives lived and from
which his ancestors came (Davies Encyclopedia 1114). Thomas's Memories of Christmas
is especially good at capturing the sights and sounds of Swansea. One Christmas at
Swansea was so much like another that Thomas, in trying to recall his Christmases as a
youth says, "I can never remember whether it snowed for six days and six nights when I
was twelve or whether it snowed for twelve days and twelve nights when I was six." What
Thomas does remember in vivid detail is that he and his friends, "went padding through
the streets, leaving huge deep footprints in the snow." He said that he, "bet people will
think there's been hippos," and then asks, "What would you do if you saw a hippo coming

down Terrace Road?" Then he asks, "What would you do if you saw two hippos?" When they passed by Mr. Daniel's house, he suggested that they should, "post Mr. Daniel a snowball through his letterbox," then he suggested further that they should write, "Mr. Daniel looks like a Spaniel" in the snow on his lawn. Davies remarks that Thomas's childhood comedies have a gentle and safe quality about them (Davies Encyclopedia 1116).

Dylan Thomas utilized many Welsh comic devices, such as the mixing of formal, solemn, pretentious speech with the coarse demotic South-Welsh vernacular. In typical Welsh fashion, Dylan Thomas would often insert a short, sometimes bizarre, passage that subverts conventional propriety and morality, into his apparently mundane account of everyday life. Another Welsh comic device which Thomas used was called "winding someone up," a device by which Thomas would develop a deceit for its own sake. This device was especially effective when used on senior people, or on people of power and prestige (Davies 1115). Another Welsh comic script which Dylan Thomas uses is to develop the beer-swilling South Walsian character who is crude and blunt. He is often presumptuous in his "matey egalitarianism." Davies notes that this type of character is now more commonly associated with Australia than with Wales, but he adds that even today, "in Wales as in Australia a subsequent brazen claim of intimate acquaintanceship with the puked-on is a standard part of the comedy" (Davies Encyclopedia 1116).

Dylan Thomas's autobiography, which is entitled Portrait of the Artist as a Young Dog (1940), is Thomas's first volume of humorous short stories (Davies Encyclopedia 1113). Its provocative chapter titles include "The Peaches," "A Visit to Grandpa's," "Patricia, Edith, and Arnold," "The Fight," "Extraordinary Little Cough," "Just Like Little Dogs," "Where Tawe Flows," "Who Do You Wish Was With Us?" "Old Garbo," and "One Warm Saturday" (Holborn 371). In Portrait of the Artist, Thomas claimed in a letter written to Vernon Watkins that he "kept the flippant title for--as the publishers advised-- money making reasons." Thomas claims that the title is not a parody of James Joyce's A Portrait of the Artist as a Young Man, but he did admit that he had been greatly influenced by Joyce's Dubliners. According to Paul Ferris, Portrait of the Artist, has, "the atmosphere of schoolboy smut and practical jokes and poetry is evoked with lingering accuracy but with nothing more." "One Warm Saturday" is the title of one of the stories in the collection. This story contains the same type of disillusionment that can be found in Joyce's "Araby." The protagonist falls in love with a girl in a park, and drinks with her and with her friends in a bar, and afterwards the entire group goes to the girl's apartment, but the protagonist loses his way in the hall after going to the bathroom, and never does find the apartment again (Holborn 375).

Deaths and Entrances (1946) is a collection of poetry which includes a poem entitled "A Refusal to Mourn the Death, by Fire, of a Child in London." The rich ambiguity of this poem is especially obvious in the last line, "After the first death, there is no other." William Tindall says that statements like this can be taken, "either as a pledge of eternal life or as a realization that death is death, that one is dead forever--or both" (Holborn 376).

"Do not go gentle into that good night" appears in Country Sleep (1952). The poem was written during an illness of Dylan Thomas's father, and it anticipates his father's death, as the son exhorts the father to affirm life in his dying (Holborn 376). Dylan Thomas held ambivalent feelings toward his father, but this late poem is written in a feeling of love and empathy, and he once commented about his father that, "A broader-minded man I have never known" (Holborn 373). The humorous stories that were written for Quite Early One Morning (1954) provided Dylan Thomas with the comic skills which he later used to write his comic radio masterpiece, Under Milk Wood. In The Growth of Milk Wood, Douglas Cleverdon tells how Dylan Thomas's most famous humorous work, Under Milk Wood, was crafted (Davies 1118). Under Milk Wood takes place in the small Welsh village of

Llareggub, which is a backwards spelling of "Bugger All." This joke illustrates, "the sly, humorous pleasure that the Welsh take in subtly winding up visitors through comic deception" (Davies Encyclopedia 1114). Dylan Thomas was skilled at the use of comic vernacular language. Consider, "Hush, the babies are sleeping, the farmers, the fishers, the tradesmen and pensioners, cobbler, school-teacher, postman and publican, the undertaker and the fancy woman, drunkard, dressmaker, preacher, policeman, the webfoot cocklewomen and the tidy wives." Here Thomas contrasts the antithetical sexual categories of "the fancy women" and "the tidy wives" (Davies Encyclopedia 1114). The "fancy women" were the women with whom someone was carrying on an affair on the side, and the "tidy wives" were the respectable, proper, and substantial women of the village. These tidy wives, "are, of course, also the censorious upholders of local morality and propriety," and they later become part of the nightmare of Mister Waldo, who is the rabbitcatcher, the barber, the herbalist, the catdoctor, and the quack (Davies Encyclopedia 1115).

Dylan Thomas described his Under Milk Wood, A Play for Voices (1954) as "prose with high blood pressure." The characters in this radio drama are Dickensian. They are flat and stereotyped, and they are drawn with energy and color rather than with subtlety. They are humours characters. There is the blind old Captain Cat, who dreams about his love Rosie Probert who is now dead. There are Miss Price and Mr. Edwards who love each other passionately even though they will never meet. There is Mrs. Ogmore-Pritchard, who nags both of her long-suffering husbands, even though they are both now deceased (Kershner 522). There is Dai Bread, who has two wives, both living and both amicable. There is Cherry Owen, the town drunkard. There is Mr. Waldo, the town rake. There is the Reverand Eli Jenkins who is both a poet and a preacher. There is "Lord Cut-Glass" who has been driven mad by time. And there is Polly Garter, the unpaid town prostitute. Except for the obvious sexuality, it is only the humor and the art that is essential in their lives. William Arrowsmith called the play, "a massive rutting masque for the listening ear" (Kershner 523).

A Prospect of the Sea (1955), and Adventures in the Skin Trade (1955) were two books of humorous writings which were published after Dylan Thomas's early death in 1953 (Davies Encyclopedia 1114). Thomas's. The Complete Recorded Stories and Humorous Essays (1972) contains such provocative titles as, "A Child's Christmas in Wales," "Quite Early One Morning," "Reminiscences of Childhood," "Return to Swansea," "A Few Words of That Kind," "A Visit to America," "An Irreverent Introduction," "A Visit to Grandpa's," "Holiday Memory," "A Story," and "Laugharne" (Holborn 372).

In an article entitled "The Writer as Drunk," Anthony Burgess compares the writing of Brendan Behan with that of Dylan Thomas. He concludes that when this comparison is made, Dylan Thomas clearly emerges as the winner in terms of creativity and style (Hutchings 127). When considering such poems as "Altarwise by Owl-light," and "And death shall have no dominion" critics often ask if Dylan Thomas is a religious writer, but this is too easy an answer. Dylan Thomas is a paradox. R. B. Kershner, Jr. said, "He has been called a pagan, a mystic, and a humanistic agnostic; his God has been identified with Nature, Sex, Love, Process, the Life Force, and with Thomas himself" (Holborn 375).

Dylan Thomas Bibliography

Brooke-Rose, Christine. A Grammar of Metaphor. New York, NY: Secker and Warburg, 1958.
Burgess, Anthony. "The Writer as Drunk." Urgent Copy: Literary Studies. London, England: Jonathan Cape, 1968, 98-102.
Cleverdon, Douglas. The Growth of Milk Wood. London, England: Dent, 1969.
Davies, Christie. "The Comic Welshman in British Literature from Shakespeare to Dylan

Thomas." Papers of the Dylan Thomas Society of Wales. Ed. Gilbert Bennett. Swansea, Wales: Dylan Thomas Society, 1982.

Davies, Christie. "Dylan Thomas." Encyclopedia of British Humorists, Volume II. Ed. Steven H. Gale. New York, NY: Garland, 1996, 1113-1118.

Davies, Christie. "Ethnic Jokes and Social Change: the Case of the Welsh." Immigrants and Minorities 4.1 (1985): 46-63.

Fromkin, Victoria, and Robert Rodman. An Introduction to Language, 3rd Edition. New York, NY: Holt, Rinehart and Winston, 1983.

Holborn, David G. "Dylan Thomas." Contemporary Authors, Volume 120. Detroit, MI: Gale Research, 1987, 371-378.

Hutchings, William. "Brendan Behan." Encyclopedia of British Humorists: Geoffrey Chaucer to John Cleese, Volume 1 A-K. Ed. Steven H. Gale. New York, NY: Garland, 1996, 118-128.

Kershner, R. B., Jr. "Dylan Thomas." Dictionary of Literary Biography, Volume Thirteen: British Dramatists Since World War II. Detroit, MI: Gale, 1982, 519-524.

Lile, Brian. Personal Letter dated April 28, 1994.

Thomas, Dylan. Collected Stories London, England, Dent, 1983.

Thomas, Dylan. The Complete Recorded Stories and Humorous Essays. New York, NY: Caedmon, 1972.

Thomas, Dylan. Portrait of the Artist as a Young Dog. New York, NY: New Directions, 1940.

Whittaker, Walter Leslie. "Welsh Humor through the Mind of Dylan Thomas." WHIMSY 6 (1988): 349.

Marganita Laski (Sarah Russell)(1915-)

Marganita Laski's Love on the Supertax (1944) tells about England in a time of war. It is a satire that assumes the form of a battle determined by class and sex roles. The two sides are represented by a Mayfair debutante on the one hand and an East End communist on the other. "The novel's conflicts between class, gender, and ideology are turned inside-out when a well-mannered working-class is feminized by its passivity while a debutante challenges the patriarchy." Laski satirizes the nostalgia of people like Waugh, whose satire is in the service of nostalgia for the past (Lassner 210).

In Toasted English (1949), Marganita Laski writes about England as a mock utopia in which the caste system is revived. C. J. Rolo praised this novel, saying that it is, "a scorching indictment of a hierarchical society." Rolo further states that the novel is a, "blandly devastating satire [that] will especially regale those well versed in the mores of Miss Laski's natives." Emmet Dedmon adds that the satire which Laski achieved in Toasted English is, "in the tradition of Jonathan Swift, that is to say, literate, enjoyable, and with a purpose" (Locher 105). The Village (1952) is a humorous novel in which two young lovers from different social classes have to contend with the snobbery of their parents. Riley Hughes considers this book to be, "a most perceptive comedy of manners in the English tradition" (Locher 276).

Marganita Laski (Sarah Russell) Bibliography

Lassner, Phyllis. " 'Between the Gaps': Sex, Class and Anarchy in the British Comic Novel of World War II." Look Who's Laughing: Gender and Comedy. Ed. Gail Finney. Amsterdam, Netherlands: Gordon and Breach, 1994, 205-220.

Locher, Frances C. "Marganita Laski." Contemporary Authors, Volume 105. Detroit, MI:

Gale Research, 1982, 276-278.

Lillian Beckwith (Lillian Comber)(1916-) SCOTLAND

The Hills is Lonely (1959) derives its name from a description which Lillian Beckwith received from an isolated Hebridean croft when she advertised for a quiet secluded place in the country: "Surely it's that quiet even the sheeps themselves on the hills is lonely." The Hills is Lonely is, "the hilarious and enchanting story of the extremely unusual rest cure that followed" (Hills back cover). The following dialogue demonstrates the nature of Lillian Beckwith's humor:

> "Come, Morag," said Lachy, pulling out a bottle of whisky from his pocket. "Give us some tots and we'll have a drink."
>
> "What'll we drink to?" someone asked.
>
> "We'll drink to the hope that the rest of the people to die here from now on will have been ailin' for three months or so before they go."
>
> "That's a terrible thing to wish for," I ejaculated. "Surely you yourself would not care to be ill all that time?"
>
> "Indeed but I would," retorted Lachy.
>
> "But why?" I asked.
>
> "Because I know fine how heavy folks are when they die suddenly," said Lachy candidly. "It's no fair on the folks who have to carry when a corpse hasn't lost a bit of weight first. Just look at Ian Moore," he continued, warming to his subject. "Seventeen stone that man was and ill less than a week. It's no right I'm tellin' you. It near killed some of us today the weight of him." (Hills 89)

Some of Beckwith's humor involves wordplay as well as social observation, as in the following dialogue:

> "Bloody fine ducks," Euan agreed blissfully
>
> "Euan!" interposed Morag in tones that shrivelled the half-wit to abjectness.
>
> "What do you feed them on?" I enquired.
>
> "Duck eggs, Missed," the reply came with prompt servility. (Euan had never made up his mind whether to address me as "Miss" or "mistress," but his compromise of "Missed" was, I suppose, as apt a designation as any other for a middle-aged spinster.)
>
> "Duck eggs?" I echoed foolishly. "Where do you get them?"
>
> Euan bestowed on Morag a look that was eloquent with pity. "The ducks lays eggs," he elucidated. "Best Bl-- Best food for ducks, Missed."
>
> "Yes, of course," I agreed wanly, faced with the eternal problem of which came first. (Hills 131)

Lillian Beckwith is a humorous writer. Inside the front cover of her The Hills is Lonely (1959) there is a list of statements which critics had made about her earlier novels. Maurice Wiggin of Sunday Times called The Sea for Breakfast (1961) "hilarious," adding, "I haven't laughed so much since Whisky Galore." The Weekly Scotsman called The Loud Halo (1964), "a sparkling book which could well become a Scottish humorous classic." The Sunday Times describes A Rope-in Case (1968) as, "delightfully and sentimentally drawn." The Oxford Mail describes Lightly Poached (1973) as "a beautiful book," adding that it smelled of earth and sea, carried the atmosphere of the crofts, and forced the reader to 'laugh aloud' " (Hills inside front cover).

The novel Beautiful Just (1975) takes place on the Hebridean island of Bruach, which provides a setting for the enchanting tales about life among the crofters. The novel is rich in incident and humor. The <u>Sunday Times</u> describes it as "hilarious," and the <u>Daily Mirror</u> says it is "absorbing," and that, "its humour is happy, easy, and natural" (<u>Beautiful</u> back cover).

Lillian Beckweth told Ann Evory, "Going to the Hebrides and taking over a croft (a small farm) proved the awakening of a desire to write. Intrigued by the simple way of life and by the toughness and humour of the islanders I felt compelled to record my experiences.... When I am asked for advice by aspiring writers I usually reply 'Put a blank sheet of paper in your typewriter and threaten it with words'" (Evory 132).

Lillian Beckwith (Lilliam Comber)Bibliography

Beckwith, Lillian. <u>The Hills is Lonely</u>, (1959). London, England: Arrow/Hutchinson, 1967.
Beckwith, Lillian. <u>Beautiful Just</u>. London, England: Arrow/Hutchinson, 1975.
Evory, Ann. "Lillian Comber." <u>Contemporary Authors, New Revision Series, Volume 3</u>.
Detroit, MI: Gale Research, 1981, 131-132.

Roald Dahl (1916-1990)

Roald Dahl's wit is frequently wickedly macabre, and his language is sometimes less than genteel. Ken Lawless says that Dahl's, "satiric wit redeems his morality tales from any taint of the merely didactic." In the <u>New Statesman</u>, Naomi Lewis wrote, "These really are moral tales. Go wrong and you get some very peculiar deserts." In Roald Dahl's short stories there is a tension between the humor on the one hand, and the grinning-skull horror on the other hand. This tension is kept alive by the "texture of the language," and by the, "subtle, inevitable tone of the secret moralist." These stores were in fact a form of "truth and consequence" (Lawless 295). Roald Dahl's fiction is bizarre, fantastic, and sometimes even grotesque. In the <u>Saturday Review</u> (20 February, 1960), Granville Hicks says, "his great gift is for telling a macabre incident in such a way that the reader shudders and smiles at the same time" (Grigsby 41). Because Roald Dahl's stories are a blend of the commonplace and the macabre, and because many of these stories appeared first in the <u>New Yorker</u>, Roald Dahl is often compared to the cartoonist Charles Addams. Dahl's "The Great Automatic Grammatisor" is a story about an author with nine starving children who will be guaranteed a "golden contract" if he will agree to put his name on some "mechanically produced drivel" which would be popular because of its mediocrity. The story ends with an ironic plea for artistic integrity, "Give us strength, oh Lord, to let our children starve" (Lawless 294).

In a juvenile story entitled, <u>The Gremlins</u> (1943), which Dahl wrote during World War II, Dahl invented the word and the concept of "gremlin." These gremlins were imps who took delight in creating mechanical problems in fighter planes (Lawless 294). "A Piece of Cake" is one of the stories in <u>Over to You: Ten Stories of Flyers and Flying</u> (1946). This surreal story is about a stunned pilot who has facial injuries and flames around his feet and who is now trying to understand how and why he hurts. He also has to figure out what he must do in order to escape from the burning plane. He must loosen the straps holding him in, and he must crawl out from under the airplane. Another surreal story is about a flier who is lying unconscious in a hospital who is imagining that he is writing jokes on his airplane to entertain the Germans. But then he realizes that the Germans won't be able to understand his jokes, because the jokes are in English. "Madame Rosette" is another story in <u>Over to You</u>. It is about three fliers on leave who arrange with Madame Rosette, a procurer, for a sexual encounter with a shop girl. But then the soldiers have second thoughts, and end up by freeing fourteen young girls that are held in bondage by Madame Rosette. Nona Balakian considers this story to be one of Dahl's most vivid, and adds that "Mr. Dahl has captured [the fliers'] spirit of mad abandon with marvelous subtle insight and genuine humor" (Grigsby 44).

In the New York Times Book Review (8 November, 1953), James Kelly praises the "satirical burlesques" which appear in Someone Like You (1953) (Grigsby 42), and reviewing the same book, Mark West is unhappy that, "Dahl's ironic criticisms of society have received little attention" (Grigsby 42). "Lamb to the Slaughter," one of the stories in Someone Like You is about a wife who, when her husband tries to leave her, strikes him with a frozen leg of lamb and kills him. Of course the police come to investigate the murder, and the wife serves them the leg of lamb, thus disposing of the evidence. As they eat the meat, they ironically comment on how the murder weapon is, "probably right under our very noses," and the wife giggles in the next room. This story illustrates the gender-warfare theme that was pointed out in A. H. Cheyer's article in the Wilson Library Bulletin (February, 1962), where it says, "the stories betray a Thurberesque glee as the author keeps score of skirmishes won and lost in the war between the sexes, in which the combatants employ a variety of ingenious dodges to get the better of their better halves" (Grigsby 45).

"The Wish," another story in Someone Like You, is about a young boy who lets his imagination run wilde. He imagines that the black parts of the carpet in his home are snakes, and that the red parts are hot coals. He tries to cross the carpet by stepping only on the yellow parts, but he falls in the process, and his hand hits a, "glittering mass of black and he gave one piercing cry of terror as it touched." Dahl adds a final touch of irony when he says, "Outside in the sunshine, far away behind the house, the mother was looking for her son" (Grigsby 45). "Mr. Feasey," still another story in Someone Like You, is a satire about Claud and his friend. Claud races dogs, and his friend is a service-station attendant. Together, they develop a scheme for racing a really slow dog over and over in order to raise the betting odds, and then substituting an identical-looking fast dog for the slow dog, and then betting large amounts of money on the fast dog they have substituted. They are successful in deceiving Mr. Feasey, the track operator. The exchange is made and the money is bet. But the bookies are not so stupid, and they refuse to pay when Claud and his Friend's dog wins because they had bet on a different dog. The satiric point which Dahl is making is that, "scheming and chicanery are so rampant in British dog racing that there is no real hope of winning, regardless of one's skill in deception" (Grigsby 45).

Mark West says that like Someone Like You, Kiss Kiss (1960) has, "tightly woven plots, macabre elements, and surprise endings," but unlike Someone Like You, even more of the stories in Kiss Kiss, "focus on tense and unhappy relationships between men and women." In both of these books, Dahl is specializing in the "horror of normality." One of the stories in Kiss Kiss is entitled "Parson's Pleasure." This story is profoundly satiric, and has a surprise ending. "Parson's Pleasure" is about an antique dealer who poses as a parson in order to buy some antique furniture at a reduced price. He discovers a Chippendale chest of drawers in the Rummins's house. In order to buy this priceless piece of furniture at a cheap price, the "parson" pretends that the piece is worthless and that he only wants its legs to attach to another piece of furniture, and the Rummins family says this is fine. When the "parson" goes to his car, Claud and Bert Rummins decide that the chest of drawers is too big to fit in the car, so they demolish the chest of drawers so that the legs can fit in the car easily. The story, which is both entertaining and ironic, satirizes the manipulative antics of antique dealers in particular, and of the upper class in general (Grigsby 46).

Switch Bitch (1974) is a collection of short fiction for adults, and is Roald Dahl's most controversial book. In Danny, The Champion of the World (1975) Claud and his son, Danny, the service-station attendant devise a scheme for poaching from Mr. Victor Hazell's wood where he grows pheasants for Easterners to come out and shoot. Mr. Hazel is a rich and arrogant landowner who manufactures pie and sausage. Claud and the attendant feed some raisins laced with sleeping potion to the pheasants, and carry off the drugged birds by the hundreds (Grigsby 46). In <u>Danny, The Champion of the World</u>, there is the following dialogue:

> "It's peculiar that a bird doesn't topple off its perch as soon as it goes to sleep. After all, if we were sitting on a branch and we went to sleep, we would fall off at once, wouldn't we?"
> "Birds have claws and long toes, dad. I expect they hold on with those."
> "I know that, Danny. But I still don't understand why the toes keep gripping the perch once the bird is asleep. Surely everything goes limp when you fall asleep."

Danny waited for his dad to go on. Then he continued,

> "I was just thinking that if a bird can keep its balance when it's asleep, then surely there isn't any reason why the pills should make it fall down."
> "It's doped. Surely it will fall down if it's doped."
> "Why should we expect it to fall down just because it's in a <u>deeper</u> sleep?"
> Then they heard the thump, thump, thump of falling pheasants (Dahl <u>Danny</u> 143).

Bessie Organ hides the birds under her child in its stroller to take to Claud the next day, but the pheasants wake up and fly away en masse, just as Mr. Hazel is due to drive past the service station. John Grigsby considers this story to be "uproariously humorous." It ends with the birds groggily walking around the station (Grigsby 46).

Although Roald Dahl's humor has always been popular with children, it has not always been accepted by adults. The mean spiritedness in <u>The Twits</u> (1980), the vulgarity in <u>The BFG</u> (1982), and the violence in <u>Matilda</u> (1988) have brought negative reactions from many parents. "Adults are apt to find children's jokes unfunny partly because the adult and the child rarely find themselves in the same emotional situation at the same time" (Wolfenstein 214). In <u>The Twits</u> (1980), Dahl introduces two of the most disgusting characters in children's literature, Mr. and Mrs. Twit. Mr. Twit is repulsive and hairy, and his disgusting beard that he rarely ever washes is a smorgasbord of moldy, rotten, leftover tidbits that have stuck to his whiskers. Children love the idea of an adult whose last priority is cleanliness. Mrs. Twit is really ugly, not because she is covered with hair, but because she is full of "ugly thoughts" (Dahl <u>Twits</u> 9).

> One morning Mrs. Twit took out her glass eye and dropped it into Mr. Twit's mug of beer when he wasn't looking. Mr. Twit sat there drinking the beer slowly. "You're plotting something," Mrs. Twit said. "When I see you starting to plot, I watch you like a wombat." "Oh, do shut up, you old hag," Mr. Twit said. He went on drinking his beer. Suddenly, as Mr. Twit tipped the last drop of beer down his throat, he caught sight of Mrs. Twit's awful glass eye staring up at him from the bottom of the mug. "I told you I was watching you," cackled Mrs. Twit. "I've got eyes everywhere so you'd better be careful." (Dahl <u>Twits</u> 1)

<u>The BFG</u> (1982) is about the night-time fear that most children have. Dahl's heroine, Sophie, cannot get to sleep, and she is snatched from her bed in the middle of the night by an ugly giant. Dahl asks, "If you can think of anything more terrifying than that happening to you in the middle of the night, then let's hear about it" (Dahl <u>BFG</u> 17). Fortunately, however, the "BFG" turns out to be a "Big Friendly Giant" who blows dreams into the bedrooms of children who are asleep. Instead of eating "human beans" as other giants would do, he eats only "icky-poo vegetables" (Dahl <u>BFG</u> 48). In <u>BFG</u>, Dahl blends words and makes fun combinations of sound for the child to pronounce like "scrumplet" (Dahl 38), "fibbling" (Dahl 45), "disgusterous" (Dahl 51), and "figglers" (Dahl 71).

Another interesting trick that Dahl plays is to spell words phonetically, thereby bringing some of the BFG's words down to the same level as the child. Thus, "elephant" becomes "elefunt" (Dahl 41), and "language" becomes "langwitch" (Dahl 44). One of the best passages in The BFG is a conversation between Sophie and the giant about "whizzpoppers" (Dahl 64). When the giant offers Sophie a drink of "frobscottle" she notices that the bubbles in the bottle, "instead of travelling upwards and bursting on the surface, were shooting downwards and bursting at the bottom" (Dahl BFG 64). It is in this way that Sophie learns about the giant's preference for farting instead of burping. According to the giant, "Whizzpopping is a sign of happiness. It is music in our ears" (Dahl BFG 67). The giant soon demonstrates this music to Sophie:

> For a few moments, the Big Friendly Giant stood quite still, and a look of absolute ecstasy began to spread over his long wrinkly face. Then suddenly the heavens opened and he let fly with a series of the loudest and rudest noises Sophie had ever hard in her life. They reverberated around the walls of the cave like thunder...; the force of the explosions actually lifted the enormous giant clear off his feet, like a rocket. (Dahl 68)

Matilda (1988) is about a girl named Matilda who has parents that are abusive and neglectful, and who think of Matilda as, "nothing more than a scab, something you have to put up with until the time comes when you can pick it off and flick it away" (Dahl Matilda 10). When Matilda is old enough to go to school, it is her misfortune to be sent to Crunchem Hall, which is run by a diabolical Headmistress named Miss Trunchbull. Dahl comically describes Miss Trunchbull as having a face like a boiled ham (Dahl 166), fingers like salamis (Dahl 144), and calve muscles as big as grapefruits (Dahl 122). Her comment, "I don't like small people" (Dahl 151) is an understatement. Miss Trunchbull likes to throw the kids out of windows like Frisbees (Dahl 110), and she likes to swing girls around by their pigtails and then let them fly (Dahl 115), and she likes to dangle little boys in the air by holding them up by their ears and proclaiming sarcastically, "I have discovered through long experience...that the ears of small boys are stuck very firmly to their heads" (Dahl 154).

Roald Dahl not only wrote the screenplay for Willy Wonka and the Chocolate Factory (Paramount, 1971), but he also wrote screen plays for two of Ian Fleming's novels, You Only Live Twice (United Artists, 1967), and Chitty Chitty Bang Bang (United Artists, 1968). In a 1997 article entitled "Dahl is Tops...," Richard Brooks sums up some children's authors' popularity polls by saying: "Roald Dahl is the favourite children's author among youngsters and for many adults. Charlie and the Chocolate Factory, BFG, Matilda, and James and the Giant Peach notched up huge numbers of votes in a joint survey by BBC Television and Waterstone's bookshops." Daisy Goodwin, Executive Editor of BBC1's The Bookworm added, "I think Dahl's popularity is that adults get their comeuppance in his books" (Brooks 3).

In The English Short Story, 1945-1980: A Critical History, Dean Baldwin said, "The best of Dahl's stories achieve a degree of palpable horror or grim irony that is at once entertaining and revealing. Explaining the id leads Dahl into fascinating territory, from which he often derives stories of great cleverness" (qtd. in Grigsby 42). Mark West concludes that in all of Dahl's work, "authoritarian figures, social institutions, and societal norms are ridiculed or at least undermined." West feels that Dahl's stories often satirize the conventional norms, institutions, and hierarchies of society from the point of view of an "outsider" (Grigsby 43).

Roald Dahl Bibliography

Baldwin, Dean. "The English Short Story in the Fifties." The English Short Story, 1945-

1980: A Critical History. Ed. Dennis Vannatta. Boston, MA: G. K. Hall, 1985, 34-74.

Brooks, Richard. "Dahl is Tops--but Children's Choice Tales are Unexpected." London Observer (August 31, 1997): 3.

Dahl, Roald. The BFG. New York, NY: Puffin, 1982.

Dahl, Roald. Danny, The Champion of the World. New York, NY: Knopf, 1975.

Dahl, Roald. Matilda. New York, NY: Puffin, 1988.

Dahl, Roald. The Twits. New York, NY: Puffin, 1980.

Grigsby, John L. "Roald Dahl." Dictionary of Literary Biography, Volume One Hundred Thirty-Nine: British Short-Fiction Writers, 1945-1980. Ed. Dean Baldwin. Detroit, MI: Gale, 1994, 40-48.

Lawless, Ken. "Roald Dahl." Encyclopedia of British Humorists, Volume I. Ed. Steven H. Gale. New York, NY: Garland, 1996, 293-296.

West, Mark. Roald Dahl. New York, NY: Twayne, 1992.

Wolfenstein, Martha. Children's Humor: A Psychological Analysis. Glencoe, IL: Free Press, 1954.

Gavin Ewart (1916-1995)

A reviewer for the Times Literary Supplement said that what makes Gavin Ewart different from other writers is that he, "isn't content with satirical pastiche or parody. He has a strong, gamey talent of his own, much concerned with the disputed territory that lies between things-as-they-are, and things-as-they-might-be, and things-as-people-say-they-are." For example, in "The Gentle Sex," Gavin ironically develops a situation in which a group of Ulster Defence Association women beat a political opponent to death in Belfast, Northern Ireland (Dear 117). Peter Reading says that Gavin Ewart had a reputation for having reintroduced an "unabashed sexual relish" to British poetry, and said further that he was, "one of the most original and influential seriocomic writers of verse in the country" (Reading 111). Ewart's poetry was light and often sexy. It has a "gentle and unpretentious wisdom", and some of his rhymes were "ingenious." Reading describes Ewart's "Officers' Mess" as funny social satire, and his "When a Beau Goes In" as "moving, light," and "elegiac" (Reading 112).

Just after Gavin Ewart's seventeenth birthday, he published his first poem. It was a long satire entitled "Phallus in Wonderland," and was published by Geoffrey Grigson in New Verse (Reading 111). This was a poem in which Ewart used word play and allusiveness to be both irreverent and sexual. Ewart often adopted the styles and mannerisms of other poets, sometimes just for parody, sometimes just as a tribute, but usually for both parody and tribute (Bennett 346). The writers who underwent his "high-spirited reworkings" include John Betjeman, Robert Browning, John Bunyan, Lord Byron, Thomas Hardy, Rudyard Kipling, Philip Larkin, Henry Wadsworth Longfellow, Samuel Pepys, Alfred, Lord Tennyson, Oscar Wilde, William Wordsworth, and Sir Thomas Wyatt. Ewart's parody of Wordsworth is written in the manner of Ogden Nash. His parody of Longfellow is called "The Meeting," and is written in the same trochaic tetrameter that "Hiawatha" is written. Ewart considered this to be the most boring of all meters:

> In the long and boring meeting,
> in the hot and boring meeting,
> there was shouting by the Chairman,
> bullying almost by the Chairman,
> people rose on points of order,
> caused chaos and points of order....

Ewart's parody continues in this manner for fifty-four more lines. Ewart's parody of Oscar Wilde's "The Importance of Being Earnest" is summed up in a series of nine limericks. John Bunyan's "The Pilgrim's Progress" has a slangy precis in which Christian is referred to as "Chris." Ewart was playful in his non-parodies as well. His "Love in a Valley" is composed entirely in Los Angeles Valley Girl "Valspeak." Every line of Ewart's forty-one-line poem entitled "The Owl Writes a Detective Story" ends with "who." Ewart also contributed to the genre the "bawdy limerick," and to the genre of the "semantic limerick," a form in which definitions taken from the Oxford English Dictionary are substituted for everyday words. Ewart also wrote Clerihews, and he credits Chambers Dictionary for giving what he considers to be the best short definition of the clerihew: "a jingle in two short couplets purporting to quintessentialise the life and character of some notable person" (Bennett 347).

In Pleasures of the Flesh (1966), Ewart has an almost Whitmanesque tone as he joyfully embraces his lust for life: "A small talent, like a small penis, / Should not be hidden lightly under a bushel, / But shine in use, or exhibitionism. / Otherwise how should one know it was there?" (Dear 117). Peter Reading says that the humorous, informal, and fantastic tone of Pleasures of the Flesh is established in "Anti-poem," the first poem in the collection (Reading 112). He furthermore considers the collection to establish the jokey, sad, serious, and compassionate tones of his future works (Reading 113). About Ewart's erotic images, Alan Brownjohn wrote in Encounter, that, "a point often forgotten...is that under the often exuberantly Rabelaisian surfaces, or between the elaborate jokes, there is a committed seriousness" (Dear 118). Ewart uses satire to express his concerns about urban social conditions and morés in The Deceptive Grin of the Gravel Porters (1968). "There are ludic, slightly Joycean, transformations of language through spelling or other irregularities." In addition, there are, "fragmented, seemingly unconnected lines put together like slogans." In Ewart's writing, as in Joyce's writing, "there is the funny, the trivial, the sad, and the thoughtful" (Reading 113).

Ewart's "So-Called Sonnets" first start appearing in The Gavin Ewart Show (1971). These "Sonnets," which Reading calls "lucubrations," are very free and informal, except that they have all been divided into octave and sestet sections. Peter Reading says that Ewart's An Imaginary Love Affair (1974) contains "charming, erotic," and "outré" hymns and lovers complaints (Reading 113). One of the sections in Or Where a Young Penguin Lies Screaming contains some inventive, curious, and comic linguistic games, such as the one in which Ballocky Bill the Sailor" is converted into formal, archaic, and pretentious phrases (Reading 114). Ewart attributes this idea of, "semantic poetry" to Stefan Themerson's novel, Bayamus (Reading 114). Be My Guest (1975) contains a number of playful parody-translations of Horatian odes, in which Ewart refuses to alter the original word order. The resulting translations have, "an amusing metamorphosed linguistic quality." Also in Be My Guest is, "The Larkin Automatic Car Wash," which parodies Larkin's "The Whitsun Weddings" by using the same stanza form as the Larkin poem (Reading 113).

The final poem in Ewart's collection of poems entitled All My Little Ones (1978), expresses the impact that Ewart's poetry might have on future generations and then says, "They'll say (if I'm lucky): 'He wrote some silly poems, and some of them were funny" (Reading 111). It was in All My Little Ones that Ewart wrote, "The world's a horrific enigma, / it's serious and sad--/ it could be a good sense of humour / that stops us [from] going mad" (Bennett 348). Robert Nye said that The Collected Ewart, 1933-1980 (1980) is witty, clever, and coarse (Dear 118). Stephen Spender considers Gavin Ewart's writing to be "compulsively readable." On the back cover to The Collected Ewart, Spender said that Ewart was able, "from a rather bitter isolation [to make] devastatingly funny comments on contemporary manners" (Ewart back cover). More Little Ones (1982) is a collection of the, "little thoughts that pass through the poet's mind" during his everyday activities. These ideas are light, and Ewart says that sometimes they turn out as silly. But he adds that, "sometimes (I think) [they have] poetic merit." Ewart has always been an advocate of lightness, and his poems are mostly funny, erotic, thoughtful, and trivial. Some are written as haikus, others as limericks, still others as Clerihews, or one-liners (Reading 114).

The title of The Ewart Quarto (1984) is an allusion to The Porter Folio (1969) by Gavin Ewart's friend, Peter Porter. It also alludes to the fact that all of the poems in the Ewart Quarto had appeared earlier in Quarto literary magazine, which consists entirely of light occasional verse (Reading 114). Robert Nye says that Ewart's Penultimate Poems (1989) is, "plenty of good filthy fun." Philip Larkin was thinking about The New Ewart (1982) when he wrote in the Quarto (May, 1982) that, "the most remarkable phenomenon of the English poetic scene during the last ten years has been the advent, or perhaps I should say the irruption, of Gavin Ewart (Reading 116).

Gavin Ewart Bibliography

Bennett, Bruce. "Gavin Ewart." Encyclopedia of British Humorists, Volume I. Ed. Steven H. Gale. New York, NY: Garland, 1996, 345-349.

Bennett, Bruce. "From Rueful to Raucous." New York Times Book Review. (August 17, 1986): 26.

Dear, Pamela S., ed. "Gavin (Buchanan) Ewart." Contemporary Authors, New Revision Series, Volume 46 (1995): 116-119.

Ewart, Gavin. Alphabet Soup. Oxford, England: Sycamore Press, 1971.

Ewart, Gavin, ed. The Batsford Book of Light Verse for Children. London, England: Batsford, 1978.

Ewart, Gavin. The Collected Ewart, 1933-1980. London, England: Hutchinson, 1980.

Ewart, Gavin. E. C. Bentley, The Complete Clerihews of E. Clerihew Bentley. Oxford, England: Oxford University Press, 1981.

Ewart, Gavin. No Fool Like an Old Fool. London, England: Victor Gollancz, 1976.

Ewart, Gavin, ed. Other People's Clerihews. Oxford, England: Oxford University Press, 1983.

Reading, Peter. "Gavin Ewart." Dictionary of Literary Biography, Poets of Great Britain and Ireland Since 1960, Volume 40. Ed. Vincent B. Sherry. Detroit, MI: Jr. Bruccoli Clark/Gale Research, 1985, 110-116.

Rubin, Stan Sanvel, ed. "'Witverse': An Interview with Gavin Ewart." Light 2 (1992): 31-34.

James Herriot (né: James Alfred Wight) (1916-1995)

In an interview for Scotsman, James Herriot told William Foster,

> Every day for twenty-five years I told my wife of something funny that had happened and said I was keeping it for the book. She usually said "Yes, dear" to humour me but one day, when I was fifty, she said: "Who are you kidding? Vets of fifty don't write first books." Well that did it. I stormed out and bought some paper and taught myself how to type. (Stanley 196)

James Herriot was born as James Alfred Wight, and he explains to Arturo F. Gonzalez in The Saturday Review how he got his pen name of "James Herriot." "So I was sitting in front of the TV tapping out one of my stories and there was this fellow James Herriot playing such a good game of soccer for Birmingham that I just took his name" (Stanley 195).

Michele Slung says that James Herriot's writing is filled with wry humor, and that the comic characters in his books include James Herriot himself as well as, "a large cast of mostly impassive furry creatures who never for an instant question the devotion they inspire or the havoc they create. Slung says that if James Herriot's Cat Stories today (1994) were to be classified as food it would have to be gingersnaps, because of their homeyness with just a hint of bite (Slung 12).

All Creatures Great and Small (1972) was an instant best seller. In fact, it made Herriot too famous, as he said to William Foster in Scotsman. "I know I should be grateful when I get as many as twenty or thirty fans waiting after surgery for me to sign their books. I am, of course, but I prefer my privacy" (Stanley 195). Phoebe Adams notes that All Creatures Great and Small is a book about, "recalcitrant cows, sinister pigs, neurotic dogs, Yorkshire weather, and pleasantly demented colleagues. It continues to be one of the funniest and most likable books around" (Stanley 196). One story in All Creatures Great and Small is about Tricky Woo, a pampered and overfed dog which Herriot had to take into his home for several weeks of diet and exercise. Herriot said that before the visit, the dog "had become hugely fat, like a bloated sausage with a leg at each corner" (Stanley 197).

Herriott writes about humorous animals, but he also writes about humorous people. In The Lord God Made Them All (1981), for example, he writes about the, "Old men doggedly doing the things they have always done for the sole reason that they have always done it" (Herriot Lord 29). Lola D. Gillebaard considers this book to contain one of the most memorable anecdotes in all of Herriot's work. It is about a new technique that had been developed for the artificial insemination of cows. Herriot flipped through a pamphlet on the subject, and he considered the process to be a relatively simple one, but he soon found himself fighting off a charging bull "with thrusts and lunges worthy of a fencing master" while wielding an eighteen-inch artificial vagina. About this story, Vic Sussman says, "This is Herriot at his best, the Buster Keaton of veterinary medicine, able to make us laugh, cry, or nod in agreement with some snippet of universal truth" (Stanley 196).

Gwyn Nichols says that James Herriot's sketches of Yorkshire farmers usually assign one feature to a customer. She suggests that this way of representing dialect is effective when the description is short, and especially effective when it is not too flattering (Nichols 7-8). For example, Mr. Pickersgill is characterized primarily by his malapropisms. When his calf was born, it bled from its "biblical cord." His pig went "bezique." Mr. Pickersgill was once charged an "absorbent price," and he believes that "trouble allus comes in cyclones" (Herriot Bright 43-44).

James Herriot (ne: James Alfred Wight) Bibliography

Herriot, James. All Things Bright and Beautiful. New York, NY: Bantam, 1975.
Herriot, James. James Herriot's Cat Stories. New York: NY: St. Martin's Press, 1994.
Herriot, James The Lord God Made Them All. New York, NY: Bantam, 1981.
Nichols, Gwyn. " 'I Don't Get No Respect': Literary Dialect and Respect for Characters." Unpublished Paper. Tempe, AZ: Arizona State University, 1988.
Slung, Michele. "Hairballs and Havoc." The New York Times Book Review (September 11, 1994): 12.
Stanley, Deborah A. "James Herriot." Contemporary Authors, New Revision Series, Volume 40. Detroit, MI: Gale Research, 1993, 194-198.

Anthony Burgess (Joseph Kell, né John Wilson) (1917-1993)

During his lifetime, Anthony Burgess was constantly lauded by his critics and peers for his imagination, his humor, his varied knowledge, and his productivity (Trenz 469). Many of Anthony Burgess's titles are enigmatic. Consider The Doctor Is Sick (1960), A Clockwork Orange (1962), Here Comes Everybody (1963), The Worm and the Ring (1970), The Land Where the Ice Cream Grows (1979), and But Do Blondes Prefer Gentlemen? Homage to QWERTYUIOP: Selected Journalism, 1978-1985 (1986) (Trenz 468). Geoffrey Aggeler considers Anthony Burgess to be one of the most versatile and prolific present-day masters of black comedy, having published seventeen novels in the twelve years preceding 1969. Burgess is a master at writing satiric farce, and has often been compared with Evelyn Waugh, but Aggeler feels that it is James Joyce who probably influenced him the most (Aggeler 235). William H. Pritchard compared Anthony Burgess with Charles Dickens because of his comic portraitures, adding that, "Crabbe's British acquaintances, such as Talbot and Nabby Adams are rather like Dickensian eccentrics" (Aggeler 236).

Another type of Burgess humor occurs when his lowest characters behave in ways which only high characters should behave. In The Right to an Answer for example, a dope-smuggling, woman-beating hoodlum justifies his life-style by making references to Shakespeare, Francis Bacon, and Graham Greene.

In 1959 Anthony Burgess was living with his wife in Borneo, and while giving a lecture to a classroom full of students he collapsed on the floor. Burgess's doctors said that he had an inoperable brain tumor, and gave Burgess only a year to live at best. Burgess was concerned for his wife's financial well being, so during his "terminal year," which turned out to be much more than a single year, Burgess wrote five novels, The Doctor Is Sick, One Hand Clapping, The Worm and the Ring, The Wanting Seed, and Inside Mr. Enderby (Trenz 470).

A Clockwork Orange (1962) was written after Anthony Burgess had read about American prisons who were using "behaviorist methods" for reforming criminals. These behaviorist methods would limit the subjects freedom of choice so that they could do only "good" things. The writing of A Clockwork Orange was also influenced by Burgess's trip to the Soviet Union where he had encountered a group of rogues called "stilyagi. These marauding thugs maintained some kind of a strange honor code. A third influence on the writing of A Clockwork Orange was the 1943 attack on Burgess's pregnant wife by a group of AWOL American soldiers. This attack sent Lynne to the hospital and caused her to abort her child, a scene which is mirrored in the novel when Alex enters the home of the writer F. Alexander and beats him up and rapes his wife (Trenz 471).

Like James Joyce and Vladimir Nabokov, Anthony Burgess is keenly aware of the auditory value of words; he is especially fond of onomatopoeia. A Clockwork Orange is narrated entirely in an invented language, very rich in onomatopoeic suggestions. Alex, the fifteen-year-old protagonist who narrates the story in a teenage underworld dialect called "nadsat" listens to "the glorious Ninth of Ludwig van" as he says, "Oh, it was gorgeosity and yumyumyum. When it came to the Scherzo I could viddy myself very clear running and running on like very mysterious nogas, carving the whole litso of the creeching world with my cut-throat britva" (Aggeler 243). This language is called "Nadsat," and it is a combination of Cockney slang and Russian. In Cosmic Satire in the Contemporary Novel, John W. Tilton explains that Burgess had three main reasons for creating "Nadsat."

> To assure the survival of the novel by creating a slang idiom for Alex that would not grow stale or outmoded as real slang does; to brainwash the reader so that he emerges from the novel with a minimal knowledge of Russian; and to cushion the reader from the violence [by presenting this violence] through a filmy curtain of an alien language that the reader would have to fight through before he could get to the violence. (Trenz 471)

Geoffrey Aggeler considers A Clockwork Orange to be a picaresque novel but in the world of an Orwellian nightmare (Aggeler 239). Aggeler considers A Clockwork Orange to be, "probably the most devastating piece of anti-utopian satire since Zamiatin's We. Orwell's most obvious target is the utopian dream suggested by such behavioral psychologists as B. F. Skinner. A Clockwork Orange seems in fact to be a direct refutation of Skinner's Walden Two, a novel which is a blueprint for a utopia in which human problems can be solved by applying the scientific technology of human behavior. Geoffrey Aggeler suggests that A Clockwork Orange is "one of the most devastating pieces of multipronged social satire in recent fiction" (Aggeler 241).

Tristram Foxe is the protagonist in The Wanting Seed (1962), a dystopia in which the world is scourged by blights and animal diseases which reduce the food supply severely. Because the inhabitants are starving they abandon all restraints imposed by society. People are murdered and devoured at "dining clubs." These cannibal feasts are often followed by heterosexual orgies, "in the ruddy light of the fat-spitting fires." The cannibal meat is placed into tin cans, which are opened before the dinner is served, because there is a widely held belief that canning makes cannibalism a "relatively civilized affair." One soldier says to Tristram, "It makes all the difference if you get it out of a tin" (Aggeler 245).

Geoffrey Aggeler considers The Wanting Seed to be a "magnificent black comedy" which, "encompasses far more than either Orwell or Huxley do in their famous dystopias." Furthermore, Burgess is "far more entertaining." The Wanting Seed is full of playful references to his fellow-novelists and other literary figures. According to Aggeler, the only major flaw of The Wanting Seed is that it tends to be, "too entertaining and too witty (Aggeler 247).

Inside Mr. Enderby (1963), written under the pseudonym of Joseph Kell, "opens with a flatulent statement that is repeated, with modifications, frequently thereafter as a kind of gaseous chorus." In fact, all of Burgess's novels are filled with sophisticated examples of word play which are best appreciated when the passages are read aloud (Aggeler 238).

Hillier, the protagonist of Tremer of Intent (1966) is a James-Bond-type character, and in fact, on one level, Tremer of Intent can be viewed as a satiric treatment of the Flemingesque spy novel. Hillier has even more exaggerated feats of appetite than does James Bond, as demonstrated by Hillier's eating contest with the super-villain Theodorescu. Hillier's greatest sin is that he refuses to serve either God or "Notgod." "If we're going to save the world," said Hillier, "we shall have to use unorthodox doctrines as well as unorthodox methods. Don't you think we'd all rather see devil-worship than bland neutrality?" (Aggeler 250). Geoffrey Aggeler considers Tremer of Intent to be a, "marvelously entertaining book, full of Burgess's wit and linguistic dexterity." But Aggeler must add that he does not find the book totally convincing (Aggeler 251).

The Clockwork Testament, or Enderby's End (1974) made it clear that the frumpy poet by the name of F. X. Enderby was becoming a mouthpiece for Burgess himself, "His comic escapades palliate for Burgess his own unhappy ventures." The autobiographical nature of the character becomes so pronounced that when Burgess is diagnosed as having a brain tumor, Enderby follows suit by going completely mad, by losing his memory, and by appropriating the name of Piggy Hogg (Trenz 470).

Geoffrey Aggeler considers the historical romance entitled Nothing Like the Sun (1975) to be one of Burgess's most entertaining novels. Part of this novel seems to have been inspired by Stephen Dedalus's discourse on Shakespeare in the ninth chapter of James Joyce's Ulysses. William Shakespeare is described as a man of boundless sexual vitality, only some of which can be channeled into his art. Before he became a writer, Shakespeare was, "a proper young man, ripely pout-mouthed and with a good leg, quiet speech but flowery withal, a fair seller of fine gloves" (qtd. in Aggeler 248).

In The Doctor is Sick, (1979) there is a catalog of great Western philosophers by a London thug, and he reflects, "It was not really surprising to hear such a parade of names from such a person. French criminals would, Edwin knew, quote Racine or Baudelaire in the act of throat-cutting; and Italian mobsters would at least know of Benedetto Croce. It was only the English who failed to see human experience as a totality." In this way Burgess is teasing his readers by playfully reminding them that, "their cultural attainments are shared by the lowliest, most depraved dregs of humanity" (Aggeler 239).

In You've Had Your Time (1990), Burgess entertains his readers with a number of apocryphal anecdotes, one of which is the famous story of how he reviewed one of his own books (Inside Mr. Enderby) in a literary supplement. He was able to do this because he had written the book under a pseudonym, Joseph Kell. Paul Bailey wrote about You've Had Your Time, "underneath the jokes and the would-be Falstaffian warmth of character, I detect a braggadocio" (Trenz 472). John Banville praised Burgess's prose by calling it, "adventurous and demanding, a wonderfully dense and inventive mock-Elizabethan that bobs along on a ceaseless ripple of word-play" (Trenz 473).

Anthony Burgess (Joseph Kell, ne John Wilson) Bibliography

Aggeler, Geoffrey. "The Comic Art of Anthony Burgess." Arizona Quarterly 25 (1969): 234-251.

Burgess, Anthony. Joysprick: An Introduction to the Language of James Joyce. New York, NY: Harcourt, Brace, Jovanovich, 1975.

Tilton, John W. Cosmic Satire in the Contemporary Novel. Lewisburg, PA: Bucknell University Press, 1977.

Trenz, Brandon. "Anthony Burgess." Contemporary Authors, New Revision Series, Volume 46. Detroit, MI: Gale Research, 1995, 467-474.

Albert Vajda (1917-1991)

In "Vajda country," Albert Vajda presented the view that anything is possible. People could grow an extra ear, or an extra limb. They could fly, or crawl fast, or speak like a machine gun, or be numb and dumb. In this way Vajda presented surreal exaggerations that highlighted the truth that he was trying to convey (Kabdebo 1163). Almost all of Vajda's writing was grounded in his own experiences but some of his stories are nevertheless satirical. In "One step forward, two all over the place," Vajda combined biting anticommunist satire with slapstick humor. In How to be a Communist (1960), and in Midsummer Night Dream (1971), he provided witty "Vademecums." Thomas Kabdebo says that Vajda helped to undermine relentless ideologies by ridiculing them relentlessly (Kabdebo 1164). Albert Vajda was going blind when he wrote Lend Me an Eye (1974), a book in which he made fun of his own helplessness and disability. "When you chop up a big bad thing, like blindness, into smaller ones, things will not get worse, they will get better" (Kabdebo 1163).

Albert Vajda Bibliography

Kabdebo, Thomas. "Albert Vajda." Encyclopedia of British Humorists, Volume II. Ed. Steven H. Gale. New York, NY: Garland, 1996, 1163-1164.

Terence Alan (Spike) Milligan (1918-)

In 1951, Spike Milligan, Peter Sellers, Harry Secombe, and Michael Bentine did a radio show called Crazy People. This show later changed its name to "The Goon Show," and was a show for which Spike Milligan was the primary scriptwriter, and which blended satire, and traditional radio comedy into surrealistic absurdity, and which was produced by the British Broadcasting Corporation. This show told the adventures of the "Goons" in their constant defense of the British Empire against the nefarious threats from outside. The show satirized many traditional British ideas. It had a zany comedy format, and a band of sturdy anti-heroes on their anti-epics, and pseudo-quests (Lesniak 317). "The Goon Show became the most popular comedy show in the history of the BBC, and it revolutionized radio comedy (Timpane 765).

Spike Milligan's humor tended to be silly, anarchic, and satirical (Timpane 765). In most of the Goon Shows, a plot is discovered whereby some dastardly villain threatens truth, justice, and the British way of life. The behavior on the Goon Shows is extremely silly. People get their teeth knocked out, or their heads shaved, or they get hit with batter puddings. Or the plot might involve the stealing of a huge Wurlitzer organ in order to set a new land speed record at Daytona Beach. Whatever the complication is, however, the listener knows that the Goon-Show regulars will come to the rescue. And these regulars consist of Eccles, the "original Goon," who is an all-purpose kindly idiot. Then there is Neddie Seagoon, a "true blue British idiot and hero always." And there is Bluebottle, Seagoon's cowardly sidekick, and Miss Minnie Barrister, who is the Spinster of the Parish. In contrast to the good Goons, there is Mr. Grytpype-Thynne, a villain, and Major Denis Bloodnok, the cowardly military idiot. Secombe played Seagoon, who either did or did not solve the mystery, and Sellers and Milligan both took on the various other roles (Timpane 766).

Some of the humor on "The Goon Show" derives from the perversion of homely clichés. "What has become of mother? Dear mother, she was like one of the family," or from the presentation of unacceptable ideas

SEAGOON: How did you get back on board?

BLOODNOK: I was molested by a lobster with a disgusting mind.

Milligan relied on the medium of radio to create outlandish visual images in the hearer's mind. Bluebottle narrates his own actions as follows: "Hurriedly wraps up captain in brown paper parcel labelled 'Explosives' and stuffs him through headquarters letter box. Jumps on to passing dustcart and exits left to buy bowler before the price goes up. Thinks--that wasn't a very big part for Bluebottle" (Timpane 766).

Spike Milligan has written much humorous literature for children, including such books as Silly Verse for Kids (1959), The Bald Twit Lion, with Carol Baker (1968), Badjelly the Witch (1971), Dip the Puppy (1974), Unspun Socks from a Children's Laundry (1981), and Sir Nobunk and the Terrible, Awful, Dreadful, Naughty, Nasty Dragon (1982). Milligan has also written adult books like his autobiography, Adolf Hitler: My Part in His Downfall (1971), and The Looney: An Irish Fantasy (1987). Milligan also published materials from "The Goon Show," such as The Goon Show Scripts (1972), More Goon Show Scripts (1973), Goon Cartoons (1982), and More Goon Cartoons (1983). Spike Milligan writes a kind of "freefall comic fantasy" in which the subconscious mind is freed and given full reign. Milligan's silly humor, "secretes a special venom against the establishment." Milligan satirically targets the army, the church, and even the BBC itself. He especially targets the aristocracy with his "idiot bigwig characters" like Major Bloodnok. Milligan's comedy is "critical comedy." It is comedy, "against bureaucracy, and on the side of human beings." It may show a man shouting gibberish in the face of an authority figure as a way of proving that, "nothing could be as mad as what passes for ordinary living."

And of course John Cleese and the other members of the Monty Python Flying Circus grew up listening to "The Goon Show." Spike Milligan said that "The Goon Show" was a show for people of all ages--especially the Ice Age, the Stone Age, and the Dark Ages (Batts 928).

Terence Alan (Spike) Milligan Bibliography

Batts, John S. "Harry Donald Secombe." Encyclopedia of British Humorists, Volume II. Ed. Steven H. Gale. New York, NY: Garland, 1996, 926-931.
Lesniak, James G., ed. Contemporary Authors,New Revision Series, Volume 33. Detroit, MI: Gale Research, 1991, 316-317.
Milligan, Spike, ed. The Book of Goons. London, England: Robson, 1974.
Milligan, Spike. The Goon Show Scripts. London, England: Woburn, 1972.
Milligan, Spike. More Goon Show Scripts. London, England: Woburn, 1973.
Timpane, John. "Spike Milligan." Encyclopedia of British Humorists, Volume II. Ed. Steven H. Gale. New York, NY: Garland, 1996, 764-770.

Penelope (Ruth) Mortimer (Penelope Dimont, Ann Temple)(1918-)

Siriol Hugh-Jones did a brief survey of wit among England's women authors, and noted the disconcerting comedy in the fiction of Penelope Mortimer and Muriel Spark. He observed that Mortimer's fiction, "can make you laugh heartily in a terrified sort of way" (qtd. in Little 20).

In The Pumpkin Eater (1962) Mrs. Armitage is a sort of caricature of an earth mother, who assumed that "it was sufficient to be alive, and make love, and have children, and behave as well as possible" (qtd. in Little 182). Perhaps Mrs. Armitage knows how many children she has, but the reader is never given a precise number. Even Mrs. Armitage thinks of her children as "kind of a lump sum" (Little 182), and observes that they often "cateracted down the stairs" to meet their father. Mrs. Armitage puzzles a journalist who assumes that such a mother figure as Mrs. Armitage will be opposed to "the bomb." During part of the interview with the journalist, Mrs. Armitage is having a telephone conversation with the husband of her own husband's current mistress. Mrs. Armitage is distressed that the mistress is pregnant, and although she has many children of her own, she says to the journalist "I think any child...any child...would be better off...dead" (Little 183).

The Handyman (1983) is an ironic and suspenseful story about Phyllis Muspratt, a middle-aged woman who suddenly becomes widowed, and who is therefore forced to face the twin challenges of solitude and old age. She meets Fred, a likable man in his fifties, who seems to be chivalrous. Fred begins to call Phyllis "Phil," and this makes her feel competent and attractive. He drinks brandy with her in the late afternoon, and when the bill is presented, Fred suggests with easy charm but disturbing consequences that sex rather than cash would be a good way to settle the account. The Handyman is filled with dark comedy (Draper and Trosky 295).

In the Spectator, Nicholas Coleridge writes that in Queen Elizabeth: A Portrait of the Queen Mother (1986), "the Queen Mother's career is deftly and wittily rehashed" (Draper and Trosky 295).

Penelope (Ruth) Mortimer (Penelope Dimont, Ann Temple) Bibliography

Draper, James P., and Susan M. Trosky. "Penelope Mortimer." Contemporary Authors,

New Revision Series, Volume 45. Detroit, MI: Gale Research, 1995, 294-296.
Little, Judy. Comedy and the Woman Writer: Woolf, Spark, and Feminism. Lincoln, NE: University of Nebraska Press, 1983.

Muriel Spark (né Muriel Sarah Camberg) (1918-) SCOTLAND

By the age of nine, Muriel Spark conceived of herself as a writer. She would write poetry and invented love letters to herself, and she would leave them where her mother could find them. The satiric and detached tone of Muriel Spark's short stories and her novels distinguished her writings from other fiction of her time (Lindquist 228). Muriel Spark has both religious and aesthetic goals as she writes a kind of cruel black comedy that would make her a "cosmic joker." But Spark also relies on puns. Melvin Maddocks said that Spark combines a technical writing virtuosity with an elegant, acerbic condescending wit that most writers find delightful. Evelyn Waugh said that the recipe of Spark's writing was one part "creamy English charm," and one part "acid wit." Nina King said, "Spark's exquisitely balanced tone proves that the richest comedy is that which explores the darkest themes." Charles Alva Hoyt said that Spark's humor is based on her conception of the novelist as a God-like figure (Hoyt 130). Barbara Grizzuti Harrison says that at heart, Spark is, "a profoundly serious comic writer whose wit advances, never undermines or diminishes, her ideas." And Jean W. Ross said that for Muriel Spark, Satire makes a more lasting impression on readers than does a straight-forward portrayal of what is wrong. Sparks herself said, "I think that a lot of the world's problems should be ridiculed, but ridiculed properly rather than, well wailed over. I do believe in satire as a very, very potent art form" (Lesniak 394).

In a chapter entitled "Satire," Jennifer Randisi indicated that as early as 1944 Muriel Spark had said she had "a satirical cast of mind" (Spark "Poet's House" 48). In 1961 Spark remarked that her conversion to Catholicism gave her, "something to work on as a satirist" (Spark "Conversion" 60), and in 1974 she said, "ridicule is the only honorable weapon we have left" (Kemp 113). Muriel Spark is especially adept at mockery, as a satiric device. In The Comforters, Caroline Rose is the voice of the mocker, a voice of "cynical lucidity," that could "overtake part of her mind." In The Hothouse by the East River, Paul observes that Elsa has become "a mocker." And in Loitering with Intent, it is Fleur Talbot who says, "I was aware of a demon inside me that rejoiced in seeing people as they were, and not only that, but more than ever as they were, and more, and more" (Randisi 16).

Derek Stanford says that much of Muriel Spark's satire is mean-spirited, wrong-minded, and destructive. He says that much of her work is a "polemic against togetherness" as she targets education in The Prime of Miss Jean Brodie, marriage in Territorial Rights, The Takeover, The Bachelors, and The Hothouse by the East River, and the church in The Abbess of Crewe (Stanford 110). Often, however, Spark's satire is meant to attack legitimate evils, such as Richard, the murderer in The Driver's Seat, the appropriately named Georgina Hogg, the beast in The Comforters, the egocentric Patrick Seton, who thinks, "she is mine.... The others were not mine but this one is mine" in The Bachelors, the egocentric Miss Jean Brodie, who says, "Give me a girl at an impressionable age, and she is mine for life" in The Prime of Miss Jean Brodie, the purely evil Sir Quentin in Loitering with Intent, the dangerous Mrs. Pettigrew in Memento Mori, the evil empire builders Lister and the Abbess of Crewe in The Abbess of Crewe, and Dougal Douglas, who is described as "a beast, a grotesque, a chameleon, and a succubus" in The Ballad of Peckham Rye (Randisi 15). Jennifer Randisi says, "Ironically enough, these people are happy." As Grace Gregory tells Anthia in Territorial Rights, "The really professional evil-doers love it.... The unhappy ones are only the guilty amateurs and the neurotics. The pros are in their element" (Randisi 14). Spark is also very conscious of names in her novels. Not only is there the beast in The Comforters named "Georgina Hogg," but there is also Beauty, Trevor Lomas's girlfriend in The Ballad of Peckham Rye. Her name is "Beauty," but Trevor calls her "snake." In Loitering with Intent, Dottie comments on the name of her husband's lover, Gray Mauser, "He's so pathetic, that Gray Mauser!" speaking as if he were a cat (Randisi 15).

Judy Little says that Muriel Spark's comic writing, like that of William Shakespeare's, is concerned with "inversion." However, unlike Shakespeare's comedies, Spark's comedies do not in the end circle back to an affirmation of the old order (Little 99). The festivity which in the comic novels of Virginia Woolf is aristocratic, and meditative, in the comic novels of Muriel Spark is loud, perhaps even impudent. Nevertheless, Spark consistently depicts playful and significant eccentricity in her novels (Little 100).

In his brief survey of wit among English authors, Siriol Hugh-Jones says that Muriel Spark causes a kind of laughter that "freezes in the throat" (Little 20). Because of Muriel Spark's playfulness, Charles Hoyt considers her to be very much like Isak Dinesen, both women being excellent stylists; both being outstanding storytellers; and both having a "superb sense of the grotesque" (Hoyt 130). Hoyt feels that Muriel Spark is a "thoroughly mischievous writer." Hoyt is not referring to the tricks she plays on her characters or upon her readers (which are there). Rather, he is referring to the fact that Spark considers the universe itself to be mischievous. "The cosmos is neither void of all sense, nor is it sentient but preoccupied: it is both aware of individuals and fond of meddling with them for its own amusement. It is, in short, mischievous" (Hoyt 126). Spark's universe reveals its playfulness in "an almost continuous flow of irony," and this irony is just as much related to comedy as it is to tragedy. In addition, Spark's writing contains an, "almost irresponsible impertinence towards everyday reality" (Hoyt 127-128).

John Glavin points out that much of what Muriel Spark writes is revisionist, and that this revisionist tendency started at an early age for Spark. At the age of nine, Spark rewrote Robert Browning's poem, "The Pied Piper." Spark's "revision" of Browning's poem began where Browning had ended and concluded with a happy ending. The Mayor and the Corporation give the Pied Piper the money he was asking for. The Pied Piper cried, "Five thousand guilders. I have won." Everyone rejoiced. In an interview with John Glavin, Muriel Spark said, "I didn't hesitate to improve on Browning, because I didn't want all the children disappearing into the mountain" (Glavin 221). Judy Little suggests that for Muriel Spark's characters "anything is possible." "In Spark's fiction possibility is assured-- in effect, guaranteed--by an absolute, eternal openness that judges and shocks any human effort at easy closure" (Little 187).

Spark's revisions are worked out, "not exclusively, but primarily through women. And at the same time she seems to be offering to feminism a model of discourse that moves out of, and into, joy" (Glavin 239). In describing why she is a Roman Catholic, Spark explains that it is so she will have "a norm to depart from." This is the same way she views literature. When she reads literature, she can always see ways that this literature could be improved. Her prize winning story, "The Seraph and the Zambesi" (1951) is a rewrite of Baudelaire's La Fanfarlo. The Comforters, her first novel, is a revision of The Book of Job in the Bible. Her Robinson (1958), as the title notes, is a rewriting of Robinson Crusoe by Daniel Defoe. In The Hothouse by the East River (1973), Spark rewrites Barrie's Peter Pan, but with sexagenarians, and with New York of the 1960s serving as the Never-Never Land. Spark's revisionist version is about, "a city filled with ghosts who refuse to grow old." The Abbess of Crewe (1974) is a retelling of Watergate in which the infamous tapes are, "transumed into a revisionary conspiracy in a cloistered convent of nuns." The Takeover (1976) is the revised edition of The Golden Bough. And

Territorial Rights (1979) is a revised version of both the Aspern Papers and The Ambassadors by Henry James. John Glavin considers Loitering With Intent to be a brilliant revision of the entire genre of autobiography, especially works by Newman and Cellini. Finally, Spark's The Only Problem (1984) is a second revision of The Book of Job, in which she revises not only the biblical text, but revises her own first novel as well. Glavin notes that Spark's, "assured, joyful, and generous rescripting shares little of the desperate, agonic processes of Harold Bloom's revisions in his The Anxiety of Influence" (Glavin 222-223). The paradoxes developed in Spark's works, even her darkest works, produce "comedy, the recovery of continuity, a fundamental reconnection to all our lost but still abundant sources of meaning and joy," For Spark, the search for Truth seems to require some sort of revision of literary history (Glavin 224). In The Faith and Fiction of Muriel Spark (1982), Ruth Whittaker further investigates the tensions and paradoxes that are part of Spark's writing (Carruthers 1050).

Frederick Karl says that Spark's novels are, "so involved with the eccentric event and the odd personality that they have virtually no content. Spark's novels are a sport, light to the point of froth. She can write about murder, betrayal, deception, and adultery as though these were the norms of a crazy-quilt society" (Karl 126). Spark felt that aggression in literature could be a good thing, and claimed that, "the only effective art of our particular time is the satirical, the harsh, the witty, the ironic and derisive." She adds that, "we have come to a moment in history when we are surrounded on all sides and oppressed by the absurd" (qtd. in Kemp 14). One of Spark's rhetorical devices is the "nevertheless principle," which is based on the overturning of expectations. As Spark herself says, "In fact I approve of the ceremonious accumulation of weather forecasts and barometer-readings that pronounce a fine day, before letting rip on the statement: 'Nevertheless, it's raining.' I find that much of my literary composition is based on the nevertheless idea" (qtd in Kemp 7)(Barreca 133, 136-137).

Patricia Stubbs castigates Spark for, "her refusal to be committed, to solve her fictional situations, for her readiness to abandon all for a jest, for her random satire" (Stubbs 33); however Regina Barreca suggests that Stubbs is evaluating Spark according to men's, not women's, literary criteria (Barreca 141). Peter Kemp comments on the jokes in Spark's writing: "Her books are never simply jokes, though they invariably contain them; they are not eccentric jeux d'esprit, ephemeral and whimsical. Comic, it has to be stressed in any approach to these novels, does not equate with trivial, any more than solemn does with valuable. It is commonplace to describe certain works as deeply serious: the books of Mrs. Spark are deeply funny" (Kemp 8). Regina Barreca adds that the "deeply funny" that Kemp is discussing, "draws on the power of the marginal and the magical" (Barreca 144). Some critics criticize Spark for being overly satirical in her writing. Her response is that "what they think is exaggeration, I think truth" (qtd in Bold 61).

All of Muriel Spark's novels have been written since she converted to Catholicism in 1954, and she feels that Catholicism has provided the norm for her satiric writings. She often portrays her Catholic characters as either ridiculous or sinister, and she writes from an author-omniscient point of view (Little 102). Spark makes a playful connection between God's world and that of the novelist. Derek Stanford has observed, "her world-picture is ours inverted" (Little 103).

The title of The Comforters (1957) is ironic because the book tells about the blundering attempts of the characters to guide each other through, "the excruciating complexities of human relationship which Mrs. Spark understands so well" (Hoyt 132). This irony is sustained throughout the entire novel, but contrasting with the irony, there is a, "curious kind of glee, that of the author revelling in her own craft. Again and again, we get a sense of fun, of exquisite playfulness, in the word-echoes and games, in the mind-reading and the tangle of mystifications" (Hoyt 133). Charles Hoyt considers The

Comforters to be a remarkable first novel, in that it treats excesses ranging from exuberance to flummery, to treachery, to witchcraft, to smuggling, to fanaticism, to thievery, to madness, to magic, to irony, to death (Hoyt 123). Hoyt considers Muriel Spark to be a surrealistic version of Jane Austen, and he supports this theory with evidence from The Comforters. In this novel there is an obnoxious woman who everyone wishes were somewhere else; this woman "literally disappears." Also in this novel are lovers who send each other identical telegrams reading, "Come immediately something mysterious going on." And Death calls on the telephone, and flying saucers enter through the window, and there are Seraphim who appear at amateur theatricals. "All the events of everyday life shade off imperceptibly into the incredible" (Hoyt 129). In The Comforters, it is Louisa Jepp who is in charge of the movements of her small band of diamond smugglers who ironically are bringing diamonds into the country in religious statues (Rowe 492).

Margaret Rowe feels that Mrs. Georgina Hogg in The Comforters is a satiric representation of the type of Catholic who delayed Spark's own conversion to Catholicism. Sharp reasoned "Good God...if I become a Catholic, will I grow like them?" Mrs. Hogg is beefy and pushy, and she specializes in manipulating people. Near the end of the novel her manipulation causes her own death. Mrs. Hogg and Caroline have traveled to the countryside, and both of them discover the same river there. Caroline, who is a good swimmer, tells Mrs. Hogg to clasp her shoulder, "but the woman in her extremity was intent on Caroline's throat." In the struggle, Caroline is rescued, but Mrs. Hogg drowns (Spark 492). John Glavin suggests that male endings have a great deal more closure than do female endings, and he feels that in this regard, The Comforters clearly has a female ending. This ending "registers with admirable panache" more than a single possible conclusion. After Laurence has snooped around Caroline's flat, he writes a letter which indicates her failings, thereby affirming his own centrality both as lover and as interpreter. Realizing that this letter does not adequately "express his objections," he tears it up into small pieces, and scatters the pieces over Hamstead Heath. Glavin notes that this is a symbolic gesture of masculine control over language. But at this point, Spark, as female novelist, intervenes in a surprising swerve that "revises the Parable of the Sower." This is the conclusion of the novel (Glavin 236). "He saw the bits of paper come to rest, some on the scrubby ground, some among the deep marsh weeds, and one piece on a thorn-bush: and he did not then foresee his later wonder, with a curious rejoicing, how the letter had got into the book" (Comforters 224).

In The Comforters the satire comes from two directions. One of Spark's characters is able to overhear certain passages of the novel as they are being typed. When she becomes aware that she herself is a character in this novel, she becomes critical of its author. "The Typing Ghost has not recorded any lively details about this hospital ward. The reason is that the author doesn't know how to describe a hospital ward. This interlude in my life is not part of the book in consequence." Just as the character in the novel complains about the author, the author, in turn complains about the character. "It was by making exasperating remarks like this that Caroline Rose continued to interfere with the book." Jennifer Randisi notes, then, that Caroline both controls the satire of the novel and is controlled by the satire. "Both character and novelist are satirists" (Randisi 16). About The Comforters, Margaret Willey says that Spark's characters, "teeter on the brink of delusion, retreating from orthodoxy into eccentric extremes of quasi-religious experience satirized with the wicked acuteness with which she later pillories spiritualism in The Bachelors, focussing on the trial of a medium for fraud" (Lesniak 393).

The Bachelors (1960) opens in the following way: "Daylight was appearing over London, the great city of bachelors. Half-pint bottles began to be stood on the doorsteps of houses containing single apartments from Hampstead Heath to Greenwich Park, and from Winstead Flats to Putney Heath; but especially in Hampstead, especially in Kensington" (qtd. in Bold 48). The bachelors in this novel are overwhelmed with triviality, as they discuss the price of frozen peas, or exchange cooking tips like how to make cod taste like halibut. The Bachelors illustrates that when they are outside of their professional City lives, men's lives tend to be banal and rootless (Bold 48). The Bachelors is about a cast of characters each of which is unstable and flawed. There is an epileptic. There is a Catholic who wants to become a Priest because he is unable to have a lasting relationship with a woman, and who is afraid of becoming a fussy and lonely old man. He says to himself, "I'm becoming a prying old maid." Then there is the grammar-school master, Ewart Thornton, who is a gossip, a fussbudget, and is even shaped like a woman ("his hips were wide for a man"). Reverend T. W. Socket is a pervert, and Martin Bowles, although he is a successful barrister, is a thirty-five-year-old mother's boy. There is also Mike Garland the transvestite, and Matthew Finch, who feels so guilty about his carnal appetites that he eats onions to repel a girl, and Patrick Seton, whose trial for forgery and false conversion connects all of the other characters. Charles Hoyt describes Seton as a, "Don Juan, with a corresponding deep-seated hatred of women" (Hoyt 138).

Vern Lindquist says that in such short-story collections as The Go-Away Bird with Other Stories (1958), Voices at Play: Stories and Ear-Pieces (1961), Collected Stories I (1967), Bang-bang You're Dead and Other Stories (1982), and The Short Stories of Muriel Spark (1985), there is a power, a wit, and an elegance. There is also a detached and ironic point of view (Lindquist 227). Charles Hoyt says that the longer the short stories are in The Go-Away Bird (1958) the better they are. Hoyt considers the very short stories to be clever, but nothing more. The longer stories, however, succeed because Spark needs room to allow her coincidences to "sprout," for her absurdities to "bloom," and for her gradual ironies to "blossom forth" uncrowded (Hoyt 137). In The Faith and Fiction of Muriel Spark (1982), Ruth Whittaker says that Spark's conversion to Catholicism, "led to a satiric view of the fallen world" (Lindquist 228). Spark's "Daisy Overend" from The Go-Away Bird tells about a girl who has two lovers. One is a political expert, and the other is a poet. Vern Lindquist suggests that this may have been to appeal to both of the sides of Muriel Spark--her literary, and her political side. The narrator finds herself in a room where a buffet has been laid, and she discovers a pair of Daisy's garters lying on the table. Daisy figures out what has happened only when she sees that the guests are having much fun at her expense. The narrator describes the situation. "I remember Daisy as she stood there, not altogether without charm, beside herself. While laughter rebounded like plunging breakers from her mouth, she guided her eyes towards myself and trained on me the missiles of her fury. For a full three minutes Daisy's mouth continued to laugh" (Lindquist 229).

"The Twins" is another story in The Go-Away Bird. This story satirizes the deceptive quality of appearances. At first, the twins seem to be sweet children, but through a series of events they show themselves to be cruel and manipulative, as they orchestrate the actions of their parents for their own amusement. They drive the narrator away, and by the end of the story they have deluded their parents into thinking that the narrator has been inconsiderate, while in truth, she has been the innocent victim of their manipulations (Lindquist 229). In "The Portobello Road" (another short story in The Go-Away Bird) there is a ghost nicknamed "Needle" because she was found murdered in a haystack. George had murdered Needle by stuffing her mouth full of hay, and had buried her in the haystack after she had threatened to tell Kathleen, George's fiancée, about his previous marriage (Lindquist 230). Needle's ghost is sighted on Portobello Road on a number of occasions, and these sightings drive George mad, not because of guilt, but because he mistakenly believes that she has come back to tell Kathleen about his bigamy (Lindquist 231). About the murder, Kathleen, Needle's friend, says, "She was at Confession only the day before she died--wasn't she lucky?" (Carruthers 1047).

Many of the short stories in Voices at Play: Stories and Ear-Pieces (1961) exhibit dramatic irony. "The Dark Glasses" is about a narrator who wears dark glasses to hide her identity as a witness of a murder until the last line: "I think it was then she recognized me." There is also dramatic irony in "A Member of the Family" and in "The Fathers' Daughters." In "A Member of the Family" there is a bizarre twist of the plot as a woman gets her wish to be invited to dinner at her boyfriend's mother's house. She discovers that all of her boyfriend's former lovers are also there, because "he never thinks romantically about any woman who has become like family" (Lindquist 232). "The First Year of My Life" is a humorously autobiographical story in Bang-bang You're Dead and Other Stories (1982). The narrator, like Muriel Spark, was born, "on the first day of the second month of the last year of the First World War, a Friday" (Lindquist 233).

The Prime of Miss Jean Brodie (1961) is set at The Marcia Blaine School for Girls. This is the territory of Miss Jean Brodie, and "the Brodie set," which consists of Monica Douglas, Rose Stanley, Eunice Gardner, Mary Macgregor, Jenny Gray, and Sandy Stranger (Rowe 496). In this novel, Miss Jean Brodie is comically eccentric, but she is also romantically dangerous. Brodie beguiles men in the same way as her girls beguile men. Two of her pupils write a fictitious story about Miss Jean Brodie in which Miss Brodie writes a letter to her lover, the music teacher, rejecting his proposal of marriage. The letter ends, "Allow me, in conclusion, to congratulate you warmly on your sexual intercourse, as well as your singing" (Carruthers 1048). The protagonist in The Prime of Miss Jean Brodie might be the most memorable character in Muriel Spark's fiction. Jean Brodie is a beautiful, vigorous, independent, unmarried protestant feminist. Jean Brodie is involved with two different men during the novel, one of them a painter, Teddy Lloyd, and she has made arrangements for one of her pupils, Rose, to be Teddy Lloyd's mistress. "I am his Muse," said Miss Brodie. "But I have renounced his love in order to dedicate my prime to the young girls in my care. I am his Muse but Rose shall take my place." But much to Jean Brodie's displeasure it is Sandy, not Rose, who actually becomes Teddy's mistress. "Yet all of Teddy's portraits, even those of Sandy, continue to look like Miss Brodie" (Hoyt 140). Jean Brodie is no longer young, but is rather "in her prime." This is her favorite phrase, and it, "resounds through the novel like a battle cry." The novel is about the war between Miss Brodie, an unorthodox teacher in a conservative girls' school, and all of the colleagues and the conventions which surround her. She has a group of supporters who have been her students, one of whom is Sandy Stranger, the novel's anti-heroine who, after absorbing all of Miss Brodie's teachings, betrays Miss Brodie's political leanings to the authorities and causes her to be dismissed. Then Sandy Stranger denies her and becomes a nun. Charles Hoyt considers The Prime of Miss Jean Brodie to be a, "wryly amusing and yet profound" novel (Hoyt 141).

The Girls of Slender Means (1963) is a comedy of manners that satirizes the, "civilized savageries of the May of Teck Club" (Rowe 498). This club is a strange club for young unmarried working girls (Hoyt 142). Some of the humor of this novel is in Muriel Spark's funny and delightful presentation of the speech patterns of young women. "Dorothy could emit, at any hour of the day or night, a waterfall of debutante chatter, which rightly gave the impression that on any occasion between talking, eating and sleeping, she did not think, except in terms of these phrase-ripples of hers: 'Filthy lunch.' 'Thee most gorgeous weddings.' 'He actually raped her, she was amazed.' 'Ghastly film.' 'I'm desperately well, thanks, how are you?'" Hoyt refers to these expressions as "chirpings and flutterings" (Hoyt 143).

Muriel Spark and Derek Stanford had lived in a close and exclusive circle of young bohemians who were incapable of understanding anyone outside of their circle. These young bohemians, "communicated with each other by using a kind of secret instinct." Most of them were unfit for active war service, and many were destined to enter into oblivion in the Soho public houses. Others had some talent but they tended to falter from lack of stamina and take jobs in advertising or publishing, and these people developed a strong dislike for real literary people (Bold 53). In The Girls of Slender Means, Jane sometimes goes to poetry readings at a rented meeting house. At other times she goes to parties to meet the kind of people she has been longing to meet--"young male poets in corduroy trousers and young female poets with waist-length hair, or at least females who typed the poetry and slept with the poets, it was nearly the same thing" (Slender 61). Alan Bold feels that by expressing Jane's eagerness to meet and interact with such people, Muriel Spark is laughing at her own younger self. Spark's depiction of this literary set is a kind of self parody (Bold 53). In The Girls of Slender Means, Spark writes, "Once you admit you can change the object [of a belief], you undermine the whole structure" (Slender 23). Regina Barreca calls this "shifting the ground." It is a device used to, "undermine the valid currency of the dominant ideology," and she feels that it is an important aspect of Spark's narrative discourse (Barreca 142).

Judy Little suggests that many critics take The Mandelbaum Gate (1965) too seriously. Ironically, these same critics then criticize the book for, "not being serious enough" (Little 144). In the novel, Barbara Vaughn says, "Every spinster should be assumed guilty before she is proved innocent; it is only common civility." At night, Joe's daughter Suzi hears something that sounds like cats, and she tells Freddy the next day, in her unidiomatic English that Ramdez, "unflowered and nearly killed Ricky." Suzi is overpowered with laughter when Ricky requests a cushion as they begin a sight-seeing drive (Little 145). Muriel Spark wrote The Mandelbaum Gate after covering the Eichmann trial in Israel as a journalist. Barbara Vaughan in The Mandelbaum Gate has many of the qualities of Muriel Spark, the author. They are both half-Jewish and half-Protestant. They are both Britons, and they have both converted to Roman Catholicism (Rowe 498). Freddy Hamilton's "conversion," on the other hand, is of a different sort (Rowe 498). When he first meets Barbara in Israel, Hamilton is annoyed by the smug way that she quotes the Bible, especially when she quotes passages which criticize his way of life. So when Barbara says, "Being what thou art, lukewarm, neither cold nor hot, thou wilt make me vomit thee out of my mouth," the words cause a dramatic change in Hamilton, a change that forces him to accompany Barbara on her dangerous pilgrimage (Rowe 499). Barbara Vaughan, who is undergoing a personal and religious pilgrimage to Israel, wanders onto the Jordanian side of Jerusalem, although she is partly Jewish. There Barbara finds a diplomatic clerk named Freddy Hamilton, and Barbara finds it humorous that Freddy is so conscious of his mother. Freddy rescues Barbara from a convent where she spends her first night in the Arab section of Jerusalem. Barbara experiences both amusement and admiration for Freddy's "madness," which she also has caught. Freddy is, "flowering in the full irrational norm of the stock she also derived from: un-self-questioning hierarchists, anarchistic imperialists, blood-sporting zoophiles, skeptical believers" (Little 101).

Frederick P. W. McDowell praised The Public Image (1968), a depiction of celebrity life in Rome, as being, "the witty, ironic, and wry development in short compass, of an ethical issue of some importance and significance" (Rowe 500-501). In The Public Image some of Spark's most desperate and defeated characters have adopted some public image, or some stereotype of themselves, and the result is a series of "completely parodic, cardboard quests" (Little 149). Annabel laughs at a "solemn American student of drama" when he scolds a telephone operator about his "priority call." She laughs again when this same student gets sick after a party and expects her to mother him.

> "But I'm sick!" he shouted at her. "I'm sick!"--so that she opened her eyes
> and saw him standing there on the rug, like a toy doll-man, his arms straight
> and sticking out from his sides as if they were made of cotton, filled with
> doll-stuffing and sewn-up. His eyes and mouth seemed completely circular

as he stared in the face of her English callousness. She laughed at him the second and last time. (qtd. in Little 151)

The Driver's Seat (1970) is Spark's harshest book, so harsh that it put the author in the hospital. Such things as the following are cruelly mocked in this novel: "a southern holiday for a desperate office worker, a macrobiotic diet, feminism, therapy for the sex-offender, civil disobedience that jams the metropolitan traffic." Judy Little says that such subjects "hardly deserve the severe beating they get in the novel" (Little 153). Regina Barreca considers Lise in The Driver's Seat to be Muriel Spark's most marginal figure, since she is on the periphery of social acceptability. She has no friends or family; she has no socially prescribed role, except that provided by her employment. She is not able to recognize deviance when she encounters it, since she has little sense of what is normal. In the following dialogue, Lise tries to hide her marginality, and this is ironic because she is unaware that the man she is talking to is also a person who lives on the margins of society:

"You know what Yin is?" he says.

She says, "Well, sort of...but it's only a snack, isn't it?"

"You understand what Yin is?"   "Well, it's a kind of slang, isn't it. You say a thing's a bit too yin...;" plainly she is groping.

"Yin," says Bill, "is the opposite of Yang." (Spark Seat 33)

Lise assumes that Bill is making sense because he's a man. Lise believes she should be able to understand him, so she pretends that she does. "Even the health-food addict appears more in control than Lise because he perceives himself as an authority" (Barreca 142-143). Regina Barreca suggests that the minor characters in Spark's novels "cackle" with the "wit of the hysteric." "They can barely contain their laughter at the absurdity of the universe before them." (Barreca 146). One such figure from The Driver's Seat, "gives out the high, hacking cough-like ancestral laughter of the streets, holding her breasts in her hands to spare them the shake-up" (Seat 176).

Patricia Meyer Spacks sees Not to Disturb (1971) as, "a Bergsonian comedy which maintains a delicate poise" (Rowe 503). Margaret Rowe says that the comic elements in this novel are "vintage Spark" (Rowe 502). Spark's black humor probably reaches its epitome in this novel about a library (Carruthers 1047). Not to Disturb has all of the elements of the gothic novel. There is a sinister house, and a butler, and an imbecile in the attic. Aristocratic intrigue and lightening are also to be found in the novel (Carruthers 1048). The name of "Victor Passerat" the illicit lover in Not to Disturb, "sounds like the successful rodent he is" (Randisi 15).

John Glavin considers The Hothouse by the East River (1973) to be mordant, baleful, and ceaselessly funny. He also considers this to be Spark's "masterfiction," and, "one of the master comicpieces of High Modernism, Finnegans Wake miniaturized, inverted, and feminized" (Glavin 230-231). Muriel Spark says that, "when we are surrounded on all sides and oppressed by the absurd, the rhetoric of our times should persuade us to contemplate the ridiculous nature of the reality before us and teach us to mock it" (qtd. in Kemp 146). Peter Kemp says that this is exactly what Spark did in The Hothouse by the East River. Spark was a master at mocking contemporary absurdities (Kemp 147).

Spark's epigraph in The Abbess of Crewe (1974) is that they "traffic in mockery." In this novel, Hubert's fakes replace Maggie's originals as a way of symbolizing that spiritualism can replace political reality. The Abbess says, "History doesn't work. Here, in the Abbey of Crewe, we have discarded history. We have entered the sphere, dear sisters, of mythology." The Abbess describes this mythology which they have entered as "history garbled," as she explains to Sister Winifrede that, "a good scenario is a garble. A bad one is a bungle. They need not be plausible, only hypnotic, like all good art" (Randisi "Satire" 9). Alexandra in The Abbess of Crewe is a nun, but she is also a self-justified aesthete in this satire about the Watergate scandal. As with the Watergate scandal, there are bugging devices, break-ins, and egomania (Rowe 503). Alexandra contrives to put electronic surveillance bugs throughout her convent in an attempt to gain information that will help her to be "elected" as Abbess (Carruthers 1048). Her opponent in this election is Sister Felicity, who divides her time between fornicating in the bushes, and attempting to democratize the abbey (Rowe 504). Alexandra is "exuberantly immoral." She feeds the nuns pet food; she robs their dowries to buy jewels for the convent's icons; and she recites classical English poetry during the most sacred hours of prayer (Carruthers 1049).

The Takeover (1976) demonstrates the inverted values of festival, as social and economic sabotage are the moving forces behind the comedy (Little 147). In The Takeover: Nancy asks, "How do you know when you're in love?" and Emilio responds, "The traffic improves and the cost of living seems very low" (Spark Takeover 34). Hubert Mallindaine sees himself as "the descendant of Caligula, the Emperor of Rome." He also sees himself as the descendant of "the Benevolent-Malign Diana of the Woods." Margaret Drabble says that the theme of The Takeover is "too large for the book," but then she praises Spark for attempting such an ambitious theme (Rowe 505). "It is certainly a theme that allows Spark scope for her considerable satiric skill, particularly in the treatment of Hubert Mallindaine" (Rowe 505).

In Territorial Rights (1979), Grace Gregory complains that she doesn't understand why the Roman Catholic church doesn't "stick to politics and keep its nose out of morals" (Spark Territorial 236). Margaret Rowe says that the interconnection among the characters of Territorial Rights "gives Spark a wide range of human behavior to satirize" (Rowe 506).

In Loitering with Intent (1981), Spark is satirizing the literary London that she knew during the 1950s (Carruthers 1049). Loitering with Intent begins with an encounter between a girl and a young policeman. The girl, Fleur Talbot, introduces herself as someone who likes going to old graveyards, and as someone who is not intimidated by the approach of a policeman. She is so accustomed to taking the initiative that she simply tells the policeman about her poem, and then she nonchalantly offers him a sandwich (Bold 62). Alan Bold feels that Spark is here presenting the reader with one of her private jokes, and Bold further feels that some of Spark's readers are irritated by her private jokes (Bold 63). In Loitering with Intent, Fleur is something of a sleuth--perhaps even a spy. She takes a top-secret job with Sir Quentin Oliver who belongs to a weird group named the "Autobiographical Association." Bold describes this group as "a kind of literary Alcoholics Anonymous," since the members are all expected to write candid memoirs which will then be hidden away for seventy years to avoid libel action. The members of the "Autobiographical Association" are dreary and banal stereotypes whose lives contain nothing to warrant the writing of memoirs, and Fleur says, "I could have realized these people with my fun and games with their life-stories, while Sir Quentin was destroying them with his needling after frankness." Alan Bold considers the central paradox of this novel to be that by choosing self-revelation as their modus operandi, the members of this club are thereby denying themselves existence. According to Bold, their "frankness produces despair and self-destruction" (Bold 66). Since Loitering with Intent is a novel about someone writing a novel, much of the fun comes from the way that Muriel Spark blurs the boundaries between reality and fiction. Alan Bold says that, "Spark manages to combine humour of a broad, sometimes farcical nature with a searching examination of the artist's freedoms--and responsibilities." He considers the novel to be, "simultaneously funny and marvelously open, in a moral sense" (Bold 64). Loitering with Intent takes place on a warm and sunny Friday, the last day of June in 1950, and Muriel Spark notes that time as a changing point in her life (Bold 56). "One day in the middle of the twentieth century I sat in an old graveyard which had not yet been demolished, in the Kensington area of London, where a young policeman stepped off the path and came over to me" (Bold

56). Elation is the tone of <u>Loitering with Intent</u>, as Fleur Talbot is still able to write entertainingly and profoundly, while at the same time being both a moralist and a comedienne. Fleur is unsentimental about sex. She shocks Dottie, the wife of one of her own lovers, by reacting nonchalantly to Dottie's suspicions that her husband is homosexual (Little 176). The ending of <u>Loitering with Intent</u> is happy and festive, in the tradition of a romantic comedy. Alan Bold considers it to be a, "parable which offers comic optimism as an alternative to existential anguish" (Bold 67). "The last action we see is Fleur kicking a football back to some small boys who are playing; as every man knows, no woman can kick a ball properly, but Fleur kicks this one with 'a chance grace' which she would probably never have managed had she been trying too hard. The moment is like an epiphany--a moment when the commonplace is made radiant" (Bold 68)"

    Margaret Rowe considers <u>Memento Mori</u> (1982) to be a, "very funny and very wise book." It is a story about some men and women who are mostly over the age of seventy, and who are in various stages of physical and/or moral decline. Jean Taylor captures the sadness of the situation when she says, "Being over seventy is like being engaged in a war. All our friends are going or gone and we survive amongst the dead and the dying as on a battlefield." These old people receive phone calls from an unidentified caller, whose identity changes for each hearer, who gives the warning, "Remember you must die" (Rowe 493). This is a surreal threat, because the caller is God, and he is attempting to make the old people aware of their sins. Thus, the novel is funny only in a macabre kind of way. The end of the novel in fact becomes a kind of "danse macabre" as one of the old people remembers the fates of his companions. Lettie Colston had fractures to the skull; Godfrey Colston had hypostatic pneumonia; Charmain Colston had uraemia; Jean Taylor had carcinoma of the cervix; Ronald Sidebottome had carcinoma of the bronchus; Guy Leet had arteriosclerosis; Henry Mortimer a coronary thrombosis (Carruthers 1048). Charles Hoyt considers <u>Memento Mori</u> to be a perfect marriage of wit, irony and fantasy. The plot is surreal, consisting of elbowings and shovings of a bunch of old English men and old English women, who cheat, lust, blackmail, and pester, but since they are getting old they are finding it increasingly difficult to hold their own: "The teapot was too heavy for his quivering fingers and fell from them on to its side, while a leafy brown sea spread from the open lid over the tablecloth and on to Godfrey's trousers." Here there is a mixture of pathos and absurdity which is presented in perfect balance (Hoyt 135). Hoyt considers the characters in <u>Memento Mori</u> to be a "superb collection of grotesques" (Hoyt 136). In <u>Memento Mori</u>, Dottie tells Fleur, the heroine, that Sir Quentin has been killed in a head-on collision, but Fleur's first concerns are for the other people who were involved in the accident. "What about the other car?" she asks, "Anyone hurt?" Dottie responds, "they were killed too." "Thank God he's dead; the man was pure evil" Dottie says, in a matter-of-fact tone that seems to indicate that the lives of the two others had been "sacrificed in a just cause" (Bold 55).

    Like <u>Loitering with Intent</u>, <u>A Far Cry from Kensington</u> (1988) satirizes the literary London that Spark had known in the 1950s (Carruthers 1049). <u>Symposium</u> (1990) is a dark comedy (Lesniak 394). Richard Jenkyns says that in <u>Open to the Public</u> (1997), Spark's crisp, dark wit, and her gift of uniqueness present a distinctive vision of the world that is an, "odd blend of the strange and the ordinary, whimsy and common sense, the straight-faced and the playful." Jenkyns says that Spark's supernatural effects can range from satisfyingly funny to unsettling, or even macabre. Two of the stories in this collection are about ghosts of murdered women. With sardonic coolness, and in a strange blend of the natural and the supernatural, Sparks has one of the ghosts say, "He looked as if he would murder me, and he did." The ghost in the other story said, "With a great joy I recognized what it was I had left behind me, my body lying strangled on the floor" (Jenkyns 18).

    Catharine Hughes says that Spark satirizes humanity's foibles and incongruities from a Catholic perspective. Patricia Stubbs notes that Spark is fascinated with the ways in which an individual varies according to different settings, or different company. Spark, "is able to create multiple ironies, arising from people's connecting and conflicting destinies" (Lesniak 392). David Worcester considers Spark's ridicule to be very close to low burlesque, which he says, "creates a standard below its victim and makes us measure him against the standard." Worcester says that Spark's characters can be considered victims, "only when viewed subjectively within the context of her satire" (Worcester 123). The controlling metaphor in Spark's later novels is the party, the holiday, or the celebration of an overthrow. In fact, parties are scattered throughout these novels. During the dancing and dining; however there are such extracurricular activities as burglary, murder, suicide, or "takeovers." Especially in Spark's later novels, the comedy becomes more satirical in force, as the "tyrannies," and the "ridiculous oppressions of our time" are mocked (Little 148).

Muriel Spark (né Muriel Sarah Camberg) Bibliography

Barreca, Regina. "The Ancestral Laughter of the Streets: Humor in Muriel Spark's Earlier Works." Untamed and Unabashed: Essays on Women and Humor in British Literature. Detroit, MI: Wayne State University Press, 1994, 133-146.

Bold, Alan, ed. Muriel Spark: An Odd Capacity for Vision. New York, NY: Vision/Barnes and Noble, 1984.

Carruthers, Gerard. "Muriel Sarah Spark." Encyclopedia of British Humorists, Volume II. Ed. Steven H. Gale. New York, NY: Garland, 1996, 1046-1050.

Glavin, John. "Muriel Spark's Unknowing Fiction." Last Laughs: Perspectives on Women and Comedy." Ed. Regina Barreca. New York, NY: Gordon and Breach, 1988, 221-242.

Hoyt, Charles Alva. "Muriel Spark: The Surrealist Jane Austen." Contemporary British Novelists. Ed. Charles Shapiro. Carbondale, IL: Southern Illinois University Press, 1965, 125-143.

Jenkyns, Richard. "Review of Muriel Spark's Open to the Public." New York Times Book Review. 26 October, 1997, 18.

Karl, Frederick. The Contemporary English Novel. New York, NY: Farrar, Strauss, and Cudahy, 1962.

Kemp, Peter. Muriel Spark. New York, NY: Barnes and Noble, 1975.

Lesniak, James G., ed. "Muriel Spark." Contemporary Authors, New Revision Series, Volume 36. Detroit, MI: Gale Research, 1992, 390-397.

Lindquist, Vern. "Muriel Spark." British Short-Fiction Writers, 1945-1980, Dictionary of Literary Biography, Volume 139, Ed. Dean Baldwin, 1994, 226-233.

Little, Judy. Comedy and the Woman Writer: Woolf, Spark, and Feminism. Lincoln, NE: University of Nebraska Press, 1983.

Randisi, Jennifer Lynn. "Muriel Spark and Satire." Muriel Spark: An Odd Capacity for Vision. Ed. Alan Bold. London, England: Barnes and Noble, 1984, 132-146.

Randisi, Jennifer Lynn. "Satire." On Her Way Rejoicing: The Fiction of Muriel Spark. Washington, DC: Catholic University of America Press, 1991, 6-18.

Rowe, Margaret Moan. "Muriel Spark." Dictionary of Literary Biography: British Novelists, 1930-1959, Volume 15, Ed. Bernard Oldsey. Detroit, MI: Bruccoli Clark/Gale Research, 1983, 490-507.

Shaw, Valerie. "Fun and Games with Life-Stories." Muriel Spark: An Odd Capacity for Vision. Ed. Alan Bold. New York, NY: Vision/Barnes and Noble, 1984, 44-70.

Spark, Muriel. The Abbess of Crewe. New York, NY: Perigee Books, 1984.

Spark, Muriel. The Bachelors. New York, NY: Perigee Books, 1984.

Spark, Muriel. The Ballad of Peckham Rye. New York, NY: Perigee Books, 1982.
Spark, Muriel. The Comforters. New York, NY: Putnam, 1957.
Spark, Muriel. The Driver's Seat. New York, NY: Putnam, 1970.
Spark, Muriel. The Girls of Slender Means. New York, NY: Alfred Knopf, 1963.
Spark, Muriel. The Hothouse by the East River. New York, NY: Penguin, 1977.
Spark, Muriel. Loitering with Intent. New York, NY: Perigee Books, 1982.
Spark, Muriel. The Mandelbaum Gate. New York, NY: Alfred A. Knopf, 1965.
Spark, Muriel. Memento Mori. New York, NY: Perigee Books, 1982.
Spark, Muriel. "My Conversion." Twentieth Century 170 (1961): 60.
Spark, Muriel. Not to Disturb. New York, NY: Penguin, 1977.
Spark, Muriel. "The Poet's House." Encounter. 30 (1968): 48.
Spark, Muriel. The Prime of Miss Jean Brodie. New York, NY: New American Library,
    1984.
Spark, Muriel. Robinson, A Novel. Philadelphia, PA: J. B. Lippincott, 1958.
Spark, Muriel. The Takeover, (1976). Middlesex, England: Penguin, 1978.
Spark, Muriel. Territorial Rights. New York, NY: Coward, McCann and Geoghegan, 1979.
Stanford, Derek. Muriel Spark: A Biographical and Critical Study. Fontwell, England:
    Centaur Press, 1963.
Stubbs, Patricia. Muriel Spark. London, England: Longman, 1973.
Worcester, David. "The Art of Satire." Satire: Modern Essays in Criticism. Ed. Ronald
    Paulson. Englewood Cliffs, NJ: Prentice-Hall, 1971.

Benedict Kiely (1919-) IRELAND

**See Nilsen, Don L. F. "Benedict Kiely." Humor in Irish Literature: A Reference
Guide. Westport, CT: Greenwood, 1996, 154, 190.**

Doris (May) Lessing (Jane Somers)(1919-)

Judy Little feels that such authors as Doris Lessing and Dorothy Richardson have
developed distinctly feminist themes in their writing. And although the writing of these
authors does not tend to be comic, it is nevertheless true that Lessing's characters often talk
about laughter (Little 20).

In A Ripple from the Storm (1958), the men treat the women with elaborate
gallantry, saying that they must help their women comrades. However, when the women
refuse their sexual advances, or choose a rival rather than choosing them, the men become
hostile and attack the women in silly ways, such as arguing whether women should be
allowed to wear lipstick. The pretty women are treated differently from the other women,
and seeing this double standard, Martha says, "there isn't one man here who doesn't think
Carrie is such a pretty girl. They all have that defensive and rather shamefaced look, and
their voices when they speak of her are different, simply because she's pretty" (Ripple 114).
When the members of the Party meet and criticize each other's performance, the men find
it difficult to criticize Jasmine because she is slender and attractive. Margie urges her
husband to treat this young woman as an equal, saying, "Go on, you old ram, she's a
human being as well, isn't she" (Ripple 120). But Piet remains quiet and protective. Marie
confronts her husband by saying, "There, you old ram, that's a piece of mind for you and
for all of you. Communist you call yourself" (Ripple 187). He pretends to cringe and to
writhe, and when he asks, "What have you got for my supper?" she suddenly gives in and
smiles back at his smile (Brown 82). Martha is enraged by the way that men demean

women as they pretend to honor them. When one of her working class comrades becomes sentimental about his mother, saying, "My mother was the salt of the earth. My dad died when I was ten and she brought up me and my two sisters on what she got by cleaning offices," Martha angrily responds, "Good, then let's arrange things so that women have to work eighteen hours a day and die at fifty, worn out so that you can go on being sentimental about us" (Ripple 94).

The Children of Violence series of novels was written between 1952 and 1969. About Martha Quest in this series, Lessing says, "Martha did not believe in violence. Yet Martha was the essence of violence, she has been conceived, bred, fed, and reared on violence because she had been born at the end of one world war, and had spent all her adolescence in the atmosphere of preparations for another" (Lesniak 266).

The play entitled Play With A Tiger was first produced in London at Comedy Theatre on March 22, 1962.

According to Little, there is "shocking laughter" in The Summer Before the Dari (1973). Kate Brown and another London housewife engaged in "cow sessions," during which "they began improvising, telling anecdotes or describing situations, in which certain words were bound to come up: wife, husband, man, woman...they laughed and laughed. 'The father of my children,' one woman would say, 'the breadwinner,' said the other, and they shrieked like harpies" (Lessing Summer 168). Judy Little notes that these women were establishing a Mardi-Gras atmosphere without the official sanction of its actually being Mardi Gras--an atmosphere in which such words as wife, husband, woman, and father are funny. These, "hilarious deviations from some unstated standard" in some way challenged that standard (Little 8).

Doris (May) Lessing (Jane Somers)Bibliography

Brown, Ruth Christiani. "Irony in Doris Lessing's A Ripple from the Storm." WHIMSY 2 (1984): 80-83.

Lesniak, James G. "Doris Lessing." Contemporary Authors, New Revision Series, Volume 33. Detroit, MI: Gale Research, 1991, 263-268.

Lessing, Doris. African Laughter: Four Visits to Zimbabwe. New York, NY: Harper Collins, 1992.

Lessing, Doris. A Ripple from the Storm. New York, NY: New American Library, 1970.

Lessing, Doris. The Summer Before the Dark. New York, NY: Alfred A. Knopf, 1973.

Little, Judy. Comedy and the Woman Writer: Woolf, Spark, and Feminism. Lincoln, NE: University of Nebraska Press, 1983.

Iris (Jean) Murdoch (1919-)

William Van O'Connor writes that Iris Murdoch, like Jean Paul Sartre, views man as a, "lonely creature in an absurd world." Man must make moral decisions, but the consequences of his decisions are very uncertain (Wilson 339). Linda Kuehl said that Iris Murdoch's novels are filled with humours characters. There is the enchanter or enchantress, who is torn between exhibitionism and introspection, egoism and generosity, cruelty and pity. There is the observer, who is trapped between love and fear of the enchanter. There is the accomplice, a strange mixture of diabolical intention and bemused charm. The accomplice has dealings with the enchanter and has power over the observers (Wilson 341). Jonathan Raban says that Murdoch is a very intelligent author, who writes with "a careless swagger." Raban also feels that Murdoch has an "astonishingly fecund, playful imagination" (Wilson 342).

Iris Murdoch feels that the novel is necessarily a comic form because an accurate description of real life has to be funny.

> I think all novels are comic forms--yes, <u>all</u> novels. If one's going to portray human life in the way that a novel does, or at least the traditional novel does, you can't avoid being funny, because human life <u>is</u> funny. Any prolonged description of anything produces something funny. Somehow any prolonged texture of a story has places for wit and places where the thing is absurd. (Nettell 13)

In Iris Murdoch's novels, the lengths to which humans are willing to go in order to protect their images of themselves is very funny indeed (Bove 193). But Iris Murdoch's style has changed during her writing career. Her first novels tend to be quaint, funny, absurd and touching, while her later comic novels tend to be dark, sad, and awful. Peter Conradi says that, "the later books are not only darker, much more confident and less anxious to charm us than the early ones--they are thereby also wiser and funnier." He adds that Murdoch's less successful novels are not the ones which are less symbolic, but rather the ones which are less comic (Conradi 28).

Judy Little places Iris Murdoch with Edna O'Brien, Penelope Mortimer, and Muriel Spark as writers who are concerned with both feminism and comedy. Little considers a typical paradigm of a Murdoch novel to be, "a character's gradual, often comic, discovery that he or she has been imposing a myth on some other person" (Little 182). Harold Bloom says that Iris Murdoch is a major student of Eros, adding that she is an, "endlessly provocative theorist of the tragicomedy of sexual love" (Bloom 2).

<u>Under the Net</u> (1954) is an inventive and funny first book which resembles Charles Dickens's <u>Pickwick Papers</u> in being, "a picaresque, charming, light and innocent first novel, an episodic account of the boozy journeyings of a quixotic, illusion-ridden knight and his cannier squire." According to Peter Conradi, the novel is filled with zest and buoyancy (Conradi 28). <u>Under the Net</u> is based on Ludwig Wittgenstein's idea that each of us builds our own "net" or system for structuring our lives. The novel contains a series of comic misadventures which have the effect of changing Jake's attitudes toward life, so that he has become able to accept the contingencies of life and the reality of other people. In effect, he throws off the net, and according to Kmetz, this is a courageous act, because, "nothing is more terrifying than freedom" (Wilson 340).

Some feminists feel that <u>The Flight from the Enchanter</u> (1956) takes an amusing and perhaps too light-hearted look at the suffragette movement in discussing the events that surround the financial difficulties of a women's journal named <u>The Artemis</u> (Bove 167). This novel is about an enigmatic enchanter whose attractiveness to others is enhanced by his mysterious origins. He is appropriately named Mischa Fox, and he has the physical and the spiritual qualities of a Gothic protagonist. He is powerful, and dark, and harsh, and he is frequently described in predatory terms. For example, Mischa has, "a sallow, hawk-like face" (Bove 168). Other features of Mischa that make him a Gothic protagonist are his age, his mysterious background, and his identification with animals. "No one knows Mischa's age. One can hardly even make a guess. It's uncanny. He could be thirty; he could be fifty-five.... No one knows where he came from either. Where was he born? What blood is in his veins? No one knows" (<u>Flight</u> 205). This "blood" reference brings in both "alien" and "vampire" associations. Furthermore, Mischa Fox is most comfortable surrounded by darkness, as when he is in his subterranean dwelling (Bove 169).

<u>A Severed Head</u> (1961) is a drawing-room comedy that shades in places into a French bedroom farce. It combines "Jungian psychoanalytic myth" with "cool philosophical wit" (Byatt 92). According to A. S. Byatt, the recurring images of the severed head, as it is sculpted, dreamed, and analyzed, are used both as a joke, and as a myth (Byatt 93). Cheryl Bove considers <u>A Severed Head</u> to be a witty, ironical and satirical comedy of

manners, "which includes the pairing and switching of partners in almost every conceivable situation among its small cast of characters." For Bove, it is a, "delightful satire of Freudian theory." At the beginning of the novel, Martin Lynch-Gibbon and his very young mistress, Georgie Hands, are discussing that Martin's wife, Antonia, does not know of their affair (Bove 135). Ironically, however, when Antonia arrives home she announces that she wants a divorce so that she will be able to marry Anderson (Severed Head 27). Somewhat later in the novel, Martin states, "With a hideous rush, like blood returning to a crushed limb, I was invaded by my old love for Georgie; and in that instant I realized how very much I had all the same, all the same, all the same, relied upon her faithfulness" (Severed Head 190).

Nevertheless, Martin is also attracted to Honor Klein, and this attraction is strengthened when he sees her in bed with her half brother. Honor Klein is at first described as repulsive and ugly with dark locks and eyes resembling those of Medusa, whose hair consisted of living snakes, and whose head was severed by the hero Persius (providing the name for Murdoch's novel). When Martin tells of his love for Honor he says, "She simply stared at me and I saw the old snake in her looking coldly out through her eyes" (Severed Head 218). But the attraction works in both directions, as Martin remarks to Honor, "I am a terrible object of fascination for you. I am a severed head such as primitive tribes and old alchemists used to use, anointing it with oil and putting a morsel of gold upon its tongue to make it utter prophecies" (Severed Head 221). Martin can see the danger in their mutual attraction, "I haven't come to torment you," but then he added, "Of course, I understand it may happen inadvertently" (Severed Head 247).

In 1964 Iris Murdoch and J. B. Priestley made A Severed Head into a play, in which there was a revolving stage which revealed a shifting of bedrooms, drawing rooms, and partners much in the mode of Restoration Comedy (comedy of manners), along with a number of Dickens-type caricatures (Martz 50). According to John Fletcher, the popular success of the play was because it, "has all the speed, elaboration and stylisation of a Restoration comedy" (Bove 139).

In places, An Unofficial Rose (1962) comes close to being a "pointed parody" (Martz 51).

The Unicorn (1963) is a Gothic novel containing an enchanted princess. It is set in a country which resembles parts of Ireland with its grim cliffs and deadly bogs (Martz 51). Nevertheless, Iris Murdoch does not consider herself to be a Gothic novelist. "I'm not a gothic novelist. This happens to be 'a gothic novel' in that it's got the form of the arrival at the mysterious castle and the monster and the captivity and the mystery and so on, and that just belongs to this novel" (Bove 166). In support of The Unicorn's being a Gothic novel, Cheryl Bove gives a number of significant details:

> The Unicorn has incident, theme, and setting characteristic of the Gothic
> novel. The Irish landscape in which it is situated includes ancient dolmens
> and megaliths. Great cliffs of black sandstone overlook a dark coastline and
> a cold, killing sea; and bogs, caves, and underground rivers give relief to the
> generally barren land. Gaze, an eighteenth-century castle surrounded by
> wrecked gardens, sequesters a beautiful lady whose cortege includes a
> courtly lover and a page. (Bove 171-172)

The Italian Girl (1964) is a Gothic novel set in D. H. Lawrence country. "Our house...was a big ugly Victorian rectory, its red brick darkened by the sour wind that blew from the nearby collieries, whose slag heaps were invisible behind the trees" (qtd. in Martz 51). The play The Italian Girl (1968) was written by James Saunders and Iris Murdoch. In fact, the play turned out to be more comic than the novel had been (Bove 183).

Iris Murdoch based The Red and the Green (1965) on the 1916 Easter uprising in Dublin (Martz 51).

Carel Fisher is the central figure of The Time of the Angels (1966). Carel Fisher is an Anglican priest, but more than that he is a larger-than-life Gothic protagonist, a fisher king gone wrong. He is an estranged "saver of souls" who rules over a wasteland (Bove 179). Darkness is an important part of The Time of the Angels. "Fisher prefers the shadows to daylight and spends much of the day lying on his bed. He keeps his drapes drawn and places a scarf over the lamp shade to dim the light. Throughout the novel the rectory is enveloped by a fog so dense that it is impossible to see outside, and the interior of the house is very dim" (Bove 180).

Part of the fun of Bruno's Dream (1969) are the vivid descriptions of various parts of London, especially that of Brompton cemetery and of the Chelsea and Battersea areas. "The 'bunchy brown granite pillars' inside the Servite Church on Fulham Road, where Miles meditates, are typical of the realistic descriptions of Murdoch's London" (Bove 184). Another humorous part of Bruno's Dream is when Nigel writes to Danby about the significance of love.

> Love is a strange thing.... It is a weird thought that anyone is permitted to love anyone and in any way he pleases. Nothing in nature forbids it. A cat may look at a king, the worthless can love the good, the good the worthless, the worthless the worthless and the good the good.... Anything can happen, so that in a way, a terrible way, there are no impossibilities. (Bruno's Dream 285-286)

In A Fairly Honourable Defeat (1970), Murdoch applies the Apollo-Marsyas myth to Simon and Axel, a homosexual couple. According to this myth, Marsyas is a mortal of outstanding musical talent who hubristically challenges Apollo, the god of music, to a contest. Marsyas of course loses, and as a penalty he is flayed and has to suffer a painful and horrible death (Dipple 132). Peter Conradi considers A Fairly Honourable Defeat to be, "both a stylishly light and a grimly dark comedy of manners, moving again from an integrated to a scattered court, and ending with the 'fairly honourable defeat' of good by evil" (Conradi 165).

The "Editor's Foreword" to The Black Prince (1973) is written by "P. Loxias," who is described by Elizabeth Dipple as, "BP's impresario, clown, harlequin and judge, and who reserves the last word for himself" (Dipple 136). In this novel BP retires from the tedium of working in a tax office in order to be a writer, but he soon discovers that he has developed writer's block, and he therefore decides to rent a cottage by the sea in order to get the privacy and silence he needs. As he prepares for his trip, he fussily checks to see if he has packed his sleeping pills, his belladonna, and his appropriate notebooks, but this is mainly a delaying tactic that reflects his inner knowledge that he is not yet ready to become a writer, and that he truly does not want to be "in silence with himself." It is at this point that three things happen. Francis Marloe announces that Christian, Bradley's former wife, has returned. Arnold phones to say that he thinks he has murdered Rachel, and Priscilla, BP's sister, arrives to announce that she has left her husband and needs to be taken care of (Dipple 145).

The primary voice in The Black Prince is that of BP, who is undergoing the experiences necessary in order to obtain knowledge. This voice represents one of Murdoch's

> ...most-highly polished comic figures. For all the grimness of the secondary persona's cogitations, he steadily reasserts that human beings are endlessly comic to each other. Defining what comedy is and how it can be played out in the middle of action which can also be seen as full of pain and horror is one of the many tasks of this novel. (Dipple 144)

In The Black Prince there is a laughable contrast between the wisdom which BP has and the tyranny of his compulsions. "It is clear from the novel that Murdoch sees this gap as the central idea of comedy and, embellished by a wit which serves to heighten the distance between personal ideas of the self and its reality" (Dipple 144-145).

The Black Prince, "illustrates the profound and essential practice of irony" (Dipple 133). The irony is produced by the contrast between "our highly developed sense of the comic on the one hand and the inevitable pain of our existence on the other." This duality is driven by the absurdity of both our obsessional prejudices and by our need to belittle other people. The Black Prince can be placed into many different genres and is therefore told from a number of different points of view. It is a love story, and an adventure story, but it is also a dramatization of a particular theory of art (Dipple 135). The Black Prince also contains highly sophisticated word play, as with the pun on "Pearson" vs. "person" vs. "persona." The B.P. ties together the name of Bradley Pearson and the title of Black Prince. Elizabeth Dipple even suspects that the name Bradley, "may be intended playfully to evoke F. H. Bradley, the English idealist philosopher whose famous book, Appearance and Reality, was really a study of the Absolute" (Dipple 135).

In The Black Prince, BP reviews Arnold Baffin's new book with a writing style that is self-serving, badly written, and filled with theory-laden criticism that tells much more about the critic than it tells about the book being reviewed. Julian Baffin's criticism of the book is much more "reliably comic" as she simply describes her father's book in rather objective terms: "He lives in a sort of rosy haze with Jesus and Mary and Buddha and Shiva and the Fisher King all chasing round and round dressed up as people in Chelsea" (qtd. in Dipple 142).

The narrator of The Black Prince discusses the use of comedy and irony in attempting to attain truth.

> Almost any tale of our doings is comic. We are bottomlessly comic to each other. Even the most adored and beloved person is comic to his lover. The novel is a comic form. Language is a comic form, and makes jokes in its sleep. God, if He existed, would laugh at His creation. Yet it is also the case that life is horrible, without metaphysical sense, wrecked by chance, pain and the close prospect of death. Out of this is born irony, our dangerous and necessary tool. (Dipple 135)

One example of the irony to be found in The Black Prince involves Arnold's phone call during which he states that he thinks has just killed Rachel, his wife, with a poker. This is ironic because later Rachel calls BP saying that she has in fact just killed Arnold, her husband, with a poker (Dipple 139).

In an article entitled "The Black Prince and the Figure of Marsyas," Elizabeth Dipple suggests that the primary function of The Black Prince is to show that the artist tends to be flawed and egocentric, and tends to expect the help of the gods. Dipple considers this entire metaphor to be "very Greek," in this case suggesting the relationship of Apollo to the Muses (Dipple 146). BP in fact thinks that Rachel might be a messenger of the god, and so he reasons that having an affair with her might take a new type of courage. "It had often, when I thought most profoundly about it, occurred to me that I was a bad artist because I was a coward. Would new courage in life prefigure and even perhaps induce courage in art?" (Dipple 147). It is ironic, though that when he actually goes to bed with her he finds himself to be impotent, so that he fails in both areas, and it becomes even more evident to him that he is, "far from ready for the creation of art" (Dipple 148).

Although Murdoch is talking about art in The Black Prince, she does not forget the ordinary world. Throughout the novel she keeps this ordinary world in focus with strong visual images ranging from the absurdly funny (such as the phallic Post Office Tower or the mad recurrences of milk chocolate) to the very serious (such as the bronze of the water buffalo lady, or the snuff box inscribed "A Friend's Gift," or the statues of Aphrodite)(Dipple 153). It may be true that the novel points to death, but this does not break its comedic frame, nor does it cause it to lose its sense of realism. In a postscript, BP expresses the central paradox of the novel, as he remembers Plato's injunction against the artist, and notes that neither Socrates nor Christ wrote anything. "And yet: I am writing these words to others who I do not know will read them. With and by this paradox I have lived, dear friend, in our sequestered peace. Perhaps it will always be for some an unavoidable paradox, but one which is only truly lived when it is also a martyrdom" (Dipple 158).

A. S. Byatt describes A Word Child (1975) as "rapid, perplexing, funny, and terrible" (Byatt 93). According to Joyce Carol Oates, much of the negative reaction of critics to Darkness Visible (1979) is because of Golding's "embarrassing fictional stereotypes, and his heavy-handedly ironic attempt to create a visionary-moron in Matty" (Lesniak 176). Rites of Passage (1980) is set in the early nineteenth century. It tells about a voyage from England to Australia (Lesniak 176). Through the eyes of Edmund Talbot, the young aristocrat who keeps a shipboard diary, Golding writes a vivid record of the ship and its characters, which include the "irascible" Captain Anderson, the "wind-machine" Mr. Brocklehand, the "whorish painted Magdaline" named Zenobia, and the "mock and ridiculous parson" Mr. Colley. Mr. Colley is satirized as mercilessly as the clerics in Henry Fielding's Joseph Andrews. Talbot describes Mr. Colley as, "the perfect victim--self-deluding, unworldly, sentimentally devout, priggish, and terrified." He is also, "ignorant of the powerful homosexual streak in his nature that impels him toward the crew and especially toward one stalwart sailor, Billy Rogers" (Lesniak 176).

Paper Men (1984) is a farce-drama novel about an aging, successful novelist's conflicts with his pushy, overbearing biographer (Lesniak 177).

On the surface, The Good Apprentice (1985) is a social comedy about the highly literate, and as such it is a "brilliant entertainment." But beneath the surface,,, there is an "astringent post-Christian Platonism" that has evolved into a negative theology that seems to offer only two alternatives--either total libertinism, or total puritanism in one's moral life. "The aesthetic puzzle is whether the comic story and the Platonic kernel can be held together" (Bloom 7).

The Wings of a Dove is a novel about a "happy resolution of the Oedipus conflict." It mixes comedy and pain as it recalls the story of Petronius's widow of Ephesus, who falls in love beside her first husband's tomb, and whose love saves her second husband's life (Conradi 265).

In conclusion, Murdoch has repeated on a number of occasions that the novel is a comic form, and that tragedy belongs only in art. Murdoch feels that when comedy fails, what we have is not tragedy, but is rather misery. Peter Conradi sums up Iris Murdoch's work by saying that, "even when they are most grim, Mordoch's novels are funny" (Conradi 263). In discussing the reasons for death and suffering in literature, Murdoch remarked that, "perhaps one of the greatest achievements of all is to join this sense of absolute mortality not to the tragic but to the comic." Iris Murdoch shares this vision with William Shakespeare. In a book entitled Iris Murdoch: The Shakespearian Interest, Richard Todd says that Iris Murdoch would agree with Anne Barton when she refers to Shakespeare's, "objective awareness that the play will continue without us." She says further, "Artistic forms which dismiss their characters into happiness, often through the solemnization or promise of marriage, are far more problematic. Such endings are not real conclusions" (Todd 70). Murdoch would agree.

Iris (Jean) Murdoch Bibliography

Barton, Ann. "As You Like It and Twelfth Night: Shakespeare's Sense of an Ending."
    Shakespearian Comedy. Ed. Malcolm Bradbury and David Palmer. London,

England: Stratford-upon-Avon Studies, 1972, 167-169.

Bloom, Harold, ed. Modern Critical Views: Iris Murdoch. New York, NY: Chelsea House, 1986.

Bove, Cheryl K. Understanding Irish Murdoch. Columbia, SC: University of South Carolina, 1993.

Byatt, A. S. "Shakespearean Plot in the Novels of Iris Murdoch." Modern Critical Views: Iris Murdoch. New York, NY: Chelsea House, 1986, 87-94.

Conradi, Peter J. Iris Murdoch: The Saint and the Artist. Hants, England: Macmillan, 1986.

Dipple, Elizabeth. "The Black Prince and the Figure of Marsyas." Modern Critical Views: Iris Murdoch. New York, NY: Chelsea House, 1986, 131-158.

Hague, Angela. Iris Murdoch's Comic Vision. London, England: Associated University Presses, 1984.

Lesniak, James G. Contemporary Authors, New Revision Series, Volume 33. Detroit, MI: Gale Research, 1991.

Little, Judy. Comedy and the Woman Writer: Woolf, Spark, and Feminism. Lincoln, NE: University of Nebraska Press, 1983.

Martz, Louis L. "The London Novels." Modern Critical Views: Iris Murdoch. New York, NY: Chelsea House, 1986, 39-58.

Murdoch, Iris. Bruno's Dream. New York, NY: Viking, 1969.

Murdoch, Iris. The Flight from the Enchanter. New York, NY: Viking, 1965.

Murdoch, Iris. A Severed Head. New York, NY: Viking, 1961.

Nettell, Stephanie. "Iris Murdoch: An Exclusive Interview." Books and Bookmen 8 (September, 1966): 13.

O'Connor, William Van. The New University Wits, and the End of Modernism. Carbondale, IL: Southern Illinois University Press, 1963.

Todd, Richard. Iris Murdoch: The Shakespearian Interest. New York, NY: Barnes and Noble/Harper and Row, 1979.

Wilson, Kathleen. "Iris Murdoch." Contemporary Authors, New Revision Series, Volume 43. Detroit, MI: Gale Research, 1994, 338-342.

Norman Frederick Simpson (1919-)

Martin Esslin considers N. F. Simpson to be a serious satirist whose humor is predicated on the Bergsonian theory of habit and social convention forcing men to act as machines (Esslin 224). Esslin sees Simpson's absurdity, "as a weapon of social criticism more powerful than the satire of the social realists." Kenneth Tynan says that Simpson is a, "dazzling new playwright and England's most gifted comic writer." George Wellwarth considers Simpson to be the literary heir of Alfred Jarry. Both Simpson and Jarry are, "pataphysicians who create a parallel fictional reality as context for existing social reality" (Rusinko 1007). Most of Simpson's plays are set in suburbia, but it is as if they are in a parallel universe to our own. Simpson's obsessive characters don't change or develop. The plot is episodic. The situations are improbable and zany. There are gross incongruities. The logic is impeccable, but is based on arbitrary premises. In addition, the plays contain a lot of coarse wit and nonsense (Zimmerman 479).

Both Rumanian-born Eugene Ionesco and English-born N. F. Simpson are satiric playwrights who specialize in the theatre of the absurd. Ionesco reduced his humans to objects or animals, such as an empty chair, or a rhinoceros. In contrast, Simpson made objects into humans, such as talking weight machines, and gave them a life of their own in his world of absurdities. Both Ionesco's and Simpson's idea of the theater of the absurd involved the paradox, the non-sequitur, and other inversions of logical processes. Like

Ionesco's characters, Simpson's characters behave mechanically, and they speak in clichés seemingly unaware of the ordinary meanings of words. The names of Simpson's plays, the names of his characters, and the puns and clichés are all clues to the fact that he is writing a special kind of satire called absurdist drama. There are visual puns, such as the elephant and the snake and the son who turns out to be a daughter in A Resounding Tinkle, and the hole in The Hole. Simpson's most outlandish collection of visual images, however, occurs in One Way Pendulum, where a miniature of the Old Bailey Courtroom is being built in a living room, and the daughter is obsessed that are arms are too short. An outlandish image that is both visual and audio in this same play is that of an assembly of weight machines singing the "Halelujah Chorus." Another clue that these plays are in the absurdist tradition is that there is often an absence of any link or progression in plot or characters (Rusinko 1001).

A Resounding Tinkle (1956) takes place at the home of Bro and Middie Paradock, and the non-sequiturs dominate the action. Act I begins with a man at the door who wants Bro to "form a government." Bro responds, "How can I start forming a government at six o'clock in the evening? It's the Prime Minister's job" (Zimmerman 476). But then Bro discovers that the proposal was a joke propounded by Uncle Ted, who was disguising his voice. But just as things are about to resolve themselves, two comedians who have been hired to be entertainers at the party, arrive, and they do a series of doctor-patient routines, after which they discuss the nature of theater and comedy. Bro is used as an example of Bergsonian theory--a human acting like a machine--and he pretends to be a computer, having himself plugged in as he gets more and more inebriated. Reminiscent of Beckett's Waiting for Godot, Act 2 of A Resounding Tinkle begins with a routine about hats, and there is another visit by the comedians, and a visit by their son, Don, who has in the meantime changed sexes, and talk about a garden that is mentioned in the house's deed of sale, but is nowhere else to be found. At this point, the Paradocks must leave the stage to make room for the Author and the critics to have a meeting (Zimmerman 477).

The characters in A Resounding Tinkle are eccentrics, or humours characters. The mother prepares large amounts of food and then must pay a neighbor to carry off the leftovers. Another character eats constantly so that eating will become a habit rather than a distraction. The son assumes that if a single weight machine can be built which can orally tell people their weights, then five hundred weight machines could be built which could sing the "Hallelujia Chorus" from George Friederic Handel's Messiah (Rusinko 1001). A Resounding Tinkle has been described by some critics not as a play, but as an "anti-play," a term that Ionesco had earlier used as the sub-title for The Bald Soprano. To impress the neighbors, the Paradocks purchase a large elephant, but their small house won't accommodate it, so they solve the problem by exchanging their elephant for a neighbor's snake. During a game of patience, a doorbell rings twice, and Middie shouts "Come in" twice, and then when it rings again she goes to the door, and discovers that there is nobody there. This is as absurd as the two comedians who try to explain the humor in a nonsensical list of figures of speech, or in the three critics, named Salt, Pepper, and Mustard, who use jargon trying to explain the nature of meaning. One of the critics concludes, that without critics, authors would be, "hard put to it to arrive anywhere at all" (Simpson Tinkle 66). One of the three critics says that a particular piece has been influenced by Bertolt Brecht (Rusinko 1002). The second critic sees no influence of Brecht at all. And the third critic sees the Brechtian technique carried well beyond Brecht. Pepper summarizes the play as, "The Comedy of Errors rewritten by Lewis Carroll to provide a part for Godot" (Simpson Tinkle 71). Simpson liked to cannibalize his own works, and he therefore wrote short plays, or skits, for revues on stage or television with such titles as Three Resounding Tinkles (1966), and Four Tall Tinkles (1967) (Zimmerman 479).

The characters in The Hole (1958) are referred to as Endo, Cerebro, Soma, and the

Visionary (Rusinko 1001). In The Hole, Simpson is satirizing, "one of the most common and singular of English habits: the queue." A Visionary, the main character, peers into a hole in which he insists that he sees a stained glass window of a cathedral being unveiled. Endo, Soma, and Cerebro also stand in the line, and also enter the debate, as they conjecture about what is in the hole. They see shadows that appear to be two people playing dominoes in boxing gloves. They see a golfer, a fish, a prisoner, and a ritual murder. Mrs. Ecto and Mrs. Meso are also in the line, but they are less concerned about the hole than they are about their husbands, one of whom is a conforming non-conformist, and the other is a nonconforming conformist (Zimmerman 477). As one of the people in line says, "each time we draw near to the cavity and together peer down into the depths, we are not only giving expression by that act to the unquenchable curiosity that is in us, but we are at the same time reaffirming the truth of the eternal and inscrutable paradox-- that it is upon this cavity that we build our faith" (Simpson Hole 54). Each of the people standing in line observing the hole feels that the hole needs to somehow be filled up, rendered knowable. In talking about The Hole, Simpson said it was about the way people like to weave all sorts of elaborately significant myths around insignificant facts. Often the process reaches the point where people believe more in the myths than in the facts on which the myths are based. The Hole is about how we create meanings, how we jump from logic into transcendental faith (Zimmerman 477).

The farce One Way Pendulum (1959) is an outrageous fantasy that combines word games, high jinx, gags, and nonsense logic (Zimmerman 478). Susan Rusinko considers One Way Pendulum to be Simpson's "funniest play." The play is about obsessions, and the title of the play describes how each person's life tends to swing only in one direction. The obsessions come together at the trial that is conducted in the replica of the Old Bailey courtroom in the home of Arthur and Mabel Groomkirby. Living in the same home was Kirby, the son; Sylvia, the daughter; and Mildred the wheelchair-bound aunt. Mr. Groomkirby takes care of parking meters; he likes to stand in front of the meters until the time runs out. As a hobby, he reads do-it-yourself books on law and carpentry, and is building a replica of the Old Bailey Courtroom in his living room. Mabel Groomkirby is equally obsessed. She is a nonstop housewife who complains that she has so little help from her family that she is forced to hire Mrs. Gantry, one of her neighbors, to eat the leftovers (Zimmerman 478). Mrs. Gantry may or may not show up at the Groomkirby's home on any particular day. Sylvia Groomkirby's obsession is her grotesquely short arms. Although her arms appear perfectly normal to other people, Sylvia says that her arms are, "too short to reach her knees without her bending." Most obsessive of all in the Groomkirby family is Kirby, who has a habit of eating only when called by a Pavlovian bell. Kirby dresses entirely in black. Even his baby things had been all black, including his shawl, his rompers, and even his bib. His sheets and pillow-cases were also black (Simpson Pendulum 88). Kirby justifies his wearing black by the funerals he attends, and he justifies the funerals by the murders he commits. Kirby has just murdered forty-three people by first telling them a joke and making them laugh, and then hitting each of them on the head (Rusinko 1004). Even Kirby's plan to make a bunch of weight machines into a chorus is related to his wearing of black. He plans to transport the weight machines to Alaska in order to lure huge numbers of people to Alaska. Once they are in Alaska, Kirby plans to make everyone jump at the same moment thus tilting the earth on its axis. The resulting deaths would be many and frequent and would provide Kirby sufficient cause for the wearing of black. When Mrs. Groomkirby hears of Kirby's plan, she responds, "Kirby has always been of a very logical turn of mind" (Zimmerman 478). The judge in the case, however, says that Kirby is innocent and argues that, "in sentencing a man for one crime, we may be putting him beyond the reach of the law in respect of those other crimes of which he might otherwise have become guilty" (Simpson Pendulum 92). The case is being tried in the replica of the Old Bailey courtroom which Mr. Groomkirby has constructed in the living room (Zimmerman 478).

In Gladly Otherwise (1959), a police inspector asks a housewife if things are as they should be. More specifically, he asks whether the shelves are supported, whether the walls are sufficiently upright, whether the sieves are letting the small stuff through, and so forth (Zimmerman 479). In Oh (1961), there is an artist who is not able to paint because he insists on having total control of the process. Among other things, he must construct his own easel, weave his own canvasses, and find his own paint pigments (Zimmerman 479). The Cresta Run (1965) has fantastic confusions and complications related to espionage and counterespionage (Zimmerman 479).

Was He Anyone? (1972) is a play about a man who is drowning in the Mediterranean Sea. He has been treading water for twenty-seven months, his predicament having been prolonged by the bureaucratic bickering about his rescue by the opposing charitable institutions (Rusinko 1005). Was He Anyone? is a play about how the National Help You Out Year Week Committee attempts not to rescue Albert Whitbrace. Although they don't rescue him, they do try to keep in comfort during his ordeal (Zimmerman 479), as they try to answer such questions as "Is he entitled to help?" "Is he using his time profitably?" and "Will rescue allow accidents to appear rewarding?" Simpson is satirizing the way that an individual's distress is so often exploited by the organizations who are designed to help them. Some critics find the play to be a deeply serious satire. Others find it to be simply good-natured and whimsical (Zimmerman 480).

Norman Frederick Simpson Bibliography

Esslin, Martin. "N. F. Simpson." Theatre of the Absurd. Garden City, NY: Doubleday, 1961, 217-224.

Froehlich, A. J. Peter. "N. F. Simpson and the Aesthetics of Nonsense." Unpublished Ph.D. Dissertation. Toronto, Canada: University of Toronto, 1976.

Galassi, Frank S. "The Absurd Theatre of Joe Orton and N. F. Simpson." Unpublished Ph.D. Dissertation. New York, NY: New York University, 1971.

Rusinko, Susan. "N. F. Simpson." Encyclopedia of British Humorists, Volume II. Ed. Steven H. Gale. New York, NY: Garland, 1996, 1000-1007.

Simpson, N. F. The Hole and Other Plays and Sketches. London, England: Faber and Faber, 1964.

Simpson, N. F. A Resounding Tinkle. London, England: Faber and Faber, 1968.

Simpson, N. F. One Way Pendulum. London, England: Faber and Faber, 1960.

Tynan, Kenneth. A View of the English Stage. London, England: Davis-Poynter, 1975.

Wellwarth, George. The Theater of Protest and Paradox. New York, NY: New York University Press, 1964.

Zimmerman, C. D. "N. F. Simpson." British Dramatists Since World War II: Dictionary of Literary Biography, Volume 13. Ed. Stanley Weintraub. Detroit, MI: Bruccoli Clark/Gale Research, 1982, 474-481.

8
Authors Born between 1920 and 1929

Richard George Adams (1920-)

Watership Down (1972) is an allegory in which animals are involved in exile and survival, heroism and political responsibility. The rabbit leaders are Hazel, along with the courageous Bigwig, the clairvoyant Fiver, and the clever Blackberry (Olendorf 3). In Watership Down there is a community, and even a complete civilization with its own government, language, and mythology. The writing style is rich and imaginative, and the chapters have cliff-hanging endings. In an interview in the Pittsburgh Press, Richard Adams may have had his tongue in his cheek as he made the following statement, "A lot of people have said this is a political fable or even a religious fable or social comment. I promise you it is not a fable, or an allegory or a parable of any kind. It is a story about rabbits, that is all" (Lesniak 3). Alison Lurie says that both Watership Down, and Shardik (1974) can be viewed as allegories and as histories of the relationships of human beings to their physical world. Arthur Cooper feels that Shardik has a rich vein of allegory and symbolism, saying that Adams is concerned with how a society worships its gods, chooses its values, and raises its children (Lesniak 4). William Safire considers The Plague Dogs (1977) to be, "a savage snarl of a satire with a clear purpose in the author's mind" (Lesniak 5). Robert Kiely is very complimentary of The Girl in a Swing (1980). He says that the love scenes between Alan and Kaethe are, "presented with lyrical beauty, a touch of humor, and increasing obsessiveness" (Lesniak 6). Traveller (1988) is a retelling of the various events of the Civil War, but the observations are made through the eyes of General Robert E. Lee's horse. The horse sees, "the follies of human beings--especially their penchant for killing one another," and Traveller thus demonstrates that animals are "ever-so-much-wiser" than are the humans who control them (Lesniak 6).

Richard George Adams Bibliography

Lesniak, James G. ed. "Richard (George) Adams." Contemporary Authors, New Revision Series, Volume 35. Detroit, MI: Gale Research, 1992, 2-6.
Olendorf, Donna, ed. "Richard Adams." Something about the Author, Volume 69. Detroit, MI: Gale Research, 1992, 1-3.

Richard Stanley (Dick) Francis (1920-)

In 1965, Dick Francis was a veteran jockey riding Devon Loch, the Queen Mother's horse, in the annual Grand National. Fifty yards from the finish line he was leading the field, and the horse suddenly faltered and fell on its stomach just ten strides from the winning post--this after clearing the last fence of the grueling four-and-a-half-mile course. Francis lost the race (MacDonald 138). Francis later explains, "Maybe he was shocked by the noise of 250,000 people screaming because the royal family's horse was winning." He continues, "if that mystery hadn't happened, I might never have written all these other ones" (Trosky 150). Francis's novels are similar to typical hard-boiled detective novels in that country truth is pitted against city vice; there is a genteel hero who is tough, hard-boiled, cynical, down-to-earth, and capable of violence; there are many red herrings to throw the detective off from the path; and there are offstage deaths and active violence. Francis's hero is someone who appears to be a common man, but who proves himself to be quite uncommon (MacDonald 139). What one character said in Slay-ride (1973) could be applied to all Francis heroes, "Give him one fact and he guesses the rest" (MacDonald 140). There is little correlation between social class and the quality of Francis's characters. Some of his upper-class figures are naïve and simplistic dabblers who place too much weight on superficial appearances.

> His university professors are out-of-date, unreliable men trying to sound like a combination of Marx and a Liverpool street punk. In fact, whenever a character resorts to polysyllabic diction and spouts unintelligibly about the nature of the universe, he should be immediately suspected of ignorance, pretension, and perhaps villainy. (MacDonald 143)

Francis's opening lines are also always clever attention getters (MacDonald, 144). The language of Dick Francis's novels is straightforward, and he especially enjoys presenting words in sets of three, such as "gentle, generous, and worried," or "bribed, bludgeoned, or blackmailed." Francis also enjoys word games and crossword puzzles, and he frequently employs puns. The title For Kicks (1965) explains not only the motivation of the protagonist's actions (he does things just for kicks), but also the physical beating he endures (kicked for kicks). Proof (1984) is the story of a wine merchant enlisted by the police to find fraudulently labeled wines. The title Proof, therefore, refers both to the nature of the evidence, and the percentage of alcohol (MacDonald 152). And the title Break In (1985) refers to the training of a horse (breaking it in), but also refers to a burglary. The title In the Frame (1976) is another play on words, as this novel deals with the "supermarket" villains who are friendly with the wealthy tourists and sell them a genuine painting, and then substitute a fake, and then recover both the original and the fake in a carefully planned burglary. So "in the frame" refers not only to the paintings, but also to the method used for stealing them (MacDonald 150). The title Reflex (1980) is still another pun, since the word "reflex" refers both to the camera type and to an involuntary response by a character in the novel (MacDonald 151).

It is the satiric treatment of class snobbery, the contrasting depictions of casual relationships, and the treatment of illusions that hide reality that cause Dead Cert (1962) to be more than just pulp fiction (MacDonald 144). In Enquiry (1969), Kelly Hughes asks the snobbish daughter of a rich trainer, "Would you consider coming down to my level?" and she responds, "Are you speaking literally, metaphorically, intellectually, financially, or socially?" (MacDonald 148). In Rat Race (1970), Matt Shore chauffeurs around the wealthy racetrack crowd, but he feels contempt for most of them. This novel is, "interspersed with brief, satiric portraits of aristocrats. Shore sees his battle for dominance over a rival company as nature's 'pecking order' at work and himself as a rat 'trapped on a treadwheel' going in circles" (MacDonald 148). In Trial Run (1978) as in other Francis novels, it is competence rather than class that makes the man. The hero in Trial Run is described as looking like, "one of those useless la-di-das in the telly ads," but he performs, "with the reflexes and coolheadedness of a professional" (MacDonald 142).

Richard Stanley (Dick) Francis Bibliography

MacDonald, Gina. "Dick Francis." British Mystery and Thriller Writers Since 1940. Detroit, MI: Gale, 1989, 136-155.
Trosky, Susan M. ed. "Dick Francis." Contemporary Authors, New Revision Series, Volume 42. Detroit, MI: Gale, 1994, 148-152.

Phyllis Dorothy James (1920-)

In an understated style, P. D. James sometimes has negative descriptions of ugly edifices, and she seems to like to subtly undermine a manor house of one of her novels. Cordelia looks at one Victorian dwelling, and wonders if, "perhaps it had replaced an earlier more agreeable house" (Benstock 222). Carla Heffner says that P. D. James's mystery novels "are like twentieth-century morality plays; the values are basic and unambiguous. Murder is wrong" (Trosky 471). P. D. James has had two significant protagonists in her mystery novels. Her male protagonist is Adam Dalgliesh (the name was spelled "Dalgleish" in the first novel, but always "Dalgliesh" thereafter) (Benstock 211). Dalgliesh is developed as an enigmatic character. His public life may be rationally understandable, but his private life is nevertheless quite incomprehensible (Benstock 213). James's female protagonist is Cordelia Gray. Many of James's romantic reviewers quickly predicted a love affair for the twenty-two-year-old Cordelia Gray, and Adam Dalgliesh who was twice her age. They saw the sparks start to fly between the two protagonists in their closing confrontation in An Unsuitable Job for a Woman (1972), but in the next two novels Cordelia Gray is hardly mentioned, and in James's eighth novel, neither Adam Dalgliesh nor Cordelia Gray plays any part. But Cordelia Gray returns in the ninth novel, and Adam Dalgliesh returns in the tenth novel, "and the sentimental reviewers and readers have remained frustrated in their anticipation of romance." In 1977, P. D. James wrote a piece for Ink: The Mystery Reader's Companion entitled, "Ought Adam to Marry Cordelia?" and in this article, James remains noncommittal, "I can only say that I have no plans at present to marry Dalgliesh to anyone. Yet even the best regulated characters are apt occasionally to escape from the sensible and controlling hand of their author and embark, however inadvisably, on a love life of their own" (Benstock 211).

The nicest murderess in all of James's canon appears in Cover Her Face (1962). She is also the nicest of all of the suspects in this particular novel. "She throttles an infuriatingly disruptive element in her household, a maid who threatens the sanctity of the family. When Dalgliesh has eliminated all of the other suspects she quietly confesses, having waited until her terminally ill husband has died so that she could be free to be imprisoned" (Benstock 224). In Cover Her Face, Dalgliesh ponders on the idea that, "every death benefitted someone, enfranchised someone, lifted a burden from someone's shoulders, whether of responsibility, the pain of vicarious suffering or the tyranny of love. Every death was a suspicious death if one looked only at motive, just as every death, at the last, was a natural death" (Benstock 224).

The opening statement in A Mind to Murder (1963) says that Dalgliesh, "had never yet known the taste of defeat," but then later in the novel Dalgliesh tracks the wrong "murderer" and he is forced to do some self analysis: "If this case doesn't cure me of conceit, nothing will" (Benstock 213).

Sergeant Masterson in <u>Shroud for a Nightingale</u> (1971) develops a case against Dalgliesh, and describes Dalgliesh as, "so uncaring about his subordinates' private life as to seem unaware that they had any." Masterson says that Dalgliesh's, "caustic wit could be as devastating as another man's bludgeon." But in <u>Shroud for a Nightingale</u>, Detective Constable Dalgliesh demonstrates his enigmatic character by saying, "I can't interest myself in anything which I not only don't understand but know that I have no prospect of ever understanding" (Benstock 216).

Adam Dalgliesh makes a brief appearance in <u>An Unsuitable Job for a Woman</u> (1972), where he comes into contact with his superior, the assistant commissioner. The relationship between these two men is presented with ironic humor: "The two men disliked each other but only one of them knew this and he was the one to whom it didn't matter" (Benstock 216).

Dalgliesh is disillusioned in <u>The Black Tower</u> (1975) when he thinks to himself, "The truth is...that I don't know what, if anything, I'm investigating, and I only spasmodically care. I haven't the stomach to do the job properly or the will and courage to leave it alone." Dalgliesh gives up trying to get the case officially opened because he has no facts to present to the police. "He couldn't say: I, Adam Dalgliesh, have had one of my famous hunches--I disagree with the coroner, with the pathologist, with the local police, with all the facts" (Benstock 215).

In <u>A Taste of Death</u> (1986) Dalgliesh's self analysis is quite mordant. He calls himself, "the poet who no longer writers poetry. The lover who substitutes technique for commitment. The policeman disillusioned with policing" (Benstock 215). In <u>A Taste for Death</u>, Dalgliesh balances his observations with a bit of irony. "It was odd, he sometimes thought, that a man morbidly sensitive about his own privacy should have chosen a job that required him to invade almost daily the privacy of others" (Benstock 217). When Dalgliesh restates the verdict of "an old detective sergeant" in <u>A Taste for Death</u>, he explains why murders are committed: "Love, Lust, Loathing, Lucre, the four Ls of murder, laddie. And the greatest of these is lucre" (Benstock 225).

Phyllis Dorothy James Bibliography

Benstock, Bernard. "P. D. James." <u>British Mystery and Thriller Writers Since 1940</u>. Eds. Bernard Benstock, and Thomas F. Staley. Detroit, MI: Gale, 1989, 210-227.
Trosky, Susan M. ed. "Phyllis Dorothy James White (P. D. James)." <u>Contemporary Authors: New Revision Series, Volume 43</u>. Detroit, MI: Gale, 1994, 468-471.

Paul Scott (1920-1978)

In <u>The Bender</u> (1963), George Spruce is a middle-aged Londoner whose life has been almost destroyed by an unexpected inheritance. This inheritance makes it unnecessary for him to get a job, but it also keeps him on the brink of poverty. "It is possible to see in the background of this mildly humorous novel and its satire of fashionable London in the 1960s Scott's preoccupation with the crucial importance of work for the definition of one's role in life and for the recognition by one's fellows of that role" (Lewis 641).

<u>The Jewel in the Crown</u> (1966) is the first novel in <u>The Raj Quartet</u>. It opens as follows: "This is the story of a rape," and this crime reverberates through all four of the novels of <u>The Raj Quartet</u>. The different characters in <u>The Raj Quartet</u> not only see this rape from very different perspectives, but they also present these perspectives through a wide variety of literary forms. "The reader must evaluate letters, memoirs, formal reports, a journal, a legal deposition, and omniscient flashbacks, all dealing with basically the same

events seen from different points of view." One of the haunting images in the four novels of The Raj Quartet is a nineteenth-century print of Queen Victoria on her throne accepting tribute from her loyal Indian subjects, and of course India was considered to be the "Jewel in the Crown" of the Empire. "In exchange for tribute the Raj offers that curious paternalistic quality known as 'manbap' by the Indians--translated to mean 'I am your father and your mother.' The print of the 'Jewel in the Crown' appears in many situations, some ironic, some poignant" (Lewis 642). A Division of the Spoils (1975) is the last novel in The Raj Quartet. Staying On (1977) is the coda to The Raj Quartet. This novel is set in 1972, and it gently satirizes the new India of sophisticated and wealthy businessmen and politicians. It also satirizes corrupt property dealers and fashionable hairdressers. Tusker and Lucy had been introduced in The Day of the Scorpion (1968), but in Staying On, Tusker and Lucy are elderly and fragile. They are still rather dull, but they are useful to the military station in Pankot, and are still making their home there after the other British have gone home (Lewis 643). "The sensitivity of the relationship between Tusker and Lucy is heightened, not destroyed, by the humorous handling of their essentially uncommunicative marriage, and the portrayal of their Muslim servant Ibrahim is a masterpiece of comedy" (Lewis 645).

Paul Scott Bibliography

Lewis, Margaret B. "Paul Scott." British Novelists Since 1960: Dictionary of Literary Biography, Volume Fourteen. Ed. Jay L. Halio., Detroit, MI: Gale, 1983, 638-645.

Sandy Wilson (1920-)

Sandy Wilson is a satiric composer and lyricist. He created many popular musicals and campy books (Ashley 1213). Camp, and nostalgic parody were Wilson's principle comic techniques. Wilson's satire tends to be more sweet than saucy. His wit tends to be genial, and his language play ranks with that of Noel Coward and Cole Porter. Like Coward and Porter, Wilson writes clever and wry lyrics (Ashley 1214). The Boy Friend (1953), which was made into an RCA Victor recording in 1955, is a parody of the light weight and stereotypical musical comedies and witty revues that were so popular on the London stage between the world wars (Ashley 1214). "The Boy friend is much more than a mere parody of the twenties." The Boy Friend, which contains the humorous ditty, "It's Never Too Late to Fall in Love," is actually, "a huge musical joke--one which visibly and audibly takes the older theater-goer back to his salad days and reminds the younger that the world was not always filled with bebop and brass-lunged baritones" (Ashley 1214). Valmouth (1959) is a recording that is, "full of fun, fantasy, and social irresponsibility as well as satire on religiosity (not religion) and promiscuity (not sex)" (Ashley 1215). Divorce Me, Darling (1964) is a fast and witty farce which B. A. Young says has some exceptionally clever songs and a stunning parody of Cole Porter. Young writes that Wilson's parody of Porter is, "funnier than anything the maestro ever did because it reduces his strength and his weakness with equal candor" (Ashley 1215). Sandy Wilson also wrote a comedy entitled, The Clapham Wonder (1978), and two satires entitled, Who's Who for Beginners (1971), and Caught in the Act (1976)(Ashley 1217).

Sandy Wilson Bibliography

Ashley, Leonard R. N. "Sandy Wilson." Encyclopedia of British Humorists, Volume II. Ed. Steven H. Gale. New York, NY: Garland, 1996, 1212-1217.

Dirk Bogarde (Derek Jules Gaspard Ulric Niven Van den Bogarde) (1921-)

Dirk Bogarde writes natural and interesting dialogue. He has a strong sense of scene, action, plot, and characterization. Bogarde's training as an actor helps him develop characters with a broad range of human emotions. Bogarde also has the ability to blend the serious with the comic (Crotzer 107).

In A Gentle Occupation (1980), a British commander by the name of General Cutts is involved with the enigmatic Miss Foto. Major Pullen is in love with a Dutch woman whose husband is missing in the beginning of the novel. But the husband is later found alive and returns home. Rooke falls in love with a half-Dutch, half-Indonesian girl who doesn't want to return to England with him because of her mixed blood. These are the kinds of relationships that must endure the confusions and the uncertainties of the novel (Crotzer 106). Many of the characters are stereotypes, but they are individuals as well. General Cutts, for example, is a typical career army officer, but he has feelings and deals with believable problems, so he is more than a stock character. It is this blend of stereotypical traits with individual traits that makes Bogarde's characters real and compelling (Crotzer 107).

In Voices in the Garden (1981) a disparate group of people are brought together in southern France at the villa of Sir Charles and Lady "Cuckoo" Peverill. All of the characters are pretending to be something that they aren't:

> Sir Charles, for instance, pretends to smoke cigarettes, even brushing imaginary ashes from his trousers and insisting that he must cut down on his smoking. Lady Peverill plays the socialite and hostess to hide the frustrations of her life and, as is revealed at the end of the novel, the fact that she is dying of leukemia. Leni Minx, the female half of the young couple who enter the Peverills' life, creates an entire personality and history to hide her true identity as Luise von Lamsfeld, a German countess. Umberto Grottorosso, the Italian film director who serves as a quasi-villain in the novel, struggles to maintain a "macho" image to mask his latent homosexuality and his sadistic tendencies. (Crotzer 107)

These pretenses offer an important challenge for Bogarde in that he must develop not only the actual characters, but he must also develop the characters that they create for themselves. The result is an interesting blend of reality and fantasy in the creation of these double characters (Crotzer 107).

Dirk Bogarde (Derek Jules Gaspard Ulric Niven Van den Bogarde) Bibliography

Crotzer, Frank. "Dirk Bogarde." British Novelists Since 1960. Ed. Jay L. Halio. Detroit, MI: Gale, 1983.

Harry Donald Secombe (1921-)

Harry Secombe's first humor success was as a member of BBC Radio's "Crazy People," a show which later became "The Goon Show." Secombe played the role of Neddy Seagoon on "The Goon Show." In this role, Secombe would weekly take on various wild-and-heroic tasks that were also quite stupid. Secombe had the central role on the show, but he was supported by a strong cast of other comedians, especially Peter Sellers with his many voices and characterizations. Spike Milligan wrote most of the scripts and also had a leading performing role with the troupe (Batts 927). Although Milligan was the main writer, he also took many suggestions from the other three primary performers. The resultant skits were fantastic and surreal. They leaned toward social satire and often poked fun at English pomposity, class consciousness, and stereotypes. The bitter-sweet perspective of the humor was consistent with the prominent perspective of post-war England looking at the remnants of the "British Empire." There was a twisted sense of logic prevalent in the dialogues of "The Goon Show" that was similar to the twisted logic of the plays of Harold Pinter, N. F. Simpson, or other contemporary playwrights in the genre of Theatre of the Absurd. "The Goon Show" scripts contained preposterous exaggerations and sound effects that reinforced Secombe's maniacal laugh, his numerous puns, and his nonsense exclamations as Seagoon (Batts 928).

In the novel, Twice Brightly (1974), Secombe is constantly punning. In Chapter 19 of Secombe's Goon for Lunch (1975), he describes a typical broadcast day at the Camden Theatre where "The Goon Show" was produced. He called the result "an anarchy in comedy" (Secombe Lunch 141). Some of Secombe's best stories are collected in Goon for Lunch, and in Goon Abroad (1982), and Secombe has more recently written what John Batts calls "a very readable autobiography" entitled Arias and Raspberries (1989) (Batts 928). The humor in Arias and Raspberries, like the humor in Secombe's other books, is broad rather than subtle, accepting rather than subversive, and benign rather than abrasive (Batts 929).

Harry Donald Secombe Bibliography

Batts, John S. "Harry Donald Secombe." Encyclopedia of British Humorists, Volume II. Ed. Steven H. Gale. New York, NY: Garland, 1996, 926-931.
Secombe, Harry. Arias and Raspberries. London, England: Robson, 1989.
Secombe, Harry. Goon for Lunch. London, England: Joseph, 1975.
Secombe, Harry. Goon Abroad. London, England: Robson, 1982.

Peter Ustinov (1921-)

A writer for the New Statesman and Nation once described Peter Ustinov as, "a tubby character with the affable, slouchy, sulky exterior of a Giant Panda." (Chapman and Dear 447). Ustinov has a wide range of imitations which includes a barking dog, a crying cat, a flamenco guitar, and a child's gastric disturbances (Chapman and Dear 448). Ustinov is part French, part Russian, and part Ethiopian, and Audrey Williamson feels that this fusion of cultures helps to explain the volatility and range of Ustinov's dramatic writings, his liberal mindedness, and his highly satiric view of politics, national character types, and international attitudes (Williamson 526). Like W. S. Gilbert, Peter Ustinov's mockery targets all sides, showing no particular allegiance to any of his targets (Williamson 529). L. Moody Simms says that Ustinov's strongest creative trait is his "civilized, mischievous wit." Ustinov himself says, "I have always been interested in the comic side of things tragic and in the melancholy side of things ribald." Ustinov's multi-cultural background probably supports his double vision, and therefore reinforces his satiric vision (Simms 1155).

Peter Ustinov wrote such plays as The House of Regrets (1942), The Banbury Nose (1944), The Love of Four Colonels (1851), No Sign of the Dove (1953), The Empty Chair (1956), Romanoff and Juliet (1956), Who's Who in Hell (1974), and Overheard (1981). The House of Regrets (1942), Ustinov's first play, is a tragi-comedy which demonstrates a brilliant sense of comic characterization (Williamson 526). L. Moody Simms says that The House of Regrets contains "brilliant comic characterizations," and shows Ustinov's "sympathetic identification with eccentrics" (Simms 1155). Since The Banbury Nose (1944) is written in reverse chronological order, the dramatic tension springs not from the playgoer's desire to know what happens next, but to know the past that has produced these results. The play is a satiric attack on the pukka-sahib tradition that was, "forced on each protesting generation of an army family." The play deals with the Hume-Banbury family, whose most distinguishing physical characteristic is the Bambury nose (Williamson 526). L. Moody Simms says that The Love of Four Colonels (1951) was Ustinov's first major comedy success. It is a wicked fairy tale set in a European state, and satirically targets various national characteristics, especially in terms of how people of different nationalities view love, the ideal woman, and war (Simms 1156). It deals with four colonels from four different countries. Each of these colonels not only represents a different point of view about international affairs, but also a different view of the military, and of love (Williamson 526). The Moment of Truth (1951) is Ustinov's satire of the tragedy of Marshall Petain. The fact that a senile marshall is brought out of retirement to be used as a figurehead by a government tottering on the edge of defeat in a civil war is a kind of political ridicule by Ustinov (Simms 1156). No Sign of the Dove (1953) is about an aging Matthew who builds an arc in the attic of his mansion, which is threatened by a flood (Williamson 526). The first act is a satire of Bloomsbury literary cliques, and the second is a bedroom farce (Williamson 527). The Empty Chair (1956) is about a sinister legend that claims that whoever sits in this chair is going to be the next victim for execution by the guillotine, and the legend comes true for Jacques Hebert, Danton, and Robespierre in their turns. But Paul Barras, a less important aristocrat is spared, but by now a new emperor is looming on the horizon (Williamson 527). Audrey Williamson shows how in The Empty Chair the wit stings by quoting one of the characters, "A revolution cannot afford a sense of humour" (Williamson 529). As L. Moody Simms states, "The irony and wit which characterize the talk of the play's protagonists is made all the more barbed by the realization that a revolution cannot bear the cost of humor" (Simms 1156). In Romanoff and Juliet (1956), Ustinov is taking a tongue-in-cheek swipe at diplomatic pomposity and political hypocrisy. It is set in the Russian and American embassies of Ruritania, during the cold-war rivalry that took place between these two super powers, and involved a Russian boy and an American girl in love, as their parents are serving as diplomats in the smallest country in Europe (Simms 1156). Romanoff and Juliet is about a delusional archbishop who marries Romanoff (an American boy), and Juliet (a Russian girl). The archbishop thinks that he is performing a symbolic marriage between two wax models (Williamson 529). L. Moody Simms says that in Who's Who in Hell (1974), "the promise of sharp political humor is undercut by, among other things, rather stale jokes" (Simms 1156). Simms says that Overheard (1981) is a comedy about an English diplomat and his wife which displays much wit and psychological insight (Simms 1157).

Peter Ustinov wrote such screenplays as Vice Versa (1947), Private Angelo (1949), and with Ira Wallach, Hot Millions (1968). Vice Versa (1947) is highly stylized, whimsical, and a bit surrealistic. It contains sly digs and witty asides as Ustinov satirizes the law, the military, the public school system, and female opportunism in Victorian England (Simms 1157). Private Angelo (1949) is a picaresque tale about an amiable chump who is caught in the War, and who drifts from one embarrassing episode to the next (Simms 1157). The film version of Romanoff and Juliet (1961) is, like the play, a satiric lampooning of national characteristics, but it is more, as the film version contains more of Ustinov's wryness, and more of his droll and whimsical humor (Simms 1157). Hot Millions (1968) was written in the witty tradition of the Alec Guinness comedies of the mid-1950s. It is an English comedy, and the humor originates from the character development. It takes sly and satiric gibes at British mores (Simms 1157).

The Loser (1961), Krumnagel (1971), The Disinformer (1989), and The Old Man and Mr. Smith: A Fable (1991) are novels. Hans Winterschild is a character in The Loser (1961) who wantonly massacres a Tuscan village and then is ironically hired as an extra by an American film company that is making a gaudy movie about the town's martyrdom. Simms says that the burlesque and satire work effectively in a number of different scenes in this tour de force (Simms 1158). Krumnagel (1971) is a satire about the contrasting ways that the British and the Americans view life, death, and the law. The humor is bitter and Ustinov makes shrewd comments on national characteristics, as Krumnagel's adventures bring him into contact with British justice, experimental prisons, American lovemaking, hard-hat types, street corner Buddhists, and forensic psychiatry. Thus Krumnagel is, "a collection of memorable and frequently humorous confrontations" (Simms 1158). The Disinformer (1989) is a satire in the form of two novellas (Simms 1158). The reviewer for Publishers Weekly said that in The Old Man and Mr. Smith: A Fable (1991), Ustinov gives, "priceless philosophical nuggets, as well as scathing satirical barbs" (qtd. in Chapman and Dear 448). L. Moody Simms considers The Old Man and Mr. Smith to be provocative, witty, and sometimes hilarious (Simms 1159).

Add a Dash of Pity (1959), and The Frontiers of the Sea (1966) are collections of short stories. In Add a Dash of Pity (1959), Ustinov's first collection of short stories, Ustinov uses wryly witty irony to develop his satire. Here the wit is astringent, but Ustinov nevertheless shows his affection for his eccentrics. "Dreams of Papua," one of the stories in The Frontiers of the Sea (1966), is about the problems of the East and the West that could be solved if only the heads of state "where harmless human beings at heart," and "could get together over some neat hobby such as stamp collecting" (Simms 1158). Ustinov wrote his autobiography, Dear Me (1977), with much intelligence and wit. It contains many amusing and entertaining anecdotes and what Simms calls "irrepressible jokiness." The writing is vivid, and at times epigrammatic (Simms 1159).

Peter Ustinov Bibliography

Chapman, Jeff, and Pamela S. Dear. Contemporary Authors, New Revision Series, Volume 51, 1996, 447-449.

Richards, Dick, ed. The Wit of Peter Ustinov. London, England: Leslie Frewin, 1969.

Simms, L. Moody Jr. "Peter Ustinov." Encyclopedia of British Humorists, Volume II. Ed. Steven H. Gale. New York, NY: Garland, 1996, 1153-1162.

Ustinov, Peter. Dear Me (autobiography). London, England: Heinemann, 1977.

Vinson, James, ed. Contemporary Dramatists. London, England: St. James Press, 1977.

Williamson, Audrey. "Peter Ustinov." Dictionary of Literary Biography, Volume Thirteen: British Dramatists Since World War II. Ed. Stanley Weintraub. Detroit, MI: Gale, 1982, 525-530.

Kingsley Amis (1922-1995)

Kingsley Amis wrote colloquial and witty anti-romantic poems, and sometimes even read his poetry on John Wain's BBC poetry program, "First Reading" (Waldhorn 5). The satire in Kingsley Amis's novels is frequently compared with the satire of Evelyn Waugh. It has also been compared with the satire of Peter DeVries, Daniel Defoe, Henry Fielding, and P. G. Wodehouse. Ironically, he has even been labeled an, "antiliberal, antigenteel, antimoralist, left-wing conservative, like Norman Mailer" (Waldhorn 4). Kingsley Amis writes dark novels, but even in his darkest novels there is much use of farce, complex Wodehousian-type linguistic jokes, black humor, and parody (Allen 20). Kenneth Allsop and other critics have placed Kingsley Amis into the group of "Angry Young Authors," along with John Braine, William Cooper, Iris Murdoch, John Osborne, Alan Sillitoe, John Wain, and Colin Wilson. What linked these writers was not so much their anger as their shared class origin (lower or middle class, but not upper class), and their unsettled social and cultural values. These authors resisted what Richard Hoggart called the "shiny barbarism" of the middle class (Waldhorn 5). In an article entitled "The Perils of Hypergamy" that appeared in Feldman and Gartenberg's The Beat Generation and the Angry Young Men, Geoffrey Gorer describes this group of authors. "Their heroes, like themselves, tend to be lower-middle-class, provincial, well-educated through grammar schools and scholarships, and generally overqualified and dissatisfied in the rigidly stratified class system that the Welfare State has failed to destroy. They aim at upward mobility, often through marriage to upper-middle-class girls" (qtd. in Allen 16). Amis himself didn't like being classed with the "Angry Young Authors," and said, "I don't like these glum chums" (Allsop 8). He further said about this group, "some of these presumptive colleagues one wouldn't like to be seen drinking with" (McDermott 21). Because Kingsley Amis's novels contain many literal interpretations of clichés and figures of speech, Brooke Allen compares Amis with P. G. Wodehouse. Allen says that Amis's writing also, "achieves superb comic effects through scrupulously exact recreations of the linguistic pretentions of recognizable social groups" (Allen 19). When critics accused Amis of changing his stance from being a left-wing radical to becoming a right-wing fascist, Amis responded, "I have not changed--I stand exactly where I was 20 or 30 years ago, opposed to totalitarianism in all its forms" (McDermott 36).

Discussing Lucky Jim (1954), That Uncertain Feeling (1955), I like it Here (1958), and Take a Girl Like You (1960), James P. Degnan says, "In the comically outraged voice of his angry young heroes--e.g., Jim Dixon of Lucky Jim and John Lewis of That Uncertain Feeling--Amis [Lampoons] what C. P. Snow...labels the 'traditional culture,' the 'culture of the literary intellectuals,' of the 'gentleman's world.'" Discussing these same four novels, James Gindin says that they are distinguished by, "a thick verbal texture that is essentially comic. The novels are full of word play and verbal jokes." Gindin then continues, "All Amis's heroes are mimics: Jim Dixon parodies the accent of Professor Welch, the phony and genteel professor in Lucky Jim; Patrick Standish, in Take a Girl Like You, deliberately echoes the Hollywood version of the Southern Negro's accent. John Lewis, the hero of That Uncertain Feeling, also mimics accents and satirically characterizes other people by the words and phrases they use" (Basil 11).

Kingsley Amis had a desire to use satire to expose recognized evil (including hypocrisy and pretension) and aggressively defend normative moral activity (Wilmes 11). He feels that it is essential for bad people to be viewed not only as bad, but as ridiculous as well (Wilmes 10). Joseph Priestly says that Kingsley Amis has the ability to be sharply droll, but adds that his desire to shock, and his brutality get in his way as a humorist (Priestley 114). Paul Fussell says that Amis is one of the best practitioners of moral satire. In this regard, Fussell goes so far as to place him in the same company as Jonathan Swift, Alexander Pope, Mark Twain, Gustave Flaubert, and H. L. Mencken (Teachout 12). Fussell's The Anti-Egotist contains numerous Amis epiphanies, many of which are outrageous and laughable, such as the following: "Twentieth-century music is like pedophilia. No matter how persuasively and persistently its champions urge their cause, it will never be accepted by the public at large, who will continue to regard it with incomprehension, outrage, and repugnance" (Teachout 12). Lucky Jim was followed quickly by three other comic novels. Kingsley Amis was quickly characterized as a comic novelist writing in the tradition of P. G. Wodehouse, and Evelyn Waugh (Basil 11).

Jim Dixon, the protagonist of Lucky Jim (1954) is a prototypical anti-hero. Jim represents the lower-middle-class drive to become part of the higher-class social system, and the guilt and self-contempt that result from abandoning one's own class. Jim is a lower-middle-class youth who earns a degree in an academic area that he neither likes nor understands. Because of his degree he gets a job as a junior lecturer in history at a provincial university, but he detests the medieval history he teaches, and he hates the cultural pretensions of the colleagues with whom he has to curry favor (Waldhorn 5). Sometimes Jim is a lout and a boor, but he is always entertaining. His mimicry is hilarious, and his slapstick debacles are uproarious. Amis uses an understated relaxed but precise vernacular prose in creating his comic spirit (Waldhorn 6). Lucky Jim is a broad farce which is anti-intellectual, frequently vulgar, and anti-Romantic in that it is grounded in the here and now (Allen 15). Lucky Jim fits very nicely into the genre of "New Comedy," with Jim in the role of "Eiron" or the self-deprecator, and the smarmy Bertrand Welch playing the role of the "Alazon" or the imposter. Professor Welch Senior is the intractable "Senex" and "Pedant" two roles which often come together in "New Comedy." The dénouement of Luck Jim is also in the tradition of "New Comedy," since the rich and powerful Gore-Urquhart is able to make the hero's fortune and unite him with the person he loves (Allen 16).

Edmund Fuller notes that Lucky Jim was, "written with the cool, detached, sardonic style which is the trademark of the British satirical novelist. Lucky Jim is funny in something approaching the Wodehouse vein, but it cuts a bit deeper." Ralph Caplan says that, "Lucky Jim never promises anything more than unmitigated pleasure and insight, and these it keeps on delivering. The book [is] not promise, but fulfillment, a commodity we confront too seldom to know how to behave when it is achieved. This seems to be true particularly when the achievement is comic. Have we forgotten how to take humor straight?" (Basil 11). Terry Teachout considers Lucky Jim to be one of the four or five funniest comic novels written during the twentieth century (Teachout 12). The four qualities that define traditional comedy can all be found in Lucky Jim, namely, 1) the use of festivity, 2) the playful tone or mood, 3) the pervasive use of comic irony, and 4) the happy ending. There are three scenes of festivity which might be said to turn into saturnalia--the arty weekend, the midsummer ball, and the Merrie England lecture, and these three scenes take up about half of the novel's total length. Jim's sense of festivity is at first private when the "festive, Yule-tide pop" of Welch's bottle of Port makes him feel "splendid." But later during the Merrie England lecture, Jim becomes the Lord of Misrule turning a pious ceremony into a living celebration of merry making (Stovel "Comic Mask" 72).

In Lucky Jim Amis uses a number of different comic devices. According to John Batts, the action is "stuffed with humor." Much of the description is also humorous, and the protagonist, as well as the characters he interacts with is also a constant source of humor. Amis frequently incorporates jokes into the text, and there is also a great deal of exaggeration, and some parody and irony. But it is the language itself and the texture of the prose, with its verbal tricks and amusing images, which provide much of the entertainment for the reader (Batts "Humor of Anger" 51). Innuendo is another comic device in Lucky Jim as on page 250 of the novel where Welch's car is seen, "parked slightly nearer one kerb than the other" (Stovel "Comic Mask" 74). Welch tells Jim that he must get his article published in order to establish his reputation in the department. Jim is amused, because he has only contempt for his article. He is contemptuous of the article's, "niggling mindlessness, its funereal parade of yawn-enforcing facts, [and] the pseudo-light it threw upon non-problems" (Lucky 20). It is especially ironic, therefore, when Jim discovers that his article has been published in translation by L. S. Caton, to whom he had originally submitted the article for consideration (Krishnan 22).

In Lucky Jim, Jim Dixon is a shy and bespectacled man in his mid-20s who is suspicious of academe in general and academic writing in particular, but he is also an ultimately fortunate picaro (Wilmes 9). He refers to academia as "this racket." As a university man, Jim considers himself to be a funny fish out of its element. He admits that he reads as little as possible, and he dislikes thinking about work. He has a habit of shelving questions, and is unable to act on decisions. He is also unable to read music, and is a poor reader of other things as well. He is socially inept, and dresses in a dirty old raincoat. He is a poor dancer. He is uninspired. He is not polite, and he keeps phone numbers in an old 1943 pocket diary. He has difficulty relating to women, and likes to stir his coffee with his fingers. Furthermore, he speaks in a "flat northern voice" (Batts "Humor of Anger" 52).

D. R. Wilmes considers Ned Welch in <u>Lucky Jim</u> to be, "a clown defeated by his own farcical ineptitude." When Welch attempts to leave the library and steps the wrong way into the revolving door, he is a fool. "Dixon stood and watched, allowing his mandrill face full play" (Wilmes 12). Ned Welch is an excruciatingly boring, inhumanly unsympathetic senior professor who insists on calling Jim by the name of his predecessor in the department. Jim is forced to laugh at Welch's jokes, but it is an anarchistic laughter that attacks, "conventional morality and stultified decorum, and is the stock-in-trade of comedy." Jim writes, "Ned Welch is a Soppy Fool with a Face Like A Pig's Bum," on Welch's steamy bathroom mirror (Bell 64). At times Jim can barely suppress his strong urge to punch Professor Welch, and Bertrand, his son. At one point in the novel Dixon has a vision of stuffing Welch into oblivion:

> He pretended to himself that he'd pick up his professor round the waist, squeeze the furry gray blue waist coat against him to expel the breath, run heavily with him up the steps, along the corridor to the Staff Cloakroom, and plunge the too-small feet in their capless shoes into a lavatory basin, pulling the plug once, twice, and again, stuffing the mouth with toilet paper. (<u>Lucky Jim</u> 9)

When Welch is playing a boring piano concerto for Jim, Jim thinks to himself,

> You ignorant clod, you stupid old sod,
> You havering slavering get.
> You wordy old turdy old scum
> You griping old piping old bum. (<u>Lucky Jim</u> 87)

Jim had similar visions about Margaret Peel. When Margaret asks Jim if he hates her, Jim wants, "to rush at her and tip her backwards in the chair, to make a deafening rude noise in her face, to push a bead up her nose" (Batts "Humor of Anger" 52).

In order to deal with his anger, Jim has manufactured a dazzling variety of faces. "He has a great repertory: a tragic mask; a half-conductor, half-boxer mask (which degenerates into a 'manic flurry of obscene gestures'); a Martian invader face; an Eskimo face; [and] a Sex Life in Ancient Rome face" (Bell 65). To this list of faces, John Batts adds the "shot-in-the-back face," the "consumptive face," the "crazy peasant face," the "tragic-mask face," the "lemon-sucking face," the "sex-maniac smile," the "Edith Sitwell face," and the "Evelyn Waugh face" (Batts 52). But with all of these, he still didn't have enough faces. "He thought what a pity it was that all his faces were designed to express rage or loathing. Now that something had happened which really deserved a face, he'd none to celebrate it with. As a kind of token, he made his Sex-Life-in-Ancient-Rome face" (<u>Lucky Jim</u> 250).

Bruce Stovel feels that <u>Lucky Jim</u> blends satire and farce into a broader comic vision, symbolized by Jim's comic faces, or comic masks. Stovel notes that the masquerade (the donning of masks) is a common theme of traditional comedy (Stovel 69), and adds that Jim is a "comic everyman" in the same way that Tom Jones is a comic everyman (Stovel "Comic Mask" 70). One of the reasons that Lucky Jim is called "Lucky" is that Gore-Urquhart offers him a job which is coveted by Bertrand (Bell 65). Urquhart explains, "It's not that you've got the qualification for this or any other work.... You haven't got the disqualifications, though, and that's much rarer" (<u>Lucky Jim</u> 234).

In <u>Lucky Jim</u> there is a double plot, and a struggle of conflicting social orders.

Gore-Urquhart is the comic deus ex machina in both of these plots. Not only does he offer Jim a new job, but he also frees Carol to tell Christine about her secret relationship with Bernard. There are a number of polar oppositions in Lucky Jim. Contrasting with the Welches, and Johns, their spy, is the comically diverse group consisting of Jim, Christine, Carol, Gore-Urquhart, and Atkinson. As in other traditional comedies, there is symmetry in the contrasting groupings. Contrasting with Margaret there is Bertrand. Contrasting with Atkinson there is Johns. On their way home from the dance, Jim tells Christine that she and Bertrand represent, "the two great classes of mankind, people I like and people I don't" (Lucky Jim 143).

Talking about Lucky Jim, Philip Gardner says, "As the novel progresses its essential subject changes from being a satire on university life and the provincial culture, fringed with snobbery represented by the Welches, and becomes Jim's search for, or at least movement toward, self-realization and self-fulfillment" (Gardner 29). R. S. Krishman says that by the end of the novel the reader is able to see how lucky Jim is. "He has vanquished his 'enemies' (The Welches, Margaret Peel, the stifling boredom of his academic position), won over Christine, his arch-rival Bertrand's erstwhile girlfriend, and, to top it all, has been blessed with the offer of a job by Christine's financier uncle, Julius Gore Urquhart." The novel ends with Lucky Jim being convulsed in laughter at the sight of Welch in a beret, and Bertrand in a fishing hat looking to Jim like, "Gide and Lytton Strachey, represented in waxwork form by a prentice hand." This goes to prove Dixon's axiom that, "nice things are nicer than nasty ones" (Krishnan 18).

Bruce Stovel considers That Uncertain Feeling (1955) to be "playful," and "remarkably funny," though most critics seem to have read the novel simply as "satirical social commentary." In this novel, Amis shows that he is not merely a satirist. Lucky Jim, and That Uncertain Feeling also establish Amis as having a larger comic vision, a vision which incorporates satire and farce and irony with humor and comedy (Stovel Uncertain Feeling 162). The novel has a double plot. John Lewis wants to win the right girl and he also wants to establish the right position in society. But at the same time he must fight for a better job and for more success in his sexual life. Since Elizabeth's husband is on the Libraries Committee, and since, "He asks my advice about a lot of things," John enters into an adulterous relationship with Elizabeth, assuming that it will bring him the promotion he needs to enable him and his family to move out of their dingy and crowded apartment (Stovel Uncertain Feeling 164). Ironically, Lewis pretends that his pursuit of Elizabeth isn't related to his getting a promotion, and he is galled when he overhears that "that librarian fellow of Elizabeth's" is an "adulterer" and a "calculating librarian." It is the expression "calculating librarian" and not the term "adulterer" that most wounds Lewis. Elizabeth does manage to make Lewis second in command, not because Lewis is a good lover, but because, "the thing that would annoy Rowlands most would be having you as his second in command. So you're going to be his second in command" (Stovel Uncertain Feeling 162). But John finally realizes that it is his wife Jean that he loves most, so he renounces both Elizabeth and her job (Stovel Uncertain Feeling 164), and in fact tells Jean the entire story about his relationship with Elizabeth. Jean somehow doesn't appreciate John's sacrifice, and rather than seeing a double victory she sees a double defeat. John has shattered their marriage bond not only by having sex with Elizabeth, but also by not getting the new job the family needed so badly. At the end of the novel, "the situation has returned, dance-like to what it had been at the outset," and John has demonstrated his bristling wit and his introspective insight. John prides himself on his intelligence, but he nevertheless must endure the, "humiliation of catching himself being thoroughly obtuse" (Stovel Uncertain Feeling 165).

I Like It Here (1958) is a parody of Henry James. I Like It Here satirizes both the xenophobic Bowen, and by extension the continent of Europe, but it also satirizes the cultural snobs, the opposites of the xenophobes, who are so often the targets of Amis's humor (Allen 17).   Amis wrote the lighthearted but serious <u>New Maps of Hell: A Survey of Science Fiction</u> (1960) in an attempt to help to legitimize the genre. Amis said that science fiction, "allows us to doff that mental and moral best behaviour with which we feel we have to treat George Eliot and James and Faulkner, and frolic like badly brought up children among the mobile jellyfishes and unstable atomic piles" (Fisher 9). In <u>Take a Girl Like You</u> (1960) Amis concentrates on the comic, social, and moral dimensions of the central conflict between Jenny Bunn and Patrick Standish (Wilmes 13). James P. Degnan says that Patrick Standish in <u>Take a Girl Like You</u> is almost an antihero because of his blasé, irresponsible, hedonistic ways. This is ironic because Amis's first three novels had attacked this kind of anti-hero. Rubin Rabinovitz suggests that the satire of <u>Take a Girl Like You</u> targets both Patrick's lechery and Jenny's persistence in preserving her virginity (Basil 12). Amis exploits the comic possibilities of circumlocution in <u>Take a Girl Like You</u> when he has Patrick Standish say to God, "I'm not trying to get credit with you by saying I know I'm a bastard. Nor by saying I'm not trying to get credit. Nor by saying I'm not trying to by saying...trying...you know what I mean" (Allen 20).

"Morale Fibre," the fourth story in <u>My Enemy's Enemy</u> (1962), is about Betty Arnulfsen whose employment has been arranged by Mair Webster, a local social worker who is married to a colleague of John Lewis. Throughout the story, Mair tries to reform Betty. John refers to Betty not as a "fallen woman," but rather as a woman who is, "rather inadmissibly inclined from the perpendicular." Betty goes back to her old hangout, and turns to prostitution, and then she returns to John and propositions him, at which point he remarks that she is, "really fallen now, right smack over full length" (Fisher 7). As "Morale Fiber" ends, John predicts that Mair will probably continue intruding into Betty's life by visiting her in jail, and more. He says that, "the people best suited to do anything about society's ills are those last likely to do so." "Interesting Things" is another ironic and humorous story in <u>My Enemy's Enemy</u>. This story is about the first date of Gloria Davies and Mr. Huws-Evans, a drab and totally conventional income-tax inspector. The story is seen through the eyes of Gloria, who makes an extensive inventory of Mr. Huws-Evans's various quirks, including his string-bag full of potato chips, and his violent admonishings against the manufacturers of razor blades. Much of the irony of the story comes from the fact that the only reason that Gloria has agreed to date Mr. Huws-Evans at all is in order to meet his brother (Fisher 8).

<u>One Fat Englishman</u> (1963) is about the adventures of forty-year-old Roger Micheldene, a lecherous British publisher on a business holiday in the United States whom Edward Kelly describes as "rotund and riotous." "Of the seven deadly sins, Roger considered himself qualified in gluttony, sloth, and lust but distinguished in anger" (Waldhorn 7). The novel is also about Irving Macher, a New York writer of "absurd literature" who nettles Roger Micheldene by calling him "Mr. Dean." "The name is Micheldene," says Roger. "It has a hyphen does it? Like Mitchell-Dean?" "No no no, it's one word" (Kelly 132). Irving Macher's name is not only a play on the English word "mocker," but it is also a play on the Yiddish word "macher," which is a pejorative slang term signifying "a phony big deal," or a "man on the make, especially in the business sense." Irving has difficulty pronouncing "St. John" (Roger Micheldene's middle name) in the correct English manner, so after failing with such pronunciations as "Sun-john" and "Sinjurn," Irving finally asks for advice and then gets it correct, saying "Sinjun. Rhymes with Honest Injun.... Will I shan't go wrong in the future." Strode Atkins, who comes from a small valley in West Virginia also has difficulty with British pronunciations but finally learns to pronounce "out" and "about" as "oat" and "aboat." It is through linguistic games such as these that Amis develops much of his satirical commentary on Americans (Kelly 133). One such significant linguistic encounter in the novel is when Roger is being

beaten in a game of Scrabble by an eight year-old. Roger becomes very angry when the boy puts down the word "niter."

"Niter? What's that supposed to mean?"
"You know, like a one nighter."
"No such word."
"Challenge me?"
"Most certainly I challenge you."
"All right."

Arthur opened a dictionary and said,

"Here we are. Niter. Potassium nitrate. A supposed nitrous element--"
"Rubbish, that's n,i,t,r,e,"
"Mm-mm. See for yourself."
"I...But this is a bloody American dictionary."
"This is bloody America." (Kelly 134)

Roger had been losing anyway because he had been drawing only A's, E's, I's, O's, and U's. Therefore, to avoid total humiliation, he upsets the Scrabble board. One of the reasons that Roger is so upset is that he considers himself so linguistically adept, and later in the novel when he is making love to Helene, he mentally parses Latin and Greek verbs, and recites passages from classical literature in order to help slow down his passion (Kelly 135).

Much of the novel revolves around an American University by the name of Budweiser College, possibly patterned after Princeton University where Amis had been a guest lecturer. Roger makes constant barbs at American pretensions to culture, but Amis's lack of familiarity with common American idioms makes some of the satire ring false (Kelly 136). But it is not only American idioms which are being satirized. Other targets of the satire include American morals, marriages, culture, and universities. "To point out that Roger himself is an immoral glutton does not exonerate the host of Americans in the novel who are as bad or worse" (Kelly 137). The humor of One Fat Englishman is developed by, "asides, slapstick, honed images, parody, mimicry, outlandish words, and highly wrought phrasing of verbal fun" (Batts "Amis Abroad" 34). Amis also uses invective in a humorous way, as can be seen in Roger Micheldene's curse of Father Colgate: "I'll confuse you, you bead-telling toad. I wouldn't take your absolution if you begged me. Try absolving yourself from the disgrace of abetting a disgrace. And stop telling me what to do, you silly little man" (Wilmes 14). One Fat Englishman makes fun of America and of Americans. Some of the descriptions are decidedly jaundiced, as when an American church is given the following description: "His eye fell at once on a building that looked like sections from a concrete battleship, with masts and turrets and portholes. It had a chromium cross stuck on its maintop to denote its function" (One Fat Englishman 80). John Batts considers this description to be a delicate mixture of the outrageous, the unusual, the flippant, and the observant (Batts "Amis Abroad" 35).

In the scrabble episode, Amis mocks American usage and spelling simply because it differs from the Queen's English. And American names are also made fun of, because they aren't like the name of Micheldene, with its upper-middle-class Englishness, and with its "great golden initials...R. H. St. J. W. M." (One Fat Englishman 131). There are times in One Fat Englishman when Amis's clever linguistic jokes, which pivot on obscure Britishisms, are in need of translation (Kelly 132). There is a double target in the satire of One Fat Englishman. English readers laugh with Micheldene at the funny language and traditions of the Americans. Micheldene puzzles over the American usage of such terms as "band," "sneakers," "tickertape," and "marquee." He frequently boasts that he cannot drive, tries to impress Americans with snuff-boxes, and snuff taking, and how to develop discriminating taste in fine cigars. He attacks America as a class-ridden society.

Eventually, however these English readers become aware of the fact that Micheldene himself is an absurd figure of pompous fatuity (Batts "Amis Abroad" 36).

The Egyptologists (1965) is a comedy about a pseudoscholarly society of Egyptologists. These Egyptologists use their seminar rooms for amorous rendezvous that are often with each other's wives (Waldhorn 8). The Anti-Death League (1966) is about a group of madcap characters. One is a lunatic psychoanalyst who denies all of the signs that he is heterosexual. Another is a charming nymphomaniac who prefers to call herself "polyandrous." Finally, there is the witty army captain who is an unashamed drunk and homosexual (Waldhorn 8). Major Ayscue is the army chaplain in The Anti-Death League who doesn't become a believer until the end of the novel. "Whenever he had prayed before it had been like talking into an empty room.... But this time it came upon him with certainty...that the room had ceased to be empty." Ironically, it is just at this time of religious conversion that Nancy, Major Ayscue's pet dog, is run down by a car (Pazereskis 30-31). James Churchill, the protagonist in The Anti-Death League tries to be a pure and idealistic knight in a modern world, but when a number of his acquaintances die, and when the woman he loves develops cancer, Churchill comes to believe that he is being trained to conduct bacteriological warfare (Wilmes 15). Churchill loses his faith, and finally concludes that only those with no sense of right and wrong could believe in God (Wilmes 16). About The Anti-Death League, Marilyn Basil says, "there is still a trace of sardonic humor, and his [Amis's] ear remains alert to the placing of details of individual speech; but Amis has here abandoned the incisive social mimicry, the memorable responses to the specificity of a person's appearance or the look of a room that have previously characterized his fiction" (Basil 12).

I Want It Now (1968) is basically a fairy tale in which a sleazy TV personality named Ronnie Appleyard, the epitome of media hypocrites, is in pursuit of an heiress named Simona Quick. Simona appears to be a troubled nymphomaniac who specializes in sexual excesses, but it turns out that her nymphomania is only a cover for her frigidity. Ronnie talks straight into the camera doing his "sincerity routine," complete with, "raised eyebrows and a lot of nodding" as he mouths fatuities about social problems that he really cares nothing about (Allen 18). Ironically, Ronnie Appleyard is able to win the madcap heiress just as she loses her inheritance, and he accepts her, as he assesses the situation, "I was shit when I met you. I still am in a lot of ways. But because of you I've had to give up trying to be a dedicated, full-time shit" (Waldhorn 9).

The Green Man (1969) is an absorbing ghost story that is both funny and grim. It is about the ghost of a murderous seventeenth-century parson who is roused by the behavior of Maurice Allington, the middle-aged owner of a pub named "The Green Man." The pub is the house where the parson had once lived (Waldhorn 9), and the depraved ghost senses an affinity with Allington, as he mistakes Allington's drunkenness and lechery for satanism. Allington, for example, arranges an orgy with his wife and his mistress only to end up as the only non-participant, as the wife and mistress take delight in each other and finally go off together (Waldhorn 10). In The Green Man, Tom Rodney Sonnenschein is like Father Colgate and Father Ayscue in being the butt of the satire (Pazereskis 30). Sonnenschein is a completely corrupt reverend who remarks, "You know, this whole immortality bit's been pretty well done to death. One's got to take the historical angle. Immortality's just a passing phase." Joyce, Allington's wife asks, "What's the point of somebody like you [Sonnenschein] being a parson when you say you don't care about things like duty and people's souls and sin? Isn't that just exactly what parsons are supposed to care about?" (Wilmes 17). Melvin Maddocks says that a "chilling fatalism" permeates The Green Man, "as though everything was predestined--jokes and all." Jonathan Yardley feels that The Green Man is, "frequently funny, tedious when the dialogue turns weighty, determinedly suave, [and] a shade too nimble in plot." Porterfield says that the tensions in The Green

Man are. "dissipated at crucial moments by cold dashes of caustic humor" (Basil 12). The Green Man ends with Allington alone, having been rejected not only by the satanic ghost, but also by his wife, and by his mistress (Waldhorn 10).

Brooke Allen considers Girl 20 (1971) to be a hilarious book. But Allen says that although Girl 20 is very funny, it is also very bitter (Allen 18). Girl 20 is, "a comic novel with serious overtones" (Basil 12). Paul Schleuter says that Girl 20 demonstrates Amis's, "talent for creating humorous situations, characters, and dialogue" (Basil 13). Sir Roy Vandervane in Girl 20 betrays his identity as a serious musician by composing and performing a piece for violin and rock band (Wilmes 11). Sir Roy Vandervane is the principle target of Girl 20, and Yandell is Vandervane's judge as well as his accomplice. "Amis launches satiric attacks left and right against Vandervane and the youth-cult, his more general target" (Wilmes 17). Vandervane adopts all of the symbolic aspects of the youthful pop culture, such as long hair, slurred speech, capricious dress, and musical fads, and he shares them with his youngest mistress, Sylvia Meera, the mindless, but sexually inventive "Girl 20" of the novel's title (Waldhorn 10). Penny has the last word in Girl 20, as she expresses the final dark joke, "We're all free now" (Wilmes 19).

Dear Illusion (1972) is a humorous and touching story about Edward Potter, who is Great Britain's leading poet but is nevertheless obscure. The story is told by Susan MacNamara, a reporter who has been sent to interview him (Fisher 8). On Drink (1972) contains short-stories with such titles as, "Aperitifs: As If You Needed Any Encouragement to Start Drinking, Here's What to Start With," and, "Stout Work: A Day in the Life of a Bottle of Guiness, Lovingly Recorded by Kingsley Amis." Collected Short Stories (1987) contains short stories with such titles as "The 2003 Claret," "The Friends of Plonk," "Too Much Trouble," and "Investing in Futures." These four stories reinforce the stories in On Drink to help develop a genre which John McDermott refers to as "Science-Fiction-Drink," or more simply as "SF-drink" (Fisher 9). "The 2003 Claret" reports on the widening gap between the pretentious snobbery of wine drinkers and the equally-pretentious anti-snobbery of beer drinkers. In "The Friends of Plonk," the year is 2145, and Simpson encounters a small group of men trying to rekindle the old ability people used to have to enjoy alcoholic beverages. People had lost this ability during the war between Wales and Mars. In "Too Much Trouble," Simpson suggests that by the year 1983, liquor will be served in packets of powder that are mixed with water to produce stout, scotch, gin, vodka, and bitter. Of the last mixture, he says that it bears, "very much the same relation to our bitter as powdered coffee to coffee." In "Investing in Futures," Simpson goes back to the Middle Ages in order to procure root cuttings from Burgundy vineyards. Mathew Fisher says that Amis's "SF-Drink" stories, "offer lighthearted satire" (Fisher 10).

There is a debate among critics about whether to read The Riverside Villas Murder (1973) as straight, or as a parody of the genre of detective stories. In this novel, Amis makes a fourteen-year-old boy the hero, and T. E. Kalem suggests that in doing this, "Amis cleverly combines, in mild parody, two ultra-British literary forms--the mystery thriller and the boyhood adventure yarn" (Basil 13). Brooke Allen says that although Ending Up (1973) is extremely funny, it is also in many ways the blackest of Amis's novels (Allen 18). The satiric target of Ending Up is modern society's attitude toward the aged, as it condemns them to the roles of the senile and the childish (Wilmes 18). Ending Up takes place at Tuppenny-hapenny Cottage, which is a closed world where five old, decrepit, and unpleasant people live, having been thrown together by accidents of their lives. Now that they are old they have come to thoroughly dislike each other and the weaknesses and bad habits that age has brought to each of them. Each of these residents begins to think how much more pleasant life would be without the others, and they therefore do what they can to inflict pain on those who have particularly irritated them. Marigold, for instance, notices that a dog's ball is lying on the stairs, but instead of picking it up, she leaves it there, "saying to herself idly that it would do one or the other of those two no harm to tread on it and take a bit of a toss." In like manner, Bernard Bastable, who used to be the homosexual lover of his servant Shorty, concocts elaborate plans to convince Shorty that his drinking is beginning to affect his bodily functions, by launching "Operation Stink and Incontinence," whereby he heats a can of urine to body temperature and pours it on him while he is asleep (Wilmes 19). Bernard Bastable is truly contemptible. He is, "malevolently witty and actively malevolent." Amis calls Bastable, "the most unpleasant of my leading characters." He is resourceful in the way he humiliates everyone.

> What diminishes the comic force of Ending Up-- and several of its set scenes are mercilessly funny--is that the other characters make poor targets for satire. Shorty is a harmless drunk and a reasonably efficient gardener and handyman. Bastable's sister Adela, the selfless housekeeper for the curious menage, is gentle, unattractive, and unloved. Her kittenish friend, the widowed Marigold, grasps at frayed fabric from her past as her memory slips away. George, an ex-professor paralyzed by a stroke, must also endure the mortification of circumlocution necessitated by nominal aphasia (an inability to recall nouns). Each of these pitiable creatures is the victim of physical frailty rather than social or moral foibles. (Waldhorn 10)

Nevertheless, Marilyn Basil says that, "despite his continual joking, and sometimes apparently callous indifference, Amis has written [in Ending Up] a very moving study of the pain of old age" (Basil 13).

Paul Gray says that The Alteration (1976), "flits quirkily between satire, science fiction, boy's adventure, and travelogue" (Basil 13). In this novel, a brilliant boy soprano is discovered by the Church, and the Church plans to preserve his gift by, "altering" his anatomy through castration. John Carey says that this novel is about, "the destructive power of the pontifical hierarchy to emasculate life and art" (Basil 13). The protagonist of The Alteration is a ten-year-old boy named Hubert Anvil who is a boy soprano of such extraordinary talent that his fame reaches Rome, where it is decided that he must be castrated in order to preserve his pure voice for singing church music. The Alteration is about the conflict between art and life, between religious and human values, between church needs and individual integrity. The resolution is devastating, and bitter in its irony. The novel has moments of good fun, such as the parody, and, "the overdrawn clergymen and the built-in comic effects incidental to an alternate world" (Waldhorn 11). Brooke Allen says that of all of Kingsley Amis's work, The Alteration is the most Swiftian. "It achieves the ruthless force and outrageous plausibility of A Modest Proposal" (Allen 19).

In Jake's Thing (1978), Jake is able to perform sexually, except that he has no desire. No one arouses him, not his third wife who is young but overweight, nor the other women that he often sleeps with. So Jake visits a sexual therapeutist who gives him the task of reading pornographic magazines while wired up to a machine that computes his level of arousal, and an all-out weekend workshop intended to, "release checks on emotion and to improve insight." But nothing works (Waldhorn 12). In Jake's Thing, a great deal of black humor and ridicule is heaped on the therapists and psychoanalysts who are trying to restore Jake's libido (Allen 18). Brooke Allen says that Amis uses much professional jargon from academia, medicine, and other professions, to satirically target these professions, and this is nicely demonstrated in Chapter 4 of Jake's Thing, where a doctor describes one of the therapies as follows: "In a non-genital sensate focusing session the couple lie down together in the nude and stroke and massage the non-genital areas of each other's bodies in turns of two or three minutes at a time for a period of up to half an hour." Another therapy is described thus, "Now we come to the use of the nocturnal mensurator. If you'd just step over here, Mr. Richardson...." Jake's Thing is a "comic diatribe" which V. S. Pritchett considers to be, "a very funny book, less for its action or its talk than its prose." Pritchett says that this book demonstrates Amis's ability to be "a master of laconic mimicry and of the vernacular drift." In the novel, Jake Richardson is referred to Dr. Proinsias Rosenberg, a sex therapist, who in turn introduces Jake Richardson to a variety of encounter groups, free love, women's liberation, and such electronic contrivances as the "nocturnal mensurator," designed to measure the level of a man's arousal while he is asleep. Christopher Lehmann-Haupt says that the novel makes the most of the comic possibilities of the situation, adding that Jake is assigned to, "study pictorial pornographic material, and to write out a sexual fantasy in not less than six hundred words." John Updike considers the satire of Jake's Thing to be "more horrifying than biting, more pathetic than amusing." Updike adds that, "Jake has more complaints than the similarly indisposed Alexander Portnoy" in Portnoy's Complaint by Philip Roth (Basil 14). At the end of Jake's Thing, his family doctor suggests a physical cure--raising his level of testosterone. Jake thinks for a few minutes, running various women through his mind, and then he tells the doctor, "No thanks." When forced to make the choice, Jake opts for misogyny rather than virility (Waldhorn 12).

Many critics consider Amis's satirical Stanley and the Women (1984) to be filled with "cranky mysogynism." Susan Fromberg Schaeffer notes, however, that in Stanley and the Women the men don't fare any better than the women, so she considers the novel to be not just misogynist, but misanthropic as well. This may be true, but some critics have argued that all comedy and all humor is "unfair," and they have further argued that the novel is valuable if it, "dramatizes thoughts that some people, somewhere, have had." Harriet Waugh, for example, argues, "Mr. Amis's portrayal of Stanley's wives as female monsters is funny and convincing. Most readers will recognize aspects of them in women they know" (Basil 15). Kingsley Amis won the Booker-McConnell Prize for Fiction for The Old Devils (1986), because of its wit, humanity, and observation. Marilyn Basil says that one significant fact about this novel is that it was written late in Amis's writing career, and is therefore masterful in its ability to conjoin the "mischievous with the mellow" (Basil 15). According to Christopher Buckley, The Russian Girl (1992) is a brilliant, mordant, and funny novel about sex, booze, and Russian intrigue. In this novel, Richard Vaisey is a 46-year-old professor at the London Institute of Slavonic Studies. Buckley describes Vaisey as

> a horny Russian-lit-loving academic whose 'idea of a perfect day was a couple of lectures and a seminar in the morning,' a little sex in the afternoon, followed by 'a catching-up on linguistic studies, a solitary dinner with a learned journal by his plate and a quiet evening trying out a possible new line on Father Zosima's stuff in 'The Brothers Karamazov,' with half an hour on Lermontov before retiring. (Buckley 11)

In a 1975 article for Contemporary Literature, Amis reflects on his excursions into new areas of fiction, and the criticism he has received for doing so:

> So I'm a funny writer, am I? Ending Up, you'll have to admit, is quite serious. Oh, so I'm primarily a comic writer with some serious overtones and undertones? Try that with The Anti-Death League and see how that fits. So I'm a writer about society, twentieth-century man and our problems? Try that one on The Green Man. Except for one satirical portrait, that of the clergyman, it is about something quite different. So there is a lot of sex? Try that on Ending Up, in which sexual things [are] referred to, but they've all taken place in the past because of the five central characters the youngest is seventy-one. So you dislike the youth of today, Mr. Amis, as in Girl 20? Try that on Ending Up where all the young people are sympathetic and all the old people are unsympathetic. This can be silly, but I think it helps to prevent one from repeating oneself, and [Robert]

Graves [said] the most dreadful thing in the world is that you're writing a book and you suddenly realize you're writing a book you've written before. Awful. I haven't quite done that yet, but it's certainly something to guard against. (Basil 16)

Kingsley Amis Bibliography

Allen, Brooke. "Kingsley Amis." Encyclopedia of British Humorists, Volume I. Ed. Steven H. Gale. New York, NY: Garland, 1996, 14-22.

Allsop, Kenneth. The Angry Decade. Wendover, England: John Goodchild, 1985.

Amis, Kingsley. The Anti-Death League. New York, NY: Harcourt, Brace and World, 1966.

Amis, Kingsley. Ending Up. New York, NY: Harcourt, Brace, Jovanovich, 1974.

Amis, Kingsley. The Green Man. New York, NY: Ballantine Books, 1971.

Amis, Kingsley. Lucky Jim. New York, NY: Viking, 1958.

Amis, Kingsley. One Fat Englishman. London, England: Victor Gollancz, 1963.

Amis, Kingsley. The Russian Girl. New York, NY: Viking, 1992.

Amis, Kingsley. Take a Girl Like You. New York, NY: New American Library/Signet, 1963.

Amis, Kingsley. That Uncertain Feeling. New York, NY: Harcourt, Brace and Company, 1955.

Basil, Marilyn K. "Kingsley Amis." Contemporary Authors, New Revision Series, Volume 28. Eds. Hal May, and James G. Lesniak. Detroit, MI: Gale Research, 1990, 9-17.

Batts, John Stuart. "Amis Abroad: American Occasions for English Humor." HUMOR: International Journal of Humor Studies 5.3 (1992): 251-266.

Batts, John Stuart. "The Humor of Anger: Looking Back at Amis and Company." WHIMSY 4 (1986): 51-54.

Bell, Robert H. " 'True Comic Edge' in Lucky Jim." American Humor 8.2 (1981): 1-7; also in WHIMSY 3 (1985): 64-66.

Buckley, Christopher. "A Little Sex, a Little Dostoyevsky--In Kingsley Amis's novel, that's the Hero's Idea of a Perfect Day." New York Times Book Review. May 15, 1994: 11-12.

Feldman, Gene and Max Gartenberg, eds. The Beat Generation and the Angry Young Men. Secaucus, NY: Citadel Press, 1984.

Fisher, Mathew David. "Kingsley Amis." Dictionary of Literary Biography, Volume One Hundred Thirty-Nine: British Short-Fiction Writers, 1945-1980. Ed. Dean Baldwin. Detroit, MI: Gale, 1994, 3-13.

Fussell, Paul. The Anti-Egotist: Kingsley Amis, Man of Letters. New York, NY: Oxford University Press, 1994.

Gardner, Philip. Kingsley Amis. Boston, MA: Twayne, 1981.

Ginden, James. Postwar British Fiction. Berkeley, CA: University of California Press, 1962.

Kelly, Edward. "Satire and Word Games in Amis's Englishman." Satire Newsletter 9 (1972): 132-138.

Krishnan, R. S. "Closure in Kingsley Amis's Lucky Jim. Studies in Contemporary Satire 18 (1991-1992): 18-25.

McDermott, John. Kingsley Amis: An English Moralist. London, England: Macmillan, 1989.

Pazeriskis, John. "Kingsley Amis--the Dark Side." Studies in Contemporary Satire 4 (1977): 28-33.

Priestley, J. B. English Humour. New York, NY: Stein and Day, 1976.

Stovel, Bruce. "A Comedy of Conscience: Kingsley Amis's The Uncertain Feeling."

International Fiction Review 4 (1977): 162-166.

Stovel, Bruce. "Traditional Comedy and the Comic Mask in Kingsley Amis's Lucky Jim."
    English Studies in Canada 4 (1978): 69-80.

Teachout, Terry. "The Old Devil Himself." The New York Times Book Review. September
    11, 1994, 12.

Waldhorn, Arthur. "Kingsley Amis." Dictionary of Literary Biography, Volume Fifteen:
    British Novelists, 1930-1959. Ed. Bernard Oldsey. Detroit, MI: Gale, 1983, 3-13.

Wilmes, D. R. "When the Curse Begins to Hurt: Kingsley Amis and Satiric Confrontation."
    Studies in Contemporary Satire 5 (1978): 9-21.

John Braine (1922-1986)

John Braine is one of England's most prominent novelists. Kenneth Allsop, Judy Simons and other critics have placed John Braine into the group of "Angry Young Men," along with Kingsley Amis, William Cooper, John Osborne, Alan Sillitoe, John Wain, and Colin Wilson (simons 47; Allsop 8).

John Braine Bibliography

Allsop, Kenneth. The Angry Decade. Wendover, England: John Goodchild, 1985.

Simons, Judy. "John Braine." British Novelists, 1930-1959: Dictionary of Literary
    Biography, Volume 15. Ed. Bernard Oldsey. Detroit, MI: Bruccoli Clark/Gale
    Research, 1983, 47-55.

(Maureen) Mollie Hunter (McIlwraith) (1922-) SCOTLAND

In Third Book of Junior Authors, Mollie Hunter writes, "My father was merry and fiery by nature; my mother merry and gentle. His tongue had a charm to it that could coax a bird out of a bush. She was like many a Borderer before her, a born storyteller. Together they set the standards that have been the main formative influence on my life" (Lesniak 249). Mollie Hunter enjoyed her English classes at Preston Lodge School, and she especially enjoyed writing essays in which she would play with language. One teacher asked her what she wanted to be when she grew up, and she replied, "a kennel maid." The teacher called the answer "nonsense," and predicted that Mollie would grow up to become a writer (Hunt 211).

Mollie Hunter enjoyed telling stories to her children, and one of her favorite subjects was an Irishman named Patrick Kintigern Keenan. Quentin, Mollie's oldest son suggested that she write the Patrick stories into a book, so that he could read them, and the result was Patrick Kintigern Keenan (1963). Mollie would read the various installments to her sons, and on one occasion she discovered that one of the boys was weeping. "Those tears, Hunter later wrote, convinced her more than ever that she should become a writer" (Hunt 212). This book was later published in the United States as The Smartest Man in Ireland (1965). The book is about a stubborn, cocky person who stands up against a supernatural force, and finally emerges victorious. Patrick, the novel's protagonist, is lazy and both stubborn and proud, thinking that he can outwit the local leprechauns. He tries to trick them into paying for a pair of their boots with false gold, and in retribution, they kidnap his son, and he must work as a slave to get his son back. The book is concerned with Patrick's change of character. Although both Patrick and his son remain stubborn to the end of the novel, Patrick learns to value his wife's common sense, and comes to realize that there are things more important than fairy gold and magical objects (Hunt 213).

Hi Johnny (1963) is a novel which features exotic characters and a series of plot twists (Hunt 213). In The Spanish Letters (1964), Jamie Morton is a "caddie," who hires himself out as a messenger or porter. Jamie is headstrong, impetuous, and at the same time romantic (Hunt 213). There are a number of exciting plot twists in The Spanish Letters (Hunt 214). Thomas, the blacksmith in Thomas and the Warlock (1967) endangers his family by believing that he is able to outwit the supernatural beings. The novel suggests that it is through unselfishness and community cooperation that we can vanquish evil foes. "When first published, Thomas and the Warlock was commended for both its humor and original characters" (Hunt 215).

You Never Knew Her as I Did! (1981) is about a page named Will Douglas. Will is the illegitimate son of Sir William Douglas. Mary, Queen of Scotts, who is being held captive at Lochleven at the time, befriends Will Douglas, and calls him "my little orphan" to soften the fact that everyone else calls him "bastard."

> The book culminates in the celebration of a holiday, in this case a festival in honor of May Day and Will's birthday, during which Will plays 'The Lord of Misrule,' pretending to be a fool. His wild antics become a cover for the queen's escape, which does not, however, prevent her eventual death years later. (Hunt 222)

Both The Knight of the Golden Plain (1983), and The Three Day Enchantment (1985) are illustrated by Marc Simont, winner of the Caldecott Medal. Both of these books mock the conventions of traditional hero tales. The hero in both is Sir Dauntless, the Knight of the Golden Plain, who spends a Saturday on a quest. The introduction, the illustrations, and the text all hint that the knight is actually a contemporary boy who is imagining these adventures (Hunt 222).

The Pied Piper Syndrome and Other Essays (1992) is an excellent fantasy story about the culture of the Shetland Islands, north of Scotland. The novel tells about the post-Christmas festival named "Up Helly Aa." It also tells about a traditional Shetland funeral, and contains many riddles and folktales (Hunt 219). Gilly Martin the Fox (1994) "retains the simplicity and humor of the original tale, once again demonstrating Hunter's power as a storyteller" (Hunt 223).

(Maureen) Mollie Hunter (McIlwraith) Bibliography

Hunt, Caroline C. Ed. British Children's Writers Since 1960. Detroit, MI: Gale, 1996.
Lesniak, James G., ed. "Mollie Hunter." Contemporary Authors: New Revision Series, Volume 37. Detroit, MI: Gale, 1992.

Philip (Arthur) Larkin (1922-1985)

Kingsley Amis said that his friend Philip Larkin was, "an almost aggressively normal undergraduate of the non-highbrow, non-sherry-sipping sort, hard-searing, hard-belching, etc., treating the college dons as fodder for obscene clerihews and the porter as a comic ogre" (Fisher 5). Philip Larkin's humor may be sarcastic, sardonic, bizarre, and witty, but it is not very funny. When he was asked what he thought he looked like he quickly replied, "Like a bald salmon" (Whalen 10). In his criticism of John Betjeman's poetry, Larkin notes a kind of flexibility and friskiness of tone which Larkin would like to achieve in his own poetry. "His texture is a subtle, a constant flickering between solemn and comic, self-mockery and self-expression...; he offers us, indeed, something we cannot find in any other writer--a gaiety, a sense of the ridiculous." Larkin's own poetry is marked by its ironic tone, which serves to restrain his more solemn intent. This ironic tone can be seen in "Church Going," "Born Yesterday," "The Old Fools," and "High Windows," and can also be seen in such sarcastic poems as "Sad Steps," where the narrator is found "groping back to bed after a piss." Terry Whalen compares the tone of "Sad Steps" with the tone of Geoffrey Chaucer's "The Millers Tale," in which Chaucer talks about people being "risen for to pisse." Larkin's poetry is punctuated, some would say punctured, by such sudden phrases as "in a pig's arse, friend," "books are a load of crap," or "stuff your pension," even though Larkin himself proclaims, "I don't think I've ever shocked for the sake of shocking" (Larkin xxxviii). Peter R. King says that there is a lucidity of language in Larkin's poetry that invites understanding even though the ideas expressed are complex or paradoxical. Peter Jones adds that Larkin's, "ironic detachment is comprehensive. Even the intense beauty that his poetry creates is created by balancing on a keen ironic edge." Larkin himself was wry in discussing his own contributions to the poetry genre, as he told the Observer the following: "I think writing about unhappiness is probably the source of my popularity, if I have any. Deprivation is for me what Daffodils were for Wordsworth" (Johnson 276).

Larkin's A Girl in Winter (1947) is considered by John Bayley to be, "a real masterpiece, a quietly gripping novel, dense with the humor that is Larkin's trademark, and also an extended prose poem" (Johnson 277). Larkin has written four volumes of poems in which he presents an unsentimental view of contemporary British life. These volumes are entitled The North Ship (1946), The Less Deceived (1955), The Whitson Weddings (1964), and High Windows (1974). Larkin's poetry, which lacks hyperbolic exaggerations about mankind, frequently uses sexual irony to detail man's diminished state (Bradley 83). Larkin uses four different perspectives in order to communicate his sexual irony. He views the single man or adolescent who longs for sex; he views the married man who is disappointed by sex; he views the ordinary citizen who is confronted by the sexual allure of modern advertising, and finally, he views the world-wise cynic who employs vulgar, sexual language in a witty defense against "larger forces" (Bradley 84).

Terry Whalen says that there is a kind of "cleansing severity" in Larkin's satirical social poems.

> When we isolate the irony and sarcasm of many of his finest poems, it becomes apparent that the poet, who is sometimes extremely sarcastic, is often debating the limits of that sarcasm himself, and laughing at his own tendency to be overly serious and severe. "Laughter," says Sartre, "is the property of man because man is the only animal that takes itself seriously." (Whalen 14)

In Anthony Thwaite's Larkin at Sixty, clive James wrote an essay about All What Jazz: A Record Diary 1961-1968 (1970) which said, "no wittier book of criticism has ever been written" (Johnson 277).

Philip (Arthur) Larkin Bibliography

Bradley, Jerry. "Sexual Irony in the Poetry of Philip Larkin." WHIMSY 2 (1984): 83-84.

Chaucer, Geoffrey. "The Millers Tale." The Works of Geoffrey Chaucer. 2nd Edition. Ed. F. N. Robinson, Cambridge, MA: The Riverside Press, 1933.

Fisher, Mathew David. "Kingsley Amis." Dictionary of Literary Biography, Volume One Hundred Thirty-Nine: British Short-Fiction Writers, 1945-1980. Ed. Dean Baldwin. Detroit, MI: Gale, 1994, 3-13.

Johnson, Anne Janette. "Philip Larkin." Contemporary Authors, New Revision Series, Volume 24. Detroit, MI: Gale Research, 1988, 274-278.

Larkin, Philip. "Introduction to John Betjeman: Collected Poems. Comp. Earl of BirkenHead. Boston, MA: Houghton Mifflin, 1971.

Whalen, Terry. " 'Being Serious and Being Funny': Philip Larkin's Irony and Sarcasm." Thalia: Studies in Literary Humor 4.1 (1982): 10-14.

Lindsay Gordon Anderson (1923-1994)

In the tradition of Ben Jonson, Lindsay Anderson's satire is, "erudite, allusive, witty, unsparing, wide-ranging, and austere" (Hutchins 32). All of Anderson's screenplays are notable for their, "innovative techniques, their fiercely satiric animus, and their witty intertextual allusiveness." They are also notable for their iconoclastic wit. Anderson's best film satires are the three "Mick Travis" films (If... [1969], O Lucky Man! [1973], and Brittania Hospital [1982]), and his Glory! Glory! (1989). Anderson directed all of these films, and he coauthored the first two with David Sherwin (Hutchings 27). If... (1969) is a scathing satirical account of a rebellion at a boy's school from the students' point of view (Hutchings 28). The satiric tension that prevails throughout If... results from a blending of interior and exterior realities. Mick is a stark inversion of the ethic developed in Rudyard Kipling's famous poem, "If." Mick, like Kim, who is greatly outnumbered by his enemy, mans his isolated barricade and fights fiercely from the battlements. Both of them keep their heads while all about them are losing theirs, and blaming it on him. The difference is that Mick deserves the blame (Hutchings 30).

O Lucky Man! (1973) is more ambitious than If... because it exposes more satiric targets. It assaults the modern business ethic, the judicial system, medical research, the military-industrial complex, and social "reformers," among many others (Hutchings 30). Brittannia Hospital (1982) contains much black, grotesque, and gruesome comedy which some critics have compared to the comedy in a "Monty Python" creation, and other critics have considered to be a gratuitous, pre-adolescent, "gross-out" type of humor (Hutchins 31). Glory! Glory! (1989), which is deftly crafted, and contains much wit, visual humor, and intelligence, exposes many of the relationships between religion and show business. The film is an "audacious institutional satire" that targets the graft, greed, hypocrisy, and sexual indulgence of the pseudo-pious American televangelists. However, the shock power of the film was weakened by the fact that when it was released its message was being eclipsed by the stories of Jimmy Swaggart, Jim and Tammy Faye Bakker, and all of the rest of the television evangelists who were in the news at the time (Hutchins 32).

Lindsay Gordon Anderson Bibliography

Hutchings, William. "Lindsay Gordon Anderson." Encyclopedia of British Humorists, Volume I. Ed. Steven H. Gale. New York, NY: Garland, 1996, 26-35.

Brendan Behan (1923-1964) IRELAND

Philip Bordinat says that both Brendan Behan and Brian Friel used comedy to humanize their characters thereby intensifying the tragic impact, even though Behan's approach is comic, while Friel's approach in The Freedom of the City is epic (Hutchings 127). Borstal Boys (1958) is a partially autobiographical novel which is influenced by the time when Brendan Behan was in London's Feltham Boys' Prison. Although Behan had been excommunicated from the Roman Catholic Church by this time, he was required by English law to attend its services in the prison chapel, and although he was not able to receive the sacraments, he was allowed to serve the Mass. Thus, in Borstal Boys, the religious services are recounted with much humor, and with occasional irreverence (Hutchings 120). At Feltham Prison, Behan enjoyed the bawdy irreverence of the other boys during the services, but he did not join in on this rowdiness. It is apparently without bitterness when Behan makes the statement that being expelled from the church was "like being pushed outside a prison and told not to come back" (Behan Borstal Boys 322). Borstal Boys is in many places a hilarious comedy that is almost devoid of bitterness. It contains many literary allusions, as well as frequent bawdy songs and humorous banter. It stresses resilience and irrepressibility. Borstal Boys has been compared to the novels of England's "Angry Young Men" of the mid-to-late-1950s--Kingsley Amis, John Braine, Alan Sillitoe, Keith Waterhouse, and others. All of these authors, including Behan, center on working-class experiences. They are all anti-authoritarian, and sometimes include coarse language and discuss taboo topics. They all have a comic vulgarity and an uninhibited frankness about the human body and its various functions. Borstal Boy contains a great deal of prison argot, including Cockney rhyming slang; the frequent obscenities contribute both to the humor, and to the frank tone of the novel, but they also are essential in the accurate portrayal of the characters (Hutchings 121).

The Quare Fellow (1956) blends naturalistic detail with raucous comedy and song. The play is about the events that happened before, during, and after the execution of a condemned man. It should be noted that in prison argot, a condemned men would be referred to as a "Quare Fellow" (Hutchings 122). When the curtain goes up on The Quare Fellow the audience hears one of the prisoners singing in defiance of the word SILENCE that is written in large block Victorian letters and dominates the wall of the stage's prison scene (Behan Complete Plays 39). This demonstrates that the authorities are not successful in their demands for conformity, as the song is subverting the silence, and swigs of methylated liniment are being drunk by the prisoners who are not able to obtain any other type of alcoholic beverage. The Bible is a cherished item in prison, because its pages can be torn out, rolled with mattress stuffing, and made into prison cigarettes. It is ironic that the quare fellow is going to be hanged for murder, while another murderer, one who had beaten his wife to death with a "silver-topped cane" has received a reprieve. But the irony becomes doubly ironic in Act 1, when the Silver-Top murderer tries to hang himself as the quare fellow is hanging onto life during his final hours. The Second Act of The Quare Fellow reveals the grave for the quare fellow that is in the process of being dug, and many of the inmates of the prison are making fun of this half-dug grave. In the third act, Behan's satire becomes even more bitter, as the petty concerns of the presiding authorities are presented in contrast to the enormity of the execution that is about to take place. There is a bitter satiric counterpoint in the scene of the teetotaling evangelist accompanying the hangman who is singing a hymn which he has written about God, mercy, and forgiveness as the hangman calculates how much of a drop is needed to accommodate the weight of the quare fellow. The final scene of the play shows the execution itself. It also shows the completed grave, and the only reminder that the prisoner had existed, his prison number carved onto the wall (Hutchings 123). But even the number is wrong, because a 7 was easier to carve than the correct number--9 (Hutchings 124).

The Hostage (1958) is a play about a grim subject, but it nevertheless demonstrates Behan's raucous, life-affirming humor, along with his acerbic satire. Even though Behan's characters are unheroic, disreputable outcasts, they nevertheless, "exuberantly affirm life through their raucous banter and their ostensibly 'immoral' activities." Catholicism is one of the satiric targets in The Hostage, as Miss Gilchrist, a social worker from St. Vincent de Paul Society, is presented as having a shallow and irrelevant piety. She has her hymns and her tracts, but totally lacks empathy for the prisoner who is about to die (Hutchings 124). Leslie and Teresa are the star-crossed lovers in The Hostage, and in the final act, as earlier, a merry song is used to heighten the tragedy. In the end, Leslie is dead, but in a controversial scene that has astonished and perplexed audiences, "a ghostly green light glows on the body," and "Leslie slowly gets up and sings, 'The bells of hell / Go ting-a-ling-a-ling. But not for you or me. / Oh death, where is thy sting-a-ling-a-ling / Or grave thy victory?'" (Behan The Hostage 236).

Later, Brendan Behan wrote and published two entertaining books of anecdotes and observations, Behan's Island: An Irish Sketchbook and Brendan Behan's New York. Flann O'Brien said that Brendan Behan was a, "...delightful rowdy, a wit, a man of action in many dangerous undertakings where he thought his duty lay, a reckless drinker, a fearless denouncer of humbug and pretence, and so a proprietor of the biggest heart that has beaten in Ireland for the past forty years" (qtd in O'Connor 318-319).
See also Nilsen, Don L. F. "Brendan Behan." Humor in Irish Literature: A Reference Guide. Westport, CT: Greenwood, 1996, 7, 130, 190-192.

Brendan Behan Bibliography

Behan, Brendan. The Complete Plays. New York, NY: Grove Press, 1978.
Bordinat, Philip. "Tragedy Through Comedy in Plays by Brendan Behan and Brian Friel." West Virginia University Philological Papers 29 (1983): 84-91.
Hutchings, William. "Brendan Behan." Encyclopedia of British Humorists, Volume I. Ed. Steven H. Gale. New York, NY: Garland, 1996, 118-128.
McCann, Sean, Ed. The Wit of Brendan Behan. London, England: Frewin, 1968.
O'Connor, Ulick. Brendan. New York, NY: Grove Press, 1973.
Waters, Maureen. "Flann O'Brien and Mad Sweeny." The Comic Irishman. Albany, NY: State Univ of New York Press, 1984, 123-136.

Thomas James Bonner Flanagan (1923-) IRELAND

See Nilsen, Don L. F. "Thomas Flanagan." Humor in Irish Literature: A Reference Guide. Westport, CT: Greenwood, 1996, 77, 192-193.

Elizabeth Jane Howard (1923-)

Robert Martin says that in After Julius (1965) Elizabeth Howard demonstrates the shallow nature of one of her characters by showing that this character could not believe in the seriousness of comedy: "Esme, as any of her friends would have said, was a practical creature; laughter meant that one was not serious, and apart from Noël Coward and P. G. Wodehouse and stories told by people about friends whom they did not really like, people who seemed to have an aimless desire to find life amusing were simply frivolous" (Martin 100).

Elizabeth Jane Howard Bibliography

Martin, Robert Bernard. The Triumph of Wit: A Study of Victorian Comic Theory. Oxford, England: Clarendon, 1974.

Wolf Mankowitz (1924-)

Make Me an Offer (1952) is about a deaf and nearly paralyzed old man who is in the care of his beautiful granddaughter. Two men want to buy a green vase from the old man, who knows that the vase is priceless, and the daughter, who does not know the value of the vase, is the go-between in the bargaining process. The narrator cheats the old man by talking directly to him rather than talking through his daughter. The daughter thinks that the old man is pleased to be getting eighty pounds for his vase, but he is actually furious, but unable to tell her so. The old man jerks for a while, trying to tell his daughter not to sell the vase, but the daughter misinterprets the jerking, "He's trying to say he's very grateful." She asks the narrator his name, and he tells her that it is "Drage." In the meantime, the old man, "made a convulsive effort and rose up shaking upon his feet." At the end of the dialogue, the narrator, "counted out sixteen fivers, smiling at him the while" (Mesher 716). David Mesher says that Make Me an Offer has a Dickensian cast of curious minor characters, and that it is a close observation and an excellent portrayal of social setting. Mesher says that the humor is, "as unlikely as it is funny" (Mesher 717).

The play entitled The Bespoke Overcoat (1954) is a sustained jewish joke. The humor and pathos of the play, which is witty and touching, comes from the tailor's commitment to his friend, even after his friend, Fender, is dead. Fender feels that all things considered, he would rather be alive than dead (Mesher 717). My Old Man's a Dustman (1956) is a bitter-sweet Post-war comedy about a shell-shocked, mute, garbage-dump scavenger who is called Arp. He gets his name from the jacket he has scrounged from the garbage which has an Air Raid Precautions insignia on it. Old Clock is the name of the blustering but kind watchman of the rubbish dump (Mesher 717). Danny Pisarov, the protagonist in Cockatrice (1963) demonstrates the fact that as Mankowitz goes from Make Me an Offer to Cockatrice, his humor becomes less and less subtle (Mesher 717). Mankowitz uses the occult for humorous effect in The Devil in Texas (1984), a novel about Dr. Stanley, who is in Texas. The novel satirizes not only American excesses, but also Dr. Stanley's search for vampires after the woman he loves has become possessed (Mesher 718).

Wolf Mankowitz Bibliography

Mesher, David. "Wolf Mankowitz." Encyclopedia of British Humorists, Volume II. Ed. Steven H. Gale. New York, NY: Garland, 1996, 714-719.

Rosamunde Pilcher (Jane Fraser) (1924-)

Rosamunde Pilcher reports in a Publishers Weekly interview with Amanda Smith that she specializes in "light reading for intelligent ladies." Pilcher is a romance writer who feels that she deserves more respect than she receives. In Publishers Weekly she explains, "All my life I've had people coming up and saying, 'Sat under the hair dryer and read one of your little stories, dear. So clever of you. Wish I had the time to do it myself.' I just say, 'Yeah, fine, pity you don't'" (Ross 376).

Rosamunde Pilcher (Jane Fraser) Bibliography

Ross, Jean W. "Rosamunde Pilcher." Contemporary Authors: New Revision Series, Volume 27. Eds. Hal May, and James G. Lesniak. Detroit, MI: Gale, 1989, 375-379.

Gerard Hoffnung (1925-1959)

Gerard Hoffnung has made a comic statement as an illustrator and cartoonist, as a story teller, and as an impresario. His work always demonstrates his artistry, wit, and charm. Joel Marks describes Hoffnung as, "jolly, concerned, highly observant, fastidious, whimsical, cherubic, arch, a superb mimic, [and] a whirlwind." Hoffnung has also created artistic comedy in two genres--cartooning and oratory (Marks 526). Hoffnung is a master at timing and emphasis as he savors every moment of his writing. He uses detail to extend his paragraphs into longer works, and he concludes with "lightening quick dénouement." In 1957, Hoffnung also conducted a series of fifty humorous chatty interviews with Charles Richardson for the BBC (Marks 527). Gerard Hoffnung said about his own contribution that he is, "probably a lunatic, but not one of the dangerous type" (Marks 528).

The Right Playmate (1952) was written by James Broughton, and illustrated by Gerard Hoffnung. The first frame has the caption, "To begin with, I was a perfectly normal boy," but the illustration shows a forlorn-looking boy skipping rope with a barbed wire instead of a rope. The humor in The Maestro (1953), like that in The Right Playmate, is quite straightforward, but it is also farcical and witty. The orchestra conductor is represented in a complete set of caricatures showing his various emotions and contortions (Marks 527). Soon after The Maestro there appeared five innovative books that contained strange comments about how musical instruments might be played. These five books were The Hoffnung Symphony Orchestra (1955), The Hoffnung Music Festival (1956), The Hoffnung Companion to Music (1957), Hoffnung's Musical Chairs (1958), and Hoffnung's Acoustics (1959), and they present Hoffnung's weird musical world in which a saxophone is stuffed with tobacco as the saxophone player lights up for a puff, and a cor anglais turns into an egg. There is the Vacuum Quartet in A Flat, sub-titled "The Hoover." There is also discussion of a jazz drummer who sweeps dust into a dustpan, and accordion caterpillars and bagpipe octopi and elephantine alphorns. And there is the kettledrum which is filled with boiling oil; this is to be used on the conductor. This is only a small part of the graphic and musical inventiveness that is presented in these five books (Marks 527).

Gerard Hoffnung Bibliography

Marks, Joel. "Gerard Hoffnung." Encyclopedia of British Humorists, Volume I. Ed. Steven H. Gale. New York, NY: Garland, 1996, 525-529.

Mary Beckett (1926-) IRELAND

See Nilsen, Don L. F. "Mary Beckett." Humor in Irish Literature: A Reference Guide. Westport, CT: Greenwood, 1996, 199.

Alun Owen (1926-)

In No Trams to Lime Street (1959) Taff and Cass are two sailors who confront difficult fathers on their first night of shore leave in Liverpool. Tass takes comic revenge by mimicking his father as a bully, but Cass is more repressed, and is therefore not able to break his feelings of animosity (Diamond 138).

Alun Owen Bibliography

Diamond, Elin F. Pinter's Comic Play. Cranbury, NJ: Associated University Presses, 1985.

Peter Levin Shaffer (1926-)

Peter Shaffer is a "brilliant, teasing farceur who targets mundane human follies" (Gianakaris 931). Elin Diamond compares Peter Shaffer's Five Finger Exercise (1958) to the plays of Noel Coward. Clive is a "neurasthenic son," who tells about his family in the following way, "...let me give you a warning. This isn't a family. It's a tribe of wild cannibals.... Between us we eat everyone we can.... Actually, we're very choosy in our victims. We only eat other members of the family" (Diamond 139).

The Private Ear (1962) is a one-act comedy which was written to be performed with The Public Eye (1962), another one-act comedy. In The Private Ear, Bob is nervous, forgetful, and extremely gauche, in contrast to Ted, who is older, more suave and experienced, and more cynical. To Ted, Doreen is just an opportunity for quick sex, but for Bob, she is an idealized pure creature. The bittersweet humor of The Private Ear comes as much from the comic attributes of Bob, Ted, and Doreen as it does from the irrationalities of first love. Comic quips can be found throughout the play (Gianakaris 932).

The Public Eye (1962) is filled with good-natured humor that is counter-balanced with a, "playful yet plausible dialectic on marriage." The eccentric trio of characters provides much clever dialogue. The title of The Public Eye is a parody both on the expression "private eye," and on the title of the companion piece The Private Ear. The plot of The Public Eye revolves around the private detective Julian Cristoforou, who is hired by a stuffy, middle-aged businessman named Charles Sidley to investigate the possible infidelity of Sidley's young wife, Belinda. Belinda is affected by her husband's stodgy values which control her life rather than freeing her spirit. Sidley is a forty-year-old accountant and an egotistical prig. He considers himself to be a Pygmalion who is charged with the task of reshaping his twenty-two-year-old bride into a socially acceptable individual. The Public Eye has sophisticated wit, and sustained good humor coming from Shaffer's fresh and clearly delineated characters. Cristoforou, one of the antagonists of the play, for example, is a free spirit. He wears a white trench coat with pockets from which he regularly retrieves packets of raisins and nuts (Gianakaris 933).

Black Comedy (1967) is a one-act comedy which was written to be performed with another one-act comedy, White Lies (1967). C. J. Gianakaris considers Black Comedy to be, "one of the most brilliant one-act farces of our era." This play is about eight very funny eccentrics, and it is filled with wit, imaginativeness, and laughter. The eight characters are involved in many misunderstandings and hilarious confusions. The pacing is "razor-sharp" as the characters barely miss running into each other, while going through their numerous pratfalls. The controlling theatrical device of the play is a reversal of dark and light, a device which can be traced to the "black comedy" of Chinese theater. The way Chinese "black comedy" works is that the stage is brilliantly lighted whenever the stage-directions would normally have complete darkness. But then there is a total blackout on stage whenever the story is taking place in a normal, lighted, ambiance. Both dark becoming light, and light becoming dark create a great deal of physical humor for the audience to enjoy, because they see what the characters assumedly cannot see during the blackout periods, and they cannot see what the characters assumedly can see during the lighted periods. The story is about Georg Bamberger, a famous art connoisseur, who is expected to come and look over Brindsley Miller's art pieces. Since it is very important for Brindsley to make a good impression, he borrows (without asking) some expensive furniture from Harold Gorringe, his gay admirer next door. In the meantime, Carol Melkert, Brindsley's fiancée, has invited her stuffy father, Colonel Melkert, to Brindsley's house to be impressed by Bamberger, and to meet Brindsley for the first time (Gianakaris 933). But just at this crucial time, a fuse blows, and this sets up the dark-light reversal. When the fuse blows, the house lights come up so that the audience can see the set for the first time. The stage remains lighted from this point until the end of the play when the fuse is replaced. The audience can thus see the characters moving around a brightly lit stage as if they were blindly operating in total darkness. When the fuse blows, Brindsley's neighbor, Miss Furnival, gropes her way into brindsley's flay, and she continues to make a pest of herself during the play. The plot is complicated still more by Clea, Brindsley's former girl-friend, who slips into his apartment in the dark. Once Clea discovers that Brindsley's new fiancée is present, she undertakes a campaign to harass Brindsley as much as possible. This is a very difficult situation which Brindsley must in some way control. First, he has to placate Clea to keep her from sabotaging his engagement with Carol. Second, he has to keep Carol from finding out about his earlier love affair with Clea. Third, he has to calm Colonel Melkert's ruffled feathers at the strange turn of events. Fourth, he has to keep Miss Furnival calm and collected. And finally, he has to delay Harold's discovery that his furniture has been borrowed. And he must do all of this while making plans for Banberger's arrival. The play ends when Schuppanzih, an eccentric electrician, replaces the broken fuse, to light up the house, but to plunge the stage into blackness, at which point the characters on stage can supposedly see what is going on, but the audience cannot. (Gianakaris 934).

The title of White Lies (1967) was later changed to The White Liars (1968). This is a play in which Tom has fallen in love with Frank's girlfriend, so Frank takes Tom to Sophie, a fortune teller, arranging in the meantime to have Sophie tell Tom a fortune that will frighten him off. Frank goes in to see Sophie to have his fortune told first. But rather than having his fortune told, he tells Sophie all about Tom, and arranges with her to go along with his plan. But earlier, Tom had deliberately misled Frank about his background, so Frank was therefore inadvertently giving Sophie false information about Tom. When Tom later has his fortune told by Sophie, therefore, he recognizes the false information that he had earlier told to Frank, and then realizes why Sophie's fortune is telling him that he should no longer see Frank's girlfriend. Tom has a hard time trying to convince Sophie that the whole thing is a charade because when Frank set up the charade with Sophie, he had not said it was to establish a relationship with Frank's girlfriend, but that it was rather to establish a relationship with Tom himself. The story ends with Sophie calling to Frank as he is leaving. Sophie tells him to take comfort, for it is not only young people who are liars. Older people are even bigger liars. And then she explains that she is not really a Baroness. She is not married to a Baron. Her mother was not a Romany noblewoman; she was a gypsy. And she wasn't even an interesting gypsy (Gianakaris 935).

The first word in the title Lettice and Lovage (1988) refers to a person, but the second word refers to a concoction of parsley and other ingredients used to make a Renaissance quaff that led Lettice Douffet and Lotte Schoen to become close friends (Gianakaris 937). Lettice and Lovage is about two middle-aged London spinsters who are quite different from each other. In the story, their temperaments at first collide, and then they are reconciled. The main protagonist is Lettice Douffet, who is not employable in a technological age because she is so flamboyant, theatrical, and artistic. Lettice has a freewheeling lifestyle and a Dionysian spirit. In contrast, Lotte Schoen, is an "Apollonian type." She operates according to cool and rational pragmatism, and believes in absolute adherence to social rules and regulations (Gianakaris 935). C. J. Gianakaris says that Lettice & Lovage blends serious thought with dazzlingly comic dialogue and great humorous characterization (Gianakaris 936).

Whom Do I Have the Honour of Addressing? (1989) is an extended playful one-act radio comedy written for BBC about a middle-aged woman named Mrs. Angela Sutcliffe. Angela is telling the various reasons she has for committing suicide into a tape recorder. She says that she will do the act as soon as she finishes her dictation. During her presentation, however, Angela is constantly being sidetracked by other thoughts. Her taping is filled with humorous digressions and chit-chat. By the end of the taped statement it has become abundantly clear that Angela will never take her own life but will instead continue to lead a buoyant life. The taping has provided the cathartic outlet that Angela needed to allow her to continue living in a flawed world (Gianakaris 937).

Peter Levin Shaffer Bibliography

Diamond, Elin F. Pinter's Comic Play. Cranbury, NJ: Associated University Presses, 1985.
Gianakaris, C. J. "Peter Levin Shaffer." Encyclopedia of British Humorists, Volume II. Ed. Steven H. Gale. New York, NY: Garland, 1996, 931-938.
Gilliatt, Penelope. Unholy Fools, Wits, Comics, Disturbers of Piece: Film and Theater. New York, NY: Viking Press, 1973.

(Patricia) Ann Jellicoe (1927-)

The Knack (1962) is a comic account of sexual conquest during the 1960s, but it is also a satiric comment on learning, teaching, and thought control. Colin and Nancy are two students who are caught in a tug-of-war between their teachers, Tom and Tolen (Snyder 569). Much of the whimsical charm of the play comes from Tom's teaching stories and games. His stories have silly aspects, such as cows that wear brassieres. Tom has concocted a fantastic game to help Colin and Nancy learn more about each other, and therefore Colin, Nancy, and the audience are surprised to discover that a mattress is really a piano, and a headboard is part of a lion's cage (Snyder 570).

Both The Knack (1962) and The Giveaway (1970) are zany satires in which the author encourages the audience to experience the play on a sensory level rather than on an intellectual level (Snyder 572). The Giveaway is a farce about consumerism, but it is also about relationships. It is about the ways that we "package ourselves," "advertise ourselves," and "sell ourselves" to a "consumer" or mate. It is also about how this consumer metaphor (like real consumerism) is based on tricks and illusions that are barriers to real human communication (Snyder 571).

(Patricia) Ann Jellico Bibliography

Snyder, Laura. "Ann Jellicoe." Encyclopedia of British Humorists, Volume I. Ed. Steven H. Gale. New York, NY: Garland, 1996, 568-573.

Thomas Ridley Sharpe (Tom Sharpe)(1928-)

Piers Brendon says that Tom Sharpe's farce is "violent, extravagant and unremitting," that it contains "a wealth of bestial ferocity and technicolor perversion," and that these two qualities give it "a distinctly manic flavour." Leonard Ashley places Sharpe into the category of British music-hall, stag-party, rugby-player authors who like to tell "loo and genitalia jokes." Sharpe tends to write a bawdy-burlesque type of humor in which the villains get their comeuppance by being exploded, eaten by lions, or otherwise taken care of in colorful-yet-appropriate ways (Ashley 953). Sharpe loves stark contrasts, rapid narrative, and eccentric people caught up in hilarious situations, as he combines startling effects with occasional deadpan humor (Ashley 954). According to a critic for Punch, Tom Sharpe is, "Britain's leading practitioner of black humour." His novels have the madcap action of the silent movies. They propel the reader into a hysterical fantasy, because Sharpe knows, "how to keep a farce moving at dazzling speed" (Ashley 955).

Sharpe says that a comic or satirical novel must have a logical plot. "Cause and effect must be seen to apply or you lose the reader. My books may seem to deal in mayhem but beneath it there has to be a carefully constructed plot if the comic elements are to be sustained" (Peters 418). Tom Sharpe is hailed as a superb satirist by both British and American critics. Alan Ryan says that Sharpe is the author of, "very possibly the funniest novels in English today." Piers Brendon talks about Sharpe's talent for "ghoulish slapstick humour" (Peters 415). Thomas Nollett says that Tom Sharpe is probably the best satirist writing in English today. His primary targets are teaching, the law, the military, the government, corporate bureaucracy, and what Nollett calls the "squirearchy" as Sharpe combines the genres of satire, comedy, and farce (Nollett Porterhouse Blue 23). Sharpe uses caricature and farce in his presentation of characters and incidents, and this type of presentation doesn't allow the assumption of knowing what rational and normal behavior is, let alone the discovery of hidden moral messages. In this respect, Sharpe's satire differs from that of Jonson, Pope, Swift and others writing in the traditional satiric mode (Nollett Porterhouse Blue 26). Nollett adds that Sharpe's works tend to be aggression mollified only slightly by, "witty exchanges, repartee, mental acuity, and verbal sleight-of-hand." Nollett doesn't believe that Sharpe is effective in purveying insights into the way people think and behave, but feels nevertheless that, "as a writer, a stylist in the satiric mode, he is indisputably brilliant" (Nollett Porterhouse Blue 28).

Angela Downing feels that Sharpe's characters are not as caricatured as are characters usually found in traditional satire, and she further feels that his use of comic incident rings more true than does the comic incident in most farce. She considers Sharpe's work to contain "original, yet plausible incongruities," and she also says that there are large doses of aggression, malice, scatology, and eroticism. In Sharpe's novels it is common for a "well-nourished lady" like Eva Wilt, Rosie Cobbett, or Lady Maud Handyman to be paired with an incongruous partner like Henry Wilt, who is indecisive and hen-pecked, or Willy Cobbett, who is a dwarf, or Sir Giles Handyman, who is a fetishist. Many of Sharpe's characters are incongruous in one way or another. Lord Petrefact is a semi-paralytic right-wing industrialist who goes around in a hearse. This hearse is in turn accompanied by an ambulance which contains a team of resuscitation doctors who are addicted to the game of Monopoly (Downing 136).

Two of Sharpe's novels are set in South Africa (Riotous Assembly, and Indecent Exposure). These South African novels demonstrate Sharpe's fondness for violence. The violence here is so mechanical, so exaggerated and so intense that it comes across as a Tom-and-Jerry cartoon. There are trigger-happy, paranoid law enforcement officers who, in Keystone-cop fashion, shoot each other and wreck their own city. "Lord Petrefact's mechanized wheel chair gets out of control, knocks over a chamber pot, smashes a priceless collection of jade, and drags its owner by his pajama cord" (McCall 60).

Riotous Assembly (1971) is a powerful attack on South Africa's apartheid system. Piers Brendon writes that this novel has done for the South African police what Catch-22 did for the United States Air Force. It targets the apparatchniks of apartheid with, "murderous ridicule infinitely more destructive than the polemical pleading or passionate abuse to which they are normally subjected in literature" (Peters 415). Riotous Assembly is a farce in which the writing style is formal and wordy, while at the same time hilarious and consistently comical and cynical. The characters in this novel are obviously caricatures of real life people (Nollett Riotous Assembly 11). The novel is filled with incongruity and mockery, two important devices of comedy; these devices serve the satiric effects, especially when the mockery takes the form of derisive laughter, and the incongruity takes on the distortions of vice and folly (Nollett Riotous Assembly 18). For example, in Riotous Assembly one character is mauled to death by a Doberman while another character is "tarred" and then "feathered" by a vulture that is shot down by a South African Army officer (Downing 137).

The slapstick and violence in <u>Riotous Assembly</u> are rendered innocuous by the fact that the ludicrous characters are remote from the reader's personal experiences. The tempo is fast-paced, and unrelenting, and there are many coincidences and surprises in a plot that comes across as very contrived. The characters in <u>Riotous Assembly</u> don't have the ability to distinguish between fantasy and reality, and this reinforces the sense of madness in the novel. The novel takes place in Piemburg, the capital of Zululand, in Africa. Sharpe's narrator comments that this city is, "half the size of New York Cemetery and twice as dead" (Nollett <u>Riotous Assembly</u> 13). The Hazelstones are a well established English family. The alcoholic Jonathan Hazelstone is the Bishop of Barotseland and the brother of Miss Hazelstone of Jacaranda House, the nymphomaniac daughter of Sir Theophilus, who runs a decaying estate on the outskirts of Piemburg, and who has been having an affair with her black cook (both Miss Hazelstone and the black cook have a rubber fetish) (Edwards 648). Jonathan and his sister are symbolic of English imperialism, and Jonathan is constantly being tormented by the imbecilic Kommandant van Heerden a senior police officer, and the bumbling Konstabel Els, the junior police officer, of the "Bureau of State Security in Pretoria," which goes by the acronym of BOSS. Jonathan has been falsely charged with the murder of Miss Hazelstone's Zulu cook, Fivepence (Nollett <u>Riotous Assembly</u> 12).

Kommandant van Heerden and Konstabel Els lay siege to Jacaranda Park so that the news about Miss Hazelstone's affair with a black cook won't leak out.

> Outrage succeeds outrage, however, when Els occupies an impregnable pillbox built by the paranoiac Sir Theophilus and, with his extraordinary armory of lethal weapons, threatens single-handedly to eliminate the whole invading local police force and army. The total confusion of the battle scene is depicted in a deadpan style, as suggested in this description of the attackers' armored cars that Els has blasted to pieces: "its occupants trickled gently but persistently through a hundred holes drilled in its side."

This is what Simon Edwards considers to be "black humor." (Edwards 648)

The action mounts, and the plot becomes complicated by a number of improbable entanglements, surprises, and coincidences. "The slapstick quality makes the acts of physical violence ludicrously unreal" (Nollett <u>Riotous Assembly</u> 14). When the Anglophiliac van Heerden is questioning Miss Hazelstone about the murder of Fivepence, she says, "People choose to follow my advice to put maroon wallpaper next to orange curtains, who am I to say them nay? People who believe that having a pink skin makes them civilized, while having a black one makes a man a savage will believe anything." Hazelstone then proceeds to show a film of Fivepence's sexual cavortings.

> "What you have just seen appears to your crude mind to be quite horrible. To me it is beautiful." She paused. "That's life, a black man pretending to be a white woman, dancing steps of a ballet he has never seen, dressed in clothes made of a material totally unsuited to a hot climate on a lawn which was imported from England, and kissing the stone face of a man who destroyed his nation, filmed by a woman who is widely regarded as the arbiter of good taste. Nothing could better express the quality of life in South Africa." (Nollett <u>Riotous Assembly</u> 15)

Later in the novel, Miss Hazelstone observed that there didn't seem to be any real difference between life in the mental hospital she was in and life in South Africa as a whole. In both places, "black madmen did all the work, while white lunatics lounged about imagining they were God" (Nollett <u>Riotous Assembly</u> 16). In a review of <u>Riotous Assembly</u>, Auberon Waugh said,

> Satirical purists would probably say that [<u>Riotous Assembly</u>] is a failure in

that it falls between two stools--savage political satire and loathing of man's brutality etc. on the one hand, slapstick on the other. They would be right to say that the book falls between two stools, but wrong to say that it is therefore a failure. It is extremely enjoyable to read and therefore a success. Its imperfections are only relative to its many excellences. (qtd. in Ashley 954)

Indecent Exposure (1973) continues the two themes of van Heerden's Anglophilia, and the stupidity and the callousness of the police. After Mrs. Heathcote-Kilkoon first seduces van Heerden, he says that he has "a stiff upper lip," to which she replies, "about the only thing stiff you have got" (McCall 61). Van Heerden thinks (wrongly) that an Englishman's heart has been transplanted into his chest, and thus he attempts to ingratiate himself with his English aristocratic compatriots (McCall 58). Verkramp is a man of excesses, and in Van Heerden's absence (he is pursuing his Anglophilic tendencies by rubbing noses with a group of English expatriates who have formed a "Dornford Yates Club," Verkramp plants explosives in a herd of ostriches by getting them to swallow gelignite. These ostriches are then released around the town to explode one by one. The Dornford Yates Club is later identified as the source of sabotage, and the police attack their country house, White Ladies. "The ubiquitous Konstabel Els, who has been acting as a servant at the house, reappears to give chase to the masquerading colonel, who is dressed in women's clothing. This brutal parody of an English fox hunt exposes the sanctimonious English justification of blood sports" (Edwards 648).

Porterhouse Blue (1974) is a broad farce, a biting satire which parodies academic life (Peters 415). It is about a college which is famous for its high living and fine cuisine. One of Sharpe's descriptions of a culinary event includes the following: "Above their heads grotesque animals pursued in plaster evidently plastered nymphs across a pastoral landscape." Porterhouse Blue is about a college which is established on the sound economic principle of admitting rich but unworthy candidates and working them through to obtain a pass degree in return for substantial endowments. It is Skullion who makes arrangements for students who know the information and who can do well on the exams to take the exams in place of the inept ones, and it is Godber Evans who becomes incensed at this procedure and is determined to put Porterhouse College on a respectable academic footing. A secondary plot in Porterhouse Blue involves Zipser, a sexually frustrated graduate student who in a fit of paranoia sends two hundred gas inflated condoms up a chimney. When Mrs. Biggs lights a fire in the chimney as a kind of foreplay in her seduction of Zipser, the gas balloons ignite and explode, and this causes the death of both Zipser and of Mrs. Biggs. Thomas Nollett considers this satiric anecdote to be pointed, witty, and incisive (Nollett Porterhouse Blue 25). Saturnalia is obvious in this seduction scene, and it is also obvious in Cathcart's costume birthday party at Coft Castle (Nollett Porterhouse Blue 26). Sharpe also plays on certain stereotypes such as the adroit schemer, which is a variation of the trickster of Greek and Roman Comedy, or the wise fool in Shakespeare's works (Nollett Porterhouse Blue 27).

As a homosexual student of Porterhouse College, Carrington is humiliated for his sexual bias by being dunked in the College fountain by undergraduate students, so Carrington wants to get revenge on the college by elaborately staging events to embarrass Porterhouse College. He further polarizes some of the ideological divisions at the college by anonymously informing the Cambridge Evening News that Scullion has been fired because he objected to the proposal that a contraceptive dispenser be installed in the Junior lavatory. He further inflames the scandal by telling the Students Radical Alliance that a particular college servant has been victimized because he has joined a trade union. And finally, he uses Pidgin English to write a note to the Bursar's Office complaining that the UNESCO expert on irrigation in Zaire has complained that his diplomatic immunity should have protected him from being ejected by the guardian of the Porterhouse gate, and should also have protected him from the accompanying obscenities (Nollett Porterhouse Blue 27).

Some of the irony of the plot revolves around the death of the Master of Porterhouse College, Sir Godber Evans, and the choice of a successor. There is a tradition that the Master's last utterance before death has the effect of naming his successor, and the Master names Skullion just as he is expiring. But he is naming him not as the Master of the College, but as his own murderer. The listeners misunderstand the Master's intended message, and Skullion becomes the new Master. Nollett says that Godber's death is, "a satiric parody of the exaggerations of tragedy" (Nollett Porterhouse Blue 25). It is ironic that Skullion, who rose from the position of Head Porter to the position of Master of Porterhouse College himself becomes partially paralyzed (Downing 136).

Skullion, the college porter in Porterhouse Blue is replaced by Blott, the gardener in Blott on the Landscape (1975). Blott is a German who used to be a prisoner of war, but who has now claimed Italian ancestry and is working as Lady Maud Lynchwood's gardener. Lady Maud is married to the impotent Sir Giles, who pays Mrs. Forthby to flog and humiliate him. It is Mrs. Forthby who says, "I may be a silly woman and not very nice but I do have my standards." Sir Giles plans to divorce her while capitalizing on his £100,000 investment in her family home in Shropshire, Handyman Hall. In order to circumvent the reversionary clause that goes into effect in case of divorce, he arranges to have a motorway built through the property. There is blackmail and counterblackmail, and Dundridge, who is in charge of the motorway scheme is so humiliated and reviled that he adopts some of the tactics of military warfare, giving this military campaign the name of "Operation Overland." Blott extends the military metaphor as he fortifies the gateway in preparing to defend the estate during a prolonged siege. (Edwards 650).

Blott on the Landscape derides environmental planners. In this novel, Sir Giles is eaten by lions in the Safari Park that Lady Maud has established on her estate. As a result, Blott wins his master's lady, his master's title, and a seat in Parliament (Peters 416). In Blott on the Landscape there is a civil servant by the name of Dundridge who designs a one-way traffic system for central London that makes it impossible to drive from Hyde Park to Picadilly except by way of the Tower Bridge and Fleet Street (McCall 63). In Blott on the Landscape, Lady Maud Handyman converts the grounds of her mansion into a Wildlife Park to keep the Ministry of Transport from running a highway through her property (Downing 136). Lady Maud's husband, Sir Giles is promoting the highway project which Lady Maud is determined to thwart in order to preserve her country estate, and she allies herself with Blott, the gardener, who is actually, "the prime mover and cause of all the disasters and havoc that take place" (Downing 137). Blott has a vague and mysterious history. Lady Maud and Blott's conspiracy involves blackmail, and the destruction of a neighboring village, and the killing of Sir Giles by a lion. In the end, Lady Maud marries Blott (McCall 59).

The Great Pursuit (1976) is an allusion to F. R. Leavis's The Great Tradition (1948) and The Common Pursuit (1952), two works which tend to define Leavisite critical orthodoxy, an orthodoxy which requires that novels present moral values that are uplifting to society. In The Great Pursuit, Dr. Louth, an old Cambridge don who believes in the Leavisite critical orthodoxy, nevertheless anonymously writes a pulp novel by the name of Pause O Men for the Virgin. She submits her manuscript to Frensic, a charming literary agent, who recognizes its market value and sells the paperback rights to Hutchmeyer, an aggressive American paperback publisher. Hutchmeyer requires that the author conduct a personal sales campaign in the United States, and since the author is anonymous, Frensic persuades Peter Piper to act as author on a book-selling tour (Edwards 651). Piper so much believes in traditional values that he uses quill pens when he writes, because they are, "the original tools of his craft," and because they, "stand as reminders of that golden age when books were written by hand, and to be a copyist was to belong to an honourable profession." Peter Piper is the kind of author who feels he must rewrite Great Expectations, and does so by writing, "'My father's family name being Pirrip, and my Christian name Philip, my infant tongue could make of both names nothing longer or more explicit than Piper....' He stopped. That wasn't right. It should have been Pip" (Edwards 652).

The Great Pursuit is a satirical assault on literary agents, publishers, authors, critics, reviewers, and even readers. F. A. Frensic is a British literary agent who receives a pulp fiction manuscript that could very well become a best seller, but the author wants to remain anonymous, so Frensic is forced to recruit a substitute author to masquerade as the real author. When Frensic and the imposter arrive in America, they encounter the sexually insatiable wife of a movie magnate, and the plot takes off in a number of humorous directions, all of them exposing the extravagant aspects of the publishing and book-reviewing business (Peters 416). Simon Edwards says that The Great Pursuit suggests a movement into a new dimension of seriousness without abandoning, "the remarkable inventiveness of comic energy that informed Sharpe's previous work (Edwards 646). The Great Pursuit is especially effective in parodying the politics of literature and publishing. It caricatures a vulgar American publisher by having Hutchmeyer say to Piper, "What I like about you is you give your readers a good fuck fantasy" (McCall 63).

Wilt (1976) is a novel which parodies academic life (Peters 415). Wilt is about Henry Wilt, who teaches Liberal Studies at Fenland Tech. Henry Wilt teaches a course to working-class butchers' apprentices, which is referred to as "Meat One." The course he teaches to secretaries is "Secs One." By the end of the novel, Henry Wilt has determined to teach his students the practical skills they need rather than the literature on which our, "culture of the word places too high a value" (Edwards 650).

Henry and his wife, Eva, become acquainted with a liberated American couple, and the wife initiates Eva into a lesbian relationship. While Eva and the wife are away, Wilt is arrested for Eva's murder, but in fact the corpse discovered is not Eva's body, but rather that of an inflatable life-sized plastic doll to which Wilt has become "attached." The most compelling part of the novel is the attempt made by Inspector Flint to force Wilt to break down and confess to a murder which has not taken place. Simon Edwards suggests that this police force is, "pertinent to recent scandals in England about police methods of interrogation" (Edwards 650).

Wilt's inadequacies are implied throughout the novel. On the first page, for example, we are told that, "he was not a decisive man." Inspector Flint in Wilt is hard and unyielding, and determined to secure Henry's conviction. Henry Wilt is like James Thurber's Walter Mitty, but more bilious. He fantasizes about disposing of his domineering wife, and in fact rehearses the murder by dumping a life-size rubber female doll into the foundation of a new college building, and this leads to an investigation by Inspector Flint who has a certain capacity for jumping to the wrong conclusions (McCall 59).

The Throwback (1978) is about Lockhart, the illegitimate son of Old Flawse's daughter. Lockhart has been raised by his grandfather, totally unaware that sex exists in the world. Lockhart's morality is based on the hodgepodge of his grandfather's reading, and it is a morality that can justify any act of violence whatsoever (Edwards 652). The Throwback derives its title from Lockhart's reversion to primitive Northumberland survival tactics, one of which is to have his grandfather stuffed and wired for sound by a taxidermist (McCall 59). There is much humorous visual imagery in The Throwback, including the ordering of a dildo and a plastic man for two old maids, the connecting of a gas line to a man's toilet, the feeding of LSD to a bull terrier, and the pumping of effluent into a house (McCall 60). The Throwback is a satire which targets bureaucrats and other authority figures, ranging from politicians and land developers to the police and the military. Francis

King considers The Throwback to be "highly entertaining," and Nigel Williams lauds its "sheer satirical bite" (Peters 416). The Throwback ends with a crazy and violent siege of Flawse Hall, which is surrounded by invading tax inspectors. But Lockhart sees them as excise men trying to get paid for debts accrued from the profits of the sale of Lockhart's wife's London estate (Edwards 653).

The main satirical target of The Wilt Alternative (1979) is law enforcement agencies (Peters 416). In this novel, Henry Wilt and his four daughters must take refuge in a compost heap at the same time that Eva Wilt battles through ditches and under barbed wire to reach her house and her children (Downing 136). Eva is determined to rescue her four daughters--quadruplets--from terrorists who have occupied her house, and in so doing she comes into conflict with the army and with the police, which are headed by Flint. Flint's tactics are derailed by Wilt's pretending that he is the leader of the People's Alternative Army (McCall 59). The climax of The Wilt Alternative involves an exploding toilet which drenches the terrorists and evokes from one onlooker the comment, "Shits in shits' clothing" (McCall 61).

Ancestral Vices (1980) is a satirical attack of the English upper classes. More specifically, it targets, "left-wing academics, right-wing capitalists, true-blue country gentry, workers, peasants, police, and lawyers" (Peters 416). The left-wing Professor of Demotic Historiography at the University of Kloon in Ancestral Vices is appropriately named Walden Yapp, and of course the name of "Kloon" for a university suggests both the word "clown," and the word "goon" (Downing 137). Professor Yap got his fellowship at the University of Kloon because of his "reputation for unthinking radicalism," and in fact more specifically because of his reputation for "unthinking thought" in general. When Professor Yapp is invited to Lord Petrefact's mansion, he decides to try out the modern Synchronized Ablution Bath, and is faced with such wonderful levers as "Wave motion," "Steam," and "Jet." It is no surprise to the reader that the bath takes over, and this is a good illustration of Henri Bergson's theory of humor as, "the mechanical encrusted upon the living."

> As Yapp tried to step into the bath, the thing suddenly lurched sideways and threw him off his feet. As he slid precipitously down it, Yapp grabbed the lever and swung it to JET. The indicator fulfilled its promise with an enthusiasm that presumably came from years of understandable neglect. Hot rusty water hurled itself from holes beneath the mahogany surround. The infernal contraption combined every mode of function its insane designer had contrived for it. It waved, it jetted, it vibrated and now it demonstrated its capacity to steam. (Downing 139)

Although Walden Yapp is not able to communicate successfully with his Synchronized Ablution Bath, he is able to communicate with a computer named Doris (McCall 63). This is the Walden Yapp who considers the word "dwarf" to be a pejorative term, and who insists instead on using the term "porg" which stands for Person Of Restricted Growth. Yapp is deaf to the unflattering sound of this word, and he is also incapable of perceiving that Willy Coppett enjoys his status as the only dwarf in Buscott (McCall 64).

Chapter Nine of Ancestral Vices begins with a parody of the sentimentally picturesque style of an English tourist guide-book. "The little town of Buscott (population 7048) nestles in the Vale of Bushampton in the heart of England. Or so the few guidebooks that bother to mention it would have the tourist believe. In fact it crouches beside the sluggish river from which it derives the first part of its name" (Peters 415). Vintage Stuff (1984) is a novel which parodies academic life (Peters 415). D. A. N. Jones compliments "the cleverness of Sharpe's plotting and the skill of the narrative" in Wilt on High (1984). Jones says that here, as in other Sharpe novels, the satire is "deliciously vicious," and he adds that, "Wilt on High is Sharpe's lewdest, raunchiest venture" (Peters

416).

In 1986, Tom Sharpe won "Le Legion d'Humour" from the Association for the Promotion of Humor in International Affairs, and in this same year, he also won the "Laureat du Grand Prix de l'Humour Noir" from Xavier Forneret (Peters 415). Many critics place the Sharpe canon squarely in the middle of the British comic tradition, describing his comedy as "zany, bawdy, and very British." Various critics have compared Tom Sharpe to Anthony Powell, Kingsley Amis, and Peter De Vries. John Sutherland says that Tom Sharpe is "the funniest novelist currently writing," as he satirizes, "incompetent authority figures, the dry rot of both elite and publicly supported educational institutions, the duplicity of literary agents, critics, writers, and publishers, the ruthless survival tactics of aristocrats, and the distorted visions of both radicals and reactionaries." He will introduce any subject for a laugh, ranging from a retired colonel who puts on a condom filled with oven cleaner to terrorists who are covered with excrement when an organic toilet explodes (McCall 57). Much of Sharpe's humor is scatological, and throughout his novels there is a running joke about organic waste disposal and the recycling of human feces (Edwards 653). Sharpe's novels are, "apocalyptic, haunted by recurring motifs of sterility, impotence, and both moral and physical perversion." They, "form a vast and grotesque counterpastoral of contemporary English life" (Edwards 654).

Thomas Ridley Sharpe (Tom Sharpe) Bibliography

Ashley, Leonard R. N. "Sharpe Criticism: Onomastics i Tom Sharpe's Satires of South Africa." Journal of the North Central Name Society (1989): 1-12.

Ashley, Leonard R. N. "Tom Sharpe." Encyclopedia of British Humorists, Volume II. Ed. Steven H. Gale. New York, NY: Garland, 1996, 950-957.

Bragg, Melvin. "[Graham] Greene, and [Tom] Sharpe." Punch 274 (1978): 505.

Brendon, Piers. "Riotous Assembly." Books and Bookmen 16.9 (1971): 42-44.

Davis, L. J. "A Farce on the Trendy Side." Washington Post Book World (March 3, 1985): 5.

Downing, Angela. "Levels of Incongruity in the Novels of Tom Sharpe." Literary and Linguistic Aspects of Humour. Barcelona, Spain: Univ of Barcelona Dept of Language, 1984, 133-140.

Downing, Angela. "Strategies of Verbal Humor in a Contemporary British Novelist." Language and Literature 8 (1983): 17-32.

Edwards, Simon. "Tom Sharpe." Dictionary of Literary Biography 14: British Novelists Since 1960. Ed. Jay L. Halio. Detroit, MI: Gale, 1983, 646-654.

Garcia, Celia Vazquez. El Humor Como Máscara del Desencanto en las Novelas de Tom Sharpe. Vigo, Spain: Universidade de Vigo, 1998.

Keates, Jonathan. "Whelk in the Soup." Observer (September 30, 1984): 20.

King, Francis. "Wise Cracks." Spectator 240.7812 (March 25, 1978): 20-21.

McCall, Raymond G. "The Comic Novels of Tom Sharpe." Critique: Studies in Modern Fiction 25.2 (1984): 57-65.

Nollet, Thomas G. "Tom Sharpe and Porterhouse Blue: The Techniques of Comedy and the Satirist's Vision." Studies in Contemporary Satire 14 (1987): 23-29.

Nollet, Thomas G. "Tom Sharpe and the Satire of Racism: Caricature and Farce in Riotous Assembly." Studies in Contemporary Satire 15 (1988): 11-19.

Nye, Robert. "Comic Violence, Violent Comedy." Guardian Weekly 121.6 (August 5, 1979): 22.

Peters, Jeanne M. "Thomas Ridley Sharpe." Contemporary Authors, Volume 122. Eds. Hal May, and Susan M. Trosky. Detroit, MI: Gale Research, 1988, 414-421.

Reynolds, Stanley. "The Sharpe End." Punch 283.7407 (November 1, 1982): 743-744.

Sharpe, Tom. Ancestral Vices. London, England: Secker and Warburg, 1980.
Sharpe, Tom. Blott on the Landscape. London, England: Secker and Warburg, 1975.
Sharpe, Tom. The Great Pursuit. London, England: Secker and Warburg, 1976.
Sharpe, Tom. Indecent Exposure. London, England: Secker and Warburg, 1973.
Sharpe, Tom. Porterhouse Blue. London, England: Secker and Warburg, 1974.
Sharpe, Tom. Riotous Assembly. London, England: Secker and Warburg, 1971.
Sharpe, Tom. Wilt. London, England: Secker and Warburg, 1976.
Sharpe, Tom. The Wilt Alternative. London, England: Secker and Warburg, 1979.
Waugh, Auberon. "Lancing Farce." Spectator 226.7455 (May 15, 1971): 671.

Alan Sillitoe (1928-)

Sillitoe's writing, "fluctuates from straight hard prose to Nottingham slang to the most literary effusions, often all on the same page." Sillitoe's characters are isolated from society; they have, "the spirit of the outsider, the dissenter, the man apart" (May and Lesniak 384). Gene Baro says that Sillitoe's writing exhibits, "lucid design, pace, a gift for salty vernacular, an unerring eye for the telling gesture, [and] a robust and yet a restrained sense of the comic." He adds that for Sillitoe, "All is achieved simply, matter-of-factly, without apparent striving for effect." James Yaffe says that Sillitoe has, "a fluent, often brilliant command of language, an acute ear for dialect, [and] a virtuoso ability to describe the sight, sound and smell of things" (May and Lesniak 385).

Saturday Night and Sunday Morning (1958) is a mock-epic adventure, a picaresque novel, a, "working-class comic epic in prose about Arthur Seaton, a lathe operator in a Nottingham bicycle factory" (Smith 668). This novel recapitulates such novels as Henry Fielding's Tom Jones, and Joseph Andrews (Hutchings Encyclopedia 987). In Arthur's factory, the workers are reduced to automatons by the monotony of their labor. But they turn to sport for status, and for identity. But even this sport is exploited by higher authority, as the athletes attempt to cash in on their athletic abilities. Sillitoe's protagonist resists this exploitation (Hutchings 1987 35-47). In The New Yorker, Anthony West says that Saturday Night and Sunday Morning has, "the true robust and earthy quality characteristic of English working-class life" (qtd. in May and Lesniak 384). Saturday Night and Sunday Morning is filled with much rowdy humor. It is about a particularly raucous Saturday Night when Arthur Seaton drinks seven gins and eleven pints of ale in a drinking contest, and then tumbles down a flight of stairs at the local pub. After winning the drinking bout, Arthur vomits twice over the newly-pressed suit of a middle-aged pub-goer whose response is the mild, "Look at this!...Oh dear!" But the woman that the middle-aged man is with utters a much more militant sort of outrage: "Look what yer've done, yer young bleeder!" (Sillitoe Saturday 13). In this way, Sillitoe skillfully differentiates her vernacular language from the man's more educated middle-class standard English. She is obviously one of the "noisy tarts" who is entertaining a middle-class client (Hutchings 985).

In Saturday Night and Sunday Morning, Arthur Seaton, the protagonist, is a twenty-one-year-old factory worker who violates decorum, despoils middle-class proprieties, and seduces other men's wives. Mrs. Bull, who lives near Arthur, is the neighborhood's foremost gossip. She has lived in the neighborhood for twenty-two years, and has become the "queen of the yard." She is bellicose, and censorious, and is called "The News of the World," and "Loudspeaker" (Sillitoe Saturday 23-24), and she confronts Arthur on his "carryin' on with married women" (Sillitoe Saturday 90). But Arthur retaliates by shooting at Mrs. Bull with his air-rifle. He snipes at her from his upstairs window, and one of his pellets hits her across her cheek as she is standing gossiping in her usual position at the corner of the yard. It should be noted that in the film version of the novel, Mrs. Bull is not shot on the cheek, but is rather shot in the rump. Winnie and Brenda are two other characters in Saturday Night..., and Arthur has a fling with each of them separately. At the Goose Fair, he also has a fling with his soon-to-be-fiancée, Doreen in an episode that shows Arthur at his "raucous, rowdy, mock-heroic best" (Hutchings 986). But in the "Sunday Morning" section of the novel, Arthur forsakes his wild and rakish ways in order to have the comfort, security, stability, and responsibilities of his impending marriage. This is the standard ending of all traditional comedies (Hutchings 987). After becoming reluctantly involved in a number of mock-heroic adventures, Arthur by the end of the novel tries to redeem himself, through "surprisingly traditional means" (Hutchings 985). By the end of the book, Arthur is a kinder, gentler character, but he even here resolves always to struggle against the, "stifling forces of conformity and deadening, mind-forged 'respectability'" against which he remains inherently opposed" (Hutchings 986).

The Loneliness of the Long-Distance Runner (1959) is about an unrepentant youth named Smith who is sentenced to a reformatory for theft. Smith deliberately loses a long distance race because the borstal director wants him to win the race for the prestige of the reformatory. Self esteem is not easy for Smith to obtain, and he therefore does not want to risk his self esteem by winning the race for the director, in the same way that a trained horse might win a race for its master. "This story explores the resentment the lower classes feel for any of the innumerable ways government, and, by extension, society, dehumanizes them" (Smith 668). One of the stories in The Loneliness of the Long-Distance Runner is entitled, "On Saturday Afternoon." It is about a sixteen-year-old boy who remembers an incident that had happened six years before in which a man tried to hang himself from a light fixture. A policeman confronts the man and asks him, "Well, what did you do it for?" The man responds, "Because I wanted to." "You'll get five years for this," says the policeman, and the man says, "That's what yo' think. I only wanted to hang myself." "Well, it's against the law, you know," says the policeman, and the man answers, "Nay, it can't be. It's my life, ain't it?" "You might think so," said the policeman, "but it ain't" (qtd. in Siegel 207).

Smith, the narrator of The Loneliness of the Long-Distance Runner is an exuberant rebel who relies on his "cunning," and his "secret subversions" to resist the standards and expectations that are imposed by society. From the beginning of the novel there is an antithesis developed between "them" and "me;" the "me" later becomes "us" (Hutchings 988). Smith is a defiant teenage anti-hero whose values are irreconcilable with those of the prevailing culture. This novel helps place Sillitoe into the class of "Angry Young Men" who, "transformed post-war fiction and drama with their forthright, vigorous, and unabashedly 'vulgar' style that combined rowdy humor and occasionally harsh satiric animus against 'respectable' society and its middle-class mores." Thus Sillitoe joins other "Angry Young Men" like Kingsley Amis, John Wain, John Braine, John Osborne, and Keith Waterhouse (Hutchings 989).

The General (1960) is an allegorical fable; Travels in Nihilon (1971) is a dystopian fantasy; The Widower's Son (1976), The Storyteller (1979), and Her Victory (1982) which are domestic character studies, all contain raucous, anarchic, and comic scenes, as well as some excellent wit and inventiveness (Hutchings 989).

The three books in the "William Posters Trilogy" are as follows: The Death of William Posters (1965), A Tree on Fire (1967), and The Flame of Life (1974). Frank Dawley, the protagonist of the "William Posters Trilogy" deserts his wife, his children, and his job in order to find freedom and a sense of identity. In his mind, Frank Dawley creates an imaginary figure and names him "William Posters." The name is suggested by the signs Dawley sees everywhere: "Bill Posters Will Be Prosecuted," and this becomes a symbol of the persecution of the underdog workmen by the authorities (Smith 670).

"Chicken," one of the stories in Guzman, Go Home, and Other Stories (1968), exhibits Sillitoe's skill at black humor. "Chicken" is about a foundry worker who steals a neighbor's chicken for Sunday dinner. He chops the chicken's head off, but the headless bird runs away from him and right back onto the neighbor's dinner table (Siegel 211).

Michael Cullen is the protagonist in A Start in Life (1970), a long picaresque novel in which Sillitoe experiments with such comic forms as satire, irony, farce, and parody. Here Sillitoe follows in the tradition of Henry Fielding, an author he very much admired. Most critics appreciate Sillitoe's humor in A Start in Life and they also appreciate his manipulation of traditional literary forms (Smith 671). Life Goes On (1985) is the sequel to A Start in Life. Life Goes On takes up the story of A Start in Life, with only a ten-year gap between the books. Both of these novels provide excellent examples of the raucous picaresque comedy that can also be found in Sillitoe's earlier novels. The protagonist is Michael Cullen, who describes himself as a, "real no-good, genuine twenty-two-carat bastard in every sense of the word" (Sillitoe A Start 71). William Hutchings considers Michael Cullen to be, "Sillitoe's most traditionally picaresque working-class rogue-hero since Arthur Seaton." He relies on cunning, wit, and trickery to succeed in life. He spends his adolescent life in what he calls the "three -ings": Reading, Working, and Fucking. In all of his comic adventures, Michael retains his resilient devil-may-care attitude. Later, when he comes back to visit his factory-working friends, he slips back into his "homeliest Redford accent," but they nevertheless realize that through his cunning and his associations, he has moved from their class into a higher class (Hutchings 990). In Life Goes On, Almanack Jack gives his personal credo as, "It's always better to act. Never stifle what you feel to be a fundamental impulse. If it causes chaos, so much the better." This is not only Almanack Jack's personal credo, it's also Alan Silitoe's sense of what makes good comedy, and is to some extent the creed of every picaro. "The eventual triumph of this 'impulse' over all of the nay-saying, life-denying forces by which it has been opposed enables 'the right sort of order and happiness' to be achieved" (Hutchings 990-991).

There are five travelers who go to Nihilon in Travels in Nihilon (1971). Nihilon is a city where the citizens value cheating and violence. They scorn honor and loyalty, and they deliberately create chaos and disaster. In the opinion of Catherine Smith, "the farce and satires of some of the adventures do not compensate for the weak multiple perspectives imposed on the novel by five protagonists" (Smith 671).

Alan Sillitoe is not easy to categorize as an author. Some critics label him an "angry young man," but other critics use the opposing label of "working-class novelist." Sillitoe himself prefers to be thought of as "simply a novelist." For Sillitoe, "Arthur Seaton is first an individual, then a representative of the working class" (Smith 674). William Hutchings says, "Sillitoe's protagonists engage in series of amoral, rakish, erotic, and even anarchic escapades that affirm (like all traditional comedy) the life-force of fertility and vitality of the body against the stifling forces of conformity and the deadening, mind-forged respectability'--a form of 'domestication' to which they are inherently opposed" (Hutchings 991).

Alan Sillitoe Bibliography

Hutchings, William. "Alan Sillitoe." Encyclopedia of British Humorists, Volume II. Ed. Steven H. Gale. New York, NY: Garland, 1996, 984-994.

Hutchings, William. "The Work of Play: Anger and the Expropriated Athletes of Alan Sillitoe and David Storey." Modern Fiction Studies 33 (Spring, 1987): 35-47.

Isaacs, N. D. "No Man in His Humour; A Note on Alan Sillitoe." Studies in Short Fiction 4.4 (1967): 350-351.

May, Hal, and James G. Lesniak, eds. "Alan Sillitoe." Contemporary Authors, New Revision Series, Volume 26. Detroit, MI: Gale Research, 1989, 383-386.

Siegel, Jennifer Semple. "Alan Sillitoe." Dictionary of Literary Biography, Volume 139:
    British Short-Fiction Writers, 1945-1980. Ed. Dean Baldwin. Detroit, MI: Gale
    Research, 1994, 203-215.
Sillitoe, Alan. Life Goes On. London, England: Granada, 1985.
Sillitoe, Alan. Saturday Night and Sunday Morning. London, England: W. H. Allen, 1958.
Sillitoe, Alan. A Start in Life. London, England: W. H. Allen, 1970.
Smith, Catherine. "Alan Sillitoe." Dictionary of Literary Biography, Volume Fourteen:
    British Novelists Since 1960. Ed. Jay L. Halio. Detroit, MI: Gale, 1983, 666-675.

John Lawrence Collins Jr. (1929-)

After traversing four continents in search of significant historical anecdotes, John
Collins co-authored four books with Dominique Lapierre: Is Paris Burning?, Or I'll Dress
You in Mourning; Freedom at Midnight; The Fifth Horseman; and O Jerusalem!. Collins
jokingly told Life magazine that his partnership with Dominique Lapiere has been so
balanced that it often frustrates their publisher. Collins says, "He wants to find out which
one of us has the talent" (Johnson 134). Is Paris Burning? (1965) is about the liberation
of Paris during the Second World War. Bernard Frizell says of this novel that the author's
"keen news sense has put them, even so long after the event, on the trail of dozens of
dramatic anecdotes, many of which they have hunted down" (Johnson 134). Or I'll Dress
You in Mourning (1967) is an exciting picaresque adventure about the life of a matador.
This novel has a tendency toward florid prose (Johnson 135). Freedom at Midnight (1975)
is about the struggle for independence in India (Johnson 134). The Fifth Horseman (1980)
is about the terrorist attack of New· York City and the explosion of an atomic bomb by
Libyan leader Moammar al-Qaddafi (Johnson 134). Collins and Lapierre were concerned
that Qaddafi's supporters might retaliate, so according to Collins, "We told some people
we were writing about nuclear proliferation, we told others it was about terrorism, and
others that it was on the oil crisis." The authors were so concerned that they sent the
completed French manuscript to the printer under a false title and a false author's name
(Johnson 135). O Jerusalem! (1972) is about the conflict between the Israelis and the
Palestinians in the Middle East (Johnson 134). David Schoenbrun says that in this novel,
         the reconstruction of events day to day, at times minute by minute, is
         skillfully and dramatically presented by two exceptional storytellers. The
         pace is so swift, the drama so heightened by alternating flashes of tragedy
         and comedy that one has to stop frequently just to catch breath and to
         marvel at the majesty and absurdity of the bloody fighting over so-called
         sacred soil (Johnson 135).

John Lawrence Collins Jr. Bibliography

Johnson, Anne Janette. "John Lawrence Collins, Jr." Contemporary Authors: New Revision
    Series, Volume 19. Ed. Linda Metzber, Detroit, MI: Gale, 1987, 133-139.

Len Deighton (1929-)

It was Len Deighton who said, "The tragedy of marriage is that while all women
marry thinking that their man will change, all men marry believing their wife will never
change. Both are invariably disappointed" (Macdonald 50). Hugh Moffet says that Len
Deighton has led an adventurous life. He has experienced a hurricane in New York and

a typhoon in Tokyo. He says he has hunted alligators in New York sewers (though this is a bit suspect), and he was taken into custody in East Berlin. He has watched blue movies in Cuba and accompanied Los Angeles policemen as they broke into a narcotics dealer's apartment. He has been a crew member on a burning airliner, and he has fallen into the Hong Kong harbor. And in 1960, when he was traveling in France with his wife, he began writing just "for a giggle." Deighton's novels, "investigate--with humor and forgiveness--the nature of man, the experiences, the values, the loyalties, and the betrayals that make him what he is" (Macdonald 38).

Nevertheless, critical response to Deighton's novels has ranged from high praise to deep contempt, with few critics taking the middle ground. This may be because of Deighton's comic departures from the standard patterns of his genre, and it may also be because of his unwillingness to take a position either in the direction of the totally serious, or in the direction of the totally popular. The criticism may also be because of Deighton's disdain for the pretensions and the snobbery of the "old boy" networks of Oxford and Cambridge graduates in particular, and upper-class English society in general (Macdonald 37). It is ironic that critics often judge Deighton in terms of the traditions of the genre, while in fact Deighton is most often, "working against the genre, using it, parodying it, transforming it to suit his own purposes" (Macdonald 41).

In his espionage novels Len Deighton blends his painstaking attention to accuracy with a light ironic touch. David Quammen says that Len Deighton is, "a talented, droll and original spy novelist." His protagonist is a nameless British intelligence officer who is cynical and full of wisecracks because he is a reluctant spy. T. J. Binyon writes that Deighton has "a gift for vivid, startling descriptions," and Peter S. Prescott says that his style is marked by "oblique narration, nervous laughter and ironic detachment" that turn his spy stories into "comedies of manners." Robin W. Winks says that Deighton, "patented a style in which every third paragraph appeared to have been left you," and Perl K. Bell agrees, saying that Deighton's, "obsessive reliance on the blurred and intangible, on loaded pauses and mysteriously disjointed dialogue, did convey the shadowy meanness of the spy's world, with its elusive loyalties, camouflaged identities and weary brutality" (Lesniak 104).

Deighton's protagonist is street-tough, self-educated, and independent. He is a man of irreverent quips, and surprising strengths. He is impudent and fallible, but he is also highly skilled and highly trained, and a survivor. Nevertheless, he lacks formal education, and is worldly, brash, insolent, and cheeky. He has a sort of working-class rudeness. He knows how to do his job more competently than better-educated workers around him, and this irritates his supervisors (Macdonald 42). He uses his wit and his charm to wage the class battle that he feels must be waged (Macdonald 43).

Anthony Boucher says that The Ipcress File (1962) is both a serious espionage novel and a parody of the genre. Boucher adds that it is, "a sharply written, ironic and realistic tale of modern spy activities." John B. Cullen comments on Deighton's humor, saying that, "Deighton writes with a tongue-in-cheek attitude." He continues that, "no one is spared the needle of subtle ridicule, but the author still tells a plausible story which holds your attention throughout." Robert Donald Spectar is being critical when he says that in The Ipcress File, "Deighton has combined picaresque satire, parody, and suspense and produced a hybrid more humorous than thrilling." And Julian Symmons calls The Ipcress File "a dazzling performance," adding, "The verve and energy, the rattle of wit in the dialogue, the side-of-the-mouth comments, the evident pleasure taken in cocking a snook at the British spy story's upper-middle-class tradition--all these together with the teasing convolutions of the plot, make it clear that a writer of remarkable talent in this field had appeared" (Lesniak 104). Robert Spector says that the nameless protagonist in The Ipcress File is a "modern picaro." It is through this nameless protagonist that Deighton satirizes and parodies modern espionage agencies and the rhetorical devices of such authors of espionage novels as Eric

Ambler, Ian Fleming, and Graham Greene (Macdonald 42). Gina Macdonald says that The Ipcress File, "combines humor and suspense in a taut story of betrayal and survival, establishing a pattern and a sensibility that has remained Deighton's hallmark throughout his literary career" (Macdonald 41).

In Funeral in Berlin (1964), Deighton attempts to disorient and suggest new ways of perceiving the Germans and Russians. Although they are portrayed as having faults, they are nevertheless humanized, and at times they are more admirable than are the English or the Americans. Colonel Stok, the Russian KGB officer, is a likeable but jaded professional who is irritated by the naïveté, the prejudice, and the mindlessness of his associates, especially the Stalinists. Stok tells amusing jokes that mock his own system, and it is only Stok and his British counterpart, the protagonist, who are able to truly determine what is going on (Macdonald 54).

Julian Symons describes Billion-Dollar Brain (1966) as having a plot, "as intricate as the lock of a good safe." The novel features George Dawlish, an unnamed cynical British protagonist, his pragmatic friend named Colonel Stock, and a neurotic American agent by the name of Harvey Newbigin. The hero becomes more and more disillusioned with modern machinery, and fears that, "it's only a matter of time before machines are pressing buttons to call people" (Macdonald 46). Julian Symons especially praises the, "characterization of the clownish double agent, Harvey Newbigin." In this novel there is an organization named "Facts for Freedom" which has a giant computer at its heart. This "horrifying menace" is called the "billion-dollar brain" (Macdonald 45).

The title of An Expensive Place to Die (1967) alludes to a quote by Oscar Wilde about the cost of dying in Paris. The novel has been praised for its, "tight construction, crisp prose, fast action, and vivid scenes" (Macdonald 46). Only When I Larf (1968), published in the United States as Only When I Laugh (1987), is a comedy thriller about three confidence tricksters--Bob Appleyard, Silas Lowther, and Liz Mason (Macdonald 46). The point of view shifts from one of these tricksters to the next as each of them assumes the narrative first person story-telling perspective (Macdonald 47).

Bomber: The Anatomy of a Holocaust (1970), "conveys as well as anything written by an Englishman what it feels like to fly, to crash, to bomb, to be bombed, to be conscious that you are experiencing the first of your last sixty seconds of life as you fall without parachute." In Bomber there is an ironic tension as the subject of the novel shifts from the battle discussions of a Spitfire reconnaissance team to the pastoral discussions of a thirteenth-century village, or shifts from the preparations for a bombing raid to the discussions of beautiful sunsets, or shifts from an unexpected revelation of love to the discussion of six hundred pounds of explosive that would annihilate the would-be lovers (Macdonald 47).

In Close-up (1972), Deighton tries to capture the essence of the motion picture industry, as he discusses the narcissism, the insecurity, the cynicism, the hypocrisy, the back-stabbing, and the pandering to youth that goes on in order to make a profit. And all of this happens beneath a gaudy and hyperactive façade (Macdonald 47). In Spy Story (1974) there is a cocky and sardonic U.S. Marine Corps colonel by the name of Schleglel who selects Deighton's unnamed narrator as his personal assistant. Patrick Armstrong, the hero, is a reluctant spy who is at odds with the world of "unintelligent intelligence." Armstrong is cynical, detached, and disenchanted. He is a fumbling and despairing character, but he is perfectly decent (Macdonald 48).

SS-GB: Nazi Occupied Britain, 1941 (1978) tells what Britain would have been like if it had lost World War II. In this portrayal, King George is a prisoner in the Tower of London, Scotland Yard is controlled by an SS-Gruppenfuhrern, and the German army is so much in competition for power with the SS that sabotage becomes a common power tool. It is in this environment that a German army band plays "Greensleeves," and a group of Americans visit the cathedral ruins, and there is a fast trade in devalued antiques (Macdonald 49). What is interesting about <u>Goodbye, Mickey Mouse</u> (1982) is that it explores the irony that parents are obligated to send their own children off to death. The book's title refers to the last words of a dying pilot to his friend, Lieutenant Morse, who is nicknamed Mickey Mouse. These dying words are also, "an expression of farewell to childhood and its trivialities, as well as what a father or mother might say to a departing son" (Lesniak 106).

It was Rudyard Kipling who first called espionage the "Great Game," and Len Deighton extends this metaphor in his trilogy based on the tennis expression, "Game, Set, and Match." The trilogy is named <u>Berlin Game</u>, <u>Mexico Set</u>, and <u>London Match</u> (Lesniak 107). This trilogy is described by Gina Macdonald as, "oblique and ironic, with a sense of humor and disillusionment and a sensitivity to manners." Deighton's writing is more serious, more credible, more fully developed, and more adept at innuendo than were his earlier works. In this trilogy, Dicky Cruyer is lazy, incompetent, and cocky. He has neat theories, but they are glib and superficial, and at odds with reality. He is insensitive to people, to places, and to atmosphere, and is often more of a "clown" than "the cool sophisticate" which is his own image of himself (Macdonald 50).

At the beginning of <u>Berlin Game</u> (1983), two agents are waiting near the Berlin Wall for a defector to cross over from East Berlin. Bernie Samson, the protagonist of the novel, asks, "How long have we been sitting here?" and his partner replies, "Near a quarter of a century." This alludes to the long-standing significance of the Berlin Wall as a symbol of East-West conflict (Lesniak 105).

In <u>Mexico Set</u> (1985), just as in the other novels in this trilogy, food is a defining metaphor. In the trilogy, British food is contrasted with French food, German food, and Russian food. Deighton uses his own knowledge of international cuisine to develop both character and plot, as in <u>Mexico Set</u> where Samson says that he has a limited capacity for the permutations of tortillas, bean mush, and chilies that numb the taste buds and sear the insides. Samson claims that he has never really trusted drinking water anywhere but Scotland, and then adds that he has never been in Scotland. Cruyer, in contrast, prides himself on sampling exotic food. He tries the <u>surtido</u> and the <u>carnitas</u> with various <u>salsas</u>, marinated cactus, and tortillas, and he lectures on their virtues. In the meantime, Samson quietly points out that it is pork ear and intestine he is consuming with such gusto. Cruyer, with cultivated condescension, pedantically explains the differences in chilies, but while doing so he mistakes cayenne for one of the very mild <u>aji</u> chilies, from the eastern provinces. Samson silently watches and enjoys Cruyer's reactions to the fiery pepper. Because he is sensitive and cautious, Samson can merge with an alien population, and he can lose himself in the crowd. But Cruyer alienates the locals, as he rushes headlong into disaster. Cruyer doesn't have a clue about the subtleties that surround him (Macdonald 40).

<u>London Match</u> (1985) is a game of wits between Bernie Samson, Fiona Samson, and the KGB (Macdonald 51). At the end of <u>London Match</u>, Samson sums up the rules of the game:

> The willingness to break rules now and again is what distinguishes free men from robots. And we spiked their guns, Werner. Forget game, set, and match. We're not playing tennis; it's a rougher game that, with more chances to cheat. We bluffed them; we bid a grand slam with a hand full of deuces and jokers, and we fooled them.... Okay, there are wounds, and there will be scars, but it's not game, set, and match to Fiona. It's not game, set, and match to anyone. It never is. (Macdonald 52)

A second of Len Deighton's trilogies is based on the fishing expression, "Hook, Line, and Sinker." The trilogy is named <u>Spy Hook</u>, <u>Spy Line</u>, and <u>Spy Sinker</u> (Macdonald

50). Spy Hook (1988) is about the cool, cynical, and detached Bernard Samson. For London Central, Bernie Samson is the, "dogsbody who got the jobs that no one else wanted" (Macdonald 53). Spy Line (1989), and Spy Sinker (1990) are two more books in the series.

Len Deighton Bibliography

Lesniak, James G., ed. "Len Deighton." Contemporary Authors, New Revision Series, Volume 33. Detroit, MI: Gale, 1991, 103-108.
Macdonald, Gina. "Len Deighton." Dictionary of Literary Biography, Volume Eighty-Seven: British Mystery and Thriller Writers Since 1940. Eds. Bernard Benstock, and Thomas F. Staley. Detroit, MI: Gale, 1989, 36-54.

Brian Friel (1929-) IRELAND

Brian Friel is very Irish in the way that he uses humor. His characters and language are humorous, but he does not develop the anglicized notion of Irish humor that is presented by George Bernard Shaw, or by Oscar Wilde. Friel's characters, and his language tend to demythologize the images and myths that have created a false view of Irish culture. In this way, Friel is hoping to rediscover a mythic Irish past that is free of the post-colonial overtones that have been imposed upon it (Haigh 407).

Philadelphia, Here I Come! (1964) is about Gareth O'Donnell who runs through his past life before moving to Philadelphia. Much of the humor of the piece comes from the revelation of his public self as contrasted with the revelation of his private self (Haigh 406). In Translations (1980), Friel uses lyrical and brutal language to show how language is both the cause and the solution of his characters' problems, and by extension, the problem of Irish identity. The characters talk in standard English, in dialectal English, and in dialectal Irish-English, depending on the person they are talking with. Some of the characters even talk in Irish, in Latin, and in Greek.

The Communication Cord (1982) is a farcical comedy about the destruction of the Irish countryside and Irish culture. In this play, the Irish middle classes with their sentimentalizing of the peasant society are shown to be just as guilty of the destruction of Irish culture as are the English with their linguistic and military tyranny. In The Communication Cord, a Catholic family comes together for the wedding of their youngest daughter in a decaying Georgian mansion named Ballybeg Hall. The characters associated with this mansion are eccentrics. There is the dying patriarch, the dotty Uncle, and the American academic. There are also some illegitimate children, and some drunken wives in what turns out to be a very moving and funny play (Haigh 406).

Dancing at Lughnasa (1990) is very autobiographical. It takes place in Northern Ireland. Friel's seven sisters are translated to the five sisters in the play. The sisters in the play even have the same first names as Brian Friel's real-life aunts. The sisters are unmarried, and they live a sparse existence, but the music of their radio transforms their existence into an ecstatic pagan celebration of the festival of Lughnasa. Dancing at Lughnasa, like many of Friel's plays, is set in the mythical town of Ballybeg. "Ballybeg speaks of the 'Irishness' of Northern Ireland in the same way that Dylan Thomas's Llareggub speaks of the 'Welshness' of South Wales" (Haigh 405).

See also Nilsen, Don L. F. "Brian Friel." Humor in Irish Literature: A Reference Guide. Westport, CT: Greenwood, 1996, 208-209.

Brian Friel Bibliography

Bordinat, Philip. "Tragedy Through Comedy in Plays by Brendan Behan and Brian Friel." West Virginia University Philological Papers 29 (1983): 84-91.

Haigh, Anthony R. "Brian Friel." Encyclopedia of British Humorists, Volume I. Ed. Steven H. Gale. New York, NY: Garland, 1996, 404-409.

Kearney, Richard. "Friel and the Politics of the Language Play." Massachusetts Review 28 (1987): 510-515.

Henry Livings (1929-)

The plays of Henry Livings are about the British working class. These plays have been placed into such categories as "Absurdist," as "Angry Young Men," and as "Kitchen Sink" (Gale 685). Livings is famous in the regional theaters of England for his working-class farces, in which his characters interact with each other in humorous ways (Gale 688). Jack's Horrible Luck (1961) is a picaresque tale about a naïve young sailor named Jack who is on shore leave in Liverpool. It is a comedy that combines broad farce with fantasy, as Livings captures the vernacular of the working class. Russell Taylor has said that the episodes are strung together in what he calls a "parable-in-farce-technique" (Gale 685). Stop It, Whoever You Are (1961) is a farcical skit that is divided into five scenes, each of which is self-contained but also related to the other scenes (Gale 685). Big Soft Nellie (1961) is a plotless farce about Stanley, a mother's boy who is the butt of jokes played on him by the employees of an electrical appliances shop. The play is again notable for its working-class cadences, and for the irony of the humor (Gale 686). Nil Carborundum (1962) is a comedy about life in the peacetime armed forces (Gale 686).

Valentine Brose is the protagonist of Eh? (1964). He is caught up in the workings of a large, modern factory. Valentine is a boiler-room attendant, and the farce of Eh? develops out of his characterization, as Val becomes so concerned with his hallucinogenic mushrooms that he neglects his boilers, and the play, which is a farce and a fantasy, ends with an explosion. Livings describes Valentine as, "pale and totally lacking in human fire. He behaves excitedly on occasion, even frenetically, and he wears gaudy cheap clothes with some dash; but he himself stays still and unaffected in the core of the fireworks. It's as if he were giving a performance of some character he's dreamed up, and his pale eyes wander in search of effect even in his apparently wildest moments" (Gale 686).

In Act I, Valentine is interviewed by Price, the works manager, for a position. At one point they discuss the thirty-four letters of reference that Valentine has accumulated. One of the letters is from a Mr. Frint, who says that Valentine is, "forsaking a brilliant academic future for a career in the Foreign Office" (Livings Eh? 30). However, a closer examination of the letter reveals that Valentine has erased the word "satisfactory" and has substituted the word "brilliant." When Mr. Frint is contacted about the letter, he says that he can remember a student named Valentine Brose, but his recollection of him is very faint. One of the other references was provided by a Mr. Oliver Broad. It consists of two newspaper clippings, the first a disclaimer stating that Mr. V. Brose of 2 Holy Bones is not the V. Brose who has been prosecuted for vagrancy in the previous day's news. The second clipping is a report telling about how the police have not been able to establish a case against V. Brose for littering offensive material on a public thoroughfare. Val is also a complainer, "It's just this getting up in the morning. I've missed my dole for the last twelve weeks because of that. They put my time for eleven o'clock. Dirty trick" (Livings Eh? 16). But Val also has a good sense of humor. When Price discovers the box of hallucinogenic mushrooms, Val denies that they are mushrooms even though the word "MUSHROOMS" is written on the box. "No. That's the maker's name. Capitals. Capital M, capital U, SHROOMS: Mervyn Ulrich Shrooms, seed merchant" (Livings Eh? 23).

Pongo Plays (1971) is a series of twelve plays about Sam Pongo, a simple but sharp-witted weaver from Lancashire, who is very much like Charles Dickens's Sam Weller in The Pickwick Papers. He is a foil for the blustering masters, and the milos glorioso military types, and like Sancho Panza and Sam Weller, he survives by his common sense and wit (Gale 688).

Henry Livings Bibliography

Gale, Steven H. "Henry Livings." Encyclopedia of British Humorists, Volume II. Ed.
    Steven H. Gale. New York, NY: Garland, 1996, 684-690.
Livings, Henry. Eh? London, England: Eyre-Methuen, 1964.

John Patrick Montague (1929-) IRELAND

See Nilsen, Don L. F. "John Patrick Montague." Humor in Irish Literature: A
    Reference Guide. Westport, CT: Greenwood, 1996, 209.

John Morgan (1929-1988) WALES

In a personal letter dated April 28, 1994, Brian Lile indicated that John Morgan's Wales is a humorous work.

John Morgan Bibliography

Lile, Brian. Personal Letter dated April 28, 1994.
Morgan, John. John Morgan's Wales. Swansea, Wales: Christopher Davies, 1993.

John (James) Osborne (1929-)

John Osborne has a predilection for epigrams which places him in the tradition of Oscar Wilde (Hirst 67). The single most important element in Osborne's style is the connection of public and private feelings. "The private layer is passionate, angry, caring, and anti-intellectual; but the public layer is satiric, and, therefore, intellectual" (Hinchliffe 54). Osborne concentrates on expressing the feelings of his hero, and this makes his work extremely subjective, and of course one of the important aspects of good satire is objectivity. Osborne is a great entertainer, and his social commentary is frequently funny and accurate; however, in the opinion of Arnold Hinchliffe it often, "tells more about the character speaking than about the object under attack" (Hinchliffe 54).

John Osborne's Look Back in Anger (1956) was the first dramatic work to give rise to the labels of "Kitchen-Sink School," and "Angry Young Men" (Athanason 377). Jimmy can neither forgive nor forget his wife Alison's upper-class social background. Jimmy is outraged by the apathy he sees around him and by his inability to enter the power structure of upper class society, so he uses his wit, and his ability to shock such gentle and nurturing people as his own wife (Athanason 378).

The Entertainer (1957) chronicles the life of a wilting, third-rate music-hall comedian by the name of Archie Rice, but Osborne was really writing about "the fate of postwar Britain, an island suffering recession and unemployment, losing its status as an empire" (Salter 340). According to Susan Salter, Osborne is capitalizing on the dramatic and the comic potential of the English music-hall tradition in The Entertainer (Salter 341). The Entertainer is a depiction of three generations of a middle-class English theatrical family. Arthur Athanason says that it is Osborne's requiem for the dying music hall tradition, and the vital aspect of English life that it represented. Its three acts are divided into an overture and thirteen short scenes reminiscent of the "turns" in the music-hall tradition. "By conceiving each scene of this play as a music-hall turn, Osborne enables the audience to see both the 'public' Archie performing his trite patter before his 'dead behind the eyes' audience and the 'private' Archie performing a different comic role of seeming nonchalance before his own family" (Athanason 379).

The World of Paul Slickey (1959) is a musical satire that targets the London Press. Osborne dedicates this play as follows:

> I dedicate this play to the liars and self-deceivers; to those who daily deal out treachery; to those who handle their professions as instruments of debasement; to those who, for a salary cheque and less, successfully betray my country; and those who will do it for no inducement at all. In this bleak time when such men have never had it so good, this entertainment is dedicated to their boredom, their incomprehension, their distaste. (Athanason 380)

The play did not get good notices. As Osborne wittily observed, it received "the worst notices since Judas Iscariot." Most critics say that the play satirized too much at once, and as a result, Osborne's efforts become excessive and futile (Athanason 381).

The Blood of the Bambergs (1962) is a crude comic satire written in the form of a revue-like one-act play. It is an experimental comedy of manners dealing with intimate marital relationship. It is about a royal wedding in a contemporary mythical kingdom between Princess Melanie and Prince Wilhelm. However Wilhelm is killed in a sports-car accident, and Heinrich, Wilhelm's younger brother, becomes the rightful successor. The problem is that Heinrich is homosexual, so to ensure that there will be heirs to the King, a plot is designed which is to prevent Heinrich's succession to the throne. Then Alan Russell is discovered. He is a bearded Australian press photographer who looks like Prince Wilhelm, and he is discovered to be the illegitimate son of the king. Against Russell's objections, the minister of culture whisks Russell to the palace to be shaved and prepared for his royal marriage to Princess Melanie on the next day. The plan is that Russell will be handsomely bribed for his service to the state, bribed for the "claustrophobia and overwhelming boredom" he will be forced to endure as monarch (Athanason 383). An example of the humor of the play is when Taft asks, "Have you ever considered Isabella, the Grand Duchess of---," Brown responds, "Yes I have. She has to shave twice a day, so she'd be able to use the Prince's razor, since he doesn't have to" (Hirst 84). Alan Brien sees The Blood of the Bambergs to be, "a satirical charade designed to clobber the monarchy industry." He also says that it is "funny, savage, and accurate" (Athanason 384).

Under Plain Cover (1962) is about a husband and wife named Tim and Jenny. They live with their two children in a little house in suburban Leicester, and are very much in love. To increase the drama of their marriage, it is firmly based on a, "highly successful sadomasochistic relationship." Tim and Jenny are role-playing clothes fetishists who order their various costumes through the mail "under plain cover." Stanley Williams is a newspaper reporter who reveals that Tim and Jenny are in fact brother and sister (though they hadn't realized it), so their happy and innocent world is quickly destroyed (Athanason 384). As soon as possible, Jenny is married off to a "decent fellow," and Tim is left on his own to shift for himself as well as he can. In the end, however, love wins out, as Jenny returns to live with Tim in seclusion (Athanason 385). Under Plain Cover is filled with witty and original dialogue, "a combination of Restoration bawdy and quick-fire repartée." At one point, Tim and Jenny talk for several minutes about knickers, and the dialogue is very creative:

> TIM: The Prime Minister's Country House--Seat: Knickers
> JENNY: Of course. Why don't you come down for the weekend?
> TIM: Open to the public on weekdays.
> JENNY: Until they pull it down. (Hirst 84)

This is a subtle erotic game which reveals how a clever manipulation of the roles in the love-making ritual is able to animate and enrich the marriage (Hirst 84).

In 1963, John Osborne wrote the screen play for Tom Jones. David Hirst feels that Osborne's screen play captures both the bucolic zest for life of the fox-hunting bon viveur Squire Western, and the subtlety of the sexual intrigue that centers on the London social circle dominated by Lady Bellaston. In the tradition of Fielding, Osborne adds delicious touches throughout the film, such as Miss Western's peremptory dismissal of a country highwayman: "Deliver! I am no wandering midwife, sir. Deliver what?" (128). Or consider Lady Bellaston's sarcastic observation about Sophie: "The girl is obviously intoxicated, and nothing less than ruin will content her" (134) (Hirst 82).

Walter Sorell says that although Osborne writes graceful lines with bite and wit, his forte is not laughter, and he goes so far as to say that the only scene of real comedy that he created with gusto can be found in A Patriot for Me (1965), where there is a "drag ball which the hero of the play, Colonel Red, attends and which is a cruel account of transvestism" (Sorell 300). In A Patriot for Me Osborne sharpens and refines his ironic dialogue. Here we get a glimpse of the terse and witty language that is present in Osborne's mature dramas. This play contains Jimmy Porter's lengthy rhetorical outbursts, and it also contains Archie Rice's clever music hall patter (Hirst 83). Act II of A Patriot for Me begins with a "Drag Ball," in which six different types of homosexuals are described as making up the complex social mixture of guests (Hirst 85).

The Hotel in Amsterdam (1968), Time Present (1968), and West of Suez (1971) are Osborne's most fully developed Comedies of Manners. The tone of the opening of The Hotel in Amsterdam is urbane as a disapproving waiter stimulates a conversation containing verbal precision and paradoxical argument with a strong echo of Oscar Wilde. The waiter, "is a descendant of Lane and Merriman from The Importance of Being Earnest."

> LAURIE: Thought you were a bit effeminate, I expect.
> GUS: Perhaps he did. I think it's these bloody trousers, darling. You said
> I should throw them away. They don't do much for me do they?
> LAURIE: Nothing desirable.
> ANNIE: Darling, you always look rather effeminate. You and Laurie both
> do in different ways.
> GUS: Ah, but Laurie carries it off somehow, I don't
> MARGARET: Especially to foreigners.
> ANNIE: It's part of your masculine charm.
> GUS: What do you mean?
> ANNIE: Oh, I don't know. A kind of mature softness.
> MARGARET: And peacockery. (Hirst 89)

The Hotel in Amsterdam contains witty conversations on such taboo subjects as menstruation and the technicalities of homosexual intercourse (Hirst 85). In The Hotel in Amsterdam, Laurie is an aggressive poseur who uses his skill at repartee as a dazzling defence to cover up his emotional unhappiness and insecurity. Laurie's animated use of language reflects both his deep sensitivity and his determination. Laurie is the central figure in a group of six people whose conversation serves to define a high level of social behavior (Hirst 88). Laurie's longer speeches, including the lengthy joke about nuns, are set pieces for the entertainment of his friends. The piece about his relatives is entertaining and witty, though there is also a substratum of guilt (Hirst 89).

In <u>Time Present</u> (1968) Pauline's criticisms act as an incentive to Pamela's wit, which ranges from the quick snub to the lengthier put down. An example of the quick snub is when Pauline says, "You kill me, you're so provincial," and Pamela responds, "Very likely. As your mother will remember, I was born in India." As an example of the lengthier put down, consider the following:

> PAULINE: Oh, you're just camp.
> PAMELA: So I've been told. Just like my father. I wish I could say the
> same for you. It's impossible to argue with someone wearing such
> cheap clothes. Take a glass of champagne down to Dave. He
> doesn't <u>need</u> to look quite so ugly, you know. I suppose he thinks
> he's beautiful, of course. (Hirst 87)

Here Pamela's responses are quick, sharp, and to the point. They are in marked contrast to Jimmy Porter's lengthy tirades (Hirst 87). Pamela's attacks on Abigail are devastating, but they are also funny and accurate. Edward points out that these attacks stem from "professional envy" (Hirst 88).

In <u>West of Suez</u> (1971) the characters are measured according to their speech. When Edward says to Frederica, "I've always been prone to being taken in, like a pussy-cat's laundry," she recognizes his insincerity, and responds, "Now you're straining." The chief arbiter of style in this play is Wyatt whose language is pleasant and avuncular, thus masking his true nature. However, his younger daughters see through this. Wyatt is older, urbane, and a supremely witty raconteur; he tends, therefore, to be the center of attention.

> WYATT: Chatter sins against language, and when we sin against the word,
> we sin against God. Gosh, I am pompous.
> FREDERICA: I wasn't going to say it.
> WYATT: Must be the Brigadier's cuddly, loving little grape. Where's your
> old man got to?
> FREDERICA: He's out there on the beach, talking to Jed.
> LAMB: Oh, <u>does</u> he talk?
> ROBERT: I think there is someone who could sin against language if he
> could bring himself to it. (Hirst 92)

Wyatt's laconic charm in the previous dialogue, however, soon gives way to the brilliant countering of a reporter's criticism. Wyatt has an iron control of the argument, and his replies have the same confident assurance as those of the dandies of Oscar Wilde or Noel Coward.

> MRS. JAMES: What do you think of man?
> WYATT: As a defect, striving for excellence.
> MRS. JAMES: Do you really think that?
> WYATT: No, but presumably you want me to say something, however dull.
> (Hirst 93)

Here it is not only Wyatt's speaking, but Osborne as well, for according to David Hirst, this is a "savage denunciation of critics" (Hirst 93).

In the <u>Guardian</u>, Michael Billington describes <u>A Sense of Detachment</u> (1973) as follows:

> How to describe John Osborne's <u>A Sense of Detachment</u> at the Royal Court?
> A thinking man's <u>Hellzapoppin</u>? A spiky, satirical, inconsequential collage?
> An attack on our own heartless, loveless, profiteering society in which
> language is corrupted daily? A moving threnody for a dying civilization?
> A paradox of this (to me) provocative, innovative and exciting work is that
> it manages to be all of these things, moving outwards from purely theatrical
> satire to an eloquent examination of the world at large...sustainedly
> entertaining. It is full of Osborne's characteristic rancid eloquence. And it

goads, provokes, and agitates its audience as only a truly vital theatrical work can. (Athanason 390)

The End of Me Old Cigar (1975) is an outrageous social satire about the widowed Lady Regine Frimley who supports herself and her young "husband," Stan, by inviting prominent men and women to her country house for intimate (but discreet) liaisons with each other (Athanason 390). Osborne's description of Kenneth Tynan in The End of Me Old Cigar is quite humorous:

> Ken Onan's face is grey-blue like a clinker
> And in his lap his boneless fingers tinker
> Dispassionately with his wilting quill.
> He has the gift, alas he lacks the will.
> The Spirit of Right Reason cries "Come Back,
> The Dunces Reign! Return to the Attack!
> Unseat triumphant Dullness from her saddle
> And put the Fear of Wit in Fiddle-Faddle!"
> But nothing takes his eye or primes his pen.
> Most self-delighting and self-damned of men! (Hirst 96)

Act I of The End of Me Old Cigar is consistently funny. "Regine's command of language is pyrotechnic, combining epigram, wisecracking rhetoric, and sarcasm to great effect" (Hirst 94). Regine sarcastically tells John Stewkes that, "Power is so sexy, as we all know.   Even more than money.   I've never had either but I can recognize it, particularly in bed" (40). This statement is complex because Regine is lying. In truth, Regine is a Jewish girl from Hackney who has gained great wealth by marrying and exploiting several husbands.   She plans to blackmail the entire male race with the compromising films she has made of various illicit sexual exploits. The humor of the piece comes more from identifying the satiric portraits than from the complexities of personal or social motivation (Hirst 94). John Osborne called The End of Me Old Cigar a, "modern comedy of modern manners, drawing attention to the fact that this genre of comedy, which had dominated the post-Restoration period, has continued to the present time as a vital genre in the English theatre" (Hirst 1). It is Len who ends the play with the statement in which the emphatic climax is printed in capital letters, "And always remember, ladies. At least in your cases: A WOMAN IS A WOMAN BUT A GOOD CIGAR IS A SMOKE" (Hirst 95).

John (James) Osborne Bibliography

Athanason, Arthur Nicholas. "John Osborne." British Dramatists Since World War II. Ed. Stanley Weintraub. Detroit, MI: Gale, 1982, 371-393.

Hinchliffe, Arnold P. "Whatever Happened to John Osborne?" Contemporary English Drama. Ed. C. W. E. Bigsby. New York, NY: Holmes and Meier, 1981.

Hirst, David L. Comedy of Manners. New York, NY: Methuen, 1979.

Salter, Susan. "John Osborne." Contemporary Authors, New Revision Series, Volume 21. Ed. Deborah A. Straub. Detroit, MI: Gale Research, 1987, 339-342.

Sorell, Walter. Facets of Comedy. New York, NY: Grosset and Dunlap, 1972.

Whelen, Christopher. The World of Paul Slickey: A Comedy of Manners with Music. London, England: Faber and Faber, 1959.

Alun Richards (1929-) WALES

In a personal letter dated April 28, 1994, Brian Lile indicated that Welsh author

Alun Richards has written two volumes of humorous short stories: The Former Miss Merlthyr Tydfil, and Dai Country.

Alun Richards Bibliography

Lile, Brian. Personal Letter dated April 28, 1994.
Richards, Alun. Dai Country. New York, NY: Michael Joseph, 1973.
Richards, Alun. The Former Miss Merthyr Tydfil. New York, NY: Penguin, 1979.

Keith Spencer Waterhouse (1929-)

Keith Waterhouse has a reputation as a humorist, and his work is tending more and more in the direction of classic farce. His humorous newspaper and magazine columns have been collected and published in The Passing of the Third-Floor Buck (1974), Mondays, Thursdays (1976), Rhubarb, Rhubarb (1979), Fanny Peculiar (1983), and Waterhouse at Large (1985). Waterhouse likes to write about the ridiculous side of things, and many of his columns are autobiographical, telling about how it was to be a youth in Yorkshire, and giving a nostalgic commentary on how much things have changed (Moseley 1174). Merritt Moseley says that Waterhouse's verbal humor is his greatest strength as a comic writer (1177).

Keith Waterhouse is best known for his novel Billy Liar (1959). Billy's work at the undertakers' place is mundane and meaningless, so he makes up for that by having a rich fantasy life, and by being a bit dishonest. He imagines that he has a job in London writing jokes for a radio comedian. He amuses himself and his friend by speaking in Yorkshire dialect, "Ah'm just about thraiped" and he also invents phantom sisters for himself, and makes believe that his mother has broken legs in order to make his life more interesting. Billy's fantasies throughout the novel are very funny. Billy Liar has a clever and convoluted plot. Billy is more or less engaged to three different girls, none of whom is known to the other two. He has just one engagement ring, which he maneuvers from girl to girl. He has to lie constantly as he keeps whisking the ring from one girl to another. The story becomes funnier and funnier as the plot moves closer to the edge of impending discovery (Moseley 1177).

Billy Liar (1960), Say Who You Are (1966), Who's Who (1974), Children's Day (1975), and Whoops a Daisy (1978) are all plays written with Willis Hall. In these plays, Waterhouse and Hall bring out the comedy of pathetic lives, and the pathos of comic lives. These plays are dramas of sexual frustration, and frustration of ambition (Moseley 1181). Merritt Moseley says that of all of Waterhouse's Yorkshire plays, Billy Liar (1960) is by far the funniest (Moseley 1176). Say Who You Are (1966) is a frenetic farce about two couples and their adulteries. On stage there is both an elevator and a stairway to allow characters to just miss each other going up or coming down. There is a great deal of mistaken identity in this old-fashioned battle of the sexes. Who's Who (1974) takes place in Brighton, where Bernard White and Timothy Black have gone for a "dirty weekend" with their lover. Helen Brown is their lover. In Act I, one man's wife goes to Brighton, and in Act II the other man's wife goes to Brighton. The result is a great deal of mistaken identity, confusion, and deception. Merritt Moseley considers Children's Day (1975) to be the best of Waterhouse's farces (Moseley 1176). The play takes place during a children's party, and there are two couples carrying on intrigues. The plot involves not only the marital complications, but also a lost rabbit, children attacking one another, and one of the children repeatedly removing his clothes. The party is going on just offstage, and an uproar is heard whenever the door to the party room is opened (Moseley 1177). In Whoops a

Daisy (1978) there is a very tight-laced family named James, Lily, and Marigold Wormald. Ken and Thelma Smedley, a crude couple from Rugby, move in next door to the Wormalds. The Smedleys are so full of life that they begin to warp James and Lily, even changing the way that they talk. Before long, everybody is using Ken's catch phrase, "whoops-a-daisy," and James, who had earlier been very prissy, is referring to his daughter as, "sitting there like a tart in a trance."

Jubb (1963) is a funny novel despite Mr. Jubb's horrible qualities and his final fate. Merritt Moseley says that it is "a genuine tragicomedy," and "a brilliant book" (Moseley 1179). Billy Liar on the Moon (1975) is a sequel to Billy Liar (1959). Billy is now a local government employee in Shepford, a town close to London. Again Billy's lying gets him into trouble. At one point he becomes bored as he is standing around the stairwell looking for Helen, so he claims that his golf clubs have been stolen, and an officious neighbor reports the theft. In truth, the clubs never existed,   Through the rest of the book he tries to fend off the police investigation. He even tries to buy some clubs so that he can claim that his clubs have turned up (Moseley 1178).

In addition to Billy Liar (1959), and Billy Liar on the Moon (1975), Merritt Moseley considers Office Life (1978), In the Mood (1983), and Bimbo (1990) to be Waterhouse's most purely comic novels. In Office Life, Waterhouse writes about British Albion, a vast company that employs an army of white-collar workers all of whom are losers. In this company, the telephones never ring, nobody does any work, and nobody seems to know exactly what British Albion does. Clement Gryce, the narrator, joins a group of conspirators who are intent in discovering the secret of British Albion. They discover that it is a shell company established to provide artificial employment to people who are unemployable. The company has been established in the assumption that if people actually realized how bad England's economy really is, there would be universal despair. This is, of course, a whimsical approach to the very serious problem of England's economic situation. This is also a good satire to show how people interact in offices, how they joke, how they laugh, who brings in candy, how often they go to the bathroom, what office supplies they steal, how late they come to work, and how early they leave for home. Life in this company is only a slight exaggeration of life in any office (Moseley 1180). In the Mood (1983) is a cheerful novel about adolescence, and about how becoming an adult (what Raymond would call a "dodo" or a "fossil") is a terrible thing from the point of view of an adolescent. Bimbo (1990) is about Debra Chase, a young, uneducated girl who becomes a Page Three pinup queen. It is written as a corrective to a sensational ghostwritten story that appears in a tabloid paper. This satire discusses the world of night clubs, of swinging photographers, and of "bonking baronets" that had recently been appearing in the tabloids, but most of the humor comes from Debra's naïve style, with its many malapropisms (Moseley 1181).

Maggie Muggins, or, Spring in Earl's Court (1981) is a terrible story about a day in the life of a drunken, sexually indiscriminate London girl who moves from one squalid room to another in the sleazy parts of the city, but it is also a funny novel. Because she is a "persona non grata," she has to make her "mail round;" that is, she has to go to all of the places she has lived to pick up her letters. She is very secretive, and never leaves a forwarding address. Maggie has a vigorous and slangy type of speech. She divides the world into two classes; she calls the ordinary people "punters," and she uses the term "faces" only for special people, like her and Sean. "Faces are marginal people who live by their wits" (Moseley 1179).

Mrs. Pooter's Diary (1983) and The Collected Letters of a Nobody, Including Mr. Pooter's Advice to His Son (1986) are continuations of George and Weedon Grossmith's The Diary of a Nobody (1892). Mrs. Pooter's Diary is said to be written by Mr. Pooter's long-suffering wife, Carrie. Carrie's diary is carefully synchronized with Charles's diary, but it provides a different view of the many events which were first revealed from Charles's point of view in 1892. The reader who is familiar with the original The Diary of a Nobody will, of course, understand much more of the humor in Waterhouse's later works (Moseley 1175).

The Theory and Practice of Lunch (1986), and The Theory and Practice of Travel (1989) are serio-comic how-to books. In The Theory and Practice of Travel there is a section about maps, one about how to complain, one on how to arrange for a "dirty weekend," and one on traveling with children. All of these sections are illustrated with cartoons and Victorian drawings.

Keith Spencer Waterhouse Bibliography

Moseley, Merritt. "Keith Spencer Waterhouse." Encyclopedia of British Humorists, Volume II. Ed. Steven H. Gale. New York, NY: Garland, 1996, 1173-1183.

9

Authors Born between
1930 and 1939

James Graham Ballard (1930-)

Sand dunes, abandoned buildings, crashed automobiles, low-flying airplanes, drained swimming pools, and beaches are recurrent themes in J. G. Ballard's stories (Trosky 15). In his first four novels, Ballard shows how the world could be destroyed by man-made global catastrophes, by high winds resulting from changed topography in The Wind from Nowhere (1962), by the melting polar ice caps in The Drowned World (1962), by the radioactive waste that has prevented evaporation of the sea, making rain a thing of the past and producing worldwide drought in The Drought (1965), and by a spreading cancerous mutation in The Crystal World (1966). Ballard's first three novels are all about worlds which punish man for tampering with nature. These three novels, but especially The Burning World, echo T. S. Eliot's The Waste Land. In The Drought a cruel new breed of men emerge in a world where money is replaced by water as the most effective currency (Fletcher 51). Ballard says that his first novels are about, "The delicate natural equipoise upon which our existence depends, the ease with which the balance may be upset, and the consequences of the resulting imbalance." Unlike T. S. Eliot, J. G. Ballard is, according to David Pringle, "a wry figure with a slight smile and melancholy eyes." Although Ballard rarely laughs, the reader nevertheless gets the impression that there is a twinkle in his eye because, "Ballard was there first." "His stories have illuminated, with tremendous insight and a truly prophetic relevance, the public moral concerns of our age." Fletcher continues, "Ballard undoubtedly sees himself as a satirist of contemporary sicknesses" (Fletcher 52).

Charles Platt writes that Ballard's heroes are, "solitary figures, courting the apocalypse and ultimately being seduced by it" (Trosky 16). In the late 1960s, Ballard became one of the leading spokesmen for the "New Wave" in science fiction, which proposed introducing experimental literary techniques, and more sophisticated subject matter into science fiction writing. In an editorial for New Worlds, Ballard wrote, "It is inner space, not outer, that needs to be explored" (Trosky 16).

Ballard says he is not interested in imaginary alien planets. He says that the only really important alien planet is Earth. Every day Ballard sees "all the extra-terrestrials we need" walking along Earth's streets. Ballard writes science fiction about the present day. He is interested in the technology of this world at this time (Fletcher 50).

Some of the stories in The Atrocity Exhibition (1970) such as "Why I Want to F---Ronald Reagan," and "The Assassination of John Fitzgerald Kennedy Considered as a Downhill Motor Race" are so strong that Joseph W. Palmer of Library Journal called this an "ugly, a nauseating, brilliant, and profound" book (Trosky 16). The Unlimited Dream Company (1971), and Hello America (1981) blend fantasy with humor (Fletcher 55). Both of these novels employ a kind of surreal humor (Fletcher 57).

Before beginning to write Crash (1973), Ballard staged an exhibition of crashed cars at the New Arts Laboratory in London, and had an opening party at the gallery. Studio International quotes Ballard as saying, "I'd never seen 100 people get drunk so quickly.... I also had a topless girl interviewing people on closed circuit TV, so that people could see themselves being interviewed around the crashed cars by this topless girl. This was clearly too much. I was the only sober person there" (Trosky 17).

In a Newsweek review of Empire of the Sun (1984), David Lehman and Donna Foote say that they would like the book placed, "on anyone's short list of outstanding novels inspired by the second world war." They continue, "It's ironic that Empire of the Sun--Ballard's first fictional foray into the past--has earned him accolades denied to his earlier 'disaster novels,' since it has more in common with them than immediately meets the eye. Like its predecessors, the book explores the zone of 'inner space.'" Empire of the Sun brings together a number of apparently irreconcilable writing notions--autobiography, naturalistic storytelling, and surrealism (Trosky 18).

James Graham Ballard Bibliography

Fletcher, John. "J. G. Ballard." Dictionary of Literary Biography, Volume 14: British Novelists Since 1960. Detroit, MI: Gale Research, 1983, 50-57.
Platt, Charles. Dream Makers: The Uncommon People Who Write Science Fiction. Berkeley, CA: Berkeley Publishing, 1980.
Pringle, David. Earth Is the Alien Planet: J. G. Ballard's Four-Dimensional Nightmare. San Bernadino, CA: Borgo, 1979.
Trosky, Susan M., ed. "J(ames) G(raham) Ballard." Contemporary Authors: New Revision Series, Volume 39. Detroit, MI: Gale Research, 1993, 14-19.

Jennifer Johnston (1930-) IRELAND

See Nilsen, Don L. F. "Jennifer Johnston." Humor in Irish Literature: A Reference Guide. Westport, CT: Greenwood, 1996, 11, 209-210.

Harold Pinter (David Baron, Harold Pinta) (1930-)

Harold Pinter's humor comes from his misunderstandings, non sequiturs, noncommunications, Yiddish phrasings, witty word play, elaborate reversals, puns, and jokes (Gale 856). David Hirst says that Pinter's predilection for the epigram places him in the tradition of Oscar Wilde, and his remorseless paring down of language along with his simple effective drama places him in the tradition of Noel Coward (Hirst 67). In his juvenile poetry Harold Pinter has some of the same features that can be found in his adult work, both his poetry and his drama--alliteration, repetition, and play with language

(Tucker 353). Martin Esslin points out that in Pinter's writing there is, "the paradox of his artistic personality." Pinter's dialogue and his characters may ring true, but the overall effect is one of mystery, uncertainty, and poetic ambiguity. Many of the dramatic elements in Pinter's work can be described as "Pinteresque." These elements include, "his characters' mysterious pasts, his theme of the intruder, and his use of language--textual and subtextual--and of silence" (Tucker 354). Stephanie Tucker says that Pinter is, "not essentially a comic writer," but she adds that, "he does write very funny dialogue" (Tucker 356). In a 1960 interview, Harold Pinter said to K. S. Guthke, "Everything is funny...the greatest earnestness is funny; even tragedy is funny. And I think what I try to do in my plays is get to this recognizable reality of the absurdity of what we do and how we behave and how we speak" (Guthke 122).

Pinter writes in the tradition of "Comedy of Menace," "Theatre of Non-Communication," "Black Comedy," "Existential Drama," "Angry Theatre," and "Theatre of the Absurd," but Frank Kastor feels that the best way to describe Pinter's writing is "Tragicomic." Pinter himself felt that in modern writing, comedy, tragedy, and farce have been blended together (Kastor 3). The conversation in Pinter's plays is mainly chitchat, banalities, and misunderstandings, and there are very many questions that go unanswered. Pinter's characters don't actually communicate. Rather, they express themselves in stammering clichés, repetitions, and contradictions. Pinter says, "Communication itself between people is so frightening that rather than do that there is a continual cross-talk, a continual talking about other things, rather than what is at the root of their relationship." As a result, actual dialogues, like the dialogues in Pinter's novels, are frequently absurdly funny and highly comic (Kastor 6).

Although Pinter does not write to entertain, his plays are funny nevertheless in their outrageous conceptions and grotesque situations. In a letter published in the London Sunday Times (August 14, 1960), Pinter admitted that absurdity is one of the features of his plays, and added, "where the comic and the tragic are closely interwoven, certain members of an audience will always give emphasis to the comic as opposed to the other, for by so doing they rationalize the other out of existence" (Sorell 297). Three of Harold Pinter's plays can be said to be written in the genre of "Comedy of Menace." These plays are The Room (1957), The Birthday Party (1957), and The Dumb Waiter (1957) (Gale 851). These contain a great deal of comedy, and the comedy is presented in a "frighteningly funny way" (Sorell 293). Pinter's plays have a haunting quality as they represent a mad world which is rotten to its core. The reader can hear an "animalistic heartbeat" beneath a very thin veneer of civilization. Pinter's obnoxious characters are, "weak in their strengths, strong in their weaknesses." They are subhuman, but they are compelling in their "fully visualized three-dimensionality" (Sorell 294). Pinter has the ability to create a maximum effect with a minimum of words. "His language is used not only to tell a story--this seems to be its secondary function--but also to stir the senses and alarm the mind" (Sorell 296). Pinter's plays don't have funny lines and funny situations as much as they have outrageous conceptions and grotesque situations (Sorell 297).

In a February 1967 interview in New Yorker, Pinter explains the genesis of three of his early plays. "I went into a room and saw one person standing up and one person sitting down, and a few weeks later I wrote The Room. I went into another room and saw two people sitting down, and a few years later I wrote The Birthday Party. I looked through a door into a third room, and saw two people standing up and I wrote The Caretaker" (Tucker 353). In a book entitled Pinter's Comic Play, Elin Diamond discusses The Room, A Slight Ache, The Birthday Party, and The Caretaker in a chapter entitled, "Posers and Losers" (Diamond Comic Play 17-88). She discusses The Dumb Waiter, The Collection, The Lover, and The Homecoming in a chapter entitled, "The Parody Plays" (Diamond Comic Play 89-158). And she discusses Old Times, No Man's Land, and

Betrayal in a chapter entitled "Playing on the Past" (Diamond Comic Play 159-210). The laughter in Pinter's plays tends to haunt the audience; at the end of the play, they're not sure whether they should be laughing or not. Pinter's plays may be happy, but they do not have happy endings. "Pinter's parody is also skewed, revealing not only the mocking spirit we expect but also noncomic tensions we do not expect. If Harold Pinter's comedy springs from traditional roots, he undercuts our laughter even as he invites it" (Diamond Comic Play 12). Pinter's plays are influenced by England's literary, popular, and theatrical comic traditions. His audiences are baffled by the "unverifiable," as they respond to the wordplay and clown staging. Pinter denies that his characters are stereotypes, but it is easy to identify the nagging wife, the belligerent father, the errant son, the foolish pedant, the wily bum, and the roaring cuckold, all of them types which date back to Greco-Roman comedy, and which continue through English domestic comedy and comedy of manners. There tends to be three significant aspects of Pinter's writing: 1). the exposure of the imposter (often the braggart), 2). verbal game playing, and 3). linguistic and theatrical parody (Diamond Comic Play 11). For Pinter, language is always at the core of his comic achievement. Throughout his writings can be found, "hectoring repetition, serial lists, rambling anecdotes, phatic inanities, and jargon parodies designed to shock and baffle his audiences. Pinter does not want his audience to become too comfortable in verifying character motives or in rationalizing play action" (Diamond Comic Play 211).

Harold Pinter is a parodist who ironically plays with and criticizes the comic tradition even as he firmly establishes himself as a significant author in that tradition (Diamond Comic Play 90). He mockingly and playfully exposes the conventions of the genre in order to define and liberate his own writing. Pinter tends to be self-reflexive, because in exposing the limitations of his models, he is commenting on his own writing as well (Diamond Comic Play 91). In his parody plays, Pinter plays games with his audience, making them think they are getting the joke, but later surprising them with an unexpected punch line (Diamond Comic Play 93). The Dumb Waiter parodies the gangster movie and the detective plot. It is filled with gangster language and guns that echo the crime world. The Collection parodies the melodrama and the soap opera. It contains furtive phone calls and middle-class interiors that cue the audience to expect melodrama, standard television soap opera, or a parody of these genres. The Lover parodies the comedy of manners with its aphoristic dialogue, and The Homecoming parodies realistic domestic family drama in its coffee-circle ceremony, etc. (Diamond Comic Play 92).

In his early plays the victims who Pinter writes about fail to control their words, and this failure often makes the reader laugh, "for it can lead to manic buffoonery" (Orr 74). John Orr feels that Pinter's plays are at the same time highly mobile, ludic, and erotic (Orr 76). David Hirst feels that the love of sport and gamesmanship are, "rarely absent from Pinter's work" (Hirst 74). In his writing, Pinter's language is like ordinary language, but from under a microscope. His plays have comic elements, but they have elements of menace as well. His wit relates to the struggles involved in intense verbal gamesmanship. His plays have in general moved away from comedy of menace to comedy of manners, as the characters shift in social status from the working-class world of the early plays to the upper-middle-class setting of Old Times and No Man's Land (Hirst 68).

In a book entitled Where Laughter Stops: Pinter's Tragicomedy (1976), Bernard Dukore says that all of Pinter's comedies from The Room (1957) to No Man's Land (1974), are not comedies at all; they are tragicomedies. These plays all begin with comic expectations, but then they move to a point where the laughter ends, and thus they, "deny the exclusiveness of comedy in the very terms they first establish to suggest comedy." These plays are not truly comfortable, since they sardonically mock the comedy they had earlier established (Dukore 72-73).

In his first play, The Room (1957), Pinter shows that he has an uncanny ear for dialogue. It has even been facetiously suggested that Pinter must have a tape recorder in his head (Hirst 67). The Room also has the rhythms of the English music hall dialogue, a dialogue that is also reminiscent of S. J. Perelman's Marx Brothers film scripts (Gale 853).   In this play, Rose Hudd alternates between being the victim and being the victimizer, as Pinter encourages the audience to laugh at the same time as he is weaving a web of fear. Rose talks to Bert, who remains silent. Rose is a nagging wife; this is a comic stereotype, and Bert is a henpecked husband who buries his nose in a magazine trying to ignore his wife; this is another comic stereotype. Although Pinter indicates pauses where Bert might respond, he never does, and although Rose is reciting a monologue, she never talks about herself. Rather, she talks about Bert's illness, Bert's food, and Bert's driving. But she never talks about Bert's silence (Diamond Comic Play 21). Rose not only has a "monologue" with Bert, she also has a "monologue" with the man at the door:

> A knock at the door. She [Rose] stands.
> ROSE: Who is it? Pause Hello! Knock repeated. Come in then. Knock
>   repeated. Who is it-- Pause. The door opens and MR. KIDD
>   comes in.
> MR. KIDD: I knocked.
> ROSE: I heard you.
> MR. KIDD: Eh? (qtd. in Diamond Comic Play 22)

The audience doesn't know whether they are laughing at Mr. Kidd's deafness, or his senility, or both (Diamond Comic Play 22). In The Room, the domestic comedy that begins the play is based mainly on a wife's waiting on her husband in a secure environment, but the play ends with the reassertion of the husband's supremacy, and the destruction of someone who has intruded into their safe haven, and the reëstablishment of the status quo, but a status quo in which harm occurs. "The comedy is negated by fear, violence, death, and the debilitation of the mainstay of security" (Dukore 9).

In The Birthday Party (1957), Stanley lives in a boarding house, where he is teased by Lulu, a neighborhood girl, is tolerated by Pete Boles, and is hovered over by Meg Boles, his landlady. At the beginning of the play Stanley is depressed and frightened. By the end of the play he's being led around, corsetted in a business suit. He has become a drooling vegetable stripped of his individuality. Stanley's disintegration is dominated by the farcical antics of Goldberg and McCann, representing an archetype which dates back to Shakespeare's time--"the Vice"--otherwise described as the trickster, the tempter, and the malicious humorist (Diamond Comic Play 45). "The Vice not only moves the action of the moralities, he explains what he is doing in comic, self-aggrandizing monologues" (Diamond Comic Play 46). In the tradition of the Vice, Pinter's Goldberg and McCann are clever schemers, able to dissemble and gull simple characters. They are characterized by their boastful monologuing, their merriment, their energy, and their motiveless malice (Diamond Comic Play 47). Not only do they gull Meg and intimidate Stanley, but in addition, Goldberg engineers a birthday party for the sole purpose of demonstrating his own cleverness. In the tradition of the Vice, Goldberg juggles identities and plays roles (Diamond Comic Play 48). Elin Diamond considers Goldberg to be one of the funniest, and also one of the most frightening characters on any stage. Stanley, Meg, and Lulu constantly and hesitantly refer to an absent father, and Goldberg picks up on this to supply anecdotes about a father, a wife, an uncle, and a dead mother, thus parodying their emotions (Diamond Comic Play 64). Goldberg is an effective con man because he is able, in the tradition of the carnival barker, to spew out old time values. He talks about the good old days with his mum, when he was a youngster and he would go for a walk down by the canal with a girl who lived down his road. This was a beautiful girl with the voice of a song bird "Good? Pure? She wasn't a Sunday school teacher for nothing" (Henkle "Pooter" 183). He would give her a little kiss on the cheek, but he never took liberties--

like other young men might have--and then he would go humming away, past the children's playground, where he would tip his hat to the toddlers and give a helping hand to a couple of stray dogs (Henkle 184). Elin Diamond considers Meg Boles to be one of Pinter's best developed comic characters, and part of her development is in her lack of pretentiousness.

> Petey enters from the door on the left with a paper and sits at the table. He begins to read. Meg's voice comes through the kitchen hatch.
>
> MEG: Is that you, Petey? Pause. Petey, is that you? Pause. Petey?
> PETEY: What?
> MEG: Is that you?
> PETEY: Yes, it's me.
> MEG: What? (Her face appears at the hatch.) Are you back?
> PETEY: Yes.
> MEG: I've got your cornflakes ready. (She disappears and reappears.) Here's your cornflakes. (Diamond Comic Play 63)

In this scene, there are many pauses and repetitions (over ten instances of the word "cornflakes") which demonstrate Pinter's particular style of linguistic humor. "Pinter has perfected a hyper-realistic version of natural speech, so unnatural in fact as to be immediately recognizable and dubbed as Pinterese or Pinteresque" (Dutton 27). In The Birthday Party, Pinter parodies the persecutors of his victims. In the tradition of the English music hall, Goldberg and McCann are travesties of Jews and Irishmen. "Their menace always seems contained by a repartée which never loses its comic rhetoric." John Orr considers The Birthday Party to be terror masquerading as fun. The only reason that the party takes place is that Meg has interrupted Goldberg's and McCann's gruelling questioning of Stanley (Orr 77). Walter Sorell says that The Birthday Party painfully echoes the cynicism of despair.

> STANLEY: (abruptly): How would you like to go away with me?
> LULU: Where?
> STANLEY: Nowhere. Still we could go.
> LULU: But where would we go?
> STANLEY: Nowhere. There's nowhere to go. So we could just go. It wouldn't matter.
> LULU: We might as well stay here.
> STANLEY: No. It's no good here.
> LULU: Where else is there?
> STANLEY: Nowhere. (Birthday Party 26)

Frank Kastor considers Act II of The Birthday Party to be especially filled with humor. There are the wildly hilarious and insane interrogations, the progressive bacchanalian growth of the birthday party, Meg's bleary post-menopause glow, Lulu's sensuality, and Goldberg's waffling between being a bon vivant and a terrorist. Then there is the violence, the sex, and the confusion of the game of Blind-Man's Bluff. Kastor consider's these scenes to be, "terrifying, hilarious, grotesque, funny, and deeply disturbing" (Kastor 7). For The Birthday Party, Pinter again establishes that it is in fact a tragicomedy rather than a simple comedy. In talking about his own stature as a concert pianist, for example, Stanley, first says that he gave concerts, "all over the world." This soon changed to, "all over the country," and finally to, "I once gave a concert" (Dukore 13). Meg's birthday gift, which starts out as a source of laughter, ends up as a source of fear. A boy's drum is funny, because it is given to an adult, and even funnier when Meg explains, "It's because you haven't got a piano." But the fun ends when Stanley beats the drum in an erratic and uncontrolled way until he stands over Meg, and both his face and his drum beat become "savage and possessed" (Dukore 14). This play does not end in a happy way.

"What had been sources of laughter at the play's start--identity, nourishment, the whereabouts of Stanley, birth, and departure--are no longer sources of laughter at its end. With each new act, the amount of comedy has decreased and the amount of terror increased" (Dukore 16-17). Shortly after The Birthday Party opened, Pinter received a letter asking him to explain a number of points in the play, as follows: "1. Who are the two men? 2. Where did Stanley come from? 3. Were they all supposed to be normal?" The letter writer continued, "You will appreciate that without the answers to my questions I cannot fully understand your play." Pinter replied to the letter writer, "Dear Madam, I would be obliged if you would kindly explain to me the meaning of your letter. These are the points which I do not understand: 1. Who are you? 2. Where do you come from? 3. Are you supposed to be normal? You will appreciate that without the answers to my questions I cannot fully understand your letter" (Tucker 354).

In The Dumb Waiter (1957), Pinter exploits and mocks the suspense of hit men who are waiting to bump off a victim. In this tense situation, Gus is anxious, and Ben is belligerent, and since they are unaware of all of the details of the crime they have been hired to commit, they are "dumb waiters" (Diamond Comic Play 94). The scene is reminiscent of a Laurel and Hardy comedy routine. Hardy blames Laurel for their catastrophes and bullies him around, Hardy becomes chastened, pauses, and then he resumes his "delicately choreographed mischief." In similar fashion, Ben and Gus are naïve about the world they live in, and Ben bullies Gus as a way of relieving his frustrations, and Gus in turn puts up with the bullying mainly by ignoring it (Diamond Comic Play 96-97). In one scene Ben is lying on the bed reading a paper and Gus is sitting on another bed having difficulty tying his shoe-laces. Finally Gus gets his shoe-laces tied but when he gets up and starts walking toward the door he stops, and looks at his feet, and then shakes his foot. Bothered by this action, Ben looks over the top of the newspaper he has been reading as Gus kneels down, takes off his shoe, and pulls out a flattened matchbox. As he examines it and shakes it, their eyes meet. Then Ben rattles his paper and starts reading again. But this exact same routine happens again, but with Gus's other foot, and this time he brings out a flattened cigarette packet. Again their eyes meet, Ben rattles his paper, and he begins reading again, as Gus puts the packet into his pocket and bends down to put on his shoes and tie the laces. At this point, Ben slams the paper down on the bed and glares at Gus. Then he picks up the paper and again begins reading. But the routine is not yet over, since Gus now goes into the lavatory, and after a while Ben hears the lavatory chain being pulled, not once, but twice. And then Gus, "re-enters, and halts at the door, scratching his head." All of this scene is done with no words being spoken in a silent-action that is clearly reminiscent of a Laurel and Hardy routine. "Like Laurel, Gus simply acts, oblivious to criticism. Like Hardy, Ben shares his irritation with the audience, glaring and rattling his newspaper. Like Hardy too, Ben's disdain makes him seem dominant" (Diamond Comic Play 97-98). Pinter's inspired use of the rising and falling of the dumb waiter in the third section of the play again supports the farcical and slapstick reading of the play providing a combination of, "parody and gamesmanship at its zaniest level" (Diamond Comic Play 104). In The Dumb Waiter, Gus and Ben are reincarnations of Didi and Gogo in Samuel Beckett's Waiting for Godot. "Uncertainty about their role matches menace with hilarity because it goes beyond caricature." Gus and Ben's uncertainty adds to the comic pathos, and supports the idea of the "dumb waiter," which here is used in both its literal and in its metaphorical sense. Gus and Ben are in the dark about what they are supposed to do, and they receive their orders from a dumb waiter, as if these orders they were receiving were restaurant orders. Like Didi and Gogo, they are playing a game which they have no control over, and like Didi and Gogo, they can do nothing more that await orders from above. Furthermore, the timing of the interventions is uncanny, as Gus and Ben are bothered at their weakest moments, "needling them to the point of exhaustion" (Orr 79). Originally the dumb waiter had been used to send food up from the kitchen, but now it was being used to send food down to the two "waiters," who, in order to entertain themselves, send up increasingly exotic menus they make up. "The dumb waiter is a superb metonymic symbol of their helplessness. It descends and rises when it wishes to and they become its frantic slaves. It moves between a room that is no longer a restaurant and a basement which is no longer a kitchen." It creates a kind of comic terror, as Wilson, the boss upstairs, becomes a modern version of Godot. Finally Gus and Ben order scampi, and when the boss refuses, Ben shouts up the tube, "WE'VE GOT NOTHING LEFT! NOTHING! DO YOU UNDERSTAND?" (Orr 80). Gus and Ben have a linguistic argument over whether it is correct to say "light the kettle," or "put on the kettle." Gus appears to win in this dispute, because Ben, who had insisted on the former, unthinkingly employs the latter. But Gus's victory is temporary, because later on, Ben triumphantly reports that the voice from the dumb waiter uses the expression "light the kettle" (Dukore 19). The Dumb Waiter ends with Ben calling for Gus to come in, and Gus coming in, but he enters as a victim, without his jacket, or holster, or revolver, and he is stooped, in an ambiguous tableau where Ben is pointing his gun at Gus. Here again they are dumb waiters, and so is the audience, which is on the edge of their seats wondering whether or not the gun will fire. The play ends with this tableau. "Comic at the opening of the play, death is not comic at its close. Comic tales of victims start the play, a noncomic vision of Gus as victim concludes it" (Dukore 21). The fact that the gun does not fire mocks their tension and reminds them that Pinter's parody is grounded in realism. "Pinter's guns and props and his characters [are] richly parodic pawns, tough and desperate but mostly funny" (Diamond Comic Play 108). It should be remembered that earlier in the play, Ben had told the complaining Gus, "You kill me." Ironically, this may come true, but it is Ben who may kill Gus. In the end, Gus no longer waits dumbly. Rather he thinks, and he questions the various aspects of his job (Dukore 18).

In A Slight Ache (1958), Edward specializes in noisy self-aggrandizing blustering, and ludicrous poses of condescension. The play opens as an English drawing-room comedy, with Edward and Flora sitting at the breakfast table not unlike the openings of countless drawing-room comedies from Sheridan to Coward. Edward has his nose buried in the newspaper, and Flora is chirping about the garden, about the lovely weather, the honeysuckle, the convolvulus, and the japonica. Edward responds with comic petulance: "I don't see why I should be expected to distinguish between these plants. It's not my job" (Diamond Comic Play 31). One of the funniest scenes in the play involves an encounter with a wasp:

> EDWARD: Cover the marmalade.
> FLORA: What?
> EDWARD: Cover the pot. There's a wasp. (He puts the paper down on
>   the table.) Don't move. Keep still. What are you doing?
> FLORA: Covering the pot.
> EDWARD: Don't move. Leave it. Keep still. (Pause) Give me the
>   "Telegraph."
> FLORA: Don't hit it. It'll bite
> EDWARD: Bite? What do you mean, bite? Keep still. (Pause)... It's
>   landing.
> FLORA: It's going in the pot.
> EDWARD: Give me the lid.
> FLORA: It's in.
> EDWARD: Give me the lid.
> FLORA: I'll do it.
> EDWARD: Give it to me! Now...slowly...

> FLORA: What are you doing?
> EDWARD: Be quiet. Slowly...carefully...on...the...pot! Ha-ha-ha. Very
>   good. He sits on a chair to the right of the table.
> FLORA: Now he's in the marmalade.
> EDWARD: Precisely. (Diamond Comic Play 32)

In A Slight Ache, Edward is the pompous gentleman scholar who lives in the privacy of his country estate. Edward is the "Alazon" whose self flattering pose foreshadows some sort of comic exposure. Edward has the ability to attain abstruse knowledge, and he uses this ability to disguise his lack of self-knowledge (Diamond Comic Play 29). In A Slight Ache there is also the Matchseller who is symbolic of the poverty that contrasts with Edward's wealth. Flora, Edward's wife, indicates that she has been raped by a red-bearded poacher, and the Matchseller becomes an instant suspect (Diamond Comic Play 30). Edward's first talk with the Matchseller is funny, because of the verbal repetitions like, "I say, can you hear me? (Pause). I said, I say, can you hear me?" It is also funny because of the sexually suggestive names of the liquor that Edward offers his guest, "Focking Orange," and "Fuchsmantel Reisling." And it is also funny because of Edward's ineffectuality in prompting a response (Dukore 23). The comedy of A Slight Ache turns to tragicomedy, and the laughter changes to tears in a series of sentences. Edward asks the Matchseller, "Ah, that's good for a guffaw, is it?" Then he continues, "That's good for a belly laugh." But then he catches his breath and recognizes the situation, "You haven't been laughing. You're crying." Summer arrives, and the flowers bloom, and the food is ready to eat, and all of these things signal comedy, "But these same manifestations at the end of A Slight Ache in the presence of an utterly defeated Edward, mock and deny comedy" (Dukore 24-25).

Earlier in A Slight Ache, it is funny as Edward and Flora argue about whether insects bite, sting, or suck. Even the destruction of the wasp is funny, as Edward pours hot water through the spoon hole of the pot "blinding him" and "destroying him" (Dukore 22). The marital bickering at the beginning of the play, together with the misunderstandings, the mutual irritation, and the correction of errors suggest a comedy. By the end of the play, however, the marriage has dissolved, and the husband and the Matchseller have exchanged places. At the beginning of the play the wife and the husband are having breakfast, at the end of the play the wife is inviting the Matchseller to lunch (Dukore 22). In A Slight Ache, Edward calls lunch "petit dejeuner" which is really the French expression for "breakfast," and he is concerned that the guest is consuming "duck," but in fact it is not "duck" that Flora has invited the matchseller to share, but rather a "mid-day goose." When it is time for Edward to offer the guest his choice of something to drink, he says, "Now look, what will you have to drink? A glass of ale? Curacao Fockink Orange? Ginger beer? Tia Maria? A Wachenheimer Fuchsmantel Reisling Beeren Auslese? Gin and it? Chateauneuf-du-Pape? A little Asti Spumanti? Or what do you say to a straightforward Piesporter Goldtropfschen Feine Auslese (Reichsgraf von Kesselstaff)?" (qtd. in Tucker 356).

In the play, this scene is consistent with the earlier provocatively named plants-- honeysuckle, convolvulus, clematis--in the garden of Edwin and Flora. These drink names are amusing both in their "sexual suggestiveness" and in their "continental inclusiveness" (Tucker 356). Edward and Flora take turns playing host and hostess to their unspeaking guest. As the play progresses, Edward grows weaker and weaker, and the Matchseller grows stronger and stronger, until Edward collapses on the floor. Flora passes the tray of wet, useless matches to her prostrate husband, and leaves with her new partner, the Matchseller (Tucker 355).

In 1959, Pinter wrote a number of humorous sketches which Stephen Grecco calls "pure comedy." Trouble in the Works and The Black and White were published in the

Disley Jones revue. One to Another (1959), and Request Stop, Last to Go, and Special Offer were published in Pieces of Eight (1989). Trouble in the Works (1959) is about two factory workers; one of them represents labor, and the other represents management. Mr. Wills, the personnel officer, tells Mr. Fibbs, his boss, that the workers are turning against the "hemi unibal spherical rod ends," and the "high speed taper shank spiral flute reamers" which the factory turns out. Pinter is here playing a game with language by using such pseudo-technical jargon (Grecco 398).

The Caretaker (1960) explores the comic and the terrifying effects of intrusion (Diamond Comic Play 65). The play opens with a silent, prologue-like scene in which Mick is alone, and is slowly surveying a room which is filled with junk. He observes each object in the room, and then sits still (Dukore 25). The action is simple. A man saves an old tramp named Davies from a scuffle, and since he wants to have a roommate he invites Davies to stay with him. But Davies's coming to live with the man causes his brother to be jealous, and this brother baits and persecutes Davies. Another complication is that Davies is ungrateful and conniving. So both brothers later agree that Davies must leave. Davies has a ragged and disheveled appearance that reminds the audience of the tramp-clowns of the circus and of early vaudeville, the ones who chase their trousers, or run from a vacuum cleaner. But Davies is most comic in his inflated self-aggrandizement, and in his fantastic posturing that is inconsistent with his bum's rags (Diamond Comic Play 66).

At the beginning of The Caretaker there is a dialogue between Aston and Davies:

ASTON: Sit down.
DAVIES: Thanks. (Looking about.) Uuh...
ASTON: Just a minute. (Aston looks around for a chair, sees one lying on its side by the rolled carpet at the fireplace, and starts to get it out.)
DAVIES: Sit down? Huh.... I haven't had a good sit down.... I haven't had a proper sit down...well, I couldn't tell you....
ASTON: (placing the chair): Here you are. (Diamond Comic Play 67)

Davies gets so involved in a conversation that he forgets that he wanted "a good sit down," and he fails to see the chair that Aston has made ready for him. Here we have a contrast between Davies's xenophobic rantings and Aston's generosity (Diamond Comic Play 68). When Aston tells a story about a woman in a pub who asked him, "How would you like me to have a look at your body," Davies responds, "They've said the same thing to me." When Aston asks incredulously, "Have they?" Davies confirms the point with, "Women? There's many a time they've come up to me and asked me more or less the same question" (Diamond Comic Play 69). In the August 14, 1960 edition of London's Sunday Times, Harold Pinter says that The Caretaker is "funny up to a point," and then he adds, "Beyond that point it ceases to be funny, and it was because of that point that I wrote it" (Sorell 297). Mick, the victimizer in The Caretaker asks his victim, "What's your game?" while in fact it is Mick himself who is playing sadistic games. Mick accuses Davies of vices which are actually more vices of Mick than they are of Davies. "Most of what you say is lies. You're violent, you're erratic, you're just completely unpredictable. You're nothing else but a wild animal, when you come down to it. You're a barbarian" (Orr 84). John Orr considers Mick's blunt comic patter to be both offensive and cumulative. Here the comic is setting the reader up for the tragic (Orr 85). Mick and Aston take turns in terrorizing Davies, one through sarcasm and aggression, and the other one through attention and compassion. Aston's revenge is to "care for" Davies, "in the way that he says he has been 'cared for' himself." "Mick's terror as naked threat, Aston's terror as muddled compassion--act like a pincer movement to exclude the outcast who entertains illusions of inclusion as a caretaker. Hence the superb dramatic irony of Aston's version of what a 'care-taker' actually is" (Orr 86). Much of the humor of the early part of the play is based on the incongruity between language and reality. Davies is a grubby, crotchety old man who is excessively preoccupied with himself. He mumbles and complains and tells about how important he is, and he is totally unresponsive to those who try to treat him kindly. The audience laughs when Davies grumbles that the shoes which Aston gives him don't fit, and he is also bothered that the laces don't match the shoes (Dukore 29). Davies says, "I've had dinner with the best," but this doesn't mesh with his appearance, or with his present situation (Dukore 27).

The comedy becomes tragicomedy when the tension increases--when the security becomes insecurity for Davies. Davies is old and pathetic, but he is not a tragic figure. Instead, he is responsible for his own folly. Aston is friendly toward Davies at the beginning of the play, but not at the end. But there is friendliness at the end, because the two brothers have become reunited. Davies is denied the job of caretaker, and Aston and Mick accept this job. Aston plans to take care of the shed by himself, and Mick will in turn protect his brother from intruders, thus taking care not of the room, but of the room's caretaker (Dukore 31). R. Dutton says of Aston and Mick that either of these men individually would not have had the same effect. It would be like Laurel without Hardy, or the Good cop without the bad cop. There are conscious, "groupings where the team is more important than the individuals involved, one physical presence setting off the other. By the same token, people often talk of them as complementary facets of the same personality, the friction between them reflecting the dualities of ego and id, or nature and nurture, or the left and right sides of the brain, or the male and female mix in all of us" (Dutton 68).

The Collection (1961) is Pinter's first TV play. It is also his first middle-class drama, and his first comedy of manners. It is almost like a play written during the Restoration, as it, "develops theatrically like a fine minuet played to threatening music and ends with a question. What is the truth?" Stella responds to this question by suggesting that there probably isn't any truth. "That's the truth...isn't it?" This is not a trick ending. Rather it is a demonstration of Pinter's atmosphere of ambiguity and uncertainty. In Pinter's program note to the Royal Court production of The Collection, Pinter says, "The desire for verification is understandable, but cannot always be satisfied. There are no hard distinctions between what is real and what is unreal, nor between what is true and what is false. The thing is not necessarily either true or false; it can be both true and false" (qtd. in Kastor 8). The Collection gets its name from Harry's antiques, but it also is concerned with two couples whose lives clash, and whose stories about what happened between Stella and Bill are contradictory (Hirst 68). The Collection is about two interlocking love triangles. There is a heterosexual couple and the woman's lover, and there is a homosexual couple and the wife of the other couple. In the first part of the play, sex, marriage, language, and the quest for truth all provide sources for laughter (Dukore 31). In The Collection James wants to know the truth about Stella's confession that she has committed adultery with Bill at a showing of dresses in Leeds. During the play there are five different versions of the adultery presented, including the possibility that it never happened at all. The Collection parodies two related dramatic styles, the nineteenth-century domestic melodrama, and the twentieth-century television soap opera (Diamond Comic Play 109). The Collection contains a large number of melodramatic signifiers, such as the flicking of cigarette ashes, the slamming of the door, the tableau of the lone figure with his gaze fixed on something other than the cause of his tension (Diamond Comic Play 112, 114). James and Stella and Harry and Bill play off from each other. Bill's verbal games mock James's trite physical games. James doesn't believe Bill's first confession, and he presses for the truth, but Bill responds with a derisive pun, saying that he wasn't sitting on the bed, but was rather "lying," and he may be lying still (Diamond Comic Play 117). James considers Bill to be a "wag," that is a jokester or an entertainer, and he considers himself in the patronizing role of the audience. Stella lies and Harry lies, and they both agree to accept their lies as truth:

> STELLA: ...my husband has suddenly dreamed up [this] fantastic story, for
> no reason at all
> HARRY: That's what I said it was. I said it was a fantastic story.
> STELLA: It is.
> HARRY: That's what I said and that's what Bill says. We both think it's
> a fantastic story. (The Collection 148)

The Collection is filled with double entendres and puns that range from fruit knives to Bill's ironic statement, "I'm going to be Minister for Home Affairs." The "collection" in the title is a reference to the dresses which are shown at Leeds, but it is also a reference to Harry's Chinese vases. "Both are fragile, expensive luxury items and serve to objectify the relationship of the characters--made for exhibit but incapable of taking stress" (Diamond Comic Play 120-121). The Collection is about the fact that truth is relative (Hirst 68). People believe what they want to believe, and what they want to believe therefore becomes the "truth" (Hirst 69). In an attempt to bully the "truth" about his wife's infidelity out of Bill, James speculates,

> You met her at ten o'clock last Friday in the lounge. You fell into
> conversation, you bought her a couple of drinks, you went upstairs together
> in the lift. In the lift you never took your eyes from her, you found you
> were both on the same floor, you helped her out by her arm. You stood
> with her in the corridor, looking at her. You touched her shoulder, said
> good night, went to your room, she went to hers, you changed into your
> yellow pyjamas and black dressing gown, you went down the passage and
> knocked on her door, you'd left your toothpaste in town.... (Hirst 69)

The humor comes from the heat of the moment contrasted with the coolness of the language. It also comes from the neat short phrases, and the master detective style of recounting events as if they had actually happened. The humor also comes from the jarring details, such as the yellow pyjamas, the black dressing gown, and the toothpaste (Hirst 70). The verbal sparring between Bill and James in the first scene of the play is funny. Bill's outrageous pun about wanting to stand for Parliament and become the "Minister for Home Affairs" is also funny. But this banter becomes unfunny even by the end of the scene, and the dialogue becomes especially unfunny when James threatens Bill with a knife at the end of the play (Dukore 32). The Collection ends with a final twist. James is still upset as he asks Stella to verify Bill's last story. "That's the truth, isn't it?" Stella in response gives a noncommittal smile that neither confirms nor denies the truth. The audience is not left with a cliffhanger ending, however, but rather is left with a parody of a cliffhanger. There will never be an answer to James's question (Diamond Comic Play 121).

The first conversation to be heard in The Lover (1963) displays a cool acceptance of adultery:

> RICHARD: (amiably) Is your lover coming today?
> SARAH: Mmnn.
> RICHARD: What time?
> SARAH: Three.
> RICHARD: Will you be going out...or staying in?
> SARAH: Oh...I think we'll stay in. (Hirst 71)

The Lover is about the "more amusing aspects of adultery." In this one-act play, Pinter parodies the comedy of manners both of the Restoration period and of the twentieth century (Diamond Comic Play 122). Richard and Sarah are playing a game in which Richard is not allowed to come home while the lover is visiting. And of course when he does return home their dialogue becomes a bit testy.

> RICHARD: What about this afternoon? Pleasant afternoon?

> SARAH: Oh yes. Quite marvelous.
> RICHARD: Your lover came, did he?
> SARAH: Mmnn. Oh yes.
> RICHARD: Did you show him the hollyhocks? Slight pause.
> SARAH: The hollyhocks? (The Lover 163)

Although she is originally taken aback, Sarah quickly, in the tradition of a Restoration wit, regains her balance and says, "Not all that interested, actually," thus intimating that her lover does more in the afternoons than just look at hollyhocks. The game metaphor expands when Sarah begins to refer to Richard's "mistress." "As Richard probed Sarah's extramarital affair she now 'discusses' his" (Diamond Comic Play 126). In the play, "teatime," a quaint English tradition, becomes the euphemism for sex under the table. The parody nature of Sarah and Richard's dialogues is emphasized by Sarah's assuming seductive B-movie gestures like arching her back, and crossing and uncrossing her legs. Together, they "scratch the drum," another parodic euphemism for sexual foreplay (Diamond Comic Play 128). In the play Richard and Sarah openly discuss their respective mistress and lover, displaying an acuteness of witty observation:

> RICHARD: What does he think of your husband? (Slight pause)
> SARAH: He respects you. (Pause)
> RICHARD: I'm rather moved by that remark, in a strange kind of way. I
>   think I can understand why you like him so much.
> SARAH: He's terribly sweet.
> RICHARD: Mmn-hmmnn.
> SARAH: He has his moods of course.
> RICHARD: Who doesn't
> SARAH: But I must say he's very loving. His whole body emanates love.
> RICHARD: How nauseating.
> SARAH: No.
> RICHARD: Manly with it, I hope?
> SARAH: Entirely
> RICHARD: Sounds tedious.
> SARAH: Not at all. (Hirst 72)

Pinter's coup de théâtre at the end of the act is the revelation that the husband and the lover are one and the same person. This knowledge places all of their previous conversation into a new perspective and throws into relief the more serious game that Richard will play in Act II. The game is much like George's game in Who's Afraid of Virginia Woolf? where George kills the child. However, in The Lovers it is Richard's mistress that gets killed, thereby forcing Sarah to accept her triple role as whore, mistress, and wife, and their love-making changes from the affairs of the afternoons, midday sexual diversions acted out in costumes, to the cozy marital context of the evenings (Hirst 72). Sarah realizes the consequences of Richard's changing of the rules of the game, and responds violently to having to kill off her lover as a reciprocating gesture:

> You paltry, stupid! Do you think he's the only one who comes! Do you?
> Do you think he's the only one I entertain? Mmmnn? Don't be silly; I
> have other visitors, all the time. When neither of you know, neither of you.
> I give them strawberries in season. With cream. Strangers, total strangers.
> But not to me, not while they're here. They come to see the hollyhocks.
> And then they stay for tea. Always. Always. (Hirst 73)

Note here the special sexual symbolism of the "strawberries," the "cream," and the "hollyhocks" (Hirst 73). The Lover is a suburban play in which the spouses verbally betray each other. Richard becomes Max, as Sarah becomes Dolores or Mary in the afternoon. "Richard/Max and Sarah/Dolores/Mary are perfectly monogamous but remain so only by swapping partners and identities at the same time" (Orr 93). But there is an imbalance in the game playing in that the lover calls her lover a "lover," while the husband calls his lover a "mistress" and a "whore," echoing the double standard in their culture. In this game, the partner who flinches less is the one who is wounded least. "The first lover to vary the game, to carry it into a new dimension and to sustain its conceit, is the winner." In this "comedy of errors" each lover must reject the other by changing his/her persona. Thus Richard and Sarah are caught in a Faustian trap by their own powers of creativity and invention. The game is painful for the players, but amusing for the audience (Orr 94):

> SARAH: You talk about me with her?
> RICHARD: Occasionally. It amuses her.
> SARAH: Amuses her?
> RICHARD: (choosing a book): Mmnn.
> SARAH: How...do you talk about me?
> RICHARD: Delicately. We discuss you as we would play an antique music box. We play it for our titillation, whenever desired. Pause.
> SARAH: I can't pretend the picture gives me great pleasure.
> RICHARD: It wasn't intended to. The pleasure is mine. (Orr 95)

Sometimes the game becomes the denial that a game is being played, but even this can become the beginning of a new game:

> SARAH: ...What are you doing, playing a game?
> MAX: A game? I don't play games.
> SARAH: Don't you? Oh, you do. You do. Usually I like them.
> MAX: I've played my last game.
> SARAH: Why? Slight pause
> MAX: The children.

This is ironic because "the children" is not in fact the end of the last game; rather, it is the start of the next game. These children may or may not actually exist, but in either case, they are still invented at a crucial point in the couples' ludic play (Orr 96). At the beginning of The Lover, Richard is able to discuss the situation with casual abandon, as if his wife's visitor were merely a maiden aunt. About half way through the play, however, Sarah's lover arrives, "to reveal himself as the husband in different costume," and the situation changes. During the second half of the play, the husband-lover and the wife-whore play a number of sexual games. These are less funny than the earlier discursive comedy, but still funny, though these scenes, "deny the exclusively comic nature of the previous discussion" (Dukore 35).

In 1964, Harold Pinter wrote five comedy sketches for BBC Radio Third Programme: That's Your Trouble, That's All, Applicant, Interview, and Dialogue. These sketches involve two men in a park who are observing a third man offstage carrying a sandwich board. Since they have nothing else to do, they argue heatedly about whether the board is giving the man a headache or a backache. They become more and more illogical and childish, as both men ignore the obvious solution to their dilemma--to ask the man himself (Grecco 398).

The Homecoming (1965) is an amusing play which treats illness, sex, and sadism in a matter-of-fact way. There are many sudden surprises and other theatrical effects. The title of The Homecoming refers to Teddy in the first act, and to Ruth in the second act. Teddy says, "I was born here," and Ruth later echoes this statement in Act 2 with, "I was born quite near here" (Dukore 38). The Homecoming is about Teddy who teaches philosophy in an American university for six years and then returns home to introduce Ruth (his wife), to Max (his father who is a former butcher), Sam (his uncle), and Lenny and Joey (his brothers--Lenny is a pimp, and Joey is a boxer). Within a day, the brothers make love with Ruth. Teddy leaves home, and Ruth stays with Teddy's family, becoming the family wife, mother, and whore (Diamond Comic Play 140). Lenny has a fear and a hatred of female sexuality, and Ruth exploits that fear by challenging him with the question, "Why don't I just take you?" Lenny assumes a moral stance, saying, "You're in love, anyway, with another man. You've had a secret liaison with another man" (Homecoming 50). Ruth's actions and statements provide a comic reversal--the attacker becomes the victimized; the biter gets bitten. The Homecoming is a powerful fusion of the ludic and the erotic. Here, the playing of sexual games for high stakes has very serious consequences (Orr 76). In The Homecoming, Pinter uses the family as a source of the "unfamiliar." This lack of recognition becomes the source of laughter, but it is not the laughter of relaxation; rather, it is the laughter of unease (Orr 96). Lenny makes up a sadistic anecdote to tell Ruth in which he casually beats her up in a tunnel by the docks. He tells the anecdote in a cheerful and callous manner, and it is clearly intended to intimidate Ruth. But Ruth holds her ground, and in fact adds an unexpected twist to Lenny's fantasy, thus making herself, "an active predatory version of the woman Lenny has dared to insult her with, turning menace back on its perpetrator."

> LENNY: ...Just give me the glass.
> RUTH: No. Pause.
> LENNY: I'll take it, then.
> RUTH: If you take the glass.... I'll take you. Pause.
> LENNY: How about me taking the glass without you taking me?
> RUTH: Why don't I just take you?

Thus Ruth refuses to flinch, and by so doing she catches Lenny off guard. Ruth has played Lenny's game, and she has played it better than Lenny was able to play it, because she has counter-attacked with greater economy. According to John Orr, Ruth's riposte is a metaphorical knee to the groin (Orr 99). Ruth is a victim who refuses to be a victim (Orr 100). In The Homecoming, Lenny also plays games with Teddy, but these games are philosophical, and Ruth echoes their philosophical differences with a parody of philosophical speech. Lenny has been using God and the table as his examples, and Ruth refers to neither of these in her parody, but rather she refers to the movement of her leg and the underwear that moves with her leg, and she asks, "Why don't you restrict your observations to that?" This is clearly a taunt, since she knows that they would rather look at her underwear moving along her thigh than talk about philosophy. To make her parody work, however, she must mimic their philosophical speech (Orr 100). Lenny and Teddy are rivals, and in one amusing episode of the play, Teddy gains his revenge on Lenny's taking his wife by eating Lenny's cheese roll (Orr 101). At one point, Max puts down Joey, the boxer, in a kind of Groucho-Marx-style statement, "I'll tell you what you've got to do. What you've got to do is you've got to learn how to defend yourself, and you've got to learn how to attack. That's your only trouble as a boxer. You don't know how to defend yourself and you don't know how to attack" (Homecoming 33). Ruth is triumphant at the end of The Homecoming, but her enjoyment mocks happiness, and, "her triumph sardonically taunts the concept of a happy ending." The Homecoming is a savage play filled with verbal and physical violence. The characters taunt each other and at the same time they mockingly amuse and shock the spectator. The characters battle for dominance over each other at the beginning of the play, and their maneuvers are laughable, but the laughter ceases as the encounters end and the victors emerge (Dukore 43).

The opening scene of Tea Party (1965) suggests that it is a sexual comedy about a husband, a wife, and a secretary. Disson hires Wendy to be his "very private secretary." She crosses, uncrosses, and recrosses her legs in a provocative manner, and she admits that she left her previous employment because "he never stopped touching me." This prompts Disson to ask, "Where?" Disson's wife is also a secretary in her husband's firm, and she says that the employers, "might not want to touch me in the way they wanted to touch her."

Thus sexuality and double entendre are sources of the verbal comedy, and the dictation scene ends when Wendy reads from her pad, "There should be no difficulty in meeting your requirements" (Dukore 44). At the beginning of <u>Tea Party</u> Disson's pride is humorous, because it suggests brag, or excessive pride, in the manufacture of bidets, not exactly a heroic job. It also suggests the absence of a realistic perspective which accounts for much comedy of manners. Disson is comically pompous as he announces, "I Don't like dithering. I don't like indulgence. I don't like self-doubt. I don't like fuzziness. I like clarity." Later in the play, however, Disson himself "dithers," and because of his failing eyesight, he doesn't see things clearly. But the laughter begins to erode when Disson's vision deteriorates beyond the laughable range (Dukore 46).

The Basement (1967) is a triangular sex comedy involving one woman and two men. Bernard Dukore calls this triangle "the girl, the stud, and the schnook." The stud and the schnook contrast with each other both verbally and physically. While the girl is undressing and getting into bed, the stud turns off the lamps and joins her while the schnook acting as an accommodating host asks, "Can I get you some cocoa? Some hot chocolate?" The visual scene which Pinter describes is also comic: "<u>Night. Law lying on the floor, a cushion at his head, covered by a blanket. His eyes are closed. Silence. A long gasp from Jane. Law's eyes open</u>" (Dukore 49). But the situation changes and the girl makes advances to Law, caressing him, and whispering to him, and urging him not to resist her. Law, in turn, primly and nervously refuses to yield. This reverses the conventional roles as the schnook takes the place of the stud. The end of the play is tragic rather than comic because the rivalry has become so bitter and violent. In the end, the stud assumes the role of a schnook, and by the last scene a happy conclusion is implied in that the schnook's desires are temporarily achieved. The male players are in the position of playing each other's roles (Dukore 48). There are many ironies in The Basement. In the milk episode, for example, Stott and Law use broken milk bottles as deadly weapons, while Jane pours milk from a bottle into a jug, and then from the jug into cups. Then she stirs the milk in the cups in a strikingly funny counterpoint to the men's dangerous confrontation. The final scene of The Basement repeats the opening scene, but the schnook and the stud have exchanged roles. Stott is in his basement flat to welcome Law in, and Jane is unseen by Stott as she stands outside. But although this is the same scene as before, it is no longer funny, because the spectators are now aware of the consequences of the men's words and actions (Dukore 50).

The interchanges between Len and Mark in The Dwarfs (1967) are filled with exaggerations, repetitions, non sequiturs, and Yiddish phrasing (Gale 854).

> MARK: What do you think of the cloth?
> LEN: The cloth? (He examines it, gasps and whistles through his teeth. At
>   a great pace.) What a piece of cloth. What a piece of cloth. What
>   a piece of cloth. What a piece of <u>cloth</u>.
> MARK: You like the cloth?
> LEN: WHAT A PIECE OF CLOTH! (Pinter <u>Dwarfs</u> 88)

This is Yiddish phrasing. It is also Yiddish phrasing when Mark does not allow himself to take anything for granted:

> LEN: Do you believe in God?
> MARK: What?
> LEN: Do you believe in God?
> MARK: Who?
> LEN: God.
> MARK: God?
> LEN: Do you believe in God?
> MARK: Do I believe in God?

LEN: Yes.
MARK: Would you say that again? (Pinter Three Plays 102-103)
Len believes in his mind that he is being pursued by tiny, dirty dwarfs, who offer him scraps of food. Eventually, Len is hospitalized, which is a good thing for Len, because he believes that the dwarfs are planning to leave him. At the very end of the play they do leave, and Len ends the play by saying, "Now all is bare. All is clean. All is scrubbed. There is a lawn. There is a shrub. There is a flower" (Grecco 402).

We Who Are About To, later revised to Mixed Doubles: An Entertainment on Marriage (1969), is about a husband and wife who recall their first encounter. But they both have difficulty in remembering the details of that fateful night. She says that they met at a party while he says it was on a bridge. She later suggests that he might have been talking about a different woman, or that they were in fact both remembering different people (Grecco 399).

Kate and Deeley are a married couple in Old Times (1971) who live in elegant seclusion, and who are visited by Kate's friend of twenty years before, Anna. The three of them reminisce about post-war London, and this becomes the fodder for sexual combat. This sexual combat is carried out by the powerful language, which is used not only to describe experience, but to create experience as well. "The fact that [Deeley and Anna] discuss something that [Deeley] says took place--even if it did not take place--actually seems to me to recreate the time and the moments vividly in the present, so that it is actually taking place before your very eyes--by the words he is using." There is in fact a sexual competition taking place here. In remembering things about Kate, Anna and Deeley are eroticizing her, and this exposes their own frustrated sexual desires (Diamond Comic Play 162). In their very different versions of the past, each person describes the other in compromising positions and places himself or herself in close proximity to Kate. Thus Kate is given the power to verify or deny these verbal images, a power which she exercises brutally at the end of the play (Diamond Comic Play 164).

In Old Times (1971), as in The Collection, there are radical disagreements in reporting the same incidents. Partly these disagreements are due to the twenty-year time gap between the incidents and the reporting of them, and the subsequent tricks played on the various memories (Hirst 69). Old Times is Pinter's most sustained example of Comedy of Manners. At the center of the plot is debate over whether the husband or the girl friend can best know the wife. Consequently, every recollection introduced by either Deeley or Anna must be countered by the other in this verbal dual (Hirst 77). As Anna says at one point in the play, "There are some things one remembers even though they may never have happened. There are things I remember which may never have happened but I recall them so they take place" (Dukore 52). Comically, Anna and Deeley contend for Kate, and in so doing they transform her from a person into an object, thereby demeaning her. Anna makes a Freudian slip when she says, "You have a wonderful casserole," but then she corrects herself, "I mean wife. So sorry" (Dukore 53). As they try to remember and reconstruct the past for their own purposes, Anna and Deeley cite relevant lines of old songs. Deeley sings the opening lines of "Lovely to Look at," and of "Blue Moon," but Anna counters with "They Can't Take That Away from Me." Deeley interrupts with the title line of this song, and Anna switches songs again and sings "The Way You Look Tonight." Deeley sings that he has a woman crazy for him, and Anna sings "I Get a Kick Out of You," but Deeley sings the final, title-line, and suggests that the kicks are his, and not Anna's. Anna and Deeley each sings a line from "These Foolish Things Remind Me of You." Dukore considers this song contest, "this comic medley of songs of love, possession, and memory," to be a play within a play (Dukore 54). "These songs within a play suggest the comedy, rivalry, ferocity of combat and conclusion of Old Times, in which Anna fails to take Kate away from Deeley" (Dukore 55). In this sparring comedy, Kate sometimes joins Anna in one-upping Deeley, and sometimes joins Deeley in one-upping Anna. The richness of the comedy is enhanced by the fact that history is seen not just from one or two perspectives, but rather from three (Diamond Comic Play 166). Deeley labels Anna as Kate's former "best friend."

KATE: She was my only friend.
DEELEY: Your best and only.
KATE: My one and only. Pause. If you have only one of something you can't say it's the best of anything.
DEELEY: Because you have nothing to compare it with?
KATE: Mmnn. Pause.
DEELEY: (Smiling): She was incomparable. (Diamond Comic Play 167)

But while the beginning of Old Times is comic, the end is tragicomic. Deeley smiles and chuckles at the beginning of the play, but at the end, he cries. The comedy at the beginning of the play is based on the happy memories about the past, but as the play progresses, the memories arouse rivalries, and a battle develops for domination of a person through participation in her past, or perhaps even through ownership of her past. Sex is a very funny subject at the beginning of the play, but this subject is no longer funny at the end of the play. "Though husband and wife reunite at the close of Old Times, their reunion denies happiness, for it involves capitulation and defeat, and whereas the start of the play recalls pleasure and sharing, the play's conclusion suggests desolation, domination, and what may be a death in life" (Dukore 51).

Monologue (1973) is about two male friends and a woman. It is a comedy which is based on friendship, sex, and family, and its verbal wit mainly derives from friendliness (Dukore 60). However, the verbal wit which appears to be a sign of self-assurance at the beginning of the play becomes a sign of desperation by the end. The friendship at the beginning of the play is undercut at the non-comic end of the play when the speaker of this "tragicomic monologue" doesn't receive the assurance and acceptance that would be consistent with comedy. Instead, the monologist is left on stage all alone (Dukore 62).

At the start of No Man's Land (1974), the comedy derives from language, from alcohol, and from security (Dukore 63). Hirst lives in Hamstead room. Hirst is a successful literary man who has Briggs and Foster as his servant-protectors. Hirst is aloof with his icy silence, and he is very resistant to change. Into this environment comes Spooner, a name reminiscent of the Reverend Spooner who provided the source for a particular kind of linguistic error called the "Spoonerism." Spooner is a shabbily dressed poet who seeks a literary relationship with Hirst. Spooner needs shelter, but he is nevertheless a comic poser, and a schemer as well. Thus Pinter's four male characters in No Man's Land play off from each other with different types of verbal creativity. Hirst is a famous poet and essayist. Spooner is a master of terza rima. Foster is a fledgling poet, and Briggs is a self-conscious raconteur, and a master of the colorful curse. As Spooner remarks, "All we have left is the English language. Can it be salvaged?" (Diamond Comic Play 180). In No Man's Land, Spooner insists on talking about his and Hirst's wives. He goads Hirst with the outrageous double entendre of an extended cricket metaphor: "Tell me with what speed she swung in the air, with what velocity she came off the wicket, whether she was responsive to finger spin, whether you could bowl a shooter with her, or an offbreak with a leg-break action. In other words, did she google?" Spooner is much more skilled than is Hirst in playing this clever verbal game because he has a paradoxical sense of, "truly accurate and therefore essentially poetic definition" (Almansi 86). No Man's Land contains numerous homosexual and obscenely comic allusions. Briggs calls Foster a "poof," a "ponce," and a "vagabond cock," all transparent slang terms for homosexuality. When he implies that he procured Foster for Hirst, Foster acknowledges that he finds the work "fruitful," but he denies being a "cunt" meaning a "fool," but later in the play Briggs uses this same label to mean both "fool" and "homosexual." In No Man's Land, Pinter mocks both women and marriage. He degrades the idealized portraits of women in Hirst's photo album, saying, "You'll be struck by the charm of the girls, their grace, the ease with which they sit, pour tea, loll" (Diamond Comic Play 196). Elin Diamond feels that No Man's Land surpasses even Old Times in its celebration of the word in the development of a "comedy of language" (Diamond Comic Play 197).

In Betrayal (1977) there is a love triangle involving a cuckolded husband who secretly loves his wife's lover more than he loves her (Orr 106). In Betrayal, Pinter goes back in time to verify the betrayals of Robert, a book publisher, Emma, Robert's wife, and Jerry, Robert's best friend, who, by the way, sleeps with Emma for seven years. Emma and Jerry thus betray Robert; however Robert also betrays Jerry by concealing that he knows about the affair, and Emma also betrays Jerry by concealing Robert's knowledge (Diamond Comic Play 198). Robert says to Emma, "I've always liked Jerry. To be honest, I've always liked him rather more than I've liked you. Maybe I should have had an affair with him myself" (Diamond Comic Play 200). Stephen Grecco says that Betrayal contains quite a bit of wit and intrigue, and that it is reminiscent of a Noel Coward play (Grecco 411).

Applicant (1980) is a comic sketch about sadism and man-hating. It depicts a young man with the appropriate name of "Lamb" entering an office for a job interview. A woman named "Piffs" determines his "psychological suitability" for the job by attaching electrodes to his palms and earphones to his head. Stephen Grecco says that this short play would be morbid if it were not for the distance provided by the cartoonlike characters (Grecco 399). Pinter's The Hothouse (1980) is set in a mental institution where the patients are known only as numbers. The characters are grotesques with names like Hogg, Lush, Peck, Lamb, and Cutts. Roote, the director of the institution, is an ex-army man. Roote and Gibbs (his immediate subordinate) spend most of their time investigating two mysteries: the death of patient number 6457, and the birth of a child to patient 6459. Their primary suspect is Lamb, who despite his innocent name, likes to do sadistic experimentation (Grecco 411). Pinter had originally started to write The Hothouse in 1958, but he abandoned his writing because the characters were so nasty, and Pinter disapproved of them so much, that he didn't want them to live. Pinter wasn't able to finish writing the novel and to publish it until 1980.

In Family Voices: A Play for Radio (1981), Pinter provides us with a wry version of the Freudian family romance. The son-protagonist writes a letter home to his mother in which he alludes to his father, but also invents a surreal family of grotesques who are a parody of his real family, and who also permit him to play out his sexual fantasies and fears. In his erotic fantasy, he is invited to Lady Withers's room for tea, and is seated next to Jane. The son becomes obsessed with buns, as Jane's toes work into his thighs. These buns are being "masticated" by the women who are, "perched surrealistically on cakestands all over the room," but he becomes especially obsessed with his own bun, which is "rock solid," and is then "juggled" by Jane's skillful toes (Diamond Comic Play 214).

In Victoria Station, a cab driver and the company controller talk at cross purposes. The driver doesn't seem to know where he is, nor does he know about the location of Victoria Station or even whether such a station actually exists or not. The comic structure of this exchange provides a conflict between the world of the driver and the world of the controller, and such conflicts persist to the end of the play. The controller pursues the rules of the old game, abusing the driver as if he were capable of finding his way to Victoria Station, provided enough pressure is placed on him to do so (Diamond Comic Play 212). In the cab itself, a passenger's reality also changes, as this passenger is first referred to as "he," then as "she" then as "true love." "I'm going to marry her in this car" (Diamond Comic Play 213).

Harold Pinter has written screenplays for three of his own books (The Birthday Party (1968), The Guest (1964) adapted from The Caretaker, and The Homecoming (1971). In addition, he has written three screenplays of books by other authors. These are The Servant (1962) from a 1965 novel by Robin Maugham, Accident (1967) from a 1965 novel by Nicholas Mosley, and The Go-Between (1969) based on L. P. Hartley's 1953 novel). All of these screenplays have been thoroughly "Pinterized" since all of them contain Pinter's special types of dialogue, humor, and situation (Grecco 411).

Harold Pinter (David Baron, Harold Pinta) Bibliography

Almansi, Guido. "Harold Pinter's Idiom of Lies." Contemporary English Drama. Ed. C. W. E. Bigsby. New York, NY: Holmes and Meier, 1981, 79-94.

Callen, A. "Comedy and Passion in the Plays of Harold Pinter." Forum for Modern Language Studies 4 (1968): 299-305.

Diamond, Elin F. "The Parody Plays." Critical Essays on Harold Pinter. Ed. Steven H. Gale. Boston, MA: G. K. Hall, 1990, 47-65.

Diamond, Elin F. "Pinter's Betrayal and the Comedy of Manners." Modern Drama 23.3 (1980): 238-245.

Diamond, Elin F. Pinter's Comic Play. Lewisburg, PA: Bucknell University Press, 1985.

Dukore, Bernard. Where Laughter Stops: Pinter's Tragicomedy. Columbia: Univ of Missouri Press, 1976.

Dutton, R. Modern Tragicomedy and The British Tradition Brighton, England: Harvester Press, 1986.

Gale, Steven H. "Harold Pinter." Encyclopedia of British Humorists, Volume II. Ed. Steven H. Gale. New York, NY: Garland, 1996, 847-862.

Grecco, Stephen. "Harold Pinter." Dictionary of Literary Biography, Volume Thirteen: British Dramatists Since World War II. Ed. Stanley Weintraub. Detroit, MI: Gale, 1982, 393-413.

Guthke, K. S. Modern Tragicomedy. New York, NY: Random House, 1966.

Henkle, Roger B. "From Pooter to Pinter: Domestic Comedy and Vulnerability." Critical Quarterly 16 (1974): 174-189.

Hewes, Henry. "Pinter's Hilarious Depth Charge." Saturday Review 50 (January 21, 1967): 61.

Hirst, David L. Comedy of Manners. New York, NY: Methuen, 1979.

Hudgins, Christopher. "Intended Audience Response, The Homecoming, and the 'Ironic Mode of Identification.'" Harold Pinter: Critical Approaches. Ed. Steven H. Gale. Madison, NJ: Fairleigh Dickinson University Press, 1986, 102-118.

Kastor, Frank S. Pinter and Modern Tragicomedy. Wichita, KS: Wichita State University, 1970.

Orr, John. "Anglo-Tragic: Pinter and the English Tradition." Tragicomedy and Contemporary Culture: Play and Performance from Beckett to Shepard. Ann Arbor, MI: University of Michigan Press, 1994, 72-87.

Orr, John. "Pinter: The Game of the Shared Experience." Tragicomedy and Contemporary Culture: Play and Performance from Beckett to Shepard. Ann Arbor, MI: University of Michigan Press, 1994, 88-108.

Pinter, Harold. "The Birthday Party" and "The Room": Two Plays. New York, NY: Grove, 1961.

Pinter, Harold. "The Caretaker" and "The Dumb Waiter": Two Plays. New York, NY: Grove, 1961.

Pinter, Harold. The Homecoming. New York, NY: Grove, 1966.

Pinter, Harold. The Lover, Tea Party, The Basement. New York, NY: Grove, 1967.

Pinter, Harold. Monologue. London, England: Gardener Press, 1973.

Pinter, Harold. Mountain Language. London, England: Faber and Faber, 1988.

Pinter, Harold. No Man's Land. New York, NY: Grove, 1975.

Pinter, Harold. Old Times. New York, NY: Grove, 1971.

Pinter, Harold. One for the Road. London, England: Methuen, 1984.

Pinter, Harold. Three Plays: "A Slight Ache," "The Collection," "The Dwarfs." New York, NY: Grove, 1962.

Sorell, Walter. Facets of Comedy. New York, NY: Grosset and Dunlap, 1972.

Tucker, Stephanie. "Harold Pinter." Contemporary Authors, New Revision Series, Volume 33. Ed. James G. Lesniak. Detroit, MI: Gale Research, 1991, 350-357.

Ruth Rendell (Barbara Vine) (1930-)

Ruth Rendell had Scandinavian grandparents who were not able to pronounce the name of "Ruth," so Ruth's mother started calling her "Barbara." For a while, Ruth's father persisted in calling her "Ruth," but then, as Ruth wrote, "since this sort of duality was impossible in one household, my father finally started calling me Barbara too" (Parr 306). When she became an author, Ruth chose "Barbara Vine" as her pseudonym, but at the same time, she does not keep her identity a secret. This ambivalence has not been a problem for her readers, but her critics have some difficulty with her double personality, and ask questions like, "Why did she do this? Who is she trying to deceive?" She responds that she is not trying to deceive anyone, and she constantly gets letters from her readers saying that they understand why she uses a pseudonym. In fact, Rendell has three sets of readers each of which likes a different set of books that Rendell writes (Ross 362).

Ruth Rendell's Chief Inspector Reginald Wexford is a middle aged father of two grown daughters. Wexford is very liberal, literate, tolerant, and sensitive. Because he is an insatiable reader, he is able to quote from a wide range of literature during his murder investigations. Rendell tells Marilyn Stasio that she thinks that Wexford is "quite witty," and she goes on to say, "He is also a big, solid type, very cool and calm. He also likes women very much and always has his time for them. What more could you want in a man?" Michael Burden is Reginald Wexford's assistant. Burden is very prim, rigid, and reactionary (Ross 362). Together, Wexford and Burden solve mysterious murders in the town of Kingsmarkham in rural Sussex, "a gritty and rather glum setting" (Ross 361).

In From Doon with Death (1964), Reginald Wexford is especially hard on Michael Burden. He speaks to him sarcastically, and he chastises him with expressions like, "Have you gone raving mad, Burden?" "Be your age," and "You make me puke" (Parr 308). In A New Lease of Death (1967), Reginald Wexford is described as, "a big man with big features and a big intimidating voice." Wexford wears a gray suit that is both shabby and wrinkled, and this was appropriate for him, because it was, "not unlike an extension of his furrowed pachydermatous skin." At this point, Michael Burden has been Wexford's assistant for five years, and he has grown immune to his teasing. He realizes that he is functioning as a safety valve for Wexford, a target on whom Wexford could, "vent his violent and sometimes shocking sense of humor" (Parr 309).

In Some Lie and Some Die (1973), Zeno Vedast (who was born as Harold Goodbody), decides to play a practical joke on Nell's first husband and Dawn Stonor. This practical joke leads the husband to a period of temporary insanity during which time he murders Dawn (Parr 314). Talking about Ruth Rendell's dénouements, David Lehman says, "few detective writers are as good at pulling such last-second rabbits out of their top hats--the last page making us see everything before it in a strange, new glare" (Ross 361).

Ruth Rendell (Barbara Vine) Bibliography

Parr, Susan Resneck. "Ruth Rendell." Dictionary of Literary Biography, Volume Eighty-
    Seven: British Mystery and Thriller Writers Since 1940. Eds. Bernard Benstock, and
    Thomas F. Staley. Detroit, MI: Gale, 1989.
Ross, Jean W. "Ruth (Barbara) Rendell." Contemporary Authors, New Revision Series:
    Volume 32. Ed. James G. Lesniak. Detroit, MI: Gale, 1991, 360-364.

Peter Barnes (1931-)

Peter Barnes's most skillful and unique dramatic device may be his use of one-liners
at the most inopportune moment. These "bad jokes" create a macabre, Kafkaesque humor
that is, despite its darkness, hysterically funny (Oberlander 77). Barnes People II (1984)
consists of seven short two-people dialogues. "The Right Time and Place" is about a
psychiatrist who tries to talk a lady out of committing suicide. The lady is so depressed
that if she bought artificial flowers, they would die on her. The psychiatrist tells the
would-be-suicide that she has convinced him that the world is terrible, so he climbs out on
his own window ledge. Of course the lady-caller must now convince the psychiatrist that
he should not jump, saying, "I came here for help and what do I get? Competition!"
(Barnes People II 37). The lady tells the psychiatrist that she now remembers that she has
a terrible fear of heights, and that she is going to be sick. The psychiatrist pleads with her
not to get sick over him. As they talk, they come to realize that their deaths will not be
taken seriously, so they decide not to commit suicide right now. For suicide, you need "the
right time and place" (Oberlander 79). "Lament for Armenians and Grey Viruses" is also
in Barnes People II. Here there is a very humorous but unconnected logic in which the
characters are drunk, and are creative with language, saying such things as, "I'm rubbishing
here," and, "I used to work, till the last sunbeam faded" (Oberlander 80). The lamenting
tramps are also smart, saying that, "honour doesn't go to the wise or success to the good--
only to those who swim with the tide." They also say that "hope is terrible torture" and
that the world will not end with a "whimper," but with a "Plop, plop...plop, plop..." (Barnes
People II 58). In "The Real Long John Silver" there are three people attending a costume
party all dressed up as Long John Silver, complete with peg leg and parrot. They argue
so much about which one of them should enter as Long John Silver that they miss the
party. "Red Noses" is about the bubonic plague, a subject which Marjorie Oberlander
finds, "about as appealing a subject as Auschwitz was in Laughter" (1987). Sheridan
Morley says that by addressing the unspeakable horror in "Red Noses" Barnes has
"achieved his usual theses about a stand-up comic being a lot more useful than a pope in
a real crisis." Barnes himself said, "the continued existence of Christianity proves that
almost anything can be made to work in the end" (Oberlander 81).

Not As Bad As They Seem (1989) is about a wife whose husband arrives home
while her lover is still in bed. The humor comes from the fact that all three of them are
blind (Oberlander 82). More Barnes People (1990) contains a story entitled "A True-Born
Englishman" in which Bray puts down the English, saying that they were born for service.
About his mother's politics, Bray contends that she was so conservative that she thought
of having her heart transplanted from the left to the right in order to make up for the
mistake originally made by the creator (Oberlander 79). The Spirit of Man (1990) contains
a story entitled "A Hand Witch of the Second Stage" in which Marie Blin is accused of
witchcraft (Oberlander 79). Barnes, who is a "humorist," wants Mary to agree to be a
witch, not a full-fledged witch, but only a hand witch of the second stage who is able to
perform magic with hand gestures, flexed fingers, and subtle wrist movements. The play

ends as follows: "Wit, cunning and endurance are more important than heroism, though heroism in small doses, helps too" (Barnes Spirit 20). Bye Bye Columbus (1993) has no heroes, but it does have a lot of aphorisms, such as, "Marriage is a funeral where you smell your own flowers," "He's a man who brightens a room just be leaving it," "Lies carry their own truth," "I'll do anything for everything," and "Learn to love yourself, it's the only affection you can count on" (Oberlander 82).

Peter Barnes Bibliography

Barker, Clive. "On Class, Christianity, and Questions of Comedy." New Theatre Quarterly 6.21 (1990): 5-24.
Barnes, Peter. Barnes People II: Seven Diologues. London, England: Heinemann, 1984.
Barnes, Peter. "The Real Long John Silver" and Other Plays. London, England: Faber and Faber, 1986.
Barnes, Peter. The Spirit of Man, and More Barnes People. London, England: Methuen, 1990.
Hiley, Jim. "Liberating Laughter: Peter Barnes and Peter Nichols in Interview." Plays and Players 6.293 (1978): 14-17.
Oberlander, Marjorie J. "Peter Barnes." Encyclopedia of British Humorists, Volume I. Ed. Steven H. Gale. New York, NY: Garland, 1996, 77-85.

David (John Moore) Cornwell (John le Carré) (1931-)

Even as a child, John le Carré felt that he was playing a role in the spy business. On the basis of his mother's cryptic comments, and his father's long absences, John and his brother concluded that their father was a spy, called away from time to time to perform dangerous missions for the good of his country (DelFattore 241). In actual fact, le Carré was working as a diplomat with the British Foreign Office in London in the early 1960s when he began writing espionage novels. He had earlier worked with the British Secret Service. Because of his diplomatic position when he began publishing his books, he was not allowed to use his own name, so he developed the pseudonym of John le Carré (Lesniak 95). Joan DelFattore notes that the expression "le carré" means "the square," and suggests that this pen name was chosen as a "slangy pun" way of showing that le Carré's books would be a realistic and unglamorous portrayal of life in the Secret Service, and therefore in stark contrast to the, "gimmicks-girls-and-guns approach of [Ian] Fleming" (DelFattore 243).

Leonard Downie Jr. quotes John le Carré as saying, "We are in the process of doing things in defense of our society which may very well produce a society which is not worth defending." Downie says that this is the controlling paradox of John le Carré's espionage novels. George Smiley is the protagonist who is featured in many of le Carré's novels. Richard W. Noland writes that Smiley is an "improbable spy master." Noland substantiates this statement by quoting le Carré's description that he is, "short, fat, quiet and wears 'really bad clothes, which hung about his squat frame like skin on a shrunken toad'" (Lesniak 95).

In Call for the Dead (1961), which was later republished as The Deadly Affair (1964), George Smiley was a brilliant but prosaic spy who is described by Joan DelFattore as

> a nearsighted, unobtrusive middle-aged man, deceptively mild and painstaking to the point of genius. Smiley is the antithesis of the glamorous spy-hero epitomized by Ian Fleming's James Bond. A timid and inexpert

driver, he wears expensive but ill-fitting clothing and is often cuckolded by his wife, who addresses him as "my darling Teddy Bear" or "Toad." His hobby, like le Carré's, is doing scholarly research on obscure seventeenth-century German poets. (DelFattore 242)

In Call for the Dead, Smiley has cleared Samuel Arthur Fennan, a member of the Foreign Office, of the charge of being a Communist sympathizer, but then he learns that Fennan has "committed suicide." When he discovers that Fennan had requested a wake-up telephone call on the night that he died, Smiley suspects that Fennan has been murdered. The novel shows the tension that develops between espionage agents and their agencies, and shows how truth is often sacrificed in the name of expediency, and how humanity is decreased in the drive for efficiency (DelFattore 242).

In A Murder of Quality (1962), as in Call for the Dead, George Smiley is persistent in seeking answers to apparently unimportant questions. In the end, however, these are the questions that needed to be asked to arrive at the proper solution. In A Murder of Quality, one of Smiley's former superiors is described as having, "the cunning of Satan and the conscience of a virgin" (DelFattore 243).

When The Spy Who Came In from the Cold (1963) was published, le Carré was the British consul in Hamburg. He is said to have laughingly told his accountant to tell him if his bank balance reached twenty thousand pounds, for if it did, he felt that he could afford to resign. The book was a best seller, and in February of 1964, le Carré became a full-time writer (DelFattore 243). Richard Noland says that in The Spy Who Came In from the Cold, the bureaucracies of the East and the West, "wage the Cold War by one simple rule--operational convenience." Noland adds that "in the name of operational convenience and alliances of expediency, any and all human values--including love and life itself--are expendable." In order to give this and his other spy novels verisimilitude, le Carré introduces many espionage slang terms, some legitimate, some not, into the novel. The expression "mole" was borrowed from the Soviet KGB, and the expression "Circus," was used as a nickname for the British Secret Service. Such jargon was used throughout the novel to allow the reader into the inner sanctum of spy operations. Le Carré himself said, "I thought it very important to give the reader the illusion of entering the secret world, and to that end I invented jargon that would be graphic and at the same time mysterious" (Lesniak 96).

In The Spy Who Came In from the Cold, the antagonist is Control, who is portrayed as being the unscrupulous and unfeeling head of the Secret Service. The protagonist is Alec Leamis, who is asked by Control to discredit Hans-Dieter Mundt, head of operations for the East German Abteilung. But Leamis discovers that the plan does not proceed as Control had said it would, and he finally realizes that Control had never intended the plan to work. Leamis finds himself in a magnificent double-cross in which nothing is as it seems to be. Whenever he carries out orders that he thinks will lead to a particular result, his actions tend to bring about the opposite result. But the irony becomes even more intense, for, "in the very act of disobeying Control's orders and taking steps to abort his plan, Leamis completes the plan, because by defying Control at that particular point he does exactly what Control had expected and hoped he would do" (DelFattore 244).

When The Spy Who Came In from the Cold was made into a movie, it was extremely faithful to the book. Furthermore, the film was made in grainy black and white in order to emphasize the harsh realism of the story. "The absence of color and the comparative slowness of the action also serve to underline the contrast between this film and the romantic spy films epitomized by the James Bond series" (DelFattore 244).

In Tinker, Tailor, Soldier, Spy (1977), George Smiley has been forced to retire from the "Circus." Oliver Lacon asks Smiley to investigate a rumor that the security of the Circus has been breached by a mole--that is by an Englishman acting as a Russian agent in England. The plot was suggested by a 1963 scandal in which a highly placed spy named Kim Philby escaped to Moscow after years of undetected treachery. In Tinker, Tailor, Soldier, Spy, George Smiley is the spy who goes after a Soviet mole in British intelligence whose code name is "Gerald." Smiley has evidence that the mole is one of five people. It is either Percy Alleline (code-named "Tinker", a Circus official destined to become chief after Control's death). Or else it is Bill Haydon (code-named "Tailor"), who is the head of the London Station. Or else it is Roy Bland (code-named "Soldier"), or it is Toby Esterhase (code-named "Poorman") who is the head of the Acton Lamp-lighters organization. Or it is George Smiley himself (code-named "Beggarman"). Because Smiley has been expelled from Circus, he must seek the aid of Peter Guillam, who is still in the Circus, but who is not in favor with the administration (DelFattore 248).

The mole has been placed by, and is controlled by Karla (Lesniak 96). It may be that George Smiley is only the protagonist, and that bureaucracy itself is the "hero." The structure of the bureaucracy imposes order to the random accumulation of facts that surround us everyday. It is the bureaucracy that provides order to this perpetual chaos. The title of Tinker, Tailor, Soldier, Spy is, of course, derived from a nursery rhyme. Holly Beth King sees the title as an, "intricately woven set of relationships between adults and children, between innocence and disillusionment, between loyalty and betrayal that gives the novel's title a deeper resonance" (Lesniak 97).

Since The Honourable Schoolboy (1977) takes place in Southeast Asia, le Carré made five visits to that part of the world in order to collect background material. At one point when he was in Cambodia, le Carré was fired on by automatic weapons, and he had to roll under a truck and lie there. During most of the incident, he was writing about his various sensations on index cards (DelFattore 251).

In Smiley's People (1980), George Smiley is called out of retirement in order to investigate Vladimir's murder. Smiley sees this as an opportunity to defeat Karla; however, in attempting this defeat, Smiley, "is forced to exploit Karla's love for his daughter even more ruthlessly than Karla once exploited Smiley's love for his wife." Therefore, it is not Karla's cruelty, but rather his affection, his humanity, that leads to his destruction (DelFattore 251). The Quest for Karla (1982) is a trilogy consisting of Tinker, Tailor, Soldier, Spy, The Honourable Schoolboy, and Smiley's People. Julian Moynihan comments on the structure of the trilogy, noting that we know that Smiley has ruined many lives, some innocent, in his tenacious pursuit of Karla; and we just don't believe that the dirty tricks are all on just one side because they were ordered up by a decent little English guy with a disarming name (Lesniak 97).

There is no George Smiley in The Little Drummer Girl (1983). When le Carré was asked why he had abandoned his famous protagonist he said that Alec Guinness's portrayal of the Smiley character on television had been so convincing that he could no longer envision Smiley apart from Guinness. The Little Drummer Girl contains le Carré's first female protagonist. Charlie is an actress who is intelligent, and sensitive, but a bit scatterbrained. Charlie is, "active in a variety of political movements that she barely understands" (DelFattore 251). The Little Drummer Girl, like other le Carré novels, blends the distinction between "them" and "us." It also blends the distinction between action and motivation, and between honor and betrayal (DelFattore 252).

A Perfect Spy (1986) is an ironic autobiography. Richard Thomas Pym is like le Carré's father, Ronald Thomas Archibald Cornwell, in a number of respects. Pym is a charming swindler, "who never quite understands why good intentions are not a fully acceptable substitute for reliable behavior." Pym has been taught that betrayal is not inconsistent with love, and is therefore quite comfortable in his role as a double agent (DelFattore 252).

Barley Blair, the protagonist in The Russia House (1989), is an innocent bystander who receives a package from a dissident Russian scientist and author code named "Goethe." The package contains detailed information on how the Soviet Union's weapons systems work, and how they fail to work. In his earlier novels, le Carré developed the theme that the West is as morally impoverished as is the East. The ironic message of The Russia House is the opposite--that the East is as technologically impoverished as is the West. Nevertheless, certain American politicians are described as "Bible-belt knuckle-draggers" who take it into their heads to pillory Goethe's material because it endangers "Fortress America." Barley Blair's code name is "Mr. Brown," and one of his interrogators drawls, "This li'l ole planet just ain't big enough for two super-powers, Mr. Brown. Which one do you favor, Mr. Brown, when poo-ush comes to sheu-uve?" (DelFattore 253). When Barley Blair meets Goethe, Goethe describes himself by saying, "I'm a moral outcast.... I trade in defiled theories." Blair responds, "Always nice to meet a writer" (DelFattore 255).

Paul Gray says that The Tailor of Panama is about some British intelligence officers in pursuit of a conspiracy that doesn't exist. Harry Pendel is the forty-year-old co-proprietor of a gentlemen's tailor shop in Panama by the name of Pendel and Braithwaite, Limitada, but in truth he is an ex-con who had torched his Uncle Benny's London garment warehouse so that they could collect the insurance. He was caught, and served his time in prison. Now, as the proprietor of a gentlemen's tailor shop, he is approached by Osnard, who says that British intelligence is reopening Panama, and asks Harry to become a spy for England. Osnard explains that not only do Panama City's elite gossip as they gather for fittings at Harry's shop, but in addition, Harry could get information in his role as the personal attendant to both the current Panamanian President and the general in charge of the U. S. Southern Command (Gray 102). This is important because on the last day of 1999, the United States is scheduled to give the control of the Panama Canal back to the Panamanians, and the British need specific details in order to bring their American allies back to their senses. Since Harry wants to save his marriage, his business, and his skin, he starts to invent the stories that the British Intelligence wants to hear, and sends these stories back to London. "Inventing conspiracies comes naturally to Harry; he is, after all, a tailor, used to dealing in loose threads, plucked from the air, woven and cut to measure." Harry is merely creating his stories "out of whole cloth" (Gray 104). Paul Gray comments on le Carré's "comic skills," and his "epigrammatic skewerings" in this intriguing spy story (Gray 104).

David (John Moore) Cornwell (John le Carré) Bibliography

DelFattore, John. "John le Carré." Dictionary of Literary Biography, Volume Eighty-Seven: British Mystery and Thriller writers Since 1940. Eds. Bernard Benstock, and Thomas F. Staley. Detroit, MI: Gale, 1989, 240-255.
Gray, Paul. "A Man, a Plan, a Canal." Time 148.20 (1996): 102-104.
Lesniak, James G. Ed. "David (John Moore) Cornwell." Contemporary Authors, New Revision Series, Volume 33. Detroit, MI: Gale, 1991, 94-99.

Malcolm Stanley Bradbury (1932-)

Malcolm Bradbury writes social satires in the tradition of Jane Austen, Tobias Smollett, Henry Fielding, Thomas Love Peacock, Charles Dickens, E. M. Forster, Evelyn Waugh, Kingsley Amis, and Simon Gray. Bradbury's special contribution is to academic satire. Alexandra Mullen lists the following as Malcolm Bradbury's "Humor" pieces: Phogey! Or, How to Have Class in a Classless Society (1960), All Dressed Up and Nowhere to Go: The Poor Man's Guide to the Affluent Society (1962), Who Do You Think

You Are? Stories and Parodies (1976), Why Come to Slaka? (1986), My Strange Quest for Mensonge: Structuralism's Hidden Hero (1987), and Unsent Letters (1988). Mullen also lists Eating People Is Wrong (1959), Stepping Westward (1965), and The History of Man (1975) as humorous novels (Mullen 152). Alexandra Mullen says that all of Bradbury's books are filled with verbal play and professional jokes that are often obscure to some of his readers. Bradbury's comic gambits, word play, allusion, and parody are reminiscent of Muriel Spark, Iris Murdoch and Evelyn Waugh (Mullen 154-155). Many of Malcolm Bradbury's readers place him into the category of "Angry Young Men," along with Kingsley Amis who five years earlier had written Lucky Jim. Bradbury responds to this classification as follows, "I was not an angry young man, perhaps, since to me the angry young men were all old, ten years older than I was. But I was a niggling one" (Bradbury Dressed 8).

Eating People Is Wrong (1959), and Stepping Westward (1965) are in the campus novel genre, a genre which includes a naïve hero, episodes such as drunken faculty meetings or lectures, a supporting cast filled with academic types, and periodic lapses from comedy into farce. Eating People Is Wrong takes place at Indiana University in the United States, and is about how a neophyte enters the system (Mullen 152).

Stepping Westward (1965), Rates of Exchange (1983), and Dr. Criminale (1992) are picaresque novels, in that they are stylistically flamboyant with haphazard plotting and flat characterization. The "heroes" in these three novels are not only unheroic; they are unheroic in a sophisticated un-real way (Mullen 153). Indiana University is renamed Benedict Arnold University in Stepping Westward (1965) (Mullen 152). In many places, Stepping Westward alludes to, borrows from, and sometimes parodies, earlier literature, including a Waugh-like shipboard scene, an Amis-like lecture on "The Writer's Dilemma," and a Nabokov-Lolita-like romp through the South West. James Walker, the novel's protagonist, was hired to teach writing as a result of a series of comic mistakes and misunderstandings. The writing he teaches is that of America's service universities: "How to underline, how to use the comma, etc." This course is designed "to enable [freshmen] to communicate with one another without sex" (Bradbury Stepping 232). In a tone of self parody, Bradbury created a composite English comic novelist by the name of Brodge in Rates of Exchange (1983). Brodge is the author of Changing Westward, about which one character says, "I think he is very funny but sometimes his ideological position is not clear" (Bradbury Rates 269). In Rates of Exchange, Bradbury creates the comical language of Slakan, a language that is so complicated that

> ...all you must know is the nouns end in "i," or sometimes two or three, but with many exceptions. We have one spoken language and one book language. Really there are only three cases, but sometimes seven. Mostly it is inflected, but also sometimes not. It is different from country to town, also from region to region, because of our confused history. Vocabulary is a little bit Latin, a little bit German, a little bit Finn. So really it is quite simple, I think you will speak it very well, soon. (Bradbury Rates 93)

The History of Man (1975) is Bradbury's only novel that is not in the campus novel genre. This is a darkly comic novel that is truly disturbing and deeply ambiguous; it needs to be read attentatively (Mullen 154). Why Come to Slaka? (1986) also demonstrates Bradbury's comic linguistic skill (Mullen 154).

Malcolm Stanley Bradbury Bibliography

Bradbury, Malcolm. All Dressed Up and Nowhere to Go, Revised Edition. London, England: Pavilion, 1982.
Bradbury, Malcolm. Rates of Exchange. London, England: Secker and Warburg, 1965.

Bradbury, Malcolm. Stepping Westward. London, England: Secker and Warburg, 1965.
Mullen, Alexandra. "Malcolm Stanley Bradbury." Encyclopedia of British Humorists,
    Volume I. Ed. Steven H. Gale. New York, NY: Garland, 1996, 151-157.

Christy Brown (1932-1981) IRELAND

See Nilsen, Don L. F. "Christy Brown." Humor in Irish Literature: A Reference
    Guide. Westport, CT: Greenwood, 1996, 210.

Alice Thomas Ellis (Anna Margaret Haycroft) (1932-) WALES

Francine Prose notes that Alice Thomas Ellis published three novels in England
under the titles of A Fly in the Ointment (1989), Clothes in the Wardrobe (1987), and
Skeleton in the Cupboard (1988). These were later published as a single volume in
America under the title of The Summer House: A Trilogy (1994).

> What makes the book remarkable may, alas, be the same qualities that cause
> it to be dismissed. Its quick humor, prickly ironies and lack of pretentious
> self-importance may lead casual readers into overlooking its true heft, its
> provocative and disturbing shrewdness.... The book's witty, acute sensibility
> may alienate those who have been schooled to distrust cleverness and are a
> bit fuzzy about the difference between facility and intelligence, a distinction
> often blurred to devalue female intelligence in particular. (Prose 13)

Alice Thomas Ellis Bibliography

Ellis, Alice Thomas. Unexplained Laughter. London, England: Duckworth, 1985.
Prose, Francine. "Life without the Wriggling." New York Times Book Review April 24,
    1994: 13-14.

Vidiadhar Surajprasad Naipaul (1932-)

Mel Gussow notes that V. S. Naipaul was a voracious reader, and that he
remembered everything he read. John Guare recalls having been at a dinner party in which
Naipaul posed three literary questions: "1). What is the only food mentioned in 'Wuthering
Heights'? [the answer is "gruel"] 2). What is the occupation of Madame Bovary's daughter?
[she works in a factory] and 3). How does Swann dispense with his mistress?" The first
two questions were greeted with stone silence, but when the third question was asked, film
director Louis Malle responded that Swann tells her he is not her type. Some years later
John Guare met V. S. Naipaul at another dinner, and Naipaul greeted Guare by asking
again the question he had asked before, "What is the only food mentioned in 'Wuthering
Heights'?" (Gussow 29).

V. S. Naipaul is a keen observer of the comedy of colonial cultures. Talking about
Rudyard Kipling and the British Raj, Naipaul said, "With one part of myself I felt the
coming together of India and England as a violation; with the other I saw it as ridiculous,
resulting in a comic mixture of costumes and the widespread use of an imperfectly
understood language" (Robinson 14-15). Naipaul's writing is filled with skepticism and
irony. It tells of how futile it is to create anything but a fragile vision of order out of the
chaos of our modern world (Morris 8). His ironies are cool, and they are cumulative, and

they communicate that, "success bought at the expense of spirit and through an evasion that means fraudulence and betrayal must count--paradoxically--as the grandest of failures." Robert Morris suggests that Naipaul may be the first contemporary author to penetrate the true psyche of the British colonial minority cultures by coming at it from the inside. Thus in many ways, Naipaul's insights about Trinidad are more representative of colonial thinking than are Forster's insights on India, Orwell's insights on Burma, or Burgess's insights on Malaya (Morris 15).

Most of V. S. Naipaul's work deals with characters who, like himself, are estranged from the societies they are supposed to belong to, and who are desperately trying to find a way to belong, or to "be someone."

> Naipaul's early work explored these themes via a West Indian variation of the comedy of manners--that is, an almost farcical portrayal of the comic aspects of an illiterate and divided society's shift from a colonial to an independent status, with an emphasis on multiracial misunderstandings and rivalries and the various ironies resulting from the sudden introduction of such democratic processes as elections. (Lesniak 328)

The Mystic Masseur (1957) is filled with crazy comic details about Trinidadians who are trying to imitate England as they try to put together an intellectual and cultural life. The comedy of The Mystic Masseur often involves their struggling with an imperfectly understood language and culture:

> "But you can't have nice wordings on a think like an invitation."
> "You is the educated man, sahib. You could think of some."
> "R.S.V.P.?"
> "What that mean?"
> "It don't mean nothing, but it nice to have it."
> "Let we have it then, man, sahib! You is a modern man and too besides, it sound as pretty wordings." (Mystic Masseur 49)

Ganish in The Mystic Masseur is a mystic who is able to cure a young boy who was tormented by a cloud that follows him and will kill him. The boy is not only frightened, but he feels helpless as well. By using some comical props and some mystical chants, Ganesh is able to cure the boy, exorcising the boy's fear by forcing him to confront this fear. What makes this scene work at the deeper comic level is that Ganesh is made to feel the boy's very real torment. "It give you a funny feeling, you know. Is like watching a theatre show and then finding afterwards that they was really killing people on the stage" (Mystic Masseur 132). This scene is more than just a makeshift sham. The "funny feeling" which Ganesh experiences, "is not that something ridiculous has occurred, but that something truly comic has." The irony of the performance has been exposed. Nevertheless, Ganesh shortly thereafter publishes his Profitable Evacuation, a book about the pleasures and profits of constipation, "as a means of strengthening the abdominal muscles" (Robinson 19).

Ganesh lives surrounded by signs of self-advertisement in both Hindi and English, and the toilet paper holder in his lavatory plays "Yankee Doodle Dandy" whenever anyone pulls the toilet paper (Morris 14). There is a comic and ironic contradiction in The Mystic Masseur between what Ganesh writes in his autobiographical books, and the actual truth, as Ganesh rises from being a mystic masseur, to being a pundit to being M.L.C., and finally to becoming M. B. E. (Robinson 20). Michael Thorpe describes the prevailing tone of The Mystic Masseur, The Suffrage of Elvira, and Miguel Street as, "that of the ironist who points up the comedy, futility, and absurdity that fill the gap between aspiration and achievement" (Lesniak 328).

The Suffrage of Elvira (1958) describes the mixed-up situation in the town of Elvira where everybody owned a Bible, whether they were Hindus, Muslims, or Christians.

Furthermore, "Hindus and Moslems celebrated Christmas and Easter. The Spaniards and some of the Negroes celebrated the Hindu festival of lights.... Everybody celebrated the Muslin festival of Hosein. In fact, when Elvira was done with religious festivals, there were few straight days left" (Morris 13). Surujpat Harbans is the protagonist of The Suffrage of Elvira, and the comic intrigue, boondoggling, and logrolling necessary on his way to the legislative council strike the reader as very humorous (Morris 14).

Miguel Street (1959), Naipaul's third novel, is also filled with crazy comic details about Trinidadians trying to act like Britishers. It is more of a satire than a comedy (Robinson 15). It is about the, "false pundits, the careless squalor, the stifling banality and the laughable ignorance of Trinidad, a society with a sense that everything is done better somewhere else." The constant theme in Miguel Street is, "Well, what can you expect in a place like this?" Here Naipaul is ridiculing; his humor is too detached to show genuine compassion (Robinson 15). Miguel Street is about a bunch of grotesques who live on Miguel Street in Port of Spain. They spend their time drinking, beating their spouses, hanging around, going to jail, and becoming obsessed by jobs they have difficulty accomplishing (Robinson 18). The lives of these grotesques are governed by poverty, frustration, un-attained ambitions, boredom, ignorance, defeat, cruelty, deceptions, superstitions, and drunkenness. But the paradox is that these characters believe Hat when he says, "Life a helluva thing," and, "You can see trouble coming and you can't do a damn thing to prevent it coming. You just go to sit and watch and wait" (Miguel Street 91). The main paradox of Miguel Street lies in the fact that there is an orderliness in the disorder, and the resulting strange coherence, in the world of Miguel Street (Morris 10). This seems to be an illustration of Henry Adam's statement in Education that, "chaos often breeds life, when order breeds habit" (Morris 11).

Fred Miller Robinson considers A House for Mr. Biswas (1961) to be an excellent example of comic realism (Robinson 14). Robinson considers this to be Naipaul's best novel, for it is here that his comic vision really flourishes. Mohan Biswas represents the "little-man" archetype. He was born with six fingers on one hand, and he was declared therefore to be an unlucky child. The family was advised to keep him away from water, and it is therefore ironic that his father drowns trying to retrieve him from a pond he is not in (Robinson 16). There is a discrepancy here between human strategies and the way fate deals with these strategies (Robinson 17). In A House for Mr. Biswas there is a comic interplay between the obstruction of reality and the liberation of Mr. Biswas's dream (Robinson 21).

In A House for Mr. Biswas much of the comedy is based on the conflict between Mr. Biswas's imaginings of a house, and the truth of the situation. The house which Biswas finally acquires by paying too much for it is a wretched dilapidated mess, not the cozy home he had imagined. There is a comic discrepancy between the romantic vision, and the actual house. Biswas and his family, "had to accommodate themselves to every peculiarity and awkwardness of the house," and much of the rhythm of the comedy is the result of making these accommodations (Robinson 17).

At one point fairly late in A House for Mr. Biswas there is a comic moment in which Mr. Biswas has finally acquired his second house, and he needs to set fire to the house and around the house in order to make a clearing. He digs trenches and prepares little nests of twigs and leaves at strategic points, and he soaks a fire brand in pitch-oil and sets it afire, and runs from nest to nest poking the fire brand into each nest and jumping back as if there were going to be an explosion. But instead of the explosion, one leaf would catch fire in one place, and a twig would catch fire in another place. They would blaze for a while, and then would shrink, smoulder, and die, leaving a trail of waning wisps of smoke, and Mr. Biswas said, "Is all right. Is all right. Fire is a funny thing. You think it out, but it blazing like hell underground" (Robinson 15). The comedy here lies in the discrepancy between Mr. Biswas's faith and enthusiasm, and the true nature of things (Robinson 15-16). The central paradox of <u>A House for Mr. Biswas</u> is based on the fact that the way up, and the way down, are actually pretty much the same (Morris 24). Naipaul wants the reader to see that Mr. Biswas is affected both from the inside (for example, by the melange of the Indian community, and especially the Tulsi sisters, cousins, and aunts) but from the outside as well (by his imperfect assimilation of Western values which end up by being aped and bastardized rather than completely understood) (Morris 26). Living with the Tulsis, Mr. Biswas is overwhelmed by a family that threatens to absorb his character, and sap his individuality, but which at the same time offers him shelter, food, protection, cures, and even assures the "success" of its passive dependents (Morris 29). For Mr. Biswas, "The world was too small, the Tulsi family too large. He felt trapped" (Morris 30). In a way, Mr. Biswas had many houses. By the end of the novel, he had memories of Hanuman House, The Chase, Green Vale, Shorthills, and the Tulsi house in Port of Spain. There is something special about Mr. Biswas's last house, however, which is described in the final chapter of the book (only eleven pages in length). Although the novel is entitled, <u>A House for Mr. Biswas</u>, this final chapter is entitled "The House," thus changing from the indefinite article "a" to the definite article "the." It was only in this last house, the house at Sikkim Street, that Mr. Biswas's dreams became a reality. "The will-o'-the-wisp, alternately glowing and guttering of forty years and three generations of Biswases, ignites with his rash, fearful, yet inspired purchase" (Morris 35). Oscar Wilde once said, that there are only two tragedies in the world. One was not getting what one wanted, and the other one was getting it. All of Mr. Biswas's earlier houses represent the first part of this epigram, and the Sikkam house represented the latter part (Morris 34).

It is ironic that in <u>The Middle Passage</u> (1962) everything that made the Indian alien in his own society also gave him his strength. This was true of his religion, but it was even more true of his family organization, because the family organization in India is, "an enclosing self-sufficient world absorbed with its quarrels and jealousies as difficult for the outsider to penetrate as for one of its members to escape" (Morris 18).

<u>Mr. Stone and the Knight's Companion</u> (1963) is set in England and has British characters. It begins with a comic scene in which Richard Stone, who is growing old, tries to lure a hated cat into his bathroom by leaving a trail of cheese cubes. He stands with a poker in his hand, waiting to attack the cat. But then he remembers that it was rats that ate cheese, not cats. So he turned on the lights and closed the front door. The next morning, Miss Millington reported that some of her cheese had disappeared from the larder, and somehow had ended up on the floor as cubes forming a wavering line from the door to the bathroom. Mr. Stone remained silent. Much of the comedy here is based on the clash between the seriousness of the plan to Mr. Stone, and the absurdity of the plan to the reader (Robinson 22).

A ludicrous and prevailing metaphor in <u>Mr. Stone and the Knight's Companion</u> relates to allusions to Camelot. "Naipaul plays off its associations with the coming and passing of Arthur and the Round Table against Mr. Stone's company, which happens to be named Excal." The Head of Mr. Stone's firm is named "Sir Harry." and there are many punning allusions to Arthurian legend which, "endows the idea with a fabled grandeur out of all proportion to its practical, or even ideal genesis." There are simple attempts to "rescue men from inactivity," "protect them from cruelty," "keep alive in them loyalty to the company" (Morris 46-47).

The Bombay bureaucracy in <u>An Area of Darkness</u> (1964), a non-fiction account of Naipaul's first visit to India, is a target of Naipaul's satire (Robinson 14-15). Naipaul is concerned with how the colonies mimic England.

Mimicry might be too harsh a word for what appears so comprehensive and profound.... But mimicry must be used...because so much of what is seen remains simple mimicry, incongruous and absurd; and because no people, by their varied physical endowments, are as capable of mimicry as the Indians. (qtd. in Morris 54)

A Flag on the Island (1967) is a novella about a middle-aged American named Frankie who served in the Caribbean during World War II, and later returns to the same spot in the Caribbean to find that it has drastically changed. A flag described as having, "rays from the yellow sun lighting up a wavy blue sea" flies where before had flown England's Union Jack, and America's Stars and Stripes. The shabby and intimate bar named "Henry's Place" which he had frequented has been turned into an expensive and garish tourist place by the name of "The Coconut Grove." Even the people have changed. When Frankie was there before, H. J. Blackwhite had been churning out romantic novels which he was not able to sell, but on his return Blackwhite has become a popular black novelist. Gary Priest had been an inept insurance salesman, now he appears as Gary Priestland in prime-time television as a revivalist on various talk-shows. And Selma, who had haunted Henry's Place as a free and uninhibited spirit, and who had been Frankie's mistress at the time, is now Mrs. Priestland, who moves with boredom among her kitchen appliances (Morris 1). Robert Morris notes that there are a number of similarities between the changes of Frankie's "fun-island-in-the-sun" and the changes of Naipaul's Trinidad which he had written about sometime earlier in The Middle Passage (1962).

Toward the end of A Flag on the Island there is a hurricane which results in the surreal world of partially sunk fishing boats, the heads and entrails of dead fish, and, "mangy pariah dogs, all rib and bone, all bleached to a nondescript fawn colour" who moved about with their tails between their legs in search of food (Morris 5). Naipaul says that a certain street was an, "aquaria, thick with life, but silent." The scene is a bizarre and grotesque series of incongruities, viewed by a bunch of brooding, hopping, circling vultures. These scenes of dereliction and abandonment are consistent with both Frankie's view, and Naipaul's view of the island (Morris 7).

The Mimic Men (1967) covers the period of 1930 to 1960, a period lasting from the time that Ralph Singh, the protagonist, is ten, until he is forty. Ironically, the closer Singh gets to the present, the more his mind blurs. Facts become opaque, and there are large gaps of time unaccounted for. Events become so shadowy, that by the end of the novel, Singh is "no more than a face peering out from behind a pillar." In contrast, Singh's childhood, adolescence, and initiation into manhood are told in vivid detail (Morris 60). Ralph Singh, whose real name is Ranjit Kripalsingh, engineers a development of condominiums named "Kripalville" in honor of his father, and of course the development is normally referred to as "Crippleville" (Morris 65). Ralph is descended from generations of idlers and failures who are generally unimaginative, unenterprising, and oppressed, and he is deeply ashamed of this genealogy. So he changes his name from Ranjit Kripalsingh to Ralph Singh (Morris 64).

It is paradoxical that Ralph Singh's desire for freedom makes him a slave. All of Singh's actions are matched by counteractions. His marriage ends in divorce. His riches end in poverty. His success ends in failure. His power ends in helplessness. His respect ends in scorn. His popularity ends in isolation. His creation ends in destruction (Morris 67-68). The more public power Singh acquires, the more isolated and impotent he becomes personally. The more he exercises control over others, the less power he has in his own life. As he becomes more in touch with the masses, he becomes less able to reënter the mainstream of society. At the end of the novel he uses the patois of Isabella to express himself, "Je vens d'lué" (Morris 62). Singh is able to describe his life in the following way, "The tragedy of power like mine is that there is no way down; there is only extinction" (Morris 69).

In a Free State (1971) represents Naipaul's most personal writing. Its theme is that we are all exiles in one way or another; we are all, "perpetually adrift in a free state" (Morris 74). The narrator of this story is Santosh, a new American citizen who is now living in Washington, D.C. (Morris 75). Santosh is disoriented in his thoughts and in his feelings, but he is delighted that he is now able to live in a pantry giving him more room than he had had in his small cupboard in Bombay. Santosh has difficulty understanding why he is chased out of a café because he is bare footed. He also is saddened when he realizes that he has spent two weeks pay for the movies and refreshments. He had been thinking in rupees rather than dollars. Santosh routinely smokes marijuana, and he is amazed that the smell of this "weed" attracts all sorts of weirdos. Finally, he is mystified by a group of hippies who are chanting Sanskrit words in praise of Lord Krishna. He is puzzled both by the fact that they are doing it, and by the fact that their accents and pronunciations are so abominable as they do it (Morris 77).

Santosh is also baffled that the blacks, which in his country would be called "hubshi," are permitted to freely roam the streets. Santosh's chaotic perceptions about Washington D.C. set up much of the satire of the novel. Santosh has a special kind of xenophobia, special because it is Santosh who is the stranger. He also has a special kind of narcissism, special because the maid finds him attractive, and this makes him think that he is like the actors on TV. His narcissism is a combination of vanity and innocence. It is rooted more in ignorance than in evil. But it leads to Santosh's fall, his comic transgression against his own ego. The black maid pulls him down onto the couch. "I saw the moment, helplessly, as one of dishonour. I saw her as Kali, goddess of death and destruction, coal-black, with a red tongue and white eyeballs and many powerful arms" (Morris 79). But for Santosh, the black maid is also the "deux ex machina." Priya advises Santosh to marry the "hubshi," because that will automatically make Santosh a citizen (Morris 81).

A Bend in the River (1979) describes life in an outpost village in Africa. One episode is an absurd sight gag about the madness of colonial change in which Naipaul mentions the rubbish heaps that are caused by the growing population. Nobody wanted to remove the rubbish, and the taxis and trucks that had to go back and forth through the rubbish stank not so much of the garbage, but of the disinfectant that was used to control the germs. It was the law that the taxis and trucks had to be disinfected, so of course the disinfectors, who made money each time they disinfected a taxi or truck, played a game of hide and seek with the taxis and the trucks among the hills of rubbish, "in a curious kind of slow motion, with the vehicles of hunters and hunted pitching up and down corrugations like launches in a heavy sea" (Robinson 23).

Tell Me Who To Kill has an Indian narrator from the West Indies who ends up in a room in London. The title comes from something the narrator says, "They [the whites] take my money, they spoil my life, they separate us. But you can't kill them. O God, show me the enemy. Once you find out who the enemy is, you can kill him." And this speech ends with the words, "Tell me who to kill" (Morris 83).

Vidiadhar Surajprasad Naipaul Bibliography

Gussow, Mel. "V. S. Naipaul in Search of Himself: A Conversation." New York Times Book Review April 24, 1994: 3, 29-30.

Lesniak, James G. "V(idiadhar) S(urajprasad) Naipaul." Contemporary Authors, New Revision Series, Volume 33. Detroit, MI: Gale, 1991, 327-331.

Morris, Robert K. Paradoxes of Order: Some Perspectives on the Fiction of V. S. Naipaul. Columbia, MO: University of Missouri Press, 1975.

Naipaul, V. S. Miguel Street. New York, NY: Penguin, 1958.

Naipaul, V. S. The Mystic Masseur. Harmondsworth, England: Penguin, 1981.
Robinson, Fred Miller. "Comic Realism and V. S. Naipaul's A House for Mr. Biswas."
Thalia: Studies in Literary Humor 5.2 (1983): 14-23.

Julia O'Faolain (1932-) IRELAND

**See Nilsen, Don L. F. "Julia O'Faolain." Humor in Irish Literature: A Reference
Guide. Westport, CT: Greenwood, 1996, 11, 210.**

Arnold Wesker (1932-)

The comedy in The Kitchen (1961) is in most situations implicit rather than explicit
(Sorell 300).
Glenda Leeming describes The Old Ones (1972) as a comedy with a sting in its tail
(Leeming 71).
The Journalists (1974), and The Wedding Feast (1977) are comedies, but they are
also satires with a corrective purpose, and the brushstrokes of these comedies are relatively
simple (Leeming 65). There are many jokes and anecdotes swapped in The Journalists, but
this doesn't necessarily make it into a comedy. Mary Mortimer is the star columnist who
is a bit destructive in her approach to journalism. Topics or people which are at odds with
her own "liberal," "tolerant," and even "idealistic" beliefs must be cut down to size. Her
grown-up children say that for Mary, puncturing pretenses has, "elevated the gutter
question, 'who does he think he is?' to a respected art form" (Leeming 72). For example,
Mary considers the views of Morton King, a Member of Parliament, to be pretentious,
patronizing, and immodest. The irony here is that his ideals are, for the most part, the
same as those of Mary. Cynthia, another journalist, asks Mary,
> Don't you ever feel uneasy, sometimes, as a journalist? We inundate people
> with depressing information and they become concerned. Then we offer
> more information and they become confused. And then we pile on more
> and more until they feel impotent but we offer them no help. No way out
> of their feelings of impotence. Don't you ever feel guilty? (Leeming 73)
The Wedding Feast (1977) is a socially satiric comedy with a sting in its tail, but
the sting of this play is different from the sting of straight drama (Leeming 71). There is
quite a bit of slapstick in The Wedding Feast. Louis falls into "blancmange" twice, and the
newly married couple's cavorting causes the couch to collapse under them. The "party"
contains a "shoe game" in which Louis is blindfolded and beaten with shoes. At first this
is fun, but as the hostility increases it becomes less fun. According to Glenda Leeming,
"the moments of discouragement and conflict rise only to submerge in the flow of comic
incident" (Leeming 72).
Wesker's The Merchant (1978) is based on William Shakespeare's The Merchant
of Venice, and Wesker's play retains most of the same names as Shakespeare had used, but
the personalities of the characters are not the same. Shakespeare's Shylock was motivated
by racial hatred, and required Antonio's pound of flesh that was due him. But Wesker's
Shylock, in this same situation, makes a joke against the anti-semitic laws of Venice that
insist on a bond. He considers such laws to be ridiculous because they force the formality
of a legal contract between friends (Leeming 74). In comparing Wesker's The Merchant
with Shakespeare's The Merchant of Venice, Richard Eder says, "Wesker has used the same
rough elements of plot and the same principal characters--all of them with a widely
different human weight and meaning--for a totally original play." He continues, "It is

provocative, generally intelligent and sometimes strained or confused. Its writing has moments of ferocious brilliance and wit" (Lesniak 449).

Arnold Wesker Bibliography

Leeming, Glenda. "Articulation and Awareness: The Modulation of Familiar Themes in Wesker's Plays in the Seventies." Contemporary English Drama. Ed. C. W. E. Bigsby. New York, NY: Holmes and Meier Publishers, 1981, 65-78.

Lesniak, James G. "Arnold Wesker." Contemporary Authors, New Revision Series, Volume 33. Detroit, MI: Gale Research, 1991, 446-450.

Sorell, Walter. Facets of Comedy. New York, NY: Grosset and Dunlap, 1972.

Beryl Bainbridge (1933-)

Beryl Bainbridge has won critical acclaim on two continents for her black humor chronicles of the lives and neuroses of English lower middle class characters. Reviewers like Julian Symons praise her, "satiric but naturalistic portrayals of the drab and desperate British poor, of the hidden springs of anarchy that bedevil the least adventurous of us, booby-trapping our lives and making them the occasion of violent and dangerous humor" (Johnson 29). Bainbridge juxtaposes horror and comedy. Anne Tyler writes, "Bainbridge addicts settle gleefully into her genteel parlors, knowing that shortly everything will fall apart. There'll be bodies in the hedge, baked apples behind the refrigerator. A grown man, in a fit of temper, will set fire to a chair arm. A woman will try to sleep while teenaged boys clamber over her bed in search of ping-pong balls" (Johnson 30). Bainbridge's female characters are alternately, "silly and wise, loving and self-absorbed, rebellious and conformist, deluded and perceptive," but they are always "accommodating and vulnerable," as they depict the image of befuddled and helpless postwar England, and the image of modern humanity perplexed in the extreme (Johnson 31). Mary Hope says that Bainbridge's writing "hides consummate technical comic skill." "Bainbridge has you crying with laughter while the blood freezes in your veins. This close relationship between farce and horror often depends on extreme physical, as well as emotional, propinquity between the characters. Her dialogue is always wildly funny, and she uses it most intricately to depict social anxiety and emotional turmoil or sterility" (Johnson 31). For Beryl Bainbridge, as for Penelope Mortimer, the comedy inverts the system, "as if all the year they were playing holiday," and it is also of a fairly extreme nature, deeply rooted in the norms which are themselves the objects of attack (Little 3). Peter Ackroyd says that Beryl Bainbridge, "has earned a well-deserved reputation as one of our funniest writers" (Johnson 32).

Young Adolf (1978) is about a family meeting in Liverpool between Adolf Hitler and his half-brother, Alois. Young Adolf is funny in a way that makes a person shudder. It is also sad in a way that astonishes the reader with unwanted feelings of sympathy (Johnson 32). Young Adolf is a Chaplinesque farce of the Nazi campaign to canonize Hitler and to dehumanize "the other." Young Adolf dehumanizes the future Fuhrer by exposing him to England's prevailing social discordances (Lassner 206). The title of this novel helps Bainbridge set the stage to deal with the life of the Fuhrer years before he has reshaped himself to be a world conqueror. Young Adolf visits his older half-brother, Alois, in Liverpool. The year is 1912, and young Adolf is a mess. He wears shapeless and tattered clothes, and he has no vocation or even sense of purpose.

The carefully wrought persona of the leader of the Third Reich is deconstructed by dramatizing its genesis in the art of burlesque and the artlessness of pure chance. His sister-in-law Bridget cannot help but laugh at "that funny walk and his ridiculously shrunken jacket" which remind her of "a pantomime." (Young Adolf 45)

Adolf's brown shirt is made out of a rag that happens to be the only salvageable cloth to dress him in so that he can interview for a job as a waiter. Bainbridge portrays young Adolf as "crazy with fear of the other, ranting incomprehensibly about vermin and redskins and men with beards" (qtd in Lassner 214). One reviewer considers Another Part of the World (1980) to be "a scrupulously detailed, wryly witty and ultimately harrowing study of manners in the British middle and working classes" (Johnson 31). Winter Garden (1980) is a satirical story about a group of artists who are invited to visit the Soviet Union (Johnson 32).

Beryl Bainbridge Bibliography

Johnson, Anne Janette. "Beryl Bainbridge." Contemporary Authors, New Revision Series, Volume 24. Detroit, MI: Gale Research, 1988, 29-33.

Lassner, Phyllis. " 'Between the Gaps': Sex, Class and Anarchy in the British Comic Novel of World War II." Look Who's Laughing: Gender and Comedy. Ed. Gail Finney. Amsterdam, Netherlands: Gordon and Breach, 1994, 205-220.

Little, Judy. Comedy and the Woman Writer: Woolf, Spark, and Feminism. Lincoln, NE: University of Nebraska Press, 1983.

Michael Frayn (1933-)

Michael Frayn has a wide range as a humorous writer--satirical journalism, documentary, the novel, metaphysical musings, and philosophical farces for the stage (Rovit 399). Frayn established himself as a social satirist as a columnist and critic for the Manchester Guardian and the London Observer. On the Guardian, Frayn had the job of writing cool and witty interviews with important film directors who were passing through Manchester. According to Terry Coleman, Frayn's interviews appeared in his "Miscellany" column, but there were never enough film directors passing through, so Frayn started making up humorous paragraphs to serve as filler. Malcolm Page says that Frayn thus invented for the column the "Don't Know Party" and such characters as the "trendy Bishop of Twicester," and the public relations consultant, Rolly Swavely, and the ambitious suburban couple who went by the names of Christopher and Lavinia Crumble. Michael Fritz believes that Frayn started developing his sense of humor at Kingston Grammar School where, to the delight of his fellow students, he developed various ways of mocking his teachers. Referring to this practice of making jokes at the expense of others, Frayn says, "I sometimes wonder if this isn't an embarrassingly exact paradigm of much that I've done since" (Salter 134).

In an interview with Barbara Isenberg, Michael Frayn says that farce is "serious business." According to Frayn, the most important element of farce is

the losing of power for coherent thought under the pressure of events. What characters in farce do traditionally is try to recover some disaster that occurred, by a course of behavior that is so ill-judged that it makes it worse. In traditional farce, people are caught in a compromising situation, try to explain it with a lie and, when they get caught, have then to explain both the original situation and the lie. And, when they're caught in that lie, they have to have another one. (Salter 135)

Michael Frayn's writing is about order and disorder. The poignancy of much of his humor comes from the confusion around his characters, and how the characters try to make order out of this confusion (Rovit 400).

Zounds! (1957) is a musical comedy. The Tin Men (1965) provides a number of important humorous insights into the complications of modern times. Michael Fritz compares Frayn's wit, sophistication, and imagination to the wit, sophistication, and imagination of S. J. Perelman, and even considers Frayn's satire to be sharper than that of Perelman. Frayn blends his satire with a sense of seriousness. The Tin Men is a story about the suitability of computers to take over the burdens of human dullness and won Frayn the Somerset Maugham Award for fiction in 1963 (Salter 134). The Russian Interpreter (1966), like The Tin Men, provides important humorous insights into the complications of modern times. The Russian Interpreter is a spy story that deals with the deceits between individuals that are greater than the deceits between nations, and Frayn won the Hawthorn Prize for this novel (Salter 134).

The Two of Us (1968) contains two two-person plays, Black and Silver and Mr. Foot, both of which rely heavily on humor of repetition. Black and Silver is about a couple on their second honeymoon who spend a night trying to compete with a crying baby as they try to communicate with each other. In the hotel room, they rush back and forth between their bed and the baby's bassinet, unable to calm the baby. Mr. Foot is about a protagonist who has an uncontrollable tic that causes his foot to jiggle. The wife tells an imaginary conversation partner that she thinks the foot is taking hold of her husband, and she doesn't think it's right for a foot to have that much control over a man. The humor in these two short plays comes both from the thwarted attempts at communication and from the characters' attempts to control things that are out of control, a baby in the one case, and a twitching foot in the other (Rovit 400).

Alphabetical Order (1975) is about a newspaper's research department. The "morgue" is changed drastically when a super-efficient young woman joins the staff. By the second act, she has changed the morgue into a model of order and efficiency, but somehow, the office has become sterile, and all of the humanity is gone. The young woman then begins to reorganize the personal lives of the other characters as well. The play asks the question, "Which is better, order or chaos" (Salter 135).

Donkey's Years: A Play (1976) is about a group of university graduates who are reunited twenty years later. When they get together, they revert to their grotesque adolescent roles and conflicts. Donkey's Years was voted the best comedy of 1982 by London's West End Theater Society. Stephen Holden said that it is a, "well-made farce that roundly twits English propriety" (Salter 135). Clouds (1976) is about the impact of Cuba, an alien culture, on three journalists, one of them American and the other two British. The humor comes from how they shift their perspectives and values, including their sexual attitudes (Rovit 400).

Balmoral (1978), and Make and Break (1980) are both social satires. Balmoral takes place in 1937 in a castle in the "Soviet Republic of Great Britain. It juxtaposes the capitalistic and the socialistic political systems" (Rovit 400). Make and Break is a grim portrayal of capitalism and industrialism and our emphasis on consumerism (Rovit 401). It is a comedy-drama about a salesman whose aggressive talent for business makes him a bit inhumane. Michael Ratcliffe describes Make and Break as, "an excessively neat, neoclassical sort of piece which draws on only a fraction of his imaginative range" (Salter 135).

Noises Off: A Play in Three Acts (1982) is a no-holds-barred slapstick farce which uses manic entrances and mistaken identities that are reminiscent of the plays of Georges Feydeau. Noises Off invites the audience to witness the turmoil that goes on behind the scenes of a touring company consisting of has-beens and never-weres, as they attempt to perform an English sex farce named "Nothing On." Frayn had developed some of his sense of theater by working for the Cambridge Footlights review, and by having a walk-on in a production of Nikolai Gogol's The Inspector General, and in fact his walk-on part was such a disaster that it provided Frayn with the insight necessary to develop the backstage slapstick for Noises Off. As Frayn explains, "I pulled instead of pushed at the door, it jammed in the frame, and there was no other way off. So I waited for what seemed like many, many hours while stagehands fought with crowbars on the other side and the audience started to slow-handclap. I've never been on the stage since" (Salter 134). Sheryl Flatow says that Noises Off was criticized for being, "nothing more than a relentless, if effective, laugh-getting machine." Then Flatow asks if this criticism isn't just a bit ridiculous, since this is the whole point of the play. She says that such criticisms don't repel audiences, and notes that Noises Off enjoyed a long run in the West End and Broadway theaters. The fun begins even before the curtain goes up, because in the Playbill there is a "program-with-the-program" (Salter 135).

Noises Off is a farce which contains numerous, "expressive looks, gestures, professional bits of miming, bodily attacks narrowly averted, [and] fiendish practical jokes like tying trouser legs together." As the actors dash off stage, they step on a rival's hand, or snatch up a weapon of defense before they dash back on stage. Because of this, eccentric props are substituted for real ones. There is a hatchet with no relevance to the plot, which appears and is passed around from actor to actor. A cactus also appears, and ends up by being plucked from the director's posterior. The total zaniness gives the play a surrealistic feel, as the inner play keeps chugging along in spite of the anarchy the actors face each time they open the door, to discover the wrong prop, or the wrong person, or nothing there when there should be something. But they are always able to improvise, and they improvise so fast that it is difficult for the audience to keep up (Worth 51). In Noises Off, Mrs. Clackett is a comic lady housekeeper who is in charge of a plate of sardines that gets lost, found, stepped on, lost again, and is all in all an excellent "red herring." The director's interruptions throughout the play serve two functions. They are funny, and they help to fix the details of the play for the audience with "a rather unusual exactness." The audience knows almost as well as the actors the exact position of everything on the set. They are aware of the four doors downstairs, the four doors upstairs, and the places where each of the characters should be at any given point in the play. A young man from a real-estate agency shows up with a dumb blond for a quick assignation in what they think is an empty house, a house which he is passing off as his own. But as soon as she has her dress off, the real owners, who are supposed to be out of the country, arrive (Worth 48). The real owners are dodging the Inland Revenue, and are stimulated by being secret visitors in their own home; they also head for the bedroom.

Noises Off, then, is a game of hide-and-seek and near misses as these four people race up and down the staircase, open and shut the doors, find objects in the wrong places, and become perturbed by the poltergeist atmosphere in which things move around as if by magic, voices of unknown people can be heard from behind doors, and the television set leaves from its appointed stand. In this farce, door handles stick, and props are mislaid, and the person most responsible for the pandemonium is the burglar who fails to appear at the appointed time, and must be searched for. When he is found, in an alcoholic stupor, he asks, "Have I missed the opening night?" It is quickly determined that the Burglar is in no condition to play his role, so understudies quickly rush to his defense by donning the Burglar's costume and doing his lines (Worth 49). The second act of Noises Off is a replaying of the first act of Nothing On, but this time it is being done "for real" (Worth 50). The audience therefore sees a set that they are already familiar with, and they also see familiar actors who are in advanced stages of exhaustion, hysteria, and inebriation. By the second act, the poltergeists are in control, and Brooke's discarded dress is mysteriously moved from place to place in much the same way as the mysterious sardines. By the second act, the audience sees not just one burglar, but three, and at one point all three of these burglars are saying the same lines in unison, much like a music-hall routine (Worth 52). There are many other humours characters in the play besides the Burglar. Dotty is a robust, noisy, humorous eccentric. The "jeune premier" is another humours character. He is appropriately named Garry Lejeune, and he is impassioned and inarticulate in his speeches. Most of his sentences work up to climaxes, but then trail off with a simple, "You know." The dumb blond seems not to be aware that there is anyone else on stage except herself. She loses her contact lens, and the whole company has to search for it with exaggerated care. Then, with a "little-girl cool," she tells everybody that she has found it-- in her eye (Worth 49). Mr. Brent, who smiles broadly as he euphorically bounds around the stage with Belinda, is always wanting rational explanations for the silly things he is asked to do in the play. He asks why he must take some parcels with him, and the director has to explain to him that the character needs the parcels because they symbolize his need for security. Mr. Brent says, "Oh, thank you, Lloyd," and picks up his parcels with renewed vigor (Worth 50).

Benefactors: A Play in Two Acts (1984) is an acerbic depiction of a 1960s couple with a failing marriage who are struggling with their ideals as they try to cope with their troubled neighbors (Salter 135). Despite the seriousness of the subject, many of the family situations are comic (Salter 136). The irony of Benefactors comes from the fact that while people are trying to change the world, the world is actually changing on its own--out of our control. In the play, David, the architect, despises modern high-rise housing complexes, but he is nevertheless forced to design one of these complex which he so much hates (Rovit 401).

Michael Frayn's Wild Honey (1984) is an adaptation of a play by Anton Chekhov; Frayn is fluent in Russian. Chekhov's play was discovered in 1920 with the title page missing. It was an unwieldy, six-hour play very much in need of revision. Platanov, the leading character in the play, is a roguish teacher who is loved by every woman in the town. About the revision, Frayn says, "I thought the only thing to do was treat it as if it were a rough draft of one of my own plays and proceed from there. If that meant giving one character's speech to another or rewriting dialogue or adding my own speeches, fine-- anything to make a better second draft." Frayn made Chekhov's play more economical, more succinct, and more witty (Salter 136).

Clockwise (1986) is Michael Frayn's first produced screenplay. It closely resembles Noises Off in its wild construction. Brian Stimpson, the protagonist, is a small-town headmaster who is obsessed with punctuality. He earns the title of "Headmaster of the Year," and has to travel by train to a distant city to deliver his acceptance speech. Brian, however, catches the wrong train, and the thought that he might arrive late to the ceremonies causes him to steal a car, invade a monastery, rob a man of his suit, and set two squadrons of police on his trail. Clockwise is a comedy which is unusual in its layered complexity, and in the way that Frayn has of working everything out. As one of the policemen pursuing Brian says, "Gonna take a bit o' sortin' out, this one." The joke here is in the understatement (Salter 135).

In Act I of Look Look (1990), the actors are part of the theater audience, watching a play. In Act II, it is discovered that the play they are watching is about themselves as individual audience members. Much of the humor of the play comes from the portrayal of self-conscious spectators. There are many recognizable comic archetypes, such as the pretentious theater buff, the doddering old man who sleeps through the first act, the innocent young boy who finds romance with the girl who is seated next to him, the lovers whose secret affair suddenly becomes public, and the author of the play, who can't help but try to manipulate and orchestrate the audience responses to his play, with such comments as, "Laugh coming up here, by the way" (Rovit 401). There is also a late-comer, who sits in the wrong seat, along with the various loud coughers, sneezers, paper rustlers, and people with digital watches that beep alarms at just the wrong time. At the end, the actors-as-spectators make witty comments about the play they have just watched (Rovit 402).

Michael Frayn has won many awards. He won the Evening Standard's Best Comedy of the Year for Alphabetical Order in 1975. He won this same award for Noises Off in 1982, and for Benefactors in 1984. He won the Society of West End Theater Award for Best Comedy of the Year for Donkeys' Years in 1976, for Noises Off in 1982, and for Benefactors in 1984 (Salter 133). Like many other writers of the 1970s and 1980s, Michael Frayn contributed a string of lively, witty comedies which raised serious philosophical questions. Malcolm Page says that Michael Frayn, "has such gifts of humor that his reputation is for comedy; however, he may be disappointed that the more solemn implications have yet to be perceived. His future may be less in comic theater, as he continues to focus mainly on people of his age, class, and education" (Salter 136).

Michael Frayn Bibliography

Rovit, Rebecca. "Michael Frayn." Encyclopedia of British Humorists, Volume I. Ed. Steven
    H. Gale. New York, NY: Garland, 1996, 398-404.
Salter, Susan. "Michael Frayn." Contemporary Authors, New Revision Series, Volume 20.
    Detroit, MI: Gale Research, 1990, 133-136.
Turner, John. "Frayn: Desperately Funny." Plays and Players 375 (1984): 8-10.
Worth, Katharine. "Farce and Michael Frayn." Modern Drama 26.1 (1983): 47-53.

Joe Orton (John Kingsley) (1933-1967)

In the tolerant theatrical climate of the 1960s Joe Orton showed that such controversial subjects as homosexuality, rape, necrophilia, and violence not only could be shown on the stage, but could be presented in an uproariously funny manner (Keller 803). "There is a husband who sympathizes with his wife's attacker, a priest who has no Christian charity, a policeman who has no respect for the law, a nurse who murders her patients for their money, and a psychiatrist who causes mental anguish rather than foster contentment" (Keller 804). The word "Ortonesque" is a special mixture of the formal and the violent with the amusing (Allen 365). In Joe Orton's work, poetic justice seldom occurs. Every aspect of bourgeois life is treated with "studied irreverence," and "a gift for parody" (Allen 368). Orton is an enemy of authority, of routine, and of sexual compartmentalization. Like Walt Whitman, he gleefully insists on man's animal nature (Allen 370). Orton is not afraid to write about illicit sex, transvestitism, homosexuality, bisexuality, and adultery, since he assumes that his audience will either laugh and join in the fun, or become a part of the strict and rigid culture that is being satirized (Keller 807).

The 1960s brought us not only Joe Orton, but also John Osborne, and Harold Pinter. They arrived on the scene to present a new refinement of expression in the rebirth of comedy of manners which coincided with a more positive critical reappraisal not only of the works of Noel Coward, but also those of the dramatists of the post-Restoration period (Hirst 67). The expression "comedy of manners" referred not only to "manner of expression," but also to "manner of behavior," and this genre was therefore considered somewhat immoral and unpleasant. Orton's Loot ends with the observation that, "people would talk; we must keep up appearances," and this is reminiscent of the following satiric lines in Pope's The Rape of the Lock when Belinda laments, "Oh hadst thou, cruel, been content to seize / Hairs less in sight, or any hairs but these!" (Hirst 2).

Joe Orton wrote comedies of manners. According to David Hirst, Orton was very aware of the morés of different social classes, and this awareness is an important aspect of Orton's moral and sexual satire (Hirst 97). Orton is a satirist who attacks from behind a polite grin. His language can be described as mock-formal. His humor is like that of Lewis Carroll in that fantastic absurdities are developed and blended with the most obvious of mundane realities. Walter Sorell says that all of Joe Orton's plays, "combine a glittering dialogue reminiscent of Oscar Wilde with black and bleak farcical material." Orton's black comedy ridicules everything that is sacred to the establishment, and Orton's characters utter, "dreadful thoughts with mock elegance worthy of the best drawing-room comedy" (Sorell 299).

Joe Orton's farces are like Oscar Wilde's, George Bernard Shaw's, and Noel Coward's in forcing audiences to confront the schizophrenic patterns of their lives rather than avoiding these patterns. John Lahr says that this is one of the things that makes Joe Orton's farces special. They are filled with black humor, and they are irreverent in questioning basic social rules of behavior. Lahr says that Orton's farces are often parodies of farce in that they make use of their own "serious and sublime comic ends." According to Lahr, "farce is an act of literary aggression which Orton carried to its logical extreme--a battle of identity that makes a spectacle of disintegration. Orton saw farce as a way of making violence and frenzy into a resonant metaphor." Marty I. Casmus says that Orton, "found farce to be a genre more commodious for his vision of the world than any form of expression he could newly carve out. It was broad enough to contain both sides of his nature, the sunny as well as the dark and anarchic. And farce could be adorned, as Oscar Wilde had proven, with glittering language." John Russell Taylor says that Orton's plays are based in the genre of camp fantasy, but these plays completely transform this camp material into a serious view of life, a view that is eccentric and comic, but a view which also carries complete conviction about something felt to be true. Keath Fraser notes that Orton had a knack for parodying, "the manners which spring from an abyss between the characters' decorous language and their indecorous actions" (Lesniak 347). Harold Clurman says, "If you open your mouth in laughter at an Orton play, a spoonful of acid is dashed into it. His jokes are a preamble to murder" (Lesniak 348).

All of Orton's villains are sincere, and they all believe in their own innocence, but there is a gap between their actions and their words, and it is this gap that establishes Orton's work as "comedy of manners." "As his plays develop they reveal a widening of that gap as speech, through wit and epigram, becomes more polished and refined" (Hirst 99). In Orton's plays, physical violence tends to give way to wit and repartée (Hirst 100). Orton's plays were controversial, but they weren't controversial enough for Orton, who would write letters to the newspapers complaining about the obscenity of his own plays. He would write grotesquely exaggerated descriptions, and he would then sign the letters with names like "Edna Welthorp (Mrs)" (Esslin 106).

The Boy Hairdresser (1963) was originally delivered to the radio-drama department of the B.B.C. in a plain brown envelope marked "H. M. Prisons." This is because at the time Joe Orton was serving a sentence in prison for having defaced public library books. He had removed the plates from a number of art books, and he had replaced illustrations with pornographic substitutes, and then Orton and his friend, Kenneth Halliwell would watch the old ladies in the public library, enjoying their shock and their indignation (Esslin 96).

Entertaining Mr. Sloane (1964) is about a middle-aged brother, and his sister, who protect their father's murderer because he is attractive, and young, and they both want to sleep with him (Lesniak 347). It was Entertaining Mr. Sloane that established Joe Orton as a shocking and subversive writer. David Hirst feels that the disturbing qualities of this play lie as much in the language and style as in the violence of the action. In a surrealistic way, Entertaining Mr. Sloane presents an incongruity between the extraordinary and improper happenings and the unruffled propriety of the conversations of the various characters (Hirst 98). Although Entertaining Mr. Sloane has the external structure of a comedy, the mechanical natures of the characters, and the explicitness of the language clearly marks it as a farce (Esslin 100).

The Good and Faithful Servant (1964) is a realistic social drama with a touch of satire in the way that the personnel officer is caricatured; nevertheless, the central characters are puppets who may be operating in a realistic world, but who have their roots in the mechanical universe of farce (Esslin 101). The play is about Buchanan who has labored diligently for fifty years, after which his company gives him only a cheap toaster as a retirement gift. Mrs. Vealfoy is the source of much humor in the play, since she intrudes into every facet of the employees' lives. She arranges the marriage of Buchanan's grandson, Ray, to his pregnant girlfriend, Debbie, but only after Debbie has informed Ray that her pregnancy is not a very good reason to get married. Mrs. Vealfoy tells Ray to join the company's work-force and start assuming responsibility, and coordinates the recreational activities of retirees like Buchanan, introducing members to each other, and ensuring that people are properly socialized. She even interferes in people's private conversations as if she were a pre-school director. At the end of the play, it is Mrs. Vealfoy who gives Buchanan's eulogy.

Ruffian on the Stair (1964) is a revision of The Boy Hairdresser. It opens with the following dialogue:

> JOYCE: Have you got an appointment today?
> MIKE: Yes. I'm to be at Kings Cross station at eleven. I'm meeting a
> man in the toilet.
> JOYCE: You always go to such interesting places. (Esslin 98)

Ruffian on the Stair is about a young man whose brother is run down and killed by a van, probably driven by gangsters. Wilson is the name of the surviving brother, and he decides to get revenge on the murderer by pretending to make love to the murderer's mistress. He realizes that the jealous murderer will kill him, and this is his way of fulfilling two different objectives simultaneously--committing suicide, and having his brother's murderer hanged as a result. But this television play, which was made for the B.B.C. was designed as a practical joke, because Orton later said that "Auntie BBC" had not even suspected that the play was in fact about, "a sexual perversion so outrageous that not even the Irish had a name for it." This perversion was "homosexual incest," and the revealing lines in the original radio version read as follows: "His fiancée won't mind. She's off already with another man.... I was more intimate with him than she was. I used to base my life round him" (Esslin 95).

Loot (1965) is the most successful of Orton's plays because of its tight dramatic construction, and because it is deeply and consistently shocking. In the play, Fay, the nurse who has been looking after the ill Mrs. McLeavy, decides to murder her so that she can marry Mr. McLeavy. Hal and Dennis take Mrs. McLeavy's corpse out of its coffin and hide it in a cupboard, so that they can use the coffin to hide some money stolen from a bank. Dennis, Hal, Fay, and Truscott, a policeman, all agree to share the loot from the bank robbery, and it is ironic that the only character in the play who is not involved in the crime, old Mr. McLeavy, is the one who is arrested and has to be removed from the scene. Fay wants to have Mr. McLeavy murdered in prison, and asks Truscott if such a thing could be arranged in prison. Truscott responds that, "anything can be arranged in prison," but then Hal responds "except pregnancy," and Truscott has to admit that Hal is right--that the prison chaperon system "defeats us there." Once it is established that the police will murder Mr. McLeavy, we hear the following dialogue:

> HAL: (with a sigh). He is a nice man. Self-effacing in his way.

DENNIS: He has an open mind. In direct contrast to the usual run of civil servant.

HAL: It's comforting to know that the police can still be relied upon when we're in trouble. (They stand beside the coffin, Fay in the middle)

FAY: We'll bury your father with your mother. That will be nice for him, won't it? (Esslin 102)

Loot thus establishes, "a farcical universe with a vengeance and at its blackest" (Esslin 101), a "satire with a truly Swiftian acerbity and savage irony." The play has a tone of contempt and derision, and all of the characters in the play are derided equally. Orton was attempting to achieve his comic effects through the contrast between the coarseness of his subject matter and the refinement of the way it was expressed (Esslin 102). In Loot there is a balance of humor and seriousness, and the satiric purpose of the play is carefully calculated to grow into a "rapidly deepening black farce" (Hirst 97). Loot is a horror story about money, in which a coffin, and a corpse move nonchalantly around the stage. Here, Orton lampoons the establishment, the banks, and the police, as he takes great pleasure in following around a Scotland Yard inspector who is more interested in finding out who robbed the bank than in who committed the murder (Sorell 300). There is a humorous epigram in Loot when the police officer is told that the death certificate is perfectly legible, and he replies, "Reading isn't an occupation we encourage among police officers. We try to keep the paper work down to a minimum" (Sorell 299).

In Loot, Dennis urges Hal to lie, and Hal responds by saying, "I can't, baby, it's my upbringing" (Hirst 101). This leads to the following confrontation between Hal and Truscott, the police officer:

TRUSCOTT: Why do you make such stupid remarks?

HAL: I'm a stupid person. That's what I'm trying to say.

TRUSCOTT: What proof have I that you're stupid? Give me an example of your stupidity.

HAL: I can't

TRUSCOTT: Why not? I don't believe you're stupid at all.

HAL: I am. I had a hand in the bank job. Fay draws a sharp breath. Hal sits frozen. Truscott takes his pipe from his mouth. (with a nervous laugh) There, that's stupid, isn't it? Telling you that.

TRUSCOTT: (also laughing) You must be stupid if you expect me to believe you. Why, if you had a hand in the bank job, you wouldn't tell me.

FAY: Not unless he was stupid. (Hirst 102)

David Hirst feels that the inverted comic logic seen in this dialogue is Loot's most outstanding feature. Inverted comic logic can also be seen in Truscott's disguise. Since he doesn't have a search warrant, he must masquerade as a Water Board Inspector in order to gain entrance to the house, but his actions are not those of a Water Board Inspector, but rather those of a Policeman--which he is. As a policeman, Truscott is a perfect stereotype:

FAY: I'm innocent until I'm proved guilty.

TRUSCOTT: Who's been filling your head with that rubbish?

FAY: I can't be had for anything. You've no proof.

TRUSCOTT: When I make out my report I shall say that you've given me a confession. It could prejudice your case if I have to forge one. (Hirst 102-103)

The Erpingham Camp (1966) is a parody of The Bacchae by Euripides, rewritten in the setting of a British holiday camp. This was, by the way, a favorite target of topical satire during the 60s. The "inmates" of this holiday camp get out of control because of the incompetence of the entertainment manager, who is both too inexperienced and too clumsy to control the evening's floor show. Dionysus of Euripides's play became Chief Redcoat Riley in Orton's play, and Pentheus became Erpingham. Erpingham dies when the floorboards of his office give way and he drops down onto the dancers on the ballroom floor below (Esslin 103).

Funeral Games (1966) is a black farce in which the satire is directed at sanctimoniousness and religious zeal (Esslin 103). In Funeral Games, Pringle is a hilarious minister who wants to murder his wife Tessa because of her alleged adultery (Keller 805). In trying to kill his wife, Pringle, a minister, demonstrates his total disregard for Christian virtues. When Caulfield reminds Pringle to "love thy neighbor," Pringle responds, "The man who said that was crucified by his" (Orton Complete Plays 340). The rest of the play is about Pringle's attempts to prove to the world that he has indeed killed his wife, and that he is, therefore, a man of great integrity (Keller 806).

What the Butler Saw (1969) is a grotesque farce in the style of Feydeau which allows Orton to expose the absurdly authoritarian logic of the new welfare state which didn't relate to the material needs of its subjects (Orr 73). What the Butler Saw is set in a lunatic asylum and Dr. Prentice, a psychiatrist, is its central figure. Dr. Prentice interviews a young woman by the name of Geraldine Barclay, who has applied for a secretarial position, and of course Dr. Prentice could not employ a secretary unless he had first had carnal knowledge of her, so he orders her to undress. She is lying naked on the couch behind a curtain when Mrs. Prentice appears. Much of the play deals with attempts to conceal the naked girl behind the curtain, and to find clothes for her, and when the only clothes that could be found are those of Nick, the bell boy, there has to be an explanation of whether she is or is not a boy, and whether Nick is or is not a girl (Esslin 105). Much of the comedy comes from the exposure of transvestitism and nudity, but there is a deeper comic plot, since both Geraldine and Nick are in fact twins (note that this is an example of classical Plautean comedy of the separated twins), who were conceived by Mr. and Mrs. Prentice before they were married, in a linen cupboard at the Station Hotel, during a post-war power outage. Geraldine and Nick are therefore not only twin siblings, but they are also the children of Dr. and Mrs. Prentice, and each has had an incestuous relationship with their respective mother and father. Dr. Rance, the inspecting psychiatrist is overjoyed by this situation, since he is working on a book on mental illness, and he knows that this case history of double incest will make his book a best seller (Esslin 105). This plot is clearly farcical in nature, but it becomes even more farcical when we learn that Geraldine had been told that her foster-mother had been killed by a gas-main explosion in which a newly erected statue of Sir Winston Churchill had fallen on the woman. According to the story, the penis of the statue had penetrated Geraldine's mother's abdomen, and later the box which Geraldine had been carrying is found to contain the missing statue part. She had thought she was merely carrying a box of old clothes belonging to her foster-mother. It is interesting that in the 1969 performance of this play, the penis was changed into Churchill's famous cigar (Esslin 105-106). In What the Butler Saw, the doctors in the private clinic for the insane are the mad people (Sorell 300). What the Butler Saw opens with a conversation between Dr. Prentice and Geraldine. This conversation is indicative of Orton's desire to write in the stimulating, but artificial, manner that was typical of Oscar Wilde.

> PRENTICE: Who was your father? Put that at the head of the page. (Geraldine puts the cardboard box she is carrying to one side, crosses her legs, rests the notebook upon her knee and makes a note.) And now the reply immediately underneath for quick reference.
> GERALDINE: I've no idea who my father was. (Dr. Prentice is perturbed by her reply although he gives no evidence of this. He gives her a kindly smile.)

>PRENTICE: I'd better be frank, Miss Barkley. I can't employ you if you're in any way miraculous. It would be contrary to established practice. You did have a father?
>
>GERALDINE: Oh, I'm sure I did. My mother was frugal in her habits, but she'd never economize unwisely. (Hirst 106)

In What the Butler Saw, there are a number of humorous marital quarrels, such as the following, which begins with Mrs. Prentice giving a nervy toss of her head and taking a drink of whisky:

>PRENTICE: She's an example of in-breeding among the lobelia-growing classes. A failure in eugenics, combined with a taste for alcohol and sexual intercourse, makes it undesirable for her to become a mother.
>
>MRS. PRENTICE: (quietly) I hardly ever have sexual intercourse.
>
>PRENTICE: You were born with your legs apart. They'll send you to the grave in a Y-shaped coffin.
>
>MRS. PRENTICE: (with a brittle laugh) My trouble stems from your inadequacy as a lover! It's embarrassing. You must have learned your technique from a Christmas cracker.

David Hirst considers this type of repartee--intellectual in form, but vehement in feeling--to be similar to the repartee of George and Martha in Who's Afraid of Virginia Woolf? (Hirst 108). But Orton is not confined to repartee in his development of comic devices. Hirst feels that Orton is brilliant in his exploitation of the potential of disguise, mistaken identity and misunderstanding in the cleverly-timed entrances of his small group of characters. Orton uses the paraphernalia of farce in a way that can shock his readers (Hirst 109). According to Walter Sorell, a controlling theme of What the Butler Saw seems to be, "when the punishment for guilt or innocence is the same, it becomes an act of logic to commit the crime" (Sorell 299). Martin Esslin feels that What the Butler Saw is a farce which contains many allusions to mythology, to classical drama, and to the anthropology of The Golden Bough (Esslin 106).

Joe Orton's plays contain a great deal of violence, and it is therefore ironic that Joe Orton was himself brutally murdered at the pinnacle of his career, at the age of thirty-four. Orton had become a very successful author, and his success had caused him to grow away from Kenneth Halliwell, another writer with whom Orton had lived for fifteen years. Halliwell became desperate and killed Orton with a hammer in the same way that Orton's character Pringle had killed his wife in Funeral Games (1966). Then Halliwell took his own life with an overdose of nembutals. John Lahr wrote, "Their deaths confirmed the vision of Orton's comedy, that reality is the ultimate outrage. Their epitaph was Orton's plays: a heritage of laughter created out of a lifetime's hunger for revenge" (Lesniak 348).

Joe Orton (John Kingsley) Bibliography

Allen, M. D. "Joe Orton." Dictionary of Literary Biography, Volume Thirteen: British Dramatists Since World War II. Ed. Stanley Weintraub. Detroit, MI: Gale, 1982, 364-370.

Casmus, Mary I. "Farce and Verbal Style in the Plays of Joe Orton." Journal of Popular Culture 23 (1980): 461-468.

Dean, Joan F. "Joe Orton and the Redefinition of Farce." Theatre Journal 34 (1982): 481-492.

Draubt, Manfred. "Comic, Tragic, or Absurd? On Some Parallels between Farces of Joe Orton and Seventeenth-Century Tragedy." English Studies 59 (1978): 202-217.

Esslin, Martin. "Joe Orton: The Comedy of (Ill) Manners." Contemporary English Drama.

Ed. C. W. E. Bigsby. New York, NY: Holmes and Meier, 1981, 95-107.

Galassi, Frank S. "The Absurd Theatre of Joe Orton and N. F. Simpson." Unpublished
     Ph.D. Dissertation. New York, NY: New York University, 1971.

Hirst, David L. Comedy of Manners. New York, NY: Methuen, 1979.

Keller, James. "Joe Orton." Encyclopedia of British Humorists, Volume II. Ed. Steven H.
     Gale. New York, NY: Garland, 1996, 803-807.

Lesniak, James G. "Joe Orton." Contemporary Authors: New Revision Series, Volume 35.
     Detroit, MI: Gale Research, 1992, 346-348.

Marcus, Frank. "Comedy or Farce?" London Magazine 6 (February 1967): 73-77.

Orr, John. Tragicomedy and Contemporary Culture: Play and Performance from Beckett
     to Shepard. Ann Arbor, MI: University of Michigan Press, 1991.

Orton, Joe. The Complete Plays. New York, NY: Grove, 1977.

Smith, Leslie. "Democratic Lunacy: The Comedies of Joe Orton." Adam: International
     Review 394-396 (1976): 73-92.

Sorell, Walter. Facets of Comedy. New York, NY: Grosset and Dunlap, 1972.

Fay Weldon (1933-)

     Fay Weldon's writing demonstrates more than just an understanding of women's
issues. More importantly, it shows an appreciation for the plight of the individual woman
(Dear 451). Agate Nesaule Krouse says that Weldon's writing demonstrates, "a rich
rendering of life with brevity and wit." John Braine says that Weldon, "possesses that very
rare quality, a sardonic, earthy, disenchanted, slightly bitter but never cruel sense of
humour" (Dear 452). Weldon feels that art is "invention and distillation mixed"; she
furthermore feels that art is "fundamentally subversive." "Art given its subversive roots,
may well provide a more effective tool against the dominant order than politics, whose
fundamental nature is conservative" (Barreca 157). Helene Cixous and Catherine Clement
argue that women, "represent the eternal threat, the anti-culture" to men because they
challenge the male mental strategies of logic, reason, and nature (Cixous and Clement 67).
Comedy and power are intimately interconnected in Weldon's writing. "The power of
comedy is to undo expectations and revise women's view of themselves in the system"
(Barreca 160).

     Fay Weldon is like other women writers in that her comedy, "is characterized by
its refusal to supply conventional comedic closure and by its emphasis on the non-absolute
nature of the universe" (Barreca 147). In Weldon's writing there is a link between comedy,
anger, refusal, and rebellion, because she likes to write humorously about her "apocalyptic
rage" (Barreca 148). "Weldon is not of the let's-present-the-best-possible-images-of-the-
modern-woman school; her women are, well, no better than her men, although they are
usually more complex, interesting and important. Her novels are intricate weavings of
politics, aphoristic commentary, romance and satire" (Barreca 150).

     Weldon's satire is wide ranging. She satirizes high culture ("museums will be very
boring places indeed. If you want to subdue the children you only have to take them on
a visit to a museum, and they will behave at once, for fear of being taken there again"), and
she also satirizes low culture ("there will be elections, but people will be expected merely
to vote for people they personally like. It will be a popularity contest. An annual 'boy or
girl most likely to run the country' jamboree")(Barreca 151). Some critics have described
Weldon's comedy as an exaggerated and humorously distorted picture of our culture;
however Regina Barreca says that it offers an, "unnervingly accurate portrait of
contemporary life." Barreca compares Weldon's humor to that of other women writers,
saying that in both cases the humor is at first presented as hyperbolic ("men pass women

around"), and this hyperbole is then associated with low-class society; but in the development of the humor, the hyperbolic notions are found to be not hyperbolic at all, but normal. "What is perceived as exaggeration is actually the product of an uncensored vision; the lower types are indeed running the system" (Barreca 152). One of the most significant aspects of Weldon's comic writing is her refusal, "to accept finality, even the finality of death or marriage." Weldon's novels frequently end with the dissolution of marriage, or with the defeat of reason, or with the triumph of the female Lucifer, or with the abandonment of children, or with the, "laying to rest of a ghost" (Barreca 152).

Fay Weldon's first novel, The Fat Woman's Joke (1967) was later published as And the Wife Ran Away (1968). In The Fat Woman's Joke, Esther says to Phyllis that, "Any woman who struggles to be accepted in a man's world makes herself ridiculous. It is a world of folly, fantasy and self-indulgence and it is not worth aspiring to. We must create our own world" (Joke 83).

For Weldon there is no such thing as "just a joke." In Down Among the Women (1971), when Weldon says, "I was only joking," she wasn't joking at all. "Joking is an important business for the very fact that comedy is part of the survival process for women" (Barreca 160). Down Among the Women is about a twenty-one-year-old unwed mother named Scarlet, who misinterprets her own feelings for Edwin, a man who is nearly forty years her senior. When she kisses him she feels something, but Weldon tells us, "it is not desire that is stirred, it is her imagination; but how can she know this? She feels she loves him. When she thinks of him kissing her, she is simply enchanted" (Women 110). In Down Among the Women, Weldon warns us all, "we see the world as we are taught to see it, not how it is" (Women 34). This implies that women are taught to find old men attractive, and tend to seek them out and then rationalize about their attraction (Barreca 149). The following anecdote appears in Down Among the Women. "Reminds me of the story of Royalty visiting the maternity hospital. Royalty inclines towards young mother. 'What lovely red hair baby has, mother. Does he take after his father?' Answer: 'Don't know, ma'am, he never took his hat off' " (Women 21). Barreca suggests that the target of this joke is not the sexually active and socially marginal woman, but is rather the authority figure who made her pregnant (Barreca 152). Down Among the Women demonstrates Weldon's ability to blend the terrible and the ridiculous, which explains why her novels, which are so filled with the pain endured by women are neither painfully depressing nor cheerfully sentimental (Dear 452).

In Female Friends (1974) when Gwyneth uses the expression, "You have to laugh...it's a funny old life," the third-person narrator responds with an ironic "Ha-ha" (Friends 47). Gwyneth is using this phrase in a way the system wants her to use it, to justify her own powerlessness (Barreca 150). Weldon often inverts normal happy endings. We can even applaud Chloe's abandonment of her husband at the end of Female Friends. Chloe is triumphant because she finally stops understanding and forgiving her narcissistic husband (Barreca 159). She says, "As for me, I no longer wait to die. I put my house...in order, and not before time. The children help. Oliver says, 'But you can't leave me with Françoise.' and I reply, 'I can, I can, and I do' " (Friends 331). Chloe's laughter at the end of Female Friends is the laugh of Medusa. It is also the laugh of Media and of Clytemnestra. But even more, it is the laugh of every woman escaping from any form of confinement. "Chloe finds she is laughing, not hysterically, or miserably, but really quite lightly and merrily; and worse, not with Oliver, but at him, and in this she is, at last, in tune with the rest of the universe" (Friends 259). Seven pages later, Weldon does a second-take. "Is she laughing at him?" And then she answers, "Yes, she is. Her victory is complete" (Friends 267). L. E. Sissman says that in Female Friends, Weldon uses "wry, cool, concise" words to develop a, "gritty replication of the gross texture of everyday life" (Dear 452).

In Remember Me (1976) the apparent vigor of the world of men pales in contrast to the real vigor of the world of women which she writes about. "Affairs of state...are child's play compared to the affairs of the home...of the intricacies of a marriage and the marriage bed" (Remember Me 203). In an interview with Regina Barreca on January 14, 1992, Weldon said, "If a corporation had to decide at what point it was feasible for a small child to ride its bicycle in the road, they would hire a dozen consultants and probably be unable to arrive at any conclusion" (Barreca 155). This illustrates a principle of women's humor developed by Nancy Walker, "Men are nearly extraneous to the 'real' lives of women; their experiences outside the home are so remote as to seem nonexistent, and their lives within the orbit of the home are trivial, insignificant, or mysterious" (Walker 13). Speaking of Remember Me, Phyllis Birnbaum says that, "precise satire, impassioned monologue, and a sense of limited human possibility make this novel a daring examination of twentieth-century discontent" (Dear 452).

In Little Sisters (1977) it is acknowledged that society considers men to be more privileged than women, but it is also shown that there is a way of inverting the system. Elsa realizes that sex outside the rules laid down for women's morality can sometimes prove to be fortifying rather than depleting, exhilarating rather than shameful (Barreca 153). Elsa says, "Man! Come to bed. Handsome, young, rich, powerful, or otherwise fortunate-- is that you? Excellent? Come inside. Because what I know and perhaps you don't is that by some mysterious but certain process of osmosis I will thereupon draw something of these qualities into myself...gaining my pleasure through your loss" (Sisters 134).

In Praxis (1978) Weldon says that society uses the expression "the nature of things" to keep women in their place. "It is nature, they say, that makes us get married. Nature, they say, that makes us crave to have babies.... It's nature that makes us love our children, clean our houses, gives us a thrill of pleasure when we please the home-coming male," but then she asks, "Who is this Nature? Nature does not know best, or if it does, it is on the man's side" (Praxis 147). Barreca notes that here Weldon is using a device often used by women authors--introducing a cliché of societal expectations, and then undercutting this cliché (Barreca 156). In Praxis, Weldon suggests that there are a number of different legitimate worlds, "each with its different ways and standards, its different framework of normality" (Praxis 190). Barreca says that it is this recognition that often leads to laughter at the standards that are arbitrarily imposed on women and the women who can never quite meet these standards (Barreca 157).

One of the messages in Praxis is that our society teaches women to fear independence. They are also taught to identify with, to desire, and to try to please men, even at the same time that they fear them. And our society teaches women to be very competitive with each other in their attempts to gain the favors of men (Barreca 149). "We betray each other. We manipulate, through sex: we fight each other for possession of the male--snap, catch, swallow, gone! Where's the next? We will quite deliberately make our sisters jealous and wretched" (Praxis 229).

At the end of Praxis there is an old woman with a broken leg who is able to laugh in delight at her own triumph. "Even here, in this horrible room, hungry and in pain, helpless, abandoned by the world in general and the social worker in particular, I can feel joy, excitation and exhilaration. I changed the world a little: yes, I did. Tilted it, minutely, on its axis. I, Praxis Duveen" (Praxis 50). Katha Pollitt sees Praxis as a collection of vignettes, polemics, epigrams which are often dazzling, and which describe the mad underbelly of our sexual politics, "with a venomous accuracy for which wit is far too mild a word" (Dear 452).

The first half of The Life and Loves of a She-Devil (1983) is an exercise in feminist thought. Fay Weldon says about the novel, "It's the feminist manifesto really: a woman must be free, independent and rich. But I found myself asking, what then? I think women are discovering that liberation isn't enough. The companionship of women is not enough. The other side of their nature is unfulfilled" (Dear 453).

The basic theme of The Life and Loves of a She-Devil is explained in the following quote from the novel: "She laughed and said she was taking up arms against God Himself. Lucifer had tried and failed, but he was male. She thought she might do better" (Barreca 147). In this novel Ruth says that women are not only denied easy access to traditional authority; they are even excluded from existence by our English language. As she says, "we are powerless, and poor, and have no importance. We are not even included in 'everyone' " (She-Devil 83). In The Life and Loves of a She-Devil, Ruth is a sorceress, and she explains how she works at this occupation:

> I make puff pastry for the chicken vol-au-vents, and when I have finished circling out the dough with the brim of a wine-glass, making wafer rounds, I take the thin curved strips of cutter left behind and mold them into a shape much like the shape of Mary Fisher, and turn the oven high, high, and crisp the figure in it until such a stench fills the kitchen that even the fan cannot remove it. (She-Devil 10)

Barreca feels that the humor in this passage is Weldon's humor at its best. She is irreverent toward domesticity and she is shamelessly furious, but at the same time she relates everything in deadpan-clean prose (Barreca 158).

In The Life and Loves of a She-Devil, Ruth loses her husband to a beautiful romance novelist, so she turns against her husband, the novelist, and everyone else who gets in her way. She undergoes extensive surgery to make her, "the very image of the former competitor." She can now begin a new life with her former husband. Carol E. Rinzler writes that "what makes this a powerfully funny and oddly powerful book is the energy that vibrates off the pages." Sybil Steinberg says the novel is filled with, "biting satire of the war between the sexes, indicting not only the male establishment's standards of beauty and feminine worthiness, but also women's own willngness to subscribe to these standards" (Dear 453).

Polaris and Other Stories (1985) is a serious, yet witty, collection of short stories (Dear 455). The Shrapnel Academy (1986) is a novel about war. The academy is named after H. Shrapnel, the British general who gave his name to the pre-World-War-I exploding artillery shell. Sarah Edworthy says that this novel is in, "quirky top form: clever, relevant, always entertaining" (Dear 453). The Heart of the Country (1987) is a satirical novel about suburban English life. Sonia, the narrator, tells the sad tale of Natalie Harris, a woman who used to be young, beautiful, and wealthy, and who used to have a nice home, "tractable" husband, and a two-day-a-week affair with an antiques dealer. But her husband is also having an affair, and he leaves Natalie to run off to Spain. So Natalie, who has now lost everything, takes up with Angus, a married man, and she exchanges sex for a job and a furnished flat. The men throughout the novel tend to be villains, and some critics say the book has a "comic-book flavor," a "willfully playful point of view," and a "silly parodic ending" (Dear 454).

Leader of the Band (1988) is a fairy tale for adults, but it also contains bits of serious thought, and messages throughout. One reviewer wrote that, "the tongue-in-cheek delivery betrays the serious thought as the frosting on the comic cake" (Dear 454). The Cloning of Joanna May (1989) is considered by Richard Eder as "faintly loony, more than faintly disquieting, and exceedingly talky satire" (Dear 454). After reading this book, Ursula K. Le Guin said that Fay Weldon, "may not be our Jane Austen, but she is making a pretty good showing as our Swift" (Dear 454).

Darcy's Utopia (1990) is about Apricot Smith who changed her name to Eleanor Darcy. Apricot Smith had been named after the color of her mother's nylon nightie. Eleanor Darcy wanted to change more than just her name. She also wanted to abolish money, and she wanted all motherhood to be preapproved by a committee of ten neighbors. She also advocated the pursuit of religion only at home, and the making, but not airing, of television programs (Dear 454).

Regina Barreca considers Darcy's Utopia (1991) to be a disturbing and fascinating comic novel which requires enormous attention. Weldon's humor, "laces these pages in a particularly wicked manner, because it plays on the role of the reader as well as the roles of the character" (Barreca 150-151). This novel is an ironic tour-de-force in which Eleanor's closest friend tells some journalists that it's, "hard to tell when she's joking and when she isn't" (Utopia 188). Regina Barreca notes that this comment is similar to a phrase in the last line of She-Devil, where she talks about, "A comic turn, turned serious" (She-Devil 241).

Moon over Minneapolis, or Why She Couldn't Stay (1991) is a collection of short stories that is both serious and witty (Dear 455). Tom Shone says that Weldon's Life Force (1992), "resembles every other Weldon novel in almost every respect--a picaresque plot that has several women dancing around a single devilish man, a bit of nudity (always 'unabashed'), some whimsical paragraph breaks, some breathless exclamation marks, and, above all, Weldon's Momsy chats with the reader." Michael Malone says about Life Force that it is, "a parable about the act of creativity" (Dear 454-455).

Fay Weldon Bibliography

Barreca, Regina. " 'Let Us Now Praise Fallen Women': Hate and Humor in Fay Weldon's Novels." Untamed and Unabashed: Essays on Women and Humor in British Literature. Detroit, MI: Wayne State University Press, 1994, 147-161.

Cixous, Helene, and Catherine Clement. The Newly Born Woman. Trans. Betsy Wing. Theory and History of Literature: 24. Minneapolis, MN: University of Minnesota Press, 1987.

Dear, Pamela S. "Fay Weldon." Contemporary Authors, New Revision Series, Volume 46. Detroit, MI: Gale Research, 1995, 449-455.

Walker, Nancy. A Very Serious Thing: Women's Humor and American Culture. Minneapolis, MN: University of Minnesota Press, 1988.

Weldon, Fay. Darcy's Utopia. New York, NY: Viking, 1991.

Weldon, Fay. Down Among the Women. Chicago, IL: Academy Chicago Publishers, 1984.

Weldon, Fay. The Fat Woman's Joke. London, England: Coronet, 1982.

Weldon, Fay. Female Friends. New York, NY: St. Martin's Press, 1974.

Weldon, Fay. The Life and Lovers of a She-Devil. New York, NY: Pantheon, 1984.

Weldon, Fay. Little Sisters. London, England: Hodder and Stoughton, 1977.

Weldon, Fay. Praxis. New York, NY: Sommit Books, 1978.

Weldon, Fay. Remember Me. New York, NY: Random House, 1976.

Edward Bond (1934-)

Edward Bond writes in the tradition of "theatre of ideas." Some critics describe him as "deliberately confusing," others describe him as "overly simplistic," some as "daringly innovative," and others as "deeply conventional." Edward Bond is an enigma (Spencer 123). In Bond's works can be found elements of the social comedy, the Noh-play, the parable, the epic, the history play, the tragedy, etc. (Spencer 124).

Early Morning (1968) is a farce in which Queen Victoria, and a lesbian by the name of Florence Nightingale, and Prince Albert, and Benjamin Disraeli are all trying to destroy each other. Their attack continues into the afterlife (Lesniak and Trosky 60). Laughter in the Dark (1969) is based on a novel by Vladimir Nabokov. The message of Bingo: Scenes of Money and Death (1971) is that if a person is an unjust person, it doesn't matter how cultured or civilized this person is, or how capable of being witty or producing wonderful jokes. Regardless of how a person looks on the surface, if a person is unjust, he will destroy himself (Lesniak and Trosky 61).

In Edward Bond's Lear (1971), the evil that the title character suffers is more horrifying than that of Shakespeare's King Lear because it is the result not of individual greed, but of, "society's collective renunciation of all natural human compassion." There is an "aprostophized humor," but otherwise it is a downbeat and grueling allegorical drama (Lesniak and Trosky 61). The Sea (1973) is a comedy that has a wider range of emotion than can be found in Bond's earlier plays. There are two scenes that are especially lively and comic in this play (Lesniak and Trosky 61).

In The Fool (1975), Bond examines the ambivalent position of the writer in society in describing the life of John Clare (Spencer 134). Clare's role as a poet is supposed to make him free, but instead it causes his lack of freedom. In Scene 5, it is the poet Lamb who is able to see that the language he uses prevents him from being understood. His role as an artist prevents him from being taken seriously, so that Mrs. Emmerson responds, "I'm proud to say I didn't understand a single word. Mr. Lamb, you're a poet. You have no call to go round putting ideas in people's heads" (Spencer 136).

Edward Bond Bibliography

Lesniak, James G., and Susan M. Trosky. "Edward Bond." Contemporary Authors, New Revision Series, Volume 38. Detroit, MI: Gale Research, 58-62.
Spencer, Jenny S. "Edward Bond's Dramatic Strategies." Contemporary English Drama. Ed. C. W. E. Bigsby, 1981, 123-137.

Aidan Chambers (Malcolm Blacklin) (1934-)

Aidan Chambers was somewhat of a loner. Nevertheless, Marion Rose was his bosom friend from the time they were in their prams until much later (Nakamura 37). As Chambers was growing up, the highlight of each week was when the council midden men came by to empty out the netties--outdoor toilets. They came up the back allies with their lorry, and raised the little door just at ground level, and shovelled the dung into their lorry. When they were finished, they threw a handful of lime onto the dung and moved on to the next house (Nakamura 38). While this was being done, all of the residents except for Aidan and Marion stayed indoors. In contrast, Aidan and Marion watched with fascinated interest, keeping as close to the men as they could, and being careful to remain upwind at all times. Then Aidan was given a quarter-sized wheel barrow as a Christmas present, and Aidan stole some flour out of the pantry, and Aidan and Marion decided to go out and clean the outdoor toilets on their own. They used their seaside spades and began to fling the dung into their wheel barrow, and cover it with the flour (surrogate lime) with great panache. Whenever the wheel barrow became full, they dumped the contents out in a vacant lot. They went all the way from House 20 to House 16 before they were discovered, but at House 16 they opened the hatch and were greeted with a scream from inside. They were undone (Nakamura 39).

Aidan didn't learn to read at first, and he called one of his teachers "a sadist." This teacher had all of the students take a book home every Friday and return it on Monday. When they brought the books back, the teacher never asked them anything about what they had read. But one evening in early 1944, Aidan looked at the book which he had brought home. He was sitting beside the kitchen stove, and his father was sitting at the other side of the stove reading a newspaper. His mother was busily ironing. All of a sudden, as he was trying to figure out the words on the page he heard voices speaking in his head. The voices were coming out of the printed words and they seemed to be talking to each other and telling a story. Aidan sat amazed as he listened to this drama which was set on a desert island and was quite adventurous. At this point, he heard his father say to his mother, "Why is he still up at this hour?" and his mother replied, "Shut up, you fool, can't you see what he's doing?" (Nakamura 42).

In 1970, Aidan and Nancy Chambers established "Thimble Press." The name is a perfect example of English understatement, since it is both modest and feminine. The press was designed to publish the magazine Signal, and whatever else might eventually be added to its list. In 1975 Aidan became bored with writing in the voice of young people and began to write in his own voice. "What I was doing had ceased to be for those pupils I used to teach and had become hackery" (Nakamura 51). "Ordering myself about like an angry school teacher, I grabbed a brand-new notebook, a brand new pencil (I usually typed everything I wrote), sat myself in an easy chair (I usually sat at a desk), and told myself to write the first thing that came into my head and to go on till I told myself to stop" (Nakamura 52). Johnny Salter (1966) is a two-and-a-half-hour comic play (Nakamura 49).

The first authorial words which Aidan Chambers wrote in his own voice were "'Literature is crap,' said Morgan." He didn't know who Morgan was. He didn't know what Morgan was talking about, or what was happening, but he kept putting onto the paper everything that came into his head. After an hour and a half, he had written a few pages. The scene was incomprehensible, but he knew it involved two boys, Morgan, and another boy he didn't know the name of, so he called him "Ditto." "These pages written out of a kind of psychic shock became, with slow and interrupted process over the next two years, the book I regard as the first of my own, the novel Breaktime (1978).

The construction of Breaktime is similar to that of James Joyce's Ulysses in that it is an account of a young man's holiday in the English countryside. Breaktime is a tour de farce, but it is more than that. Richard Yates says that Chambers's verbal tricks in Breaktime, "come close to swamping the novel." Yates adds that Chambers, "is attempting to write a Joycean novel as an adolescent would, with all the energy and none of the moderation of age." Margery Fisher writes that Breaktime is written "with humour and wit, with ingenuity and candour, and adds that, "the author has offered one piece of one kind of truth in a spirit of technical and emotional investigation" (Telgen 61).

Margery Fisher considers Dance on My Grave (1982) to be, "a book that makes its point through raucous humour and implied feeling, through the sharp observation of a boy and his blundering apprehensions of the way others observe him" (Telgen 61). A reviewer named Cech says that Booktalk: Occasional Writing on Children and Literature (1985) is "chock-full of good ideas." He continues that it is, "insightful, patient, funny, moving, and always aware of the authors and readers who are taking part in the dialogue of its pages" (Telgen 61).

Aidan Chambers (Malcolm Blacklin) Bibliography

Nakamura, Joyce. "Aidan Chambers." Something about the Author. Detroit, MI: Gale, 1991, 37-55.

Olendorf, Donna, ed. "Aidan Chambers." Something about the Author, Volume 69. Detroit, MI: Gale Research, 1992, 29-33.

Telgen, Diane. "Aidan Chambers." Contemporary Authors: New Revision Series, Volume 31. Ed. James G. Lesniak. Detroit, MI: Gale, 1990, 60-61.

Trevor Griffiths (Ben Rae) (1935-)

According to Christian W. Thomsen, Trevor Griffiths is a socialist playwright whose plays are multi-layered, and whose technique relies on multiple perspectives (Thomsen 172). Trevor Griffiths has a predilection for ambiguous titles as can be seen by the double meaning in the title of the play The Party (1973), a double meaning which throws an ironic slant on a play which, "alternates between seriousness, comedy, frustration, and impotence" (Thomsen 172). The Party is filled with clever puns, nicely coined phrases, and, "convincing aphorisms of a kind which show Griffiths to be a master of language." There is a prevailing irony in The Party which makes the speeches and statements a bit inconclusive. In The Party, there is a comprehensive analysis of the Left that is imbedded in the, "complex structures of present-day society" (Thomsen 173). The end of the play echoes the prologue, in which the melancholy clown says, "Je suis Marxiste, Tendance Groucho" (Thomsen 174).

Trevor Griffiths is very fond of stand-up comedy, and his Comedians (1975) is a play about comedy and about comedians. One of the functions of the play is to be a tribute to the forms of entertainment that are associated with working-class culture. In the play there is a class which teaches about comic methods. Waters, a veteran comedian, is the teacher in the class, and there are six students. Waters explains to his students that he stopped being a comedian and became a teacher because he was "afraid of success." Waters considers comedy to be a cathartic way of liberating the fears and anxieties of the audience, a way that is free from prejudice, clichés, or hardened patterns of thinking. The play has a number of racial stereotypes, and is filled with sophisticated humor, such as Gethin Price's tragi-comic mime, which is presented in the style of Grock. But the mime collapses into violence as he plays the role of a football hooligan and attacks two dummies who are dressed up as members of the bourgeoisie. Price also approaches a lady and wants to pin a marigold between her breasts. He does so, and then steps back to look at his work, saying, "No need for thanks. My pleasure entirely. Believe me." But then there is silence as a dark red stain suddenly appears beneath the flower and gets bigger and bigger. Price remarks, "Aagh, aagh, aagh, aagh." This is the type of humor which borders between, "comedy, black humour, and anarchic madness" (Thomsen 174).

Most critics regard Comedians as Griffiths's best play. Comedians is a comedy about comedy and politics, but it is also a comedy about life. It focuses on six comedians who graduate from a comedy program, and do their debut performances in a Manchester working men's club. A conflict develops between their teacher and a talent scout, who have differing conceptions of comedy; in the comedian's various nightclub routines, he exposes various aspects of humanity. Clive Barnes called Comedians one of the funniest comedies to appear in some time, and described it as, "comedy with an esthetic, moral, and above all, political purpose. Martin Gottfried claimed that Griffiths, "has warmth, he has vigor, he has an affirming attitude. In this play he is affirming quality above shoddiness, high standards not just in stand-up comedy but of course in all of art and finally in all of life" (Cuthbertson 167).

Trevor Griffiths (Ben Rae) Bibliography

Cuthbertson, Ken. "Trevor Griffiths." Contemporary Authors, New Revision Series, Volume 45. Eds. James P. Draper and Susan M. Trosky. Detroit, MI: Gale Research, 1995): 165-168.

Thomsen, Christian W. "Three Socialist Playwrights: John McGrath, Caryl Churchill, Trevor Griffiths." Contemporary English Drama. Ed. C. W. E. Bigsby. New York, NY: Holmes and Meier, 1981, 157-176.

David (John) Lodge (1935-)

David Lodge's novels tend to be set in the academic world. They tend to employ "metafictional games," and "stylistic experiments." And their structure and details tend to come from one or more works in the canon of English literature. Therefore, their greatest appeal is to an academic audience (Mellown 694). Elgin Mellown lists the following as humorous David-Lodge novels: The British Museum Is Falling Down (1965), Changing Places: A Tale of Two Campuses (1975), How Far Can You Go? (1980), Small World (1984), Nice Work (1988), and Paradise News (1991). The Picturegoers (1960), Ginger, You're Barmy (1962), and Out of the Shelter (1970) are serious or realistic novels, in which the comedy is incidental rather than a structural element of the plot. In all of his novels, Lodge makes use of humor only when it is pertinent to the real-life situations, but it is these real-life situations that really concern him. Much of the humor in his humorous novels comes from Lodge's specialized knowledge of English literature, the same knowledge that he uses in his scholarly works (Mellown 692). Lodge's university characters are usually individual with comic eccentricities that are especially appreciated by readers who are aware of the archetypes they represent. Unlike Kingsley Amis, whose university characters are drawn in broad strokes, and represent stereotypes to be mocked and satirized, Lodge likes to depict more specific characters and situations (Mellown 695). Michael Rosenthal says that David Lodge is a novelist whose themes tend to be exuberant and "marvelously funny" (qtd. in Marecki 298). David Lodge assesses his own writing as follows:

> I don't think the novels are destructive satires, but they are undermining the accepted pretensions of scholarship. Any institution or profession is likely to claim an exaggerated importance for itself. I see comedy as a way of puncturing that, and I think it's what comedy always has done. It's done it to politicians and journalists and all kinds of other professions as well as academics. (Marecki 301)

The Picturegoers (1960) focuses mostly on Michael Underwood, a promising young literature student who has fallen away from the church. During the last part of his schooling, Michael boards with the Mallory family and falls in love with Clare Mallory, a former convent novice. As Michael tries to seduce Clare, she tries to reawaken Michael's faith. The ironic conclusion to the novel is that Clare falls in love with Michael and offers herself to him, but he rejects her advances "in order to join the priesthood." Maurice Richardson says that a lot of The Picturegoers is "quite funny" (Marecki 298).

The British Museum Is Falling Down (1965) is the first of the, "highly comic, satiric novels which were to become David Lodge's trademark." A theme which recurs in this and other Lodge novels is about a sincere Catholic struggling with the difficulties imposed on him by the rigid doctrines of the church, especially the problems connected with the "rhythm" method of birth control. The novel depicts one day in the life of Adam Appleby, a graduate student who is already the father of three children because he couldn't master the rhythm method. When Adam awakes on the day that the novel tells about, Adam's wife, Barbara, tells Adam that she may again be pregnant, and this sends Adam out into a day of pandemonium similar to that of Leopold Bloom in James Joyce's Ulysses. Lodge has the ability to blend humor and serious matters that is described by one critic as "unceasingly and vigorously funny." But this same critic continues,

> yet throughout the book serious undertones give emphasis and point to the author's general levity. His comic and satiric treatment of the current Catholic indecision over family planning is not a frontal attack on the church itself but rather a good-natured tickling meant to evoke laughter and a serious new consideration of the effect of the Catholic ban on artificial

contraception on couples such as the Applebys. (Marecki 299)

When Adam gets to the museum, he is so preoccupied with the possibility of his wife's fourth pregnancy, that he doesn't watch where he is going, and is knocked to the floor. When he gets knocked to the floor a second time, he considers having a nervous breakdown as a solution to his problems, but thinks this solution might be too drastic. Then he considers getting a special dispensation from the pope to practice artificial conception, or if this dispensation was not granted, when he died he imagined that his tragic case could be brought to the attention of the Vatican Council, and, "the doctrine of Natural Law revised as a result" (Lodge British 54).

One of the strongest characters in The British Museum Is Falling Down is the British Museum itself. To Adam, the Museum is a woman, both a wife and a mother. It is a symbol of fertility. It is pregnant with scholars. The scene of Adam going into the Reading Room, reads as follows: "He passed through the narrow vaginal passage, and entered the huge womb of the Reading Room. Across the floor, dispersed along the radiating desks, scholars curled, foetus-like, over their books, little buds of intellectual life thrown off by some gigantic act of generation performed upon that nest of knowledge, those inexhaustible ovaries of learning, the concentric inner rings of the catalogue shelves" (Lodge British 50).

The British Museum Is Falling Down is a parody of a Romance. At a party, Adam places a finger in his ear to answer the phone.

> As he walked unsteadily away from the phone, the people in the corridor falling back before him, he thought of himself as a man set apart by a dangerous quest. For what was that house in Bayswater, dismal of aspect and shrouded in fog, with its mad, key-rattling old queen, raven-haired, honey-tongued daughter, and murderous minions insecurely pent in the dungeon below, but a Castle Perilous from which, mounted on his trusty scooter, he, intrepid Sir Adam, sought to snatch the unholy grail of Egbert Merrymarch's scrofulous novel? If the success of his quest, contrary to the old story, necessitated his fall from grace in the arms of the seductive maiden [A virgin named "Virginia"], then so much the better. He had had enough of continence. (Lodge British 141)

The structure of The British Museum Is Falling Down is based on James Joyce's Ulysses. It is the story of a Ph.D. candidate in English Literature (Adam Appleby) who is writing his dissertation in the Reading Room of the British Museum (Mellown 694). Adam Appleby is the modern equivalent of Leopold Bloom, and his wife Barbara is the equivalent of Molly. Barbara, like Molly, must remain at home during her husband's wanderings, and the novel ends with a monologue that is a parody of the Penelope section of Joyce's novel. When Adam's fellow students accuse Appleby of no longer being able to distinguish between life and literature, Lodge is telling a metafictional joke at his own expense, as Adam defends himself by saying, "Literature is mostly about having sex and not much about having children. Life is the other way round" (Lodge British 50). In the 1981 edition of The British Museum Is Falling Down, Lodge identifies a number of literary references, and names ten different authors he parodies, including not only Joyce, but Baron Corvo, Virginia Woolf, Graham Greene, and especially Henry James (Mellown 695). The result is a kind of parody literary pastiche. "There was, in particular, the danger of puzzling and alienating the reader who wouldn't recognize the allusions. My aim was to make the narrative and its frequent shifts of style fully intelligible and satisfying to such a reader, while offering the more literary reader the extra entertainment of spotting the parodies" (Lodge British xix).

In Out of the Shelter (1970), Timothy's observations often produce a wry or sardonic smile from the reader. In this novel, the contrast between the innocent and sheltered sixteen-year-old narrator, and the situations he finds himself in, sets Lodge up for his comic slant on life (Mellown 693).

Elgin Mellown says that the primary allusion in Changing Places: A Tale of Two Campuses (1975) is to Aspects of the Novel (1927) by E. M. Forster. The novel is about a university exchange program in which the aggressive and flamboyant Morris Zapp leaves his position at the State University of Euphoria, which is located in Plotinus (actually Berkeley, California) just across the bay from "Esseph" (San Francisco) in order to trade places with a timid and unambitious Philip Swallow from the University of Rummidge in the English Midlands. The English city of Rummidge is large and industrial, and is located at the intersection of three motorways, twenty-six railway lines and six stagnant canals (Mellown 696). Zapp and Swallow exchange cars, homes, and even wives. Before the switch, both Zapp and Swallow had suffered from failing marriages and uninspiring careers, but each person flourishes in his new surroundings and new identity. Neil Hepburn says that, "no funnier or more penetrating account of the special relationship is likely to come your way for a long time" (Marecki 299). Much of the humor of Changing Places comes from seeing the Englishman's point of view projected onto the American landscape, and vice versa. In discussing the laughter in Changing Places, Isaac Asimov says that some of it comes from feeling superior to the people in the joke, and some comes from the sudden realization of incongruity, or sudden relief from tension, or a sudden reinterpretation of events (Lafuente 227). Mellown indicates that Changing Places is more of a caricature of academic life than it is a satire of this life. Mellown says that Lodge is an "internationalist" who sees that students on both sides of the Atlantic behave in equally irrational ways. Although the behaviors may be different, they are equally ridiculous whether it happens in California or in England (Mellown 697).

How Far Can You Go? (1980) was published in the United States under the title of Souls and Bodies (1982). This novel is about the sexual and religious evolution of a group of English Catholics, characters who are treated by Lodge in a comic fashion (Marecki 299). About this book, Le Anne Schreiber says, "Mr. Lodge has written a book full of his own energy, intelligence, wit, compassion and anger" (Marecki 300). The real hero of this novel is the pill, and Nicholas Shrimpton says, "Lodge's picture of these couples struggling to come to terms with it [the pill] hovers delicately between tragedy and farce" (Marecki 300). How Far Can You Go? is about a group of young Catholic students at the University of London. The humor of the novel comes chiefly from the sexual dilemmas these devout Catholics face. Even though their sexual inclinations range widely, they all share the inhibitions instilled in them by the Catholic Church. Lodge has all of the members of the group tell about their sexual experiences over the past twenty-five years of great religious change, and by doing this he can humorously present the stark contrast between sexual attitudes of 1950 and those of 1975 (Mellown 697). Lodge tells about a Catholic couple of 1953 that are so inexperienced and inhibited that they have trouble consummating their relationship. The husband suggests that some ointment would help: "She did, as it happened, have some Vaseline with her, which she used for the preventing of chapped lips. Applied to her nether lips it produced almost magical results. Afterwards, Michael put his hands behind his head and smiled beatifically at the ceiling. 'From now on,' he said, 'I'm always going to give Vaseline for wedding presents'" (Lodge Changing 64).

Even though Lodge describes a variety of sexual scenes in How Far Can You Go? his sense of humor keeps the scenes from becoming lascivious or pornographic. Lodge is discussing how sexual license in the Roman Catholic church changes over time, and his emphasis on religious values gives the events a sense of depth and meaning to the events that could otherwise be viewed as ridiculous. For example Ruth, who obtains permission to visit various Catholic orders, finds herself in California where she becomes involved in strikes by exploited workers who refer to the police as "Mean-looking mothers." Because of Ruth's upbringing in the Catholic Church, she interpreted this term of abuse to be a shortened form of "Mother Superiors" (Mellown 698).

In Small World: An Academic Romance (1984), the reader is reintroduced to Morris Zapp and Philip Swallow (from Changing Places), and of course Small World is another campus novel. But in Small World, Zap and Swallow are only two of the many characters who jet around the world from one academic conference to the next, in search of glory, and romantic encounters. Each of them would also like to become the UNESCO chair of literary criticism, because this is a position which carries with it virtually no responsibilities, and a $100,000 tax-free salary. Michael Rosenthal says that this novel is "exuberant," and "marvelously funny," and that it, "demonstrates [that] no one is better able to treat the peripatetic quality of current academic life than the British writer David Lodge." Despite the breathless pace of the novel, with its profusion of incident and of geographical scope, Lodge remains in control of his material, according to Rosenthal (Marecki 299). When Morris Zapp is kidnapped his captors expect his ex-wife to pay the ransom demand; however, when the kidnappers telephone her she asks, "How much do I have to pay to make you keep him?" (Lodge Small World 276).

According to Elgin Mellown, "every detail and twist of the plot [of Small World] even the names of the characters, are taken from romance literature." The most important source is Edmund Spenser's The Faerie Queene (Mellown 699). Lodge has a keen ear for language, and likes to develop sustained parodies. In Small World he parodies Raymond Chandler (Lodge Small World 278), and T. S. Eliot's The Waste Land (Lodge Small World 261-263). Like Changing Places, the setting of Small World is Rummidge University. "They had appraised the stained and broken furniture, explored the dusty interiors of cupboards in vain for coat-hangers, and tested the narrow beds, whose springs sagged dejectedly in the middle, deprived of all resilience by the battering of a decades's horseplay and copulation. Each room had a washbasin, though not every washbasin had a plug, or every plug a chain" (Lodge Small World 3). Small World is set in the world of international literary conferences. It has three plots. One is the quest of Persse McGarrigle to find the beautiful Angelica Pabst. Another is Philip Swallow's attempt to divorce his wife, Hilary, and marry Joy. And the third is the competition of a number of literature professors for a UNESCO chair for which the recipient is paid $100,000 per year and has no duties to perform. It is a "conceptual chair" (Easthope 5). Small World both exaggerates and parodies its characters, and in addition, the three narratives draw on some rather elaborate coincidences (Easthope 6). There is also some gross humor, as when a connection is made between eating and excreting. The novel tracks food and drink as it passes from an aircraft's refrigerated cabinet, into the microwave oven, then into the "bellies" of the passengers, and finally into the plane's "septic tank" (Lodge Small World 88).

In Small World, Persse McGarrigle is an Irish poet, and until page 325 of the novel, he is also a virgin (Easthope 7). Early in the novel there is an explanation of how McGarrigle received his lectureship at Limerick: "They really meant to interview another fellow called McGarrigle--some high-flying prize scholar from Trinity. But the letter was addressed to me--someone slipped up in the Registry--and they were too embarrassed to retract the invitation" (Lodge Small World 15). Later in the novel Angelica tells McGarrigle to secretly come to her room so that he can watch her undress. He does so, and hides in the wardrobe, but it is Robin Dempsey who comes into the room and undresses, sniffing himself under both of his armpits in the process. When Persse coughs, Dempsey thinks that it is Angelica, who has come to see him (Lodge Small World 54-55).

There is much humorous visual imagery in Small World, as when Felix Skinner and his secretary drink too much liquor during lunch, and he takes her back to the office and down to the storeroom in the basement, where they make love while leaning over some boxes. At the moment of climax, they fall together, "in a heap of crushed cardboard and spilled books." The books turn out to be copies of Philip Swallow's book on Hazlitt, which Skinner has forgotten to send out for review. In the meantime, Philip Swallow takes off for Turkey where he is scheduled to give a lecture on Hazlitt, but he forgets to take toilet paper with him. When he gets to Turkey, there is a power outage, and since Philip is suffering from diarrhoea because of eating some tainted food, he must find his way to the lavatory in the dark. When he finds that there is no toilet paper in the lavatory, he uses some paper out of his briefcase. "When the lights came on of their own accord he found he was up to page five of his lecture on 'the legacy of Hazlitt'" (Lodge Small World 190). When the traditional Swallow asks the avant-garde Zapp the "point" of all of the academic posturing, Zapp responds as follows: "The point, of course, is to uphold the institution of academic literary studies. We maintain our position in society by publicly performing a certain ritual, just like any other group of workers in the realm of discourse--lawyers, politicians, journalists" (Lodge Small World 29).

Nice Work (1988) is about Robyn Penrose, a lecturer in the English Department of the local university who is asked, in the name of town-gown cooperation, to shadow Victor Wilcox, the Managing Director of J. Pringle and Sons, a local foundry, but the situation becomes reversed, and the executive becomes the shadower of the lecturer. He can always be found at her side as she lectures, conducts tutorials, and interviews students. Much of the humor comes from the contrasting attitudes of the academic in the workplace and the businessman in the academy (Mellown 693).

In Paradise News (1991), Ursula is divorced, is in her seventies, is dying of cancer, and is living in Hawaii, far from her family, so she pays for Bernard and his father to fly out to see her. The irony of the novel is based on the different meanings of "paradise" for different people. As tourists, the Walshes are looking for an earthly paradise in Hawaii, while Ursula is looking for the paradise of their company (Mellown 694).

David (John) Lodge Bibliography

Easthope, Antony. "The English Sense of Humor." Unpublished Paper. Manchester, England: Manchester Polytechnic University, 1997.

Lafuente, Maria Socorro Suarez. "La Tecnica Humoristica de David Lodge en Changing Places." Literary and Linguistic Aspects of Humour. Barcelona, Spain: Univ of Barcelona Dept of Languages, 1984, 227-232.

Lodge, David. The British Museum Is Falling Down. London, England: Martin Secker and Warburg, 1981.

Lodge, David. Changing Places: A Tale of Two Campuses. London, England: Secker and Warburg, 1975.

Lodge, David. How Far Can You Go? London, England: Secker and Warburg, 1980.

Lodge, David. Small World: An Academic Romance. London, England: Secker and Warburg, 1984.

Marecki, Joan E. "David Lodge." Contemporary Authors, New Revision Series, Volume 19. Ed. Linda Metzger. Detroit, MI: Gale Research, 1987, 297-303.

Mellown, Elgin W. "David Lodge." Encyclopedia of British Humorists, Volume II. Ed. Steven H. Gale. New York, NY: Garland, 1996, 691-701.

John (Peter) McGrath (1935-) SCOTLAND

John McGrath is the founder, and the long-time director of two popular theater companies, one in Scotland, and one in England, but both with the same name, "7:84."

The name comes from the common assumption that eighty-four percent of the wealth lies in the hands of seven percent of the population. McGrath's plays incorporate the tragic and the comic elements of modern life as seen through the eyes of a working-class audience (Brennan 288-289). According to Christian W. Thomsen, John McGrath is a socialist playwright who, "attacks capitalism and the ruling class, satirizing them and exposing their deeds through carefully researched facts" (Thomsen 172).

Writing about A Man Has Two Fathers (1958), but extending his statement to other plays as well, John Bull says, "McGrath's clear awareness of the dangers of arguing for an impossibly simple solution to a highly complex problem--the dilemma of all revolutionaries living in a non-revolutionary age--is brilliantly articulated in the humour and wit of the plays, frequently inviting the audience into the never self-contained discourse" (Brennan 289).

Soft or a Girl (1971) was revised as My Pal and Me for its Edinburgh production in 1975. It is a musical comedy that is set during the fire watch over the city of Liverpool during a particular World War II air raid. It is a comedy that is lively and diverting. It is also a study of life that is thoughtfully conceived (Brennan 290). The characters in Soft or a Girl are out of the tradition of humours comedy. Mary takes everything seriously and has a sensitive feel for the dark and poetic side of life. Fiona is the family genius who has ambitions to be a student and to climb the social ladder. Sandra is the sensuous working-class girl with a sense that happiness is relative and is probably short lived. Maconochie is the father with straightforward socialist convictions. Yorry is an intellectual and enthusiastic communist. Willie is being converted to socialism. And Andy is an anarchist (Thomsen 162).

The title of Fish in the Sea (1973) comes from Mao Tse Tung's famous analogy in which he compared the Communist Party to a fish, and the members of the Communist Party to the water in which the fish swims around (Thomsen 161). In this play there are three Labour MPs who are modelled after the three Gods in The Good Woman of Setzuan, and the potential political complexity is undercut by the fact that McGrath is poking fun at these figures. McGrath is here developing a dramatic form of his own as he draws from the traditions of the documentary, the music hall, the pop and pub tradition, and realistic comedy. His blend of these influences produces something which is both powerful and original, something which Christian Thomsen calls a "semi-realistic tragi-comedy" (Thomsen 162). Boom (1974), The Game's a Bogey (1974), and Little Red Hen (1975) are fiercely satirical. They are also what Thomsen calls "agit-prop" (Thomsen 164). McGrath realizes that Yobbo Nowt (1975) is not exactly a musical comedy, even though, "it is definitely musical and a comedy" (Thomsen 164).

John (Peter) McGrath Bibliography

Brennan, Carol. "John McGrath." Contemporary Authors, Volume 145. Ed. Kathleen J. Edgar. Detroit, MI: Gale Research, 1995, 286-291.

Thomsen, Christian W. "Three Socialist Playwrights: John McGrath, Caryl Churchill, Trevor Griffiths." Contemporary English Drama. Ed. C. W. E. Bigsby. New York, NY: Holmes and Meier, 1981, 157-176.

Andrew (Annandale) Sinclair (1935-)

In general, critics praised the gentle social satire presented in Andrew Sinclair's early novels (Vincent 675). Gog (1967) is a picaresque novel that takes place just after the end of World War II. A seven-foot naked man is washed ashore on the coast of Scotland.

He is suffering from amnesia, but tatooed on the backs of his hands are the words Gog and Magog (Vincent 678). He sets out for London hoping to learn more about his identity. During his journey, Gog meets a variety of fictional, historical, and mythological characters (Lesniak and Trosky 393). Some critics consider Gog to be an attempt at sophisticated satire, and they are not sure that the satire is successful. Kenneth Trodd says that Gog is, "a series of funny production numbers: droll, but the laughs are hollow where they need to be edgy; the wrong sort of punch." Frank McGuinness also believes that Gog packs the wrong sort of punch, and says that the book exhibits, "perhaps more satirical pretensions than the author's talent for ribald and extravagant inventiveness can finally support." McGuinness feels that Sinclair's satirical aims are, "lost in a welter of scholarly clowning, crude farce, and the sort of glib cynicism that is so often mistaken for cold, hard-headed intellectualism." J. D. Scott considers Gog to be a, "monument of myth and slapstick, violence and parody, drama-of-evil and custard-pie comedy" (Lesniak and Trosky 394).

Patricia Meyer Spacks describes Magog (1972) as consisting of, "gobbling great hunks of time, a vast dramatis personae; tossing off puns, inside jokes, bits of mythology; insisting that the life of a man and of an empire have much in common." She feels that Magog, "trivializes all it touches." She concludes that it is, "funny sometimes, sometimes even sad, but the lack of sharp authorial perspective makes it seem purposeless" (Lesniak and Trosky 394). Oswell Blakeston likes the beginning of the novel, "but then, alas, [Sinclair] plunges into farce." As Blakeston puts it, "after one has laughed at a well-aimed poisoned dart of brilliant criticism, it's hard to accept the old custard pie as a devastating weapon" (Lesniak and Trosky 395).

The inspiration for The Surrey Cat (1976) came from newspaper reports in the early 1970s that a large black cat had been sighted roaming the Surrey countryside. It is true that these newspaper reports were unconfirmed, and that the cat was never found, but Sinclair nevertheless had the grounding for his story about a small community that was terrorized by the cat. In the novel, Peter Gwynvor is responsible for destroying the cat and protecting the village, and Gwynvor is faced with the choice of whether he would prefer a slow death by cancer, or a fast death by confronting the cat. "It is hard to tell whether or not the evocation of D. H. Lawrence in the scene in which Mister Spring, Gwynvor's butler-cum-gamekeeper, makes love to Gwynvor's girl friend, Claudia, as she lies naked in the moonlight upon a pile of dead rabbits, is intended as some kind of literary joke" (Vincent 680).

In The Facts in the Case of E. A. Poe (1979), Sinclair is the editor and compiler of notes left by Ernest Albert Pons. Pons believes that he is a twentieth-century reincarnation of Edgar Allan Poe. Pons visits a psychiatrist even though he has no desire to be cured of this belief, and in fact he selects a psychiatrist by the name of "Dupin" because he has the same name as Poe's fictional detective, C. Auguste Dupin" (Vincent 680).

King Ludd (1988), the last novel of the trilogy Gog, Magog, and King Ludd, is the story of the nineteenth century Luddites. These were the British laborers who were displaced by machines in their factories. They began a rebellion against mechanization, and King Ludd was the name given to the mythical leader of this rebellion. In Sinclair's version, Gog discovers that the idea of King Ludd was in fact based on one of his ancestors (Lesniak and Trosky 395).

Andrew (Annandale) Sinclair Bibliography

Lesniak, James G., and Susan M. Trosky, Eds. "Andrew (Annandale) Sinclair."
     Contemporary Authors, New Revision Series, Volume 38. Detroit, MI: Gale, 1993,
     392-396.
Vincent, Judith. "Andrew Sinclair." Dictionary of Literary Biography, Volume Fourteen:

British Novelists Since 1960. Ed. Jay L. Halio. Detroit, MI: Gale, 1993, 675-681.

Donald Michael Thomas (1935-)

In The White Hotel (1981), D. M. Thomas uses erotic poetry, and a prose rendering of this erotic poetry to reveal the soul of Lisa Erdman. George Levine says that the writing in this novel, "is full of dislocation and surprise; it is seductive, frightening, and beautifully alive." Levine continues that, "such language immediately established the mysterious 'Anna G.' as a powerful presence" (Draper and Trosky 436).

William French suggests that Thomas had a lot of fun in writing Summit (1988), a satirical farce written in the tradition of following a trilogy of serious works with a light and farcical coda. In Summit, there is a meeting in Geneva of two superpower leaders who are referred to as Grobichov and "Tiger" O'Reilly. O'Reilly is the U.S. President who had been a movie star before he became president, and he is accompanied by his vice-president, Shrub. Michiko Kakutani says that Summit is, "a clever and often hilarious entertainment that opens a small window on the absurdities and perils of modern history" (Draper and Trosky 439).

Richard Erder says that Memories and Hallucinations (1988) is so absurd that it almost comes across as self-parody. Rosemary Dinnage says that it is richly imaginative, as it veers from humor to pretentiousness and back to humor (Draper and Trosky 440).

Donald Michael Thomas Bibliography

Draper, James P., and Susan M. Trosky, eds. "D(onald) M(ichael) Thomas." Contemporary Authors: New Revision Series, Volume 45. New York, NY: Gale, 1995, 433-441.

Stephen Frears (1936-) IRELAND

See Nilsen, Don L. F. "Stephen Frears." Humor in Irish Literature: A Reference Guide. Westport, CT: Greenwood, 1996, 210.

Simon Gray (1936-)

Wise Child (1967), Dutch Uncle (1969), and Spoiled (1970) are a blend of Georges Feydeau farce, and Agatha Christie mystery. These early plays have fast-moving turns of plot, wildly funny suspense, and ambiguous sexual identity as they exploit both verbal and visual humor. Wise Child was originally written as a television script, and contains a complex farcical plot, and much dark humor. The play starred Alex Guinness in drag, and because of this and because of the two adjoining bedrooms in the classical farcical setting, it caused something of a scandal (Bednerick 465-466). Dutch Uncle contains many visual jokes, such as the oversized wardrobe which Mr. Godboy has bought as a way of murdering May, his wife, thereby allowing him to have an affair with his neighbor's wife. He is not concerned about the notoriety that this will get him because he knows his action will attract Inspector Hawkins, whom he idolizes (Bednerick 466). These three plays were written just after the abolition of stage censorship in Britain, and they therefore flirt with once taboo subjects. Spoiled, for example, deals with erotic relationships between teachers and students (Bednerick 466).

Butley (1971) is a witty play which details a very bad day in the life of Ben Butley.

His wife Anne has left him, and Joey, his former prize student who has been both his office mate and his apartment mate, has taken on a new lover, Reg, a London publisher. Ben is trying to confirm his suspicions by getting the details of Joey's new relationship. As he is asking Reg questions, Ben is comically interrupted by students who are asking about tutorials, and by college administrators and colleagues who have various complaints, and by Anne, who wants a divorce so that she will be able to marry, "the most boring man in London" (Bednerick 466). Ben Butley is a complex anti-hero parodying the structure of Greek tragedy and at the same time maintaining the classical unities as Gray contrasts the repartée among True Wits, Would-be Wits, and the Witless (Bednerick 467). Ben Butley wins the verbal games and the one-upmanship because he is a master improviser, and changes the rules of the game, resulting in, "a triple game--one within the play, another which parodies social, literary, and theatrical traditions, and yet another which the playwright is simultaneously playing with his audience" (Bednerick 467).

> BEN: Does Reg's mother work in the shop too?
> JOEY: No.
> BEN: Oh. Where is she then, in the daytime?
> JOEY: Out.
> BEN: Out where?
> JOEY: Just out.
> BEN: She has a job then?
> JOEY: Yes.
> BEN: And where does she do this job? On the streets?
> JOEY: You could put it like that, yes.
> BEN: What does she do? Sweep them?
> JOEY: No.
> BEN: She walks them?
> JOEY: Yes, in point of fact.
> BEN: The precise suburb is irrelevant. (pause) So Reg's mother is a prostitute.
> JOEY: No, she's a--traffic warden. (Gray Butley 18-19)

In Plays: One, Simon Gray was asked whether or not he based the character of Ben Butley on his own life. He responded, "I now realize that it was far more likely that, for a time at least, I based myself on Butley--or more precisely, Alan Bates's performance of it" (Gray Plays ix). Quartermaine's Terms (1979) is a play about a lovable teacher of English to foreign students named St. John Quartermaine, who is both submissive and mediocre (Bednerick 468). The Holy Terror and Tartuffe (1990) is a revision of Melon (1987) in which the comedy lies not so much in the story of a psychological breakdown as in the complexity of the central character, the social satire, the funny events, and the very funny lines (Bednerick 470). Hidden Laughter (1990) is a play about a vicar named Ronnie, and a recent widower named Ben. Ben is not in Ronnie's Parish. Instead, in a sort of role reversal, Ronnie is Ben's gardener, both literally and metaphorically. Ben tells Ronnie that he has difficulty believing in a God who allows madness and death to occur, and Ronnie agrees, but then reasons, "There's no point in believing in him unless it's impossible to believe in him, if you follow, because if he existed, and we all knew he existed there'd be no difficulty at all in believing in him and what'd be the point in that?" Ronnie continues that faith is, "a matter of believing what's impossible to believe. Do you, um, see? Otherwise it's not faith. It's certainty" (Gray Hidden 10).

Simon Gray Bibliography

Bednerik, Marya. "Simon Gray." Encyclopedia of British Humorists, Volume I. Ed. Steven

H. Gale. New York, NY: Garland, 1996, 465-473.

Blaydes, Sophia B. "Literary Allusion as Satire in Simon Gray's Butley." Midwest Quarterly 18 (1977): 374-391.

Burkman, Katherine H. "The Fool as Hero: Simon Gray's Butley and Otherwise Engaged." Theatre Journal 33 (1981): 163-172.

Gray, Simon. Butley. London, England: Methuen, 1971.

Gray, Simon. Hidden Laughter. London, England: Faber and Faber, 1990.

Gray, Simon. Plays: One. London, England: Methuen, 1986.

Nothof, Anne. "Simon Gray's Comedy of Bad Manners." Essays in Theatre 6.2 (1988): 109-122.

Shafer, Yvonne. "Aristophanic and Chekhovian Structure in the Plays of Simon Gray." Theatre Studies 31/32 (1984-1986): 32-40.

Smith, Carolyn. "Simon Gray and the Grotesque." Within the Dramatic Spectrum. Ed. Karelisa Hartigan. New York, NY: University of America Presses, 1986, 168-176.

Peter Tinniswood (1936-)

In the early 1960s, Peter Tinniswood's was writing for That Was the Week That Was, the BBC television satirical series. After this, Tinniswood wrote many satiric novels which chiefly targeted the materialism of modern culture (Turton 1120). Glyn Turton considers Tinniswood's first novel, A Touch of Daniel (1969), to be, "one of the most accomplished works of comic fiction since World War II." In this novel, Tinniswood created the Brandon family, a family which would continue into I Didn't Know You Cared (1973), Except You're a Bird (1974), and Call it a Canary (1985). It should be noted that unlike the humor in the other Brandon books, the humor in Call it a Canary (1985) is grim rather than uproarious (Turton 1120). These three novels are about Mr. and Mrs. Leslie Brandon, their son Carter, and Mrs. Brandon's brother Mort. The way that these characters interrelate with each other "imitates, to brilliant comic effect, the way of life and speech of the North of England." These novels are comedies of manners, but they are also a kind of humorous magical realism. In A Touch of Daniel, the protagonist (Daniel), who has the power to heal, is adopted by the Brandon family. Daniel is the offspring of the elderly Uncle Mort and Auntie Lil. Although Daniel dies of pneumonia in a "surge of black comedy" at the end of A Touch of Daniel, his spirit and his voice live on in Carter's head throughout the next three Brandon-family novels. Much of Tinniswood's humor derives from the contradictions of the working-class hero (or anti-hero) Carter. Carter is a stock character in post-war British fiction in that, although he is trapped in his social class, he nevertheless struggles to articulate his identity (Turton 1119). Uncle Mort's North Country (1986) and Uncle Mort's South Country (1989) are sequels to the Brandon family novels. In these two novels, Carter and Uncle Mort become picaresque heroes in a series of episodes that place them across the north and south of England respectively. Turton considers Uncle Mort to be, "one of the great comic creations of Modern English writing. His mind is a rag-bag of folk memories and lovingly nurtured prejudices." He is a dour Northerner who is blunt to the point of rudeness. He is enthusiastic, passionate, vulgar, and abusive (Turton 1120).

Tinniswood's The Stirk of Stirk (1974), and Shemerelda (1981) are also comic novels. In these novels, Tinniswood is able to observe the ludicrous aspects of everyday life while at the same time creating a "darkly tinged lyrical fantasy." The Stirk of Stirk is a parody retelling of the Robin Hood legend, in which Robin Hood is transformed into a mincing, camp, figure of fun. The novel not only parodies the Robin Hood legend in particular, but it also parodies the romance, the lyricism, and the dramatic elements that are associated with this genre. "It is precisely the playing off of a lyrical impulse against the farcical, vulgar, and bathetic elements of the everyday which gives his writing its richness and individuality" (Turton 1120).

Tinniswood's Brigadier books are also very humorous. They include, Tales from a Long Room (1981), More Tales from a Long Room (1982), Collected Tales from a Long Room (1982), The Brigadier Down Under (1983), The Home Front (1983), The Brigadier in Season (1984), The Brigadier's Tour (1985), The Brigadier's Brief Lives (1985), and Tales from Witney Scrotum (1987). Much of the humor in the Brigadier books comes from Tinniswood's love of ornithology and sport. Like that of many other Englishmen, the Brigadier's love of cricket transcends social class. The Brigadier's failing memory is another device which Tinniswood uses for comic effect, and still another is England's class consciousness. In fact, Tinniswood brings these three satiric targets together. As Glyn Turton states it, "In his rambling reminiscences, the game is turned into a whimsical portmanteau metaphor for modern England" (Turton 1121).

Two of Tinniswood's comic novels to come out of his writing for radio are Hayballs (1989), and Winston (1991). Winston is a Rabelaisian character. He is the

> lustful, low-life version of the Admirable Crichton, amorous companion and counselor to the middle-class Nancy, who finds in his embraces consolation from her vexatious, eccentric family. Winston, part bucolic, hedonistic preacher of traditional popular imaging, part social security scrounger of contemporary political mythology, is a character for our times and a fitting addition to the comic gallery of Tinniswood's work. (Turton 1121)

Peter Tinniswood Bibliography

Turton, Glyn. "Peter Tinniswood." Encyclopedia of British Humorists, Volume II. Ed. Steven H. Gale. New York, NY: Garland, 1996, 1118-1122.

Tom Stoppard (William Boot)(1937-)

Tom Stoppard is our "brightest university wit" even though he left school at the early age of seventeen. His plays sparkle with puns, polysyllables, language games, quid pro quos, and distorted quotations. His satiric parodies target academic lectures, sports reports, news broadcasts, theatre reviews, detective stories, and aesthetic problems of all sorts. He especially likes to target the classics and celebrities. Ruby Cohn considers the "light drama" which Stoppard writes to be akin to the genre of "light verse" (Cohn 109). Stoppard has the audacity of Aristophanes as he writes travesties that target logic, philosophy, politics, science, criticism, and art. Stoppard's plays are absurd, illogical, philosophical, and filled with jokes. Stoppard is able to demonstrate Wittgenstein's famous statement that, "a serious and good philosophical work could be written that would consist entirely of jokes" (Davidson 39). Stoppard says that the two writers who may have influenced him the most are Beckett and Joyce, and both Beckett and Joyce are aware of the highly serious use of jokes. Stoppard, like Beckett, especially enjoyed the broadly theatrical jokes of farce, jokes that involve the dislocation of our assumptions and expectations and challenge our ability to distinguish between appearance and reality. Stoppard says that the funniest joke he knows is one also used by Beckett which consists of a confident statement followed by immediate refutation in the same voice (Hayman 10).

Anne Wright says that Tom Stoppard has been a leading figure of British drama since the mid-1960s and that he, "ranks as a dramatist of brilliant and original comic genius." He is a master of "philosophical farce," "dazzling theatricality," and "wit with a profound exploration of metaphysical concerns" (Wright 483). His plays are steeped in theatrical convention and stock comic situations that include mistaken identities, verbal misunderstandings, innuendo, farcical incongruity, visual and verbal jokes, puns, and language games (Wright 484). He is able to fuse the frivolous with the serious (Wright 485). John Gardner says that Stoppard writes a kind of farce where the tone can be described as "ultra-theatrical pizzazz." Gardner says that Stoppard's "delightfully flashy language" is unique. But Gardner may be a bit puritanical when he indicates that Stoppard's, "theatricalism, farce, and verbal wit are incompatible with or at least inappropriate to great art" (Gardner 58-59). Stoppard likes to anchor his plays in real-life events such as the events of Elsinore, or Churchill's funeral, or a <u>coup d'etat</u> by Radical Liberals, or Zurich in ferment. Stoppard is reminding us all that historical events always look slightly ridiculous when seen from the margins (Billington 122). Stoppard writes in the tradition of "the absurd." But Stoppard is not content just to leave his audience in an "absurdist void."

> He explores man coping with the artistic world in such plays as <u>Rosencrantz and Guildenstern Are Dead</u>, <u>Artist Descending a Staircase</u>, <u>The Real Inspector Hound</u>, and <u>Travesties</u>. He explores man coping with political systems in <u>If You're Glad I'll be Frank</u>, <u>Travesties</u>, and <u>Every Good Boy Deserves Favour</u>. He explores man coping in society in such plays as <u>Enter a Free Man</u>, <u>Albert's Bridge</u>, <u>Where Are They Now</u>, and <u>Professional Foul</u>. He explores man and his faith, both religious and secular, in such plays as <u>Jumpers</u>, and <u>Travesties</u>. (Cahn 156)

By having competing characters, Tom Stoppard argues with himself in his plays. Stoppard said, "I write plays because dialogue is the most respectable way of contradicting myself." He continues,

> The element which I find most valuable [in my work] is the one that other people are put off by--that is, that there is very often no single, clear statement in my plays. What there is, is a series of conflicting statements made by conflicting characters, and they tend to play a sort of infinite leap-frog. You know, an argument, a refutation, then a rebuttal of the refutation, then a counter-rebuttal, so that there is never any point in this intellectual leap-frog at which I feel <u>that</u> is the speech to stop it on, <u>that</u> is the last word. (Zeifman "Tomfoolery" 186; Dean 4)

Stoppard likes the pun because the pun is "language arguing with itself." When there is a pun, one character assumes one meaning, while another character assumes a different meaning. A pun is, "quintessentially dialectical, containing within itself its own thesis and antithesis." "It is a deliciously funny and effective form of aggression, at one and the same time ostensibly inoffensive and yet teasingly (or viciously) hostile" (Zeifman "Tomfoolery" 187). Stoppard's puns are intended to amuse, but they are also used, "carefully and deliberately as structural devices in his plays, as an integral part of the play's basic 'meaning'" (Zeifman "Tomfoolery" 175).

Alice Rayner notes that the paradoxes of George Bernard Shaw tend to be in the "indicative mood," and that the world which Shaw created was also "indicative," having the appearance of the real and the concrete. In contrast, Stoppard's paradoxes are in the "subjunctive mood," and Stoppard's world is hypothetical, potential, possible, and non-existent, based on the establishment of an "if." Victor Cahn notes that critics often consider Stoppard's writing to be philosophical and erudite, and he is sometimes considered to be a "university wit," even though he never attended a university (Cahn 24). Stoppard loves all forms of wordplay, but especially puns, and he often refers to himself as a "bounced Czech" (Wright 1074).

A Walk on the Water (1963) is a domestic comedy which was later transformed into Enter a Free Man (1964)(Cahn 25). In this play, George Riley is a dreamer who considers himself to be an inventor even though all of his inventions have failed. Nevertheless, he is unwilling to accept unemployment compensation because he is employed--as an inventor (Cahn 26). George's ideas are so whimsical that they are doomed to failure. One of his inventions, for example, is an envelope which has the edges of the flap gummed on both sides. Such ideas are so quixotic, and pathetic, and ridiculous that they cause the audience to laugh (Cahn 28).

> However, an additional irony dominates the play. Because much of the play is comic, the audience expects the type of ending appropriate to a comedy, where conflicts are resolved in favor of the hero. But in the final scene in the pub, as Harry demonstrates the obvious futility of the invention, our disappointment is doubly painful. We knew that the invention was hopeless, and that in life George would have no chance of selling it. But somehow we had hoped that in a comedy the inevitable might be avoided. Our illusions collapse with George's. (Cahn 29)

Stoppard has fun creating linguistic trickery and double meanings in his writings, as in the following dialogue:

> RILEY: (calling up to Harry): A man is born free and everywhere he is in
>   chains. Who said that?
> ABLE: Houdini?
> RILEY: (turning): Who?
> ABLE: --dini.
> RILEY: Houdini. No. (Enter 33)

"Life, Times: Fragments" (1964) is the first of Stoppard's works to be founded on the principles of parody and literary allusion (Cahn 78). It is a short story about a writer who applies for a job as a political reporter, but is rejected because he doesn't know the name of the Foreign Secretary. So he turns to writing fiction, saying, "Then I can make the Foreign Secretary anybody I bloody well like" (Cahn 76).

The Real Thing (1964) further develops the paradox which Henry James suggested in his story by the same name, whereby we prefer to become informed from literature rather than from real life (Kelly 144). Stoppard blends his literature with real life. The characters in The Real Thing all have careers in the theater; we are nevertheless surprised when the opening scene turns out to have been the performance of a play. House of Cards is the name of the play within the play, and once we are aware that it is a play within a play, we can now observe the action through two frames as we watch actors playing actors who also play multiple roles (Kelly 145). The Real Thing may attempt to present a "sacramental view of language," but it does so ironically.

> The Annie-Henry debate on writing ends, as all such debates do in Stoppard's plays, at an impasse. In exasperation, Henry echoes the husband of the opening of House of Cards by implicitly accusing Annie of caring for Brodie: "Why Brodie. Do you fancy him or what?" When he realizes his error, Annie refuses to let him take back his words. "Too late," she tells him, a phrase that his daughter will repeat later as she leaves to follow her lover on his fairground tour. (Kelly 148)

"The Story" (1964) is a short story about a newspaper reporter who covers out-of-town court sessions for a press service. One story concerns a case of child molestation, and the reporter promises the defendant that the story won't be publicized. But one of his associates insists that the details of the story be sent to the wire service, and a week after the story is published, the defendant, who is a schoolteacher named Blake, commits suicide (Cahn 78-79). In this story, the narrator is as powerless as is Blake: "The bloke was pleading guilty. He was red and tweedy and too fat but the main thing about him was that he kept grinning. I really mean grinning but there was nothing there. It was just a shape he put his mouth into. He was too fat and altogether sick with where he had got himself" (Cahn 79).

Stoppard wrote the play, If You're Glad I'll be Frank (1966) for BBC radio. It was aired as part of a series on Strange Occupations, a series about bizarre and nonexistent jobs. The main joke of the job is about the voice that tells the time when a person dials in. The voice is not a mechanical recording, but belongs to a real woman (Wright 487). If You're Glad I'll be Frank (1966) is a one-act radio play in which Frank calls up the telephone company to ask for the correct time. But he recognizes the answering voice to be that of his wife, Gladys. Gladys is mindlessly reciting the precise time every ten seconds (Cahn 81). In order to preserve her sanity in such a boring job, she allows her mind to wander through her memory to look for any joyous experiences she has had in the past: "Yes, we met dancing. I liked him from the first. He said, 'If you're Glad I'll be Frank....'" There was time to laugh then but when I laughed a bumblebee fluttered its wings a million times. How can one compete?..." (Cahn 85). Gladys's mind gradually deteriorates until she begins to giggle madly at the thought of whispering an obscenity into the phone that will, "leave ten thousand coronaries sprawled across their telephone tables." Gladys feels she needs to, "perform a gratuitous act that will demonstrate her scorn for the conventions of an absurd world." Because he is a bus driver and is tied to his schedule, Frank also has to battle against the mechanized world. When he reaches the front of the building where Gladys works, he is faced with yet another barrier when the Porter says, "You can't park there after seven if the month's got an R in it or before nine if it hasn't except on Christmas and the Chairman's birthday should it fall in Lent" (Cahn 88).

In a radio play entitled, "M" is for Moon and Other Things (1964), Alfred and Constance are shown to be a middle-aged and middle-class couple, who are reading at the beginning of the play. Alfred is reading the newspaper, and Constance is reading a mail-order encyclopedia. Alfred finishes reading, and turns on the television set to discover that the thriller Dial "M" for Murder is just finishing. The news that follows is about the death of Marilyn Monroe, and by coincidence, Constance has by this time reached the letter "M" in her encyclopedia (Wright 486).

Lord Malquist and Mr. Moon (1966) is a blend of serious contemplation and extravagant comedy involving persistent paradox and wordplay. In this novel, the author is very conscious of narrative method and style. Anne Wright considers Malquist to be a Wildean figure, and says that the novel parodies many of Wilde's comic techniques. Mr. Moon, who is hired as a secretary and companion to Lord Malquist, is quite insecure and very much tormented by his wife's infidelity. The fact that Mr. Moon is carrying a bomb around in his pocket also adds suspense to the novel (Wright 488). Lord Malquist and Mr. Moon is a tour de force of absurdist black humor, in which incredible and horrific events are reported with vacuous tranquility (Cahn 66). Mr. Moon is a secretary to Lord Malquist, but he is constantly forgetting dialogue when he tries to write down each day's proceedings. As a secretary, he doesn't take enough notes in his diary, and the notes he does take down are mostly vapid trivia. Mr. Moon states at the end of the opening chapter that. "Tomorrow I hope to do better justice to Lord Malquist's conversation--I did in fact make some notes today but unfortunately my notebook was destroyed in a small fire later on" (Cahn 70). In Lord Malquist and Mr. Moon there are constant accounts of death and destruction, but they are always reported with utter calm. There are many allusions to the funeral of a national hero. Lord Malquist inadvertently kills a woman as he is driving his coach. Mr. Moon murders a general. Marie, Jane's maid, is accidentally shot by a cowboy and dies, after which she lies unattended for a long period of time (Cahn 71). Jane, Mr. Moon's wife in the novel is nicknamed "Fertility Jane" (Cahn 72). She has a parade of lovers, and she sensually moves from bed to bath to bed throughout the novel (Cahn 69). At the end of <u>Lord Malquist and Mr. Moon</u>, an explosion destroys Mr. Moon's coach, "dispersing Moon and O'Hara and bits of pink and yellow wreckage at various points along the road between the Palace and Parliament Square" (Cahn 67).

According to Susan Rusinko, the writing of <u>Rosencrantz and Guildenstern Are Dead</u> (1966) places Tom Stoppard into the ranks of such dramatists as Oscar Wilde and George Bernard Shaw, and other great writers of comedy of ideas. Such dramatists are noted for "(1) the dazzling wit and vivid imagery of the playwright's language, (2) the daringly plagiaristic usage of other writers' plots and characters, and (3) the incongruous situations that stem from a disjointedness between the characters and their times" (Wright 1068). In the tradition of <u>commedia dell'arte</u>, the play, <u>Rosencrantz and Guildenstern Are Dead</u>, contains questions that remain unanswered, and courtly characters who burst onto stage and then out of sight, and corpses which are revived (Cohn 113). Here, Stoppard is using the same dramatic comic devices which Beckett had used--puns, sight gags, poses, jokes, games, aphorisms, double takes, double talk, cross-conversation, and asides to the audience; still, neither Stoppard nor Beckett consider their plays to be farces (Cohn 114). As <u>Rosencrantz and Guildenstern Are Dead</u> opens, Rosencrantz and Guildenstern are spinning coins. The audience becomes quickly aware that the coin has been spun eighty-nine times, and has come up heads exactly eighty-nine times. Rosencrantz and Guildenstern are confused by this, and they try to use logic to reason things out. At one point Guildenstern discusses individual probability in the following way: "A spectacular vindication of the principle that each individual coin spun individually (he spins one) is as likely to come down heads as tails and therefore should cause no surprise each individual time as it does" (<u>Rosencrantz</u> 16). Guildenstern's attempt to rationalize the long string of "heads" becomes more and more intense with each toss, and he begins to fear that this one particular experience cannot be rationalized. But his fear is based on an even-more global realization: "All the games with logic...are desperate fending off of the silence in which nameless fears can possess our imaginations" (Cave 65). The Player doesn't check the last flip of the coin, because he knows without checking that it is heads. But when the Player removes his foot, and the coin is revealed, it turns out to be tails. Victor Cahn points out that this is not only the turning point in the coin toss, it is also the turning point in the play, because logic and order are suddenly restored, and Rosencrantz and Guildenstern, and their audience are now in the "real world" (Cahn 44).

<u>Rosencrantz and Guildenstern Are Dead</u> is a parody of Shakespeare's <u>Hamlet</u>, and whenever the characters from <u>Hamlet</u> are on the stage, they speak in Elizabethan English.

> Not only do they use the style of language, but Stoppard maintains the integrity of Shakespeare's language by using the exact dialogue from the play when the characters interact together. If this were not contradiction enough, Stoppard uses lines from Shakespeare when Rosencrantz and Guildenstern interact with characters from <u>Hamlet</u>; yet as soon as that interaction is finished, Rosencrantz and Guildenstern return to speaking in colloquial [20th century] English. (Presto 4)

<u>Rosencrantz and Guildenstern Are Dead</u> is not only a parody of Shakespeare's <u>Hamlet</u>; it is a parody of Beckett's <u>Waiting for Godot</u> as well (Sorell 301). Like Vladimir and Estragon, Rosencrantz and Guildenstern are nonentities, and like Vladimir and Estragon, Rosencrantz and Guildenstern are masters of, "the <u>non sequitur</u>, philosophical, illogical reasoning, and surrealistic, [and] automatic reactions." Few people who have seen <u>Hamlet</u> are able to distinguish between Rosencrantz and Guildenstern, and in the Stoppard play their personalities are so interchangeable that they even get their own names confused. At Elsinore, Rosencrantz and Guildenstern are required to shadow Hamlet in order to find out details relating to his madness. To get more information, they decide to interview

Hamlet in a rapid-fire question-answer game where each person must answer a question with a question. This turns out to be fun on the surface, but the scene is both tragic and comic in its effect (Sorell 302). Stoppard's parody of the mad scene in Hamlet is especially masterful:

> GUILDENSTERN: I think I have it. A man talking sense to himself is no
> madder than a man talking nonsense not to himself.
> ROSENCRANTZ: Or just as mad.
> GUILDENSTERN: Or just as mad.
> ROSENCRANTZ: And he does both.
> GUILDENSTERN: So there you are.
> ROSENCRANTZ: Stark raving sane. (Rosencrantz 67-68)

One of the ironies of Rosencrantz and Guildenstern Are Dead is that the two title characters seem to be able to choose between life and death by reading the letter which asks the King of England to execute them. Having read the letter, they could destroy it and not show it to the king, but Rosencrantz notes, "There must have been a point somewhere at the beginning when we could have said no. But somehow we missed it" (Sorell 303).

Hersh Zeifman notes that Guildenstern is the first in a long line of Stoppard compulsive punsters. "We laugh at the agility of his mind and the nimbleness of his wit: he is having fun with language, playing with it and we share his pleasure" (Zeifman "Tomfoolery" 176). "In Stoppard's plays words are, more often than not, puns: ambiguous, confusing, enigmatic" (Zeifman "Tomfoolery" 177).

> GUILDENSTERN: And receive such thanks as fits a king's remembrance.
> ROSENCRANTZ: I like the sound of that. What do you think he means by
> remembrance?"
> GUILDENSTERN: He doesn't forget his friends.
> ROSENCRANTZ: Would you care to estimate?
> GUILDENSTERN: Difficult to say, really--some kings tend to be amnesiac,
> others I suppose the opposite, whatever that is...
> ROSENCRANTZ: Yes--but--
> GUILDENSTERN: Elephantine...?
> ROSENCRANTZ: Not how long--how much?
> GUILDENSTERN: Retentive--he's a very retentive king, a royal retainer.
> (qtd. in Zeifman "Tomfoolery" 176)

When Rosencrantz says "What are you playing at?" Guildenstern responds, "Words, words. They're all we have to go on" (Zeifman "Tomfoolery" 176). The punning in Rosencrantz and Guildenstern Are Dead is extensive. Hersh Zeifman points out that a linguistic pun occurs whenever two concepts are referred to by a single word, and goes on to say that this same thing happens with the two title characters, since they share a single name--Rosencrantzandguildenstern. As with all puns, this sharing of a single sound-form causes confusion (Zeifman "Tomfoolery" 178).

The soliloquies of Guildenstern and Rosencrantz make perfectly good sense, though Guildenstern's soliloquies are much more the intelligent of the two. Guildenstern describes death in the following way:

> Because you'd be helpless, wouldn't you? Stuffed in a box like that, I mean
> you'd be in there for ever. Even taking into account the fact that you're
> dead, it isn't a pleasant thought. Especially if you're dead, really...ask
> yourself, if I asked you straight off--I'm going to stuff you in this box now,
> would you rather be alive or dead? Naturally, you'd prefer to be alive. Life
> in a box is better than no life at all, I expect. You'd have a chance at least.
> You could lie there thinking--well, at least I'm not dead! (Rosencrantz 70-
> 71)

Contrast Guildenstern's soliloquy about death with Rosencrantz soliloquy about the same subject: "It's what actors do best. They have to exploit whatever talent is given them, and their talent is dying. They can die heroically, comically, ironically, slowly, suddenly, disgustingly, charmingly, or from a great height" (Rosencrantz 83). It should be noted that Guildenstern's description of death is actually an ironic foreshadowing of his own death at the end of the play (Cahn 58).

When Rosencrantz and Guildenstern get into a rapid dialogue with each other, their separate ideas, which may be coherent by themselves, become incoherent in the context of the other.

PLAYER: Why?
GUILDENSTERN: Ah. (To Rosencrantz) Why?
ROSENCRANTZ: Exactly.
GUILDENSTERN: Exactly what?
ROSENCRANTZ: Exactly why.
GUILDENSTERN: Exactly why <u>what</u>?
ROSENCRANTZ: What?
GUILDENSTERN: Why?
ROSENCRANTZ: Why what, exactly?
GUILDENSTERN: Why is he mad?!
ROSENCRANTZ: I don't know! (Rosencrantz 68)

Over the years, critics have written hundreds of commentaries in an attempt to investigate the essence of Shakespeare's Hamlet, and hundreds more to investigate the essence of Stoppard's Rosencrantz and Guildenstern Are Dead, and this is ironic, because one of the targets of the satire is this literary criticism. Rosencrantz is able to sum up both plays with only a very few words. Speaking to Hamlet, he says, "your father, whom you love, dies; you are his heir; you come back to find that hardly was the corpse cold before his young brother popped onto his throne and into his sheets, thereby offending both legal and natural practice" (Rosencrantz 50-51). This effective reduction of the plot is a parody of the huge stacks of critical inquiry that have been written (Cahn 50). Anne Wright says that by focusing on Shakespeare's minor characters in Rosencrantz and Guildenstern Are Dead, Stoppard does not expand their roles, but rather, "extends their thinness" (Trosky 407).

In A Separate Peace (1966) John Brown registers at a hospital not because he is ill, but because he needs a place to stay. He explains, "It's the privacy I'm after--that and the clean linen" (Cahn 87). When he is asked why he chose a hospital rather than a hotel, he responds, "I want to do nothing, and have nothing expected of me. That isn't possible out there. It worries them. They want to know what you're at--staying in your room all the time--they want to know what you're <u>doing</u>" (Cahn 87). Maggie Coates is his confidante, and he tells her, "I came for the white calm, meals on trays and quiet efficiency, time passing and bringing nothing." He remembers that the only other time in his life when he was happy was when he was a prisoner of war. "The war was going on but I wasn't going to it any more. They gave us food, life was regulated, in a box of earth and wire and sky, and sometimes you'd hear an aeroplane miles up, but it couldn't touch you" (Cahn 88). John Brown thought that he'd become a monk, but they wouldn't have him because he wasn't a believer. He asked them if he could stay without being a "proper monk" but they wouldn't let him, so he said, "What I need is a sort of monastery for agnostics" (Cahn 89).

Albert's Bridge (1967) is a play which begins with the scene of four men painting a bridge. Of the four, only Albert is happy at his work. Dan expresses the opinion of the other three men: "I've spread my life over those girders, and in five minutes I could scrape down to my prime." In contrast, Albert expresses his opinion of the bridge: "That bridge was--separate--complete--removed, defined by principles of engineering...the whole thing utterly fixed by rules that make it stay up. It's complete, and a man can give his life to its maintenance, a very fine bargain." Albert at first admires the bridge, but this admiration turns to affection, and finally to an obsession that interferes with his personal relationships with his father, his mother, and his wife Kate. Finally, Albert has transferred all of his love to the bridge (Cahn 90). At the beginning of the novel we see four men who must paint the bridge every two years, but then a new paint is invented which can last for eight years, and this prompts the leaders of Clufton Bay to fire three of the painters. Only Albert, the happy painter, is asked to continue, "I was happy up there, doing something simple but so grand" (Cahn 91). When Albert is left alone on the bridge, to work all by himself, Stoppard changes the language from prose to poetry (Cahn 92). But then the company that has hired Albert as the single painter changes its policy, and decides to finish the bridge painting in a single day. So at the end of the play, an army of 1,800 painters marches toward Albert, who is waiting on the bridge, and who says, "Eighteen-hundred men flung against me by a madman! Was I so important? Here they come." But under the pressure of all of this weight, the bridge collapses, and Albert cries, "To go to such lengths! I didn't do them any harm! What did I have that they wanted?" (Cahn 94).

Another Moon Called Earth (1967), Teeth (1967), and Neutral Ground (1968) are three television farces. Teeth is a thirty-minute BBC production that takes place in the office of Harry Dunn, a dentist, who discovers that he has George, his wife's lover, in his dental chair. He takes revenge on George by staining his teeth green, and by seducing his wife, who happens to be Harry's receptionist (Wright 488).

The Real Inspector Hound (1968) burlesques a particular Agatha Christie mystery in which the detective proves to be the murderer (Cohn 110). Stoppard also got some suggestions for this play from Arthur Conan Doyle's The Hound of the Baskervilles, such as a repeated crime, a false Sherlock Holmes, and a disguised corpse (Whitaker 114). The title of Stoppard's play is derived from Major Magnus's accusing Moon of killing the unknown stranger, cutting the telephone wires, and returning as Inspector Hound. At this point, Major Magnus removes his moustaches, leaps out of his wheelchair, and declares himself to be "the real Inspector Hound." Inside of the play The Real Inspector Hound, there is a reënactment of the murder--a play within a play. This is based on Agatha Christie's The Mousetrap, but it is also based on Shakespeare's "The Mousetrap" which is the name of the play within the play used by Hamlet to convict Claudius of his guilt (Stoppard later used a play-within-a-play to half-convict Rosencrantz and Guildenstern of their treachery). It is Trotter who has all of the characters go to the positions that they had occupied when the murder occurred, at which point Trotter says, "The same actions will be performed, but not necessarily by the same people" (Whitaker 113).

The Real Inspector Hound is a one-act farce in which Mrs. Drudge answers the telephone by saying, "Hello, the drawing-room of Lady Muldoon's country residence one morning in early spring?" (Whitaker 111). In the play, Moon and Birdboot sit in seats that are visible to the audience (Cahn 95). The name "Moon" implies a touch of madness, but it also conjures up the image of one body in space floating around another body in space, and that is exactly what Moon does. He is a second-rate critic floating around a world of theatre that considers him to be of minor importance. The name "Birdboot" also suggests total triviality. Throughout the performance, both Birdboot and Moon offer a running commentary about the "hilariously bad play" they are reviewing, a play whose primary tension comes from the knowledge that a madman, who might have appeared on stage under the name of Simon Gascoyne, has escaped, and is in the vicinity of the isolated Muldoon Manor (Cahn 96-97). The radio sends such cryptic messages as "Essex County police are still searching in vain for the madman who is at large in the deadly marshes of the coastal region.... Meanwhile police and volunteers are combing the swamps with loud-hailers, shouting, 'Don't be a madman, give yourself up.'" So this is sort of a play within a play (Cahn 97) in the tradition of the "trilogy of the theatre," which is part of Pirandello's Six Characters in Search of an Author (Whitaker 111).

The Real Inspector Hound is not only a satirical farce; it is a parable and a parody as well. It is a parody of an Agatha Christie thriller, but exaggerated. In the second act of this melodramatic farce a critic jumps up from his seat in the audience and hurtles over the footlights onto the stage to answer the phone. Walter Sorell considers The Real Inspector Hound to be a witty and highly entertaining play (Sorell 301). There is much verbal play in the dialogue. Lord Magnus, who is confined to a wheelchair, nearly runs over Simon, and Magnus asks, "How long have you been a pedestrian?" Simon responds, "Ever since I could walk."

At another moment of crisis, Inspector Hound is conducting a search for the escaped madman, and when he becomes panicked he snatches the phone and says, "I'll call the police!" Cynthia says, "But you are the police!" and Hound responds, "Thank God I'm here--" (Cahn 97). At another point in The Real Inspector Hound, Detective Inspector Foot misinterprets the mother's innocent request to be allowed to play the tuba:

> MOTHER: Is it all right for me to practice?
>
> FOOT: No, it is not all right! Ministry standards may be lax but we draw the line at Home Surgery to bring in the little luxuries of life.
>
> MOTHER: I only practice on the tuba.
>
> FOOT: Tuba, femur, fibula--it takes more than a penchant for rubber gloves to get a license nowadays. (Zeifman "Tomfoolery" 180)

Tom Stoppard used to be a drama critic, and he is therefore having some fun at the expense of his former profession when he writes about two of the drama critics in The Real Inspector Hound named Moon and Birdboot. Their use of drama-critic jargon and catch phrases greatly helps in the development of the parody. But despite the parodic nature of Stoppard's play, and despite the fact that it is a farce, the deaths of Moon and Birdboot are both moving and shocking because they felt that in their positions as critics they were invulnerable (Cahn 100-101).

After Magritte (1970) gets its title from Rene Magritte (1898-1967) the quintessential surrealist painter (Cahn 106). After attending an exhibit of Magritte's paintings the family of three passes a man who might have just committed a crime, and the play is devoted to the different accounts of just who this man was, what he was wearing, and the nature of his identity. The title of the play is ambiguous, since it could refer to actions encountered after seeing a Magritte exhibit, or it could refer to something in the style of Magritte, and could therefore refer to this sense as well. After looking at a Magritte exhibit the three would of course be seeing the world through surrealistic eyes. The person passing the three is bizarre. "Thelma imagines him to have been a one-legged football player, clad in a striped uniform, wearing a white beard, and carrying a football under his arm. Reginald insists that the figure was an old bearded man wearing his pajamas, with a face covered with shaving cream, and carrying a tortoise. Inspector Foot is sure that it was a one-legged minstrel carrying a crutch and a stolen cash-box" (Whitaker 116). The uncertainty is characteristic of surrealist art (Cahn 108). The play contains both verbal and visual puns. The audience must suspect the meaning of nearly every item in the play, from the title of the play itself to such words, images, and objects as "foot," "tuba," "language," and "light," all of which turn out to be disconcertingly plural in meaning (Whitaker 117).

The opening tableau of After Magritte shows Harris, in fishing waders, standing on a chair, blowing into a heavy metal lampshade which is suspended over his head. A shoeless woman in a full-length gown is on her hands and knees staring at the floor, and another woman is lying on an ironing board, covered by a white bath towel; she is wearing a black rubber bathing cap that conceals much of her head and face. A bowler hat is resting on her stomach. Against the door is a pile of furniture, including a setee, chairs, a TV set, a cupboard, and a gramophone with an old-fashioned horn. Through the window the audience can see the totally motionless shoulders, face, and helmet of a police constable. At first all of these elements appear bizarre, but the audience is gradually given evidence to help interpret the scene as perfectly rational and even commonplace (Whitaker 115). Reginald in trying to repair a light fixture must counterbalance the fixture by one hundred and fifty lead slugs that Thelma is gathering up from the floor.   The counterbalancing weight is equal to a basket of fruit, with the subtraction of a bite from an apple, or the addition of a hat to maintain its equilibrium. The opening dialogue is provoked by Reginald Harris's blowing on the hot bulb, and contains both deliberate and inadvertent puns:

> THELMA: It's electric, dear.
> HARRIS: (mildly) I didn't thinking it was a flaming torch.
> THELMA: There's no need to use language. That's what I always say.
>   (Whitaker 117).

Harris has used the word "flaming" not as an obscenity, but as a literal expression, that is, he was saying that he didn't thinking it was a "fire-torch," and when Thelma refers to the "language" that Harris is using, she means "bad language" (Zeifman "Tomfoolery" 179). Later in the play Harris and Thelma again misunderstand each other, when Harris says, "The most--the very most--I am prepared to concede is that he may have been a sort of street arab making off with his lute...," and Thelma misunderstands "lute" as "loot," so Harris expands on his original meaning by saying, "Or his mandolin--Who's to say?" (Zeifman "Tomfoolery" 179).

In After Magritte, Harris says he saw a mysterious one-legged white-bearded man hopping down the street who was blind, and who was wearing striped pajamas, and carrying a turtle under one arm as he brandished a white stick. Harris says, "I happened to see him with my own eyes," and his wife says, "We all saw him," but his wife's description of what she saw is totally at odds with the description of her husband (Zeifman "Tomfoolery" 178). At the end of the play Foot tells how he was shaving when he saw Harris in his car pulling away from the curb outside of his residence on Ponsonby Place. He rushed outdoors with both feet jammed in the same pajama leg, while carrying his wife's handbag an unopened parasol, hoping that he might move his own car before it received a parking ticket (Whitaker 116).

When Mother calls "Lights!" Holmes enters and turns on the central light fixture which discloses the final tableau (Whitaker 118). The closing tableau of After Magritte looks just as weird to the audience as the opening tableau had once looked. But now the audience has been made to understand how, "the apparently irrefutable evidence of our senses can frequently be misleading" (Zeifman "Tomfoolery" 179). The play comes full cycle, and ends with a tableau that gives Holmes still another riddle to solve. The mother is balancing on a chair, standing precariously on one foot, as she is playing her tuba. Reginald has a cushion-cover over his eyes, and is wearing his wife's gown. He is also standing on one foot, and is counting. Thelma is crawling on the floor in her underwear sniffing, and Foot himself has one foot bare, and his eyes are covered by sun-glasses, as he eats a banana (Whitaker 116). The lampshade of the light fixture has lost a few ounces of the counterweight that had been provided by the banana now being eaten by Foot in order to relieve his migraine, so that the fixture descends until it touches the top of the table and leaves the stage in total darkness (Whitaker 118).

The Engagement is an expansion of The Dissolution of Dominic Boot (1970) which is a television farce. Where Are They Now (1970) is about how the past becomes distorted, and therefore how people's recollections of the past are often contradictory. Some graduates return yearly for a dinner-reunion talk about their school days, recalling their miseries with good-humored nostalgia. Their nostalgia allows them to have delusions of constant happiness, and this hypocrisy is underscored by flashbacks during the dinner (Cahn 110). One of the characters who does not blend in to the group is named Jenkins, and his problem is that his memories are not the same as those of the other characters. He can't remember the names and the other details as well, and only at the end, when he starts to sing his school song, do we realize that he has been attending the wrong reunion (Cahn 111). Gale, another character in Where Are They Now who has become a journalist of some reputation, reflects on how the dinner is progressing, and makes the following observation, "I suppose it's not very important, but at least we would have been happier children, and childhood is Last Chance Gulch for happiness. After that, you know too much" (Cahn 111).

Artist Descending a Staircase (1972) is about artists, one of whom is Beauchamp who says about artists, "The artist is a lucky dog. That is all there is to say about him. In any community of a thousand souls there will be nine hundred doing the work, ninety doing well, nine doing good, and one lucky dog painting or writing about the other nine hundred and ninety-nine" (Cahn 126). Martello, an artist living with Beauchamp is working on a statue which he calls "The Cripple." It is composed of a wooden man with a real leg (Cahn 127). Martello and Donner are trying to create the artistically perfect female body by attempting various media--plaster, sugar, paint, wheat, even ripe pears. They want to create the ideal female beauty as described in the Song of Solomon: "her navel as a round goblet which wanteth not liquor, her belly like a field of wheat set about with lilies, yea, her two breasts will be like two young roes that are twins" (Davidson 47).

The title of Artist Descending a Staircase is a pun based on Marcel Duchamp's cubist masterpiece named, Nude Descending a Staircase. Another pun in this play occurs when Martello criticizes Donner's outrageous edible art, by saying about a statue made out of sugar that, "it will give cubism a new lease on life" (Zeifman "Tomfoolery" 187). In the beginning of Artist Descending a Staircase, Beauchamp and Martello are listening to an audiotape which has recorded the final minutes in the life of Donner, their friend and fellow artist. The audience joins Beauchamp and Martello in trying to interpret what the sounds on the tape mean. Evidently Donner, the murder victim, was expecting his assailant, for he exclaimed, "Ah! There you are...." Since Donner was a semi-recluse who for years had only seen Beauchamp and Martello, Beauchamp assumes Martello to be the murderer, and Martello accuses Beauchamp of the crime (Zeifman "Tomfoolery" 181). Martello says, "Beauchamp, there you are. [meaning: that "Ah" on the tape was Donner's response to your arrival]. Unless we can agree on that I can't even begin to help you clear up this mess." But Beauchamp misinterprets the expression "clear up this mess" and Martello must explain, "I didn't mean clear up Donner!--honestly, Beauchamp, you buffoon!" (Zeifman "Tomfoolery" 182).

By the end of Artist Descending a Staircase, Beauchamp and Martello and the audience realize that they have been misinterpreting the evidence. What they assume to have been Donner's snoring turns out to have been the buzzing of a fly. What they assumed to have been Donner's reaction to the appearance of a close friend was instead his feeling of triumph at having located the fly. And what they assumed to have been Donner's friend striking Donner was instead Donner's attempt to swat the fly. Thus his subsequent fall was not a murder, but rather an accidental death, and the revelation of these ironic misconceptions comes as a shock to everyone (Cahn 126).

The opening scene of Jumpers (1972) shows an empty stage with a screen at the back. Dotty enters and struggles to sing "Shine On, Harvest Moon," but fails. This is followed by the entrance of a female trapeze artist, who gradually takes off her clothes to the approval of her unseen admirers. Then a company of gymnasts in yellow jumpsuits enter, and they perform a series of complicated gymnastic routines (Cahn 113). One of these routines is to leap over moving letters that sometimes spell their names (Davidson 43). The jumpers also form a human pyramid, which they hold until a gunshot blows one jumper out of the bottom row (Davidson 44). These gymnasts later turn out to be members of the Radical-Liberal Party, and they are celebrating their seizure of the British government. Dotty comments on the way that they have come into power, "It's not the voting that's democracy, it's the counting" (Cahn 115). In Jumpers, Stoppard's "Dotty" is similar to Sheridan's "Mrs. Malaprop" in her confusion of words. She confuses "panache" for "panacea," "rationalize" for "nationalize." But it is Inspector Bones who confuses the word "magician" with "logician" (Cohn 115). Sam Clegthorpe is the agricultural spokesman for the Radical Liberals, and he is an acknowledged agnostic who has been named to be the Archbishop of Canterbury in the new government. Sir Archibald Jumper is the leader of the group; he is, "a doctor of medicine, philosophy, literature, and law, with diplomas in psychological medicine and P.T. including gym" (Cahn 115). George Moore, Dotty's husband in Jumpers, is a professor of philosophy, and is the intellect of the group. The lecture he is working on is comically incoherent, and discusses the irrational, the emotional, and the whimsical, saying that these three, "are the stamp of humanity which makes reason a civilizing force. In a wholly rational society the moralist will be a variety of crank, haranguing the bus queue with a demented certitude of one blessed with privileged information" (Perrett 90). When the agnostic veterinarian Clegthorpe is appointed as Archbishop of Canterbury, George exclaims, "How the hell do I know what I find incredible? Credibility is an expanding field" (Perrett 91).

Jumpers is a satiric play that is mainly without plot, exposition, development, or dénouement. It is instead, a "synchronization of events," and is clearly in the genre of "absurd drama" (Cahn 117). The opening scene is an extravaganza which includes in rapid succession, a naked woman swinging from a chandelier, a troupe of acrobats, and a murder. It is quickly established that the play is a farce, and that the theme deals with the disparity between appearance and reality. It is a comedy of confusion and cross-purposes (Perrett 88). Bones comes to investigate an anonymous complaint about the shooting of an acrobat. He considers the report to be a hoax, but he wants to investigate in order to "pay his respects" to Dotty, but the opening of a door reveals George with his face covered with shaving cream. He is holding a bow and arrow in one hand, and a tortoise in the other hand. George's appearance is bizarre to Bones, but is perfectly understandable to the audience, because they know that the bow and arrow and the tortoise are props for his lecture, and that he was shaving when he was interrupted. The scene is therefore an investigation of appearances vs. reality. This theme continues into the second act where George observes Archie making love with Dotty, but this later turns out to be nothing more than the performance of a charade (Perrett 91). This appearance-vs-reality theme is also demonstrated by George's philosophical stance: "There are many things I know which are not verifiable but nobody can tell me I don't know them." George guarantees this statement by saying that he is just as certain of this statement as he is certain of the fact that Dotty has killed Thumper. The real truth is, however, that it is George who has killed Thumper, without realizing it (Perrett 93).

Throughout Jumpers, George ruminates in philosophical fashion as he prepares for the annual university debate, but he is constantly being interrupted by Dotty's cries for help. In the first scene she shouts about "Wolves" and "Rape" and "Murder," but George only responds by saying, "Dorothy, I will not have my work interrupted by these gratuitous acts of lupine delinquency." George is constantly playing charades and word games with Dotty. When he walks into her bedroom and finds her nude body sprawled face down on the bed he remarks that she is "the naked and the dead." When Dotty puts a goldfish bowl on her head and walks around with the leaden gate of a moonwalker, and then stoops down to pick up a small coin, George recognizes "The Moon and Sixpence." But George is too philosophical to be able to see the real Dotty at all (Davidson 46). George's constant ruminating is a parody of the philosophical thinking in the real world. A. J. Ayer, the British philosopher, said that he felt that this parody was, "exceedingly funny and even affectionate." Ayer adds, "This is very fine parody, and like all the best parodies could quite often be mistaken for the original" (Cahn 116).

George Moore's apartment is fashionable, but it is a place of chaos ranging from a secretary who strips and swings on a trapeze, a neurotic wife, and a murdered colleague hung on a bedroom door who constantly interrupts George's thinking (Dean 11). George Moore, the central character of Jumpers, suspects that his wife Dotty is having an affair with Archie, the Vice-Chancellor of the University at which George is a Professor of Ethics (Zeifman "Tomfoolery" 183). George "looks for logical inferences" as he "examines the data," and he becomes convinced that Dotty killed McFee. In fact, he's just as sure that Dotty killed McFee as he is that Dotty killed Thumper, George's pet rabbit. But Dotty in fact did not kill Thumper; George killed him--by accident of course. So George's "logical inferences" are not as "certain" as he thinks they are. George, by the way, is also trying to use "logical inferences" to prove the existence of God (Zeifman "Tomfoolery" 184). There are many puns in Jumpers which echo the puns in the plays of Samuel Beckett, but especially one in the coda--"Wham, bam, thank you Sam" (Zeifman "Tomfoolery" 192). George ruminates throughout the play, trying to determine the meaning of life. "I don't claim to know that God exists, I only claim that he does without my knowing it, and while I claim as much I do not claim to know as much; indeed I cannot know and God knows I cannot" (Cahn 120). George is very philosophical. He considers both the National Gallery, and a home for stray dogs to be monuments to irrationality. "If rationality were the criterion for things allowed to exist, the world would be one gigantic field of soya beans" (Davidson 45).

George is a comic figure in Jumpers. He is a caricature of a professor with his "flannels and shabby smoking jacket, hair awry, his expression and manner signifying remonstrance." George ponders a paradox about Achilles and the Tortoise. If Achilles is the fleetest of Greek warriors, and if the tortoise is given a headstart, then, Zeno argues, Achilles can never catch up with the tortoise no matter how fast he runs. because no matter what point Achilles arrives at, the tortoise has already been there. George has obtained a hare in order to test his hypothesis, but the hare has wandered off. George has become attached to the hare and has given him the nickname of "Thumper." Earlier in the play, George had been trying to test another of Zeno's paradoxes--that an arrow in flight is always at rest at any given instant, and had fired an arrow into the air to test this hypothesis. Toward the end of the play, George is still searching for Thumper, and he notices a spot of blood on his secretary's coat and realizes it must have dripped from the top of the wardrobe. He reaches up there and finds Thumper, impaled on an arrow. As he steps down from the wardrobe he crushes the pet turtle with his foot. The impact of this moment involves many sensations. There is horror and shock at the sudden death. But there is also the humor associated with George's clumsiness and his helplessness as he attempts to bring order to an unordered world. "The audience scarcely knows whether to scream, cry, or laugh" (Cahn 122).

In Jumpers, Stoppard has the stock characters of classical comedy. George Moore is the "Eiron" who is not able to take himself seriously. Sir Archibald Jumper is the "Alazon" since he is an imposter who poses as a learned doctor, lawyer, coroner, acrobat, or Vice Chancellor. Crouch, the Porter, is the clever servant who succeeds in challenging George Moore's logic. And Dotty is the Young Woman (Davidson 43). In the tradition of Aristophanes, Jumpers includes a procession, a debate, a sacrifice, a feast, and a concluding festive union. The procession is the procession of acrobats at the beginning of the play; the debate is a continuing one on whether ethics are relative or absolute; the sacrifice involves the carrying out of Duncan McFee's dead body by the acrobats; the feast has hints that the person who has been sacrificed is also providing the main course at the dinner, and the festive union occurs when Dotty appears like a goddess on a spangled crescent moon and sings to George, to Archie, and to the chorus of <u>Jumpers</u>. In writing his plays, Stoppard was always aware of classical dramatic traditions, and he describes <u>Jumpers</u> and <u>Travesties</u> in the following way: "You start with a prologue which is slightly strange. Then you have an interminable monologue which is rather funny. Then you have scenes. Then you end up with another monologue. And unexpected bits of music and dance, and at the same time people are playing ping-pong with various intellectual arguments" (Davidson 42). In terms of dénouement, there is a difference between New Comedy and Old Comedy. In New Comedy, the boy gets the girl, but in Old Comedy, everybody gets the girl. Since <u>Jumpers</u> is written in the tradition of Old Comedy, it "does not end with a clinch between George and Dotty but with Dotty's public appearance to the entire cast" (Davidson 50).

    <u>Travesties</u> (1975) is a blend of satire and burlesque (Cohn 116). Ruby Cohn considers this play to represent Stoppard at his best, with its, "puns, games, jargon, pastiche, sight gags, limericks, vaudeville, misquotations, cross-conversations" and "mistaken identities" (Cohn 119). In <u>Travesties</u>, James Joyce, Lenin, and Tristan Tzara, a famous Dada poet all find themselves in Zurich, Switzerland at the same time during World War I (Cahn 128). In <u>Travesties</u>, Stoppard discusses the three ways of becoming an artist. The first way is to do things by which is meant art; this is exemplified by Joyce. The second way is to make art mean the things you do; this is exemplified by Tzara. The third way is to subjugate art to social utility; this is exemplified by Lenin (Cohn 117). The travesties which are discussed in this play involve some of Stoppard's favorite subjects--the unverifiability of truth, the fluidity of art and of life, the grace and skill of art, the inscrutability of fate, the unpredictability of memory, and the charm of the vulnerable non-hero (Cohn 117).

At one point they are all together at the Zurich public library. Tristan Tzara is sitting at a table cutting slips of paper from books and arranging them at random as he is composing some poetry in Dadaist fashion. The poem he is composing reads, "Eel at enormous appletzara / key dairy chef's hat he'll learn oomparah! / Ill raced alas whispers kill later nut east, / noon avuncular ill day Clara!" At the next table is sitting Joyce, dictating the opening lines from the "Oxen of the Sun" episode of <u>Ulysses</u> to his loyal, but puzzled, secretary, Gwendolyn:

        JOYCE: Hoopsa, boyaboy, hoopsa!
        GWEN: Hoopsa, boyaboy, hoopsa!
        JOYCE: Hoopsa, boyaboy, hoopsa!
        GWEN: Likewise thrice?
        JOYCE: Uh-hum. (Cahn 129)

    Both Tristan Tzara and James Joyce are indulging in a travesty, Tzara a travesty of the nature of poetry, and Joyce a travesty of prose (Cahn 129). Lenin is sitting at a third table. He is talking excitedly in Russian about news of the Revolution that has been brought to him by his wife, Nadya. His dignity becomes lessened as his cries of "Dah, dah" become inextricably tied to Tristan Tzara's poetry (Cahn 130). Henry Carr is an ex-army officer who is serving as a minor officer in the British Consulate during this time (Cahn 128). Carr's performance of Oscar Wilde's <u>The Importance of Being Earnest</u> has affected his memories, so that he thinks of himself and Tristan Tzara as both being characters in the play. He is Algernon, and Tristan is Jack/Ernest. The plot of Stoppard's play is surrealistic: "Carr is romantically entwined with Cecily who helps Lenin with his book on Imperialism. Tzara is enthralled by Carr's sister Gwendolyn who helps Joyce with his work in progress, <u>Ulysses</u> (Cohn 117). In the Stoppard version of <u>The Importance of</u>

Being Earnest, Tzara's English becomes garbled with French: "Eel ate enormous appletzara...noon avuncular ill day Clara!" can be translated into proper French as "Il est un homme s'appelle Tzara.... Nous n'avons que l'art, il declara" (Cohn 118).

The invectives in Travesties are funny. Carr calls Joyce, "a liar and a hypocrite, a tight-fisted, sponging, fornicating drunk," and Carr says to Tzara, "you little Rumanian wog--you bloody dago--you jumped up phrase-making smart-alecky arty-intellectual Balkan turd."   Tzara says to Carr, "you bloody English philistine--you ignorant smart-arse bogus bourgeois Anglo-Saxon prick!" And Tzara says to Joyce, "you supercilious streak of Irish puke! You four-eyed, bog-ignorant, potato-eating ponce!" (Cohn 118).

Henry Carr likes Ernest's costume in The Importance of Being Earnest, and decides he wants to play that part. "You enter in a bottle-green velvet smoking jacket with black frogging--hose white, cravat perfect, boots elastic-side, trousers of your own choice." Ruby Cohn feels that Henry Carr is funnier than his predecessor George Moore because of his clothes fetish. She describes Carr as being a, "memorialist, jingoist, fashion-plate philistine, defender of the artist though he ignores the arts."   She considers Henry Carr to be Stoppard's "most endearing character" (Cohn 119).

Both Carr and Tzara are dandies right out of Wilde's play, and their dialogue is very reminiscent of Wilde, filled with epigrams and stylized word usage, as the world becomes a showcase for their particular elegance (Cahn 132). Carr, the narrator, presents Joyce as a, "convivial song-and-dance man, given to limericks, folk songs, and outrageous puns" (Cahn 134).   In Carr's mind, Joyce has come to Carr's home in order to enlist him to play Algernon in The Importance of Being Earnest (Cahn 135). As The Importance of Being Earnest progresses, the script reflects Carr's surrealistic confusions:

> GWEN: That's my brother.
> CECILY: Your brother?
> GWEN: Yes, My brother, Henry Carr.
> CECILY: Do you mean that he is not Tristan Tzara the artist?
> GWEN: Quite the contrary: He is the British Consul.
> BENNETT: Mr. Tzara....
> GWEN: Tristan! My Tristan!
> CECILY: Comrade Jack. (Cahn 142)

The second act of Travesties deals with Lenin's ideas of political revolution as opposed to the artistic revolution of the Dadaists, and the Joycean revolution involved with investing man's life with some dignity (Cahn 137). After his experiences, Carr says, "I learned three things in Zurich during the war. I wrote them down. Firstly, you're either a revolutionary or you're not, and if you're not you might as well be an artist as anything else. Secondly, if you can't be an artist, you might as well be a revolutionary.... I forget the third thing" (Cahn 143). Thus, Carr expresses the main theme of the play, that both the artist and the revolutionary have difficult and uncertain roles (Cahn 143).

Hersh Zeifman considers Travesties to be Stoppard's most sustained work of "theatrical punning."   In this play, Henry Carr is a "punster's dream" (Zeifman "Tomfoolery" 188). The cumulative effect on the audience of all these puns is one of "helpless, giddy laughter," but the important point to remember is that Stoppard is using these puns structurally to shape the audience's response to the play's larger issues (Zeifman "Tomfoolery" 189). On the surface it appears that everything Carr says about James Joyce is meant to ridicule and discredit him, but the dazzling, exhilarating play with words, reminiscent of James Joyce's writing, does the opposite of what it appears to do. It has the effect of revering and vindicating Joyce (Zeifman "Tomfoolery" 190).

Dirty Linen (1976) is a farce about a sex scandal in the British Parliament. The farce takes place in a meeting room of the House of Commons, where a special committee has been convened to investigate a number of sordid rumors (Davidson 51). The plot revolves around various newspaper stories that a particular "lawnmower in nickers" has seduced more than one hundred Members of Parliament and other government officials. This person is named Maddie (Madeleine) Gotobed, and she is, in fact, the secretary to the Select Committee on Promiscuity in High Places. As the play opens, Maddie has already slept with five of the six members of the committee, and during the recess for the division bell, she will make it six of the six (Dean 86).

In Dirty Linen, Maddie Gotobed is the first character onto the scene; she is the secretary who has just been assigned to the committee (Cahn 101). The first time the audience sees Maddie, she is alone on the stage trying on her new silk knickers (Davidson 51). Her French silk knickers alternate flashes of emerald green, shocking pink, and peacock as she walks across the stage (Davidson 52). Maddie recites the sexual conquests she has made and then says, "I wouldn't have bothered if I'd know it was supposed to be a secret" (Davidson 53). Then enters Cocklebury-Smythe, and McTeazle, two hopelessly stuffy members of the committee. These entrances are followed by the entrances of the other members of the committee until finally all of them are on stage, and it soon becomes clear that all of them have had affairs with Maddie, and in fact that Maddie is the "mystery woman" they are all investigating (Cahn 102-103). In the play, drawers and other undergarments appear from parcels at the most inopportune moments, and are passed around, sat on, and tossed aside with great speed (Cahn 103). The dialogue is also witty:

> WITHENSHAW: I can see you know your way around these committees, Miss Gotobed. You do speedwriting, I suppose?
>
> MADDIE: Yes, if I'm given enough time.

or,

> FRENCH: What is that?
> WITHENSHAW: Pair of briefs.
> FRENCH: What are they doing there?
> WITHENSHAW: It's a brief case. (Cahn 104)

The puns in Dirty Linen are used by Stoppard to keep the truth hidden. Zeifman says that Stoppard is using puns to "pull the wool over people's ears." At one point in Dirty Linen, McTeazle is trying to have a private conversation with Maddie, but he is constantly being interrupted by Cocklebury-Smythe's flitting into and out of the room. In McTeazle's speech below, the italicization corresponds to Cocklebury-Smythe's momentary reappearances, at which times McTeazle is forced to shift into puns as a way of deceiving Cocklebury-Smythe:

> Maddening the way one is kept waiting for ours is a very tricky position, my dear. In normal times one can count on chaps being quite sympathetic to the sight of a Member of Parliament having dinner with a lovely young woman in some out-of-the-way nook--it could be a case of constituency business, they're not necessarily screw-oo-ooge is, I think you'll find, not in "David Copperfield" at all, still less in "The Old Curiosity Sho"--cking though it is, the sight of a Member of Parliament having some out-of-the-way nookie with a lovely young woman might well be a case of a genuine love match. (Zeifman "Tomfoolery" 190).

What is impressive here is the inventiveness of McTeazle's mind, and the speed with which he is able to extricate himself from a potentially embarrassing situation (Zeifman "Tomfoolery" 190). In Dirty Linen Withenshaw must also recover from a potentially embarrassing situation by using language cleverly. He is saying, "You can't have a committee washing dirty linen in the corridors of power unless every member is above suspicion," when all of a sudden he inadvertently pulls from an envelope a pair of Y-front female panties. He quickly puts the panties back into the envelope, saying, "the wheres and Y-fronts, the whys and wherefores of this Committee are clear to you all." "Wheres and

Y-fronts" is an outrageous pun that immediately grabs our attention. Withenshaw claims that he has never seen Maddie before, but without prompting, he knows her first name. He is able to salvage the situation, however, by changing the expression "Maddie" into "Maddiemoiselle." Some of the wordplay in Dirty Linen is even more scatological, as when Cocklebury-Smythe asks McTeazle, "Why don't you go and see if you can raise those great tits--boobs--those boobies, absolute tits, don't you agree, Malcolm and Douglas--though good men as well" (Zeifman "Tomfoolery" 191). Such puns as the ones mentioned above are important for their amusement value, but they are even more important in leading us into the heart of the play's theme and structure (Zeifman "Tomfoolery" 192). Maddie's last line in Dirty Linen is also the last line of the play. "Finita La Commedia," and this, "certainly emphasizes the theatrical nature of the life here presented" (Cahn 105). After the production of Dirty Linen, Stoppard received a tongue-in-cheek letter from the Clerks' Department of the House of Commons, inviting him for a drink and pointing out a number of discrepancies between the play and the reality it was supposed to represent (Perrett 89).

New-Found-Land (1976) is a parody about a British Parliamentarian's discovery of the United States (Cohn 111). The monologue begins, "My America!--my new-found-land!" which is a line from John Donne's Elegy 19, entitled, "To His Mistris Going to Bed" (Davidson 54). One of the Characters in New-Found-Land is a man named Arthur. He is "a very junior Home Office Official." Another character is named Bernard, and he is "a very senior Home Office Official." Bernard is partly deaf, and partly senile, and he rambles on about how he won a bet from Lloyd George. It is clear that he has recounted this story hundreds of times, and that it is probably the only important event that has ever happened to him. In the story, Lloyd George had thought that Big Ben was the name of a famous clock, and not the name of the bell inside of the clock, and Bernard had won a five-pound note, a note which he is happy to produce triumphantly to accompany his story (Cahn 105).

Every Good Boy Deserves Favour (1978) is described by Victor Cahn as, "a witty, yet tragic, one-act play" (Cahn 147). The cast includes both "actors" and "orchestra" (Cahn 143). It was the London Symphony Orchestra conductor André Previn who convinced Stoppard to write Every Good Boy Deserves Favour which contains a brief excerpt of Tchaikovsky's "1812 Overture," included to mock Ivanov's Napoleonic posturing as he threatens Alexander (Kelly 116-117). Mel Gussow suggests that, "much of the comedy comes from the contrast between the small reality--two men in a tiny cell--and the enormity of the delusion" (Trosky 409). Every Good Boy Deserves Favour opens with the symphony musicians appearing to tune their instruments, but there are no sounds coming from the orchestra. Our first impression is to laugh at this musicless music, but we soon learn that Ivanov hears the instruments even though the audience does not. "The musical score also moves between comic parody (instruments imitating people) and satiric exposure (particular scores being cited ironically to suggest particular characters' follies)" (Kelly 133). The play takes place in a cell which holds two men, both with the same name, Alexander Ivanov (Cahn 143). In the play, the one who is called "Ivanov" is a mental patient, and the one called "Alexander" is a political prisoner (Cahn 144). Ruby Cohn notes that, "since the mad musician makes no political statements, and the sane dissident hears no orchestra, both are freed" (Cohn 111).

The opening scene of the play establishes the difference. It is Ivanov who plays the triangle in a mimed performance that includes an orchestra that is visible to the audience, but is known by the audience to be a figment of Ivanov's imagination. When the audience finally hears real music, this music is known to come from Ivanov's mind rather than from a real orchestra (Cahn 144). The idea of having a full orchestra on stage is a very dramatic gesture (Cahn 147). Alexander tells how he came to be in the cell with Ivanov:

They arrested a couple of writers, A and B, who had published some stories under different names. Under their own names they got five years and seven years hard labor. I thought this was most peculiar. My friend, C, demonstrated against the arrest of A land B. I told him he was crazy to do it, and they put him back into the mental hospital.... M compiled a book on the trials of C, I, J, K, and L, and with his colleagues N, O, P, Q, R, and S attended the trial of T who had written a book about his experiences, and who got a year in labor camp. (Cahn 145)

The Chief Doctor in charge of Alexander's case is not a Doctor of Medicine, but is rather a Doctor of Philosophy who is seeking to control Alex's language and his thinking. The Doctor tells Alexander, "Your opinions are your symptoms. Your disease is dissent" (Cahn 146). Alexander doesn't protest his imprisonment nor does he speak against injustice. Rather, he gives, "identical answers to the same questions asked of the lunatic Ivanov." Then all four of the major characters, Ivanov, Alexander, the Doctor, and the Colonel join Ivanov's orchestra. Sacha wants to get his father, Alexander, out of prison.

> SACHA: (not singing) Tell them lies. Tell them they've cured you. Tell them you're grateful.
> ALEX: How can that be right?
> SACHA: If they're wicked how can it be wrong?
> ALEX: It helps them to go on being wicked. It helps people to think they're not so wicked after all.
> SACHA: It doesn't matter. I want you to come home.
> ALEX: And what about the other fathers? And mothers?
> SACHA: (shouts) It's wicked to let yourself die! (Cahn 147)

In Every Good Boy Deserves Favour, not only does Alexander have the same name as does his hostile cellmate (called Ivanov), but Alexander's son is called Sacha, which is the diminutive form of Alexander, so that Alexander actually has the same name as both his cellmate and his son. By putting Alexander senior into the same cell as his insane double, Ivanov, the prison authorities had hoped to undermine Alexander senior's sanity, thereby proving that he was justly imprisoned. "Sacha plays Ivanov's (and Stoppard's) instrument, the triangle [called in the play the 'subversive triangle'] in the school orchestra. Ivanov's triangle playing is lunatic and involuntary, while Sacha's is compulsory" (Kelly 118). In Every Good Boy Deserves Favour, Ivanov imagines that he is conducting an orchestra, but the play is really about the fact that both Alexander and Ivanov are conforming to the score that the state has designated for them to play. The fact that the three major characters in the play are all named Alexander Ivanov allows for the sleight-of-hand dénouement, since this name sameness is what saves them from the Soviet system (Dean 95). The play ends when the Colonel releases the two prisoners and therefore forfeits the reconciliation scene expected in comedy because of an ominous suggestion of further trouble to come. Sacha wishes that, "everything can be all right," but this suggestion is to the accompaniment of a musical score that is disturbingly menacing (Kelly 122).

As the play Professional Foul (1978) opens, Professor Anderson is on his way to Prague to attend a philosophical convention, where he is scheduled to deliver a paper entitled, "Ethical Fictions as Ethical Foundations." Professor Anderson is visited in his hotel room by one of his former students in England, a Czech by the name of Pavel Hollar.

> ANDERSON: You got a decent degree, too, didn't you?
> HOLLAR: Yes, I got a first.
> ANDERSON: Of course you did. Well done, well done. Are you still in philosophy?
> HOLLAR: No, unfortunately.

ANDERSON: Ah. What are you doing now?

HOLLAR: I am a cleaner at the bus station.

ANDERSON: You wash buses?

HOLLAR: No, not buses--the lavatories, the floors where people walk and
     so. (Cahn 148)

At this point, Hollar starts to talk about a doctoral dissertation he has written about inherent individual rights. These rights "may or may not include, for example, the right to publish something. In that situation, the individual ethic would flow from the collective ethic, just as the State says it does. Hollar wants Anderson to take his manuscript out of the country and get it published for him outside of Czechoslovakia (Cahn 149). Hollar's controversial thesis is about the conflicting rights of the individual and the rights of the community, and Anderson plants Hollar's thesis in McKendrick's luggage. As expected, when they go through customs, Anderson's and Chetwyn's luggage are thoroughly searched by the authorities, while McKendrick, who is a Marxist, goes through customs with no inspection at all (Dean 92-93).

Three of the four philosophers attending the convention in Professional Foul are Englishmen--Chetwyn, Anderson, and McKendrick. The fourth, Stone, is an American whose pursuits as a "linguistic philosopher" are openly mocked. His, "epistimological observations verge on the tautological." Anderson and McKendrick consider Stone's field to be a "linguistic quirk," since Stone feels that, "through misunderstanding, language's inherent ambiguity, or the oddities of idiomatic expression, old can be young and young, old." Ironically Stoppard's writings have proven Stone's thesis to be true, for Stoppard himself is a great manipulator of language and wit. For example, McKendrick's last line in the first scene is an illustration of the ambiguity inherent in language. When he asks himself, "I wonder if there'll be any decent women," he does not mean "decent" in the sense of morality or respectability, but rather, just the opposite (Dean 90).

Professional Foul contains several scenes that are based on Stoppard's personal knowledge of actual events in the arrest of Czech playwright and President of Czechoslovakia, Vaclav Havel (Pavel Hollar in the play), based on the testimony of Vaclav Havel's wife with whom Stoppard spoke during his 1977 tour. In this play, three events are linked--the approaching colloquium, the World Cup Soccer Match, and the oppression of Czech artists and intellectuals (Kelly 123). In one scene of the play, one man is going through the books, leafing through each book and looking at each book's spine. Another man is sorting out fluff from the carpet sweeper. Still another man is standing on a chair looking for something inside of the ventilation grating. In the meantime, Pavel Hollar is listening to the soccer game on his wife's radio because he was forced to relinquish his performance tickets to a plainclothes policeman. Hollar is being charged with a trumped-up currency offence, the radio is announcing that Broadbent, a British player, has fouled Deml, a Czech player, and has thus prevented him from scoring a certain goal. At this moment of high suspense, Stoppard, "invites us to compare the ethos of professional soccer with that of the communist-controlled Czech regime: both require that when an individual player's sense of 'natural' justice conflicts with the team's need to win, the group ethic will prevail over the individual's sense of fair play" (Kelly 127). Katherine Kelly explains: "In choosing to help Hollar by smuggling out his thesis in McKendrick's briefcase and by altering his colloquium talk to reflect the gist of Hollar's argument, Anderson reverses a principle--that of respect for one's colleague and host--after experiencing his host's treachery" (Kelly 128). Stoppard says that in football a player is committed to make an intentional foul in order to stop a goal, and this is called a "professional foul." The question which Stoppard is asking is whether or not the same commitment is necessary in politics as in football. Must a person deliberately break the rules of the game, if the breaking of these rules is not only justified, but even almost required (Cahn 151). The issue is related to the balance of ethics between individual and collective rights. "The implications are serious for a collective state or State ethic, which finds itself in conflict with individual rights and seeks, in the name of the people, to impose its values on the very individuals who comprise the State" (Cahn 152).

The title of Dogg's Our Pet (1979) is an anagram of "Dogg's Troupe" (Whitaker 118). In Dogg's Our Pet, the characters are given the names of code-words used in the military to represent the first four letters of the English alphabet. There are schoolboys named "Able," and "Baker"; there is a workman named "Charlie," and there is a schoolmaster named "Dogg" (Cohn 110). It is Charlie who is shouting to someone offstage for objects to aid in the building of a speaker's platform for a ceremony that is about to happen. He calls for a plank, a slab, a block, a brick, and a cube. But the rhythm of building the platform is interrupted whenever Able, Baker, or Dogg violate the linguistic code. Despite the confusion, Charlie is able to build a wall which contains lettered slabs and blocks with insulting messages written in a coded language called "Dogg." After the platform is built, and the Lady has delivered her speech on the wobbly platform, Charlie says,

> Three points only while I have the platform. Firstly, just because it's been opened, there's no need to run amok kicking footballs through windows and writing on the walls. It's me who's got to keep this place looking new so let's start by leaving it as we find it. Secondly, I can take a joke as well as any man, but I've noticed a lot of language about the place and if there's one thing I can't stand it's language. I forgot what the third point is.

At this point, Charlie rebuilds the wall to read: "DOGGS TROUPE THE END" (Whitaker 119).

Night and Day (1978) is set in a mythical African country in the late 1970s, and represents the international political situation of that place and time (Dean 97). Night and Day is a loose parody of Evelyn Waugh's Scoop, a satire about Fleet Street (Kelly 138). Mageeba's idea for a "free press" is to support a press edited by one of his relatives (Dean 100). The audience gradually comes to realize that what they had thought was reality, was actually Guthrie's prophetic dream, but there is a period of time when the audience straddles between reality and Guthrie's dream world, the world of night (dreams) and of day (reality) (Kelly 139). The play is about three journalists, but especially about Guthrie, a quiet and retiring photographer. Guthrie is the least overtly egotistical even though he is probably the most experienced of the group. Wagner is egotistical, competitive, and crude. Milne (possibly an echo of A. A. Milne) is the youngest, the highest born, the best educated, and the most naïve member of the trio (Kelly 141). It is Milne who says, "Junk journalism is the evidence of a society that has got at least one thing right, that there should be nobody with the power to dictate where responsible journalism begins" (Kelly 142).

Ruth Carson, the protagonist in Night and Day, plays hostess and mistress while her husband and three British reporters go on with their political revolution. It is Ruth who provides the structure of the play with her asides and soliloquies that are not heard by the other characters on stage (Dean 11). Whenever Ruth is supposed to speak out loud, her speech is noted in the script as RUTH, but whenever her speech is an aside to the audience, the "RUTH" is surrounded by quotes. This produces two different characters--the public RUTH, and the private "RUTH," and whenever she speaks an aside, Ruth is supposed to turn full-face to the audience. Ruth has a one-night stand with a reporter named Richard Wagner. She explains her "moment of weakness" by saying, "I let you take me to dinner because there was no danger of going to bed with you. And then, because there was no danger of going to bed a second time, I went to bed with you" (Dean 98).

Ruth is aware of the paradox of a "free press." She realizes that only without governmental intervention is the press truly free to publish the truth, but without government intervention, the press must rely upon a readership that will financially support the expense of determining the truth.   Thus, she realizes that "intellectual freedom sometimes entails unpleasant and even reprehensible practices." Night and Day is an ironic attack on the entire journalistic system. It is an attack of the unions that can deprive the public of the news through labor actions. It is an attack of the journalists who squander their talents in order to produce titillating copy. And it is an attack of the reading public which supports and rewards these misdirected efforts (Dean 101).

Dogg's Hamlet (1980) condenses Shakespeare's Hamlet down to thirteen minutes, and then this is followed by a two-minute condensation of the condensation to be given as an encore (Whitaker 120). In this parody, Stoppard's mini-Hamlet preserves the outline of the plot and the clichés of the major soliloquies, but the speed with which it is produced gives the impression of a slapstick speed-through of Shakespeare's play.   In Dogg's Hamlet, Stoppard is mocking the compulsory recitations of Shakespeare by captive schoolchildren (Kelly 131). In Dogg's Hamlet, the stage is prepared for a production of Hamlet by three schoolboys whose native language is Dogg. Dogg uses English words, but these words have entirely different meanings than regular English. For example, when a dignified matron offers a ceremonial greeting in Dogg, she says, "Scabs. slobs, black yobs, yids, spicks, wops" which has the same effect as the regular English expression, "Your grace, ladies and gentlemen, boys and girls" (Dean 103).

Cahoot's Macbeth (1980) is dedicated to the Czech playwright Pavel Kohout, and presents an underground performance of Shakespeare's Macbeth which is so often interrupted by government censors that they switch to an artificial language called "Dogg," to avoid being arrested (Trosky 409). In Cahoot's Macbeth Stoppard uses parody to expose the Czech harassment of dissenting artists and intellectuals. The abbreviated Macbeth is presented in the form of living room theater, and takes place inside of a private home. It is performed by actors who have been banned from performing on the public Czech stage, and the play is heard by the secret police, who are doing their job of appropriately eavesdropping (Kelly 129). Cahoot's Macbeth is a mocking parody. Dogg's Hamlet is also a parody, but the tone is not mocking--it is more serious than that. Cahoot's Macbeth is about the clandestine recitation of Shakespeare by censored artists in the East. "Here the play has been collapsed not to dispatch it as quickly as possible but to preserve it without detection. Its compression serves to remind us of the danger of performing it at all" (Kelly 131). The Inspector in Cahoot's Macbeth has a strong stage presence. In fact, part of his comic persona comes from his constantly attempting to upstage the other actors:

INSPECTOR:...Would you care to make a statement?
CAHOOT: "Thou hast it now: King, Cawdor, Glamis, all
        As the weird sister promised...."
INSPECTOR: Kindly leave my wife's family out of this....
CAHOOT: "...and I fear I thou playest most foully for't...." (Kelly 132)

The actors in Cahoot's Macbeth have learned the basics of the strange language called "Dogg," and they use this alternate language as they construct a stage, in order to evade the state censors. "Rafters Birnam cakehops hobble Dunsinane, / fry counterpane nit crossly window-framed, / fancifully oblong!...." This is translated into regular English as "Though Birnam Wood be come to Dunsinane / And thou opposed, being of no woman born, / Yet will I try the last" (Kelly 133).

At one point in Cahoot's Macbeth there is an incessant knocking on the door which is reminiscent of the Porter scene in Shakespeare's Macbeth. When the door opens, an Inspector from the state police enters and says, "Oh- I'm sorry--is this the National Theatre?" This statement reminds the audience of the repression of theatrical freedom in communist countries. The Inspector demonstrates a sadistic and sinister wit. He has a stinging rejoinder for almost every sentence uttered by his victims. The Inspector says to

Lady Macbeth, "Darling, you were marvelous." Lady Macbeth replies "I'm not your darling," and the Inspector says, "I know, and you were'nt marvelous either" (Dean 104).

Stoppard's On the Razzle (1981) has an intricate farcical plot that involves the adventures of Weinberl and Christopher, two assistants to the master grocer Herr Zangler. When Herr Zangler decides to go to Vienna to entertain his fiancée, he leaves Weinberl and Christopher in charge of his shop. Weinberl and Christopher also decide to go "on a razzle" to Vienna, and complications develop when they encounter Zangler in the city during their once-in-a-lifetime illicit spree (Wright 498). The play contains an unbroken sequence of jokes, in which, "each word is squeezed for its maximum comic mileage."

> The central figure, Zangler, is provided with a running gag in his constant malapropisms and parapraxes, laboriously assisted by the other characters in his search for the correct word or phrase. The large cast is grouped into pairs, recalling the routines of stand-up comics and music-hall patter: the grocer and his new servant; the fiancée and her female friend; the young lovers; and the two assistants, senior and junior. (Wright 499)

Stoppard's Squaring the Circle (1984) has the flavor of a documentary; however it also contains many comic ironies that resulted from the war between the British director and the American producers (Wright 1073). Stoppard's use of twins in Hapgood (1988) (he has three sets) is a comic device of long standing. His baroquely convoluted spy plot is another comic device, especially in that this plot demonstrates that people do things for multiple reasons--often for conflicting reasons. In Hapgood there is no absolute morality, nor is there straight causality that explains human behavior (Kelly 153). Because it is a post-Newtonian parody of the spy formula, there is some question among critics as to whether to class it as a spy thriller, a poetic metaphor, or a joking Nabokovian spoof. The author Stoppard has thought about the junction of scientific observation, and aesthetic contemplation, and the character Kerner has also thought about it. "When I have learned the [spy] language I will write my own book. The traitor will be the one you don't like very much, it will be a scandal. Also I will reveal him at the beginning. I don't understand this mania for surprises. If the author knows, it's rude not to tell" (Kelly 154).

Isabel Florence Hapgood in Hapgood has the code name of "Mother," which is a pun on the connotations of motherhood in Russia and in England. Isabel received her name as she was a green agent because at tea time she always acted as a "mother" in her all-male office. So now she is the "mother" of her own unit, as she pours the tea and makes significant operative decisions. There are numerous doppelgangers in Hapgood. There are the nameless Russian Twins. There are Ridley and his twin brother, and there are Hapgood and her pseudo-twin, Celia Newton. By having a twin--either real or imagined--the agent is able to be in two different places at the same time, and this is a distinct advantage in the world of espionage. "Twins defeat surveillance because when you know what one of them is doing you can't be certain where she is, and when you know where she is, you can't be certain what she's doing" (Kelly 151).

In Hapgood, Joseph Kerner is a scientist and a spy. He is trained as a theoretical physicist, but he likes games, especially the spy game and verbal games. He specializes in puns, tactical stratagems, sports, and mathematics. He talks to Blair and Hapgood, his spy colleagues, in a language which Stoppard adapted from The Feynman Lectures on Physics, especially the chapter on "Quantum Behavior." His similes are a covert way of telling how spies should behave, and how they should view reality. He develops a playful metaphor that compares human behavior to the behavior of subatomic particles: "You can't make a picture of what Bohr proposed, an electron does not go round like a planet, it is like a moth which was there a moment ago, it gains or loses a quantum of energy and it jumps, and at the moment of the quantum jump it is like two moths, one to be here and one to stop being there; an electron is like twins, each one unique, a unique twin" (Kelly 152).

In <u>Hapgood</u>, Stoppard is trying to reestablish his powers as a comic playwright, by establishing a, "total theatrical metaphor for post-Newtonian morality and epistemology in comic terms." <u>Hapgood</u> illustrates how a scientific paper and a work of art differ, and how they overlap (Kelly 155). Hapgood is a perfect demonstration of post-Newtonian flexibility. She balks at equating the KGB with "the opposition," saying, "We're just keeping each other in business." She also begins using the off-color language of her twin sister to express her frustrations. Since <u>Hapgood</u> is a post-Newtonian spy thriller, the concluding scene is indeterminate. Kerner's interest in language and games is rekindled by his son's rugby match, and even though he says that he will return to Russia, he nevertheless remains fixed on stage (Kelly 157).

In a chapter entitled "Silence and the Turn toward Satire," Katherine Kelly says that Stoppard's satires, "fend off, expose, debunk, and deny, the political culture oppressing them. In <u>Every Good Boy Deserves Favour</u> the hero Alexander refuses to play an instrument; <u>Professional Foul</u>'s Pavel Hollar refuses to place the ethic of the state over that of the individual; and actor Cahoot of <u>Cahoot's Macbeth</u> refuses to remain silent" (Kelly 115). In all of his plays, Stoppard is creative in his use of linear movement, flashbacks, plots within plots, and copious references to other literary works. In Stoppard's plays there is clutter and much episodic action, but there is also structure, and Stoppard expects his audiences to grasp that structure (Cahn 156). In Stoppard's plays, the pace is brisk, there are constant literary allusions, and double and triple meanings. His language is amusing, and richly woven with ideas. Stoppard marks the beginning of the "post-absurdist" movement (Cahn 157).

Stoppard has demonstrated a penchant for recycled names.

> The most celebrated example of Stoppard's recurrent names are the Moons of <u>Lord Malquist and Mr. Moon</u> and <u>The Real Inspector Hound</u>, and the Boots of "The Dissolution of Dominic Boot" and <u>The Real Inspector Hound</u> (in which the character is actually named Birdboot.) The Georges of his plays (Riley from <u>Enter a Free Man</u> and Moore from <u>Jumpers</u>) also have more in common than a cursory glance might suggest. (Dean 12)

Stoppard has demonstrated a penchant for word play, witty repartée, and tour-de-force conclusions which are partly the result of his having read Oscar Wilde (Dean 7-8). Stoppard has also demonstrated a penchant for allusion. His plays contain many famous characters or characters which were made famous in other plays. In his plays, Stoppard has reintroduced characters from <u>Hamlet</u>, from <u>Macbeth</u>, and from <u>The Importance of Being Earnest</u>. He has reintroduced such characters from contemporary life as Vladimir Bukovsky, Pavel Kohout, and Alfred J. Ayer, and such characters from history as V. I. Lenin, Henry Carr, and James Joyce (Dean 10). But Stoppard never allows the expectations of his audiences to be fully realized. As soon as he has developed a stereotype to the extent that everyone knows what type of behavior to expect for that stereotype, Stoppard breathes new life into these stereotypical characters. Joan Fitzpatrick Dean says that Stoppard seems to be committed to ambushing his audiences (Dean 9). Stoppard has also demonstrated a penchant for parody of popular genres such as the whodunnit, the historical play, or the music comedy. The clichés, the suspense, and the intrigue of the whodunnit, for example, are used to generate <u>The Real Inspector Hound, Jumpers</u>, and <u>Artist Descending a Staircase</u>. Ironically, this strong sense of parody is responsible both for Stoppard's commercial success and for the critical attacks which he has received (Dean 6).

Dean comments on Stoppard's special use of language:

> Stoppard's treatment of language allies him not only with the absurdists but also with the wittiest if not greatest writers of the English Language. Like Conrad, Stoppard may have had the advantage of learning English as a

second language and thus a greater sensitivity to the ironies and nuances of its idiom. His use of puns, quid pro quo, and other forms of wordplay is perhaps his most acclaimed and best known characteristic.... Stoppard indulges himself as well as his audience in the shear pleasure of experiencing the density and richness of which the language is capable. Moreover, his attention to language results not only in humor but also precision. (Dean 107)

Dean says that Stoppard is something of an anomaly in that he is a serious comic writer with an interest in theatrical realism who was born into an age of tragicomedy (Trosky 407). Dean says that, "Stoppard's faith in man and his characters' persistent, if battered, optimism are aptly suited to his comic mode" (Dean 108).

Tom Stoppard (William Boot) Bibliography

Ariztia, Pilar Zozaya. "Tom Stoppard: 'A Fellow of Infinite Jest....'" Literary and Linguistic Aspects of Humour. Barcelona, Spain: Univ of Barcelona Dept of Languages, 1984, 305-311.

Barker, Clive. "Contemporary Shakespearean Parody in British Theatre." Shakespeare Jahrbuch 105 (1969): 104-120.

Billington, Michael. "Travesties." Critical Essays on Tom Stoppard. Ed. Anthony Jenkins. Boston, MA: G. K. Hall, 1990, 121-128.

Bradshaw, Jon. "Tom Stoppard, Nonstop: Word Games with a Hit Playwright." Tom Stoppard in Conversation. Ed. Paul Delaney. Ann Arbor, MI: University of Michigan Press, 1994, 95ff.

Cahn, Victor L. Beyond Absurdity: The Plays of Tom Stoppard. Rutherford, NJ: Fairleigh Dickinson University Press, 1979.

Cave, Richard Allen. "An Art of Literary Travesty: Rosencrantz and Guildenstern Are Dead, Jumpers." Critical Essays on Tom Stoppard. Ed. Anthony Jenkins. Boston, MA: G. K. Hall, 1990, 162-72.

Cohn, Ruby. "Tom Stoppard: Light Drama and Dirges in Marriage." Contemporary English Drama. Ed. C. W. E. Bigsby. New York, NY: Holmes and Meier, 1981, 109-120.

Davidson, Mary R. "Transcending Logic: Stoppard, Wittgenstein, and Aristophanes." Analogical Modern Drama. Ed. Kenneth S. White. Amsterdam, Netherlands: Rodopi, 1982, 39-60.

Dean, Joan Fitzpatrick. Tom Stoppard: Comedy as a Moral Matrix. Columbia, MO: Univ of Missouri Press, 1981.

Gardner, John. On Moral Fiction. New York, NY: Basic Books, 1978.

Ginakaris, C. J. "Absurdism Altered: Rosencrantz and Guildenstern Are Dead." Drama Survey 7 (1969): 52-58.

Hayman, Ronald. Tom Stoppard. London, England: Heinemann, 1977.

Kelly, Katherine E. Tom Stoppard and the Craft of Comedy--Medium and Genre at Play. Ann Arbor, MI: University of Michigan Press, 1991.

Orta, Ignacio Vazquez. "Rosencrantz and Guildenstern Are Dead: A Linguistic Game." 1984, 265-268.

Perrett, Roy W. "Philosophy as Farce, or Farce as Philosophy." Critical Essays on Tom Stoppard. Ed. Anthony Jenkins. Boston, MA: G. K. Hall, 1990, 87-96.

Presto, Nina. "To Be or Not To Be...." Unpublished Paper. Tempe, AZ: Arizona State University, 1995.

Rayner, Alice. "Stoppard's Paradox: Delight in Utopia." Comic Persuasion: Moral Structure in British Comedy from Shakespeare to Stoppard. Berkeley, CA: Univ of California Press, 1987, 129-151.

Rusinko, Susan. "Tom Stoppard." Encyclopedia of British Humorists, Volume II. Ed. Steven H. Gale. New York, NY: Garland, 1996, 1067-1075.

Sorell, Walter. Facets of Comedy. New York, NY: Grosset and Dunlap 1972.

Stoppard, Tom. After Magritte. London, England: Faber and Faber, 1971.

Stoppard, Tom. Albert's Bridge and If You're Glad I'll Be Frank. London, England: Faber and Faber, 1969.

Stoppard, Tom. "Ambushes for the Audience: Towards a High Comedy of Ideas." Theatre Quarterly 4 (1974): 3-17.

Stoppard, Tom. Artist Descending a Staircase and Where Are They Now? London, England: Faber and Faber, 1973.

Stoppard, Tom. Dirty Linen and New-Found-Land. New York, NY: Grove, 1976.

Stoppard, Tom. Enter a Free Man. New York, NY: Grove, 1972.

Stoppard, Tom. Every Good Boy Deserves Favour and Professional Foul. New York, NY: Grove, 1978.

Stoppard, Tom. Jumpers. New York, NY: Grove, 1971.

Stoppard, Tom. Lord Malquist and Mr. Moon. 1966. London, England: Faber and Faber, 1974.

Stoppard, Tom. The Real Inspector Hound. New York, NY: Grove, 1969.

Stoppard, Tom. Rosencrantz and Guildenstern Are Dead. New York, NY: Grove Press, 1967.

Stoppard, Tom. Travesties. London, England: Faber and Faber, 1975.

Stoppard, Tom. "A Very Satirical Thing Happened to Me on the Way to the Theatre Tonight." Encore 10 (1973): 33-36.

Trosky, Susan M. "Tom Stoppard." Contemporary Authors: New Revision Series, Volume 39. Detroit, MI: Gale, 1993, 405-413.

Weightman, John. "A Metaphysical Comedy." Encounter 38 (1972): 44-46.

Whitaker, Thomas R. "Logics of the Absurd." Critical Essays on Tom Stoppard. Ed. Anthony Jenkins. Boston, MA: G. K. Hall, 1990, 110-120.

Wright, Anne. "Tom Stoppard." Dictionary of Literary Biography, Volume Thirteen: British Dramatists Since World War II. Ed. Stanley Weintraub. Detroit, MI: Gale, 1982, 482-500.

Zabalbeascoa, Jose Antonio. "Rosencrantz and Guildenstern Are Alive and Well." Literary and Linguistic Aspects of Humour. Barcelona, Spain: Univ of Barcelona Dept of Languages, 1984, 297-303.

Zeifman, Hersh. "Comedy of Ambush: Tom Stoppard's The Real Thing." Modern Drama 26 (1983): 139-149.

Zeifman, Hersh. "Tomfoolery: Stoppard's Theatrical Puns." Critical Essays on Tom Stoppard. Ed. Anthony Jenkins. Boston, MA: G. K. Hall, 1990, 175-193.

David Benedictus (1938-)

The Fourth of June (1962) is David Benedictus's first novel. In this novel he satirized life at Eton and Balliol, two exclusive English schools which he had attended. T. Winnifrith says that, "the timing of Benedictus's first novel was admirable, as it coincided with a wave of satire directed against the Macmillan government, full of old Etonions and racked by sexual scandals" (Straub 52). The novel contains a wide array of eccentric characters, both young and old, and Benedictus's presentation of these characters is genuinely funny. The novel centers on a lower-middle-class boy by the name of Scarfe, who is brought to Eton as part of an educational experiment. Berwick is a bullying athlete who has a doting nymphomaniac mother known as "Lady Hormones." For Berwick's seventeenth birthday, she presents him with a chorus girl. Another character in the novel is a "bloody funny Bishop" who encourages Scarfe to visit him whenever he is in religious trouble. But on one of these visits, Scarfe catches the Bishop peeping through a window at the Chaplain's daughter who is undressing in front of an uncurtained window. Scarfe is a squat, ugly, grammar-school boy with a number of unattractive qualities. He is, "pathetic, whining, boorish, and afflicted with adolescent religiosity." John Batts says that The Fourth of June "glitters with images, and these are a rich store of humour." He also says that much of the humor is based on a kind of anger that produces laughter. Some critics consider the novel to be classical; others consider it to be pop; still others consider it mock-heroic, or fanciful, or conceited, or absurd, but they all agree that it is humorous (Batts 53).

David Benedictus Bibliography

Batts, John. "The Humor of Anger: Looking Back at Amis and Company." WHIMSY 4 (1986): 51-54.
Straub, Deborah A. "David Benedictus." Contemporary Authors: New Revision Series, Volume 24. Detroit, MI: Gale, 1988, 52.

Caryl Churchill (1938-)

According to Christian W. Thomsen, Caryl Churchill is a feminist socialist playwright who, "proceeds with irony and sarcasm, aiming at a double target--the ideology of male supremacy and of the ruling classes" (Thomsen 172). Caryl Churchill, whose father was a cartoonist, tells about the impact that cartooning had on her work: "Cartoons are really so much like plays. An image with somebody saying something. I grew up with his cartoons of the war--of Goebbels and Mussolini" (Weintraub 119).

Owners (1972) is a play about ownership. The characters, "own, or want to own, property, human relations, human bodies, with a fierce, petrified heartlessness that points out the psychological defects and reified humanity which are the product of a society which regards ownership with a quasi-religious awe" (Thomsen 166). In Traps (1977) the audience is given ambiguous clues as to whether the play is meant to be a serious alternative to bourgeois living, or a parody targeting alternative forms of living (Thomsen 168). Traps is about how a group of six people in a room relate interpersonally. The setting of the play changes from the city to the country, from the past to the present, as the play questions our perceptions of reality. Churchill compares this play to a painting by Dutch artist M. C. Escher, where objects exist in relationships that would be impossible in real life (Weintraub 122).

Sylvie Drake says that Cloud Nine (1979) has been described as a sexual comedy, as a feminist tract, as a satire on sexual politics, as a paean to androgyny, as a dream play, and as a reality play (Dear 69). Act I takes place in British colonial Africa in the year 1880, and Act II takes place in London a hundred years later. But the characters in Act II are merely twenty-five years older than they were in Act I, rather than the 100-years older that they should be. Richard Christensen notes that the seven actors change roles for the second act, and don't necessarily play characters of their own age or gender. "Betty, the sweet little wife, is played by a man; Edward, the son and heir, is played by a girl. And Joshua, the black servant, is played by a white man." Some critics suggest that Cloud Nine is an old-fashioned satire because there is really nothing at stake, since no-one today would defend the racist and sexist attitudes of the Victorian colonials being targeted in the play (Dear 70). Cloud Nine is an outspoken satiric play in which the farcical roles establish enough distance to allow the audience to enjoy a riot of laughter (Bermel 189). No-one in the audience feels threatened because of the juggling of the roles, the softening of the "hard edges of the material," and the good-natured banter (Bermel 190). Churchill uses a great deal of experimental language and subtle ambiguities. The plays on words are actually traps for both the audience and for the actors. Christian Thomsen considers Cloud Nine to be a "polished exuberant farce," which uses dramatic devices which appear on the surface to be experimental, but which are in fact, "firmly rooted in the tradition of farce" (Thomsen 168). The characters in Cloud Nine are caricatures of Victorian types, and Churchill is here especially attacking the, "self-ordained godlike superiority of the British male" (Thomsen 169). The title of Cloud Nine comes from a song lyric which is repeated with varying effects throughout the play. The song discusses various unusual sexual orientations including sex between two men, sex between two women, and sex between a sixty-five-year-old bride, and a seventeen-year-old groom. The song also discusses smoking dope on some playground swings, with the resultant description of, "higher and higher on true love's wings." The last line of the song is also surrealistic: "Upside down when you reach Cloud Nine" (Bermel 181).

Cloud Nine is a fantasy in which current affairs, history, and other aspects of realism overlap. The first act takes place during Victorian times in a British colony in Africa (Bermel 181). The scene is described tersely: "Low bright sun. Verandah, Flagpole with Union Jack." There are four members in the inner family, three of them named after British royalty. The young Victoria is represented by a dummy. Edward, her brother, is represented by a grown woman. Betty (a shortened form of Elizabeth), their mother, is played by a man. Clive is the fourth member of the inner family. He is strongly colonial in his leanings. He is also very macho and feels that it is his duty to hold his family in line.

> Clive heads a household of intersecting opposites: a woman for a son, a man for a wife, and a dummy for a daughter. Clive announces, "I am the father to the natives here," and his personal family includes, by extension, Joshua, his African "boy" for the past eight years, played by a white actor; Ellen, Edward's gay governess, and Maud, Betty's prim mother, who taught her the formulas of self-suppression. (Bermel 182)

Joshua is "whiter than white." He sings "In the Deep Midwinter," which is a British carol associated with the boys' and girls' schools of England, and which is totally inappropriate in Africa, especially when sung by a black. Joshua also calls an African creation myth a "bad story," and prefers the story about Adam and Eve, saying that, "God made man white like him and gave him the bad woman who liked the snake and gave us all this trouble" (Bermel 183).

In Cloud Nine, one of the characters outside of the inner family is the gay, Harry. When Clive says, "There is something dark about women, that threatens what is best in us. Between men that light burns brightly," Harry responds, "I didn't know you felt like that." When Clive continues, by saying, "Women are irrational, demanding, inconsistent, treacherous, lustful, and they smell different from us," Harry misinterprets what Clive is saying, and he grabs hold of Clive in order to show some affection. But although Clive is a misogynist, he is also a homophobe, and he is bewildered by Harry's actions and considers these actions to be a "most revolting perversion," adding that, "Rome fell, Harry, and this sin can destroy an empire. My God, what a betrayal of the Queen.... I cannot keep a secret like this. Rivers will be named after you.... You must save yourself from depravity. You must get married" (Bermel 184). Clive even suggests that Caroline Saunders would be a good person to marry. Harry responds, in "one of the many glints of comic agony," that, "I suppose getting married wouldn't be any worse than killing myself" (Bermel 184).

The scene and the characters change remarkably for the second half of Cloud Nine. Whereas the first act was set in 1880-colonial Africa, the second act is set in 1980-postcolonial England. "Victoria and Betty are now played by women, Edward by a man. Clive, Maud, Harry, Ellen, and Mrs. Saunders (the last two roles doubled) have given way to four newcomers: Victoria's husband Martin, Edward's promiscuous lover, Gerry, a young lesbian mother named Lin, and her small daughter, Cathy (performed by a male actor), who sings dirty skipping rhymes" (Bermel 185). Cathy has grown up between the sexes. She wears boys' clothes, and she plays with boy's toys, and uses boys' strong language. But she's also very fond of jewelry and ornaments, and in scene ii, she enters, "wearing a pink dress and carrying a rifle" (Bermel 187). In Cloud Nine, Martin, the father, says that he just wants to make Victoria, his wife, happy, and says, "I'm not like whatever percentage of American men have become impotent as a direct result of women's liberation, which I am totally in favour of.... My one aim is to give you rolling orgasms like I do other women. So why the hell don't you have them?" (Bermel 187). Jack Kroll of Newsweek called Cloud Nine "a riotously humane farce," while John Barber of the Daily Telegraph described the first act, with its straightlaced family, as "a nest of Tartuffes," and says that the first act is far funnier than the second act, which is about, "who did what, and with which, and to whom" (Weintraub 123).

Ned Chaillet said in the London Times that Three More Sleepless Nights (1980) is a humorous play (Weintraub 123). In Top Girls (1982), Churchill demonstrates considerable wit and intelligence that are at the same time resonant, and dramatically riveting (Dear 70). Fen (1983) is a series of linked vignettes where there are six actors, but these six actors portray twenty-two different characters of differing ages. The pungent language, and the eerie events of these twenty-two characters take the audience into an exotic world (Dear 71).

Serious Money (1987) demonstrates Churchill's ability to write acid satire that exposes the greed and amorality of London's recently deregulated (1986) stock exchange. At the end of the first act there is a controversial "Futures Song" which contains outrageously obscene lyrics, and on-stage antics. "Future Song" brings into question traditional attitudes about gender, and it mocks the crassly sexual way that capitalists equate money and women (Dear 71). In 1987, Caryl Churchill won the London Evening Standard award for best comedy of the year (Dear 68).

Ice Cream (1989) is a short play which was later added to Hot Fudge (1990) another short play, so that the two plays can be billed as "Ice Cream with Hot Fudge" (Dear 71). Frank Rich says that these two short plays, "hurtle forward in mysterious, strobe-bright, snapshot-quick vignettes of acidic, verbal wit and oblique events" (Dear 72). Mel Gussow explains that the name of the play Mad Forest (1990) comes from a forest near Bucharest which is referred to as "Mad Forest" because it is considered to be impenetrable for the foreigner who doesn't know the paths. In other words, Churchill believes that one would have to be Romanian to understand the Romanian events of the year described by the play (Dear 72).

Caryl Churchill Bibliography

Bermel, Albert. Comic Agony: Mixed Impressions in the Modern Theatre. Evanston, IL: Northwestern University Press, 1993.

Dear, Pamela S. "Caryl Churchill." Contemporary Authors, New Revision Series, Volume 46. Detroit, MI: Gale, 1995, 68-73.

Thomsen, Christian W. "Three Socialist Playwrights: John McGrath, Caryl Churchill, Trevor Griffiths." Contemporary English Drama. Ed. C. W. E. Bigsby. New York, NY: Holmes and Meier, 1981, 157-176.

Thurman, Judith. "Caryl Churchill: The Playwright Who Makes You Laugh about Orgasm,

Racism, Class Struggle, Homophobia, Woman-Hating, the British Empire, and the Irrepressible Strangeness of the Human Heart." Ms (May, 1972): 51-54, 57.

Weintraub, Erica Beth. "Caryl Churchill." Dictionary of Literary Bibliography, Volume Thirteen: British Dramatists Since World War II. Ed. Stanley Weintraub. Detroit, MI: Gale, 1982, 118-124.

Alan Coren (1938-)

During the nine years that Alan Coren was the editor of Punch, he increased its circulation, lowered the average age of its readers, and increased its concentration on humor (before Coren, Punch had been a bit stodgy) (Moseley 275). Many of Coren's satires targeted the state of Britain. He targeted the decline of education (both secondary and university), increasing governmental inefficiencies, bureaucratization, the acceptance of failure in English life, the silliness that is on television, the pretentions of what he called the "chattering classes" of leftist intellectuals, and the vulgarity of popular tastes. Coren had a favorite series that features a bunch of people in a pub as they talk about the royal family, science, and the economy. They display a combination of ignorance, complacency, and intolerance (Moseley 276).

The Dog It Was That Died (1965) was originally published as separate pieces in The Atlantic Monthly, The Listener, and Punch. These pieces are divided into sections called "Us," "Them," and "Me." In the "Us" section, he writes about England and English, as contrasted with the "Them" section which are about America and Americans. The "Me" section, "features a personna in which physical haplessness, frustrated elegance, and linguistic playfulness coincide." This section has a strong tinge of S. J. Perelman (Moseley 275). In All Except the Bastard (1969) there is a series of articles about various parts of England, and another series called "American Dreams" that is mostly about the war in Vietnam (Moseley 275). Other sections include "Behind the Curtains," which is about Communist countries, and "The Chronicles of Magoon," which is a collection of "heavy-handed satires" (Moseley 276).

The Sanity Inspector (1974) contains thirty-one pieces that were originally printed in Punch. These essays are about British urban and suburban life, and articles on so-called "literary subjects." Many of Coren's articles originate in something which he has read in the newspapers, but others are pure fantasy. His "Suffer Little Children" has samples of children's literature as if they had been written by Feodor Dostoyevsky, William Shakespeare, and Ernest Hemingway. The irreverent tone which Coren established in The Sanity Inspector was continued into Golfing for Cats (1975), The Lady from Stalingrad Mansions (1977), The Rhinestone as Bit as the Ritz (1979), Tissues for Men (1981), The Cricklewood Diet (1982), Bumf (1984), Something for the Weekend (1986), and Bin Ends (1987). The Best of Alan Coren (1980) is a collection of the first five of these books. Alan Coren likes people to buy his books, therefore he did research on which subjects sold the most books. He discovered that in Britain, the three most popular subjects were golf, cats, and the Third Reich; therefore, he wrote Golfing for Cats, and had the publisher put a swastika on the cover. Alan Coren's books tend to be sharp parodies both of individual writers and of genres of writing.

Alan Coren also targeted America and Americans in his satires. He targeted the stupidity of American presidents (especially Gerald Ford and Ronald Reagan), and the smug ignorance of Americans traveling in Europe. Coren's The Peanut Papers (1977) is a satire of the Jimmy Carter family, especially their more trivial follies. It pretends to have been written by "Miz" Lillian Carter. Because the book unfairly mocks attitudes and educational deficiencies that are not legitimately true for the Carter family, Merritt Moseley feels that the book should best be read as if it were about entirely fictional people rather than real human beings (Moseley 275).

Alan Coren Bibliography

Coren, Alan. Present Laughter: A Personal Anthology of Modern Humour. London, England: Robson, 1982.

Coren, Alan. The Punch Book of Kids. London, England: Robson, 1983.

Coren, Alan. The Penguin Book of Modern Humour. Harmondsworth, England: Penguin, 1983.

Coren, Alan. "Humor's Death and Other Exaggerations." World Press Review 27 (1980): 35-37.

Moseley, Merritt. "Alan Coren." Encyclopedia of British Humorists, Volume I. Ed. Steven H. Gale. New York, NY: Garland, 1996, 274-278.

Frederick Forsyth (1938-)

As a genre, Frederick Forsyth chose to write a fiction that is made realistic by the conventions of journalism (Macdonald 135). Forsyth's characters travel constantly. "If their movements were represented on road maps, the opponents would begin in widely separated locations, zigzag with increasing rapidity across the map, sometimes, ironically, crossing paths, and then finally head inexorably toward one another for the dénouement as the masterminds quietly manipulate affairs to their liking" (Macdonald 126). Forsyth told John Mortimer that he likes, "to write about immoral people doing immoral things. I want to show that the establishment's as immoral as the criminals" (Lesniak and Trosky 136). Even though Forsyth's novels are grim, some critics such as Mel Watkins and Margaret Cannon also find them at times very funny (Macdonald 133).

In his novels, Forsyth develops very powerful visual imagery. In The Odessa File (1972), Peter Miller sees a dead man's face that reminds him of, "the shrunken skull from the Amazon basin he had once seen, whose lips had been sewn together by the natives." In The Dogs of War (1974), there is a broken pier whose supports had crumbled away, and Forsyth describes these supports as "sticking up like broken teeth." There is a short story in No Comebacks: Collected Short Stories (1982) in which someone is described as being "as harmless as a calf in the byre," and in "A Careful Man" in the same book, a character looks at a pile of money, "with the indifference of a satyr observing a virgin." The Fourth Protocol (1984) also has vivid imagery, as in the description of the general secretary of the Communist Party of the Soviet Union. This character, "blinks rarely, and then slowly, like a bird of prey," and he "nods like an old lizard." His, "hooded eyes brooded behind the glittering glasses." But in spite of these picturesque images, Forsyth's understated style is spare and laconic. "Anyone stopping those four [nine millimeter machine-gun] rounds will speedily feel very unwell" (Macdonald 127). Stanley Elkin considers The Day of the Jackal (1971) not only plausible, but also so well written that, "even saintly readers will be hard put not to cheer this particular villain along with his devious way" (Macdonald 127).

The Dogs of War became a very controversial book when a writer for the London Times accused Forsyth of paying $200,000 to mercenaries to attempt a coup against the President of Equatorial Guinea, Francisco Marcias Nguema. Forsyth at first denied the allegations, but he later admitted to David Butler and Anthony Collins of Newsweek that he had, "organized a coup attempt for research purposes." He added, however that he had, "never intended to go through with it" (Lesniak and Trosky 137).

Andrew Macdonald says that in No Comebacks, Forsyth, "reveals an unexpected wit and a deft, O. Henry-like skill at ironic final reversal (Macdonald 131). Most critics find Forsyth's short stories "diverting" (Macdonald 133). The Negotiator (1989) is about the kidnapping of the son of an American President. John Katzenbach says that The Negotiator is a bit thin on characterization and dialogue, but adds that the plot has, "enough twists to fill a pretzel factory" (Lesniak and Trosky 138).

Frederick Forsyth Bibliography

Lesniak, James G., and Susan M. Trosky, Eds. "Frederick Forsyth." Contemporary Authors, New Revision Series, Volume 38. Detroit, MI: Gale, 1993, 135-138.
Macdonald, Andrew F. "Frederick Forsyth." Dictionary of Literary Biography, Volume Eighty-Seven: British Mystery and Thriller Writers Since 1940. Eds. Bernard Benstock, and Thomas F. Staley. Detroit, MI: Gale, 1989, 125-135.

Alan Ayckbourn (Roland Allen)(1939-)

Bryan Appleyard quotes Alan Ayckbourn as having said, "What the extreme left and the extreme right have in common is absolutely no sense of humour," and he adds, "perhaps I can spread a sense of balance through comedy" (Marowski 47). Appleyard notes that Ayckbourn's words, "have a habit of pursuing themselves back and forth between jokes and semi-visionary worries about a collapsing society" (Marowski and Stine 46). John Peter says that Ayckbourn's plays are, "about families or small communities engaged in the great tribal rituals of Christmas party, cricket, tennis, selling the car, funeral, picnic--scenes in which he observes the English Middle Class in the bizarre activity it calls Life" (Kalson "Ayckbourn" 32). Ayckbourn gets so much of his material from his home life that Christine Ayckbourn, who lives in Leeds with Alan and their two sons Steven and Philip, once said that she would, "be among the richest women in the world if she claimed royalties for all the fodder she has provided for his bitter, biting domestic comedies." Ayckbourn hates to write. He requires a deadline, and he also requires constant reminders of the approach of that deadline. Very often the posters are printed, the parts are assigned, and the tickets are sold before Ayckbourn ever begins to write a particular play (Kalson "Ayckbourn" 18).

John Russell Taylor says that Ayckbourn specializes in the "comedy of embarrassment" (Riley and Mendelson 34), as his characters try desperately to continue to live normal and respectable private lives in very eccentric public conditions (Riley and Mendelson 35). Harold Clurman says that Ayckbourn is, "a master hand at turning the bitter apathy, the stale absurdity which most English playwrights now find characteristic of Britain's lower-middle-class existence into hilarious comedy." Albert E. Kalson says that a typical Ayckbourn play is an, "intricately staged domestic comedy with a half-dozen intertwined characters who reflect the audience's own unattainable dreams and disappointments while moving them to laughter with at least a suggestion of a tear" (Johnson 18). Alan Brien says that what is funny to Ayckbourn's audiences can be tragic to the characters in the plays, and that, "there is no lump in the throat to equal a swallowed laugh which turns sour" (Johnson 19). Gerard Raymond agrees with Brien noting that Ayckbourn operated under the assumption that, "bad relationships make good theatre." Raymond says that this is why Ayckbourn has tended to keep married couples in the forefront of his comedies (Raymond 26). Ayckbourn feels that, "a comedy is just a tragedy interrupted" (qtd. in Londre 71).

Early in his career, Ayckbourn would label his plays as comedies or as farces, but in 1981 when he published Sisterly Feelings and Taking Steps together in a single volume, he abandoned this labeling, because he had labeled the first a comedy and the second a farce, and this labeling had provoked a great deal of lengthy and tedious discussion as to where and when the boundaries should be drawn between these two designations. For Ayckbourn, comedies are, "straight plays with a sense of humour, often saying much the same thing only more enjoyable and therefore to a wider audience." Farces, on the other hand are, "out to be, and often are, funnier than comedies, though in order to achieve this, the author has necessarily had to jettison one or two things like deep character analysis or Serious Things" (Kalson Laughter 11).

Before he was a playwright, Ayckbourn was an actor. Albert E. Kalson says that Ayckbourn needed the experience of being an actor to prepare him for being a good playwright. "Beyond the easy jokes, the mistaken identities, the intricate staging, Ayckbourn was learning a craft that would enable him always within the framework of bourgeois comedy, to illuminate the tedium, the pain, even the horror of daily life recognizable not only in England's Home Counties..., or in gruffer, heartier northern England..., but all over the world" (Johnson 19).

At one point in his acting career, Ayckbourn complained about a bad play that the company was rehearsing, so his director challenged him to write a better one. In response to this challenge, Ayckbourn wrote The Square Cat (1959), and of course he wrote a good acting part into the play for himself, as a guitar-playing pop singer. This tradition of writing himself good parts continued. As Ayckbourn recalls, "I wrote a second one for me in which I played four parts, and then I wrote a third one for me in which I played eight parts. But I was starting to write better than I could act, so I then wrote myself a super part and gave it to someone else. Then I gave up acting altogether" (Kalson "Ayckbourn" 17).

Daniel Marowski and Jean Stine describe Alan Ayckbourn's creative staging as follows:

> Ayckbourn's staging techniques often allow his characters to transcend space and time. In How the Other Half Loves (1969), for example, two separate settings are superimposed onstage so that actions which occur in different places, at different times, are seen simultaneously. Similarly in Bedroom Farce (1975), three bedrooms in three different homes are the setting for continuous, cross-cutting action. In Taking Steps (1979), multiple levels of a house are thrust from a single-level stage, and Way Upstream (1981) is performed on a boat suspended in a fiberglass tank of water. (Marowski and Stine 39)

Standing Room Only (1961) is a comic nightmare which details the lives of a family living on a London bus which is stranded in a twenty-year traffic jam on Shaftesbury Avenue. The mood is lightened by a number of pleasant jokes. One passenger remarks, for example, that the British government is experimenting in what it calls a "Pause in Birth Increase," and another passenger remarks that this is a "Pregnant Pause" (Kalson "Ayckbourn" 18). The time of the play is stated as "early twenty-first century," and the bus has been in the traffic jam so long that the driver's two daughters have grown up on the bus, and have never known any other home. The destination board in the bus announces the bus driver's name, "Hammersmith," and this is followed by the destination, "BRDWY," which the driver interprets as meaning "Best Ruddy Driver We've 'ad Yet" (Blistein 26-27). Albert Kalson describes The Sparrow (1967) as a "conventional comedy" (Kalson "Ayckbourn" 19).

Guido Almansi says that plays like Relatively Speaking (1968), How the Other Half Loves (1969), and Absurd Person Singular (1972), "abound with the basic element of theatrical humor, that is incongruity, or association of unassociable elements" (Johnson 19). Relatively Speaking is an "undiluted farce" based on, "a prolonged equivocation about

Greg's visiting his fiancée's former mature lover while incorrectly believing that he is her father. In the tradition of comedy of errors, the play develops all embarrassments possible through this mistake" (Gunton 28). Ayckbourn wrote Relatively Speaking when Stephen Joseph, owner of the Stephen Joseph Theatre in Scarborough, asked him for, "a play which would make people laugh when their seaside summer holidays were spoiled by the rain and they came into the theatre to get dry before trudging back to their landladies" (Kalson "Ayckbourn" 18). According to Oleg Kerensky, Relatively Speaking is a mild social satire as well as an ingenious farcical comedy containing good dialogue and complex situations, numerous misunderstandings, and ingenious plots (Marowski and Stine 40). In this play, Ayckbourn is deliberately making the most out of the least, as he sees just how far one farcical joke can be extended. The joke involves a misunderstanding in which a girl's older fiancé is taken to be her father. According to John Russell Taylor, "this is your basic stuff of farce" (Marowski and Stine 44).

Relatively Speaking is modeled on one of the most perfect of all of the well-made comedies, Oscar Wilde's The Importance of Being Earnest (1895). Both plays are metaphysical explorations on the question of identity. Early in Relatively Speaking, Greg is terrified that he may lose his identity during the night, and each morning when he awakes, he is unsure of who he is. A difference between these two plays, however, is that Wilde's play dazzles with epigrams and aphorisms, while Ayckbourn's offers the "serviceable joke." When Sheila is asked what prize she won in school for Memory and Elocution, she responds simply, "I've forgotten" (Kalson "Ayckbourn 19). The mistaken identities in Relatively Speaking would be incredible except for the fact that Ayckbourn carefully works out the plots so that they at the same time have a special kind of credibility:

> On a Sunday morning, Gilly--telling her current lover, Greg, that she is off to visit her parents--goes to the country house of her older lover, Philip, to break off their relationship. Greg finds the address, travels there himself, and takes Philip and his wife Sheila to be Ginny's parents. Philip, however, assumes that Greg is Sheila's young lover who hopes to seduce her away. Ginny is forced to play Philip's daughter in front of Greg while behaving like Philip's secretary in front of Sheila. (Londre 69)

Felicia Londre feels that despite the complexity of this plot, "the dramatic soufflé does not fall, and the comic spirit prevails" (Londre 69).

There is some cruelty in How the Other Half Loves (1969), in that whenever the foolish wife makes a stupid remark, her husband slaps her on the wrists. The humiliation of a perfectly harmless woman being punished in front of her friends delighted the audience and disgusted critic Harold Hobson. He does not enjoy seeing a woman being made to look ridiculous in public (Marowski and Stine 47). In How the Other Half Loves, Ayckbourn combines two households into a single set, super-imposing and intertwining the actions of the two families. Half of the set is elegant, with damask wallpaper and Harrods' traditional furniture, but the other half of the set shows a struggling Guardian reader with distemper, and there are nappies hanging around, drying. There are two links between the two households. The first is that the two husbands work for the same firm; the second is that the grand Mrs. Foster is having an affair with the ambitious Mr. Phillips (Marowski and Stine 45).

How the Other Half Loves is a highly inventive farce which takes place both in the living room of the tasteful Foster home and the living room of the cluttered and uncared-for Phillips home both presented superimposed on the same stage at the same time. The lush and expensive period furniture of the Fosters shares a one-room stage with the modern, and trendy Phillips furniture (Kalson "Ayckbourn" 19). One of the most hilarious scenes in all of the Ayckbourn canon occurs Thursday night at the Fosters' home and Friday night at the Phillips's home when two contrasting dinner parties are staged simultaneously at an extended dining table. The Featherstones are invited to both of these dinner parties, and at the home of the Fosters, they are properly served an elegant meal with linen table napkins and crystal. But at the home of the Phillipses a casual supper is "slopped together" for them, and they eat it with half paper napkins and tumblers from the local supermarket. "The suspense in <u>How the Other Half Loves</u> transcends plot in involving the audience's appreciation of the characters as actors negotiating the onstage traffic jams to which they must seem to be oblivious" (Kalson "Ayckbourn" 20).

Albert Kalson considers <u>Time and Time Again</u> (1971) to be a "comedy of quiet desperation" (Kalson "Ayckbourn" 21). In this play, Ayckbourn develops a total vacuum of a central character. This central character makes no decisions, and does nothing. Everything is done for him, and it is his total lack of action that affects the whole course of the play. "Doing nothing, he upsets five lives" (Nasso 44). According to Oleg Kerensky, Leonard, the central character, is, "a pale, alert, darting young man who is bored by the idle chit-chat of those around him, and who has a disturbing effect on them with his mixture of selfishness and naïveté." Leonard talks to the garden gnome. He hides in cupboards and lusts after Joan, who is the fiancée of Graham's employee, Peter (Marowski and Stine 40).

<u>Absurd Person Singular</u> (1972) won the <u>Evening Standard</u> Drama Award for best comedy of the year. The play is about three unhappily married couples who entertain themselves on three consecutive Christmas Eves. The play is not set in sitting rooms, or in drawing rooms, but rather in kitchens, and each act takes us to a different kitchen. In Act I we are in the Hopcroft's small suburban home, where the guests seek sanctuary in the kitchen in order to avoid the terrible jokes of the unseen Potters. In Act II we are in the Jackson's fourth floor apartment, where the guests are held hostage in the kitchen by George, the Jackson's large dog, which has just bitten Mr. Potter in an adjoining room (Kalson "Ayckbourn" 21). And in Act III, we are in the Brewster-Wrights's Victorian mansion, where the Brewster-Wrights and the Jacksons are hiding unsuccessfully from the uninvited Hopcrofts (Kalson "Ayckbourn" 22). <u>Absurd Person Singular</u> is a masterpiece of dark comedy in which the hostess of the party drinks herself into a stupor and gets buried offstage underneath a pile of coats thrown over her by her uncomprehending guests (Marowski and Stine 39).

In the second act of <u>Absurd Person Singular</u>, Eva is attempting to commit suicide, and she has taken so many pills that she is in a zombie state, and is unaware that her guests are going to be arriving soon. She is still in her dressing gown as she tries in many ways to commit suicide. When Jane finds her with her head stuck in the oven, Jane assumes that she is trying to clean it and happily takes over the job. Eva also tries to jump to her death, to stab herself to death, to electrocute herself, to hang herself, not to mention her attempting an overdose, but everything fails, as her guests shunt her from one corner of the kitchen to another. On one occasion, they use her suicide note to draw up plans for unclogging the sink and on another occasion they use her suicide note to help in the changing of an electrical fixture. Harold Hobson contrasts the audience's reaction to the wife's suicide attempts with his own reaction: "Every means she attempted ludicrously failed to succeed. No matter how hard she tried, she failed every time to kill herself. This seemed very funny to the audience, but it did not seem funny to me" (Marowski and Stine 47). <u>Absurd Person Singular</u> ends with a "dance macabre." Sydney forces the others into a game of forfeits which involves apples under the chin, oranges between the knees, pears on spoons in the mouth. And he hysterically exhorts them to "Dance. Dance. Keep dancing. Dance...." This is black farce at its best. Life is a frantic game, chaotically played. "One dances or dies" (Kalson "Ayckbourn" 22).

<u>Confusions</u> (1973) is a series of five one-act plays which are loosely strung together

to produce a two-hour evening. Oleg Kerensky notes that <u>Confusions</u> uses only three actors and two actresses to play twenty-one characters, and these five people must arrange their costume and make-up changes so that one play can follow the next with scarcely any break in the action (Marowski and Stine 40). <u>Mother Figure</u>, the first of these five sketches, is about a woman who has lived alone with her children for such a long time that she has started talking to her neighbors as children as well. "Her conversation is full of choccy bics, smack the botty, toothypegs, lovely choccy, and Mr. Poddle." Guido Almansi says that, "In the adult context I found each word from this baby language terrifying" (Gunton 28). Kerensky explains that <u>Drinking Companions</u>, the second sketch is about Lucy's husband, who is trying to pick up two girls in the bar of a provincial hotel. During the entire sketch he thinks that they are going to come to his bedroom, as he gets drunker and drunker, but in the dénouement of the sketch, they both walk out on him (Marowski and Stine 40). <u>Between Mouthfuls</u> employs a typical Ayckbourn gimmick that the audience can hear only as much of the various conversations as the waiter can hear. As soon as the waiter leaves one of the tables, the conversation at that table reverts to dumb show. "A great deal of the laughter is extracted in this situation, from the sudden interruptions of conversation as the waiter moves from table to table and to the kitchen, and from the waiter's 'tactful' hoverings and occasional deft intrusions with the food and wine" (Marowski and Stine 41). <u>Gosforth's Fête</u>, is the funniest of the five sketches; everything goes wrong. One couple discusses their affair and the girl's pregnancy, unaware that what they are saying is being announced over the public address system. The lady councillor who opens the fête gets her dress ruined in the mud; in addition, the tea urn can't be turned off, so there is a manic procession of tea cups being carried to it to catch the tea, and this is during the councillor's speech. Another problem is that the sound system short-circuits and nearly electrocutes the councillor. In the mean time, the pregnant girl's fiancé gets drunk and bawls obscene songs into a megaphone. The chaos is hilarious. There are five characters in <u>A Talk in The Park</u> who complain to their neighbors that they have been bored to death by their other neighbors (Marowski and Stine 41).

The Norman Conquests (1973) is a rueful comedy which gently mocks the characters as they reveal themselves to the audience (Bermel 124). <u>The Norman Conquests</u> is actually a series of three two-act plays that are designed to be played on three consecutive evenings. The titles of the three plays are: <u>Living Together</u>, <u>Table Manners</u>, and <u>Round and Round the Garden</u> (Bermel 124). Ian Watson describes this trilogy as, "three self-contained plays, featuring the same people at the same house over the same weekend. Each play stands as a complete entity and can be performed independently of the other two; although in practice, all three are usually played on consecutive nights, to be seen in any order" (Blistein 28). Richard Christiansen says that the three plays in <u>The Norman Conquest</u> trilogy

> fit together like Chinese boxes. Each comedy has the same cast of characters, the same time frame and the same house as a setting; but what the audience sees on stage in the dining room in one play may happen off stage in the living room in another, and vice versa. though each play can be enjoyed on its own, much of the fun relies on the audience knowing what is going on in the other two plays. (Johnson 20)

The unnamed matron of <u>The Norman Conquests</u> has three offspring. One member of the Dewers family is named Reg, and is a real-estate agent who loves games, riddles, and jokes; Reg is married to Sarah, who is completely devoid of any sense of fun. Sarah is Reg's shrewish and domineering wife. Sarah seeks perfection in an imperfect world (Blistein 28). Sarah accuses Norman of stealing Annie away from Tom, and Norman objects to her calling this a "theft."

NORMAN: I wasn't stealing her, I was borrowing her. For the week-end.

SARAH: [You] make her sound like one of your library books. (qtd. in Blistein 31)

Reg's older sister in The Norman Conquests is named Ruth, and she is a business executive and the best-looking person in the family, but one reason she is so good looking is that she will not wear the glasses needed to correct her nearsightedness. Ruth says that not wearing glasses is not because she is vain, but because the glasses squeeze her sinus passages, and make her sneeze (Bermel 134). Ruth has a sharp wit, and needs it in order to counterattack the philandering of her husband Norman. Norman is a latter-day Dionysus who masquerades sometimes as an assistant librarian and sometimes as a gigolo (Bermel 124). At one point Ruth depersonifies Norman when she says to Sarah, "I think I must be rather fond of him. It's a bit like owning an oversized unmanageable dog, being married to Norman. He's not very well house-trained, he needs exercising--mental and physical-- and it's sensible to lock him up if you have visitors. Otherwise he mauls them. But I'd hate to get rid of him" (Blistein 30). Ruth further depersonifies Norman, making him not into an animal but into a thing, when she says to Annie, "I always feel with Norman that I have him on loan from somewhere. Like one of his library books. I'll get a card one day informing me he's overdue and there's a fine to pay on him" (Blistein 31). The Norman Conquests is a Comedy of Humours in which five of the six roles are straightforward, comic-farce types. Reg is a downtrodden spouse. Reg tries to arouse laughter with his gags, but his punch lines have a way of turning soggy since they tend to fall on uncomprehending ears such as Tom's. Sarah is a nagging and exacting "hausfrau." Sarah specializes in sarcasm, especially sarcasm aimed at her husband, Reg. Ruth is an icy career woman, who is also a wit. It is Ruth who says, "Other people's marriages are invariably a source of amazement." Norman also uses sarcasm. It is Norman who says, "Is this lettuce leaf all for me? I can hardly believe my good fortune." Norman and Ruth are constantly bickering:

RUTH: Norman, what is going on here? What are you up to?

NORMAN: Since when have you cared what I'm up to?

RUTH: Well, I don't normally. You know you're perfectly free to come and go. Not that I could stop you. But I do object to having my Saturday nights ruined. (qtd. in Bermel 130)

Ruth's Saturday nights are ruined not because she would like to have them for rest or for pleasure, but because she needs them for more work. It is Ruth's salary that pays the household expenses. Norman responds by saying, "All right, I'm a kept man, A married ponce." And Ruth tells about Norman's constantly bursting into her office while she is seeing clients, and about his behaving abominably when she brings business associates home for dinner, and about his scrawling obscenities all over her business papers. Norman admits that he does all of these things, but says that he does them because he loves her (Bermel 130).

Tom, the fifth character in The Norman Conquests, is a bachelor and dimwitted veterinarian, who likes Annie (Blistein 29). It is Tom who suddenly remembers the only joke he knows, but he tells it so badly that the others continue their separate conversations across his snatches of recollection, and he never finishes the joke (Bermel 125). Tom is either the source, or the object of nearly every misunderstanding in the play. Because of her nearsightedness, Ruth has difficulty unfolding a folding chair, and finally gives up and decides to sit on the side of the folding chair, unfolded. When Tom finds Ruth sitting on the side of the folding chair, he politely assumes that she is doing it on purpose, and sits on another folding chair the same way, unfolded (Bermel 134).

Playing off all of the other five characters in The Norman Conquests, is Annie, the spinster who seeks love and escape, but not necessarily in that order (Blistein 28). Annie is the frumpish virgin whom Norman tempts into an assignation. Norman and Annie are scheduled to spend a "sordid weekend" at Hastings, the 1066 battleground of the original "Norman Conquest" (Bermel 127). But Hastings is all booked up, so Norman makes reservations for East Grinstead where he plans to make one of his "conquests." On Annie's suggestion, he purchases a new pair of pyjamas because, as Annie points out, "just because you're unfaithful there's no need for your pyjamas to be as well" (Blistein 29).

At one point in the play, the dialogue goes as follows:

> NORMAN: I love you.
> ANNIE: Oh Norman.... When you look like that, I almost believe you. You look like a--what are those things...?
> NORMAN: Greek gods?
> ANNIE: Old English sheepdogs. (Bermel 138)

Albert Bermel concludes that in The Norman Conquests, "Ayckbourn conceives of another of his middle-income, lower-middlebrow households and into it injects a spirit of mischief, of appetite, of spontaneity" (Bermel 137)

In The Norman Conquests, Norman repeats one line about half a dozen times. This line has to do with Norman's desire to make people, especially women, happy (Blistein 31). Norman has a reconciliation with his wife, but he still has an assignation pending with Sarah, and another one with Annie.

> NORMAN: Ah. (Brightening) Well, since we're all here, we ought to make the most of it, eh? What do you say? Norman smiles round at the women in turn. Ruth gets up and without another word goes into the house. Ruth.... He turns to Annie but she too, rises and goes into the house. Annie.... He turns to Sarah. She, likewise, rises and follows the others. Sarah! Norman is left alone, bewildered, then genuinely hurt and indignant (Shouting after them) I only wanted to make you happy.
> CURTAIN. (Blistein 33)

John Simon says that in Bedroom Farce (1975) the characters are, "funny not because they are smarter or more foolish than the rest of us, but because they are exactly like us, only in a slightly tightened, sharpened version" (Gunton 29). This play is a comedy of manners about disappointed expectations. It contains neither the titillation nor the frenzy that its title suggests (Kalson "Ayckbourn" 24). Actually, the funniest scene in the play involves an elderly couple who are in bed with each other trying to salvage a disappointing anniversary dinner by savoring pinchards on toast (Kalson "Ayckbourn" 25).

Just between Ourselves (1976) is a very bleak comedy which bewilders audiences which have come to the theatre to be entertained because it forces them to laugh in the wrong places and then feel embarrassed about it. Albert Kalson says that this play is written in the Chekhovian manner, but that it lacks "Chekhovian humanity" (Kalson "Ayckbourn" 26). Malcolm Page says that Just between Ourselves demonstrates how a well-meaning husband can drive his wife insane through his relentless cheerfulness and optimism. In the first scene, the audience laughs twice at Dennis's amusing lines about his wife's nervous clumsiness, but then we wince when we recognize the implications of being always on the receiving end of put-down humor. In the second scene there is a disastrous tea-party during which everyone tries not to notice that the birthday cake is not there. The end of the third scene is an episode which is at the same time wildly funny and deeply tragic, as Vera goes insane.

> While Dennis has become entangled inside the car with the steering-wheel, seat-belts, and neighbouring woman Pam, to whom he is demonstrating the car, Vera quarrels with her mother-in-law and pursues her with a roaring electric drill. Then Pam slumps onto the car horn, which "blasts loudly and continuously." and Neil comes in with a birthday cake, switching on lights,

thus "bathing the scene in a glorious technicolour." and singing "Happy birthday to you."
This is hilariously dark humor (Marowski and Stine 49).

Ten Times Table (1977) is a, "sedentary farce with faintly allegorical overtones." It is Ayckbourn's farcical study of the "committee person." The play is set at the ballroom of the "awful Swan Hotel," where a committee meets over a period of several months to plan a pageant which is based on a questionable historic event that had occurred two centuries earlier. This event was called the Massacre of the Pendon Twelve, and involved a local farmer named John Cockle who was so vigorous in protesting against unfair taxation that the militia was summoned to quell the disturbance. The militia mortally wounded John Cockle and a number of his followers. When the pageant finally takes place, it becomes a shambles. Nevertheless, everyone has a good time and the committee begins contemplating next year's event--a battle between the Romans and the ancient Britons (Kalson "Ayckbourn" 27). Felicia Londre says that Ten Times Table is possibly the last of Ayckbourn's plays in which hilarity predominates over bitterness (Londre 70).

In Absent Friends (1978), Diana pours a jar of cream over her husband's head, and recalls wanting to be a member of the Canadian Royal Mounted Police when she was a child in a parody of Mary Tyrone's final speech in Eugene O'Neill's Long Day's Journey Into Night (1956). This play contains much "bitchy, witty dialogue" which carries the audience past its initial distaste for the subject matter--death (Kalson "Ayckbourn" 24). Family Circles (1978) is about a wedding anniversary where two daughters bring their husbands, and the third daughter brings her latest lay. As they are celebrating the anniversary, their parents may or may not be trying to murder each other, while each of the three daughters spends some time attached to one after another of the three men (Marowski and Stine 41).

Anthony Curtis says that in Joking Apart (1978), Ayckbourn uses comic strategies to expose serious issues (Gunton 30). This play is about Brian and Anthea--and others. One of Ayckbourn's gimmicks is that the same actress plays all three of Brian's girlfriends, and also plays Anthea's daughter Debbie, Brian's last hope for an Anthea substitute (Kalson "Ayckbourn" 27). There is much action, but few words in Mr. Whatnot (1979), a play which is reminiscent of a Harpo-Marx routine. According to Ronald Hayman, in this play, the eponymous piano-tuner never talks; instead, he, "mimes his farcically anarchic way into marrying the daughter of a lord" (Marowski and Stine 41).

The subtitle of Sisterly Feelings (1979) is "A Related Comedy," and this is a pun, similar to the pun in Relatively Speaking which encompasses content, form, and theme. The flip of the coin or whim of the actress which determines the action in this play, suggests that for the central characters, the only truth is a "relative truth" (Kalson "Ayckbourn" 29). Sisterly Feelings is a "New Comedy" which demonstrates Ayckbourn's sense of "comic determinism" in that there is a toss of a coin at one point in the play, and an actress's whim at another point in the play that dictate what is to follow. These fate-determining actions are billed as "Chances," and some performances contain these chances while at other performances these decisions have been predetermined (Kalson "Ayckbourn" 28). According to John Peter, Ayckbourn investigates how things would turn out if the rangy and athletic Simon had walked home with Dorcas instead of her sister Abigail. Ayckbourn also investigates how things would turn out if he walks home with Abigail, starts an affair with her, and later her husband surprises them at a family picnic which ends in confusion and pouring rain (Marowski and Stine 42). Of the two "chances," the Abigail option is richer in comic invention, but the Dorcas option suggests that it is more than just fate that rules our lives (Kalson "Ayckbourn" 30). Regardless of what decisions are made earlier in the play, the final scene remains unchanged, and this demonstrates Ayckbourn's point that frequently important decisions made early in life only appear to actually change people's lives (Marowski and Stine 40). Eric Shorter feels that in <u>Sisterly Feelings</u>, Ayckbourn is a master not so much of wit as of the "witty situation, of the witty twisting of situation and making it all turn on character" (Gunton 29). Talking about <u>Sisterly Feelings</u>, Benedict Nightingale says that, "no other playwright has managed to extract so much wry and disenchanted humour from the glum rituals of middle-class life" (Gunton 31).

Taking Steps (1979) is a farce that is described by Ayckbourn as, "an attic, a bedroom, a lounge, a wife in a quandary and a fiancée in a cupboard, a devious builder, a nervous solicitor, a ponderous personnel officer, and a drunken manufacturer all embroiled in a tale of love, confusion, and freedom" (Kalson "Ayckbourn" 30). This play is a situational comedy that represents society in transition. Kitty and Elizabeth would like to be part of a nuclear family; however, they also want to be independent. Neither of them is especially well trained to strike out alone; however, they need breathing room. The title of the play, "Taking Steps" refers to this transitional situation. The two women want to become liberated; however, they both realize that they will need to "take certain steps" in order to achieve this status. The play opens with Elizabeth writing a letter to her husband, Roland, that she's going to run off and pursue her career as a dancer. Her brother, Mark, is saying, "This is one hell of a step you're taking, Lizzie, and if you were to ask me, you're walking right into it" (<u>Taking</u> 151). Later on in the play, Elizabeth is trying to escape the house when her husband, Roland, comes in with his lawyer, Tristram. Elizabeth is coming down the stairs at the time, when she freezes. She "stands stock still, then slowly begins to back up the stairs again with her suitcases" (<u>Taking</u> 171). She remains in this transitional situation for quite some time, providing a visual pun to reinforce both the metaphorical and literal meanings of the title, "Taking Steps."

In <u>Taking Steps</u>, Roland doesn't want Elizabeth to run off and become a dancer. In order to keep her home and in a supportive role, he places her on a pedestal. Elizabeth says, "I daren't do anything normal in front of him now in case it shatters some illusions he's got. I have to leave the room to scratch" (<u>Taking</u> 155)). Later in the play, we get Roland's perspective of Elizabeth's perfection: "The whole time I've lived with that woman, I have never seen her scratch herself. Not once. I'd call that unnatural, wouldn't you? Grounds for divorce, don't you think so, Mr. Watson? Failure to itch" (<u>Taking</u> 192).

Much of the comedy of <u>Taking Steps</u> seems to be based on various types of ambiguity and resultant misinterpretations. This occurs at the linguistic level, the metaphorical level, the characterization level, and the who's-who level. Some of the ambiguity and resultant confusion is based on the fact that things are too visually similar to be distinguishable. All the rooms in the house are painted brown. In order to distinguish between one room and another, therefore, a person must refer to "the Dark Brown, the Patch Brown, the Mouldy Brown, the Nasty Brown, the Dirty Brown, and the Yucky-Awful-Foul-Brown" (<u>Taking</u> 162). To add to the visual ambiguity and confusion, all of the men are using the pajamas of the manor, and all of these pajamas are exactly the same. At other times the ambiguity and resultant confusion in <u>Taking Steps</u> is based on the fact that the characters are not always paying attention when they are told to do things. Mark says, "I'm chatting away and people just seem to doze off" (<u>Taking</u> 160). This happens throughout the play. Some of the ambiguity and resultant confusion is based on Roland's strange use of terms. He says "the real McKay" instead of "the real McCoy," and he talks about his wife "lumbering up" instead of "limbering up." That he is doing this intentionally does not make it any less confusing. In fact, Tristram Watson, the lawyer, makes the same type of linguistic blunders, but does so unintentionally (Nilsen 6).

In <u>Taking Steps</u>, there is also much humor based on the British propensity for understatement, as in "Oh, damn it. Damn it. I beg your pardon but damn it" (<u>Taking</u> 190), or "he's gone an improbable colour" (<u>Taking</u> 191). When Mark runs over Leslie's

Yamaha, Leslie asks if the damage is serious, and Mark responds, "No. A bit fell off it. But it didn't look vital. It's now a Yama, or possibly a Maha, depending on which end I hit" (Taking 195). Another example of language play occurs when Mark is reading Elizabeth's letter telling her husband Roland that she is leaving him. Mark reads, "I only wish I could have had the cabbage--that can't be right...." Elizabeth corrects, "'courage.' It's perfectly clear." Mark starts over, and when he comes to "courage," he says, "Looks more like 'carnage' now. I only wish I could have had the carnage" (Taking 153). This "carnage" which Mark persists on seeing in Elizabeth's letter extends to his metaphors as well. He tells Elizabeth, "Roland'll be absolutely poleaxed." He continues, "He'll be scythed legless, Lizzie." Mark extends the metaphor even further, "No, he'll be absolutely steam-pressed" (Taking 153). Later on, Elizabeth does a reciprocating metaphor on Mark: "I don't happen to rate your views on marriage extremely highly. It's intended as a thirty year marathon. Not a three month sprint" (Taking 156). Another extended metaphor in Taking Steps is the word and the concept of "bucket." There's something funny about this word, and about this product, and furthermore, it is a natural for punning. Talking about Roland, Leslie says, "He made all his money in buckets, you know." Tristram says, "Really," and Leslie continues, "Cast iron, polythene, plastic, you name it." In the play, buckets are used to catch water from the leaky ceiling, and are referred to constantly in ambiguous ways, like "buckets are whatever you put into them" (Taking 174).

Taking Steps is written in the Gothic dark-and-stormy-night tradition. The play begins, "It is a cold Friday evening in February around 6 p.m. It is already dark and looks like rain. The house overall seems grey and gloomy" (Taking 150). Tristram, the landlord, arrives in full motorcycle gear (including helmet) in order to show an old mansion to Roland. In the mansion, the roof leaks, and the floorboards squeak. Roland bounces on the floorboards to show Tristram that they sway, and says, "I don't want some housekeeper falling on top of me while I'm in bed" (Taking 178). Taking Steps is a "Gothic Play" set in modern times--or rather, it is a parody of a Gothic play. It is dark. It is stormy. We are hearing strange noises and seeing strange things. Our imaginations are running rampant. Tristram, the landlord in Taking Steps, has lived in this village for many years, and he remembers that this mansion was once a grand and elegant brothel. He also remembers that there were many unhappy people when the brothel was condemned, one of them being Scarlet Lucy, a ghost of one of the ladies of the "dark and stormy evening," who was said to still haunt the house. When Tristram is downstairs, he hears Elizabeth walking upstairs, but no-one is supposed to be upstairs, so he assumes it must be Scarlet Lucy. Because the night is dark and stormy, Tristram decides to spend the night in the mansion, but by now Roland has read Elizabeth's note, and doesn't want to sleep in the Master Bedroom because of too many reminders, so he goes to the attic, and Tristram sleeps in the Master Bedroom. But then Elizabeth decides she wants to come back to her husband, so in the middle of the night she climbs into bed with Tristram and hugs him tightly throughout the night. Tristram had caught a glimpse of Elizabeth during the thunderstorm, in her flowing nightdress, and he doesn't tell Elizabeth that he is not her husband, because he thinks Elizabeth is Scarlet Lucy (Nilsen 9-10).

In Taking Steps, Ayckbourn develops the tension necessary in a Gothic play in many ways. He does it by developing ambiguities and confusions, but he also does it by having people be interrupted at crucial points. When Tristram finds Elizabeth's "Dear John" note, he says, "Er...excuse me. There's a note. Here. Seems to be a note" (Taking 183). But his speech is interrupted by Kitty's noises from the closet in the attic. Some time later, Roland remembers the note, and starts to read it, but the phone rings. Roland tells Leslie to read the note while he answers the phone. Leslie does, and his dialogue goes, "Oh, dear." "Oh, dear." "Oh, dear," with the other people saying other things in between. His last "Oh, dear," is followed by, "I think we may have problems here" (Taking

186), as he hands the note to Tristram. Leslie and Tristram decide to protect Roland from the news, and merely tell him, "Ah, she says she's getting you a surprise but she'll be back shortly" (Taking 186). Tristram, "in a rather reflex action, tucks the note he is holding under his cushion," and later Roland ironically remarks, "I'm afraid there's some rather grim news." When Leslie says, "What?" Roland continues, "We appear to be running out of scotch" (Taking 188). In the Gothic tradition, Taking Steps takes place on a night that is dark and stormy. In the Gothic tradition, it is about people being in the wrong places--people being present when they are expected to be absent and absent when they are expected to be present. There are ambiguous notes, an old and creaky mansion, strange noises, a story about the house having been a brothel, and especially the story about Scarlet Lucy's revenge of giving someone a night of torrid love before he died--all add to the development not of a Gothic novel, but of the parody of one (Nilsen 10).

According to John Russell Taylor, Season's Greetings (1981) tells about the many mishaps of an uncomfortable family Christmas which leads up to an irresistible scene in which the wife's attempts to entice her sister's boy friend into bed (or onto the rug in the hall) are constantly being thwarted (Marowski and Stine 43). Season's Greetings contains a full range of comic devices, including children's toys under the Christmas tree where a seduction takes place, and a bumbling husband who insists presenting his boring puppet shows on anyone who happens to be around. In Season's Greetings there is a powerful mixture of merriment and pain (Londre 70).

According to Linda Brown, Suburban Strains (1981) makes devastating fun of dinner parties, especially dinner parties where the husband insists in doing all of the cooking, because he likes to. He enters in a navy-blue striped apron with matching oven gloves which flap about nervously when the lateness of the guests threatens to ruin his poulet l'estragon (Marowski and Stine 44). John Russell Taylor notes that in this play, the past and the present are staged simultaneously, with two different actions cunningly intercutting each other. Its being a musical enables the audience through song to know what the characters are thinking, even though they might be saying something quite different, or saying nothing at all (Marowski and Stine 44).

Paul Allen says that Way Upstream (1981) is a comic and slightly cynical play that is very difficult to stage because the set consists of a cabin cruiser floating in murky water, and moored to a towpath. After the couples come aboard, the boat moves out into the stream and a bow wave indicates that the boat is moving forward. Allen says that the first mooring is, "as funny as any set-piece Ayckbourn has given us" (Marowski and Stine 45). Bryan Appleyard says that the villain and hero of Way Upstream contrast markedly. Vince is "a very dangerous smiling villain," and Alistar is "a man who is forced eventually to make a decision and wins...just" (Marowski and Stine 46). Woman in Mind (1985) begins with Susan stepping on the end of a garden rake and knocking herself out. Her resulting head injury causes her to hallucinate that the insensitive characters with whom she lives are actually an ideal family, and the counterpoint of the reality and the fantasy collide and overlap as Susan slips into madness (Londre 70).

Henceforward (1987) is a frightening comedy of progress and loss, set in a reclusive composer's North London apartment in the near future. Jerome, the composer, is struggling against rampant technology, and human isolation as he tries to gain custody of his daughter. Ayckbourn is raising the contradiction that technology and convenience are frequently at variance with human interaction and community. Jerome's walls are filled with high-tech synthesizers, video phones, and ultra-modern musical contrivances, but in contrast, his apartment is an "island of creature comforts," and the life outside of his apartment is "mired in a sea of civic chaos." These North London streets outside of his apartment "team with anarchy," as, "citizens shuttle from here to there in insulated high-tech comfort." This play uses comedy to address serious themes. The play is, "peppered with the kind of quirky human behavior that lends itself to laughter" (Grady 7). Henceforward is a dystopia in which gangs of marauding feminists control the streets, and artistic creativity has been replaced by technology. One of the cleverest aspects of the play is Jerome's robot named Nan. She was designed as a child-care robot, but Jerome uses her for household management, which she does, but with a great independence of spirit. She persists in presenting mugs of coffee and glasses of orange juice upside down. Felicia Londre says that the robot Nan is a metaphor for the changing roles of women (Londre 71).

Body Language (1990) has been labeled by some critics as a farce, by others as a comedy-farce, by still others as black comedy. Albert Kalson says that it might even be labeled a "tragical-comical psycho-medical entertainment" (Kalson Laughter 11).

Harold Hobson sums up Alan Ayckbourn's contribution to the theater as follows:

> The things that the public appreciates in Ayckbourn--the jokes, the leger-de-main, the farce, the high spirits--are all worth appreciating. They are first-class theatre. But they are not, in my opinion, the things which are most valuable in him.... Behind all his foolery he has this sad conviction that marriage is a thing that will not endure.... It is when Ayckbourn sees the tears of life, its underlying, ineradicable sadness, that he is at his superb best. (Marowski and Stine 47)

Alan Ayckbourn has shown critics that he can make people laugh without resorting to one-liners. "His comedy depends upon the adroit juxtaposition of episodes, the clever manipulation of time, the dexterous use of props. In Ayckbourn's plays, a lawn chair, a biscuit tin, a rug, an easy-to-assemble-yourself dressing table, a wastepaper basket are all more important than a clever line" (Blistein 34). Guido Alamsi says that Ayckbourn's major contribution to the theatre is his constant recourse to off-stage action. "It is like a Velásquez painting which focuses on a peripheral point of reference--the kitchen table with a scullery maid for instance--while the real action is taking place elsewhere in an inconspicuous corner of the canvas" (Gunton 28). Albert E. Kalson sums up Ayckbourn's life as follows:

> If he had been a happier man, he wouldn't have wanted to write plays. If he had been a more successful actor, he would have had no need to do so. If he'd known happier people in his early life, his plays wouldn't be so interesting. And if he had not been an actor at all, it would have taken him much longer to learn how to construct his plots, prepare his effects and time his jokes. (Johnson 19)

Alan Ayckbourn (Roland Allen) Bibliography

Ayckbourn, Alan. Sisterly Feelings and Taking Steps. London, England: Chatto and Windus, 1981.

Bermel, Albert. Comic Agony: Mixed Impressions in the Modern Theatre. Evanston, IL: Northwestern University Press, 1993.

Blistein, Elmer M. "Alan Ayckbourn. Few Jokes, Much Comedy." Modern Drama 26 (1983): 26-35.

Connell, Brian. "Playing for Laughs to a Lady Typist: A Times Profile." Times January 5, 1976, 5.

Dukore, Bernard F. "Craft, Character, Comedy: Ayckbourn's Woman in Mind." Twentieth Century Literature 32 (1986): 23-39.

Grady, Michael. "ASU Theatre Opens Season with Scary Science Fiction Comedy." ASU Insight October 7, 1994, 7.

Gunton, Sharon R. "Alan Ayckbourn." Contemporary Literary Criticism, Volume 18. Detroit, MI: Gale, 1981, 27-31.

Johnson, Anne Janette. "Alan Ayckbourn." Contemporary Authors, New Revision Series, Volume 31. Ed. James G. Lesniak. Detroit, MI: Gale, 1990, 17-21.

Kalson, Albert E. "Alan Ayckbourn." British Dramatists Since World War II: Part I: A-L. Ed. Stanley Weintraub. Detroit, MI: Gale, 1982, 15-32.

Kalson, Albert E. Laughter in the Dark: The Plays of Alan Ayckbourn. Rutherford, NJ: Fairleigh Dickinson University Press, 1993.

Londre, Felicia Hardison. "Alan Ayckbourn." Encyclopedia of British Humorists, Volume I. Ed. Steven H. Gale. New York, NY: Garland, 1996, 66-72.

Marowski, Daniel G., and Jean C. Stine. "Alan Ayckbourn." Contemporary Literary Criticism, Volume 33. Detroit, MI: Gale, 1985, 39-50.

Nasso, Christine. "Alan Ayckbourn." Contemporary Authors, First Revision, Volumes 21-24. Detroit, MI: Gale, 1977, 43-44.

Nilsen, Alleen Pace, and Don L. F. Nilsen. "Humorous Aspects of Alan Ayckbourn's British Comedy, Taking Steps. Unpublished Paper, 1996.

Raymond, Gerard. "Alan Ayckbourn Takes Manhattan." Theater Week (Grntusty 36, 2992): 33-37.

Riley, Carolyn, and Phyllis Carmel Mendelson. "Alan Ayckbourn." Contemporary Literary Criticism. Detroit, MI: Gale, 1976, 34-38.

Thornber, Robin. "A Farceur, Relatively Speaking." Guardian August 7, 1970, 8.

John (Marwood) Cleese (Monty Python) (1939-)

John Cleese is a tall actor-comedian who excels in invective. He portrays such people as a high official in the "Ministry of Silly Walks," or an Army sergeant who teaches recruits how to defend themselves against someone armed with a piece of fresh fruit. He also plays a person trying to sell albatrosses for refreshment. His confection is named "Stormy petrel on a stick" (Telgen 98). The Monty-Python format began with Cleese's At Last, the 1948 Show, which was filled with hilarious madcap antics and weird logic. Spike Milligan and Peter Sellers joined John Cleese in the 1950s and the Python group added people and energy as they traveled into the 1960s. In 1969, BBC offered Cleese a series, and he telephoned the other members of the group and they ended up with carte blanche power for their thirteen late-night spots on BBC2. They specialized in stream-of-consciousness sketches, and a circus atmosphere featuring their Bonzo Dog Doo Dah Band. Much of their humor was visual, with Graham Chapman providing the animation. John Cleese gives credit to Marty Feldman for helping him with his signature sketch. "When I first met Marty, he went on at great length about what he used to call the internal logic of a sketch, which is that you could have everybody sitting in dustbins or dressed as carrots, but if somebody walks into the room who isn't dressed as a carrot or who isn't wheeled in in a dustbin, then you have to explain why not. It's got to be founded on that, on solid logic. It's all got to fit internally" (Athey 253). Some of the jokes in the skits were intellectual, but others were purely visual, and involved men in drag, or an English barrister in a bowler hat carrying a briefcase strutting in a way that with each step his feet were lifted higher than his waist. One of the sketches was about a waitress who had only one major item on the menu--Spam. There was even Spam salad and finally, "Spam, Spam, Spam, Spam." This Spam scene was the inspiration for a similar scene on Saturday Night Live in which John Belushi played a short-order cook, but was able to serve only two items--Cheeseburgers and Pepsi. In another sketch, an interviewer is interviewing three guests, one who speaks only the beginnings of words (Cleese), another the middles of words, and the third the ends of words. Cleese was especially skilled at playing authority figures of the tall, decent, stiff-upper-lip English type (Athey 254).

With Graham Chapman, Peter Sellers, and Terry Southern, John Cleese is the author of The Magic Christian (1970). With Graham Chapman, Peter Cook, and Kevin Billington, he is the author of The Rise and Rise of Michael Rimmer (1970). With Jack Hobbs and Joe McGrath, he is the author of The Strange Case of the End of Civilization as We Know It (1977). With Connie Booth he is the author of Fawlty Towers (1989). And with Charles Crichton, he is the author of A Fish Called Wanda (1988). Along with Graham Chapman, Terry Gilliam, Eric Idle, Terence Jones, and Michael Palin, John Cleese is a member of the Monty Python group, which has written And Now for Something Completely Different (1972), Monty Python and the Holy Grail (1975), Monty Python's Life of Brian (1979), Monty Python Live at the Hollywood Bowl (1982), The Meaning of Life (1983), and Monty Python's Flying Circus: All the Words (1989).

Thomas Meehan writes that the authors in the Monty-Python group have a genius for, "making nonsensical fun of all who are pompous, pretentious, humorless, or boring, or who take themselves too seriously." (Telgen 98). Harry F. Waters hails Monty Python's Flying Circus (1974) as, "the most improbably successful program in the history of American public television." He refers to the cult status of the program as "Pythonmania." Meehan says that this group is willing to attempt almost anything and to lampoon almost anybody. Meehan feels that watching this program, "is a bit like making a dizzying journey through a surreal fun house. Mixing filmed sketches that rarely last longer than a minute or two with bizarre pieces of animation, the program leaps wildly about in time and place. A sketch may begin in rural 17th-century England, for instance, and a moment later its characters are browsing in a modern-day London pornographic bookshop" (Telgen 98).

John Cleese told Laurence Shames that the group wanted to satirize attitudes rather than individuals: "We were more interested in a web of comic logic than a string of separate jokes." Cleese continues that, "I think the great thing about Python is that it was funny in a way that was really about the way people actually are." Commenting on why the group is so popular around the world, Cleese said, "We must have had some sort of insight into certain types of people that transcended boundaries" (Telgen 98).

Monty Python and the Holy Grail (1975) is a parody of the legend of King Arthur, in which King Arthur's knights have a number of episodic ludicrous adventures that include a battle in which the king's adversaries hurl muddied animal carcasses at the grail seekers from the top of a castle wall. There are many incongruities in Monty Python and the Holy Grail, such as knights that are travelling, but not on horses, who go hopping along clapping coconut halves together to simulate the sounds of horses' hooves. There are soldiers who debate whether a five-ounce European swallow could possibly have transported a one-pound coconut to England, or whether it was instead the larger non-migratory African swallow. They conclude that it might have been two swallows working in tandem. This is followed by the equally incongruous attack of the Killer Rabbit (Athey 255).

Monty Python's Life of Brian (1979) is a parody of such Hollywood biblical productions as The Greatest Story Ever Told, and King of Kings. It tells of the misadventures of Brian Cohen of Nazareth who happens to share his birthday with the infant Jesus and is therefore mistaken for the Christchild by three wise men bearing gifts. Most of Brian's life is spent dodging his followers, who claim that he is the Messiah. This is a parody of the way people usually follow religious leaders, but at the same time discard the messages that the religious leaders are telling them, so that religion ends up by serving the followers' needs to feel more righteous and religiously pure. Gene Siskel calls Life of Brian a, "gentle but very funny parody whose humor is light and very clever" (qtd. in Telgen 99). The Life of Brian is a satirical attack on blind followers of religion (Athey 255).

Sheila Benson says that The Meaning of Life (1983) is a well constructed social satire, but not quite of the order of a Jonathan Swift satire. Nevertheless, it is, "very fast indeed, and pungently and acidly observed." Canby considers <u>The Meaning of Life</u> to be, "sometimes hilarious and colossally rude but, as often as it evokes laughs, it overwhelms us by the majesty of its production and special effects" (qtd. in Telgen 99).

Sheila Benson says that <u>A Fish Called Wanda</u> (1988), "pretends to be a caper movie about a smooth London jewel heist and its infinitely complex aftermath. Actually, it's a smart farce about ingrained cultural differences, playing the clenched respectability of the Brits against the hearty spontaneity--some might call it vulgarity--of the Yanks." Cathleen McGuigan says that <u>A Fish Called Wanda</u>, "is a weird kettle of you-know-what," and Rita Kempley says that is "dark and strange, even sadistic." She says that Cleese has created an, "inventive, happily demented script," and she calls the result a "sex farce for consenting adults" (qtd. in Telgen 100). In <u>A Fish Called Wanda</u>, Cleese plays a respectable authority figure, a barrister, who unwittingly becomes involved in a number of farcical intrigues (Athey 255).

With his actress wife, Connie Booth, John Cleese developed and played in a television series named <u>Fawlty Towers</u> (1989), a story about a Torquay resort hotel which is run by a man who hates people. Fawlty is the archetype of the British misanthrope and fool, and the show is a study in the "hilarity of humiliation." In <u>Fawlty Towers</u>, Cleese and Booth play, "with devastating effect seething, angry, mentally volcanic characters who if they are pushed just one more inch will erupt in a ranting, fist-shaking, quavering rage--and then, of course, are pushed that one inch" (Telgen 98). When a stuffy matron who is partly deaf asks for a refund because from her room all she can see is the town of Torquay, the irritable Basil Fawlty responds, "When one looks out the window of a Torquay hotel, what does one expect to see other than Torquay? The Sidney Opera House? the Hanging Gardens of Babylon? Herds of wildebeests sweeping majestically across the horizon? Are you disappointed because Krakatoa isn't erupting within your view?" In another episode, Basil's wife hints about their anniversary, Basil responds, "Anniversary of what? The battle of Agincourt? Crecy? Trafalgar?" Unlike the Monty Python shows, <u>Fawlty Towers</u> is concerned very much with British behavior and emotions. Basil Fawlty is the kind of person that the English can identify with. They live in a society in which they are not able to say, "I'm sorry, this food is not good enough," or "I bought this pair of shoes and I want you to replace them" because such acts of simple assertion are looked down on in England, so according to Cleese, England is filled with people who on the surface display a kind of brittle politeness, but underneath there is a lot of seething rage (Athey 255).

For Americans, John Cleese epitomizes the eccentric Englishman who is very intellectual, but also somewhat daft. His wit is zany and unpredictable, and contains much that is absurd. Cleese is such a popular figure that he has become a television pitchman for Sony, Schweppes, American Express, Magnavox, and other commercial products. Cleese remarks, "The sillier the activity, the more they seem to pay" (Athey 256).

See also Graham Chapman, Terry Gilliam, Eric Idle, Terry Jones, and Michael Palin.

John (Marwood) Cleese (Monty Python) Bibliography

Athey, Joel. "John Cleese." <u>Encyclopedia of British Humorists, Volume I</u>. Ed. Steven H. Gale. New York, NY: Garland, 1996, 252-256.
Telgen, Diane. "John (Marwood) Cleese." <u>Contemporary Authors, New Revision Series, Volume 35</u>. Ed. James G. Lesniak, Detroit, MI: Gale, 1992, 96-100.

Margaret Drabble (1939-)

Margaret Drabble used to be a contributor to Punch (Lesniak 133), and she uses both humor and wit to spice up her satiric novels (Lightfoot Garrick 167). Drabble has a deep conviction that if a person could get high enough over the world, this person would see that the things that look like coincidence are, in fact, part of a pattern, and this conviction makes her, "prepared to bet on the existence of God" (Lightfoot Ice 69). Gail Cunningham has stated that the typical Margaret Drabble heroine either is able to make many appropriate literary references, or she is sexually immature. In Margaret Drabble: Puritanism and Permissiveness, Valerie Myer has called this the "brains and breasts dichotomy" (Lesniak 133).

Like Margaret Drabble, Sarah Bennet of A Summer Bird-Cage (1963) is a graduate of Oxbridge. Sarah has given up the idea of going on to pursue a higher degree, because in her words, "you can't be a sexy don" (Lesniak 133).

The Garrick Year (1964) is a domestic novel about a young woman trying to cope with her husband, her children, and her inability to figure out her identity and her goals. The novel contains extraordinary accidents and strange parallels of coincidence, as Emma Evans ruminates on her recent past in an attempt to examine her priorities as a woman, as a wife, and as a mother. But Margaret Drabble's insights are greater than are those of her protagonist, as Drabble provides ironies in this novel that Emma is not aware of. Emma is an insecure modern feminist who plans to work as a newsreader on television, but she gives up her plans in order to follow her husband to the Garrick Theatre Festival in Hereford. As David pursues his acting career, Emma becomes bored and jealous, and in a self-mocking tone says, "My tastes are shallow, my life is shallow, and I like anonymity, change, and fame. In Hereford, I could have none of these things: I was condemned to familiarity, which, beyond anything I find hard to maintain with ease." In order to spice up her life, she decides to have an affair with Wyndham Farrar, David's director, but the affair ironically turns into a domestic routine: "The thought of myself in an apron asking him if he liked his eggs hard or soft or fried on both sides did not accord easily with my ideas of passion." In addition, Wyndham had a cold. The existential accidents that keep happening in The Garrick Year help to keep life unpredictable, bewildering, challenging, exciting, and funny (Lightfoot Garrick 168). This is a comedy of manners as told from Emma's first-person point of view, in which humor and wit are blended with a critical attitude (Lightfoot Garrick 169).

In The Realms of Gold (1975), Drabble combines witty satire with serious existential angst. The novel asks whether or not an individual by himself or herself can make the world into the "realms of gold" or whether Keats was right in suggesting that the "realms of gold" are attainable only through the imagination provided by good literature (Lightfoot Realms 86). The constant allusion to "teeth" in the novel is a reminder of decay and mortality presented metaphorically and satirically, and these allusions range from Frances's painful wisdom teeth, to Karel's spare pair of false teeth, to the perfect teeth of a sheep skull and Karel's "anxiety-ridden tooth, lost in Prague" (Lightfoot Realms 88). In the novel, Frances Wingate is a successful archeologist who knows a great deal about the lives and cultures of ancient peoples, but ironically knows very little about modern life (Lightfoot Realms 87). Frances wants to visit the city for two days with her lover, Karel Schmidt, and she also envisages making love by the sea. But sometimes expectations and reality are not the same. Frances and Karel end up with their car stuck in a flat yellow swamp. They are covered with mud, and they hear the "honk, honk, koax, koax" of the frogs in a nearby drainpipe. "So they lay down in the mud and made love, which was, after all, the purpose of the expedition" (Lightfoot Realms 88).

Janet Bird in The Realms of Gold derives satisfaction in being able to contemplate disaster. Janet's husband is immature and domineering, but Janet does not leave him; however, she does like to fantasize disasters, as she tries to imagine something that will improve her life--"a cataclysm, a volcano, a fire, an outbreak of war, anything to break the unremitting nothingness of her existence" (Little 184). The narrator of the novel considers how the "myth of sacrificial domesticity" limits Janet: "Society offers Pyrex dishes and silver teaspoons as bribes, as bargains, as anesthesia against self-sacrifice" (Little 184). Janet is an "underground figure" who likes to read books about military eruptions or books about war and concentration camps. One novel she is reading is about a Jewish woman who tosses her baby from the window of a train that is going toward a concentration camp:

> She had thrown the baby into the arms of a Polish peasant woman, who was hoeing the turnip field, and as the train moved on inexorably to extinction, the Polish woman and the Jewish woman had exchanged looks of profound significance, and the Polish woman had picked up the baby and had embraced and kissed it with a promise of devotion as the train moved out of sight. (Little 185)

Janet likes such stories but she is not sure why. Is it because of the death and destruction, or because the baby is, "salvaged and harvested like a turnip from the field"? The inappropriateness of comparing a baby to a turnip, especially in these painful circumstances, is Janet's wry way of distancing herself from her own despair. "She feels that she would almost like to toss away her own baby, Hugh; she suspects that she is not the best mother for him, but she knows too that there is 'no way of getting off this train.'" She will have to raise her turnip herself (Little 185).

Drabble explains the title of The Ice Age (1977) as, "shorthand for economic depression--everything frozen including wages." But the satire, the wit, and the symbolism of the title extend further. Drabble is suggesting that the twentieth century is cold and inadequate, like a new ice age. The people and the institutions, and the nations have lost the power to care and to be interconnected. The protagonist, Kitty Friedmann, is a shallow optimist who is afraid to admit that evil exists. But in fact, she has lost both her husband and her foot to an I.R.A. bomb, and ironically she lost them while dining out to celebrate her Ruby wedding anniversary. This is black comedy. Anthony Keating is the central character of the novel. Anthony identifies with the pheasant who was flying over Anthony's duck pond when it died of a heart attack. Anthony ends up in Wallacian prison where, "there's something rather consoling about the lack of options" (Lightfoot Ice 69). When Anthony writes from his prison to Alison that she should do what she wished with his house, adding that God would advise her, Alison was extremely perplexed. "Who was God? Was it a code name for Giles Peterson or Len Wincobank?" Ellen Rose feels that the above sentence might be the funniest line in the novel, but adds that it also might be the most serious (120).

Marjorie Lightfoot sums up Margaret Drabble's contribution to satire as follows:

> Drabble's use of satire has shifted remarkably. The Garrick Year's realistic world was lightly touched by satire, as Emma told her own story. The Realms of Gold presented a self-conscious satirical treatment of a realistic world, examined through shifts in points of view held by the characters and narrator. If Emma was not a very insightful protagonist responding to an existential world, Stephen and Frances were more thoughtful and articulate, though with faith, still bewildered, one choosing suicide, the other, faith. But The Ice Age insists on a pseudo-realistic world, constructed for the sake of demonstration of an apparent existential dilemma through shifting third person points of view and the narrator's. Artificial characters, often dealt with harshly through satire, mock the notion of choice. (Lightfoot Ice 69-70)

There is still a small group of critics who don't take Margaret Drabble's writing seriously. Drabble explains that the main reason for this is that she has chosen to write, "at the end of a dying tradition, which I admire, [rather] than at the beginning of a tradition which I deplore." Michael F. Harper says that Drabble is frequently viewed, "as a late twentieth-century novelist who writes what many reviewers have taken to be good, solid nineteenth-century novels" (Lesniak 137). According to James Lesniak, Drabble is a "post Romantic ironist," and reading her novels requires a compromise to take place between the ideal world of the imagination and the limiting world of reality (Lesniak 138).

Margaret Drabble Bibliography

Lesniak, James G. "Margaret Drabble." Contemporary Authors, New Revision Series, Volume 35. Detroit, MI: Gale, 1992, 132-139.

Lightfoot, Marjorie J. "Margaret Drabble's Satire in The Ice Age: Existentialism or Determinism?" WHIMSY 3 (1985): 68-70.

Lightfoot, Marjorie J. "The Realms of Gold: Margaret Drabble's Satirical Imagery." WHIMSY 3 (1985): 86-88.

Lightfoot, Marjorie J. "Satire in Margaret Drabble's Existential Novel, The Garrick Year." WHIMSY 1 (1983): 167-169.

Little, Judy. Comedy and the Woman Writer: Woolf, Spark, and Feminism. Lincoln, NE: University of Nebraska Press, 1983.

Myer, Valerie. Margaret Drabble: Puritanism and Permissiveness. New York, NY: Vision Press, 1974.

Rose, Ellen. The Novels of Margaret Drabble. Totowa, NJ: Barnes and Noble, 1980.

Seamus Heaney (1939-) IRELAND

In an interview with Seamus Heaney's regarding The Spirit Level (1996), Seamus Heaney asks the reader to "hoard and praise the verity of gravel." He tells of the "gems for the undeluded," and about the "milt of earth," and about the earth's "plain, champing song against the shovel," and about "soundtests and sandblasts words like 'honest worth.'" About this kind of writing, Richard Tillinghast says,

> The Anglo-Saxon pith of "gravel" and "milt" rubs shoulders with the biblical and Latinate "verity." And notice the satisfying consonant rhyme of "gravel" and "shovel," and the elegant music of the feminine half-rhymes "soundtests" and "sandblasts" tucked into the last line. If you can't hear the "champing song" when shovel digs into gravel, you don't have ears. (Tillinghast 6)

See also Nilsen, Don L. F. "Seamus Heaney." Humor in Irish Literature: A Reference Guide. Westport, CT: Greenwood, 1996, 4, 6.

Seamus Heaney Bibliography:

Tillinghast, Richard. "Poems into Plowshares." The New York Times Book Review July 21, 1996, 6.

Clive James (Vivian Leopold)(1939-)

Clive James attended Sydney University on a scholarship for war orphans, but he didn't like school because it was so perplexing. He later said that he had difficulty figuring out what kind of a car was a "Ford Madox Ford," and what kind of conflict was an "Evelyn War" (DeKane 205).

        James has written four books of mock-heroic epic verse which display alliterative
titles: The Fate of Felicity Fark in the Land of the Media: A Moral Poem in Rhyming
Couplets (1975), Peregrine Prykke's Pilgrimage Through the London Literary World
(1976), Brittania Bright's Bewilderment in the Wilderness of Westminster: A Political
Poem in Rhyming Couplets (1976), and Charles Charming's Challenges on the Pathway to
the Throne: A Royal Poem in Rhyming Couplets (1981). The following quote from The
Fate of Felicity Fark in the Land of the Media demonstrates Clive James's subtle command
of language. There is a sharp accuracy in these satiric vignettes. James was successful in
presenting a standard by which the achievements of his figures should be judged (Hirst 95).
James's description of Kenneth Tynan is humorous and memorable. Tynan's face is grey-
blue like a clinker, and his boneless fingers fidget in his lap. As he tries to write it
becomes obvious that although he has the gift of a writer, he lacks the will as he becomes
"Most self-delighting" and yet "self-damned" of men (Hirst 96).
        In his mock epic verses, James satirizes the television medium as well as print
journalism. He also satirizes national politics, and British royalty. More specifically,
Peregrine Prykke's Pilgrimage takes on the publishing industry, and prompted Auberon
Waugh to write in Books and Bookmen that James's satire displays a "robust, knockabout
talent," and also demonstrates a, "wit and original perception, not to mention an amiable
eccentricity of judgment." The Fate of Felicity Fark is a poetic satire of print and broadcast
journalism. Britannia Bright's Bewilderment is a commentary on national politics. Charles
Charming's Challengers is a guide to the wedding of Prince Charles to Lady Diana
Seethrough-Spiffing, and introduces such guests as Prime Minister Margo Hatbox, historian
A. J. P. Tailspin, and romance writer Barbara Heartburn. Some critics contend that James
was not critical enough of the royal family, but Evelyn Waugh said that James is, "one of
the funniest and most formidable writers around" (DeKane 206).
        Clive James's weekly columns in the London Observer were described by Laurie
Taylor as filled with acerbic self-consciousness, and a sense of the ridiculous. These
columns, which were noted for both the reality and unreality of the images were originally
read by more than one-million readers daily, and were later published in the form of three
books: Visions Before Midnight: Television Criticism from the Observer: 1972-1976.
(1977), The Crystal Bucket: Television Criticism from the Observer: 1976-1979 (1981), and
Glued to the Box: Television Criticism from the Observer: 1979-1982 (1983). About the
original articles in the Observer, and the books that were published later, Richard Gilman
said that, "Mr. James makes the programmes so much more enjoyable than they can ever
have been to watch." Christopher Warman said that the television columns in Glued to the
Box are, "sharply observed and highly intelligent, but best of all they are funny" (DeKane
206).
        David Leitch considers Unreliable Memoirs (1980) to be, "a hilarious and
unexpectedly sentimental journey along roads lined with hibiscus and (mainly untouchable)
girls named Nola, Gail, and Velma." James's humor is often raucous, crass, and
adolescent, but Jeffrey Scheuer says that his comic sense is, "bound up with a pathos that
is never mawkish," and that this is what, "makes this a moving and funny book."
Unreliable Memoirs documents the fact that during school, James was known as the class
clown. He compensated for his small stature by being an entertainer, and later said, "I
cultivated the knack of exaggeration. Lying outrageously, I inflated rumour and hearsay
into saga and legend." At one point James claimed to be a close personal acquaintance of
German Field Marshall Erwin Rommell, and when certain people didn't believe that he was
telling the truth, he produced a pair of old sand goggles (DeKane 205).
        Brilliant Creatures: A First Novel (1983) satirizes the book-publishing industry
(DeKane 206). Richard Caseby says that Falling Toward England: (Unreliable Memoirs
Continued) (1985), the second installment in Clive James's autobiography, is filled with,

"wickedly funny jokes and jibes that make you laugh out loud and feel warm to the man." Whitney Balliett says that the book is a funny, light, laughter-producing book that is a streamlined version of George Orwell's Down and Out in Paris and London (DeKane 205).

Clive James (Vivian Leopold) Bibliography

DeKane, Carol Lynn. "Clive James." Contemporary Authors, Volume 128. Ed. Susan M.
    Trosky. Detroit, MI: Gale, 1990, 204-207.
Hirst, David L. Comedy of Manners. New York, NY: Methuen, 1979.

Auberon Alexander Waugh (1939-)

Auberon Waugh's novels are amusing and satirical as they target all sorts of pretensions, especially those relating to major trends in the twentieth century (Moseley 1184). Peter Hebblethwaite says that Auberon Waugh's writing exhibits, "a brusque common sense, a savage irony, and a disregard for the niceties of lit. crit. that have made him enemies" (Hebblethwaite 534). In Will This Do? Waugh says that he has a special gift for, "making the comment, at any given time, which people least wish to hear" (Waugh 214-215).

The Foxglove Saga (1960) is about Martin Foxglove, a charming but unscrupulous young man from a "good family," and his ugly and unappealing companion, Kenneth Stoat. It begins with a group of monks discussing the imminent death of one of their members. Rather than being concerned with religious issues, the monks are most interested in who will get his typewriter and special mattress. It is delightfully comic and witty (Moseley 1184).

Jamey Sligger is the protagonist of Path of Dalliance (1963), and Auberon Waugh has said that it is autobiographical in nature. Waugh takes incidents that have happened in his life, and exaggerates them for comic effect. Jamey, who is the friend of Frazer-Robinson, is always treated well because his family is rich, but his friend Jamey is treated badly and is marginalized by society because he doesn't have any money. Jamey is a comic eccentric who is sent down from Oxford for no very good reason. He goes to live with his mother. Jamey's brother, who had been away in prison, comes home at the same time as Jamey comes home, and he brings a fellow inmate home to stay with them. Mrs. Sligger, whom Waugh presents as the parody of an unthinking liberal, falls in love with the former convict (Moseley 1184). Some of the humor in Path of Dalliance is rather sophomoric. This is especially true of the name of a man--Creepy Crawley, the name of a group--The Rapists, and the name of a woman--Mrs. Droppings (Moseley 1185).

Arthur Friendship is a character is Waugh's third novel, Who Are the Violets Now? (1965). He works for Woman's Dream magazine, and in the evenings he works for an organization named "Education for Peace," but the leader of this organization turns out to be a Nazi who is finally kidnapped and taken to Israel for a trial. In the novel, Arthur bravely goes into a burning room. He is attempting to save a baby, but he accidentally saves a bundle of laundry instead, while at the same time becoming totally disfigured. The satirical targets of Who Are the Violets Now? include women's magazines, the peace movement, attitudes toward black people, as well as black people themselves, especially the flamboyant ones (Moseley 1185).

Consider the Lilies (1968) is probably Auberon Waugh's best novel. Appropriately enough, it is narrated by Nicholas Trumpeter, a modern Anglican clergyman. The book is about Nicholas, who went into the ministry as the easiest way he could think of to make a living; Nicholas is completely without scruples. All of the clergy in the novel are misfits

and eccentrics. One of them thinks that he is Christ; another has a pet fettish; and still
another refuses to hold services, even on Easter Sunday (Moseley 1185). A Bed of
Flowers; Or As You Like It (1972) is a take off from Shakespeare's As You Like It, and
has Oliver, Orlando, Rosalind, and Celia as principle characters (Moseley 1185).

Between 1970 and 1986, Auberon Waugh wrote for Private Eye, the satirical and
investigative magazine, and A. N. Wilson's chapter on "Satire" in Penfriends from Porlock
sheds some light on the humor in Private Eye, and some light on Auberon Waugh as well
(Moseley 1189). The mock diary which Waugh published in Private Eye was written with
"unfettered freedom of commentary." Waugh even invented his own supposed activities.
He writes about the frequent visits of his friends with the royal family, and about the
advice he gave to Prince Charles about the choice of a marriage partner. He also gives full
accounts of trips to Japan, Libya, and Uruguay that he never took, and invents books,
events, and nicknames at will (Moseley 1186).

The diaries which Waugh published in Private Eye were later compiled into The
Diaries of Auberon Waugh: A Turbulent Decade, 1976-1985 (1985). These diaries claim
that Prince Andrew has never learned to speak, that Princess Anne's son actually has four
legs, that Lord Mountbatten is a gay Communist spy, that Lord Snowdon is Welsh, half
Jewish, and a dwarf, and that Marshal Tito is a woman. Of course Waugh has been sued
many times for libel, but only one of these suits was upheld. This was when he was sued
by a woman whom he claimed had gone to bed with half the members of the Cabinet.
Waugh said that even though this had happened, no impropriety had occurred (Koenig 92).
Merritt Mosely says that by using the genre of the diary, "Waugh has made comic, fictional
characters of real people, not the least of whom is himself" (Moseley 1187).

Auberon Alexander Waugh Bibliography

Hebblethwaite, Peter. "Son of Waugh." America 126 (May 20, 1972): 534-536.
Koenig, Rhoda. "A Handful of Mud: Auberon Waugh's War on Manners." Harper's 261
     (December, 1980): 86-92.
Moseley, Merritt. "Auberon Alexander Waugh." Encyclopedia of British Humorists,
     Volume II. Ed. Steven H. Gale. New York, NY: Garland, 1996, 1183-1189.
Waugh, Auberon. The Diaries of Auberon Waugh: A Turbulent Decade, 1976-1985.
     London, England: André Deutsch, 1985.
Waugh, Auberon. Will This Do?: Memoirs. London, England: Century, 1991.
Wilson, A. N. "Satire." Penfriends from Porlock. London, England: Hamilton, 1988 254-
     266.

10
Authors Born between 1940 and 1949

Jeffrey (Howard) Archer (1940-)

The plots of Jeffrey Archer's novels are very much grounded in Archer's real life. Archer was a star athlete who graduated from Oxford and earned a million dollars in business. Still in his 20s, he married a brilliant chemist, and was elected to the House of Commons. But then one of his investments failed, and he lost his money and resigned from Parliament. At this point he wrote a novel about four young men who were bilked out of a million dollars, and who think up a scheme to get the money back. This is what happened to Archer, and it is also what inspired Not a Penny More, Not a Penny Less, a novel that became an instant best-seller in the United States, and which made Archer rich again (Gonsior 26).

Jean W. Ross asked Archer how he managed the sheer energy to keep up with all of his various interests and activities. Archer responded, "People underestimate energy. If you have one gift plus energy, you'll go to the very top. I've always said the formula is: one gift plus energy, you'll be a king; energy and no gift, you're a prince; a gift and no energy, you're a pauper" (Gonsior 27).

Jeffrey (Howard) Archer Bibliography

Gonsior, Marion. "Jeffrey (Howard) Archer." Contemporary Authors, New Revision Series, Volume 22. Ed. Deborah A. Straub. Detroit, MI: Gale, 1988, 25-29.

Angela Carter (1940-1992)

Shadow Dance (1966) is a Gothic detective novel in which the main setting is a junk shop that sells fashionable Victorian rubbish. In this novel there is a threesome that can be variably interpreted. The most impressionable of the three is Morris. His hippie partner in the antique business is the attractive and vicious Honeybuzzard. And finally, there is Honeybuzzard's self-mutilated girl friend named Ghislaine (Sage 206).

The Magic Toyshop (1967), like Shadow Dance, focuses on the culture of play--the culture that trades on dreams. In The Magic Toyshop, there is fifteen-year-old Melanie, and there is Melanie's younger brother and sister (Sage 206). All three are "bleakly orphaned," by being "whisked unceremoniously from their comfortable middle-class home in the country to the dirty, sinister South London shop where unknown Uncle Philip makes his all-two-lifelike toys" (Sage 207).

Several Perceptions (1968) is also about play. Here there is a geriatric music-hall performer who plays an imaginary fiddle. There is also a richly aging call girl, a bisexual self-appointed master of the revelry, who uses his house to collect misfits. And there is his mother, who lies in bed in a coma, listening to 1930s show tunes. There is also Joseph, an analyst who says things like, "You're wedged in the gap between art and life." The climax of Several Perceptions occurs at a Christmas party and involves a series of ironic miracles, with the result being that the fiddler is suddenly playing a real violin, and the call girl's wartime boyfriend comes back, etc. (Sage 207).

Heroes and Villains (1969) is a fantasy set in the "Dark Ages" not of the past, but of the future. The opening of this Gothic science-fiction novel is a parody of Jane Austen's Emma (1816), but with the writing being more aggressive. Carter's Dark Ages of the future, "is divided between Professors, who wryly mull over history's disasters in their high towers, and Barbarians, vagrant, predatory scavengers who threaten the outposts of rationalism" (Sage 207).

Love (1971) is, "an immaculately ironic salute to the passing of the 1960s." Love is set in hippie Bristol, and is about a sexual triangle. "Love is altogether blacker, more erotic and more lucidly nasty than is Shadow Dance." In Love, Buzz, Lee, and Annabel live in an atmosphere polluted with images. An especially telling point in the novel is when Lee accepts Annabel's challenge to, "have his heart tattooed on his chest--in green, the most painful pigment" (Sage 208).

Like Jonathan Swift, Angela Carter belongs to Northrop Frye's "third phase" of satire; her characters are set in a world so zany and unpredictable that common sense and ordinary associations are no longer able to explain the action. In The Infernal Desire Machines of Doctor Hoffman, and Nights at the Circus, Carter creates, "weirdly logical fantasies of debauch, dream, and delirium" (Hallab 108). Desiderio in The Infernal Desire Machines, and Jack Walser in Nights at the Circus are bemused and slightly cynical characters who are lured into their journeys of discovery by a desire for a dream-like woman, and also by a practical quest for knowledge. Desiderio is the spy, and Jack Walser is the journalist. Another reason that they undertake the journey is that they are beset by a kind of youthful restlessness and boredom. Both Desiderio and Walser encounter various fairs, circuses, and odd cultures, and are forced to share the environments, and the goals of the various freaks and monsters (Hallab 109). These freaks and monsters fall into three general categories. There are the real or possible freaks, who have oddities so great that they cast doubt on the traditional definitions of what it is to be human. There are the impossible or fantastic freaks, who blur the distinction between reality and illusion. And there are the various kinds of monsters, who test the boundaries of human reason and appetite (Hallab 110). Leslie Fiedler says that people tend to be both fascinated and repelled by freaks, and that this is because these freaks violate our accepted norms of definition. In freaks, we are unable to determine if something is human or animal, male or female, even alive or dead. Fiedler says, "The true freak...stirs both supernatural terror and natural sympathy, since, unlike the fabulous monsters, he is one of us, the human child of human parents, however altered by forces we do not quite understand into something mythic and mysterious" (Fiedler 24).

The Infernal Desire Machines of Doctor Hoffman (1972) was retitled The War of Dreams when it came to the United States. The entire novel is about the clash between the reality principle and the pleasure principle. In his search for the Doctor, Desiderio, the narrator, comes upon a community of River Indians who adopt him into their tribe and acquaint him with their rituals in exchange for Desiderio's knowledge of how to read and write. "It is only with the greatest reluctance that he realizes, on the eve of his marriage and final absorption, that of course they mean to eat him at his own wedding feast, in order to imbibe his unnatural skill." In the manner of Swift's Gulliver's Travels, Desiderio discovers a surreal brothel in which the android prostitutes transform flesh into vegetable, into animal, and into machine. He also discovers a community of rational centaurs who worship a Great Stallion, and who punish their human livestock with pain and repression. The structure of The Infernal Desire Machines of Doctor Hoffman, like that of Heroes and Villains, is picaresque, but it is, "tighter and more informed in its depiction of alternative societies" (Sage 209).

In The Infernal Desire Machines of Doctor Hoffman Desiderio spends some time at a fair as he is in pursuit of Dr. Hoffman and his dream woman, Albertina. At the fair, Desiderio becomes friends with Alligator Boy, the Bearded Woman, and an androgynous Sharpshooter much like Calamity Jane (Hallab 110). In Desire Machines there is a Sleeping Maiden, and there are Moroccan acrobats whose performance ends with a wild tossing about of heads and arms and eyes (Hallab 112). There is also Albertina/Albert, who is "ambiguously gendered," and who in both reality and dream appears in various forms and disguises throughout the novel, thereby suggesting magical powers. The Minister of the City is a "monster of rationalism" in that he rigidly insists on ordering reality to fit his preconceived theory of symmetry. Dr. Hoffman is the Minister's enemy, and Dr. Hoffman is equally mad in his intention to impose, "the chaotic imaginings of desire onto reality" (Hallab 113). Another "monster" in Desire Machines is the Count, who is a, "self-created Sadean monster of sexual prowess and cruelty." Mary Hallab feels that the River People in Desire Machines can also be considered "cultural monstrosities." Finally, there are the fabulous Centaurs who inhabit Nebulous Time, a place where they can make their very own world, and who have done nothing more than to bind themselves to a rigid and unimaginative ethnocentric horror of history and tradition (Hallab 114). By the end of the novel, Desiderio is on the verge of becoming a "perpetually copulating cog" in Dr. Hoffman's infernal desire machine, when he reclaims his rational self; nevertheless, he has certain regrets as he chooses to side with the more normal human community. And Dr. Hoffman turns out to be a cold-hearted and ridiculous old charlatan (Hallab 116).

In the "Afterward" of Fireworks (1974), Carter said, "We live in Gothic times." She means by this that the, "sub-genres are now the appropriate and (paradoxically) central ones, since the times themselves are splintered and fraught with violent mythology" (Sage 205). There is a passage entitled "A Souvenir of Japan" which illustrates how Carter is able to mingle pleasure with dread.

> Speaking of mirrors, the Japanese have a great respect for them and, in old-fashioned inns, one often finds them hooded with fabric covers when not in use...; as if in celebration of the thing they feared, they seemed to have made the entire city into a cold hall of mirrors which continually proliferated whole galleries of constantly changing appearances, all marvelous but none tangible. If they did not lock up the real looking-glasses it would be hard to tell what was real and what was not. (Sage 209)

The Passion of New Eve (1977) is primitive and picaresque in structure.

> The writing retains a mocking charm. Tristessa's absurd hobby, for instance--"sculpting" glass teardrops by plopping barrowloads of molten glass into her swimming pool from the diving board--is at once satirically accurate (in the fan magazines, all stars had a hobby) and mythically suggestive, the contemporary symbol of all the crystal tears shed by suffering Gothic heroines from the eighteenth century on. (Sage 211)

The Sadeian Woman (1979) is, "a polemical exploration of the uses of pornography, which itself boldly exploits Sade." Lorna Sage says that Carter's choice of Sade as a "collaborator," "has an edge of vengeful humor about it" (Sage 212). The main theme of

The Bloody Chamber (1979) is the blend of the artificial and the animal nature of man. It is a development of the "Beauty and the Beast" antithetical qualities (Sage 212).

In Nights at the Circus (1984), Jack Walser is a journalist who joins the circus as an objective recorder of the oddities there, but he finds himself being treated contemptuously because of his "normalness." So in order to gain acceptance into the circus group, he becomes a painted clown and loses his "very self, as he had known it." But in this new guise, he becomes an outcast from ordinary society, as he is hooted at by the children in the streets and becomes a perpetual joke. He dresses as "the Human Chicken" and has to cry "cock-a-doodle-do," until he is involved in a train wreck and loses his memory and can recall very little more than his role as a chicken (Hallab 115).

In Circus there is a Sleeping Maiden, and an Intelligent pig, and there are also Educated Apes (Hallab 112). Sophia Fevvers is a winged woman who can actually fly. She is '...a gargantuan eater, a hard drinker, a straight and often bawdy talker, and a cold-blooded gold-digger who can never resist an opportunity to add another diamond bracelet to her collection. On the other hand, she is a bird, an 'angel,' 'the Cockney Venus,' 'the Winged Victory,' a 'goddess,' a 'miracle,' even the sheltering 'Madonna of Misericordia'" (Hallab 113). In Circus there is also Madame Schreck, a monster of greed, and Buffo the Clown, who is ironically a monster of misanthropy and hopelessness, and there are also a number of creepy perverts in Circus, who pay to stare at Madame Schreck's "Abyss" of unhappy prostitutes. Hallab considers the woodsmen in Circus to be "cultural monstrosities" (Hallab 114). Nights at the Circus concludes on a positive note, as a, "giant comedy, wafted over by the spiralling tornado of Fevver's laughter" (Circus 295). Mary Hallab considers this ending to be, "a joyous acceptance of the multiplicity of life" (Hallab 117).

Angela Carter's critics note that there are four recurring themes in her fiction: lush prose, violence, Gothic suspense, and eroticism (Lesniak 72). Carter stretches the boundaries of contemporary fiction as she blends reality with the bizarre to create her imaginary worlds. James Brockway says that like all geniuses, Carter, "walks the tightrope on one side of which yawns the chasm of madness, and the other the chasm of bathos." Brockway considers Carter to be "Our Lady Edgar Allan Poe." Carter herself regards the fantasy aspect of her works to be one of the ways that she establishes them as social satire, and adds, "I have always felt that one person's fantasy is another person's everyday life" (Lesniak 73). In 1979 Carter published Comic and Curious Cats, and in 1987 she edited Don't Bet on the Prince: Contemporary Feminist Fairy Tales in North America and Europe (Lesniak 72).

Angela Carter Bibliography:

Carter, Angela. Nights at the Circus, 1984, New York, NY: Penguin, 1986.
Fiedler, Leslie. Freaks: Myths and Images of the Secret Self. New York, NY: Anchor/Doubleday, 1978.
Hallab, Mary Y. "'Human Diversity' in the Novels of Angela Carter: Which Ones Are the Freaks?" Studies in Contemporary Satire 19 (1995): 108-117.
Lesniak, James G. "Angela Carter." Contemporary Authors, New Revision Series, Volume 36. Detroit, MI: Gale Research, 1992, 72-73.
Sage, Lorna. "Angela Carter." Dictionary of Literary Biography, Volume Fourteen: British Novelists Since 1960. Ed. Jay L. Halio. Detroit, MI: Gale, 1983, 205-212.

Terry (Vance) Gilliam (Monty Python) (1940-)

From 1962 until 1964, Terry Gilliam was the associate editor of a New York satirical magazine named Help!, and from 1964 until 1965 he was a free-lance cartoonist. By 1968 he was a sketch writer and creator of animated films for Do Not Adjust Your Set, a television series on the BBC, and at this same time he was a resident cartoonist for another television series entitled, We Have Ways of Making You Laugh, and an animator for a third television series named Marty. Finally, in 1969, Gilliam became a member of the Monty Python comedy troupe (Telgen 167). Gilliam is the only American member of the Monty Python group. He had met John Cleese while illustrating for Help!. Gilliam's bizarre animations in Monty Python's Flying Circus (1969-1974) followed no set form. Some of the sketches would change into, "something completely different. Some would end in the middle, or be interrupted by other sketches" (Telgen 91).

Lewis Grossberger said that Monty Python consists of "six hardened perpetrators of silliness, comedy recidivists who'd stop at nothing to tickle an innocent victim" (Telgen 168). Python sketches contain a great deal of visual imagery, and can often be remembered for a long time. Examples include, "The Ministry of Silly Walks," "The Upper-Class Twit of the Year Contest," "The All England Summarize Proust Competition," "The Dead Parrot," "The Lumberjack Song," and "Spam."

Gilliam recalls that a lot of the cartoons for Monty Python were very disturbing. "There's a lot of anger, anarchy and nihilism along with the bright colors and silly pictures." He said that this was because, "you hope you can reach people on different levels." Various critics have compared Gilliam's work to that of such surrealist painters as René Magritte, Salvador Dali, and Max Ernst. Terry Gilliam may have been more intense than the other members of the Monty Python group. Michael Palin once remarked that, "if Python was made up of six Gilliams, there would be this total explosion of creativity and bits of Pythons spattered all over the walls" (Telgen 169).

Judith Crist feels that Gilliam's Jabberwocky (1977) becomes a bit wearing despite its, "intermittent moments of wild satire and inventive comedy." Penelope Gilliatt, however, believes that if Lewis Carroll had seen Gilliam's Jabberwocky monster, he "would have rejoiced in [the film's] nincompoop wit and the blue-sky reaches of its nonsense. Not often has the rude been so recklessly funny" (Telgen 169).

Brazil (1984), written with Tom Stoppard and Charles McKeown, is a mixture of comedy, satire, and horror. Sheila Benson describes it as a, "brilliant, exhausting, savagely funny post-Orwellian satire." In this film, Gilliam targets modern technology, terrorists, repairmen, bureaucrats, plastic surgeons, ad men, and sticklers for detail (Telgen 170). Desson Howe says that The Adventures of Baron Munchausen (1989) is a, "brilliantly inventive epic of fantasy and satire" (Telgen 171).

See also Graham Chapman, John Cleese, Eric Idle, Terry Jones, and Michael Palin.

Terry (Vance) Gilliam (Monty Python) Bibliography

Telgen, Diane. "Graham Chapman." Contemporary Authors, New Revision Series, Volume 35. Ed. James G. Lesniak. Detroit, MI: Gale, 1992, 90-94.
Telgen, Diane. "Terry (Vance) Gilliam." Contemporary Authors, New Revision Series, Volume 35. Ed. James G. Lesniak. Detroit, MI: Gale, 1992, 167-172.

Graham Chapman (Monty Python) (1941-1989)

Graham Chapman attended Cambridge University, completed his medical studies and became a licensed doctor. But he liked writing and performing better. In Monty

Python's Flying Circus (1969-1974), Graham Chapman would play an Army colonel who would stop a sketch in the middle and complain that it was "too silly." Very often Chapman would appear in skits as a confused upper-class husband, or an officious executive, or he might appear in drag as an assortment of strange women (Telgen 91). In real life, he would usually take a couple of drinks to see him through the afternoon, and he would frequently be the first person in the bar in the evenings. "I must have insulted a lot of people dreadfully and even assaulted quite a few. I went through a period of feeling women's breasts at the bar, using the excuse, 'It's all right, I'm a doctor'" (Telgen 92).

Graham Chapman played King Arthur in Monty Python and the Holy Grail (1977) (Telgen 91). Chapman also played the title role in Monty Python's Life of Brian (1979) (Telgen 91). This is a spoof on Hollywood biblical epics in which Brian is a mild-mannered person who was born on the same day as Christ, and who is therefore mistaken for the Messiah. Some religious people have become upset that the Monty Python troupe is mocking religion; however, Barry Took notes that true religion is not being mocked. What is being mocked is the "bogus, catchpenny and lunatic fringe" of religion. Took continues that in the film, the targets are not the religious figures, bur are rather, "a puzzled and anxious proletariat, incompetent rules, ineffective revolutionary committees, property developers, snobbism and bigotry, a mass of minorities jockeying for their own petty advantage. In short, civilization as we know it today" (Telgen 92).

Graham Chapman's Yellowbeard (1983) is a pirate film written and performed with John Cleese and Eric Idle. It stars Chapman as Yellowbeard, and it, "attacks the pirate genre with a mad comedic thrust" (Telgen 92).

See also John Cleese, Terry Gilliam, Eric Idle, Terry Jones, and Michael Palin.

Graham Chapman (Monty Python) Bibliography

Telgen, Diane. "Graham Chapman." Contemporary Authors, New Revision Series, Volume 35. Ed. James G. Lesniak. Detroit, MI: Gale, 1992, 90-94.

Derek Mahon (1941-) IRELAND

See Nilsen, Don L. F. "Derek Mahon." Humor in Irish Literature: A Reference Guide. Westport, CT: Greenwood, 1996, 211.

Piers Paul Read (1941-)

Philip Flynn says that the themes in the novels of Piers Paul Read include "the emptiness of secular society," "the danger of social stagnation," "the importance of marital fidelity," and "the strange connection between Communist and Christian ideals." Flynn notes, however, that Read's tone is ironic, and that many critics have found a certain cynicism and nihilism pervading his work. Malcolm Bradbury says that Read uses realism to develop his irony, saying that for Read, "the social world, which demands attention, is also a delusion, a source of inexhaustible hypocrisies." This is the irony that drives The Professor's Daughter (1971), The Upstart (1973), and A Season in the West (1989) (Johnson 354). "Read adopted the idioms of his time--the idioms of cynicism, nihilism, sociological/biological determinism. Until the writing of Alive: The Story of the Andes Survivors (1974), he would play games with his readers: fiction's truth and Read's own truths would be veiled" (Flynn 624).

In Game in Heaven with Tussy Marx (1966), the reader sees a dowager duchess, the narrator, and Karl Marx's daughter, Tussy, looking down on the processions of people on the mountaintops and the highlands of Britain. These processions are seeking a leader, or a hero. The word "game" in the title refers to the narrator's attempt to construct a fictional history about "Hereward," a revolutionary saint who could be the hero that the men and women are seeking.

> Read here employs themes that mean much to him: the emptiness of secular society [he can see the despair of his fellow countrymen who have lost hope in their community, their empire, their nation or even their welfare state]; the danger of social stagnation [their instincts are clogged by customs no longer relevant to their society]; the importance of marital fidelity [he can see no logic in this concept, but he nevertheless knows that fidelity is a good thing for the "measure of a man's calibre"]; and the strange connection between Communist and Christian ideals [even though these two sets of ideals are so different they represent an interweaving body and soul, of heaven and earth]. (Flynn 623)

But Read uses an ironic tone in treating these themes, because an ironic tone is, "the tone of a young novelist not wishing to be laughed at as too earnest." Even though Hereward is speaking the truth, he is doing it in terms of irony, cynicism, and contempt (Flynn 623).

The Junkers (1968) is a complex horror story about Naziism, the twentieth-century's great symbol for evil. The Junkers, "plays upon the paradigm of comedy, with lovers from different worlds overcoming obstacles to give birth to a "brave new world" in a wedding feast at the end of the novel (Flynn 624).

Critics in both Britain and in America have praised The Professor's Daughter (1971) for its intelligence and its wit, but they agree that Read "mucked up" the resolution "in mere melodrama." The critics in Russia, on the other hand, were delighted by Read's "condemnation of capitalist values" (Flynn 626).

The Upstart (1973) is a blend of two genres, the rogue/criminal autobiography, and the account of spiritual conversion. It is in London, that Hilary, the rogue hero of the novel, leads a double life. He is a burglar who preys upon the rich, and he is also a painter who preys upon the rich. "The parvenus who buy his fraudulent paintings are the very men whose town houses he loots." Hilary joins forces with a band of fences, deviants, and pimps, all of them alumni of the public school he attended (Flynn 627).

Alive: The Story of the Andes Survivors (1974) provides a Christian spin on the survival of a Rugby team whose plane wrecked in the Andes. The epigraph of Alive is taken from John 15:13: "Greater love hath no man than this, that a man lay down his life for his friends." This quote, and the sacrament of Holy Communion become the central symbols for the survivors. "The young men of the amateur rugby team had overcome their horror at eating human flesh by connecting their experience to Christ's first Eucharist. In deciding to eat those already dead, each of the young men offered his own body to his surviving comrades in the event of his own death. They later remembered that at nightly prayers they had felt a mystical unity" (Flynn 628).

Philip Flynn concludes that Piers Paul Read's books contain "calm, graceful prose," and that his writing style exhibits a "cool, wry, and tough intelligence." "If his own mature religious certainty does not limit his imaginative sympathy with varied human sinners, he soon may join the thin ranks of major modern moral satirists" (Flynn 631).

Piers Paul Read Bibliography

Flynn, Philip. "Piers Paul Read." Dictionary of Literary Biography, Volume Fourteen: British Novelists Since 1960. Ed. Jay L. Halio. Detroit, MI: Gale, 1983, 622-631.

Johnson, Anne Janette. "Piers Paul Read." Contemporary Authors, New Revision Series,
    Volume 38. Eds. James G. Lesniak, and Susan M. Trosky. Detroit, MI: Gale, 1993,
    353-355.

Eric Cross (1942-) IRELAND

**See Nilsen, Don L. F. "Eric Cross." Humor in Irish Literature: A Reference Guide.
Westport, CT: Greenwood, 1996, 211.**

Susan Elizabeth Hill (1942-)

Jonathan Raban writes in London Magazine that Susan Hill has, "a fine sense of
pace and timing and a delicious eye for incongruous detail" (qtd. in May and Lesniak 201).
Gentleman and Ladies (1968) is written in a lightly ironic tone (Cole 396). Writing for
London Magazine, Jonathan Raban called A Change for the Better (1969) a "rueful comedy
of manners" (Cole 397).

Susan Elizabeth Hill Bibliography

Cole, Catherine Wells. "Susan Hill." Dictionary of Literary Biography, Volume Fourteen:
    British Novelists Since 1960. Ed. Jay L. Halio. Detroit, MI: Gale Research, 1983,
    394-400.
May, Hal, and James G. Lesniak, Eds. "Susan (Elizabeth) Hill." Contemporary Authors,
    New Revision Series, Volume 29. Detroit, MI: Gale Research, 1990, 200-202.

Terence Graham Parry Jones (Monty Python) (1942-)

In the Monty Python troupe, Terry Jones is the short, dark Welshman who dresses
up in women's clothes and screeches. Terry Jones plays women in many Monty Python
sketches; however, he is not limited to such roles. He also plays a perverse vicar, a nude
organist, an overzealous bicycle repairman, and Mr. Creosote, a grotesquely overweight
man who is very skilled at projectile vomiting (Telgen 251). Carol Van Strum places Terry
Jones into the same category as Hans Christian Anderson and the Brothers Grimm, saying
that Jones adds, "new color and his own wacky sense of humor to the classic style and
form of the fairy tale." Van Strum considers Jones to be a wizard of a story teller
(Olendorf 100).
        Terry Jones and Terry Gilliam are the co-directors of Monty Python and the Holy
Grail (1975). Richard Schickel says that, "Grail is as funny as a movie can get, but it is
also a tough-minded picture--as outraged about the human propensity for violence as it is
in its attack on that propensity" (Telgen 251).
        Terry Jones and Michael Palin wrote a television series entitled Ripping Yarns
(1976-1977). One of the yarns is about an amphibian which crosses a mountain. Another
is about a murder where each of the four suspects insists on his own guilt, not innocence.
Still another is about two parents who run away from their boring son (Telgen 252). Terry
Jones was the director of Monty Python's Life of Brian (1979), a parody of the Bible. In
the movie, Jones plays Mandy, the mother of Brian. Mandy is a "pragmatic madonna
figure" who stops off on her way to a stoning to buy some stones. She asks the stone
merchant for "two with points, a big flat one, and a package of gravel." The Life of Brian

is a satirical treatment of religious fanatics and overblown biblical extravaganzas. Although some people feel that Jesus Christ is the target of the satire, Bruce Smith explains that, "Christ's ideas and what Christ was saying weren't what we wanted to make fun of. Our target was the way human beings have interpreted Christ's ideas" (Telgen 251).

Terry Jones wrote Chaucer's Knight: The Portrait of a Medieval Mercenary (1980), a book in which Jones challenges the traditional view that the Knight in Chaucer's Canterbury Tales is a "militant Christian idealist." Jones suggests instead that he is a, "shabby mercenary without morals or scruples--the typical product of an age which saw war turned into a business" (Telgen 252). Andrea Chambers describes Fairy Tales (1981) as a "series of satirical yet light-hearted tales." Brian Patten says that these tales are often very dark, but he adds that Jones's "lunatic sense of humour makes them unique" (Telgen 252). Fairy Tales includes a story about a ferocious beast who has a thousand teeth, but who loses them to sweets. It includes another story about a slightly deaf princess who is so beautiful that the birds sing and wake her up. And still another story is about a little girl who turns a monster into a rabbit merely by standing up to it (Olendorf 99).

In Monty Python Live at the Hollywood Bowl (1982), Terry Jones appears as a demented housewife who serves her family a rat tart for supper (Telgen 251). Terry Jones is the director of the final film which the Monty Pythons made as a group, The Meaning of Life (1983). The Meaning of Life discusses the various stages in the human life span. There is a song-and-dance number entitled, "Every Sperm Is Sacred" which lampoons the Catholic stance on birth control. In this film there is also a depiction of a live organ donation, and the vomit-spewing explosion of a gluttonous restaurant diner (Telgen 251).

Terry Jones wrote, directed, and performed in The Saga of Erik the Viking (1983) for children, a story about a hero's search for, "the land where the sun goes at night." Andrew Wawn considers the book to be, "an intriguing sequence of tales, full of wit and invention" (Olendorf 100). In 1984 Jones won the Children's Book Award for the book form of Erik the Viking, which is a humorous look at the Viking conquest. Erik discovers that raping and pillaging isn't all it's cracked up to be (Telgen 252). The Saga of Erik the Viking is a funny piece of writing and it is also filled with weird and wonderful characters (Telgen 252). The title character in Nicobobinus (1985) sets out to find the Land of the Dragons. During his journey, he has one of his hands and both of his feet turned into gold; he and Rosie meet pirates who specialize in kidnapping, and they also meet evil monks, a no-good doctor, a ship that steers itself, some dragons, and most mysterious of all, the "Basilcat" (Olendorf 100). Terry Jones also wrote a poetry volume for children entitled, The Curse of the Vampire Socks (1988).

See also Graham Chapman, John Cleese, Terry Gilliam, Eric Idle, and Michael Palin.

Terence Graham Parry Jones (Monty Python) Bibliography

Olendorf, Donna, ed. "Terry Jones." Something about the Author. Detroit, MI: Gale, 1992, 97-100.

Telgen, Diane. "Terence Graham Parry Jones." Contemporary Authors, New Revision Series, Volume 35. Ed. James G. Lesniak. Detroit, MI: Gale, 1992, 249-253.

Jonathan Raban (1942-)

When Jonathan Raban was seven years old, he read Mark Twain's Adventures of Huckleberry Finn, and dreamed that Norfolk England was transformed into the Mississippi River Valley. Later Raban wrote up his thoughts and published them in the form of Old

Glory: An American Voyage (1981). Raban did research for this novel, but Noel Perrin points out in the New York Times Book Review (September 6, 1981) that, unlike Huck and Jim who slept on the raft, caught catfish, and drank river water, Raban stayed in hotels and motels all the way down the Mississippi, except when inhabitants of the river towns took him off to their homes (Salter 380). Salter notes that on one occasion Raban forgot his packed lunch, and he became so hungry that he pulled a catfish out of the river with the idea of eating it. But he was overwhelmed with disgust at the, "sad, spotty, limp-whiskered thing." Nevertheless, he forced himself to clean it and cook it, and he ate one bite, but then "Mild hunger seemed far preferable to dead catfish" (qtd. in Salter 381).

Jonathan Raban Bibliography

Salter, Susan. "Jonathan Raban." Contemporary Authors, New Revision Series, Volume 17. Eds. Linda Metzger, and Deborah A. Straub. Detroit, MI: Gale Research, 1986, 380-381.

Eric Idle (Monty Python) (1943-)

As part of the Monty Python troupe, Eric Idle takes on the roles of leering rogues, obsequious television hosts, and fussy old women. He is the editor of The Brand New Monty Python Book (1973), and of Monty Python's Big Red Book (1975), which is actually blue in color (Telgen 233).

Rutland Weekend Television (1974) is a parody of small independent television stations (Telgen 233). In Monty Python and the Holy Grail (1975), Eric Idle plays the role of Sir Robin the Not-So-Brave. At the first sign of danger, he wets his armor, and he is accompanied by a troupe of minstrels who sing odes to his cowardice. Penelope Gilliatt says that the entire film is, "recklessly funny and sometimes a matter of comic genius." It is, "a triumph of errancy and muddle" (Telgen 233). Howard Smith and Leslie Harlib say that All You Need Is Cash (1978) has a kind of "sneaky power" in its satire. They especially praise its, "fifteen slyly brilliant parody songs of well-known Beatles tunes" (Telgen 234). In Monty Python's Life of Brian (1979), Eric Idle is a nonchalant crucifixion victim who jokes with his executioners and leads them all in a sing-along from the crosses entitled, "Always Look on the Bright Side of Life" (Telgen 234). In The Meaning of Life (1983), Idle is clad in a pink long-tailed tuxedo as he emerges from a refrigerator to interrupt a live-organ transplant by serenading the unwilling donor with facts about the universe (Telgen 234).

See also Graham Chapman, John Cleese, Terry Gilliam, Terry Jones, and Michael Palin.

Eric Idle (Monty Python) Bibliography

Telgen, Diane. "Eric Idle." Contemporary Authors. Ed. James G. Lesniak. Detroit, MI: Gale, 1992, 232-235.

Michael (Edward) Palin (Monty Python) (1943-)

Michael Palin not only brought his unique sense of humor to the various Monty Python projects he was associated with, but he brought this unique sense of humor to his books, his television shows, and his films as well. In the Monty Python troupe, it was frequently Michael Palin who could make weird connections between things that were not normally thought to be connected in any way. He told John Fitzgerald, "I conjure surreal images and I don't like comedy which is forced." It was Palin who played such memorable characters as Queen Victoria, and a pet shop owner who sells a dead parrot, and a bedraggled man who can only say "It's..." (Telgen 369).

In Monty Python and the Holy Grail (1975), Palin was Sir Galahad the Chaste. He is challenged by a castle full of beautiful, eager, young women (Telgen 369).

Michael Palin teamed with Terry Jones to write The Complete and Utter History of Britain (1969), Secrets (1973), Bert Fegg's Nasty Book for Boys and Girls (1974), Their Finest Hours (1976), Ripping Yarns (1978), and More Ripping Yarns (1978). Ripping Yarns is an attempt to capture the contrast between gentility on the one hand, and bizarre disruptive forces on the other hand that existed during the period of King Edward (Telgen 370). More Ripping Yarns is a sequel to Ripping Yarns and like the earlier book, it features satirical stories of British pluck and adventure (Olendorf 150).

Michael Palin and Terry Gilliam teamed up to write Time Bandits (1981), which is described by Vincent Canby as "a cheerfully irreverent lark" about a young boy whose bedroom is invaded by six time-travelling dwarfs. He joins the six dwarfs in their travels, and together they use a map that shows the holes in the universe, as they embark on a trip through time in search of riches and adventure. Along the way, they meet historical figures like Agamemnon, Robin Hood and Napoleon. They also meet fantastic creatures like an ogre, a giant, and the "embodiment of Evil." David Ansen says that Time Bandits "is a teeming and original stew that stirs in many genres and moods" (Olendorf 151). He also says that it has an earthy, satirical tone similar to that found in the writings of Jonathan Swift. Palin's writing also contains strong doses of absurdism, and surrealism similar to that found in the European theatre (Telgen 370).

In 1981, Michael Palin wrote his first book for younger children. It is entitled, Small Harry and the Toothache Pills (1981) (Telgen 151). Michael Palin wrote, produced, and starred in The Missionary (1983), which Pat H. Broeske describes as, "a sly comedy of manners in which a young Edwardian idealist dispenses religion--and sex--with equal fervor." David Ansen says that The Missionary is, "a sunny attack on the upper classes," but it is furthermore "a happily unfashionable tribute to downard mobility and [is also] a sort of back-handed love story." Ansen concludes that it is, "that rare comedy that never strains for a laugh" (Telgen 370). Finally, in Terry Gilliam's Brazil (1986), it is Michael Palin who is the "smiling torturer" (Telgen 371).

See also Graham Chapman, John Cleese, Terry Gilliam, Eric Idle, and Terry Jones.

Michael (Edward) Palin (Monty Python) Bibliography

Olendorf, Donna, ed. "Michael (Edward) Palin." Something about the Author. Detroit, MI: Gale, 1992, 149-151.

Telgen, Diane. "Michael (Edward) Palin." Contemporary Authors, New Revision Series, Volume 35. Ed. James G. Lesniak. Detroit, MI: Gale, 1992, 367-372.

John Banville (1945-) IRELAND

George O'Brien considers John Banville to be, "the most interesting and resourceful Irish novelist of his generation" (O'Brien 58). John Banville's novels contain careful historical documentation, extensive metaphors, and complex literary allusions; they have been compared to the writings of James Joyce and Samuel Beckett (Drane 31).

Nightspawn (1971) is filled with tricks and literary sleights of hand, and what

George O'Brien describes as "fireworks displays" (O'Brien 59). It is a surrealistic novel about love, murder, and political intrigue. The novel contains many doppelgangers and veiled figures dimly seen hiding under things. <u>Nightspawn</u> is, "a parody of several genres in which Banville attempts to expose the limitations of the traditional novel through a deliberately confusing narrative." Many critics are baffled by the novel, and they have called it everything from a thriller, to a black comedy to a simple study in decadence. The novel contains much dry humor and is rich in its use of words and language (Drane 31).

J. A. Cuddon says that <u>Birchwood</u> (1973) is "witty and exuberant," and adds that, "its originality springs for the most part from Mr. Banville's lyrical gifts as a dexterous stringer together of words." Cuddon says that <u>Birchwood</u> is a moral tale, "which is continuously alive with Mr. Banville's sardonic humour, invention and verbal ingenuity" (Drane 31). Gabriel Godkin, the protagonist of <u>Birchwood</u> returns home to confront his incestuously begotten half brother, Michael. They are in conflict over who is to possess the family home, and Gabriel says, "There is no form, no order, only echoes and coincidences, sleight of hand, dark laughter. I accept it." <u>Birchwood</u> is a provocative novel that is, "sufficiently close to concerns in Irish literary culture to have difficulty in being a critique (in the form of a parable) or a rejection (in the form of a black comedy)" (O'Brien 60).

<u>Doctor Copernicus</u> (1976) and <u>Kepler</u> (1981) are both historical novels. About these two novels, Banville said the following:

> Copernicus and Kepler certainly were obsessed with the notion that they could find the secret order of the universe, and it seems to me that this is what artists try to do all the time. It's an absolutely impossible task. It can't be done, because I don't really believe that there is any order. But it's the pathos of that quest that fascinates me, the pathos of highly intelligent human beings who know that the world is built on chance but are still going ahead, saying, I will not accept this. I'm going to manufacture order, if necessary, and impose it on the chaos. (Drane 33)

Banville continues, saying that Kepler's life,

> ...was so extraordinary and fraught with so much grotesque comedy that fiction simply wouldn't be able to sustain it; only life could sustain that kind of fictional invention. For instance, in my Kepler book, the time that he spends defending his mother against the charge of witchcraft is quite short. In fact, Kepler gave something like eight years of his life to that. And then the old lady upped and died about six months after he got her off anyway. (Drane 33)

Sir Isaac Newton, the narrator in <u>The Newton Letter</u> (1982), remarks, "It wasn't the exotic I was after, but the <u>ordinary</u>, that strangest and most elusive of enigmas" (O'Brien 61). About his writing, John Banville said, "You take something and you give it an intensity which in its own life in the world it doesn't have." Then he gives an example: "A chair is standing there looking at you saying 'goodness, I never realized that about myself.' It's the thing that keeps you writing" (O'Brien 62).

John Banville Bibliography

Drane, Janice E. "John Banville." <u>Contemporary Authors, Volume 128</u>. Ed. Susan M. Trosky. Detroit, MI: Gale, 1990.

O'Brien, George. "John Banville." <u>Dictionary of Literary Biography, Volume Fourteen: British Novelists Since 1960</u>. Ed. Jay L. Halio. Detroit, MI: Gale, 1983, 58-62.

Michael Rosen (1946-)

Michael Rosen says that in his poems he either tries to have fun with the sounds of words, or he tries to explore the ironies of small events. John Fuller says that in Wouldn't You Like to Know (1977), "Rosen satisfies most of the demands that children make of poems, playing for family sentiment, inventing silly phrases, insulting authority" (Lesniak 376). Roy Blatchford describes Rosen's I See a Voice (1981) as, "chirpy, relaxed and good-humoured" (Lesniak 376). In his stories, to be found in Silly Stories (1988), or in Kingfisher Book of Funny Stories (1988), Rosen either tries to adapt folk stories that he likes, or else he explores how certain kinds of ignorance or oppression can be dealt with (Lesniak 376).

Michael Rosen Bibliography

Lesniak, James G., ed. "Michael Rosen." Contemporary Authors: New Revision Series, Volume 32. Detroit, MI: Gale, 1991.

Sue Townsend (1946-)

Adrian Mole is Townsend's popular diary-writing character. Much of the humor in Secret Diary (1982) comes from Adrian's inability to distinguish the trivial from the essential, and it also comes from his inability to see anything funny in his situation (Wills 1132). Adrian is an incurable worrier, and he often overreacts to his problems. Most of his concerns turn out to be totally unfounded. Secret Diary is a vivid satire about Margaret Thatcher's England. It targets joblessness in Adrian's father, cutbacks in social programs in the elimination of school lunches, and inadequate care for the elderly in the neglect of Bert Baxter. Adrian is a conscientious innocent who takes responsibility not only for himself, but for his parents and for Bert as well. Much of the humor in Secret Diary comes from the struggles of Townsend's characters to rise above the mundane annoyances that clutter their lives. In order to get out of his dreary existence, Adrian, for example, reads The Female Eunuch while his mother is flirting not only with feminism, but with Mr. Lucas as well. When his electricity is cut off, Adrian reads Hard Times. "Such comic incongruity underlines the tawdriness of his life while poking gentle fun at his attempts to take himself too seriously" (Wills 1134). The light satiric tone of Secret Diary carries over also into The Growing Pains of Adrian Mole (1984)(Wills 1133).

Groping for Words (1983) is a play that struggles with the problems of illiteracy. The play opens in a literacy class in a kindergarten setting, where big people have to sit in tiny chairs and put their legs under tiny tables, reminding the adults there that they are "misfits" (Wills 1133). Bazaar and Rummage (1982) is a play about agoraphobia, in which three women leave their homes for the first time in years in order to hold a rummage sale. They become involved in a number of different comic situations as their frailties, their fears, and their hopes are revealed. Here again, Townsend juxtaposes the serious and the trivial for comic effect. One woman cries, for example not only because the world is wicked, but also because her vacuum cleaner has broken down (Townsend Bazaar 37).

The Great Celestial Cow (1984) investigates the culture shock of Sita, an East Indian woman, as she is uprooted from her rural homeland in order to live in Leicester (Wills 1133). Rebuilding Coventry (1988) is about a woman named Coventry who accidentally kills her neighbor with an Action-Figure doll. She leaves her husband and her children, whom she calls the "dreary" people, and enters into a series of picaresque adventures in London. Here again, Prime Minister Thatcher is a target of the satire, as

Townsend tells about how Thatcher's policies have isolated and hardened the people of London regardless of their social status. Rebuilding Coventry is a sharp satire on social conditions in contemporary Britain, in which Townsend exposes the wretched conditions of the homeless and the heartlessness of those who have the power to bring about change (Wills 1134). As Coventry is looking for shelter in London, she finds a Cardboard City, where she shares a shelter with Dodo. Ironically, Dodo expresses her nostalgia for the mental hospital that she was forced to leave, saying, "You could be as mad as you liked.... And it was warm and safe" (Townsend Rebuilding 93).

Sue Townsend Bibliography

Townsend, Sue. Bazaar and Rummage, Groping for Words, and Womberang. London, England: Methuen, 1990.
Townsend, Sue. Rebuilding Coventry: A Tale of Two Cities. London, England: Methuen, 1988.
Wills, Deborah. "Sue Townsend." Encyclopedia of British Humorists, Volume II. Ed. Steven H. Gale. New York, NY: Garland, 1996, 1132-1136.

Salman Rushdie (1947-)

M. D. Fletcher's Reading Rushdie: Perspectives on the Fiction of Salman Rushdie discusses Rushdie's fiction in terms of Rushdie's political stance, and also in terms of specific metafictional, satiric, and other literary devices which Rushdie uses to comment on political history. As a satirist, Rushdie was influenced greatly by François Rabelais, by Laurence Stern, by Gunter Grass, and by Gabriel Garcia Marquez. Rushdie himself feels that two major influences were Charles Dickens and Jonathan Swift, but he also acknowledges the influence of Sterne, Grass, and Marquez (Fletcher 3). In his writings, Rushdie undertakes the "chutnification" of English as he creates an ironic hybrid language that in a sense decolonizes the English (Fletcher 4). Rushdie's writing is "postmodern" in that it destabilizes the center, but it is not "post-colonial" in that it does not privilege the margins. Rushdie uses irony to overcome the complicity of writing in English (Fletcher 6). In his satiric and critical stance, Rushdie uses the parodic and the ironic aspects of postmodernistic intertextuality to make very serious points (Fletcher 7, 11). M. D. Fletcher considers Rushdie's fiction to be postmodern writing of an especially humorous and biting variety. "In Rushdie's view, satire is cleansing and therefore potentially recuperative in its own way. Primarily parodic, and thus textual, the postmodern may yet satirize through other historical and literary texts, as well as satirizing textual explanations of historical events" (Fletcher 8).

Rushdie uses many different satiric techniques in his writing. The parody, the obscenity, the ribald humor, and the carnivalesque atmosphere all have the effect of bringing down the serious and lofty while at the same time claiming a place for the sensual and the corporeal. In Rushdie's writing there is a "domestication of grand events," as important historical events and figures are brought down into everyday perspective. Fletcher calls this the "worm's-eye view" of the culture (Fletcher 15). Another satiric technique is the unreliable narrator. Rushdie uses this technique in Midnight's Children, in Shame, and in Haroun (Fletcher 16). In addition, jokes, and puns, and misused folk sayings, and ironic depictions of the commercialization of religion also add to the satire, as does the giving of names and nicknames, and wordplay in general (Fletcher 16). Targets of Rushdie's satires include London's treatment of immigrants, the Asian and the black communities of London, and the Indian bias in favor of light skin. Rushdie is also critical of indigenous post-colonial governments in India and Pakistan (Fletcher 17). Rushdie's postmodern writing is filled with, "riotous comedy, exuberant play, and irrepressible carnival. All normal boundaries and prohibitions are turned on their head, and all normal social hierarchies are mixed and jostled together in a carnivalized space" (Engblom 295).

Grimus (1975) contains imaginative flights of science fiction, as well as extravagant fantasy, and clever twists of sexual humor in what Uma Parameswaran considers to be "typical of Rushdie." Grimus becomes surreal because of the disorientation in time, the dislocation in space, the distortion of reality, and what Gunther Anders calls "the literal metaphor" (Parameswaran 36). In Grimus there are also many types of word play, with the anagram being the most prevalent. "The Gorfic obsession with anagram-making ranges from simple rearrangement of word-forms to the exalted level of the Divine Game of Order. The vast mental powers of the Gorfs make it possible for them anagrammatically to alter their very environment" (Grimus 68). Anagrams provide the basic framework of this novel in which the Gorfs (Frogs) inhabit the planet Thera (Earth), which orbits around the star Nus (Sun) in the Yawy Klim (Milky Way) galaxy of the Gorfic Nirveesu (Universe). The Gorfs (Frogs) are described by Parameswaran as, "very highly evolved frog-like creatures of rock." Even the title of the novel is an anagram, since "Grimus" is an anagram of Simurg. The longest and most complex anagram in the novel relates the question, "And are we actually to be the least intelligent race in our Endimion?" to its answer, "Determine how catalytic an elite is; use our talent and learning lobe" (Parameswaran 39). "By choosing an anagram of Simurg, Grimus proclaims that he would use Simurg's qualities but distort them to create something else. This could be the central metaphor of the novel" (Parameswaran 37).

The names in Grimus also demonstrate Rushdie's ability at word play. Kama(la) Sutra and Lee Kok Fook are specialists in the House of the Rising Son, and Pissov, Sodov, Burgov, and Phukov are the names of four Russian generals (Parameswaran 37). Other characters are given names that demonstrate their most prevalent quality. Bird-Dog has a dog-like devotion to "the Great Bird," and Axona (Ax Owner), Liv Sylwan (Swanly), and Livia Cramm (Live 'ere Cram) are also appropriately named. Still another type of word play is based on the frequent allusions to earlier literature, as when Khallit and Mallit toss coins and banter meaninglessly in a scene that is highly reminiscent of a scene in Tom Stoppard's Rosencrantz and Guildenstern Are Dead. In a similar way, the isolation of Axona Plateau and Bird'Dog's visit to the plain (with its juke boxes and cars) reminds the reader of Garcia Marquez's One Hundred Years of Solitude (Parameswaran 38). And René Descartes's "I think, therefore I am" is changed in Grimus to "I think, therefore it is" (Parameswaran 40). There are also allusions to the Bible, as when Grimus, like Satan, tempts Eagle three times. Furthermore, the first part of the Dance gives a person the power to choose his manner of death, and the second is a Dance of Veils associated with the dance of Salome in the Bible. The third dance is the power of Conceptualization (Parameswaran 41).

Linda Hutcheon says that Midnight's Children (1981) is a postmodern metafiction that parodies as it alludes to other fiction. This novel ironically distances itself from earlier texts (both literary and historical) such as Stern's Tristram Shandy, and Marquez's One Hundred Years of Solitude (Fletcher 6). It is possible to consider Midnight's Children either a satire, or a comic epic, but in either case, the satiric elements are quite prominent (Fletcher 8). Midnight's Children takes place in India and offers a commentary on Indian political history (Fletcher 10). There is much diversity in Midnight's Children. The literary styles range from straight forward narrative to fairy-tale style, to newspaper reporter style, to court evidence style, to school essay style, to public speech style. The genre itself is sometimes fantasy, sometimes satire, sometimes parody, sometimes allegory, and sometimes merely reportage (Fletcher 13).

According to M. D. Fletcher, <u>Shame</u> (1983) is a special kind of satire which is organized as a fictional example of truth of a formula statement. This special kind of satire is called an "Apologue" (Fletcher 97). In <u>Shame</u>, the ridicule and the techniques of satire constitute only two of the aspects of the development (Fletcher 98). <u>Shame</u> satirizes the political history of Pakistan, and focuses on the feudalistic family rivalry that is basic to Pakistani politics as the civilians and the military compete with each other in ways that are both ruthless and ridiculous. The satire targets the pernicious effect of fundamental religion and fundamental politics (Fletcher 10). <u>Shame</u> is the most directly satirical of Rushdie's novels, even though satiric devices appear in all five of Rushdie's novels. In <u>Shame</u>, the intertextual parody is used for satiric purposes. Rushdie says this about <u>Shame</u>: "They're gangsters, clowns, hoodlums who somehow got into the cast of a high tragedy. And what you had to do was take the plot of tragedy and write it like farce, a kind of macabre, black farce" (Fletcher 14). In <u>Shame</u>, the post-colonial leaders bear the brunt of the satire. As Bilquis says, "Once giants walked the earth. Now the pygmies have taken over, however" (Fletcher 17).

Salman Rushdie says that because the first draft of <u>Shame</u> was "very very depressing," and "unbelievably morbid," he changed later drafts to work in "the language of comedy" (Brennan 109). Timothy Brennan says that <u>Shame</u> parodies the style of sacred texts in many ways. Brennan mentions genealogical trees, and they he goes on to say that <u>Shame</u>

> is riddled with pretentious capitalization ("Rim of Things"), elliptical utterances, and absurdly elaborate number symbolism. But the details of style sometimes suggest the Qur'an specifically. For example, the novel's run-on words ("wentwithoutsaying," "whichwhichwhich," "nothing-that-you-will-be-unwilling-to-do") probably mimic the practice of Arabic calligraphers, who often connected adjacent letters when copying the Arabic in order to create a pleasing visual effect from the continuously patterned line. (Brennan 112)

Much of this parody is based on the tendency of the writers of religious texts to use colloquial devices. Rushdie says, for example, that no one would find the anecdotal breaks in the narrative unusual if they were hearing the story recited orally. "What seems like a calculated literary device, he claims, is only the written simulation of the very common practice among storytellers of interrupting themselves" (Brennan 113).

Brennan points out that the central irony of <u>Shame</u> is that, "the progress supposedly represented by Pakistan's escape from European control had the accidental effect of exiling it from the rights and protections developed on the European continent" (Brennan 118). There are also contributing ironies--that Rushdie is a Bombay Muslim who has lived in England from the age of fourteen, that he is a writer whose family moved to Pakistan only a little bit more than ten years ago, and that he is nevertheless called a "Pakistani" writer. Thus, <u>Shame</u> is an extraordinary document: "for it reveals a critique so completely 'felt' that it could only have come from a native, and yet is so imbued with English points of reference that it could not possibly have" (Brennan 121).

The major function of <u>The Satanic Verses</u> (1988) is to expose the dangerous nature of closed and absolutist belief systems. It is ironic, therefore, that much of the hostility towards this book comes from those about whom, and for whom the book was written (Fletcher 1-2). M. Keith Booker compares <u>The Satanic Verses</u> to James Joyce's <u>Finnegans Wake</u>, and Sadik Jalal Al-Azm gives strong evidence that there is a direct influence not only from Joyce, but from Rabelais as well (Fletcher 4). According to Stephen Sleman, "<u>The Satanic Verses</u> includes both the 'root-metaphors of postmodernism'--'pastiche, parody and history'--and the 'culture-specific knowledges, the privileged position of the native reader, the absence of orientalist glossary and those obvious stylistic nuances which mark the text's post-coloniality'" (Fletcher 8). In an article entitled "Being God's Postman is no Fun, Yaar," Srinivas Aravamudan emphasizes the satiric nature of The Satanic Verses (Fletcher 8). The Satanic Verses explores the experiences of immigrants, especially Eastern immigrants, to England, as they attempt to develop a power base and a new sense of self (Fletcher 10). This novel raises basic questions about the nature of revelation, faith, and skepticism, and focuses especially on Islam. The novel asks whether or not absolute beliefs are justified when these beliefs may very well be inspired not by God but by Satan, or may merely be a figment of someone's overactive imagination (Fletcher 11). Agha Shahid Ali objects to The Satanic Verses because of its insulting tone and gratuitousness, but M. D. Fletcher notes, that, "the very nature of satire/carnivalesque involves an insulting tone and gratuitousness" (Fletcher 18).

Sadik Jalal Al-Azm suggests that Salman Rushdie and François Rabelais are alike in a number of important respects. "Rabelais created the famous Abbey of Thélème as an anti-monastery open to both sexes (under the motto 'do as you will') where life is no longer regulated by bells, walls and suffocating rules. In comparison, Rushdie creates the by now equally famous Meccan bordello, Hijab, as an anti-harem emancipated from Mahound's newly instituted rule-book and where, perhaps, something of the Thélème spirit lives on" (Al-Azm 259). But the comparison does not end here. Rabelais's Gargantua and Pantagruel was condemned by established religion as being sacrilegious, blasphemous, and obscene, and Rabelais himself was considered to be an apostate. Rabelais narrowly escaped the stake on more than one occasion either by hiding, or by relying on the help of very powerful patrons and admirers. Both Rabelais and Rushdie used the novel to shock, bewilder, and awaken, while at the same time developing ironies, parodies, and criticisms underneath the exaggerations, and thereby revealing important-but-painful truths about their respective ages and societies (Al-Azm 258). Al-Azm also compares Rushdie with Joyce, saying that Joyce's relationship to Ireland is similar to Rushdie's relationship with India. "Joyce rejects the idea of an Ireland subservient to 'medicinemen,' priests and Empire. Rushdie rejects with equal strength the idea of an India no less subservient to her 'magicmen,' priest-mullahs and the new representatives of Empire (the new Raj)" (Al-Azm 267).

In The Satanic Verses the Qur'an is parodied, and the Islamic proscriptions against women are ridiculed by depicting the parallels between prostitutes at the Curtain or Veil and Muhammad's wives. The female characters in this novel are very strong (Fletcher 14). In The Satanic Verses, Chamcha is an anglophile who has shortened his name from Chamchawala so that the English can pronounce it more easily, and Chamcha's lover says about this, "You name yourself Mister Toady and you expect us not to laugh" (Fletcher 16).

Satire has a special significance in Arabic culture. In The Satanic Verses, a particularly Arabic rhetorical device called "Jahilia," is described as, "minstrels singing vicious satires, vitriolic odes commissioned by one chief against another, by one tribe against its neighbor" (Aravamudan 194). It is reported that the prophet Muhammad said after one particular battle that the satire of three poets caused more damage than all of the other weapons, and it is said that on two different occasions Muhammad ordered female satirists to be executed. In fact, the English word "lampoon" is rendered into Arabic as "hija," and this is also the Arabic word for "spear" (Aravamudan 195). One of the sections of The Satanic Verses that has especially incensed Muslims is the dream about the impersonation of the Prophet Muhammad and his twelve wives by Baal and twelve prostitutes in a Jahilian brothel. "The brothel, known as "Hijab, or the Curtain," is a further provocation, as it alludes to Muhammad's divinely inspired decree instigating the separation of his women from visitors by a curtain, or a veil, a practice extended to society at large" (Aravamudan 196). In The Satanic Verses, Margaret Thatcher is lampooned as "Mrs. Torture," and as "Maggie the Bitch," and it is therefore ironic that publicly Thatcher had to defend Rushdie and give him police protection in spite of the fact that she didn't like the book's politics (Aravamudan 199).

Haroun and the Sea of Stories (1990) is a children's fantasy story that demonstrates the importance of stories, of language, and of free speech (Fletcher 11), but it is also the type of children's story that only adults can really understand (Durix 343). It is Mali's job to keep the stories in good condition. The word "Mali" literally means "gardener of stories." Iff explains to Haroun that, "without Mali's intervention, certain popular romances [would] have become just long lists of shopping expeditions" (Durix 348). Haroun and the Sea of Stories owes much to the earlier Tales of the Arabian Nights, and in fact Haroun and Rashid have a houseboat named "Arabian Nights Plus One," because, as Snooty Buttoo announces, "it is better than the real Arabian Nights. Like the Arabian Nights, Haroun and the Sea of Stories is filled with genies, and, "a thousand and one becomes a paradigm for beauty, perfection or abundance; there are 1001 violin strings, 1001 currents, and 1001 islands on which the city of Kahani is built" (Durix 350).

Haroun tells a story about "Moody Land," a place where the atmosphere is constantly changing according to the mood of the protagonist. In this "Moody Land," characters other than the protagonist also have a less-profound effect on the atmosphere. For example, the atmosphere can be so full of hot air that a burning wind can result when Snooty Buttoo comes around (Durix 344).

Haroun and the Sea of Stories has an appendix which gives the meanings of the Hindustani names of the characters allowing the reader to share in the side-jokes or meaningful associations. In Haroun, Rushdie strings metaphors or advertising jingles together to produce a comic affect. He also echoes patterns and motifs which makes the novel reminiscent of Carroll's Alice in Wonderland, or Through the Looking Glass. The names of the characters are also humorous for English speakers. The bus driver is named "Butt," and so is the Hoopoe, whom Durix describes as "a mad driver." There is also "Buttoo," the corrupt politician. This recycling of names can also be seen in the fact that The Moon Kahani has the same name as Haroun's ill-fated city. Even when the names are not the same, the characters might be. For example, Khattam-Shud and Mr. Sengupta have a strong resemblance each to the other (Durix 344).

In Haroun, the "Plentimaw Fishes" always go about in twos, and speak in rhyme. The followers of Bezaban have somehow become disconnected from their own shadows, and Khattam-Shud bears a strong resemblance to the Ayatollah Khomeini. "Khattam-Shud," by the way, is a Hindustani word which is uttered by storytellers to signal the ends of their stories, and in Haroun, Khattam Shud is described as, "the Prince of Silence and the Foe of Speech." The Chupwalas are the followers of Khattam Shud, and they are described by Durix as "quiet fellows." The Chapwalas hate the light so much that they have invented something called "darkbulbs," which they can use to "turn the darkness on." In contrast to Khattam-Shud and the Chupwalas, there are the Guppies, who are gentle and democratic in nature. In Gup City, the punishments are very mild. For example, when Rashid is captured as a spy, the Guppies try to determine what his punishment should be. "Maybe we should scold him. Or make him stand in the corner. Or write I must not spy one thousand and one times. Or is that too severe?" (Durix 345). The Chupwalas are finally defeated by Haroun's magic trick (given him by a genie). By this trick, Haroun is able to make the sun shine over the Chupwala's dark world. Since this dark world is based on frozen structures, the shining sun melts everything to nothing, and there is a, "triumph of light over darkness, of freedom over tyranny, of life over rigidity and sterility" (Durix 346).

Salman Rushdie Bibliography

Al-Azm, Sadik Jalal. "The Importance of Being Earnest About Salman Rushdie." Reading
    Rushdie. Ed. M. D. Fletcher. Atlanta, GA: Rodopi, 1994, 255-292.
Aravamudan, Srinivas. "Being God's Postman is no Fun, Yaar." Reading Rushdie. Ed. M.
    D. Fletcher. Atlanta, GA: Rodopi, 1994, 187-208.
Brennan, Timothy. "Shame's Holy Book." Reading Rushdie. Ed. M. D. Fletcher. Atlanta,
    GA: Rodopi, 1994, 109-122.
Durix, Jean-Pierre. "'The Gardener of Stories': Salman Rushdie's Haroun and the Sea of
    Stories. Reading Rushdie. Ed. M. D. Fletcher. Atlanta, GA: Rodopi, 1994, 343-351.
Engblom, Philip. "A Multitude of Voices: Carnivalization and Dialogicality in the Novels
    of Salman Rushdie." Reading Rushdie. Ed. M. D. Fletcher. Atlanta, GA: Rodopi,
    1994, 293-304.
Fletcher, M. D., ed. Reading Rushdie: Perspectives on the Fiction of Salman Rushdie.
    Atlanta, GA: Rodopi, 1994.
Parameswaran, Uma. "New Dimensions Courtesy of the Whirling Demons: Word-Play in
    Grimus." Reading Rushdie. Ed. M. D. Fletcher. Atlanta, GA: Rodopi, 1994, 35-44.
Rushdie, Salman. Grimus. London, England: Granada/Panther, 1981.

Willy Russell (1947-)

Willy Russell calls John, Paul, George, Ringo... and Bert (1974) his "Beatles play."
It was a smashing success at the Everyman Theater and later when it was transferred to
London's West End, it won the prize for "Best Musical" (Free 913). When the British
ambassador to the United States tells his wife that they are going to have a reception for
the Beatles, she replies, "The who?" and the ambassador responds, "No, the Beatles." This
is a communication error, because the ambassador had thought that his wife was asking
about a competing rock-and-roll band, the "Who" (Free 914).

In One for the Road (1976), Jane tells her friend Pauline how important a
satisfactory sex life is for a happy marriage, and worrying about Pauline's problem she
asks, "Premature is he? Premature? Far more common than you think." Pauline
misunderstands what Jane means by "premature," and responds that that is not Dennis's
problem, adding that, "he was carried for the full nine months" (Free 914). The satiric
targets of One for the Road are pretentiousness and one-upmanship. Dennis has just turned
forty, and he takes his revenge on his privileged, but meaningless and routine life by
decapitating the concrete garden gnomes, by spray-painting graffiti on the walls, and by
refusing to participate in the various organizations associated with his estate. He mocks his
wife Pauline, and their best friends Roger and Jane when they use the words "Hachis au
parmentier" to describe a simple cottage pie. Dennis also observes, "Before I met Jane I
thought lasagna was a Swedish actress; I thought Jane Fonda was a cheese dip; I thought
Prunella Scales was a skin disease" (Free 915).

Breezeblock Party (1978) is a satirical treatment of class differences, as the sisters
Betty and Reeny constantly one-up each other (Free 915). Betty is given a phallic vibrator
as a joke Christmas gift, but she does not recognize it as such, and therefore misses the
double entendre when she is told that it is "an electric organ." She thinks instead that it
is a drinks mixer, and proudly displays it on her television set (Free 914). Stags and Hens
(1978) satirizes the way culture dictates behavior. At her "hen party," Linda disappoints
her friends and disgusts her fiancé's friends by refusing to drink "a proper tart's drink" like
Babychams (Free 915).

Willy Russell likes to create situations in which conflicting sets of class values are
rubbed against each other, thus exposing the foibles of each. The result is hilarious
repartée. The title character in the play Educating Rita (1980) goes about innocently

deflating the pedantry of the academic world by writing an essay on how to stage Henrik Ibsen's Peer Gynt with the glib, "do it on the radio" (Free 913). When Rita discovers a copy of E. M. Forster's Howards End, she says that it "sounds filthy," and when Frank asks if she knows Yeats, she responds in character, "The wine lodge?" One of the ironies of the play is that by the end, both Frank and Rita have become educated. The play ends with verbal comedy and a sight gag, as Rita says to Frank, "I never thought there was anythin' I could give you. But there is." She seats Frank in a chair, but instead of the implied sex, Rita picks up a pair of scissors and announces, "'I'm gonna take ten years off of you,'" a perfect reward for one who she called 'a geriatric hippie' in act 1, scene 1" (Free 914).

Our Day Out (1983) is a musical about a day's outing in an amusement park by what Russell calls, the "Progress Class." Much of the comedy comes from the clash of children with their bus driver, with cafe owners, and with Briggs. At one of the potential bus stops, the owners see the bus coming, and quickly change the "Coaches Welcome" sign with another sign which reads, "Absolutely no Coaches." At the next bus stop, the new management marks all of the prices up before they allow the children to enter. This is ironic, because the children still win the battle by stealing more than they pay for (Free 915). Shirley Valentine (1986) is about escaping from mundane and stereotyped existence both by talking about taking chances and by actually taking chances. In this play, Shirley Valentine has a neighbor with a vegetarian bloodhound, but Shirley feeds minced beef to the dog, reasoning, "if God had wanted to create it as a vegetarian dog he wouldn't have created it as a bloodhound would he? He would have made it as a grapejuice hound" (Free 914).

The musical Blood Brothers (1988) was a twelve-year hit in London's West End. It opened in New York in 1993 and received four Tony nominations. In this play, Mrs. Johnstone is a welfare mother who works as a cleaning lady for an upper-middle-class couple. When she has twins, she gives one of them to the couple she works for. But the boys later meet each other, and become playmates, and ironically become "blood brothers." Much of the comedy derives from class differences. The twin who remained with the poor family tells the twin who was given away to the rich family that he plays games with the police. When a policeman asks him to give his name and explain what he is doing there, he responds, "Adolf Hitler," and "waitin' for the ninety-two bus" (Free 916).

Willy Russell Bibliography

Free, Mary. "Willy Russell." Encyclopedia of British Humorists, Volume II. Ed. Steven H.
    Gale. New York, NY: Garland, 1996, 912-917.

Carson Ciaran (1948-) IRELAND

See Nilsen, Don L. F. "Carson Ciaran." Humor in Irish Literature: A Reference Guide. Westport, CT: Greenwood, 1996, 211.

Martin Louis Amis (1949-)

Gerard Carruthers says that Martin Amis is "one of the most vicious satirists of the modern urban world" (Carruthers 23). Marla Levy says that Amis, "has a curious way of extracting laughs at the expense of human baseness and poverty; even the pathetic appears funny when he describes it." When critics say that Amis's books are sexist, he responds that his books are satires, and that the apparent sexism is "a parody of the egotistical male disposition" (Levy 29). In a 1978 interview, Amis told Angela Neustatter of <u>Cosmopolitan</u>, "Looked at seriously, of course, my books are ghastly, but the point is they are satire.... I'm not writing social comment. My books are playful literature. I'm after laughs." Amis says that "sanity" is one of his primary concerns; however, he also notes, "I'm more interested in rival versions of sanity--one person saying to another, 'My sanity is saner than yours'" (Levy 30).

In <u>The Rachel Papers</u> (1973), Charles Highway is a prolific writer who has written a number of pads and notebooks about Rachel Noyes, his former girl friend. By referring to these notes, and by recalling other memories, Charles, who is the first-person narrator, gives an entertaining and witty account of growing up (Levy 30). <u>The Rachel Papers</u> is a picaresque novel that highlights Charles Highway's sexual appetites (Carruthers 23).

<u>Dead Babies</u> (1975) is a Menippean satire (Carruthers 23). It is also a cleverly dark comedy of manners which, not only showcases Amis's ability to use humor and satire successfully, but also depicts the bizarre violence that takes place in his decadent setting of a drug-filled weekend involving six young people who share a large house which is named Appleseed Rectory, and which is located just outside of London. The entire novel takes place between Friday and Sunday; however Amis uses flashbacks extensively to flesh out his development of each of his six characters, all of whom are connected in some way with the University of London (Levy 31). Throughout the weekend, there is a mysterious stranger who plays a number of nasty practical jokes on everyone and leaves notes signed "Johnny." The title of the paperback edition was changed from <u>Dead Babies</u> to <u>Dark Secrets</u>, because the original title was considered, "too morbid to have any popular appeal" (Levy 32).

<u>Success</u> (1978) contains both the dark humor of <u>Dead Babies</u> and the sheer hilarity of <u>The Rachel Papers</u>. Although it is written in first person, the point of view changes, since the foster brothers Terence (Terry) and Gregory alternate in narrating the chapters. As the title suggests, the novel is basically concerned with "success," but the amusing point of the novel is that the same events, and the evaluation of these events, can change drastically when described by two different people (Levy 32). <u>Success</u> is like <u>Dead Babies</u> in that the comedic effect of both of these novels derives from, "a grim explosion of the hedonistic façade of human life" (Carruthers 24).

The dust jacket of <u>Other People: A Mystery Story</u> (1981) contains Dennis Potter's proclamation that this novel is written with, "wit and talent and mordant perception" (Levy 29). <u>Other People</u> is a Post-Modern comedy in which the artifice of the novel ironically comments on the artifice of the real world (Carruthers 24). <u>Money: A Suicide Note</u> (1984) is Amis's most explicit satire about how large financial interests control our personal lives. The novel is a satiric refutation to the economics proposed by Reagan and Thatcher during the 1980s.

In <u>London Fields</u> (1989), Nicola Six (the "Six" stands for "Sex") is so disgusted with the neuroses of the modern world that she decides to commit suicide, but then she becomes involved with a low-life by the ironic name of Keith Talent (Carruthers 24). Nicola doesn't like Keith's philandering, and in some reptilian imagery, Nicola sees the reptile house in Keith Talent's brain, and in her vision, "it wouldn't be her who romped and basked with Keith and rolled with him in the mud. It would be Enola, Enola Gay." This is a bit of comic exaggeration in which the visual image of the bomber that was used to drop the atomic bomb on Japan is hyperbolically evoked (Carruthers 25).

Martin Louis Amis Bibliography

Carruthers, Gerard. "Martin Louis Amis." <u>Encyclopedia of British Humorists, Volume I</u>. Ed. Steven H. Gale. New York, NY: Garland, 1996, 22-26.

Levy, Marla. "Martin Amis." Dictionary of Literary Biography, Volume Fourteen: British Novelists Since 1960. Ed. Jay L. Halio. Detroit, MI: Gale Research, 1983, 29-32.

Morrison, Susan. "The Wit and Fury of Martin Amis." Rolling Stone 578 (May 17, 1990): 95-102.

Neustatter, Angela. "Amis and Connolly--The Best-Seller Boys." Cosmopolitan 185 (August, 1978): 71-72.

Ken Follett (1949-)

Ken Follett wants his books to inform and to delight. In his books, he wants to blend the serious with the popular (Macdonald and Macdonald 115). He learned how to write good books by writing mediocre books and then asking himself what was wrong with them. Andrew and Gina Macdonald say that one of Follett's strengths lies in his ability to humanize his villains. "All are well rounded and complete, with credible motives and understandable passions--if anything, they are sometimes so sympathetic that they jeopardize the reader's relationship with the hero" (Johnson 150). Michael Demarest considers Ken Follett to be, "an expert in the art of ransacking history for thrills," because each of his novels is based on news stories and historical events. His works tend to follow a hunter-hunted format that leads to exciting chase scenes and games of wit and brinkmanship (Macdonald and Macdonald 113).

The Modigliani Scandal (1976) has been praised by various critics as "sprightly, ebullient, light, bright, cheery, and fizzy." It is a, "classic caper novel, the kind that focuses on myriads of characters dashing around romantic European locations in search of a big score." The plot is, "amusing, refreshing, a bit amoral and risqué, and likeable, and ultimately quite forgettable." "The humor comes from the polished and mostly privileged characters using art and artists as their main chance, betraying others and corrupting themselves not for the love of beauty but for monetary leverage, reputation, and academic or social success" (Macdonald and Macdonald 117).

Peter Prescott calls The Eye of the Needle (1978), "rubbish of the very best sort, a triumph of invention over convention." The Eye of the Needle is about a German spy in England. His German name is Heinrich von Müller, and his English name is Henry Faber. He is code-named "Die Nadel" (The Needle) (Macdonald and Macdonald 117). Throughout the novel, Faber is fearful and tense, and he is incredibly lonely. At night he has nightmares about giving away his cover by using German sentence construction, or by wearing swastika-adorned socks. By the end of the novel, Faber is charming, witty, and ingenious, and he is also disdainful of the German high command and of the National Socialist party (Macdonald and Macdonald 119).

Triple (1979) is about three students at Oxford University. David Rostov, who later becomes a Soviet Intelligence Officer; Yasif Hassan, a Palestinian who becomes a triple agent for the Egyptians, the Soviets, and the Fedayeen; and Nathaniel Dickstein (Nat), a cockney Jew who later becomes an immigrant in Israel. Dickstein is a very successful spy, but nevertheless a reluctant one. It is ironic that this same group meets again later when they learn that Egypt is building a nuclear reactor in the western desert. After Dickstein blows his cover, his steps come to be anticipated, and his movements become traceable. His objective therefore becomes thwarted, and his companion quips, "You wouldn't think we were the chosen people, with our luck." By the end of the novel, it is clear that Follett is sympathetic to Dickstein, and therefore sides with the Israelis. But it is also clear that Follett can appreciate and present the motives of PLO outrage and extremism. "If an understanding of and a tolerance for paradox and ambiguity is a defining characteristic of both civilized behavior and literary art, then the novel's attempt to balance motives by humanizing villains and questioning the heroics of its protagonist qualifies the book as literary" (Macdonald and Macdonald 120).

Follett's skill at setting up a chain of events in chronological sequence, is illustrated in the theft scene of The Key to Rebecca (1980) where Wolff, the master spy and villain, creates a diversion for the theft of a British Army briefcase by shouting "thief" and by pointing at a small boy who seems to be running away. This creates total pandemonium:

> The crowd from the bus stop, the acrobats' audience, and most of the people in the cafe surged forward and began to attack one or another of the drivers- -Arabs assuming the Greek was the culprit and everyone else assuming it was the Arab.... Everyone yelled at everyone else in five languages. Passing cars halted to watch the melée, the traffic backed up in three directions, and every stopped car sounded its horn. A dog struggled free of its leash and started biting people's legs in a frenzy of excitement. (Macdonald and Macdonald 114)

Lieutenant Colonel Reggie Bogge is one of the satirical targets in The Key to Rebecca. Bogge represents the British pukka sahib. Such sahibs spend their time polishing their cricket game, deriding the natives, and closing their eyes to anything which is awkward or dangerous. In the novel, Rommel's forces have moved close to victory, as the British and the Egyptians search frantically for Wolff's code book. The "key" in the title of the novel is a marked copy of Daphne Du Maurier's Rebecca (1938) which can provide the key to the breaking of Wolff's code. Andrew and Gina Macdonald say that, "all the main characters in The Key to Rebecca, female and male, heroes and villains, are memorable and individualized, just quirky enough to persuade readers of their reality" (Macdonald and Macdonald 121).

In Lie Down with Lions (1985) Jane's

> attractiveness as a character palls when Follett's plot has her submit to her childishly obsessive and shallow husband, mothering him as he wishes in spite of his beating her, his betrayal of her friends to Russian execution, and his inability to confront the truth. Are readers to see Jane as a sympathetic, liberated female character or as a satiric portrait of the excesses and dishonesties perpetrated by the personally warped in the name of the women's movement? (Macdonald and Macdonald 123)

It is ironic that Jane is not able to blow up some Russians because they are so young, and so innocent, and because it would have been "murder." But most of all, she couldn't blow them away, "because they have mothers." Andrew and Gina Macdonald say that, "such bathos calls into question readers' previous sympathies toward Jane," since this makes Jane's portrait, "inconsistent with her earlier good sense and stability" (Macdonald and Macdonald 123).

Ken Follett Bibliography

Johnson, Anne Janette. "Ken(neth Martin) Follett." Contemporary Authors, New Revision Series, Volume 33. Ed. James G. Lesniak. Detroit, MI: Gale, 1991, 149-153.
Macdonald, Andrew F., and Gina Macdonald. "Ken Follett." Dictionary of Literary Biography, Volume Eighty-Seven: British Mystery and Thriller Writers Since 1940. Eds. Bernard Benstock and Thomas F. Staley. Detroit, MI: Gale, 1989, 113-124.

11
Authors Born after 1949

Bryan MacMahon (1950-) IRELAND

See Nilsen, Don L. F. "Bryan MacMahon." Humor in Irish Literature: A Reference
Guide. **Westport, CT: Greenwood, 1996, 1-2, 211-212.**

Andrew Norman Wilson (1950-)

A. N. Wilson has a reputation for writing farcical novels which mock British life.
He began writing in the late 1970s with some intricately plotted works that exploit the
absurdities of England's social institutions (Stone 482). Wilson's satirical targets include
particular figures in academic, in religious, and in political life, and he also targets fads of
all kinds (Hollinghurst 776). Brian Murray says that A. N. Wilson is one of Britain's most
prolific and visible literary figures, and that his writing tends to be erudite, witty, and
provocative (Murray 321). Wilson became famous for mocking and teasing various
prominent figures such as Salman Rushdie, and Robert Runcie, the former archbishop of
Canterbury. In 1990, Wilson wrote an article in the Spectator in which he revealed the
unflattering details of private conversations with the Queen Mother and other members of
the Royal Family. His comments sparked an intense controversy. It is ironic that A. N.
Wilson was also on the receiving end of a number of barbs and denunciations, especially
in Britain's satiric magazine Private Eye (Murray 323).
Les Stone says that in The Sweets of Pimlico (1977), Wilson reveals, "a marked
penchant for mining both the eccentric and the banal to comic advantage." Paul Abelman
says that this novel is a work of, "intrinsic elegance as well as great charm and wit" (Stone
482). The relationship between Evelyn Tradescant and Baron Theo Gormann lies at the
base of this novel. At the beginning of the novel, Evelyn spends her time nurturing her
passion for beetles. In fact, coleoptery becomes a central metaphor to demonstrate how
Evelyn understands English society. Her understanding is both satirical and sociological:
"The Whirligig Beetles, Gyrini natatores, she recalled, swim about in crowds, in endless
circles and gyrations on the surface of still water. How one distinguished their sex; she
rather forgot" (Hollinghurst 777). Evelyn's brother, Jeremy has had a relationship with
"Pimlico" Price, who is a gay manufacturer of sweets. Gormann supports Pimlico, but
Pimlico is jealous of Gormann's attention to the girl. "Wilson here contrives the
catastrophe first in a manner which is farcical (when Jeremy posts letters to his parents, his
sister, and his boyfriend in the wrong envelopes), and second in a sad and ironic coda in
which Gormann dies and Evelyn, with a passivity which becomes typical of Wilson's
characters, accepts 'Pimlico' Price's offer of marriage" (Hollinghurst 778). The critic for
the Daily Telegraph said that The Sweets of Pimlico is "a witty novel of manners." It won
the Rhys Memorial Prize for fiction (Murray 321).

Unguarded Hours (1978) tells about the misadventures of a hapless protagonist by the name of Norman Shotover. Norman, "muddles his way through the worlds of academe and organized religion, encountering several well-drawn eccentrics and comic types along the way." Unguarded Hours won wide praise from reviewers who noted the "tight pacing" and the "deft use of farce" (Murray 321). Norman Shotover is a passive innocent who brings to mind Paul Pennyfeather in Evelyn Waugh's Decline and Fall (1928), and in fact, the satirical mode of both Unguarded Hours and Kindly Light has been compared to the satirical mode of Waugh's early novels (Hollinghurst 778). Unguarded Hours begins, "Had the Dean's daughter worn a bra that afternoon, Norman Shotover might never have found out about the Church of England; still less about how to fly." A lot of the humor in Unguarded Hours comes from the various outrageous characters who Norman comes into contact with. There is Mr. Skeggs, an alcoholic electrician who claims to be a bishop. Mr. Skeggs has an interest in the legal profession, but he has even more of an interest in magnificent titles. Mr. Skeggs gets Norman drunk and ordains him to a host of titles (Hollinghurst 778). And there is Mungo, the aristocratic "Dundee of Caik," who is given to impulsive statements like, "I don't hold with the Lake District." And there is the dean, who is a rabble-rousing clergyman with incendiary books like Chuck It, God. And throughout the novel, Shotover wanders among such eccentrics as these (Stone 482). One of the devices of the novel is based on moments of shock when unexpecting people stumble onto unsuspected sexual acts involving unexpected people or practices (Hollinghurst 779).

Kindly Light (1979) is again about Norman Shotover, and in fact contains many of the same characters as are to be found in Unguarded Hours, but here they are subjected to, "a more farcical and bizarre story and are refracted through a sketchier and funnier manner" (Hollinghurst 779). In Kindly Light, Shotover is portrayed as an unwilling member of the Catholic Institute of Alfonso, otherwise known as the "CIA." Most critics say that Kindly Light is frequently hilarious, and some critics consider this to be Wilson's funniest work. Susan Kennedy says that Kindly Light compares favorably with the comedies of Evelyn Waugh. She adds that they are, "very very funny: deadly accurate black comedy" (Stone 482). The paradox of Kindly Light is that, "in many ways, religion was so obviously an admirable and necessary thing. And yet it never seemed to make anyone any better. The reverse was often the case" (Hollinghurst 779).

The Healing Art (1980) is a sentimental comedy about a middle-aged woman named Pamela Cowper, who learns that she is dying of cancer. Pamela is told that she would be able to live much longer if she agreed to submit her body to chemotherapy, but she refuses the treatment. Nevertheless, her health doesn't deteriorate. The health of her ward mate, on the other hand, deteriorates noticeably. Finally, Pamela suspects that Doctor Tulloch, their physician, might have accidentally switched their x-rays. This is the scenario that Wilson uses to satirically target both the medical world and the world of academia (Stone 482). Simon Blow was very impressed with Wilson's comic achievement in The Healing Art, saying that, even though the theme of the novel is deeply tragic, Wilson was successful, "at playing black comedy that can make us laugh just when we should cry" (Stone 483). Alan Hollinghurst notes that the novel's initial device, in which the X-rays of two women suffering from cancer are confused, is potentially farcical, but the lightness of the farce is subverted by the gravity of the issues. It is a tragi-comedy, containing, "almost libellously satirical elements," and the novel has a gratuitous satirical climax in which Pamela's friend's Oxford college is gutted by fire (Hollinghurst 779).

Who Was Oswald Fish? (1981) is about an eccentric celebrity named Fanny Williams and her attempts to restore a Gothic Victorian church which had been designed by Oswald Fish. The novel contains much mayhem during which Fish's memoirs are discovered, and they prove to be very sexual in nature. This situation gives Wilson the opportunity to contrast Victorian and contemporary British society. Tim Heald says that

<u>Who Was Oswald Fish?</u> is, "an enjoyable, clever piece of black comedy" (Stone 483). Oswald Fish was a late Victorian architect and designer whose masterpiece, St. Aidan's Purgstall Heath, Birmingham, is going to be demolished. Fish's elderly daughter finds and reads Fish's journal, and discovers the details of Fish's adulteries, and the complex blood relationships running among many of the principal characters. Alan Hollinghurst sums up the novel as follows: "Despite passages as funny as any Wilson has written, the tone of the book is increasingly sinister and unhappy" (Hollinghurst 780).

    <u>Wise Virgin</u> (1982) is a novel about Giles Fox, a blind scholar who is obsessed with editing a medieval text that advocates virginity. Michiko Kakatuni says that in <u>Wise Virgin</u>, Wilson, "successfully balanced his gift for wicked comedy with caring and compassion." Martha Duffy agreed, saying that in this novel Wilson found, "his own balance between light and dark comedy" (Stone 483).

    <u>Scandal: or, Priscilla's Kindness</u> (1983) is a comedy about sexual hijinks and British politics. Derek Blore, the novel's protagonist, is a Member of Parliament who enjoys sadomasochistic sex. Les Stone feels that in this novel, as in many Wilson novels, the cast of secondary eccentric characters rival the hero in terms of outrageousness. For example, there is Blore's wife, Priscilla, who commits adultery out of kindness. And there is Feathers, the despicable journalist who craves alcohol, and amuses others. And there is Bernadette, a dull prostitute who fills Blore's need for regular floggings. Jonathan Yardley considers the novel to be "deliciously witty," and Elaine Kendall especially liked Wilson's skill at characterization. "Where else will you find a hoodlum who changes his name from Costigan to Costigano for professional reasons?" Kendall says that <u>Scandal</u> is a, "comic novel in the classic English tradition" (Stone 483).

    <u>Gentlemen in England</u> (1985) is a successful lampoon of the repressive Victorian period of England's history. Michiko Kakatuni says that this novel marks Wilson's "continued development as a comic writer" (Stone 483). <u>Love Unknown</u> (1986) also has its share of eccentric characters. This is a novel which targets such institutions as organized religion, feminism, and infidelity (Stone 483). George Sayer says that Wilson's <u>C. S. Lewis: A Biography</u> (1990), "has great merits." He says that this biography is "a good piece of narrative, enlivened by sharp observation, neat vignettes of character, bizarre incidents, and quite a lot of humor" (Murray 326).

Andrew Norman Wilson Bibliography

Hollinghurst, Alan. "A. N. Wilson." <u>Dictionary of Literary Biography, Volume Fourteen: British Novelists Since 1960</u>. Detroit, MI: Gale, 1983, 776-780.

Murray, Brian. "A. N. Wilson." <u>Dictionary of Literary Biography, Volume One Hundred Fifty-Five: Twentieth-Century British Literary Biographies</u>. Ed. Steven Serafin. Detroit, MI: Bruccoli Clark Layman/Gale Research, 1995, 320-337.

Stone, Les. "A(ndrew) N(orman) Wilson." <u>Contemporary Authors, Volume 122</u>. Eds. Hal May and Susan M. Trosky. Detroit, MI: Gale, 1988, 481-484.

Bill Bryson (c1951-)

    In 1987, Bill Bryson and his family took their blue Rambler station wagon on a vacation trip. Their goal was to find the perfect small town. In <u>The Lost Continent: Travels in Small-Town America</u> (1989), Bryson describes this perfect small town as follows: "Bing Crosby would be the priest, Jimmy Stewart mayor, Fred MacMurray the high school principal. Henry Fonda a Quaker farmer. Walter Brennan would run the gas station, a boyish Mickey Rooney would deliver groceries, and somewhere, at an open window, Deanna Durbin would sing" (Olendorf 51).

Bill Bryson Bibliography

Olendorf, Donna, ed. "Bill Bryson." <u>Contemporary Authors, Volume 142</u>. Detroit, MI: Gale
    Research, 1994, 51-53.

Douglas (Noel) Adams (1952-)

    Douglas Adams writes in such popular genres as mystery, science fiction, and the
fantasy novel, and he does so with a distinctively and sophisticatedly humorous style
(Donnelly 9). Adams writes science fiction as social satire; or more precisely, he writes
parodies of science fiction. His novels have a kind of surrealistic audacity, as Adams
searches for the ironies that are involved in "epistemological verities." Adams creates
bizarre characters with preposterous names who quickly become involved in improbable
twists of plot (Donnelly 7). One of the most entertaining aspects of Adams's style is that
he introduces seemingly irrelevant factors which later prove to be integral to the plot
(Donnelly 8).
    Richard Brown says that much of Douglas Adams's comedy comes from his mis-
applications of pseudo-high-tech concepts. Adams's writing constantly demonstrates
Murphy's law--that anything that can go wrong will go wrong. John Clute says that in
Adams's writing, "there is enough joy throughout, enough tooth to the zaniness, and enough
rude knowingness about media-hype versions of science fiction, to make <u>Hitchhiker</u> one of
the genre's rare genuinely funny books." Philip Howard adds, "Adams has fun with the
trendy manners of our time, from worship of the motor car to jogging, and from the
pedantry of committee meetings, Point of Order Madam Chairperson, to religious
enthusiasm and, engagingly, Sci-Fi itself." Peter Kemp sees hints of Lewis Carroll and
Edward Lear in the <u>Hitchhiker</u> series: "There are logical extensions of mad premises,
grotesque creatures with crazily evocative names, chattering objects, moments of satiric
farce, and picturesquely absurd landscapes." Michael Adams notes that Douglas Adams's
satiric targets include, "bureaucracies, bad poets, literary critics, scientific theories,
nightclub entertainers, religion, philosophy, labor unions, economists, tax laws, clichés,
structural linguistics, rock 'n' roll, sentimentality, cricket commentators, and Paul
McCartney's wealth" (Lesniak 3).
    In 1978, Douglas Adams wrote a series of comic science-fiction radio dramas
entitled <u>The Hitchhiker's Guide to the Galaxy</u>. These radio scripts were later expanded and
revised to become <u>Hitchhikers Guide</u> (1979), and <u>The Restaurant at the End of the Universe</u>
(1980). These books later became record albums, a computer game, and a six-episode BBC
television series named <u>Hitchhiker's Guide to the Galaxy</u> (1981). Adams later collaborated
on <u>The Utterly, Utterly Merry Comic Relief Christmas Book</u> (1986) (Donnelly 7).
    <u>Hitchhiker's Guide to the Galaxy</u> (1979), <u>Life, the Universe, and Everything</u> (1980),
<u>The Restaurant at the End of the Universe</u> (1980), <u>So Long, and Thanks for All the Fish</u>
(1984) and <u>Mostly Harmless</u> (1992) are the five books in the cosmic satiric series Douglas
Adams calls <u>The Hitchhiker's Trilogy</u> (1984), and this illustrates Douglas Adams's
propensity for breaking rules. It is interesting to note that while there are five books in <u>The
Hitchhiker's Trilogy</u>, there are only two books in Douglas Adams's more recent trilogy
which makes up the Dirk Gently series (Wilcox 9). In <u>The Hitchhiker's Trilogy</u>, Arthur
Dent is a bungling British Everyman who is on a "heroic" quest in search of a drinkable
cup of tea (Kropf 62).
    <u>Hitchhiker's Guide to the Galaxy</u>, has inspired a number of novels, a television

series, and even an interactive computer game. Adams came up for the idea of <u>The Hitchhiker's Guide to the Galaxy</u> while he was in Innsbruck, Austria. At the time, he was lying in a field, drunk, and was gazing at the stars. In his hand was a copy of <u>The Hitchhiker's Guide to Europe</u>. It is therefore ironic and coincidental, when Arthur Dent lies down in front of a bulldozer as he tries to keep his house from being bulldozed in order to make room for a freeway. His friend, Ford Prefect, approaches him and tells him they both have to go to the pub and get drunk because the earth is scheduled to end in five minutes. At this point, a large yellow spaceship hovers over them and announces, "Citizens of the Earth, I am sorry but your planet must be destroyed to make way for the new interstellar highway" (Alexander 4).

Chad Nilep points out that a regular guide book explains the location of an unknown place by locating it next to known places. One clue to the parody nature of <u>The Hitchhiker's Guide</u>, therefore comes from that fact that it locates one unknown place in reference to another unknown place: "Beyond what used to be called the Limitless Lightfields of Flanux until the Gray Binding Fiefdoms of Saxaquine were discovered lying behind them lie the Gray Binding Fiefdoms of Saxaquine" (Douglas Adams 606). This is a tautology based on a reference that no longer exists, and never did. The, "incongruity is produced by describing two unknown locations solely in terms of their relative positions. This incongruity, when presented in colloquial language, is easily read as humorous." Thus, although it does nothing to increase the reader's knowledge of the places being alluded to, it does, "further the text's comedic tendencies" (Nilep 7). One of the ironies of <u>Hitchhiker's Guide</u> is that the Earth is destroyed in the first chapter by the subhuman Vogons who are clearing the way for a hyperspace bypass. But the reader later finds out that "Earth" is not Earth, but is actually a supercomputer that is being run by mice, who are trying to find out the meaning of Life, the Universe, and Everything. The supercomputer tells them the answer to this question is "42," however, this raises more questions than it answers. Almost every chapter in <u>Hitchhiker's Guide</u> ends with an imminent cataclysm which is always averted by some improbable new plot development at the very last moment (Donnelly 7).

In order to develop his science-fiction parody, Adams turns all of the science fiction clichés inside out. For example, he destroys the earth in the opening pages of the first novel in <u>The Hitchhiker's Trilogy</u>. As Douglas Adams recounts, "Most science fiction seems to have for the climax the great concern: is the earth going to be destroyed? Everybody knows the hero is going to save it, so I thought, why not get past that one straight off?" (Adams 176). It should be noted that although the earth is destroyed in the first novel of the Hitchhiker series, it miraculously still exists in the final novel of the series. Lisa Tuttle says that <u>The Hitchhiker's Trilogy</u> is, "inspired lunacy that leaves hardly a science fiction cliché alive." The trilogy chronicles the adventures of Arthur Dent a constantly-bewildered and out-of-control Englishman, and his alien-friend Ford Prefect, who has been posing for the past fifteen years as an unemployed actor. When they discover that the Earth is going to be demolished to make room for an interstellar bypass, they hitch a ride on a space vehicle and thereby narrowly escape the calamity. With the aid of a computer travel guide, they travel through the galaxy and encounter a motley array of characters which includes Marvin, a terminally depressed robot, Zaphod Beeblebrox, the three-armed and two-headed president of the galaxy, and Slartibartfast, a planet designer who specializes in fjords. <u>The Hitchhiker's Trilogy</u> is unlike most other science fiction in that it demonstrates an uncommon sense of humor (Lesniak 3).

Nilep notes that much of <u>So Long, and Thanks for All the Fish</u> (1984) deals with forms that are familiar to people living on earth, but unfamiliar if a larger perspective is assumed. On earth we refer to the Sun as "the Sun," but in the Introduction to <u>So Long, and Thanks for All the Fish</u> it is described differently, as, "Far out in the uncharted backwaters of the unfashionable end of the Western Spiral arm of the Galaxy lies a small unregarded yellow sun" (Douglas Adams 475). Nilep notes that part of the humor of this statement lies in the conflicting metaphors.

> In this passage, the author cues the reader to consider certain semantic frames. The words "uncharted," "backwaters," and, to a lesser extent, "far out" are all reminiscent of sailing and exploring, and bring to mind a tradition of naval fiction. Other elements of the sentence, "galaxy," "sun," and "spiral arm" are not compatible with a naval tale, however. They bring to mind space and space exploration. This incongruity can easily be reconciled by calling to mind the metaphor SPACE TRAVEL IS SAILING, and its associated gestalt, relating planets to ports, astronauts to sailors, etc. This metaphor is a common one in the Science Fiction genre, and allows the reader to adjust expectations quickly and easily. (Nilep 4)

Nilep says that there is also another metaphor at work in this sentence, indicated by the words "far out," "unfashionable," "unregarded," and "Western." This metaphor is not easily reconcilable with the other two. The image of fashion and style requires an additional metaphorical extension, since the metaphor of "The Fashion World" has to be reconfigured to "The Fashion Galaxy," and the metaphorical components of "world" must be remapped to cover the entire "galaxy." (Nilep 4-5)

In this same introduction, there is a sentence that violates a number of H. P. Grice's conversational implicatures. The sentence reads, "And then, one Thursday, nearly two thousand years after one man had been nailed to a tree for saying how great it would be to be nice to people for a change, a girl sitting on her own in a small café in Rickmansworth suddenly realized what it was that had gone wrong all this time, and she finally knew how the world could be made a good and happy place" (Douglas Adams 475). Nilep says that some of the humor here comes from the reduction in the significance of the crucifixion by relating Christ's crucifixion to an unknown character being presented in the novel. "Beyond the reduction of Christ, the sentence gains additional humor from the novel interplay of general and specific descriptions: 'one Thursday, nearly two thousand years later' 'in a small café in Ricksmansworth,' versus 'the world,' and 'all this time.'" Nilep says that these notions placed side-by-side, "calls for the reader to reconcile the images via humorous interpretation" (Nilep 6).

Dirk Gently's Holistic Detective Agency (1987) features Dirk Gently, and employs a time-machine, a spaceship, an Electric Monk, and Samuel Taylor Coleridge's ghost in solving the murder of a computer executive. This novel is filled with coincidence and humor. John Nicholson says, "What signifies most here is the quality of the writing, the asides and allusions, and--above all--the jokes. Mr. Adams scores very high on all counts" (Lesniak 4). Dirk Gently lives in a, "chaotic quantum universe abuzz with the uncertainty principle, clouded with fuzzy logic, awash in low probability events." Gently's theory is that, "since everything is contingent upon everything else, everything is a clue and that wherever he happens to go and whatever he might be inclined to do all amount to working on the case" (Donnelly 8). Perhaps the six-foot-five Adams is thinking about himself in Dirk Gently's Holistic Detective Agency as he describes Richard MacDuff as "Tall. Tall and absurdly thin. And good-natured. A bit like a preying mantis that doesn't prey. A non-preying mantis if you like. A sort of pleasant genial mantis that's given up preying and taken up tennis instead" (Donnelly 7).

In The Long Dark Tea-Time of the Soul (1988), Adams says, "every particle of the universe affects every other particle, however faintly or obliquely" (Long Dark 110). Adams likes to introduce five or six disparate plots, and then bring them crashing together in an unexpected dénouement (Donnelly 7). Cathleen Shine says that The Long Dark Tea-Time of the Soul is, "a clever and funny novel about an English detective, an American girl in a bad mood and a Norse god who sells his soul to an advertising executive." Dirk Gently has only one client, and this one client is murdered, after which Dirk turns his attention to a mysterious explosion that takes place at the check-in-counter of an airport. Since he is a "holistic detective," he is convinced that there is some connection between these two seemingly unrelated events. Jess Bravin says that this novel demonstrates a skewed imagination and an ironic wit. Cathleen Shine says that in this novel, Adams's humor is crisp and intelligent, and that his prose is filled with elegant, absurdly literal-minded overstatements, and she adds that this writing is, "a pleasure to read" (Lesniak 4). Last Chance to See (1991) is the book form of a series of BBC radio programs which began in 1988 about nearly extinct animals. Both the radio series and the book have the title, "Last Chance to See" (Donnelly 7).

Douglas (Noel) Adams Bibliography

Adams, Douglas. The Long Dark Tea-Time of the Soul. New York, NY: Simon and Schuster, 1988.

Adams, Douglas. The More Than Complete Hitchhiker's Guide. New York, NY: Wings Books, 1986.

Adams, Michael. "Douglas Adams." Dictionary of Literary Biography Yearbook: 1983. Eds. Mary Bruccoli, and Jean W. Ross. Detroit, MI: Gale, 1984, 176.

Alexander, Edward. "Satire...Why?." Unpublished Paper. Tempe, AZ: Arizona State University, 1989.

Donnelly, William. "Douglas (Noel) Adams." Encyclopedia of British Humorists, Volume I. Ed. Steven H. Gale. New York, NY: Garland, 1996, 6-10.

Kropf, Carl R. "Douglas Adams's Hitchhiker Novels as Mock Science Fiction." Science Fiction Studies March, 1988: 61-70.

Lesniak, James G. "Douglas Adams." Contemporary Authors: New Revision Series, Volume 34. Detroit, MI: Gale, 1991, 2-5.

Nilep, Chad. "Toward an Understanding of Fictional-World Semantics: Semantic and Pragmatic Frames in Adams's So Long and Thanks for All the Fish. Unpublished Paper. Tempe, AZ: Arizona State University, 1996.

Wilcox, Christine M. "Douglas Adams: An Eclectic Style Generates Humor." Unpublished Paper. Tempe, AZ: Arizona State University, 1990.

Ellis Ni Dhuibhe-Almquist (1954-) IRELAND

See Nilsen, Don L. F. "Ellis Ni Dhuibhe-Almquist." Humor in Irish Literature: A Reference Guide. Westport, CT: Greenwood, 1996, 212.

Maura O'Halloran (1955-1982) IRELAND

See Nilsen, Don L. F. "Maura O'Halloran." Humor in Irish Literature: A Reference Guide. Westport, CT: Greenwood, 1996, 212.

Paul Muldoon (1956-) IRELAND

See Nilsen, Don L. F. "Paul Muldoon." Humor in Irish Literature: A Reference Guide. Westport, CT: Greenwood, 1996, 212.

Roddy Doyle (1958-) IRELAND

See Nilsen, Don L. F. "Roddy Doyle." <u>Humor in Irish Literature: A Reference Guide</u>. Westport, CT: Greenwood, 1996, 213.

Index